CHAMBERS

ADULT LEARNERS' DICTIONARY

CHAMBERS

An imprint of Chambers Harrap Publishers Ltd
7 Hopetoun Crescent
Edinburgh, EH7 4AY

First published by Chambers Harrap Publishers Ltd 2005

A CIP catalogue record for this book is available from the British Library.

ISBN 0550 10182 9

Designed and typeset by Chambers Harrap Publishers Ltd, Edinburgh
Printed in Italy by Legoprint

Contents

Contributors

Editors
Ian Brookes
Pat Bulhosen
Lucy Hollingworth
Mary O'Neill

Publishing manager
Patrick White

Prepress manager
Sharon McTeir

Prepress controller
Clair Simpson

The editors would like to acknowledge with thanks the assistance and advice of:

Gail Blackwood; Janice Booker; Hilary Bryant; Fay Dayns; Margaret Dennehy; Louise Eyer; Yvonne Gibson; Val Golding; Joanne Gregory; Christopher Harris; Trish Jacobs; Jackie Kowalewski; Ruth Lane; Leighton Nugent; Janet Ravensdale; Katherine Redmond; Ann Stewart; Colette Sweeney; Joseph Whyte; Jean Wilkinson.

Looking up a word in the dictionary

A dictionary is a list of words and their meanings, in alphabetical order. You can use it to find out what a word means, but also to check that you have spelt or used a word properly.

Each word and all the information around it is called a dictionary **entry**.

Say, for instance, that you want to look up the entry for the word **edge**. To work out its alphabetical order, you just have to decide where the letters of the word come in the alphabet.

1 Look at the **first letter** of the word. Letter **e** comes after letter **d** and before letter **f** in the alphabet, so the word **edge** will come after words beginning with **d** and before words beginning with **f** in the dictionary.

The capital and small letter at the side of the page shows you the letter that begins the words on that page so, if you are looking up **edge**, you can look for the pages where **Ee** is marked.

Ee

2 Then you have to look at the **second letter** of the word, which in **edge** is letter **d**. This comes after **c** and before **e** in the alphabet. Therefore, the word **edge** will come somewhere after any words beginning with **ec** and before any words beginning with **ee** in the dictionary.

eczema
→ **edge**
edible
edit
educate
-ee
eel

3 If there is more than one entry in the dictionary beginning with **ed**, you then look at the **third letter** of the word, and decide on its alphabetical order to work out where it will appear in the list of words.

The words at the top of the page show you the series of words that appears in alphabetical order on that page:

ECG → edible

Preface

Chambers Adult Learners' Dictionary has been developed in response to demand from teachers of adult literacy for a dictionary presented in more straightforward terms than traditional 'adult' dictionaries, but which recognizes and addresses the vocabulary needs of adult learners.

Compiled and designed with the benefit of advice from a number of tutors, the dictionary offers exceptionally clear and accessible definitions, with the focus on practical vocabulary encountered in modern life, including, for example, *direct debit, meningitis, National Insurance, ombudsman, paternity* and *warranty.* Examples of the word in context are included in many entries, helping to identify both the meaning of the word and how it is used.

Further assistance with language is provided by clear part-of-speech labels (noun, verb, etc), designed to increase awareness and understanding of the concepts. The inclusion of full-out forms such as the plurals of nouns and past tenses of verbs makes such inflections easy to identify and spell. Extra pieces of important and interesting information, such as homophones that can be confused, pronunciations and word histories, are included in short, eye-catching boxes. As well as making the page attractive, this ensures that the main entry itself remains uncluttered and easy to follow.

Particularly useful for adult learners is the series of *Language for Life* panels, each dealing with a language topic such as *computers* or *insurance.* These panels have been specially written to provide full but simple explanations of vocabulary which can be complicated, but which is essential to understanding today's world.

The two-colour layout is open and attractive, and the typeface has the approval of the British Dyslexia Association. To make them immediately identifiable, the entry words are picked out in colour. An identifying letter is printed at the side of the page, helping the user to find their way to the correct alphabetical place.

All these features make *Chambers Adult Learners' Dictionary* an invaluable resource for adult students of literacy, for both structured dictionary work and everyday reference.

Here are some special cases, and how to look them up.

•A word beginning with a capital letter

Sometimes a word begins with a capital letter. This may be the case if it is the proper name of someone or something, a trademark or an abbreviation:

BC   **Biro**   **Boxing Day**

This is just a different form of the letter, so it is treated the same as a small letter in alphabetical order:

   bazaar
→ **BC**
   be

However, if two words are exactly the same except that one starts with a capital letter, then the one with the capital letter is put first:

   VAT
   vat

•A word containing an apostrophe

A word might contain an apostrophe if it is a shortened form:

haven't   **I'm**   **we'll**

The apostrophe is ignored because it is not a letter of the alphabet, and the rest of the word is put in alphabetical order:

   haven
→ **haven't**
   haversack

If two words have the same letters, but one is a shortened form with an apostrophe, then the one without the apostrophe is put first:

   well
   we'll

•A prefix or a suffix

In this book you can also look up prefixes and suffixes. These are small parts of words that can be added to the beginning or end of a word to change what it means.

Prefixes and suffixes are shown with a hyphen at the beginning or the end:

   after-   **dis-**   **-ee**   **-ness**

The hyphen is ignored because it is not a letter of the alphabet, and the rest of the word is put in alphabetical order:

> **educate**
> → **-ee**
> **eel**

If two words have the same letters, but one is a prefix or a suffix and is shown with a hyphen, then the one without the hyphen is put first:

> **after**
> **after-**

• A word spelt the same as another word

Sometimes there are two entries for what looks like the same word. This is because although the words are spelt the same, they have different meanings and word histories. These words have small numbers beside them so you know they are different:

> **bear**[1]
> **bear**[2]

What is in a dictionary entry

The entry word

The word type

Adjective forms
Words after **adjective:** are the forms you use when you are making a comparison and you want to say something is 'more' or 'the most' compared to something else.

A phrase or idiom
This is a group of words that always appear together and have a special meaning. If you look up the main word in the phrase, then you should find its meaning in the entry.

A member of the word family
For more about word families, see page xi.

Another member of the word family
The arrow means that you have to look this up at its own place. For more about word families, see page xi.

Plural of a noun
A word after **noun:** is the plural, which is the form you use when you are talking about more than one of something.

Information box
For more about information boxes, see page xii.

Examples
These show you how you might use the word, and help to explain the meaning even more.

Verb forms
Any words after **verb:** are the different forms of the verb that you use depending on who did the action, or when it happened.

vagrant [noun: **vagrants**] someone who has no permanent place to live

vague [adjective: **vaguer, vaguest**] not very clear or definite: *I have a vague idea where he lives.*
♦ **vaguely** [adverb] not clearly or precisely: *He looked vaguely familiar.*
vain [adjective: **vainer, vainest**]
1 too proud of yourself and thinking too much about the way you look
2 useless: *He made a vain attempt to get up.*
[noun] if you do something **in vain,** you do it without success: *He tried in vain to get out through the bars of the cage.*
♦ **vainly** [adverb] without achieving what you want to do: *I tossed about in bed, vainly trying to get comfortable.*
➞ **vanity**
valentine [noun: **valentines**]
1 a card that you send on Saint Valentine's Day (14 February) to show that you love someone
2 the person you send a valentine to
valet [noun: **valets**] a male servant who works for another man and looks after his clothes
[verb: **valets, valeting, valeted**] to clean out a car

ⓘ The noun is pronounced **va**-lay, with a silent *t.*

valiant [adjective] brave: *She made a valiant attempt to rescue the cat.*
♦ **valiantly** [adverb] in a brave way
valid [adjective]
1 legally or officially acceptable and able to be used: *a valid passport*
2 reasonable and acceptable: *a valid excuse*
♦ **validate** [verb: **validates, validating, validated**] to validate something such as a ticket is to make it valid

Word types

This is a list of the various groups that words belong to, depending on the type of word it is and the job that it does in a sentence. These are used in this dictionary to label words.

abbreviation
An abbreviation is a short form of a word or phrase. For example, **St** is an abbreviation of **Street**, and **UK** is an abbreviation of **United Kingdom**.

adjective
An adjective is a word that tells you something about a noun. For example, **difficult, good** and **stupid** are adjectives: *a **difficult** sum* • *That film was **good**.* • *a **stupid** mistake*

adverb
An adverb is a word that tells you something about a verb, an adjective or another adverb. For example, **badly, abroad** and **really** are adverbs: *He played **badly**.* • *I lived **abroad**.* • *I am **really** sorry.* • *He played **really badly**.*

conjunction
A conjunction is a word that links other words or parts of a sentence. For example, **and, but** and **or** are conjunctions: *salt **and** pepper* • *I like butter **but** I hate cheese.* • *do **or** die*

interjection
An interjection is a word or phrase used to express a strong feeling such as surprise, shock or anger. For example, **Oh!** and **Hooray!** are interjections.

noun
A noun is a word that refers to a person or a thing. For example, **tree, Sue**, and **idea** are nouns.

plural noun
A plural noun refers to more than one person or thing, so you have to use the plural form of a verb with it – the verb has to agree. For example, **trousers** is a plural noun, so you would say *The trousers fit me* rather than *The trousers fits me*.

prefix
A prefix is a letter or a group of letters that is added to the beginning of a word to change its meaning and make another word. For example, the prefix **pre-** adds the meaning 'before' to a word, so a *preview* is a look or view of something in advance.

preposition
A preposition is a word put before a noun or pronoun to show how something is related or connected to it. For example, the word **in** is a preposition in the sentence *I put my shopping **in** my bag*. It shows the relationship between 'the shopping' and 'my bag'.

pronoun
A pronoun is a word that can be used in place of a noun. For example, **he** and **it** are pronouns. In the sentence *Gary ate the ice cream,* **Gary** and **the ice cream** could be changed to pronouns and the sentence would be *He ate it.*

short form
This is used in this dictionary to label two words that have been joined together using an apostrophe. For example, the word **couldn't** is a short form of **could not**.

suffix
A suffix is a letter or a group of letters that is added to the end of a word to change the job it does and to make another word. For example, the suffix **–ful** makes a word into an adjective meaning 'full of', so **joyful** means 'full of joy'.

verb
A verb is the word in a sentence that tells you what someone or something does. For example, **be**, **eat** and **speak** are verbs.

Word families

A word family is a group of words that come from a single word called the **root**. You will notice that the meanings of the words in a word family are connected in some way. You will also notice that the words in the group have parts that are similar in spelling, but usually have different endings.

Here are some examples of word families:

danger	**dangerous**	**dangerously**	
hope	**hopeful**	**hopefully**	**hopefulness**
vain	**vainly**	**vanity**	

Dictionary entries that are very close together are often part of the same family. Sometimes, words from the word family are included in the entry for the root word:

 ◆ **vainly** [adverb]

Sometimes, however, words from the same family are separated by other entries, so an arrow is used to tell you that there is a connected word in another part of the dictionary:

 ⟶ **vanity**

Information boxes

Sometimes after an entry there will be a small box that looks like this:

> ⓘ _____

The ⓘ sign tells you that there is extra information in the box.

These boxes may tell you how to use a word properly, for example by not getting the word mixed up with another one that sounds the same:

> ⓘ Remember the difference between
> **especially** and **specially**.
> **Especially** means 'particularly': *I like all of the*
> *characters, especially Harry.*
> **Specially** means 'for a special purpose': *I*
> *cooked this meal specially for you.*

They may tell you whether it is a very formal or informal word:

> ⓘ The first sense of **perceive** is a formal word.

Some tell you where the word comes from:

> ⓘ **Braille** is named after the man who invented
> it, Louis *Braille*, who was a teacher in France.

Some tell you how to say a word. Many of these boxes show the word divided into chunks called **syllables**. The one in bold is the one with **stress**, which means you pronounce it more strongly:

> ⓘ The noun is pronounced **va**-lay, with a
> silent *t*.

Some tell you how to pronounce a word by giving a word that rhymes with it:

> ⓘ This word rhymes with **cow**.

Language for Life boxes

Below is a list of the boxes in this book with the heading **Language for Life**, and the pages where you will find them. These boxes explain words and terms you might come across in different areas of life.

Glossary of dictionary terms

Some of the words you may come across in this dictionary are special terms to describe language and how it is used. Some of them may be unfamiliar. Here is a glossary to explain what they mean.

consonant
A consonant is any letter of the alphabet except **a, e, i, o** or **u**. It is also a speech sound you make when you use your lips, teeth or tongue to stop the flow of air.

formal
Formal language and words follow rules strictly, and are suitable for writing or when you are being very polite. For example, **forsake** is a formal word meaning to leave someone or something for ever.

future tense
The future tense of a verb is the form that you use when you are talking about something that has still to happen. Usually, the future tense is made up of more than one word. For example, **will finish** in *I will finish the job next week* is a future tense form of the verb **finish**.

informal
Informal language and words might be used when you are speaking to your friends, but they are not as suitable for writing. For example, **comfy** is an informal word for 'comfortable'.

past tense
The past tense of a verb is the form that you use when you are talking about what has happened in the past. For example, **relaxed** in *I relaxed after the race* is a past tense form of the verb **relax**.

phrase
A phrase is a group of words expressing a single meaning or idea. A phrase might be used on its own or as part of a sentence. For example, **now and then** in *I go swimming now and then* is a phrase.

plural
A plural is the form of a word that you use when there is more than one person, thing or group. For example, **families** is the plural of **family**.

possessive
A possessive is a word that shows who or what a person or thing belongs to. For example, **my**, **yours** and **theirs**, and nouns with **'s** added at the end, are possessives.

present tense
The present tense of a verb is the form that you use when you are talking about what is happening now. For example, **throw** and **throws** in *I throw the ball and he throws it back* are present tense forms of the verb **throw**.

singular
A singular is the form of a word that you use when there is one person, thing or group, rather than two or more. For example, the singular of **buses** is **bus**.

slang
Slang is very informal words or expressions that you use in everyday speech, but not in writing or when you are being polite. For example, **push off** is a slang term meaning 'go away'.

stress
Stress is extra weight that is put on part of a word, so you pronounce it more strongly. For example, in the word **bedroom** the stress is on **bed**.

syllable
A syllable is a word or part of a word that is a single sound. For example, **pen** has one syllable, **pen-cil** has two syllables, and **com-pu-ter** has three.

vowel
A vowel is one of the letters of the alphabet **a**, **e**, **i**, **o** or **u**. It is also a speech sound you make that does not use your lips, teeth or tongue to stop the flow of air.

a or **an** [adjective]
 1 one: *a hundred miles*
 2 any: *I need a pen.*
 3 each: *He gets £5 a week.*

ⓘ **A** is used before words beginning with a consonant, for example *a horse*. It is also used before words beginning with **u** if they are pronounced like 'you', for example *a uniform*. **An** is used before words beginning with a vowel (**a**, **e**, **i**, **o**, **u**) or **h** when it is not pronounced, for example *an eye, an hour*.

aback [adverb] if someone is **taken aback**, they are rather shocked: *I was taken aback by the change in Dan.*

abandon [verb: **abandons, abandoning, abandoned**]
 1 if you abandon someone or something, you go away, leaving them behind on purpose: *He'll abandon the getaway car as soon as possible.* • *How could she abandon her family like that?*
 2 to give up something such as an idea or plan: *If it rains, we'll just abandon the whole trip.*

abashed [adjective] shy and embarrassed

abattoir [noun: **abattoirs**] a place where animals are killed for food

abbey [noun: **abbeys**]
 1 the home of a group of Christian monks or nuns
 2 a church that was built for monks or nuns to use

abbot [noun: **abbots**] a monk who is in charge of an abbey

abbreviate [verb: **abbreviates, abbreviating, abbreviated**] to abbreviate a word or phrase is to make it shorter:

Everyone abbreviates Alistair James's name to A.J.
 ◆ **abbreviation** [noun: **abbreviations**] a short form of a word or phrase. For example, *UK* is an abbreviation for *United Kingdom*

LANGUAGE FOR LIFE

abbreviations

Abbreviations are often used in advertisements and on official forms, which can sometimes make these difficult to understand. You may see the following:
 • **approx** stands for 'approximately'
 • **exp** stands for 'experience'
 • **f/t** stands for 'full-time'
 • **k** stands for 'thousand'
 • **n/a** stands for 'not applicable' (used if a question on a form does not apply to you)
 • **ono** stands for 'or nearest offer' (used to say that the person selling something may accept less than the advertised price)
 • **pa** stands for 'per annum' (= per year)
 • **pcm** stands for 'per calendar month'
 • **p/t** stands for 'part-time'
 • **tbc** stands for 'to be confirmed'
 • **reqd** stands for 'required'
 • **w/e** stands for 'week ending'

abdicate [verb: **abdicates, abdicating, abdicated**] if a king or queen abdicates, they give up their position to someone else
 ◆ **abdication** [noun: **abdications**] an abdication is when someone gives up a position of power or responsibility

abdomen [noun: **abdomens**]
 1 the part of an animal's body that contains the stomach

Aa

2 the back part of an insect's body

✦ **abdominal** [adjective] to do with the area of your body that contains your stomach: *abdominal exercises* • *abdominal pain*

abduct [verb: **abducts, abducting, abducted**] to take someone away by using force: *Two more tourists have been abducted from their hotel room.*

✦ **abduction** [noun: **abductions**] taking someone away using force: *He faces charges of child abduction and murder.*

abhor [verb: **abhors, abhorring, abhorred**] to abhor someone or something is to hate them: *I abhor violence.*

abide [verb: **abides, abiding, abode** or **abided**]

1 if you **can't abide** something or someone, you can't stand them: *I can't abide people who smoke in restaurants.*

2 to **abide by** a rule or decision is to keep to it: *Please abide by the rules of the game.*

✦ **abiding** [adjective] an abiding feeling or memory lasts for a long time

ability [noun: **abilities**]

1 someone who has the ability to do something is able to do it: *Not everyone has the ability to keep a secret.*

2 talent: *a pupil with great ability*

ablaze [adjective and adverb]

1 on fire: *The bomb set several buildings ablaze.*

2 shining very brightly: *The children's eyes were ablaze with excitement.*

able [adjective: **abler, ablest**]

1 if you are able to do something, you can do it: *He wasn't able to run fast enough.* • *Will you be able to help me?*

2 an able person is good at doing something: *an able student*

⟶ **ability, ably**

-able or **-ible** [suffix] if **-able** or **-ible** comes at the end of a word, it is an adjective that means 'able to be'. For example, *manageable* means 'able to be managed'

able-bodied [adjective]

1 fit and healthy

2 able-bodied is sometimes used to describe people who are not disabled

ably [adverb] if you do something ably, you do it well: *an unusual film, ably directed by George Clooney*

abnormal [adjective] not normal, especially in a worrying way: *abnormal behaviour for a five-year-old*

✦ **abnormality** [noun: **abnormalities**] something that is not normal

✦ **abnormally** [adverb] unusually: *an abnormally fast heartbeat*

aboard [preposition and adverb] on or onto a bus, train, ship or aeroplane: *one of the team aboard the shuttle* • *We all climbed aboard the boat.* • *Everyone should go aboard now.*

abode [noun] an old or formal word for the place where someone lives: *He had no fixed abode and had to sleep on the street.*

abolish [verb: **abolishes, abolishing, abolished**] to abolish a rule or a way of doing something is to get rid of it: *a plan to abolish fishing licences*

✦ **abolition** [noun] getting rid of something such as a law or system of doing something: *the abolition of free eye tests*

Aboriginal or **Aborigine** [noun: **Aboriginals** or **Aborigines**] one of the people who lived in Australia before anyone arrived from other countries

abort [verb: **aborts, aborting, aborted**]

1 if a foetus aborts or is aborted from its mother's body, it is born when it is too young to survive

2 to abort a plan or process is to stop it after it has already started: *Severe storms forced NASA to abort the launch of the space shuttle.*

✦ **abortion** [noun: **abortions**] an operation to prevent a baby from developing and being born

abound [verb: **abounds, abounding, abounded**] if things abound, there are a lot of them: *Stories abound of girls spotted in supermarkets and turned into top models.*

about [preposition]

1 on the subject of: *a book about bats* • *a talk about Spain*

2 around: *Clothes were scattered about the room.*

[adverb]

1 in or to one place and then another: *move things about* • *running about all day*

2 not exactly but nearly the number given: *about five years ago* • *about four centimetres*
3 in the opposite direction: *He turned about and walked away.*
4 if you are **about to** do something, you are going to do it now: *I was about to leave when the phone rang.* • *I think it's about to rain.*
5 about turn is an order to turn around and face in the opposite direction

above [preposition]
1 over: *the shelf above the sink* • *two degrees above zero* • *in the class above me*
2 if someone feels they are above a feeling or action, they think it is not worth their time: *James was not above asking for his ten pence back.*
3 above all is an expression meaning more than anything else: *We were, above all, hungry.*
[adverb]
1 higher up: *clouds in the sky above*
2 earlier in a piece of writing: *See instruction 5 above.*

abrasion [noun: **abrasions**] a graze on the skin
✦ **abrasive** [adjective] an abrasive material is rough when you touch it: *Rub the dirt off with abrasive paper.*

abreast [adverb]
1 side by side: *walking three abreast*
2 if someone **keeps abreast** of developments, they make sure they know about any changes that happen

abridge [verb: **abridges, abridging, abridged**] to make a book or story shorter: *a novel abridged for television*
✦ **abridgement** or **abridgment** [noun: **abridgements** or **abridgments**] a book or story that has been made shorter

abroad [adverb] in or to a foreign country: *travel abroad*

abrupt [adjective]
1 sudden: *an abrupt change of direction*
2 an abrupt person speaks sharply and rudely
3 an abrupt statement or question is sudden and short
✦ **abruptly** [adverb]
1 suddenly: *He turned abruptly and walked out.*
2 if someone speaks abruptly, they say something sharply

abscess [noun: **abscesses**] a lump inside your body that is painful and filled with liquid

abseil [verb: **abseils, abseiling, abseiled**] to let yourself down a rope with your feet against a wall or cliff
✦ **abseiling** [noun] a sport in which you go down a cliff on a rope

absence [noun: **absences**] being away from a place: *Your absence from the meeting was noticed.*

absent [adjective] away for a short time: *Is anyone absent today?* • *Two people were absent from the rehearsal.*

absent-minded [adjective] an absent-minded person often forgets things

absolute [adjective] complete: *absolute rubbish*
✦ **absolutely** [adverb]
1 completely: *absolutely ridiculous*
2 yes, certainly: *'Please can I have one of those?' 'Absolutely.'*

absorb [verb: **absorbs, absorbing, absorbed**]
1 to soak up liquid: *The bath mat will absorb the splashes.*
2 if you are **absorbed in** something, you are giving it all your attention: *We were so absorbed in our game, we didn't hear the bell.*
✦ **absorbent** [adjective] an absorbent material is able to soak up liquid: *absorbent kitchen towels*
✦ **absorbing** [adjective] very interesting and taking all your attention: *an absorbing puzzle*

abstain [verb: **abstains, abstaining, abstained**]
1 to choose not to vote: *If you can't make up your mind, why don't you just abstain?*
2 if you **abstain from** something, you stop yourself from doing it: *Pregnant women are advised to abstain from alcohol.*
✦ **abstention** [noun: **abstentions**] when someone refuses to vote: *Three said 'yes', two said 'no', and there were two abstentions.*
✦ **abstinence** [noun] when you stop yourself from doing something, especially eating, drinking or having sex

abstract [adjective] something that is abstract cannot be seen or touched, for example *honesty* and *an argument*

ⓘ The opposite of **abstract** is **concrete**.

absurd [adjective] ridiculous: *What an absurd idea!*

✦ **absurdity** [noun: **absurdities**] something that is ridiculous: *I can't listen to any more of these absurdities!*

✦ **absurdly** [adverb] in a ridiculous way: *an absurdly easy question*

abundance [noun]

1 an abundance of something is a lot of it: *an abundance of information on the subject*

2 if there is something **in abundance**, there is plenty of it: *There was food in abundance.*

✦ **abundant** [adjective] existing in large amounts: *an abundant harvest* • *abundant red hair*

✦ **abundantly** [adverb]

1 in large amounts: *Fruit is abundantly available in the market.*

2 very: *It is abundantly clear that you are very angry.*

abuse [noun: **abuses**]

1 using something the wrong way on purpose: *alcohol abuse*

2 bad treatment: *child abuse*

3 insults: *shouting abuse at us in the street*

[verb: **abuses, abusing, abused**]

1 to abuse something such as a position is to use it the wrong way on purpose: *a bank manager who abused people's trust and stole their money*

2 to abuse someone or something is to treat them badly: *people who abuse animals*

✦ **abusive** [adjective] rude or insulting

ⓘ The verb **abuse** ends with a **z** sound. The noun **abuse** ends with an **ss** sound.

abysmal [adjective] very bad: *abysmal exam results*

✦ **abysmally** [adverb] very badly: *The team played abysmally.*

abyss [noun: **abysses**] a very deep or bottomless hole

academic [adjective]

1 to do with studying and education: *academic qualifications* • *the academic year*

2 good at studying and learning: *He loves school but he isn't very academic.*

[noun: **academics**] a teacher at a college or university

✦ **academically** [adverb] in a way that is to do with studying and learning: *Not all students can succeed academically.*

academy [noun: **academies**] a school or college where you learn about a particular subject: *an academy of music*

accelerate [verb: **accelerates, accelerating, accelerated**] to go faster

✦ **acceleration** [noun]

1 acceleration is increasing speed: *You'll be pushed back into your seat during acceleration.*

2 a vehicle's acceleration is its power to go faster: *This car has amazing acceleration!*

✦ **accelerator** [noun: **accelerators**] the pedal or lever that you press to make a vehicle go faster: *Press the accelerator gently and move off.*

accent [noun: **accents**]

1 the way people from a particular area pronounce words: *I have a Scottish accent.* • *I speak German with a strong English accent.*

2 a mark over a letter in a foreign language that shows how to pronounce it, for example over e in the word *café*

3 a stress that makes one part of a word or a sentence, or one note in music, stand out more than the others: *Put the accent on the third syllable in the word 'preparation'.*

accentuate [verb: **accentuates, accentuating, accentuated**] to make something more obvious

accept [verb: **accepts, accepting, accepted**]

1 to take something that someone offers you

2 you accept an invitation when you say 'yes' to it

3 you accept something like an idea if you agree that it is true: *I accept that I was wrong and I'm sorry.*

4 a school or university accepts someone when they agree that they can study there: *Ray has been accepted to study medicine.*

✦ **acceptable** [adjective] good enough: *This kind of behaviour just isn't acceptable!*

✦ **acceptance** [noun]

1 taking something that is given to you: *Most*

actors make an acceptance speech when they win an Oscar.

2 a written answer accepting an offer: *a letter of acceptance*

access [noun: **accesses**] a way of getting to or into a place: *The builders will need access to the house while you're out at work.*
[verb: **accesses, accessing, accessed**] to get and be able to use information on a computer: *This file was last accessed yesterday.*
♦ **accessible** [adjective] easy to get to: *The house is not very accessible.*

accessory [noun: **accessories**]
1 an extra part that can be used with something bigger: *a hair-drier with lots of accessories*
2 something like a bag, a scarf or jewellery, that goes with your clothes: *a little black dress with shocking pink accessories*
3 a person who helps someone to do something bad: *an accessory to murder*

accident [noun: **accidents**]
1 a bad thing that happens by chance: *We had an accident with the glue and now it's everywhere.*
2 a road accident is when a vehicle crashes into something on a road
3 something happens **by accident** when it happens by chance: *I dropped the glass by accident and it smashed.*
♦ **accidental** [adjective] if something is accidental, it happens by mistake
♦ **accidentally** [adverb] by accident: *I accidentally shut the car door and locked my keys inside.*

Accident and Emergency [noun] the hospital department that deals with people who have been injured and need medical attention

acclaim [noun] praise
♦ **acclaimed** [adjective] if something is acclaimed, it has had a lot of praise: *an acclaimed television show*

accommodate [verb: **accommodates, accommodating, accommodated**]
1 to find a place to stay for someone: *The whole group can be accommodated in the same hotel.*
2 to be big enough for someone or something:

This room could easily accommodate ten people.
♦ **accommodating** [adjective] being helpful
♦ **accommodation** [noun] somewhere to stay or live: *We'll look for accommodation as soon as we arrive.*

accompaniment [noun: **accompaniments**] the music that someone plays for a person to sing or play an instrument to: *a love song with a guitar accompaniment*

accompany [verb: **accompanies, accompanying, accompanied**]
1 to go with someone to where they are going: *Would you mind accompanying me to the station, sir?*
2 to play an instrument, especially the piano, while someone else sings a song or plays music: *Her sister usually accompanies her on the piano.*

accomplice [noun: **accomplices**] someone who helps a person to do something bad

accomplish [verb: **accomplishes, accomplishing, accomplished**] to manage to do something: *Most children accomplished the task in a few minutes.*
♦ **accomplished** [adjective] talented: *an accomplished goalkeeper*
♦ **accomplishment** [noun: **accomplishments**]
1 an accomplishment is something you are very good at: *Cooking is just one of her many accomplishments.*
2 accomplishment is completing or finishing something

accord [noun] if you do something **of your own accord**, you do it without being asked or told: *I was surprised that he thanked me of his own accord.*
♦ **accordingly** [adverb] in a way that suits what has just been said or what is happening: *The sun was shining and Jake dressed accordingly.*

according to [preposition]
1 information according to someone is what that person says: *Hannah's ill, according to Lucy.*
2 if one thing is measured according to another, they are compared with each other:

You'll be paid *according to how much work you have done.* • *Did everything go according to plan?*

accordion [noun: **accordions**] a musical instrument that you play by pressing in and out a folding box with a small keyboard like a piano on its side

account [noun: **accounts**]

1 a description of something that happened: *His account of the journey made us laugh.*

2 an arrangement with a bank to keep money there: *Which account do you want to pay this cheque into?*

3 an agreement with a shop for you to pay at the end of each month for what you have bought during the month

4 a bill showing how much someone has paid and how much they must still pay

5 to **take something into account** is to consider it: *Will they take my age into account when they decide who can go?*

6 on account of means 'because of': *I can't run very well on account of my bad leg.*

7 on no account means 'definitely not': *You are on no account to stay out after ten o'clock.*

[verb: **accounts, accounting, accounted**] to account for something is to explain it: *The fact that it's her birthday accounts for all the visitors she's had today.*

LANGUAGE FOR LIFE

bank accounts

There are different types of bank account.

• A **current account** allows you to take money out at any time.

• A **deposit account**, sometimes called a **savings account**, pays you more interest than a current account, but you have to leave your money in the account for longer.

• A **joint account** is an account for two people who can both take money out and put money into it.

accountancy [noun] the job of organizing and keeping records of a person's or a company's money

accountant [noun: **accountants**] someone whose job is to write and keep in order a person's or company's money accounts

accounts [plural noun] written records of the money received and spent by a person or company

accumulate [verb: **accumulates, accumulating, accumulated**]

1 you have accumulated things when you have collected a lot of them

2 things accumulate when they pile up: *A pile of bills had accumulated on my desk.*

♦ **accumulation** [noun: **accumulations**] a lot of things that have come together in one place: *an accumulation of empty boxes in the hall*

accuracy [noun] being exactly right: *Please check the accuracy of this measurement.*

accurate [adjective] exactly right: *an accurate guess*

♦ **accurately** [adverb] exactly: *Copy the shape as accurately as possible.*

accusation [noun: **accusations**] a statement saying that someone has done something wrong: *Jude has made a very serious accusation against you.*

accuse [verb: **accuses, accusing, accused**] you accuse someone when you say they have done something wrong: *Are you accusing me of lying?*

♦ **accused** [noun] **the accused** is the person in a court who is supposed to have committed a crime: *Do you recognize the accused?*

ⓘ **The accused** can mean more than one person: *The accused are all pupils at the same school.*

accustomed [adjective] used to: *We've all become accustomed to his strange way of talking.*

ace [noun: **aces**]

1 a playing-card with one symbol on it and a letter 'A' in the corner: *the ace of spades*

2 an expert: *a Brazilian soccer ace*

3 in tennis, a serve that the other player cannot reach

[adjective] an informal word meaning very good: *The food was ace.* • *an ace detective*

ache [noun: **aches**] a pain that goes on and on: *an ache behind my eyes*

[verb: **aches, aching, ached**] to hurt for a long time, especially in a dull, heavy sort of way: *My arm aches from playing too much tennis.*

achieve [verb: **achieves, achieving, achieved**]
1 to succeed in doing something: *We have achieved everything we set out to do.*
2 to get something, especially by trying hard: *She has achieved a very high standard.*
◆ **achievement** [noun: **achievements**]
1 an achievement is a success or good result: *a list of his achievements so far*
2 achievement is having success: *a high level of achievement in this class*

acid [noun: **acids**] a type of chemical. Strong acids can dissolve metals
◆ **acidic** [adjective]
1 containing acid
2 with a sharp, sour taste
◆ **acidity** [noun] how acid something is

acid rain [noun] rain that contains pollution that factories and cities have released into the air

acknowledge [verb: **acknowledges, acknowledging, acknowledged**]
1 to admit that something is true: *I acknowledge that you were right.*
2 to tell someone that you have received something they sent you: *They never acknowledge my letters.*
◆ **acknowledgement** [noun: **acknowledgements**] a note to tell someone that you have received something: *I sent two letters but only got one acknowledgement.*

acne [noun] a skin problem that causes spots, usually on someone's face. Acne is common among teenagers

acorn [noun: **acorns**] a kind of nut that grows on oak trees

acoustic [adjective]
1 to do with sound and hearing: *an acoustic signal*
2 an acoustic musical instrument does not need electrical equipment to work
◆ **acoustics** [plural noun] the way a room can make music or speech sound better or worse: *The Tudor Hall has wonderful acoustics.*

acquaint [verb: **acquaints, acquainting, acquainted**]
1 to acquaint someone with something is to tell them about it: *Let me acquaint you with the facts of the case.*

2 if you are acquainted with something or someone, you know them
◆ **acquaintance** [noun: **acquaintances**]
1 someone you have met
2 to **make someone's acquaintance** is to meet them for the first time

acquire [verb: **acquires, acquiring, acquired**] to get something: *I see you've acquired a new jacket.*

acquit [verb: **acquits, acquitting, acquitted**]
1 to acquit someone of a crime is to decide in a court that they did not do it
2 to **acquit yourself well** or **badly** is to do well or badly
◆ **acquittal** [noun: **acquittals**] when someone is acquitted of a crime

acre [noun: **acres**] an area of land of about 4047 square metres

acrobat [noun: **acrobats**] someone who performs gymnastic tricks like somersaults and tightrope-walking
◆ **acrobatic** [adjective] to do with gymnastic movements, especially jumping
◆ **acrobatics** [plural noun] clever physical movements like skilful jumping and balancing

acronym [noun: **acronyms**] a word made from the first letters of other words. For example, the second part of *CD-ROM* is an acronym for *Read Only Memory*

across [preposition]
1 on or to the other side: *Their house is across the river from ours.* • *I ran across the road.*
2 from one side of something to the other: *a bridge across the river* • *clouds moving across the sky*
[adverb] to the other side of something: *Don't run, but walk across quickly.*

acrylic [noun] a substance used for making some paints, fabrics and different kinds of plastic materials
[adjective] made with acrylic: *an acrylic sweater*

act [verb: **acts, acting, acted**]
1 to perform in a play or film
2 to behave in a certain way: *Do stop acting like a baby.*
3 to do something: *We must act now to save the planet!*

Aa

4 to **act up** is to behave badly

[noun: **acts**]

1 something that someone does: *a brave act*

2 a law: *an act of parliament*

3 a section of a play

4 a short piece of entertainment or the people involved: *a comedy act*

✦ **acting** [noun] performing in plays or films [adjective] doing someone else's job for a time while they are away: *the acting headmaster*

⇒ **actor, actress**

action [noun: **actions**]

1 an action is a movement someone or something makes: *Hit the ball with a swinging action.*

2 action is moving or doing something: *Let's see some action around here!*

3 the action of a film, book or play is what happens in the story: *Most of the action takes place in America.*

4 action is fighting in a war: *a soldier killed in action*

5 if a machine is **out of action**, it is not working: *My car's out of action at the moment.*

action replay [noun: **action replays**] a repeat of a bit of film, especially part of a sports match, often shown in slow-motion

action stations [plural noun] the positions soldiers take up when they get ready to fight

activate [verb: **activates, activating, activated**] to make something start working: *Activate all emergency systems now!*

active [adjective]

1 busy doing a lot of things: *Her mum's very active in the drama club.*

2 moving around a lot: *Try to keep active in order to keep fit.*

3 in grammar, an active verb or sentence has a subject that performs the action of the verb, for example in the sentence *The cat chased the mouse*

✦ **actively** [adverb] in a way that involves doing a lot of things: *actively helping people with problems*

activist [noun: **activists**] someone who is an active member of a political party or protest group: *animal rights activists*

activity [noun: **activities**]

1 an activity is something you do, especially something you do for fun, in an organized way: *a variety of sporting activities*

2 activity is being active or busy

actor [noun: **actors**] someone who performs in a play or film

actress [noun: **actresses**] a woman who performs in a play or film

actual [adjective] real: *We guessed there were about 100 people but the actual number was 110.*

✦ **actually** [adverb] in fact: *Actually, there are a lot of things you don't know.*

acupuncture [noun] a treatment for pain and illness where the points of very thin needles are put into your skin at different places on your body

acute [adjective]

1 an acute problem, especially a pain or illness, is very bad: *acute appendicitis • an acute shortage of nurses*

2 quick to realize or understand something: *an acute mind • acute eyesight*

3 if two lines are at an acute angle, they point in almost the same direction

✦ **acutely** [adverb] extremely: *I felt acutely embarrassed.*

AD [abbreviation] **AD** is used before or after a date to show that the date was after the birth of Jesus Christ, for example *2000 AD*. Look up and compare **BC**

ⓘ **AD** is short for **Anno Domini**, which is Latin for 'in the year of our Lord'.

ad [noun: **ads**] an informal word for an **advertisement**

adamant [adjective] very firm and not likely to give in: *Her father was adamant about going home immediately.*

Adam's apple [noun: **Adam's apples**] the lump you can see at the front of a man's neck

adapt [verb: **adapts, adapting, adapted**]

1 to change something to make it more suitable: *Can you adapt your wedding speech for Jody's birthday?*

2 if you adapt to something, you get used to it: *It didn't take long to adapt to the heat when we moved south.*

✦ **adaptable** [adjective] an adaptable

person can easily fit in with new or different situations

◆ **adaptation** [noun: **adaptations**] an old story that is told in a new way: *a television adaptation of Roald Dahl's novel*

◆ **adaptor** [noun: **adaptors**] a kind of plug you use to connect a plug of one type to a socket of another, or to connect several plugs to one socket

add [verb: **adds, adding, added**]

1 to put things together: *Add two and two. • Add the milk and sugar to the mixture.*

2 to say or write something else: *'If you don't mind?' he added.*

3 to **add up** is to find the total of numbers put together: *Can you add these numbers up in your head?*

4 if things **add up**, they grow into a large amount: *£5 a week soon adds up.*

→ **addition**

adder [noun: **adders**] a poisonous snake with a black zigzag pattern on its back which is found in the north of Europe and Asia

addict [noun: **addicts**] someone who cannot stop taking something: *a drug addict*

◆ **addicted** [adjective] if you are addicted to something, you cannot manage without it

◆ **addiction** [noun: **addictions**] not being able to stop taking something: *alcohol addiction*

◆ **addictive** [adjective] if something is addictive, it makes you want to do it more and more: *an addictive computer game*

addition [noun: **additions**]

1 addition is adding up numbers: *some addition exercises*

2 an addition is something that has been added: *I noticed a new addition to the collection.*

3 if you do one thing **in addition** to another, you do it as well

◆ **additional** [adjective] extra: *We're having three additional rooms built on the back of the building.*

◆ **additionally** [adverb] as well as that: *Additionally, you have to pay to get in.*

additive [noun: **additives**] a substance that is added to food or drinks to make them taste

better or stay fresh for longer: *Our organic cheeses are free from additives.*

address [noun: **addresses**]

1 your address is the name or number of the house, the street and the town where you live: *What's your new address?*

2 a formal speech

[verb: **addresses, addressing, addressed**]

1 to write an address on an envelope or parcel

2 to speak to someone: *Were you addressing me?*

adept [adjective] very clever at something

adequate [adjective] enough: *Three rooms should be adequate for our family.*

adhesive [noun: **adhesives**] glue

[adjective] sticky: *adhesive tape*

Adi Granth [noun] the holy book of the Sikh religion

adjacent [adjective] next to: *The park is adjacent to the hospital. • A policeman was in the adjacent room.*

adjective [part of speech: **adjectives**] a word that tells you something about a noun. For example, *difficult, good* and *stupid* are adjectives

adjoin [verb: **adjoins, adjoining, adjoined**] a formal word that means to be joined to: *The bathroom adjoins the bedroom.*

◆ **adjoining** [adjective] an adjoining room is the next room along

adjourn [verb: **adjourns, adjourning, adjourned**] to adjourn a meeting is to stop it but intend to continue it at another time

adjust [verb: **adjusts, adjusting, adjusted**]

1 to adjust something is to change it a little bit: *I adjusted the clock by two minutes.*

2 if someone adjusts to something, they get used to it: *It was difficult to adjust to living in a flat.*

◆ **adjustable** [adjective] something adjustable can be changed to fit: *adjustable seat belts*

◆ **adjustment** [noun: **adjustments**]

1 an adjustment is a slight change: *We've made a few adjustments to the schedule this week.*

2 adjustment is making changes to suit a new situation: *You'll be fine after a short period of adjustment.*

Aa

administer [verb: **administers, administering, administered**] to administer a medicine is to give it to someone

administrate [verb: **administrates, administrating, administrated**] to run an organization

♦ **administration** [noun: **administrations**]

1 administration is running an organization

2 the administration in an organization is the group of people who run it

♦ **administrative** [adjective] to do with running a business or country: *an administrative job*

♦ **administrator** [noun: **administrators**] someone who runs or helps to run an organization

admirable [adjective] if something is admirable, a lot of people think it is very good: *The way he behaved was admirable.*

♦ **admirably** [adverb] very well: *I thought you spoke admirably.*

admiral [noun: **admirals**] one of the most important officers in the navy

admiration [noun] a feeling of liking someone or something very much because you think they are good: *He looked at the boy with admiration.*

admire [verb: **admires, admiring, admired**]

1 to like someone or something very much

2 to enjoy looking at something: *I've been admiring your new hat.*

♦ **admirer** [noun: **admirers**] a person who likes someone or something very much

admission [noun: **admissions**]

1 being allowed into a place: *A sign on the door said 'No admission'.*

2 the cost of getting in: *We don't charge admission here.*

3 an admission is when you agree that something bad is true: *We were surprised by his admission that he had done it.*

admit [verb: **admits, admitting, admitted**]

1 to agree that you have done something bad: *I admit that I should have told you sooner.*

2 to agree that something is true: *I admit that this is a difficult exercise, but do your best.*

3 to let someone in: *They won't admit anyone wearing trainers.*

♦ **admittance** [noun] being allowed to go in somewhere: *No admittance for anyone under 18.*

♦ **admittedly** [adverb] it must be agreed: *Admittedly, I wasn't there at the time. But I believe him.*

ado [noun] **without further ado** means right now, without doing anything else

adolescence [noun] the time between childhood and being an adult

♦ **adolescent** [noun: **adolescents**] someone older than a child, but not yet an adult

♦ **adolescent** [adjective] to do with someone who is older than a child but not yet an adult

adopt [verb: **adopts, adopting, adopted**]

1 to adopt a child is to take them into your own family and legally become their parent

2 to adopt a way of doing something is to start to do it that way: *We must adopt new methods of fighting crime.*

♦ **adoption** [noun]

1 taking a child into a new family: *Adoption can take a long time.*

2 taking on something new: *the adoption of a new transport policy*

♦ **adoptive** [adjective] adoptive parents are the new parents of a child who goes into a new family

adorable [adjective] a thing or person is adorable if you cannot help liking them very much

adoration [noun] loving someone or something very much: *a look of adoration*

adore [verb: **adores, adoring, adored**] to think something or someone is wonderful: *She just adores her father.*

adorn [verb: **adorns, adorning, adorned**] to decorate something: *Their hair was adorned with flowers.*

adrenalin or **adrenaline** [noun] a chemical in your body that is produced when you are afraid, angry or excited

adrift [adjective] a boat that is adrift is not tied up and is probably moving in the wind [adverb] if a boat goes adrift, it floats too far from the shore

adulation [noun] a lot of praise from people

adult [noun: **adults**] a grown-up
[adjective] to do with or for grown-ups: *adult sizes*
→ **adulthood**

adultery [noun] having sex with someone when you are married to someone else: *to commit adultery*

adulthood [noun] the period of time in your life when you are an adult

advance [noun: **advances**]
1 progress or movement forward: *technological advances*
2 a payment made before it is due: *I asked for an advance of £50 on my salary.*
3 if something happens **in advance** of something else, it happens before it: *I arrived in advance to make sure everything was ready.*
4 if someone **makes advances** to someone else, they try to develop a sexual relationship with them
[verb: **advances, advancing, advanced**] to move forwards: *a crowd advancing towards us*
[adjective] happening before an event: *an advance booking for the show*
♦ **advanced** [adjective] high level: *an advanced Spanish course*

advantage [noun: **advantages**]
1 a benefit or good quality: *the advantages of working from home*
2 in tennis scoring, advantage is the point after deuce (40-40)
3 if you **have an advantage over** someone else, things are better for you for some reason: *Max had an advantage over the others as he already spoke Italian. • Her long legs give her an advantage in the high jump.*
4 to **take advantage of** a situation is to use it well: *We took advantage of the sunshine to get the clothes dry.*
5 if you **take advantage of** someone, you take more of their kindness than you really should

advent [noun]
1 the arrival of something: *the advent of the steam engine*
2 the season of **Advent** is the four weeks before Christmas

adventure [noun: **adventures**] something exciting that happens or is going to happen to you: *A jungle visit would be a real adventure for us.*
♦ **adventurous** [adjective] an adventurous person likes to do exciting new things

adverb [part of speech: **adverbs**] a word that you use to describe verbs, adjectives or other adverbs. For example, *really, badly, abroad* and *often* are adverbs

adversary [noun: **adversaries**] an enemy or somebody who is against you in a competition

advert [noun: **adverts**] advert is short for **advertisement**

advertise [verb: **advertises, advertising, advertised**] to tell as many people as possible about something: *Nobody will come unless we advertise the concert.*
♦ **advertisement** [noun: **advertisements**] a notice, newspaper announcement or short film about something that somebody is trying to sell: *I saw an advertisement for a new chocolate bar.*
♦ **advertising** [noun] the business of making advertisements: *Seeta works in advertising.*

advice [noun] someone who gives you advice tells you what they think you should do: *If I follow her advice, I won't have any money left!*

ⓘ Remember that **advice** with a **c** is a noun: *Can you give me some advice?*
Advise with an **s** is a verb: *Can you advise me?*

advisable [adjective] something that is advisable is probably a sensible thing to do

advise [verb: **advises, advising, advised**] to tell someone what you think they should do
♦ **adviser** or **advisor** [noun: **advisers** or **advisors**] someone who tells people the best thing to do
♦ **advisory** [adjective] to do with giving advice: *an advisory body*

advocate [verb: **advocates, advocating, advocated**] to recommend or support an idea [noun: **advocates**]
1 someone who supports an idea: *He's an advocate of higher taxes.*
2 in Scotland, an advocate is a lawyer

aerate [verb: **aerates, aerating, aerated**] to put air into something such as soil or a liquid

aerial [noun: **aerials**] equipment made of metal, especially wire, for getting or sending radio or television signals: *a TV aerial on the roof*

[adjective] from up in the air: *an aerial photo*

aero- [prefix] if a word starts with **aero-**, it has something to do with air or flying. For example, an *aeroplane* is a machine for flying

aerobatics [plural noun] flying stunts in an aeroplane

aerobics [plural noun] exercises for the whole body that make your heart and lungs work hard

aerodrome [noun: **aerodromes**] a place where private aeroplanes are kept, with an area of land for taking off and landing

aeroplane [noun: **aeroplanes**] a machine for flying that has fixed wings

aerosol [noun: **aerosols**] a container with a button on top that you press to let out a spray of liquid

afar [adverb] a long way away: *The visitors had travelled from afar.*

affair [noun: **affairs**]
1 a group of events that make up a situation: *We need to investigate this affair of the missing ticket money.*
2 business or concern: *financial affairs* • *I'm not going to tell you because it's my own affair.*
3 a sexual relationship between two people, when one or both of them is married to someone else

affect [verb: **affects, affecting, affected**] to change a thing or person in some way or cause them some harm: *The accident affected his eyesight.* • *Were you affected by the floods?*

ⓘ You have to be careful not to confuse **affect**, which is a verb, with **effect**, which is a noun.
✓ One thing **affects** another.
✓ One thing has an **effect** on another.

affection [noun] a strong feeling of liking someone
♦ **affectionate** [adjective] an affectionate person shows that they like or love someone:

Her mother gave her an affectionate kiss.
♦ **affectionately** [adverb] in a kind, loving sort of way: *Joe scratched the cat's head affectionately.*

affiliated [adjective] if one organization is affiliated to or with another, they are connected in some kind of partnership: *The school is affiliated to the local technical college.*
♦ **affiliation** [noun: **affiliations**] a connection between two or more organizations

affinity [noun: **affinities**] a feeling that different things or people have a close connection: *Flo had always had a deep affinity with horses.*

affix [verb: **affixes, affixing, affixed**] to attach something: *Affix stamp here.*

afflict [verb: **afflicts, afflicting, afflicted**] if an illness afflicts someone, they suffer from it: *This is a disease that can afflict anyone.*
♦ **affliction** [noun: **afflictions**] an illness or problem that makes someone miserable

affluence [noun] having a lot of money to spend: *There was greater affluence after the war.*

affluent [adjective] having a lot of money and possessions: *an affluent lifestyle*

afford [verb: **affords, affording, afforded**]
1 if you can afford something, you have enough money to pay for it: *I can't afford a new dress.* • *We couldn't afford to go abroad.*
2 if you can afford the time for something, you have enough time to do it: *I can't afford to stay any longer or I'll be late.*
♦ **affordable** [adjective] at a low enough price to buy

affront [verb: **affronts, affronting, affronted**] if you are affronted, you are offended and angry: *Brenda was affronted by his remark.*
[noun: **affronts**] a remark or action that offends someone

afloat [adverb] floating: *Donny held on to a piece of wood to stay afloat.*

afraid [adjective]
1 frightened: *There's no need to be afraid.* • *Small children are often afraid of dogs.* • *I was*

afraid that I'd fall. • *Don't be afraid to tell me if you don't understand.*
2 sorry: *I'm afraid I don't know.*

afresh [adverb] once again: *Throw that away and begin afresh.*

after [preposition]
1 following or later than something: *I'll do it after dinner.* • *Your name's after mine on the list.* • *It rained day after day.*
2 if you were named after someone, you were given their name: *Gordon was named after his uncle.*
3 to ask after someone is ask how they are: *Mrs Young was asking after you.*
4 if something happens **after all**, it happens in spite of everything that went before: *I decided to go to the party after all.*
[adverb] later: *Can you come the week after?*
[conjunction] following in time: *Mrs Shaw died after we moved.* • *After we'd said goodbye, we felt quite sad.*

after- [prefix] if a word starts with **after-**, it adds the meaning 'after' or 'later' to the word. For example, the *afternoon* is the part of the day after noon or midday

after-effects [plural noun] the bad things that follow on from something you do or something that happens: *the after-effects of the conflict*

afternoon [noun: **afternoons**] the time between midday and the evening
[adjective] happening in the afternoon: *afternoon classes*

aftershave [noun] a liquid for men to put on their skin after shaving

afterwards [adverb] later on: *He's busy now but I'll speak to him afterwards.*

again [adverb]
1 once more: *Do it again!*
2 to the place you started from: *Can we go home again now?*
3 on the other hand: *There again, I could be wrong.*
4 if you do something **again and again**, you do it a lot of times

against [preposition]
1 leaning on, touching or hitting something: *throwing a ball against the wall* • *sitting with his back against a tree*

2 competing with someone: *We're playing against you next.*
3 opposed to something: *I'm against the ban on hunting.* • *Smoking on the train is against the law.*

age [noun: **ages**]
1 someone's age is how old they are: *Zoe will start school at the age of four.*
2 an age is a very long time: *We had to wait an age for him to come out.* • *You took ages to finish.*
3 a time in history: *the Stone Age*
4 if someone **comes of age**, they become an adult
5 if someone is **under age**, they are not legally old enough do something: *You can't buy beer — you're under age.*
[verb: **ages, aging** or **ageing, aged**] to look older or to make someone look older: *She's aged a lot recently.* • *We'll age you with make-up for your part in the play.*
✦ **aged** [noun] **the aged** are old people
✦ **ageism** [noun] treating old people unfairly because of their age

ⓘ Aged is pronounced with two syllables: **ayj**-id.

agency [noun: **agencies**] an office or business that organizes things: *an employment agency*

agenda [noun: **agendas**] a list of things that will be discussed at a meeting: *What's on the agenda today?*

agent [noun: **agents**]
1 a spy: *a secret agent*
2 someone whose job is arranging things for someone else or for an organization: *The travel agent will send you the tickets before you leave.*
3 a cleaning agent is a substance that you use to clean things

aggravate [verb: **aggravates, aggravating, aggravated**] to make something worse: *Don't scratch or you'll simply aggravate the infection.*
✦ **aggravation** [noun] irritating kind of trouble: *That man has caused a lot of aggravation today.*

aggregate [noun: **aggregates**] a total

aggression [noun] a way of behaving that is angry and threatening

aggressive [adjective] angry and ready to attack

♦ **aggressively** [adverb] in a threatening way: *'What do you think you're looking at?' he asked aggressively.*

aggrieved [adjective] feeling that someone has been unfair to you

aghast [adjective] horrified

agile [adjective] good at moving about quickly and easily: *Those children were as agile as monkeys.*

♦ **agility** [noun] being able to move about and change direction quickly

agitate [verb: **agitates, agitating, agitated**]

1 something agitates you if it makes you nervous and worried: *This news will agitate her.*

2 to **agitate for** something is to try to get something or make something happen: *We must agitate for a change in the law.*

♦ **agitated** [adjective] nervous and worried: *I started to get agitated when nobody answered the door.*

♦ **agitation** [noun] getting nervous and upset: *She tried to hide her agitation.*

agnostic [noun: **agnostics**] someone who believes nobody can tell if God exists or not

ago [adverb] in the past: *I last saw Lily ten years ago.*

agog [adjective] excited and interested

agony [noun] very great pain: *You could see he was in agony.*

agoraphobia [noun] people who have agoraphobia are afraid of being in open spaces or of going outside at all

♦ **agoraphobic** [adjective] afraid of leaving a place that feels safe

agree [verb: **agrees, agreeing, agreed**]

1 to agree with someone is to think the same as them about something: *Don't you agree? • She never agrees with him about anything. • I agree with everything you've said.*

2 to agree to do something is to say that you will do what someone has asked you to: *I only agreed to come if you came too.*

3 if some food or drink does not agree with you, it upsets your stomach

♦ **agreeable** [adjective] pleasant

♦ **agreement** [noun: **agreements**]

1 when you make an agreement, you and someone else decide to do something: *These countries now have an agreement to work together for peace.*

2 agreement is when things such as opinions or answers are the same: *I am happy to say that we are in complete agreement about this.*

agricultural [adjective] to do with growing crops and rearing animals

agriculture [noun] growing crops and rearing animals

ahead [adverb] in front: *Run on ahead and tell them we're coming. • Our house is straight ahead. • We've got a long journey ahead of us.*

aid [noun]

1 help: *He can walk with the aid of a stick. • Mr Oliver came to our aid. • Many countries will send aid to the disaster area.*

2 if you collect money **in aid of** a charity, group or organization, you do it to help them: *a collection in aid of the crash victims*

[verb: **aids, aiding, aided**] to help someone

AIDS [noun] a condition that destroys the body's immune system. AIDS stands for Acquired Immune Deficiency Syndrome

ailment [noun: **ailments**] something wrong with you, like an illness

aim [verb: **aims, aiming, aimed**]

1 to point something such as a weapon at a particular person or thing: *Paul was aiming at the target but missed it completely.*

2 to aim to do something is to intend to do it: *We aim to help all our customers.*

[noun: **aims**]

1 your aim is what you are trying to do: *Here's a list of our aims for the year.*

2 if your aim is good, you can hit a target well

♦ **aimless** [adjective] having no goal or purpose: *an aimless stroll*

♦ **aimlessly** [adverb] without a reason: *walking aimlessly around the house*

air [noun]

1 the gases around us that we breathe in: *Kelly left the room to get some air. • The air carries the seeds for miles.*

2 an air of secrecy or mystery is a feeling that there is a secret or mystery
3 if you travel **by air**, you go in a plane or helicopter
4 if a programme is **on the air**, it is being broadcast on radio or television
5 if a decision is **up in the air**, it has not been definitely decided yet: *Our holiday plans are still up in the air.*
[verb: **airs, airing, aired**]
1 to air washing is to make it completely dry
2 to air a room is to let some fresh air into it
3 to air your views or opinions is to tell people what you think

airbag [noun: **airbags**] a bag that blows up like a balloon in front of a driver or passenger to protect them if their vehicle crashes

airbed [noun: **airbeds**] a mattress filled with air

airborne [adjective] moving in the air: *airborne diseases*

air-conditioned [adjective] an air-conditioned room or car has a system to keep it at a certain temperature

air conditioning [noun] a system of keeping a room at a certain temperature

aircraft [noun: **aircraft**] a vehicle that you can fly in

aircraft carrier [noun: **aircraft carriers**] a warship that aircraft can take off from and land on

air force [noun: **air forces**] the part of an army that uses aircraft

airgun [noun: **airguns**] a gun that fires using the power of compressed air

airless [adjective] an airless room is stuffy

airline [noun: **airlines**] a company that takes people to places by plane: *an airline ticket*

airlock [noun: **airlocks**]
1 a bubble in a pipe that stops liquid flowing through it
2 a compartment with two doors for getting in and out of a spaceship or submarine

airport [noun: **airports**] a place where passengers can get on and off aircraft

air raid [noun: **air raids**] an attack by aircraft

airship [noun: **airships**] a large balloon with engines for carrying things or people

airtight [adjective] made so that air cannot pass in or out: *an airtight container*

airy [adjective: **airier, airiest**]
1 with lots of fresh air: *an airy balcony*
2 not very serious: *an airy way of talking*

aisle [noun: **aisles**] the space that you can walk along between rows of seats or shelves

ajar [adverb] slightly open: *David left the door ajar on purpose.*

aka [abbreviation] short for **also known as**: *William H Bonney, aka Billy the Kid*

akimbo [adverb] if you stand with your arms akimbo, you have your hands on your hips and your elbows pointing outwards

alarm [noun: **alarms**]
1 an alarm is a way of warning people: *the fire alarm*
2 alarm is a sudden feeling of fear: *Freddie jumped back in alarm.*
[verb: **alarms, alarming, alarmed**] to frighten someone, especially suddenly
♦ **alarming** [adjective] scary: *an alarming sight*

alas [interjection] an old way of saying you are sad and regret something

albatross [noun: **albatrosses**] a large white sea bird

albino [noun: **albinos**] a person or animal with no natural colour in their hair, skin or eyes

album [noun: **albums**]
1 a book for keeping a collection of something such as photos, stamps or autographs
2 a collection of songs or pieces of music put on a CD, tape or record and given a title: *an old Beatles album*

albumen [noun] the white part of an egg

alcohol [noun] drinks like wine, beer and spirits, that can make you drunk if you drink too much of them
♦ **alcoholic** [adjective] containing alcohol: *alcoholic drinks*
[noun: **alcoholics**] an alcoholic is someone whose health is affected by regularly drinking too much alcohol

alcove [noun: **alcoves**] a space in a room where part of the wall is further back than the rest: *an alcove filled with shelves*

ale [noun: **ales**] a kind of beer

alert [adjective] wide awake and ready for action

[verb: **alerts, alerting, alerted**] to warn someone about a danger

[noun: **alerts**]

1 an alarm

2 if you are **on the alert**, you are ready to deal with possible problems

algae [plural noun] plants that grow near or in water and do not have stems, leaves or flowers, for example seaweed

> ⓘ **Algae** is the plural of **alga**. The singular, **alga**, is not often used.

algebra [noun] a type of mathematics that has letters and signs instead of numbers

alias [adverb] also known as: *Norman Cook, alias Fatboy Slim*

[noun: **aliases**] another name that someone uses: *She uses an alias when she travels abroad.*

alibi [noun: **alibis**] proof that someone could not have committed a particular crime, because they were somewhere else at the time: *Taylor has a great alibi — he was in prison when the robbery took place.*

alien [noun: **aliens**]

1 a foreigner

2 a creature from another planet

[adjective] strange: *an alien idea*

alight [adjective] on fire: *eyes alight with excitement*

[adverb] on fire: *She set the building alight.*

[verb: **alights, alighting, alighted**]

1 to get off a train or bus

2 to settle or land: *A seagull will always alight on the highest point.*

align [verb: **aligns, aligning, aligned**] to bring things into line with each other: *Align the words down the left side of the page.*

♦ **alignment** [noun] the arrangement of things in a straight line: *The wheels need to be in alignment to work properly.*

alike [adjective] like one another: *The twins aren't at all alike in character.*

[adverb] the same way: *Dad treats us both alike.*

alive [adjective]

1 living: *the greatest ballerina alive*

2 lively: *The whole town was alive with the news.*

3 if you are **alive to** something, you know about it: *We are all alive to the dangers of the situation.*

alkali [noun: **alkalis**] the type of chemical that behaves in the opposite way to acids and can cancel them out. It is used in substances such as soap and dye

♦ **alkaline** [adjective] containing an alkali

all [adjective]

1 every one: *All the children stood up.*

2 every part: *We ate all the cake.*

[pronoun]

1 every one: *I want to see them all.*

2 every part of something: *Don't spend it all.*

[adverb]

1 completely: *His shirt was all dirty.*

2 if you are **all in**, you are tired out: *We were all in after the race.*

3 if something is **all over**, it is finished: *I'll be glad when it's all over.*

4 if things are **all over** somewhere, they are in every part of it: *His clothes were all over the place.*

Allah [noun] the Muslim name for the creator of the world

allegation [noun: **allegations**] to make an allegation against someone is to claim that they have done something wrong

allege [verb: **alleges, alleging, alleged**] to say that someone has done something wrong: *The boys allege that they are being bullied.*

♦ **allegedly** [adverb] if something is allegedly true, people say it but there is no proof: *He allegedly stole money out of the till but he still works there.*

allegiance [noun] loyalty: *The soldiers all swear allegiance to their country.*

allergic [adjective] to be allergic to something is to become uncomfortable or ill because your body is sensitive to it: *an allergic reaction* • *I'm allergic to cats.*

allergy [noun: **allergies**] a condition where your body reacts badly to something you touch, breathe, eat or drink: *a peanut allergy*

alley [noun: **alleys**]

1 a narrow passage between buildings

2 a place where you can play games like skittles: *a bowling alley*

alliance [noun: **alliances**] an agreement between people or countries to be on the same side if there is an argument or war

alligator [noun: **alligators**] a large reptile like a crocodile, with thick skin, a long tail and large jaws

allocate [verb: **allocates, allocating, allocated**] to give someone something or part of something that is for them to use: *Now we'll allocate the rooms you will be staying in.*

♦ **allocation** [noun]
1 allocation is giving or sharing something out
2 an allocation is something that has been given out: *Both teams have the same allocation of tickets for the cup final.*

allot [verb: **allots, allotting, allotted**] to allot something is to share something out: *It was hard to finish the exam in the time allotted.*

♦ **allotment** [noun: **allotments**] an allotment is a small piece of land that someone can rent for growing vegetables

allow [verb: **allows, allowing, allowed**]
1 to allow someone to do something is to let them do it: *Will you allow me to come in now?*
2 to allow something is to let it happen: *We do not allow smoking in the house.*
3 to allow someone something is to give it to them: *Ben's parents allowed him £40 a week while he was a student.*
4 to **allow for** something is to take it into account in your plans or calculations: *Add 5% to allow for inflation.*

♦ **allowance** [noun: **allowances**]
1 the amount that anyone can have of something: *There's a baggage allowance that you mustn't go over.*
2 an amount of money that someone is given regularly: *Adam gets an allowance of £50 a month from his father.*
3 to **make allowances for** something is to expect less from someone because of it: *We'll make allowances for the fact that you've never done anything like this before.*

alloy [noun: **alloys**] a mixture of two or more metals

all right [adverb]
1 reasonably good: *The party was all right I suppose.*
2 safe or well: *I'm glad you're all right — we heard there had been an accident.*
3 satisfactory: *Is it all right if I go out tonight?*
[interjection] you can say 'all right' when you agree to something: *All right, I'll go then.*

allure [noun] something that you find attractive about a thing or person: *the allure of life at sea*
♦ **alluring** [adjective] tempting: *an alluring idea*

ally [noun: **allies**] a country, business or person that is joined to or supports another
[verb: **allies, allying, allied**] if a country or business is allied to another, they are joined as partners
⇒ **alliance**

almighty [adjective]
1 very powerful: *almighty God*
2 very big: *There was an almighty row.*
[noun] **the Almighty** is God

almond [noun: **almonds**] a long narrow nut with a hard shell

almost [adverb] very nearly but not quite: *She is almost ten years old.*

aloft [adverb] high up: *Bernard held the cup aloft.*

alone [adjective] without anyone else: *Kate was alone in the house.*
[adverb]
1 not with others: *I live alone.*
2 without other things: *The ticket alone will use up all my money.*

along [preposition]
1 from one end to the other: *Shona walked along the street.*
2 on the length of: *Hari's house is somewhere along this street.*
[adverb]
1 onwards: *Move along, please.*
2 to a particular place: *I'll come along later.*
3 **along with** means together with: *We'd packed drinks along with the sandwiches.*

alongside [preposition] beside: *A police car pulled up alongside us.*

aloof [adjective] staying apart from other people and not being interested in them

Aa

aloud [adverb] so that someone can hear: *It's much slower to count aloud.*

alp [noun: **alps**] a high mountain, especially one in or near Switzerland
→ **alpine**

alphabet [noun: **alphabets**] all the letters of a language arranged in a particular order
♦ **alphabetical** [adjective]
1 with the first letters in the order of the alphabet: *an alphabetical index*
2 something that is arranged **in alphabetical order** is arranged so that words beginning with 'A' come first, then 'B' and so on: *This dictionary is in alphabetical order.*
♦ **alphabetically** [adverb] with the letters in the order of the alphabet: *The list has been arranged alphabetically.*

alpine [adjective] to do with high parts of mountains: *an alpine meadow*

already [adverb]
1 before a particular time: *I had already gone when Bob arrived.*
2 now, before the expected time: *Is he here already?*

ⓘ If you write **all ready** as two words, then it means 'completely prepared', for example: *Are you all ready to go?*

alright [adverb] another spelling of **all right**

ⓘ It is a good idea to write this as two words, as many people think the spelling **alright** is wrong.

alsatian [noun: **alsatians**] a large breed of dog with a short brown and black coat. An alsatian can also be called a **German shepherd dog**

also [adverb] in addition: *Bernie speaks French and also Italian.* • *My sister also attends this school.*

altar [noun: **altars**] a raised place or table for offerings to a god

alter [verb: **alters, altering, altered**]
1 to alter something is to change it: *Can you alter this skirt to fit me?*
2 to alter is to change: *The town has altered a lot recently.*
♦ **alteration** [noun: **alterations**]
1 an alteration is a change: *There have been a few alterations to our plans.*

2 alteration is change: *The museum is closed for alteration.*

alternate [verb: **alternates, alternating, alternated**] to do or happen in turn: *Rain and sun alternated throughout the day.*
[adjective] alternate things are in turn, first one then the other: *a fence with alternate stripes of red and green*

alternative [adjective] giving you another choice or possibility: *If you cannot come on Tuesday you can suggest an alternative day.*
[noun: **alternatives**] another possibility: *Is there an alternative to chips on the menu?*
♦ **alternatively** [adverb] you can use 'alternatively' when you are offering another suggestion: *Alternatively, we could go to the cinema.*

alternative medicine [noun] treating diseases with methods such as acupuncture and homeopathy rather than conventional drugs and surgery

alternator [noun: **alternators**] an electricity generator that produces an electric current that keeps changing its direction

although [conjunction] in spite of the fact that: *I did go to the show, although I'd said I wouldn't.*

altitude [noun: **altitudes**] the altitude of a place is its height above the level of the sea: *We are flying at an altitude of 20,000 metres.*

alto [noun: **altos**]
1 the lowest singing voice for a woman
2 the highest singing voice for a man

altogether [adverb]
1 completely: *I'm not altogether happy.*
2 in total: *We raised £100 altogether.*

ⓘ If you write **all together** as two words, it has the different meaning of 'together in a group', for example, *It's good that we're all together again.*

aluminium [noun] a very light metal that is silver-coloured

ⓘ **Aluminium** is spelled **aluminum** in the United States, and pronounced a-**loom**-in-um.

always [adverb]
1 at all times: *I always work hard.*
2 continually: *I'm always getting this wrong.*

3 forever: *I'll always remember that day.*

Alzheimer's disease [noun] a serious illness that affects your brain and makes you forget things and become more and more confused. It is often known as just **Alzheimer's**

am[1] [verb]

1 the form of the verb **be** in the present tense that you use with **I**: *I am happy.*

2 am is also used as a helping verb along with a main verb: *I am going out.*

am[2] or **a.m.** [abbreviation] **am** is added after the time to show that the time is in the morning, for example *7am.* Look up and compare **pm**

(i) **am** is short for **ante meridiem**, which is Latin for 'before midday'.

amalgamate [verb: **amalgamates, amalgamating, amalgamated**] to join with something else: *The two firms amalgamated last year.*

◆ **amalgamation** [noun]

1 amalgamation is the joining of two or more things, especially organizations

2 an amalgamation is two or more things joined together

amass [verb: **amasses, amassing, amassed**] to collect a large quantity of something: *The family has amassed a lot of furniture over the years.*

amateur [noun: **amateurs**]

1 someone who takes part in a sport without being paid for it

2 someone who does something because they enjoy it, not because they are paid for it: *Holly's an excellent actress even though she's an amateur.*

[adjective]

1 not paid: *an amateur disc-jockey*

2 not involving payment: *amateur athletics*

amaze [verb: **amazes, amazing, amazed**] to surprise someone very much: *It amazes me how stupid you can be.*

◆ **amazed** [adjective] very surprised: *We were all amazed.*

◆ **amazement** [noun] great surprise: *To my amazement, Dad agreed with me.*

◆ **amazing** [adjective] very surprising: *an amazing sight*

◆ **amazingly** [adverb] very surprisingly: *The cake was amazingly good.* • *Amazingly, it didn't rain for our picnic.*

ambassador [noun: **ambassadors**] an official who represents their own government in a foreign country: *the British ambassador to Japan*

amber [noun]

1 a clear yellow-brown substance that is used to make jewellery and may contain fossils

2 the colour of the middle traffic light, between red and green

ambi- [prefix] if a word starts with **ambi-**, it is to do with both parts or two of something. For example, if you are *ambivalent* you have two different feelings at the same time about something

ambidextrous [adjective] an ambidextrous person can use either of their hands equally well

ambience [noun] the ambience of a place is the atmosphere it has: *The restaurant has a pleasant ambience.*

◆ **ambient** [adjective] to do with the atmosphere in a place: *The ambient temperature is twenty degrees Celsius.*

ambiguity [noun: **ambiguities**]

1 an ambiguity is something with more than one meaning

2 ambiguity is uncertainty

ambiguous [adjective] with two possible meanings: *This question is ambiguous.*

◆ **ambiguously** [adverb] without one clear meaning: *The book ends ambiguously — we have to decide ourselves what really happened.*

ambition [noun: **ambitions**]

1 an ambition is something that you have wanted to do for a long time: *I have an ambition to see the pyramids.*

2 ambition is wanting to be very successful

◆ **ambitious** [adjective]

1 an ambitious person wants to be very successful in life

2 an ambitious project is one that you know will be difficult for you

amble [verb: **ambles, ambling, ambled**] to walk slowly in a relaxed way

ambulance [noun: **ambulances**] a vehicle

Aa

for taking sick or injured people to hospital

ambush [noun: **ambushes**] an ambush is when someone hides so that they can make a surprise attack on someone else
[verb: **ambushes, ambushing, ambushed**] to attack someone from a hiding place

amend [verb: **amends, amending, amended**] to improve something you have said or written by making small changes
◆ **amendment** [noun: **amendments**] a slight change to something such as a law
◆ **amends** [plural noun] if you **make amends**, you make up for having done something wrong: Now we'll see if he can make amends for letting in that goal.

amenity [noun: **amenities**] something such as a shop or park that makes life easier or more pleasant for people in that area

amethyst [noun: **amethysts**] a precious purple or violet stone: a necklace of amethysts

amiable [adjective] friendly and relaxed: a very amiable man
◆ **amiably** [adverb] in a friendly, relaxed way

amicable [adjective] you reach an amicable agreement without any argument
◆ **amicably** [adverb] in a friendly way

amid or **amidst** [adverb] in the middle of: a moment of calm amid great excitement

amiss [adverb] if something is amiss, there is something wrong

ammonia [noun] a substance that can be a gas or a liquid and has a very strong smell

ammunition [noun] bullets, bombs or shells that you can fire from a weapon

amnesia [noun] amnesia is losing your memory

amnesty [noun: **amnesties**] a period of time when the usual punishments for crimes do not apply: an amnesty for people who owe parking fines

amok [adverb] if someone **runs amok**, they go mad and do a lot of damage

among or **amongst** [preposition]
1 surrounded by or in the middle of: You are among friends.
2 one of a group of: Among all my books, this is my favourite.
3 in shares or parts: Divide the chocolate among yourselves.

ⓘ If you are talking about more than two people, you should use **among** or **amongst**, for example The work was divided **among** the pupils.
If you are talking about two people, you should use **between**, for example Carl and Sue divided the sweets **between** them.

amount [noun: **amounts**] a quantity: a small amount of money • large amounts of land
[verb: **amounts, amounting, amounted**]
1 to amount to a particular number is to add up to that much: What I've spent amounts to exactly $10.
2 if one thing amounts to another, it is just about the same thing: His speech amounted to a description of how clever he was.

amp [noun: **amps**]
1 the usual word for an **ampere**, the unit used to measure how strong an electric current is
2 a short form of the word **amplifier**

ampersand [noun: **ampersands**] the sign &, which means 'and'

amphibian [noun: **amphibians**]
1 an animal that lives on land and in water: Frogs are amphibians.
2 a vehicle that can travel on land and on water
◆ **amphibious** [adjective] able to go or live on land and in water

amphitheatre [noun: **amphitheatres**] a theatre that has seats in a circle around an area in the centre

ample [adjective] plenty or more than enough: We had ample opportunity to ask questions.
→ **amply**

amplifier [noun: **amplifiers**] a machine that makes sounds from a musical instrument or sound system louder

amplify [verb: **amplifies, amplifying, amplified**] to make something louder

amply [adverb] very well or even more than necessary: We were amply rewarded with tea and chocolate cake.

amputate [verb: **amputates, amputating, amputated**] to cut off a part of the body
◆ **amputation** [noun: **amputations**]

1 amputation is cutting off part of the body

2 an amputation is an operation to cut off part of the body

amuse [verb: **amuses, amusing, amused**]
1 to make someone laugh
2 to keep someone happy for a while: *Would you amuse the children for half an hour?*
♦ **amusement** [noun: **amusements**]
1 amusement is the feeling that makes you laugh
2 amusement is entertainment: *What did you do for amusement on holiday?*
3 an amusement is a machine or activity that you enjoy: *There were amusements, food stalls and talent shows.*

an [adjective] you use **an** instead of **a** before words beginning with a vowel or 'h' when it is not pronounced: *an elephant • an honest person*

anaemia [noun] a condition where someone does not have enough red blood cells and looks pale
♦ **anaemic** [adjective]
1 suffering from anaemia
2 looking pale or ill

anaesthesia [noun] giving someone a drug to stop them feeling any pain

anaesthetic [noun: **anaesthetics**] a drug that stops you feeling pain or makes you unconscious: *The operation will be carried out under general anaesthetic.*
♦ **anaesthetist** [noun: **anaesthetists**] a doctor whose job is to give people anaesthetics

anagram [noun: **anagrams**] a word or sentence that has the same letters as another word or sentence, but in a different order. For example, *tape* is an anagram of *peat*

analogue [adjective] an analogue watch or clock has hands that move around a clock face to show the time

analogy [noun: **analogies**] something that is similar to something else and therefore helps to explain it

analyse [verb: **analyses, analysing, analysed**] to examine the different parts of something: *We are looking for someone who can quickly analyse and evaluate data.*
♦ **analysis** [noun: **analyses**] an examination

of the different parts of something
♦ **analyst** [noun: **analysts**]
1 someone who examines the different parts of something
2 someone whose job is to talk to a person and try to find out what is making them unhappy

anarchist [noun: **anarchists**] someone who believes it isn't necessary to have any government in a country

anarchy [noun] a situation where people do not obey laws and there is no organization

anatomy [noun] all the parts of the body

ancestor [noun: **ancestors**] your ancestors are all the past members of your family
♦ **ancestral** [adjective] belonging to someone's family in the past: *the Duke's ancestral home*
♦ **ancestry** [noun] your ancestry is your family's past: *We can trace our ancestry back to the twelfth century.*

anchor [noun: **anchors**] a heavy piece of metal on a rope or chain that is attached to a boat or ship and that stops it from moving away
[verb: **anchors, anchoring, anchored**]
1 to drop the anchor of a boat or ship to stop it moving away
2 to fix something firmly to the spot
♦ **anchorage** [noun: **anchorages**] a place where ships can stop

anchovy [noun: **anchovies**] a type of small fish with a very salty taste

ancient [adjective]
1 belonging to a very long time ago: *ancient history*
2 very old

and [conjunction]
1 a word that is used to join parts of sentences: *We'll have bread and butter. • pink and blue striped paper • Go and get ready.*
2 plus: *2 and 2 make 4*

android [noun: **androids**] a robot that looks like a human being

anecdote [noun: **anecdotes**] a short story that someone tells, often about something that happened to them: *a very funny speech, full of anecdotes about his journey*

anemone [noun: **anemones**] a kind of flower that often grows in woodland

Aa

angel [noun: **angels**]
1 a messenger from God
2 a very good person
♦ **angelic** [adjective] very beautiful and good
anger [noun] the violent feeling you get about someone or something that annoys you
[verb: **angers, angering, angered**] to make someone feel angry
angle [noun]
1 the shape that is made at the point where two straight lines meet
2 a point of view: *What's your angle on this?*
[verb: **angles, angling, angled**] to try to get something by making hints: *Did you hear her angling to borrow my new coat?*
♦ **angler** [noun: **anglers**] someone who enjoys fishing with a fishing-rod
Anglican [adjective] to do with or belonging to the Church of England
[noun: **Anglicans**] a member of the Church of England
angling [noun] the sport of fishing with a fishing-rod
Anglo-Saxon [noun: **Anglo-Saxons**]
1 Anglo-Saxons were the peoples who came to live in England and parts of Scotland in the 5th century
2 Old English, the English language before about 1150
[adjective] belonging to or to do with the Anglo-Saxon people or their language, Old English
angrily [adverb] in an angry way: *A young woman came in, shouting angrily.*
angry [adjective: **angrier, angriest**] cross or very cross: *Then Mike got very angry.* • *an angry crowd* • *The second article made us even angrier.*
anguish [noun] a terrible feeling of unhappiness and suffering
♦ **anguished** [adjective] miserable and suffering: *an anguished look*
angular [adjective] an angular body or face is thin and pointed
animal [noun: **animals**]
1 a living being that can feel and move: *Humans and insects — we're all animals.*
2 a living being that is not a human: *a hospital for sick animals* • *a pet animal*

animated [adjective]
1 in an animated film, things appear to move and be alive when they are really only pictures or objects
2 behaving or talking in a lively way: *He had never seen them so animated.*
♦ **animatedly** [adverb] in a lively way
animation [noun: **animations**]
1 an animation is a film where pictures or objects appear to move by themselves
2 animation is energy and liveliness
♦ **animator** [noun: **animators**] someone who makes films from drawings or objects that are moved around
animosity [noun] a feeling of strong dislike towards someone
aniseed [noun] a seed that tastes like liquorice and is used in making sweets, drinks and medicines
ankle [noun: **ankles**] the joint where your foot joins your leg
annex or **annexe** [noun: **annexes**] an extra part of a building that may be added on to it or may be in a separate place
[verb: **annexes, annexing, annexed**] to annex something such as land is to take it and use it like your own

ⓘ The spelling **annexe**, with an **e** at the end, can only be used for the noun. The verb is always spelt **annex**.

annihilate [verb: **annihilates, annihilating, annihilated**] to destroy somebody or something completely
♦ **annihilation** [noun] destroying somebody or something completely
anniversary [noun: **anniversaries**] a day that has the same date as an event in the past: *a wedding anniversary* • *Today is the anniversary of the King's death.*
announce [verb: **announces, announcing, announced**] to tell everyone something: *Have they announced their engagement yet?* • *The minister has announced that he is retiring.*
♦ **announcement** [noun: **announcements**] something that everybody is told, either in a special speech or on a notice: *Listen everyone; I want to make an announcement.* • *the wedding*

announcements in the daily paper

• **announcer** [noun: **announcers**] someone who introduces programmes on television or the radio

annoy [verb: **annoys, annoying, annoyed**] to annoy someone is to make them feel rather angry: *The way she never listens to me really annoys me.*

• **annoyance** [noun: **annoyances**]
1 annoyance is a feeling of irritation: *a look of annoyance*
2 an annoyance is something that irritates you

• **annoyed** [adjective] rather angry: *annoyed that it was raining* • *feeling annoyed about being kept waiting*

• **annoying** [adjective] making you feel rather angry: *an annoying habit* • *Jo can be so annoying!*

annual [adjective]
1 an annual event happens once every year: *an annual meeting of shareholders*
2 an annual amount is the amount calculated over one year: *annual rainfall* • *What is your annual income?*

[noun: **annuals**]
1 a book that is published every year
2 a plant that lives for only one year

• **annually** [adverb] happening once every year

anoint [verb: **anoints, anointing, anointed**] to put oil on someone's head in a ceremony as a sign that they are specially chosen for something

anon [noun] people sometimes sign a note or letter as 'anon' if they do not want to their proper name to be known

anonymous [adjective]
1 an anonymous letter or book is written by an unknown writer
2 an anonymous telephone call is made by someone who does not give their name

• **anonymously** [adverb] by someone who does not give their name: *The money has been given anonymously.*

anorak [noun: **anoraks**] a waterproof jacket, usually with a hood

anorexia [noun] an illness in which someone refuses to eat and becomes so thin that they might die

• **anorexic** [adjective] suffering from anorexia and very thin

another [adjective]
1 one more: *Have another piece of chocolate.*
2 a different: *Another day we'll walk further.*
[pronoun]
1 one more: *He had two gold medals and now he has another.*
2 a different one: *If that's broken, use another.*

answer [noun: **answers**]
1 an answer is what you reply when someone asks you a question
2 the answer to a problem is the solution
[verb: **answers, answering, answered**]
1 to reply when someone asks you a question or sends a letter: *Answer each question on a different page.* • *Answer me now please.* • *I'm just going to answer his letter.*
2 to pick up the phone when it rings: *A child answered the telephone.*
3 to open the door when someone rings or knocks: *Would you answer the door please?*
4 if you **answer back**, you are cheeky or rude to someone who has told you off

answerphone or **answering machine** [noun: **answerphones** or **answering machines**] a machine that automatically answers your phone and allows people to leave messages for you

ant [noun: **ants**] a tiny insect that usually has no wings

antagonism [noun] a feeling of wanting to fight against someone or an idea

• **antagonistic** [adjective] wanting to fight or argue with someone or something

• **antagonize** or **antagonise** [verb: **antagonizes, antagonizing, antagonized**] to make someone want to fight or argue with you

ante- [prefix] if a word starts with **ante-**, it often adds the meaning 'before' to the word. For example, an *anteroom* is a room you go into before you enter a larger room

anteater [noun: **anteaters**] an animal with a long nose and no teeth, that mainly eats ants

antelope [noun: **antelope** or **antelopes**] an animal like a deer, that has long horns and runs very fast

antenatal [adjective] to do with the time

when a woman is pregnant, before the baby is born: *antenatal classes*

antenna [noun: **antennae** or **antennas**]
1 a long thin feeler on the head of an insect or shellfish
2 an aerial, for example, for a television

(i) The plural of **antenna** when it means 'a feeler' is **antennae** (pronounced an-**ten**-ee). The plural form when it means 'an aerial' is **antennas**.

anthem [noun: **anthems**] a song that praises someone or something, for example a national anthem, which praises a country or its ruler

ant-hill [noun: **ant-hills**] a pile of earth that ants build up over their nest

anthology [noun: **anthologies**] a book of stories, poems or songs by different writers

anthropology [noun] the study of the way human beings live

anti- [prefix] if a word starts with **anti-**, it often adds the meaning 'against' to the word. For example, *anti-war* means against war

antibiotic [noun: **antibiotics**] a medicine that fights bacteria that can cause infections: *Penicillin is an antibiotic.*

antibody [noun: **antibodies**] a substance that your body produces in your blood to fight harmful bacteria

anticipate [verb: **anticipates, anticipating, anticipated**] to anticipate something is to expect it to happen and even to do something about it before it happens: *We don't anticipate any problems.* • *A couple of reporters had anticipated his early arrival.*
◆ **anticipation** [noun]
1 anticipation is excitement about something that is going to happen
2 if you act **in anticipation of** something, you do it because you expect that thing to happen: *The school has closed in anticipation of the heavy snow forecast for tomorrow.*

anticlimax [noun: **anticlimaxes**]
1 an anticlimax is a dull end to an exciting story
2 you get a feeling of anticlimax when some excitement is over and things calm down again

anticlockwise [adverb] going in the opposite direction to the hands of a clock: *Turn the top of the bottle anticlockwise.*

[adjective] in the opposite direction to the hands of a clock: *an anticlockwise movement*

antics [plural noun] someone's antics are the funny things that they do

antidote [noun: **antidotes**] a medicine that stops a poison being harmful

antifreeze [noun] a chemical that you can add to a liquid such as the water in a car radiator to stop it from freezing

antihistamine [noun: **antihistamines**] a drug that you take if you have an allergy or hay fever

antiperspirant [noun: **antiperspirants**] a substance that stops you sweating

antiquated [adjective] old-fashioned

antique [noun: **antiques**] an object that is old and valuable: *a collector of antiques*
[adjective] old and valuable

antiseptic [noun: **antiseptics**] a substance that kills germs

antisocial [adjective]
1 antisocial behaviour is unpleasant or harmful to other people
2 antisocial people do not enjoy being with other people

antler [noun: **antlers**] a horn that divides like branches and grows on the head of a deer, especially a stag

antonym [noun: **antonyms**] a word that means the opposite of another word. For example, *big* is an antonym of *small*. Look up and compare **synonym**

anus [noun] the opening in your bottom through which you get rid of solid waste from your body

anvil [noun: **anvils**] a heavy metal block that a blacksmith holds hot metal against while he is hammering it into shape

anxiety [noun: **anxieties**]
1 anxiety is worrying, especially about what may happen
2 an anxiety is something you are worried about

anxious [adjective]
1 worried: *an anxious face*
2 nervous and uncomfortable: *an anxious time*
3 keen: *I'm anxious to get there on time to get a good seat.*

Aa

✦ **anxiously** [adverb] in a worried way: *He looked anxiously at his watch.*

any [adjective]
1 every: *Any child would know that answer.*
2 one, but not a particular one: *It'll be here any day now.*
3 some: *Have we got any sweets?*
[adverb] at all: *Are you feeling any better?*
[pronoun]
1 one: *Ask any of them.*
2 some: *We haven't got any left.*

anybody [pronoun]
1 any person at all: *Anybody is allowed to enter.*
2 an important person: *Don't listen to her — she isn't anybody.*

anyhow [adverb]
1 anyway: *I missed lunch but I wasn't hungry anyhow.*
2 in an untidy, careless way: *The books had been left anyhow all over the floor.*

anyone [pronoun] any person at all: *There isn't anyone left.*

anything [pronoun] something of any kind: *He hasn't eaten anything.* • *Did Louise say anything?* • *Has anything happened?*

anyway [adverb]
1 in any case: *Leon couldn't go with me but I enjoyed the party anyway.*
2 a word you use to change the subject in a conversation: *Anyway, how have you been lately?*

anywhere [adverb] in or to any place: *I'm not going anywhere.* • *I can't find my keys anywhere.*
[pronoun] any place: *Anywhere would be better than this.*

ⓘ **Any place** (two words) is used in American English instead of **anywhere**.

apart [adverb]
1 separated by distance or time: *with your feet apart* • *two classes, a week apart*
2 into pieces: *Take the lamp apart.*
3 **apart from** means except for: *Apart from us, nobody's interested.*

apartheid [noun] the system that used to operate in South Africa, where black and white people were treated differently by law

apartment [noun: **apartments**]
1 a set of rooms on one level of a building
2 a room in a building

apathetic [adjective] someone who is apathetic is not interested in anything

apathy [noun] not being interested in anything

ape [noun: **apes**] a kind of monkey that is large and has no tail
[verb: **apes, aping, aped**] to copy what someone else does

apex [noun: **apexes** or **apices**] the top point of something, especially a triangle

aphid [noun: **aphids**] a small insect, for example a greenfly, that feeds on plants

apiary [noun: **apiaries**] a place where bees are kept

apiece [adverb] an old-fashioned word for **each**: *five packets at £1 apiece*

apologetic [adjective] if you are apologetic, you show that you are sorry for something you have done
✦ **apologetically** [adverb] showing that you are sorry

apologize or **apologise** [verb: **apologizes, apologizing, apologized**] to say sorry for doing something wrong: *I had to apologize to my boss for being late.*
✦ **apology** [noun: **apologies**] an apology is when you say you are sorry for something you have done: *a public apology for his disgraceful behaviour*

apostle [noun: **apostles**] one of the first twelve followers of Jesus Christ

apostrophe [noun: **apostrophes**] the mark (') that shows where a letter or letters have been missed out, for example in *don't* or *he's*. It also shows who owns something when it is used with *'s* as in *Nicky's desk*

appal [verb: **appals, appalling, appalled**] if you are appalled, you are shocked because something is so bad: *I was appalled by her language.*
✦ **appalling** [adjective]
1 shocking: *an appalling accident*
2 very bad: *appalling weather*

apparatus [noun] the equipment that you need for a particular task: *breathing apparatus for the divers*

apparent [adjective]
1 easy to see: *Then, for no apparent reason, he began to cry.*
2 appearing to be true: *Make a list of the apparent problems.*
◆ **apparently** [adverb] it appears or seems: *David is apparently off sick today.*

appeal [verb: **appeals, appealing, appealed**]
1 to appeal for something is to ask everyone for what you badly need: *The police have appealed to the public for more information.*
2 to appeal to someone is to be attractive to them: *Bungee jumping doesn't appeal to me one bit.*
3 to appeal against a decision is to ask someone to change their mind
[noun: **appeals**]
1 an appeal is a request for something you want very much
2 appeal is what makes a thing or person attractive and interesting: *I don't understand the appeal of stamp collecting.*
3 an appeal is asking someone to change a decision, especially in a court of law: *His appeal was rejected.*

appear [verb: **appears, appearing, appeared**]
1 a thing or person appears when you can suddenly see them: *Then Greta appeared round the corner.* • *A black mark has appeared on the wall.*
2 to seem: *Jill appeared to be getting very cross.* • *You don't appear to be ready yet.*
3 to have to be in front of other people, for example in a court of law or on the stage: *Tom is appearing as Hamlet at the Globe Theatre.* • *The president had to appear before the finance committee.*
◆ **appearance** [noun: **appearances**]
1 arriving: *Until Mina's appearance, the evening had been very dull.*
2 the way a thing or person looks: *Change your appearance with a new hairstyle.*
3 being in front of people for a performance or interview: *This is Mel's second appearance in a comedy.*
4 appearances are the way things seem to be, but possibly not the way they really are

appease [verb: **appeases, appeasing, appeased**] to make someone feel better by giving them what they want

appendicitis [noun] an illness where your appendix is painful and usually has to be removed

appendix [noun: **appendices** or **appendixes**]
1 a small tube inside your body that is a useless part of the human intestines
2 an extra section at the end of a book or document that gives more details about something

---

ⓘ The plural of **appendix** when it is a part of the body is **appendixes**: *The doctor removed two appendixes that day.*
The plural when it is part of a book is **appendices**: *The appendices begin on page 430.*

---

appetite [noun: **appetites**] your appetite, usually for food, is how much you want some: *Elly has lost her appetite since she's been ill.*
◆ **appetizer** or **appetiser** [noun: **appetizers**] something small to eat or drink before a meal
◆ **appetizing** or **appetising** [adjective] making you want to eat: *an appetizing smell*

applaud [verb: **applauds, applauding, applauded**] to clap your hands to show your approval of someone or something: *The audience applauded Nancy loudly.* • *For a moment we didn't think anyone would applaud.*
◆ **applause** [noun] clapping

apple [noun: **apples**]
1 a hard, round fruit with red, green or yellow skin
2 if someone is **the apple of your eye**, you are very proud of them

appliance [noun: **appliances**] a piece of equipment: *kitchen appliances*

applicable [adjective]
1 a rule that is applicable to you applies to you
2 a question that is not applicable to you is one that you do not have to answer

applicant [noun: **applicants**] someone who applies for something such as a job or university place

application [noun: **applications**]
1 an application is a letter or a form asking for something such as a job
2 application is an effort to do something well: *He could pass the exam with a little more application.*
3 when you put something such as paint or cream on a surface: *Let the paint dry between applications.*
4 an application is a computer program that does a particular kind of job, for example, a word processing program

applicator [noun: **applicators**] a tool or device that helps you to spread a product in exactly the right place: *Spread the glue with the applicator on the top.*

applied [adjective] an applied science is one that has a practical use

apply [verb: **applies, applying, applied**]
1 to ask for something such as a job, usually by a letter or a form: *Maria's applying to university this year.*
2 to apply something to a surface is to put or spread it on: *Apply the cream to your skin three times a day.*
3 if something applies to you, it affects you: *Do these rules apply to all of us?*
4 to **apply yourself** is to try hard

appoint [verb: **appoints, appointing, appointed**]
1 to give someone a job: *The committee appointed Mrs Burns as manager.*
2 an appointed time or place is one arranged in advance: *Lizzie was the only one there at the appointed time.*
♦ appointment [noun: **appointments**]
1 an appointment is a time and place that you must meet someone: *I have a doctor's appointment at 2 o'clock tomorrow.*
2 an appointment is a job
3 choosing someone for a job: *the appointment of a new music teacher*

appraisal [noun: **appraisals**] a method of estimating how well someone is doing in their job

appreciate [verb: **appreciates, appreciating, appreciated**]
1 to think that something is valuable, useful, important or kind: *I'd appreciate your advice about this.*

2 to understand something: *Martha appreciates that she won't live forever.*
3 to become more valuable: *The painting has appreciated in value over the years.*
♦ appreciation [noun]
1 understanding: *the appreciation of art*
2 thanks: *a gift in appreciation of your help*
3 increasing value
♦ appreciative [adjective] an appreciative person shows that they are grateful or pleased by something: *an appreciative audience*

apprehension [noun]
1 worry about the future: *in a state of apprehension*
2 catching someone, for example a criminal

apprehensive [adjective] nervous and afraid: *apprehensive about the future*
♦ apprehensively [adverb] in a nervous way

apprentice [noun: **apprentices**] someone who is learning how to do a skilled job from someone who can already do it
♦ apprenticeship [noun: **apprenticeships**] the time when someone is learning their job

approach [verb: **approaches, approaching, approached**]
1 to come towards a place, person or thing: *approach the animals very slowly • a plane approaching Paris from the south*
2 to go to someone with a suggestion: *If you want more money you'll have to approach your boss.*
[noun: **approaches**]
1 the way up to a building: *a tree-lined approach*
2 a way of trying to deal with something: *the logical approach*
♦ approachable [adjective] an approachable person is easy to talk to

appropriate [adjective] suitable: *Please wear appropriate clothing.*

approval [noun] approval is when someone thinks something is good or satisfactory: *We need your approval before we can send the money.*

approve [verb: **approves, approving, approved**]
1 to **approve of** something is to think it is

good: *He did not approve of noisy children.*
2 to approve something is to agree to it

approximate [adjective] not exact: *Can you tell me the approximate number of chairs we'll need?*

♦ **approximately** [adverb] more or less: *approximately one thousand people*

apricot [noun: **apricots**]
1 a small orange-coloured fruit with a soft skin and a stone inside
2 a soft orange colour

April [noun] the fourth month of the year, after March and before May

apron [noun: **aprons**] you wear an apron if you want to keep the front of your clothes clean or dry

apt [adjective]
1 likely: *apt to fly into a temper*
2 suitable: *an apt description*
→ **aptly**

aptitude [noun] talent: *Sylvia shows plenty of aptitude for the piano.*

aptly [adverb] suitably: *a house by the river, very aptly named 'River's Edge'*

aqua- [prefix] if a word starts with **aqua-**, it has something to do with water. For example, an *aqualung* is a piece of equipment that lets you breathe under water

aquamarine [adjective] blue-green

aquarium [noun: **aquariums** or **aquaria**] a glass tank or a building, for example in a zoo, for keeping fish or water animals

aquatic [adjective] to do with water: *aquatic sports • Aquatic plants live in water.*

aqueduct [noun: **aqueducts**] a bridge that carries a river or canal across a valley

arable [adjective] arable land is farming land where crops grow

arbitrary [adjective] an arbitrary decision or choice is one that you make without a good reason: *Our choice of hotel was purely arbitrary.*

arbitrate [verb: **arbitrates, arbitrating, arbitrated**] to be a judge when people are arguing

♦ **arbitration** [noun] trying to settle an argument between other people

arc [noun: **arcs**] a curve that is like part of a circle

arcade [noun: **arcades**] a covered walk, especially with shops along the side

arch [noun: **arches**]
1 the curved top of a doorway or between the supports of a bridge
2 the curved part underneath your foot
[verb: **arches, arching, arched**] to curve over: *a cat arching its back*

arch- [prefix] if a word starts with **arch-**, it adds the meaning 'most important' to the word. For example, your *arch-enemy* is your main enemy

archaeological [adjective] to do with studying things left by people in the past

archaeologist [noun: **archaeologists**] someone who studies things left in the ground by people in the past

archaeology [noun] the study of what is on or in the ground, left there by people in the past

archaic [adjective] dating from a very long time ago

archangel [noun: **archangels**] a chief angel

archbishop [noun: **archbishops**] a chief bishop

archer [noun: **archers**] someone who shoots with a bow and arrow

archery [noun] the sport of shooting with a bow and arrow

archipelago [noun: **archipelagoes** or **archipelagos**] a group of small islands

architect [noun: **architects**] someone whose job is to design buildings

♦ **architectural** [adjective] to do with the way buildings are designed: *architectural features like pillars and arches*

♦ **architecturally** [adverb] in a way that is to do with building design: *Architecturally, the city is very interesting.*

♦ **architecture** [noun]
1 designing buildings: *Safari had given up architecture to become an artist.*
2 a style of building: *Norman architecture*

archives [plural noun]
1 the historical records of a place or organization: *Search the archives for some information about the fire in 1900.*
2 a place on a computer hard disk where files that are not often used are stored

ardent [adjective] having strong feelings: *an ardent football fan*

arduous [adjective] difficult or hard-going: *an arduous climb to the top of the hill*

are [verb]
1 the form of the verb **be** in the present tense that is used with **you, we, they** and plural nouns: *We are all here today.* • *What are the best places to visit?*
2 are is also used as a helping verb along with a main verb: *We are leaving tomorrow.*

area [noun: **areas**]
1 a part or region: *a children's play area* • *There are a lot of farms in this area.*
2 a part of a subject or activity: *Education is an area that Gavin knows a lot about.*
3 the size of a surface, that you measure in **square** units: *A carpet that is 5 metres by 5 metres has an area of 25 square metres.*

arena [noun: **arenas**] a large space for sports or other entertainments with seats all around it

aren't [short form] a short way to say and write **are not**: *These aren't my boots.*

arguable [adjective] if something is arguable, some people say that it is true: *It is arguable that he is the best player we've ever had.*
✦ **arguably** [adverb] something is arguably true if it is possible to believe it: *It is arguably a very good thing that Hussein lost his job.*

argue [verb: **argues, arguing, argued**]
1 to **argue with** someone is to tell them how you disagree with what they have said: *The children never stop arguing with each other.*
2 to argue a point of view is to give reasons for having it: *The manager argued that the shop would have to close.*
✦ **argument** [noun: **arguments**]
1 a discussion where people do not agree with each other: *The kids were having an argument about what to watch on TV.*
2 the reasons for a point of view: *My argument against the plan is that we just don't have the money.*
✦ **argumentative** [adjective] an argumentative person often has disagreements with other people

arid [adjective] very dry: *the arid deserts of Arizona*

arise [verb: **arises, arising, arose, arisen**] to happen: *A small problem has arisen.*

aristocracy [noun] people from a country's oldest families that were often close to the royal families of the past: *Only members of the aristocracy are invited to these occasions.*
✦ **aristocrat** [noun: **aristocrats**] someone from an old family who often has a title like *Lord* or *Lady*
✦ **aristocratic** [adjective]
1 belonging to a country's upper class
2 looking like a member of the upper class

arithmetic [noun] adding, subtracting, dividing and multiplying numbers
✦ **arithmetical** [adjective] to do with calculating numbers

ark [noun: **arks**] the boat that carried Noah, his family and two of every animal during the flood in the Bible story

arm[1] [noun: **arms**]
1 your arm is the part of your body between your shoulder and your hand: *Alan slowly folded his arms.*
2 the arm of a piece of clothing is a sleeve
3 a part of something that sticks out of its side, usually with a bend or angle in it: *the arm of a chair*
4 if people are **arm-in-arm**, they have their arms linked together

arm[2] [verb: **arms, arming, armed**] to arm someone is to give them a weapon to fight with
➡ **armed, arms**

armada [noun] a fleet of ships going to war

armadillo [noun: **armadillos**] a small animal from America that has a kind of protective shell made of small plates of bone

armaments [plural noun] weapons and other war equipment

armchair [noun: **armchairs**] a comfortable chair with sides for resting your arms on

armed [adjective] someone who is armed has a weapon with them: *When the burglar was arrested, the police found that he had been heavily armed.*

armistice [noun] a time when enemies agree to stop fighting for a while, especially to talk about stopping for ever

Aa

armour [noun] a hard cover, usually made from metal, that protects someone or something in a battle: *a knight wearing a suit of armour*
♦ **armoured** [adjective] protected by a hard layer of something such as metal: *an armoured vehicle*

armpit [noun: **armpits**] the angle under your arm where it joins your body

arms [plural noun]
1 weapons
2 to **take up arms** is to begin fighting

army [noun: **armies**] an organization of a lot of people, usually soldiers, who will fight against an enemy

aroma [noun: **aromas**] a nice smell, especially of food

aromatherapy [noun] using the oils of plants and flowers that have different smells to treat people who are not well

aromatic [adjective] having a good smell: *aromatic plants*

arose [verb] a way of changing the verb **arise** to make a past tense: *Several problems arose at the meeting.*

around [preposition]
1 on all sides: *sitting around the table*
2 in a circle: *hold hands around the tree*
3 at or to different parts of a place: *walking around the city*
4 about: *at around 4 o'clock* • *around sixty kilos* • *She lives somewhere around here.*
[adverb] all about in different places: *clothes lying all around* • *children running around*

arouse [verb: **arouses, arousing, aroused**]
1 to arouse someone is to wake them up
2 to arouse a feeling in someone is to make them have that feeling: *His strange behaviour aroused my curiosity.*

arrange [verb: **arranges, arranging, arranged**]
1 to set things out carefully: *Arrange the knives and forks on the table.*
2 to make plans so that something happens: *Who is arranging the wedding?*
♦ **arrangement** [noun: **arrangements**]
1 arrangement is putting or planning things the way you want them: *classes in flower arrangement*

2 an arrangement is the position that things are put in: *a flower arrangement*
3 an arrangement is a plan or set of plans that are made so that something can happen the way you want it to: *The arrangement was that we should meet back at the car.*

array [noun: **arrays**] a lot of things set out for people to see: *The table was spread with an array of different salads.*

arrears [plural noun] to be **in arrears** is to be behind with payments that should have been made: *I don't like being in arrears with the rent.*

arrest [verb: **arrests, arresting, arrested**] to arrest someone is to catch them and take them to be charged with a crime
[noun: **arrests**]
1 an arrest is when the police take someone to be charged with a crime
2 someone is **under arrest** when the police hold them before charging them with a crime

arrival [noun: **arrivals**]
1 when someone reaches a place: *We are all looking forward to Alice's arrival.* • *Please report to reception on arrival.*
2 an arrival is a person or thing that has come to a place: *Come and meet the new arrivals.*

arrive [verb: **arrives, arriving, arrived**]
1 to arrive at a place is to reach it: *Please arrive at the station by 5.30.* • *If they don't arrive soon, we'll have to go without them.*
2 when a time or event arrives, it happens: *Would her birthday ever arrive?*
3 to **arrive at** a decision is to finally make a decision

arrogance [noun] a feeling of being more important or better than other people

arrogant [adjective] an arrogant person thinks they are better than other people

arrow [noun: **arrows**]
1 a pointed stick that you can shoot from a bow
2 a pointed shape that shows a particular direction: *Follow the red arrows to the X-ray department.*

arsenal [noun: **arsenals**] a store for weapons

arsenic [noun] a strong poison

arson [noun] the crime of setting fire to a building on purpose

 ✦ **arsonist** [noun: **arsonists**] someone who sets fire to a building on purpose

art [noun: **arts**]

1 art is the beautiful things that people do and invent in painting, sculpture, music and literature

2 an art is a skill that you use to do or make something beautiful: *the art of tapestry*

3 the arts are subjects that you can study that are not sciences

artery [noun: **arteries**] a tube that takes blood around your body from your heart

artful [adjective] clever in a sneaky, dishonest way

arthritic [adjective] swollen and painful because of arthritis

arthritis [noun] a disease that causes swollen joints that are painful and make moving difficult

artichoke [noun: **artichokes**] a vegetable that grows on a long stem and looks a bit like a pineapple

article [noun: **articles**]

1 a thing or item: *articles of clothing*

2 a piece of writing in a magazine or newspaper: *an article about farming*

3 in grammar, the words **a** and **the** are called articles

articulate [verb: **articulates, articulating, articulated**] to say something clearly

 ✦ **articulated** [adjective] an articulated lorry has a joint between the cab and the trailer that makes turning easier

 ✦ **articulation** [noun] speaking very clearly

artificial [adjective] looking natural, but actually made by humans or by a machine: *artificial snow*

 ✦ **artificially** [adverb] not naturally

artificial respiration [noun] forcing air into and out of someone's lungs when they have stopped breathing

artillery [noun] big guns that an army uses

artist [noun: **artists**]

1 someone who paints, draws or makes sculptures

2 someone who does something very skilfully, especially some kind of performing

artiste [noun: **artistes**] a stage performer such as a dancer, singer or actor

artistic [adjective]

1 an artistic person is creative and enjoys art

2 something artistic is creative and skilful: *a very artistic interpretation*

 ✦ **artistically** [adverb] skilfully done in a way that is pleasing to look at: *an artistically decorated room*

as [conjunction]

1 a word you use when you compare things or people: *Are you as tall as me? • This one's not as cheap as that one.*

2 while: *As we climbed, the air got colder.*

3 because: *I went first as I was the youngest.*

4 like: *As I thought, most people had already left.*

asbestos [noun] a grey–white poisonous material that does not burn and is used in buildings and clothes as protection against fire

ascend [verb: **ascends, ascending, ascended**]

1 to ascend something such as a hill is to climb it

2 to ascend is to go upwards: *a bird ascending into the sky*

 ✦ **ascent** [noun: **ascents**] an upward movement or climb: *The plane will now begin its ascent to 50,000 feet.*

ash [noun: **ashes**] the white powder that remains after something is burnt

ash [noun: **ashes**] a tree with a silvery–grey bark

ashamed [adjective]

1 to be ashamed of yourself is to feel bad about something that you have done: *I'm ashamed of my behaviour today.*

2 to be ashamed of a thing or person is to feel bad because they are not good enough: *I'm ashamed of my Dad's rotten old car but he likes it.*

ashore [adverb] on or on to dry land: *We went ashore for dinner and returned to the ship later.*

ashtray [noun: **ashtrays**] a small dish for the ash from people's cigarettes

aside [adverb] to or on one side: *Please stand aside and let us through.*

ask [verb: **asks, asking, asked**]

1 to ask a question is to say it so that you get an answer from someone: *They asked us about our families.*

Aa

2 to ask someone for something is to tell them that you want them to give it to you: *I asked Joanne for a match.*

3 to ask someone to an event like a party is to invite them: *We've asked twenty people but they won't all turn up.*

4 to ask something of someone is to expect it: *I think you're asking too much of these children.*

5 to **ask after someone** is to ask how they are

6 if you **ask for it**, you do something that will definitely get you into trouble

7 if you **ask for trouble**, you do something stupid that will probably end badly

askew [adverb] not straight: *Dom's collar was open and his tie was askew.*

asleep [adjective]

1 sleeping: *Don't wake her if she's asleep.*

2 if your arm or leg is asleep, you cannot feel it because it's been in the same position for too long

[adverb] into sleep: *I fell asleep after a while.*

asparagus [noun] a plant with fat, pale green stems that can be cooked and eaten as a vegetable

aspect [noun: **aspects**]

1 a part of a situation or problem: *Many aspects of this plan bother me.*

2 the direction a building faces: *a house with a northern aspect*

asphalt [noun] a surface for roads and paths that looks like gravel mixed with tar

aspiration [noun: **aspirations**] a hope that you will have or achieve something

aspire [verb: **aspires, aspiring, aspired**] to aspire to something is to hope that you will have it

aspirin [noun] medicine for stopping pain, usually made into tablets

ass [noun: **asses**]

1 a donkey

2 a stupid person

assail [verb: **assails, assailing, assailed**] to attack someone

♦ **assailant** [noun: **assailants**] an attacker

assassin [noun: **assassins**] a person who kills someone on purpose

♦ **assassinate** [verb: **assassinates, assassinating, assassinated**] to kill someone, especially a politician

♦ **assassination** [noun: **assassinations**] a planned killing, especially of a politician

assault [noun: **assaults**] an attack

[verb: **assaults, assaulting, assaulted**] to attack someone

assault course [noun: **assault courses**] a set of obstacles in a row that people, especially soldiers, have to climb, jump or crawl over in order to get fit, or prove that they are fit

assemble [verb: **assembles, assembling, assembled**]

1 to get several things or people together: *We've assembled a choir for the concert.*

2 to put something together from several parts: *instructions for assembling the bookcase*

3 if people assemble, they come together in a group: *Please assemble in the hall after the show.*

♦ **assembly** [noun: **assemblies**]

1 putting something together from different parts: *instructions for assembly*

2 coming together to form a group: *notices for morning assembly at school*

3 an assembly is a group of important people such as politicians, who make decisions for other people: *the General Assembly of the United Nations*

assembly line [noun: **assembly lines**] a conveyor belt in a factory which a line of products travels down. People standing beside it add a different part to each product until it is complete

assent [verb: **assents, assenting, assented**] to agree

[noun] agreement

assert [verb: **asserts, asserting, asserted**]

1 to claim that something is true

2 to **assert yourself** is to act or speak out confidently

♦ **assertion** [noun: **assertions**] something that someone claims as true: *We know Nigel did it in spite of his assertions that he didn't.*

♦ **assertive** [adjective] confident and not afraid to speak out

♦ **assertiveness** [noun] being confident and not afraid to speak out

assess [verb: **assesses, assessing,**

assessed] to consider and decide how good, valuable or important something is: *One of our agents will assess the damage to your car.*
◆ **assessment** [noun: **assessments**] an opinion about something from someone who has considered it carefully: *What is your assessment of the situation now?*

asset [noun: **assets**]
1 an asset is something that is useful: *Our team's chief asset is Tom.* • *Paula's voice is her best asset.*
2 someone's assets are the valuable things they own: *The company must sell some of its assets.*

assign [verb: **assigns, assigning, assigned]** to assign a job or task to someone is to give it to them to do
◆ **assignment** [noun: **assignments**] a job or task for a particular person to do: *I've got three homework assignments to finish by Friday.*

assist [verb: **assists, assisting, assisted**] to help someone to do something
◆ **assistance** [noun] help for someone who is trying to do something
◆ **assistant** [noun: **assistants**]
1 someone whose job is to help someone else: *My assistant will take some notes.*
2 a **shop assistant**

associate [verb: **associates, associating, associated**]
1 to associate with someone is to spend time with them: *Frank associates with a lot of very important people.*
2 to associate things such as words is to make connections between them in your mind
[noun: **associates**] your associates are the people you mix with
◆ **associated** [adjective] connected in some way: *a disease with associated problems*

association [noun: **associations**]
1 an association is a club or society
2 association is putting things or people together: *a word association game*

assorted [adjective] mixed: *assorted flavours*
◆ **assortment** [noun: **assortments**] a mixture: *a strange assortment of people*

assume [verb: **assumes, assuming, assumed**]

1 to suppose something: *Oh sorry, I assumed that you had met each other before.*
2 to assume something such as a look or attitude is to begin to have it: *He assumed a puzzled look but of course he knew the answer.*
3 to assume a new name is to change your name
◆ **assumption** [noun: **assumptions**] something you suppose

assurance [noun: **assurances**]
1 assurance is being confident: *Tim plays tennis with complete assurance.*
2 an assurance is a promise: *I had his assurance that it would be done.*
3 another word for **life assurance**

assure [verb: **assures, assuring, assured**] to try to make someone feel certain about what you are telling them: *I'd like to assure you we are doing all we can.* • *Mr Harris has assured us that the car will be ready tomorrow.*
◆ **assured** [adjective]
1 confident: *an assured manner*
2 if you say someone can **rest assured**, it means they can be confident that it is true or that it will happen: *Pupils can rest assured that the school will be open soon.*

asterisk [noun: **asterisks**] a star (*), used in a piece of text to show that there is a note, with another star beside it, often at the bottom of the page

asteroid [noun: **asteroids**] one of the rocky objects that circle the Sun, mostly between Jupiter and Mars

asthma [noun] an illness that people may suffer from for a long time and that makes breathing difficult
◆ **asthmatic** [adjective] someone who is asthmatic sometimes finds it very difficult to breathe and usually has medicine with them in case this happens suddenly
[noun: **asthmatics**] someone who has trouble breathing because they suffer from asthma

astonish [verb: **astonishes, astonishing, astonished]** to surprise someone very much: *What he said simply astonished me!*
◆ **astonished** [adjective] you are astonished when you are extremely surprised: *I'm astonished that you think that about me.*

Aa

♦ **astonishing** [adjective] extremely surprising: *an astonishing outburst* • *It was astonishing just how quickly we finished.*

astound [verb: **astounds, astounding, astounded**] to surprise or shock someone very much: *The information astounded us all.*

♦ **astounded** [adjective] you are astounded when you are very surprised and shocked

♦ **astounding** [adjective] amazing: *an astounding revelation*

astray [adverb]
1 to **go astray** is to go to the wrong place or in the wrong direction: *Your letter still hasn't arrived. It must have gone astray.*
2 to **be led astray** is to start behaving badly because other people do: *He's the kind of boy who is easily led astray.*

astride [preposition] with one leg on each side: *sitting astride a horse*

astro- [prefix] if a word starts with **astro-**, it has something to do with the stars or space. For example, *astronautics* is the science of travelling in space

astrologer [noun: **astrologers**] someone who studies the stars and suggests how their movements might affect our lives

astrology [noun] the study of how the stars and the way they move may affect our lives

astronaut [noun: **astronauts**] a member of the crew of a spacecraft

astronomer [noun: **astronomers**] someone who studies the stars

astronomical [adjective]
1 to do with the stars: *the American Astronomical Society*
2 very large: *an astronomical number*
♦ **astronomically** [adverb] very much: *Prices have risen astronomically.*

astronomy [noun] the study of the stars and the way they move

astute [adjective] clever in getting the best out of a situation: *an astute politician*

asylum [noun: **asylums**]
1 asylum is safety and protection, especially for people who do not feel safe in their own country: *people who seek political asylum in this country*
2 an old-fashioned word for a home for people with mental illnesses

asymmetrical [adjective] something asymmetrical has two sides of different shapes. Asymmetrical is the opposite of **symmetrical**

at [preposition]
1 showing where or when you mean: *Look at me!* • *Meet at the station.* • *School finishes at 4 o'clock.*
2 costing: *four bottles at 75p each*

ate [verb] a way of changing the verb **eat** to make a past tense: *The dog ate most of my dinner last night.*

atheism [noun] the belief that there is no god

atheist [noun: **atheists**] someone who does not believe in a god

athlete [noun: **athletes**] someone who is very fit and good at sport
♦ **athletic** [adjective]
1 fit and strong
2 to do with the sports of running, jumping and throwing
♦ **athletics** [noun] the group of sports that include running, jumping and throwing

atlas [noun: **atlases**] a book of maps

atmosphere [noun: **atmospheres**]
1 the air around a planet: *the Earth's atmosphere*
2 a feeling around where you are: *The club has a nice friendly atmosphere.*
♦ **atmospheric** [adjective]
1 to do with the air
2 with a very strong feeling in the air: *a very atmospheric experience*

atom [noun: **atoms**] the tiniest possible part of a substance. More than one atom can make up a **molecule**

atomic [adjective] using the power that is created when atoms are broken: *atomic weapons*

atrocious [adjective] very bad
♦ **atrocity** [noun: **atrocities**] a terrible, violent crime

attach [verb: **attaches, attaching, attached**]
1 to attach one thing to another is to fix it there: *attached to the wall with a nail*
2 if you attach a document to an e-mail message, you send it with it
♦ **attached** [adjective] if you are attached

to someone, you are very fond of them
+ **attachment** [noun: **attachments**]
1 a friendship
2 an extra part that you can add to a machine to make it do something different: *a grating attachment for the food processor*
3 something like a document or picture that you send with an e-mail message: *Save the attachment before opening it.*

attack [verb: **attacks, attacking, attacked**]
1 to attack someone is to suddenly try to hurt them: *A man was attacked and robbed on Friday.*
2 to attack a person or thing is to say bad things about them: *The newspapers have all attacked the minister's story.*
3 to attack a place is to fire at it or drop bombs on it: *The airfield is being attacked by enemy bombers.*
[noun: **attacks**]
1 a violent act against a place or person: *an attack on the west of the city*
2 an attempt to hurt someone by writing or saying bad things about them: *an attack on his honesty*
3 a sudden pain or illness: *an attack of hay fever*
+ **attacker** [noun: **attackers**] a person who tries to hurt someone violently: *Ravi said he didn't know his attackers.*

attain [verb: **attains, attaining, attained**]
to achieve something: *75% of students attained GCSEs in grades A to C.*
+ **attainment** [noun: **attainments**]
1 attainment is how much you have achieved: *the attainment of an objective*
2 an attainment is something you have achieved

attempt [verb: **attempt, attempting, attempted**] to attempt something or to attempt to do something is to try to do it: *attempting a very steep climb to the top • Nobody has ever attempted to do this before.*
[noun: **attempts**]
1 when you make an attempt, you try to do something: *an attempt to break the record*
2 to make **an attempt on someone's life** is to try to kill them

attend [verb: **attends, attending, attended**]
1 to attend an event is to go to it: *Thousands of people attended the concert in the park.*
2 to **attend to** a thing is to deal with it: *I've got a lot of jobs to attend to this morning.*
3 to **attend to** someone is to do what they need you to do for them: *The doctor will attend to the children first.*
+ **attendance** [noun]
1 being present somewhere: *the attendance register*
2 the number of people who are present somewhere: *poor attendance*
3 if someone is **in attendance**, they are in a place with someone else: *a general with two other officers in attendance*
+ **attendant** [noun: **attendants**] someone whose job is to help: *a petrol-pump attendant*

attention [noun]
1 you pay attention to something when you think about it, listen to it or look at it
2 attention is care or concentration: *medical attention • I found it difficult to hold the audience's attention for long.*
3 if someone **stands to attention**, they stand up straight like a soldier
+ **attentive** [adjective] giving a lot of thought and care: *an attentive student*
+ **attentively** [adverb] carefully, with a lot of consideration: *Graeme looked after me very attentively when I was ill.*

attic [noun: **attics**] the space in the roof of a house

attitude [noun: **attitudes**]
1 the way someone thinks about something: *John's attitude to work is not helpful.*
2 if someone has attitude, they are very confident, sometimes in a rude way

attract [verb: **attracts, attracting, attracted**]
1 if someone or something attracts you, they make you interested in them and like them: *It was his smile that first attracted me.*
2 to attract someone's attention is to get them to look or listen: *trying to attract his attention from the other side of the room*
3 things are attracted to each other when they move towards each other without any

help: *A magnet attracts iron filings.*

+ **attraction** [noun: **attractions**]
1 attraction is the way things seem to pull together without any help
2 an attraction is something that you want to see or do: *What do you think are the main attractions here?*

+ **attractive** [adjective]
1 an attractive thing or person looks nice
2 an attractive idea sounds like a good idea

+ **attractively** [adverb] in a pleasant way

aubergine [noun: **aubergines**] an oval vegetable with a smooth, shiny, dark purple skin

auburn [adjective] auburn hair is reddish-brown

auction [noun: **auctions**] a sale where the person who offers the highest price for something is able to buy it
[verb: **auctions, auctioning, auctioned**] to auction something is to sell it to the person who offers the most money for it

+ **auctioneer** [noun: **auctioneers**] someone whose job is to sell things to the person who offers the most money for them

audacious [adjective] brave and daring: *an audacious plan • an audacious young man*

+ **audacity** [noun] boldness

audible [adjective] an audible sound can be heard easily

+ **audibly** [adverb] in a way that people can hear: *Douglas gasped audibly.*

audience [noun: **audiences**]
1 the people who listen to or watch a performance: *My father was in the audience tonight. • a television audience of millions*
2 an interview with an important person: *an audience with the Queen*

audio- [prefix] if a word starts with **audio-**, it has something to do with hearing. For example, an *audiologist* studies how people hear

audio-visual [adjective] to do with both hearing and seeing: *The tour begins with an audio-visual presentation.*

audition [noun: **auditions**] a short performance in front of one or more people to show what you can do: *an audition for the Royal Ballet*
[verb: **auditions, auditioning, auditioned**]

1 to try to get a place in a show or a musical group by showing how well you can do
2 to watch and listen to performers and try to choose the best ones for something like a choir or play: *We auditioned over 100 actors for the part.*

auditorium [noun: **auditoriums**] the part of a theatre where the audience sits

August [noun] the eighth month of the year, after July and before September

aunt [noun: **aunts**]
1 the sister of one of your parents
2 your uncle's wife

au pair [noun: **au pairs**] a person, usually a young woman, who lives with a family in another country and works for them in return for pocket money

aural [adjective] to do with your ears or hearing: *an aural examination*

austere [adjective]
1 something that is austere looks plain and undecorated: *an austere waiting-room*
2 a person who is austere is hard and unfriendly

+ **austerity** [noun]
1 a plain, hard appearance
2 strictness

authentic [adjective] real: *an authentic wartime uniform*

+ **authenticity** [noun] how real or true something is: *It's difficult to prove the authenticity of this story.*

author [noun: **authors**] a writer of something such as a book: *Atkinson is the author of four novels.*

authority [noun: **authorities**]
1 authority is power and control: *You have no authority in this building.*
2 an authority is the group of people who control an activity or area: *The local authority is the district council.*
3 an authority on a subject is an expert: *She's a world authority on butterflies.*

+ **authorization** or **authorisation** [noun] official permission for someone to do something: *authorization to perform surgery*

+ **authorize** or **authorise** [verb: **authorizes, authorizing, authorized**]
1 to give someone permission to do something:

Can you authorize us to continue?
2 to officially allow something to happen: *The chief has authorized the use of riot police.*

autism [noun] a condition where someone finds it very difficult to communicate and mix with other people and the world outside themselves
♦ **autistic** [adjective] an autistic person suffers from autism

auto- [prefix] if a word starts with **auto-**, it has something to do with yourself. For example, an *autobiography* is a book about yourself that you write yourself

autobiographical [adjective] to do with someone's own life: *Many of the events in Barrie's story are autobiographical.*

autobiography [noun: **autobiographies**] the story of someone's own life

autograph [noun: **autographs**] someone's name that they wrote themselves: *Please can I have your autograph?*
[verb: **autographs, autographing, autographed**] to sign your name on something like your photograph or a book that you have written

automatic [adjective]
1 an automatic machine only needs to be switched on and then it works by itself: *an automatic washing machine*
2 an automatic action is something you do without thinking
[noun: **automatics**] a machine such as a car or a rifle, that does certain things by itself
♦ **automatically** [adverb] working or happening without being controlled all the time: *When I saw the stone coming I automatically ducked.*
♦ **automation** [noun] using machines to do things instead of people

automobile [noun: **automobiles**] the American English word for **car**

autopsy [noun: **autopsies**] an examination of a dead person's body, usually to find out why they died

autumn [noun: **autumns**] the season after summer, when the leaves change colour and fall, and it gets dark earlier
♦ **autumnal** [adjective] happening in the

season after summer: *trees in their autumnal colours*

auxiliary [noun: **auxiliaries**]
1 a helper: *He's a hospital auxiliary.*
2 an **auxiliary verb**
[adjective] helping, additional: *an auxiliary worker*

auxiliary verb [part of speech: **auxiliary verbs**] a short verb like *should, will* or *have* that you use with a main verb to make slight differences of meaning, for example a past tense in *I have finished.* These words are sometimes called **helping verbs**

avail [noun] if something is **to no avail**, it is no use: *Our attempt to hide was to no avail.*
[verb: **avails, availing, availed**] if you **avail yourself of** something, you make good use of it: *Make sure you avail yourself of every opportunity that comes your way.*

availability [noun]
1 how possible it is to get something: *Please can you check the availability of tickets for Thursday?*
2 how free someone is to do something

available [adjective]
1 if something is available, you can get it, usually by buying it
2 if someone is available, they are free to do something: *I'm sorry, Mr Wright isn't available just now.*

avalanche [noun: **avalanches**] a huge amount of snow and ice sliding down the side of a mountain

avarice [noun] greed
♦ **avaricious** [adjective] greedy
ⓘ This is a formal word.

avenge [verb: **avenges, avenging, avenged**] to take revenge on someone for something they did to someone you care about

avenue [noun: **avenues**] a street, usually with trees on both sides

average [noun: **averages**]
1 the number you get if you add amounts together and then divide that total by the number of amounts: *The average of 3, 4 and 8 is 5.*
2 the normal level or standard: *We spend an*

average of £100 a week on food.
[adjective] usual or ordinary: *How much do you earn in an average week?*

avert [verb: **averts, averting, averted**]
1 to turn away: *Avert your eyes for a moment please.*
2 to manage to stop something happening: *desperately trying to avert war*

aviary [noun: **aviaries**] a large cage or building for keeping birds

aviation [noun] flying in aircraft

avid [adjective] keen: *an avid reader*

avocado [noun: **avocados** or **avocadoes**]
1 a pear-shaped fruit with dark green skin and a large stone in the middle
2 a light green colour

avoid [verb: **avoids, avoiding, avoided**] to keep out of the way of a thing or person: *avoid being seen* • *Have you been avoiding me for some reason?*
✦ **avoidable** [adjective] something that is avoidable is not necessary or does not need to happen

await [verb: **awaits, awaiting, awaited**] to wait for a thing or person: *A surprise was awaiting me at home.*

awake [adjective] not sleeping: *Are you still awake?*
[verb: **awakes, awaking, awoke, awoken**] to wake up: *Gloria awoke early.* • *Something had awoken me.*
✦ **awaken** [verb: **awakens, awakening, awakened**] to wake someone up: *We were awakened by the bombs.*

award [noun: **awards**] a prize: *Joe won the award for Man of the Match.*
[verb: **awards, awarding, awarded**] to award someone something is to give it to them because they deserve it: *We have been awarded the title of 'School of the Year'.*

aware [adjective] if you are **aware of** something, you know about it or know that it exists: *Derek became aware of someone else in the room.* • *I'm perfectly aware that you've been waiting a long time.*
✦ **awareness** [noun] realizing and understanding: *safety awareness week*

away [adverb]
1 somewhere else: *Go away!* • *Throw that away.*

2 at a distance: *How far away is the school?* • *only a week away*
3 in the opposite direction: *Peter turned away.* • *Please make sure you put everything away when you've finished.*
4 continuously: *working away all night*
5 right away means immediately
[adjective] an away game or match is one your team has to travel to. Look up and compare **home**

awe [noun] a feeling that a thing or person is wonderful but a little frightening: *The children gazed at their hero in awe.*
✦ **awesome** [adjective]
1 very good or impressive
2 making you feel very small and scared: *the awesome possibility of war*

awestruck [adjective] filled with feelings of wonder mixed with fear

awful [adjective]
1 very bad: *an awful headache*
2 very great: *That won't make an awful lot of difference.*
✦ **awfully** [adverb]
1 very: *It's an awfully long way.*
2 very badly: *We played awfully.*

awkward [adjective]
1 difficult to manage or use: *That's an awkward question.* • *I find this keyboard a bit awkward.*
2 someone who is being awkward is not being helpful: *Just stop being awkward and say you'll come.*
3 if you feel awkward, you feel uncomfortable or embarrassed: *I began to feel awkward when they started to talk about me.*
✦ **awkwardly** [adverb] in a difficult or uncomfortable way

awning [noun: **awnings**] a cover like a soft roof that protects something from rain or sun

awoke [verb] a way of changing the verb **awake** to make a past tense: *I awoke next morning to the sound of birds singing.*

awoken [verb] a form of the verb **awake** that is used with a helping verb to show that something happened in the past: *I had awoken late that morning.*

axe [noun: **axes**] a tool for chopping wood
[verb: **axes, axing, axed**]

1 if a plan or service is axed, it is stopped

2 if jobs are axed, the people doing them are no longer needed

axis [noun: **axes**]

1 the imaginary line through something like a planet that it seems to spin around

2 in a graph, the line up the side or along the bottom that you measure against

axle [noun: **axles**] in a vehicle, an axle is a rod that has a wheel at each end

ayatollah [noun: **ayatollahs**] a Muslim religious leader in Iran

aye [interjection] another word for **yes**

azalea [noun: **azaleas**] a bush that has bright white, cream or pink flowers

azure [noun] the blue colour of the sky

Aa

B

babble [verb: **babbles, babbling, babbled**]

1 to talk or say something quickly without making very much sense: *Carol was babbling on about some book she'd read.*

2 running water babbles when it makes a pleasant bubbling sound: *The stream babbled and sparkled as it flowed over the rocks.*

baboon [noun: **baboons**] a type of large monkey with a long pointed nose and long teeth, found in Africa and parts of Asia

baby [noun: **babies**]

1 a very young child

2 an older child or an adult who is crying or behaving like a baby: *Don't be such a baby, it's only a little spider.*

[adjective] very young: *a baby elephant*

♦ **babyish** [adjective]

1 like a baby: *a smooth babyish face*

2 suitable for babies or younger children: *This game is probably too babyish for ten-year-olds.*

babysit [verb: **babysits, babysitting, babysat**] to look after a baby or child when its parents are out: *My niece sometimes babysits for me at the weekend.* • *Would you babysit the boys next Saturday?*

♦ **babysitter** [noun: **babysitters**] someone who looks after a baby or a child when its parents are out

bachelor [noun: **bachelors**] a man who has never married

ⓘ Remember there is no **t** before the **c** in **bachelor**.

back [noun: **backs**]

1 the back of something is the side that is opposite to or furthest away from its front: *Nina hid her diary at the back of a drawer.*

2 the part of your body that stretches from the back of your neck to your bottom: *I always sleep on my back.*

3 in football and hockey, a back is a player who mostly tries to stop the other team scoring a goal. Look up and compare **forward**

4 to **put someone's back up** is to annoy them: *Don't be so cheeky. You'll put Dad's back up and he won't let us go out.*

[adjective] behind or opposite the front: *Ben's had one of his back teeth out.*

[adverb]

1 farther away in distance: *Stand back and make more room.*

2 to the place, person or state from which someone or something came: *We won't be able to get there and back in a day.* • *I lent him my book and he hasn't given it back yet.*

3 towards the back of something or on your back: *Sit back and enjoy the show.* • *He lay back on the bed.*

4 in or to an earlier time: *Think back and try to remember exactly what happened.*

[verb: **backs, backing, backed**]

1 to move backwards: *When Lucy saw what was in the box, she backed away in fear.*

2 to back someone is to give them support or help, often money: *It's a great invention and I'm sure you'll soon find someone to back you.*

3 someone **backs down** when they admit they are beaten or have lost an argument: *Ryan knows he can't win, but he's still refusing to back down.*

4 to **back up** computer information is to make

a separate copy of it so that the information is not lost if the computer breaks down

backbone [noun: **backbones**] the row of bones down the middle of your back that forms your spine

backdate [verb: **backdates, backdating, backdated**] if you backdate something such as a cheque or a payment, you make it effective from an earlier date: *Claims for benefit can be backdated for up to 52 weeks.*

backfire [verb: **backfires, backfiring, backfired**]
1 if a motor vehicle backfires, its fuel burns too soon and causes a loud bang in its exhaust pipe
2 if a plan backfires, it has the opposite effect from what you intended

backgammon [noun] a game where you throw dice and move round pieces on a patterned board

background [noun: **backgrounds**]
1 the part of a picture, pattern, etc behind the main figures or objects: *white flowers on a green background* • *Here's a photo of us with Ben Nevis in the background.*
2 a person's background is their family, the kind of life they have had and the things they have done in the past: *children from poorer backgrounds* • *Her husband has an army background.*
3 the background of an event is anything that happened before it that helps to explain how the event came about: *the background to the English Civil War*

backhand [noun] in games like tennis or squash, a way of hitting the ball by holding the racket across the front of your body with the back of your hand facing towards the ball

backlog [noun] a large amount of something such as work or letters that has gathered and needs to dealt with: *The strike has led to a huge backlog of mail.* • *We've got to work this weekend to try to clear the backlog.*

backstroke [noun] a way of swimming where you lie on your back, kick your legs and swing your arms backwards over your shoulders

backup [noun: **backups**]
1 additional people or equipment that you can use when you need them: *I've booked the babysitter and got mum as a backup just in case.*
2 a separate copy of information on a computer so that it is not lost if the computer breaks down

backward [adjective]
1 facing or aimed towards the back: *a backward look*
2 slow to learn or develop
[adverb] backwards: *She was looking backward over her shoulder.*

backwards [adverb]
1 in the direction opposite to the one you are facing: *Stepping backwards without looking, he fell down the manhole.*
2 towards the past: *If we move further backwards in time, we come to the age of the dinosaurs.*
3 in the opposite way to the usual way: *Tom can say the alphabet backwards.*

bacon [noun] salted meat from a pig, usually eaten in thin strips called rashers

bacteria [noun] very small creatures living in air, water, living animals and plants, and in dead and decaying things. Some types of bacteria can cause diseases or illness in humans and animals

ⓘ **Bacteria** is the plural of **bacterium**. The singular, **bacterium**, is not often used. Because **bacteria** is the plural it should be used with a plural verb:
✓ The bacteria **have** not been identified.
✗ The bacteria **has** not been identified.

bad [adjective: **worse, worst**]
1 wicked or naughty: *You're a bad influence on me.* • *Get out, you bad dog!*
2 not of a good standard: *His handwriting is bad, and his spelling is worse.*
3 nasty or upsetting: *a bad storm* • *very bad news*
4 harmful to your health: *Eating too many fatty foods can be bad for you.*
5 if someone is bad at doing something they do not do it well: *I'm very bad at maths.*
6 something is bad or has gone bad if it is rotten or decaying: *Don't eat that pear — it's bad.* • *Your teeth will go bad if you don't brush them regularly.*

Bb

7 you say '**not bad**' or '**not too bad**' to mean quite good: '*How are you feeling today?*' '*Not too bad, thanks.*'
➙ **badly**

ⓘ Comparing how **bad** things are: *The weather was **bad** yesterday, but it was **worse** the day before, and last Friday was **worst** of all.*

bade [verb] a way of changing the verb **bid²** to make a past tense: *I bade him goodbye.*

badge [noun: **badges**] a small object with words or pictures printed on it that you pin or sew on to your clothing to show, for example, that you are a member of a group or club

badger [noun: **badgers**] an animal with a pointed black-and-white striped face and grey fur on the rest of its body. Badgers live underground and come out at night to feed

badly [adverb: **worse, worst**]
1 not well: *The work was done very badly.*
2 seriously: *The car was badly damaged in the crash.*
3 very much: *I badly wanted a new pair of trainers.*

badminton [noun] a game in which two or four players use rackets to hit a light object called a shuttlecock across a net

bad-tempered [adjective] speaking or behaving angrily or rudely: *Perhaps you wouldn't be so bad-tempered in the morning if you got more sleep.*

baffle [verb: **baffles, baffling, baffled**] if a problem baffles you, you cannot work out what it is about or how to solve it: *The robbers tried to baffle the local police by leaving false clues.*
♦ **baffling** [adjective] puzzling: *a baffling problem*

bag [noun: **bags**]
1 an object made of paper, plastic, cloth or leather used to carry things in: *a bag of crisps*
2 if you've got **bags of** something, you have a lot of it: *We've got bags of time before the bus comes.*
[verb: **bags, bagging, bagged**] to put things into a bag or bags: *We helped Dad bag all the garden rubbish.*

bagel [noun: **bagels**] a type of bread roll shaped like a ring

bagful [noun: **bagfuls**] the amount that a bag holds: *Adam must have eaten four or five bagfuls of sweets.*

baggage [noun] the cases and bags that a person takes with them when they travel: *The baggage is stored in the back of the coach.*

baggy [adjective: **baggier, baggiest**] baggy clothes are too big for the person wearing them and hang loosely from their body: *I like wearing baggy jumpers because they're comfortable.*

bagpipes [plural noun] a musical instrument made up of a cloth or leather bag with pipes attached to it that you play by blowing down a pipe

baguette [noun: **baguettes**] a long narrow loaf of French bread, also called a **French stick**

ⓘ This word is pronounced bag-**ett**.

bail¹ [noun] money that has to be paid to a court so that someone who has been arrested for a crime can be let out of prison until their trial
[verb: **bails, bailing, bailed**] a prisoner is bailed or **bailed out** when a sum of money is paid to the court and they are set free until their trial

ⓘ Be careful not to confuse the spellings or meanings of **bail** and **bale**.

bail² [noun: **bails**] in cricket, the bails are the short pieces of wood that lie across the top of the stumps

bailiff [noun: **bailiffs**] someone whose job is to take away the possessions of a person who has not paid money they owe

bairn [noun: **bairns**] a Scottish word for **child**

bait [noun] food put on a hook to catch fish or put in a trap to catch animals
[verb: **baits, baiting, baited**] to bait a hook or trap is to put food on it to attract and catch fish or animals

bake [verb: **bakes, baking, baked**]
1 to bake is to cook things like cakes, biscuits or bread in an oven: *Mum does a lot of cooking but she doesn't bake very often.*
2 to bake food is to cook it in an oven: *Bake the lasagne in a medium oven until it is golden brown.*

3 to bake things that are soft is to harden them in the sun or in an oven: *The bricks have to be baked before they can be used to build with.*

baker [noun: **bakers**]
1 someone who bakes bread and cakes: *My grandmother was a brilliant baker.*
2 a baker's is a shop selling freshly baked bread and cakes

bakery [noun: **bakeries**] a shop or factory where bread and cakes are made

balance [noun: **balances**]
1 you have your balance when you are in a steady enough position not to fall: *I lost my balance and fell over.*
2 a situation when things are in a satisfactory relationship with each other: *Try to achieve a balance between work and family life.*
3 the balance of a bank or building society account is the amount of money in it
[verb: **balances, balancing, balanced**]
1 to balance something is to make or keep it steady: *Lisa balanced the book on her head.*
2 to **balance the books** is to make sure that the amount of money spent isn't bigger than the amount received

balcony [noun: **balconies**]
1 a platform built out from the wall of a building, usually with a railing around it
2 the balcony in a theatre or cinema is the area upstairs where the seats are above the rest of the audience

bald [adjective: **balder, baldest**]
1 someone who is bald has very little or no hair: *My uncle is completely bald.*
2 something that is bald has very little covering: *We'll have to hide that bald patch in the middle of the rug somehow.*
 ✦ **balding** [adjective] going bald: *a balding elderly gentleman*
 ✦ **baldness** [noun] being bald

bale [noun: **bales**] a bundle of hay, cloth or paper that has been tied up tightly
[verb: **bales, baling, baled**] to bale hay, cloth or paper is to tie it tightly in bundles

bale² [verb: **bales, baling, baled**] to **bale out** of a dangerous place or an emergency situation is to escape from it: *The pilot had to bale out of the burning aeroplane and parachute to the ground.*

ball¹ [noun: **balls**]
1 a round object that you use for playing games like football, hockey, cricket and tennis
2 anything that has a round shape: *a ball of string* • *The hedgehog had rolled itself into a tight ball.*
3 if someone is **on the ball**, they are alert and quick to act

ball² [noun: **balls**]
1 a big formal party where people dance: *Cinderella couldn't go to the ball.*
2 to **have a ball** is to have a very good time

ballad [noun: **ballads**] a love song

ball bearings [plural noun] small metal balls that are placed in grooves in some machine parts and allow the parts to move easily over each other

ballerina [noun: **ballerinas**] a female ballet dancer

ballet [noun: **ballets**]
1 ballet is a type of dancing that uses graceful steps and movements: *Emily prefers ballet to tap dancing.*
2 a ballet is a story told using dance: *My favourite ballets are The Nutcracker and Swan Lake.*

balloon [noun: **balloons**] a very light object made of thin rubber that expands and floats when it is filled with air or gas
[verb: **balloons, ballooning, ballooned**] to balloon is to expand or swell like a balloon does when it is filled with air or gas: *The sail ballooned out in the breeze.*

ballot [noun: **ballots**] a way of voting in secret by marking a paper and putting it into a special box
[verb: **ballots, balloting, balloted**] to ballot a group of people is to get votes from them by ballot: *The workers were balloted and voted to strike.*

ballpoint or **ballpoint pen** [noun: **ballpoints** or **ballpoint pens**] a pen with a small metal ball as the tip

balm [noun: **balms**] a soothing ointment used to help heal burns and damaged skin
 ✦ **balmy** [adjective: **balmier, balmiest**] warm and soothing: *hot days followed by balmy nights*

balsa or **balsa wood** [noun] a very light

wood that is often used to make model boats and aircraft

bamboo [noun]
1 a type of Asian grass that can grow very tall and has hard round hollow stems
2 bamboo is the stems of this plant that are used to make furniture, baskets, etc

bamboozle [verb: **bamboozle, bamboozling, bamboozled**] to bamboozle someone is to confuse or trick them: *The instructions for the video completely bamboozled me.*

ban [verb: **bans, banning, banned**] to ban something is to not allow it: *Cycling is banned in the park.*
[noun: **bans**] an order that something is not allowed: *a ban on smoking*

banana [noun: **bananas**] a long, curved, yellow fruit that you peel to eat and that grows in hot countries

band [noun: **bands**]
1 a strip of material to put round something: *a rubber band • a headband*
2 a stripe: *a broad band of colour*
3 a group: *a band of robbers*
4 a group of musicians who play together: *a rock band*
[verb: **bands, banding, banded**] to **band together** is to join together to do something as a group: *All the parents banded together to campaign for a new school crossing.*

bandage [noun: **bandages**] a strip of cloth for wrapping round a part of your body that has been cut or hurt
[verb: **bandages, bandaging, bandaged**] to bandage a part of your body is to wrap it in a bandage

bandit [noun: **bandits**] an armed criminal who attacks and robs travellers

bandwagon [noun] people who **jump** or **climb on the bandwagon** join something only because it is fashionable or successful, not because it is right or worthwhile

bandy [adjective: **bandier, bandiest**] bandy legs curve outwards at the knees

bane [noun] the **bane of your life** is the thing that most annoys you or that causes you the most trouble: *Hay fever is the bane of my life.*

bang [noun: **bangs**]

1 a sudden loud noise: *There was a loud bang and all the lights went out.*
2 a hard knock: *She's had a bang on the head and is feeling a bit dizzy.*
3 if a party or other event **goes with a bang**, everyone there has a very good time
[verb: **bangs, banging, banged**]
1 a door or window bangs when it closes or is shut roughly so that it makes a loud noise: *The door banged shut in the wind.*
2 to bang something is to knock it hard against something else: *Neil banged his head on the shelf.*

banger [noun: **bangers**]
1 a type of firework that makes loud banging noises when it is set off
2 a sausage: *bangers and mash*
3 a rusty car that is falling to pieces

bangle [noun: **bangles**] a ring of metal, wood or plastic that you wear on your wrist

banish [verb: **banishes, banishing, banished**]
1 to banish someone is to make them leave the country or their home as a punishment
2 to banish a feeling is to make it go away: *His exam results banished any doubts about his ability.*
✦ **banishment** [noun] being banished

banisters [plural noun] the rail and its supports that you can hold on to as you go up and down stairs

banjo [noun: **banjos** or **banjoes**] an instrument with a round body and a long neck that you play by plucking the strings

bank [noun: **banks**]
1 a business that looks after and lends money: *Most people keep their money in a bank for safety. • I have to go to the bank this morning.*
2 a place where a particular thing is stored so that it can be used later: *a computer data bank • a blood bank*
3 the banks of a river or a lake are the areas of ground beside it: *We camped on the banks of Loch Lomond.*
4 a mound or a raised area of ground: *There's a steep wooded bank behind the house.*
[verb: **banks, banking, banked**]
1 to bank money is to put it in a bank: *I'm going to spend half the £100 I won and bank the rest.*
2 if you **bank on** something, you depend on it:

You can't bank on the weather staying dry, so take an umbrella.
3 an aeroplane banks when it tips over to one side as it changes direction

LANGUAGE FOR LIFE
banks
Here are some important words that you may come across being used by banks:
• Your **balance** is the amount of money you have in your account.
• A **credit** is a word for money that you have paid into the bank.
• A **debit** is a word for money that you have taken out of the bank.
• A **deposit** is when you pay money into the bank.
• **Interest** is extra money that you have to pay back when you have borrowed money, or that a bank puts into your account regularly.
• Your **PIN** is the secret number that you use to take money out of your account, for example at a cash machine.
• A **statement** is a letter that the bank sends you that shows how much money you have in your account and what you have spent.
• A **withdrawal** is when you take money out of the bank.

bank card [noun: **bank cards**] a small piece of plastic that you can use to pay for things or to get money out of a cash machine
banker [noun: **bankers**] someone who runs a business that looks after and lends money
bank holiday [noun: **bank holidays**] a public holiday when the banks are closed
banking [noun] the business that banks do
banknote [noun: **banknotes**] a piece of paper money issued by a bank
bankrupt [adjective] a person or a business is bankrupt or goes bankrupt if they are not able to pay the money they owe: *The business went bankrupt because overheads rose.*
♦ **bankruptcy** [noun: **bankruptcies**] being bankrupt: *The business is facing bankruptcy.* • *The number of bankruptcies went up last year.*
banner [noun: **banners**] a large piece of cloth with printing or writing on it which is carried on poles: *protestors carrying anti-war banners*

banquet [noun: **banquets**] a formal dinner that a lot of people attend where guests often make speeches and toasts
ⓘ This word is pronounced **bang**-kwit.

banter [noun] banter is talk where people tease each other in fun or make funny remarks to each other
baptism [noun: **baptisms**] a Christian ceremony where someone has water sprinkled on their head as a sign they are to become part of the Church
baptize or **baptise** [verb: **baptizes, baptizing, baptized**] to baptize someone is to make them part of the Christian Church by the ceremony of sprinkling water on their head
bar [noun: **bars**]
1 a piece of hard material: *an iron bar*
2 a bar of something is a solid piece of it: *a bar of chocolate*
3 a broad line or band: *a brown bird with black bars on its wings*
4 a room or counter serving drinks or food: *a burger bar*
5 one of the sections of equal time into which a piece of music is divided: *four beats to the bar*
[verb: **bars, barring, barred**]
1 to bar a door, a window or a gate is to put metal or wooden bars across it so that no one can get in or out
2 if people are barred from a place or from doing something, they are not allowed in or are not allowed to do it: *Anyone over the age of 12 is barred from the competition.*
barb [noun: **barbs**] a point on an arrow or a fish hook that faces backwards and makes the arrow or hook stick firmly
barbarian [noun: **barbarians**] a savage or uncivilized person
barbaric [adjective] cruel or uncivilized: *a barbaric custom*
barbecue [noun: **barbecues**]
1 a grill used for cooking food outdoors
2 an outdoor party where food is grilled on a barbecue
[verb: **barbecues, barbecuing, barbecued**] to barbecue food is to grill it on a barbecue
barbed wire [noun] wire that has sharp

spikes twisted round it. Barbed wire is used on walls and fences to stop people and animals climbing over

barber [noun: **barbers**]
1 a man whose job is to cut men's hair
2 a barber's is a shop where men have their hair cut

bar chart [noun: **bar charts**] a diagram in which various amounts are shown using coloured or shaded blocks of different heights

bar code [noun: **bar codes**] a code made up of lines and spaces which is printed on an item for sale so that it can be identified by a computer

bare [adjective: **barer, barest**] naked or without any covering: *It's a bit too cold to be going out with bare legs.* • *Without the posters on the walls the bedroom looks really bare.*

barefaced [adjective] something that is barefaced is done without feeling any guilt or embarrassment: *a barefaced lie*

barely [adverb] hardly or almost not: *They had barely arrived when they had to leave again.* • *The truck barely avoided hitting us when it skidded across the road.*

bargain [noun: **bargains**]
1 an agreement people make between themselves
2 if something is a bargain, it is cheap or cheaper than usual: *These jeans were a real bargain.*
3 **into the bargain** means as well or besides: *It's a good warm jacket and waterproof into the bargain.*
[verb: **bargains, bargaining, bargained**]
1 to bargain is to argue about the price you will pay for something
2 if you **get more than you bargain for**, you get something extra, usually something bad, that you didn't expect

barge [noun: **barges**] a flat-bottomed boat used on canals and rivers
[verb: **barges, barging, barged**]
1 to barge into a place or a person is to rush, push or bump into them clumsily: *Matt barged into the room knocking all the books over as he came.*
2 to barge against people or barge through a crowd is to push against or through them

roughly and rudely: *Hannah barged past us to get to the front of the queue.*

baritone [noun: **baritones**]
1 a male singing voice between the lowest and highest pitch
2 a man with this singing voice

bark¹ [noun: **barks**] the short, loud sound that a dog or fox makes
[verb: **barks, barking, barked**]
1 animals bark when they make this sound
2 if a person barks, they speak loudly and sharply: *'Hurry up, you lot!' he barked.*
3 if someone **barks up the wrong tree**, they make a mistake that leads them to think something that is not correct

bark² [noun] the bark of a tree is the rough outer covering of its trunk and branches

barley [noun] a grain used for food and for making beer

barman [noun: **barmen**] a man who serves drinks at a bar

bar mitzvah [noun: **bar mitzvahs**] a religious ceremony for Jewish boys to mark the time, at about age 13, when they are expected to take some of the responsibilities of an adult

barn [noun: **barns**] a large building on a farm for storing grain or hay

barnacle [noun: **barnacles**] a type of small shellfish that fastens itself on to rocks and the bottoms of boats

barometer [noun: **barometers**] an instrument for measuring the pressure of air and showing changes in the weather

baron [noun: **barons**] a type of nobleman

baroness [noun: **baronesses**] a female baron or a baron's wife: *Baroness Thatcher*

barracks [noun: **barracks**] a place where soldiers live or are based

barracuda [noun: **barracudas**] a large fierce sea fish with big teeth, found in the Caribbean and other warm seas

barrel [noun: **barrels**]
1 a wooden or metal container with curved sides used for holding liquids such as beer and wine
2 the barrel of a gun is the metal tube through which the shot or bullet is fired

barren [adjective] a barren landscape has very little or nothing growing on it

Bb

barricade [noun: **barricades**] a barrier put up in a street to stop people passing through [verb: **barricades, barricading, barricaded**] to barricade a place is to put up a barrier to stop people getting in or passing through: *They've barricaded themselves inside the house.*

barrier [noun: **barriers**]
1 a gate or fence used to stop people getting past
2 a barrier is anything that stops you getting ahead: *Nowadays, being a girl isn't any barrier to a career in the navy.*

barrister [noun: **barristers**] a lawyer who presents people's cases in court

barrow [noun: **barrows**] a type of small cart that you push

barter [verb: **barters, bartering, bartered**] to give one thing in exchange for another, without using any money

base [noun: **bases**]
1 the surface or part on which something rests or stands: *a bronze statue on a black marble base*
2 the lowest part of something: *the base of the mountain*
3 a headquarters: *The soldiers went back to base.*
[verb: **bases, basing, based**]
1 to base one thing on another is to create it using the other thing as a start: *a story based on fact*
2 if a person or organization is based in a particular place, that is where they live or do their work

ⓘ Though the words **base** and **bass** sound the same, remember that they have different spellings.

baseball [noun: **baseballs**]
1 a game played with a long rounded bat and a ball by two teams
2 a baseball is a small ball used in the game of baseball

basement [noun: **basements**] the lowest floor of a building, under the ground

bases [noun] the plural form of **basis** and **base**

bash [verb: **bashes, bashing, bashed**] to bash something is to hit it hard: *The door closed suddenly and bashed me on the nose.*
[noun: **bashes**]
1 a hard hit: *He gave the nail a couple of good bashes.*
2 to **have a bash** is to have a try: *I don't know exactly how to do it, but I'll have a bash at it anyway.*

basic [adjective]
1 basic describes things that are at the most essential or simple level: *basic driving skills*
2 something is basic if it does not include anything unnecessary or too fancy: *The cottage was pretty basic – it didn't even have a proper bath.*

basically [adverb] in the most important or essential way: *Joe's basically a good person.* • *Basically, I was sick of the job.*

ⓘ Remember the correct spelling:
✓ basic**ally**
✗ basicly

basics [plural noun] the basics are the most essential or important facts, skills or knowledge you need to have about a subject: *To be a good writer you need to know the basics of grammar and punctuation.*

basil [noun] a herb with sweet-smelling leaves that are used in cookery

basin [noun: **basins**]
1 a sink for washing your hands and face in
2 a bowl used in the kitchen for holding liquids or food: *a pudding basin*
3 an area of land from which water flows into a river: *the Amazon basin*

basis [noun: **bases**] the basis of something is what it is built on or what it is based on: *We've always been on a very friendly basis until now.* • *You'll be paid on an hourly basis.*

bask [verb: **basks, basking, basked**]
1 to bask is to sit or lie enjoying warmth: *We basked in the warm sunshine.*
2 to bask in other people's praise or attention is to enjoy it: *Amrish had scored the winning goal and was basking in the admiration of his friends.*

basket [noun: **baskets**] a container made of strips of wood or canes woven together

basketball [noun: **basketballs**]

1 basketball is a game played by two teams who try to score points by throwing a ball through a hoop fixed high above the ground on a post
2 a basketball is a large ball used to play basketball

bass [noun: **basses**]
1 in music, the bass is the lowest range of notes
2 a musical instrument with a low tone, such as a bass guitar or double bass
3 a man with the deepest kind of singing or speaking voice
[adjective] of or making the lowest range of musical notes: *singing the bass part*

bass clef [noun: **bass clefs**] a musical sign that shows you that the pitch of the following notes should be bass

bassoon [noun: **bassoons**] a long wooden instrument that you play by blowing into it to make a low sound

bastard [noun: **bastards**] someone whose parents were not married when he or she was born

bat[1] [noun: **bats**]
1 a shaped piece of wood that you use to hit the ball in games like cricket and baseball
2 if you do something **off your own bat**, you do it without anyone telling you that you have to do it
[verb: **bats, batting, batted**] to bat is to use the bat in games such as cricket and rounders: *It's Gary's turn to bat next.*

bat[2] [noun: **bats**] a flying animal that comes out at night to feed

batch [noun: **batches**]
1 a number of things, especially pieces of food, all made at one time: *a batch of scones*
2 a group of people that arrive or are dealt with at one time: *A new batch of hotel guests arrives tomorrow.*

bated [adjective] if you are waiting **with bated breath**, you are excited or anxious to find out what will happen next: *We were all waiting with bated breath to see how the film would end.*

ⓘ Try not to confuse the spelling of **bated** with **baited**, the past tense form of **bait**.

bath [noun: **baths**]

1 a bath is a large container that you fill with water and sit in to wash yourself: *You're filthy! When did you last have a bath?*
2 baths are a building which contains a public swimming pool: *I learnt to swim in the local baths.*
[verb: **baths, bathing, bathed**] to bath someone is to wash them in a bath: *Will you bath the baby for me, please?*

bathe [verb: **bathes, bathing, bathed**]
1 to wash yourself in a bath
2 to swim in water: *They always bathe in the sea before breakfast.*
3 you bathe a sore part of your body when you wash it gently with water or some other liquid: *I'm going to bathe my aching feet as soon as I get home.*

bathroom [noun: **bathrooms**] a room for washing yourself in, usually containing a bath or a shower, a basin and a lavatory

bat mitzvah [noun: **bat mitzvahs**] a religious ceremony for Jewish girls to mark the time, at about age 12, when they are expected to start taking some of the responsibilites of an adult

baton [noun: **batons**] a short thin stick used, for example, by someone who is conducting music or by runners in a relay race

batsman [noun: **batsmen**] a man who bats in cricket

battalion [noun: **battalions**] a large group of soldiers that is part of a regiment

batten [verb: **battens, battening, battened**] to **batten something down** is to fasten it down firmly and make it secure: *He'd battened down the edges of the tent to stop them flapping in the wind.*

batter [verb: **batters, battering, battered**] to hit something hard over and over again: *The rain battered down on the metal roof.*
[noun] batter is a mixture of flour, milk and eggs used to coat fish and other food before it is fried in oil: *cod in batter*

battering ram [noun: **battering rams**] a large heavy log hit against a door or gate to break it down

battery [noun: **batteries**]
1 a device used to supply electrical power to things like watches, cameras and car engines:

Did you remember to buy a new battery for the smoke alarm? • *The car wouldn't start because its battery was flat.*

2 a set of cages that hens are kept in so that their eggs can be collected easily

battle [noun: **battles**]

1 a fight between two armies: *the Battle of Hastings*

2 any fight or struggle: *a battle for power* [verb: **battles, battling, battled**] to battle is to fight or struggle: *The ship battled bravely through the storm.*

battlements [plural noun] a wall around the top of a castle or fort that has spaces cut in it for the people inside to shoot at people outside

battleship [noun: **battleships**] a very large ship that has big guns

bauble [noun: **baubles**] a shiny or glittery decoration

bawl [verb: **bawls, bawling, bawled**] to cry or shout very loudly: *You'll have to bawl at him to make him hear you.*

ⓘ Try not to confuse **bawl** and **ball**, which sound the same when you say them.

bay [noun: **bays**]

1 a piece of land on the coast or on the shore of a lake that bends inwards: *the Bay of Biscay*

2 an area that is marked out for a particular use: *a loading bay*

3 if you keep or hold something **at bay**, you do not let it come near you or harm you: *Vitamin C helps to keep colds at bay.*

bayonet [noun: **bayonets**] a long sharp blade that can be fixed on to the end of a soldier's rifle

bazaar [noun: **bazaars**]

1 an event where goods are sold to raise money, especially for a good cause

2 a type of Middle Eastern market, usually with small shops or stalls selling different goods

BC [abbreviation] short for **before Christ**. BC is added after a date to show that the date was before the birth of Jesus Christ, for example, *450 BC*. Look up and compare **AD**

be [verb]

1 to be is to exist: *There may be a very good reason for it.*

2 to be something is to have that position or to do that job: *What do you want to be when you grow up?* • *Her brother's an accountant.*

3 to be a particular thing is to have that feeling or quality: *Try to be happy.* • *We can't all be as clever as you.*

ⓘ There are many different forms of the verb **be**.

If you are talking about something that is happening at this moment, you use the present tense forms. These are *I* **am**, *you* or *they* **are**, *he, she,* or *it* **is**.

You can also say *I* **am being**, *you, we,* or *they* **are being**, *he, she,* or *it* **is being**.

If you are talking about something that was the case in the past, you use the past tense forms. These are *I, he, she,* or *it* **was**, *you, we,* or *they* **were**.

You can also say *I, you, we,* or *they* **have been**, *he, she,* or *it* **has been**.

beach [noun: **beaches**] the shore of the sea, especially an area of sand or pebbles that have been left on the shore by the waves

beacon [noun: **beacons**] a light or a fire that can be seen from a long distance away and is lit as a warning or a signal

bead [noun: **beads**]

1 a small round piece of glass, plastic or wood with a hole through the middle, used to make necklaces or sewn on to clothes as decoration

2 a round drop of liquid: *There were beads of sweat on his forehead.*

beady [adjective: **beadier, beadiest**] beady eyes are round and shiny

beagle [noun: **beagles**] a type of dog with a black, white and brown coat and long ears

beak [noun: **beaks**] a bird's beak is the hard, pointed part of its mouth that it uses to pick up food

beaker [noun: **beakers**] a type of drinking cup, usually without a handle

beam [noun: **beams**]

1 a long thick piece of wood or metal used to support a building or bridge

2 a line of light

[verb: **beams, beaming, beamed**]

1 to shine: *The sun beamed down all day.*

2 if someone beams, they have a big smile on their face

Bb

bean [noun: **beans**]
1 a type of seed that grows in a pod and is eaten as a vegetable
2 if someone is **full of beans**, they have lots of energy

bear[1] [noun: **bears**] a large, heavy animal with a thick coat and hooked claws

bear[2] [verb: **bears, bearing, bore, born** or **borne**]
1 to bear something is to put up with it: *She couldn't bear the cold winters.* • *Stephen just can't bear to part with his old toys.*
2 to bear something is to carry it or have it: *Hassan appeared, bearing a steaming cup.* • *The door bore the family's name.*
3 women bear children and animals bear young when they give birth to them
4 if you **bear something in mind**, you remember that it is important: *Please bear in mind that you only have an hour to write your essay.*
• **bearable** [adjective] if something is bearable, you are able to put up with it: *'Is the pain bad?' 'Just now it's bearable.'*

ⓘ If you are talking about the birth of a child or young animal, you use the spelling **born**: *He was **born** at midnight on New Year's Eve.*
If you mean that something is carried, or someone has put up with something, or a woman has given birth to a child, you use the spelling **borne**:
*She had **borne** five children.* • *I couldn't have **borne** much more of the heat.* • *The seeds are **borne** on the wind.*

beard [noun: **beards**] the hair that grows on a man's chin and cheeks: *He'd shaved off his beard.*
• **bearded** [adjective] having a beard: *a tall bearded man*

bearing [noun: **bearings**]
1 a person's bearing is the way they behave, especially the way they stand and walk: *an old gentleman with a dignified bearing*
2 something that has a bearing on a situation affects it in some way: *His age will have a bearing on how quickly he recovers from his illness.*
3 to **get your bearings** is to find your way or to find out where you are

4 if you **lose your bearings**, you lose your way and don't know where you are

beast [noun: **beasts**]
1 a four-footed animal
2 a cruel or nasty person: *Don't do that, you beast!*
• **beastly** [adjective: **beastlier, beastliest**] horrible or nasty: *Stop being so beastly to her.*

beat [verb: **beats, beating, beat, beaten**]
1 to hit someone or something over and over again: *He beat his fists on the table.*
2 to beat someone is to defeat them or win against them: *Do you think Manchester United can beat Real Madrid?*
3 to make a regular sound or movement: *He could hear his heart beating.*
4 to beat food is to stir or mix it by making quick regular movements through it with a spoon, fork or whisk
5 to **beat someone up** is to injure them by hitting them over and over again
[noun: **beats**]
1 a beat is a regular sound or movement like that made by your heart or your pulse: *A low moan from nearby made my heart skip a beat.*
2 music with a beat has a regular rhythm
3 a police officer's beat is the regular route he or she takes around an area

beautiful [adjective]
1 a beautiful person is very pretty or handsome
2 very pleasant to see, hear or smell: *a beautiful sunset* • *a beautiful voice* • *a rose with a beautiful scent*
3 the weather is beautiful when it is very pleasant, especially if it is bright, dry and sunny: *It's a beautiful morning.*
• **beautifully** [adverb] in a beautiful way: *She is always beautifully dressed.*

ⓘ Remember that beautiful starts **b-e-a-u**.

beauty [noun: **beauties**]
1 beauty is being very attractive and pleasant to see or hear: *the beauty of the alpine scenery*
2 a beauty is a person who is beautiful to look at: *Her grandmother was a famous beauty.*
3 a beauty is a thing you think is very good: *Just look at the fish he caught. Isn't it a beauty?*

beaver [noun: **beavers**]
1 an animal with a soft brown coat and a large flat tail that lives in dams it builds across rivers using tree branches
2 a beaver is a member of the most junior branch of the Scout Association
[verb: **beavers, beavering, beavered**] to **beaver away** is to work very hard: *Sanjay's been beavering away at that science project for days now.*

became [verb] a way of changing the verb **become** to make a past tense: *It became obvious that he was lying.*

because [conjunction]
1 for the reason that: • *You can't borrow my bike because there's something wrong with the brakes.* • *Just because it's raining, it doesn't mean you should do nothing all day.*
2 because of means as a result of: *The match was postponed because of bad weather.*

beckon [verb: **beckons, beckoning, beckoned**] to beckon to someone is to make a sign with your hand to show them that you want them to come nearer: *Alice beckoned to the waiter to come over.*

become [verb: **becomes, becoming, became, become**]
1 to come to be: *She'd become old and frail.* • *Tony Blair became prime minister in 1997.*
2 to happen to someone or something: *I wonder what became of her?*
• **becoming** [adjective] something that is becoming looks nice on the person wearing it

bed [noun: **beds**]
1 a piece of furniture or place to sleep on: *Each night, chimpanzees make beds of twigs high up in the trees.* • *Time to get ready for bed.*
2 the bottom of a river, a lake or the sea
3 an area in a garden that contains flowers and other plants: *a bed of lilies*
[verb: **beds, bedding, bedded**] you **bed down** somewhere when you get ready to go to sleep there

bedclothes [plural noun] things like sheets, blankets or a duvet used to cover a bed

bedding [noun] anything used to make a bed with, such as a mattress, sheets and pillows, or for animals, straw or hay

bedlam [noun] a place full of confusion and noise: *The railway station was bedlam with thousands of people stranded.*

bedraggled [adjective] untidy and dirty: *The kitten had been caught in the rain and its fur was all bedraggled.*

bedridden [adjective] someone who is bedridden stays in bed all the time, usually because they are too ill or frail to get up

bedroom [noun: **bedrooms**] a room with a bed or beds used for sleeping in

bedspread [noun: **bedspreads**] a cover that goes over the top of the other bedclothes on a bed

bedstead [noun: **bedsteads**] the metal or wooden framework of a bed

bee [noun: **bees**]
1 a small winged insect that can sting you. Bees fly from flower to flower collecting nectar to make honey
2 if you **have a bee in your bonnet** about something, you believe it is so important that you think or talk about it all the time

beech [noun: **beeches**] a tree with grey, smooth bark and rounded leaves

beef [noun] meat from a cow

beefburger [noun: **beefburgers**] a flattened cake of minced beef that is fried or grilled and eaten in a bread roll

beefeater [noun: **beefeaters**] one of the guards at the Tower of London, who wear an old-fashioned red uniform

beehive [noun: **beehives**] a box or container where bees are kept so that the honey they make can be collected

beeline [noun] if you **make a beeline for something**, you go straight towards it: *As soon as the doors opened we made a beeline for the sale rail.*

been [verb] a form of the verb **be** that is used with a helping verb to show that something happened in the past: *Thank you, you've been very helpful.*

beer [noun: **beers**] an alcoholic drink made from barley and often flavoured with hops

beetle [noun: **beetles**] an insect with two pairs of wings. Its front wings are hard and cover its back wings when the beetle is not flying

beetroot [noun: **beetroots**] a small, round,

dark red vegetable that grows under the ground

befall [verb: **befalls, befalling, befell, befallen**] if something befalls you, it happens to you: *If some accident should befall me, please get in touch with my relatives in Australia.*

ⓘ **Befall** is a word that isn't used very often nowadays, but you might come across it in older stories.

before [preposition]
1 earlier than something: *Let's go for a walk before lunch.* • *I sent the letter the day before yesterday.*
2 before long means soon: *If you can wait a while, the boss will be back before long.*
[adverb] at an earlier time: *I don't think we've met before.* • *We had all been to the beach the day before.*
[conjunction]
1 earlier than the time when something will happen: *Wash your hands before you come to the table.*
2 rather than: *Ali would die before he would admit he was wrong.*

beforehand [adverb] before the time when something else happens: *If you're coming to the party next week, would you let me know beforehand.*

beg [verb: **begs, begging, begged**]
1 if someone begs, they ask other people to give them money or food, because they are poor or have no job: *children begging in the streets*
2 if you beg for something, you ask someone very eagerly for it because you want it very much: *Kitty begged her father to buy her the shoes.*

began [verb] a way of changing the verb **begin** to make a past tense: *It began to rain and we stayed in.*

beggar [noun: **beggars**] someone who lives by begging for money or food from people who pass by

begin [verb: **begins, beginning, began, begun**]
1 to begin is to start: *The concert began at 7.30 and finished at about 9.30.* • *Marie had*
begun to enjoy being at the new school.
2 to begin with means at first: *Lorna didn't like her new school to begin with.*

♦ **beginner** [noun: **beginners**] someone who has only just started to do or to learn something: *a guitar class for beginners*

♦ **beginning** [noun: **beginnings**]
1 the start of something: *He led from the beginning of the race.*
2 the early part of a period of time: *In the beginning, I didn't like her much.* • *My birthday is at the beginning of July.*
3 the beginnings of something are the first things that happen before it gets bigger: *the beginnings of a really successful company*

begrudge [verb: **begrudges, begrudging, begrudged**] to be jealous of someone because of something they have got or done: *I don't begrudge him his success.*

beguiling [adjective] seeming to be attractive: *Winning millions on the lottery is a very beguiling idea, but it isn't very likely to happen.*

begun [verb] a form of the verb **begin** that is used with a helping verb to show that something happened in the past: *I had just begun the ironing when James phoned.*

behalf [noun]
1 you do something **on behalf of** a person or an organization when you act as their representative: *I'm here on behalf of the Premium Insurance Company.*
2 to do something **on someone's behalf** is to do it for them or because of them: *Please don't go to any trouble on my behalf.*

behave [verb: **behaves, behaving, behaved**]
1 to behave in a certain way is to act in that way: *If you behave badly today, you won't get any sweets.* • *They were all behaving very strangely.*
2 if you behave or behave yourself, you are good and don't do anything that you shouldn't

behaviour [noun]
1 the way you behave: *Gold stars are awarded for good behaviour.* • *His behaviour was really awful that day.*
2 the way an animal or other living thing normally behaves: *Clare wants to study the behaviour of gorillas.*

behead [verb: **beheads, beheading, beheaded**] to behead someone is to cut their head off: *King Charles I was beheaded in 1649.*

behind [preposition]
1 at or to the back of something or someone: *Look behind the sofa.* • *Shut the door behind you, please.*
2 staying after someone or something: *The steam train left a trail of sooty smoke behind it.*
3 not as far ahead as other people: *Robert's fallen behind the rest of the class.*
4 helping or encouraging someone or something: *The crowd really got behind him and cheered and clapped as he ran to the finishing line.*
5 responsible for something: *We want to find out who was behind the robbery.*
6 an experience is behind you when it happened in the past: *That's all behind him now.*
7 if something is done **behind your back**, it is done without you knowing about it: *I don't like people talking about me behind my back.*
[adverb]
1 at or to the back: *an engine with six carriages behind*
2 late or not up to date: *She's fallen behind with her work.*
3 if you stay behind or remain behind, you do not leave when other people leave: *My sister left. I stayed behind to pack her things along with mine.*
[noun: **behinds**] your bottom: *Get up off your behind and do some work!*

behold [verb: **beholds, beholding, beheld**] to behold something is to see it: *He beheld a huge, tawny lion, with great glistening white teeth.*

ⓘ **Behold** is an old-fashioned word.

beige [noun] a very light brown colour, like the colour of milky coffee or tea

ⓘ This word is pronounced **bayj**.

being [verb] the form of the verb **be** that is used to make certain tenses: *I am being good today.* • *He was just being kind.*
[noun: **beings**] a being is something that lives

or exists: *a science-fiction story about beings from other planets*

belated [adjective] arriving late: *a belated birthday present*
♦ **belatedly** [adverb] late: *He did it rather belatedly, but at least he did thank me.*

belch [verb: **belches, belching, belched**] to belch is to let air from your stomach come out of your mouth with a loud noise
[noun: **belches**] the noise made when you let air from your stomach come out of your mouth

belfry [noun: **belfries**] a tower, especially on a church, where a bell is hung

belief [noun: **beliefs**] something you believe, especially something that you think is true or exists

believable [adjective] if something is believable, it can be believed because it could happen: *a believable excuse*

believe [verb: **believes, believing, believed**]
1 to be sure that something is true or real: *I believed his story.*
2 to think that something is true though you are not completely sure: *I believe he was once a famous film star.*
3 if you **believe in** something, you accept that it is right or it exists: *I don't believe in ghosts.* • *His parents didn't believe in smacking children when they were naughty.*
♦ **believer** [noun: **believers**] someone who believes something, especially someone who believes in a particular religion

bell [noun: **bells**]
1 a hollow metal object with a long piece of metal inside that swings and hits the sides of the bell making a ringing sound
2 any device that makes a ringing sound: *a doorbell* • *a bicycle bell*

bellow [verb: **bellows, bellowing, bellowed**] to bellow is to roar like a bull: *He bellowed at us to stop what we were doing.*
[noun: **bellows**] a roar

belly [noun: **bellies**]
1 the front part of your body between your chest and the tops of your legs
2 your stomach
3 the part underneath an animal's body between its front legs and its back legs

belly-button [noun: **belly-buttons**] your navel

belly-flop [noun: **belly-flops**] someone diving does a belly-flop when they hit the surface of the water with the front of their body

belong [verb: **belongs, belonging, belonged**]
1 if something belongs to you, you own it: *Who does this suitcase belong to?*
2 you belong to the place where you feel at home: *She felt as if she didn't belong there.*
3 if you belong to a club or organization, you are a member: *Peter belongs to the local tennis club.*
4 something belongs in a particular place if that is where it is usually kept: *That big chair belongs over there by the fireplace.*
5 people or things that belong with each other match each other, fit together or make a pair: *These socks don't belong together.*
• **belongings** [plural noun] your belongings are the things you own: *Omar just packed up all his belongings and moved out.*

beloved [adjective] loved very much: *her beloved old teddy bear*
[noun] the person that someone is in love with: *He sent a red rose to his beloved.*

ⓘ This word is pronounced be-**luv**-id.

below [preposition] lower than or under something: *The plane was flying below the clouds.* • *Simon was below me in school.*
[adverb] at or to a lower place: *We climbed to the top of the hill and looked down on the valley below.* • *Fill in the tear-off strip below.*

belt [noun: **belts**]
1 a band of leather, cloth or plastic that you wear around your waist
2 a loop of material in a machine that moves round and round: *a conveyor belt* • *a fan belt*
[verb: **belts, belting, belted**]
1 to belt someone is to hit them hard: *The branch sprang back and belted him on the nose.*
2 to belt is to go very fast: *The boys came belting down the hill on their bikes.*

bench [noun: **benches**]
1 a long seat: *We sat on a wooden bench in the park.*

2 a table used to make things on: *a carpenter's bench*

bend [verb: **bends, bending, bent**]
1 you bend or bend down when you lower your body by making your back curve: *She bent down to look more closely at the tiny insects.*
2 to curve: *He bent the wire around the post.* • *The road bends to the right up ahead.*
3 if you **bend over backwards** to do something, you try your hardest to do it
4 if someone **bends the rules**, they break the rules in a way that will not be noticed or is not very important
[noun: **bends**] a curve: *a bend in the road*

beneath [preposition] below or under something: *Atlantis, the lost city beneath the sea*
[adverb] below or under: *the sky above and the earth beneath* • *I hadn't realized there was a second layer of chocolates beneath.*

benefit [noun: **benefits**]
1 a benefit is something that helps you: *Having a mobile phone can be a real benefit in an emergency.*
2 people on benefit get money from the government to help them with their living expenses
[verb: **benefits, benefiting** or **benefitting, benefited** or **benefitted**] if you benefit from something, or if something benefits you, it helps you: *I think you'll benefit from the extra lessons.*

benevolent [adjective] full of kindness: *The old man gave the children a benevolent smile.*

benign [adjective]
1 a benign tumour will not cause you any harm
2 kind and gentle

bent [verb] a way of changing the verb **bend** to make a past tense. It can be used with or without a helping verb: *The striker bent the ball round the defenders.* • *I have bent this fork.*
[adjective]
1 not straight: *a bent pin*
2 if someone is **bent on** doing something, they are determined to do it

bequeath [verb: **bequeaths, bequeathing, bequeathed**] to bequeath your money or property to someone is to arrange for them to be given it after you die

bequest [noun: **bequests**] money or property that someone gives to you after they have died

bereaved [adjective] someone is bereaved if one of their close relatives or friends has died: *the bereaved families of the accident victims* [plural noun] the bereaved are the close relatives or friends of someone who has died: *an organization offering counselling to the bereaved*

♦ **bereavement** [noun: **bereavements**] someone suffers a bereavement when a relative or close friend dies

beret [noun: **berets**] a flat round hat made of felt or some other kind of soft fabric

ⓘ This word is pronounced **ber**-ay.

berry [noun: **berries**] a small fruit containing seeds that grows on certain types of plant: *Holly has red berries.*

ⓘ Do not confuse the spellings of **berry**, **beret** and **bury**, which can sound the same.

berserk [adjective] to go berserk is to become very angry or violent: *Dad went berserk when he saw the damage to the car.*

berth [noun: **berths**]
1 a bed on a boat or a train
2 a place in a harbour where a boat or ship can tie up or anchor
[verb: **berths, berthing, berthed**] a ship berths when it reaches the end of a journey and ties up or anchors in a harbour

beside [preposition]
1 next to or at the side of someone or something: *We do like to be beside the sea.* • *Go and stand beside Billy.*
2 compared with: *Beside that tiny kitten the dog looks enormous.*
3 if something is **beside the point**, it has nothing to do with the thing being talked about or dealt with
4 if you are **beside yourself**, you are very upset: *Her parents are beside themselves with grief.*

ⓘ Be careful not to use **besides** when you should use **beside**:
✓ *That's beside the point.*
✗ *That's besides the point.*

besides [preposition] as well as: *He isn't really interested in anything besides football.* [adverb] also: *It's too wet to go out. Besides, I have a lot of marking to do.*

besiege [verb: **besieges, besieging, besieged**] to besiege a place is to surround it so that no one or nothing can get out: *The castle was besieged for three weeks by the English army.*

best [adjective] better than all the rest: *the best film they'd ever seen*
[adverb] in the most suitable or pleasing way: *I know it's difficult but just do it as best you can.* • *The city is best seen at night when all the skyscrapers are lit up.*
[noun]
1 the most excellent things: *Parents want the best for their children.*
2 if you **do your best**, you do something as well as you can
3 to **make the best of** something is to enjoy it or do as well as you can with it, even if it is not very good: *Although it was raining, we made the best of our trip to the seaside.*

best man [noun] the best man at a wedding is the man who helps the bridegroom and stands beside him during the ceremony

bet [noun: **bets**] a bet is money that you risk on the result of something before the result is known. If the result is the way you have said it would be you win more money, but if the result is different you lose the money you bet
[verb: **bets, betting, bet** or **betted**]
1 to make a bet: *I'll bet you £5 that Sophie wins.*
2 to bet is to say that something will happen because you are pretty sure that it will: *I bet that Jackie will be late again.*

betray [verb: **betrays, betraying, betrayed**] to betray someone who trusts you is to do something to harm them or help their opponents: *He betrayed his country by selling secrets to the enemy.*

♦ **betrayal** [noun: **betrayals**] doing something to harm someone who trusts you

betrothed [adjective] one person is betrothed to another when they are engaged to be married

better [adjective]

1 of a higher standard: *This is a better way to do it.*

2 not as bad or as ill: *My cold's much better today.* • *Don't go back to work until you're better.*

[adverb]

1 in a more pleasing way or to a higher degree: *Which do you like better, the green one or the blue one?* • *Try to do better next time.*

2 better off means richer or in a better position: *We'd be better off taking the plane. We'd get there quicker.*

3 if you **had better** do something, you must or ought to do it: *I had better hurry, or I'll be late.*

[noun]

1 something of a higher standard than others: *Of the two tennis players, Federer was definitely the better.*

2 if you **get the better of** someone, you defeat them: *You'll never get the better of him, no matter how long you argue.*

between [preposition]

1 in the area or space that divides two people, things or places: *What letter comes between Q and S in the alphabet?* • *the road between San Francisco and Los Angeles*

2 giving each a part or a piece: *Colin and Russell divided the work between them.*

3 including or involving each one: *They'll have to sort it out between them. We're not getting mixed up in it.*

4 one and not the other: *I had to decide between going to the concert or staying to watch the fireworks.*

[adverb] things between or in between are in the middle: *He'd had a big breakfast, an enormous lunch and lots of snacks in between.*

beverage [noun: **beverages**] a drink

beware [verb] to tell someone to beware or beware of something is to warn them that there is danger: *The sign on the gate said 'Beware of the dog'.*

ⓘ The verb **beware** does not have different forms or tenses like other verbs, because it is only used when you are telling people what to do or giving them a warning.

bewilder [verb: **bewilders, bewildering, bewildered**] to bewilder someone is to confuse them

• **bewildering** [adjective] confusing: *a bewildering set of instructions*

• **bewilderment** [noun] being bewildered: *'What on earth is this?' exclaimed Leo in bewilderment.*

bewitch [verb: **bewitches, bewitching, bewitched**] to bewitch someone is to put a magic spell on them

• **bewitching** [adjective] so attractive that you feel as if you are under a magic spell: *a bewitching smile*

beyond [preposition]

1 on the far side of something: *Turn right just beyond the bridge.*

2 more than or greater than something: *The noise level was beyond anything I'd ever experienced before.*

3 if something is beyond someone, it is too difficult or confusing for them to understand: *It's beyond me why he didn't grab the opportunity when he had it.*

[adverb] further away: *We could see right across the valley to the mountains beyond.*

bi- [prefix] if a word starts with **bi-**, it adds the meaning 'two' or 'twice' to the word. For example, a *bicycle* has two wheels and *bimonthly* means twice a month

bias [noun: **biases**] if you have a bias towards a person or thing, you prefer them, often without thinking about whether someone or something else may be just as good: *There is a definite bias against change of any sort in the local council.*

• **biased** or **biassed** [adjective] favouring one person or thing unfairly: *a biased point of view*

bib [noun: **bibs**] a piece of cloth or plastic tied around a baby's neck to protect the front of its clothes while it is eating

Bible [noun: **Bibles**] the holy book of the Christian and Jewish religions

• **biblical** [adjective] to do with or in the Bible: *a biblical character*

biblio- [prefix] if a word starts with **biblio-**, it has something to do with books. For example, a *bibliography* is a list of books

biceps [noun: **biceps**] the big muscles at the top of your arms that bulge when you bend your arms upwards

bicker [verb: **bickers, bickering, bickered**] if two people bicker, they argue about things that are not very important: *Let's not waste time bickering about who will pay for it. It's only 50p.*

bicycle [noun: **bicycles**] a machine you ride on, made up of a metal frame with two wheels that you move by pressing down on pedals with your feet

bid¹ [noun: **bids**]
1 a bid is an offer of the price you are prepared to pay for something at an auction
2 a bid is a try: *They made a final desperate bid for freedom.*
[verb: **bids, bidding, bid**] to make an offer of a price: *Will someone bid £5 for this beautiful old chair?*

bid² [verb: **bids, bidding, bid** or **bade, bidden** or **bid**]
1 to make a greeting to someone: *He bade me goodnight.*
2 to tell someone to do something: *The headmaster bade them come to his office next morning.*

bidet [noun: **bidets**] a bidet is a small low bowl that you sit on to wash your bottom

ⓘ This word is pronounced **bee**-day.

bifocals [plural noun] glasses that allow you to focus on close-up objects as well as distant objects. Look up and compare **varifocals**

big [adjective: **bigger, biggest**]
1 large: *a big lorry* • *It was the biggest fish he'd ever seen.*
2 older: *My big brother is 15.* • *When you're bigger you can walk to school on your own.*
3 important: *Are you going to watch the big match on TV?*
4 successful, popular or famous: *He used to be big in the United States.*

bigamy [noun] being married to two people at the same time

bigot [noun: **bigots**] someone who thinks people who have different beliefs or belong to a different group are wrong

♦ **bigoted** [adjective] prejudiced against anyone with different beliefs or anyone from a different group

♦ **bigotry** [noun] being bigoted

bike [noun: **bikes**] a bicycle

bikini [noun: **bikinis**] a kind of swimsuit for girls and women made up of a bra top and pants

bile [noun] a liquid made in your liver that helps you to digest food

bilingual [adjective] using, knowing or dealing with two different languages: *She's bilingual in French and German.*

bill¹ [noun: **bills**]
1 a piece of paper showing how much is owed for something, such as a meal in a restaurant or the supply of goods or services: *an electricity bill*
2 a poster or printed sheet listing or advertising something
3 a suggestion for a new law that people in parliament discuss and vote for or against

LANGUAGE FOR LIFE
bills
Here are some important words that you may come across when people send you a bill:
• An **account** is a bill showing how much you have paid and how much you must still pay.
• If you pay by **direct debit**, you tell your bank to give money regularly to a person or organization to pay your bills.
• An **invoice** is a piece of paper that lists the things you have bought and says how much you must pay.
• **Outstanding** means 'still to be paid'.
• The **quantity** of something is the number of that thing that you have bought.
• A **quarter** is a period of one-quarter of the year, or three months.
• **Settlement** means paying the amount that you owe.
• A **standing charge** is a fixed amount that you have to pay to an organization whether or not you use their services.
• **VAT** is a tax which is added to the cost of the things you have bought.

bill² [noun: **bills**] a bird's beak

billiards [noun] a game you play by hitting three balls on a large cloth-covered table with the tip of a long stick called a cue

Bb

billion [noun: **billions**] a thousand million, written in numbers as 1,000,000,000 or 1000000000: *The government gets billions of pounds a year from taxes.*

billow [verb: **billows, billowing, billowed**] to billow is to rise in curving shapes like waves: *storm clouds billowing landward from the west*

bin [noun: **bins**] a container for putting rubbish in or for storing food or wine
[verb: **bins, binning, binned**] to bin something is to get rid of it

binary [adjective] made up of two parts: *a binary star*

binary number [noun: **binary numbers**] a number that is made up of the digits 0 and 1 only, used to stand for the amount of units, twos, fours and so on in the number. Computers use these numbers to operate

bind [verb: **binds, binding, bound**]
1 to tie or fasten things together: *They'd bound his hands and feet with tape.*
2 if you are bound to do something, you are obliged to do it: *You are legally bound to reply to this letter.*
[noun] a nuisance: *It was a bit of a bind having to take two buses to get to work.*

binge [verb: **binges, bingeing** or **binging, binged**] to eat or drink too much, especially in a short time
[noun: **binges**] a period of eating or drinking too much

bingo [noun] a gambling game where you match the numbers on your card against numbers picked out at random and called out

binoculars [plural noun] an instrument that is like a telescope but has a lens for each eye: *a pair of binoculars*

bio- [prefix] if a word starts with **bio-**, it has something to do with life or living things. For example, *biology* is the study of living things

biodegradable [adjective] a biodegradable substance does not harm the environment much because it decays quickly and naturally when you throw it away

biographical [adjective] about a person's life: *biographical details* • *a biographical film*

biography [noun: **biographies**] a story about a real person's life

biological [adjective] to do with living things

and the way they grow and behave: *a biological process*

biologist [noun: **biologists**] a person who studies biology

biology [noun] the study of living things

biopsy [noun: **biopsies**] a medical process where some cells are taken from your body to be looked at to see if they are healthy

biosphere [noun] the area on and above the Earth where living things exist

birch [noun: **birches**] a kind of tree with grey or silvery bark and small leaves

bird [noun: **birds**] a creature with wings and feathers that lays eggs: *Penguins are flightless birds.*

bird of prey [noun: **birds of prey**] a bird that kills and eats small animals or birds

birdwatching [noun] the hobby of looking at birds in their natural surroundings

Biro [noun: **Biros**] a kind of ballpoint pen. This word is a trademark

birth [noun: **births**]
1 birth is the process of being born: *Life is the time between birth and death.* • *the birth of nations*
2 a birth is the time when a particular person or animal is born

birth control [noun] methods used to avoid getting pregnant

birthday [noun: **birthdays**] your birthday is the anniversary of the date when you were born

birthmark [noun: **birthmarks**] a mark on someone's skin that they have had since they were born

biscuit [noun: **biscuits**] a kind of hard, baked cake made from dough

bisect [verb: **bisects, bisecting, bisected**] a line bisects something when it cuts it into two parts

bisexual [adjective] sexually attracted to both men and women
[noun: **bisexuals**] someone who is sexually attracted to both men and women

bishop [noun: **bishops**]
1 in some Christian churches such as the Catholic Church and the Church of England, a bishop is a member of the clergy in charge of a district

2 in the game of chess, a bishop is a piece which has a bishop's hat

bison [noun: **bison** or **bisons**] a kind of wild ox with a long shaggy coat

bit[1] [noun: **bits**]

1 a piece or a part: *There were some bits of the book that I really enjoyed.*

2 a metal bar on a horse's bridle that the horse holds in its mouth

3 the smallest piece of computer information

4 a bit is a short time: *Let's wait a bit longer.*

5 a bit of is a small amount: *I need a bit of help with this work.*

6 to do something **bit by bit** is to do it gradually

7 if you **do your bit**, you do your share of work that has to be done

8 if something **comes to bits** or **falls to bits**, it breaks into pieces or falls apart: *The toy came to bits in my hand.* • *This car is falling to bits.*

bit[2] [verb] a way of changing the verb **bite** to make a past tense: *Your dog bit me!*

bitch [noun: **bitches**]

1 a female dog

2 an offensive word for an unpleasant or spiteful woman

✦ **bitchy** [adjective: **bitchier, bitchiest**] nasty or spiteful: *a bitchy remark* • *Don't be bitchy.*

bite [verb: **bites, biting, bit, bitten**]

1 you bite something when you cut through it by bringing your top and bottom teeth together: *Connor bit his tongue when he fell.*

2 if an animal bites, it uses its teeth to attack or injure: *Be careful! The cat sometimes bites.*

[noun: **bites**] a cut or injury made with your teeth, or the part cut off by biting: *The dog gave the postman a nasty bite.* • *Can I have a bite of your apple?*

bitmap [noun: **bitmaps**] a bitmap is a way of displaying an image on a computer. The image is broken up into small pieces of information called pixels that can be stored as units in the computer memory

[verb: **bitmaps, bitmapping, bitmapped**] to create or display an image on a computer in this way

bitter [adjective]

1 bitter things have a sour rather than a sweet taste: *Lemon juice is bitter.*

2 if the weather is bitter, it is uncomfortably cold: *a bitter winter's night*

3 to be bitter is to be angry and resentful because of disappointment: *He turned into a bitter old man who hated the world.*

bizarre [adjective] very odd or strange

black [noun]

1 the darkest colour, the colour of coal or a dark night

2 a black person has dark skin: *black Britons*

[verb: **blacks, blacking, blacked**] if someone **blacks out**, they become unconscious for a short time

black-and-blue [adjective] badly bruised or covered with bruises: *The forwards are often black-and-blue the day after a rugby match.*

blackberry [noun: **blackberries**] a small, very dark purple or black fruit that grows on a plant with prickly stems

blackbird [noun: **blackbirds**] a bird with black feathers and an orange beak. Female blackbirds are dark brown

blackboard [noun: **blackboards**] a dark surface for writing on with chalk

blacken [verb: **blackens, blackening, blackened**]

1 to make something black or dark: *The soldiers blackened their faces so that they wouldn't be seen.*

2 to blacken someone's character is to damage it by saying something bad about it

black eye [noun: **black eyes**] an injury that has bruised the skin around your eye

black hole [noun: **black holes**] an area in outer space that draws everything into it by gravity. Nothing can escape from a black hole

black ice [noun] clear ice on roads that is difficult to see and so is dangerous for drivers

blacklist [noun: **blacklists**] a list of people who are not to be given something, for example jobs

[verb: **blacklists, blacklisting, blacklisted**] to blacklist someone is to put their name on a blacklist, so that they are not given something

black magic [noun] magic which is meant to do harm

blackmail [verb: **blackmails, blackmailing, blackmailed**] if you blackmail someone, you get money from them by threatening to tell people something they have kept secret or to hurt someone they care about

[noun] the crime of blackmailing someone

◆ **blackmailer** [noun: **blackmailers**] a criminal who blackmails someone

black market [noun] something bought or sold on the black market is bought or sold illegally or dishonestly

blackout [noun: **blackouts**]
1 if there is a blackout somewhere, there is total darkness with no lights on or to be seen
2 if someone has a blackout, they become unconscious for a short time and don't remember anything about it

black pudding [noun: **black puddings**] a kind of sausage made from animal's blood mixed with spices

black sheep [noun: **black sheep**] a member of a family or group who gets into trouble a lot

blacksmith [noun: **blacksmiths**] someone who makes and repairs things made of iron, especially horseshoes

bladder [noun: **bladders**] the organ in your body where urine is collected

blade [noun: **blades**]
1 the cutting part of a knife, sword or razor that has a thin sharp edge
2 a long thin leaf of grass

blame [verb: **blames, blaming, blamed**]
1 to say that something is someone's fault: *It's not my fault so don't try to blame me.* • *He's been made to look silly, so you can't blame him for being angry.*
2 you are to blame for something bad if you are responsible for it: *Who is to blame for this mess?*
[noun] blame is fault or responsibility for something bad that has happened: *They were made to take the blame.*

◆ **blameless** [adjective] with no faults or having done nothing wrong: *She has led a blameless life.*

bland [adjective: **blander, blandest**]
1 bland food is mild and doesn't have any strong flavours or spices

2 bland means mild and not causing any offence or annoyance: *a bland smile*

blank [adjective: **blanker, blankest**]
1 if something like a sheet of paper is blank, it has nothing marked or written on it: *a blank cheque*
2 if someone's face is blank, their face or eyes show nothing, either because they don't understand or because they don't want to show any feeling: *a blank stare*
[noun: **blanks**]
1 an empty space: *I can't remember anything. The whole of last week is a complete blank.*
2 a cartridge for a gun that contains an explosive but no bullet: *The actors used blanks in their rifles when the battle scenes were being filmed.*

blanket [noun: **blankets**]
1 a covering for a bed, usually made of wool or some other warm fabric
2 a layer that covers everything: *a blanket of snow*

blare [verb: **blares, blaring, blared**] to blare is to sound loudly: *music blaring from the loudspeakers*
[noun: **blares**] a loud sound like the sound made by a trumpet or horn

blaspheme [verb: **blasphemes, blaspheming, blasphemed**] to blaspheme is to curse using words that offend people who believe in God or a god

◆ **blasphemous** [adjective] using curses or swearwords that are disrespectful to God or a god

◆ **blasphemy** [noun: **blasphemies**] cursing or swearing that is disrespectful to God or a god

blast [noun: **blasts**]
1 a loud violent explosion: *The bomb went off and many people were injured in the blast.*
2 a strong wind or gust of wind: *They stood shivering in the icy blast.*
3 a loud sound from a trumpet or horn: *The lorry driver gave a couple of blasts on his horn.*
4 if something is playing **full blast**, it is playing as loudly as possible: *The radio was on full blast.*
[verb: **blasts, blasting, blasted**]
1 to blast is to use explosives or an explosion to

break up or destroy something solid such as rock: *They were blasting in the quarry again yesterday.*

2 to blast is to make a loud noise: *music blasting out of the open windows*

3 to blast something is to strongly criticize it: *The mayor made a speech blasting all his opponents.*

4 a rocket **blasts off** when its fuel is ignited and it starts to rise into the air

blast-off [noun: **blast-offs**] the moment when a rocket is launched

blatant [adjective] bad behaviour is blatant when it is very obvious and the person doing it doesn't seem to care that it is obvious: *It was a blatant lie.*

♦ **blatantly** [adverb] in a very obvious way: *They were quite blatantly dropping litter all over the park.*

blaze [noun: **blazes**]

1 the bright flames from a fire: *The firemen put out the blaze.*

2 something that glows like a fire: *a blaze of colour* • *a blaze of glory*

[verb: **blazes, blazing, blazed**] to glow brightly with, or as if with, flames: *Katie was blazing with anger.*

blazer [noun: **blazers**] a kind of jacket worn as part of a school uniform or by members of a club

bleach [noun] a chemical used to whiten or lighten fabrics or as a household cleaner

[verb: **bleaches, bleaching, bleached**] to lighten or whiten something with bleach or sunlight

♦ **bleached** [adjective] made white or blond by bleach or sunlight: *bleached hair*

bleak [adjective: **bleaker, bleakest**]

1 cold, bare and miserable: *a bleak winter landscape*

2 hopeless and miserable: *Our chances of winning the football match looked bleak.*

♦ **bleakly** [adverb] in a cold or miserable way: *He smiled bleakly.*

♦ **bleakness** [noun] being bleak: *the bleakness of the dark hills*

bleary [adjective: **blearier, bleariest**] if your eyes are bleary, they are red and tired and you can't see clearly

bleat [noun: **bleats**] the sound a sheep or goat makes

[verb: **bleats, bleating, bleated**]

1 a sheep or goat bleats when it makes its usual sound

2 to speak in an annoying complaining way: *She was bleating on about how unfair it all was.*

bleed [verb: **bleeds, bleeding, bled**]

1 you bleed when you lose blood, especially from a cut or injury

2 if a person's heart bleeds, they are feeling very sad

♦ **bleeding** [noun] a flow of blood: *First try to stop the bleeding and then ring for an ambulance.*

bleep [noun: **bleeps**] a short high-pitched sound made by an electronic device as a signal

[verb: **bleeps, bleeping, bleeped**]

1 to make this sound

2 to signal to someone using an electronic device: *If you need to get in touch, you can have me bleeped.*

♦ **bleeper** [noun: **bleepers**] an electronic device used to contact someone by signalling them with a bleeping sound

blemish [noun: **blemishes**]

1 a mark that spoils something's appearance: *an apple covered with blemishes*

2 something that spoils someone's good reputation: *a blemish on his character*

blend [verb: **blends, blending, blended**]

1 to put things together so that they are mixed in with each other: *Blend the butter and the sugar.*

2 if people or things **blend in** somewhere, they fit in well with the people or things around them

[noun: **blends**] a mixture of two or more things: *Banana milkshake is a blend of milk, banana and ice cream.*

♦ **blender** [noun: **blenders**] a machine with a blade that turns quickly, used for mixing foods or liquids together

bless [verb: **blesses, blessing, blessed**]

1 if someone is blessed, they are made happy or they have good luck: *They've been blessed with two beautiful children.*

2 to bless someone or something is to ask God to look after them: *The cardinal blessed the poor.*

♦ **blessing** [noun: **blessings**]
1 a wish for happiness: *He gave the young couple his blessing.*
2 something that brings happiness or relief: *The rain will be a blessing for everyone who has been suffering in the drought.*
3 if something is **a blessing in disguise**, it doesn't seem to be good but it has a good or useful effect

blew [verb] a way of changing the verb **blow** to make a past tense: *Her hat blew off in the wind.*

blind [adjective] not able to see: *New-born kittens are blind.*
[verb: **blinds, blinding, blinded**] to make someone blind: *He was blinded in the war.* • *The light blinded me for a moment.*
[noun: **blinds**] a covering for a window used instead of curtains or used to keep out strong sunlight: *Pull down the blinds.*

blindfold [noun: **blindfolds**] a cover put over someone's eyes to stop them seeing
[verb: **blindfolds, blindfolding, blindfolded**] to put a blindfold on someone

blinding [adjective] something blinding is dazzling or causes blindness for a short time: *a blinding flash*

blink [verb: **blinks, blinking, blinked**] to close your eyes for a short time: *blinking in the strong sunlight* • *It will all be over before you can blink.*
[noun: **blinks**] the short time taken to close and open your eyes: *It was all over in the blink of an eye.*

blinkers [plural noun] blinkers are two pieces of leather put over a horse's eyes to stop it seeing in any direction except to the front

bliss [noun] bliss is a feeling of very great happiness: *It was bliss not to have to go to work for a couple of days.*

♦ **blissful** [adjective] lovely: *We spent a blissful day at the seaside.*

♦ **blissfully** [adverb] happily: *Pete was blissfully unaware of the trouble he had caused.*

blister [noun: **blisters**] a thin bubble on your skin where it has been burned or rubbed
[verb: **blisters, blistering, blistered**] to form blisters

♦ **blistering** [adjective]
1 a blistering pace is a very fast pace
2 blistering weather is uncomfortably hot

blithe [adjective] happy and carefree
♦ **blithely** [adjective] happily and without worry or care: *Paul blithely imagines he can pass the exam without doing any work.*

blitz [noun: **blitzes**]
1 an attack made by many military aircraft dropping bombs
2 a quick burst of activity, for example, to get through tidying or other work that needs to be done

blizzard [noun: **blizzards**] a storm with wind and heavy snow

bloated [adjective] swollen: *His stomach felt bloated after the huge meal.*

blob [noun: **blobs**] a round lump of something soft or liquid: *blobs of paint*

block [noun: **blocks**]
1 a solid lump of something: *Cut the wood into blocks.* • *a block of ice cream*
2 a group of buildings or houses that are joined together: *a block of flats* • *Go down a couple of blocks and turn the corner.*
3 a barrier or obstacle that stops people or things getting through: *a road block*
[verb: **blocks, blocking, blocked**]
1 to block something is to close it up so that nothing can get through: *The fallen leaves had blocked the drain.* • *The road was blocked by an overturned lorry.*
2 to block something is to get in its way: *There were lots of taller people in front blocking our view.*

blockade [noun: **blockades**] when a place is surrounded by soldiers or ships to stop people or things getting in and out: *a blockade of French ports*
[verb: **blockades, blockading, blockaded**] to surround a place to stop people or things getting in and out

blockage [noun: **blockages**] something that blocks a road, channel or pipe: *The fallen tree had caused a blockage.*

block capitals [plural noun] you use block capitals when you use capital letters to write every letter in every word, LIKE THIS

block graph [noun: **block graphs**] a graph with piles of blocks that show the number of things in different groups

blond or **blonde** [adjective: **blonder, blondest**] fair-haired
[noun: **blonds** or **blondes**] a person with fair hair

ⓘ The spelling **blonde**, with an **e**, is used for girls and women.
The spelling **blond**, without an **e**, is used for boys and men.

blood [noun] the red liquid that carries nutrients, oxygen and other substances round your body in veins

blood donor [noun: **blood donors**] someone who gives some of their blood to be used for other people who have lost blood in an accident or operation and need a blood transfusion

blood group [noun: **blood groups**] your blood group is the type of blood you have. If you ever need a blood transfusion the blood used will come from someone with the same blood group

bloodhound [noun: **bloodhounds**] a kind of hunting dog with long ears, a wrinkled face and a very good sense of smell

bloodshed [noun] bloodshed is violence in which people are injured or killed

bloodshot [adjective] if your eyes are bloodshot, the white parts are red

bloodstream [noun] your bloodstream is the blood moving round your body inside a system of veins: *If the infection gets into the bloodstream it is carried quickly round the body.*

bloodthirsty [adjective: **bloodthirstier, bloodthirstiest**] a bloodthirsty person is eager to kill or enjoys seeing people or animals being killed

blood transfusion [noun: **blood transfusions**] when some blood from a donor is injected into your bloodstream

blood vessel [noun: **blood vessels**] one of the tubes that carry blood around the body, for example an artery, vein or capillary, and that form a network throughout the whole body

bloody [adjective: **bloodier, bloodiest**] covered in or full of blood: *a bloody nose*

bloom [noun: **blooms**] a flower: *a rose bush with many blooms*
[verb: **blooms, blooming, bloomed**] to flower: *Many plants in the garden have bloomed early this year.*

blossom [noun: **blossoms**] the flowers that appear on a fruit tree before the fruit
[verb: **blossoms, blossoming, blossomed**]
1 a tree or bush blossoms when it flowers before producing fruit
2 a person blossoms when they become more successful or attractive: *Under the teacher's guidance, his musical talent blossomed.*

blot [noun: **blots**]
1 an inky stain
2 something unpleasant or ugly: *a blot on his character*
[verb: **blots, blotting, blotted**]
1 to make an inky stain on paper
2 if you blot or **blot up** something that has spilled, you dab at it to dry it and prevent it smearing
3 if you **blot out** an unpleasant thought or memory, you put it out of your mind completely

blotch [noun: **blotches**] a spot or patch of a different colour: *Maddy's skin was covered with red blotches.*
♦ **blotchy** [adjective: **blotchier, blotchiest**] marked with blotches

blouse [noun: **blouses**] a woman's shirt

blow [noun: **blows**]
1 a hard knock: *a blow to the face*
2 a sudden piece of bad luck: *It was a bit of a blow not being able to go to the concert.*
[verb: **blows, blowing, blew, blown**]
1 wind blows when it moves around: *a breeze blowing from the west*
2 to blow something is to force air on to it or into it: *Blow on the hot soup so that you don't burn your mouth.*
3 to blow a musical instrument is to breathe into it to make a sound: *blow a horn*
4 when something unpleasant **blows over**, it passes and is forgotten: *I hope your work problems soon blow over.*

Bb

5 to **blow something up** is to destroy it with an explosion: *Guy Fawkes plotted to blow up the Houses of Parliament.*

blowlamp [noun: **blowlamps**] a tool for aiming a very hot flame at something to heat it up and melt it

blubber [noun] the fat from whales and other sea animals

blue [noun: **blues**]
1 the colour of the sky in the day time if there are no clouds
2 if something comes **out of the blue**, it happens without anyone expecting it
3 if someone **has the blues**, they are feeling unhappy or depressed
[adjective]
1 of the colour blue: *a blue jersey*
2 unhappy or depressed: *Poor Brendan is feeling a bit blue today.*

bluebell [noun: **bluebells**] a flower with blue bell-shaped flowers

bluebottle [noun: **bluebottle**] a large fly with a shiny blue body

blueprint [noun: **blueprints**] a plan of work that is to be done, especially of something that is to be built

bluff [verb: **bluffs, bluffing, bluffed**] to bluff is to make people think that you know something when you don't, or that you are going to do something that you have no intention of doing
[noun: **bluffs**] a trick or deception: *They weren't going to attack. It was only a bluff.*

blunder [noun: **blunders**] a bad or embarrassing mistake
[verb: **blunders, blundering, blundered**]
1 to make a bad or embarrassing mistake
2 to move around in an awkward or clumsy way: *He couldn't see where he was going and blundered into a ditch.*

blunt [adjective: **blunter, bluntest**]
1 with an edge or point that is not sharp: *This knife is blunt.*
2 someone who is blunt says what they think without trying to be polite: *Nick is always blunt and to the point.*
◆ bluntly [adverb] without trying to be polite: *'I hate it,' she said bluntly.*

blur [noun: **blurs**]

1 something with edges that can't be seen clearly: *a blur of faces*
2 something that you can't remember clearly: *I don't really know what happened. It was all a blur.*

blurt [verb: **blurts, blurting, blurted**] to **blurt something out** is to say it suddenly without thinking: *Kenny told us about the party. He just blurted it out and totally spoiled the surprise.*

blush [noun: **blushes**] a bright pink glow on the face from embarrassment
[verb: **blushes, blushing, blushed**] to go pink in the face with embarrassment: *Everyone turned to look at Philip, who blushed.*

bluster [noun] loud angry talk or boasting
◆ blustery [adjective] if the weather is blustery, the wind is blowing in strong gusts

boa constrictor [noun: **boa constrictors**] a very large South American snake that kills its prey by coiling round it and crushing it

boar [noun: **boars**]
1 a male pig
2 a wild pig

board [noun: **boards**]
1 a flat piece of cut wood
2 a flat piece of material with a pattern or divisions marked on it, used to play a game: *a backgammon board*
3 if board is provided somewhere where people stay, they are given their meals there: *The company gives us £25 a day for board.*
4 a group of people who manage a business company or other organization: *a board of directors*
5 **on board** means on a ship, aircraft or other public transport vehicle
[verb: **boards, boarding, boarded**]
1 if someone boards, they are provided with their meals and lodging somewhere: *The boys will board during term time while their parents are away.*
2 to board a ship or an aircraft is to get on it to make a journey: *The astronauts boarded the spaceship.*
◆ boarder [noun: **boarders**]
1 someone who stays in a boarding house
2 a pupil who stays at a boarding school: *The school has both day pupils and boarders.*

boarding house [noun: **boarding houses**] a house where guests pay a fixed price for meals and their room

boarding school [noun: **boarding schools**] a school where some or all of the pupils live during term time

boast [verb: **boasts, boasting, boasted**] to boast is to talk proudly about things you own or things you have done, in a way that other people find annoying: *He's always boasting about his big house and his fancy car.*
[noun: **boasts**] a boast is something you say when you boast: *It was her proud boast that she'd never failed an exam.*

boat [noun: **boats**]
1 a vehicle for travelling over the surface of water. A boat is smaller than a ship
2 if two or more people are **in the same boat**, they have the same problems or face the same difficulties

bob [verb: **bobs, bobbing, bobbed**] to bob is to move up and down quickly above the surface or top of something: *little boats bobbing on the lake • I saw their heads bob up from behind the hedge.*

bobbin [noun: **bobbins**] a round object on which thread is wound, often so that it can be used in a sewing machine

bobble [noun: **bobbles**] a small round piece of soft material used for decoration on clothing, especially on hats

bobsleigh [noun: **bobsleighs**] a kind of long sledge which has a compartment for the riders and is used for racing down ice slopes

bode [verb: **bodes**] if something bodes well, or bodes ill, it shows that something good, or something bad, is likely to happen

bodice [noun: **bodices**] the part of a dress that fits tightly on the body above the waist

bodily [adjective] bodily means of the body: *Blood and saliva are bodily fluids.*
[adverb] by or with your whole body: *He was carried bodily down the river by the current.*

body [noun: **bodies**]
1 the whole of a human being or an animal: *I had a rash all over my body.*
2 a dead person or animal: *They found the bodies of hundreds of dead birds on the shore.*

bodyguard [noun: **bodyguards**] someone whose job is to protect an important or famous person

bog [noun: **bogs**] an area of land that is very wet and where the ground is so soft that you sink into it
[verb: **bogs, bogging, bogged**] if you get **bogged down** in something, you can't continue it or make any progress: *She got bogged down in her sums and couldn't finish the exercise.*
→ **boggy**

boggle [verb: **boggles, boggling, boggled**] your mind boggles when you are not able to understand or imagine something

boggy [adjective: **boggier, boggiest**] boggy ground is wet and sinks under you when you step on it

bogus [adjective]
1 pretending to be something they are not: *Old people must be careful of bogus salesmen.*
2 false: *The documents turned out to be bogus.*

boil[1] [verb: **boils, boiling, boiled**]
1 something boils when it is heated until it bubbles and turns into gas or vapour: *Is the water boiling yet?*
2 to boil a liquid is to heat it until it bubbles: *Boil some water in a saucepan and add the pasta.*
3 to boil food is to cook it in boiling water: *Are you going to boil or fry the eggs?*
[noun] a state of boiling: *Bring the water to the boil.*
→ **boiling**

boil[2] [noun: **boils**] a boil is a red painful swelling on your skin caused by an infection

boiling [adjective] very hot: *It's boiling in here.*

boiling point [noun: **boiling points**] the temperature at which a particular liquid boils: *The boiling point of water is 100 degrees Celsius.*

boisterous [adjective] very active and full of energy, especially playing roughly and noisily: *a boisterous two-year-old*

bold [adjective: **bolder, boldest**]
1 daring or fearless: *a bold leader • It was rather bold of him to ask that question.*
2 standing out clearly: *a bold swirly pattern*
3 bold type or print is thick dark letters **like this**
♦ **boldly** [adjective]
1 fearlessly: *Samuel walked boldly into the*

Bb

room, which was full of strangers.
2 clearly: *The bright red flowers stood out boldly against the green leaves.*

bollard [noun: **bollards**] a short post placed on a road to stop cars from driving into or on an area

bolster [verb: **bolsters, bolstering, bolstered**] to bolster something, or to **bolster it up**, is to do something to support or strengthen it: *We were bolstered up by the people cheering us on along the route.*
[noun: **bolsters**] a long pillow

bolt [noun: **bolts**]
1 a metal bar that slides across to fasten a door
2 a kind of heavy screw that is held in place by a nut
3 a streak of lightning
[verb: **bolts, bolting, bolted**]
1 to bolt a door is to fasten it securely with a bolt
2 to bolt is to run away very fast: *There was a loud bang and Beth's pony bolted.*

bomb [noun: **bombs**] a hollow metal case containing explosives that can be set off
[verb: **bombs, bombing, bombed**] to bomb a place is to drop bombs on it

bombard [verb: **bombard, bombarding, bombarded**]
1 an army bombards a place when it attacks it with lots of missiles
2 if you are bombarded with things, they come at you very quickly all together or one after the other: *The press bombarded him with questions.*

bombshell [noun: **bombshells**] a piece of news that takes you completely by surprise: *Lily dropped a bombshell the other day when she said she was getting married.*

bond [noun: **bonds**]
1 something that brings or keeps people together: *a bond of friendship*
2 something used for tying someone up or taking away their freedom: *the bonds of slavery*
3 a bond is the strong force that holds two atoms together: *a chemical bond*
[verb: **bonds, bonding, bonded**]
1 to bond one thing to another is to make the first thing stick firmly to the second thing: *Use*

glue to bond the two pieces together.
2 if two people bond, they feel close to each other, usually because they have something in common

bone [noun: **bones**]
1 bone is the hard substance that forms a skeleton and supports the flesh and muscle in your body
2 a bone is one of the pieces of a skeleton: *Brian broke a bone in his arm.*
→ **bony**

bonfire [noun: **bonfires**] a large fire built outside: *We made a bonfire of all the garden rubbish.*

bonnet [noun: **bonnets**]
1 the piece at the front of a car that covers the engine
2 a hat that ties under the chin

bonny [adjective: **bonnier, bonniest**] pretty: *a bonny baby*

bonsai [noun: **bonsai**] a very small tree grown in a pot

bonus [noun: **bonuses**]
1 something extra that is good to get: *We were lucky enough to see the whales and as a bonus one of them jumped right out of the water.*
2 extra money that employees are given in addition to their salary: *a Christmas bonus*

bony [adjective: **bonier, boniest**]
1 so thin that the shape of the bones can be seen through the skin: *long bony fingers*
2 full of bones: *a bony piece of fish*

boo [verb: **boos, booing, booed**] people in an audience boo when they make loud rude noises because they don't like what they have seen or heard: *He was booed off the stage.*
[noun: **boos**] a word that people in an audience shout when they are not pleased

booby prize [noun: **booby prizes**] the booby prize is a prize sometimes given to the person who has come last

booby trap [noun: **booby traps**] a booby trap is a trap or bomb that people don't know is there until it is too late

book [noun: **books**] pages joined together and given a cover: *a picture book • a book about Mexico* [verb: **books, booking, booked**] you book a table in a restaurant or tickets for an event or a holiday when you tell the restaurant or the company selling the tickets that you want them kept for you: *We've booked a family holiday in France in July.*

book-keeping [noun] book-keeping is the keeping of records that show all the money that a business or organization makes and spends

booklet [noun: **booklets**] a small book, usually with only a few pages, that gives information about something

bookmaker [noun: **bookmakers**]
1 someone whose job is to take bets on things like horse races and pay out money to the people who have won
2 a bookmaker's is a shop where people can make bets

bookmark [noun: **bookmarks**]
1 a strip of paper or other material that you put between the pages of a book so that you can go back later to the place where you had stopped reading
2 an electronic way of marking a website so that you can find it again

bookworm [noun: **bookworms**] someone who likes reading lots of books

boom [noun: **booms**]
1 a boom is a loud noise like the sound a big drum makes: *We could hear the boom of thunder in the distance.*
2 if there is a boom in business or in a country, a lot more things are bought and sold, and more money is made
[verb: **booms, booming, boomed**]
1 to boom is to make a loud sound
2 business booms when a lot more things are sold

boomerang [noun: **boomerangs**] a boomerang is a curved piece of wood that you throw away from you and which turns in the air and comes back towards you

boon [noun: **boons**] a boon is something good that happens that you are grateful for: *It would be a real boon if we got hot weather for the barbecue next Saturday.*

boost [noun: **boosts**] something that helps to improve something or raise it to a higher or better level: *The school funds got a boost from the money raised at the summer fair.*
[verb: **boosts, boosting, boosted**] to boost something is to help raise it to a higher or better level: *Playing in the concert will boost her confidence.*

boot [noun: **boots**] a kind of shoe that covers the ankle and often part of the leg
[verb: **boots, booting, booted**]
1 to boot something is to kick it: *Georgie booted the ball right over the bar.*
2 to **boot someone out** is to force them to leave: *Becky was booted out of the club for breaking the rules.*
3 to **boot up** a computer is to start its operating system, the program that controls all the other programs

booth [noun: **booths**] a small enclosed compartment used for a particular purpose, for example to make a phone call or have your photo taken, or where people mark their voting paper in an election

booty [noun] booty is the things that thieves, pirates or invading soldiers steal or take by force and keep for themselves

border [noun: **borders**]
1 the border between two countries or areas is the line on the map which separates them: *They settled near the Canadian and United States border.*
2 an edge of something or a strip round its edge: *a pillowcase with a lace border*
[verb: **borders, bordering, bordered**] one thing **borders on** another when the first thing is very close to the second thing: *Jumping off that wall borders on stupidity.*

borderline [noun: **borderlines**]
1 a line that separates two places or things
2 something that is **on the borderline** is very close to the line or division between two things
[adjective] something that is borderline is so close to two different things that it is difficult to decide which it is: *Your work is borderline. You might get a pass or a fail.*

bore [verb: **bores, boring, bored**] if something bores you, it makes you feel tired and fed up because it doesn't interest you: *The speech bored him.*
[noun: **bores**] someone or something that

makes you feel tired and fed up: *It was a real bore having to sort all the papers.*

→ **bored, boredom, boring**

ⓘ Be careful not to confuse the spellings of the noun **boar** meaning a male pig, and the verb and noun **bore**.

bore ² [verb: **bores, boring, bored**] to bore something is to use a drill, or something that works like a drill, to make a hole in or through it: *The insect bores a tiny hole in the fruit.*

bore ³ [verb] a way of changing the verb **bear** to make a past tense: *Our hard work bore fruit.*

bored [adjective] if you are bored, you feel tired and fed up because you are doing something that isn't interesting, or because you have nothing to do: *I'm bored. Let's go out and play.*

boredom [noun] being bored

boring [adjective] not at all interesting: *a long boring journey*

born [verb]
1 a form of the verb **bear** that you use if you are talking about the birth of a baby or animal: *My sister was born three years ago.*
2 to be born is to come into existence: *A new star was born.*
[adjective] having a talent you seem to have been born with: *Zoe's a born entertainer.*

borne [verb] a form of the verb **bear** that is used with a helping verb to show that something happened in the past: *He had borne the hardships of his life without complaining.*

borough [noun: **boroughs**] a town that elects members of parliament

borrow [verb: **borrows, borrowing, borrowed**] to borrow something is to take it with the owner's permission and give it back to them later: *Can I borrow your pencil for a minute, please?*

♦ **borrower** [noun: **borrowers**] a person who borrows something, especially money from a bank

ⓘ Try not to confuse **borrowing** and **lending**. If you **borrow** something *from* someone, you get it from them, and if you **lend** something *to* someone, you give it to them.

bosom [noun: **bosoms**] someone's bosom is their breast
[adjective] a bosom friend is a very close friend

boss [noun: **bosses**]
1 a manager in a workplace who is in charge of other people working there: *Her boss gave her a pay rise.*
2 the most important person in a group, who orders the others about: *I'm the boss, so you've got to do what I tell you.*
[verb: **bosses, bossing, bossed**] to boss people, or to **boss them around**, is to tell them what to do

bossy [adjective: **bossier, bossiest**] someone who is bossy likes telling other people what to do: *Stop being so bossy. You're not in charge here.*

botanic or **botanical** [adjective] to do with plants or the study of plants: *We visited the city's botanic gardens.* • *a botanical specimen*

botany [noun] the study of plants

botch [verb: **botches, botching, botched**] to botch something is to make a mess of it or do it wrongly: *Carrie was really worried that she'd botched the exam.*

both [adjective] both is used to refer to two people or things when you mean the one and also the other: *She ate both cakes, and I didn't get one.* • *Both the boys are good at tennis.*
[pronoun] you can say both to talk about two people or things together: *I bought both because they were so pretty.* • *Both of you are good at tennis.*

bother [verb: **bothers, bothering, bothered**]
1 if you bother someone, you do something that annoys them or interrupts them: *Stop bothering me, I'm busy.*
2 if something bothers you, it makes you feel unhappy or worried: *He said it didn't bother him that he hadn't won.*
3 to bother to do something is to take the time or trouble to do it: *Don't bother to tidy up yet.*
[noun] nuisance or trouble: *The address book saves you the bother of having to remember e-mail addresses.* • *It was no bother to help you out.*

bottle [noun: **bottles**] a container with a narrow neck used for holding liquids like milk, lemonade or wine
[verb: **bottles, bottling, bottled**]
1 to bottle a liquid is to put it in a bottle
2 if someone **bottles up** unpleasant memories or feelings, they aren't able to talk about them to anyone even though it would probably make them feel better if they did

bottle bank [noun: **bottle banks**] a container where empty glass bottles can be put so that the glass can be recycled

bottleneck [noun: **bottlenecks**] a place where traffic cannot move properly because there is too much of it and the road is too narrow

bottom [noun: **bottoms**]
1 the lowest part of something: *the bottom of the stairs* • *the bottom of the sea*
2 the part of your body that you sit on
[adjective] in the lowest position, with other things above: *the bottom shelf*
◆ **bottomless** [adjective] very deep, as if having no bottom: *a bottomless pit*

bough [noun: **boughs**] one of the bigger branches that grows from the trunk of a tree

ⓘ This word rhymes with **cow**.

bought [verb] a way of changing the verb **buy** to make a past tense. It can be used with or without a helping verb: *Suzie bought me an ice cream.* • *Hari has bought the land on which his shop stands.*

boulder [noun: **boulders**] a big piece of stone or rock

ⓘ Be careful not to confuse the spellings of **bolder** meaning 'more bold' and **boulder** meaning 'a large rock'.

bounce [verb: **bounces, bouncing, bounced**]
1 to bounce is to jump up and down quickly on a springy surface: *We bounced on the trampoline.*
2 a ball bounces when it hits something hard and moves away again in another direction
3 if someone **bounces back**, they recover quickly from a failure or disappointment
◆ **bouncing** [adjective] a bouncing baby is strong and healthy

◆ **bouncy** [adjective] springy and able to move up and down: *a bouncy castle*

bound¹ [noun: **bounds**] a leap or jumping movement: *The deer was over the fence in a single bound.*
[verb: **bounds, bounding, bounded**] to run with jumping movements: *The dogs bounded into the room, barking excitedly.*

bound² [verb: **bounds, bounding, bounded**] the place where one area bounds another is the place which marks the boundary between them: *The farm is bounded in the east by a forest and in the west by a large lake.*
[noun: **bounds**] if a place is **out of bounds**, you are not allowed to go there: *The riverbank is out of bounds for the younger children.*
⟶ **boundless**

bound³ [adjective]
1 going in a particular direction: *We were homeward bound.*
2 to be bound for a place is to be on your way there or planning to go there: *ships bound for the Far East*
3 to be bound to do something is to be certain or very likely to do it: *The plants are bound to grow if you keep them well watered.*

bound⁴ [verb] a way of changing the verb **bind** to make a past tense. It can be used with or without a helping verb: *He bound the boat to the wall.* • *The nurse has bound her ankle up.*

boundary [noun: **boundaries**] a line that divides a place or thing from what is next to it: *the boundary between the city and the countryside*

boundless [adjective] having no limit: *Granny still has boundless energy.*

bountiful [adjective] giving or providing something generously: *a bountiful harvest*

bounty [noun: **bounties**]
1 bounty is generosity: *The harvest festival is a celebration of nature's bounty.*
2 a bounty is money paid as a reward, especially for capturing or killing a person or animal

bouquet [noun: **bouquets**] a bunch of flowers

ⓘ This word is pronounced boo–**kay**.

bout [noun: **bouts**] a period of something unpleasant, especially illness: *a bout of flu*

boutique [noun: **boutiques**] a small shop selling fashionable clothes

bow [verb: **bows, bowing, bowed**]
1 if you bow to someone, you bend your head or the top half of your body forward to greet them or show them respect: *Everyone bowed to the king and queen.*
2 to bow is to bend: *He walked with his head bowed in shame.*
3 if someone **bows to** something, they give in to it: *We all had to bow to his demands.*
4 to **bow out** of something that you have been doing before, or that you have said you would do, is to stop doing it or not to take part in it: *Smith may bow out of politics altogether.*
[noun: **bows**] when you bend your head or body forward: *The pianist took a bow when the audience clapped.*

bow² [noun: **bows**]
1 a weapon for shooting arrows
2 a wooden rod with horse hair stretched along it, used for playing a musical instrument such as a violin or cello
3 a knot made with loops on either side: *Tie the ribbon in a bow.*
[verb: **bows, bowing, bowed**]
1 to use a bow to play a stringed musical instrument
2 to bend: *The shelf bowed under the weight of the books.*
[adjective] bent: *bow legs • bow-legged*

bow³ [noun: **bows**] the pointed front part of a ship or boat: *The anchor is stored in the bow. • The bows of the ship hit the pier.*

ⓘ **bow¹** and **bow³** rhyme with **cow**. **bow²** is pronounced to rhyme with **low**.

bowel [noun: **bowels**] your bowels are long tubes inside the lower part of your body that food goes through after leaving your stomach

bowl [noun: **bowls**]
1 a wide container open at the top and used for holding various things: *a soup bowl*
2 anything round and hollow that is shaped like this kind of container, for example a sports stadium

3 a heavy ball used in games like bowls and skittles
[verb: **bowls, bowling, bowled**]
1 to bowl is to throw the ball towards the person batting in cricket and rounders
2 to bowl is to play the game of bowls
3 if something **bowls you over**, it overwhelms you: *Wendy was bowled over by their generosity.*

bowler¹ [noun: **bowlers**]
1 someone who bowls in cricket and rounders
2 someone who plays the game of bowls

bowler² or **bowler hat** [noun: **bowlers** or **bowler hats**] a kind of smart hat worn by men, especially businessmen, that has a hard rounded top and narrow brim

bowling [noun]
1 the game of tenpin bowling, played with skittles
2 the game of bowls, played on a bowling green

bowls [noun] a game in which heavy balls are rolled along a special flat surface called a bowling green

bow tie [noun: **bow ties**] a tie that is shaped like a small bow and is sometimes worn by men on formal occasions

box [noun: **boxes**] a container, sometimes with a lid, used for holding or storing things
[verb: **boxes, boxing, boxed**]
1 to box something is to put it in a box or boxes
2 people box when they hit each other with their fists
◆ **boxer** [noun: **boxers**] someone who does the sport of boxing
◆ **boxing** [noun] a sport in which two people hit each other with their fists, usually while wearing heavy leather gloves

Boxing Day [noun] the day after Christmas Day

box office [noun] a box office is the place at a theatre or cinema where you can buy tickets

boy [noun: **boys**] a male child

boycott [verb: **boycotts, boycotting, boycotted**] if you boycott a person, organization or product, you refuse to have anything to do with them
[noun: **boycotts**] a refusal to have anything to do with a person, organization or product

boyfriend [noun: **boyfriends**] a male friend, especially someone you are having a romantic relationship with

boyhood [noun] the period in your life when you are a boy

boyish [adjective]
1 behaving like a boy: *She's always been boyish and full of mischief.*
2 looking like a young boy: *Now almost 60, he still has the same boyish face.*

bra [noun: **bras**] a piece of underwear that women wear to support their breasts

brace [noun: **braces**]
1 a device that forces or holds two things together tightly
2 a piece of wire put on teeth to straighten them

bracelet [noun: **bracelets**] a piece of jewellery that you wear around your wrist

braces [plural noun] two pieces of elastic or stretchy fabric that are fastened to the back and front of the waistband of trousers to hold the trousers up

bracing [adjective] a bracing wind or walk is healthy and fresh: *a bracing walk by the sea*

bracken [noun] a wild plant like a fern that grows in clumps in woods and on hillsides

bracket [noun: **brackets**]
1 a punctuation symbol usually written or printed in pairs like this ( ) or this [ ] to show that the words, letters, or numbers inside them are separated from the writing coming before or after
2 a grouping or category: *Holidays to the Caribbean are in a much higher price bracket than holidays to Spain.*
3 a piece of metal used to attach a shelf to a wall

brag [verb: **brags, bragging, bragged**] to brag is to boast: *Kat's always bragging about her fashionable clothes.*

braid [noun: **braids**]
1 braid is a thick kind of fancy ribbon used to trim things with
2 a braid is a plait of hair
[verb: **braids, braiding, braided**] to plait hair, wool or ribbon by weaving strands in and out

braille [noun] a writing system for blind people which instead of printed letters has groups of raised dots which can be read by touching them

(i) **Braille** is named after the man who invented it, Louis *Braille*, who was a teacher in France.

brain [noun: **brains**] the organ inside your skull that controls all the other parts of your body and that you think with

brainwash [verb: **brainwashes, brainwashing, brainwashed**] to brainwash someone is to make them believe something by telling them over and over again that it is true

brainwave [noun: **brainwaves**] if you have a brainwave, you suddenly have a very good idea

brainy [adjective: **brainier, brainiest**] clever: *Caitlin is definitely brainy enough to be a doctor.*

brake [noun: **brakes**] a device or system in a vehicle that is used for stopping or slowing down: *Always check your brakes before you go out on a long bike ride.*
[verb: **brakes, braking, braked**] to brake is to use a brake to slow down or stop: *Dad braked suddenly and we were all thrown forward.*

bramble [noun: **brambles**] a blackberry plant

bran [noun] the brown parts that cover wheat grains

branch [noun: **branches**]
1 any of the parts of a tree that grow out from the trunk: *Rooks build their nests high in the branches of trees.*
2 one of the shops or businesses that belong to a larger organization: *the local branch of the bank*
[verb: **branches, branching, branched**]
1 to form branches or to separate into different parts like the branches of a tree: *The road branches to the north and west.*
2 to **branch out** is to develop in different ways: *We're trying to branch out into selling on the Internet.*

brand [noun: **brands**] a name given to a particular product by the company that makes it: *This isn't my usual brand of shampoo, but it's just as good.*

Bb

brandish [verb: **brandishes, brandishing, brandished**] to brandish a weapon is to wave it about in a threatening way: *Three robbers burst in brandishing guns.*

brand-new [adjective] completely new: *a brand-new car*

brandy [noun: **brandies**] a kind of very strong alcoholic drink that you drink after a meal

brass [noun]
1 a metal made by mixing copper and zinc
2 musical instruments made of brass, like trumpets and tubas, that form part of a bigger orchestra or are used in a brass band
[adjective] made of brass: *a brass name plate*

brass band [noun: **brass bands**] a musical group in which wind instruments made of brass are played

brassy [adjective: **brassier, brassiest**]
1 yellowish in colour like brass: *brassy blonde hair*
2 having a loud harsh sound like a musical instrument made of brass: *a brassy voice*

brat [noun: **brats**] a child who is rude or naughty

bravado [noun] behaviour intended to make people believe that you are brave and confident, but which is only done for show

brave [adjective: **braver, bravest**] able to face danger without being afraid or suffer pain without complaining: *It was brave of you to chase away that bull.*
[noun: **braves**] a young warrior belonging to a Native American tribe

♦ **bravely** [adverb] courageously: *She smiled bravely, though she was in pain.*

♦ **bravery** [noun] being brave: *an award for bravery*

bravo [interjection] a word that people say or shout when they think something is well done: *There were calls of 'Bravo!' from the audience.*

brawl [noun: **brawls**] a noisy fight or quarrel, especially in a public place
[verb: **brawls, brawling, brawled**] to brawl is to fight or quarrel noisily, especially in a public place

brawn [noun] big, strong muscles or the strength these give

♦ **brawny** [adjective: **brawnier, brawniest**] having strong muscles: *A brawny young man lifted the boxes out of the van.*

bray [noun: **brays**] the loud harsh sound a donkey or ass makes
[verb: **brays, braying, brayed**] a donkey or ass brays when it makes this sound

brazen [adjective] bold and impudent
[verb: **brazens, brazening, brazened**] if someone **brazens it out**, they keep on doing something that other people would find too embarrassing or difficult to continue with

♦ **brazenly** [adverb] boldly and impudently

brazier [noun: **braziers**] a metal container in which people burn coal to keep themselves warm when they are standing outside for a long time in cold weather

breach [noun: **breaches**]
1 a gap or hole made in something solid like a wall: *A breach in the dam caused flooding in the valley below.*
2 a breaking of an agreement or a relationship: *a breach of the peace agreement*
[verb: **breaches, breaching, breached**] to break or make a hole in something: *The explosion breached the castle wall.*

bread [noun] a food whose main ingredient is flour. Bread is baked in an oven and is often cut into slices for making sandwiches and toast

breadth [noun: **breadths**] the size of something measured from one side to the other: *Measure the length and the breadth and multiply the two to get the area.*

breadwinner [noun: **breadwinners**] the person in a family who earns the money

break [verb: **breaks, breaking, broke, broken**]
1 something breaks when it falls to pieces: *The vase fell over and broke.*
2 to break something is to cause it to fall to pieces, usually by dropping it or hitting it against something: *Careful, or you'll break that glass.*
3 to break a law is to do something that the law forbids
4 to break news is to tell it: *I didn't want to break the bad news to them before they had finished their holiday.*

5 a boy's voice breaks when it gets deeper and becomes like a man's
6 if a machine **breaks down**, it stops working
7 if you **break off** what you are doing, you stop doing it for a while
8 fire, fighting or a disease **breaks out** when it starts suddenly
9 school **breaks up** when the term finishes and the teachers and pupils go on holiday
[noun: **breaks**]
1 a opening or crack in something: *a break in the clouds* • *David had a bad break in his leg.*
2 a pause: *a break in her studies*
3 a piece of good luck: *It was a lucky break finding someone to buy your old bike.*
♦ breakable [adjective] something breakable can be broken if you don't handle it carefully

ⓘ Be careful not to confuse the spellings of **break** meaning 'to damage' and **brake** meaning 'to slow down or stop'.

breakdown [noun: **breakdowns**]
1 a breakdown happens when a machine breaks or stops working: *We had a breakdown on the motorway.*
2 someone has a breakdown if they become depressed and anxious and can't cope with everyday life

breaker [noun: **breakers**] a large wave that breaks on the shore

breakfast [noun: **breakfasts**] a meal people eat in the morning soon after getting out of bed

break-in [noun: **break-ins**] when someone gets into a house or other building illegally, to cause damage or steal things

breakthrough [noun: **breakthroughs**] a sudden success after working for a long time: *a breakthrough in the treatment of cancer*

breakwater [noun: **breakwaters**] a barrier built in or near the sea to protect the land from the force of the waves

breast [noun: **breasts**]
1 the part of the front of your body that is between your neck and your waist
2 either of the two organs on the front of a woman's body that are used to feed milk to her baby

3 someone **makes a clean breast of it** when they tell the whole truth, especially about something they have done wrong

breastbone [noun: **breastbones**] the bone that goes down the front of your chest between your ribs

breaststroke [noun] a way of swimming where you hold your hands together in front of you and then push forwards and sideways with your arms, while moving your legs like a frog

breath [noun: **breaths**]
1 you take a breath when you fill your lungs with air and then let the air out again: *Take a few deep breaths.*
2 your breath is the air that comes out of your mouth: *We could see our breath in the freezing air.*
3 if you say something **under your breath**, you say it very quietly

breathe [verb: **breathes, breathing, breathed**] to take in air through your mouth or nose into your lungs so that your body gets the oxygen it needs, and to blow air back out through your mouth or nose to get rid of carbon dioxide: *He was so quiet I thought he wasn't breathing.*

ⓘ Remember that the verb **breathe** has an **e** at the end, while the noun **breath** does not. Be careful not to confuse the spellings of the verb **breathes** and the noun plural **breaths**.

breathless [adjective] if you are breathless, you are finding it difficult to breathe, usually because of hard exercise or an illness like asthma

breathtaking [adjective] very impressive, surprising or exciting: *The scenery was breathtaking.*

breed [verb: **breeds, breeding, bred**]
1 animals breed when they mate and have babies or young
2 to breed animals is to allow them to mate and have young: *a farmer who breeds rare types of cattle*
[noun: **breeds**] a particular type of animal: *The Aberdeen Angus is a famous Scottish breed of cattle.*
♦ breeder [noun: **breeders**] someone who

Bb

breeds animals: *a dog breeder*

breeze [noun: **breezes**] a light wind

✦ **breezy** [adjective: **breezier, breeziest**]
1 if the weather is breezy, there is a light wind blowing
2 someone who is breezy is cheerful and light-hearted: *Shona's always bright and breezy in the mornings.*

brevity [noun] saying or writing only the few words you need: *Aim for brevity when you are e-mailing people.*

brew [verb: **brews, brewing, brewed**]
1 to brew beer is to make it
2 to brew tea is to make it by letting tea leaves soak in boiling water
3 if a storm or trouble is brewing, it is about to begin
✦ **brewer** [noun: **brewers**] a person or business that makes beer
✦ **brewery** [noun: **breweries**] a factory where beer is made

briar or **brier** [noun: **briars** or **briers**] a wild rose bush

bribe [noun: **bribes**] a bribe is money or a gift offered to someone to get them to do something: *He was accused of taking bribes.*
[verb: **bribes, bribing, bribed**] to bribe someone is to offer them money or a gift to get them to do something: *You were a fool to try to bribe the policeman.*
✦ **bribery** [noun] offering or taking bribes

bric-a-brac [noun] small ornaments that are interesting or attractive but aren't worth very much

brick [noun: **bricks**] a block of baked clay used for building

bricklayer [noun: **bricklayers**] a worker whose job is to build things with bricks, especially walls

bridal [adjective] used by a bride or having to do with brides: *a bridal bouquet* • *a white bridal car*

bride [noun: **brides**] a bride is a woman on her wedding day

bridegroom [noun: **bridegrooms**] a bridegroom is a man on his wedding day

bridesmaid [noun: **bridesmaids**] a bridesmaid is a girl or unmarried woman who helps a bride on her wedding day

bridge [noun: **bridges**]
1 a structure built over a river, road or valley to allow people or vehicles to cross from one side to the other
2 a platform on a ship where the captain usually stands
3 the bridge of your nose is the bony part
4 a card game for four people playing in pairs

bridle [noun: **bridles**] a horse's bridle is the part of its harness that goes around its head: *Mike attached the reins to the horse's bridle.*

brief [adjective: **briefer, briefest**] short: *The interview was much briefer than Malcolm thought it was going to be.*
[verb: **briefs, briefing, briefed**] to brief someone is to give them information or instructions about something: *Our coach always briefs us before a match on the other team's strengths.*
[noun: **briefs**] someone, especially a lawyer, given a brief when they are given the information or instructions they need to do their work

briefcase [noun: **briefcases**] a flat case for carrying business papers in

briefly [adverb] in a short form or for a short time: *Tell us briefly what you want us to do.* • *They stopped briefly to get more petrol.*

briefs [plural noun] briefs are short underpants

brier [noun: **briers**] another spelling of **briar**

brigade [noun: **brigades**]
1 a group of soldiers that forms part of an army division
2 a group of people who do a special job: *the fire brigade*

brigadier [noun: **brigadiers**] an army officer in command of a brigade

bright [adjective: **brighter, brightest**]
1 giving out a lot of light or having a lot of light: *the bright lights of the city* • *a nice bright bedroom*
2 a bright colour is strong and clear: *His eyes were bright blue.*
3 to feel bright is to feel cheerful and happy, and to be interested in what is going on around you: *Grandad was a lot brighter this morning when I saw him.*
4 a bright person is clever: *She's bright but she's a bit lazy.*

◆ **brighten** [verb: **brightens, brightening, brightened**]

1 to make or become lighter or sunnier: *A coat of paint would brighten the walls.* • *The weather brightened up and we went out for a walk.*

2 to make or become more cheerful and happy: *The good news brightened her up.* • *Jack brightened a bit when I suggested a game of cricket.*

◆ **brightly** [adverb] in a bright way: *The sun shone brightly.*

◆ **brightness** [noun] being bright

brilliance [noun]

1 being very bright or giving out strong light: *the brilliance of the crown jewels*

2 impressiveness or cleverness: *She shows brilliance as an actress.*

brilliant [adjective]

1 very bright or giving out strong light: *brilliant sunshine*

2 very clever or impressive: *Fiona gave a brilliant speech.*

◆ **brilliantly** [adverb]

1 very brightly: *The arena was brilliantly lit.*

2 very cleverly or impressively: *In the school play, Sanjay plays the bad-tempered old king brilliantly.*

brim [noun: **brims**]

1 the edge of a container: *His glass was filled right up to the brim.*

2 the lower part of a hat that sticks out: *Val wore a big felt hat with the brim turned up.*

[verb: **brims, brimming, brimmed**] a container brims when it is full up to its top edge: *Her eyes were brimming with tears.*

brine [noun] water with salt in it, often used to keep food in

bring [verb: **brings, bringing, brought**]

1 to bring is to take, lead or carry a person or thing with you: *You can bring all your friends to the party.* • *He'd brought a couple of jigsaws downstairs.*

2 if one thing brings another, the first thing causes the second to come: *The drought brought famine to the area.*

3 if one event **brings about** another, the first causes the second: *The changes in climate were thought to have been brought about by global warming.*

4 if someone **brings something off**, they manage to do it successfully

5 if you **bring someone round**, you persuade them to change their opinion and agree with you: *We have to bring him round to our point of view.*

6 to **bring someone round** when they are unconscious is to make them wake up

7 to **bring up** a subject is to mention it: *You shouldn't have brought up the subject of money.*

8 to **bring up** children or young animals is to look after them until they are old enough to look after themselves: *Oliver Twist was brought up in an orphanage.*

9 if someone **brings up** their food, they vomit

brink [noun]

1 the edge of something high or deep, like a cliff or river: *The boat stopped right on the brink of a waterfall.*

2 if you are **on the brink** of something, it is about to happen: *We could see that Noreen was on the brink of tears.*

brisk [adjective: **brisker, briskest**] quick and lively: *walking at a brisk pace*

◆ **briskly** [adverb] quickly

bristle [noun: **bristles**] a short stiff hair: *This brush is losing its bristles.*

◆ **bristly** [adjective: **bristlier, bristliest**] having or covered with bristles: *Dan had a bristly chin because he hadn't shaved.*

brittle [adjective] hard but easily broken: *Eggshells are brittle.*

broach [verb: **broaches, broaching, broached**] to broach a subject or question is to begin to talk about it

broad [adjective: **broader, broadest**]

1 having a relatively large width: *a broad avenue* • *My feet are small but broad.*

2 a broad accent or dialect is strong or noticeable: *He wrote poetry in broad Scots.*

broadband [adjective] a broadband Internet connection can carry data from the telephone, computer, TV, etc all at the same time

broadcast [verb: **broadcasts, broadcasting, broadcast**]

1 a TV or radio station broadcasts when it sends out programmes which people can

Bb

receive on their televisions or radios
2 to broadcast something is to tell it to a lot of people: *Someone's been broadcasting lies about him.*
[noun: **broadcasts**] a programme sent out by a TV or radio station
• **broadcaster** [noun: **broadcasters**] someone whose job is to speak on TV or radio programmes
• **broadcasting** [noun] the work or business of TV and radio stations

broaden [verb: **broadens, broadening, broadened**] to make or become wider: *They'd broadened the road and made two lanes.* • *At this point, the river broadens.*

broadly [adverb]
1 widely: *He was smiling broadly, so we knew everything was okay.*
2 generally: *Your essay is broadly right, but not detailed enough.*

broad-minded [adjective] someone who is broad-minded thinks other people should be free to think or act as they want to

broadness [noun] how broad something is

broadsheet [noun: **broadsheets**] a newspaper printed on large sheets of paper folded in the middle, especially a newspaper that deals with news in a serious way

broccoli [noun] a vegetable with lots of tiny tightly-packed green or purple flowerheads growing from a thick stalk

brochure [noun: **brochures**] a booklet with information about a particular range of products, often with pictures: *a holiday brochure*

broke [verb] a way of changing the verb **break** to make a past tense: *I broke two mugs this morning.*

broke² [adjective] having no money: *I can't afford a holiday, I'm completely broke.*

broken [verb] a form of the verb **break** that is used with a helping verb to show that something happened in the past: *A curious crack sounded, as if something had broken.*
[adjective]
1 with a break or breaks: *a broken window*
2 a broken home is a home in which one of the parents has left to live somewhere else

broker [noun: **brokers**] someone whose job

is to act as an agent buying or selling goods or services for other people: *an insurance broker*

bronchitis [noun] a lung disease which makes breathing difficult

bronze [noun]
1 a metal that is a mixture of copper and tin: *The statue was cast in bronze.*
2 a red-brown colour like this metal
[adjective] made of, or the colour of, bronze: *a bronze sculpture*
• **bronzed** [adjective] covered with bronze or of a red-brown colour like bronze: *bronzed skin*

bronze medal [noun: **bronze medals**] a medal made of bronze awarded to the person who comes third in a sporting event

brooch [noun: **brooches**] a piece of jewellery with a pin or clasp that you fasten on to your collar or the front of your dress or jacket

ⓘ This word rhymes with **coach**.

brood [noun: **broods**] a brood is several young birds or reptiles with the same mother that hatch out of their eggs at the same time
[verb: **broods, brooding, brooded**]
1 a bird broods when it sits on its eggs to hatch them
2 to **brood over** or **about** something is to think hard or worry about it for a long time: *Gabriel's brooding over the goal he gave away in the final.*
• **broody** [adjective]
1 a broody hen is sitting on eggs to hatch them
2 if someone is broody, they are thinking long and hard about something

brook [noun: **brooks**] a small stream

broom [noun: **brooms**] a brush with a long handle, used for sweeping floors

broomstick [noun: **broomsticks**] a long handle with thin sticks tied to one end that witches are supposed to ride on

broth [noun: **broths**] a kind of soup made with vegetables and sometimes meat

brothel [noun: **brothels**] a house where men can go to have sex with prostitutes

brother [noun: **brothers**] your brother is a boy or man who has the same parents as you do
• **brotherhood** [noun: **brotherhoods**]

1 brotherhood is a feeling of friendship among boys and men

2 a brotherhood is a group or society for men

brother-in-law [noun: **brothers-in-law**] your sister's husband, your husband's or wife's brother, or your husband's or wife's sister's husband

brought [verb] a way of changing the verb **bring** to make a past tense. It can be used with or without a helping verb: *Jeremy brought me a cup of hot tea.* • *I have brought a box of chocolates for you.*

brow [noun: **brows**]

1 your brow is your forehead

2 your brows are your eyebrows

3 the brow of a hill is the point at the top from where it slopes down

browbeat [verb: **browbeats, browbeating, browbeat, browbeaten**] to browbeat someone is to bully them with words

brown [noun] the colour of soil and most kinds of wood, made by mixing red, yellow and blue

Brownie [noun: **Brownies**] a Brownie is a member of the Brownie Guides, the junior branch of the Guide Association

browse [verb: **browses, browsing, browsed**] to browse is to look quickly through a range of different things, for example the books in a shop, to see if there is anything you want or like

♦ **browser** [noun: **browsers**] a browser is a computer program that lets you search and move around the Internet

bruise [noun: **bruises**] a mark on the skin caused by a knock or blow: *Joe's got a big bruise just under his eye.*

[verb: **bruises, bruising, bruised**] to make a bruise on someone's or something's skin: *Daniel bruised his knees when he fell.* • *Be careful not to bruise the peaches when you handle them.*

brunette [adjective] having brown hair [noun: **brunettes**] someone with brown hair

brunt [noun] to **bear** or **take the brunt of** something is to take its full force: *The side of the bus bore the brunt of the impact.*

brush [noun: **brushes**]

1 a thing with tufts of bristles used to smooth hair, paint with, or clean dirt or dust away

2 to give something a brush is to brush it [verb: **brushes, brushing, brushed**]

1 to brush something is to move a brush over it: *Have you brushed your teeth?*

2 to **brush against** something is to touch it lightly with part of your body

Brussels sprout [noun: **Brussels sprouts**] a vegetable that looks like a tiny cabbage

brutal [adjective] very cruel: *a brutal murder*

♦ **brutality** [noun] violent cruelty

♦ **brutally** [adverb] cruelly, savagely: *The poor horses had been brutally beaten.*

brute [noun: **brutes**]

1 an animal, especially a big strong animal like a bull or a horse

2 a very cruel or savage man

BSE [abbreviation] short for *bovine spongiform encephalopathy*, a disease that affects the brains of cattle. Many people call it mad cow disease

bubble [noun: **bubbles**]

1 a very thin light ball of liquid filled with air: *soap bubbles*

2 a small ball of air inside a liquid: *We could see the air bubbles in the water.*

[verb: **bubbles, bubbling, bubbled**]

1 something bubbles when small balls of air form in it: *A big pot of soup was bubbling on the stove.*

2 if something **bubbles up**, it is forced up to the surface like bubbles rising in a liquid: *Excitement was bubbling up inside her.*

♦ **bubbly** [adjective: **bubblier, bubbliest**]

1 full of bubbles: *The paint had gone all bubbly in the heat of the sun.*

2 full of energy and life: *a bubbly personality*

buccaneer [noun: **buccaneers**] someone who attacks ships while they are at sea and steals things from them: *an adventure story about pirates and buccaneers*

buck [noun: **bucks**]

1 a male rabbit, hare or deer

2 an informal word for an American dollar: *It cost twenty bucks.*

[verb: **bucks, bucking, bucked**] a horse bucks when it jumps into the air kicking its back legs outwards

bucket [noun: **buckets**]

1 a container, usually with a handle, used for

Bb

carrying water or things like earth, sand or cement

2 the amount that a bucket will hold: *four buckets of water*

bucketful [noun: **bucketfuls**] the amount that a bucket will hold: *We'll need a couple more bucketfuls of cement to finish the path.*

buckle [noun: **buckles**] a clip for fastening a belt or a strap

[verb: **buckles, buckling, buckled**]

1 to buckle something is to fasten it with a buckle

2 to **buckle down** is to start working hard or with determination: *You'll have to buckle down to work when you go back to college.*

bud [noun: **buds**] the part of a tree or plant from which a leaf or flower develops

[verb: **buds, budding, budded**] a plant buds when its buds start to show

Buddhism [noun] a religion, practised in many parts of the world, that follows the teachings of Buddha

• **Buddhist** [noun: **Buddhists**] someone who follows the teachings of Buddha

[adjective] to do with Buddhism or Buddhists

budding [adjective] in the early stages of becoming something: *Henry's a budding scientist.*

budge [verb: **budges, budging, budged**] to budge means to move slightly: *We all tried to turn the key in the lock, but it wouldn't budge.*

budgerigar [noun: **budgerigars**] a small bird with brightly coloured feathers that is often kept as a pet

budget [noun: **budgets**] a plan for spending, usually for a certain time period: *We had a monthly budget of £300 for food and bus fares.*

[verb: **budgets, budgeting, budgeted**] to budget is to decide what you are able to spend money on: *You'll have to budget very carefully to make your money last a fortnight.*

[adjective] not costing very much: *budget flights*

budgie [noun: **budgies**] a budgerigar: *We've taught our budgie to talk.*

buff [noun: **buffs**]

1 buff is a light brown colour

2 a buff is someone who is interested in a

particular subject and knows a lot about it: *a film buff* • *a computer buff*

[verb: **buffs, buffing, buffed**] to buff a surface, or to **buff it up**, is to rub it with a soft dry cloth to make it shiny

buffalo [noun: **buffalos** or **buffaloes**]

1 a large ox with big curved horns, found in Asia and Africa

2 a bison

buffer [noun: **buffers**] something designed to reduce the force of a collision, especially the metal posts on a railway barrier that help bring a moving train to a stop

buffet[1] [noun: **buffets**]

1 a compartment on a train where food and drinks are served

2 various types of food set out on a table at a party for people to help themselves

buffet[2] [verb: **buffets, buffeting, buffeted**] to buffet something is to knock it about roughly: *The little boat was buffeted by the storm.*

ⓘ **buffet**[1] is pronounced **boof**-ay, with a silent **t** a the end.
buffet[2] is pronounced **buf**-it.

---

buffoon [noun: **buffoons**] a clown or a fool

bug [noun: **bugs**]

1 a small insect, especially one that bites

2 a germ that causes illness: *She had a tummy bug.*

3 a tiny hidden microphone used to record secretly what people say

4 a fault in a computer program that stops it working properly

[verb: **bugs, bugging, bugged**]

1 to bug someone is to annoy them

2 to bug a room or a telephone is to put a hidden microphone in it to record what people say

buggy [noun: **buggies**] a baby's pushchair

bugle [noun: **bugles**] an instrument like a small trumpet, used for military signals

build [verb: **builds, building, built**]

1 to build something is to put together its parts bit by bit: *He's building a wall.* • *Milk builds healthy teeth and bones.*

2 if something **builds you up**, it makes you stronger

[noun] your build is the shape of your body: *a man with a strong, muscular build*

builder [noun: **builders**] someone whose job is to build and repair houses and other structures

building [noun: **buildings**]
1 building is the trade or action of making houses and other structures: *There is a lot of building going on in this street.*
2 a building is a house or other structure: *New York has lots of tall buildings.*

building society [noun: **building societies**] an organization, rather like a bank, whose main business is lending money so that people can buy houses

bulb [noun: **bulbs**]
1 the rounded part of plants like onions or tulips that the rest grows out of: *daffodil bulbs*
2 a glass globe with an electrical part inside that gives out light: *The bulb's gone in my bedside lamp.*

bulge [noun: **bulges**] a swelling or lump
[verb: **bulges, bulging, bulged**] to bulge is to stick out: *His eyes bulged in horror.*

bulimia or **bulimia nervosa** [noun] an eating disorder in which people eat too much and then make themselves vomit
◆ **bulimic** [adjective] suffering from bulimia

bulk [noun]
1 something's bulk is its size, especially if it is large and heavy: *Wrestlers use their bulk to throw their opponents.*
2 the bulk of something is most of it: *The bulk of his pocket money was spent on computer games.*
3 if you buy **in bulk**, you buy large quantities at one time: *It's much cheaper to buy household goods in bulk.*
◆ **bulky** [adjective: **bulkier, bulkiest**] large or taking up a lot of space: *a bulky package*

bull [noun: **bulls**]
1 the male of a type of cattle or ox: *Don't go into that field. There's a bull in it.*
2 a male elephant or a male whale
3 a bull in a china shop is a very clumsy person
4 if you **take the bull by the horns**, you deal with a difficult problem in a very determined way

bulldog [noun: **bulldogs**] a kind of dog with short legs, a strong body and a wrinkled face

bulldozer [noun: **bulldozers**] a large machine with a heavy metal shovel at the front used to move big amounts of earth and stones

bullet [noun: **bullets**]
1 a piece of shaped metal fired from a gun
2 if you **bite the bullet**, you make a decision to do something that you don't really want to do

bulletin [noun: **bulletins**] a report of the latest news: *The next bulletin will be at 6 p.m.*

bullet-proof [adjective] specially strengthened so that bullets cannot go through: *a bullet-proof vest*

bullfight [noun: **bullfights**] a kind of entertainment held in Spain and some other countries, in which a bull charges at men on horseback or on foot, and is usually killed with a sword by a man called a matador
◆ **bullfighter** [noun: **bullfighters**] someone who fights bulls as part of this entertainment

bullion [noun] brick-shaped bars of gold or silver

bullock [noun: **bullocks**] a young bull

bull's-eye [noun: **bull's-eyes**] the mark in the centre of an archery target or dartboard that you score very high points for hitting

bully [noun: **bullies**] a person who is cruel to people smaller or weaker than they are
[verb: **bullies, bullying, bullied**] to be cruel to smaller or weaker people
◆ **bullying** [noun] what bullies do to people smaller or weaker than they are

bum¹ [noun: **bums**] a very informal word for your bottom

bum² [noun: **bums**] an American English word for a **tramp** or **beggar**

bumbag [noun: **bumbags**] a small bag that hangs from a strap tied around your waist

bumblebee [noun: **bumblebees**] a kind of bee with a fat yellow and black striped body

bump [noun: **bumps**]
1 a knock or blow: *He got a bump on the head and was knocked unconscious.*
2 a raised or swollen part on the surface of something: *a road with speed bumps to slow the traffic down*
[verb: **bumps, bumping, bumped**]
1 to bump something is to knock it by accident:

Try not to bump my arm when I'm writing. • The baby bumped her head on the table.

2 if you **bump into** someone, you meet them by chance: *I bumped into Helen in the street yesterday.*

bumper [noun: **bumpers**] a car's bumper is the piece of metal or plastic around the front or back that protects it from knocks

[adjective] bigger than usual: *a bumper harvest • a bumper pack of toilet rolls*

bumpy [adjective: **bumpier, bumpiest**] full of bumps: *a very bumpy ride across the fields*

bun [noun: **buns**] a kind of cake made with sweet dough: *a currant bun*

bunch [noun: **bunches**] a group of things tied or growing together: *a bunch of grapes • The warder had a big bunch of keys.*

[verb: **bunches, bunching, bunched**] to **bunch together**, or to **bunch up**, is to be or move close together: *The sheep bunched together and the sheepdog couldn't separate them.*

bundle [noun: **bundles**] a number of things fastened or tied up together: *a bundle of newspapers*

[verb: **bundles, bundling, bundled**]
1 to bundle things is to tie them up in a bundle
2 to bundle someone into something is to push them roughly into it: *He was bundled into a taxi before the photographers could see him.*

bung [noun: **bungs**] something used to block a hole so that liquid does not get in or out

[verb: **bungs, bunging, bunged**] to **bung something up** is to block it: *His voice sounded funny because his nose was all bunged up.*

bungalow [noun: **bunglalows**] a house with only one storey

bungee jumping [noun] a sport where you jump from a high place with strong rubber ropes attached to your ankles so that you bounce back up again before you reach the ground

bungle [verb: **bungles, bungling, bungled**] to bungle something is to do it badly or clumsily

♦ **bungler** [noun: **bunglers**] someone who makes a mess of doing something

♦ **bungling** [adjective] making mistakes or clumsy

bunk [noun: **bunks**]
1 a narrow bed fitted against a wall like the bed in a ship's cabin
2 if someone **does a bunk**, they run away, usually to escape something unpleasant

bunk bed [noun: **bunk beds**] two or more beds built one above the other

bunker [noun: **bunkers**]
1 a pit filled with sand on a golf course that players try to avoid because it is difficult to hit the ball out of
2 a large box or container for storing coal
3 an underground shelter used to escape from bombs during a war

bunny [noun: **bunnies**] a rabbit

Bunsen burner [noun: **Bunsen burners**] a gas burner with an open flame used to heat things up in science laboratories

bunting [noun] a row of little flags tied to a length of rope and used to decorate ships or streets during celebrations

buoy [noun: **buoys**] a large floating object anchored to the seabed and used to mark a shipping channel or to warn ships that there is shallow water

(i) Lots of people get the spelling of **buoy** wrong. Remember the **u**, which comes before the **o**, not after it.

buoyant [adjective] able to float

burden [noun: **burdens**] something that has to be carried: *donkeys with heavy burdens on their backs*

[verb: **burdens, burdening, burdened**] to burden someone is to give them a load to carry: *I was burdened with all the suitcases.*

bureau [noun: **bureaux**]
1 an office where you can get information: *a travel bureau*
2 a writing desk with drawers

bureaucracy [noun] all the rules and complicated systems that office staff have to follow, especially those that cause delays and are sometimes unnecessary

burglar [noun: **burglars**] a criminal who breaks into a house or other building to steal things

♦ **burglary** [noun: **burglaries**] the crime of breaking into houses to steal things

Bb

burgle [verb: **burgles, burgling, burgled**] to break into a house or other building to steal things

burial [noun: **burials**] putting a dead person in the ground

burly [adjective: **burlier, burliest**] a burly person is big, strong and heavy: *two burly policemen*

burn [verb: **burns, burning, burnt** or **burned**]
1 to burn something is to set fire to it: *Be careful with that wok or you'll burn the house down.*
2 to burn is to be on fire: *We could see the grass burning from miles away.*
3 if something burns you, it injures you by burning or being very hot: *The soup burnt his tongue.*
[noun: **burns**] an injury or mark left after touching fire or something very hot

burp [verb: **burps, burping, burped**] to burp is to make a rude sound by letting air come out of your stomach through your mouth
[noun: **burps**] this sound

burrow [noun: **burrows**] a hole in the ground made by a rabbit or other animal
[verb: **burrows, burrowing, burrowed**] to burrow is to make a hole in the ground

burst [verb: **bursts, bursting, burst**]
1 to break or tear, especially from being put under too much pressure: *He blew and blew until the balloon burst.*
2 to **burst in** is to come in suddenly and noisily: *Anna burst in just as I was falling asleep.*
[adjective] having burst: *a burst tyre*

bury [verb: **buries, burying, buried**]
1 to bury a dead person is to put their body in the ground
2 to bury something is to cover or hide it: *She buried her face in her hands.*
3 people who have been fighting or quarrelling **bury the hatchet** when they make up
➡ **burial**

bus [noun: **buses**] a large vehicle with lots of seats for passengers

bush [noun: **bushes**] a woody plant that has many leaves and is smaller than a tree: *a rose bush*

◆ **bushy** [adjective: **bushier, bushiest**]
1 covered with bushes
2 growing thickly: *a long bushy tail*

busily [adverb] in a busy, hard-working way: *He was busily trying to persuade all his friends to join the club.*

business [noun: **businesses**]
1 business is buying and selling, and the work of producing things that people want to buy: *Len went into business with his brother.*
2 a business is any company that makes and sells goods, or that sells services
3 someone's business is their work or trade: *What business are you in?*
4 a company **goes out of business** when it stops trading
5 to **mind your own business** is to pay attention only to your own personal affairs or things that concern you directly

businesslike [adjective] someone who is businesslike deals with things in a practical and efficient way

businessman [noun: **businessmen**] a man whose work is in a business

businesswoman [noun: **businesswomen**] a woman whose work is in a business

busker [noun: **buskers**] a musician who plays in the street and gets money from passers-by

bus stop [noun: **bus stops**] a place where a bus stops on its route to let passengers get on and off

bust [noun: **busts**]
1 a woman's bust is her breasts
2 a bust is a sculpture of a person's head and shoulders
[adjective]
1 broken: *The video's bust.*
2 bankrupt: *The business is almost bust.*
[adverb] if a person or business goes bust, they become bankrupt

bustle [verb: **bustles, bustling, bustled**] to bustle is to hurry or make yourself busy: *She was bustling around trying to make lunch.*

busy [adjective: **busier, busiest**]
1 someone is busy when they have a lot to do: *You'll need something to keep you busy during the school holidays.*

Bb

2 if a place or a road is busy, there is a lot of people or traffic in it: *London's busy streets*
→ **busily**

busybody [noun: **busybodies**] a nosy person who tries to find out everyone else's business

but [conjunction]
1 but is used between parts of a sentence to show that there is a difference between the first part and the second part: *I can cycle but I can't drive.* • *He'd like to have gone to the pictures but he doesn't have any money.*
2 but is also used between parts of a sentence to mean 'except': *You've done nothing but moan.*
[preposition] except: *No one but me turned up.*

butcher [noun: **butchers**]
1 someone whose job is to carve up raw meat
2 a butcher's is a shop that sells meat

butler [noun: **butlers**] a male servant who looks after a rich person or who is in charge of the other servants in a rich person's house

butt [noun: **butts**]
1 the butt of a gun or rifle is the thick part furthest away from the barrel
2 if you are the butt of other people's jokes, they all make jokes about you or laugh at you
[verb: **butts, butting, butted**]
1 to butt something is to hit it using your head: *The goat butted me when I tried to stroke it.*
2 to **butt in** is to interrupt other people while they are talking together

butter [noun] a yellow fatty food made from milk and used to spread on bread or for cooking
[verb: **butters, buttering, buttered**]
1 to spread butter on bread or toast: *I must have buttered and filled two hundred sandwiches for the party.*
2 if you **butter someone up**, you say flattering things to them so that they will help you or be nice to you
→ **buttery**

buttercup [noun: **buttercups**] a common wild flower with yellow petals

butterfly [noun: **butterflies**] a kind of insect with brightly coloured patterned wings

buttermilk [noun] the part of milk that is left after making butter

butterscotch [noun: **butterscotches**] a type of hard toffee made with butter

buttery [adjective] covered with butter, or tasting or looking like butter: *buttery toast* • *a buttery paste*

buttocks [plural noun] your buttocks are your bottom

button [noun: **buttons**]
1 a round object used to fasten clothes
2 something you press to make a machine work
[verb: **buttons, buttoning, buttoned**] to fasten with buttons: *Button up your coat.* • *The dress buttons at the back.*

buttonhole [noun: **buttonholes**] a hole that you push a button through to fasten your clothes

buttress [noun: **buttresses**] a support built against a wall

buy [verb: **buys, buying, bought**] to buy something is to give money so that it becomes yours: *I've bought all their albums.*
♦ **buyer** [noun: **buyers**] someone who buys something: *We couldn't find a buyer for our old computer.*

buzz [verb: **buzzes, buzzing, buzzed**]
1 to make a sound like a bee: *Flies buzzed round our heads.*
2 to **buzz about** or **around** is to move about busily and quickly: *Pam was buzzing about trying to organize everyone.*
[noun: **buzzes**]
1 the sound a bee makes when it is flying
2 a murmuring sound made by lots of people talking at once: *a buzz of excitement*
3 a pleasant feeling you get when you do something exciting or successful: *I always get a buzz out of performing on stage.*
4 a call using the telephone: *Give me a buzz tomorrow.*

buzzard [noun: **buzzards**] a large bird which kills and eats small animals

buzzer [noun: **buzzers**] a device that makes a buzzing noise

by [preposition]
1 near to or next to something: *the big house by the station*
2 past someone or something: *A tall boy ran by me.*

3 through, along or across something: *We came by the north road.*
4 something is by someone when they are the person who has created it: *a painting by Turner*
5 something happens or is done by a certain time when it happens or is done no later than that time: *I'll be home by 7.30.*
6 by means of something: *go by train*
7 to the extent of something: *White Dancer won by a head.*
8 by is used when giving measurements of length and width: *The room is 5 metres by 3 metres.*
9 by is used to say how much or how often: *Will he be paid by the week or by the month?*
10 you say '**by the way**' when you want to add something to what you have just said: *I've made soup for later, I've fed the cat, and by the way, there's no milk left.*
[adverb]
1 near: *They all stood by, watching but doing nothing to help.*
2 past: *The cars went whizzing by.*
3 aside: *Try to put some money by for an emergency.*
4 by and by means after some time: *By and by, they came to a little house in the middle of the wood.*
by- [prefix] if a word starts with **by-**, it adds the meaning 'at or to the side' to the word. For example, a *bypass* passes around the outside of a town

bye [noun: **byes**]
1 a short way of saying **goodbye**
2 in competitions, you get a bye if you have no opponent in a round and automatically go into the next round
bye-bye [interjection] a more informal way of saying **goodbye**
by-election [noun: **by-elections**] an election to vote in a new member of parliament that happens between general elections
bygone [adjective] bygone days are in the past: *in bygone days, when there were no telephones or computers*
by-law [noun: **by-laws**] a law made by a local council rather than by a national parliament
bypass [noun: **bypasses**] a road built around a town or city so that traffic does not need to pass through the town or city
[verb: **bypasses, bypassing, bypassed**] to go round something rather than through it
by-product [noun: **by-products**] something useful that is produced when making something else
bystander [noun: **bystanders**] someone who watches something happening but isn't involved in it
byte [noun: **bytes**] a unit used to measure computer memory or data

ⓘ Remember that a computer **byte** is spelt with a **y**.

C

C [abbreviation] short for **Celsius** or **centigrade**

cab [noun: **cabs**]

1 a taxi: *We took a cab to the airport.*

2 a compartment at the front of a lorry or bus where the driver sits

cabaret [noun: **cabarets**] a show in a club or restaurant, which usually includes singers, dancers and comedians

ⓘ This word is pronounced **cab**-a-ray.

cabbage [noun: **cabbages**] a large round green vegetable with layers of leaves packed close together

cabin [noun: **cabins**]

1 a wooden hut or house: *a log cabin*

2 one of the small rooms in a ship used by passengers or crew members to sleep in

3 the part of an aeroplane where the passengers sit

cabin crew [noun: **cabin crews**] the people whose job it is to look after the passengers on an aeroplane

cabinet [noun: **cabinets**]

1 a cupboard with shelves and doors that is used for storing things: *a bathroom cabinet*

2 a group of government ministers who decide what the government will do

cable [noun: **cables**]

1 strong metal rope used for tying up ships or for supporting heavy loads: *Miles of cable were used to build the bridge.* • *The tent collapsed when a cable snapped.*

2 a tube with wires inside that carry electronic signals or electric current: *a telephone cable*

3 cable is cable television: *We can't get cable or satellite here.*

4 a telegram: *He sent a cable saying he would be arriving home at midnight the next day.*

cable car [noun: **cable cars**] a vehicle used to carry people up mountains. The cable car hangs in the air from strong wires and is moved by pulleys

cable television [noun] a television service in which programmes are transmitted along underground cables to people's houses

cackle [noun: **cackles**]

1 a loud sound made by a hen or a goose

2 a loud harsh-sounding laugh

[verb: **cackles, cackling, cackled**]

1 a hen or goose cackles when it makes this sound

2 if someone cackles, they laugh loudly and harshly

cactus [noun: **cactuses** or **cacti**] a kind of prickly plant that grows mainly in deserts and very dry places. Cactuses store water in their thick leaves

CAD [abbreviation] short for **computer-aided design**, where computers are used to help draw plans for things like buildings or machines: *a new CAD program*

caddie [noun: **caddies**] someone whose job is to carry a golfer's clubs around the golf course

caddy [noun: **caddies**] a box for keeping tea in

cadet [noun: **cadets**]

1 a young person training to be an officer in the armed forces or the police

2 a school pupil who is doing military training

cadge [verb: **cadges, cadging, cadged**] to cadge something from someone is to get it by begging or asking them for it: *Phil missed the bus so had to cadge a lift from his neighbour.*

Caesarean section or **Caesarean**
[noun: **Caesarean sections** or **Caesareans**]
a surgical operation in which a pregnant woman's stomach is cut so that the baby inside her womb can be taken out

ⓘ The word **Caesarean** is used because the Roman emperor Julius *Caesar* was supposed to have been born this way.

café [noun: **cafés**] a small restaurant that serves drinks and snacks

cafeteria [noun: **cafeterias**] a restaurant where the customers serve themselves from a counter

cafetière [noun: **cafetières**] a type of jug that you make coffee in by pressing down a plunger to separate the coffee grounds from the liquid

caffeine [noun] caffeine is a substance that makes you feel more alert and active. Tea and coffee and some fizzy drinks contain caffeine

caftan [noun: **caftans**] a loose, long-sleeved piece of clothing that comes down to your ankles, worn in some Middle Eastern countries

cage [noun: **cages**] a box or enclosure with bars where a bird or animal is kept so that it can't escape
[verb: **cages, caging, caged**] to cage an animal or bird is to put it in a cage
♦ **caged** [adjective] kept in a cage: *caged birds*

cagoule [noun: **cagoules**] a hooded waterproof jacket like a light anorak but without an opening all the way down the front

cajole [verb: **cajoles, cajoling, cajoled**] to cajole someone is to get them to do something by being nice to them
♦ **cajolery** [noun] persuasion by flattery

cake [noun: **cakes**] a food made from a mixture of flour, eggs, sugar, butter and other ingredients, baked in an oven until it is firm: *Do you like cake? • a Christmas cake*

calamine [noun] a pink powder used in a lotion that soothes burns or sore skin

calamity [noun: **calamities**] something terrible that happens, a disaster

calcium [noun] a chemical found in chalk and lime and in bones and teeth

calculate [verb: **calculates, calculating, calculated**]
1 to calculate something is to count it up or work it out using numbers or mathematics: *One apple costs 13p. Calculate the cost of 174 apples.*
2 if you calculate something, you make a guess about it using all the facts that you have: *The robbers had calculated that no one would realize that anything was missing until they were long gone.*
♦ **calculating** [adjective] a calculating person works out what is going to benefit them
♦ **calculation** [noun: **calculations**] something you work out, either using numbers or what you know: *By my calculation, we should be finished by Tuesday.*
♦ **calculator** [noun: **calculators**] an electronic machine that you use to do mathematical calculations quickly

calendar [noun: **calendars**] a table or list that shows the days of the year with their dates, divided into weeks and months

calf[1] [noun: **calves**]
1 a young cow or ox: *a bull calf*
2 a young elephant, whale or deer: *a red deer calf*

calf[2] [noun: **calves**] the back part of your leg just below the knee, where there is a big muscle

call [verb: **calls, calling, called**]
1 to call is to shout: *I heard him calling my name.*
2 to call someone is to ask them to come to you: *Call the children in from the garden.*
3 to call someone is to speak to them on the telephone: *Have you called your mother yet?*
4 to call someone something is to give them that name: *He's called Jonathan James. • How dare you call me a liar!*
5 to **call at** a place is to stop there for a short time: *We drove to Ipswich, calling at my sister's house on the way.*
[noun: **calls**]
1 a shout: *calls for help*
2 a telephone conversation: *I had a call from David yesterday.*
3 a short visit: *I've got a couple of calls to make on the way home.*

Cc

callous [adjective] cruel or unkind to other people: *a callous murderer*

ⓘ Do not confuse the spelling of the adjective **callous** with the noun **callus**.

callus [noun: **calluses**] an area of hard skin on your hands or feet, caused by constant rubbing

calm [adjective: **calmer, calmest**]
1 still and quiet: *a calm sea*
2 not anxious, excited or upset
[verb: **calms, calming, calmed**]
1 to calm or to **calm down** is to become quiet and still again after being noisy or disturbed: *The boats can sail when the weather calms down.*
2 to calm someone, or to **calm someone down**, is to stop them being excited or upset, and to **calm down** is to stop being excited or upset: *She took a couple of deep breaths to calm herself down.* • *After such a shock, it will take him a few minutes to calm down.*
♦ **calmly** [adverb] without showing any anxiety or excitement: *Grace walked calmly on to the stage.*
♦ **calmness** [noun] being calm: *We were impressed by his calmness under pressure.*

calorie [noun: **calories**] a unit of heat used to measure how much energy a food gives

calypso [noun: **calypsos**] a type of West Indian popular song, usually with words that are made up as it is sung

camber [noun: **cambers**] a curve on the surface of a road which slopes down on each side from a high point in the middle

camcorder [noun: **camcorders**] a video camera that also records sound

came [verb] a way of changing the verb **come** to make a past tense: *They came downstairs, laughing and shouting.*

camel [noun: **camels**] a desert animal with a long neck and one or two humps on its back for storing water

cameo [noun: **cameos**] a stone, usually part of a piece of jewellery, with a pattern cut out of a different coloured background so that it stands out

camera [noun: **cameras**] a device for taking photographs, or for making television programmes or films

camisole [noun: **camisoles**] a woman's light vest or top with thin shoulder straps

camomile [noun] a kind of plant with yellow flowers, used to make herbal tea and medicines

camouflage [noun: **camouflages**] a way of disguising things so that they are not easy to see, especially by making them blend in with their background
[verb: **camouflages, camouflaging, camouflaged**] to camouflage something is to disguise it so that it will not be noticed easily: *The stick insect camouflages itself by sitting very still on a twig.*

camp [noun: **camps**] a place where people live in tents, huts or caravans, usually for a short time: *a refugee camp*
[verb: **camps, camping, camped**] to camp is to stay somewhere for a short time in a tent, hut or caravan: *We camped in a clearing in the woods.*
➡ **camper, camping**

campaign [noun: **campaigns**] a campaign is a series of activities to try to achieve a particular thing, for example selling a product or getting someone elected: *an advertising campaign*
[verb: **campaigns, campaigning, campaigned**] to campaign for something is to organize support for it: *They've been campaigning to have a new theatre built.*
♦ **campaigner** [noun: **campaigners**] someone who organizes support for something

camper [noun: **campers**]
1 someone who stays in a tent or hut, usually while they are on holiday
2 a type of vehicle that you can live in, usually while you are on holiday

camping [noun] if you go camping, you go somewhere where you stay in a shelter like a tent, hut or caravan

campsite [noun: **campsites**] a place where people camp in tents

campus [noun: **campuses**] the buildings and grounds of a college or university

can[1] [verb]
1 to have the ability to: *Can you swim? Yes, I can.*

Cc

2 to be allowed to: *Can I go swimming? Yes, you can.*

ⓘ **Can** is the present tense form. You use **could** for the past tense.

can [noun: **cans**] a container made of tin or some other metal, especially one that is sealed to keep a food or drink from going bad [verb: **cans, canning, canned**] to can food is to seal it in cans

canal [noun: **canals**] a long channel filled with water and built so that boats can travel across an area of land: *the Panama Canal*

canary [noun: **canaries**] a small singing bird with yellow feathers, often kept as a pet

cancel [verb: **cancels, cancelling, cancelled**]
1 to cancel an arrangement is to say that it will not happen: *The match was cancelled because of the snow.*
2 to cancel a cheque or a payment is to stop it being paid
♦ **cancellation** [noun: **cancellations**] a cancellation is something that had been booked in advance and has then been cancelled: *You'll get a seat on the flight if there are any last-minute cancellations.*

cancer [noun: **cancers**] a serious disease in which some cells in the body start to grow very quickly and form lumps

candid [adjective] honest and truthful: *Sheena was very candid about her past mistakes.*
→ **candidly**

candidate [noun: **candidates**]
1 someone who is taking an exam
2 someone who is trying to get a particular job or position

candidly [adverb] openly and truthfully: *He spoke candidly about what had gone wrong.*

candle [noun: **candles**] a stick of wax with a piece of string called a wick through the middle, which is lit so that it burns and gives out light

candlestick [noun: **candlesticks**] a holder for keeping a candle upright

candy [noun: **candies**]
1 candy is sugar that has been boiled and has then become solid
2 a candy is a sweet

candyfloss [noun] candyfloss is sugar that has been heated and spun into fluff which you eat off a stick

cane [noun: **canes**]
1 the hollow, hard stem of bamboo and some other plants
2 a walking stick: *The old man carried a silver-topped cane.*
[verb: **canes, caning, caned**] to cane someone is to hit them with a long stick as a punishment

canine [adjective]
1 to do with dogs or like a dog: *canine behaviour*
2 canine teeth are sharp and pointed. Humans have four canine teeth

canister [noun: **canisters**] a container, often made of metal, used for storing things: *a canister of tea*

cannabis [noun] a drug that some people smoke to make them feel relaxed

cannibal [noun: **cannibals**] a person who eats other people, or an animal that eats animals of the same species
♦ **cannibalism** [noun] eating other people, or eating other animals of the same species

cannon [noun: **cannons**] a type of large gun that fires cannonballs or heavy shells

cannonball [noun: **cannonballs**] a heavy ball of metal or stone fired from a cannon

cannot [verb]
1 cannot is used with another verb to say that you are not able to do something: *I cannot read your writing.*
2 cannot is used with another verb when you are not giving permission for something: *No, you cannot have another slice of cake.*

canoe [noun: **canoes**] a light boat that is pointed at both ends and that you move through the water using a paddle [verb: **canoes, canoeing, canoed**] to canoe is to paddle, or to travel in, a canoe

canon [noun: **canons**]
1 a rule or law
2 a title given to some Christian priests, especially a priest that works in a cathedral

canopy [noun: **canopies**] a covering that is hung above something: *a canopy over a bed*

can't [short form] a short way to say and write **cannot**: *I can't hear you.*

Cc

canteen [noun: **canteens**] a restaurant in a school, office or factory where pupils or workers can get meals and snacks

canter [noun] a gentle running pace of a horse that is faster than a trot and slower than a gallop

[verb: **canters, cantering, cantered**] to canter is to go at a pace between a trot and a gallop

canvas [noun: **canvases**]
1 canvas is a strong cloth used to make tents and sails
2 a canvas is a piece of this cloth stretched and used for painting on

canvass [verb: **canvasses, canvassing, canvassed**] to canvass opinion or support is to go round asking people for it: *He's canvassing for the Green Party.*

ⓘ Notice the different spellings of the noun **canvas** and the verb **canvass**.

canyon [noun: **canyons**] a deep river valley with steep sides: *the Grand Canyon*

cap [noun: **caps**]
1 a soft hat that often has a peak at the front
2 a small top for a bottle, tube or pen
[verb: **caps, capping, capped**]
1 to cap something is to put a covering or lid on it: *mountains capped with snow*
2 a sportsman is capped when he or she is chosen to play in the team representing their country

capable [adjective]
1 a capable person is able to deal with problems or difficulties without help
2 if you are capable of something, you are able to do it or achieve it: *The old lady isn't capable of looking after herself any more.*
♦ **capably** [adverb] to do something capably is to deal with it well or efficiently: *I'm sure you'll do the job very capably.*

capacity [noun: **capacities**]
1 the capacity of a container or building is the total amount that it will hold: *a barrel with a capacity of 100 litres* • *The hall has a seating capacity of 300.*
2 someone's capacity to do something is their ability to do it: *Flynn has the capacity to be a great leader.*

3 to do something in your capacity as something is to do it as part of a job you have: *Mrs Jones came to the meeting in her capacity as head teacher.*

cape¹ [noun: **capes**] a kind of coat with no sleeves which is tied at the neck

cape² [noun: **capes**] a piece of land that sticks out into the sea: *He's sailed round the Cape of Good Hope and Cape Horn.*

caper [verb: **capers, capering, capered**] to caper is to leap and dance about in an amusing way: *The clown capered round the stage.*
[noun: **capers**] an adventure or an amusing activity: *Joe's off on one of his climbing capers.*

capillary [noun: **capillaries**] the narrowest type of blood vessel

capital [adjective]
1 most important: *a capital city*
2 punishable by death: *Murder is still a capital crime in some states in the US.*
[noun: **capitals**]
1 the capital of a country or state is the city where its government is based: *What's the capital of Sweden?* • *Sacramento is the state capital of California.*
2 a capital is a capital letter: *Write your name in capitals at the top of the page.*
3 capital is money that can be invested, for example in a business or a savings account, to make more money

capital city [noun: **capital cities**] a city in a state or country where its government is based

capitalism [noun] a system in which businesses are owned and run by individuals rather than being controlled by the government of a country
♦ **capitalist** [noun: **capitalists**] someone who believes in capitalism
[adjective] having a system of capitalism: *capitalist countries*

capitalize or **capitalise** [verb: **capitalizes, capitalizing, capitalized**]
1 to capitalize a letter is to write or print it as a capital letter
2 to **capitalize on** something is to use it to your advantage or benefit

capital letter [noun: **capital letters**] a

letter like the larger one you write at the start of your name, as in CAPITAL LETTERS

capital punishment [noun] capital punishment is being killed as a punishment for a crime, for example murder

cappuccino [noun: **cappuccinos**] coffee made with frothy hot milk and often served with powdered chocolate on the top

capsize [verb: **capsizes, capsizing, capsized**] when a boat capsizes, it turns upside down: *The little sailing boat capsized.*

capsule [noun: **capsules**]
1 a small pill filled with a dose of medicine
2 a part of a spacecraft, especially the part that the astronauts live and work in, that can be separated from the rest of the spacecraft

captain [noun: **captains**]
1 an officer in charge of a ship, an aircraft or a company of soldiers
2 the leader of a sports team or a sports club [verb: **captains, captaining, captained**] to captain a ship or an aircraft, or a sports team, is to be its captain

caption [noun: **captions**] a piece of writing above, below or beside a picture or photograph that explains or describes what is in it

captivate [verb: **captivates, captivating, captivated**] to captivate someone is to fascinate them and hold all their attention
♦ **captivating** [adjective] charming or fascinating: *a captivating smile*

captive [noun: **captives**] a person who has been caught and is being held prisoner [adjective]
1 caught and held prisoner: *a captive bird*
2 not able to escape: *The other passengers were a captive audience when she started singing on the train.*
♦ **captivity** [noun]
1 being a prisoner
2 animals in captivity are kept in a zoo or some other enclosed space, rather than living in the wild

capture [verb: **captures, capturing, captured**]
1 to capture someone is to take them prisoner: *Many soldiers were captured by the enemy.*
2 to capture something belonging to someone

else is to take it from them by force: *They captured many Spanish ships loaded with gold and silver.*

car [noun: **cars**] a vehicle with an engine and seats for a small number of passengers

LANGUAGE FOR LIFE

cars

Here are some important words that you may come across when you are buying or looking after a car:

• **Insurance** is an arrangement in which you pay a company money each year and they pay the costs if your car is damaged or stolen, or if it damages another car.

• The **logbook** is the official document that shows when a car was made and who has owned it. It is properly called the Vehicle Registration Document.

• The **MOT test** is a test done by qualified mechanics to find out if your car is safe to be driven. All cars over three years old have to pass an MOT test every year.

• **Road tax** is a tax that you pay if you want to drive your car on the road. It is properly called Vehicle Excise Duty.

• A **service** is a regular check to make sure your car is working properly.

caramel [noun: **caramels**]
1 caramel is sugar that has been heated until it goes brown
2 a caramel is a sweet made with browned sugar

carat [noun: **carats**] a measurement of the weight of gems and of the purity of gold

caravan [noun: **caravans**] a vehicle for living in which can be towed behind a car

carbohydrate [noun: **carbohydrates**] a mixture of sugar, hydrogen and oxygen that is found in certain foods and gives the body energy

carbon [noun] a chemical element found in all living things as well as in substances like coal, oil, charcoal and diamond

carbonated [adjective] a carbonated drink has carbon dioxide gas added to it to make it fizzy

carbon dioxide [noun] a gas found in air and breathed out by humans and animals

Cc

carbon monoxide [noun] a poisonous gas with no smell which is made when carbon is burned

carbon paper [noun] a special type of paper coated with ink on one side that is used to make copies of documents as they are being written or typed

carbuncle [noun: **carbuncles**] a painful swelling under the skin

carburettor [noun: **carburettors**] the part inside an engine where air and the fuel are mixed to produce a gas that will burn to give power to the engine

carcass [noun: **carcasses**] a dead body of an animal

card [noun: **cards**]
1 card is thick stiff paper
2 a card is a piece of this used to give a greeting or information to someone: *a birthday card* • *a business card*
3 cards or playing cards are a set of rectangular pieces of card with numbers and symbols printed on one side, that are used for playing games
4 cards or card games are games like bridge that are played with a set of playing cards
5 something that is **on the cards** is likely to happen

cardboard [noun] cardboard is very stiff, thick paper used to make boxes and packaging

cardiac [adjective] to do with the heart: *a cardiac surgeon*

cardigan [noun: **cardigans**] a knitted sweater that has buttons down the front

ⓘ Cardigans were named after the Earl of Cardigan, whose soldiers wore woollen jackets with buttons.

cardinal [noun: **cardinals**] a high-ranking priest in the Roman Catholic Church

cardiology [noun] the area of medicine that deals with the heart and diseases that affect it

care [noun: **cares**]
1 care is worry or anxiety: *We all want a life with as little care and trouble as possible.*
2 a care is a cause for worry or anxiety: *She was humming to herself as if she didn't have a care in the world.*
3 care is close attention paid to something: *Meg does her work with great care.* • *Take care! It's slippery here.*
4 if children are **in care**, they are looked after by the local social services because their parents cannot look after them
5 if you **take care of** someone or something, you look after them: *Their aunt took care of them after their parents died.* • *Can you take care of the arrangements for the meeting?*
[verb: **cares, caring, cared**]
1 to care is to be concerned or interested: *He said he didn't care what happened.*
2 if you care for a child, a person who is ill, etc, you look after them: *Sarah wants to be a vet so that she can care for sick animals.*
3 if you say you care for something, you mean that you like it or want it: *I don't care much for fish.*
→ **carer**

career [noun: **careers**] a person's career is the job or profession they have trained for and which they can move up in as they go through their working life: *a career in the police force*
[verb: **careers, careering, careered**] to career is to move very quickly and without proper control: *The car careered into a lamppost.*

carefree [adjective] having no worries: *a carefree life*

careful [adjective] making sure that you do something properly without making a mistake or causing an accident: *Dad is always careful to lock all the doors.* • *Be careful when you cross the road.*
♦ **carefully** [adverb] without making mistakes or causing damage: *Gretta wrapped up the ornament carefully in tissue paper.*

careless [adjective] not being careful or not paying close attention: *a careless mistake* • *Alex is a bit careless with his money.*
♦ **carelessly** [adverb] in a careless way
♦ **carelessness** [noun] being careless

carer [noun: **carers**] someone who looks after an old or ill person, especially in their home

caress [verb: **caresses, caressing, caressed**] to caress something is to touch it or stroke it lovingly: *A gentle breeze caressed her face.*

caretaker [noun: **caretakers**] someone whose job is to look after a building

cargo [noun: **cargoes**] the things carried by a ship or aeroplane: *a cargo of iron ore*

caricature [noun: **caricatures**] a caricature of a person is a drawing of them that makes their features look funny or ridiculous
[verb: **caricatures, caricaturing, caricatured**] to caricature someone is to draw them or describe them to make them seem funny or ridiculous

caries [noun] the medical name for decayed parts of the teeth: *Brushing your teeth will help to prevent caries.*

carnage [noun] carnage is the killing or wounding of a lot of people

carnation [noun: **carnations**] a garden plant that has long stems and brightly coloured pink, red or white flowers with lots of petals

carnival [noun: **carnivals**] carnival or a carnival is a celebration for which people get dressed up in costumes and sing and dance outdoors

carnivore [noun: **carnivores**] any animal that eats meat. Look up and compare **herbivore** and **omnivore**
♦ **carnivorous** [adjective] eating meat: *Tyrannosaurus rex was a huge carnivorous dinosaur.*

carol [noun: **carols**] a song sung at Christmas time

carp [noun: **carp** or **carps**] a kind of fish with a wide body, often kept in ponds

car park [noun: **car parks**] a place where cars can be left for a short time: *a multi-storey car park*

carpenter [noun: **carpenters**] someone who works at making things from wood
♦ **carpentry** [noun] making things from wood

carpet [noun: **carpets**]
1 a covering for a floor made of wool or some other soft strong fabric
2 anything that forms a covering on the ground: *a carpet of primroses and bluebells*
[verb: **carpets, carpeting, carpeted**] to carpet something is to cover it, either with a carpet or with something that covers like a carpet

carriage [noun: **carriages**]
1 one of the long sections of a train where passengers sit or sleep
2 a vehicle that can carry passengers and is pulled by horses
3 carriage is carrying anything or the cost of carrying something

carrion [noun] carrion is rotting flesh from animals that have died, which is often eaten by other animals or birds such as crows

carrot [noun: **carrots**] a long orange vegetable that grows under the ground

ⓘ Be careful not to confuse the spellings of the words **carat** and **carrot**.

carry [verb: **carries, carrying, carried**]
1 if you carry something, you pick it up and take it somewhere: *This bag is too heavy for me to carry.*
2 when sound carries, it travels over a long distance: *He has the sort of voice that carries.*
3 to **carry on** is to continue: *Carry on with your work while I go and see the headmaster.*
4 to **carry on** is to behave in a certain way, especially badly: *Will you two stop carrying on like children, please.*
5 to **carry something out** is to do it: *The surgeon will carry out the operation tomorrow morning.*
6 if someone **gets carried away**, they get too excited by something: *He got a bit carried away by the music and started jumping up and down.*

carrycot [noun: **carrycots**] a light cot with handles for carrying a baby in

carry-on [noun: **carry-ons**] a fuss

cart [noun: **carts**] a vehicle pulled by a horse and used for carrying loads

cartilage [noun] cartilage is a strong stretchy type of body tissue found between certain bones and in the nose and ears

cartography [noun] making maps and charts

carton [noun: **cartons**] a box or container made of cardboard: *a carton of milk*

cartoon [noun: **cartoons**]
1 a drawing or a series of drawings printed in a newspaper or magazine, often making fun of someone famous

Cc

Cc

2 a film made by drawing the characters and action

♦ **cartoonist** [noun: **cartoonists**] someone who draws cartoons

cartridge [noun: **cartridges**] a small case holding, for example, film for a camera, ink for a pen or printer, or the bullet for a gun. A cartridge can be removed and replaced easily

cartwheel [noun: **cartwheels**] a movement in which you take your weight on your hands and turn your whole body sideways in a circle through the air to land on your feet

carve [verb: **carves, carving, carved**]
1 to carve something is to make or shape it using a cutting tool: *The faces of the presidents are carved out of the rock.*
2 to carve meat is to cut it into slices or pieces using a sharp knife

cascade [noun: **cascades**] a waterfall [verb: **cascades, cascading, cascaded**] to cascade is to tumble downwards like water in a waterfall

case[1] [noun: **cases**]
1 a suitcase: *Have you unpacked your cases yet?*
2 a container or covering: *The crown jewels are kept in a glass case.*

case[2] [noun: **cases**]
1 a particular example of something happening: *It was a case of having to wait until the train arrived.*
2 a problem that is dealt with by a lawyer, a doctor or the police: *a court case* • *There had been no cases of smallpox for many years.*
3 you do something **in case** something else happens when you want to take care because the second thing might happen: *Take an umbrella in case it rains.*

casement [noun: **casements**] a type of window frame in which the window opens sideways by swinging on hinges

cash [noun] cash is banknotes and coins: *I didn't have enough cash to pay the fare, so I had to go to the cashpoint.*
[verb: **cashes, cashing, cashed**]
1 to cash a cheque is to change it for banknotes or coins
2 to **cash in on** something is to profit from it

cashew [noun: **cashews**] a kind of kidney-shaped nut with a buttery taste

cashier [noun: **cashiers**] someone whose job is to take in and pay out money, for example in a bank

cash machine or **cashpoint** [noun: **cash machines** or **cashpoints**] a machine where you can take money out of your bank account by putting in your bank card

cash register [noun: **cash registers**] a machine used in a shop that records and stores the money paid by customers

casino [noun: **casinos**] a building where people can gamble

cask [noun: **casks**] a barrel for holding wine or beer

casket [noun: **caskets**]
1 a wooden or metal box for keeping things in, especially jewels
2 a coffin

casserole [noun: **casseroles**]
1 a dish with a cover for cooking and serving food
2 the food cooked in a casserole: *a beef casserole*
[verb: **casseroles, casseroling, casseroled**] to casserole food is to cook it in the oven in a covered dish

cassette [noun: **cassettes**] a small case holding a long piece of recording tape or film that moves around a spool when it is fitted into a tape recorder or camera

cassette player or **cassette recorder** [noun: **cassette players** or **cassette recorders**] a machine that plays and makes recordings on tape

cassock [noun: **cassocks**] a long-sleeved robe that goes from the shoulders down to the ankles and is worn by priests

cast [verb: **casts, casting, cast**]
1 to cast a play or a film is to choose the actors who will be in it
2 to cast an object in metal or plaster is to shape it in a mould
3 to cast something is to throw it: *They'd been cast into prison.*
[noun: **casts**]
1 the cast of a play or film are the actors in it
2 an object formed in a mould: *The policeman made a plaster cast of the footprints.*

castanets [plural noun] castanets are a

musical instrument made up of two pieces of hard wood or plastic that you hold in your hand and hit together to make a loud clicking sound

castaway [noun: **castaways**] someone who has been left in a lonely place, for example a desert island, usually after a shipwreck

caste [noun: **castes**] a class or rank of people

caster [noun] another spelling of **castor**

castle [noun: **castles**]
1 a type of large building with thick, high walls and usually towers and battlements, which was built to protect the people inside from attack
2 a piece with a top like a castle in chess

castor or **caster** [noun: **castors** or **casters**] one of a set of small wheels attached to the bottom of a piece of furniture so that it can be moved about easily

castor oil [noun] a yellow oil from a kind of palm that is used as medicine

castor sugar [noun] a kind of sugar in the form of very fine granules that is used in cooking and baking

casual [adjective]
1 not suitable for formal occasions: *casual clothes*
2 not serious, not caring or not taking much interest: *Sarita's a bit too casual in her attitude to her work.*
♦ **casually** [adverb] in a casual way: *casually dressed*

casualty [noun: **casualties**]
1 a casualty is someone who has been injured or killed: *Ambulances ferried the casualties to hospital.*
2 casualty is the old name for **Accident and Emergency**, the hospital department that deals with people who have been injured and need medical attention

cat [noun: **cats**]
1 an animal, often kept as a pet, that has soft fur and claws
2 any animal that belongs to the family of animals that includes cats, lions, leopards and tigers
3 if you **let the cat out of the bag**, you tell people something that they aren't supposed to know

catalogue [noun: **catalogues**] a book showing a company's products or a list in a library giving details of all the books available [verb: **catalogues, cataloguing, catalogued**] to catalogue things is to put details about them in a list

catalyst [noun: **catalysts**]
1 a substance which starts a chemical reaction but which does not itself react or change
2 something that makes a change take place

catalytic converter [noun: **catalytic converters**] a device in a car that stops harmful substances getting into the air from the car's exhaust

catamaran [noun: **catamarans**] a type of sailing boat with two hulls beside each other

catapult [noun: **catapults**] a small weapon made of a forked stick with a piece of elastic stretched across the fork, used for firing small stones [verb: **catapults, catapulting, catapulted**] to be catapulted is to be thrown forward forcefully: *The bike hit a rock and he was catapulted over the handlebars.*

cataract [noun: **cataracts**] an eye disease in which the lens in your eye becomes gradually thicker so that it becomes more and more difficult to see

catastrophe [noun: **catastrophes**] a sudden terrible disaster
♦ **catastrophic** [adjective] absolutely terrible: *the catastrophic effects of the earthquake*

ⓘ **Catastrophe** is pronounced cat-**as**-tro-fi. **Catastrophic** is pronounced cat-as-**trof**-ik.

catch [verb: **catches, catching, caught**]
1 to catch something is to hold it and stop it from escaping: *Throw the ball and I'll try to catch it.*
• *Les caught a fish but let it go again.*
2 to catch an illness is to get it: *Be careful not to catch a cold.*
3 to catch a bus or train is to be in time to get on to it: *I left early so that I would catch the 8.30 train.*
4 to catch someone doing something, especially something bad, is to surprise or discover them while they are doing it: *My neighbour caught me making faces at her.*

Cc

Cc

5 if you catch part of your body or your clothing, you injure or damage it on something: *Sam caught his sleeve on the door as he was coming in.*

6 to **catch up**, or **catch up with** people who are ahead of you, is to reach the place where they are

7 to **catch fire** is to start to burn and produce flames

[noun: **catches**]

1 a fastening: *The catch on my bracelet has broken.*

2 a fisherman's catch is the number of fish he has caught

3 something that seems good at first has a catch if it has a disadvantage that you didn't know about: *The holiday was supposed to be free, but there was a catch, of course.*

♦ **catching** [adjective] if an illness or disease is catching, it is infectious: *I hope that sore throat you have isn't catching.*

catchment area [noun: **catchment areas**] an area from which a particular school gets its pupils

catchphrase [noun: **catchphrases**] a phrase that is used by someone again and again, especially an entertainer or comedian, so that you remember it

catchy [adjective: **catchier, catchiest**] a catchy tune is one that you remember easily

categorize or **categorise** [verb: **categorizes, categorizing, categorized**] to categorize people or things is to group them together according to what type, size or age they are

category [noun: **categories**] a grouping of people or things of the same type: *different categories of fiction*

cater [verb: **caters, catering, catered**]
1 to cater is to prepare and supply food
2 to cater for something or someone is to provide what is wanted or needed: *an exhibition that caters for every type of gardener*

♦ **caterer** [noun: **caterers**] a person or business whose job is to prepare and provide food for people, for example at a conference or wedding

caterpillar [noun: **caterpillars**] a small creature with a soft body that feeds on plants and leaves and which turns into a moth or butterfly

caterwaul [verb: **caterwauls, caterwauling, caterwauled**] to caterwaul is to make a horrible howling or screeching noise like a cat

cat flap [noun: **cat flaps**] a small door cut in a door through which a pet cat can come in or go out

cathedral [noun: **cathedrals**] the main church in an area, where a bishop preaches

catherine wheel [noun: **catherine wheels**] a firework that spins round and round as it burns

Catholic [adjective] having to do with, or belonging to, the Roman Catholic Church
[noun: **Catholics**] a Roman Catholic

catkin [noun: **catkins**] a small tightly-packed flower that hangs from a short stem and grows on some trees, like willow and hazel

catseye [noun: **catseyes**] catseyes are small objects fixed in a road surface which reflect light and guide drivers at night. This word is a trademark

cattle [plural noun] cows, bulls and oxen and any other grass-eating animals of this family

caught [verb] a way of changing the verb **catch** to make a past tense. It can be used with or without a helping verb: *Emily caught a cold.*
• *She must have caught it from Sophie.*

cauldron [noun: **cauldrons**] a big pot heated over a fire and used to cook things in

cauliflower [noun: **cauliflowers**] a round vegetable related to the cabbage and made up of tightly packed white flowers or florets

cause [verb: **causes, causing, caused**] to cause something is to make it happen: *The leak in the roof caused damp in the bedroom.*
[noun: **causes**]
1 a cause of something is what makes it happen: *the causes of poverty*
2 a cause is something that people support because they believe it is right: *She supports many good causes.*

causeway [noun: **causeways**] a causeway is a raised road over shallow water or wet ground

caustic [adjective] a caustic substance burns or causes rust

cauterize or **cauterise** [verb: **cauterizes, cauterizing, cauterized**] to cauterize a wound is to burn it with hot metal so that it heals well

caution [noun: **cautions**]
1 caution is taking care to avoid danger or risk: *Please drive with caution.*
2 a caution is a warning: *The police let him off with a caution.*
♦ **cautionary** [adjective] a cautionary story or tale is one that gives a warning
♦ **cautious** [adjective] to be cautious is to be very careful to avoid danger or risk

cavalcade [noun: **cavalcades**] a long line of people on horseback or in vehicles moving along a route to celebrate something

cavalry [noun] cavalry or the cavalry are soldiers on horseback: *He joined the cavalry.*

cave [noun: **caves**] a large hole in the side of a hill, cliff or mountain or under the ground

caveman [noun: **cavemen**] a male human from prehistoric times who lived in a cave

cavern [noun: **caverns**] a large cave
♦ **cavernous** [adjective] deep and wide, like a cavern: *inside the whale's cavernous mouth*

cavewoman [noun: **cavewomen**] a female human from prehistoric times who lived in a cave

caviare or **caviar** [noun] an expensive food that is the eggs of a large fish called a sturgeon

cavity [noun: **cavities**]
1 a hollow space or hole
2 a hollow in a tooth caused by decay

caw [verb: **caws, cawing, cawed**] a crow caws when it makes a loud harsh sound
[noun: **caws**] the sound a crow makes

cc [abbreviation] short for **cubic centimetre** or **cubic centimetres**

CCTV [abbreviation] short for **closed circuit television**, a television system used for security in a building or in a particular area

CD [abbreviation: **CD's** or **CDs**] short for **compact disc**: *I got two CD's for my birthday.*

CD-ROM [abbreviation: **CD-ROMs**] short for **compact disc read-only memory**, a system by which optical information on a compact disc can be viewed on the visual display unit of a computer, but cannot be

altered: *This game is available on CD-ROM.*

cease [verb: **ceases, ceasing, ceased**] to cease is to stop

ceasefire [noun: **ceasefires**]
1 an order given to stop firing weapons
2 an agreement made between two armies or fighting groups to stop fighting for a time

ceaseless [adjective] not stopping: *a ceaseless thump, thump, thump*

cedar [noun: **cedars**] a kind of tall evergreen tree

ceilidh [noun: **ceilidhs**] a social event with Scottish dancing and music

ⓘ This word is pronounced **kay**-li.

ceiling [noun: **ceilings**]
1 the inner roof of a room
2 an upper limit: *They'd set a ceiling of 7% on pay rises.*

celebrate [verb: **celebrates, celebrating, celebrated**] to celebrate something is to have a party or do something special because of it: *Everyone was celebrating the New Year.*
♦ **celebration** [noun: **celebrations**] celebration or a celebration is something done to celebrate an event: *They've won money on the lottery and are having a celebration.*

celebrity [noun: **celebrities**]
1 celebrity is fame
2 a celebrity is someone who is famous

celery [noun] a kind of vegetable with long light-green ridged stalks with feathery leaves growing at the top

cell [noun: **cells**]
1 the smallest part of a living thing. The cells in most living things divide so that the animal or plant can grow or repair any part that has been damaged or injured
2 a small room that a prisoner is kept in or that a monk lives in
3 a device in a battery that produces electrical energy using chemicals

cellar [noun: **cellars**] an underground room used for storing things

cellist [noun: **cellists**] someone who plays the cello

cello [noun: **cellos**] an instrument like a large violin that is held upright on the floor and played with a bow

Cc

ⓘ This word is pronounced **chel**-o.

cellophane [noun] cellophane is a thin transparent material used for wrapping things in. This word is a trademark

cellular [adjective]
1 made up of or having cells: *the cellular structure of a honeycomb*
2 a cellular phone uses a system of radio transmitters called cells. A phone message is sent between the transmitters until it reaches the one nearest the phone that is to receive the message

cellulose [noun] a substance that makes up the cell walls of plants and is used to make paper and textiles

Celsius [adjective] of the temperature scale at which water freezes at 0 degrees and boils at 100 degrees, or measured using this scale: *57 degrees Celsius*

cement [noun]
1 a grey powder that is mixed with sand and water and used to stick bricks together in a wall or to make concrete
2 any type of strong glue that sticks things together firmly: *plastic cement*
[verb: **cements, cementing, cemented**]
1 to cement things is to join or stick them with cement
2 to cement something such as a relationship is to make it stronger: *an exchange of gifts to cement their new friendship*

cemetery [noun: **cemeteries**] a place where dead people are buried

cenotaph [noun: **cenotaphs**] a monument to people who are buried somewhere else, especially soldiers, sailors and pilots who have died in a war

censor [noun: **censors**] someone whose job is to cut any offensive parts out of books and films before they are seen by the public
[verb: **censors, censoring, censored**] to censor something is stop it being sold or shown to the public

census [noun: **censuses**] an official survey carried out every few years to find out how many people are living in a particular country: *The last census in Britain was in 2001.*

cent [noun: **cents**] a unit of money worth one hundredth of a larger unit of money, for example the American or Australian dollar or the euro

centaur [noun: **centaurs**] a creature from old stories or myths which was half man and half horse

centenary [noun: **centenaries**] the hundredth anniversary of an event: *a special edition to celebrate the centenary of Beatrix Potter's birth*

centennial [adjective]
1 having lasted for a hundred years
2 happening every hundred years
[noun: **centennials**] a centenary

centi- or **cent-** [prefix] if a word starts with **centi-** or **cent-**, it has something to do with a hundred or a hundredth part of. For example, a *century* is a hundred years and a *centimetre* is a hundredth part of a metre

centigrade [adjective]
1 of temperature or a temperature scale that is measured in or made up of a hundred degrees
2 another name for Celsius

centigram or **centigramme** [noun: **centigrams** or **centigrammes**] a measurement of weight that is a hundredth part of a gram. This is often shortened to **cg**

centilitre [noun: **centilitres**] a measurement used for liquids that is a hundredth part of a litre. This is often shortened to **cl**

centimetre [noun: **centimetres**] a measurement of length that is a hundredth part of a metre. This is often shortened to **cm**

centipede [noun: **centipedes**] a crawling insect with a long body and lots of pairs of legs

central [adjective] near or at the centre

central heating [noun] a system used for heating houses where water is heated in a boiler and sent through pipes to radiators in each room

central locking [noun] a system in a car where you lock or unlock the locks on all the doors by turning a key in one lock

centre [noun: **centres**]
1 the centre of something is its middle point or part: *the centre of a circle • chocolates with soft centres*
2 a centre is a building or group of buildings used for a particular activity: *a sports centre*

[verb: **centres, centring, centred**] to centre something is to put it in the centre
➡ **central**

century [noun: **centuries**]
1 a hundred years
2 if a cricketer scores a century, he or she scores a hundred runs in a match

ceramic [adjective] made of clay that is baked until hard in a very hot oven called a kiln: *a ceramic dish*
[noun: **ceramics**] an object made of pottery: *She makes beautiful sculptures and ceramics.*
◆ **ceramics** [noun] ceramics is the art or craft of making things with clay which are then baked in a kiln

cereal [noun: **cereals**]
1 a cereal is a grain that is used as food, for example wheat, maize, oats, barley and rice
2 cereal or a cereal is this food, especially one that is eaten for breakfast

ⓘ Be careful not to confuse the spellings of **cereal** and **serial**.

ceremonial [adjective] to do with ceremony or a particular ceremony: *Opening Parliament is one of the monarch's ceremonial duties.*
[noun: **ceremonials**] ceremonial or ceremonials are the actions that form part of an official or traditional ceremony

ceremonious [adjective] ceremonious behaviour is very correct and polite: *He gave a ceremonious bow.*
◆ **ceremoniously** [adverb] with grand gestures or actions: *A huge cake was placed ceremoniously in the centre of the table.*

ceremony [noun: **ceremonies**]
1 ceremony is formal behaviour at a grand or important occasion: *all the ceremony of a coronation*
2 a ceremony is an event where special forms or customs are used: *a wedding ceremony*

certain [adjective]
1 if something is certain, it will definitely happen or be the case: *There's certain to be someone there who can help you.*
2 if you are certain about something, you are sure about it: *I'm almost certain I saw a light in the old mill.*
3 for certain means definitely or surely: *How*

can you say for certain that this is a dinosaur bone?
4 to **make certain** is to make sure: *Make certain that rope is tied tightly.*
◆ **certainly** [adverb] definitely: *Joe certainly impressed us with his acting.*
◆ **certainty** [noun: **certainties**]
1 certainty is feeling or being certain
2 a certainty is something that will definitely happen

certificate [noun: **certificates**] an official piece of paper that gives written details of something, for example a person's birth or death, or an exam they have passed: *Peter got first prize for English and Sheila got a certificate of merit.*
◆ **certify** [verb: **certifies, certifying, certified**] to certify something is to put it down in writing as an official statement or promise: *This is to certify that John Braddick took part in the Science Challenge.*

CFC [abbreviation: **CFCs**] short for **chlorofluorocarbon**, a chemical that can damage the Earth's ozone layer and which was used in the past in refrigerators

cg [abbreviation] short for **centigram** or **centigrams**

chador or **chadar** or **chudder** [noun: **chadors** or **chadars** or **chudders**] a thick veil worn by Muslim women that covers their head and shoulders

chafe [verb: **chafes, chafing, chafed**] to rub your skin and make it sore or warm: *Toby's wellington boots were chafing his legs.*

chaff [noun] chaff is the husks from corn left after the corn has been threshed

chaffinch [noun: **chaffinches**] a small singing bird with black, white and brown stripes on its wings

chain [noun: **chains**]
1 chain, or a chain, is several rings that are linked together
2 a chain of things is several things that are linked or connected: *a chain of events*
3 a chain of shops is several similar shops owned by the same person or company

chain letter [noun: **chain letters**] a letter that asks the person receiving it to send a copy to several other people, promising or threatening that something will happen if they do or do not

chain mail [noun] chain mail is armour made up of small iron links

chain reaction [noun: **chain reactions**] a chain reaction happens when one event causes another event to happen and so on

chain saw [noun: **chain saws**] a motorized saw that has cutting teeth on the edge of a chain which rotates very quickly

chain store [noun: **chain stores**] a shop or store that is part of a group of similar stores, all owned by the same company

chair [noun: **chairs**] a chair is a piece of furniture that has a back and which one person sits on

[verb: **chairs, chairing, chaired**] to chair a meeting is to be officially in charge of it

chairlift [noun: **chairlifts**] a system that has chairs or seats hanging from a moving wire, used to carry skiers and walkers up mountains

chairperson [noun: **chairpeople**] a person who is in charge of a meeting. If it is a man, he may be called a **chairman**, and if it is a woman, she may be called a **chairwoman**

chalet [noun: **chalets**] a small wooden house

ⓘ This word is pronounced **shal**-ay.

chalice [noun: **chalices**] a cup for wine used in church services, for example when taking communion

chalk [noun: **chalks**]
1 chalk is a kind of soft white limestone
2 a chalk is a piece of this, often with a colour mixed through it, that you can use to draw with

♦ **chalky** [adjective: **chalkier, chalkiest**]
1 tasting or feeling like chalk
2 pale or white like chalk: *unhealthy-looking chalky skin*

challenge [verb: **challenges, challenging, challenged**]
1 to challenge a person or their actions is to question whether they are right: *The border guards challenged anyone who they thought was trying to get into the country.*
2 to challenge someone is to ask them to compete or fight: *He challenged his enemy to a duel.*
3 if something challenges you, you have to

work hard or use all your abilities to get it done: *This exam will challenge even the ablest pupil.* [noun: **challenges**]
1 a challenge is something that needs all your ability to do it: *Her new job is going to be a challenge for her.*
2 a challenge is an invitation to fight or compete with someone

♦ **challenger** [noun: **challengers**] someone who invites another person to compete with them, especially a sportsman who wants to compete against a champion

♦ **challenging** [adjective] something challenging is difficult to do

chamber [noun: **chambers**]
1 a large room for meetings: *the council chamber*
2 an enclosed space: *a dark underground chamber*
3 an old-fashioned word for a room: *in the king's chamber*

chamber music [noun] classical music for a small group of players that is performed in a room rather than a large hall

chameleon [noun: **chameleons**] a small lizard that can change its colour to match its surroundings

chamois [noun: **chamois**]
1 a small goat-like mountain deer that lives in Europe and parts of Asia
2 soft thin leather made from the skin of this animal, used to make gloves or for polishing things

ⓘ When you are talking about the deer this word is pronounced **sham**-wah.
When you are talking about the leather it is pronounced **sham**-my.

champ [verb: **champs, champing, champed**] to champ is to chew noisily

champagne [noun] a type of sparkling wine produced in the Champagne area of France

champion [noun: **champions**]
1 someone who has beaten all the others in a contest or competition: *the world boxing champion*
2 someone who is a champion of a cause is a strong supporter of that cause: *Mrs Pankhurst, the champion of women's right to vote*

[verb: **champions, championing, championed**] to champion something is to support it strongly

♦ **championship** [noun: **championships**] a competition or contest to decide who is the champion

chance [noun: **chances**]

1 a possibility: *Is there any chance that we'll be picked for the team, do you think? • Bolton have no chance of winning the match.*

2 to take a chance is to take a risk: *We took a chance that we would find accommodation when we got there.*

3 an opportunity: *You didn't give me a chance to answer.*

4 chance is luck or fortune: *games of chance*

5 something that happens **by chance** happens by accident: *I saw him quite by chance parking his van up the street.*

[verb: **chances, chancing, chanced**] if you chance something, you take a risk: *It would probably have been all right, but we didn't want to chance it.*

[adjective] happening by accident: *a chance meeting*

➡ **chancy**

chancellor [noun: **chancellors**]

1 a high-ranking government official or minister: *the Chancellor of the Exchequer*

2 the head of a university

chancy [adjective: **chancier, chanciest**] rather risky: *It was a bit chancy taking a route we didn't know well.*

chandelier [noun: **chandeliers**] a light fitting that hangs from the ceiling and holds several lights

change [verb: **changes, changing, changed**]

1 to change is to become different or make something different: *The leaves changed from green to golden brown. • You've changed the curtains in here, haven't you?*

2 if you change, you put on different clothes

3 if you change schools, jobs or houses, you leave one and go to another

4 to change money is to exchange one type of money for another: *Can you change a £5 note for me?*

5 if you change your mind, you start to have a

different intention or opinion about something [noun: **changes**]

1 a change is a difference: *I'm afraid there's no change in your father's condition.*

2 a change of clothes is a different set of clothes

3 change is money in the form of coins: *Have you got any change?*

4 change is any extra money that you have given to a seller that is more than the price of the item you want to buy and which the seller gives back to you: *I told the taxi-driver to keep the change.*

changeable [adjective] the weather is changeable when it changes often or is likely to change

channel [noun: **channels**]

1 a groove or passage that water can travel along, or part of a sea or river that is deep enough for ships to travel along: *a drainage channel • a shipping channel*

2 a narrow sea or part of a sea: *the English Channel*

3 a television or radio station that is broadcast on a particular frequency: *Let's turn over to the other channel.*

[verb: **channels, channelling, channelled**] to channel something is to make it go in a particular direction: *They should channel their energies into something more useful.*

chant [verb: **chants, chanting, chanted**] to chant something is to say it or repeat it as if you were singing

[noun: **chants**] a chant is something that is repeated again and again in a singing voice

Chanukah [noun] another spelling of **Hanukkah**, a Jewish festival

chaos [noun] great disorder and confusion

♦ **chaotic** [adjective] completely disorganized: *The traffic was chaotic.*

ⓘ This word is pronounced **kay**-os.

chap [noun: **chaps**] a man: *He's a nice chap.*

chapatti [noun: **chapattis**] a kind of flat Indian bread

chapel [noun: **chapels**]

1 a small church or a small part of a larger church

Cc

2 a room inside a building that is used for worship: *the hospital chapel*

chaperone [noun: **chaperones**] a woman who accompanies an unmarried girl or young woman when she is out in public

chaplain [noun: **chaplains**] someone, often a priest or minister of the church, who conducts religious services in a hospital, school, or prison, or for the army

chapped [adjective] chapped skin is dry, red and sore: *chapped lips*

chapter [noun: **chapters**] one of the sections of a book: *Turn to chapter three in your history books.*

char [verb: **chars, charring, charred**] if something chars or is charred, it is burnt black

character [noun: **characters**]
1 your character is the type of nature you have or the good and bad points that make you the way you are
2 a person that a writer creates for a story, film or play: *Sam Weller, Mr Micawber and other Dickens characters*
3 a letter, symbol, etc used in writing or printing: *Chinese characters*
• **characteristic** [noun: **characteristics**] a person's or thing's characteristics are the features or qualities that you notice or that make them what they are
[adjective] a characteristic feature or quality is one that is typical of a particular person or thing
• **characterization** or **characterisation** [noun] characterization is the creation of different characters by a writer and the way the writer makes these characters change and develop during the story
• **characterize** or **characterise** [verb: **characterizes, characterizing, characterized**]
1 a quality or feature that characterizes someone or something is one that is typical of them or by which they can be recognized
2 to characterize someone in a certain way is to describe them in that way: *He'd been characterized as a villain.*

charade [noun: **charades**] a pretence
• **charades** [noun] charades is a game

where players have to guess the title of a book, film or television programme when one of them acts it out

charcoal [noun] charcoal is wood that has been burnt until it is black. Charcoal is used to draw with and as fuel

charge [verb: **charges, charging, charged**]
1 to charge someone with a crime is to accuse them of it: *He was charged with rape.*
2 to charge a certain price for something is to ask that amount of money for it: *The shopkeeper charged me $20 too much.*
3 to charge is to move forward in a sudden rush: *The demonstrators suddenly charged forward.*
4 to charge a battery or piece of electrical equipment is to fill it with electricity: *Where can I charge my phone?*
[noun: **charges**]
1 an accusation: *arrested on a charge of robbery*
2 a price or fee: *There will be a small extra charge for postage and packing.*
3 a sudden rush to attack: *The forwards should have reached the ten-yard line with that last charge.*
4 an amount of electricity in something
5 to be **in charge** is to be the person controlling or managing something: *Ms Handy is in charge of the sales department.*

charge card [noun: **charge cards**] a plastic card issued by a store that you can use to buy goods there and pay for them later

charger [noun: **chargers**] a piece of electrical equipment that you plug a mobile phone into to charge it

chariot [noun: **chariots**] a chariot was a two-wheeled open vehicle pulled by one or more horses. Chariots were used by the ancient Egyptians, Greeks and Romans for racing and fighting

charisma [noun] charisma is a personal quality that charms and impresses people: *a politician with lots of charisma*
• **charismatic** [adjective] a charismatic person attracts or impresses people by the way they speak or act: *a charismatic leader*

charitable [adjective]

Cc

1 a charitable person or a charitable act is kind and generous without asking anything in return
2 a charitable organization is one that gives money or help to the poor

charity [noun: **charities**]
1 charity is giving to the poor and people in need without asking anything in return
2 a charity is an organization that raises money to give to the poor

charm [noun: **charms**]
1 charm is a quality some people have that attracts and delights other people
2 a charm is a magic spell or something that is believed to have magical powers
[verb: **charms, charming, charmed**]
1 to charm someone is to attract and delight them
2 to charm someone or something is to put a magic spell on them: *The Pied Piper charmed the rats with his playing.*
♦ **charming** [adjective] delightful: *What a charming young man your son is.*

chart [noun: **charts**]
1 a chart is a table or diagram showing various measurements usually taken at different times: *a chart showing the rate of population growth*
2 a chart is a map of the sea or the coast used by sailors
3 a chart is a list of the most popular CDs, tapes and records

charter [noun: **charters**] an official document listing rights that people have
[verb: **charters, chartering, chartered**] to charter a boat or an aeroplane is to hire it

charter flight [noun: **charter flights**] a plane journey arranged by a travel agency that has bought all the seats and sells the tickets more cheaply than usual

chase [verb: **chases, chasing, chased**] to chase someone or something is to run after them
[noun: **chases**] a chase is a hunt or pursuit

chasm [noun: **chasms**] a deep narrow opening between rocks

chassis [noun: **chassis**] a vehicle's chassis is the frame and wheels that support its body

ⓘ This word is pronounced **shass**–i, with a silent **s** at the end.

chaste [adjective] a chaste person is very good and virtuous

chat [verb: **chats, chatting, chatted**]
1 people chat when they talk to each other in a friendly way about everyday things
2 to **chat someone up** is to try to attract them sexually by talking to them in a friendly way
[noun: **chats**] a friendly talk
→ **chatty**

chateau [noun: **chateaux**] a castle or large house in France

chat room [noun: **chat rooms**] an area on the Internet where people can exchange messages

chatter [verb: **chatters, chattering, chattered**]
1 if animals or birds chatter, they make loud cries quickly one after the other: *monkeys chattering in the treetops*
2 to chatter is to talk about silly or unimportant things: *Stop chattering, you two, and get on with your work.*
3 if your teeth chatter, they rattle against each other, usually because you are cold or frightened

chatty [adjective: **chattier, chattiest**] if someone is chatty, they like to talk or chat to other people: *At first she was shy, but now she's become quite chatty.*

chauffeur [noun: **chauffeurs**] someone whose job is to drive a car, especially a big expensive car belonging to a rich person

chauvinism [noun] chauvinism is a belief that your own country or your own sex is the best or the most important
♦ **chauvinist** [noun: **chauvinists**] someone who believes that their own sex or their own country is superior: *a male chauvinist*
[adjective] showing chauvinism: *a chauvinist attitude*

ⓘ **Chauvinism** is named after Nicholas Chauvin, a French soldier who was very proud of his country.

cheap [adjective: **cheaper, cheapest**]
1 something cheap does not cost a lot: *a cheap fare*
2 something that is cheap is not worth much money: *a cheap imitation diamond*

Cc

◆ **cheapen** [verb: **cheapens, cheapening, cheapened**] to cheapen something is to make it seem to have no value

◆ **cheaply** [adverb] inexpensively: *You can eat quite cheaply at these cafés.*

cheat [verb: **cheats, cheating, cheated**]
1 to cheat someone is to deceive them: *The men cheated the old lady out of all her savings.*
2 to cheat in a game or exam is to behave dishonestly so that you gain an advantage: *It's cheating to look at someone else's cards.*
[noun: **cheats**] a cheat is someone who deceives people or tries to gain an advantage by behaving dishonestly

check [verb: **checks, checking, checked**]
1 to check something is to make sure that it is correct or that it is working properly: *Can you check the tyre pressure, too, please?*
2 to check something is to hold it back or bring it to a stop: *He tried to check the bleeding by tying a handkerchief round his leg.*
3 if you **check in** at a hotel or airport, you tell the people there that you have arrived
4 if you **check something out**, you find out about it: *I'm just going to check out the times of the trains on the Internet.*
[noun: **checks**] a test to see that something is correct or is working properly: *a health check*

check [noun: **checks**] a pattern of squares: *trousers with a bold check*

◆ **checked** [adjective] having a pattern of squares: *a checked skirt*

checkmate [noun] checkmate is a position in chess from which the king cannot escape

checkout [noun: **checkouts**] a checkout is the place where you pay at a supermarket or self-service shop

check-up [noun: **check-ups**] an examination by a doctor or dentist to make sure you or your teeth are healthy

cheek [noun: **cheeks**]
1 your cheeks are the two areas of your face that stretch from below your eyes to your chin
2 cheek, or a cheek, is rudeness to someone who should be given more respect: *He said I was the worst goalie he'd ever seen. What a cheek!*

◆ **cheekily** [adverb] rudely and disrespectfully

◆ **cheeky** [adjective: **cheekier, cheekiest**] rude and showing lack of respect: *Don't be cheeky to your father!*

cheer [noun: **cheers**] a cheer is a loud shout to encourage someone or show that you think they are doing well
[verb: **cheers, cheering, cheered**]
1 to cheer is to shout encouragement or approval: *They cheered each runner as he ran into the stadium.*
2 to **cheer someone up** is to make them feel happier
➡ **cheers, cheery**

cheerful [adjective]
1 a cheerful person behaves in a happy way
2 a cheerful place is bright and pleasant and makes you feel comfortable or happy

cheerio [interjection] a word people use instead of 'goodbye' when they are talking to their friends: *Cheerio, see you tomorrow.*

cheers [interjection]
1 a word people use as a toast: *Cheers, everyone. Happy New Year!*
2 a word people use when they want to say 'thank you': *'Here's your book back.' 'Cheers.'*

cheery [adjective: **cheerier, cheeriest**] a cheery person or thing is bright and merry: *Scott gave me a cheery smile as he drove away.*

cheese [noun: **cheeses**] a white or yellow food made from milk, which can be solid or soft
[adjective] made with or containing cheese: *a cheese sandwich*

cheesecake [noun: **cheesecakes**] a dessert which has a crisp biscuit base with a sweet mixture containing cream cheese on top

cheesy [adjective: **cheesier, cheesiest**]
1 tasting or smelling of cheese
2 a cheesy grin is a very broad smile

cheetah [noun: **cheetahs**] a spotted African animal, related to the cat, that can run very fast over short distances

chef [noun: **chefs**] someone with special training whose job is to cook in the kitchen of a restaurant or hotel

chemical [noun: **chemicals**] a chemical is a substance formed by or used in chemistry
[adjective] formed by, using, or containing a chemical or chemicals: *a chemical reaction*

chemist [noun: **chemists**]
  1 someone who studies chemistry
  2 someone who makes up medicines and medical prescriptions
  3 a chemist's is a shop where medicines and toiletries are sold
chemistry [noun]
  1 chemistry is the study of chemical elements and the way they combine and react with each other
  2 the chemistry between people is the way they act or react to each other
chemotherapy [noun] a treatment for cancer using powerful chemicals or combinations of chemicals
cheque [noun: **cheques**] a piece of printed paper used to pay for things with money from a bank account

---

ⓘ In North America, the spelling of this word is **check**.

---

chequered or **checkered** [adjective] having a pattern of different coloured squares, like a chessboard
chequers or **checkers** [plural noun]
  1 black and white squares like those on a chessboard
  2 another name for the game of **draughts**
cherish [verb: **cherishes, cherishing, cherished**] to cherish someone or something is to care for and look after them
cherry [noun: **cherries**]
  1 a kind of small round red fruit with a large stone inside
  2 the tree that this fruit grows on
cherub [noun: **cherubs** or **cherubim**] an angel that looks like a plump baby with wings
chess [noun] a game played on a chequered board, the chessboard, by two players. Each player has a set of chess pieces, or chessmen, which are moved in various ways to capture the other player's pieces
chest [noun: **chests**]
  1 your chest is the front of your body from the bottom of your neck to your stomach
  2 a large box for storing or carrying things: *a treasure chest*
chestnut [noun: **chestnuts**]
  1 a shiny reddish-brown nut that grows inside a prickly skin
  2 a tree that chestnuts grow on
  3 a reddish-brown colour
chew [verb: **chews, chewing, chewed**]
  1 to chew is to break up food with your teeth before swallowing it
  2 to **chew on** something, or to **chew something over**, is to think about it carefully for a while
  ✦ **chewy** [adjective: **chewier, chewiest**] a chewy food has to be chewed a lot to make it soft
chick [noun: **chicks**] a baby bird
chicken [noun: **chickens**]
  1 a chicken is a hen, especially a young hen
  2 chicken is the meat from a hen: *roast chicken*
  3 a coward: *Jump! Don't be such a chicken.*
  4 if you **count your chickens before they're hatched**, you expect something that you might not actually get
chickenpox [noun] an infectious disease which causes itchy spots to appear on your skin
chickpea [noun: **chickpeas**] a type of light brown pea that can be boiled and eaten in sauces or salads
chicory [noun] a plant with bitter-tasting leaves that are eaten in salads
chide [verb: **chides, chiding, chided**] to chide someone is to scold or criticize them: *Max is always chiding me about my forgetfulness.*
chief [noun: **chiefs**]
  1 a ruler or leader: *the chief of an African tribe*
  2 a boss: *the chiefs of industry*
  [adjective] main or most important: *the chief city of the region*
  ✦ **chiefly** [adverb] mainly: *They ate some meat but chiefly their diet consisted of roots and berries.*
chiffon [noun] a thin transparent material made of silk or nylon
chihuahua [noun: **chihuahuas**] a tiny breed of dog, originally from Mexico
child [noun: **children**]
  1 a young human being: *a child's view of the world*
  2 a son or daughter: *Their children are grown up.*

Cc

103

Cc

childhood [noun] the period of time in your life when you are a child: *memories of childhood*

childish [adjective] behaving in a silly way, like a child: *Don't be so childish!*

✦ **childishly** [adverb] in a silly way

childlike [adjective] innocent, like a child: *childlike innocence*

childminder [noun: **childminders**] someone who looks after a child or children when their parents are at work

childproof [adjective] designed so that it can't be opened, operated or damaged by a child: *a childproof lock*

children [noun] the plural of **child**: *One child was late and the rest of the children had to wait.*

chill [noun: **chills**]
1 if there is a chill in the air, it feels cold
2 if you get a chill, you suffer from a fever and shivering
[adjective] cold: *a chill wind blowing from the mountains*
[verb: **chills, chilling, chilled**] to chill something is to make it cold
➝ **chilly**

chilli [noun: **chillis**] a pod from a type of pepper that has a hot fiery taste and is used in cooking

chilly [adjective: **chillier, chilliest**] cold: *Shut the window. It's a bit chilly in here.*

chime [noun: **chimes**] a chime is the sound of a bell or bells ringing
[verb: **chimes, chiming, chimed**]
1 bells chime when they make ringing sounds
2 a clock chimes when it makes a ringing or musical sound as it strikes the hour or any part of the hour

chimney [noun: **chimneys**] a passage above a fire that allows smoke to escape

chimneysweep [noun: **chimneysweeps**] someone who clears the soot out of chimneys

chimpanzee [noun: **chimpanzees**] a small African ape with black fur, a flat face and large brown eyes

chin [noun: **chins**] your chin is the part of your face that sticks out below your mouth

china [noun] china is porcelain, a high quality material used to make things like cups, plates and ornaments

chink [noun: **chinks**]
1 a small gap: *a shaft of sunlight coming through a chink in the curtains*
2 a sound made when coins or other small metal objects hit each other

chip [verb: **chips, chipping, chipped**]
1 to chip something is to break a small piece off it: *Roy chipped one of his teeth playing rugby.*
2 if someone **chips in**, they contribute to a discussion, usually with a suggestion or comment
[noun: **chips**]
1 a small piece broken off a hard object, or the place where a small piece has been broken off: *The bowl had a few chips and cracks, but it was still worth a lot of money.*
2 chips are potatoes cut into strips and fried: *chips with everything*
3 in the United States, chips are potato crisps
4 if someone is **a chip off the old block**, they look like or behave like one of their parents, especially their father

chip and PIN [noun] chip and PIN is a system of paying for goods in a shop with a credit card or a debit card, where you type the secret number for your card into a machine

chipmunk [noun: **chipmunks**] a small North American animal with a long bushy tail and stripes on its back

chiropodist [noun: **chiropodists**] someone whose job is to treat problems and diseases of people's feet

✦ **chiropody** [noun] the care and treatment of people's feet, especially problems like corns and verrucas

chiropractor [noun: **chiropractors**] someone whose job is to relieve pain by pressing on bones in your body, especially your spine

chirp or **chirrup** [verb: **chirps, chirping, chirped** or **chirrups, chirruping, chirruped**] to chirp is to make a short shrill sound or sounds: *sparrows chirping*
[noun: **chirps**] a short shrill sound: *the chirp of baby birds*

✦ **chirpy** [adjective: **chirpier, chirpiest**] happy and cheerful: *You sound very chirpy this morning.*

chisel [noun: **chisels**] a very sharp tool used

for cutting pieces off wood, stone or metal [verb: **chisels, chiselling, chiselled**] to chisel something is to cut it using a chisel: *Josh chiselled his name in the stone.*

chive [noun: **chives**] a herb with long thin hollow shoots that have a flavour like a mild onion

chlorinate [verb: **chlorinates, chlorinating, chlorinated**] to chlorinate water is to add chlorine to it to kill any bacteria

chlorine [noun] a gas with a harsh smell which is used as a bleach and disinfectant

chloroform [noun] a liquid that makes you become unconscious if you inhale its vapour

chlorophyll [noun] a green substance in the leaves of a plant that allows the plant to use energy from the sun in a process called photosynthesis

chock-a-block [adjective] if something is chock-a-block, it is very full or crowded: *All the roads into the city were chock-a-block with rush-hour traffic.*

chocolate [noun: **chocolates**]
1 chocolate is a sweet food or drink made from the seeds of a tropical tree: *a bar of chocolate* • *Richard always has a cup of hot chocolate before going to bed.*
2 a chocolate is a sweet or a drink made with chocolate

choice [noun: **choices**] there is choice, or a choice, when you are able to decide which thing you will have because there is more than one thing available or on offer: *We were given a choice of meat or fish.* • *He had to do it; he had no choice in the matter.*
[adjective: **choicer, choicest**] choice things are of the best quality available: *the choicest vegetables*

choir [noun: **choirs**]
1 a group of singers: *Val sings in the church choir.*
2 part of a church where the choir sings
→ **choral, chorus**

choke [verb: **chokes, choking, choked**]
1 to choke on something is to have your breathing tubes blocked, especially by a piece of food that has got stuck in your throat: *She choked on a fish bone.*
2 if someone chokes, or something chokes

them, they cough and gasp because they can't breathe properly: *This collar's far too tight; it's choking me.*
3 if a drain or something similar is choked, it is blocked up with things: *gutters choked with leaves*

cholesterol [noun] a substance found in your body that helps to carry fats in your blood to the body tissues

chomp [verb: **chomps, chomping, chomped**] to chomp is to chew noisily

choose [verb: **chooses, choosing, chose, chosen**] to take one particular person or thing from a group of people or things that are available: *If you could have only one of them, which would you choose?*

chop [verb: **chops, chopping, chopped**]
1 to chop something is to cut it with an axe or a sharp tool like an axe: *Mr Willis was busy chopping a tree down.*
2 to chop something or chop something up is to cut it into pieces: *Chop the onion into fairly large chunks.*
3 to **chop and change** is to keep changing things
[noun: **chops**] a chop is a piece of meat, usually with a bit of bone, that has been cut off a larger piece of meat: *pork chops with apple sauce*

chopper [noun: **choppers**]
1 a small axe used for chopping wood
2 a helicopter

choppy [adjective: **choppier, choppiest**] if the sea is choppy, it is rough with lots of little waves

chopsticks [plural noun] chopsticks are two thin pieces of wood or plastic held in one hand and used to pick up food and put it in your mouth. Chopsticks are used in the Far East, in places like China and Japan

choral [adjective] sung by or written for a choir: *choral music*

chord [noun: **chords**] a musical sound made by playing several notes together: *Andy can play a few chords on the guitar.*

chore [noun: **chores**] a job, often one that is difficult or boring and has to be done regularly

choreographer [noun: **choreographers**] someone who designs and arranges dances and dance steps, especially for a ballet or musical

✦ **choreography** [noun] the design and arrangement of dances and dance steps

chorus [noun: **choruses**]
1 the part of a song that is repeated after every verse
2 the chorus in a play or musical is a group of singers that perform together on the stage
3 a choir
4 lots of people speaking or shouting together: *a chorus of protest*
[verb: **choruses, chorusing, chorused**] to chorus is to speak or sing all together: *'Happy birthday to you,' they chorused.*

chose [verb] a way of changing the verb **choose** to make a past tense: *I wasn't made to do it; I chose to do it.*

chosen [verb] a form of the verb **choose** that is used with a helping verb to show that something happened in the past: *Banking was the career he had chosen.*
[adjective] being your choice: *your chosen career*

christen [verb: **christens, christening, christened**] to christen a child is to baptize it and give it a name

✦ **christening** [noun: **christenings**] a ceremony at which a child is baptized

Christian [noun: **Christians**] someone who is a believer in Christianity and follows the teachings of Jesus Christ
[adjective] to do with Christianity or Christians

✦ **Christianity** [noun] a religion, practised in many parts of the world, that follows the teachings of Jesus Christ

Christian name [noun: **Christian names**] a first name or personal name. Look up and compare **surname**

Christmas [noun] a Christian festival celebrating the birth of Christ and held on 25 December each year
[adjective] for or to do with Christmas: *a Christmas tree*

Christmas Eve [noun] 24 December, the day before Christmas Day

chromosome [noun: **chromosomes**] a rod-shaped part found in every body cell of living things. Chromosomes contain the special

chemical patterns, or genes, that control what an individual living thing is like

chronic [adjective]
1 a chronic disease is one that goes on for a long time
2 an informal way of saying that something is very bad: *The smell from the gasworks was really chronic.*

chronicle [noun: **chronicles**] a record of things in the order that they happened
[verb: **chronicles, chronicling, chronicled**] to chronicle events is to write them down in the order that they happen

chronological [adjective] if a record of events is chronological, or in chronological order, it is arranged in the order in which the events happened

chrysalis [noun: **chrysalises**] an insect such as a moth or butterfly at the stage of its life when it covers itself with a case

chrysanthemum [noun: **chrysanthemums**] a garden plant which either has clusters of small flowers or one or two large flowers with lots of petals

chubby [adjective: **chubbier, chubbiest**] rather fat, but in an attractive way: *the baby's chubby little legs*

chuck [verb: **chucks, chucking, chucked**] to chuck something is to throw it or toss it: *He ran in, chucking his shopping bags down on the floor.*

chuckle [verb: **chuckles, chuckling, chuckled**] to chuckle is to laugh softly: *The story made me chuckle to myself.*
[noun: **chuckles**] a low or quiet laugh

chug [verb: **chugs, chugging, chugged**] to chug is to make a noise like a slowly moving engine, or to move along slowly: *The little steam train came chugging up the hill.*

chum [noun: **chums**] a friend: *an old school chum*

chump [noun: **chumps**] a fool: *I felt such a chump when I found out I'd been tricked.*

chunk [noun: **chunks**]
1 a thick or uneven lump of something: *a chunk of cheese* • *pineapple chunks*
2 a large part of something: *We had to use quite a chunk of our savings to pay for the damage to the car.*

chunky [adjective: **chunkier, chunkiest**]
1 thick and heavy: *a warm chunky sweater*
2 broad and heavy: *a chunky body*

church [noun: **churches**] a building where people, especially Christians, go to worship

churchyard [noun: **churchyards**] the area of land around a church, where people are buried

churlish [adjective] bad-mannered or rude: *It would be churlish to refuse his generous offer.*

churn [noun: **churns**] a special container for making butter from milk. The milk inside is moved about quickly by paddles until the fat separates
[verb: **churns, churning, churned**]
1 to churn milk is to make it into butter inside a churn
2 if something churns, it moves about violently: *I was so nervous my stomach was churning.*

chute [noun: **chutes**]
1 a long sloping channel that water, objects or people slide down
2 a piece of playground equipment with a sloping part that children can slide down

chutney [noun] chutney is a thick sauce made from fruit or vegetables, vinegar and spices and eaten cold with meat or cheese

cider [noun] cider is an alcoholic drink made from apples

cigar [noun: **cigars**] a thick tube made from tobacco leaves that people smoke

cigarette [noun: **cigarettes**] a tube of thin paper filled with chopped tobacco that people smoke

cinder [noun: **cinders**] a small piece of burnt coal or wood that is left at the bottom of a fire

cine camera [noun: **cine cameras**] a type of camera for making films

cinema [noun: **cinemas**]
1 a cinema is a place where films are shown on a big screen
2 cinema is films as an industry or an art form: *a career in cinema*

cinnamon [noun] a brown sweet-tasting spice used in puddings and cakes

cipher [noun: **ciphers**] a secret written code: *They wrote messages to each other in cipher.*

circa [preposition] if circa is used before a date, it means 'about' or 'approximately': *circa 1850*

circle [noun: **circles**]
1 a shape whose outside edge is an endless curving line which is always the same distance away from a central point: *Draw one circle for the head and another for the body.* • *Form a circle in the centre of the room.*
2 a circle of people is a group of people who know each other, have something in common, or do a particular thing together: *a sewing circle* • *He's not part of my circle of friends.*
3 the circle in a theatre is the seats in one of the upper floors
4 if something **comes full circle**, it returns to the point where it began
[verb: **circles, circling, circled**]
1 to circle is to go round and round: *vultures circling overhead* • *planes circling the airport*
2 to circle something is draw a circle round it: *She circled the area on the map with a red marker.*

circuit [noun: **circuits**]
1 if you do a circuit of something, you go right round it, often arriving back at or near the place where you started
2 a racing circuit is a track that racing cars and motorbikes race round
3 an electrical circuit is the path that electricity follows between two points
4 a connected group of events, especially of a particular sport: *the international golf circuit*

circular [adjective] round, in the shape of a circle: *a circular window*
[noun: **circulars**] a letter or notice that is sent round to a lot of different people

circulate [verb: **circulates, circulating, circulated**]
1 to circulate is to move round or through something: *water circulating in the central heating system*
2 to circulate something is to send it round: *Details of the meeting will be circulated to all members of staff.*

circulation [noun]
1 circulation is movement round or through something
2 your circulation is the movement of blood round your body, pumped by your heart through your veins and arteries

Cc

Cc

3 a particular newspaper's or magazine's circulation is the number of copies that are sold

circumcise [verb: **circumcises, circumcising, circumcised**] to cut away the part covering the end of the penis called the foreskin, either for medical or religious reasons
♦ **circumcision** [noun: **circumcisions**] an operation to cut away the foreskin from the penis

circumference [noun: **circumferences**]
1 the length of the outside edge of a circle: *What's the circumference of this coin?*
2 the outside edge of a circle: *Mark a point on the circumference of the circle and draw a line through it.*

circumstance [noun: **circumstances**]
1 an event or fact: *Is there any circumstance that might alter your decision?*
2 the circumstances of a situation are the events or conditions that affect or led up to that situation
3 your circumstances are the condition of your life, especially how much money or wealth you have
♦ **circumstantial** [adjective] circumstantial evidence is evidence that makes you believe something though there is no actual proof

circus [noun: **circuses**] a type of travelling entertainment that usually includes clowns, acrobats, trapeze artistes, and often performing animals

ⓘ It is called a **circus** because it takes place inside a ring, and **circus** is the Latin word for a *circle* or *ring*.

cistern [noun: **cisterns**] a tank for storing water

citadel [noun: **citadels**] a fort inside a city where the people from the city can go if they are attacked

cite [verb: **cites, citing, cited**] to cite something is to mention it as an example or to quote it as proof: *Try to cite some examples of good environmental schemes in your essay.*

citizen [noun: **citizens**]
1 someone who lives in a particular town, state or country: *citizens of Paris*
2 someone who belongs officially to a particular country: *He lives in Singapore but he's an Australian citizen.*
♦ **citizenship** [noun]
1 to have citizenship of a country is to belong officially to that country: *She's applied for Canadian citizenship.*
2 citizenship is the responsibilities and duties you have by being a citizen of a particular state or country: *Children should be taught good citizenship.*

citrus fruit [noun: **citrus fruits**] a fruit with a thick skin and a sharp flavour, for example an orange, lemon, lime or grapefruit

city [noun: **cities**] a large important town, especially one that has a cathedral: *What's the biggest city in Europe?*

civic [adjective] to do with a city or citizens: *civic pride* • *a civic centre*

civil [adjective]
1 if a person is civil, they talk or behave in a polite way
2 civil means involving or having to do with the citizens of a country: *civil unrest*
3 civil means having to do with ordinary people or civilians, not the military or the church: *civil life* • *a civil marriage ceremony*

civil engineer [noun: **civil engineers**] someone whose job is to plan and build public buildings and things like roads and bridges

civilian [noun: **civilians**] a person who is not in the armed forces

civilization [noun: **civilizations**]
1 civilization is being or becoming civilized
2 a civilization is a particular society or culture at a particular period in time: *He spent his life studying ancient civilizations in Central and South America.*

civilize or **civilise** [verb: **civilizes, civilizing, civilized**]
1 to civilize primitive people is to teach them how things are done in more advanced cultures or societies, so that their society becomes more developed
2 to civilize someone is to teach them good behaviour
♦ **civilized** [adjective] behaving well or politely, without arguing or being aggressive: *Let's try and have a civilized discussion instead of all shouting at once.*

civil rights [plural noun] civil rights are your rights to be treated fairly in society no matter what sex, colour or religion you are

civil servant [noun: **civil servants**] someone who works in the civil service of a country

• **civil service** [noun] the civil service is all the departments of the government that organize the running of the country, rather than the law-making or military branches of the government

civil war [noun: **civil wars**] a war between two groups within the same country

CJD [abbreviation] short for **Creutzfeldt-Jacob Disease**, a serious illness that destroys your brain cells and can kill you. Some cases may have been caused by eating beef infected with BSE

cl [abbreviation] short for **centilitre** or **centilitres**

clad [adjective] clothed or covered: *Robin Hood and his merry men, all clad in Lincoln green* • *mountains clad in snow*

claim [verb: **claims, claiming, claimed**]
1 to claim that something is true is to state that it is a fact, even though there is no real proof: *Marco claims he saw a flying saucer.*
2 to claim something is to demand it as your right or to state that it is yours: *You'll need to fill in this form to claim unemployment benefit.* • *If no one claims any of the lost items they will be sold for charity.*
[noun: **claims**]
1 a statement that something is a fact: *No one listened to his repeated claims that he was innocent.*
2 a demand or request for something that you have a right to or that you say you own: *an insurance claim* • *the family's historical claim to the land*

• **claimant** [noun: **claimants**] someone who makes a claim

clairvoyant [adjective] able to see into the future
[noun: **clairvoyants**] someone who claims that they can see things that will happen in the future

clam [noun: **clams**] a large shellfish with two shells that are joined at one side and which can

be closed tightly for protection
[verb: **clams, clamming, clammed**] if someone **clams up**, they stop talking or won't give any more information

clamber [verb: **clambers, clambering, clambered**] to clamber is to climb up or over things using your hands and feet: *They tried to clamber up the steep and slippery slope.*

clammy [adjective: **clammier, clammiest**] damp in a sticky, unpleasant way: *His hands became clammy and his hair stood on end with fear.*

clamour [verb: **clamours, clamouring, clamoured**] to clamour for something is to try to get it by making noisy demands: *All the children were clamouring to see what was in the box.*
[noun] clamour, or a clamour, is noisy shouts or demands

clamp [noun: **clamps**] a device for holding things together tightly or a device attached tightly to something to stop it moving: *a wheel clamp*
[verb: **clamps, clamping, clamped**]
1 to clamp something is to put a clamp on it: *Clamp the two pieces of wood together until the glue dries.* • *Oh no! My car's been clamped.*
2 to **clamp down** on something is to stop it happening by controlling it more strictly: *We will have to clamp down on litter if we want to clean up the city.*

clan [noun: **clans**] a group of families all descended from the same family and usually all having the same name

clandestine [adjective] if something is clandestine, it is kept secret or hidden, especially because it is not allowed: *The plotters held a series of clandestine meetings.*

clang [verb: **clangs, clanging, clanged**] to clang is to make a loud ringing sound, like a heavy piece of metal hitting against a hard material: *The prison gate clanged shut behind them.*
[noun: **clangs**] a loud ringing sound

clank [verb: **clanks, clanking, clanked**] to make a loud dull sound, like metal hitting metal: *Strange machines were clanking in the gloomy shed.*

Cc

Cc

[noun: **clanks**] a loud dull sound: *the clank of heavy chains*

clap [verb: **claps, clapping, clapped**]

1 you clap when you hit the palms of your hands together making a slapping sound: *The audience clapped and cheered.* • *We all clapped in time to the music.*

2 to hit someone or something lightly with a slapping movement: *He clapped his friend on the back.*

[noun: **claps**]

1 a short slapping sound made when you hit your hands together or when you hit someone lightly with the flat of your hand

2 a sudden very loud sound made by thunder

• clapper [noun: **clappers**] the part of a bell that strikes against the inside to make the ringing sound

claptrap [noun] nonsense or meaningless talk

clarify [verb: **clarifies, clarifying, clarified**] to clarify something is to make it clearer or easier to understand

clarinet [noun: **clarinets**] a musical instrument made of wood that you play by blowing through it and pressing keys with your fingers

• clarinettist [noun: **clarinettists**] someone who plays the clarinet

clarity [noun] clearness: *the clarity of the image*

clash [verb: **clashes, clashing, clashed**]

1 if two pieces of hard material clash, they make a loud sound as they hit each other: *cymbals clashing*

2 if two people clash, they disagree or argue angrily with each other

3 if two colours clash, they do not go well together: *The purple clashes with the red.*

[noun: **clashes**]

1 a sound made when two things hit against each other: *the clash of cymbals*

2 an angry disagreement between people: *They've had a few clashes over the years.*

clasp [verb: **clasps, clasping, clasped**] to clasp something is to hold it tightly or closely: *Jenny was clasping a little child in her arms.*

[noun: **clasps**]

1 a hook or pin for holding things together: *The clasp's broken on this brooch.*

2 a grasp

class [noun: **classes**]

1 a group of schoolchildren or students who are taught together, or a period of time during which a particular subject is taught: *It was Maureen's first day in Miss Smith's class.* • *Leyla is going to her aerobics class tonight.*

2 a grouping of people who have similar backgrounds or who belong to the same rank in society: *the working class*

3 a division of things according to how good they are: *Abby's a first class student.*

4 a grouping of animals or plants that are related to each other or have something in common

[verb: **classes, classing, classed**] to class people or things is to put them in a grouping with others of the same type or rank: *Anyone under 16 is classed as a junior member.*

→ classify, classy

classic [noun: **classics**] a great book or other work of art that goes on being admired long after it was written or made

[adjective]

1 recognized as great for all time: *classic children's stories*

2 a classic example of something is typical: *He made the classic mistake of thinking that he could do all his studying in the week before the exam.*

• classical [adjective]

1 belonging to the style or culture of ancient Greece or Rome: *classical architecture*

2 traditional: *classical ballet*

classical music [noun] traditional, serious music that goes on being played or listened to for a long time after it has been composed

classics [noun] the study of the ancient Greek and Latin languages, and the work of ancient Greek and Roman writers

classification [noun: **classifications**]

1 classification is putting things into groups of different types

2 a classification is a group that includes people or things of the same type

classified [adjective] classified information is information that the government keeps secret from the public

classify [verb: **classifies, classifying, classified**] to classify people or things is to put them into groups or classes according to what type they are

classmate [noun: **classmates**] your classmates are the people in your school or college class

classroom [noun: **classrooms**] a room where lessons are given in a school or college

classy [adjective: **classier, classiest**] stylish and expensive: *Imogen always looks classy.*

clatter [verb: **clatters, clattering, clattered**] to clatter is to make a loud noise like hard objects falling or hitting each other: *He came clattering downstairs in his ski boots.* [noun] a sound made when hard objects fall or hit against each other: *the clatter of dishes being washed*

clause [noun: **clauses**]
1 a group of words that makes up a sentence or part of a sentence
2 a part of an official document or contract

claustrophobia [noun] people who have claustrophobia are afraid of small, enclosed or crowded spaces
  ◆ claustrophobic [adjective] afraid of small, enclosed or crowded spaces

claw [noun: **claws**]
1 one of the long pointed nails on some animals' paws
2 a part on the end of a crab's or lobster's leg that it uses for gripping things
[verb: **claws, clawing, clawed**] to **claw at** something is to scratch it with claws or fingernails

clay [noun] soft sticky material found in the ground and used for making pottery

clean [adjective: **cleaner, cleanest**]
1 if something is clean, it has no dirt or germs on or in it: *a clean face and hands • There was no clean water to drink.*
2 complete: *She wanted a clean break from her past.*
3 straight, without any jagged or rough edges: *It is a clean break so the bone should heal well.*
4 unused: *Take a clean sheet of paper and start again.*
5 fair and honest: *a clean game of football*
[adverb]

1 completely: *It went clean through and out the other side. • He's gone clean mad.*
2 if someone **comes clean**, they tell the truth
[verb: **cleans, cleaning, cleaned**]
1 to clean something is to remove the dirt from it
2 to **clean up** is to tidy a place, removing any dirt and rubbish
  ◆ cleaner [noun: **cleaners**]
1 a person whose job is to clean houses, offices or other buildings
2 a product for cleaning things: *lavatory cleaner*
  ◆ cleanliness [noun] being clean: *Cleanliness helps prevent germs spreading.*

cleanse [verb: **cleanses, cleansing, cleansed**] to cleanse something such as your skin or a cut is to make it clean: *Cleanse the wound with an antiseptic.*
  ◆ cleanser [noun: **cleansers**] a product that cleanses something, especially your skin

clear [adjective: **clearer, clearest**]
1 easy to see, hear or understand: *a clear view • She spoke in a clear voice. • His explanation wasn't very clear.*
2 see-through: *clear glass*
3 not blocked or marked by anything: *a clear sky • The road was clear.*
4 without meeting any difficulties or obstacles: *The way is clear for him to win the title.*
[adverb] not near something or not touching it: *Stand clear of the gates.*
[verb: **clears, clearing, cleared**]
1 to clear is to make or become clear: *The sky cleared and the sun came out. • Police cleared the streets around the car bomb.*
2 to clear things is to move them or tidy them away: *Whose turn is it to clear the dirty supper dishes?*
3 if someone is cleared of something, a judge or other person in authority decides they are not guilty or not to blame
4 to clear something is to jump over it without touching it: *Jamie's pony cleared all the fences.*
5 to **clear off** is to go right away from somewhere: *We had wandered on to his land and he told us to clear off.*
6 if something such as a rash **clears up**, it goes away
  ◆ clearance [noun: **clearances**]

Cc

Cc

1 clearing something away: *the clearance of the land to make room for housing*
2 the amount of space between one thing and another passing beside it or under it: *There isn't enough clearance for the lorry to go through that gap.*
3 if someone or something has clearance to do something, they have permission to do it: *Air traffic controllers give aeroplanes clearance to land.*
♦ **clearing** [noun: **clearings**] a gap in a forest where there are no trees
♦ **clearly** [adverb]
1 in a clear way: *I can't see it very clearly.*
2 obviously: *Clearly, we couldn't continue without proper equipment.*
♦ **clearness** [noun] being clear
→ **clarify, clarity**

cleave [verb: **cleaves, cleaving, clove** or **cleft** or **cleaved, cloven** or **cleft** or **cleaved**] to cleave something is to split it
♦ **cleaver** [noun: **cleavers**] a cutting tool with a large square blade fitted to a handle

clef [noun: **clefs**] a symbol used at the beginning of a piece of music to show how high or low the notes should be

cleft [noun: **clefts**] a split or opening: *A jagged cleft had opened up in the rocks.*
[adjective] split: *a cleft stick*

cleft palate [noun: **cleft palates**] a split in the roof of the mouth that some people have when they are born

clench [verb: **clenches, clenching, clenched**] to clench something is to hold it tightly or press it tightly together: *Clenching his teeth, he jumped out of the plane.*

clergy [plural noun] the clergy are priests or ministers in the Christian church

clergyman [noun: **clergymen**] a man who is a priest or minister of the church

clergywoman [noun: **clergywomen**] a woman who is a priest or minister of the church

cleric [noun: **clerics**] a member of the clergy
♦ **clerical** [adjective]
1 of or used by the clergy: *The man was wearing a clerical collar.*
2 to do with office work: *a clerical assistant*

clerk [noun: **clerks**] an office worker whose job is to write letters, do filing or keep accounts

clever [adjective: **cleverer, cleverest**]
1 quick to learn and understand things: *He's the cleverest boy in his class.*
2 skilful: *She's always been clever with her hands.*

cliché [noun: **clichés**] a phrase that has been used so often it no longer has the effect it once had

ⓘ This word is pronounced **klee**–shay.

click [noun: **clicks**] a short, sharp sound like the sound made when a door lock is closed gently
[verb: **clicks, clicking, clicked**]
1 to make this sound: *We could hear her heels clicking on the stone floor.*
2 if you click on something that appears on a computer screen, you choose it by pressing the button on the mouse

client [noun: **clients**]
1 someone who uses the services of a person like a lawyer or accountant
2 a customer

cliff [noun: **cliffs**] a high, steep, rocky slope, usually facing the sea

cliffhanger [noun: **cliffhangers**] a situation or story that is exciting because you don't know how it will turn out until the very end

climate [noun: **climates**] the usual sort of weather there is in a region or area: *The Earth's climate is getting warmer.* • *plants that only grow in hot climates*

climax [noun: **climaxes**] the most important, most exciting or most interesting point in a story or situation

climb [verb: **climbs, climbing, climbed**]
1 to climb is to go up or to go towards the top: *He likes to climb mountains.*
2 if someone involved in an argument or disagreement **climbs down**, they eventually admit that they were wrong
[noun: **climbs**] an act of climbing: *We had a steep climb to the top.*
♦ **climber** [noun: **climbers**]
1 someone who climbs, often as a pastime or sport
2 a plant that climbs up things like walls and fences

clinch [verb: **clinches, clinching, clinched**]

to clinch a bargain or argument is to settle it

cling [verb: **clings, clinging, clung**] to cling to something is to stick to it or hang on to it tightly: *shellfish clinging to the rocks*

clingfilm [noun] clingfilm is a very thin sheet of plastic that is used to cover food

clinic [noun: **clinics**] a place where people can be seen by doctors to get treatment and advice: *an eye clinic*

clink [noun: **clinks**] a sharp ringing sound like the sound made when glasses or coins are hit together
[verb: **clinks, clinking, clinked**] to clink is to make this sound

clip [verb: **clips, clipping, clipped**]
1 to clip something is to cut small or short parts off it: *clipping the hedge with shears*
2 to clip something is to fasten it with a clip: *a badge clipped on to his lapel*
[noun: **clips**] a small fastening device: *a paper clip*

clipboard [noun: **clipboards**] a piece of strong card with a clip at the top that you fasten paper to and write on

clipper [noun: **clippers**]
1 a type of fast sailing ship
2 clippers are an instrument used for clipping things: *nail clippers*

clique [noun: **cliques**] a small group of people who are friendly to each other but keep other people out of the group
• cliquey [adjective: **cliquier, cliquiest**] a cliquey group of people are friendly to each other but keep other people out

cloak [noun: **cloaks**]
1 a piece of clothing without sleeves that is worn over other clothes and hangs down loosely from the shoulders
2 anything that covers or hides: *the cloak of darkness*
[verb: **cloaks, cloaking, cloaked**] to cloak something is to cover or hide it: *hills cloaked in mist*

cloakroom [noun: **cloakrooms**] a room or area in a building where visitors can leave their coats, hats and bags

clobber [verb: **clobbers, clobbering, clobbered**] to clobber someone is to hit them hard

clock [noun: **clocks**] a machine for measuring time
[verb: **clocks, clocking, clocked**] to **clock up** a certain number of points, for example, is to achieve that number over a period of time

clockwise [adjective] turning or moving in the same direction as the hands of a clock

clockwork [noun]
1 the machinery of an old-fashioned clock with a spring that you wind up
2 if something goes or works **like clockwork**, it goes or works smoothly without any problems

clod [noun: **clods**] a solid lump of earth

clog [noun: **clogs**] a shoe with a wooden sole
[verb: **clogs, clogging, clogged**] to clog something, or to **clog it up**, is to block it: *drains clogged up with fallen leaves and litter*

cloister [noun: **cloisters**] a covered passageway that is open on one side and goes round a courtyard in a monastery, cathedral or college

clone [noun: **clones**] an exact copy of a plant or animal, made artificially by taking cells from it
[verb: **clones, cloning, cloned**] to make an exact copy of a plant or animal in this way

close¹ [adjective]
1 near in distance or time: *They are quite close in age.*
2 very dear or intimate: *a close friendship*
3 tight: *a close fit*
4 thorough or careful: *Pay close attention.*
5 having no fresh air: *a close atmosphere*
[adverb: **closer, closest**] near: *He came close to winning.* • *She stood close by.*
→ **closely**

ⓘ This use of **close** is pronounced **close** with an **ss** sound.

close² [verb: **closes, closing, closed**]
1 to shut: *Close the door behind you.*
2 to finish: *They closed the concert by singing the national anthem.*
[noun: **closes**]
1 the end of something: *at the close of day*
2 a street that is blocked at one end
→ **closure**

Cc

Cc

ⓘ If you are talking about the **close** of something, you pronounce it **cloze**. If you are talking about a street, you pronounce **close** with an **ss** sound.

closely [adverb]
1 at a close distance: *He came into the room, closely followed by his two friends.*
2 tightly: *closely packed sardines*

closet [noun: **closets**] a cupboard

close-up [noun: **close-ups**] a photograph or a shot in a film that has been taken very close to something so that all the details can be seen

closure [noun: **closures**] an act of closing: *school closures*

clot [noun: **clots**] a lump or clump that forms in liquids, especially in cream or blood
[verb: **clots, clotting, clotted**] to form clots

cloth [noun: **cloths**]
1 cloth is material made by weaving threads of wool, silk, cotton or some other fibre
2 a cloth is a piece of fabric

clothe [verb: **clothes, clothing, clothed**] to clothe someone is to put clothes on them or provide them with clothes: *They need money to feed and clothe themselves.*
✦ **clothes** [plural noun] clothes are the things people wear to cover their bodies
✦ **clothing** [noun] clothing is clothes

cloud [noun: **clouds**]
1 clouds are masses of tiny water drops floating in the sky
2 a cloud of something is a mass of it in the air: *a cloud of flies*
3 if you are **on cloud nine**, you are very happy
[verb: **clouds, clouding, clouded**] to become cloudy: *The sky clouded over and it started to rain.*

cloudburst [noun: **cloudbursts**] a sudden spell of very heavy rain

cloudy [adjective: **cloudier, cloudiest**]
1 filled with clouds: *a cloudy sky*
2 not clear: *a cloudy liquid*

clout [noun: **clouts**]
1 a clout is a blow with the hand
2 clout is influence and power: *an organization with a lot of political clout*
[verb: **clouts, clouting, clouted**] to hit someone with the hand

clove[1] [noun: **cloves**] a small dried bud of a tropical plant, used in cooking as a spice
clove[2] [noun: **cloves**] one of the sections into which a plant bulb splits: *a clove of garlic*

cloven hoof [noun: **cloven hooves**] a hoof divided into two parts, like that of cows, sheep, pigs and goats

clover [noun] a small flowering plant that grows amongst grass

clown [noun: **clowns**] someone who works in a circus and does funny acts dressed up in ridiculous clothes
[verb: **clowns, clowning, clowned**] to clown or **clown around** is to act in a funny or silly way

cloying [adjective] sweet in a sickly way

club [noun: **clubs**]
1 an organized group of people who meet regularly to take part in an activity, or the place where they meet
2 a place where people go in the evening to dance and have a drink
3 one of the metal sticks used in golf to hit the ball
4 a heavy piece of wood or metal used as a weapon
5 clubs is one of the four suits of playing cards, which have the symbol (♣) printed on them
[verb: **clubs, clubbing, clubbed**]
1 if people **go clubbing**, they go out dancing and drinking in clubs
2 if people **club together**, they each contribute some money to buy something

cluck [noun: **clucks**] a sound made by a hen
[verb: **clucks, clucking, clucked**] to make this sound

clue [noun: **clues**]
1 a sign or piece of evidence that helps solve a puzzle, mystery or crime
2 if someone **doesn't have a clue**, they don't know anything or they don't know how to do something

clump [noun: **clumps**] a group of plants growing close together: *a clump of bluebells*

clumsy [adjective: **clumsier, clumsiest**] a clumsy person is awkward in the way they move or act, especially by dropping things or bumping into things

clung [verb] a way of changing the verb **cling**

to make a past tense. It can be used with or without a helping verb: *Barnacles and mussels clung to the rocks.* • *The little girl had clung on to her teddy bear all day.*

cluster [noun: **clusters**] several things placed or growing very close together: *clusters of grapes*
[verb: **clusters, clustering, clustered**] to cluster is to move or be very close together: *The children clustered round the teacher.*

clutch [verb: **clutches, clutching, clutched**]
1 to clutch something is to hold it tightly in your hand or hands
2 to clutch at something is to try to get hold of it
3 to **clutch at straws** is to try hard to find a way out of a bad situation or to think of a way of solving it, even though it has very little chance of being successful
[noun: **clutches**]
1 the part of a car's engine that you operate with a pedal to control the gears
2 to be **in someone's clutches** is to be in their grasp, especially if they have control or power over you

clutter [noun] clutter is lots of things that cover or fill a space so that it looks untidy or disorganized
[verb: **clutters, cluttering, cluttered**] to clutter or to **clutter up** a space is to fill it with lots of things and make it untidy: *Books cluttered every surface.*

cm [abbreviation] short for **centimetre** or **centimetres**

Co. [abbreviation] short for **Company** when it is part of a business name: *Reginald Bloggs & Co., Ironmongers*

co-, com- or **con-** [prefix] if a word starts with **co-, com-** or **con-**, it adds the meaning 'working with' or 'together with' to the word. For example, a *co-author* is someone who has written a book with another writer

coach [noun: **coaches**]
1 a single-decker bus used to carry passengers over long distances
2 a person who trains someone in a particular skill or prepares them for a competition or performance: *a rugby coach* • *a singing coach*
3 a type of large four-wheeled carriage

pulled by horses and used to carry passengers
4 a railway carriage for passengers
[verb: **coaches, coaching, coached**] to coach someone is to prepare them for a competition, exam or performance

coal [noun] a hard black substance containing carbon that is dug out of the ground and burnt as fuel

coal gas [noun] a mixture of gases that come from coal, used as a fuel for lighting and heating

coalmine [noun: **coalmines**] a mine where coal is dug out of the earth

coarse [adjective: **coarser, coarsest**]
1 feeling rough or harsh: *coarse cloth*
2 vulgar: *coarse language*

coast [noun: **coasts**]
1 the coast is the area of land next to the sea
2 if **the coast is clear**, there is no one around to see you or stop you doing something
[verb: **coasts, coasting, coasted**] to coast, or to **coast along**, is to go along without making much effort

coastguard [noun: **coastguards**] someone whose job is to guard the coast of a country against smugglers and to help ships in danger

coat [noun: **coats**]
1 a piece of clothing with sleeves that usually reaches to your knees and that you wear over your other clothes
2 a layer: *three coats of paint*
[verb: **coats, coating, coated**] to coat something is to cover it with a layer of something: *They'd coated their bodies with mud.*

coat of arms [noun: **coats of arms**] a coat of arms is the badge or crest used by a particular family

coax [verb: **coaxes, coaxing, coaxed**] to coax someone to do something is to persuade them gently to do it

cob [noun: **cobs**] a long round solid part of a maize plant that the seeds grow on

cobble or **cobblestone** [noun: **cobbles** or **cobblestones**] cobbles are rounded stones set into a road
• **cobbled** [adjective] covered with cobbles

cobbler [noun: **cobblers**] someone whose job is making and repairing shoes

cobra [noun: **cobras**] a type of poisonous snake that raises itself up before it bites

cobweb [noun: **cobwebs**] a criss-cross pattern of thin threads that a spider makes to catch insects

cocaine [noun] a very addictive illegal drug

cock [noun: **cocks**] a male bird
[verb: **cocks, cocking, cocked**]
1 an animal cocks its ears when it makes its ears stand upright so that it can hear better
2 you cock your head when you tilt it to one side

cockatoo [noun: **cockatoos**] a type of large parrot with a crest on top of its head that it can raise and lower

cockerel [noun: **cockerels**] a male chicken

cocker spaniel [noun: **cocker spaniels**] a breed of small dog with a long silky coat and ears that hang down

cockle [noun: **cockles**] a type of small round edible shellfish that lives in the sea

cockney [noun: **cockneys**]
1 someone who comes from the east end of London
2 the accent or way of speaking of people who come from around the east end of London

cockpit [noun: **cockpits**] the space in an aeroplane where the pilot sits

cockroach [noun: **cockroaches**] a large crawling insect usually found in damp or dirty places

cocktail [noun: **cocktails**]
1 a drink made with one or more alcoholic drinks that are often also mixed with fruit juice and ice
2 a mixture made with several different ingredients: *a fruit cocktail*

cocky [adjective: **cockier, cockiest**] a cocky person is cheeky and confident

cocoa [noun: **cocoas**] a hot drink made with the powdered seeds of a tropical tree, which are also used to make chocolate

coconut [noun: **coconuts**] a large hairy nut from a tropical palm tree that has white firm flesh and a thin liquid called coconut milk inside

cocoon [noun: **cocoons**] a case made by a caterpillar inside which it changes into an adult moth or butterfly

cod [noun: **cod**] a large sea fish found in northern seas of the world and caught for food

coddle [verb: **coddles, coddling, coddled**] to coddle someone is to protect them and treat them like a baby

code [noun: **codes**]
1 code, or a code, is a set of signs or letters used for signalling or writing: *a message written in secret code*
2 a set of rules or laws: *a code of honour*
[verb: **codes, coding, coded**] to code something is to put it in a particular code of letters or signs: *All messages were coded before being sent.*

coed [adjective] a short form of the word **coeducational**

coeducation [noun] the teaching of boys and girls in the same school or college
♦ **coeducational** [adjective] teaching both male and female students: *a coeducational school*

coexist [verb: **coexists, coexisting, coexisted**] if two or more people or things coexist, they live or exist together at the same time and sometimes also in the same place

coffee [noun: **coffees**]
1 coffee is a drink made from the roasted and ground-up beans of a tropical plant
2 a coffee is a cup of this drink

coffer [noun: **coffers**]
1 a coffer is a large strong box used to store things in, especially money or valuables
2 a company's or organization's coffers is the store of money it has

coffin [noun: **coffins**] a long wooden box that a dead body is put into

cog [noun: **cogs**] one of the pointed parts, looking rather like teeth, that are round the edge of a cogwheel in an engine or machine

cognac [noun] cognac is a kind of French brandy

cogwheel [noun: **cogwheels**] a metal disc with cogs cut out of its edge, used to turn other cogwheels or parts inside a machine such as a clock or watch

cohere [verb: **coheres, cohering, cohered**] if things cohere, they stick together
♦ **coherence** [noun] connection between things, especially thoughts or ideas
♦ **coherent** [adjective]

1 coherent speech is clear and easy to understand
2 coherent thoughts or ideas are connected in a logical way
• **coherently** [adverb] clearly or logically: *He argued forcibly and coherently against the changes.*

coil [verb: **coils, coiling, coiled**] to coil is to twist or wind to form rings or loops: *The huge snake coiled itself round the branch.*
[noun: **coils**] a loop or series of loops in something long such as rope or hair: *a coil of thin wire*

coin [noun: **coins**] a piece of metal money
[verb: **coins, coining, coined**]
1 to make metal into money
2 to coin a new word or phrase is to invent it

coinage [noun: **coinages**] a country's coinage is all the coins used in its particular money system

coincide [verb: **coincides, coinciding, coincided**] events coincide with each other when they happen at the same time: *The carnival will coincide with the beginning of the school holidays.*

coincidence [noun: **coincidences**] a coincidence is when two things happen at the same time, without being planned: *Both families booked holidays at the same resort by sheer coincidence.*
• **coincidental** [adjective] happening at the same time by chance

coke [noun]
1 a type of fuel made from coal
2 a slang word for **cocaine**

cola [noun: **colas**] a dark brown fizzy drink

colander [noun: **colanders**] a container with holes in the bottom used to drain water from food

cold [adjective: **colder, coldest**]
1 low in temperature: *a cold drink • It's too cold to go outside.*
2 unfriendly: *a cold stare*
[noun: **colds**]
1 the cold is cold weather or coldness: *Granny doesn't like the cold.*
2 a cold is an illness caused by a virus which makes you sneeze and cough, and makes your nose run

cold-blooded [adjective]
1 a cold-blooded animal is not able to store heat in its body. Reptiles and snakes are cold-blooded
2 a cold-blooded person is unfeeling and cruel

coldly [adverb] in an unfriendly way: *She treated them coldly.*

coldness [noun] being cold

cold sore [noun: **cold sores**] a blister, usually somewhere on your lip or mouth, caused by a virus

coleslaw [noun] a salad made from sliced raw cabbage mixed with mayonnaise

colic [noun] a sudden and severe pain in your stomach

collaborate [verb: **collaborates, collaborating**]
1 if two or more people collaborate, they help each other by sharing information and ideas
2 if someone collaborates, they give an enemy information or help
• **collaboration** [noun] sharing information or ideas
• **collaborator** [noun: **collaborators**] someone who shares information with another person

collage [noun: **collages**] a picture or design made by sticking different materials, for example bits of paper, photographs or small objects, on to a sheet of card or wood

collapse [verb: **collapses, collapsing, collapsed**] to fall down from being under too much weight or because of lack of strength: *The bridge collapsed under the lorry's weight. • The runner collapsed, exhausted, just before the finish line.*
[noun: **collapses**] a falling down or caving in
• **collapsible** [adjective] collapsible furniture or equipment can be folded or taken down so that it fits into a smaller space

collar [noun: **collars**]
1 the piece of material on a shirt or other piece of clothing that fits round your neck
2 a band of leather or other material fastened round an animal's neck
[verb: **collars, collaring, collared**] to collar someone or something is to get hold of them

collarbone [noun: **collarbones**] one of two

Cc

bones in your body that stretch from your shoulder to just under the front of your neck

collate [verb: **collates, collating, collated**] to collate different pieces of information or pieces of paper is to bring them together and arrange them in order

colleague [noun: **colleagues**] a person's colleagues are the people they work with

collect [verb: **collects, collecting, collected**]
1 to collect things is to find them and gather them together: *Ted collects unusual postcards.*
2 to collect someone or something from a place is to go there and pick them up: *George collected me from the airport.*

♦ **collection** [noun: **collections**]
1 collection is picking someone or something up from a place: *There were two parcels waiting for collection.*
2 a collection is a number of things that have been gathered together by one person or in one place: *a stamp collection*
3 a collection is money collected from different people, for example in church or in order to buy someone a present

♦ **collective** [adjective] done by several people or groups, not just one: *a collective decision*

collective noun [noun: **collective nouns**] a collective noun is a word used to refer to a group or collection of people or things. The words *family, team, staff, government, police, herd, flock, cattle, luggage* and *furniture* are examples of collective nouns

collector [noun: **collectors**] someone who finds and gathers several things of the same type to make a collection: *a collector of antiques*

college [noun: **colleges**] a place where people go to learn or be trained after they have left school: *He's going to sixth form college.*

collide [verb: **collides, colliding, collided**] moving objects collide when they hit each other
➡ **collision**

collie [noun: **collies**] a kind of sheepdog

colliery [noun: **collieries**] a coal mine

collision [noun: **collisions**] a crash between moving vehicles or objects: *a collision between two lorries on the motorway*

colloquial [adjective] colloquial language is used in everyday speech but not in formal speaking or writing. For example, *ta-ta* is a colloquial expression for 'goodbye'

♦ **colloquially** [adverb] informally

collude [verb: **colludes, colluding, colluded**] if people collude, they make agreements with each other in secret

♦ **collusion** [noun] collusion is secret cooperation between people

cologne [noun] cologne is a kind of light perfume

colon[1] [noun: **colons**] a colon is a punctuation mark (:) used to separate parts of a sentence or used before items in a list, for example in *There are three things you will need: paper, scissors and glue.*

colon[2] [noun: **colons**] your colon is part of your bowel

colonel [noun: **colonels**] a high-ranking officer in the army or air force

ⓘ This word is pronounced **kir**–nil.

colonial [adjective] to do with a country's colonies abroad

colonist [noun: **colonists**] someone who goes to another country to set up a colony

colonize or **colonise** [verb: **colonizes, colonizing, colonized**]
1 people, animals or plants colonize an area when they move into it and begin to live or grow there
2 if a country colonizes another part of the world, it takes it over and controls it

colony [noun: **colonies**]
1 a group of people who have settled in another part of the world, or the new settlement they have made: *The Pilgrim Fathers set up colonies on the east coast of America.*
2 a group of people, animals or plants of the same type living together: *a colony of ants*
3 a country's foreign colonies were the parts of the world that it controlled: *Hong Kong used to be a British colony.*

colossal [adjective] enormous: *a colossal appetite*

colour [noun: **colours**]
1 colour, or a colour, is a quality that shows up when light hits an object, for example, redness, blueness, yellowness, and so on: *What colour are your eyes?* • *The sea was a lovely blue colour.*
2 a person's colour is the shade of their skin
3 if someone is **off colour**, they are not feeling very well
4 when you pass a test or exam **with flying colours**, you get a high mark or you do very well in it
[adjective] having or using colour: *colour TV*
[verb: **colours, colouring, coloured**] to colour a picture is to add colours to it with paints or crayons
colour-blind [adjective] not able to tell the difference between certain colours, especially red and green
coloured [adjective] having a colour: *a brightly coloured scarf*
colourful [adjective]
1 having lots of bright colours: *colourful clothing*
2 interesting or exciting: *Her uncle's a colourful character.*
colouring [noun: **colourings**]
1 colouring is a substance used to give something a colour: *red food colouring*
2 someone's colouring is the colour of their skin and hair: *That shade of green suits her dark colouring.*
colourless [adjective]
1 having no colour: *Water is a colourless liquid.*
2 dull and uninteresting: *She had a flat colourless voice.*
colt [noun: **colts**] a young horse
column [noun: **columns**]
1 a stone or wooden pillar
2 something with a long or tall narrow shape: *Columns of smoke and dust rose from the erupting volcano.*
3 a long line of people one behind the other or things one below the other: *a column of marching soldiers* • *a column of figures*
4 a section in a newspaper that appears regularly and is usually written by the same person

♦ **columnist** [noun: **columnists**] a person who writes an article in a newspaper
com- [prefix] look at the entry for **co-**
coma [noun: **comas**] if someone is in a coma, they are unconscious for a long period of time
♦ **comatose** [adjective] in a coma or seeming to be in a coma
comb [noun: **combs**]
1 an object with a row of teeth along one side that you use to make your hair tidy
2 a part that sticks up on the top of some birds' heads
[verb: **combs, combing, combed**]
1 to comb hair is to make it tidy using a comb
2 to comb a place is to search it carefully and thoroughly: *Detectives were combing the area for clues.*
combat [noun] combat is fighting: *soldiers in combat*
[verb: **combats, combatting, combatted**] to combat something is to fight or struggle against it: *a superhero who combats crime*
combination [noun: **combinations**]
1 combination is the joining or mixing of two or more things
2 a combination is several things that have been joined or mixed
combination lock [noun: **combination locks**] a lock that can only be opened when a particular sequence of numbers is selected on a keypad or by turning a dial
combine [verb: **combines, combining, combined**] to combine things is to join or mix them together: *Combine all the ingredients in a mixing bowl.*
combine harvester [noun: **combine harvesters**] a large farm machine that both cuts and threshes crops
combustible [adjective] a combustible substance will burn or catch fire: *a highly combustible gas found in coal mines*
combustion [noun] burning: *the combustion of gases*
come [verb: **comes, coming, came**]
1 to move towards the person speaking or to move to the place where they are: *Are you coming with us or not?* • *They came by boat and train.*
2 to arrive, happen or exist: *Has my parcel*

Cc

come yet? • *The mountains came into view.* •
People come in all shapes and sizes.

3 to **come about** is to happen: *How did this
disagreement come about?*

4 to **come across** a person or thing is to meet
or find them by accident: *I came across a letter
I had written on 28 June, 1964.*

5 to **come by** something is to get it: *Work was
becoming harder and harder to come by.*

6 someone who has been unconscious or has
fainted **comes round** or **comes to** when they
wake up

comedian [noun: **comedians**] a performer
who tells jokes and funny stories or who acts in
comedies

comedy [noun: **comedies**]
1 comedy is the art of making people laugh
2 a comedy is a funny play or film
→ **comic**

comet [noun: **comets**] a kind of star that
travels across the sky trailing a tail of light
behind it

comfort [noun: **comforts**]
1 comfort is a pleasant feeling you get if you
are relaxed, happy, warm or secure
2 comforts are luxuries or pleasant
surroundings: *a hotel with all the comforts of
home*
[verb: **comforts, comforting, comforted**] to
comfort someone who is sad or upset is to
make them feel happier by saying or doing
nice things

comfortable [adjective] having no pain,
worry or trouble
♦ **comfortably** [adverb] in a comfortable
way: *Are you all sitting comfortably?*

comfy [adjective: **comfier, comfiest**] an
informal word for **comfortable**: *a comfy chair*

comic [adjective]
1 having to do with or involved in comedy: *a
comic actor*
2 funny, amusing: *His face had a really comic
expression.*
[noun: **comics**]
1 a magazine, especially for children, that has
funny stories told in pictures
2 someone who is funny, especially a comedian
♦ **comical** [adjective] funny: *The kitten's
antics were comical.*

comic strip [noun: **comic strips**] a series of
drawings that tell a funny story

comma [noun: **commas**] a punctuation mark
(,) used to show a slight pause in a sentence or
to separate off parts of a sentence to make it
easier to read and understand

command [verb: **commands,
commanding, commanded**]
1 to command someone to do something is to
order them to do it: *'I command you to kneel
before me,' shouted the king.*
2 to command something is to be in control or in
charge of it: *He commanded the Roman
legions.*
[noun: **commands**]
1 a command is an order: *by royal command*
2 to be **in command** is to be in charge or in
control: *Who's the officer in command?*
♦ **commandeer** [verb: **commandeers,
commandeering, commandeered**] if
something is commandeered, it is taken
especially by an army for their use
♦ **commander** [noun: **commanders**]
someone who commands or is in command,
especially an officer in the police or navy
♦ **commandment** [noun:
commandments] a command or order,
especially one of the ten commandments given
to Moses by God

commando [noun: **commandos** or
commandoes] a soldier who works with
others in a small group and is specially trained
to do difficult or dangerous tasks

commemorate [verb: **commemorates,
commemorating, commemorated**] to
commemorate something, for example a battle
or some other famous event, is to remember it
by holding a ceremony or putting up a
monument
♦ **commemoration** [noun:
commemorations] a commemoration of a
person or event is something that is done to
remember and celebrate that person or event

commence [verb: **commences,
commencing, commenced**] to commence is
to begin: *The meeting will commence at 3
o'clock precisely.*
♦ **commencement** [noun] a formal way of
saying the beginning of something

commend [verb: **commends, commending, commended**] to praise someone or something or to say that they deserve praise
* **commendable** [adjective] deserving praise: *commendable bravery*
* **commendation** [noun: **commendations**] an honour or praise given to someone who has done something well

comment [noun: **comments**] a remark or opinion about someone or something: *I'd welcome any comments about the revised schedule.*
[verb: **comments, commenting, commented**] to comment, or comment on something, is to make a remark or give your opinion about it: *'That was a waste of time,' Sally commented.*
* **commentary** [noun: **commentaries**] a description or explanation of an event as it happens by someone who is there
* **commentator** [noun: **commentators**] someone who gives a commentary: *a cricket commentator*

commerce [noun] commerce is the buying and selling of goods and services: *international commerce*
* **commercial** [adjective]
1 to do with trade or making money by selling goods and services
2 paid for by selling advertising space or time: *commercial TV*
[noun: **commercials**] an advertisement for a product on TV or radio
* **commercialized** or **commercialised** [adjective] too concerned with making money: *Christmas has become so commercialized.*

commiserate [verb: **commiserates, commiserating, commiserated**] to commiserate with someone is to sympathize with them about something that is making them unhappy
* **commiserations** [plural noun] when you offer someone your commiserations, you let them know you are sorry about a disappointment or upset they have suffered

commission [noun: **commissions**]
1 someone who is paid commission is paid a fee for each thing they sell

2 a commission is a group of people who investigate something or have authority over something: *the Commission for Racial Equality*
3 an order to do or produce something for payment: *a commission to paint her portrait*
[verb: **commissions, commissioning, commissioned**] to commission something, or to commission someone to do something, is to give an instruction or order for it to be done: *He'd been commissioned to write a book.*

commit [verb: **commits, committing, committed**]
1 to commit a crime is to do something that breaks the law
2 to commit yourself to something is to say, promise or decide that you will do it
* **commitment** [noun: **commitments**] a promise or duty: *Viran made a definite commitment to be there.*
* **committed** [adjective] having strong beliefs: *a committed Christian*

committee [noun: **committees**] a number of people chosen to deal with a task or special business: *the organizing committee for the summer fair*

commodity [noun: **commodities**] anything that can be bought and sold

common [adjective: **commoner, commonest**]
1 seen or happening often and in many places: *Traffic jams are a common occurrence in cities.*
• *one of the commonest childhood diseases*
2 ordinary: *the common people*
3 shared by many: *Their common goal was to make the Games a success.*
[noun: **commons**]
1 a common is a piece of land that belongs to and can be used by all the people in a town: *Wimbledon Common*
2 if people or things **have something in common**, they are similar in some way

Common Market [noun] the Common Market is an old-fashioned name for the European Economic Community or European Union

commonplace [adjective] not at all unusual

common room [noun: **common rooms**] a room in a school or college where a group of

Cc

teachers or students can relax together between classes

common sense [noun] the ability to think and behave sensibly

commonwealth [noun] a group of countries or states that cooperate with each other, especially in trade

commotion [noun] a noisy disturbance

communal [adjective] shared by several people: *a communal garden*

commune [noun: **communes**] a group of people who live together and share work, possessions and expenses

communicable [adjective] a communicable disease can be passed from one person to another

communicate [verb: **communicates, communicating, communicated**]

1 to communicate is to give information to others, for example by making sounds or by writing: *The monkeys communicate with loud barking calls.*

2 to communicate with someone is to get in touch with them: *We communicate mainly by telephone and e-mail.*

♦ **communication** [noun: **communications**]

1 communication is conveying information: *Text messaging is a common form of communication.*

2 a communication is a message: *We've received an urgent communication from head office.*

♦ **communicative** [adjective] a communicative person is willing to talk to others and give them information

Communion [noun] in the Christian Church, Communion is the ceremony celebrating the Last Supper of Jesus and his disciples

communism [noun] communism is the belief that all the wealth created by industry should be shared by everyone in society

♦ **communist** [noun: **communists**] someone who believes in communism [adjective] believing in communism or to do with communists: *a communist country*

community [noun: **communities**]

1 a group living in a particular area or a group sharing the same background: *a school serving the local community*

2 the community is all of society or all the people of the world

commute [verb: **commutes, commuting, commuted**] to travel regularly between two places, especially between home and the place where you work

♦ **commuter** [noun: **commuters**] someone who commutes

compact [adjective] with all its parts fitted tightly or closely together so that they take up very little space: *a compact little kitchen*

compact disc [noun: **compact discs**] a small metal disc on which sound and images are recorded in digital form. The information on a compact disc is read by a laser beam in a compact disc player or computer

companion [noun: **companions**] someone who spends a lot of time with another person

♦ **companionship** [noun] being with each other and having a friendly relationship

company [noun: **companies**]

1 a company is a business firm: *They've formed a company to design video games.*

2 company is companionship: *He's very good company.*

3 a group of people who spend time together: *She got into bad company and started going out late.*

4 if you **keep someone company**, you stay with them or go somewhere with them

5 to **part company** is to leave each other

comparable [adjective] similar: *The two games are comparable in difficulty.*

comparative [adjective]

1 judged by comparing with something else: *He had not lived here as long as the rest of us and was a comparative stranger.*

2 in grammar, a comparative form of an adjective or adverb is the form that usually ends with –er or is used with *more*. For example *better, worse, luckier, braver* and *more dangerous* are comparative forms [noun: **comparatives**] a comparative form of an adjective or adverb

♦ **comparatively** [adverb] compared with something else: *The house was noisy, and the garden was comparatively quiet.*

compare [verb: **compares, comparing, compared**]

1 to put two or more things together to show how similar or different they are, or which is better: *The weather today is lovely compared to last week.*
2 to describe someone or something as like another person or thing: *She compared him to a mad dog.*
✦ **comparison** [noun: **comparisons**] putting two or more things together to show how they are similar or different
compartment [noun: **compartments**] a separate enclosed part within a larger thing: *a secret compartment at the back of the desk*
compass [noun: **compasses**] an instrument that shows the direction of north with a magnet and which you can use to find your way
compasses [plural noun] compasses, or a pair of compasses, are an instrument with two hinged legs used to draw circles or to measure out distances between two points
compassion [noun] if you have or show compassion for people, you feel pity for their suffering
✦ **compassionate** [adjective] showing pity or mercy for people who are suffering or in trouble
compatibility [noun] the quality that allows people or things to get on or work well together
compatible [noun] able to exist or work well together: *The two computer programs weren't compatible.*
compatriot [noun: **compatriots**] your compatriots are people who come from the same country as you do
compel [verb: **compels, compelling, compelled**] to compel someone to do something is to force them to do it
✦ **compelling** [adjective]
1 so interesting or exciting that you are forced to go on reading, watching or listening
2 a compelling argument is so strong that you cannot disagree with it
⇢ **compulsion**
compendium [noun: **compendiums** or **compendia**]
1 a book in which lots of different information about a particular subject is brought together
2 a box that contains several different board games

compensate [verb: **compensates, compensating, compensated**]
1 to compensate someone is to give them something, especially money, in exchange for loss or damage they have suffered
2 if one thing compensates for another, it makes up for it: *His ability to get on with people compensates for his lack of experience.*
✦ **compensation** [noun] compensation is something given to make up for loss or damage
compère [noun: **compères**] someone who introduces the different acts in an entertainment show
compete [verb: **competes, competing, competed**] to compete is to try to beat or be more successful than others: *athletes competing in the Olympics*
⇢ **competition**
competence [noun] the ability or skill to do something properly or well
✦ **competent** [adjective] capable, efficient or skilled: *a very competent pianist*
✦ **competently** [adverb] efficiently or skilfully
competition [noun: **competitions**]
1 a competition is a contest between people who are each trying to win or be better than the others
2 the competition is the people or organizations you are competing against
✦ **competitive** [adjective] a competitive person likes to compete and win against other people
✦ **competitor** [noun: **competitors**] someone taking part in a competition
compilation [noun: **compilations**]
1 compilation is the process of compiling something
2 a compilation is a collection of pieces of writing, music or information: *The album is a compilation of the band's greatest hits.*
compile [verb: **compiles, compiling, compiled**] to compile something such as an encyclopedia is to make it using information that has been collected together
✦ **compiler** [noun: **compilers**] a person or machine that compiles
complacency [noun] an attitude in which

you become lazy because you think you have done all that you need to

• **complacent** [adjective] too satisfied with what you do

complain [verb: **complains, complaining, complained**] to say or write that you are not happy or satisfied: *He complained that it was too hot and that he hated the food.*

• **complaint** [noun: **complaints**]

1 a statement that lets people know that you are not happy or satisfied

2 an illness

complement [noun: **complements**]

1 something that is added to make something complete

2 something that goes very well with another thing: *The sauce is a lovely complement to the meal.*

[verb: **complements, complementing, complemented**] if two things complement each other, they go very well together

• **complementary** [adjective]

1 going well together

2 together making up a whole

ⓘ Try not to confuse **complement** with **compliment**. Remember that the meaning of **complement** is related to **complete**, and so their first six letters are the same.

---

complementary medicine [noun] types of medical treatment not provided by most ordinary doctors, that treat the causes of an illness rather than the symptoms.

Acupuncture and **homeopathy** are types of complementary medicine

complete [verb: **completes, completing, completed**] to complete something is to finish it or make it whole: *You must complete the test in 15 minutes.*

[adjective]

1 with nothing missing: *a complete set of golf clubs*

2 finished: *When the dam is complete it will be over 150 metres high.*

3 total: *I felt a complete fool.*

• **completely** [adverb] totally: *I agree completely.*

• **completeness** [noun] wholeness

• **completion** [noun] when something is finished: *The filming is nearing completion.*

complex [adjective]

1 made up of many parts: *a complex network of streets*

2 difficult to understand or work out: *a complex problem*

[noun: **complexes**]

1 a group of buildings all with the same use: *a sports complex*

2 if someone has a complex, there is something that they are very sensitive about: *She has a real complex about her weight.*

→ **complexity**

complexion [noun: **complexions**] your complexion is the colouring of your skin: *a rosy complexion*

complexity [noun: **complexities**]

1 complexity is being complicated or difficult

2 the complexities of something are the things that make it complicated or difficult: *the complexities of the tax system*

compliance [noun] compliance is obeying someone else's wishes

• **compliant** [adjective]

1 a compliant person is someone who does what another person wants

2 a compliant piece of equipment is designed to work with a particular system or set of instructions: *Our software is compliant with most types of PC.*

complicate [verb: **complicates, complicating, complicated**] to complicate something is to make it more difficult

• **complicated** [adjective] difficult to work out or understand: *a complicated sum*

• **complication** [noun: **complications**] something that creates a problem or difficulty

compliment [noun: **compliments**]

1 a compliment is something that you say that praises someone: *Otto paid me a compliment for once.*

2 to give your compliments to someone is to give them your good wishes

[verb: **compliments, complimenting, complimented**] to compliment someone is to praise them: *Leo complimented her on her good taste.*

• **complimentary** [adjective]

1 flattering or praising: *The article she wrote was very complimentary.*

2 given free: *complimentary tickets for the show*

comply [verb: **complies, complying, complied**] to comply is to obey or agree to do something: *It is impossible to comply with such demands.*
→ **compliance**

component [noun: **components**] one of the parts that are put together to make a whole, for example one of the different parts that make up a machine

compose [verb: **composes, composing, composed**]
1 to write a piece of music, a speech, etc
2 to compose yourself is to become calm
♦ **composed** [adjective]
1 if you are composed, you are in control of your feelings
2 **composed of** means made up of: *a team composed of three men and three women*
♦ **composer** [noun: **composers**] someone who writes music
♦ **composition** [noun: **compositions**]
1 composition is composing: *a lesson in spelling and composition*
2 a composition is something made up, for example a piece of writing or music
→ **composure**

compost [noun] compost is a mixture made up of decayed plants and manure that is spread on soil

composure [noun] being in control of your feelings so that you are calm

compound [noun: **compounds**]
1 something formed from two or more parts: *a chemical compound*
2 an area enclosed by a fence or wall, for example at a factory or prison
3 a word made up from two or more other words. The words *airport, tape recorder* and *bird-bath* are compounds
[verb: **compounds, compounding, compounded**] to compound a problem is to make it worse by adding to it

comprehend [verb: **comprehends, comprehending, comprehended**] to understand
♦ **comprehensible** [adjective] if something is comprehensible, it can be understood

♦ **comprehension** [noun] comprehension is understanding: *a test of reading and comprehension*
♦ **comprehensive** [adjective] dealing with everything: *a comprehensive report*
[noun: **comprehensives**] a comprehensive school

comprehensive school [noun: **comprehensive schools**] a secondary school run by the state where pupils of all abilities are educated in all subjects

compress [verb: **compresses, compressing, compressed**] to compress something is to make it fit into a smaller space, often by squeezing it or shortening it
[noun: **compresses**] a compress is a thick pad of material pressed on a wound or painful area

ⓘ The verb **compress** is pronounced com-**press**, with the stress at the end.
The noun **compress** is pronounced **com**-press, with the stress at the beginning.

comprise [verb: **comprises, comprising, comprised**] to contain or be made up of: *The test will comprise two parts.*

compromise [verb: **compromises, compromising, compromised**] to compromise is to give up some part of what you want so that an agreement can be made
[noun: **compromises**] an agreement in which each person or side involved gives up something they originally asked for: *We've finally reached a compromise on where to go on holiday.*

compulsion [noun: **compulsions**]
1 compulsion is being forced to do something
2 a compulsion is a feeling that you must do something: *a compulsion to eat chocolate*
♦ **compulsive** [adjective] if you are compulsive, you cannot help doing something: *a compulsive liar*
♦ **compulsory** [adjective] something that is compulsory must be done: *Subjects like Maths and English are compulsory.*

computer [noun: **computers**] an electronic machine that can store and deal with very large amounts of information
♦ **computerize** or **computerise** [verb: **computerizes, computerizing,**

computerized] to computerize a system or a set of information is to organize it so that it can be held in a computer's memory

♦ **computerized** [adjective] stored in or dealt with by a computer: *computerized records of fingerprints*

♦ **computing** [noun] the operation of computers or the skill of working with computers

LANGUAGE FOR LIFE

computers

Here are some important words that you may come across when you are buying or using a computer:

• The **CPU** or **central processing unit** is the part of the computer that controls all the other parts.

• A **disk drive** is part of a computer that can read data that is stored on a disk.

• A **graphics card** stores data and allows you to see it as pictures.

• A **hard drive** is part of a computer that can read data that is stored inside the computer.

• A **modem** is used to send information from a computer to other computers on a network down a telephone line.

• A **monitor** is a screen attached to a computer which allows you to see the file or program you are working on. It is sometimes called a **VDU** or **visual display unit**.

• A **mouse** is a device that you move with your hand to point to places on the screen. It has a button or buttons that you press to instruct the computer to do something.

• A **sound card** stores data and allows you to hear it through speakers or headphones.

comrade [noun: **comrades**] a friend or close companion, for example a soldier who is in the same army in a war

con [verb: **cons, conning, conned**] to con someone is to trick them into doing something or thinking something is true

[noun: **cons**] a trick used to deceive someone

con- [prefix] look at the entry for **co-**

concave [adjective] curving inwards or downwards. Look up and compare **convex**: *a concave lens*

conceal [verb: **conceals, concealing,**

concealed] to conceal something is to hide it carefully or keep it secret: *She concealed herself behind a bush.*

♦ **concealment** [noun] concealment is the careful hiding of something: *concealment of his true feelings*

concede [verb: **concedes, conceding, conceded**]

1 to concede something is to admit that it is true: *'It may be possible,' he conceded.*

2 to concede defeat is to accept that you have lost

➡ **concession**

conceit [noun] conceit is having a very good opinion of yourself and what you can do: *She was amazed at the actor's total lack of conceit.*

♦ **conceited** [adjective] having a very good opinion of yourself and what you can do

conceivable [adjective] something that is conceivable is possible to imagine or believe

♦ **conceivably** [adverb] possibly

conceive [verb: **conceives, conceiving, conceived**]

1 to conceive something is to form an idea of it in your mind: *He couldn't conceive how he was going to do it.*

2 if a woman conceives, she becomes pregnant

➡ **concept, conception**

concentrate [verb: **concentrates, concentrating, concentrated**]

1 if you concentrate, or concentrate on something, you give all your attention to it: *Try to concentrate on one thing at a time.*

2 if things are concentrated in one place, they are all together in that place

♦ **concentrated** [adjective] a concentrated liquid is stronger and thicker because some of the water in it has been taken out

♦ **concentration** [noun] concentration is giving all your attention to something

concentration camp [noun: **concentration camps**] a camp where certain types of people are kept prisoner, especially during a war

concentric [adjective] concentric circles are inside each other and have the same centre

concept [noun: **concepts**] an idea or picture in your mind: *He doesn't seem to have any concept of right and wrong.*

conception [noun: **conceptions**]
1 conception is the forming of ideas or pictures in your mind
2 a conception is an idea you form in your mind
3 conception happens when a woman becomes pregnant

concern [verb: **concerns, concerning, concerned**]
1 if something concerns you, it worries you or is important to you: *His disappearance was beginning to concern us.*
2 if something concerns you, it affects or involves you: *Don't interfere in things that don't concern you.*
[noun: **concerns**]
1 concern is caring about something: *They showed no concern for the law.*
2 a concern is a worry or doubt: *If you have any concerns about the exam, you should speak to your class teacher.*
3 a concern is a business: *The garage has always been a family concern.*
• **concerned** [adjective] worried or caring about someone or something: *concerned parents*
• **concerning** [preposition] about or involving someone or something: *a matter concerning your divorce*

concert [noun: **concerts**] a performance by musicians or singers
• **concerted** [adjective] done by a group of people working together: *We must make a concerted effort to win this match.*

concertina [noun: **concertinas**] a musical instrument that you hold in both hands and play by squeezing it inwards while pressing buttons to make the notes

concerto [noun: **concertos**] a piece of music to be played by a solo instrument and an orchestra: *a piano concerto*

concession [noun: **concessions**] something that you allow someone to have so that an argument or protest can be ended: *The company refused to make any concessions and the strike continued.*

concise [adjective] short and containing all the information without unnecessary details

conclude [verb: **concludes, concluding, concluded**]

1 to end: *That concludes today's lesson.*
2 to decide: *He concluded that she was lying.*
• **concluding** [adjective] last: *the concluding chapter of the novel*
• **conclusion** [noun: **conclusions**]
1 an end: *I just have to write the conclusion of my essay.*
2 a decision you make after thinking about something: *I've come to the conclusion that she just doesn't care.*
3 if you **jump to conclusions**, you make your mind up about something too quickly, without knowing all the facts
• **conclusive** [adjective] conclusive proof or evidence shows that something is definitely true
• **conclusively** [adverb] without any doubt: *The videotape proved conclusively that he was the person who had broken in.*

concoct [verb: **concocts, concocting, concocted**]
1 to concoct something is to make it by mixing different things together
2 to concoct a story or plan is to make it up
• **concoction** [noun: **concoctions**] something made by mixing different things together: *The drink is a concoction of fruit juices.*

concourse [noun: **concourses**] a large hall where people can gather, for example at an airport or station building

concrete [noun] concrete is a strong, hard building material made by mixing sand, cement, tiny stones and water
[adjective]
1 made of concrete: *a concrete floor*
2 something that is concrete can be seen or touched: *A table is a concrete object.*
3 something that is concrete is definite: *Do you have any concrete proposals to make?*
[verb: **concretes, concreting, concreted**] to concrete something is to put concrete on it: *Dan's going to concrete the driveway this weekend.*

ⓘ The opposite of meaning 2 of **concrete** is **abstract**.

concussion [noun] injury to the brain that is caused by a blow to the head and makes a person feel dizzy or become unconscious for a while

condemn [verb: **condemns, condemning, condemned**]

1 to condemn someone or something is to say that they are wrong or bad

2 someone condemned to a punishment is sentenced by a court to that punishment: *Mary Queen of Scots was condemned to death.*

♦ **condemnation** [noun: **condemnations**] saying that something is wrong or bad

condensation [noun] condensation happens when moisture in the air cools and becomes liquid, for example when water in the air in a warm room cools and forms drops on the cooler surface of a window

condense [verb: **condenses, condensing, condensed**]

1 vapour condenses when it turns to liquid

2 to condense something is to make it shorter

condescending [adjective] if you are condescending, you act like you are better than other people

condiment [noun: **condiments**] condiments are things that you add to food to give it more flavour, for example salt, pepper and mustard

condition [noun: **conditions**]

1 the state or circumstances a person or thing is in: *The building is in a dangerous condition.*

2 something that has to happen before something else does: *I'll go on the condition that you come too.*

♦ **conditional** [adjective] depending on something else happening: *a conditional offer of a place at university*

♦ **conditionally** [adverb] only if something else happens

♦ **conditioner** [noun: **conditioners**] conditioner is a liquid that improves the texture and condition of your hair or of things washed in a machine

condolences [plural noun] you give or send your condolences to someone to show your sympathy when someone close to them has died

condom [noun: **condoms**] a thin rubber covering a man wears on his penis during sex to prevent a woman from getting pregnant and protect them from passing on sexual diseases

condone [verb: **condones, condoning, condoned**] to condone bad behaviour is to allow it to happen without saying that it is wrong

conduct [verb: **conducts, conducting, conducted**]

1 to conduct someone or something is to guide, manage or control them: *The butler conducted us into the library.* • *Sarah Hobbs conducts the orchestra.*

2 if you conduct yourself in a certain way, you behave in that way: *We expect you to conduct yourselves well at the match.*

3 if a material conducts electricity or heat, it allows electricity or heat to flow through it or be transferred from one place to another by it [noun] your conduct is the way you behave

♦ **conduction** [noun] conduction is the transfer of electricity or heat through something

♦ **conductor** [noun: **conductors**]

1 someone who leads the musicians in an orchestra

2 an object that conducts electricity: *a lightning conductor*

(i) The verb **conduct** is pronounced con–**dukt**, with the stress at the end.
The noun **conduct** is pronounced **con**–dukt, with the stress at the beginning.

cone [noun: **cones**]

1 a solid shape with a round base and sides that slope up to a point at the top

2 a fruit of a pine or fir tree containing its seeds

3 a container of this shape made of wafer and used to hold ice cream

➡ **conical**

confectioner [noun: **confectioners**]

1 someone who makes cakes and sweets

2 a confectioner's is a shop selling cakes and sweets

♦ **confectionery** [noun] cakes and sweets

confederate [noun: **confederates**] someone's confederates are the people who help them, especially to do something illegal

♦ **confederation** [noun: **confederations**] several groups who have united so that they can work together

confer [verb: **confers, conferring,**

conferred] people confer when they discuss something together

◆ **conference** [noun: **conferences**] a meeting of people to discuss a particular subject

confess [verb: **confesses, confessing, confessed**] to confess is to admit to other people that you have done something, especially something wrong: *I don't mind confessing that I was terrified.*

◆ **confession** [noun: **confessions**] confession is admitting you are guilty of a crime or some other bad thing: *He made a full confession to the police.*

confetti [noun] tiny pieces of coloured paper that are thrown over a married couple after the wedding ceremony

confide [verb: **confides, confiding, confided**] to confide in someone is to tell them your secrets

confidence [noun: **confidences**]
1 confidence is being sure of yourself
2 a confidence is a secret
3 if you tell someone something **in confidence**, you expect them not to tell it to anyone else

confidence trick [noun: **confidence tricks**] a trick that is meant to deceive people, especially in order to get their money

confident [adjective]
1 sure of yourself or of your ability to do something: *She's a very confident swimmer.*
2 sure that something will happen the way you expect it to: *I'm confident we'll find the lost children safe and well.*

confidential [adjective] confidential information should not be told to other people

◆ **confidentially** [adverb] in confidence

confine [verb: **confines, confining, confined**] to confine something or someone is to keep them within limits or shut up inside a place: *The soldiers were confined to barracks.*

◆ **confined** [adjective] a confined space is very small and restricted

◆ **confinement** [noun] being locked up or confined

confirm [verb: **confirms, confirming, confirmed**] to confirm something is to say or make sure that it is correct or true: *Please*

confirm that you will be able to come to the meeting.

◆ **confirmation** [noun] something that confirms: *Have you had confirmation of your appointment yet?*

confiscate [verb: **confiscates, confiscating, confiscated**] to confiscate something is to take it away from someone as a punishment

◆ **confiscation** [noun] taking something away as a punishment

conflagration [noun: **conflagrations**] a fierce fire that spreads and destroys a lot of things

conflict [noun: **conflicts**]
1 conflict is argument or disagreement
2 a conflict is a battle or war: *the conflict in the Balkans*
3 if there is a conflict between two things, they cannot work together: *a conflict of ideas*

◆ **conflicting** [adjective] two conflicting things contradict each other or compete with each other

conform [verb: **conforms, conforming, conformed**] to conform is to behave in a way that obeys the rules or laws that most other people obey

confound [verb: **confounds, confounding, confounded**] if something confounds you, it puzzles you

confront [verb: **confronts, confronting, confronted**]
1 to confront something unpleasant is to deal with it in a determined way
2 to confront a person is to meet them as an enemy or to accuse them of something: *He turned and confronted his attackers.* ◆ *You should confront her and ask her about the missing money.*

◆ **confrontation** [noun: **confrontations**] a face-to-face argument or fight between two people or sides

confuse [verb: **confuses, confusing, confused**]
1 to confuse things is to mix them up so that you think one thing is the other
2 if something confuses you, you aren't able to think clearly and don't know what to do or say next

* **confusing** [adjective] difficult to follow or understand
* **confusion** [noun] being confused or mixed up

congeal [verb: **congeals, congealing, congealed**] if a liquid congeals, it forms a thick jelly-like mass

congested [adjective] a congested road or passageway is crowded or blocked up so people or things can't move through easily
* **congestion** [noun] crowding or blocking

congratulate [verb: **congratulates, congratulating, congratulated**] to congratulate someone is to tell them you are happy about something they have achieved: *I congratulated her on her exam results.*
* **congratulations** [plural noun] you say 'congratulations' to someone when you want to show them that you are happy at their success

congregate [verb: **congregates, congregating, congregated**] to congregate is to gather together somewhere in a group or crowd
* **congregation** [noun: **congregations**] a church congregation is all the people who have gathered to hear a church service

congress [noun: **congresses**]
1 a meeting of many different people: *an international congress to discuss refugees*
2 Congress is the parliament of the United States, made up of the Senate and the House of Representatives

conical [adjective] shaped like a cone

conifer [noun: **conifers**] a type of tree with long thin leaves shaped like needles and seeds inside cones
* **coniferous** [adjective] coniferous trees grow cones

conjunction [noun] something that happens or is done **in conjunction with** something else happens or is done at the same time
[part of speech: **conjunctions**] in grammar, a conjunction is a word that links other words or parts of a sentence. For example, the words *and, but* and *or* are conjunctions

conjure [verb: **conjures, conjuring, conjured**]
1 to conjure is to do magic tricks that seem to make things appear or disappear

2 if something **conjures something up**, it makes it appear in your mind: *The smell of new hay conjured up a picture of the countryside.*
* **conjuror** [noun: **conjurors**] someone who does tricks that make things seem to appear or disappear by magic

conker [noun: **conkers**] a large brown seed of the horse chestnut tree

conman [noun: **conmen**] someone who tricks or deceives other people, usually to get money

connect [verb: **connects, connecting, connected**] to connect things is to join them: *How do you connect the PC to the Internet?* • *The detective hadn't connected the two events in his mind.*
* **connection** [noun: **connections**]
1 something that joins two things together
2 a train, bus or plane that you need to catch so that you can continue a journey: *We missed our connection to Stansted because the train was late.*
3 in connection with means to do with: *He is wanted by the police in connection with a theft.*

connotation [noun: **connotations**] what is suggested by a word as well as its obvious meaning

conquer [verb: **conquers, conquering, conquered**] to conquer is to defeat: *Napoleon tried to conquer Egypt.* • *Claire seems to have finally conquered her shyness.*
* **conqueror** [noun: **conquerors**] someone who conquers a country or people
* **conquest** [noun: **conquests**] something that is won by great effort or force

conscience [noun] your conscience is your sense of right and wrong
* **conscientious** [adjective] a conscientious person works hard and carefully to get things right
* **conscientiously** [adverb] carefully and diligently

ⓘ Be careful how you spell this word. Remember it is spelt **con** + **science**.

conscious [adjective]
1 you are conscious when you are awake and aware of your surroundings

2 you are conscious of something happening when you are aware of it
3 a conscious act or decision is one that you have thought about
• **consciously** [adverb] deliberately or being aware of what you are doing
• **consciousness** [noun] the state of being aware of yourself and what is going on around you: *She lost consciousness and woke up in hospital.*

conscript [verb: **conscripts, conscripting, conscripted**] to force someone by law to join the armed forces: *The government conscripted young men.*
[noun: **conscripts**] someone who is forced by law to join the armed forces
• **conscription** [noun] forcing people to join the armed forces

ⓘ The verb **conscript** is pronounced con-**script**, with the stress at the end.
The noun **conscript** is pronounced **con**-script, with the stress at the beginning.

consecrate [verb: **consecrates, consecrating, consecrated**] to consecrate something is to put it aside for a religious or holy use
• **consecration** [noun] giving something a religious use

consecutive [adjective] one after the other: *It snowed on three consecutive days.*

consensus [noun] consensus, or a consensus, is agreement or a feeling shared by most people

consent [verb: **consents, consenting, consented**] someone consents to something when they agree to it
[noun] to give consent for something is to allow it

consequence [noun: **consequences**]
1 consequence is importance: *It was of no consequence.*
2 a consequence is something that follows as a result of something else: *He did no work and the consequence was that he failed all his exams.*
3 if you **take** or **suffer the consequences** for something, you have to accept anything unpleasant that results from it: *If you break the*

law you have to take the consequences.
• **consequent** [adjective] following as a result
• **consequently** [adverb] as a result

conservation [noun] looking after things such as old buildings, works of art or the environment and working to prevent them being damaged or destroyed
• **conservationist** [noun: **conservationists**] a conservationist is someone who works to stop old buildings, works of art or the environment being ruined

conservative [adjective]
1 a conservative person does not like changes or new fashions: *He's a very conservative dresser.*
2 a conservative estimate or guess is cautious and is usually less than the actual amount

conservatory [noun: **conservatories**] a room or building which has walls and a roof made of glass and often holds a lot of plants

conserve [verb: **conserves, conserving, conserved**] to conserve things is to keep them from being wasted or lost: *Close the windows to conserve heat.*
➝ **conservation, conservative**

consider [verb: **considers, considering, considered**]
1 to consider something is to think about it carefully: *I'll consider your idea.*
2 to consider someone or something as being something is to think of them like that: *I consider him to be a true friend.*
3 to consider other people is to think about what they want or need

considerable [adjective] quite big: *a considerable distance*
• **considerably** [adverb] quite a lot: *John earns considerably more than I do.*

considerate [adjective] thinking of other people and what they want: *It was considerate of you to help me.*

consideration [noun: **considerations**]
1 consideration is thinking carefully about things
2 a consideration is something that you take into account when you are making a decision
3 to **take something into consideration** is to think about it while you are making a decision

Cc

considering [preposition] taking into account: *Considering how clever you are, I think you should have done better.*

consignment [noun: **consignments**] a load of goods sent from one place to another

consist [verb: **consists, consisting, consisted**] to be made up of something: *a simple meal consisting of a small loaf and cheese*

consistency [noun: **consistencies**]
1 consistency is being always the same
2 something's consistency is its thickness or firmness: *a sauce with the consistency of cream*
♦ **consistent** [adjective] staying the same all the way through: *Keep the style of your essay consistent.*
♦ **consistently** [adverb] without changing: *He has consistently turned up for work late.*

consolation [noun: **consolations**] something that makes a disappointment seem less bad

consolation prize [noun: **consolation prizes**] a prize given to someone who has come second in a competition

console¹ [verb: **consoles, consoling, consoled**] to console someone is to comfort them
→ **consolation**

console² [noun: **consoles**]
1 a small piece of electronic equipment that you connect to a television to play video games on: *a games console*
2 a console is a board or box with the controls for a machine arranged on it

ⓘ Console meaning 'to comfort' is pronounced con-**sole**, with the stress at the end.
Console meaning 'a piece of equipment' is pronounced **con**-sole, with the stress at the beginning.

consolidate [verb: **consolidates, consolidating, consolidated**] to consolidate something is to strengthen it or make it more solid

consonant [noun: **consonants**] a consonant is any letter of the alphabet except *a, e, i, o,* or *u*

consort [verb: **consorts, consorting, consorted**] to consort with people is to be in their company
[noun: **consorts**] a husband or wife

conspicuous [adjective] very obvious or easily seen

conspiracy [noun: **conspiracies**] a secret plot between several people to commit a crime together
♦ **conspirator** [noun: **conspirators**] someone who plots with others to commit a crime

conspire [verb: **conspires, conspiring, conspired**]
1 to conspire is to plot with other people to commit a crime
2 if things conspire against you, they come together to stop you doing something you want to do

constable [noun: **constables**] an ordinary police officer

constancy [noun] never changing or stopping

constant [adjective] never stopping: *constant sunshine*
♦ **constantly** [adverb] all the time: *It rained constantly for a week.*

constellation [noun: **constellations**] a large group of stars that can be seen in the sky at night

constipated [adjective] someone is constipated when their bowels don't work well and they can't get rid of the waste from their body
♦ **constipation** [noun] being constipated

constituency [noun: **constituencies**] a district of the country that has a member of parliament
♦ **constituent** [noun: **constituents**]
1 something that is a part of a larger thing: *The main constituent of the human body is water.*
2 a voter in a constituency

constitute [verb: **constitutes, constituting, constituted**] to constitute is to be or to form something: *Global warming constitutes a risk to the environment.*
♦ **constitution** [noun: **constitutions**]
1 a constitution is a set of rules or laws by

which a country or organization is governed

2 your constitution is the health and strength of your body, especially its ability to fight off illness or injury

◆ **constitutional** [adjective] to do with a constitution

constrain [verb: **constrains, constraining, constrained**] to constrain someone or something is to stop them making progress or developing

◆ **constraint** [noun: **constraints**] something that prevents progress or development

constrict [verb: **constricts, constricting, constricted**] to constrict something is to squeeze it tightly

construct [verb: **constructs, constructing, constructed**] to build something up from several parts: *construct a model*

◆ **construction** [noun: **constructions**]
1 construction is building
2 a construction is something built up from several parts

◆ **constructive** [adjective] helpful: *constructive criticism*

consul [noun: **consuls**] someone whose job is to represent his or her government in a foreign country and help people from his or her own country who are there

◆ **consulate** [noun: **consulates**] the office of a consul

consult [verb: **consults, consulting, consulted**] to consult is to ask advice or get information from someone or something: *If the headache persists, consult a doctor.*

◆ **consultant** [noun: **consultants**]
1 someone whose job is to give advice on a subject that they know a lot about: *a marketing consultant*
2 a hospital doctor who is an expert in a particular type of illness

◆ **consultation** [noun: **consultations**] a meeting with an expert who can give you advice and information

consume [verb: **consumes, consuming, consumed**]
1 to consume something is to use it up
2 to consume food is to eat it
3 to consume something is to destroy it: *The fire consumed the forest.*

◆ **consumer** [noun: **consumers**] someone who buys and uses things

◆ **consumption** [noun] consuming or the amount that is consumed: *the world's consumption of oil*

contact [verb: **contacts, contacting, contacted**]
1 to contact someone is to get in touch with them
2 things contact each other when they touch or come together
[noun: **contacts**]
1 contact is being in touch or touching: *I've lost contact with almost all the people I went to school with.*
2 your contacts are the people you keep in touch with

contact lens [noun: **contact lenses**] a thin piece of plastic worn on the front of your eye to help you see better

contagious [adjective] a contagious disease can be spread between people

contain [verb: **contains, containing, contained**]
1 to contain something is to hold it or have it inside: *How much does this bucket contain?*
2 to contain yourself is to hold back your feelings: *Annie couldn't contain her excitement.*

◆ **container** [noun: **containers**] something for putting things in, for example a box or jar

contaminate [verb: **contaminates, contaminating, contaminated**] to contaminate something clean or pure is to make it dirty or poisonous by putting something in it: *water contaminated with chemicals*

◆ **contaminated** [adjective] not clean or pure because something dirty or dangerous has been added

◆ **contamination** [noun] making something dirty or poisonous

contemplate [verb: **contemplates, contemplating, contemplated**] to contemplate is to think about something or look at something for a long time: *The possibility is just too horrible to contemplate.*

◆ **contemplation** [noun: **contemplations**] thinking in a quiet, serious way

◆ **contemplative** [adjective] spending time thinking

Cc

contemporary [adjective]
1 belonging to the time now: *contemporary art*
2 if one thing is contemporary with another, they exist at the same time
[noun: **contemporaries**] your contemporaries are people who are living at the same time as you

contempt [noun] if you have contempt for someone or something, you have a very poor opinion of them and don't think they deserve any respect

contend [verb: **contends, contending, contended**] to contend with something is to struggle with it: *She has enough to contend with, working and bringing up four kids on her own.*
◆ **contender** [noun: **contenders**] someone who has entered a competition
➡ **contention**

content[1] [adjective] to be content is to be happy and satisfied
➡ **contented, contentment**

ⓘ This word is pronounced con-**tent**, with the stress at the end.

content[2] [noun: **contents**] the content or contents of something are the things that it contains

ⓘ This word is pronounced **con**-tent, with the stress at the beginning.

contented [adjective] a contented person is happy and satisfied

contention [noun] disagreement or quarrelling between people

contentment [noun] being content

contest [noun: **contests**] a competition: *a contest of strength*
◆ **contestant** [noun: **contestants**] someone involved in a contest

context [noun: **contexts**] the context of a word or sentence is what is said or written before and after it and which makes its meaning clear

continent [noun: **continents**]
1 one of the large areas that the Earth's land is divided into. The continents are Africa, Antarctica, North America, South America, Asia, Australia and Europe
2 the Continent is a British name for the

European mainland: *They always go to the Continent on holiday.*
◆ **continental** [adjective] to do with a continent, especially the European continent seen from the point of view of people living in Britain

continual [adjective]
1 going on without stopping: *the continual noise of traffic*
2 happening again and again: *I'm tired of your continual bad behaviour.*
◆ **continually** [adverb] all the time or again and again: *Matt is continually rude to me.*

continue [verb: **continues, continuing, continued**]
1 to continue is to go on in the same way or in the same direction as before
2 to continue with something is to go on with it
◆ **continuity** [noun] having no breaks or stops
◆ **continuous** [adjective] going on without a break or stop: *a continuous line from north to south*

contorted [adjective] twisted in an unnatural way
◆ **contortion** [noun: **contortions**] a twist

contour [noun: **contours**]
1 the contours of something are its shape seen in outline: *a car with sleek contours*
2 a line on a map which links points of the same height and shows the shape of a hill or mountain

contra- [prefix] if a word starts with **contra-**, it adds the meaning 'against' or 'opposite to' to the word. For example, a *contraflow* is a flow in the opposite direction

contraception [noun] preventing pregnancy: *various methods of contraception*

contraceptive [noun: **contraceptives**] a pill or other device that is used to prevent a woman becoming pregnant

contract [noun: **contracts**] a contract is a written agreement
[verb: **contracts, contracting, contracted**]
1 to contract work out to someone is to make an agreement with them that they will do the work
2 to contract is to get smaller: *As the muscle contracts your arm is raised.*

3 to contract a disease is to catch it: *People who contracted polio were often left crippled.*
◆ **contraction** [noun]
1 contraction is getting smaller or shorter
2 when a muscle gets tighter, especially the painful movement of a woman's womb as her baby is born
◆ **contractor** [noun: **contractors**] someone who is given a contract to do a particular job: *a building contractor*

contradict [verb: **contradicts, contradicting, contradicted**] to contradict someone is to say that what they have just said is not correct
◆ **contradiction** [noun: **contradictions**] something that makes a statement or fact seem untrue because it shows the opposite
◆ **contradictory** [adjective] a contradictory statement is one that states the opposite of what has just been said

contraflow [noun: **contraflows**] a contraflow is a line of traffic that goes in the opposite direction to another line of traffic on the same side of a main road

contraption [noun: **contraptions**] a contraption is an odd-looking machine or instrument

contrary [adjective] opposite or opposed to each other: *They have contrary views on the subject.*
[noun] you say '**on the contrary**' when you want to say that the opposite is true: *There will be no tax rises. On the contrary, some tax bills may fall.*

contrast [noun: **contrasts**] if there is a contrast between things, they are different in some way
[verb: **contrasts, contrasting, contrasted**] to contrast one thing with another is to show the differences between them

ⓘ The noun **contrast** is pronounced **con**-trast, with the stress at the beginning.
The verb **contrast** is pronounced con-**trast**, with the stress at the end.

contravene [verb: **contravenes, contravening, contravened**] if something contravenes a rule, it breaks it or goes against it
◆ **contravention** [noun: **contraventions**]

breaking or going against a rule, or something that does this

contribute [verb: **contributes, contributing, contributed**]
1 to contribute money or time is to give it: *We each had to contribute towards Paul's present.*
2 if one thing contributes to another, it is one of its causes: *People driving too close to the car in front contributed to the accident.*
◆ **contribution** [noun: **contributions**] something that is given or done to help to achieve something
◆ **contributor** [noun: **contributors**] someone who makes a contribution

contrite [adjective] if someone is contrite, they feel or show that they are sorry for something bad they have done
◆ **contrition** [noun] feeling or showing that you are sorry

contrive [verb: **contrives, contriving, contrived**]
1 to contrive something is to make it, especially from things that are available: *He'd contrived a sort of ladder out of pieces of wood.*
2 to contrive to do something is to try to do it: *She contrived to hide her disappointment.*
◆ **contrived** [adjective] something that is contrived is false and unnatural: *a contrived story about things that would never happen*

control [noun: **controls**]
1 control is the power someone has to rule or make decisions
2 if you have control over someone or something, you are able to make them behave in the way you want: *She keeps tight control over her class.*
3 if someone is **in control**, they are in charge of a situation
4 if someone or something is **out of control**, they are behaving or working in a way that can't be controlled
[verb: **controls, controlling, controlled**]
1 to control something is to have power over it or to run it
2 to control yourself is to stay calm and not show your feelings
◆ **controller** [noun: **controllers**] a person or thing that controls or directs something

Cc

♦ **controls** [plural noun] the controls of a vehicle or other machine are the buttons, levers and pedals that make it go or work

control tower [noun: **control towers**] a tall building at an airport where air traffic controllers direct the planes that are taking off and landing

controversial [adjective] if something is controversial, it causes arguments because some people don't agree with it

♦ **controversy** [noun: **controversies**] something that causes arguments or discussions because some people agree with it and some people don't

conundrum [noun: **conundrums**] a puzzling question or riddle

conurbation [noun: **conurbations**] two towns or cities that have been joined by building on the land between them

convalesce [verb: **convalesces, convalescing, convalesced**] someone who has been ill convalesces when they rest and recover their health

♦ **convalescence** [noun] the time taken by someone to recover their health and strength after an illness

♦ **convalescent** [noun: **convalescents**] someone recovering from an illness

convection [noun] convection is the spreading of heat through air or water

♦ **convector** [noun: **convectors**] a heater that works by convection

convene [verb: **convenes, convening, convened**] to convene is to come together or to call people to come together: *convene a meeting*

♦ **convener** [noun: **conveners**]
1 someone who calls a meeting
2 someone who is the chairperson of a committee

convenience [noun: **conveniences**]
1 convenience is being easy to use, reach or do, or being suitable: *I like the convenience of living so close to the shops.* • *For everyone's convenience, we will meet after work.*
2 a convenience is something that makes people's lives easy or comfortable: *The hotel has every modern convenience.*
3 a convenience is a lavatory

4 to do something **at your convenience** is to do it when it suits you

♦ **convenient** [adjective] handy or suitable: *If it isn't convenient just now, I can call round later.*

♦ **conveniently** [adverb] in a convenient way

convent [noun: **convents**] a building where a group of nuns lives

convention [noun: **conventions**]
1 convention, or a convention, is a way of behaving that has become normal because people have been doing it for a long time
2 a convention is a meeting of people, usually to discuss a particular subject: *a science fiction convention*

♦ **conventional** [adjective] if something is conventional, it is traditional and not at all unusual

♦ **conventionally** [adverb] by custom or tradition

converge [verb: **converges, converging, converged**] to converge is to come together at a certain point: *The two roads converge just beyond the bridge.*

conversation [noun: **conversations**] talk or a talk between people: *Stuart's not very good at making conversation.* • *We had a long conversation about music.*

♦ **conversational** [adjective] to do with conversation: *written in a conversational tone*

converse [1] [verb: **converses, conversing, conversed**] when people converse, they talk to each other

converse [2] [noun] the converse of something is its opposite

♦ **conversely** [adverb] in the opposite way or from the opposite point of view

conversion [noun: **conversions**] changing from one thing to another

convert [verb: **converts, converting, converted**] to convert something is to change it into something else: *Convert this sum of money from pounds into dollars.*
[noun: **converts**] a convert is someone who has changed one set of opinions or beliefs for another

♦ **convertible** [adjective] able to be changed from one thing to another

ⓘ The verb **convert** is pronounced con-**vert**, with the stress at the end.
The noun **convert** is pronounced **con**-vert, with the stress at the beginning.

---

convex [adjective] curving outwards or upwards. Look up and compare **concave**

convey [verb: **conveys, conveying, conveyed**]
1 to convey something or someone is to carry or transport them: *A bus conveyed us to the lecture theatre.*
2 to convey a meaning is to pass it on to other people: *What are you trying to convey in this poem?*

conveyor belt [noun: **conveyor belts**] a moving surface used to carry things from one place to another, especially in a factory

convict [verb: **convicts, convicting, convicted**] to convict someone is to say in a court of law that they are guilty of a crime
[noun: **convicts**] someone who has been found guilty of a crime and sent to prison
♦ **conviction** [noun: **convictions**]
1 conviction is strong belief
2 a conviction is a sentence given to someone who has been found guilty of a crime: *Greene has had many convictions for theft.*

ⓘ The verb **convict** is pronounced con-**vict**, with the stress at the end.
The noun **convict** is pronounced **con**-vict, with the stress at the beginning.

---

convince [verb: **convinces, convincing, convinced**] to convince someone of something is to make them believe that it is true or real: *Vijay found it hard to convince his parents that he was too ill to go to school.*
♦ **convinced** [adjective] certain that something is true or real: *David's convinced that he saw a ghost.*

convoy [noun: **convoys**] a number of ships, lorries or other vehicles travelling along together in a line

convulse [verb: **convulses, convulsing, convulsed**] to convulse is to twist or shake violently: *We were convulsed with laughter.*
♦ **convulsion** [noun: **convulsions**] a sudden jerking, twisting or shaking, especially caused by muscle movements that you can't control

coo [noun: **coos**] a soft gentle sound made by a dove or a pigeon
[verb: **coos, cooing, cooed**] to make this sound

cook [verb: **cooks, cooking, cooked**]
1 to cook food is to heat it by baking, frying, roasting or boiling
2 food cooks when it heats up and becomes ready to eat
[noun: **cooks**] a cook is someone who prepares and cooks food
♦ **cooker** [noun: **cookers**] a large piece of kitchen equipment used for cooking food: *a gas cooker*
♦ **cookery** [noun] the skill or activity of cooking food

cookie [noun: **cookies**] a biscuit

cool [adjective: **cooler, coolest**]
1 slightly cold: *a cool drink*
2 calm and controlled: *If you find yourself in a dangerous situation, try to stay cool.*
3 not friendly: *He gave a cool reply.*
4 an informal way of describing someone or something you think is great: *He has a really cool haircut.* • *'I've got a new mobile.' 'Cool!'*
♦ **coolly** [adverb]
1 calmly
2 in an unfriendly way
♦ **coolness** [noun] being cool

coop [noun: **coops**] a cage where chickens are kept
[verb: **coops, cooping, cooped**] if you are **cooped up** somewhere, you are inside or in a small space that you would like to escape from

cooperate [verb: **cooperates, cooperating, cooperated**]
1 people cooperate when they work together to do or achieve something
2 to cooperate with someone is to do what they want you to do
♦ **cooperation** [noun]
1 working with others so that something can be done or achieved
2 doing what someone asks or tells you to do
♦ **cooperative** [adjective]
1 willing to do something someone asks you or tells you to do
2 a cooperative business or organization is

Cc

Cc

one that is managed or owned by everyone who works in it or uses it

coordinate [verb: **coordinates, coordinating, coordinated**] to coordinate movements or actions is to make them fit in with each other or work smoothly together

✦ **coordinates** [plural noun] two sets of numbers or letters used to show a position on a graph or find a place on a map

✦ **coordination** [noun]

1 the organization of different people or things so that they work together smoothly or well

2 the ability to control your body so that different parts work well together: *hand and eye coordination*

cop[1] [verb: **cops, copping, copped**] to **cop out** of something that is your responsibility is to avoid doing it

cop[2] [noun: **cops**] an informal word for a police officer: *a New York cop*

cope [verb: **copes, coping, coped**] to cope with something is to manage to deal with it: *She said she couldn't cope with any more work.*

copious [adjective] in large quantities: *He made copious notes during the interview.*

copper[1] [noun]

1 copper is a red-brown metal

2 a red-brown colour

3 a coin that is made of copper and which usually has a low value: *He gave the beggar a few coppers.*

copper[2] [noun: **coppers**] an informal word for a police officer

copse or **coppice** [noun: **copses** or **coppices**] a wood made up of small or low-growing trees

copy [verb: **copies, copying, copied**]

1 to copy something is to make another thing that looks exactly the same or nearly the same

2 to copy something down is to write it down

3 to copy someone is to do the same thing that they do: *Conrad copies everything his big brother does.*

[noun: **copies**]

1 a copy is something that has been copied from something else

2 a copy of a book, magazine or newspaper is one of several that have been printed

copyright [noun] copyright is the right a person or organization has to copy or publish a book, a piece of music, a film or a video game

coral [noun] a hard pink material made up of the skeletons of tiny sea creatures

[adjective] made of coral: *a coral island • a coral necklace*

coral reef [noun: **coral reefs**] a hard rock-like mass of coral that builds up over many years on the seabed

cord [noun: **cords**]

1 cord is thin rope or thick string: *The prisoner's hands were tied with cord.*

2 a cord is a thin rope: *a window cord*

3 an electric cable or flex

ⓘ Do not confuse the spellings of **cord** and **chord**, which have different meanings.

cordial [adjective] polite and friendly in a formal way: *Their discussions were perfectly cordial.*

[noun: **cordials**] a fruit juice that you drink diluted with water: *lime cordial*

cordon [noun: **cordons**] a line of police, soldiers or guards standing around an area to keep people back

[verb: **cordons, cordoning, cordoned**] to **cordon off** an area is to put up a barrier of some sort around it to stop people going there

corduroy [noun] a cotton cloth with rows of soft velvety ridges on the outer surface

core [noun: **cores**] the inner part of something, for example a fruit or the Earth: *an apple core*

[verb: **cores, coring, cored**] to core an apple is to take out the inner part that you don't normally eat

corgi [noun: **corgis**] a breed of dog with short legs and upright ears

cork [noun: **corks**]

1 cork is a light substance that floats, which comes from the bark of a type of oak tree

2 a cork is a piece of this used as a stopper for a bottle

corkscrew [noun: **corkscrews**] a device with a twisted metal spike used to pull corks from wine bottles

cormorant [noun: **cormorants**] a type of large black sea bird with a long curved beak

corn[1] [noun]
  1 wheat or a similar crop
  2 maize
corn[2] [noun: **corns**] a sore, hard lump on your foot caused by your shoe rubbing your skin
cornea [noun: **corneas**] the see-through covering at the front of your eyeball
corned beef [noun] beef that has been salted and packed into tins
corner [noun: **corners**]
  1 a point where two roads, walls, edges or lines meet: *I'll meet you at the corner of George Street and Alexander Road.*
  2 a place away from the main part or far away: *a secluded corner in the garden • travelling to the far corners of the world*
  3 in soccer and hockey, a kick or hit that you take from one of the corners at the opposing team's end of the pitch
  [verb: **corners, cornering, cornered**] to corner a person or animal is to force them into a position they can't escape from
cornerstone [noun: **cornerstones**]
  1 a stone at one corner of a building's foundations used as a support for other stones built on top
  2 something on which everything else depends: *the cornerstone of his argument*
cornet [noun: **cornets**]
  1 a musical instrument that looks like a small trumpet
  2 a cornet-shaped wafer which is used to contain ice cream
cornflour [noun] a white powder made from ground maize and used in cooking, for example to thicken sauces
cornflower [noun: **cornflowers**] a plant with bright blue flowers that grows wild in fields
corny [adjective: **cornier, corniest**]
  1 weak or silly, or heard many times before: *a corny joke*
  2 sentimental: *a corny old film*
coronary [noun: **coronaries**] a heart attack
coronation [noun: **coronations**] the crowning of a king, queen or emperor
coronet [noun: **coronets**] a small crown, especially one worn by a duke
corporal[1] [noun: **corporals**] a soldier with a rank between private and sergeant

corporal[2] [adjective] to do with the body
corporal punishment [noun] punishment in which the person being punished is hit or beaten
corporation [noun: **corporations**] a corporation is a large business or a group of businesses
corps [noun: **corps**] a division of the army, especially one that does a special job: *the Army Medical Corps*

ⓘ This word is pronounced **cor**.

corpse [noun: **corpses**] a dead body
corral [noun: **corrals**] an enclosure, usually surrounded by a wooden fence, where animals such as cattle and horses are kept
correct [adjective]
  1 right, not wrong: *The correct answer is 15.*
  2 correct behaviour is the sort of behaviour that people find acceptable
  [verb: **corrects, correcting, corrected**]
  1 to correct something is to mark or change any mistakes or faults in it: *Your tutor will correct this exercise.*
  2 to correct someone is to tell them that what they have said or done is wrong
  • correction [noun: **corrections**]
  1 a correction is a mark or change made to correct a mistake
  2 correction is checking and altering something to make it better or more accurate
correspond [verb: **corresponds, corresponding, corresponded**]
  1 if two things correspond, they are the same
  2 people correspond when they write to each other
  • correspondence [noun]
  1 letters
  2 likeness or similarity: *There was no correspondence between their two stories.*
  • correspondent [noun: **correspondents**] a journalist who writes news reports about a particular subject: *a war correspondent*
corridor [noun: **corridors**] a corridor is a passageway in a building or train
corrode [verb: **corrodes, corroding, corroded**] metal corrodes when it rusts or is eaten away by a chemical

Cc

+ **corrosion** [noun] corroding

+ **corrosive** [adjective] able to destroy or wear away metal: *a corrosive acid*

corrugated [adjective] folded or shaped into a series of ridges: *a corrugated iron roof*

corrupt [verb: **corrupts, corrupting, corrupted**] to corrupt someone is to make them dishonest or evil
[adjective] someone who is corrupt behaves dishonestly, usually by taking bribes: *corrupt officials*

+ **corruption** [noun] dishonesty by people in positions where they are expected to behave honestly

corset [noun: **corsets**] a stiff garment that fits tightly around the middle part of your body and is worn under other clothes to support your back or give your body a better shape

cosh [noun: **coshes**] a short heavy stick used for hitting people

cosmetic [noun: **cosmetics**] cosmetics are things like lipstick, powder and face cream that people use to make themselves look better

cosmetic surgery [noun] surgery done to change a person's appearance rather than for any medical reason

cosmic [adjective] to do with the universe and outer space

cosmonaut [noun: **cosmonauts**] a Russian astronaut

cosmopolitan [adjective] including people or ideas from many parts of the world: *cosmopolitan cities like London and New York*

cosmos [noun] the cosmos is the universe
→ **cosmic**

cost [verb: **costs, costing, cost**]
1 if something costs a certain amount of money, that is the amount you have to pay for it: *How much does a litre of milk cost?*
2 to cost someone something is to make them lose that thing: *His heroism cost him his life.*
[noun: **costs**]
1 the cost of something is the amount of money that has to be spent to buy it or make it
2 the cost of something is what has to be suffered to do it or get it
3 at all costs means no matter what cost or suffering may be involved: *Yushi was determined to succeed at all costs.*

+ **costly** [adverb] costing a lot: *a costly item of jewellery*

costume [noun: **costumes**]
1 a special set of clothes worn by an actor in a play or film
2 the clothes worn by the people of a particular country or in a particular period of history: *The children were dressed in national costume for the parade.* • *Elizabethan costumes*
3 fancy dress

cosy [adjective: **cosier, cosiest**] warm and comfortable: *a cosy little bedroom* • *I'm nice and cosy sitting here by the fire.*

cot [noun: **cots**] a bed with high sides for a baby or young child to sleep in

cot death [noun] an old-fashioned name for **sudden infant death syndrome**

cottage [noun: **cottages**] a small house in the country or in a village

cottage cheese [noun] a soft white lumpy type of cheese

cotton [noun] a type of cloth made from the fibres inside the seeds of a plant that is grown in warm climates

cotton wool [noun] a mass of soft loose fibres of cotton used to clean wounds or take off make-up

couch [noun: **couches**] a sofa

couch potato [noun: **couch potatoes**] a person who is not active enough, especially someone who sits watching television a lot

cougar [noun: **cougars**] a large wild animal of the cat family that lives in America. Another name for the cougar is the **mountain lion**

cough [verb: **coughs, coughing, coughed**] you cough when you make a loud rough sound in your throat as you force air out of your lungs
[noun: **coughs**]
1 the noise you make when you cough
2 an illness that causes you to cough

could [verb]
1 could is used with another verb to say that something is or might be possible, or to ask politely if something is possible: *He could do it if he tried hard enough.* • *Could I have a drink of water, please?*
2 could is used as a past tense form of the verb **can**: *He could run fast when he was young.*

couldn't [short form] a short way to say and write **could not**

council [noun: **councils**] a group of people who are elected to discuss and manage the affairs of a town or city

♦ **councillor** [noun: **councillors**] someone elected to a town or city council

ⓘ Be careful not to confuse the noun **council** with the noun and verb **counsel**.

council tax [noun] in Britain, a tax that you pay for local services such as schools and libraries, based on how much your house is worth

counsel [verb: **counsels, counselling, counselled**] to counsel someone is to give them advice

[noun: **counsels**]

1 advice

2 a lawyer who presents evidence at a trial: *the counsel for the defence*

♦ **counselling** [noun] giving special advice to people: *the student counselling service*

♦ **counsellor** [noun: **counsellors**] someone who gives advice

count [verb: **counts, counting, counted**]

1 to count is to say numbers in order: *Can you count backwards from 10?*

2 to count something, or to **count things up**, is to work out the total: *He was busy counting his money.*

3 if something counts, it is important or has value: *They tried to make every day they were together count.*

4 if you can **count on** someone or something you can rely on them

[noun: **counts**]

1 a count is a number of things to be counted: *The teacher did a head count before we left.*

2 to **keep count** is to know how many there are or have been

3 to **lose count** is to forget how many you have already counted

→ **countless**

count [noun: **counts**] a nobleman in certain countries

countdown [noun] a countdown is counting backwards to the exact time when something will happen, for example a rocket will be launched

counter [verb: **counters, countering, countered**] to counter something is to respond to it by fighting back or saying or doing the opposite

[adverb] against or in the opposite direction: *Counter to our advice, he wants to be a racing driver.*

counter [noun: **counters**]

1 a table or surface across which customers are served, for example in a shop, a bank or a café

2 a small plastic or metal disc used in some board games

counter- [prefix] if a word starts with **counter-**, it adds the meaning 'opposite' to the word. For example, in American English, *counterclockwise* means going round in the opposite direction to clockwise

counteract [verb: **counteracts, counteracting, counteracted**] if one thing counteracts another thing, it reduces or takes away the effect of that other thing by doing the opposite: *a face cream that is supposed to counteract wrinkles*

counterattack [noun: **counterattacks**] a counterattack is an attack made against an enemy who has attacked first

counterfeit [adjective] not real or genuine: *a counterfeit stamp*

[noun: **counterfeits**] a counterfeit is a copy made to look like the real thing

counterfoil [noun: **counterfoils**] the counterfoil of a cheque or ticket is the part left behind when you tear off the cheque or ticket, that you keep as a record

counterpart [noun: **counterparts**] someone's counterpart is a person who has a similar job in a different place: *The British Prime Minister will be meeting his European counterparts.*

countersign [verb: **countersigns, countersigning, countersigned**] to sign a document that has already been signed by someone else

countess [noun: **countesses**]

1 a woman with the same rank as a count or earl

2 the wife of a count

countless [adjective] too many to count: *I've done this countless times.*

Cc

Cc

country [noun: **countries**]
1 a nation or one of the areas of the world controlled by its own government
2 the land where certain people or animals live: *This is grizzly bear country.*
3 an area: *the West Country*
4 the country is the parts of the land away from towns and cities: *They live in the country.*

countryman [noun: **countrymen**]
1 a man who lives and works in the countryside
2 your countrymen are men who come from the same country as you do

countryside [noun] the countryside is land away from towns and cities

countrywoman [noun: **countrywomen**]
1 a woman who lives and works in the countryside
2 your countrywomen are the women who come from the same country as you do

county [noun: **counties**] a county is one of the areas that some countries or states are divided into, which each have their own local government

coup [noun: **coups**] a coup is a sudden change of government in which new people take power without an election being held

ⓘ This word is pronounced **coo**.

couple [noun: **couples**]
1 two or approximately two: *I hadn't seen him for a couple of months.*
2 a husband and wife or two people who have a similar close relationship: *an elderly couple*
[verb: **couples, coupling, coupled**] to couple things is to join one to the other

coupon [noun: **coupons**] a coupon is a piece of paper that you can use to claim a free gift or get money off something

courage [noun]
1 courage is the quality some people have that allows them to do dangerous or frightening things
2 to **pluck up** or **screw up your courage** is to force yourself to be brave
◆ **courageous** [adjective] brave

courgette [noun: **courgettes**] a type of vegetable that looks like a small cucumber but is eaten cooked

courier [noun: **couriers**] someone who carries messages or packages from one place to another
[verb: **couriers, couriering, couriered**] to courier something is to send it using a courier

course [noun: **courses**]
1 a number of lessons on a particular subject: *a French course*
2 a course of treatment is medical treatment given in stages or over a period of time
3 a course is the ground that a race is run over or a game is played on: *a racecourse* • *a golf course*
4 one of the parts of a meal: *We had soup for the first course.*
5 the route or direction that something moves or travels along: *following the river's course for several miles*
6 in due course means after a while or at its proper time
7 in the course of means during something
8 you say '**of course**' when you want to agree to a request someone has made in a polite way or when you want to show that something was expected: *'Can I borrow that book for a few days?' 'Of course you can.'* • *We went on holiday and of course it rained the whole time.*

ⓘ Do not confuse the spelling of the noun **course** with the adjective **coarse**.

court [noun: **courts**]
1 a court is a building or room where judges or magistrates make decisions on legal subjects or where trials are held
2 a royal court is the place where a king or queen and the people who attend to them have their official home
3 a court is an area marked out with lines where a game such as tennis, basketball or squash is played: *an indoor tennis court*
[verb: **courts, courting, courted**] to court someone is to try to win their love or friendship
⟶ **courtship**

courteous [adjective] polite and respectful towards other people
◆ **courtesy** [noun: **courtesies**]
1 courtesy is polite behaviour towards other people
2 a courtesy is a polite action

courtier [noun: **courtiers**] someone who attends a king or queen at their official home

court-martial [noun: **court-martials** or **courts-martial**] a military trial [verb: **court-martials, court-martialling, court-martialled**] to court-martial someone in the armed forces is to put them on trial for breaking military law

courtship [noun: **courtships**] courtship is the process of or time spent winning the love of someone you want to marry

courtyard [noun: **courtyards**] an open area inside a building surrounded on all sides by walls

cousin [noun: **cousins**] the son or daughter of your aunt or uncle

cove [noun: **coves**] a small bay on the sea coast

coven [noun: **covens**] a group of witches

covenant [noun: **covenants**] a solemn agreement that people make to do or not to do something

cover [verb: **covers, covering, covered**]
1 to cover something is to put or spread something else on or over it so that it is hidden: *Mum had covered the table with a clean cloth.*
2 to cover a distance or period of time is to travel over that distance or stretch over that period of time: *We covered ten miles in three hours.* • *The history book covers the whole of Queen Victoria's reign.*
3 to cover something is to deal with it: *The local newspaper covered the story.* • *We'll need some cash to cover our expenses.*
4 to cover or **cover something up** is to hide it completely: *His actions since then had been designed to cover up the crime.*
[noun: **covers**] something that covers, hides or protects: *a bed cover* • *We had to increase our insurance cover after the extension was built.*
  ♦ **coverage** [noun] coverage is the amount of space or time given to an item of news in a newspaper or on a TV or radio programme

covert [adjective] covert actions are done in secret

covet [verb: **covets, coveting, coveted**] to covet something is to want it for yourself

  ♦ **covetous** [adjective] a covetous person wants very much to own or get things

cow [noun: **cows**]
1 a large animal kept on farms for its milk: *a dairy cow*
2 a female animal of the ox family or a female elephant or whale

coward [noun: **cowards**] someone who has no courage
  ♦ **cowardice** [noun] being a coward
  ♦ **cowardly** [adjective] behaving like a coward

cowboy [noun: **cowboys**] a man who herds cattle while on horseback, especially in the western United States

cower [verb: **cowers, cowering, cowered**] to cower is to move back because you are afraid

cowgirl [noun: **cowgirls**] a woman who herds cattle while on horseback

cowl [noun: **cowls**] a monk's hood

cowslip [noun: **cowslips**] a wild plant with yellow sweet-smelling flowers that grow on long stalks

cox [noun: **coxes**] the cox of a rowing boat or a lifeboat is the person whose job it is to steer [verb: **coxes, coxing, coxed**] to cox a boat is to steer it

coy [adjective: **coyer, coyest**] pretending to be shy: *a coy smile*

coyote [noun: **coyotes**] a type of wild dog that lives in North America

crab [noun: **crabs**] a sea animal with a broad shell and five pairs of legs. A crab has claws on its front pair of legs

crack [noun: **cracks**]
1 a narrow break or split: *This mug has a crack in it.*
2 a sudden sharp sound: *the crack of a whip*
3 to **have a crack at** something is to make an attempt to do it
[verb: **cracks, cracking, cracked**]
1 to crack is to split or break so that a small gap appears: *I'm sorry, I've cracked this cup.* • *The mirror suddenly cracked.*
2 to crack a joke is to make a joke

crackdown [noun: **crackdowns**] firm action taken against someone or something: *a crackdown on illegal street traders*

cracker [noun: **crackers**]
1 a Christmas toy made up of a paper tube which two people pull and which makes a bang or crack when it comes apart
2 a thin crisp biscuit: *cheese and crackers*

crackle [verb: **crackles, crackling, crackled**] to make a series of short cracking noises: *The fire crackled in the grate.*
[noun] these noises: *the crackle of twigs underfoot*

cradle [noun: **cradles**] a baby's bed, especially one that can be rocked from side to side
[verb: **cradles, cradling, cradled**] to cradle something is to hold it gently: *She cradled the baby in her arms.*

craft [noun: **crafts**]
1 a skill, like pottery or wood carving, in which you make something with your hands
2 a boat, ship, aeroplane or spaceship

craftsman [noun: **craftsmen**] a man who is skilled at making things with his hands
♦ **craftsmanship** [noun] the skill of a craftsman or craftswoman

craftswoman [noun: **craftswomen**] a woman who is skilled at making things with her hands

crafty [adjective: **craftier, craftiest**] a crafty person is clever at getting things done in the way they want, often by tricking or deceiving people

crag [noun: **crags**] a high steep rock or rough mass of rocks
♦ **craggy** [adjective: **craggier, craggiest**]
1 steep and rough: *a great craggy mountain*
2 someone with craggy features has lots of lines on their face

cram [verb: **crams, cramming, crammed**]
1 to cram things somewhere is to push or force them into a space that is too small: *Elizabeth tried to cram even more crisps into her mouth.*
2 if a place or container is crammed with things, it is filled very full: *All the shelves were crammed with books of every size.*
3 to cram for an exam is to learn as much as possible in the short time before you have to sit the exam

cramp [noun: **cramps**]
1 cramp is pain somewhere in your body

caused when a muscle suddenly tightens
2 cramps are pains in a muscle or muscles, especially in your stomach
[verb: **cramps, cramping, cramped**] muscles cramp when they tighten up suddenly causing pain
♦ **cramped** [adjective] a cramped space is uncomfortable because it is too small to move about in or because it is crowded with people or things

cranberry [noun: **cranberries**] a cranberry is a small red fruit with a sour taste, used to make sauces and drinks

crane [noun: **cranes**]
1 a tall machine used to lift heavy weights, for example pieces of cargo that have to be taken off a ship
2 a type of large bird with a long neck and long thin legs
[verb: **cranes, craning, craned**] if you crane your neck, you stretch your neck as far as possible so that you can get a better view of something

crane fly [noun: **crane flies**] an insect with a thin body and very long legs. Another name for a crane fly is a **daddy-long-legs**

cranium [noun: **crania** or **craniums**] your cranium is your skull

crank [noun: **cranks**]
1 a crank is a lever that you turn to make an engine or a piece of machinery move or work
2 a crank is someone who has strange ideas or behaves in an odd way
[verb: **cranks, cranking, cranked**] to crank an engine or a piece of machinery, or to **crank it up**, is to turn a lever over and over again to make it move or work
♦ **cranky** [adjective: **crankier, crankiest**] if someone is cranky, they are bad-tempered

cranny [noun: **crannies**] a narrow opening or crack, especially in a rock or wall

crash [noun: **crashes**]
1 a loud noise, especially one made when something hard hits another hard thing and causes damage: *the crash of breaking glass*
2 a crash between two vehicles is an accidental collision between them while one or both are moving: *Her parents were killed in a plane crash.*

3 a computer crash is when the computer fails because it can't process information properly or the system has been damaged

[verb: **crashes, crashing, crashed**]

1 to crash is to make a loud noise: *The crystal vase crashed to the floor.*

2 if vehicles crash, or you crash them, they are involved in an accidental collision: *A plane had crashed into the mountain.* • *Jane crashed her car last night.*

3 if a computer crashes, it stops working because it can't process information or because it has been damaged

[adjective] done in a short time to get results quickly: *a crash diet* • *a crash course in French*

crash helmet [noun: **crash helmets**] a hard helmet worn by motorcyclists or racing drivers to protect their head

crash-land [verb: **crash-lands, crash-landing, crash-landed**] if an aeroplane crash-lands, it hits the ground hard, either because it is out of control or because the pilot has to land in an emergency

• **crash-landing** [noun: **crash-landings**] an aeroplane makes a crash-landing when there is an emergency or it is out of control

crate [noun: **crates**] a wooden or plastic box used for carrying things, especially breakable things like bottles

crater [noun: **craters**]

1 a bowl-shaped hole in the ground where a bomb has exploded or a meteor has landed

2 a bowl-shaped hollow at the top of a volcano where it has erupted

cravat [noun: **cravats**] a wide strip of thin cloth that is folded and tied around the neck. Men sometimes wear cravats instead of ties

crave [verb: **craves, craving, craved**] to crave something is to want it very much

• **craving** [noun: **cravings**] if you have a craving for something, you have a strong urge to have it: *When she was pregnant she developed a craving for salty foods.*

crawl [verb: **crawls, crawling, crawled**]

1 if a person crawls, they move forwards on their hands and knees: *Pat had to crawl under the desk to get the pen she'd dropped.*

2 insects or reptiles crawl when they move

about on their legs: *Look! There's a spider crawling up the wall behind you.*

3 to crawl is to move at a very slow pace: *The traffic was crawling along at about 2 miles per hour.*

[noun]

1 a crawl is a very slow pace: *We were moving forward at a crawl.*

2 the crawl is a way of swimming where you kick your legs and swing first one arm and then the other into the water ahead of you

crayon [noun: **crayons**] a stick of coloured wax or a coloured pencil for drawing with

craze [noun: **crazes**] a fashion or pastime that is very popular for a short time: *a craze for wearing second-hand clothes*

crazy [adjective: **crazier, craziest**]

1 mad: *a crazy idea* • *I think he's gone crazy.*

2 if you are crazy about someone or something, you love them or like them very much

creak [verb: **creaks, creaking, creaked**] to creak is to make a squeaking or grating noise: *The floorboards creaked as he tried to tiptoe along the corridor.*

[noun: **creaks**] a squeaking or grating noise

• **creaky** [adjective: **creakier, creakiest**] making squeaking or grating noises: *a creaky old bed*

cream [noun: **creams**]

1 cream is a thick yellow-white liquid that forms on top of milk

2 a cream is a thick liquid that you put on your skin or hair: *suntan cream*

3 cream is a yellowish-white colour

• **creamy** [adjective: **creamier, creamiest**] containing cream or thick like cream: *a creamy dessert*

crease [noun: **creases**] a wrinkle, line or fold made by bending or crushing fabric or paper: *Always fold your trousers along the creases before you hang them up.*

[verb: **creases, creasing, creased**]

1 material that creases will crush easily so that lines or wrinkles form in it

2 to crease material or paper is to press it or bend it into lines or folds

create [verb: **creates, creating, created**] to create something is to make it or invent it, or to

make it happen or exist: *They created a big fuss until they got what they wanted.*
* **creation** [noun: **creations**]
1 the creation of something is making it: *the creation of the universe*
2 a creation is something new that has been made: *one of the designer's latest creations*
* **creative** [adjective] a creative person has the skill and imagination to make new things, especially works of art
* **creativity** [noun] creativity is the talent or imagination to make or invent things
* **creator** [noun: **creators**] someone who makes something new
creature [noun: **creatures**] a living thing that is able to move about. Animals are creatures, but plants are not
crèche [noun: **crèches**] a place where very young children are looked after together while their parents are elsewhere
credible [adjective] something credible can be believed
credit [noun: **credits**]
1 credit is a system used in shops and businesses where customers can get things now and pay for them later
2 your bank account is in credit when you have money in it
3 if people give you credit for something good, they give you praise or approval because of it
4 the credits are the list at the end of a film or television programme of all the people who worked on it
[verb: **credits, crediting, credited**]
1 to credit some money to an account is to put it there: *The phone company will credit my account with £25 to apologize for their mistake.*
2 to credit someone with an achievement or a good quality is to say that they have done it or have it
3 to credit something is to believe it: *You wouldn't credit how many times we got lost.*
* **creditable** [adjective] good enough to deserve praise or respect: *a very creditable performance*
credit card [noun: **credit cards**] a small plastic card that allows you to buy things when you want them and to pay for them later

credit cards

Here are some important words and expressions that you may come across when you are using a credit card:
• An **account** is an arrangement you have with a company that gives you a credit card that allows you to buy things and pay the company later.
• An **annual fee** is an amount of money you may have to pay every year to the company that gives you a credit card.
• The **APR** or **annual percentage rate** is a figure that shows you how much interest you would pay over a whole year if you borrow money. It is best to use this figure to compare the cost of using different cards, because sometimes the figures that companies use in their adverts are based on shorter periods and can be misleading.
• Your **balance** is the amount that you owe the credit-card company.
• A **charge** is a payment that you have to make to the credit-card company.
• Your **credit limit** is the amount of money you can spend using the card.
• **Interest** is extra money that you have to pay to the company if you borrow money.
• The **interest rate** is the amount of extra money you have to pay back for each £100 that you borrow.
• The **minimum payment** is the smallest amount that you have to pay when the company sends you a statement.
• A **statement** is a letter that the credit-card company sends you telling you how much you have spent and how much you have to pay them.

creed [noun: **creeds**] something that you believe in, especially the religious beliefs that you have
creek [noun: **creeks**] a short or narrow river
creep [verb: **creeps, creeping, crept**]
1 to creep is to move forwards slowly and quietly: *He crept downstairs in the middle of the night.*
2 animals that creep move slowly with their bodies close to the ground
[noun: **creeps**]

1 someone who is unpleasant or weird
2 if someone or something **gives you the creeps**, they make you shiver with disgust or fear

♦ **creeper** [noun: **creepers**] a plant that grows over the ground or up a wall

♦ **creepy** [adjective: **creepier, creepiest**] a creepy place or person makes you shiver with fear or disgust

cremate [verb: **cremates, cremating, cremated**] to cremate a dead person is to burn their body rather than bury it

♦ **cremation** [noun: **cremations**] the burning of a dead body or dead bodies

♦ **crematorium** [noun: **crematoriums** or **crematoria**] a building where dead people's bodies are burned

creosote [noun] a type of thick dark brown paint made from wood tar and used to stop wood rotting

crêpe [noun] a thin fabric with a wrinkled surface: *a crêpe bandage*

crêpe paper [noun] a type of thin wrinkled paper used for decoration or for wrapping things in

crept [verb] a way of changing the verb **creep** to make a past tense. It can be used with or without a helping verb: *They crept up on him and said 'Boo!'. • We had crept in unnoticed.*

crescendo [noun: **crescendos**]
1 if sounds reach a crescendo, they grow louder and louder until they are at their loudest
2 in a piece of music, a crescendo is a place where the music gets louder

crescent [noun: **crescents**]
1 a curved shape which comes to a point at each end and is wider in the middle, like the shape of the moon at certain times of the month
2 a curved street

cress [noun] a small green plant with peppery-tasting leaves which are used in salads and sandwiches

crest [noun: **crests**]
1 the crest of a wave or hill is its highest point
2 the feathers that stick up on the top of some birds' heads
3 a family's or organization's badge or emblem

crestfallen [adjective] if someone is crestfallen, they look sad and disappointed

because something they had hoped for or had being trying to do has not turned out well

crevasse [noun: **crevasses**] a deep crack in ice

crevice [noun: **crevices**] a thin crack or opening in rock

crew [1] [noun: **crews**] a group of people who work together, especially on a ship or aeroplane: *The lifeboat has a crew of five. • The film crew were busy setting up lights and cameras.*
[verb: **crews, crewing, crewed**] to crew a boat or ship is to work as a member of its crew

crew [2] [verb] a way of changing the verb **crow** to make a past tense: *The cock crew.*

crewcut [noun: **crewcuts**] a very short hairstyle for men and boys, first used in the army and navy

crib [noun: **cribs**] a small cot for a baby
[verb: **cribs, cribbing, cribbed**] to crib is to copy someone else's work and pretend it is your own

crick [noun: **cricks**] if you have a crick in your neck, your neck feels stiff and painful because the muscles have tightened up

cricket [1] [noun] a game played outdoors between two sides of eleven players with a wooden bat and ball

cricket [2] [noun: **crickets**] a small insect that lives in grass. A cricket makes a high-pitched whirring sound by rubbing its wings together

cricketer [noun: **cricketers**] someone who plays cricket

cried [verb] a way of changing the verb **cry** to make a past tense. It can be used with or without a helping verb: *The baby cried and cried. • He had cried all day.*

cries [noun] the plural of the noun **cry**: *No one heard their cries for help.*
[verb] the form of the verb **cry** in the present tense that you use with **he**, **she**, or **it**: *She always cries when she watches romantic films.*

crime [noun: **crimes**]
1 a crime is an illegal activity such as robbery, murder, assault or dangerous driving
Someone who has committed a crime can be punished by law
2 crime is all these activities

Cc

✦ **criminal** [noun: **criminals**] someone who has committed a crime
[adjective]
1 to do with crime or criminals: *a criminal court*
2 against the law or very wrong: *a criminal act*

crimson [noun] a bright red colour

cringe [verb: **cringes, cringing, cringed**]
1 to cringe is to crouch or back away from something in fear: *The dog cringed and showed its teeth.*
2 if something you or someone else has done makes you cringe, it makes you feel very embarrassed

crinkle [noun: **crinkles**] a small crease or wrinkle
[verb: **crinkles, crinkling, crinkled**] to crinkle something is to form small creases or wrinkles in it
✦ **crinkly** [adjective: **crinklier, crinkliest**] having lots of small creases or wrinkles

cripple [verb: **cripples, crippling, crippled**]
1 an injury or disease cripples someone if it causes damage to their body, or part of their body, which stops them moving about normally
2 to cripple something is to damage it so that it cannot function properly: *The long war had crippled the country.*
✦ **crippled** [adjective]
1 unable to move about normally: *a crippled bird with a broken wing*
2 so badly damaged it cannot work normally: *The crippled warship limped back into port.*

crisis [noun: **crises**] a very difficult or dangerous time or event

crisp [adjective: **crisper, crispest**]
1 stiff or hard and easily broken: *nice crisp salad leaves*
2 crisp weather is frosty and dry
[noun: **crisps**] a thin slice of potato that has been fried in oil until it is crisp: *a bag of crisps*
✦ **crispness** [noun] being crisp
✦ **crispy** [adjective: **crispier, crispiest**] hard or firm enough to break easily: *a crispy sugar topping*

criss-cross [verb: **criss-crosses, criss-crossing, criss-crossed**] things criss-cross when they cross each other again and again to form a pattern of crossed lines

critic [noun: **critics**]
1 someone who finds faults in something: *a critic of the government*
2 someone who writes about new books, films, music or shows and says what is good or bad about them
✦ **critical** [adjective] to be critical of something is to say what you think its faults are
✦ **criticism** [noun: **criticisms**]
1 criticism is pointing out faults: *Try not to be hurt by criticism.*
2 a criticism is a statement about a fault you think someone or something has: *My only criticism is the story is too long.*
✦ **criticize** or **criticise** [verb: **criticizes, criticizing, criticized**] to criticize something is to say what you think its faults are: *It always hurts when you criticize me.*

croak [verb: **croaks, croaking, croaked**]
1 to croak is to speak in a hoarse voice because your throat is sore or dry
2 a frog croaks when it makes its deep harsh sound
[noun: **croaks**]
1 the sound made by a frog or toad
2 a low hoarse voice
✦ **croaky** [adjective: **croakier, croakiest**] a croaky voice is deep and hoarse

crochet [noun] crochet is a type of knitting in which stitches are made by twisting thread or wool around a single needle with a hook on the end
[verb: **crochets, crocheting, crocheted**] to crochet is to make something out of wool or thread using a single needle to make the stitches

ⓘ This word is pronounced **cro**-shay.

crockery [noun] crockery is plates, bowls and cups used for eating food

crocodile [noun: **crocodiles**]
1 a large reptile with thick skin, a long tail and big jaws. Crocodiles are found mainly in Africa and Australia and live in rivers and lakes
2 if you **cry** or **shed crocodile tears**, you pretend to be sorry about something when you are really quite pleased about it

crocus [noun: **crocuses**] a small plant that grows from a bulb and has white, purple or yellow flowers that come out in the spring

croft [noun: **crofts**] a small farm in the Scottish Highlands with a cottage and a small amount of land

♦ **crofter** [noun: **crofters**] someone who lives and works on a croft

croissant [noun: **croissants**] a flaky crescent-shaped bread roll

crook [noun: **crooks**]
1 a crook is a criminal or someone who behaves dishonestly
2 the crook of your arm or leg is the part at the inside of your elbow or the back of your knee that curves inwards
3 a stick carried by a shepherd, which has a curved top that he uses for catching sheep by their necks
[verb: **crooks, crooking, crooked**] to crook something is to bend it or form it into a curve: *He crooked one eyebrow and looked at me.*

♦ **crooked** [adjective] bent or forming a curve

ⓘ **Crooked** is pronounced **crook**-id.

crop [noun: **crops**]
1 crops are plants that are gathered or harvested for food from fields, trees or bushes
2 a crop is a particular kind of plant or fruit that grows and is harvested at one time: *We'll get a good crop of apples this year.*
3 a riding crop is a short whip used by jockeys and horse riders
[verb: **crops, cropping, cropped**]
1 to crop something is to cut it short
2 when something **crops up**, it happens without being expected or planned

cropper [noun] if you are doing something dangerous or illegal and you **come a cropper**, you have an accident or you are caught out

croquet [noun] a game played on a lawn with wooden balls that the players hit through metal hoops using long wooden hammers called mallets

ⓘ This word is pronounced **kro**-kay.

cross [noun: **crosses**]
1 a shape made when two straight lines go over each other at a point in the middle, ✗ or +

2 a symbol used in the Christian religion to stand for the cross on which Christ was crucified
3 a mixture of two things, especially an animal or plant that has been bred from two different animals or plants: *A mule is a cross between a donkey and a horse.*
[verb: **crosses, crossing, crossed**]
1 to cross something is to go over it from one side to the other: *cross a bridge*
2 if one thing crosses another, they meet at a certain point and go on beyond it: *at the place where the road crosses the railway line*
3 to cross things is to put one across and on top of the other: *cross your fingers*
4 to **cross something out** is to draw a line or lines through it because you want to get rid of it or to replace it with something else: *He crossed out John's name and wrote in his own.*
[adjective: **crosser, crossest**] annoyed or angry: *I got very cross when he didn't turn up.*

crossbar [noun: **crossbars**]
1 the crossbar on a man's bike is the horizontal piece of metal between the saddle and the handlebars
2 the crossbar on a goal is the horizontal piece of wood between the uprights

crossbow [noun: **crossbows**] a weapon for shooting arrows with a bow string stretched horizontally on a cross-shaped frame

cross-country [adjective] a cross-country race is one where the runners go across the countryside rather than along a road or track

cross-examination [noun: **cross-examinations**] a series of questions asked to check whether earlier answers are the same

cross-examine [verb: **cross-examines, cross-examining, cross-examined**] to cross-examine someone is to ask them questions so that their answers can be compared with answers they had given earlier

cross-eyed [adjective] a cross-eyed person has eyes that look towards their nose instead of straight ahead

crossfire [noun] crossfire is gunfire coming from different directions

crossing [noun: **crossings**]
1 a place where a road or river can be crossed
2 a journey made by a ship between two

pieces of land: *a short ferry crossing from Mull to Iona*

crossly [adverb] angrily

cross-purposes [plural noun] if two people are at cross-purposes, they are talking about different things though they think they mean the same thing

cross-reference [noun: **cross-references**] a note in a dictionary or encyclopedia that tells you to look at another entry for more information

crossroads [noun] a place where two or more roads meet

cross-section [noun: **cross-sections**]
1 a cut made through a solid object so that you can see the structure inside, or a picture of this
2 a cross-section of a group of people or things is a sample that includes all the different types of people or things: *a cross-section of the public*

crossword [noun: **crosswords**] a word game where you fill in words or letters on a grid by solving clues

crotch [noun: **crotches**] the area of your body or of your trousers that is between your legs where the tops of your legs join your body

crouch [verb: **crouches, crouching, crouched**] you crouch when you bend your legs and back so that your body is close to the ground

crow[1] [noun: **crows**] a large black bird that makes a loud, harsh sound

crow[2] [verb: **crows, crowing, crowed** or **crew**]
1 when a cock crows, it makes a loud sound, especially early in the morning
2 to crow is to boast: *He was crowing about his success.*

crowbar [noun: **crowbars**] a heavy metal bar curved at one end that is used as a lever

crowd [noun: **crowds**] a large number of people or things gathered in one place: *a football crowd • crowds of shoppers*
[verb: **crowds, crowding, crowded**] if people or things crowd in, or crowd into a place, they fill it up so that there is hardly any space left
• **crowded** [adjective] full of people or things: *a crowded street*

crown [noun: **crowns**]
1 an ornament, often made of gold and studded with jewels, worn by a king or queen on their head during formal occasions
2 the top of something such as your head or a hill
[verb: **crowns, crowning, crowned**]
1 a king or queen is crowned when they are made the monarch of a country in a ceremony where a crown is put on their head
2 to crown something is to add something on top: *We had a very long tiring journey and, to crown it all, our luggage was lost at the airport.*
⟶ **coronation**

crow's-nest [noun: **crow's nests**] the place at the top of a ship's mast where a sailor goes to get a view of things far away

crucial [adjective] of great importance: *a crucial exam*

crucifix [noun: **crucifixes**] a cross with a figure of Christ on it, used as a symbol of the Christian religion
• **crucifixion** [noun: **crucifixions**] fastening someone's hands and feet to a large wooden cross and leaving them to die. Crucifixion was often used as a punishment by the ancient Romans and Christ was killed in this way
• **crucify** [verb: **crucifies, crucifying, crucified**] to crucify someone is to fasten their hands and feet to a large wooden cross and leave them to die

crude [adjective: **cruder, crudest**]
1 made or done in a rough or simple way: *a crude map drawn on the back of an envelope*
2 crude oil is as it is when it came out of the ground and has not been refined
3 rude or vulgar: *a crude joke*
• **crudely** [adverb] roughly or simply: *a crudely made table*

cruel [adjective: **crueller, cruellest**] someone who is cruel causes pain or suffering to other people without showing any pity
• **cruelly** [adverb] in a cruel way or with cruelty
• **cruelty** [noun] being cruel

cruet [noun: **cruets**] a container for holding small jars of pepper, salt and mustard put on a table during meals

cruise [verb: **cruises, cruising, cruised**] to

cruise is to travel by ship, plane or car at a steady speed
[noun: **cruises**] a holiday spent on a ship, travelling from one port to another
♦ **cruiser** [noun: **cruisers**] a kind of fast warship

crumb [noun: **crumbs**]
1 crumbs are small pieces of bread, cake or biscuit
2 a crumb of something is a tiny piece of it: *a crumb of comfort*

crumble [verb: **crumbles, crumbling, crumbled**] to crumble is to break down into small pieces: *The walls of the old house were crumbling.* • *Crumble the biscuit on top of the fruit.*
♦ **crumbly** [adjective: **crumblier, crumbliest**] breaking down easily into small pieces the size of crumbs: *dry crumbly soil*

crumpet [noun: **crumpets**] a type of small thick pancake with holes in the top

crumple [verb: **crumples, crumpling, crumpled**] to crumple something is to crush it or squeeze it so that lots of wrinkles or folds are made in it: *He crumpled the piece of paper and threw it in the bin.*

crunch [verb: **crunches, crunching, crunched**]
1 if you crunch food, you make a crushing noise as you break it up with your teeth
2 to crunch is to make a crushing or grinding noise: *The snow crunched under our feet.*
[noun: **crunches**]
1 a crushing or grinding noise: *the crunch of feet on the gravel path*
2 to **come to the crunch** is to reach the point when you must make a decision of some kind
♦ **crunchy** [adjective: **crunchier, crunchiest**] crunchy food is hard and brittle: *a crunchy biscuit*

crusade [noun: **crusades**] a campaign, often over a long period of time, in which people try to achieve something that they feel strongly about
♦ **crusader** [noun: **crusaders**] someone who goes on a crusade

crush [verb: **crushes, crushing, crushed**]
1 to crush something is to press it or squash it so that it is broken or damaged: *His leg was crushed by a falling rock.*

2 to crush something is to grind it or press it into a pulp or powder: *Crush two cloves of garlic.*
[noun: **crushes**]
1 a crush is a crowd of people squeezed tightly together
2 to **have a crush on** someone, especially someone older, is to feel love for them, usually only for a short time
♦ **crushed** [adjective]
1 broken or squashed by a heavy weight: *crushed ice*
2 completely defeated and miserable: *Mayssa felt crushed by their criticism.*

crust [noun: **crusts**]
1 a crisp top or surface that forms on something, for example on bread or pastry as it bakes in the oven: *Cut the crusts off two slices of bread.*
2 the Earth's crust is its outside surface
➡ **crusty**

crustacean [noun: **crustaceans**] a sea animal with a hard outer shell, for example a crab, lobster or shrimp

crusty [adjective: **crustier, crustiest**] having a crisp baked crust: *a delicious crusty pie*

crutch [noun: **crutches**] a stick held under your armpit or elbow to support you if you have an injured leg or foot

cry [verb: **cries, crying, cried**]
1 to cry is to shout: *She cried out in pain.*
2 you cry when tears fall from your eyes, and often you make a sobbing or wailing sound at the same time
[noun: **cries**]
1 a shout
2 if people say that one thing is **a far cry** from another, they mean it comes nowhere near or is nothing like that other thing

crypt [noun: **crypts**] an underground room built beneath a church

cryptic [adjective] having a hidden meaning or answer that is difficult to work out: *a cryptic crossword clue*

crystal [noun: **crystals**]
1 a small, shaped part of a solid material that is formed naturally, for example in salt or ice or a mineral
2 a kind of high-quality glass
♦ **crystallize** or **crystallise** [verb:

Cc

crystallizes, crystallizing, crystallized] a substance crystallizes when it forms crystals

cub [noun: **cubs**]
1 a baby lion, tiger, bear or wolf
2 a member of the Cub Scouts, the junior branch of the Scout Association

cube [noun: **cubes**] a solid shape with six equally sized square sides

cubic [adjective]
1 shaped like a cube
2 a cubic measurement is one used to measure volume. For example, a cubic metre is a space one metre long, one metre wide and one metre high

cubicle [noun: **cubicles**] a small enclosed area that has enough space for one person to stand in, for example when they are changing their clothes

cuboid [noun: **cuboids**] a solid shape with six faces that are all rectangular

cuckoo [noun: **cuckoos**] a bird that gets its name from the call it makes. The female cuckoo lays her eggs in other birds' nests

cucumber [noun: **cucumbers**] a long green vegetable that is usually sliced and eaten raw in salads

cud [noun] a cow, goat or deer chews the cud when it brings partly digested food back up from its stomach to chew again

cuddle [verb: **cuddles, cuddling, cuddled**] to cuddle someone is to hold them in your arms to show your love and affection for them
[noun: **cuddles**] if you give someone a cuddle, you put your arms around them and hold them closely
✦ **cuddly** [adjective: **cuddlier, cuddliest**] a cuddly person or thing makes you want to cuddle them

cudgel [noun: **cudgels**] a heavy stick

cue[1] [noun: **cues**]
1 a signal to a performer to start doing something
2 if something happens **on cue**, it happens at exactly the right moment

cue[2] [noun: **cues**] a long tapered stick used to play snooker and billiards

cuff [noun: **cuffs**] a cuff is the end of a sleeve where it fits tightly around your wrist
[verb: **cuffs, cuffing, cuffed**] to cuff someone is to hit them with your hand

cufflinks [plural noun] cufflinks are decorative fasteners for shirt cuffs

cuisine [noun: **cuisines**] a particular style of cooking: *French cuisine*

cul-de-sac [noun: **cul-de-sacs**] a street that is blocked at one end

cull [noun: **culls**] a cull is the organized killing of a number of animals: *a badger cull*
[verb: **culls, culling, culled**] to cull animals is to kill them

culminate [verb: **culminates, culminating, culminated**] if an event culminates in something, that is its final or most important point: *The celebrations culminated in a fireworks display.*
✦ **culmination** [noun] the end of something

culprit [noun: **culprits**] someone who is responsible for doing something bad

cult [noun: **cults**]
1 a religion, especially one with secret or strange beliefs and rituals
2 someone or something that becomes very popular or fashionable
[adjective] very popular or fashionable with a particular group of people: *a cult TV show* • *a band with a cult following*

cultivate [verb: **cultivates, cultivating, cultivated**]
1 to cultivate land is to prepare it so that you can grow things on it
2 to cultivate a crop is to grow it and look after it
3 to cultivate something is to work at it so that it grows or develops: *cultivate a friendship*
✦ **cultivation** [noun] preparing land to grow crops, or growing and looking after crops

cultural [adjective] to do with culture, especially art, music and literature

culture [noun: **cultures**]
1 a culture is a society with its own customs and beliefs that make it different from other people or societies
2 culture is things like music, literature and painting that you learn about to develop your mind
✦ **cultured** [adjective] a cultured person is well educated in things like art, music and literature

cumbersome [adjective] awkward to carry or awkward to deal with

cunning [noun] someone who has cunning has the ability to get what they want by secret and clever planning
[adjective] sly and clever: *I have a cunning plan.*

cup [noun: **cups**]
1 a small container with a handle that you drink out of: *cups and saucers*
2 a decorated metal object or container used as a prize in a competition: *the World Cup*
[verb: **cups, cupping, cupped**] to cup your hands is to put them together and bend them into a bowl shape

cupboard [noun: **cupboards**] a box with shelves, either built into a wall or standing on the floor, used to store things in

cupful [noun: **cupfuls**] the amount a cup will hold

curable [adjective] a curable disease can be cured

curate [noun: **curates**] a priest whose job is to help a parish priest

curator [noun: **curators**] a person in charge of a museum or gallery

curb [verb: **curbs, curbing, curbed**] to curb something is to control it or hold it back: *He tried hard to curb his spending.*

curd [noun: **curds**]
1 curd is milk that has been thickened by adding acid to it
2 curds are the slightly solid lumps separated out from milk and used to make cheese. The liquid left over is called **whey**

curdle [verb: **curdles, curdling, curdled**]
1 milk curdles when it thickens because it has gone bad
2 if something makes your blood curdle, it terrifies you

cure [verb: **cures, curing, cured**]
1 to cure a disease or illness is to make it go away
2 to cure a problem is to solve it and make it go away
3 to cure meat is to put salt on it or dry it to make it last longer
[noun: **cures**] something that makes a disease or illness go away: *a cure for cancer*
➝ **curable**

curfew [noun: **curfews**] an official order that people must stay inside their houses after a certain time or between certain hours

curiosity [noun: **curiosities**]
1 curiosity is being eager to find out about something
2 a curiosity is something strange and interesting

curious [adjective]
1 if you are curious about something, you want to know about it: *I was curious to hear her side of the story.*
2 if something is curious, it is strange or difficult to understand

curl [noun: **curls**] a soft twist or ring of hair: *blonde curls*
[verb: **curls, curling, curled**]
1 to curl hair is to form soft twists or rings in it
2 smoke curls when it moves upwards in twisted or curving shapes
3 to **curl up** is to tuck your legs and arms in close to your body and bend your back in a curve
✦ **curler** [noun: **curlers**]
1 a tube of plastic or sponge that hair is wound around to make it curly
2 someone who plays the game of curling

curling [noun] a game played by sliding heavy round stones over ice towards a target

curly [adjective: **curlier, curliest**] having a curl or curls: *a curly tail* • *curly hair*

currant [noun: **currants**] a small dried grape

currency [noun: **currencies**] the money used in a particular country: *The euro is the new European currency.*

current [adjective] something is current if it exists or is happening now: *the current job market*
[noun: **currents**]
1 a current is a flow of water or air going in one direction
2 an electric current is a flow of electricity through a wire or circuit

ⓘ Be careful not to confuse the spellings of **current** and **currant**.

current account [noun: **current accounts**] a bank account that allows you to take money out at any time

Cc

Cc

current affairs [plural noun] important political events that are happening at the present time

curriculum [noun: **curriculums** or **curricula**] a curriculum is a course of study or all the courses of study at a school or college

curry [noun: **curries**] a type of food cooked with spices: *chicken curry*

curse [noun: **curses**]
1 a swear word
2 if someone puts a curse on you, they say a magic spell that will make you have bad luck
3 something you have to put up with even though it is hard
[verb: **curses, cursing, cursed**]
1 to curse is to use swear words
2 to curse someone or something is to complain angrily about them

cursor [noun: **cursors**] a flashing mark on a computer screen that shows you where to start keying in information

curt [adjective] short and sounding unfriendly: *a curt reply*

curtain [noun: **curtains**] a long piece of material that can be drawn or dropped across a window, stage or cinema screen

curtsy or **curtsey** [verb: **curtsies, curtsying, curtsied** or **curtseys, curtseying, curtseyed**] a woman or girl curtsies when she bends her knees with one leg behind the other: *All the girls curtsied to the princess.*
[noun: **curtsies**] a curtsy is this movement, made to show respect to someone

curve [noun: **curves**] a curve is a line that bends
[verb: **curves, curving, curved**] to curve is to bend

cushion [noun: **cushions**]
1 a soft plump pad of material that you sit on, rest against or kneel on
2 something that gives protection or keeps something off a hard surface: *The hovercraft moves along on a cushion of air.*
[verb: **cushions, cushioning, cushioned**] to cushion a blow is to make it less painful

cushy [adjective: **cushier, cushiest**] easy to do: *a cushy job*

custard [noun] a thick dessert made from eggs, milk or cream, and sugar

custody [noun]
1 someone who is in custody is being kept in a cell until they can be charged with a crime
2 to have custody of children is to be responsible for looking after them: *After the divorce Kathy was granted custody of their two children.*

custom [noun: **customs**]
1 a custom is something that people usually or traditionally do: *Japanese customs • It is my custom to walk to the station each morning.*
2 you give a shop your custom when you buy things from it
✦ **customary** [adjective] something that is customary is usual or is done by custom

custom-built or **custom-made** [adjective] something that is custom-built is built for a particular purpose

customer [noun: **customers**] a person who buys things or services from a shop or business

customize or **customise** [verb: **customizes, customizing, customized**] to customize something is to make changes to it so that it suits an individual person: *The company customizes cars for disabled people.*

customs [noun] customs is the place where you have your luggage inspected when you travel to and from a foreign country

cut [verb: **cuts, cutting, cut**]
1 to cut something is to divide it, separate it, make a hole in it or shape it, using scissors, a knife or some other sharp instrument
2 to make something less: *My salary has been cut.*
3 to **cut off** something such as gas or electricity is to stop it being supplied to a home
4 if someone tells you to **cut it out**, they are telling you to stop doing something
[noun]
1 a split or small wound made by something sharp
2 a reduction: *a price cut*
3 a share of something
➡ **cutting**

cute [adjective: **cuter, cutest**]
1 attractive or pretty: *a cute little puppy*
2 smart or clever: *Don't try to be cute with me.*

cutlass [noun: **cutlasses**] a curved sword that is sharp along only one edge

cutlery [noun] cutlery is knives, forks and spoons

cutlet [noun: **cutlets**] a piece of meat cut from a larger piece: *lamb cutlets*

cutting [noun: **cuttings**]
1 an article cut out of a newspaper or magazine
2 a piece cut off a plant from which a new plant will grow
[adjective] meant to hurt someone's feelings: *a cutting remark*

CV [abbreviation: **CVs**] short for **curriculum vitae**. Someone's curriculum vitae is a document that gives details of their education and working career

cyanide [noun] a kind of deadly poison

cyber- [prefix] if a word starts with **cyber-** it has something to do with communication by computers and other electronic devices, as happens on the Internet. For example, *cyberspace* is the space used in electronic communication rather than real space

cycle [verb: **cycles, cycling, cycled**] to cycle is to ride a bicycle
[noun: **cycles**]
1 a bicycle
2 a series of things that happen one after the other and then start again: *the cycle of the seasons*

◆ **cyclist** [noun: **cyclists**] someone riding a bicycle

cyclone [noun: **cyclones**] a large storm that happens in tropical countries, with high winds circling round a calm centre called the eye of the storm

cygnet [noun: **cygnets**] a baby swan

cylinder [noun: **cylinders**] a solid shape with a round top and bottom and straight sides
◆ **cylindrical** [adjective] shaped like a cylinder

cymbals [plural noun] a musical instrument made up of two circles of brass that you play by banging them together to make a musical sound

cynic [noun: **cynics**] someone who sees something bad in everyone and everything no matter how good they may be
◆ **cynical** [adjective] a cynical person believes the worst about everyone and everything
◆ **cynicism** [noun] believing bad things about everyone and everything, no matter how good they may seem

cypress [noun: **cypresses**] a type of tall tree with dark green needles

cyst [noun: **cysts**] a lump filled with liquid on or just under the skin

czar [noun: **czars**] another spelling of **tsar**

czarina [noun: **czarinas**] another spelling of **tsarina**

D

dab [verb: **dabs, dabbing, dabbed**] to touch something lightly with your fingers or with something soft: *Dab your eyes with a tissue.*
[noun: **dabs**] a light touch of something: *a dab of blusher on each cheek*

dabble [verb: **dabbles, dabbling, dabbled**] to dabble in an activity is to do it for fun but not very seriously: *He was a rich man who dabbled in many hobbies that happened to take his fancy.*

dachshund [noun: **dachshunds**] a type of dog with short legs and a long body

dad or **daddy** [noun: **dads** or **daddies**] a word that people use for **father**, especially when speaking. Daddy is mainly used by children: *Thanks to all the mums and dads who have helped.* • *Give daddy a hug.*

daffodil [noun: **daffodils**] a yellow flower that grows from a bulb and blooms in spring

daft [adjective: **dafter, daftest**] silly: *a daft thing to do* • *Don't be daft!*

dagger [noun: **daggers**] a knife like a small sword

daily [adjective] happening or done every day: *a daily newspaper*
[adverb] every day: *We met daily for a month.*
[noun: **dailies**] a newspaper that is published every weekday

dainty [adjective: **daintier, daintiest**] small and neat

dairy [noun: **dairies**] a place where products like butter and cheese are made from milk
[adjective] dairy farming is keeping cows to produce milk

daisy [noun: **daisies**] a type of small white flower with a yellow centre. Daisies often grow wild in grass

dale [noun: **dales**] a valley

Dalmatian [noun: **Dalmatians**] a type of large dog that has a white coat with dark spots

dam [noun: **dams**] a wall across a river that holds a lot of the water back
[verb: **dams, damming, dammed**] to build a wall across a river to stop it from flowing naturally

damage [noun] damage is any kind of harm that has been done: *The storm caused a lot of damage.*
[verb: **damages, damaging, damaged**] to hurt, spoil or break something: *The book was damaged in the post.*
♦ **damages** [plural noun] an amount of money that someone gets to make up for a loss or injury they have suffered: *She was awarded damages of £5000.*

dame [noun: **dames**]
1 in Britain, a title that the government or the Queen can give to a woman who has done something very good
2 the character of an old woman in a pantomime. It is usually played by a man

damn [interjection] an impolite word that someone who is very irritated might use
[verb: **damns, damning, damned**] to blame someone or say that they are very bad

damp [adjective: **damper, dampest**] a bit wet: *Wipe with a damp cloth.*
[noun] slight wetness: *a patch of damp on the wall*

damp course or **damp-proof course**

[noun: **damp courses** or **damp-proof courses**] a layer of waterproof material put into a wall near the bottom to stop damp rising up the wall

dampen [verb: **dampens, dampening, dampened**] to make something a bit wet: *Dampen the brush before using it.*

damson [noun: **damsons**] a type of small plum

dance [verb: **dances, dancing, danced**] to move your feet to a rhythm, usually in music
[noun: **dances**]
1 a set of steps that you do to some kind of music
2 a party for dancing
♦ **dancer** [noun: **dancers**] someone who dances

dandelion [noun: **dandelions**] a yellow flower that is a common weed in people's gardens

dandruff [noun] tiny dry flakes of dead skin that can collect near the roots of your hair: *an anti-dandruff shampoo*

danger [noun: **dangers**]
1 a danger is something that may harm or injure you: *the dangers of skiing*
2 danger is a situation when something may harm or injure you: *He knew that his life was in danger.*
♦ **dangerous** [adjective]
1 likely to hurt someone: *a dangerous substance*
2 risky: *It's dangerous to play near the railway.*
♦ **dangerously** [adverb] in a way that could be harmful: *driving dangerously close to the edge*

dangle [verb: **dangles, dangling, dangled**] to hang down loosely: *Her hair dangled in her eyes.* • *We sat on the edge, dangling our legs in the water.*

dank [adjective: **danker, dankest**] a dank place is wet and cold

dappled [adjective] covered with patches of light or colour: *a dappled horse*

dare [verb: **dares, daring, dared**]
1 to dare someone to do something is to challenge them to do it: *I dare you to do that again!*
2 to dare or **dare to** do something is to be

brave enough to do it: *Rachel wouldn't dare argue with the boss.* • *Only a fool would to dare to do that.*
3 if you **dare not** or **daren't** do something, you are not brave enough to do it: *I daren't tell you what happened.*

daredevil [noun: **daredevils**] a person who enjoys danger and taking risks
[adjective] dangerous or risky: *a daredevil project*

daring [adjective] bold and brave: *a daring rescue attempt*

dark [adjective: **darker, darkest**]
1 without light: *a dark room*
2 strong or deep in colour: *dark blue* • *dark hair*
3 gloomy, sad or miserable
[noun]
1 where there is no light: *I'm not afraid of the dark.*
2 nightfall: *Don't go out after dark without a torch.*
3 if you are **in the dark** about something, you know nothing about it
♦ **darken** [verb: **darkens, darkening, darkened**] to get or make darker: *The sky darkened as the rain moved nearer.*
♦ **darkness** [noun] where there is no light: *a tiny point of light in the darkness*

darling [noun: **darlings**]
1 someone you care very much about: *Darling, what's the matter?*
2 someone's favourite: *The child had been her darling since his first day in the class.*

darn [verb: **darns, darning, darned**] to mend a hole, for example in a sock, by sewing long stitches in one direction and weaving more stitches through them

dart [verb: **darts, darting, darted**] to move somewhere fast: *A child darted out of the door as I entered.*
[noun: **darts**] a little arrow that can be fired as a weapon or thrown in a game
♦ **darts** [noun] a game where you throw small arrow-shaped objects at a round board called a dartboard that has scores on it

dash [verb: **dashes, dashing, dashed**] to hurry somewhere: *I've got to dash to the shops.*
[noun: **dashes**]
1 a rush to get somewhere: *a mad dash to the airport*

Dd

Dd

2 a small amount of something that you add to food or drink: *Add a dash of vinegar.*

3 a short line (–), sometimes used between words in a text as a punctuation mark: *You could use a dash instead of a colon there.*

dashboard [noun: **dashboards**] the panel in front of the driver in a car, containing dials or gauges for things like speed, petrol and oil

data [noun] information or facts

ⓘ **Data** is the plural of **datum**. The singular, **datum**, is not often used. In fact, **data** is usually used with a singular verb, although it is a plural noun: *The data is clear.*

database [noun: **databases**] information that is stored on a computer in lists or tables

date¹ [noun: **dates**]

1 the number of the day of the month, the month and the year: *The date today is 30 July.*

2 a particular day of a particular month and year: *What is your date of birth?*

3 an arrangement to go out with someone: *Polly's got another date with Chris tonight.*

[verb: **dates, dating, dated**]

1 to write a date on a letter or other document: *The letter was dated 3rd May.*

2 to belong to a certain time: *Our house dates from the nineteenth century.*

3 to decide how old something is: *The ring's very old but I couldn't date it exactly.*

4 to look old-fashioned: *Shoes always date very quickly.*

date² [noun: **dates**] a small, dark fruit with a stone that grows on some palm trees

daub [verb: **daubs, daubing, daubed**] to spread something like paint on a surface untidily and unevenly

daughter [noun: **daughters**] someone's female child: *She was the daughter of a poet.*

daughter-in-law [noun: **daughters-in-law**] your son's wife

daunt [verb: **daunts, daunting, daunted**] if something daunts you, it puts you off because it is big, dangerous or difficult: *daunted by the cost of the project*

♦ **daunting** [adjective] so big, dangerous or difficult that it puts you off: *the daunting height of the next jump*

dawdle [verb: **dawdles, dawdling, dawdled**] if you dawdle, you walk or do something slowly

dawn [noun: **dawns**] the beginning of the day, when it gets light

[verb: **dawns, dawning, dawned**]

1 to start: *A new age has dawned.*

2 if something **dawns on** you, you suddenly realize it: *It dawned on him that he could pay someone else to do this.*

day [noun: **days**]

1 the time when it is light between sunrise and sunset: *We spent the whole day on the beach.*

2 the twenty-four hours between one midnight and another: *There are 365 days in a year.*

3 a time or period: *in my grandfather's day*

day centre [noun: **day centres**] a place where people, especially old and disabled people, can go during the day to be cared for or for social activities

daydream [verb: **daydreams, daydreaming, daydreamed**] to think about things you would like to happen instead of concentrating on what you are supposed to be doing

daylight [noun] the light that comes from the sun during the day

daze [verb: **dazes, dazing, dazed**] to make someone feel confused and unable to see or think straight: *He was dazed by the blow.*
[noun: **dazes**] to be **in a daze** is to be confused or unable to think clearly: *I stood there in a daze, not knowing what to do.*

dazzle [verb: **dazzles, dazzling, dazzled**] a light dazzles you when it shines so brightly that you cannot see properly

de- [prefix]

1 if a word starts with **de-** it can have something to do with removing. For example, *de-icer* is a substance that removes the ice from a car

2 if a word starts with **de-** it may add the meaning 'away from'. For example, to *deprive* someone of something is to take it away from them

3 if a word starts with **de-** it may also add the meaning 'down'. For example, to *descend* is to go down

dead [adjective]

1 no longer living: *a dead poet*

2 no longer working or active: *The telephone line's dead.*
[adverb]
1 completely: *He just stopped dead in front of me.*
2 exactly: *standing dead in the centre of the circle*
[noun]
1 the dead are all the people who have died
2 the dead of night is the darkest and quietest part of it

dead end [noun: **dead ends**] a road or path that does not lead anywhere

dead heat [noun: **dead heats**] a race that two people finish at exactly the same time

deadline [noun: **deadlines**] the time when something, such as a piece of work, must be finished

deadly [adjective: **deadlier, deadliest**] able to kill: *a deadly poison*

deaf [adjective: **deafer, deafest**] not able to hear properly: *Grandma grew deafer and deafer as she got older.*

• **deafen** [verb: **deafens, deafening, deafened**] to deafen someone is to make them deaf or unable to hear for a short time: *The explosion deafened us for a moment.*

• **deafening** [adjective] unpleasantly loud: *The music was deafening and we had to leave.*

• **deafness** [noun] being deaf

deal [noun: **deals**]
1 an agreement, especially in business: *I think that's a fair deal.*
2 an amount of something: *a great deal of money*
3 a handing out of something, especially playing cards: *It's your deal.*
[verb: **deals, dealing, dealt**]
1 to give small amounts of something to a lot of people: *You deal the cards this time.*
2 if you **deal in** something, you buy and sell it: *They deal in luxury fabrics.*
3 to **deal with** a person or situation, especially a problem, is to do something about it: *The manager deals with all complaints personally.*
4 if a text or speech **deals with** a subject, it is about it: *a book dealing with DIY*

• **dealer** [noun: **dealers**] someone who

buys and sells things: *an antiques dealer*

• **dealings** [plural noun] someone's dealings are the business arrangements they make

dear [adjective: **dearer, dearest**]
1 a thing or person that is dear to you is important because you love them: *my dear old teddy*
2 expensive: *too dear for me to buy*
3 the word you use with a name or title at the beginning of a letter: *Dear Mary • Dear Sir*
[noun: **dears**] a person that is very lovable: *Nancy is such a dear.*

• **dearly** [adverb] very much: *Of course she loves him dearly.*

dearth [noun] a shortage of something: *a dearth of good maths teachers*

death [noun: **deaths**] the time when a person or animal stops living: *written just before the artist's death*

• **deathly** [adjective] like a thing or person that is dead: *deathly pale*

debate [noun: **debates**] a public discussion or argument, for example on television or in parliament
[verb: **debates, debating, debated**] to discuss a lot of different aspects of something

debit [noun: **debits**] an amount of money that is taken out of a bank account
[verb: **debits, debiting, debited**] to take money out of a bank account: *The amount of your bill will be debited from your account on 1st April.*

debit card [noun: **debit cards**] a small plastic card that you can use to pay for things by having money moved directly from your bank account into the account of the person or company you are paying

debris [noun] debris is the bits of something that has broken up: *the debris of a wrecked ship*

debt [noun: **debts**]
1 something, especially money, that one person owes another
2 if you are **in debt**, you owe someone money

début [noun: **débuts**] the first time a performer appears in public: *The pair made their début at the King's Theatre in 1999.*

dec- or **deca-** [prefix] if a word starts with **dec-** or **deca-** it often has something to do with the number ten. For example, a *decagon* is a shape with ten sides

decade [noun: **decades**] a period of ten years: *the third decade of the twentieth century*

decaff [noun: **decaffs**] an informal word for decaffeinated coffee: *Have you got any decaff?*

decaffeinated [adjective] decaffeinated coffee has had the caffeine removed

decagon [noun: **decagons**] a flat shape with ten straight sides

decathlon [noun: **decathlons**] an athletics contest in which each athlete competes in ten different sporting events

decay [verb: **decays, decaying, decayed**] to go rotten
[noun] going bad or rotting: *tooth decay*

deceased [adjective] a formal word meaning **dead**
[noun] **the deceased** is the dead person that has already been mentioned: *It's clear that the deceased did not know his attacker.*

deceit [noun] deceit is lies and trickery
  ♦ **deceitful** [adjective] not telling the truth

deceive [verb: **deceives, deceiving, deceived**] to fool or trick someone by telling lies or making them think something is true: *The sun deceived me into thinking it was warm outside.*
  ♦ **deceiver** [noun: **deceivers**] someone who deceives another person
  → **deception**

December [noun] the twelfth month of the year, after November and before January

decency [noun] decency is respectable and reasonable behaviour
  ♦ **decent** [adjective]
  1 good, honest and respectable: *a decent family*
  2 acceptable or good enough: *a decent salary*

deception [noun: **deceptions**]
  1 deception is not telling the truth
  2 a deception is a trick or lie
  ♦ **deceptive** [adjective] not showing the true situation: *The photo's deceptive — I'm actually much older than I look there.*

decibel [noun: **decibels**] a unit that is used for measuring how loud a sound is

decide [verb: **decides, deciding, decided**]
  1 to make up your mind to do something: *Greg decided to buy a computer.*
  2 to choose: *I can't decide between the blue one and the green one.*
  3 to bring about a result in a competition: *Amrish's goal decided the match.*
  ♦ **decided** [adjective] definite: *a decided improvement*
  ♦ **decidedly** [adverb] very much: *You will feel decidedly better after a rest.*
  → **decision**

deciduous [adjective] a deciduous plant does not have leaves in the winter. Look up and compare **evergreen**

decimal [adjective] based on a system of tens or tenths: *decimal fractions*
[noun: **decimals**] a fraction shown as a number of tenths and hundredths: *A half, written as a decimal, is 0.5.*

decimal point [noun: **decimal points**] the dot after the whole units and before the tenths in a decimal: *To multiply by ten, just move the decimal point to the right.*

decipher [verb: **deciphers, deciphering, deciphered**] to make sense of something, such as a coded message: *Philip's handwriting has always been difficult to decipher.*

decision [noun: **decisions**] something that you have decided: *It was a very difficult decision to make.*
  ♦ **decisive** [adjective]
  1 a decisive person is good at making up their mind quickly and firmly
  2 a decisive action is firm and makes a difference to a result: *a decisive attack by the home team*

deck [noun: **decks**]
  1 a deck of a boat is one of its levels or the part you can walk on outside
  2 a pack of playing cards
  3 the turning part of a record player or tape recorder: *a stereo with a double tape deck*

deckchair [noun: **deckchairs**] a folding chair for sitting outside and relaxing in

declaration [noun: **declarations**] a clear or official announcement: *a declaration of war*

declare [verb: **declares, declaring, declared**]

1 to announce something firmly: *She suddenly declared that she was leaving.*

2 to make an official statement to people in authority that you have goods that you should pay duty on or income that you should pay tax on

decline [verb: **declines, declining, declined**]

1 to refuse an offer or invitation

2 to get weaker, worse or less: *The president's popularity has sharply declined.*

decode [verb: **decodes, decoding, decoded**] to work out the meaning of a coded message

decompose [verb: **decomposes, decomposing, decomposed**] to rot

decorate [verb: **decorates, decorating, decorated**]

1 to add something fancy to something plain to make it look nicer: *We'll decorate the cake with sugar roses.*

2 to paint or paper the inside of a room

3 to give someone a medal or an award for doing something special: *He was decorated for bravery in the war.*

♦ **decoration** [noun: **decorations**]

1 decoration is adding things to improve the look of something

2 a decoration is an ornament that makes something look better: *Christmas decorations*

♦ **decorative** [adjective] a decorative object is intended to make something look better: *a decorative picture frame*

♦ **decorator** [noun: **decorators**] someone whose job is to paint and paper rooms

decoy [noun: **decoys**] a thing or person that leads someone into a trap

decrease [verb: **decreases, decreasing, decreased**] to make or become less: *Josh's interest in football has decreased as he's got older.* • *A healthy diet helps to decrease the risk of heart disease.*

[noun: **decreases**] the amount that something decreases

decree [verb: **decrees, decreeing, decreed**] to announce publicly that something should happen

[noun: **decrees**] an official order or statement that something should happen

decrepit [adjective] old and in bad condition

dedicate [verb: **dedicates, dedicating, dedicated**]

1 to dedicate time to something is to spend time doing only that: *She dedicated her whole life to music.*

2 to mention someone's name right at the beginning of a work you have written, because they are important to you: *The author dedicated his play to his daughter.*

deduce [verb: **deduces, deducing, deduced**] to work something out from a lot of pieces of information

→ **deduction**

deduct [verb: **deducts, deducting, deducted**] to take an amount away from a larger figure: *My wages have already had tax deducted from them.*

deduction [noun: **deductions**]

1 an amount that you take away from a bigger figure

2 something that you work out from all the information you have

deed [noun: **deeds**]

1 something that someone has done: *my good deed for the day*

2 an official document that shows who owns something

deep [adjective: **deeper, deepest**]

1 going a long way down: *Is the pond very deep?*

2 very low in tone: *a deep voice*

3 reaching a long way back: *a deep cupboard*

4 very strong or dark: *deep blue* • *deep dislike*

[adverb: **deeper, deepest**]

1 in a downward direction: *a hole a metre deep*

2 from front to back: *rows of soldiers standing four deep*

♦ **deepen** [verb: **deepens, deepening, deepened**]

1 to go further down or back: *The river deepens here to more than 2 metres.*

2 to get stronger: *a deepening gloom*

♦ **deeply** [adverb] very or very much: *deeply shocked* • *deeply in love*

→ **depth**

deer [noun: **deer**] an animal with four thin legs

Dd

that runs very fast and gracefully. A male deer has antlers like branches that grow on its head

ⓘ The singular and plural forms of **deer** are the same: *a deer in the woods* • *two deer in the park.*

Dd

deface [verb: **defaces, defacing, defaced**] to spoil the way something looks

defeat [verb: **defeats, defeating, defeated**] to beat someone in a competition or war

[noun: **defeats**]

1 a defeat is a game or a battle that you have lost

2 defeat is being beaten at something

defect[1] [noun: **defects**] a fault that stops something from working properly: *a heart defect*

➡ **defective**

defect[2] [verb: **defects, defecting, defected**] to go over to the other side, for example to a different political party or an enemy country: *The spy defected to the United States.*

✦ **defection** [noun: **defections**] going over to the other side

➡ **defector**

ⓘ Remember that the noun **defect** is pronounced **dee**-fekt, with the stress at the beginning, but the verb **defect** is pronounced di-**fekt**, with the stress at the end.

defective [adjective] having something wrong with it: *a defective computer program*

defector [noun: **defectors**] someone who defects

defence [noun: **defences**]

1 protection against attack: *The wall was the city's main defence.*

2 protecting yourself against attack or criticism: *In my defence, I was only doing what I was told.*

3 in a court case, the side that tries to help a person who is accused of doing something wrong

defenceless [adjective] defenceless people, animals or places have no way of protecting themselves: *a defenceless baby seal*

defend [verb: **defends, defending,**

defended] to protect someone or something from being attacked or criticized: *Kim always defends his brother if people say he's too quiet.*

✦ **defendant** [noun: **defendants**] a person that is accused of committing a crime in a court case

✦ **defensive** [adjective]

1 designed to protect: *defensive weapons*

2 worried about being criticized: *a defensive look*

defer [verb: **defers, deferring, deferred**] to put something off until later: *The meeting has been deferred until more people can come.*

defiance [noun] openly disobeying someone or something: *Pamela went out, in defiance of her parents' instructions.*

✦ **defiant** [adjective] refusing to obey: *a defiant child*

✦ **defiantly** [adverb] purposely not obeying: *John defiantly refused to go.*

deficiency [noun: **deficiencies**] an amount that is less than it should be: *a deficiency of B vitamins*

✦ **deficient** [adjective] without enough of something: *The team is deficient in communication skills.*

deficit [noun: **deficits**] how much less money you really have than you expected to have: *The accounts show a deficit of several pounds.*

define [verb: **defines, defining, defined**]

1 to give the exact meaning of something like a word or phrase

2 to show the exact outline of something: *The edges of the car park are clearly defined by white lines.*

➡ **definition**

definite [adjective] certain: *It's not definite, but the wedding will probably be in August.*

definite article [noun: **definite articles**] the name used in grammar for the word **the**

ⓘ There are two kinds of article in English grammar: **the** is the *definite article* and **a** or **an** is the *indefinite article.*

definitely [adverb] certainly, without a doubt: *We'll definitely be back by 10 o'clock.*

definition [noun: **definitions**] the meaning of a word or phrase

deflate [verb: **deflates, deflating, deflated**]
1 to let the air out of something that has been blown up, like a tyre or balloon
2 to make someone feel less confident or enthusiastic: *He felt deflated after losing the match.*

deflect [verb: **deflects, deflecting, deflected**] to change the direction that something is supposed to be travelling in: *Craig deflected the ball into the net.*
♦ **deflection** [noun: **deflections**] a change of direction

deforestation [noun] cutting down large numbers of trees in an area

deform [verb: **deforms, deforming, deformed**] to spoil the shape of something
♦ **deformed** [adjective] not shaped normally: *a deformed arm*
♦ **deformity** [noun: **deformities**] when something is not shaped normally

defrost [verb: **defrosts, defrosting, defrosted**]
1 to defrost frozen food is to make it ready to cook or eat: *Do not refreeze this product after defrosting it.*
2 to defrost a fridge or freezer is to remove the ice from it

deft [adjective: **defter, deftest**]
1 a deft movement is quick and clever
2 a deft person moves neatly and skilfully
♦ **deftly** [adverb] quickly and skilfully: *Hannah caught the ball deftly.*

defy [verb: **defies, defying, defied**]
1 to defy a person or something like a rule is to openly disobey them
2 to defy someone to do something is to challenge them to do it: *I defy you to do that again!*
3 to make something impossible: *a scene that defies description*
➡ **defiance**

degenerate [verb: **degenerates, degenerating, degenerated**] to get worse: *After the accident, Jacob's health degenerated sharply.*

degrade [verb: **degrades, degrading, degraded**] to make someone feel that they are not important or not worth anything

♦ **degrading** [adjective] making a person feel worthless

degree [noun: **degrees**]
1 a unit for measuring temperature, shown by the symbol °: *It's 30° (degrees) here today.*
2 a unit for measuring angles, shown by the symbol °: *An angle of 90° (degrees) is a right angle.*
3 a very small amount: *improving slowly by degrees*
4 a qualification that students can study for at a university or college

dehydrate [verb: **dehydrates, dehydrating, dehydrated**] to dry out
♦ **dehydrated** [adjective]
1 dehydrated foods are dried by having the water removed: *dehydrated vegetables*
2 someone who is dehydrated is weak and ill because they have not had enough water to drink
♦ **dehydration** [noun] being dried up because of not containing as much water as usual

déjà vu [noun] a strange feeling of having had the very same experience before

---

ⓘ This is pronounced day-zha **voo**.

---

dejected [adjective] feeling very fed up
♦ **dejection** [noun] a depressed feeling

delay [noun: **delays**] the extra time you have to wait if something happens later than expected: *There was a delay of half an hour before take-off.*
[verb: **delays, delaying, delayed**]
1 to put something off until later: *Apply now! Don't delay!* • *We delayed our holidays until after the strike.*
2 to make someone or something late: *I was delayed by the arrival of an unexpected visitor.*

delegate [verb: **delegates, delegating, delegated**] to give someone a job to do, especially one that is your responsibility
[noun: **delegates**] a person who represents someone else at a meeting
♦ **delegation** [noun: **delegations**] a group of representatives at a meeting or conference

delete [verb: **deletes, deleting, deleted**] to cross out or remove something from a piece of text

Dd

Dd

• **deletion** [noun: **deletions**] a deletion is a part of a text that has been removed

deliberate [adjective] not accidental, but done on purpose: *a deliberate lie*
[verb: **deliberates, deliberating, deliberated**] to think seriously about something for a while: *We're still deliberating about what to do next.*

• **deliberately** [adverb] on purpose, not by accident: *They deliberately left the door open so that the mice could escape.*

delicacy [noun: **delicacies**] something delicious and unusual to eat: *These eggs are regarded as a great delicacy in some countries.*

delicate [adjective]
1 a delicate object can easily be broken
2 a delicate situation needs careful attention to avoid a problem arising
3 a delicate pattern is fine and dainty
4 a delicate person is often ill

delicatessen [noun: **delicatessens**] a shop that sells cooked meat, cheese and other prepared foods

delicious [adjective] very good to eat, drink or smell: *a delicious meal*

delight [noun: **delights**] great pleasure: *The baby squealed with delight when she saw her mother.*
[verb: **delights, delighting, delighted**] to please someone very much

• **delighted** [adjective] very pleased: *We'd be delighted to come to the party.*

• **delightful** [adjective] very pleasing

delinquency [noun] bad behaviour or law-breaking

delinquent [noun: **delinquents**] someone who behaves badly in the community, especially by breaking the law

delirious [adjective]
1 if you are delirious, you are confused and unable to think normally because you have a high temperature
2 extremely happy or excited: *Martha was delirious when she found she'd passed her exam.*

deliver [verb: **delivers, delivering, delivered**]
1 to deliver something is to take it to the door of

someone's home or workplace: *We're delivering leaflets to all the houses in this area.*
2 to deliver a speech is to say it out loud
3 to deliver a baby is to help with its birth

• **delivery** [noun: **deliveries**] when or how something is delivered

delta [noun: **deltas**] the area like a triangle that is formed if a river splits into separate branches where it flows into the sea

delude [verb: **deludes, deluding, deluded**] to delude someone is to make them believe something that is not true
→ **delusion**

deluge [noun: **deluges**]
1 a downpour or flood
2 a large amount of anything: *a deluge of complaints*
[verb: **deluges, deluging, deluged**] to be deluged with something is to receive lots and lots of them: *We have been deluged with entries for our latest competition.*

delusion [noun: **delusions**] something that a person believes that is not true

delve [verb: **delves, delving, delved**] to look for something as if you are digging for it: *Nan was delving into her handbag for something.*

demand [verb: **demands, demanding, demanded**]
1 to ask for something as if you are giving an order: *I demand to know where you've been!*
2 to need: *This work demanded all our skills.*
[noun: **demands**]
1 a request that is almost an order
2 a need: *There is not much demand for sun cream at this time of year.*

• **demanding** [adjective] needing a lot of time or effort: *a very demanding job*

demeanour [noun] the way you behave: *Something in his demeanour made me suspicious.*

demented [adjective] out of your mind: *demented with worry*

democracy [noun: **democracies**]
1 a form of government where people elect representatives to lead them
2 a country that has an elected government

• democrat [noun: **democrats**] someone who believes that people should be allowed to vote for their government

• democratic [adjective] involving a system where people elect the government

demolish [verb: **demolishes, demolishing, demolished**] to knock something down: *The flats will be demolished immediately.*

• demolition [noun] knocking a building down

demon [noun: **demons**] an evil spirit

demonstrate [verb: **demonstrates, demonstrating, demonstrated**]
1 to show someone how to do something or how something works: *Can you demonstrate how to turn the machine on?*
2 to let people know how you feel about something, especially by marching or waving signs in public

• demonstration [noun: **demonstrations**]
1 an explanation of how to do something or how something works: *a cookery demonstration*
2 an expression of how someone feels about something, especially by marching in public to protest about it: *a demonstration against nuclear weapons*

• demonstrative [adjective] a demonstrative person often or easily shows how they are feeling

• demonstrator [noun: **demonstrators**]
1 someone who takes part in a protest march or public expression of feeling
2 someone who shows people how something is done

demoralize or **demoralise** [verb: **demoralizes, demoralizing, demoralized**] to take away someone's confidence or courage

demure [adjective] a demure person is quiet, shy and modest

den [noun: **dens**] the home of a wild animal: *a lion's den*

denial [noun: **denials**] saying that something is not true

denim [noun] a tough cotton fabric that jeans and other clothes are made out of

denominator [noun: **denominators**] the number below the line in a fraction

denounce [verb: **denounces, denouncing, denounced**] to say publicly that something is bad or that someone has done something bad: *He was denounced as a cheat.*

dense [adjective: **denser, densest**]
1 thick or very closely packed together: *dense fog • a dense forest*
2 someone who is dense does not understand things quickly

• density [noun: **densities**] how thick or closely packed something is

dent [noun: **dents**] a hollow in a surface caused by hitting: *a dent in the side of the car* [verb: **dents, denting, dented**] to hit something and make a hollow shape in it

dental [adjective] to do with teeth: *dental hygiene*

dentist [noun: **dentists**] a doctor whose job is to look after people's teeth

• dentistry [noun] the work of a dentist

dentures [plural noun] a set of false teeth

deny [verb: **denies, denying, denied**]
1 to deny something is to say that it is not true: *Nina denied that she had stolen anything.*
2 to deny a request is to say 'no' to it
3 to deny yourself something is to do without something you want or need
➡ denial

deodorant [noun: **deodorants**] a product, such as a spray, that stops unpleasant smells

depart [verb: **departs, departing, departed**] to leave: *The train departs at 9.15.*
➡ departure

department [noun: **departments**] a section of a school, shop, business or government: *the new head of the Sales department*

departure [noun: **departures**] a time when a thing or person leaves a place: *All departures are shown on the left of the timetable.*

depend [verb: **depends, depending, depended**]
1 to depend on someone or something is to rely on them: *Our mother depends on us to do the shopping.*

2 if a situation depends on something, it will be changed by that thing: *The price of our fruit depends on the weather.*

♦ **dependable** [adjective] if someone is dependable, you can rely on them

♦ **dependant** [noun: **dependants**] someone who is looked after by someone else who pays for everything they need: *Fill in the names of all your dependants.*

♦ **dependence** [noun] not being able to do without something: *dependence on drugs*

♦ **dependent** [adjective] relying on something or someone: *She became dependent on her aunt.*

depict [verb: **depicts, depicting, depicted**] to show or describe: *The sketch depicts a railway station.*

deplete [verb: **depletes, depleting, depleted**] if a supply becomes depleted, it gets smaller or less: *The food stocks were being depleted.*

deplorable [adjective] very bad

deplore [verb: **deplores, deploring, deplored**] if you deplore something, you say or think that it is wrong or very bad

deport [verb: **deports, deporting, deported**] if a government deports someone, they send them out of the country

♦ **deportation** [noun: **deportations**] sending someone out of a country

depose [verb: **deposes, deposing, deposed**] if someone is deposed, they are removed from an important position: *The president has been deposed.*

deposit [noun: **deposits**]
1 part of the price of something that you pay in advance: *We had to pay a deposit of £100 on the cooker.*
2 an amount of money that you pay into a bank or building society account
3 a layer of something that is left behind or that forms over a long time
[verb: **deposits, depositing, deposited**]
1 to put money in an account
2 to leave something behind: *Deposit your luggage here and pick it up later.*

deposit account [noun: **deposit accounts**] a bank account that you use to save money in

depot [noun: **depots**]
1 a place where vehicles like buses or trains are kept when they are not in use
2 a store: *a weapons depot*

ⓘ The final *t* of **depot** is silent.

depress [verb: **depresses, depressing, depressed**] to make someone gloomy or unhappy

♦ **depressed** [adjective] unhappy or fed up

♦ **depressing** [adjective] making a person feel unhappy: *depressing weather*

♦ **depression** [noun: **depressions**]
1 feeling unhappy or fed up
2 a bad time when things are not going as well as usual
3 a hollow or dip in a surface: *a depression left where he'd been sitting in the sand*
4 a patch of low air pressure that often brings bad weather

deprivation [noun] not having the basic things that people need

deprive [verb: **deprives, depriving, deprived**] to deprive someone of something is to take it away from them: *She's been deprived of sleep since the noisy neighbours moved in.*

♦ **deprived** [adjective] not having all the things that are necessary for a basically good life: *a deprived area of the inner city*

depth [noun: **depths**]
1 how deep something is: *measure the depth of the water*
2 a deep place: *the depths of the ocean*
3 how strong something is: *the depth of the colour*
4 if you study or discuss a subject **in depth**, you look at it in a lot of detail
5 if you feel **out of your depth** in a situation, you are involved in things that are too difficult for you to understand

deputy [noun: **deputies**]
1 someone who takes over when the person in charge is not there: *the deputy head teacher*
2 someone's assistant: *the sheriff and all his deputies*

derail [verb: **derails, derailing, derailed**] if a train derails or is derailed, it comes off the track

♦ **derailment** [noun: **derailments**] a

derailment happens when a train comes off the track

deranged [adjective] mad

derby [noun: **derbies**] a sports match between two teams from the same town or area

derelict [adjective] deserted and falling apart: *a derelict factory building*

deride [verb: **derides, deriding, derided**] to laugh at someone or something because you think they are ridiculous
  • **derision** [noun] mocking laughter

derogatory [adjective] a derogatory remark is rude or critical of someone or something

derrick [noun: **derricks**]
  1 a crane, especially at docks
  2 a tower over an oil well that supports the drilling machinery

descend [verb: **descends, descending, descended**]
  1 to go or climb downwards
  2 if you are descended from someone, you come after them in the same family
  • **descendant** [noun: **descendants**] someone's descendants are their children, grandchildren, great-grandchildren, and so on
  • **descent** [noun: **descents**]
  1 going or climbing downwards: *the descent of the mountain*
  2 a downward slope

describe [verb: **describes, describing, described**] to say what happened or what someone or something is like: *Can you describe what you saw?*
  • **description** [noun: **descriptions**]
  1 description is explaining what someone or something is like: *an author who's good at description*
  2 a description is the way someone describes a someone or something: *a very funny description of what happened*
  3 a sort, type or kind: *people of all descriptions*
  • **descriptive** [adjective] describing someone or something: *a descriptive poem*

desert[1] [verb: **deserts, deserting, deserted**] to go away and leave someone or something, especially the army: *The soldier was shot for deserting.* • *She deserted her young family.*

desert[2] [noun: **deserts**] an area of land where it does not rain much, so the earth is very dry and not many plants will grow

---

(i) The verb **desert**, meaning to leave something, is pronounced diz–**ert**, with the stress at the end.
The noun **desert**, meaning an area of dry land, is pronounced **dez**–ert, with the stress at the beginning.

Dd

desert island [noun: **desert islands**] a tropical island where nobody lives

deserve [verb: **deserves, deserving, deserved**] to deserve something is to have earned it because of the way you are or something you have done: *Samir deserves to be promoted.*
  • **deservedly** [adverb] rightly
  • **deserving** [adjective] a deserving person or cause is good and should be helped

desiccated [adjective] dried: *desiccated coconut*

design [verb: **designs, designing, designed**]
  1 to plan a building or product before it is built or made
  2 if something is designed for a particular purpose, it is intended to do it: *This dictionary is designed to be used by adult learners.*
  [noun: **designs**]
  1 design is planning new shapes and ideas: *studying craft and design*
  2 a design is a plan or diagram of something that could be made: *a design for a new racing car*
  3 a pattern: *a geometric design*
  ⇒ **designer**

designate [verb: **designates, designating, designated**] to choose someone or something for a particular purpose
  • **designation** [noun: **designations**] a name or title

designer [noun: **designers**] someone whose job is to create things and decide what shape or style they will have: *a car designer*

desirable [adjective] something desirable is worth having and you want it very much: *a desirable house by the sea*

desire [verb: **desires, desiring, desired**] to

want something very much: *all the riches you could desire*

[noun: **desires**] a longing or something you want very much: *a secret desire*

desk [noun: **desks**] a table for writing at

desolate [adjective]

1 a desolate place is empty of people

2 a desolate person is lonely and very unhappy

♦ **desolation** [noun] a feeling of unhappiness and emptiness

despair [noun] no hope

[verb: **despairs, despairing, despaired**] to give up hope: *He despaired of ever seeing his son again.*

♦ **despairing** [adjective] feeling that there is no hope

despatch [verb] another spelling of **dispatch**

desperate [adjective]

1 extremely bad or serious: *a desperate situation*

2 needing something very much: *desperate for food*

♦ **desperately** [adverb] extremely or very much: *desperately in need*

♦ **desperation** [noun] a feeling that you will do anything to make things better

despicable [adjective] hateful

despise [verb: **despises, despising, despised**] to hate someone or something very much

despite [preposition] despite someone or something means without taking any notice of them: *Despite the rain, we enjoyed the picnic.*

despondency [noun] feeling fed up

♦ **despondent** [adjective] fed up or depressed

dessert [noun: **desserts**] a pudding or sweet at the end of a meal

ⓘ **Dessert** (with a double **s**), meaning a part of a meal, is pronounced diz–**ert**, with the stress at the end.

destination [noun: **destinations**] the place someone is on the way to

destined [adjective] if something is destined, it will happen: *destined to become a star*

destiny [noun: **destinies**] what will happen

in the future: *I believe you can change your own destiny.*

destitute [adjective] with no money, food or a place to live

destroy [verb: **destroys, destroying, destroyed**]

1 to wreck or ruin something: *a city destroyed in the war*

2 to destroy an animal is to kill it: *cattle that had to be destroyed*

♦ **destroyer** [noun: **destroyers**]

1 someone who destroys something

2 a fast warship

♦ **destruction** [noun] completely destroying something

♦ **destructive** [adjective] doing a lot of damage: *Her children are so destructive!*

detach [verb: **detaches, detaching, detached**] to separate things from each other: *You can detach the hood from the jacket.*

♦ **detached** [adjective]

1 a detached house stands all by itself

2 a detached person is not involved or interested in either side of an argument

♦ **detachment** [noun: **detachments**]

1 detachment is not feeling involved in something other people have strong opinions about

2 a detachment is a group of people, especially soldiers, chosen for a special job

detail [noun: **details**]

1 a small part, fact or item: *Draw the outline and then fill in the details.*

2 if you describe something **in detail**, you leave nothing out

♦ **detailed** [adjective] including all the small facts or the smallest parts of something: *a detailed drawing*

detain [verb: **detains, detaining, detained**]

1 to make someone stay somewhere: *detained by the police for 24 hours*

2 to delay someone: *I'm sorry to have detained you.*

detect [verb: **detects, detecting, detected**]

1 to discover something that is not obvious

2 to notice: *I detected a hint of annoyance in his voice.*

♦ **detection** [noun] finding out or noticing

things: *Early detection of this illness is very important.*

• **detective** [noun: **detectives**] someone whose job is to try to find out information in order to solve crimes and find criminals

• **detector** [noun: **detectors**] a piece of equipment that is used to detect something: *a smoke detector*

detention [noun: **detentions**] making a person stay in a place, especially in prison or in school after everyone else has left, as a punishment

deter [verb: **deters, deterring, deterred**] to put someone off doing something
→ **deterrent**

detergent [noun: **detergents**] a chemical for cleaning things: *washing-up detergent*

deteriorate [verb: **deteriorates, deteriorating, deteriorated**] to get worse: *Joe's health is deteriorating rapidly.*

• **deterioration** [noun] growing worse: *a deterioration in her condition*

determination [noun] the fixed idea that you will do something, however difficult it may be: *a determination to win*

• **determine** [verb: **determines, determining, determined**] to control or influence what happens: *The weather will determine how long the event lasts.*

• **determined** [adjective] with a fixed idea that you are going to do something: *The team was determined to finish first if they possibly could.*

deterrent [noun: **deterrents**] something that puts people off doing something

detest [verb: **detests, detesting, detested**] to hate someone or something very much

detonate [verb: **detonates, detonating, detonated**] to explode or make something explode: *The shell could detonate at any moment.* • *The bomb was detonated from across the street.*

• **detonator** [noun: **detonators**] something that sets off an explosive device

detour [noun: **detours**] a different and longer way of getting somewhere

detract [verb: **detracts, detracting, detracted**] to take something away or make something less: *The repair detracted from the value of the vase.*

deuce [noun] the tennis score of 40–40

devastate [verb: **devastates, devastating, devastated**] to ruin a place completely

• **devastated** [adjective] very shocked and upset: *We were devastated by the news.*

• **devastation** [noun]
1 ruin and destruction: *scenes of devastation after the explosion*
2 a feeling of being very badly shocked

develop [verb: **develops, developing, developed**]
1 to grow or make something grow bigger, better or more complicated: *The young animals develop very quickly.* • *plans to develop tourism in the area*
2 to make a photograph on a film into a picture
3 to put up new buildings: *This land is to be developed.*

• **development** [noun: **developments**]
1 there is development or a development when something grows bigger, better or more advanced or more complicated: *recent developments in mobile-phone technology*
2 a development is a new event in a story
3 an area of land with new buildings on it: *a housing development*

deviate [verb: **deviates, deviating, deviated**] to do something different or go in a different direction from what you might expect or predict

• **deviation** [noun: **deviations**] something that is different from what is normal

device [noun: **devices**] a tool, instrument or piece of equipment: *a device for cleaning keyboards*

devil [noun: **devils**]
1 an evil spirit
2 a wicked person

devious [adjective] clever in a sly way

devise [verb: **devises, devising, devised**] to think up a plan or way of doing something

devolution [noun] giving some government power to smaller areas

devote [verb: **devotes, devoting, devoted**]
1 to devote time to someone or something is to spend that time with them
2 to devote yourself to someone or something

Dd

is to be interested in and involved with only them
* **devoted** [adjective] extremely loving: *a devoted daughter*
* **devotion** [noun] great love

devour [verb: **devours, devouring, devoured**] to eat up or swallow very quickly

devout [adjective] a devout person takes the rules and beliefs of a religion very seriously

dew [noun] tiny drops of water that form on the ground at night

dhoti [noun: **dhotis**] a long piece of cloth that Hindu men wear wrapped around the lower half of their bodies

di- [prefix] if a word starts with **di-** it usually has something to do with two, twice or double. For example, a *dioxide* has two atoms of oxygen

diabetes [noun] a serious illness in which your body doesn't produce enough insulin to control the amount of sugar in your blood

diabetic [adjective] someone who is diabetic has diabetes
[noun: **diabetics**] a diabetic is someone who has diabetes

diabolical [adjective] very wicked

diagnose [verb: **diagnoses, diagnosing, diagnosed**] to decide what is wrong with a thing or person
* **diagnosis** [noun: **diagnoses**] a decision about what is wrong with someone: *The doctor made a diagnosis from one look at the patient.*

diagonal [adjective] going from one corner straight to the opposite corner

diagram [noun: **diagrams**] a drawing that explains something

dial [noun: **dials**] a circle of numbers that often has a central pointer that moves around it to show a measurement
[verb: **dials, dialling, dialled**] to dial a telephone number is to call it

dialect [noun: **dialects**] the form of a language that is used by people who live in a particular area

(i) People who speak different **dialects** use different words from each other. People who have different **accents** pronounce the same words differently.

dialogue [noun: **dialogues**]
1 dialogue is talk between people
2 a dialogue is a conversation

diameter [noun: **diameters**] a straight line from one side of a circle to the other and through its centre

diamond [noun: **diamonds**]
1 a very hard, clear precious stone that is a form of carbon
2 a four-sided pointed shape (◆)
3 diamonds is one of the four suits of playing cards, which have the symbol ◆ printed on them

diaper [noun: **diapers**] the American English word for a **nappy**

diaphragm [noun: **diaphragms**] a layer of muscle that separates your stomach from your chest and that moves up and down when you breathe

diarrhoea [noun] if you have diarrhoea, you go to the toilet very often and the solid waste from your body is too watery

diary [noun: **diaries**] a book listing the dates of the year where you can write down your appointments and things you have done each day

dice [noun: **dice**] a small cube with different numbers of dots on each side. You throw a dice and use the number of dots as a score when it's your turn in a game

dictate [verb: **dictates, dictating, dictated**]
1 to dictate something is to say words for someone to write down: *I have to type the letters that my boss dictates.*
2 to dictate to someone is to order them to do things
* **dictation** [noun: **dictations**] a piece of text that someone speaks and another person writes down
* **dictator** [noun: **dictators**] a person who has complete power over everyone else

dictionary [noun: **dictionaries**] a book that gives words in alphabetical order and their meanings: *a French dictionary • a dictionary of medical words*

did [verb] a way of changing the verb **do** to make a past tense: *I did the dishes yesterday, it's your turn today.*

didn't [short form] a short way to say and write **did not**

die [verb: **dies, dying, died**]
1 to stop living
2 to **die away** is to fade away: *The wail of the siren gradually died away.*
3 to **die down** is to become less strong: *wait for the fuss to die down*
4 to **die out** is to disappear gradually: *More and more species of animal are dying out.*

diesel [noun] a heavy type of oil that is used as fuel for engines and boilers

diet [noun: **diets**]
1 the food that a person eats: *Do you have a healthy diet?*
2 a special course of foods for a person who, for example, has an illness or wants to lose weight: *Maybe you need to go on a diet.*
[verb: **diets, dieting, dieted**] to eat only certain foods so as to lose weight

differ [verb: **differs, differing, differed**]
1 to differ from something is not to be the same as it
2 to differ is to disagree with someone: *They differ over just about everything.*
• **difference** [noun: **differences**]
1 the way that something is not the same as something else
2 the amount between two numbers: *The difference between 6 and 10 is 4.*
• **different** [adjective] a thing or person is different from another if they are not the same

ⓘ Many people think it is wrong if you say **different to**, so you should say **different from**: *This pencil is **different from** that one.* In American English, people use **different than**.

difficult [adjective]
1 not easy
2 a difficult person is hard to please: *a difficult customer*
• **difficulty** [noun: **difficulties**]
1 difficulty is not being easy: *You should be able to do this without difficulty.*
2 a difficulty is something that causes a problem: *We had a few difficulties at the beginning of the day.*

diffuse [verb: **diffuses, diffusing, diffused**] to spread something, especially light, widely and evenly

dig [verb: **digs, digging, dug**]
1 to lift up and turn over earth with a spade
2 to make a hole, especially in the ground
3 to poke someone: *She dug Adam in the ribs and giggled.*
[noun: **digs**]
1 a poke: *a dig in the ribs*
2 a remark that you make to irritate someone deliberately: *I pretended not to hear her dig about dieting.*
3 a place where archaeologists remove earth to look for ancient remains
→ **digger**

digest [verb: **digests, digesting, digested**] to break down food in your stomach so that your body can use it properly
• **digestion** [noun] the way your body breaks down what you eat so that your body can use it

digger [noun: **diggers**] a machine that can move or break up large amounts of earth

digit [noun: **digits**]
1 a number from 0 to 9
2 a finger or toe

digital [adjective]
1 based on the use of numbers
2 a digital clock or watch shows the time as a row of numbers, rather than on a round face. Look up and compare **analogue**
3 digital technology stores sounds and pictures as sets of numbers or electronic signals

digital television [noun] a method of broadcasting that uses digital technology

dignified [adjective] calm and serious

dignitary [noun: **dignitaries**] someone with an important job or position

dignity [noun]
1 a calm manner: *He told them to be quiet, to behave with some dignity.*
2 pride and self-respect

dike or **dyke** [noun: **dikes** or **dykes**]
1 a wall that holds water back
2 a ditch that water runs along

dilapidated [adjective] falling to pieces: *a dilapidated old car*

dilate [verb: **dilates, dilating, dilated**] to

make or get larger or wider: *The pupils of your eyes dilate in the dark.*

dilemma [noun: **dilemmas**] a situation when you have to make a difficult choice between two options

diligence [noun] a serious and careful attitude to work

• **diligent** [adjective] hard-working

dilute [verb: **dilutes, diluting, diluted**] to add water to a liquid so that it is not as strong: *Try diluting the juice with fizzy water.*

• **diluted** [adjective] a diluted liquid is weaker because water has been added to it

• **dilution** [noun] adding water to a strong liquid to make it weaker

dim [adjective: **dimmer, dimmest**]
1 a dim light or colour is not bright or clear
2 a dim person is not very quick at understanding
[verb: **dims, dimming, dimmed**] if the lights dim or you dim the lights, it gets darker or more difficult to see

dime [noun: **dimes**] one tenth of a US or Canadian dollar, which is ten cents

dimension [noun: **dimensions**] a measurement such as the length, width or area of something: *Please give the dimensions of the doorway.*

diminish [verb: **diminishes, diminishing, diminished**] to get or make less or smaller

dimple [noun: **dimples**] a small hollow like a dent in the flesh of your chin or cheek: *Harry has dimples when he smiles.*

din [noun] a very loud noise

dine [verb: **dines, dining, dined**] to have dinner

• **diner** [noun: **diners**]
1 someone who is eating dinner, especially in a restaurant
2 in the US, a cheap restaurant

dinghy [noun: **dinghies**] a small boat for rowing or sailing

dinner [noun: **dinners**] a main meal in the evening or in the middle of the day

dinosaur [noun: **dinosaurs**] an extinct prehistoric giant reptile

dip [verb: **dips, dipping, dipped**]
1 to put something in and out of a liquid quickly: *Dip the clothes in the dye.*

2 to slope downwards: *The field dips down towards the bottom of the valley.*
3 to dip a vehicle's headlights is to lower them so that they do not dazzle other drivers
[noun: **dips**]
1 a soft food that you eat by dipping things in it
2 a slope downwards in the land
3 a quick swim
4 a liquid that something can be put into for a short time

diploma [noun: **diplomas**] a qualification that someone can study for in a particular subject

diplomacy [noun]
1 the job of keeping friendly relationships between countries
2 managing to deal with people without offending them

• **diplomat** [noun: **diplomats**] someone whose job is to keep good relationships and communications between countries

• **diplomatic** [adjective]
1 to do with the relationships between countries: *the diplomatic service*
2 tactful and able to keep people happy

dire [adjective: **direr, direst**] dreadful: *in dire need*

direct [adjective]
1 straight, or as straight as possible: *a direct route to the airport*
2 frank and honest
[verb: **directs, directing, directed**]
1 to aim or make something go a particular way: *His remarks were directed at me.*
2 to tell someone how to get somewhere: *Could you please direct me to the post office?*
3 to control or guide: *The police direct the traffic when it's busy.*

direct debit [noun: **direct debits**] a direct debit is an instruction to your bank to pay money regularly to a person or organization

direction [noun: **directions**]
1 a direction is the place or point a thing or person goes towards or faces: *Which direction is the library?*
2 a direction is an order or instruction: *directions for use*
3 directions are instructions for getting somewhere: *Try to follow my directions to the hidden treasure.*

4 direction is controlling or organizing things

directly [adverb]
1 straight away: *The manager will see you directly.*
2 straight: *looking directly at me*

director [noun: **directors**]
1 the manager of a business
2 someone who makes a film or organizes a stage show

direct speech [noun] in a story or report, the exact words that a person said

dirt [noun] dirt is any substance that is not clean or makes something unclean, such as mud or dust
◆ **dirty** [adjective: **dirtier, dirtiest**]
1 not clean: *dirty floors*
2 not polite: *dirty language*
3 unfair or dishonest: *a dirty trick*

dis- [prefix]
1 if a word starts with **dis-** it can have something to do with separation and moving apart. For example, *disjointed* means 'not connected properly'
2 if a word starts with **dis-** it may also mean 'not' something. For example, *dislike* means 'not to like'

disability [noun: **disabilities**] a physical or mental problem that makes some aspects of life difficult

disabled [adjective] having a physical or mental problem that makes some aspects of life difficult

disadvantage [noun: **disadvantages**] something that is not helpful or desirable: *The only disadvantage of the plan is that it could be too expensive.*

disagree [verb: **disagrees, disagreeing, disagreed**]
1 to have a different opinion about something: *I completely disagree with you about that.*
2 to make you feel ill: *The prawns in the curry disagreed with me.*
◆ **disagreeable** [adjective] unpleasant
◆ **disagreement** [noun: **disagreements**]
1 disagreement is having different opinions
2 a disagreement is an argument: *We've had several disagreements on this subject.*

disallow [verb: **disallows, disallowing, disallowed**] to disallow a goal or point in sport is to say that it does not count: *Our next shot was disallowed by the referee.*

disappear [verb: **disappears, disappearing, disappeared**] to vanish or go out of sight
◆ **disappearance** [noun: **disappearances**] when something or someone vanishes: *The police are investigating the disappearance of the businessman.*

disappoint [verb: **disappoints, disappointing, disappointed**] to let someone down: *I'm sorry to disappoint you, but I can't come to your party.*
◆ **disappointed** [adjective] feeling let down
◆ **disappointment** [noun: **disappointments**] a feeling of being let down because something does not happen or turns out worse than you expected: *It was a disappointment to find that all the tickets had already been sold.*

disapproval [noun] thinking something is not good
◆ **disapprove** [verb: **disapproves, disapproving, disapproved**] to disapprove of someone or something is to think that they are bad, wrong or unsuitable: *My parents definitely disapproved of my new friend.*

disarm [verb: **disarms, disarming, disarmed**]
1 to disarm someone is to take a weapon away from them: *A security guard managed to disarm the intruder.*
2 to disarm is to give up weapons that you have
◆ **disarmament** [noun] getting rid of weapons of war

disaster [noun: **disasters**] something terrible that happens, especially if there is a lot of damage or people hurt
◆ **disastrous** [adjective] causing a lot of damage or injuries

disbelief [noun] not believing something: *an expression of complete disbelief*
◆ **disbelieve** [verb: **disbelieves, disbelieving, disbelieved**] to think someone is lying or something is untrue

disc [noun: **discs**]

Dd

1 something flat and round

2 a CD

discard [verb: **discards, discarding, discarded**] to throw something away: *a discarded wrapper*

discern [verb: **discerns, discerning, discerned**] to see or understand something

discharge [verb: **discharges, discharging, discharged**]

1 to discharge a prisoner or patient in a hospital is to let them go

2 to discharge a substance like a liquid or gas is to give it off or let it out: *a factory that discharges dangerous products into the environment*

[noun: **discharges**]

1 carrying out an order or duty: *injured in the discharge of his duty*

2 letting someone go: *an honourable discharge from the army*

3 a substance that comes or leaks out of something

disciple [noun: **disciples**]

1 a person who follows and believes in someone else's ideas

2 one of the original followers of Jesus Christ

disciplinarian [noun: **disciplinarians**] someone who is very strict

disciplinary [adjective] to do with rules for how to behave and with punishment for breaking rules

discipline [noun] strict training or rules for how to behave and punishment for breaking them

disclose [verb: **discloses, disclosing, disclosed**] to tell someone a secret or something private

disco [noun: **discos**] a place or party where people dance to recorded music

discolour [verb: **discolours, discolouring, discoloured**] to go or make something go a strange or unpleasant colour: *teeth discoloured by tobacco*

discomfort [noun] being uncomfortable: *The doctor asked if I had felt any discomfort.*

disconnect [verb: **disconnects, disconnecting, disconnected**]

1 to cut off the supply of something such as gas or electricity: *The phone has been disconnected.*

2 to separate things that were joined together

discontent [noun] a feeling of not being happy or satisfied with a situation

♦ **discontented** [adjective] not satisfied and wanting to change a situation

discontinue [verb: **discontinues, discontinuing, discontinued**] to stop making or selling a product: *That model has been discontinued.*

discount [noun: **discounts**] some money taken off a price to make it cheaper: *10% discount on all goods*

discourage [verb: **discourages, discouraging, discouraged**] to put someone off doing something: *Don't be discouraged by what he said.*

♦ **discouragement** [noun]

1 a feeling of disappointment that puts you off doing something

2 an effort to put you off something that you want to do

♦ **discouraging** [adjective] making you feel less hopeful or confident about something: *discouraging news*

discover [verb: **discovers, discovering, discovered**] to find information, a place or an object, especially for the first time: *The settlers discovered gold in the mountains.* • *We discovered that the paint wouldn't mix with water.*

♦ **discoverer** [noun: **discoverers**] a person who finds something for the first time

♦ **discovery** [noun: **discoveries**] finding something, especially by accident: *the discovery of America*

discreet [adjective] careful not to say things that might embarrass people or cause trouble: *A good solicitor has to be discreet.*

discriminate [verb: **discriminates, discriminating, discriminated**]

1 to treat different people or groups differently in the same situation, often because of their colour, religion or sex

2 to see differences between things and prefer one to another

♦ **discrimination** [noun]

1 treating people differently because of their colour, religion or sex: *sexual discrimination*

2 being able to see differences in things and decide if they are good or bad

discus [noun: **discuses**] a heavy disc that athletes throw as far as they can in a competition

discuss [verb: **discusses, discussing, discussed**] to talk about something: *You should try to discuss this with your wife.*

• **discussion** [noun: **discussions**] talks or conversations between people: *discussions between world leaders*

disdain [noun] not liking a thing or person because you do not think they are good or interesting enough

• **disdainful** [adjective] looking down on a thing or person as not good or interesting enough

disease [noun: **diseases**] an illness: *heart disease*

• **diseased** [adjective] not healthy, especially because of an illness: *diseased leaves on the roses*

disfigure [verb: **disfigures, disfiguring, disfigured**] to spoil the look of something

disgrace [noun]
1 something that makes you feel ashamed: *It's no disgrace to come last if you tried hard.*
2 if you are in disgrace, other people do not approve of what you have done: *Debbie's in disgrace for staying out all night.*

• **disgraceful** [adjective] shameful or very bad

disguise [noun: **disguises**]
1 disguise is make-up and clothing that you wear to change your appearance so that people do not recognize you
2 if you are in disguise, you have changed your appearance in this way
[verb: **disguises, disguising, disguised**]
1 to disguise yourself as another person is to dress and behave like them: *She disguised herself as a tourist.*
2 to disguise something such as your voice or your handwriting is to change it so that people will not recognize it

disgust [noun] a strong feeling that you do not like or approve of something: *The sight of the worms filled Luisa with disgust.*

• **disgusted** [adjective] sickened by

something bad, wrong or unpleasant

• **disgusting** [adjective] extremely unpleasant: *That tastes disgusting!*

dish [noun: **dishes**]
1 a plate or bowl for food
2 food that has been prepared for eating: *a fish dish*
3 a large disc that is an aerial for receiving satellite signals, especially for television broadcasts
[verb: **dishes, dishing, dished**] to **dish out** food is to serve it to people

dishearten [verb: **disheartens, disheartening, disheartened**] to make someone feel less hopeful or confident

dishevelled [adjective] with messed-up hair and untidy clothes

dishonest [adjective] not telling the truth and cheating people: *a dishonest way of doing business*

• **dishonesty** [noun] cheating or not being honest

dishwasher [noun: **dishwashers**] a machine for washing things such as plates, cups and cutlery after a meal

disinfect [verb: **disinfects, disinfecting, disinfected**] to disinfect something is to destroy germs on it that might cause disease: *disinfect the bathroom once a week*

• **disinfectant** [noun: **disinfectants**] a product that kills germs

disintegrate [verb: **disintegrates, disintegrating, disintegrated**] to fall to pieces

• **disintegration** [noun] falling apart

disinterested [adjective] not having personal feelings for or against someone or something: *A disinterested judge will make a fair decision.*

disk [noun: **disks**] a round flat object that computers use to store information on: *Save the file on a floppy disk.* • *The virus could infect your hard disk.*

disk drive [noun: **disk drives**] the part of a computer that holds and operates the disks that store information

dislike [verb: **dislikes, disliking, disliked**] not to like someone or something: *I dislike having to get up early, but I have to do it.*

Dd

Dd

dislocate [verb: **dislocates, dislocating, dislocated**] to dislocate a joint is to put a bone out of its correct position: *Tom dislocated his shoulder in a rugby match.*
+ **dislocation** [noun] when something, especially a bone, gets moved from its correct position

dislodge [verb: **dislodges, dislodging, dislodged**] to move something, especially when it is stuck, from its place

disloyal [adjective] not loyal or faithful
+ **disloyalty** [noun] not being loyal or faithful to someone you should be supporting

dismal [adjective] gloomy and not at all bright or attractive: *dismal weather*

dismantle [verb: **dismantles, dismantling, dismantled**] to take something apart

dismay [noun] an unpleasant feeling of surprise and worry: *We watched in dismay as Ted fell into the water.*

dismiss [verb: **dismisses, dismissing, dismissed**]
1 to dismiss someone is to send them away: *The class were dismissed by the teacher early today.*
2 to dismiss someone from their job is to sack them
+ **dismissal** [noun: **dismissals**] when someone gets sent away, especially being sacked from their job: *an unfair dismissal*

dismount [verb: **dismounts, dismounting, dismounted**] to get off a bicycle or horse

disobedience [noun] when someone does not do what they are told to do
+ **disobedient** [adjective] not doing as you are told
+ **disobey** [verb: **disobeys, disobeying, disobeyed**] not to do what you are told to do: *How dare you disobey me!*

disorder [noun]
1 disorder is a state of confusion or a disturbance
2 a disorder is an illness
+ **disorderly** [adjective] behaving badly: *a disorderly crowd*

disorganized or **disorganised** [adjective]
1 things are disorganized if they are in a mess

or a state of confusion: *Her clothes lay in a disorganized heap.*
2 a person is disorganized if they are bad at making plans or doing things efficiently: *I found him a very disorganized person to work with.*

disown [verb: **disowns, disowning, disowned**] to claim that you do not have any connection with someone: *I'll disown you completely if you make a scene.*

dispatch or **despatch** [verb: **dispatches, dispatching, dispatched** or **despatches, despatching, despatched**] to send off: *a parcel dispatched on the 29th*

dispense [verb: **dispenses, dispensing, dispensed**]
1 to give something out, especially medicine
2 to **dispense with** something is to decide to do without it
+ **dispenser** [noun: **dispensers**] a machine or container that you can get measured amounts of something from: *a cash dispenser*

disperse [verb: **disperses, dispersing, dispersed**] to scatter or send things or people off in different directions: *The crowd is now beginning to disperse.*

displace [verb: **displaces, displacing, displaced**] to put or take something or someone out of the place they seemed to be fixed in: *Thousands of people were displaced during the war.*

display [noun: **displays**]
1 a show or exhibition: *a display of the children's work • an air display*
2 the way you see things on a computer screen: *You can change the display so that it's bigger.*
3 something that is **on display** is arranged for people to see
[verb: **displays, displaying, displayed**] to set things out for an exhibition or to show something for people to see: *The treasure will be displayed in the museum for two months.*

displease [verb: **displeases, displeasing, displeased**] to annoy someone
+ **displeasure** [noun] annoyance

disposable [adjective] a disposable product is meant to be used and then thrown away: *disposable nappies*

disposal [noun]

1 getting rid of something: *a waste-disposal unit in the kitchen*
2 a thing or person that is **at your disposal** is available for you to use: *There will be a car at your disposal.*

dispose [verb: **disposes, disposing, disposed**] to dispose of something is to get rid of it: *Where can I dispose of my old fridge?*

disprove [verb: **disproves, disproving, disproved**] to prove that something is not true

dispute [noun: **disputes**] an argument, especially about work or between countries [verb: **disputes, disputing, disputed**] to argue about something: *They dispute that they have been treated fairly.*

disqualification [noun] stopping someone from driving or taking part in a competition because they have done something wrong [verb: **disqualifies, disqualifying, disqualified**] to prevent someone from doing something because they have broken the rules or the law: *Three contestants have been disqualified for wearing the wrong kind of shoes.* • *He has been disqualified from driving for 12 months.*

disregard [verb: **disregards, disregarding, disregarded**] to take no notice of something: *They have completely disregarded my instructions.*

disrepair [noun] disrepair is a bad state or condition: *a building that had fallen into disrepair*

disrespect [noun] being rude and behaving without respect towards someone
• **disrespectful** [adjective] not polite towards someone: *disrespectful language*

disrupt [verb: **disrupts, disrupting, disrupted**] to disturb the normal way things run: *Traffic was disrupted because of the march.*
• **disruption** [noun: **disruptions**] disturbance of the smooth running of something: *disruption in the town centre caused by a burst water pipe*
• **disruptive** [adjective] causing disturbance and disorder: *Disruptive pupils will be excluded.*

dissatisfaction [noun] irritation or not being pleased about something

• **dissatisfied** [adjective] to be dissatisfied with something is not to be pleased about it

dissect [verb: **dissects, dissecting, dissected**] to cut something up so that you can examine it
• **dissection** [noun] cutting something up so that you can see all its parts in detail

dissimilar [adjective] not the same

dissolve [verb: **dissolves, dissolving, dissolved**] to melt or be melted in liquid: *Keep stirring until the sugar dissolves completely.*

dissuade [verb: **dissuades, dissuading, dissuaded**] to dissuade someone from doing something is to persuade them not to do it

distance [noun: **distances**]
1 the space between things: *Measure the distance between the lines accurately.*
2 if something is **in the distance**, it is a long way away: *the sound of a train in the distance*
3 if you **keep your distance**, you keep back or away from someone or something
• **distant** [adjective]
1 far off, not close: *a distant shout* • *a distant cousin*
2 cold and unfriendly: *behaving in a distant manner*

distil [verb: **distils, distilling, distilled**] to make a liquid pure by boiling it and cooling the vapour that is produced
• **distillery** [noun: **distilleries**] a factory that makes strong alcoholic drinks like whisky and brandy

distinct [adjective]
1 clear: *a distinct improvement*
2 different: *two languages that are quite distinct*
• **distinction** [noun: **distinctions**]
1 a difference: *We have to make a distinction between the low-paid and the unemployed.*
2 an honour: *She had the distinction of being the first woman airline pilot.*
3 a high mark in an examination: *Sandy always got distinctions in his piano exams.*
• **distinctive** [adjective] different and easy to recognize: *a distinctive singing voice*

distinguish [verb: **distinguishes, distinguishing, distinguished**]
1 to see a difference between things: *Jamie can't distinguish green from brown because he's colour blind.*

Dd

2 to make something out, either by seeing or hearing it

♦ **distinguished** [adjective] famous and respected: *a distinguished novelist*

distort [verb: **distorts, distorting, distorted**]

1 to twist something out of shape: *a face distorted with pain*

2 to express information so that it seems to mean something different: *a newspaper report that distorts the truth*

3 to make a sound strange and unclear: *A microphone can distort your voice.*

♦ **distortion** [noun] changing something so that it is noticeably different

distract [verb: **distracts, distracting, distracted**] to take your attention away: *Try not to be distracted by the noise outside.*

♦ **distraction** [noun: **distractions**] something that takes your attention away from what you are doing: *I've had so many distractions today that I haven't finished.*

distraught [adjective] extremely worried or upset

distress [noun] pain, sadness or worry [verb: **distresses, distressing, distressed**] to upset someone

♦ **distressed** [adjective] upset

♦ **distressing** [adjective] making someone feel very upset: *distressing pictures of the famine area*

distribute [verb: **distributes, distributing, distributed**] to give something out to lots of people: *Please distribute the leaflets to your friends.* • *a company that distributes products to shops*

♦ **distribution** [noun] when something goes or is taken out to different places

district [noun: **districts**] one part of a country or town: *a country district*

distrust [verb: **distrusts, distrusting, distrusted**] not to trust someone or something [noun] suspecting, or not trusting someone or something: *a look of distrust*

disturb [verb: **disturbs, disturbing, disturbed**]

1 to interrupt something that is going on, or someone who is doing something: *I'm sorry to disturb you, but I need to ask you a question.*

2 to disturb something is to change the way it has been arranged: *I knew that someone had been at my desk because the papers had been disturbed.*

3 if something disturbs you, it upsets or worries you

♦ **disturbance** [noun: **disturbances**] noise or noisy behaviour: *disturbances in the street during the night*

♦ **disturbing** [adjective] upsetting: *disturbing scenes of violence*

disused [adjective] not used any more: *a disused railway station*

ditch [noun: **ditches**] a long narrow hole in the ground, especially one that has water in it

[verb: **ditches, ditching, ditched**] to ditch something is to get rid of it

dither [verb: **dithers, dithering, dithered**] if you dither, you hesitate and can't make a decision

divan [noun: **divans**] a bed that has no headboard at the top

dive [verb: **dives, diving, dived**]

1 to go into water headfirst

2 to go down steeply and quickly: *an eagle diving down into a field*

[noun: **dives**] a downwards movement, especially headfirst into water

diverse [adjective] different or varied: *a diverse selection of cheeses*

➡ **diversity**

diversion [noun: **diversions**]

1 an alternative route to the usual one: *There was a diversion because the bridge was closed.*

2 something that takes your attention away, especially an amusement: *The little boys created a diversion while the big ones stole our bikes.* • *The puppet show was a welcome diversion.*

diversity [noun] variety: *the great diversity of plants in this region*

divert [verb: **diverts, diverting, diverted**] to divert something such as traffic is to make it go a different way

➡ **diversion**

divide [verb: **divides, dividing, divided**]

1 to separate into parts: *divide the boys into*

teams of five • a single cell that divides and becomes two cells

2 in maths, to find how many times one number contains another: *If you divide 12 by 3, you get 4.* • *12 divided by 3 is 4.*
→ **divisible, division**

dividend [noun: **dividends**] part of the profits that a company makes, which is paid to people who own shares in the company

divine [adjective] belonging to a god or like a god

divisible [adjective] able to be divided exactly: *12 is divisible by 2, 3, 4 and 6.*

division [noun: **divisions**]
1 dividing things, numbers or people: *long division*
2 something that divides
3 a section of something: *There are eight teams in each division of the league.*

divorce [noun: **divorces**] the official end of a marriage
[verb: **divorces, divorcing, divorced**] to end a marriage with someone: *His parents divorced when he was 6.* • *Julia is divorcing her husband.*

divulge [verb: **divulges, divulging, divulged**] to reveal some information, for example a secret

Diwali [noun] the Hindu or Sikh religious festival of lights that takes place in October or November

DIY [abbreviation] short for **do-it-yourself**, making or repairing things yourself for your home rather than paying someone else to do it

dizzy [adjective: **dizzier, dizziest**] giddy: *Spinning round like that will make you dizzy.*

DJ [abbreviation] short for **disc jockey**, someone who plays CDs and records in a club or on the radio

DNA [abbreviation] short for **deoxyribonucleic acid**, the substance in living things that holds information about your individual genes

do [verb: **does, doing, did, done**]
1 to carry out an action or deal with a task: *always doing something* • *Do your homework.*
2 to get along: *How are you doing?*
3 to be enough: *Will a pound do?*
4 to swindle someone: *They'll do you if they*

can, so make sure you check your change.
5 to **do away with** something or someone is to get rid of them or kill them
6 to **do something up** is to fasten it: *Do your jacket up — it's cold out there.*
7 to **do something up** is to decorate it: *We're doing up our hall.*
[noun: **dos**] a party: *The wedding's at 3 and there's an evening do afterwards.*

ⓘ The verb **do** is very important in making good English sentences.
Use it to avoid repeating a verb: *We rarely have a picnic, but when we **do**, it always rains.*
Use it with a more important verb:
(1) in questions: ***Do** you understand?*
(2) in sentences with **not**: *I **don't** know.*
(3) to stress something: *I **do** like your dress.*

docile [adjective] tame and easy to manage: *a docile pet*

dock[1] [noun: **docks**] part of a harbour where ships can load and unload
[verb: **docks, docking, docked**]
1 a ship docks when it goes into a dock: *When we've docked, a crane will unload the containers.*
2 a spacecraft docks when it joins another craft during a flight
→ **docker**

dock[2] [verb: **docks, docking, docked**]
1 to dock someone's pay is to make it less
2 to dock an animal's tail is to cut it short

dock[3] [noun: **docks**] part of a law court where the person accused of a crime stands or sits

docker [noun: **dockers**] someone who works at the docks, loading and unloading ships

doctor [noun: **doctors**] someone who has been trained in medicine and whose job is to treat people when they are ill

document [noun: **documents**] a paper with official information on it: *Keep this document for your records.*

documentary [noun: **documentaries**] a film or television programme that is about real people and events

dodge [verb: **dodges, dodging, dodged**] to avoid something by a quick or clever

Dd

movement: *Graeme managed to dodge out of the way before the ball hit him.*
[noun: **dodges**] a movement or trick to avoid something

doe [noun: **does**] the female of certain animals like deer, rabbits or hares

does [verb] the form of the verb **do** that is used with **he**, **she** and **it**

doesn't [short form] a short way to say and write **does not**

dog [noun: **dogs**] a four-legged animal that barks and that people often keep as a pet
[verb: **dogs, dogging, dogged**] to follow and trouble someone: *The group were dogged by technical problems on their latest tour.*

dog-eared [adjective] a dog-eared page has a curled or bent corner

dogged [adjective] determined or stubborn

ⓘ This word is pronounced **dog**-id.

dogsbody [noun: **dogsbodies**] someone who gets all the small, uninteresting jobs to do

doily or **doyley** [noun: **doilies** or **doyleys**] a piece of paper with a pattern of holes in it that is put under cakes or biscuits on a plate

doldrums [plural noun] someone who is **in the doldrums** is fed up

dole [noun] someone who is **on the dole** has no job and is getting payments from the government
[verb: **doles, doling, doled**] to **dole something out** is to give it out in small amounts

doll [noun: **dolls**] a toy in the shape of a person

dollar [noun: **dollars**] the main unit of money in many countries including the United States, Canada, Australia and New Zealand

dolphin [noun: **dolphins**] a very intelligent sea mammal of the whale family that has a long pointed mouth

-dom [suffix]
1 if **-dom** comes at the end of a word, it is a noun that refers to a particular state or condition. For example, *wisdom* is the state of being wise
2 when **-dom** comes at the end of some words, they are nouns that refer to a particular area. For example, a *kingdom* is land ruled by a king

domain [noun: **domains**] the area that one person or government rules over

dome [noun: **domes**] the roof of a building in the shape of the top half of a ball

domestic [adjective]
1 to do with homes and houses: *domestic tasks like cleaning and cooking*
2 a domestic animal is not wild, but kept as a pet or on a farm
♦ **domesticated** [adjective]
1 a domesticated animal is one that lives in contact with humans, either as a pet or on a farm
2 a domesticated person likes looking after their home and family

dominant [adjective] stronger or more noticeable than others: *The dominant feature of this illness is a rash.*

dominate [verb: **dominates, dominating, dominated**] to control others by being strongest or most powerful: *Paul dominates every conversation.*
♦ **domination** [noun] when a powerful person controls everyone else

dominoes [noun] a game played with small rectangular blocks that have different numbers of dots on them

donate [verb: **donates, donating, donated**] to give something, especially money, as a gift: *Would you donate something to our charity?*
♦ **donation** [noun: **donations**] something that someone gives without getting anything back
⇒ **donor**

done [verb] a form of the verb **do** that is used with a helping verb to show that something happened in the past: *I've done the dishes.*

donkey [noun: **donkeys**] a type of animal that looks like a small horse with long ears

donor [noun: **donors**] someone who gives something that someone else can use: *Blood donors are urgently needed.*

donor card [noun: **donor cards**] a card that you carry to show that you are willing for parts of your body to be used to help someone else after you are dead

don't [short form] a short way to say and write **do not**

doom [noun] an unpleasant end like ruin or death
♦ **doomed** [adjective] bound to fail: *The project was doomed from the start.*
door [noun: **doors**] a panel, often on a hinge, that you can open and close to cover the entrance to a building, room or cupboard
doorstep [noun: **doorsteps**] the step in front of the door of a house
doorway [noun: **doorways**] the entrance to a room, house or other building
dope [noun: **dopes**]
1 an illegal drug, especially cannabis
2 an idiot
[verb: **dopes, doping, doped**] to drug someone
dormant [adjective] not active at the moment: *a dormant volcano*
dormitory [noun: **dormitories**] a bedroom for several people, especially in a school
dosage [noun: **dosages**] the amount of a medicine that you should take: *the correct dosage of a drug*
dose [noun: **doses**] an amount of medicine that you take at one time
dossier [noun: **dossiers**] a set of papers with information about a particular person or subject
dot [noun: **dots**]
1 a small round mark
2 if something happens **on the dot**, it happens exactly on time: *Belinda arrived at three o'clock on the dot, just as she'd promised.*
dote [verb: **dotes, doting, doted**] to **dote on** someone is to be extremely fond of them
double [adjective]
1 containing twice as much: *a double dose of antibiotics*
2 made up of two of the same sort: *double doors*
3 suitable for two: *a double room*
[noun: **doubles**]
1 twice as much: *Jan earns double what I get.*
2 a thing or person that looks exactly like another one: *I saw your double in the street yesterday.*
3 if you do something **at the double**, you do it very quickly
[verb: **doubles, doubling, doubled**]

1 to multiply something by two
2 to **double up** is to bend over in laughter or pain
double bass [noun: **double basses**] the largest instrument in the violin family, which plays very low notes
double-cross [verb: **double-crosses, double-crossing, double-crossed**] if you double-cross someone, you cheat them
double-decker [noun: **double-deckers**] a bus with an upper floor
doubly [adverb] extra: *Make doubly sure that the door's locked.*
doubt [noun: **doubts**] a feeling of not being sure about something: *Leo had his doubts about the plan.* • *I have no doubt you are quite right.*
[verb: **doubts, doubting, doubted**] to be unsure about something: *I doubt that you will understand.*
doubtful [adjective]
1 to be doubtful about something is to be unsure about it
2 something that is doubtful is not likely: *It was doubtful that they would ever be found now.*
dough [noun] a mixture of flour and water for making bread

ⓘ The word **dough** sounds the same as the word **doe** (a female deer), and rhymes with **slow**.

doughnut [noun: **doughnuts**] a round cake that is deep-fried. It may have a hole in the middle or be filled with something such as jam or chocolate
dour [adjective: **dourer, dourest**] stern and unhappy: *a dour expression*
dove [noun: **doves**] a kind of pigeon that is usually white
dowdy [adjective: **dowdier, dowdiest**] looking dull, uninteresting and unfashionable
down[1] [adverb]
1 towards or in a lower position: *get down* • *She was sitting down.*
2 to a smaller size: *cut the picture down to fit the frame*
3 along: *go down to the post office*
4 if you **go down with** something, you

Dd

become ill with it: *Fran's gone down with flu.*
[preposition]

1 towards or in a lower part: *tears running down his face*

2 along: *walking down the road*

down² [noun] light, soft feathers

downcast [adjective] feeling sad

downfall [noun: **downfalls**] ruin or defeat: *the downfall of a powerful leader*

downhill [adjective] going downwards: *a downhill path*
[adverb] down a slope: *We travelled downhill for several hours.*

download [verb: **downloads, downloading, downloaded**] to transfer information, such as pictures or music, onto your computer from the Internet or another computer: *The file is downloading now.* • *You can download music for free.*

down-market [adjective] low in quality and price: *a down-market shopping centre*

downpour [noun: **downpours**] a heavy fall of rain

downs [plural noun] low grassy hills

downstairs [adverb] to a lower floor of a building: *go downstairs*
[adjective] on a lower floor: *the downstairs bathroom*

downstream [adverb] further down a river in the direction that it flows, usually towards the sea

downward [adjective] towards a lower place or position: *a downward slope*
✦ **downwards** or **downward** [adverb] moving or leading to a lower place or position: *The path winds downwards to the lakeside.*

dowry [noun: **dowries**] money and property that a woman brings to her marriage from her family

doze [verb: **dozes, dozing, dozed**]

1 to doze is to sleep lightly

2 to **doze off** is to fall into a light sleep
[noun: **dozes**] a light sleep: *I had a doze after lunch.*

dozen [noun: **dozens**] twelve: *a dozen eggs*

drab [adjective: **drabber, drabbest**] uninteresting and without any bright colours

draft [noun: **drafts**] a rough experimental

outline of something: *This is just the first draft of my essay.*
[verb: **drafts, drafting, drafted**] to make a rough plan of something

draftsman or **draftswoman** [noun: **draftsmen** or **draftswomen**] another spelling of **draughtsman** or **draughtswoman**

drag [verb: **drags, dragging, dragged**]

1 to pull something along roughly: *Thomas came out dragging his schoolbag behind him.*

2 to move too slowly: *The play seemed to drag on for hours.*

3 to drag a river or lake is to search it with a net
[noun]

1 a boring task or event: *Choir practice was always such a drag.*

2 if a man is **in drag**, he is wearing women's clothes

dragon [noun: **dragons**] an imaginary, fire-breathing reptile with wings

dragonfly [noun: **dragonflies**] a long thin insect with double wings

drain [verb: **drains, draining, drained**]

1 to drain something is to let the water run out of it: *They must drain the reservoir to repair the dam.* • *Drain the pasta well.*

2 to drain is to flow away: *watching the liquid drain down the sink*

3 to drain a container of drink is to drink it all

4 if something drains someone, it makes them very tired
[noun: **drains**]

1 a pipe or ditch for waste water to flow away in

2 something that uses up your energy or money: *Our holiday was a big drain on our finances.*
✦ **drainage** [noun] removing waste water by systems of pipes and rivers
✦ **drained** [adjective] with no strength left: *After being in court all day, I felt completely drained.*

drake [noun: **drakes**] a male duck

drama [noun: **dramas**]

1 drama is acting, directing and producing plays

2 a drama is a play for the theatre or television

3 drama is something exciting happening

◆ dramatic [adjective]
1 to do with plays and the theatre: *a dramatic production*
2 exciting
3 sudden and unexpected: *a dramatic rise in exam passes*
◆ dramatist [noun: **dramatists**] someone who writes plays
◆ dramatization or **dramatisation** [noun: **dramatizations**] a dramatization is a play based on an existing story or book
◆ dramatize or **dramatise** [verb: **dramatizes, dramatizing, dramatized**]
1 to turn something into a play for the theatre or television: *This story has been dramatized several times.*
2 to make a story or report more exciting than the actual event

drank [verb] a way of changing the verb **drink** to make a past tense: *We drank our tea and left as quickly as possible.*

drape [verb: **drapes, draping, draped**] to arrange cloth so that it hangs gracefully: *Sue draped the shawl around her shoulders.*

draper [noun: **drapers**] someone who owns a shop that sells curtains and cloth
◆ drapery [noun] fabric and cloth that hangs, such as curtains

drapes [plural noun] an American English word for curtains

drastic [adjective] a drastic action has an extreme effect: *We need to do something drastic here.*
◆ drastically [adverb] in a sudden and extreme way: *Nora has changed drastically in the last few months.*

draught [noun: **draughts**] a current of air
→ draughty

draughts [noun] a game for two people who move round black or white pieces on a checked board

draughtsman [noun: **draughtsmen**] a man whose job is to draw plans

draughtswoman [noun: **draughtswomen**] a woman whose job is to draw plans

draughty [adjective: **draughtier, draughtiest**] a draughty place is cold and full of moving air currents

draw [verb: **draws, drawing, drew, drawn**]
1 to make a picture with a pencil or pen
2 to pull something along behind: *Horses drew the carriage.*
3 to attract: *The circus always draws huge audiences.*
4 to bring something near: *Draw your chair up to the table.*
5 to score equal points in a game: *These two have drawn every match they've played so far.* • *We drew 2–2.*
[noun: **draws**]
1 an equal score: *The game ended in a draw.*
2 a lottery or raffle
→ drawing

drawback [noun: **drawbacks**] a disadvantage: *The main drawback of the plan is that it's expensive.*

drawbridge [noun: **drawbridges**] a bridge at the entrance to a castle that can be raised or lowered

drawer [noun: **drawers**] a sliding box in a table, chest or cupboard

drawing [noun: **drawings**] a picture drawn with a pencil or pen

drawing pin [noun: **drawing pins**] a short pin with a large flat head that you use to fix paper to an upright surface like a board

drawl [verb: **drawls, drawling, drawled**] to speak slowly and lazily
[noun: **drawls**] a slow, lazy way of speaking

drawn [verb] a form of the verb **draw** that is used with a helping verb to show that something happened in the past: *I've drawn several styles for you to choose from.*

dread [verb: **dreads, dreading, dreaded**] to be very afraid and worried about something that is going to happen: *We're all dreading the exams.*
[noun] a feeling of great fear: *The thought of flying fills me with dread.*

dreadful [adjective] terrible: *dreadful news* • *a dreadful film*
◆ dreadfully [adverb]
1 very badly: *The children have been behaving dreadfully all day.*
2 very much: *I'm dreadfully sorry.*

Dd

dreadlocks [plural noun] hair that is worn in long twisted strands

dream [noun: **dreams**]
1 the things you think while you are asleep: *I had a very strange dream last night.*
2 a hope or ambition: *It was always her dream to go to Hollywood.*
3 if you are **in a dream**, you are concentrating on your thoughts and not on what is going on around you
[verb: **dreams, dreaming, dreamt** or **dreamed**] to imagine something: *Did you say that or did I dream it?*

dreary [adjective: **drearier, dreariest**] dull and boring

dredge [verb: **dredges, dredging, dredged**] to scrape mud or waste off the bottom of a lake or river
✦ **dredger** [noun: **dredgers**] a ship that digs a channel in a river or seabed

drench [verb: **drenches, drenching, drenched**] to be drenched is to be completely wet

dress [noun: **dresses**]
1 a dress is a piece of clothing for girls or women like a top and skirt joined together
2 dress is clothing: *dancers in traditional dress*
[verb: **dresses, dressing, dressed**]
1 to put clothes on: *The doorbell rang while I was dressing.* • *You dress the children and I'll get the breakfast.* • *Hurry up and get dressed!*
2 to put salt and pepper or a sauce on food ready for eating: *I just need to dress the salad.*
3 to put a bandage or plaster on a wound
4 to **dress up** is to put on special clothes: *Colin always loved to dress up as a pirate.*
✦ **dresser** [noun: **dressers**] a kitchen cupboard with open shelves at the top
✦ **dressing** [noun: **dressings**]
1 a light sauce for food, especially salad
2 a bandage or plaster for a wound

dressing-gown [noun: **dressing-gowns**] a piece of clothing like a loose coat that you wear over your pyjamas

dressmaker [noun: **dressmakers**] someone who makes clothes for women

dress rehearsal [noun: **dress rehearsals**] the final rehearsal for a stage show when the actors wear their costumes

drew [verb] a way of changing the verb **draw** to make a past tense: *Who drew this face on the board?*

dribble [verb: **dribbles, dribbling, dribbled**]
1 to let liquid leak out of your mouth
2 in football, to kick the ball gently along in front of you as you run

dried [verb] a way of changing the verb **dry** to make a past tense. It can be used with or without a helping verb: *Jill dried the glasses with a soft cloth.* • *After the fruit has been dried, it will keep for months.*

drift [verb: **drifts, drifting, drifted**]
1 to move with the tide or current of flowing water: *The boat drifted for days before being found.*
2 to wander about or live with no clear purpose: *He just seems to drift through life.*
[noun: **drifts**]
1 a pile of snow or sand that has been blown by the wind
2 the general meaning of what someone says: *I think I get your drift.*

driftwood [noun] wood that the sea washes up on to beaches

drill [verb: **drills, drilling, drilled**]
1 to make a hole in something hard
2 to do repeated exercises, especially in the army
[noun: **drills**]
1 a tool for making holes in hard materials like wood or stone
2 an exercise that is repeated frequently: *a fire drill*

drink [verb: **drinks, drinking, drank, drunk**]
1 to swallow a liquid
2 to drink alcohol: *I refused the wine because I don't drink.*
[noun: **drinks**]
1 a liquid that you swallow when you are thirsty: *a drink of water*
2 alcoholic liquids: *Please do not bring drink into the hostel.*

drip [noun: **drips**]
1 a drop of liquid: *We're trying to catch the drips in a bucket.*
2 a series of falling drops of liquid: *I could hear*

the drip of the bathroom tap all night.
3 a piece of equipment for slowly giving a hospital patient a liquid that their body needs
[verb: **drips, dripping, dripped**]
1 to fall in drops: *water dripping from the trees*
2 to let a liquid fall in drops: *I can hear a tap dripping somewhere.*

dripping [noun] the fat that comes out of roasting meat

drive [verb: **drives, driving, drove, driven**]
1 to control a vehicle such as a car: *Can you drive?* • *He drove the van into a tree.*
2 to hit a ball very hard, especially in golf
3 to force someone into a certain state: *That tune's driving me crazy.*
[noun: **drives**]
1 a journey in a car: *Let's go for a drive.*
2 another word for a **driveway**
3 drive is energy and enthusiasm: *someone with a lot of drive*
⟶ **driver**

drivel [noun] written or spoken nonsense

driven [verb] a form of the verb **drive** that is used with a helping verb to show that something happened in the past: *Have you ever driven a car like this before?*

driver [noun: **drivers**] a person who drives a vehicle

driveway or **drive** [noun: **driveways** or **drives**] a private road up to a house: *a car parked in the driveway*

drizzle [noun] light rain
[verb: **drizzles, drizzling, drizzled**] to rain gently
♦ **drizzly** [adjective] drizzly weather is when it is dull and raining gently

drone [verb: **drones, droning, droned**]
1 to speak in a dull, boring voice: *The man seemed to drone on and on.*
2 to make a low humming sound
[noun: **drones**]
1 a low humming sound: *the drone of a plane overhead*
2 a male bee

drool [verb: **drools, drooling, drooled**]
1 to dribble
2 to **drool over** someone or something is to be enthusiastic about them in a silly way: *We stood drooling over the dresses in the window.*

droop [verb: **droops, drooping, drooped**]
to bend weakly or hang down: *The flowers are drooping.*

drop [noun: **drops**]
1 a small blob of liquid: *drops of water on the window*
2 a small quantity: *only a drop of milk left in the bottle*
3 a fall or decrease: *Kevin's new job will mean a drop in pay.*
[verb: **drops, dropping, dropped**]
1 to let something fall: *Drop the gun now!*
2 to fall suddenly: *The temperature drops a lot in the evening.*

drought [noun: **droughts**] a time when very little rain falls

ⓘ This word is pronounced **drowt**.

drove [verb] a way of changing the verb **drive** to make a past tense: *We drove to London down the M1.*

drown [verb: **drowns, drowning, drowned**]
1 to drown is to die because of not being able to breathe under water
2 to kill someone by keeping them under water so that they cannot breathe
3 to block out a sound with a louder one: *The music in the club drowned out our conversation.*

drowsy [adjective: **drowsier, drowsiest**] sleepy

drudgery [noun] boring, hard work

drug [noun: **drugs**]
1 a medicine: *a new drug for curing colds*
2 a chemical that people take to make them feel or think differently, or because they cannot stop using it
[verb: **drugs, drugging, drugged**] to give someone a drug that will make them unconscious

drum [noun: **drums**]
1 an instrument that is round and has a skin stretched over it that you hit to make a rhythm
2 a container in the shape of a cylinder: *an oil drum*
[verb: **drums, drumming, drummed**]
1 to beat a drum
2 to tap your fingers repeatedly

Dd

◆ **drummer** [noun: **drummers**] someone who plays the drums

drunk [verb] a form of the verb **drink** that is used with a helping verb to show that something happened in the past: *Haven't you drunk your cup of tea yet?*

[adjective] someone who is drunk is suffering from the effects of drinking too much alcohol: *He was so drunk he couldn't stand up straight.*

[noun: **drunks**] someone who is always drinking too much alcohol

dry [adjective: **drier, driest**]
1 not wet or damp: *clean, dry clothes*
2 not lively or interesting: *a dry book*
3 dry humour is funny in a way that is not obvious
4 dry wine is not sweet
[verb: **dries, drying, dried**] to remove or lose all the liquid from something

dry cleaning [noun] a way of cleaning clothes with special chemicals instead of water

dryer [noun: **dryers**] a machine that dries washing

dual [adjective] made up of two of something: *Our plan has a dual purpose.*

dual carriageway [noun: **dual carriageways**] a road where the traffic going in each direction is separated by some kind of barrier

dub [verb: **dubs, dubbing, dubbed**]
1 to add new sound to a film: *We watched Robin Hood, dubbed into Italian.*
2 to give someone another name, especially a nickname: *He's been dubbed 'The Eye' by his students.*

dubious [adjective]
1 feeling doubtful about something: *I'm a bit dubious about this wallpaper.*
2 probably dishonest: *a dubious character*

duchess [noun: **duchesses**]
1 the title of a woman who has the same rank as a duke
2 the wife of a duke

duck [noun: **ducks**] a water bird with webbed feet, short legs and a wide, flat beak
[verb: **ducks, ducking, ducked**]
1 to duck is to lower your head quickly, as if you were avoiding being hit

2 to duck someone is to push them under water

duckling [noun: **ducklings**] a baby duck

duct [noun: **ducts**] a tube or pipe: *tear duct*

dud [noun: **duds**] something that is faulty or does not work properly

due [adjective]
1 expected to arrive: *Their plane is due in ten minutes.*
2 needing to be paid: *The rent is due at the beginning of the month.*
3 if something that happens is **due to** something else, it is caused by it: *The delay was due to roadworks on the motorway.*
[adverb] directly: *due south of here*
→ duly

duel [noun: **duels**] a fight between two people that they arrange to settle an argument
[verb: **duels, duelling, duelled**] to fight another person to decide an argument

duet [noun: **duets**] a piece of music for two singers or players

dug [verb] a way of changing the verb **dig** to make a past tense. It can be used with or without a helping verb: *The children dug a hole under the apple tree.* • *A huge hole had been dug.*

dugout [noun: **dugouts**] a shelter at the side of a football pitch where the manager and substitutes can sit

duke [noun: **dukes**] a nobleman of high rank

dull [adjective: **duller, dullest**]
1 not bright: *a dull day* • *a dull blue colour*
2 not lively or interesting: *a dreadfully dull speech*
3 not clear or ringing: *a dull thump on the door*
◆ **dullness** [noun] being dull
◆ **dully** [adverb]
1 in a boring and uninteresting way
2 not brightly: *lights shining dully in the distance*

duly [adverb] as expected: *We duly handed over our gifts to the birthday girl.*

dumb [adjective: **dumber, dumbest**]
1 not able to speak
2 stupid: *That's the dumbest idea you've ever had.*

dumbfounded [adjective] to be dumbfounded is to be speechless with amazement

dummy [noun: **dummies**]
1 a model of a person, especially for displaying clothes in a shop: *The cars are crash-tested with dummies in them.*
2 an imitation teat that a baby sucks for comfort
3 an imitation of anything

dump [verb: **dumps, dumping, dumped**]
1 to unload and leave rubbish or something you do not want
2 to drop something heavily: *The kids dumped their schoolbags in the hall.*
[noun: **dumps**]
1 a place for leaving rubbish
2 an informal word for a messy or dirty place: *This flat is such a dump.*

dumpling [noun: **dumplings**] a cooked ball of dough that may be served with meat dishes

dumpy [adjective: **dumpier, dumpiest**] a dumpy person is short and fat

dunce [noun: **dunces**] someone who finds learning difficult

dune [noun: **dunes**] a low hill of sand

dung [noun] the solid waste of animals

dungarees [plural noun] a pair of trousers with a bib and braces attached

dungeon [noun: **dungeons**] a dark underground prison

duo [noun: **duos**] two people, especially a pair of musicians

dupe [verb: **dupes, duping, duped**] to trick or cheat someone: *The tourists were duped into handing over their money.*

duplicate [verb: **duplicates, duplicating, duplicated**] to make a copy or copies of something
[adjective] exactly the same: *a duplicate key*
[noun: **duplicates**] an exact copy
♦ **duplication** [noun] copying something exactly

durability [noun] how long-lasting something is: *We do tests on the products for durability.*

durable [adjective] lasting a long time: *a durable fabric for work clothes*

duration [noun] how long something lasts or continues: *a play of two hours' duration*

during [preposition] while something else is happening: *We left during the interval.*

dusk [noun] twilight, when night is falling in the evening

dust [noun] a fine powder of something, especially household dirt
[verb: **dusts, dusting, dusted**]
1 to clean dry dirt from surfaces: *The books have to be dusted regularly.*
2 to cover something with a fine powder: *Dust the cake with icing sugar.*

dustbin [noun: **dustbins**] a large container for household rubbish

duster [noun: **dusters**] a cloth for removing dust from surfaces

dustman [noun: **dustmen**] someone whose job is to collect household rubbish

dustpan [noun: **dustpans**] a flat container with a handle, used for sweeping dust into

dutiful [adjective] a dutiful person does what is expected of them: *Amir tried to be a dutiful son.*

duty [noun: **duties**]
1 something a person should do, especially as part of their job: *It's your duty to check the doors are locked.*
2 a tax: *raising the duty on imports*

duty-free [adjective] products that are duty-free are cheaper because the price does not include tax

duvet [noun: **duvets**] a quilt stuffed with feathers or artificial fibres that is used instead of blankets on a bed

ⓘ This word is pronounced **doo**-vay.

DVD [abbreviation] short for **digital versatile disk**, a type of disk that pictures and sounds can be recorded on, and which can hold more information than a CD

dwarf [noun: **dwarfs** or **dwarves**] a person or thing that is much smaller than normal
[verb: **dwarfs, dwarfing, dwarfed**] to make something else look small: *The new hotel dwarfs the old shops that surround it.*

dwell [verb: **dwells, dwelling, dwelt**]
1 to live somewhere
2 to **dwell on** something is to think or speak about it for a long time: *There's no point in dwelling on your mistakes now.*

dwindle [verb: **dwindles, dwindling, dwindled**] to grow less and less: *our dwindling supplies*

Dd

Dd

dye [noun: **dyes**] a powder or liquid that you use to change the colour of fabric or hair
[verb: **dyes, dyeing, dyed**] to make something such as fabric or hair a different colour: *I dyed my white shirt black.*

(i) When you add **-ing** to the verb **dye**, you keep the **e** to make **dyeing**. The word **dying**, without an **e**, comes from the verb **die**.

dying [verb] a way of changing the verb **die** when it is combined with a helping verb or to make it into a noun: *I'm dying to see that film.* • *He says he isn't afraid of dying.*

dyke [noun: **dykes**] another spelling of **dike**

dynamic [adjective] full of energy and new ideas: *a dynamic young manager*

dynamite [noun] a type of powerful explosive

dynamo [noun: **dynamos**] a machine that converts the energy of movement into electricity

dynasty [noun: **dynasties**] a series of rulers or leaders from the same family

dyslexia [noun] difficulty in learning to read and spell
• **dyslexic** [adjective] a dyslexic person has difficulty in learning to recognize and form written words correctly

E

Ee

E [abbreviation] short for **east**

each [adjective]

1 each person or thing in a group or pair is every one as an individual: *He had a heavy suitcase in each hand.*

2 each other is used to show that each person or thing in a group does something to the others: *The team all hugged each other.* • *The cat and dog don't like each other much.*

[pronoun] every one individually: *Each of the girls had a different costume.*

eager [adjective] very keen to do or have something: *Imran seems eager to learn.*

♦ **eagerly** [adverb] keenly, enthusiastically: *All her fans were eagerly waiting for the next book.*

♦ **eagerness** [noun] being eager: *In his eagerness to get there, he fell over.*

eagle [noun: **eagles**] a large bird with a hooked beak and sharp claws that attacks small creatures

ear¹ [noun: **ears**] your ears are the two parts of your body on each side of your head that you hear with

ear² [noun: **ears**] an ear of corn or wheat is the part at the top of the plant's stem where the grains or seeds grow

earache [noun] pain inside your ear

eardrum [noun: **eardrums**] the part inside your ear that vibrates when sound hits it

earl [noun: **earls**] a British nobleman

earlobe [noun: **earlobes**] the soft rounded part that hangs down at the bottom of your ear

early [adjective and adverb: **earlier, earliest**]

1 happening or arriving before others or before the expected or normal time: *Nick had taken an earlier train.* • *I'm tired so I'm going to bed early tonight.*

2 near the beginning of something: *It's so quiet here in the early morning.* • *She showed musical talent early in life.*

earmark [verb: **earmarks, earmarking, earmarked**] to earmark something is to select it to be used for a special purpose: *That money's been earmarked for a new car.*

earn [verb: **earns, earning, earned**]

1 to earn money is to get it in return for work: *Sophie is trying to earn her living as an artist.*

2 to earn something good, such as praise, is to get it because you have done something well

earnest [adjective] serious about, or really meaning, what you do or say

[noun] if someone is **in earnest**, they are serious or sincere about something

earnings [plural noun] your earnings are all the money that you get from working or by investing money

earphones [plural noun] two small speakers that you wear in or on your ears so that you can listen to music or other sounds

earplugs [plural noun] small plugs that you put in your ears to block out loud noises

earring [noun: **earrings**] a piece of jewellery worn on your ear

earshot [noun] if a sound is in earshot, it is within the range of your hearing: *I couldn't hear what they were saying because they were just out of earshot.*

earth [noun: **earths**]

1 the Earth is the planet we live on

2 earth is the ground or soil: *digging in the earth*

189

Ee

3 the earth is the wire in an electrical circuit or piece of equipment that channels the electric current into the ground and makes it safe to use
4 a fox's earth is the burrow or hole it lives in
♦ **earthly** [adjective] to do with the Earth, rather than the sky or heaven

earthquake [noun: **earthquakes**] a situation when the ground shakes because of pressure that has built up in the rocks of the Earth's surface

earthworm [noun: **earthworms**] a common type of worm found in soil

earwig [noun: **earwigs**] a common garden insect with pincers at its tail

ease [verb: **eases, easing, eased**]
1 to ease is to make or become less difficult or painful: *These tablets will help to ease the pain.* • *Tensions in the area have gradually eased.*
2 to ease something into or out of a place is to move it there gently or gradually: *They eased the last big block into position.*
[noun]
1 ease is rest: *Gary was taking his ease in a hammock in the garden.*
2 if you are **at ease** with something, you feel comfortable about it: *He's never completely at ease talking to strangers.*
3 to do something **with ease** is to do it without any effort or difficulty: *Lorna won the race with ease.*

easel [noun: **easels**] a frame used by an artist to support the picture he or she is working on

easily [adverb]
1 without a lot of effort or difficulty: *Chelsea won easily.*
2 by a long way: *She's easily the most successful female pop singer today.*
3 very possibly: *It could easily be two weeks before you get a replacement.*

east [noun]
1 the direction where you see the sun rising in the morning, opposite to west
2 the East and the Far East are the countries in Asia
[adjective] in, from, or towards the east: *an east wind* • *East London*
[adverb] to the east: *We headed east.*
➡ **easterly, eastern, eastward**

Easter [noun] a Christian festival to remember Christ's rising from the dead, celebrated in spring

easterly [adjective] coming from, or going towards, the east: *an easterly breeze* • *They set off in an easterly direction.*

eastern [adjective] belonging to, or coming from, the east: *an eastern custom*

eastward or **eastwards** [adverb] to or towards the east: *sailing eastwards towards the rising sun*

easy [adjective: **easier, easiest**]
1 not difficult or hard to do: *an easy exam paper*
2 you **take it easy** when you relax or don't work too hard
➡ **easily**

eat [verb: **eats, eating, ate, eaten**]
1 to eat food is to chew and swallow it
2 to eat is to have a meal: *What time would you like to eat?*
3 to **eat something away** is to destroy it gradually: *The cliffs were being eaten away by the sea.*
4 to **eat something up** is to eat it all or to use it all up: *Eat up your greens.* • *The repairs had eaten up all their savings.*

eaves [plural noun] the eaves of a building are the parts where the roof sticks out over the walls

eavesdrop [verb: **eavesdrops, eavesdropping, eavesdropped**] to eavesdrop is to listen to other people's conversations without them knowing

ebb [verb: **ebbs, ebbing, ebbed**]
1 the tide ebbs when the water in the sea goes back from the land. Look up and compare **flow**
2 something **ebbs away** when it gradually gets less and less until it disappears
[noun] if something is **at a low ebb**, it is at a low level: *Her confidence was at a low ebb.*

ebony [noun] a very hard black wood from an African tree

eccentric [adjective] an eccentric person behaves in a way that is slightly odd or different from most people
♦ **eccentricity** [noun: **eccentricities**] odd behaviour

ECG [noun: **ECGs**] a test when you are wired

up to a machine that measures how well your heart is beating. The diagram that the machine produces is also called an ECG

ⓘ **ECG** is short for **electrocardiogram** or **electrocardiograph**.

echo [noun: **echoes**] a sound that you hear again after it has travelled away from you, bounced off a surface and come back towards you
[verb: **echoes, echoing, echoed**]
1 a sound echoes when it is comes back and you hear it again
2 to echo what someone has said is to repeat it
éclair [noun: **éclairs**] a long thin cake made of special light pastry filled with cream and with chocolate on top
eclipse [noun: **eclipses**]
1 an eclipse of the sun happens when the sun disappears behind the moon and the sky goes dark for a few minutes
2 an eclipse of the moon happens when the Earth comes between the moon and the sun, and the Earth's shadow falls on the moon
eco- [prefix] if a word starts with **eco-**, it has something to do with the environment. For example, *eco-friendly* means not damaging to the environment
ecological [adjective]
1 to do with ecology or the ecology of a particular area
2 not harmful to the environment: *an ecological detergent*
ecology [noun]
1 ecology is the study of how plants and animals exist together in their environment and how they are affected by their environment
2 the ecology of a particular area is all the plants and animals in that area and how they depend on each other and on the special conditions there to exist
economic [adjective]
1 to do with an economy: *an economic forecast*
2 making money or profit: *The business was no longer economic and closed down.*
• **economical** [adjective] not wasting money: *an economical car that doesn't use a lot of fuel*

• **economics** [noun] economics is the study of how money is created and spent
• **economist** [noun: **economists**] someone who studies economics
• **economize** or **economise** [verb: **economizes, economizing, economized**] to economize is to be careful about spending money
economy [noun: **economies**]
1 a country's economy is all the wealth it creates through producing and selling goods, and the way that wealth is used
2 economy is using something, especially money, carefully to avoid waste
3 to make economies is to make savings
ecosystem [noun: **ecosystems**] a system in which plants and animals exist together, depending on each other and on the surrounding conditions for survival
ecstasy [noun]
1 ecstasy is a feeling of wild joy or pleasure
2 Ecstasy is an illegal drug that can cause hallucinations
ecstatic [adjective] if someone is ecstatic, they are as happy as it is possible to be: *She was ecstatic to see her missing son again.*
eczema [noun] a disease in which dry, itchy, red patches develop on your skin
edge [noun: **edges**]
1 the end of something: *the edge of the cliff • the edge of the table*
2 a side of something that is sharp enough to cut: *The knives have sharp edges.*
3 if someone is **on edge**, they are nervous and easily irritated: *Adam's a bit on edge because he's waiting for his exam results.*
[verb: **edges, edging, edged**]
1 to move slowly and carefully: *Harry edged along the narrow ledge.*
2 to form a border around something: *pillowcases edged with lace*
• **edging** [noun: **edgings**] something that forms a border around something else
• **edgy** [adjective: **edgier, edgiest**] to be edgy is to feel nervous and a bit bad-tempered
edible [adjective] if something is edible, it can be eaten: *edible mushrooms*
edit [verb: **edits, editing, edited**]

Ee

1 to edit a book, magazine or newspaper is to prepare it to be published or printed by correcting the text or putting all its parts together in order

2 to edit a film or tape recording is to cut it or alter it so that it is ready to be broadcast

♦ **edition** [noun: **editions**] an edition of a book, magazine or newspaper is all the copies that are printed at the same time

♦ **editor** [noun: **editors**]

1 someone who corrects or brings together all the parts of a book, magazine, newspaper or film

2 someone in charge of what goes into a newspaper or part of a newspaper

educate [verb: **educates, educating, educated**] to educate people is to teach them and to help them learn things

♦ **educated** [adjective] an educated person is someone who knows a lot because they have had a good education

♦ **education** [noun] education is teaching, especially in schools or colleges

♦ **educational** [adjective] to do with teaching and learning

-ee [suffix]

1 if **-ee** comes at the end of a word, it is a noun that refers to someone who is 'receiving' an action. For example, an *interviewee* is someone who is being interviewed

2 if **-ee** comes at the end of other words, they are nouns that refer to someone who has done an action. For example, an *escapee* is someone who has escaped

eel [noun: **eels**] a type of fish that has a long thin body like a snake

eerie [adjective] if something is eerie, it is strange in a frightening way: *a dark and eerie old house*

♦ **eerily** [adverb] strangely or weirdly: *The forest suddenly became eerily silent.*

effect [noun: **effects**]

1 if one thing has an effect on another, it influences it or causes something to happen to it: *His asthma has no effect on his ability as a footballer.*

2 the effect of something is the result it has: *She was suffering from the effects of a long plane journey.*

3 if a law or rule **comes into effect**, it begins to be used: *The law came into effect in July.*

♦ **effective** [adjective] working well or producing the results you want: *an effective treatment for the common cold*

ⓘ You have to be careful not to confuse **effect**, which is a noun, with **affect**, which is a verb. *One thing has an **effect** on another. One thing **affects** another.*

effeminate [adjective] an effeminate man behaves more like a woman than a man

effervescent [adjective]

1 an effervescent liquid bubbles or fizzes because it is full of gas: *an effervescent drink*

2 someone with an effervescent personality seems to bubble with enthusiasm and energy

efficiency [noun] efficiency is working well

efficient [adjective] an efficient process, system or person is one that works quickly and well

effort [noun: **efforts**]

1 effort is hard work: *It needs a lot of effort to be an athlete.*

2 an effort is a try: *That was a really good effort, Sonia.*

♦ **effortless** [adjective] not needing, or seeming not to need, a lot of hard work or energy: *A good ballet dancer makes it look effortless.*

eg or **e.g.** [abbreviation] You use **eg** when you are giving an example of what you mean: *animals found in Africa, eg the lion and the giraffe*

ⓘ **eg** is short for **exempli gratia**, which is Latin for 'for example'.

egg [noun: **eggs**]

1 an egg is a shell or case with a developing baby bird, reptile or fish inside

2 an egg is one of these laid by a hen or other bird that we eat as food: *a hard-boiled egg*

3 an egg is a special cell stored inside the body of a female mammal which can grow into a baby

4 if you **put all your eggs in one basket**, you put all your money or effort into one thing, and if it fails you will lose everything

[verb: **eggs, egging, egged**] to **egg**

Ee

someone on is to encourage them, usually to do something bad

ego [noun: **egos**] your ego is the opinion you have of your own importance: *All the attention and praise was good for her ego.*

Eid [noun] Eid is an Arabic word meaning *festival*. The **Eid-ul-Fitr** is a Muslim festival held each year to celebrate the end of **Ramadan**, when there is a feast and people give each other presents

eiderdown [noun: **eiderdowns**] a warm top covering for a bed, filled with feathers or some other light material

eight [noun: **eights**] the number 8

eighteen [noun] the number 18

eighteenth [adjective and adverb] after seventeenth and before nineteenth: *my cousin's eighteenth birthday party*

eighth [adjective and adverb] after seventh and before ninth: *the eighth book in the series* • *Our team finished eighth.*
[noun: **eighths**] the fraction $\frac{1}{8}$, which means one of eight equal parts of something: *an eighth of a mile*

eighty [noun: **eighties**] the number 80

either [adjective]
1 the one or the other: *She can write with either hand.*
2 both: *goalposts at either end of the pitch*
[pronoun] the one or the other of two: *I can't afford either of them.*
[adverb] as well: *If you don't go, I won't go either.*
[conjunction] **either** is used with **or** to show a choice or alternative: *You can have either a video game or a CD.*

ⓘ Remember that the verb that follows **either** and **or** should be singular if a singular noun comes before it, and the verb should be plural if a plural noun comes before it.
*Either George or his brother **was** telling lies.*
*Either George or his brothers **were** telling lies.*

eject [verb: **ejects, ejecting, ejected**]
1 to eject something is to throw it out with sudden force: *The octopus ejected a cloud of black ink.*
2 if a pilot ejects from an aircraft in an emergency, he or she operates a special seat which is fired out of the cockpit

elaborate [adjective] involving complicated detail or decoration: *an elaborate plan* • *elaborate costumes*
[verb: **elaborates, elaborating, elaborated**] to **elaborate on** something is to explain it more fully or in more detail: *Would you like to elaborate on that statement?*

elastic [adjective] able to stretch and then spring back: *an elastic band*
[noun] elastic is a strip of fabric with rubber or some other stretchy material woven into it to make it stretch and spring back
• **elasticity** [noun] the quality of being stretchy or springy

elated [adjective] very pleased and excited: *They were elated after winning the cup.*

elbow [noun: **elbows**] the joint in the middle of your arm that bends
[verb: **elbows, elbowing, elbowed**] to elbow someone is to poke or push them with your elbow

elder [adjective] older: *elder brothers and sisters*
[noun: **elders**] your elders are people who are older than you
• **elderly** [adjective] an elderly person is old
• **eldest** [adjective] oldest: *his eldest child*

elect [verb: **elects, electing, elected**] to elect someone is to choose them by voting: *elect a president*
• **election** [noun: **elections**] when people choose someone by voting: *standing for election* • *a presidential election*
• **elector** [noun: **electors**] someone who votes in an election
• **electorate** [noun: **electorates**] all the people who can vote in an election

electric [adjective] made or worked by electricity: *an electric spark* • *an electric light*
• **electrical** [adjective] to do with electricity: *an electrical circuit* • *an electrical storm*

electrician [noun: **electricians**] someone whose job is to fit or repair electrical equipment

electricity [noun] a form of energy used to make light and heat and to power machinery

electrify [verb: **electrifies, electrifying, electrified**]

Ee

Ee

1 to electrify machinery or equipment is to make it work on electric power

2 if something electrifies you, it excites, shocks or startles you

electro- [prefix] if a word starts with **electro-**, it has something to do with electricity. For example, an *electromagnet* is a magnet that is worked by an electric current

electrocute [verb: **electrocutes, electrocuting, electrocuted**] to be electrocuted is to be killed by a strong electric current which passes through your body: *He was electrocuted while he was trying to fix the lights.*

• **electrocution** [noun] electrocuting someone or being electrocuted

electrode [noun: **electrodes**] a small metal device that allows electric current to pass from a source of power, such as a battery, to a piece of equipment

electromagnet [noun: **electromagnets**] a magnet that works when an electric current passes through it

electronic [adjective]

1 electronic equipment uses very small electrical circuits such as silicon chips and transistors

2 to do with electronics

• **electronics** [noun] the study of how particles with electric charges flow and how they can be used in machinery

elegance [noun] being graceful and tastefully dressed

• **elegant** [adjective] stylish and smart: *an elegant lady*

element [noun: **elements**]

1 a chemical element is a substance which cannot be split into separate or simpler substances. Hydrogen, oxygen, nitrogen and carbon are elements

2 the elements of something are the basic parts that make it up: *the elements of mathematics*

3 the elements are things like rain and wind that make the weather, especially bad weather: *They were stuck on a bare hillside, completely exposed to the elements.*

4 a small part or bit of something: *There is an element of truth in what he said.*

5 a bent or coiled piece of metal containing an electric wire that heats an electric kettle or oven

6 if you are **in your element**, you are doing the thing that you are best at or that you enjoy the most

• **elementary** [adjective] at the simplest or most basic level: *an elementary particle* • *an elementary school*

elephant [noun: **elephants**] a very large animal with a long trunk, large flapping ears, thick grey skin and tusks made of ivory

elevate [verb: **elevates, elevating, elevated**] to elevate something is to raise it

• **elevator** [noun: **elevators**] an elevator is a lift for carrying people between the floors in a building

eleven [noun: **elevens**] the number 11

eleventh [adjective] after tenth and before twelfth: *the eleventh day of the eleventh month*

elf [noun: **elves**] in stories, a tiny fairy that gets up to mischief. An elf is often described as having a thin face with pointed ears

• **elfin** [adjective] like an elf: *a small elfin face*

eligible [adjective] an eligible person is suitable for or allowed to do something: *Am I eligible for a payment?*

eliminate [verb: **eliminates, eliminating, eliminated**] to eliminate something is to get rid of it completely: *steps to eliminate poverty*

• **elimination** [noun] getting rid of something completely

elite [noun: **elites**] the elite in a society or group are the best or most important people in it: *the sporting elite*
[adjective] belonging to an elite: *an elite force*

elk [noun: **elk** or **elks**] a type of very large deer with large horns that is found in northern Europe and Asia

ellipse [noun: **ellipses**] an oval shape

• **elliptical** [adjective] shaped like an oval: *a planet with an elliptical orbit*

elm [noun: **elms**] a type of tall tree with broad round leaves

elocution [noun] elocution is the art of speaking correctly and clearly

elongate [verb: **elongates, elongating, elongated**] to get longer or make something longer

eloquent [adjective] able to talk and express yourself well

else [adverb]
1 other than or besides the thing or person already talked about: *They didn't have anywhere else to go.*
2 or else means otherwise: *Put on a jumper or else you'll catch cold.*

elsewhere [adverb] in another place: *Luckily, he'd been elsewhere when his house was destroyed.*

elude [verb: **eludes, eluding, eluded**]
1 to elude someone who is looking for you is to get away from them without being seen or caught
2 if something eludes you, you can't get hold of it or remember it: *The phrase he wanted eluded him.*
 • **elusive** [adjective] difficult to see or find

em- [prefix] look at the entry for **en-**

e-mail or **email** [noun: **e-mails** or **emails**] short for **electronic mail**, a message or messages that are sent between computers: *They keep in touch by e-mail.* • *He sends me an e-mail every day.*
[verb: **e-mails, e-mailing, e-mailed** or **emails, emailing, emailed**] to e-mail someone is to send them an e-mail

embankment [noun: **embankments**] a steep bank of earth or rock built up along the sides of a railway, canal or motorway

embark [verb: **embarks, embarking, embarked**]
1 to embark is to get on a ship at the beginning of a journey
2 to **embark on** something is to begin it: *We're about to embark on an exciting new project.*

embarrass [verb: **embarrasses, embarrassing, embarrassed**] to embarrass someone is to make them feel uncomfortable or ashamed
 • **embarrassed** [adjective] looking or feeling ashamed or self-conscious
 • **embarrassing** [adjective] making you feel embarrassed
 • **embarrassment** [noun] being embarrassed

embassy [noun: **embassies**] a building where an ambassador lives and works

embellish [verb: **embellishes, embellishing, embellished**] to embellish something is to add details to it to make it more fancy or more interesting
 • **embellishment** [noun: **embellishments**] an embellishment is something added as decoration or to make something more interesting

embers [plural noun] the small hot pieces left when coal or wood is burnt in a fire

emblem [noun: **emblems**] an object or image that is used as a symbol for something else: *The thistle is the emblem of Scotland.*

embrace [verb: **embraces, embracing, embraced**]
1 to embrace someone is to put your arms round them and hold them tight
2 to embrace something, such as an idea or belief, is to accept it or adopt it
3 to embrace something is to include it: *a subject that embraces both maths and science*
[noun: **embraces**] a hug

embroider [verb: **embroiders, embroidering, embroidered**] to embroider is to stitch patterns with coloured threads
 • **embroidery** [noun] decorative stitching

embryo [noun: **embryos**] a baby animal or bird at the very earliest stages of its development when it starts growing inside its mother's womb or inside an egg

emerald [noun: **emeralds**]
1 a green precious stone
2 a bright green colour

emerge [verb: **emerges, emerging, emerged**] to emerge is to come out: *The baby crocodiles emerge from the eggs.*

emergency [noun: **emergencies**] an emergency is a sudden, unexpected event, often one that puts people's lives or property in danger

emigrant [noun: **emigrants**] someone who leaves one country to go and live in another

emigrate [verb: **emigrates, emigrating, emigrated**] to emigrate is to leave your country to go and live in another country

ⓘ Do not confuse this with the word **immigrate**. You **emigrate** if you leave your country, but you **immigrate** if you come into a new country.

Ee

eminent [adjective] an eminent person is famous and well-respected: *an eminent lawyer*

emission [noun: **emissions**]
1 emission is emitting something
2 an emission is something that is sent out, such as the fumes from a car's exhaust or smoke from a factory chimney

Ee

emit [verb: **emits, emitting, emitted**] to emit something, such as light, heat, gas or a sound, is to produce it and send it out: *The machine emitted a high-pitched screech.*

emotion [noun: **emotions**] an emotion is a strong feeling, such as love, hate, fear, jealousy or anger: *He showed no emotion as he was sentenced to jail. • Anya struggled to control her emotions.*

♦ **emotional** [adjective] showing or having strong feelings: *an emotional farewell*

empathize or **empathise** [verb: **empathizes, empathizing, empathized**] to empathize with someone is to feel close to them because you have experienced the same things they have

♦ **empathy** [noun] empathy is feeling close to someone because you know how they feel

emperor [noun: **emperors**] the ruler of an empire

emphasis [noun: **emphases**] emphasis is special importance given to something or extra stress put on something to make it stand out: *Say the line with a bit more emphasis.*

♦ **emphasize** or **emphasise** [verb: **emphasizes, emphasizing, emphasized**] to emphasize something is to make it stand out: *I want to emphasize the importance of road safety.*

♦ **emphatic** [adjective] an emphatic statement is made strongly or firmly

empire [noun: **empires**]
1 an empire is a group of countries governed by a single ruler
2 a business empire is a group of companies or businesses controlled by one person or organization

employ [verb: **employs, employing, employed**] you employ someone who works for you, usually in return for pay: *The company employs skilled workers.*

♦ **employee** [noun: **employees**] someone who works for a company or another person

♦ **employer** [noun: **employers**] a company or person who employs people

♦ **employment** [noun] employment is work, especially for pay

empress [noun: **empresses**] a female ruler of an empire

emptiness [noun] being empty

empty [adjective: **emptier, emptiest**] having nothing or no one inside: *an empty glass • an empty classroom*
[verb: **empties, emptying, emptied**]
1 to empty is to make or become empty: *Empty your pockets. • The theatre slowly emptied.*
2 to empty something is to tip or pour it out of a container: *The dustmen were emptying the rubbish out of the bins.*

emu [noun: **emus**] a large Australian bird that cannot fly and looks similar to, but is smaller than, an ostrich

emulate [verb: **emulates, emulating, emulated**] to emulate someone is to copy them because you admire them

emulsion [noun: **emulsions**] a type of paint that produces a surface that is not shiny: *a tin of emulsion*

en- or **em-** [prefix] if a word begins with **en-** or **em-**, it adds the meaning 'into' to the word. For example, to *enclose* something is to close it in, and to *embark* is to go into a ship

enable [verb: **enables, enabling, enabled**] if something enables you to do something, it makes it possible for you to do it: *Sponsorship would enable more young athletes to develop.*

enamel [noun: **enamels**]
1 a hard shiny coating that is baked on to metal in a very hot oven to protect or decorate it
2 the hard white coating on teeth
[adjective] made of or covered with enamel: *an enamel plate*

enchant [verb: **enchants, enchanting, enchanted**]
1 if something enchants you, it delights or charms you
2 fairies and witches in stories enchant people when they put a magic spell or charm on them

+ **enchanted** [adjective] magical or under a magic spell: *an enchanted forest*
+ **enchanting** [adjective] delightful or charming: *an enchanting smile*
+ **enchantment** [noun] a feeling of delight or wonder

enclose [verb: **encloses, enclosing, enclosed**]
1 to enclose something in an envelope or package is to put it inside with your letter
2 to enclose a piece of land is to surround it with a fence or wall
+ **enclosure** [noun: **enclosures**]
1 something you put in an envelope or package with a letter
2 an area of land with a wall or fence around it

encore [noun: **encores**] an extra song or dance performed at the end of a stage show because the audience has shown that they want more

ⓘ This word is pronounced **on**-kor.

encounter [verb: **encounters, encountering, encountered**]
1 to encounter something is to experience it: *They encountered many difficulties on their journey.*
2 to encounter someone is to meet them by chance
[noun: **encounters**] a meeting: *an encounter with enemy troops*

encourage [verb: **encourages, encouraging, encouraged**]
1 to encourage someone is to support them and make them feel confident about what they are doing or are planning to do
2 to encourage something is to do something that will make it more likely to happen
+ **encouragement** [noun] supporting or giving confidence to someone or something: *The crowd roared, all shouting encouragement to the team they favoured.*
+ **encouraging** [adjective] giving confidence or hope: *an encouraging sign*

encyclopedia or **encyclopaedia** [noun: **encyclopedias** or **encyclopaedias**] a book with information about many subjects, or on a particular subject: *an encyclopedia of art*

+ **encyclopedic** [adjective] giving or having a lot of facts and information about many things

end [noun: **ends**]
1 the end of something is its last part or the place where it finishes: *the end of the day* • *I read the book from beginning to end.*
2 the ends of something are the parts farthest away from the middle: *The boys had to run from one end of the pitch to the other.*
3 an end is a result that you aim for or a purpose that you have: *They used their power for their own private ends.*
4 to **make ends meet** is to have enough money to buy what you need
5 if something happens for hours, days or months **on end**, it continues without stopping for that length of time: *The rain seemed to go on for weeks on end.*
[verb: **ends, ending, ended**]
1 to finish: *Our holiday ends tomorrow.* • *He ended his speech with a joke.*
2 to **end up** somewhere is to finish there or come to a stop there: *I always knew he'd end up in prison.*
➞ **ending**

endanger [verb: **endangers, endangering, endangered**] to endanger something is to put it in danger or at risk

endangered species [noun: **endangered species**] an endangered species is a type of animal or plant that is in danger of dying out

endeavour [verb: **endeavours, endeavouring, endeavoured**] to endeavour to do something is to try to do it, especially in a serious or determined way
[noun: **endeavours**]
1 endeavour is the effort or energy people put into doing things: *human endeavour*
2 an endeavour is an attempt to do something which needs effort or energy: *I wish you luck in all your endeavours.*

ending [noun: **endings**] the last part: *The story had a happy ending.*

endorse [verb: **endorses, endorsing, endorsed**] to endorse something is to give it your support
+ **endorsement** [noun: **endorsements**]

Ee

197

1 support or confirmation of a person, plan or idea: *endorsement of the new plan*
2 an endorsement is an official note of something a driver has done wrong that is written on their driving licence

endowment mortgage [noun: **endowment mortgages**] a type of mortgage that is linked to an endowment policy that should eventually pay off the amount of the loan

endowment policy [noun: **endowment policies**] a type of insurance policy that you pay into for an agreed number of years, after which the money is paid back to you with interest. It is often sold with a mortgage and the money is used to pay off the loan

endurance [noun] the ability to last or to survive long periods of strain: *a test of endurance*

endure [verb: **endures, enduring, endured**]
1 to endure something is to put up with it over a long period of time: *He didn't know if he could endure the loneliness any more.*
2 to endure is to last: *Her work endures only in our memories.*

enemy [noun: **enemies**]
1 someone or something that is against you or wants to do you harm
2 in a war, the enemy is the people or country you are fighting against
[adjective] to do with the enemy: *enemy troops*

energetic [adjective] very active and lively: *an energetic dance*

energy [noun: **energies**]
1 the strength or power to work or be active: *Most toddlers have bags of energy.*
2 a form of power, such as heat or electricity: *trying to save energy • nuclear energy*

enforce [verb: **enforces, enforcing, enforced**] to enforce a rule or law is to use it and make sure people obey it

engage [verb: **engages, engaging, engaged**]
1 to engage someone is to start to employ them
2 to engage in an activity is to do it or keep busy doing it

✦ **engaged** [adjective]
1 if two people are engaged, they have promised to marry each other
2 a telephone or toilet is engaged when it is being used

✦ **engagement** [noun: **engagements**]
1 a promise to marry someone
2 an appointment to meet someone or to do something for a certain period of time

engine [noun: **engines**]
1 a machine that turns the energy made by burning fuel into movement: *a car with a diesel engine*
2 the vehicle at the front of a train that pulls the coaches: *a steam engine*

engineer [noun: **engineers**]
1 someone who works with or designs engines and machines: *a telephone engineer*
2 someone who designs and makes things like bridges and roads: *a civil engineer*
[verb: **engineers, engineering, engineered**] to engineer something is to make it happen by clever planning: *Josh tried to engineer a meeting between the two sides.*

✦ **engineering** [noun] engineering is the science or work of designing and making machinery, or of designing roads and bridges

engrave [verb: **engraves, engraving, engraved**] to engrave a design or lettering is to carve it into a hard surface, such as metal or glass

✦ **engraving** [noun: **engravings**]
1 engraving is the process or skill of carving designs or lettering into metal or glass
2 an engraving is a picture made by doing this

engrossed [adjective] if you are engrossed in something it takes your whole attention or interest

enhance [verb: **enhances, enhancing, enhanced**] to enhance something is to make it better or greater

enjoy [verb: **enjoys, enjoying, enjoyed**]
1 to enjoy something is to get a feeling of pleasure from it: *They seemed to enjoy the concert.*
2 to enjoy yourself is to have a good time: *We enjoyed ourselves at the party.*

✦ **enjoyable** [adjective] making you feel happy

✦ **enjoyment** [noun] pleasure

enlarge [verb: **enlarges, enlarging, enlarged**] to enlarge something is to make it bigger
  ◆ **enlargement** [noun: **enlargements**]
  1 enlargement is increasing in size
  2 an enlargement is a larger photograph made from a smaller one

enlist [verb: **enlists, enlisting, enlisted**]
  1 to enlist is to join the army, navy or air force
  2 if you enlist someone's help or support, you ask for it and get it

enormous [adjective] very big: *an enormous tree*
  ◆ **enormously** [adverb]
  1 very greatly: *They all enjoyed themselves enormously.*
  2 extremely: *enormously grateful*

enough [adjective] as much or as many as you need, want or can put up with: *I've got enough problems without this!*
  [pronoun] as much as you need, want or can put up with: *Have you all had enough to eat and drink?*
  [adverb] as much as is needed or wanted: *You've gone far enough.*

enquire [verb: **enquires, enquiring, enquired**] another spelling of **inquire**
  ◆ **enquiry** [noun: **enquiries**] another spelling of **inquiry**

enrage [verb: **enrages, enraging, enraged**] if something enrages you, it makes you very angry

enrich [verb: **enriches, enriching, enriched**] to enrich something is to improve it by adding something to it: *Art enriches people's lives.*

enrol or **enroll** [verb: **enrols** or **enrolls, enrolling, enrolled**] to enrol is to put your name on a register or list: *Jackie's just enrolled at a stage school.*
  ◆ **enrolment** [noun] enrolling or the number of people enrolled

ensue [verb: **ensues, ensuing, ensued**] to ensue is to come after or as a result of something else: *Hundreds of people came into the shop and chaos ensued.*

ensure [verb: **ensures, ensuring, ensured**] to ensure is to make certain: *Please ensure you have all your belongings with you.*

entail [verb: **entails, entailing, entailed**]
  1 one thing entails another when it makes that other thing necessary: *Learning the piano entails hours of practice.*
  2 what something entails is what is involved in doing it: *Can you tell me what the job will entail?*

entangled [adjective] if things are entangled, they are wound around each other so that it is difficult to separate them

enter [verb: **enters, entering, entered**]
  1 to go in or into a place: *Please enter.* • *A tall man entered the room.*
  2 to enter a competition is to take part in it
  3 to enter something in a book, list or computer is to write it in the book or list, or type it into the computer

enterprise [noun: **enterprises**]
  1 enterprise is the ability to think of and try out new ideas and find ways to carry them out: *We're looking for someone with enterprise for this job.*
  2 an enterprise is something that involves planning and risk, such as a business
  ◆ **enterprising** [adjective] an enterprising person is able to think of new ways of doing things and is not frightened of taking risks

entertain [verb: **entertains, entertaining, entertained**]
  1 to entertain people is to amuse them: *Emily entertained us by telling a few jokes.*
  2 to entertain people is to invite them as your guests for a meal or a drink
  ◆ **entertainer** [noun: **entertainers**] someone who dances, sings or tells jokes to entertain people
  ◆ **entertaining** [adjective] amusing
  ◆ **entertainment** [noun: **entertainments**] something that amuses people or gives them pleasure

enthral [verb: **enthrals, enthralling, enthralled**] if something enthrals you, it fascinates you and holds your attention completely

enthusiasm [noun] if someone has enthusiasm, they are very keen to do or try things or they show a great deal of interest in something
  ◆ **enthusiast** [noun: **enthusiasts**] someone

Ee

who is very interested or involved in a particular thing: *James is a great cycling enthusiast.*

◆ **enthusiastic** [adjective] eager and showing keenness: *enthusiastic applause*

entire [adjective] an entire thing is the whole of it: *Connor spent the entire day paddling in the sea.*

◆ **entirely** [adverb] totally or completely: *It was my fault entirely.*

entitle [verb: **entitles, entitling, entitled**] if something entitles you to something, it gives you the right to have it or do it: *You are entitled to five weeks' holiday per year.*

◆ **entitlement** [noun] something you are entitled to: *holiday entitlement*

entrance [noun: **entrances**]
1 a place where you can go in or out: *The prince left by a side entrance.*
2 to make an entrance is to come into a room or come on to a stage

◆ **entrant** [noun: **entrants**] someone who enters a competition or contest

entry [noun: **entries**]
1 entry is going in or entering: *his entry into politics* • *There was a high iron gate barring our entry.*
2 an entry in a diary or book is one of the items written or printed in it
3 someone or something that enters a competition: *The competition attracted thousands of entries.*

envelop [verb: **envelops, enveloping, enveloped**] if one thing envelops another, it surrounds it and covers it completely: *A thick fog enveloped the hills.*

envelope [noun: **envelopes**] a folded paper covering for a letter or other document, especially one that is to be sent by post

envious [adjective] if you are envious of someone, you want something that they have

environment [noun: **environments**]
1 a person's or animal's environment is their surroundings where they live
2 the environment is all the things, such as air, land, sea, animals and plants, that make up the natural world around us

◆ **environmental** [adjective] to do with the environment

◆ **environmentalist** [noun: **environmentalists**] someone who tries to protect the environment from damage

envy [noun] if you feel envy, you want what someone else has
[verb: **envies, envying, envied**] to envy someone is to want what they have: *We envied him, because he did not have to go to school.*
⟶ **envious**

enzyme [noun: **enzymes**] one of a group of chemical substances made in both animals and plants, which make certain chemical changes begin or which control the speed of chemical changes

epic [noun: **epics**] an epic is a long story, poem or film about great events or exciting and heroic adventures

epicentre [noun: **epicentres**] the epicentre of an earthquake is the point on the ground just above where the earthquake starts and where it is strongest

epidemic [noun: **epidemics**] an epidemic happens when an illness or disease spreads and many people get it: *a flu epidemic*

epidural [noun: **epidurals**] an injection of an anaesthetic into your lower back so that you do not feel any pain. It is often given to women who are having a baby

epilepsy [noun] epilepsy is an illness that affects the brain and which causes short spells of unconsciousness and uncontrolled movements of the body called convulsions

◆ **epileptic** [adjective] caused by epilepsy: *an epileptic fit*
[noun: **epileptics**] someone who suffers from epilepsy

episode [noun: **episodes**]
1 an episode is one of the parts of a story or one of the programmes in a radio or TV series
2 an episode is an event: *It was one of the most embarrassing episodes of his life.*

epitaph [noun: **epitaphs**] a dead person's epitaph is what is written about them on their gravestone

equal [adjective]
1 two or more things are equal when they are of the same size, value or amount: *Cut the cake into four equal slices.*

2 if you are equal to a task, you are fit or able to do it

[verb: **equals, equalling, equalled**] one thing equals another when they are the same in size, value or amount

[noun: **equals**] a person's equal is someone who is as good as they are

+ **equality** [noun] being equal

+ **equalize** or **equalise** [verb: **equalizes, equalizing, equalized**]

1 to equalize things is to make them equal

2 to equalize is to score a goal to make each team's score the same: *Rooney equalized just before half-time.*

+ **equalizer** or **equaliser** [noun: **equalizers**] something that makes things equal, especially a goal that makes two teams' scores equal

+ **equally** [adverb]

1 in the same way or to the same degree: *The two drivers were equally to blame for the accident.*

2 in a way that is fair: *Share the sweets out equally.*

equation [noun: **equations**] in maths, a statement that two things are equal with the two parts written on either side of an equals sign, for example $15 + 4 = 25 - 6$

equator [noun] the equator is the line drawn on maps that goes around the Earth halfway between the North Pole and the South Pole

equilibrium [noun] equal balance between two things

equip [verb: **equips, equipping, equipped**] to equip someone is to provide them with all the things they will need to do a particular job: *They equipped themselves with ropes, crampons, ice axes and oxygen for the ascent of Everest.*

+ **equipment** [noun] the tools and special clothing needed to do a particular activity or job: *a shop selling camping equipment*

-er[1] [suffix] if **-er** comes at the end of a word, it may be an adjective that means 'more'. For example, *higher* means 'more high' than something else

-er[2] or **-or** [suffix] if **-er** or **-or** comes at the end of a word, it may be a noun that refers to someone or something that does an

action. For example, a *writer* is someone who or something that writes, and a *conductor* is someone who or something that conducts

equivalent [adjective] if two or more things are equivalent, they have the same value, use, meaning or effect

[noun: **equivalents**] something that is equivalent to something else: *Two sixes are the equivalent of three fours.*

era [noun: **eras**] a particular period in history: *the era of the dinosaurs*

erase [verb: **erases, erasing, erased**] to erase something is to rub it out or make it disappear

+ **eraser** [noun: **erasers**] an eraser is a rubber used to remove writing or marks made in pencil or ink

erect [adjective] upright: *an erect posture*

[verb: **erects, erecting, erected**] to erect something is to put it up: *They erected their tents.*

+ **erection** [noun: **erections**]

1 an erection is when a man's penis becomes stiff because he is sexually aroused

2 erection is the building of something

erode [verb: **erodes, eroding, eroded**] if something erodes or is eroded, it is slowly worn away

+ **erosion** [noun] the gradual wearing away of something, such as stone or soil

erotic [adjective] making someone feel sexually aroused

errand [noun: **errands**] if you go on an errand for someone, you go somewhere to do something for them

error [noun: **errors**] a mistake: *There's an error in this column of figures.*

erupt [verb: **erupts, erupting, erupted**]

1 if a volcano erupts, hot lava, ash and dust is thrown out of it

2 something erupts when it suddenly bursts or breaks out: *Violence erupted at the demonstration.*

+ **eruption** [noun: **eruptions**] an eruption is the throwing out of lava, ash and dust by a volcano

escalate [verb: **escalates, escalating, escalated**] if something escalates, it increases or gets more intense

Ee

♦ **escalator** [noun: **escalators**] a moving staircase for carrying people between the floors of a building

escapade [noun: **escapades**] an adventure, often one where rules or laws are broken

escape [verb: **escapes, escaping, escaped**]

1 to escape is to get out or away to safety or freedom: *The lion had escaped from its cage.*

2 to escape something is to avoid it: *You're lucky to have escaped punishment.*

3 if something escapes you, you can't remember it

[noun: **escapes**]

1 escaping: *an escape of gas*

2 a way to get free or get away to safety: *There was no escape from her boring life.*

escort [verb: **escorts, escorting, escorted**] to escort someone is to go somewhere with them: *We were escorted into the room by the butler.*

[noun: **escorts**] someone who escorts another person

Eskimo [noun: **Eskimos**] Eskimos are the Inuit people, who live in cold places such as Greenland, Canada and Alaska

ⓘ Nowadays, the Inuit prefer not to be called Eskimos.

especially [adverb] particularly: *It was especially cold that morning.*

ⓘ Remember the difference between **especially** and **specially**.
Especially means 'particularly': *I like all of the characters, especially Harry.*
Specially means 'for a special purpose': *I cooked this meal specially for you.*

espionage [noun] spying to find out another country's or company's secrets

esplanade [noun: **esplanades**] a long level road, especially along the seafront in a town

-ess [suffix] if **-ess** comes at the end of a word, it is a noun that refers to the female of something. For example, a *lioness* is a female lion

essay [noun: **essays**] a long piece of writing about a particular subject

essence [noun: **essences**]

1 the essence of something is its most important part or its true character

2 essence is a concentrated liquid, often taken from a plant and containing its flavour or scent: *vanilla essence*

essential [adjective] if something is essential, it is absolutely necessary and you must have it or do it

[noun: **essentials**] an essential is something that you must have

-est [suffix] if **-est** comes at the end of a word, it is an adjective that means 'the most'. For example, *highest* means 'most high' compared to other things

establish [verb: **establishes, establishing, established**]

1 to establish something is to set it up: *He established a small bakery business.*

2 to establish something is to find it out and prove it: *establishing the truth*

♦ **establishment** [noun: **establishments**]

1 the establishment of something is setting it up or proving it

2 an establishment is a place where a business is set up and is operating

estate [noun: **estates**]

1 a large piece of land belonging to one person or one family

2 a large area with lots of houses or factories and businesses built on it: *a housing estate* • *an industrial estate*

3 a person's estate is all the things they have or own, such as property and money, especially when they die

estate agent [noun: **estate agents**] someone who is employed to sell people's houses and who charges them a fee for doing so

estate car [noun: **estate cars**] a large type of car with a lot of space behind the seats for carrying things

esteem [noun] esteem is great respect for someone: *He was held in high esteem by his colleagues.*

[verb: **esteems, esteeming, esteemed**] to esteem someone or something is to respect them a lot

estimate [verb: **estimates, estimating, estimated**] to estimate something is to try to judge what its size, amount or value is without measuring it accurately

[noun: **estimates**] a rough judgement of what something's size, amount or value is

◆ **estimation** [noun] estimating or roughly judging without having accurate measurements or all the facts

estuary [noun: **estuaries**] the wide part of a river where it meets the sea

etc or **etc.** [abbreviation] you can add **etc** after a list to show that there are other things that have not been named: *an art shop selling paints, canvases, brushes, etc*

ⓘ **etc** is short for **et cetera**, which is Latin for 'and the rest'.

etch [verb: **etches, etching, etched**] to draw lines and patterns on metal and glass by letting acid eat away the places where you want the lines to be

◆ **etching** [noun: **etchings**] an etching is a print made from a metal plate that has the picture etched on to it

eternal [adjective] lasting for ever or seeming to last for ever: *the eternal cycle of the seasons*

◆ **eternally** [adverb] for ever

◆ **eternity** [noun] eternity is time that never ends

ethic [noun: **ethics**]

1 an ethic is a rule or principle by which someone lives: *the work ethic*

2 ethics are rules or principles about what is right and wrong

◆ **ethical** [adjective] to do with ethics or what is morally right

ethnic [adjective] ethnic is used to refer to the particular race or culture that someone belongs to: *an ethnic group*

etiquette [noun] a set of rules about good manners

eucalyptus [noun: **eucalyptuses** or **eucalypti**] a type of Australian tree that is evergreen and whose leaves contain a strong-smelling oil that is used as a flavouring

euphemism [noun: **euphemisms**] a word or phrase that you use instead of one that might offend or shock people. For example, euphemisms such as *to pass on* or *to slip away*

are used when people want to avoid mentioning death or dying

euphoria [noun] a feeling of great excitement and happiness

◆ **euphoric** [adjective] feeling very excited and happy

euro [noun: **euros**] the main unit of money in many European countries

European [adjective] to do with or belonging to the continent of Europe [noun: **Europeans**] someone who comes from Europe

euthanasia [noun] euthanasia is helping someone who is suffering from an incurable disease to die

evacuate [verb: **evacuates, evacuating, evacuated**]

1 if people evacuate a place, they leave it because it has become dangerous

2 to evacuate people from a place is to help or order them to leave because it has become dangerous

◆ **evacuation** [noun: **evacuations**] leaving or emptying a place, especially because it has become dangerous

◆ **evacuee** [noun: **evacuees**] someone who has been evacuated from a place, especially during a war

evade [verb: **evades, evading, evaded**] to evade something is to avoid it or avoid dealing with it directly

➡ **evasion**

evaluate [verb: **evaluates, evaluating, evaluated**] to evaluate something is to decide how good or useful it is

evaporate [verb: **evaporates, evaporating, evaporated**] if liquid evaporates, it turns into a gas or vapour and disappears

◆ **evaporation** [noun] turning into a vapour or gas

evasion [noun: **evasions**] evasion is purposely avoiding something

eve [noun: **eves**] the eve of a particular day is the day or evening before

even [adjective]

1 an even surface is level and smooth

2 things are even when they are equal: *The scores were even.*

3 an even number is one that can be divided by 2 without a remainder, for example 12 and 6000. Look up and compare **odd**

4 someone who has an even temper is calm and doesn't suddenly change their mood

5 if you **get even with** someone who has done something to harm you, you get your revenge on them

[adverb]

1 even is used to emphasize another word: *It was even colder the next morning.*

2 even so is used before a statement that is surprising after what you have just said: *It looks like the right one, but even so, I'd like to check.*

[verb: **evens, evening, evened**]

1 if something **evens out**, it becomes level: *The track evened out once we got over the hill.*

2 if two or more things **even out**, they become equal or balanced

evening [noun: **evenings**] evening is the last part of the day and the early part of the night

evenly [adverb]

1 levelly or smoothly: *Spread the icing evenly over the top of the cake.*

2 equally: *evenly balanced*

event [noun: **events**]

1 something that happens that stands out or is important for some reason: *events in history*

2 one of the items in a programme of sports or entertainment: *The next event is the men's relay.*

♦ **eventful** [adjective] full of action, excitement and interesting events: *She's led an eventful life.*

eventual [adjective] happening at the end of a period of time or as a result of some process: *the eventual winner*

♦ **eventually** [adverb] finally

ever [adverb]

1 at any time or at all: *Have you ever been to France?*

2 always: *ever ready to help*

3 of all time or on record: *the biggest pizza ever*

4 ever after is used in stories to mean from that time onwards or for always: *They got married and lived happily ever after.*

5 ever so is used for emphasis, to mean extremely: *It's ever so kind of you.*

evergreen [adjective] evergreen plants do not lose their leaves in the winter. Look up and compare **deciduous**

[noun: **evergreens**] an evergreen tree or shrub

everlasting [adjective] going on or lasting for ever

every [adjective]

1 all the people or things of a particular kind without leaving any out: *Every runner will get a medal for taking part.* • *He does 200 press-ups every day.*

2 if something happens or is done **every so often**, it happens or is done occasionally but not regularly or all the time

everybody or **everyone** [pronoun] all people or every person: *I thought everybody liked ice cream.*

everyday [adjective] not special or unusual: *an everyday occurrence*

everything [pronoun] all things: *Everything in the room was covered in dust.*

everywhere [adverb] in every place: *We looked for him everywhere.*

evict [verb: **evicts, evicting, evicted**] to evict someone from a house or land is to force them to leave it

♦ **eviction** [noun: **evictions**] evicting someone from their home or land

evidence [noun]

1 evidence is anything that makes people believe that something is true or has happened

2 someone gives evidence in court when they tell the jury or judge what they know about the case

♦ **evident** [adjective] obvious or easily understood: *It was evident that he was not going to speak.*

♦ **evidently** [adverb] seemingly: *Evidently, there was some sort of argument.*

evil [adjective] an evil person or an evil act is wicked and causes great harm

[noun: **evils**]

1 evil is wickedness

2 an evil is something that causes great harm or destruction: *the evils of drink*

evolution [noun] evolution is the long slow process by which animals and plants change over hundreds and thousands of years to adapt better to their environment

evolve [verb: **evolves, evolving, evolved**]
to evolve is to change very gradually

ewe [noun: **ewes**] an adult female sheep

ex- [prefix] if **ex-** comes at the beginning of a word it adds the meaning 'outside' or 'former' to the rest of the word. For example, the *exterior* of something is its outside surface and an *ex-president* is someone who used to be president but isn't any longer

exact [adjective]
1 an exact amount has nothing left out or nothing left over
2 to be exact is to be correct, accurate and precise
♦ **exactly** [adverb] correctly or in an exact way: *That comes to £10 exactly.*

exaggerate [verb: **exaggerates, exaggerating, exaggerated**] to exaggerate is to make something seem better, bigger or more important than it really is: *You're exaggerating! She can't be that fat.*
♦ **exaggeration** [noun: **exaggerations**] exaggerating or a statement that exaggerates

exam [noun: **exams**] an examination: *GCSE exams*

examination [noun: **examinations**]
1 an examination is a formal test of someone's knowledge or ability
2 examination is looking carefully at something

examine [verb: **examines, examining, examined**]
1 to examine something is to look at it carefully
2 to examine pupils or students is to test their knowledge by asking them questions
3 if a doctor examines you, he or she looks carefully at you to check that you are healthy

example [noun: **examples**]
1 an example of something is a thing of that kind
2 if someone is or sets a good example they behave in a way that others should copy

exasperate [verb: **exasperates, exasperating, exasperated**] something exasperates you when it makes you feel very annoyed and frustrated
♦ **exasperated** [adjective] extremely annoyed
♦ **exasperating** [adjective] extremely annoying

♦ **exasperation** [noun] a feeling of frustrated anger

excavate [verb: **excavates, excavating, excavated**] to excavate is to dig in the ground or dig something out of the ground: *They'd excavated tons of rock to build the foundations.*
♦ **excavation** [noun: **excavations**] a hole made by digging in the ground or something dug out of the ground
♦ **excavator** [noun: **excavators**] a machine that is used for digging

exceed [verb: **exceeds, exceeding, exceeded**] to exceed something is to go beyond or above it: *This year's profit exceeded our expectations.*
♦ **exceedingly** [adverb] a formal word for very: *an exceedingly boring journey*

excel [verb: **excels, excelling, excelled**] to excel at something is to be extremely good at it and better than most other people

excellence [noun] excellence is very high quality or great ability

excellent [adjective] extremely good or of a very high standard: *an excellent piece of work*

except [preposition and conjunction] other than, apart from, or not including: *He works every day except Sunday.*
♦ **exception** [noun: **exceptions**] something that is not the same as the others in a group or something that a statement does not apply to: *an exception to the rule*
♦ **exceptional** [adjective] unusual or outstanding: *Gail has an exceptional gift for writing.*
♦ **exceptionally** [adverb] unusually: *exceptionally fine weather*

excerpt [noun: **excerpts**] a short piece of writing, music or film that has been taken from a larger complete work

excess [noun: **excesses**]
1 an excess of something is too much of it
2 a sum of money that you have to pay towards the cost of something when you claim the rest of the cost from an insurance company: *There's a £100 excess on my car insurance policy.*
3 if an amount is **in excess of** another amount, it is greater than it: *The football club has debts in excess of £10 million.*

Ee

[adjective] extra: *excess baggage*
+ **excessive** [adjective] too much or too great

exchange [verb: **exchanges, exchanging, exchanged**] to exchange things is to swap them or to give one and take the other instead [noun: **exchanges**] a swap

excite [verb: **excites, exciting, excited**] to excite someone is to make them feel very eager or to give them a pleasant feeling of danger
+ **excited** [adjective] not calm because you are looking forward very much to something
+ **excitement** [noun] being excited
+ **exciting** [adjective] thrilling or full of lively action

exclaim [verb: **exclaims, exclaiming, exclaimed**] to exclaim is to say something suddenly or loudly: *'What a wonderful surprise!' she exclaimed.*
+ **exclamation** [noun: **exclamations**] an exclamation is a word, phrase or sentence spoken suddenly or loudly and expressing strong feelings and emotions, such as surprise, anger, pain, admiration or frustration

exclamation mark [noun: **exclamation marks**] a punctuation mark (!) used instead of a full stop after an exclamation

exclude [verb: **excludes, excluding, excluded**] to exclude someone or something is to not include them or to prevent them from taking part: *Paul was excluded from school for a week as a punishment.*
+ **exclusion** [noun: **exclusions**]
1 exclusion is not including someone or something
2 preventing a pupil from going to school because they have behaved badly
+ **exclusive** [adjective]
1 an exclusive place is meant for or used by only a certain special group of people, such as the rich
2 if something is exclusive, it is found in only one place and you can't get it anywhere else: *an exclusive offer*
3 if one thing is exclusive of another, it does not include that other thing: *It costs £20, exclusive of postage.*
+ **exclusively** [adverb] only: *The stadium is*

used exclusively for big international events.

excrement [noun] excrement is the solid waste that comes out of the bodies of humans and animals

excrete [verb: **excretes, excreting, excreted**] to excrete waste or some other substance is to send it out of your body
+ **excretion** [noun] sending out waste from your body

excruciating [adjective] excruciating pain is extremely severe

excursion [noun: **excursions**] a trip somewhere for pleasure

excuse [verb: **excuses, excusing, excused**]
1 to forgive someone for doing something, especially if there is a good reason for it: *Such behaviour cannot be excused.*
2 to be excused from doing something is to be let off doing it
[noun: **excuses**] something you say to explain something you have done wrong: *I'm sick of you making excuses about your work.*

execute [verb: **executes, executing, executed**]
1 to execute someone is to kill them as an official punishment
2 to execute an order or plan is to carry it out
+ **execution** [noun: **executions**] killing someone by order of the law
+ **executioner** [noun: **executioners**] someone who executes people who have been condemned to death

executive [noun: **executives**] a senior manager in a business or organization

exempt [adjective] if someone or something is exempt from a law, tax or obligation, it does not apply to them
+ **exemption** [noun: **exemptions**] being exempt from a law, tax or obligation

exercise [noun: **exercises**]
1 exercise is movements or games done to keep your body fit and healthy: *We should all take more exercise.*
2 an exercise is something you do to practise something
[verb: **exercises, exercising, exercised**] to exercise is to move around and be active so that you use your muscles and keep fit and healthy

Ee

exert [verb: **exerts, exerting, exerted**] to exert yourself is to make an effort
+ **exertion** [noun: **exertions**] exertion is hard physical work or effort

exhale [verb: **exhales, exhaling, exhaled**] to breath air out of your lungs through your nose and mouth. Look up and compare **inhale**

exhaust [verb: **exhausts, exhausting, exhausted**]
1 if something exhausts you, it uses up all your strength or energy
2 to exhaust a supply of something is to use it all up
[noun: **exhausts**] the pipes that carry the fumes out of a vehicle's engine
+ **exhausted** [adjective] very tired or worn out: *She was completely exhausted by the time she got home.*
+ **exhausting** [adjective] very tiring
+ **exhaustion** [noun] a feeling of great tiredness

exhibit [noun: **exhibits**] something that is put on display in a gallery or museum
[verb: **exhibits, exhibiting, exhibited**] to exhibit something is to show it: *Julia exhibits her paintings at a small local gallery.*
+ **exhibition** [noun: **exhibitions**] a public show or open display: *an exhibition of wildlife photographs*
+ **exhibitor** [noun: **exhibitors**] someone who exhibits their work or products at a public gallery or show

exhilarating [adjective] making you feel happy and full of energy: *an exhilarating ride across the fields*

exile [verb: **exiles, exiling, exiled**] to exile someone from their country is to drive them away and make them live in another country
[noun: **exiles**]
1 an exile is someone who has been forced to leave their country
2 exile is a time spent living in a country that is not your own

exist [verb: **exists, existing, existed**]
1 to exist is to be or to live: *Do fairies really exist, do you think?*
2 to exist is to stay alive: *How do they exist on such a low wage?*
+ **existence** [noun]

1 being or being alive
2 a way of living: *a solitary existence*

exit [verb: **exits, exiting, exited**] to go out: *They exited the stadium by the west gate.*
[noun: **exits**]
1 a way out of somewhere: *Leave the motorway by the next exit.*
2 to make an exit is to leave: *He made a hasty exit.*

exorcism [noun: **exorcisms**] a spell or ritual to drive out an evil spirit from a place or a person
+ **exorcist** [noun: **exorcists**] someone who performs an exorcism
+ **exorcize** or **exorcise** [verb: **exorcizes, exorcizing, exorcizing**] to exorcize an evil spirit is to drive it out

exotic [adjective] something exotic is interesting, colourful or strange, usually because it comes from a foreign country that is very different from your own

expand [verb: **expands, expanding, expanded**] something expands when it grows bigger or wider or opens out to become bigger or wider

expanse [noun: **expanses**] an area of land, sea or sky that stretches over a big distance: *a wide expanse of desert*

expansion [noun] getting bigger or wider: *the expansion of metal when it is heated*

expect [verb: **expects, expecting, expected**]
1 to expect something is to believe that it will happen or it will be the case: *I expect it will be warm in Portugal.*
2 if you are expecting something, you are waiting for it to happen or arrive: *I'm expecting a parcel.*
3 to expect something is to think that it ought to happen or that you have a right to it: *I expected a bit more gratitude.*
+ **expectant** [adjective]
1 to be expectant is to be hopeful that something good will happen
2 an expectant mother is a pregnant woman
+ **expectation** [noun: **expectations**] something you expect to happen at some time in the future

expedition [noun: **expeditions**] a journey

made for a purpose, especially one made by a group of people: *an expedition to the South Pole*

expel [verb: **expels, expelling, expelled**]
1 to expel something is to drive or force it out
2 to expel a pupil from school is to make them leave the school in disgrace
➟ **expulsion**

expense [noun: **expenses**]
1 expense is the cost of something in money
2 your expenses are the sums of money you have to spend in order to live or do your job
✦ **expensive** [adjective] costing a lot of money

experience [noun: **experiences**]
1 experience is knowledge and skill that a person gains by doing something or doing it for a long time
2 an experience is an event that you are involved in
[verb: **experiences, experiencing, experienced**]
1 if you experience a situation or problem, you are in that situation or have that problem: *Many elderly people experience poverty.*
2 if you experience a feeling or emotion, you feel it: *He had never experienced such pain.*
✦ **experienced** [adjective] an experienced person knows about something because they have done it already: *an experienced teacher*

experiment [noun: **experiments**]
1 a scientific test to discover something unknown or to check that an idea is true
2 something done to find out what will happen or what its effect will be
[verb: **experiments, experimenting, experimented**] to experiment is to do scientific experiments or to try something to find out what the result will be
✦ **experimental** [adjective] as a test or trial

expert [noun: **experts**] someone who knows a lot about a particular subject
[adjective] very knowledgeable or skilled at something: *an expert chess-player*
✦ **expertise** [noun] skill or knowledge

expire [verb: **expires, expiring, expired**] something expires when it runs out or becomes out of date: *Your passport expired last month.*
✦ **expiry** [noun] running out or becoming out of date

explain [verb: **explains, explaining, explained**]
1 to explain something is to give more or simpler information or instructions so that it is easier to understand or do: *Could you explain what you mean?*
2 to explain yourself is to give someone reasons for your behaviour
✦ **explanation** [noun: **explanations**] something that explains
✦ **explanatory** [adjective] intended to explain

explicit [adjective] shown or said very clearly and frankly

explode [verb: **explodes, exploding, exploded**]
1 to explode is to blow up like a bomb with a loud noise
2 if someone explodes, they suddenly lose their temper
➟ **explosion**

exploit [verb: **exploits, exploiting, exploited**] to exploit someone or a situation is to use them to get some benefit for yourself
[noun: **exploits**] a daring action or adventure
✦ **exploitation** [noun] exploiting someone or something

exploration [noun: **explorations**] exploration is exploring a place or thing: *space exploration*

explore [verb: **explores, exploring, explored**]
1 to explore a place is to look around it and find out what it is like: *They set off to explore the island.*
2 to explore something is to study it to discover things about it or find out how good it might be: *I'm exploring the possibility of working abroad.*
✦ **explorer** [noun: **explorers**] someone who travels to a remote or unknown place to find out what it is like

explosion [noun: **explosions**] a very loud noise made, for example, when a bomb goes off or something is blown up
✦ **explosive** [adjective] likely to explode: *a highly explosive gas*
[noun: **explosives**] a substance, such as gunpowder, that is used to blow things up

export [verb: **exports, exporting, exported**] to export goods is to send them out of your country to be sold abroad
[noun: **exports**] exports are goods that are sent and sold abroad

expose [verb: **exposes, exposing, exposed**]
1 to expose something is to uncover it so that it is seen
2 to expose someone is to show people what or who they really are: *He resigned after being exposed by the tabloids.*
3 to expose someone to something is to let them experience it or suffer it: *How could you expose your own child to danger?*

♦ **exposure** [noun: **exposures**]
1 exposure is exposing someone or something
2 an exposure is a piece of film that has been exposed to light and will become a photograph when it is developed

express [verb: **expresses, expressing, expressed**] to express a thought or feeling is to put it into words or show it by your actions: *Alex expresses himself well.*
[adjective] travelling fast from one place to another: *an express train • an express package*
[noun: **expresses**] an express train: *We caught the express to Leeds.*

♦ **expression** [noun: **expressions**]
1 a look on your face that shows how you are feeling: *a bored expression*
2 a group of words that have a particular meaning
3 showing how you feel or think by what you do or say

♦ **expressive** [adjective] having the ability to express meaning or feelings clearly

expulsion [noun: **expulsions**] being driven out or expelled

exquisite [adjective] very beautiful

extend [verb: **extends, extending, extended**]
1 to extend a building is to make it larger: *We're having our kitchen extended.*
2 to extend something is to make it longer or last longer: *It might be possible to extend the length of your mortgage.*
3 to extend a part of your body is to hold it out

♦ **extension** [noun: **extensions**]
1 a telephone line from a main line to a room or office: *Extension 4321, please.*
2 a part added on, for example to a building: *They've added on an extension behind the garage.*
3 something that adds length or more time to something: *Can I have an extension to finish my project?*
4 extending something

♦ **extensive** [adjective] covering a large space or wide area: *extensive gardens*

♦ **extent** [noun]
1 the space something covers
2 an amount or degree: *It was, to a great extent, his own fault. • What's the extent of the damage?*

exterior [adjective] at, on or for the outside: *exterior walls*
[noun: **exteriors**] the exterior of something is its outside: *The exterior of the house was painted bright blue.*

exterminate [verb: **exterminates, exterminating, exterminated**] to exterminate living things, especially pests, is to kill them all and get rid of them

external [adjective] outside or on the outside: *an external wall*

extinct [adjective]
1 extinct animals or plants have died out completely and no longer exist
2 an extinct volcano stopped erupting a long time ago

♦ **extinction** [noun] being destroyed completely or dying out completely

extinguish [verb: **extinguishes, extinguishing, extinguished**] to extinguish a light or flame is to stop it burning: *Please extinguish your cigarettes.*

♦ **extinguisher** [noun: **extinguishers**] a device used to spray foam or chemicals on to a fire to put it out

extortionate [adjective] far too expensive: *an extortionate price*

extra [adjective] an extra thing or amount is more than is usual or necessary: *Here's an extra blanket in case you're cold.*
[adverb] very: *extra large*
[noun: **extras**]

Ee

Ee

1 something extra, especially a charge that is not included in the original price

2 an actor who appears for a short time in a film as one of a crowd in the background

extra- [prefix] if a word begins with **extra-**, it adds the meaning 'more' or 'beyond' to the word. For example, an *extraterrestrial* being comes from a place beyond the Earth

extract [verb: **extracts, extracting, extracted**] to extract something is to take it out: *extract a tooth* • *extracting oil from the sea bed*

[noun: **extracts**]

1 a substance that has been extracted

2 a short piece from a book or film

✦ **extraction** [noun: **extractions**]

1 being extracted or something that is extracted, especially a tooth

2 your extraction is the country where your family originally came from: *Joe is of Italian extraction.*

extraordinarily [adverb] very unusually or surprisingly: *extraordinarily tall*

extraordinary [adjective] very special or unusual: *an extraordinary child*

extraterrestrial [adjective] from a planet or place other than the Earth

[noun: **extraterrestrials**] a being from another planet

extravagance [noun: **extravagances**] being extravagant

extravagant [adjective] spending too much money or using too much of something: *Don't be too extravagant with the paper — we haven't much left.*

extravaganza [noun: **extravaganzas**] a spectacular public show

extreme [adjective]

1 far from being ordinary or usual: *His reaction to the news was a bit extreme.*

2 far away from the centre or middle: *The boy on the extreme right of the picture.*

3 very great: *extreme cold*

[noun: **extremes**]

1 something that is extreme: *extremes of temperature*

2 if you **go to extremes**, you do or say extraordinary things

✦ **extremely** [adverb] very: *extremely naughty*

extrovert or **extravert** [noun: **extroverts** or **extraverts**] someone who has an outgoing personality and is interested in other people and the outside world. Look up and compare **introvert**

exuberant [adjective] happy, excited and full of energy: *The players were exuberant when they won.*

eye [noun: **eyes**]

1 your eyes are the two parts of your body at the front of your head that you see with

2 the eye of a needle is the hole that you put the thread through

3 people who don't **see eye to eye** disagree or do not get on well together

[verb: **eyes, eyeing, eyed**] to eye someone or something is to look at them, especially because you are interested in them

eyeball [noun: **eyeballs**] the round part that makes up your whole eye

eyebrow [noun: **eyebrows**] your eyebrows are the lines of hair above your eyes

eyelash [noun: **eyelashes**] your eyelashes are the hairs round the edges of your eyes

eyelet [noun: **eyelets**] a small round hole in leather or cloth, used, for example, to thread a lace through

eyelid [noun: **eyelids**] your eyelids are the pieces of skin that cover your eyes when your eyes are closed

eyeliner [noun: **eyeliners**] make-up that you use to draw a line around your eyes

eyeshadow [noun: **eyeshadows**] coloured make-up that you put on your eyelids

eyesight [noun] the ability to see: *Her eyesight is poor so she wears contact lenses.*

eyesore [noun: **eyesores**] something ugly that spoils a view or scene

eyewitness [noun: **eyewitnesses**] someone who has seen something happen, for example a crime being committed: *Police are appealing for eyewitnesses.*

F

F [abbreviation] short for **Fahrenheit**

fable [noun: **fables**] a story, usually about animals, that teaches a lesson about how people behave

fabric [noun: **fabrics**] cloth: *natural fabrics such as cotton or linen*

fabulous [adjective] extremely good: *The weather was fabulous.*

façade [noun: **façades**]
1 the front of a building
2 a false impression that someone or something gives: *His happiness was just a façade.*

face [noun: **faces**]
1 the front of your head where your eyes, nose, and mouth are
2 the part of a clock or watch where the numbers are
3 the steep side of a mountain or cliff
4 one of the flat outside surfaces of a shape
5 to **make** or **pull a face** is to twist your face into a strange expression
[verb: **faces, facing, faced**]
1 to be opposite someone or something: *My house faces the park.*
2 to look or turn in the direction of someone or something: *They turned and faced each other.*
3 to have to deal with a difficult situation: *She has faced many difficulties in her life.*
4 to **face up to** a problem is to accept and deal with it: *You must face up to your responsibilities.*

facelift [noun: **facelifts**] a medical operation to remove the lines on someone's face and make them look younger

facial [adjective] relating to your face: *a facial expression*
[noun: **facials**] a beauty treatment that is done to your face

facility [noun: **facilities**]
1 an ability: *He has a great facility for solving problems.*
2 a building or piece of equipment that you can use for doing something: *a mobile phone with an Internet facility • sports facilities*

fact [noun: **facts**]
1 something that you know is true
2 you say '**in fact**' when you are going to give more exact information: *They know each other well; in fact they went to school together.*
➡ **factual**

factor [noun: **factors**] something that causes or influences a situation: *The weather is often one of the main factors in choosing where to go for a holiday.*

factory [noun: **factories**] a building where something is made in large quantities: *a chocolate factory*

factual [adjective] based on facts: *factual information*

faculty [noun: **faculties**]
1 a natural ability that people have: *the faculty of speech*
2 a department of a university: *the Faculty of Law*

fad [noun: **fads**] something that is popular or fashionable for a short time: *a passing fad for skateboarding*

fade [verb: **fades, fading, faded**]
1 to disappear gradually: *Hopes of finding him were starting to fade.*
2 to lose colour and brightness: *These jeans have faded.*

faeces [plural noun] a formal word for solid waste from people's or animal's bodies

Fahrenheit [noun] a system for measuring temperature in which water freezes at 32 degrees and boils at 212 degrees

ⓘ This word is pronounced **far**-un-hite.

fail [verb: **fails, failing, failed**]
1 if you fail an exam or test, you do not pass it: *My brother failed his driving test.*
2 if you fail in something you are trying to do, you are unsuccessful in doing it: *They failed in their attempt to sail round the world.*
3 if something fails or fails to do something, it does not do what you expect or need it to do: *The parcel failed to arrive.* • *The brakes failed.*
♦ **failing** [noun: **failings**] a fault
♦ **failure** [noun: **failures**]
1 a failure is someone or something that is not successful: *She felt like a failure.*
2 failure is the act of failing: *Their first attempt ended in failure.*

faint [adjective: **fainter, faintest**]
1 difficult to see, hear or smell: *There's a faint mark on the carpet.* • *the faint sound of footsteps*
2 if you feel faint, you feel as though you might become unconscious
[verb: **faints, fainting, fainted**] to suddenly become unconscious and fall to the ground: *Richard fainted when he saw the blood.*
♦ **faintly** [adverb]
1 in a way that is difficult to see, hear or smell: *'Yes,' she said faintly.*
2 slightly: *He looked faintly ridiculous.*

fair [adjective: **fairer, fairest**]
1 treating everyone equally: *a fair trial*
2 fair skin or hair is very light in colour
3 fair weather is very pleasant, with no rain
4 quite good but not very good: *Joe's work is only fair.*
5 quite large in size or amount: *Nadia lives a fair distance away from here.*
→ **fairly, fairness**

fair [noun: **fairs**]
1 a collection of rides that you can go on for entertainment, which moves from town to town
2 an event with lots of stalls where you can buy things: *the village fair*

fairly [adverb]
1 quite: *I was fairly nervous about the test.*
2 in a way that is reasonable: *We were treated very fairly.*

fairness [noun] being fair

fairy [noun: **fairies**] an imaginary creature which has magical powers and looks like a small person with wings

fairy lights [plural noun] coloured lights for decoration, especially on a Christmas tree

fairy story or **fairy tale** [noun: **fairy stories** or **fairy tales**] a traditional story in which magic things happen

faith [noun: **faiths**]
1 faith is great trust: *I have a lot of faith in him.*
2 religious belief: *people of different faiths*
♦ **faithful** [adjective] loyal and keeping your promises: *a faithful friend* • *He was faithful to his wife.*
♦ **faithfully** [adverb]
1 trustfully and loyally: *She promised faithfully to come.*
2 you write **Yours faithfully** at the end of a formal letter that begins with 'Dear Sir' or 'Dear Madam'

fake [adjective] not real, but copying something else: *fake fur*
[noun: **fakes**] a copy of something rather than the real thing
[verb: **fakes, faking, faked**]
1 to pretend something in order to trick someone: *faking a German accent*
2 to make a copy of something and pretend it is real

falcon [noun: **falcons**] a bird that kills other animals for food

fall [verb: **falls, falling, fell, fallen**]
1 if something falls, it drops down to the ground: *The apples fell from the tree.*
2 if you fall, you have an accident and hit the ground: *Ben fell downstairs.*
3 if an amount, price or temperature falls, it goes down
4 to enter a particular state: *They fell in love.* • *I often fall asleep at the cinema.*
5 to **fall out** is to stop being friends with someone: *Jane and Anne have fallen out.*
[noun: **falls**]
1 an accident in which you hit the ground: *My*

grandmother had a fall last week.

2 a drop in a price, amount or temperature: *a fall in prices*

3 the American English word for **autumn**

fallout [noun] radioactive dust from a nuclear explosion

false [adjective]

1 if something you say or believe is false, it is not true or correct: *He made a false statement to the police.*

2 an object that is false is not real or natural: *false teeth*

 ✦ **falsely** [adverb] incorrectly: *I was falsely accused of theft.*

 ✦ **falseness** [noun] being false

fame [noun] being known by a lot of people: *young actors looking for fame*

familiar [adjective]

1 if someone or something is familiar, you know them very well: *His voice sounded familiar.*

2 if you are familiar with something, you have seen it or used it before: *I'm not familiar with this software.*

 ✦ **familiarize** or **familiarise** [verb: **familiarizes, familiarizing, familiarized**] to familiarize yourself is to make sure you know something: *Try to familiarize yourself with the rules.*

family [noun: **families**]

1 a group of people who are related to each other: *Most people in my family have brown hair.*

2 a group of animals, plants or languages that are related to each other

ⓘ **Family** can be used with a singular or plural verb in British English, for example:
The family next door has a dog.
The family next door have a dog.

family planning [noun] controlling how many children you have, for example by using contraceptives

famine [noun: **famines**] a situation in which many people do not have enough food and may die

famished [adjective] extremely hungry

famous [adjective] known by many people: *a famous actor*

fan [superscript]1[/superscript] [noun: **fans**] someone who likes a person

or thing very much: *football fans* • *a fan of Brad Pitt*

fan [superscript]2[/superscript] [noun: **fans**]

1 a machine with thin blades that spin round and make the air cooler

2 something that you hold and wave in front of your face to make you feel cooler

[verb: **fans, fanning, fanned**] to fan yourself is to use a fan to cool yourself down

fanatic [noun: **fanatics**] someone who likes someone or something in an extreme way: *a cycling fanatic*

 ✦ **fanatical** [adjective] extremely enthusiastic about something

 ✦ **fanaticism** [noun] very strong enthusiasm that can sometimes make people behave unreasonably

fancy [verb: **fancies, fancying, fancied**]

1 to like the idea of having or doing something: *Do you fancy going to the cinema?* • *I really fancy a bacon sandwich.*

2 an informal word meaning to be attracted to someone: *My friend fancies you.*

[adjective: **fancier, fanciest**] decorated and not plain: *fancy cakes*

fancy dress [noun] clothes that you wear to a party to make you look like someone or something else

fanfare [noun: **fanfares**] a short, loud piece of music played on a trumpet

fang [noun: **fangs**] a long, sharp tooth of a fierce animal or a snake

fantastic [adjective] extremely good: *We had a fantastic time in Rome.* • *You look fantastic!*

fantasy [noun: **fantasies**] something good that you imagine might happen but that probably will not happen: *He has a fantasy about being rich and famous.*

FAQ [abbreviation] short for **frequently asked questions**, a list of questions about a particular topic

ⓘ This term is used mainly in computing and on the Internet.

far [adverb: **farther** or **further**, **farthest** or **furthest**]

1 a long distance: *We have walked quite far.* • *I haven't got far with my homework.*

Ff

Ff

2 much: *She's a far better swimmer than I am.*

3 so far means until now: *I've only read ten pages so far.*

[adjective] the far part of something is the part that is the greatest distance from you: *a house on the far side of the lake*

farce [noun: **farces**]
1 a situation that is funny or stupid
2 a play in which funny and unlikely things happen

fare [noun: **fares**] the price of a journey by bus, train or aeroplane: *The train fare to London is £33.*

farewell [interjection] an old-fashioned word for **goodbye**

far-fetched [adjective] extremely unlikely to be true

farm [noun: **farms**] an area of land where crops are grown and animals are kept
• **farmer** [noun: **farmers**] someone who owns and works on a farm

farmhouse [noun: **farmhouses**] a house on a farm where the farmer lives

farming [noun] the business of running a farm

farmyard [noun: **farmyards**] an area surrounded by buildings on a farm

fascinate [verb: **fascinates, fascinating, fascinated**] to interest someone very much
• **fascinating** [adjective] extremely interesting: *a fascinating story*
• **fascination** [noun] a great interest in something: *I've always had a fascination for unusual animals.*

fashion [noun: **fashions**]
1 something that is very popular at a particular time: *a fashion for tight jeans*
2 something that is **in fashion** is fashionable: *Short skirts were in fashion then.*
3 something that is **out of fashion** is not fashionable
• **fashionable** [adjective] liked by many people at a particular time: *a fashionable restaurant*

fast¹ [adjective: **faster, fastest**]
1 quick: *a fast car*
2 if a clock or watch is fast, it shows a time that is later than the correct time
[adverb: **faster, fastest**] quickly: *She can run very fast.*

fast² [verb: **fasts, fasting, fasted**] if you fast, you do not eat any food, particularly for religious or medical reasons: *I am fasting because it is Ramadan.*
[noun: **fasts**] a time when you do not eat any food

fasten [verb: **fastens, fastening, fastened**] to join or tie two things together
• **fastener** [noun: **fasteners**] something that is used to join two things together

fast food [noun] food that can be prepared quickly, such as hamburgers

fat [adjective: **fatter, fattest**] a fat person has a wide heavy body
[noun: **fats**]
1 an oily substance that forms a layer under your skin which keeps you warm
2 an oily substance in food or used in cooking
➡ **fatten, fatty**

fatal [adjective]
1 a fatal accident or illness is one that causes someone's death
2 causing serious problems: *a fatal mistake*
• **fatality** [noun: **fatalities**] a death in an accident
• **fatally** [adverb] in a way which causes someone's death: *He was fatally wounded.*

fate [noun]
1 a power that seems to control what happens
2 the things that will happen to someone, especially unpleasant things: *It was his fate to be captured again after his escape.*

father [noun: **fathers**] your male parent
• **fatherhood** [noun] being a father

father-in-law [noun: **father-in-laws** or **fathers-in-law**] the father of your wife or husband

fatherly [adjective] kindly and protective: *a fatherly hug*

fathom [verb: **fathoms, fathoming, fathomed**] to understand something after thinking about it: *I still can't fathom why he didn't tell me.*

fatigue [noun] extreme tiredness

fatten [verb: **fattens, fattening, fattened**] to make an animal fatter so it can be eaten
• **fattening** [adjective] fattening foods make you fatter: *Chocolate is quite fattening.*

fatty [adjective: **fattier, fattiest**] fatty food contains a lot of fat

faucet [noun: **faucets**] the American English word for a water tap

fault [noun: **faults**]
1 a mistake or something that is wrong: *There's a fault in the engine.*
2 if something bad is your fault, you are responsible for it: *Whose fault is it that we lost the keys?*
3 a long crack in the Earth's surface which causes an earthquake if it moves
♦ **faultless** [adjective] perfect
♦ **faulty** [adjective] something that is faulty has something wrong with it: *a faulty computer*

favour [noun: **favours**]
1 something you do for someone to help them: *Could you do me a favour and check my homework?*
2 if you are **in favour** of something, you think that it is a good idea: *I'm in favour of higher pay for nurses.*
♦ **favourable** [adjective] good and suitable: *favourable weather conditions*
♦ **favourably** [adverb] in a way that makes something seem good: *This DVD player compares favourably with others.*

favourite [adjective] your favourite person or thing is the one you like best: *My favourite colour is purple.* • *Who's your favourite player?*
♦ **favouritism** [noun] favouritism is treating one person or group better than others

fawn [noun: **fawns**] a young deer

fax [noun: **faxes**]
1 a message that is sent and printed by a special machine attached to a telephone line
2 a machine used for sending a message like this
[verb: **faxes, faxing, faxed**] to send someone a fax

fear [noun: **fears**]
1 fear is the feeling of being very frightened: *She was shaking with fear.*
2 a fear is a frightened feeling that you have about something: *John has a fear of spiders.*
[verb: **fears, fearing, feared**] to be afraid of someone or something

♦ **fearful** [adjective] feeling frightened about something
♦ **fearless** [adjective] not frightened by anything

feast [noun: **feasts**] a large meal for a special occasion

feat [noun: **feats**] something someone does that impresses you because it needs a lot of skill, strength or courage

feather [noun: **feathers**] one of the long light things that cover a bird's body
♦ **feathery** [adjective] soft and light like a feather

feature [noun: **features**]
1 a part or quality of something: *a house with many interesting features*
2 a part of your face, such as your eyes, nose or mouth
[verb: **features, featuring, featured**] to have as an important part: *a film featuring exotic locations*

February [noun] the second month of the year, after January and before March

fed [verb] a way of changing the verb **feed** to make a past tense. It can be used with or without a helping verb: *Anna fed the dog.* • *Have you fed the cat?*
→ **fed up**

federal [adjective] relating to a group of states which have their own government
♦ **federation** [noun: **federations**] a group of states or organizations which have joined together

fed up [adjective] slightly annoyed or bored: *I'm fed up with this work.*

fee [noun: **fees**] an amount of money that you must pay for a service: *university tuition fees*

feeble [adjective: **feebler, feeblest**] very weak
♦ **feebly** [adverb] in a weak way

feed [verb: **feeds, feeding, fed**]
1 to feed a person or animal is to give them food: *Dad was feeding the baby.*
2 to feed on something is to eat it: *Rabbits feed on grass.*

feedback [noun] comments from people about work you are doing, intended to help you do it better

feel [verb: **feels, feeling, felt**]

Ff

Ff

1 to have a particular feeling: *I feel tired.* • *Do you feel better today?*

2 to touch something with your fingers to see what it is like

3 to experience something touching you or happening to you: *Suddenly, she felt a hand on her shoulder.* • *He could feel himself falling.*

4 if something feels a certain way, such as hot, smooth or dry, that is how it seems when you touch it: *Your forehead feels hot.*

5 to think or believe something: *I feel he should have asked my opinion first.*

6 if you **feel like** something, you want it or want to do it: *Do you feel like going for a swim?*

♦ **feeler** [noun: **feelers**] one of the two long things on an insect's head

♦ **feeling** [noun: **feelings**]

1 something that you experience in your mind or body: *a feeling of excitement*

2 if you **hurt someone's feelings**, you make them feel upset

feet [noun] the plural of **foot**

feline [adjective] to do with cats

fell¹ [verb] a way of changing the verb **fall** to make a past tense: *Suddenly, she fell off the chair.*

fell² [verb: **fells, felling, felled**] if you fell a tree, you cut it down

fellow [noun: **fellows**] an informal word for a boy or man: *He's an unusual fellow.*

[adjective] your fellow students or workers are the people who study or work with you

♦ **fellowship** [noun]

1 a feeling of friendliness between people who have similar interests

2 a club or organization

felt¹ [noun] a type of cloth made of rolled and pressed wool

felt² [verb] a way of changing the verb **feel** to make a past tense. It can be used with or without a helping verb: *He felt very tired.* • *Have you felt how soft this fur is?*

female [adjective] belonging to the sex which can give birth or lay eggs: *A female lion is called a lioness.*

[noun: **females**] a female animal or person

feminine [adjective]

1 to do with women, or having qualities that are typical of a woman

2 in English grammar, feminine forms of words refer to females. For example, *she* is a feminine pronoun

♦ **femininity** [noun] being like a woman

feminism [noun] the belief that women should have the same rights and opportunities as men

♦ **feminist** [noun: **feminists**] someone who has this belief

fence [noun: **fences**] a wooden or metal barrier

fencing [noun] a sport in which people fight with swords

fend [verb: **fends, fending, fended**] if you **fend for yourself**, you look after yourself

fender [noun: **fenders**] the American English word for **bumper**

ferment [verb: **ferments, fermented, fermenting**] when beer or wine ferments, it is changed chemically because of the effect of yeast or bacteria

fern [noun: **ferns**] a plant with long leaves like feathers

ferocious [adjective] extremely fierce: *a ferocious dog*

♦ **ferociously** [adverb] in a fierce way

♦ **ferocity** [noun] being fierce

ferret [noun: **ferrets**] a small animal with a long body, used to hunt rabbits

ferry [noun: **ferries**] a boat that carries people and vehicles

fertile [adjective]

1 fertile land is good for growing crops on

2 a fertile person or animal is able to produce children or young animals

♦ **fertility** [noun] being fertile

♦ **fertilization** or **fertilisation** [noun] the act of fertilizing something

♦ **fertilize** or **fertilise** [verb: **fertilizes, fertilizing, fertilized**]

1 to add a substance to soil so that plants grow better

2 to put male and female cells together so that a baby or a young plant or animal is produced

♦ **fertilizer** or **fertiliser** [noun: **fertilizers**] a substance you put on soil to make plants grow better

fervent [adjective] extremely enthusiastic: *a fervent hope* • *a fervent football fan*

festival [noun: **festivals**]
1 a special time when people have a holiday to celebrate something: *a religious festival*
2 a time when there are a lot of special events of a particular type: *a film festival*
• **festive** [adjective] to do with happy celebrations
• **festivities** [plural noun] the things you do to celebrate a special event

festoon [verb: **festoons, festooning, festooned**] to decorate a place with lots of ribbons, balloons or flowers

fetch [verb: **fetches, fetching, fetched**] to go somewhere and bring something or someone back with you: *Could you fetch the newspaper for me, please?*

fete or **fête** [noun: **fetes** or **fêtes**] a special event with stalls and games, for example to raise money for a school or church

fetus [noun: **fetuses**] another spelling of **foetus**

feud [noun: **feuds**] an argument between two people or groups that continues for a very long time
[verb: **feuds, feuding, feuded**] to have a feud with someone

ⓘ This word is pronounced **fyood**.

fever [noun: **fevers**] if you have a fever, your body temperature is higher than normal because you are ill
• **feverish** [adjective] feeling very hot because you are ill

few [adjective: **fewer, fewest**] not many: *She has few friends in the village.*
[noun] a small number: *'Did you take any photos?' 'Only a few.'*

fiancé [noun: **fiancés**] a woman's fiancé is the man she is engaged to

fiancée [noun: **fiancées**] a man's fiancée is the woman he is engaged to

fiasco [noun: **fiascos**] a situation that is a complete failure

fib [noun: **fibs**] a lie that is not about anything important: *He's telling fibs again.*
[verb: **fibs, fibbing, fibbed**] to tell a harmless lie

fibre [noun: **fibres**]
1 a thin thread of something

2 a cloth made up of thin threads
3 a substance in food which humans cannot digest and which helps your bowels work properly

fibreglass [noun] a strong material made from tiny pieces of glass and plastic

fickle [adjective] not staying loyal to one particular thing

fiction [noun] books that describe imaginary people and situations rather than real ones
• **fictional** [adjective] to do with fiction
• **fictitious** [adjective] imaginary and not true

fiddle [noun: **fiddles**] a violin
[verb: **fiddles, fiddling, fiddled**]
1 to play or interfere with something in an annoying way: *Stop fiddling with your hair.*
2 to play a violin
• **fiddly** [adjective] something that is fiddly is difficult to do or use because it is so small

fidget [verb: **fidgets, fidgeting, fidgeted**] to keep moving because you are nervous or bored

field [noun: **fields**]
1 an area of ground used for growing crops or keeping animals on
2 an area of grass used for playing sport on
[verb: **fields, fielding, fielded**] in games like cricket and baseball, if you field, you are the person or team that tries to stop the ball and throw it back after someone has hit it

fieldwork [noun] research that is done outside and not in a classroom or laboratory

fiend [noun: **fiends**]
1 an evil spirit
2 someone who is very keen on something: *a computer games fiend*

fierce [adjective: **fiercer, fiercest**] violent and angry: *a fierce animal* • *a fierce storm*
• **fiercely** [adverb] in a fierce way

fiery [adjective]
1 like fire
2 becoming angry very easily: *a fiery temper*

fifteen [noun] the number 15

fifteenth [adjective and adverb] after fourteenth and before sixteenth: *the fifteenth of November*

fifth [adjective and adverb] after fourth and before sixth: *the fifth day of my holiday*

Ff

[noun: **fifths**] the fraction $\frac{1}{5}$, which means one of five equal parts of something: *A fifth of the money is mine.*

fiftieth [adjective and adverb] after forty-ninth and before fifty-first: *It's my husband's fiftieth birthday tomorrow.*

fifty [noun: **fifties**] the number 50

fig [noun: **figs**] a fruit with a lot of seeds in it, which can be dried

fight [verb: **fights, fighting, fought**]
1 to use your body or weapons to try to hurt someone who is doing the same to you
2 to argue with someone
[noun: **fights**]
1 the act of fighting with someone: *There was a fight in the pub.*
2 strong action to achieve something: *the long fight for justice*
♦ **fighter** [noun: **fighters**]
1 someone who is fighting
2 a fast military plane used for attacking

figment [noun: **figments**] a **figment of your imagination** is something you have imagined that does not really exist

figure [noun: **figures**]
1 a number
2 the shape of a person: *There was a dark figure in the doorway.*
[verb: **figures, figuring, figured**] if you **figure something out**, you understand it: *I just can't figure out how the burglar got in.*

figure of speech [noun: **figures of speech**] a word or phrase used in a different way from usual to create a particular picture. For example, if you say someone is a *lion*, you mean that they are as brave or fierce as a lion

file[1] [noun: **files**]
1 a folder for keeping papers in
2 a place for storing information together in a computer
3 if people walk **in single file**, they walk one behind another
[verb: **files, filing, filed**] to put papers into a file

file[2] [noun: **files**] a tool with a rough edge, used for making things smooth: *a nail file*
[verb: **files, filing, filed**] to shape something and make it smooth using a file

fill [verb: **fills, filling, filled**]

1 to fill a container is to make it full: *The waiter filled our glasses with wine.*
2 if a place fills, it becomes full: *The concert hall quickly filled with people.*
3 to **fill in** a form is to write information on it

fillet [noun: **fillets**] a piece of meat or fish with no bones in it
[verb: **fillets, filleting, filleted**] to fillet a fish or a piece of meat is to remove the bones from it

filling [noun: **fillings**]
1 something used to fill a hole in your tooth: *Ben hasn't got any fillings.*
2 something used to fill something such as a cake or pie: *pancakes with a chocolate filling*

filling station [noun: **filling stations**] a place where you buy petrol

filly [noun: **fillies**] a young female horse

film [noun: **films**]
1 a story that you watch in a cinema or on television
2 something you put inside a camera so you can take photographs
[verb: **films, filming, filmed**] to make a film of something

filter [noun: **filters**] something that traps solid material and lets liquid or gas pass through: *a water filter*
[verb: **filters, filtered, filtering**] to put something through a filter

filth [noun]
1 dirt
2 rude words or behaviour
♦ **filthy** [adjective]
1 very dirty
2 very rude: *filthy language*

fin [noun: **fins**] one of the parts on a fish that help it to balance and swim

final [adjective] coming at the end: *the final chapter of a book*
[noun: **finals**] the last game in a competition, which decides who will win

finale [noun: **finales**] the last part of a show or piece of music

ⓘ This word is pronounced fin-**ah**-lee.

finalize or **finalise** [verb: **finalizes, finalizing, finalized**] to arrange the last details of something, such as a plan or trip

finally [adverb]
1 after a long time: *When he finally arrived, it was after midnight.*
2 used to introduce the last in a list of things: *Finally, I would like to thank everyone who has helped.*

finance [noun: **finances**]
1 finance is affairs to do with money: *John is an expert in finance.*
2 finance is the money needed for something: *finance for a new theatre*
3 your finances are the amount of money that you have: *Our finances are in a healthy state.*
[verb: **finances, financing, financed**] to give someone money to pay for a plan or business
◆ **financial** [adjective] to do with money

finch [noun: **finches**] a small bird with a short beak

find [verb: **finds, finding, found**]
1 to get or see something accidentally, or after you have been looking for it: *I can't find my pencil case.* • *I found a £10 note in the street.*
2 to discover something: *Have you found the answer yet?*
3 to have a particular opinion about someone or something: *I found him very rude.*
4 to **find something out** is to discover information about it: *I'll try and find out the train times.*

fine [noun: **fines**] money that someone must pay as a punishment: *a parking fine*
[verb: **fines, fined, fining**] to make someone pay a fine: *He was fined for dropping litter.*

fine [adjective: **finer, finest**]
1 if you are fine, you are healthy and well
2 good or acceptable: *'Shall we meet at 4 o'clock?' 'Yes, that's fine.'* • *fine weather*
3 very thin or delicate: *a fine line*
◆ **finely** [adverb]
1 in very thin small pieces: *Chop the onion finely.*
2 in a beautiful or impressive way: *a finely decorated room*

finger [noun: **fingers**] one of the long parts at the end of your hand

fingerprint [noun: **fingerprints**] the mark that the tip of your finger leaves when you touch something: *The police took his fingerprints.*

finish [verb: **finishes, finishing, finished**]
1 if something finishes, it ends: *What time did the film finish?*
2 if you finish something, you stop doing it or complete it: *Have you finished your homework?* • *I'll just finish my drink.*
3 to **finish with** something is to stop using it because you do not need it any more
[noun: **finishes**] the end of something, such as a race: *a close finish*

fir [noun: **firs**] a type of tree that keeps its leaves in winter

fire [noun: **fires**]
1 flames and heat that burn and destroy something: *The building was destroyed by fire.* • *There was a fire at the school last night.*
2 a pile of wood or coal that is burning to give heat
3 a device that heats a room using gas or electricity: *Put the fire on if you're cold.*
4 if something is **on fire**, it is burning and producing flames: *The house was on fire.*
[verb: **fires, firing, fired**]
1 to fire a gun is to shoot a bullet from it
2 to fire someone from their job is to dismiss them from it so they no longer have it

fire alarm [noun: **fire alarms**] a bell that rings to warn you of a fire

firearm [noun: **firearms**] a gun

fire brigade [noun: **fire brigades**] the group of people whose job is to put out fires

fire engine [noun: **fire engines**] a vehicle that carries firefighters and equipment to put out a fire

fire escape [noun: **fire escapes**] a way out, such as stairs on the outside of a building, that you use if there is a fire

firefighter [noun: **firefighters**] someone whose job is to put out a fire

firefly [noun: **fireflies**] a fly with a tail that shines in the dark

fireguard [noun: **fireguards**] something you put round a fire to protect people from it

fireman [noun: **firemen**] a less formal name for a **firefighter**

fireplace [noun: **fireplaces**] the space for a fire in the wall of a room

firewood [noun] wood for burning as fuel

firework [noun: **fireworks**] fireworks are

Ff

things that explode and make bright lights in the sky for entertainment

firm[1] [adjective: **firmer, firmest**]
1 not soft: *a firm bed*
2 strict and not changing your mind: *She is a very firm leader.*

firm[2] [noun: **firms**] a company: *She works for a firm in the City.*

first [adjective] coming before everyone or everything else: *the first name on the list*
[adverb]
1 before anyone or anything else: *I finished the exam first.* • *Eat your dinner first.*
2 doing better than everyone else: *Philip came first in the cookery competition.*
[pronoun]
1 the person or thing that comes before all others: *Who is first in the queue?*
2 at first means at the start of a period of time: *I didn't like Rob at first.*

first aid [noun] simple medical treatment that you give to someone who is injured or ill

first-class [adjective]
1 something that is first class is the best or most expensive type: *a first-class compartment on the train*
2 to do with a standard of the mail service that is the quickest but more expensive: *a first-class stamp*
[adverb] using the best or most expensive type: *Len always travels first-class.*

first-hand [adjective] learned through personal experience or involvement and not from being told by other people

firstly [adverb] used for introducing the first of several points or items: *Firstly, I'd like to welcome everybody.*

first name [noun: **first names**] the name that is before your surname or before your middle name

first-rate [adjective] excellent: *a first-rate doctor*

fish [noun: **fish or fishes**] a creature that lives and swims in water, which people often eat as food
[verb: **fishes, fishing, fished**] to catch fish

fisherman [noun: **fishermen**] someone who catches fish as a job or sport

fishing [noun] the sport of catching fish

fishmonger [noun: **fishmongers**]
1 someone who sells fish
2 a fishmonger's is a shop that sells fish

fission [noun] fission is splitting up the nucleus of an atom so that energy is given out

fissure [noun: **fissures**] a long, deep crack in something, especially in rock

fist [noun: **fists**] your hand when it is closed tightly: *Don't shake your fist at me!*

fit[1] [adjective: **fitter, fittest**]
1 healthy and active because you do exercise: *I'm trying to get fit.*
2 good enough: *This food isn't fit to eat.*
[verb: **fits, fitting, fitted**]
1 to be the right size for someone or something: *The dress fits you perfectly.* • *The cupboard will fit in the corner.*
2 to fix something in a place: *We're having new kitchen units fitted next week.*
3 to have space to put people or things: *I can't fit any more into the suitcase.*
➟ **fitness, fitting**

fit[2] [noun: **fits**] if someone has a fit they suddenly become unconscious and may make movements they can't control

fitness [noun] how healthy and well someone is: *exercises to improve fitness*

fitting [adjective] suitable: *a fitting end to the day*

five [noun: **fives**] the number 5

fix [verb: **fixes, fixing, fixed**]
1 to attach something to something else: *She fixed the shelves to the wall.*
2 to mend something: *He's trying to fix my computer.*
3 to arrange something: *Have you fixed a date for the wedding?*
♦ **fixed** [adjective] not changing or moving: *a fixed expression*

fizz [verb: **fizzes, fizzing, fizzed**] if liquid fizzes, it produces a lot of bubbles
♦ **fizzy** [adjective: **fizzier, fizziest**] a fizzy drink has bubbles in it

fjord [noun: **fjords**] a narrow area of water surrounded by cliffs, especially in Norway
ⓘ This word is pronounced **fee**-ord.

flabbergasted [adjective] extremely surprised or shocked

flabby [adjective: **flabbier, flabbiest**] fat, with too much flesh that is not firm

flag [noun: **flags**] a piece of cloth with a pattern on it, used as the symbol of a country or organization: *The American flag has stars and stripes on it.*

flagpole [noun: **flagpoles**] a tall pole that a flag is hung from

flagstone [noun: **flagstones**] a flat piece of stone used for making a path or floor

flake [noun: **flakes**] a small thin piece of something
• **flaky** [adjective: **flakier, flakiest**] breaking up easily into small thin pieces: *flaky pastry*

flamboyant [adjective]
1 confident and lively: *a flamboyant actor*
2 bright and colourful: *flamboyant clothes*

flame [noun: **flames**]
1 the bright burning gas that you see in a fire
2 something that is **in flames** is burning: *The building was in flames.*

flamingo [noun: **flamingoes** or **flamingos**] a large pink bird with long legs

flammable [adjective] something that is flammable burns easily

ⓘ **Inflammable** means the same as **flammable**.

flan [noun: **flans**] a pie that is not covered on the top: *a lemon flan*

flank [noun: **flanks**] the side of an animal's body, especially a horse's
[verb: **flanks, flanking, flanked**] if you are flanked by two people, you have one of them on each side of you: *She left the courtroom flanked by police officers.*

flannel [noun: **flannels**]
1 a soft, light cloth
2 a piece of cloth used for washing yourself

flap [verb: **flaps, flapping, flapped**] if a bird flaps its wings, it moves them up and down
[noun: **flaps**]
1 a movement up and down, like that of a bird's wings
2 a piece of something that hangs down over an opening

flapjack [noun: **flapjacks**] a thick biscuit made from oats, butter and sugar

flare [verb: **flares, flared, flaring**]
1 if a fire flares or **flares up**, it burns with a sudden bright light
2 if someone **flares up**, they suddenly become angry
3 if an illness or injury **flares up**, it suddenly starts again or becomes worse

flash [verb: **flashes, flashing, flashed**] to shine quickly
[noun: **flashes**] a sudden bright light: *a flash of lightning*

flashlight [noun: **flashlights**] the American English word for **torch**

flashy [adjective: **flashier, flashiest**] expensive and meant to impress people: *a flashy car*

flask [noun: **flasks**]
1 a bottle or other container for liquid
2 a special container for keeping drinks hot or cold

flat [adjective: **flatter, flattest**]
1 level and not sloping: *a flat roof*
2 a flat tyre does not have any air in it
3 a flat battery has no more power in it
[adverb]
1 stretched out: *Omar was lying flat on his back.*
2 if you do something **flat out**, you do it as quickly as possible: *We worked flat out to get it finished.*
[noun: **flats**]
1 a set of rooms that someone lives in, which are part of a larger building
2 in written music, a sign (♭) that makes a note lower by half a tone
• **flatly** [adverb] in a definite way: *He flatly refused to do it.*
• **flatten** [verb: **flattens, flattening, flattened**] to make something become flat

flatter [verb: **flatters, flattering, flattered**] to say nice things about someone, often because you want them to do something for you
• **flattery** [noun] nice things you say to someone because you want to please them

flavour [noun: **flavours**] the taste that something has: *Chocolate is my favourite ice-cream flavour.*
• **flavouring** [noun: **flavourings**]

Ff

something added to food to give it a particular taste

flaw [noun: **flaws**] a fault in someone or something

♦ **flawed** [adjective] not perfect

♦ **flawless** [adjective] perfect, with no faults: *a flawless performance*

flea [noun: **fleas**] a very small insect that jumps and bites people or animals

fleck [noun: **flecks**] a very small mark or dot of colour

♦ **flecked** [adjective] marked with flecks

fled [verb] a way of changing the verb **flee** to make a past tense. It can be used with or without a helping verb: *The burglar fled through the front door.* • *She had fled when she heard us coming.*

fledgling [noun: **fledglings**] a young bird that has just learned to fly

flee [verb: **flees, fleeing, fled**] to run away or escape: *Nina turned and fled.*

fleece [noun: **fleeces**]
1 the wool on a sheep
2 a soft, warm material
3 a jacket or top made from this soft, warm material

♦ **fleecy** [adjective] soft and warm, like wool

fleet [noun: **fleets**] a large number of ships or vehicles: *a fleet of boats*

fleeting [adjective] lasting for only a short time: *a fleeting smile*

flesh [noun]
1 the soft part of your body that covers your bones
2 the soft inside part of fruit and vegetables

flew [verb] a way of changing the verb **fly** to make a past tense: *The bird flew away.*

flex [noun: **flexes**] a piece of wire covered in plastic, which carries electricity to a piece of equipment
[verb: **flexes, flexing, flexed**] to bend

flexibility [noun] the quality of being flexible

flexible [adjective]
1 able to bend without breaking
2 able to change to suit different people or situations: *flexible arrangements*

flexitime [noun] a system in which you can choose what time you start and finish work each day

flick [verb: **flicks, flicking, flicked**] to hit something suddenly and quickly

flicker [verb: **flickers, flickering, flickered**] if a light or flame flickers, it does not burn steadily but seems to get darker then lighter

flight [noun: **flights**]
1 a flight is a journey on a plane or helicopter
2 flight is the action of flying: *a flock of geese in flight*
3 a flight of stairs is a set of stairs

flimsy [adjective: **flimsier, flimsiest**] likely to break or tear

flinch [verb: **flinches, flinching, flinched**] to move part of your body suddenly, for example because you are frightened or in pain

fling [verb: **flings, flinging, flung**] to throw something using a lot of force: *He flung his racket down.*

flint [noun: **flints**] a hard, grey stone that can produce a spark

flip [verb: **flips, flipped, flipping**] to throw something so that it turns in the air: *flipping a pancake*

flippant [adjective] not serious enough: *a flippant answer*

flipper [noun: **flippers**]
1 one of the large flat feet that some animals such as seals and turtles have to help them swim
2 a wide, long, flat shoe that you wear to help you swim underwater

flirt [verb: **flirts, flirting, flirted**] to behave as though you think someone is attractive: *Emma was flirting with her sister's boyfriend.*
[noun: **flirts**] someone who often flirts with people

♦ **flirtation** [noun] behaviour in which someone flirts

♦ **flirtatious** [adjective] flirting a lot

flit [verb: **flits, flitting, flitted**] to move quickly and lightly from one place to another: *His eyes flitted round the room.*

float [verb: **floats, floating, floated**] to move along or stay on the surface of water and not sink
[noun: **floats**]
1 something that is designed to float, such as a raft or something you hold when you are learning to swim

2 an electric van used for delivering milk

3 a decorated platform that is pulled along by a vehicle in a parade

flock [noun: **flocks**] a group of sheep, goats or birds

flog [verb: **flogs, flogging, flogged**]

1 to hit someone several times, especially with a whip or cane

2 an informal word meaning to sell something

flood [noun: **floods**] a lot of water in a place that is usually dry

[verb: **floods, flooding, flooded**] if water floods a place, it covers it in large amounts

floodlight [noun: **floodlights**] a bright light used at night for lighting a sports field or the outside of a building

• **floodlit** [adjective] lit by a floodlight

floor [noun: **floors**]

1 the surface that you stand on in a room: *There were toys all over the bedroom floor.*

2 one of the levels in a building: *Which floor is your apartment on?*

flop [verb: **flops, flopping, flopped**]

1 to fall or sit down suddenly and heavily: *She flopped into the nearest armchair.*

2 to hang in a loose and untidy way: *His hair flopped over his eyes.*

• **floppy** [adjective: **floppier, floppiest**] soft and able to bend easily

floppy disk [noun: **floppy disks**] a piece of plastic that you put in a computer, which can store information

floral [adjective]

1 made of flowers: *a floral arrangement*

2 decorated with pictures of flowers: *floral wallpaper*

florist [noun: **florists**]

1 someone who sells flowers

2 a florist's is a shop selling flowers

floss [noun]

1 a mass of fine, silky threads: *candy floss*

2 floss or dental floss is thread you use for cleaning between your teeth

[verb: **flosses, flossing, flossed**] to clean your teeth using floss

flounce [verb: **flounces, flouncing, flounced**] to walk away suddenly, for example because you are angry or upset: *Kat flounced out of the room and slammed the door.*

flounder [verb: **flounders, floundering, floundered**] to struggle or move in a clumsy way

flour [noun] powder made from wheat, used for making bread and cakes

flourish [verb: **flourishes, flourishing, flourished**] to develop quickly and well: *Her new business is flourishing.*

flout [verb: **flouts, flouting, flouted**] if you flout a law or rule, you do not obey it

flow [verb: **flows, flowing, flowed**]

1 if a liquid flows, it moves along: *The River Thames flows through London.*

2 the tide flows when the water in the sea moves towards the land. Look up and compare **ebb**

[noun: **flows**] a steady movement of something

flow chart [noun: **flow charts**] a chart showing the different steps you have to take to make something work, for example a computer program

flower [noun: **flowers**] the part of a plant that has coloured petals: *Tulips are my favourite flower.*

[verb: **flowers, flowering, flowered**] to produce flowers: *Bluebells usually flower in May.*

flu [noun] an illness like a very bad cold with muscle pains and weakness. Flu is short for **influenza**

flue [noun: **flues**] a chimney that takes air or smoke away from a fire or heater

fluent [adjective] speaking a language clearly, easily and well: *She speaks fluent German.* • *Ben is fluent in French.*

• **fluently** [adverb] clearly and well: *Hannah speaks Italian fluently.*

fluff [noun] small, soft pieces that come off wool or other material

• **fluffy** [adjective: **fluffier, fluffiest**] soft like fluff: *a fluffy toy*

fluid [noun: **fluids**] a liquid

[adjective] able to flow like a liquid: *Blood is a fluid substance.*

fluke [noun: **flukes**] a lucky or unusual thing that happens by accident

flume [noun: **flumes**] a channel carrying water that you can slide down at a swimming pool

Ff

flung [verb] a way of changing the verb **fling** to form a past tense. It can be used with or without a helping verb: *Adam flung his bag down on the floor.* • *Katie had flung herself on the ground.*

fluorescent [adjective]
1 very bright: *fluorescent yellow socks*
2 a fluorescent light is a tube filled with a gas that gives off rays of light when electricity is passed through it

fluoride [noun] a chemical added to toothpaste or water to protect your teeth

flurry [noun: **flurries**] a small amount of something that happens quickly over a short period of time: *a flurry of activity* • *snow flurries*

flush [verb: **flushes, flushing, flushed**]
1 to press or pull a handle to make water go down a toilet
2 if you flush, you become red in the face

fluster [verb: **flusters, flustering, flustered**] to make someone feel nervous and confused

flute [noun: **flutes**] an instrument you play by holding it sideways to your mouth and blowing into it

flutter [verb: **flutters, fluttering, fluttered**] to move lightly and quickly through the air

fly [verb: **flies, flying, flew, flown**]
1 to move through the air: *A robin flew across the garden.*
2 to move very quickly: *The days flew by.*
[noun: **flies**] a small insect that flies

flyer [noun: **flyers**] a small piece of paper that advertises something

flyover [noun: **flyovers**] a road that is built on pillars so as to cross over another road

flywheel [noun: **flywheels**] a heavy wheel in a machine or engine

foal [noun: **foals**] a young horse

foam [noun]
1 a mass of small bubbles on top of a liquid
2 a soft material that is full of small holes and used in mattresses and chairs

fob [noun: **fobs**] a decoration attached to a bunch of keys

fob [verb: **fobs, fobbing, fobbed**] to **fob someone off** is to try to stop someone asking questions or complaining by telling them a lie

focus [verb: **focuses, focusing, focused**]
1 to concentrate on one particular thing: *The report focused on the need to improve standards.*
2 to adjust the way you look at something or a camera lens so you get a clear picture

fodder [noun] food for horses or farm animals

foe [noun: **foes**] a formal word for an enemy

foetus or **fetus** [noun: **foetuses** or **fetuses**] a baby before it is born

ⓘ This word is pronounced **fee**-tus.

fog [noun] thick, damp cloud that makes it difficult to see
♦ **foggy** [adjective] having a lot of fog: *a foggy day*

foghorn [noun: **foghorns**] something that makes a loud noise to warn ships of danger at sea when it is foggy

foil [noun] metal in very thin sheets, used for wrapping food

fold [verb: **folds, folding, folded**]
1 to bend one part of something so that it covers another part: *Dan folded the letter and put it in the envelope.*
2 to **fold your arms** is to cross your arms over your chest

folder [noun: **folders**]
1 a cardboard cover for holding papers
2 a place where you keep documents on a computer

foliage [noun] the leaves on a tree or plant

folk [plural noun] people
[adjective] belonging to the people of a country or area or their traditions: *an Irish folk song* • *Russian folk tales*

folk music [noun] traditional music from a particular country or area

follow [verb: **follows, following, followed**]
1 to go after someone or something: *He followed her down the street.*
2 to happen after something: *The meal was followed by a dance.*
3 if you follow a road, you go along it: *Follow the path to the end and turn right.*
4 to understand what someone is saying: *Do you follow me?*
5 to obey instructions or advice: *I followed his advice and arrived early.*

Ff

+ **follower** [noun: **followers**] someone who supports or admires someone or something

+ **following** [adjective] the following day, week or year is the next one: *I finished work on Friday and we went on holiday the following Wednesday.*

fond [adjective: **fonder, fondest**] if you are **fond of** someone or something, you like them very much

+ **fondly** [adverb] in a way that shows you like someone or something

+ **fondness** [noun] being fond of someone or something

font [noun: **fonts**]
1 a style of letters used in printing or computer documents
2 in a church, a large stone bowl for holding water during a baptism ceremony

food [noun] things that you eat to stay alive: *What's your favourite food?*

LANGUAGE FOR LIFE

food

The food we eat should contain a range of different substances which the body needs to stay healthy:
• **Carbohydrate** is a substance in foods that the body uses to store energy.
• **Fat** is a substance in foods that the body stores to keep you warm and provide energy.
• **Fibre** or **roughage** helps food move quickly through the body.
• **Protein** is a substance in foods that the body needs to perform the chemical changes that make it work.
• **Vitamins** are substances in foods that the body uses to help it grow and to fight against disease.
You should also look at the information after the entry for **vitamin**.

food chain [noun] a series of creatures where each type is eaten in turn by the next type in the series

food processor [noun: **food processors**] an electric machine for chopping, slicing or mixing food

fool [noun: **fools**]
1 a stupid or silly person
2 if you **make a fool of yourself**, you do something that makes people think you are silly [verb: **fools, fooling, fooled**]
1 to fool someone is to trick them
2 to **fool about** or **fool around** is to behave in a silly way

+ **foolish** [adjective] silly or stupid

foot [noun: **feet**]
1 your feet are the parts of your body that you stand on
2 the bottom of something: *the foot of a mountain*
3 a unit of length equal to 12 inches or about 30 centimetres
4 if you travel **on foot**, you walk

football [noun: **footballs**]
1 football is a game played by two teams who try to kick a ball into a goal
2 a football is a ball used for playing football

foothill [noun: **foothills**] a hill at the bottom of a higher mountain

foothold [noun: **footholds**] a place where you can put your foot when you are climbing

footing [noun]
1 your balance on your feet: *I lost my footing and fell.*
2 the relationship between two people or groups: *two groups on an equal footing*

footpath [noun: **footpaths**] a path you can walk on, especially in the countryside

footprint [noun: **footprints**] a mark that your foot leaves: *footprints in the snow*

footstep [noun: **footsteps**] the sound of someone walking: *I could hear footsteps.*

footwear [noun] things such as shoes and boots that you wear on your feet

for [preposition]
1 intended to be received by someone: *There's a letter for you.*
2 intended to do something: *What's this switch for?*
3 used to show a certain amount: *I've lived here for eight years.* • *We walked for two miles.* • *I got these trainers for £30.*
4 showing who a feeling is about: *I felt very sorry for him.*
5 used to show a reason: *He was arrested for shoplifting.*
6 meaning: *What's the word for 'girl' in French?*

Ff

Ff

7 in favour of something: *Are you for or against the new plan?*

forbid [verb: **forbids, forbidding, forbade, forbidden**] to tell someone that they must not do something

♦ **forbidden** [adjective] not allowed: *Smoking is forbidden throughout the hospital.*

force [verb: **forces, forcing, forced**]

1 to make someone do something: *He forced me to give him money.*

2 to make something move by using your strength: *The police had to force the door open.* [noun]

1 power or strength: *The force of the explosion damaged many buildings.*

2 a group of people, such as police or soldiers, who are trained to work together: *the air force*

3 if a law or rule is **in force**, it applies at that time and people must obey it

4 if people do something **in force**, a lot of them are involved: *Police arrived in force to stop the demonstration.*

♦ **forceful** [adjective] powerful: *a forceful argument*

ford [noun: **fords**] a shallow part of a river that you can drive across

fore- [prefix] if a word starts with **fore-**, it adds the meaning 'before' or 'at the front of'. For example, your *forehead* is at the front of your head

forearm [noun: **forearms**] the part of your arm between your elbow and your wrist

foreboding [noun] if you have a sense of foreboding, you feel that something bad is going to happen

forecast [noun: **forecasts**] a statement about what is going to happen, especially with the weather

forecourt [noun: **forecourts**] an open area in front of a building such as a petrol station

forefather [noun: **forefathers**] someone in your family who lived a long time ago

forefinger [noun: **forefingers**] the finger that is next to your thumb

foregone [adjective] a **foregone conclusion** is something that is certain to happen

foreground [noun] the part of a view or picture that is nearest to you

forehand [noun: **forehands**] in games such as tennis or squash, a way of hitting the ball with the palm of your hand facing forward

forehead [noun: **foreheads**] the part of your face above your eyebrows

foreign [adjective] a foreign person or custom comes from a country that is not your country: *foreign languages*

♦ **foreigner** [noun: **foreigners**] someone who comes from a country that is not your country

foreleg [noun: **forelegs**] one of the front legs of an animal that has four legs

foreman [noun: **foremen**] someone who is in charge of a group of factory workers or builders

foremost [adjective] the most famous or important

forename [noun: **forenames**] a formal word for the name or names that come before your surname

forensic [adjective] to do with using science in criminal investigations: *forensic medicine*

foresee [verb: **foresees, foreseeing, foresaw, foreseen**] to know about something before it happens

foresight [noun] the ability to know what will happen in the future

forest [noun: **forests**] a place where a lot of trees are growing together

♦ **forestry** [noun] planting and looking after trees and forests

forever [noun] always: *You can't stay in your room forever.*

foreword [noun: **forewords**] an introduction at the start of a book

forfeit [verb: **forfeits, forfeiting, forfeited**] to have something taken away from you because of something you have done: *If you refuse alternative employment, you may forfeit the right to redundancy pay.*

forge [verb: **forges, forging, forged**]

1 to make an illegal copy of something: *He was sent to prison for forging passports.*

2 to forge hot metal is to hammer it into a shape [noun: **forges**] a place where metal is heated and shaped, for example a blacksmith's

♦ **forgery** [noun: **forgeries**]

1 forgery is the crime of copying something and trying to make it look real

2 a forgery is an illegal copy of something

forget [verb: **forgets, forgetting, forgot, forgotten**]

1 not to remember something: *I forgot to send Dad a birthday card.*

2 to leave something behind by accident: *Val's forgotten her umbrella.*

◆ **forgetful** [adjective] often forgetting things

forgive [verb: **forgives, forgiving, forgave, forgiven**] to stop being angry with someone: *Have you forgiven him for breaking the window?*

◆ **forgiveness** [noun] forgiving someone

◆ **forgiving** [adjective] willing to forgive

forgot [verb] a way of changing the verb **forget** to make a past tense: *I forgot to ask what time we were meeting.*

forgotten [verb] a form of the verb **forget** that is used with a helping verb to show that something happened in the past: *I had forgotten to lock the door.*

[adjective] not remembered by anyone: *forgotten heroes*

fork [noun: **forks**]

1 something with a handle and points that you use for lifting food to your mouth

2 a point where a road or river divides and goes off in two different directions

fork-lift truck [noun: **fork-lift trucks**] a vehicle with two flat pointed arms on the front for lifting and moving heavy things

forlorn [adjective] looking lonely and unhappy

form [noun: **forms**]

1 a type of something: *a form of transport*

2 a piece of paper with questions and spaces to write your answers: *You have to fill in a form to get a passport.*

3 a class at school: *Which form are you in?*

4 a shape something has or makes: *The chairs had been arranged in the form of a circle.*

[verb: **forms, forming, formed**]

1 to start or make something start to appear or exist: *How was the Earth formed? • An idea formed in his mind.*

2 to form a particular shape is to make it: *The children held hands and formed a circle.*

3 to form an organization or club is to start it

LANGUAGE FOR LIFE

forms

You may find these words on official forms:

• Your **forename** means your first name, as opposed to your surname.

• Your **marital status** means whether you are married, single, divorced or separated.

• Your **occupation** is your usual job.

• Your **position** means the title of your job within the organization you work for, such as 'Administrator' or 'Sales Assistant'.

• Your **title** is the word you place in front of your name, such as 'Mr' or 'Ms'.

formal [adjective]

1 done according to rules about what is polite: *a formal dinner party*

2 suitable for an official or important situation: *formal dress*

3 formal language and words follow rules strictly and are suitable for writing

◆ **formality** [noun: **formalities**] something that must be done but does not have much meaning

format [noun: **formats**] the way something is designed or arranged: *The album is available in cassette or CD format.*

[verb: **formats, formatting, formatted**] to prepare a computer disk so that you can store information on it

formation [noun: **formations**]

1 formation is forming something: *the formation of a new government*

2 a formation is a shape made by the way people or things are arranged

former [adjective] before but not now: *the former President • In former times, people did not travel so much.*

[noun] the former is the first of two people or things you are mentioning. The second one is the **latter**: *We visited America and Canada but stayed longer in the former.*

◆ **formerly** [adverb] once, in the past: *Their house was formerly a shop.*

formidable [adjective] difficult or frightening: *a formidable task*

formula [noun: **formulas** or **formulae**]

1 in maths or chemistry, a set of letters, numbers or symbols that stand for an idea or chemical

Ff

Ff

compound: *What's the formula for calculating the area of a circle?*

2 the way to make something and the substances used in it

◆ **formulate** [verb: **formulates, formulating, formulated**] to invent and develop a plan or idea

forsake [verb: **forsakes, forsaking, forsook, forsaken**] a formal word meaning to leave someone or something for ever

fort [noun: **forts**] a strong building designed to be easy to defend against attack

forth [adverb]

1 forwards or onwards: *They went forth into the desert.*

2 if you move **back and forth**, you go first in one direction then in the opposite direction

forthcoming [adjective] happening soon: *forthcoming events*

forthright [adjective] very honest and direct: *a forthright chat* • *John was forthright in his criticism.*

fortieth [adjective and adverb] after thirty-ninth and before forty-first: *It's Claire's fortieth birthday tomorrow.*

fortification [noun: **fortifications**] something that is built to defend a place against attack

fortify [verb: **fortifies, fortifying, fortified**] to strengthen someone or something

fortnight [noun] a period of two weeks: *We're going to Greece for a fortnight.*

◆ **fortnightly** [adverb] happening every two weeks

[adjective] every two weeks: *a fortnightly magazine*

fortress [noun: **fortresses**] a fort or town that has been protected against attack

fortunate [adjective] lucky: *We were fortunate to catch our train, we were so late.*

◆ **fortunately** [adverb] luckily: *Fortunately, nobody was injured.*

fortune [noun: **fortunes**]

1 a fortune is a lot of money: *His uncle died and left him a fortune.*

2 fortune is luck: *Sue had the good fortune to win first prize.*

forty [noun: **forties**] the number 40

forward [adjective] in the direction that is in

front of you: *a forward movement*

[verb: **forward, forwarding, forwarded**] to send a letter or e-mail you have received to someone else

[noun: **forwards**] in football and hockey, a forward is a player who mostly plays in the front line of a team and tries to score goals. In rugby, a forward is one of the players that makes up a scrum. Look up and compare **back**

◆ **forwards** or **forward** [adverb] in the direction that is in front of you: *The car moved slowly forwards.*

fossil [noun: **fossils**] the remains of an animal or plant that have hardened into rock after a very long time

fossil fuel [noun: **fossil fuels**] a fuel that is made from the remains of animals and plants. Coal, crude oil and natural gas are fossil fuels

fossilize or **fossilise** [verb: **fossilizes, fossilizing, fossilized**] to become a fossil

foster [verb: **fosters, fostering, fostered**]

1 if you foster a child, they live as part of your family for a period of time while their parents cannot look after them

2 to foster an idea or feeling is to encourage it to develop

foster child [noun: **foster children**] a child who is looked after for a period of time when its parents cannot look after it

foster parent [noun: **foster parents**] someone who looks after children that are not their own

fought [verb] a way of changing the verb **fight** to make a past tense. It can be used with or without a helping verb: *He fought with his brother.* • *They had fought for freedom and lost.*

foul [adjective: **fouler, foulest**] extremely unpleasant: *a foul smell*

[noun: **fouls**] in sport, a foul is an action that is against the rules

found [verb: **founds, founding, founded**] to start an organization: *The college was founded in 1950.*

foundations [plural noun] the foundations of a building are its solid base under the ground

founder [noun: **founders**] someone who starts an organization

foundry [noun: **foundries**] a factory where metal or glass is melted and made into things

fountain [noun: **fountains**] a structure that produces a jet of water which is used for decoration in a garden or park

fountain pen [noun: **fountain pens**] a pen full of ink that flows out through a nib

four [noun: **fours**] the number 4

fourteen [noun] the number 14

fourteenth [adjective and adverb] after thirteenth and before fifteenth: *It's my son's fourteenth birthday tomorrow.*

fourth [adjective and adverb] after third and before fifth: *Mario finished fourth in the race.*

fowl [noun: **fowl** or **fowls**] a bird that is kept for its meat and eggs, for example, a chicken

fox [noun: **foxes**] a wild animal that looks like a dog, with red fur and a thick tail

foxglove [noun: **foxgloves**] a tall plant with purple bell–shaped flowers

foyer [noun: **foyers**] the entrance hall in a large building such as a theatre or office block

fraction [noun: **fractions**] an amount, such as $\frac{1}{2}$ or $\frac{3}{8}$, that is part of a whole number

fracture [verb: **fractures, fracturing, fractured**] to crack or break something, especially a bone in your body: *Emma's fractured her arm.*
[noun: **fractures**] a crack or break in something, especially a bone in your body

fragile [adjective] not very strong and likely to break
 • **fragility** [noun] the state of being fragile

fragment [noun: **fragments**] a fragment of something is a small piece that has broken off

fragrance [noun: **fragrances**] a pleasant smell
 • **fragrant** [adjective] something that is fragrant smells very pleasant

frail [adjective: **frailer, frailest**] weak: *a frail old lady*
 • **frailty** [noun] weakness

frame [noun: **frames**]
1 a piece of wood or metal around the edge of a picture or mirror
2 the part that holds the lenses in a pair of glasses
3 the structure around which something is built or made: *the frame of a house*

4 your **frame of mind** is your mood

framework [noun: **frameworks**] the structure on which something is planned or built

franchise [noun: **franchises**] a right to sell the goods of a particular company

frank [adjective: **franker, frankest**] honest and saying what you think
 • **frankly** [adverb] as an honest opinion: *Frankly, I don't think he's good enough for the job.*

frantic [adjective] very worried or excited and doing things quickly: *a frantic search* • *His mother was frantic with worry.*
 • **frantically** [adverb] in a frantic way

fraud [noun: **frauds**]
1 fraud is the crime of deceiving people to get money
2 a fraud is someone who deceives other people by pretending

fraught [adjective]
1 if you are fraught, you are anxious and tense
2 if something such as a situation is fraught, it makes you worry
3 if a situation is **fraught with** something such as danger, it is full of danger or problems

frayed [adjective] frayed material is starting to come apart at the edges

freak [noun: **freaks**]
1 a strange person
2 someone who is very interested in something: *a health freak*
[adjective] extremely unusual: *a freak accident*

freckle [noun: **freckles**] a small brown mark on your skin, especially your face
 • **freckled** [adjective] covered in freckles

free [adjective]
1 not costing any money: *It's free to get into the museum.*
2 available: *Is this seat free?* • *Are you free this evening?*
3 if you are free to do something, you are allowed to do it: *You are free to go anywhere you like.*
[verb: **frees, freeing, freed**] to give someone the right to do what they want
 • **freedom** [noun] the right to do what you want
 → **freely**

Ff

229

freelance [adjective and adverb] working for yourself and not as an employee of a company or organization: *a freelance journalist* • *Sally works freelance as a writer.*

freely [adverb] without being limited or blocked: *You can speak freely to me.* • *I freely admit I was wrong.*

free-range [adjective]
1 free-range animals are allowed to move freely around a farm
2 free-range eggs come from chickens that are allowed to move around freely

freeway [noun: **freeways**] in the United States, a freeway is a fast road with many lanes

freewheel [verb: **freewheels, freewheeling, freewheeled**] to ride a bicycle without turning the pedals

freeze [verb: **freezes, freezing, froze, frozen**]
1 if something freezes, it becomes very cold and goes hard or turns into ice
2 if you freeze food, you store it at a very cold temperature so it keeps for a long time
3 if you freeze, you stop moving suddenly: *He froze when he saw the big dog.*
♦ **freezer** [noun: **freezers**] a machine for keeping food very cold
♦ **freezing** [adjective] very cold: *It's freezing in here.*

freezing point [noun: **freezing points**] the temperature at which a liquid becomes solid

freight [noun] goods that are being carried by a lorry, ship or plane
♦ **freighter** [noun: **freighters**] a large ship or plane for carrying goods

French fries [plural noun] long thin pieces of potato, fried in deep fat

French window [noun: **French windows**] a tall glass door that opens onto a garden or patio

frenzy [noun] a state of great excitement, activity and emotion

frequency [noun: **frequencies**]
1 the frequency of something is the number of times it happens
2 the frequency of sound or radio waves is the number that pass the same point in one second. Human beings cannot hear sounds that have extremely high frequencies
♦ **frequent** [adjective] happening often: *Dave makes frequent visits to his grandmother.*
♦ **frequently** [adverb] often: *Lee is frequently late for work.*

fresh [adjective: **fresher, freshest**]
1 just made or collected: *fresh orange juice*
2 clean: *I'll put some fresh sheets on the bed.*
3 cool and refreshing: *fresh air*
♦ **freshen** [verb: **freshens, freshening, freshened**] to make something fresher
♦ **freshly** [adverb] only just made or done: *freshly baked bread*

freshwater [adjective] a freshwater fish lives in rivers and lakes, rather than in the sea

fret [verb: **frets, fretting, fretted**] to feel worried, unhappy and unable to relax

friction [noun]
1 the rubbing of one surface against another surface
2 disagreement or arguing

Friday [noun: **Fridays**] the day of the week after Thursday and before Saturday: *It's my birthday on Friday.*

fridge [noun: **fridges**] a machine for keeping food cool. Fridge is short for **refrigerator**

fried [verb] a way of changing the verb **fry** to make a past tense. It can be used with or without a helping verb: *She fried the fish in butter.* • *Have you fried the chicken?*
[adjective] cooked in hot oil or fat: *a fried egg*

friend [noun: **friends**] someone who you know and like: *Lindsay is my best friend.*
♦ **friendly** [adjective: **friendlier, friendliest**] kind and welcoming: *She's very friendly to everyone.*
♦ **friendship** [noun: **friendships**] the relationship you have with a friend

frieze [noun: **friezes**] a long narrow strip of decorated paper that you put on a wall

frigate [noun: **frigates**] a small warship

fright [noun] a sudden feeling of fear: *You gave me a fright, jumping out like that!*
♦ **frighten** [verb: **frightens, frightening, frightened**] to frighten someone is to make them feel scared
♦ **frightened** [adjective] scared: *I felt very frightened.*

frightening [adjective] something that is frightening makes you feel scared: *a frightening experience*

frightful [adjective] very bad

frightfully [adverb] an old-fashioned word for **very**: *I'm frightfully sorry.*

frill [noun: **frills**] a narrow strip of cloth pulled into folds that is attached to something along one edge as a decoration

frilly [adjective] decorated with frills: *a frilly skirt*

fringe [noun: **fringes**]
1 hair that hangs down over your forehead
2 loose threads that form an edge on something such as a scarf or rug

frisky [adjective: **friskier, friskiest**] lively and full of energy: *a frisky puppy*

fritter [verb: **fritters, frittering, frittered**] if you **fritter away** money or time, you waste it

frivolous [adjective] a frivolous person is playful and not serious

frizzy [adjective: **frizzier, frizziest**] frizzy hair has very tight curls in it

frock [noun: **frocks**] an old-fashioned word for a dress

frog [noun: **frogs**] a small brown or green animal that can jump and lives near water

frogman [noun: **frogmen**] someone whose job is to swim underwater wearing a rubber suit and using special breathing equipment

frolic [verb: **frolics, frolicking, frolicked**] to play in a lively and happy way: *lambs frolicking in the fields*

from [preposition]
1 showing where something started: *She's driving up from London.* • *Read the poem from the beginning.*
2 showing what has made something happen: *Yogurt is made from milk.* • *He was shivering from the cold.*
3 out of a place or away: *Ali took a notebook from the drawer.* • *Take those sweets from her before she eats them all!*

front [noun: **fronts**]
1 the front of something is the part of it that faces forwards: *a house with a red front* • *The front of the car was badly damaged.*
2 an area where fighting takes place during a war
3 a weather front is the warm or cold edge of a mass of air
4 if you are **in front of** someone or something, you are facing them: *He stood in front of the class and started to speak.*
[adjective] at the front of something: *the front door*

frontier [noun: **frontiers**] a dividing line between two countries

frost [noun] a very thin layer of white ice crystals that forms on surfaces outside when the weather is cold

frosted [adjective] frosted glass has been specially treated so you cannot see through it

frosty [adjective: **frostier, frostiest**]
1 when it is frosty, everything is covered in frost
2 not very friendly: *a frosty welcome*

froth [noun] foam on top of a liquid

frothy [adjective: **frothier, frothiest**] a frothy liquid has foam on top

frown [verb: **frowns, frowning, frowned**] to wrinkle your forehead because you are thinking very hard or because you are worried or angry
[noun: **frowns**] an expression in which your forehead is wrinkled

froze [verb] a way of changing the verb **freeze** to make a past tense: *The milk froze in the fridge.*

frozen [verb] a form of the verb **freeze** that is used with a helping verb to show that something happened in the past: *It was so cold that the lake had frozen.*
[adjective] frozen food is stored at a very cold temperature to make it keep for a long time: *a packet of frozen peas*

frugal [adjective] if you are frugal, you are careful with your money and save it rather than spending a lot

fruit [noun] the part of a plant that contains the seeds and that you can sometimes eat: *Grapes are my favourite fruit.*

fruitful [adjective] something that is fruitful has good results: *a fruitful meeting*

fruitless [adjective] not producing the result you wanted: *a fruitless search*

frustrate [verb: **frustrates, frustrating, frustrated**] if something frustrates you, it

Ff

makes you feel annoyed because you cannot do or achieve what you want

• **frustration** [noun: **frustrations**] a feeling of being annoyed because you cannot do or achieve what you want

fry [verb: **fries, frying, fried**] to cook something in hot oil or fat

fudge [noun] a soft sweet made from butter and sugar

fuel [noun: **fuels**] a substance such as gas, wood or coal that burns to give heat, light or power

fugitive [noun: **fugitives**] someone who has escaped from the police

-ful [suffix]

1 if **-ful** comes at the end of a word, it is an adjective that means 'full of'. For example, *joyful* means full of joy

2 when **-ful** comes at the end of other words, they are nouns that refer to the amount that something holds. For example, a *spoonful* is the amount of something that a spoon can hold

fulfil [verb: **fulfils, fulfilling, fulfilled**] to do what you want to do or what you are expected to do: *The team fulfilled all our expectations.*

• **fulfilling** [adjective] making you feel that you have achieved something good: *Being a youth worker is a fulfilling job.*

• **fulfilment** [noun] a feeling of having achieved something successfully

full [adjective: **fuller, fullest**]

1 containing as much as possible: *The train was full.* • *a full bottle of milk* • *The room was full of children.*

2 if something is full, it is complete and has nothing missed out: *He told me the full story.*

3 if you are full or **full up**, you cannot eat any more.

4 if a room or building is **full up**, there is no space for anyone or anything else: *I'm sorry, the hotel is full up.*

full moon [noun: **full moons**] the moon when it is a complete circle

full stop [noun: **full stops**] the mark (.) used for showing where a sentence ends and after an abbreviation

full-time [adjective and adverb] if you work full-time or have a full-time job, you work for all the hours of a normal job

fully [adverb] completely: *He hasn't fully recovered from the accident.*

fumble [verb: **fumbles, fumbling, fumbled**] to use your hands in an awkward way: *Raj fumbled in his pocket for the key.*

fume [verb: **fumes, fuming, fumed**] to be very angry

• **fumes** [plural noun] smoke or gas that is unpleasant to breathe in

fun [noun]

1 enjoyment and pleasure: *Skateboarding is good fun.* • *We had a lot of fun at the party.*

2 if you **make fun of** someone, you tease them or make others laugh at them

function [noun: **functions**]

1 the purpose of someone or something: *The function of an iron is to press the creases out of clothes.*

2 a function is an important social event [verb: **functions, functioning, functioned**] to work in the correct way

• **functional** [adjective] practical and useful

fund [noun: **funds**] an amount of money for a particular purpose [verb: **funds, funding, funded**] to provide money for a particular purpose

fundamental [adjective] basic and important: *the fundamental rules of management*

funeral [noun: **funerals**] a ceremony that people have when someone dies

funfair [noun: **funfairs**] a collection of rides that you can go on for entertainment

fungus [noun: **fungi**] a plant with no leaves or flowers, for example a mushroom

funnel [noun: **funnels**]

1 something that is wide at the top and narrow at the bottom, used for pouring liquids or powder into a narrow opening

2 a chimney through which smoke leaves a ship

funnily [adverb] in a way that is odd: *Funnily enough, we were born at the same time on the same day.*

funny [adjective: **funnier, funniest**]

1 a funny person or thing makes you laugh: *a funny story*

2 strange or unusual: *There was a funny noise coming from the engine.*

funny bone [noun: **funny bones**] a part of your elbow that tingles when you bang it

fur [noun] the soft hair on some animals
➡ **furry**

furious [adjective] extremely angry

furnace [noun: **furnaces**] a large oven for melting metal or glass

furnish [verb: **furnishes, furnishing, furnished**] to put furniture in a house or room
◆ **furnishings** [plural noun] the furniture, carpets and curtains that you put in a house or room

furniture [noun] furniture is the objects such as beds, tables and chairs that you put in a room

furrow [noun: **furrows**] a long narrow cut made in the ground by a plough

furry [adjective: **furrier, furriest**] covered in fur

further [adjective]
1 a greater distance: *Which is further from here, London or Aberdeen?*
2 more: *If you need further information, please ask.*
[adverb] for a greater distance: *I walked further than I needed.*

furthermore [adverb] a formal word that is used when you are adding something to what you have just said: *I don't want to go, and furthermore, I won't go.*

furthest [adverb] to the greatest distance or degree: *Who can throw the ball the furthest?*

furtive [adjective] an action that is furtive is done secretly: *a furtive glance*
◆ **furtively** [adverb] in a secret way

fury [noun] great anger
➡ **furious**

fuse [noun: **fuses**] a wire inside a plug or piece of electrical equipment that melts if too much electricity passes through it, and stops the equipment from working
[verb: **fuses, fusing, fused**]
1 if two things fuse or are fused, they join together because they melt
2 if a piece of electrical equipment fuses, it stops working because the fuse has melted

fuselage [noun: **fuselages**] the main body of an aeroplane

fusion [noun] joining things together, such as the nuclei of atoms

fuss [noun]
1 unnecessary worry or excitement about something: *I don't know what all the fuss is about.*
2 if you **make a fuss of** someone, you give them a lot of attention
[verb: **fusses, fussing, fussed**] to worry too much about something or give it too much attention: *She fusses over her pet dog.*
◆ **fussy** [adjective: **fussier, fussiest**] someone who is fussy worries too much about small details that are not important

futile [adjective] useless and having no effect

futon [noun: **futons**] a mattress on a wooden frame that you can use as a bed or a seat

future [noun]
1 the future is the time that will come: *You can't know what will happen to you in the future.*
2 **in future** means in the time from now on: *In future, please be more careful.*

future tense [noun] the form of a verb that you use when you are talking about what will happen in the future

fuzz [noun] fine, light hair or feathers
◆ **fuzzy** [adjective: **fuzzier, fuzziest**]
1 a fuzzy picture is unclear
2 fuzzy hair is soft and curly

Ff

G

g [abbreviation] short for **gram** or **grams**

gab [noun] if someone has **the gift of the gab**, they are good at talking

gabble [verb: **gabbles, gabbling, gabbled**] to gabble is to talk so quickly it is difficult for other people to understand what you are saying

gable [noun: **gables**] an end of a house or building where the wall and the roof form a triangular shape

gadget [noun: **gadgets**] a tool or small piece of equipment

gag [noun: **gags**]
1 something put round, in or over someone's mouth to stop them speaking
2 a joke or funny story told by a comedian
[verb: **gags, gagging, gagged**] to gag someone is to stop them speaking

gaggle [noun: **gaggles**] a group of geese

gaily [adjective] if you do something gaily, you do it in a lively happy way

gain [verb: **gains, gaining, gained**]
1 to gain something is to win it, get it or earn it: *You gain twenty extra points for that move.*
2 to **gain on** someone is to get closer to them
3 if a clock or watch gains, it goes faster than it should and shows a later time than the real time
[noun: **gains**] something that you get that is more than you had before: *Her loss was my gain.*
• *The party made big gains in the local elections.*

gala [noun: **galas**] a special public event or entertainment: *a swimming gala* • *a fund-raising gala*

galaxy [noun: **galaxies**] a huge group of stars in the universe. Our galaxy is the Milky Way

gale [noun: **gales**] a very strong wind

gall [verb: **galls, galling, galled**] if something galls you, it annoys you
[noun] if you **have the gall to** do something, you are brave or cheeky enough to do it: *He wouldn't have the gall to call me that to my face.*

gallant [adjective]
1 gallant behaviour shows courage and honour: *a gallant effort*
2 very polite and considerate: *a gallant young man*
• **gallantry** [noun] bravery: *an award for gallantry*

gall bladder [noun: **gall bladders**] an organ near your liver where bile is stored

galleon [noun: **galleons**] a large Spanish sailing ship used in the sixteenth and seventeenth centuries for making long sea journeys

gallery [noun: **galleries**]
1 a large building or a shop where works of art are displayed to the public
2 a high open balcony at the back or side of a church, theatre or law court

galley [noun: **galleys**]
1 a type of ship used in ancient times that was moved through the water by lots of large oars
2 a kitchen on a boat or aeroplane

gallon [noun: **gallons**] a measurement of liquids equal to about 4.55 litres. There are 8 pints in a gallon

gallop [noun: **gallops**]
1 a fast running pace
2 a ride on a horse going at this pace: *a morning gallop on the sands*

[verb: **gallops, galloping, galloped**]
1 a horse gallops when it runs at its fastest pace with all four feet off the ground at the same time
2 if you **gallop through** something, you do it very quickly: *We seem to be galloping through the work today.*

gallows [noun] a high wooden frame where criminals used to be hanged: *sent to the gallows*

galore [adjective] you can use **galore** to emphasize there is a lot of something: *There were presents galore.*

(i) **Galore** is one of the adjectives that is always placed immediately after the noun it is describing.

galvanize or **galvanise** [verb: **galvanizes, galvanizing, galvanized**]
1 to galvanize iron or steel is to coat it with zinc to stop it rusting
2 if something galvanizes you into doing something, it gives you the urge to do it: *His father's death galvanized him into action.*

gamble [verb: **gambles, gambling, gambled**]
1 to bet money on the result of something, for example a card game or horse race
2 to take a risk or chance
[noun: **gambles**] something you decide to do that may not turn out the way you want
♦ **gambler** [noun: **gamblers**] someone who gambles money on the result of a race or game

game [noun: **games**]
1 a game is any activity or contest with a set of rules in which players try to do better than others or try to get points: *a computer game • card games*
2 in some sports, a game is one of the parts of a complete match: *He won the first set 7 games to 5.*
3 game is wild animals and birds that are hunted for sport
4 if you **give the game away**, you let other people know about something you have been trying to hide or keep secret
[adjective] someone who is game is ready to do things, especially things that involve risk: *Ask Harry, he's game for anything.*

gamekeeper [noun: **gamekeepers**] someone whose job is to look after wild animals and birds on private land in the countryside and stop people hunting them without permission

gammon [noun] gammon is the salted and smoked meat from the leg of a pig

gander [noun: **ganders**] a male goose

gang [noun: **gangs**]
1 a group of friends who meet regularly or go around together
2 a group of criminals or other troublemakers
[verb: **gangs, ganging, ganged**] if several people **gang up on** another person, they get together to frighten or hurt that person

gangling [adjective] tall and thin: *a gangling youth*

gangrene [noun] when tissue in the body decays because blood isn't getting to it

gangster [noun: **gangsters**] a member of a gang of criminals

gangway [noun: **gangways**]
1 a narrow passage, for example where people can walk between rows of seats
2 a narrow platform or bridge used to get on and off a ship, which can be moved away when the ship sails

gantry [noun: **gantries**] a high metal frame used to support heavy machines such as cranes

gaol [noun: **gaols**] another spelling of **jail**
♦ **gaoler** [noun: **gaolers**] another spelling of **jailer**

gap [noun: **gaps**]
1 an opening or space in the middle of something or between things: *a gap in the wall • a gap between his front teeth*
2 something missing: *a gap in his memory*
3 a difference between two things: *the gap between rich and poor*

gape [verb: **gapes, gaping, gaped**]
1 to gape is to stare with your mouth open, usually because you are very surprised or impressed
2 something that gapes is wide open

garage [noun: **garages**]
1 a building, often a small one beside a house, for storing a car or other vehicle
2 a place where vehicles are repaired, or a

Gg

shop selling petrol and often other items for vehicles or road journeys

garbage [noun] rubbish

garbled [adjective] garbled words or messages are mixed up and hard to understand

garden [noun: **gardens**] a piece of land where flowers, trees and vegetables are grown
+ **gardener** [noun: **gardeners**] someone who does gardening
+ **gardening** [noun] working in and taking care of a garden

gargle [verb: **gargles, gargling, gargled**] to rinse your mouth and throat with a liquid by holding it in your mouth and letting air from your throat bubble through it

gargoyle [noun: **gargoyles**] a stone carving of an ugly creature's head, with an open mouth forming a spout, used to carry rainwater that comes off the roof of a building

garish [adjective] garish colours or patterns are too bright

garland [noun: **garlands**] flowers or leaves woven together into a circle

garlic [noun] a plant related to the onion with bulbs that divide into sections called cloves, which are used in cooking to add flavour

garment [noun: **garments**] a piece of clothing

garnet [noun: **garnets**] a hard red precious stone

garnish [verb: **garnishes, garnishing, garnished**] to garnish food is to decorate it [noun: **garnishes**] something used to decorate food, for example herbs or nuts: *served with a garnish of wild parsley*

garret [noun: **garrets**] a room in an attic

garrison [noun: **garrisons**] a group of soldiers guarding a town or fortress, or the building they live in

garter [noun: **garters**] a broad band of elastic used to keep a stocking or sock up

gas [noun: **gases** or **gasses**]
1 a substance that is not liquid or solid and that moves about like air: *Oxygen and carbon dioxide are two of the gases that make up air.*
2 any natural or manufactured gas that burns easily and is used as fuel: *natural gas • coal gas*

3 a short form of the word **gasoline**

gash [noun: **gashes**] a deep open cut [verb: **gashes, gashing, gashed**] to gash something is to make a long deep cut in it

gasket [noun: **gaskets**] a ring or flat strip of padding or rubber used to seal joints between two pieces of metal to stop gas or steam from escaping

gas mask [noun: **gas masks**] a mask that covers your nose and mouth so that you do not breathe in poisonous gas

gasoline [noun] the American English word for **petrol**

gasp [verb: **gasps, gasping, gasped**]
1 to gasp is to take a short sudden breath in through your open mouth making a sound as you do so: *They all gasped in horror.*
2 to gasp for air is to take sudden short breaths because you need to get oxygen into your lungs quickly
[noun: **gasps**] the sound of a sudden short breath

gastric [adjective] to do with the stomach: *a gastric ulcer*

gastroenteritis [noun] a painful stomach illness caused by a virus or by bacteria in food

gasworks [noun] a gasworks is a place where gas is made, especially from coal

gate [noun: **gates**]
1 a structure like a door that is used to close an opening in a wall or fence: *Please close the gate.*
2 the place where passengers get on a plane at an airport
3 the number of people attending a sports event or the total amount of money they pay to get in

gateau [noun: **gateaus** or **gateaux**] a large cake made in layers, usually with cream or chocolate filling

gatecrash [verb: **gatecrashes, gatecrashing, gatecrashed**] if someone gatecrashes a party or other event, they go to it although they haven't been invited
+ **gatecrasher** [noun: **gatecrashers**] someone who goes to a party without being invited

gateway [noun: **gateways**]
1 an opening with a gate across it

2 anything that is an entrance or like an entrance: *a gateway to the future*

3 a connection between two computer networks that allows information to be passed between them

gather [verb: **gathers, gathering, gathered**]

1 to meet or come together in a group: *A crowd gathered at the airport.*

2 to gather things is to collect them or bring them together

3 to gather speed is to get faster and faster

4 to gather something is to hear or read about it: *I gather he's lived here for more than fifty years.*

♦ **gathering** [noun: **gatherings**] a meeting of people

gaudy [adjective: **gaudier, gaudiest**] gaudy colours are very strong and bright

gauge [noun: **gauges**]

1 an instrument for measuring things such as temperature, depth or height

2 the distance between railway tracks

[verb: **gauges, gauging, gauged**]

1 to gauge something is to measure it

2 to gauge something is to make a guess at it: *I can never gauge what his reaction will be.*

gaunt [adjective] a gaunt person is thin and bony, often because they are ill

gauntlet [noun: **gauntlets**]

1 a type of thick glove with a part that covers the wrist and lower part of the arm

2 if you **throw down the gauntlet**, you challenge someone, especially to a fight

gauze [noun] a very thin material that you can see through. Gauze is sometimes used to cover cuts and scratches

gave [verb] a way of changing the verb **give** to make a past tense: *Jane gave Rob her phone number.*

gawky [adjective: **gawkier, gawkiest**] a gawky person is tall and awkward-looking

gay [adjective: **gayer, gayest**]

1 someone who is gay is homosexual

2 a gay bar or club is one where gay people go

3 lively and full of fun: *happy and gay*

4 brightly coloured: *gay banners*

[noun: **gays**] someone who is homosexual

gaze [verb: **gazes, gazing, gazed**] to look at something steadily

[noun: **gazes**] a long steady look

gazelle [noun: **gazelles**] a type of African or Asian animal that looks like a small deer and that can move quickly and gracefully

GB [abbreviation] short for **gigabyte**

gear [noun: **gears**]

1 gear is the clothes and equipment you need or use for a particular sport or job: *tennis gear*

2 a gear is a mechanism made up of connecting toothed wheels that transfers power to the moving parts of a machine, for example from a car's engine to its wheels

[verb: **gears, gearing, geared**]

1 to gear things to a particular group of people is to adapt things for that group: *The course is geared to more advanced students.*

2 to **gear up** for something is to get ready for it

gearbox [noun: **gearboxes**] the part of a motor vehicle that contains a set of gears

geese [noun] the plural of **goose**

gel [noun: **gels**] gel is a thick substance that looks like jelly and is used to hold your hair in a certain style

[verb: **gels, gelling, gelled**] if you gel your hair, you put gel onto it to shape it into different styles

gelatine [noun] a clear substance used in cooking that sets to form jelly

gem [noun: **gems**] a valuable stone or mineral, for example a diamond or emerald, that can be cut and polished and used in jewellery

gender [noun: **genders**]

1 gender is being male or female

2 in grammar, the gender of a word tells you if it is masculine, feminine or neuter

gene [noun: **genes**] a part of a living cell of an animal or plant that contains information inherited from its parents and that affects things like hair or skin colour

genealogy [noun: **genealogies**] the history of how people in a family are linked from one generation to the next

genera [noun] the plural of **genus**

general [adjective]

1 involving everyone or most things: *a general feeling of gloom* • *general knowledge*

Gg

2 broad and not detailed: *Can you give me a general idea of what it will cost?*

3 if something happens or is true **in general**, it usually happens or is true: *Schools are achieving better results in general.*

[noun: **generals**] an important army officer

general anaesthetic [noun: **general anaesthetics**] a drug that makes you go to sleep while a doctor operates on you

general election [noun: **general elections**] an election in which all the voters in a country elect the members of parliament

generalize or **generalise** [verb: **generalizes, generalizing, generalized**] to make a statement that does not go into any detail

generally [adverb] usually: *Children generally start school at about age five.*

general practitioner [noun: **general practitioners**] a doctor who sees sick people from a particular area at a local clinic or surgery, or visits them at home. This is often shortened to **GP**

generate [verb: **generates, generating, generated**] to generate something is to create it: *His work generated a lot of interest.*

◆ **generation** [noun: **generations**]
1 generation is creating something: *the generation of electricity*
2 a generation is a single step in a family tree. For example, your parents are from one generation and you are from the next generation

◆ **generator** [noun: **generators**] a machine that makes power, especially electricity

generosity [noun] being kind and giving unselfishly to people

generous [adjective]
1 a generous person is kind and gives to other people in an unselfish way
2 a generous gift is bigger or more than expected

◆ **generously** [adverb] in a generous way: *Please give generously.*

genetic [adjective] to do with genes, or inherited through the genes: *a genetic defect*

genetically modified [adjective] genetically modified plants or animals have had one or more of their genes changed

artificially so that their natural characteristics are changed or improved. This is often shortened to **GM**

genetics [noun] the study of genes and how they work

genial [adjective] a genial person is good-natured
◆ **geniality** [noun] being good-natured
◆ **genially** [adverb] in a good-natured way

genie [noun: **genies** or **genii**] in Arabian and Persian stories, a magical spirit who watches over and grants the wishes of the person who controls it

genitals [plural noun] a person's genitals are their sexual organs

genius [noun: **geniuses**]
1 a genius is someone who is unusually clever or skilful
2 genius is extraordinary cleverness or skill

genteel [adjective] if someone is genteel, they think it is important to appear very polite and well-mannered

gentle [adjective: **gentler, gentlest**]
1 a gentle person is kind and calm: *a gentle giant*
2 soft and light: *a gentle breeze • a gentle tap on his shoulder*

gentleman [noun: **gentlemen**]
1 a word used to refer politely to a man: *Good morning, gentlemen.*
2 a man who is very polite and good-mannered: *He's a real gentleman.*
◆ **gentlemanly** [adjective] gentlemanly behaviour is polite and good-mannered

gentleness [noun] being gentle

gently [adjective] in a gentle way

gentry [noun] an old-fashioned word for people from one of the higher classes of society

gents [noun] the gents is a public toilet for boys and men: *Where is the gents, please?*

genuine [adjective]
1 real, not fake: *a genuine work of art*
2 honest and not pretending: *a genuine person*
◆ **genuinely** [adverb] really or honestly: *I was genuinely impressed.*
◆ **genuineness** [noun] being real or honest

genus [noun: **genera**] a genus is a class of animals or plants which usually includes several different species

geo- [prefix] if a word starts with **geo-**, it has something to do with the Earth. For example, *geology* is the study of the Earth's rocks

geographic or **geographical** [adjective] to do with geography and where things are situated on the Earth's surface

geography [noun] geography is the study of the Earth's surface and the people on it

geologist [noun: **geologists**] someone who studies geology

geology [noun] the study of the Earth's rocks, minerals and soil, what they are made up of, and how they were created

geometric or **geometrical** [adjective] a geometric shape is made up of straight lines and angles

geometry [noun] geometry is a type of mathematics which deals with the study of angles, lines, curves and shapes

geranium [noun: **geraniums**] a kind of bushy garden plant that has red, pink, purple or white flowers

gerbil [noun: **gerbils**] a small animal similar to a rat, but with long back legs, that is often kept as a pet

geriatric [adjective] to do with old people and the illnesses they suffer from: *a geriatric care unit*

germ [noun: **germs**] a tiny living thing that can cause disease

German measles [noun] a minor disease children sometimes get. If a pregnant woman catches it, it can seriously harm her unborn baby

germinate [verb: **germinates, germinating, germinated**] a seed germinates when it begins to sprout or grow
 ✦ **germination** [noun] germinating

gesticulate [verb: **gesticulates, gesticulating, gesticulated**] to gesticulate is to wave your hands or arms to express something

gesture [noun: **gestures**] a movement made with part of your body which expresses a meaning or feeling, for example pointing at something, nodding or winking
 [verb: **gestures, gesturing, gestured**] to make a gesture with part of your body, especially your hand, arm or head

get [verb: **gets, getting, got**]
 1 you get something when someone gives it to you or you fetch it: *Isabel got lots of birthday presents.*
 2 you have got something when you have it or own it: *Have you got £10 I could borrow? • They haven't got a TV.*
 3 you get someone to do something for you when you ask or persuade them to do it: *Get Raymond to help you lift that big box.*
 4 you get somewhere when you arrive there: *We got to New York at 5 o'clock in the morning.*
 5 to become: *The baby's getting bigger every day. • I got wet in the rain.*
 6 you get a bus or some other form of transport when you travel on it: *I usually get the train to work.*
 7 if you get a disease or illness, you catch it: *They had an injection to stop them getting measles.*
 8 if you get something such as a joke, you understand it: *I don't get it: why's he so late?*
 9 to **get something across** is to make people understand it: *The government is struggling to get its message across.*
 10 to **get at** someone is to criticize them
 11 to **get away with** something is to manage to do something wrong or illegal without being caught or punished
 12 to **get by** is to manage, especially with the money you have: *It's hard to get by on a nurse's wage.*
 13 to **get on** is to make progress or to do well in your career: *You have to study hard if you want to get on. • I've got to get on with this report.*
 14 if people **get on** or **get on with** each other, they like each other and are friendly to each other: *Phil and Mike seem to get on really well.*
 15 to **get out of** something is to avoid doing it
 16 to **get over** something is to recover from it: *It took her a long time to get over the shock.*

geyser [noun: **geysers**] a spout of hot water that comes out of the ground

ghastly [adjective: **ghastlier, ghastliest**] horrible or very ugly: *a ghastly smell*

gherkin [noun: **gherkins**] a kind of pickled vegetable that looks like a small cucumber

Gg

ghetto [noun: **ghettos**] an area in a town or city where a certain group of people live, especially poor people

ghost [noun: **ghosts**] the spirit of a dead person

✦ **ghostly** [adjective: **ghostlier, ghostliest**]
1 like a ghost
2 very pale

ghoul [noun: **ghouls**]
1 in Muslim folk tales, an evil spirit that steals and eats dead bodies
2 someone who is very interested in death and disaster

✦ **ghoulish** [adjective] unnaturally interested in death and disaster

giant [noun: **giants**]
1 in stories, an imaginary being like a huge person that is often evil or frightening
2 a very large or important thing: *an industrial giant*
[adjective] huge or bigger than normal: *a giant crane • a giant tortoise*

gibberish [noun] gibberish is fast talk that has no meaning or is hard to understand

gibbon [noun: **gibbons**] a type of ape with long thin arms and legs

giblets [plural noun] the internal parts of a chicken or turkey that are used in cooking to make stock for soup or gravy, especially the neck, heart and lungs

giddiness [noun] a feeling of dizziness

giddy [adjective: **giddier, giddiest**] if you feel giddy, you feel dizzy

gift [noun: **gifts**]
1 a present
2 a natural ability: *Adam has a gift for languages.*

✦ **gifted** [adjective] a gifted person is extremely good at something or extremely clever

gig [noun: **gigs**] a gig is a concert of pop or jazz music

gigabyte [noun: **gigabytes**] a unit used to measure computer memory or data, equal to approximately a thousand megabytes. This is often shortened to **GB**

gigantic [adjective] huge, like a giant

giggle [verb: **giggles, giggling, giggled**] to giggle is to laugh in a silly or nervous way

[noun: **giggles**] a silly or nervous laugh

gild [verb: **gilds, gilding, gilded**] to gild something is to cover it with gold

gills [plural noun] a fish's gills are the openings at each side of its body just behind its head, which allow it to breathe

gilt [noun] gilt is a thin layer of gold that is used to decorate something
[adjective] decorated with gilt: *a gilt frame*

gimmick [noun: **gimmicks**] something that is meant to attract people's attention, but has no real value

gin [noun] an alcoholic drink made with grain and flavoured with juniper berries

ginger [noun] the knobbly root of a tropical plant which has a spicy taste and is used in cooking
[adjective] ginger hair is a reddish-brown colour

gingerbread [noun] a kind of cake flavoured with powdered ginger

gingerly [adverb] if you do something gingerly, you do it very slowly and carefully because you are nervous: *He stepped gingerly onto the wobbly bridge.*

Gipsy [noun: **Gipsies**] another spelling of **Gypsy**

giraffe [noun: **giraffes**] an African animal with a spotted coat, long legs and a very long neck

girder [noun: **girders**] a beam made of iron, steel or wood, used as a support in bridges and buildings

girdle [noun: **girdles**] a tight piece of underwear that makes your hips and stomach look slimmer

girl [noun: **girls**] a female child or young woman

girlfriend [noun: **girlfriends**]
1 a female friend
2 a girl or woman that someone is having a romantic or sexual relationship with

gist [noun] the gist of a story or argument is its basic meaning or its main point

give [verb: **gives, giving, gave, given**]
1 to give something to someone is to let them have it or to pass it on to them: *Let me give you some advice. • Give your bags to the porter.*

2 if someone gives a party or performance, they hold a party or they perform in front of other people

3 to give a cry, shout or laugh is to make that sound out loud: *He gave a whoop of joy.*

4 if something gives, it bends, sags or collapses when too much weight is put on top of it: *The rotten floorboard gave under him and his foot went through.*

5 to **give away** a secret is to tell it to someone without meaning to

6 to **give in** is to admit defeat

7 if a machine or a part of your body **gives out**, it stops working

8 to **give up** is to stop trying to do something because it has become too difficult

9 something **gives way** when it breaks or collapses

10 drivers **give way** when they stop at a junction or roundabout and allow other traffic to pass in front of them

♦ **given** [adjective] decided or selected: *On any given day, there are several dozen accidents.*

glacier [noun: **glaciers**] a huge mass of ice moving slowly down a valley

glad [adjective: **gladder, gladdest**] pleased or happy: *We're very glad you could make it to the party.* • *I'd be glad to help you.*

♦ **gladden** [verb: **gladdens, gladdening, gladdened**] if something gladdens someone, it makes them happy: *a sight to gladden your heart*

➡ **gladly**

glade [noun: **glades**] an open space in a wood or forest

gladiator [noun: **gladiators**] in ancient Rome, a man trained to fight with other men or with wild animals to entertain spectators

gladly [adverb] happily or with pleasure: *I'll gladly do what you ask.*

glamorous [adjective] attractive, fashionable and exciting

glamour [noun]

1 extravagant beauty, especially if it is rather false

2 the excitement of being rich, fashionable or famous

glance [verb: **glances, glancing, glanced**]

1 to look quickly at something and then look away again

2 if something moving **glances off** another thing, it hits that thing then flies off sideways

[noun: **glances**]

1 a short quick look

2 if you see or understand something **at a glance**, you see or understand it immediately

gland [noun: **glands**] an organ in your body that stores substances that it can use later or can get rid of

♦ **glandular** [adjective] to do with a gland or glands

glare [verb: **glares, glaring, glared**]

1 if someone glares, they look at someone or something angrily

2 if a light glares, it shines very brightly and hurts your eyes

[noun: **glares**]

1 a fierce or angry look

2 very strong bright light that dazzles you

♦ **glaring** [adjective] standing out in a very obvious way: *a glaring mistake*

♦ **glaringly** [adverb] very clearly: *It was glaringly obvious that he was lying.*

glass [noun: **glasses**]

1 glass is a hard breakable material that lets light through

2 a glass is a container for drinks made of this material, or the amount it will hold: *a tall glass* • *She drank three glasses of milk.*

[adjective] made of glass: *a glass bowl*

♦ **glasses** [plural noun] glasses are a pair of clear lenses inside a frame that you wear over your eyes to help you see more clearly

♦ **glassy** [adjective: **glassier, glassiest**]

1 shiny like glass, or transparent like glass

2 if someone's eyes are glassy, they have no expression in them

glaze [verb: **glazes, glazing, glazed**]

1 to glaze a window is to fit a sheet or sheets of glass into it

2 to glaze pots is to bake a hard shiny covering on their surface

3 if someone's eyes **glaze over**, they lose all expression

[noun: **glazes**] a shiny covering

♦ **glazier** [noun: **glaziers**] someone whose job is to put glass in windows

Gg

gleam [verb: **gleams, gleaming, gleamed**] to shine or glow brightly: *A light gleamed in the distance.*
[noun: **gleams**]
1 a beam or flash of light: *the gleam of headlights in the distance*
2 brightness or shininess: *the gleam of newly polished furniture*

glee [noun] joyful excitement or pleasure
♦ **gleeful** [adjective] joyful
♦ **gleefully** [adverb] happily or joyfully

glen [noun: **glens**] a valley in Scotland

glide [verb: **glides, gliding, glided**]
1 to move smoothly, especially over a surface
2 to fly in a glider
♦ **glider** [noun: **gliders**] a light aeroplane with no engine that is towed into the air by another aeroplane, then floats on air currents

glimmer [verb: **glimmers, glimmering, glimmered**] to burn or shine weakly or faintly
[noun: **glimmers**]
1 a faint light
2 a glimmer of something such as hope is a slight amount or sign of it

glimpse [noun: **glimpses**] a brief look at something
[verb: **glimpses, glimpsing, glimpsed**] to glimpse something is to see it for a very short time

glint [verb: **glints, glinting, glinted**] to reflect flashes of light
[noun: **glints**] a flash of light reflected off a surface

glisten [verb: **glistens, glistening, glistened**] if a surface glistens, light reflects off it, because it is shiny or wet: *Her eyes glistened with tears.*

glitter [verb: **glitters, glittering, glittered**] to shine or sparkle with small flashes of light
[noun] glitter is tiny pieces of shiny material used for decoration
♦ **glittery** [adjective] shining with little sparks of light or tiny pieces of shiny material: *glittery make-up*

gloat [verb: **gloats, gloating, gloated**] to show too much pleasure at your own success or at someone else's failure

global [adjective]
1 to do with or involving the whole world: *global businesses*
2 involving everyone or everything: *a global increase in pay*
♦ **globally** [adverb] worldwide or generally

global warming [noun] the gradual warming of the Earth's surface and atmosphere as a result of the greenhouse effect, causing sea temperatures to rise and weather to change around the world

globe [noun: **globes**]
1 the globe is the Earth: *people from around the globe*
2 a globe is a large ball with a map of the Earth printed on it that can be turned on a stand
3 a globe is anything shaped like a ball or sphere

glockenspiel [noun: **glockenspiels**] a musical instrument made up of a row of metal bars that you play by hitting them with sticks to make different notes

gloom [noun]
1 darkness or near-darkness: *A shape appeared out of the gloom.*
2 sadness or depression: *They were filled with gloom when they heard the news.*
♦ **gloominess** [noun]
1 being dark, nearly dark or dull: *the gloominess of a winter's morning*
2 being sad or depressed: *Her gloominess made us all feel bad.*
♦ **gloomy** [adjective: **gloomier, gloomiest**]
1 dark or nearly dark: *a gloomy passageway*
2 sad or depressing: *a gloomy picture of the future*

glorify [verb: **glorifies, glorifying, glorified**] to glorify someone or something is to praise them very highly, in a way that makes them seem impressive: *glorify God • The book glorifies war.*

glorious [adjective]
1 splendidly beautiful: *glorious singing*
2 deserving or bringing glory: *a glorious victory*

glory [noun: **glories**]
1 honour and praise
2 a splendidly beautiful thing: *the glories of medieval architecture*

[verb: **glories, glorying, gloried**] if you **glory in** something, you feel or show that you are proud and delighted about it: *They gloried in their unexpected victory.*

gloss [noun]
  1 gloss is the brightness of a surface
  2 a type of paint that produces a shiny surface: *a tin of gloss*
  → **glossy**

glossary [noun: **glossaries**] a list of words, with explanations of their meanings

glossy [adjective: **glossier, glossiest**] smooth and shiny: *a glossy surface • glossy hair*

glove [noun: **gloves**] gloves are two matching pieces of clothing that you wear on your hands

glow [verb: **glows, glowing, glowed**] to burn or shine with a warm or soft light
  [noun] warm or soft light: *the glow of the fire*
  → **glowing**

glower [verb: **glowers, glowering, glowered**] to stare at something or somebody with a frown

glowing [adjective]
  1 burning or shining with a warm or soft light: *glowing embers*
  2 full of praise and admiration: *He got a glowing appraisal from his manager.*

glow-worm [noun: **glow-worms**] a kind of beetle that glows in the dark

glucose [noun] a kind of sugar that is found in certain foods, like fruit, and which gives you energy

glue [noun: **glues**] a substance used for sticking things together
  [verb: **glues, gluing** or **glueing, glued**] to glue something is to stick it with glue
  ◆ **gluey** [adjective] covered with glue or sticky like glue

glum [adjective: **glummer, glummest**] looking or feeling sad and depressed

gluten [noun] a sticky protein found in wheat and some other cereals

glutton [noun: **gluttons**]
  1 someone who is very greedy and eats too much
  2 someone who is very eager for something, especially something that is not pleasant: *a glutton for punishment*

◆ **gluttony** [noun] eating too much

GM [abbreviation] short for **genetically modified**

gnarled [adjective] twisted and knobbly: *gnarled fingers • The branches of the tree were gnarled with age.*

gnash [verb: **gnashes, gnashing, gnashed**] if someone gnashes their teeth, they grind them together, especially because they are angry

gnat [noun: **gnats**] a small flying insect that bites and sucks blood

gnaw [verb: **gnaws, gnawing, gnawed**] to chew something hard or scrape at it with the teeth: *The dog was gnawing at a bone.*

gnome [noun: **gnomes**]
  1 in stories, a small fairy creature that looks like a little old man wearing a soft pointed hat
  2 a figure like this that some people put in their gardens as a decoration

go [verb: **goes, going, went, gone**]
  1 if you go somewhere, you travel or move there: *I'm going home now.*
  2 if a road or path goes somewhere, it leads to that place: *Does this road go to Inverness?*
  3 to leave: *It's six o'clock, so I'll have to go soon.*
  4 the place where something goes is the place where it fits or is kept: *That piece of the jigsaw goes at the top.*
  5 to become: *Her face went pale. • Your soup's gone cold.*
  6 to **go in for** something is to take part in it
  7 food **goes off** when it becomes bad
  8 a bomb **goes off** when it explodes
  9 to **go on** is to continue: *Go on with your work. • The baby went on crying.*
  10 if you **go through with** something, you do it although it is difficult or unpleasant: *They persuaded her to go through with the operation.*
  11 if you are **going to** do something, you are about to do it: *What were you going to say?*
  [noun: **goes**]
  1 a go is a try or an attempt
  2 if someone is **on the go**, they are busy or active

goad [verb: **goads, goading, goaded**] to goad someone is to annoy them until they do something that you want them to do

go-ahead [noun] if something **gets the go-ahead**, it is allowed to begin
[adjective] a go-ahead person is someone who is full of ideas and plans for the future

goal [noun: **goals**]
1 in games like football and hockey, the goal is the area where you have to put the ball to score a point
2 a goal is a point scored when a ball goes into this area
3 an aim that you want to achieve

goat [noun: **goats**] an animal with horns and long rough hair. Goats are kept for their milk, meat and hair

gobble [verb: **gobbles, gobbling, gobbled**]
1 if someone gobbles their food, they eat it very quickly
2 a turkey gobbles when it makes a series of loud sounds

goblet [noun: **goblets**] a drinking cup with a stem and a rounded bowl

goblin [noun: **goblins**] in fairy stories, an evil and ugly creature in the form of a little man

god [noun: **gods**]
1 a god is one of several beings that some people believe have the power to change or affect nature or what happens to individuals: *Greek and Roman gods • the god of war*
2 **God** is the being that Christians, Muslims, Jews and members of other religions worship

godchild [noun: **godchildren**] a god-daughter or godson

god-daughter [noun: **god-daughters**] someone's god-daughter is a girl that they are godmother or godfather to

goddess [noun: **goddesses**] a female god

godfather [noun: **godfathers**] a child's godfather is a man who has agreed to help make sure that the child is brought up as a Christian

godmother [noun: **godmothers**] a child's godmother is a woman who has agreed to help make sure that the child is brought up as a Christian

godparent [noun: **godparents**] a godfather or godmother

godsend [noun: **godsends**] something

good that happens unexpectedly just when you need it

godson [noun: **godsons**] someone's godson is a boy that they are godmother or godfather to

goggles [plural noun] people wear goggles over their eyes to protect them, for example when they are swimming underwater or working with materials that might damage their eyes

go-kart [noun: **go-karts**] a small low vehicle that is used for racing, but which has a much less powerful engine than a real racing car

gold [noun]
1 a pale yellow precious metal
2 a yellow colour
• **golden** [adjective] gold-coloured or made of gold: *golden hair • a golden crown*

golden wedding [noun: **golden weddings**] the 50th anniversary of a couple's marriage

goldfish [noun: **goldfish**] a small fish with golden or orange scales that is kept as a pet

gold medal [noun: **gold medals**] a medal made of gold awarded to the person who comes first in a sporting event

golf [noun] a game played on a large, specially designed area of land. The players hit a small ball with long clubs into a series of small holes
• **golfer** [noun: **golfers**] someone who plays golf

gondola [noun: **gondolas**] a type of open boat used on the canals and waterways of Venice and rowed by a single oar at the back
• **gondolier** [noun: **gondoliers**] someone who rows a gondola

gone [verb] the form of the verb **go** that is used with a helping verb to show that something happened in the past: *I tried to catch him before he left, but he had gone.*

gong [noun: **gongs**] a large round piece of metal that is hit with a stick to make a ringing sound

good [adjective: **better, best**]
1 something good is enjoyable or pleasant, or is of a high standard: *Did you have a good holiday?*

2 a good person is kind and thoughtful: *My grandparents are very good to me.*
3 good behaviour is correct or proper: *Sue has very good manners.*
4 to be good at something is to be able to do it well: *Mark's very good at fixing cars.*
5 satisfactory or substantial: *He earns a good salary.*
6 something is good for you when it benefits you in some way, especially by keeping you healthy
[noun]
1 what is proper and correct: *the difference between good and evil*
2 if something is done **for good**, it will stay that way for ever: *He won't be coming back — he's gone for good.*
➞ **better, best**

goodbye [interjection] you say 'goodbye' to people you are leaving or who are leaving you

goodness [noun]
1 being good and kind
2 the goodness in food is the things in it that will make you healthy when you eat it

goods [plural noun] goods are things for sale: *goods from other countries*

goodwill [noun] goodwill is kind wishes: *The King and Queen sent him a message of goodwill.*

goose [noun: **geese**] a bird with a long neck and webbed feet

gooseberry [noun: **gooseberries**] a small round pale green fruit with a hairy skin that grows on a low bush

goosebumps or **goosepimples** [plural noun] if you get **goosebumps** or **goosepimples**, tiny lumps appear on your skin, usually because you are cold or have had a fright

gore [verb: **gores, goring, gored**] if a bull or other animal gores someone, it injures them with its horns or tusks
[noun] gore is lots of blood
➞ **gory**

gorge [noun: **gorges**] a deep narrow valley between hills

gorgeous [adjective] beautiful: *The baby's absolutely gorgeous.* • *lots of gorgeous food*

gorilla [noun: **gorillas**] a kind of West African ape with a large head, long arms and a strong heavy body

ⓘ Be careful not to confuse the spellings of **gorilla** and **guerilla**, a type of fighter.

gorse [noun] gorse is a type of wild shrub with yellow flowers and sharp spines on its stems
gory [adjective: **gorier, goriest**] with lots of blood: *a gory film*
gosling [noun: **goslings**] a baby goose
gospel [noun: **gospels**]
1 the gospel is the teachings of Christ
2 the Gospels are the parts of the Christian Bible describing the teachings of Christ
3 the truth: *He swore that what he had told me was gospel.*
gossip [verb: **gossips, gossiping, gossiped**] to gossip is to have a conversation with someone about what other people are doing
[noun: **gossips**]
1 gossip is informal talk, often about what other people are doing
2 a gossip is someone who gossips a lot
got [verb] a way of changing the verb **get** to make a past tense. It can be used with or without a helping verb: *Kathy got a bike for her birthday.* • *She had got a pony the previous year.*

ⓘ In North America and Australia another form, **gotten**, is also used with a helping verb: *She had gotten a pony the previous year.*

gouge [verb: **gouges, gouging, gouged**] to gouge something out is to dig it out using your fingernails or a sharp tool
govern [verb: **governs, governing, governed**] to govern something such as a country is to control it and decide its rules
✦ **governess** [noun: **governesses**] especially in the past, a woman employed by parents to teach their children at home
✦ **government** [noun: **governments**] a government is the group of people who put the laws of a country into effect
✦ **governor** [noun: **governors**]
1 someone who is the head of government in some countries or states

Gg

2 school governors are the group of people who manage a particular school's business

gown [noun: **gowns**] a long formal dress that women wear on special occasions

GP [abbreviation: **GPs**] short for **general practitioner**

grab [verb: **grabs, grabbing, grabbed**]
1 to grasp something suddenly or roughly: *He grabbed my bag and ran away.*
2 to take something eagerly or in a hurry: *Let's stop and grab a bite to eat.*

grace [noun: **graces**]
1 grace is beauty or elegance in the way you move
2 if someone behaves with grace they are gentle, pleasant and thoughtful
3 approval or favour: *with the grace of God*
4 if you do something **with bad grace**, you do it unwillingly or in a grudging way
5 if you do something **with good grace**, you do it willingly and without complaining

graceful [adjective] graceful movements are elegant and attractive
✦ **gracefully** [adverb] with grace

gracious [adjective] behaving in a polite and kind way: *a gracious lady* • *It was very gracious of you to apologize.*
✦ **graciously** [adverb] politely and kindly

grade [noun: **grades**]
1 a grade is a placing or stage on a scale of quality or rank
2 if someone or something **makes the grade**, they reach the necessary standard
[verb: **grades, grading, graded**] to grade things is to sort them according to their size or quality, or to mark them according to how good they are

gradient [noun: **gradients**] a measure of how steep a slope is, which is shown as a percentage or a number out of ten

gradual [adjective] going or changing slowly and steadily: *a gradual increase*
✦ **gradually** [adverb] slowly and steadily: *The weather gradually got colder.*

graduate [verb: **graduates, graduating, graduated**] to graduate from college or university is to successfully finish your course and get a degree or diploma

[noun: **graduates**] someone who has a degree from a university or college
✦ **graduation** [noun: **graduations**] the ceremony held when students at a college or university are given degrees or diplomas

graffiti [noun] words or pictures painted or drawn on a wall

graft [verb: **grafts, grafting, grafted**] to attach one thing on to another, for example a piece of skin that has been taken from one part of the body for sewing on to another damaged part
[noun: **grafts**] something such as the stem of a plant or a piece of skin that has been attached to another plant or another part of the body so that it can begin to grow there

grain [noun: **grains**]
1 a grain is a single seed from a cereal plant like wheat or maize
2 grain is the seeds of cereal plants
3 a tiny piece of something: *a grain of pollen*
4 the grain on wood is the pattern of lines that run along or across its surface

gram or **gramme** [noun: **grams** or **grammes**] the basic measurement of weight in the metric system, equal to about 0.035 ounces. This is often shortened to **g**

grammar [noun]
1 grammar is the correct use of words in speech and writing, and the rules about putting them together: *It's bad grammar to say 'I done'.*
2 the rules that apply to how words are formed and used in a particular language: *French grammar*

grammar school [noun: **grammar schools**] in Britain, a type of secondary school

grammatical [adjective] grammatical speech or writing is correct according to the rules of grammar

gramme [noun: **grammes**] another spelling of **gram**

gran [noun: **grans**] an informal word for **grandmother**

grand [adjective: **grander, grandest**]
1 great or fine: *a grand house*
2 noble: *She's a very grand old lady.*

grandchild [noun: **grandchildren**] a child of your son or daughter

grand-daughter [noun: **grand-**

Gg

daughters] the daughter of your son or daughter

grandfather [noun: **grandfathers**] your father's or mother's father

grandmother [noun: **grandmothers**] your father's or mother's mother

grandparent [noun: **grandparents**] a parent of your father or mother

grandson [noun: **grandsons**] the son of your son or daughter

grandstand [noun: **grandstands**] a place for spectators at a sports stadium or race ground with rows of seats built in tiers one above the other

granite [noun] a very hard grey or red rock

granny [noun: **grannies**] an informal word for **grandmother**

grant [verb: **grants, granting, granted**]
1 to grant something that someone has asked for is to allow it or give it: *grant permission*
2 to admit that something is true: *It's very difficult, I grant you.*
[noun: **grants**] a sum of money that has been given or awarded for a special purpose: *a repair grant*

granule [noun: **granules**] a very small grain or part: *sugar granules*

grape [noun: **grapes**] a small green or dark red berry that grows in bunches and is used to make wine

grapefruit [noun: **grapefruit** or **grapefruits**] a large citrus fruit with thick yellow skin and yellow or pink flesh

graph [noun: **graphs**] a diagram with lines drawn between different points on squared paper, used to show how things compare to each other

graphic [adjective]
1 to do with drawing, painting or writing: *the graphic arts*
2 showing or giving a lot of detail, often too much detail: *a graphic description of the robbery*
♦ **graphics** [plural noun] pictures, drawings and decorative lettering, especially those done on a computer or used in computer games or Web pages

grapple [verb: **grapples, grappling, grappled**]
1 to grapple with someone is to wrestle or struggle with them
2 to grapple with a difficult problem is to try hard to deal with it

grasp [verb: **grasps, grasping, grasped**]
1 to grasp something is to take hold of it or hold it tightly
2 to grasp something is to understand it: *I still couldn't grasp what he was trying to tell me.*

grass [noun: **grasses**] a plant with long thin leaves called blades, which covers lawns and fields

grasshopper [noun: **grasshoppers**] a brown or green insect with long back legs that can hop or jump long distances

grassland [noun: **grasslands**] a large area covered with grass

grassy [adjective: **grassier, grassiest**] covered with grass: *a grassy field*

grate [superscript] 1 [verb: **grates, grating, grated**]
1 to grate food is to cut it into fine strands or shreds using a grater
2 something grates when it makes an unpleasant squeaking or scratching noise as it rubs, or is rubbed, against something
⟶ **grater**

grate [superscript] 2 [noun: **grates**] a framework of metal bars in a fireplace, where the fuel is burned

grateful [adjective] feeling thankful or showing or giving thanks: *I'm very grateful for all your kindness.*
♦ **gratefully** [adverb] thankfully

grater [noun: **graters**] a kitchen tool that has lots of small holes with sharp edges on its surface, used for grating things like cheese or vegetables

grating [noun: **gratings**] a covering for a window or an outside drain with holes in it so that water or air can pass through

gratitude [noun] if you feel gratitude towards someone, you want to repay them for something kind that they have done

grave [superscript] 1 [noun: **graves**] a place where a dead body is buried

grave [superscript] 2 [adjective: **graver, gravest**]
1 very serious: *a grave mistake*
2 solemn-looking

gravel [noun] small stones used to cover roads, paths and driveways

Gg

gravestone [noun: **gravestones**] a piece of stone with writing on it which says who is buried in a grave

graveyard [noun: **graveyards**] a place where dead people or animals are buried

gravity [noun]
1 gravity is the force that pulls things towards the earth and makes them fall to the ground
2 gravity is seriousness: *the gravity of the crime*

gravy [noun] a sauce made from the juices that come out of meat while it is cooking

graze [verb: **grazes, grazing, grazed**]
1 animals graze when they move around eating grass and other plants
2 to graze your skin is to scratch it by dragging it against something hard
3 if something grazes you, it touches you lightly as it goes past
[noun: **grazes**] a graze is a scratch or scratches on your skin made by something hard and rough

grease [noun] thick fat or oil, or any oily substance
[verb: **greases, greasing, greased**] to grease something is to rub grease on it: *Grease the pan well.*
♦ **greasy** [adjective: **greasier, greasiest**] oily or fatty

great [adjective: **greater, greatest**]
1 very important or special: *a great day for the school*
2 very talented or distinguished: *one of the greatest scientists of all time*
3 very large: *The elephant lifted one of its great feet.*
4 very enjoyable or very good: *It was a great film.*
[noun: **greats**] an extremely famous, special or important person or thing: *one of Hollywood's greats*

great-grandchild [noun: **great-grandchildren**] your grandson's or grand-daughter's child

great-grand-daughter [noun: **great-grand-daughters**] your grandson's or grand-daughter's daughter

great-grandfather [noun: **great-grandfathers**] your grandmother's or grandfather's father

great-grandmother [noun: **great-grandmothers**] your grandmother's or grandfather's mother

great-grandparent [noun: **great-grandparents**] a parent of your grandmother or grandfather

great-grandson [noun: **great-grandsons**] your grandson's or grand-daughter's son

greatly [adverb] very much: *She wasn't greatly pleased.*

greatness [noun] being very impressive, important or talented

greed [noun] great or selfish desire for more of something than you need, especially food or money
♦ **greedily** [adverb] in a greedy way
♦ **greediness** [noun] being greedy
♦ **greedy** [adjective: **greedier, greediest**] wanting more of something than you actually need

green [noun] the colour of grass and the leaves of most plants

green belt [noun] an area of green fields around a city where you are not allowed to put up buildings

greenery [noun] plants with green leaves

green fingers [plural noun] someone who has green fingers is good at gardening and making plants grow

greengrocer [noun: **greengrocers**]
1 someone who sells fruit and vegetables to the public
2 a greengrocer's is a shop selling fruit and vegetables

greenhouse [noun: **greenhouses**] a shed with glass walls and a glass roof that gets warm when the sun shines and is used for growing plants in

greenhouse effect [noun] the greenhouse effect is the heating of the Earth's surface caused by pollution in the atmosphere which traps the heat from the sun

greens [plural noun] green vegetables such as cabbage: *Be sure to eat all your greens.*

greet [verb: **greets, greeting, greeted**]
1 to greet someone is to say something to them when they arrive or when you meet them
2 if something is greeted in a certain way,

people react to it in that way: *The announcement was greeted with howls of protest.*

• **greeting** [noun: **greetings**] something that you say when you meet someone, for example 'hello' or 'hi' or 'good morning'

grenade [noun: **grenades**] a small bomb that is timed to explode a few seconds after someone throws it

grew [verb] a way of changing the verb **grow** to make a past tense: *Stephen grew three centimetres last summer.*

grey [noun] a colour between black and white

greyhound [noun: **greyhounds**] a type of dog with a slim body and narrow head, which can run very fast over short distances and is used for racing

grid [noun: **grids**]
1 a pattern of lines that cross each other horizontally and vertically and form squares in between
2 a map or chart with a set of numbered lines
3 a grating made up of bars that cross each other like a grid
4 a network of electricity lines over a wide area

grid reference [noun: **grid references**] a set of numbers or letters used to show a place on a grid

grief [noun]
1 great sorrow, especially when someone has died
2 if you **come to grief**, you fail or have an accident

grievance [noun: **grievances**] something that you think is wrong and that you complain about

grieve [verb: **grieves, grieving, grieved**] to grieve is to feel very sad for a while, especially because someone has died or because you miss something that you have lost

grievous [adjective]
1 a grievous wound or injury is very serious
2 something grievous causes sorrow or sadness

grill [verb: **grills, grilling, grilled**]
1 to grill food is to cook it by putting it close to something hot: *Grill the fish for a couple of minutes on each side.*

2 to grill someone is to ask them lots of questions
[noun: **grills**] the part of a cooker where food can be grilled

grille [noun: **grilles**] a metal grating covering a door, window or other space in a wall

grim [adjective: **grimmer, grimmest**]
1 if someone looks grim, they have a serious and slightly fierce expression on their face
2 something grim is dreadful, upsetting or shocking

grimace [verb: **grimaces, grimacing, grimaced**] to twist your face in an ugly way, because you are in pain or you are disgusted at something
[noun: **grimaces**] an ugly twisted expression

grime [noun] dirt that has been on a surface for a long time and is difficult to get off
• **grimy** [adjective: **grimier, grimiest**] covered with grime

grin [verb: **grins, grinning, grinned**] to grin is to smile broadly showing your teeth
[noun: **grins**] a wide smile

grind [verb: **grinds, grinding, ground**]
1 to grind something solid is to crush it into a powder between two hard surfaces
2 to grind something is to sharpen or polish it against a hard or rough surface
3 to grind your teeth is to rub them together sideways
[noun] something that is difficult and boring to do: *the daily grind of work*
• **grinder** [noun: **grinders**] a machine that grinds things such as coffee beans

grindstone [noun: **grindstones**]
1 a circular stone that turns on top of another stone and is used in mills to grind corn
2 if you **have your nose to the grindstone**, you are working very hard, usually for long periods of time

grip [verb: **grips, gripping, gripped**]
1 if you grip something, you hold it tightly
2 if something grips you, it holds your attention completely
[noun: **grips**]
1 a hold or grasp: *a tight grip* • *in the grip of winter*
2 a small U-shaped wire used to keep hair in place

Gg

Gg

♦ **gripping** [adjective] holding your attention completely: *the climax of a gripping film*

grisly [adjective] frightful or ghastly: *a grisly story about a mad axeman*

gristle [noun] a kind of tough stretchy tissue that is sometimes found in meat

♦ **gristly** [adjective] gristly meat is tough and chewy because it has pieces of gristle in it

grit [noun]
1 grit is tiny sharp pieces of stone or sand
2 if someone has grit, they are brave and determined

♦ **gritty** [adjective: **grittier, grittiest**]
1 having a rough texture like grit
2 brave and determined: *a gritty fighter*
3 showing life as being harsh and difficult: *a gritty television drama*

grizzly [noun: **grizzlies**] a grizzly bear

grizzly bear [noun: **grizzly bears**] a type of large brown bear with grey-brown hair on its head and back. Grizzly bears are found in parts of the United States and Canada

groan [verb: **groans, groaning, groaned**]
1 if someone groans, they make a long deep sound because they are in pain or they think something is bad
2 if something groans, it makes a sound like a groan: *The trees creaked and groaned.*
[noun: **groans**] a deep moan made in the back of your throat

grocer [noun: **grocers**]
1 someone who runs a shop or supermarket selling groceries
2 a grocer's is a shop selling groceries

♦ **groceries** [plural noun] groceries are foods and other household goods that you buy in a shop or supermarket

groggy [adjective: **groggier, groggiest**] if you feel groggy, you can't think clearly, for example because you are weak after an illness

groin [noun] your groin is the place where your legs join the rest of your body

groom [verb: **grooms, grooming, groomed**]
1 to groom an animal is to look after it, especially by brushing or combing its coat
2 animals groom each other when they clean each other's coats by licking or picking through the hair

3 to groom yourself is to make yourself look neat and smart
[noun: **grooms**]
1 someone who looks after horses
2 a bridegroom

groove [noun: **grooves**] a long narrow channel cut into a surface

grope [verb: **gropes, groping, groped**]
1 to grope for something you can't see is to feel about with your hand to try to find it
2 to grope for an answer, or for the right word, is to try to find it without being sure how to do so

gross [adjective: **grosser, grossest**]
1 coarse, vulgar and bad-mannered
2 very bad: *gross ignorance*
3 an informal word for disgusting
4 very fat
5 a gross amount is the total amount without anything being taken away: *The gross weight of the parcel includes all the packaging.*
[noun: **gross** or **grosses**] a gross is 12 dozen or 144

♦ **grossly** [adverb] hugely: *grossly inflated prices*

grotesque [adjective] very strange and ugly-looking: *grotesque masks*

grotty [adjective: **grottier, grottiest**] an informal word for dirty and run-down: *a grotty little apartment*

ground[1] [noun: **grounds**]
1 the ground is the Earth's surface: *fall to the ground • on higher ground*
2 ground is earth or soil: *stony ground*
3 a ground is a sports field, especially one belonging to a particular club: *What's the name of Arsenal's ground?*
4 to **get something off the ground** is to get it started
5 if something **suits someone down to the ground**, it suits them very well indeed
➡ **grounded, grounds**

ground[2] [verb] a way of changing the verb **grind** to make a past tense. It can be used with or without a helping verb: *The miller ground the corn. • The coffee has been ground too finely.*

grounded [adjective]
1 a child is grounded when they aren't allowed out, as a punishment

2 a pilot or plane is grounded when they aren't allowed to fly

grounds [plural noun]
1 the grounds of a large house or building are the areas of land that surround it and are part of the same property
2 to have grounds for doing something is to have reasons for doing it
3 grounds are tiny pieces or powder made by grinding: *coffee grounds*

group [noun: **groups**] a number of people or things that are together or that belong together [verb: **groups, grouping, grouped**] to bring people or things together in a group or groups

grouse¹ [noun: **grouse**] a type of plump speckled bird that lives on moorland and is hunted for sport

grouse² [noun: **grouses**] a complaint [verb: **grouses, grousing, groused**] to grouse about something is to complain about it

grove [noun: **groves**] a small group of trees growing close together: *an olive grove*

grovel [verb: **grovels, grovelling, grovelled**]
1 to grovel is to crawl or lie on the ground
2 to grovel to someone is to be over-respectful to them, usually in an effort to make them like you: *I wish he wouldn't grovel to the boss like that.*

grow [verb: **grows, growing, grew, grown**]
1 to grow is to get bigger, taller, wider or stronger: *He's grown as tall as his father.*
2 to grow plants is to look after them while they grow: *We grow vegetables in our garden.*
3 to become: *It was growing dark.*
4 if you **grow out of** something you used to do or wear when you were younger, you become too old or big for it
➡ **growth**

growl [verb: **growls, growling, growled**]
1 an animal such as a dog or lion growls when it makes a deep threatening noise in its throat
2 a person growls when they talk in a deep voice, often because they are angry [noun: **growls**] a deep threatening sound: *The dog let out a low growl.*

growth [noun: **growths**]
1 growing or getting bigger: *the rapid growth of computer technology*
2 the process by which things grow: *Warmth brings about growth in the garden.*
3 a lump that grows on the body: *A growth developed on his hand.*

grub [noun: **grubs**]
1 a grub is the soft-bodied form of an insect just after it has hatched from the egg
2 grub is an informal word for food

grubby [adjective: **grubbier, grubbiest**] dirty: *Go and wash those grubby hands!*

grudge [verb: **grudges, grudging, grudged**] if you grudge giving something to someone, you feel annoyed because you think they don't deserve it: *We did not grudge them their good fortune, after all their problems.* [noun: **grudges**] if you have a grudge against someone, they have done something to you that you are angry about and haven't forgiven

gruelling [adjective] very difficult and tiring: *a gruelling climb to the summit of the mountain*

gruesome [adjective] horrible or sickening: *a gruesome murder*

gruff [adjective: **gruffer, gruffest**] a gruff voice is deep and sounds harsh

grumble [verb: **grumbles, grumbling, grumbled**] to grumble is to complain in a bad-tempered way

grumpy [adjective: **grumpier, grumpiest**] bad-tempered: *He's grumpy in the morning.*

grunt [verb: **grunts, grunting, grunted**] to make a deep snorting noise like a pig [noun: **grunts**] a deep snorting noise

guarantee [noun: **guarantees**] a promise that something will definitely be done or that something will be replaced free of charge if it goes wrong [verb: **guarantees, guaranteeing, guaranteed**] to guarantee something is to make a promise that it will happen or be done

guard [noun: **guards**]
1 someone, or a group of people, whose job is to watch over or protect a person or place, or to make sure that prisoners don't escape
2 something that protects you or a part of your body from damage or accidents: *a fire guard • a mouth guard*
3 someone who is in charge of a train or coach

Gg

4 to **keep** or **stand guard** is to watch over someone or something

5 if you **catch someone off guard**, you say or do something that they weren't prepared for [verb: **guards, guarding, guarded**]

1 to guard a person or place is to watch over them

2 to **guard against** something is to take care not to let it happen

♦ **guardian** [noun: **guardians**]

1 someone who watches over and protects

2 a child's or young person's guardian is someone with the legal right and duty to take care of them

guerrilla [noun: **guerrillas**] a fighter who is a member of a small or unofficial army which makes surprise attacks on larger armies

guess [verb: **guesses, guessing, guessed**] to guess is to give an answer or opinion without knowing or being sure of all or any of the facts [noun: **guesses**] an answer or opinion made by guessing

guest [noun: **guests**]

1 someone you invite to your house or to a party

2 someone staying in a hotel

guesthouse [noun: **guesthouses**] a small hotel

guffaw [verb: **guffaws, guffawing, guffawed**] to laugh loudly [noun: **guffaws**] a loud laugh

guidance [noun] if someone gives you guidance, they give you advice about how you should do something

guide [verb: **guides, guiding, guided**]

1 to guide someone is to show them the way or how to do something

2 to guide something is to make it go in a certain direction [noun: **guides**]

1 someone who shows tourists around or who leads travellers

2 a book that gives information about a place

3 a Guide is a young person who is a member of the Guide Association

guide dog [noun: **guide dogs**] a specially trained dog used by a blind person to help them get around

guild [noun: **guilds**]

1 a society of craftsmen or tradesmen

2 a society or social club

guile [noun] guile is being cunning and clever

guillotine [noun: **guillotines**]

1 an instrument with a blade that falls very quickly from a height and which was used in the past, especially in France, to execute people by cutting off their heads

2 a machine with a very sharp blade used for cutting paper

guilt [noun]

1 an uneasy feeling you get when you know you have done something wrong: *She felt no guilt at what she had done.*

2 the fact that you have done something wrong: *He admitted his guilt and accepted the punishment.*

♦ **guilty** [adjective: **guiltier, guiltiest**]

1 you feel guilty when you feel that you have done something wrong

2 if someone is guilty of something, other people think that something they do is wrong: *She's guilty of neglecting her duties as a mother.*

3 someone is found guilty of a crime when a jury or judge decides that they did it

guinea pig [noun: **guinea pigs**]

1 a small animal with small round ears and long hair that children often keep as a pet

2 someone who is used as part of an experiment

guitar [noun: **guitars**] an instrument with a rounded body, a long neck and strings that you play with your fingers

gulf [noun: **gulfs**]

1 a large bay filled by the sea

2 if there is a gulf between people or things, they are very far apart or very different from each other

gull [noun: **gulls**] a common sea bird

gullet [noun: **gullets**] your gullet is the tube that food goes down into your stomach

gullible [adjective] a gullible person believes what they are told and is easily tricked

gully [noun: **gullies**] a deep channel worn away by a river or stream

gulp [verb: **gulps, gulping, gulped**] to gulp is to swallow air or liquid quickly in large mouthfuls: *He gulped down his tea.* [noun: **gulps**]

1 the sound made when you gulp
2 a large mouthful

gum [noun: **gums**]
1 a type of glue used to stick paper or card
2 chewing gum
3 a sticky jelly-like sweet: *fruit gums*
4 your gums are the parts inside your mouth just above your top teeth and below your bottom teeth
[verb: **gums, gumming, gummed**] to stick something with gum
♦ **gummy** [adjective: **gummier, gummiest**] sticky like gum

gum tree [noun: **gum trees**]
1 a tree that produces gum, especially the eucalyptus tree
2 if you are **up a gum tree**, you are in a very difficult situation

gun [noun: **guns**]
1 a weapon that fires bullets or shells from a metal tube
2 if you **jump the gun**, you start before you should
3 if you **stick to your guns**, you refuse to change your mind about something

gunfire [noun]
1 the firing of guns
2 the sound of bullets being fired from a gun

gunpowder [noun] a powder that explodes when it is lit

gurgle [verb: **gurgles, gurgling, gurgled**]
1 water gurgles when it makes a pleasant bubbling sound as it flows
2 to make small bubbling sounds in your throat with saliva or some other liquid
[noun: **gurgles**] a bubbling sound

guru [noun: **gurus**]
1 a Hindu or Sikh religious leader and teacher
2 any greatly respected teacher or leader: *a tennis guru*

gush [verb: **gushes, gushing, gushed**]
1 water or other liquid gushes when it flows out suddenly and strongly
2 to gush is to talk with exaggerated emotion

gust [noun: **gusts**] a sudden rush of wind
♦ **gusty** [adjective: **gustier, gustiest**] gusty weather has sudden rushes of wind

gut [noun: **guts**] your gut is your stomach and intestines
[verb: **guts, gutting, gutted**]
1 to gut a dead fish or animal is to remove the organs from inside its body
2 to gut a place is to destroy or remove everything inside it: *The building was gutted by fire.*
♦ **guts** [plural noun]
1 guts are intestines
2 someone who has guts has courage

gutter [noun: **gutters**] a channel for carrying water, especially one fixed to the edge of a roof or by the side of the road for carrying away rainwater into the underground drains

guy [noun: **guys**]
1 an informal word for a man or boy
2 a type of large doll made to represent Guy Fawkes, which is burnt on a bonfire on 5 November, Guy Fawkes Night

guzzle [verb: **guzzles, guzzling, guzzled**] to eat or drink quickly and greedily

gym [noun: **gyms**]
1 a short form of the word **gymnasium**
2 gym is the exercises and games that you do in a school gymnasium

gymkhana [noun: **gymkhanas**] a horse-riding event which includes races and jumping competitions

gymnasium [noun: **gymnasiums** or **gymnasia**] a large room in a school or sports centre with equipment for doing exercises

gymnast [noun: **gymnasts**] someone trained to do gymnastics
♦ **gymnastic** [adjective] to do with gymnastics, or strong and graceful like the exercises done by a gymnast
♦ **gymnastics** [noun] exercises done indoors in a gymnasium using special equipment like bars, ropes and beams

Gypsy or **Gipsy** [noun: **Gypsies** or **Gipsies**] a member of a race of people who travel from place to place and have no fixed home

Gg

H

habit [noun: **habits**] a habit is something that you do regularly: *Tommy has a bad habit of grinding his teeth.*
➡ **habitual**

habitat [noun: **habitats**] an animal's or plant's habitat is the place where it lives or grows

habitual [adjective]
1 doing something again and again: *a habitual criminal*
2 done regularly, as a habit: *her habitual morning cup of coffee*

hack [verb: **hacks, hacking, hacked**]
1 to chop, or to chop up, roughly: *They hacked their way through the thick jungle.*
2 to get access to the information in a computer without the user's permission

hacker [noun: **hackers**] someone who uses their computer skills to get access to information in other people's computers illegally or without permission

hacksaw [noun: **hacksaws**] a saw with a thin blade used to cut metal

had [verb]
1 a way of changing the verb **have** to make a past tense. It can be used with or without a helping verb: *Omar had a steak and I had salmon.* • *Have you had chickenpox?*
2 had is also used as a helping verb along with a main verb: *I had enjoyed my stay in France.* • *He had had enough.*

haddock [noun: **haddock** or **haddocks**] a type of sea fish with firm, white, flaky flesh

hadn't [short form] a short way to say and write **had not**: *Laura hadn't expected to win.*

haemorrhage [noun: **haemorrhages**] very serious bleeding that it is difficult to stop
[verb: **haemorrhages, haemorrhaging, haemorrhaged**] to bleed very heavily and suddenly

hag [noun: **hags**] an ugly old woman

haggard [adjective] tired and ill-looking

haggis [noun: **haggises**] a Scottish food made with minced sheep's heart mixed with oatmeal and spices

haggle [verb: **haggles, haggling, haggled**] to bargain over something you want to buy, trying to lower the price that the seller first asks for

hail[1] [verb: **hails, hailing, hailed**]
1 to hail someone is to shout or wave to get their attention: *I hailed a taxi on the main road.*
2 to **hail from** a place is to come from that place: *Liz hails from Manchester.*

hail[2] [noun] hailstones falling from the sky
[verb: **hails, hailing, hailed**] it hails when hailstones fall

hailstones [plural noun] small white balls of frozen water that fall in showers from the sky

hair [noun: **hairs**]
1 a hair is one of the thread-like things that grow on the surface of the skin of animals and humans
2 your hair is the mass of hairs that grow on your head
3 to **split hairs** is to give too much importance to small and unimportant details

hairdresser [noun: **hairdressers**]
1 someone whose job is to cut, style and colour people's hair
2 a hairdresser's is a place where a hairdresser cuts, colours and styles your hair
♦ **hairdressing** [noun] the art, skill or work of a hairdresser

hair-drier [noun: **hair-driers**] a piece of electrical equipment that dries your hair by blowing hot air over it

hairgrip [noun: **hairgrips**] a narrow piece of bent metal that you can push into your hair to keep it in place

hairline [noun: **hairlines**] your hairline is the line along your forehead where your hair starts to grow

hair-raising [adjective] terrifying or dangerous: *a hair-raising ride on the Big Dipper*

hairstyle [noun: **hairstyles**] a way of cutting or wearing your hair

hairy [adjective: **hairier, hairiest**]
1 covered with hair: *A hobbit is a small creature with hairy feet.*
2 terrifying or dangerous: *If it is stormy, the ferry crossing can get a bit hairy.*

halal or **hallal** [adjective] halal meat is from animals killed and prepared according to the laws of Islam

half [noun: **halves**]
1 a half is one of two equal parts that together make up the whole of something: *He ate half and I ate the other half.*
2 the fraction $\frac{1}{2}$, equivalent to the decimal fraction 0.5 and equal to one divided by two
[adjective]
1 being one of two equal parts: *a half brick*
2 not full or complete: *a half smile*
3 if you say that someone is, for example, too clever **by half**, you mean that their cleverness is annoying
4 people say '**not half**' when they want to emphasize that they agree completely with what someone else has just said: *'That was a great goal, wasn't it?' 'Not half.'*
[adverb]
1 to the level or extent of a half: *This glass is only half full.*
2 partly or almost: *a half-open door*
3 nearly: *It wasn't half as scary as I expected it to be.*
➡ **halve**

half-baked [adjective] a half-baked idea or plan is one that has not been properly thought out

half-brother [noun: **half-brothers**] your half-brother has either the same father or the same mother as you do

half day [noun: **half days**] a holiday for half the working or school day, either for the morning or the afternoon

half-hearted [adjective] without much enthusiasm or effort
♦ **half-heartedly** [adverb] not very enthusiastically: *Thomas joined in half-heartedly with the chorus.*

half-mast [noun] if a flag is at half-mast, it is flown from a position halfway up the flagpole, usually as a sign of mourning for someone who has died

half moon [noun: **half moons**] the moon when it looks like a semicircle

half-sister [noun: **half-sisters**] your half-sister has either the same father or the same mother as you do

half-term [noun: **half-terms**] a short holiday from school about halfway through the school term

half-time [noun] in games like football, hockey and rugby, a break from play in the middle of the match, after which the teams usually change ends

halfway [adverb and adjective] in the middle between two points, or between the beginning and the end: *the halfway mark • halfway through the lesson*

hall [noun: **halls**]
1 an area just inside the entrance to a house that you go through to get to other rooms or to the stairs
2 a large building or room where meetings, concerts and other events are held

hallelujah [interjection] a shout or exclamation of praise to God

hallmark [noun: **hallmarks**]
1 a mark stamped on things made of gold or silver to show their quality
2 the hallmark of something is its main feature: *The hallmark of a good writer is the ability to hold the reader's attention.*

hallo [interjection] another spelling of **hello**

Hallowe'en [noun] October 31, the time when ghosts and witches are traditionally supposed to wander about, and when people get dressed up in costumes and masks

Hh

Hh

hallucinate [verb: **hallucinates, hallucinating, hallucinated**] to see things that aren't really there: *The drugs made him hallucinate.*

• **hallucination** [noun: **hallucinations**] a vision someone has of something that doesn't really exist

hallway [noun: **hallways**] an entrance hall in a house or building

halo [noun: **haloes**] a ring of light round the head of an angel or saint in pictures and paintings, showing that they are holy

halt [verb: **halts, halting, halted**] to stop moving and stand still
[noun: **halts**] a stop: *The train came to a halt and we got off.*

halter [noun: **halters**] a rope or strap you put over a horse's head, so that you can hold it or lead it

halve [verb: **halves, halving, halved**]
1 to divide, split or cut something into two equal parts
2 if something is halved, it is reduced to half its original size or amount

halves [noun] the plural of **half**

ham[1] [noun: **hams**] ham is smoked and salted meat from the leg of a pig

ham[2] [noun: **hams**]
1 a ham is an actor who overacts
2 a radio ham is someone who operates a radio transmitter and receiver as a hobby

hamburger [noun: **hamburgers**] a round flat cake of minced meat that is fried and usually eaten in a bun

hammer [noun: **hammers**] a tool with a heavy metal or wooden head at the end of a handle, used for knocking nails in or for breaking up hard material like stones and concrete
[verb: **hammers, hammering, hammered**]
1 to hit something with a hammer: *hammering the nails in one by one*
2 to hit something hard: *hammering on the door with his fists*
3 to beat someone severely or completely: *We hammered the other team 10–0.*
4 to **hammer something out** is to discuss it until everyone is satisfied: *hammer out an agreement*

hammock [noun: **hammocks**] a kind of bed made up of a long piece of fabric which is hung from ropes at either end so that it swings above the ground

hamper[1] [noun: **hampers**] a large basket with a lid used for carrying food, plates and cutlery, especially for picnics

hamper[2] [verb: **hampers, hampering, hampered**] to hamper someone or something is to stop them making progress

hamster [noun: **hamsters**] a small animal with soft fur and a short tail, often kept as a pet

hand [noun: **hands**]
1 your hand is the part of your body at the end of your arm just below your wrist
2 a narrow pointer on a clock or watch that moves round and shows the time: *the minute hand*
3 if you give or lend someone a hand, you help them: *I'll give you a hand with your luggage.*
4 a set of playing cards dealt to a player in a card game: *Both my partner and I had good hands.*
5 a worker on a farm, in a factory or on a ship: *The captain gave the order 'All hands on deck!'*
6 a unit, equal to 4 inches or about 10 centimetres, used for measuring the height of horses: *a huge horse of almost 16 hands*
7 to give a performer a big hand is to clap or applaud them loudly and enthusiastically
8 something that is **at hand** is available quickly: *Help is at hand.*
9 you do or make something **by hand** when you use your hands to do or make it
10 something is **in hand** when it is being dealt with
11 if someone or something is **on hand**, they are ready and available to help or be used
12 if things get **out of hand**, they get out of control
13 if something is **to hand**, it is near you and you are able to reach it or use it easily
[verb: **hands, handing, handed**] to hand something to someone is to pass it to them

handbag [noun: **handbags**] a small bag for carrying personal belongings like your purse and keys

handbook [noun: **handbooks**] a book of instructions on how to do something: *an* *illustrated handbook on first aid*

handbrake [noun: **handbrakes**] a brake in a vehicle that is operated by the driver pulling a lever

handcuffs [plural noun] a pair of metal rings joined by a chain which the police use to lock around the wrists of someone they have arrested

handful [noun: **handfuls**]
1 an amount that you can hold in your hand: *a handful of rice*
2 a small number: *Only a handful of people turned up.*
3 a person or animal whose behaviour makes them difficult to deal with: *Greta can be quite a handful.*

handicap [noun: **handicaps**] a physical or mental injury or disability that prevents someone from living normally
[verb: **handicaps, handicapping, handicapped**] to handicap someone is to give them a disability or make them unable to do something properly
♦ **handicapped** [adjective] disabled, either mentally or physically

handicraft [noun: **handicrafts**] a craft done using your hands, such as sewing, knitting or pottery

handiwork [noun] someone's handiwork is something that they have made or done

handkerchief [noun: **handkerchiefs**] a small piece of cloth or tissue paper used for wiping your nose

handle [noun: **handles**]
1 a part of an object that you use to pick it up and hold it: *a brush with a long handle*
2 a lever or knob on a door that you hold when you open and close the door
3 if someone **flies off the handle**, they lose their temper
[verb: **handles, handling, handled**]
1 to touch something or hold it with your hands: *Try not to handle the fruit too much.*
2 to deal or cope with something: *Mr Peters is handling all the arrangements for the trip.*

handlebars [plural noun] the curved part at the front of a bicycle that you rest your hands on and use to steer the bicycle

handler [noun: **handlers**]

1 someone who trains or controls an animal: *police dogs and their handlers*
2 someone whose job is to move or carry things: *a baggage handler at the airport*

hand-me-downs [plural noun] clothes that older brothers or sisters have worn and grown out of and that have been passed on to younger brothers or sisters

handout [noun: **handouts**]
1 a sheet of paper or booklet containing information that is given out free to people at a class or lecture
2 money, food or clothing that is given free to poor people

handrail [noun: **handrails**] a narrow rail that people can hold on to for safety

handsome [adjective: **handsomer, handsomest**]
1 good looking: *a handsome young actor*
2 large or generous: *They made a handsome profit.*

hands-on [adjective] hands-on experience involves you doing something yourself rather than reading about it or watching others do it

handstand [noun: **handstands**] a gymnastic movement in which you balance your body upside-down carrying your weight on your hands and holding your legs straight up in the air

handwriting [noun] writing done with a pen or pencil
♦ **handwritten** [adjective] written with a pen or pencil, not typed or printed

handy [adjective: **handier, handiest**]
1 useful and easy to use: *a handy size for carrying in your pocket*
2 nearby and easily reached: *The house is handy both for the station and the bus stop.*

handyman [noun: **handymen**] someone who does small building and repair jobs

hang [verb: **hangs, hanging, hung** or **hanged**]
1 to hang something is to attach it or support it at the top so that most of it is held loosely above the ground: *Hang your jackets up on the pegs.*
2 something hangs when it is supported near the top and is held above the ground: *Joe was hanging upside down by his feet.*

Hh

3 to hang someone is to kill them by tying a rope around their neck and removing a support from under their feet

4 to **hang about** or **hang around** is to stay in one place doing nothing: *Don't let's hang about any more. Let's get started.*

[noun] to **get the hang of** something is to understand it or learn how to do it after a bit of practice

➡ **hanger**

ⓘ **Hung** is the usual form of the past tense of the verb **hang**. However, you use **hanged** instead of **hung** to refer to someone who dies by hanging.

hangar [noun: **hangars**] a big shed that aeroplanes are kept in

hangdog [adjective] someone with a hangdog expression looks very guilty and ashamed

hanger [noun: **hangers**] a shaped piece of metal, wood or plastic with a hook, used to hang clothes on

hang-glider [noun: **hang-gliders**] a type of vehicle that flies using air currents, with the pilot strapped in a harness that hangs beneath a large frame like a kite

♦ **hang-gliding** [noun] the sport or pastime of flying in hang-gliders

hangman [noun: **hangmen**] someone whose job is to hang people who are condemned to death

hangover [noun: **hangovers**]

1 a sick feeling, often with an aching head, that people sometimes get after they have drunk too much alcohol

2 something that remains after an event or period of time is over: *a hangover from the 1960s*

hang-up [noun: **hang-ups**] something that makes you feel anxious or embarrassed, especially something not very important: *She's always had a hang-up about her nose.*

hank [noun: **hanks**] a small loose bundle made up of strands of hair, wool or thread

hanker [verb: **hankers, hankering, hankered**] to hanker for or after something is to long to have it

hankie or **hanky** [noun: **hankies**] an

informal short form of the word **handkerchief**

Hanukkah or **Chanukah** [noun]
Hanukkah is a Jewish festival lasting for eight days in December. It is also called the Feast of Dedication or the Festival of Lights, because a candle is lit on each of the eight days

haphazard [adjective] with no organization or planning

happen [verb: **happens, happening, happened**]

1 if something happens, it takes place or occurs: *When did this happen?* • *I pressed the button but nothing happened.*

2 if something happens to a person or thing, an event or situation affects or involves them: *Do you know what's happened to the front door key?*

3 if you happen to do or see something, you do or see it by chance: *She just happened to be there and saw the whole thing.*

♦ **happening** [noun: **happenings**] an event

happily [adverb]

1 joyfully or contentedly: *smiling happily*

2 luckily: *Happily, it all turned out well.*

happiness [noun] being happy

happy [adjective: **happier, happiest**]

1 joyful: *the happiest day of her life*

2 pleased or contented: *I'd be happy to help.*

3 lucky: *a happy coincidence*

happy-go-lucky [adjective] a happy-go-lucky person is cheerful, enjoying anything good that happens to come along and not worrying about the future

harass [verb: **harasses, harassing, harassed**] to harass someone is to keep annoying them, pestering them or interfering with their life

♦ **harassed** [adjective] feeling worried and anxious because you have too much to do

♦ **harassment** [noun] harassing someone or being harassed

harbour [noun: **harbours**] a place protected from wind and rough seas where ships and boats can shelter and dock

[verb: **harbours, harbouring, harboured**]

1 to harbour a feeling is to keep it in your mind for a long time: *She'd harboured a grudge against them for years.*

2 to harbour a criminal is to protect them from

Hh

being found or arrested by the police

hard [adjective: **harder, hardest**]
1 feeling firm and solid when touched and not easily broken or bent out of shape: *hard as rock • a hard bed*
2 difficult: *a very hard problem • He's had a hard life.*
3 needing a lot of effort: *hard work*
4 tough or not easy to deal with: *hard luck • They drive a hard bargain.*
5 hard water doesn't form a good lather when you add soap to it, and it contains minerals that form deposits in equipment such as kettles
6 someone who is **hard of hearing** is nearly deaf

[adverb: **harder, hardest**]
1 strongly or violently: *It was raining hard when we got there.*
2 with more effort: *You must work harder.*

hardback [noun: **hardbacks**] a book that has a stiff hard cover. Look up and compare **paperback**

hardboard [noun] thin strong board made from wood pulp that has been softened and pressed together

hard disk [noun: **hard disks**] a disk inside a computer where large amounts of information are stored

harden [verb: **hardens, hardening, hardened**]
1 to become firm or solid: *The molten lava hardens to form rock.*
2 to become tougher or less sympathetic: *His heart had been hardened by constant rejection.*

hard-hearted [adjective] tough and unsympathetic to other people's feelings or problems

hardline [adjective] people with hardline attitudes or opinions stick to what they believe and refuse to change or compromise

hardly [adverb]
1 only just or almost not: *I hardly know him. • He'd hardly put the key in the door when down came the rain.*
2 hardly is used for emphasis to mean 'not at all': *She's hardly likely to want him at the party after the way he insulted her.*

hardship [noun: **hardships**] something that is very difficult to cope with: *financial hardship*

hard shoulder [noun] the hard shoulder is the strip at either side of a motorway for use in an emergency, for example if your car has broken down

hard up [adjective] poor: *His family is too hard up to be able to afford the fees.*

hardware [noun]
1 hardware is tools and equipment used, for example, in the house and garden
2 computer hardware is electronic machinery like the processor and disk drives. Look up and compare **software**

hardy [adjective: **hardier, hardiest**] strong and tough and able to cope with difficult and uncomfortable conditions

hare [noun: **hares**] an animal similar to a rabbit, but larger and with longer back legs and bigger ears

hare-brained [adjective] a hare-brained idea or plan is mad or foolish

hare lip [noun: **hare lips**] a deformity that some babies are born with in which the top lip is split

hark [verb: **harks, harking, harked**]
1 an old-fashioned word meaning listen: *Hark, the herald angels sing. • Hark at him!*
2 to **hark back** to some event in the past is to refer to it or return to it

harlequin [noun: **harlequins**] a comic pantomime character who wears a costume that has many bright colours

harm [verb: **harms, harming, harmed**] to harm someone or something is to hurt or damage them: *You might harm your eyes if you sit too close to the TV.*
[noun] damage or injury: *No harm will come to you. • It would do no harm to ask.*
✦ **harmful** [adjective] causing damage or injury: *protecting your skin from the sun's harmful rays*
✦ **harmless** [adjective] not dangerous or not causing any damage or annoyance: *a harmless little insect*

harmonica [noun: **harmonicas**] an instrument that you hold to your mouth and play by blowing and sucking air through it

harmonious [adjective]

Hh

Hh

1 harmonious sound or music is pleasant to listen to

2 harmonious colours or designs go well together and don't clash

3 people who have a harmonious relationship cooperate with each other and don't have disagreements

• harmoniously [adverb] in a pleasant or peaceful way

harmonize or **harmonise** [verb: **harmonizes, harmonizing, harmonized**]

1 singers or musicians harmonize when they sing or play together using notes that combine pleasantly with the main tune

2 things harmonize when they fit or combine well together

harmony [noun: **harmonies**]

1 harmony is combining notes or colours in a way that sounds or looks pleasant

2 a harmony is a musical part that combines pleasantly with the main melody

3 harmony is peaceful agreement and cooperation between people: *living in harmony with our neighbours*

harness [noun: **harnesses**]

1 a set of leather straps that attach a horse to a cart so that it can pull it

2 a similar set of straps for attaching someone to something, for example for holding a child who is learning to walk

harp [noun: **harps**] an instrument with strings stretched across an open triangular frame. A harp stands upright and you play it by plucking the strings with your fingers

[verb: **harps, harping, harped**] to **harp on** or **harp on about** something is to keep on talking about it in an annoying way

• harpist [noun: **harpists**] someone who plays the harp

harpoon [noun: **harpoons**] a spear with a rope attached at one end that is used to kill fish and whales

harpsichord [noun: **harpsichords**] an instrument with keys similar to a piano but with strings that are plucked when you press the keys

harrowing [adjective] very upsetting or disturbing: *a harrowing experience*

harsh [adjective: **harsher, harshest**]

1 very uncomfortable: *a harsh climate*

2 unpleasantly strong or loud: *harsh light* • *the harsh cry of a raven*

3 cruel and unkind: *a harsh punishment*

• harshly [adverb] roughly, severely or cruelly

• harshness [noun] being harsh

harvest [noun: **harvests**]

1 harvest is the time of year when ripe crops are gathered

2 a harvest is the amount of a crop that is gathered: *This year's coffee harvest was very poor.*

[verb: **harvests, harvesting, harvested**] to gather a crop when it is ripe: *harvesting grapes*

• harvester [noun: **harvesters**]

1 a piece of machinery that gathers in a crop of a particular type

2 someone whose job is to pick, cut or gather in a crop

has [verb]

1 the form of the verb **have** that is used with *he, she* and *it* to make a present tense: *He has brown eyes.*

2 has is also used as a helping verb along with a main verb: *She has gone home.*

has-been [noun: **has-beens**] someone who used to be famous or successful but who isn't any more

hash [noun: **hashes**]

1 a dish made with cooked meat and vegetables that have been chopped up and recooked

2 to make a hash of something is to make a mess of it

hasn't [short form] a short way to say and write **has not**: *Hasn't it been a lovely day?*

hassle [verb: **hassles, hassling, hassled**] to hassle someone is to put pressure on them or cause them problems

[noun: **hassles**] hassle, or a hassle, is something that causes you problems or inconvenience

haste [noun]

1 haste is hurry or speed: *In her haste she almost dropped the basket.*

2 to make haste is to hurry

• hasten [verb: **hastens, hastening, hastened**] to hasten is to hurry or push forward: *We saw him hastening towards us.*

• **hastily** [adverb] in a hurried way: *Hastily, he hid the sweets he had stolen.*

• **hasty** [adjective: **hastier, hastiest**] a hasty action is one that is done too quickly without enough thought

hat [noun: **hats**] a covering for your head

hatch[1] [verb: **hatches, hatching, hatched**]
1 baby birds and reptiles hatch when they break out of their eggs: *We watched the chicks hatching out of the eggs.*
2 to hatch a plot is to think of it and develop its details, especially in secret

hatch[2] [noun: **hatches**] a door or covering over an opening in a floor, wall or ship's deck

hatchback [noun: **hatchbacks**] a car with a sloping door at the back that opens upwards

hatchet [noun: **hatchets**]
1 a small axe
2 people who have been fighting or quarrelling **bury the hatchet** when they make up

hate [verb: **hates, hating, hated**] to dislike something or someone very much: *Pete hates tidying his bedroom.*
[noun: **hates**]
1 hate is very strong dislike: *Her eyes were full of hate and disappointment.*
2 your hates are the things that you dislike very much: *It's one of his pet hates.*

• **hateful** [adjective] very nasty or very bad: *a hateful thing to say*

• **hatred** [noun] hatred is a very strong feeling of dislike

hat-trick [noun: **hat-tricks**]
1 in games like football and hockey, a hat-trick is three goals scored by one player in a single match
2 in cricket, a bowler gets a hat-trick when he or she gets three batsmen out with three balls bowled one after the other

haughty [adjective: **haughtier, haughtiest**] a haughty person is proud and thinks they are better or more important than other people

haul [verb: **hauls, hauling, hauled**] to haul something heavy is to pull it or drag it using a lot of effort: *He managed to haul himself up on to a narrow ledge.*
[noun: **hauls**]

1 a quantity gathered or caught at one time: *a huge haul of cod and haddock*
2 a strong tug or pull: *Give the rope one more good haul.*
3 a **long haul** is a long and difficult journey, job or process

haulage [noun] people or companies involved in haulage carry goods from one place to another for payment

haunch [noun: **haunches**] your haunches are your bottom and the upper part of your thighs: *He squatted down on his haunches in the dust.*

haunt [verb: **haunts, haunting, haunted**]
1 if people believe a ghost haunts a place, they think it is present there or appears there
2 if someone haunts a place, they go there again and again: *Bob haunts the football ground, trying to get a glimpse of his heroes.*
3 if a bad feeling or memory haunts you, you can't stop thinking about it
[noun: **haunts**] a place where you go again and again: *This club is one of my old haunts.*

• **haunted** [adjective] a haunted place is somewhere where people believe there are ghosts

have [verb: **has, having, had**]
1 to have something is to own or possess it: *I'll look at your essay as soon as I have a free moment.* • *He has a limp.*
2 to have an illness is to suffer from it: *Carol's had measles.* • *I have a terrible headache.*
3 to have something is to get or receive it: *I had a phone call from him last week.*
4 to have a baby is to give birth to it: *The cat had kittens.*
5 to have food or drink is to eat it or drink it: *You'll have lunch with us, won't you?*
6 to have something done is to get it done: *He's having a tooth out.*
7 if you have to do something, you must do it: *You have to tell me what was said.*
8 **have** is also used as a helping verb along with a main verb: *I have left some money for you.*
9 to **have it out** with someone is to talk to them to settle an argument or disagreement
10 to **have someone on** is to tell them something is true when it isn't

haven [noun: **havens**] a place where people can go to be safe or quiet

Hh

haven't [short form] a short way to say and write **have not**: *I haven't seen the film.*

haversack [noun: **haversacks**] a canvas bag with shoulder straps that you use to carry things on your back when you are walking or marching

havoc [noun] to cause havoc is to cause damage, destruction or confusion

hawk [noun: **hawks**] a bird of prey with a short, strong hooked beak and very good eyesight

hawthorn [noun: **hawthorns**] a small tree with thorny stems, white flowers and small red berries

hay [noun] grass that has been cut and dried and is used to feed animals

hay fever [noun] an allergy to pollen that some people have, which makes them sneeze and have watery or itchy eyes and a runny nose

haystack [noun: **haystacks**] a large pile of cut hay stacked up in layers and stored until it is needed

haywire [adjective] if something **goes haywire**, it goes out of control

hazard [noun: **hazards**] a risk of harm or danger
[verb: **hazards, hazarding, hazarded**]
1 to hazard something is to risk it
2 to hazard a guess is to make a guess that is quite likely to be wrong
• hazardous [adjective] dangerous or risky: *hazardous driving conditions*

haze [noun: **hazes**] thin mist: *a heat haze* → **hazy**

hazel [noun: **hazels**]
1 a small tree on which round nuts grow
2 a light green-brown colour: *hazel eyes*

hazelnut [noun: **hazelnuts**] an edible nut that grows on a hazel tree

hazy [adjective: **hazier, haziest**]
1 with a thin mist: *hazy sunshine*
2 vague and unclear: *He only has hazy memories of his parents.*

he [pronoun] a word you use to talk about a man, boy, or male animal that has already been mentioned or pointed out: *Everyone likes Ted because he is so funny.*

head [noun: **heads**]

1 the part of a human's or animal's body that contains the brain, eyes and mouth
2 your mind or intelligence: *The idea just popped into my head.*
3 the head of a group or organization is the person in charge
4 the top of something: *the title at the head of the page*
5 if someone **goes over your head**, they talk to the person who is your boss instead of you
6 if praise or success **goes to someone's head**, they become conceited
7 to be **head over heels** is to be very much in love with someone
8 if you are **in over your head**, you are involved in something that is too complicated or serious for you to cope with or control
9 if you say someone is **off their head**, you mean they are mad
[verb: **heads, heading, headed**]
1 if you head a group of people, you lead them or are in charge of them
2 to head somewhere is to go towards that place
3 to head a ball is to hit it with your head
4 to **head someone** or **something off** is to get in front of them to stop them going any further

headache [noun: **headaches**] a pain in your head

headboard [noun: **headboards**] the upright part at the top of a bed

headdress [noun: **headdresses**] a decoration worn on your head, for example as part of a costume

header [noun: **headers**] in football, a header is when you hit the ball with your head

headfirst [adverb] you jump or fall headfirst when you jump or fall forwards with your head in front of the rest of your body

heading [noun: **headings**] a title at the top or beginning of a page or a section of writing

headland [noun: **headlands**] a piece of land that sticks out into the sea

headlight [noun: **headlights**] one of a pair of lights at the front of a car, van or lorry

headline [noun: **headlines**] a line printed in large letters at the top of a newspaper page or article

headlong [adverb and adjective]
1 headfirst or in an uncontrolled way: *Sally dived headlong into the muddy stream.* • *a headlong dash towards the finish line*
2 without giving yourself enough time to think: *You shouldn't rush headlong into a big decision like that.*

headmaster [noun: **headmasters**] a male teacher in charge of running a school

headmistress [noun: **headmistresses**] a female teacher in charge of running a school

head-on [adjective and adverb]
1 with the head or front first: *The other car hit us head-on.* • *a head-on collision*
2 directly, without trying to avoid what may be unpleasant: *tackling their problems head-on*

headphones [plural noun] two small speakers that you wear in or on your ears so that you can listen to music or other sounds

headquarters [plural noun]
1 the central office from which a large business or organization is controlled
2 a place from which an army, navy, air force or police force is controlled

ⓘ **Headquarters** can be used with a singular or plural verb, for example:
*The company headquarters **is** in London.*
*The company headquarters **are** in London.*

heads [plural noun] the side of a coin that has a person's head stamped on it: *Call heads or tails when I toss the coin.*

headset [noun: **headsets**] a pair of headphones, often with a microphone attached

headstart [noun] if you get a headstart, you get an advantage by starting or beginning before other people

headstrong [adjective] a headstrong person is determined to do what they want to do and won't take advice from other people

head teacher [noun: **head teachers**] a teacher in charge of running a school

headway [noun] to make headway is to make forward progress

heal [verb: **heals, healing, healed**]
1 a wound or injury heals when it gets better
2 to heal someone or heal a wound is to make them better or healthy again

• **healer** [noun: **healers**] someone or something that heals people who are sick

health [noun]
1 your health is the condition of your body or mind, and how well you are: *Myra's health is not good.* • *mental health*
2 the health of something is how good or bad its condition is: *the health of the economy*

health centre [noun: **health centres**] a place where doctors and nurses look after people from a particular area and hold clinics

health food [noun: **health foods**] a food that people believe is good for their health

healthily [adverb] in a way that is good for your health: *eat healthily*

healthiness [noun] being healthy

health visitor [noun: **health visitors**] a nurse who visits ill or old people, or newly born babies, in their homes

healthy [adjective: **healthier, healthiest**]
1 fit and well: *a healthy baby*
2 good for you: *lots of healthy exercise*
3 in a good state or condition: *a healthy bank balance*

heap [noun: **heaps**]
1 an untidy pile of things: *a heap of dirty clothes*
2 if you have **heaps** of something, you have a lot of it: *There's heaps of time before the match starts.*
[verb: **heaps, heaping, heaped**] to heap things is to pile them up: *His plate was heaped with food.*

hear [verb: **hears, hearing, heard**]
1 to hear sounds is to be aware of them through your ears: *Can you hear that clicking noise?*
2 to hear news is to be told it: *I heard that she had got into the next round of the competition.*
3 to have heard of someone or something is to know that they exist: *I'd never heard of him before.*
4 you hear from someone when they get in touch with you: *We haven't heard from him for over a month.*

• **hearer** [noun: **hearers**] your hearers are the people who are listening to you when you are speaking

• **hearing** [noun: **hearings**]

Hh

1 your hearing is your ability to hear

2 if something is said in your hearing, you can hear it

3 a hearing is a court trial

hearing aid [noun: **hearing aids**] a small device that is fitted into or at the back of a deaf person's ear to help them hear

hearsay [noun] hearsay is things other people have told you, which may or may not be true: *Someone told me Jason had run away, but I think it's only hearsay.*

hearse [noun: **hearses**] a specially designed car used to carry the coffin at a funeral

heart [noun: **hearts**]

1 your heart is the organ inside your chest that pumps blood around your body

2 someone's heart is their feelings and emotions: *She captured the hearts of the audience.* • *Ken has a kind heart.*

3 a heart is a shape, ♥, that represents the human heart and human love

4 hearts is one of the four suits of playing cards, which have the symbol ♥ printed on them

5 the heart of something is its central or most important part: *getting to the heart of the problem*

6 if you learn something **by heart**, you learn it so that you can repeat it exactly
➙ **hearty**

heart attack [noun: **heart attacks**] if someone has a heart attack, their heart suddenly stops working properly and they feel very ill and may die

heartbeat [noun: **heartbeats**] the regular sound that your heart makes as it pumps blood round your body

heartbreak [noun] great sadness
• **heartbreaking** [adjective] making someone very sad
• **heartbroken** [adjective] feeling very sad: *Kay was heartbroken when he left her.*

hearten [verb: **heartens, heartening, heartened**] something heartens you when it makes you feel happier or more hopeful

heartfelt [adjective] heartfelt feelings or words are completely sincere: *my heartfelt thanks*

hearth [noun: **hearths**] the floor of a fireplace or the area just in front of it

heartily [adverb]

1 loudly and enthusiastically: *They laughed heartily at all his jokes.*

2 sincerely or completely: *I'm heartily sick of their constant complaints.*

heartless [adjective] unkind and cruel

heart-rending [adjective] something heart-rending makes you feel very sad or sorry for someone

heart-throb [noun: **heart-throbs**] a very attractive person with whom lots of people fall in love

heart-to-heart [noun: **heart-to-hearts**] a talk with someone in which you discuss private or intimate things

hearty [adjective: **heartier, heartiest**]

1 strong and healthy

2 cheerful, loud and friendly: *a hearty welcome*

3 a hearty meal is a large and satisfying meal
➙ **heartily**

heat [noun: **heats**]

1 heat is high temperature or the warmth that something hot gives out: *the heat from the sun*

2 heat is anger or strong feelings: *She tried to calm them down and take the heat out of the situation.*

3 a heat is a round in a competition or race: *Ian won his heat and went through to the semi-final.*

[verb: **heats, heating, heated**]

1 to heat something, or heat it up, is to raise its temperature or make it warm or hot

2 if something heats up, it becomes warmer or hotter
• **heated** [adjective] full of anger or strong feelings: *a heated discussion*
• **heater** [noun: **heaters**] a piece of equipment used to heat a space, such as a room or the inside of a car
➙ **heating**

heath [noun: **heaths**] a high wild area of land covered with grass and low bushes

heathen [noun: **heathens**] someone who doesn't believe in God and is not a member of one of the main world religions

heather [noun: **heathers**] a small shrub that

grows close to the ground on hills and moors and has tiny purple or white flowers

heating [noun] the system or machinery used to heat a building

heatwave [noun: **heatwaves**] a spell of unusually hot weather, usually lasting for several days or weeks

heave [verb: **heaves, heaving, heaved**]
1 to heave something heavy is to lift, pull or throw it using a lot of effort: *The men heaved the bags of coal on to their shoulders.* • *Both teams heaved at the rope.*
2 you heave a sigh when you sigh deeply making your shoulders and chest rise up

heaven [noun: **heavens**]
1 the place where good people are supposed to go when they die and where God and the angels are believed to live
2 the sky is sometimes called the heavens: *The heavens opened and the rain came lashing down.*
3 a very pleasant place or thing: *This chocolate cake is just heaven.*
♦ **heavenly** [adjective]
1 to do with heaven: *the heavenly choir of angels*
2 very pleasant: *It was heavenly just lying in the sunshine.*

heavily [adverb] with a lot of force or weight

heaviness [noun] being heavy or how heavy something is

heavy [adjective: **heavier, heaviest**]
1 something that is heavy weighs a lot
2 the amount that something weighs is how heavy it is
3 heavy rain or a heavy blow has a lot of force
4 a heavy smoker smokes a lot and a heavy drinker drinks a lot of alcohol
5 if your heart is heavy, you feel sad

heavy-duty [adjective] heavy-duty material or machinery can stand up to a lot of very hard use: *heavy-duty plastic sacks*

heavy industry [noun: **heavy industries**] an industry or industries such as coal-mining, steel-making and ship-building

Hebrew [noun] Hebrew is the ancient language of the Jewish people, which is used in a modern form in Israel
[adjective] in, or to do with, ancient or modern Hebrew

heckle [verb: **heckles, heckling, heckled**] to interrupt a speaker or performer with loud comments or questions
♦ **heckler** [noun: **hecklers**] a member of an audience who heckles a speaker or performer

hectare [noun: **hectares**] a unit of area equal to 10,000 square metres or approximately 2½ acres

hectic [adjective] very busy or having too much to do in too short a time: *Today has been absolutely hectic.*

he'd [short form] a short way to say and write **he had** or **he would**: *He'd never been there before.* • *He'd never have guessed.*

hedge [noun: **hedges**] a line of bushes, trees or shrubs planted close together and growing into each other to form a boundary
[verb: **hedges, hedging, hedged**] to hedge is to avoid answering a question

hedgehog [noun: **hedgehogs**] a small wild mammal with prickles all over its body

hedgerow [noun: **hedgerows**] a line of shrubs and small trees growing close together along the side of a road or field

heed [verb: **heeds, heeding, heeded**] to heed something is to pay attention to it
[noun] if you pay heed to something, or take heed of it, you pay attention to it
♦ **heedless** [adjective] if you are heedless of something, you take no notice of it

heel [noun: **heels**]
1 your heels are the back parts of your feet
2 the heel of a shoe or boot is the part under the back of your foot
3 the heel of a sock or stocking is the part that covers your heel
4 if you **take to your heels**, you start running

hefty [adjective: **heftier, heftiest**]
1 big and heavily or strongly built: *a hefty wrestler*
2 powerful: *a hefty blow*
3 large in amount: *a hefty sum of money*

height [noun: **heights**]
1 how tall or high someone or something is: *What height is Mount Everest?*
2 the highest, greatest or strongest point something reaches or can reach: *It is the height of stupidity to throw a lighted firework.*
3 a high place: *looking down from the heights*

Hh

Hh

◆ **heighten** [verb: **heightens, heightening, heightened**]
1 to make something higher: *We'll have to heighten the seat of the bike a little.*
2 something heightens, or is heightened, when it increases or is increased: *The music heightens the tension of the film.*

heir [noun: **heirs**] someone who is entitled by law to get money, property or a title from someone when they die

heiress [noun: **heiresses**] a girl or woman who is entitled by law to get money, property or a title from someone when they die

heirloom [noun: **heirlooms**] something valuable that has been handed down in a family from parents or grandparents to their children or grandchildren

held [verb] a way of changing the verb **hold** to make a past tense. It can be used with or without a helping verb: *I held my breath and waited.* ◆ *Turner had held the job for ten years.*

helicopter [noun: **helicopters**] a flying machine without wings that is lifted into the air by large propellers on top which spin round very fast

helix [noun: **helixes** or **helices**] a screw-shaped coil or spiral

hell [noun]
1 hell is the place where people who have sinned are supposed to go when they die and where the Devil is believed to live
2 an evil or very unpleasant place

he'll [short form] a short way to say and write **he will** or **he shall**: *He'll be here soon.*

hello [interjection] you say 'hello' as a greeting when you meet someone or begin talking to them

helm [noun: **helms**] the wheel or handle used to steer a ship or boat

helmet [noun: **helmets**] a hard covering worn to protect the head, for example by soldiers, cyclists and firemen

help [verb: **helps, helping, helped**]
1 to do something useful for someone: *I find a warm bath helps to relax me.*
2 if you can't help something, you can't stop yourself from doing it, or you can't stop it happening: *She couldn't help laughing when she saw his face.*
3 if you **help yourself**, you take something without waiting for someone to give it to you
[noun: **helps**]
1 you give someone help when you do something useful for them: *Could you give me some help with the gardening?*
2 a help is someone or something that helps: *Thanks for the tip. It was a great help.*
[interjection] people shout 'Help!' when they are in danger and want someone to come and help them

◆ **helper** [noun: **helpers**] someone who helps another person

helpful [adjective] willing to help, or giving help

◆ **helpfully** [adverb] in a helpful way

helping [noun: **helpings**] a portion or serving of food: *Paolo always has second helpings.*

helping verb [noun: **helping verbs**] a short verb like *should, will* or *can* that you use with a main verb to make slight differences of meaning, for example a past tense in *Have you finished?* The helping verbs are also called **auxiliary verbs**

helpless [adjective] not able to do anything for yourself, or to help other people in trouble
◆ **helplessly** [adverb] in a helpless way: *I stared helplessly as the dog ran towards me.*

helpline [noun: **helplines**] a telephone number that you can ring when you have a problem to talk to people who are qualified to give you advice about that particular subject

helter-skelter [noun: **helter-skelters**] a tall slide that goes round and round in a spiral
[adverb] to go helter-skelter is to go very fast in an uncontrolled way

hem [noun: **hems**] the edge of a piece of material that has been folded over and sewn down
[verb: **hems, hemming, hemmed**]
1 to hem a piece of cloth is to sew a hem on its edge
2 if people or things **hem you in**, they surround you and stop you moving in any direction

hemisphere [noun: **hemispheres**]
1 half the Earth, either divided around the equator or from the north to the south pole: *the northern hemisphere*

2 a shape which is half a sphere or ball

hemline [noun: **hemlines**] the point on your legs that a coat, dress or skirt reaches down to: *Short hemlines are fashionable again.*

hemp [noun] a plant grown for the fibres it produces, which are used to make ropes and rough cloth for sacks

hen [noun: **hens**] a female chicken

hence [adverb]
1 for this reason: *He's just got some bad news, hence his glum expression.*
2 from this time or from this place: *five years hence*

henna [noun] a reddish-brown dye that comes from a plant and that you can use to colour your hair or decorate your body

hen party or **hen night** [noun: **hen parties** or **hen nights**] a celebration for a group of women, especially one held just before one of them gets married

her [pronoun] a word you use to talk about a woman, a girl, a female animal or a vehicle or ship that has already been mentioned or pointed out: *I'm looking for Mrs Peters. Have you seen her?*
[adjective] belonging to her: *Her hair is blonde.*

herald [noun: **heralds**]
1 in the past, someone who made important announcements or carried important messages for a king or queen
2 something that is a sign of something that is going to happen or come soon: *snowdrops, the herald of spring*
[verb: **heralds, heralding, heralded**] to herald something is to announce it or show that it will come soon

heraldry [noun] heraldry is the study of coats of arms and family crests

herb [noun: **herbs**] a plant, such as camomile, parsley, rosemary or thyme, that is used for making medicines or for flavouring food: *herbs and spices*
♦ **herbal** [adjective] using herbs or to do with herbs: *herbal medicines* • *herbal tea*

herbivore [noun: **herbivores**] an animal that eats only grass and plants. Look up and compare **carnivore** and **omnivore**
♦ **herbivorous** [adjective] eating only grass and plants: *Deer are herbivorous.*

herd [noun: **herds**] a large group of animals of one type: *a herd of buffalo*
[verb: **herds, herding, herded**] to herd animals or people is to gather them together and make them go somewhere in a group: *We were herded into a small room at the back.*

here [adverb]
1 at, in or to this place or time: *I like it here.*
2 things that are **here and there** are in several different places
[interjection]
1 people say 'Here!' to express surprise or anger at something someone is doing: *Here! You aren't supposed to do that!*
2 you say 'here' when you are offering something to someone: *Here, take this one. It's better than the one you have.*

hereafter [adverb] after this or from this time on
[noun] the hereafter is life after death

hereby [adverb] hereby is used in an official or legal statement to announce what you are going to do and how it will be done: *We hereby promise to abide by this agreement.*

hereditary [adjective] passed down from one generation to the next: *a hereditary disease*

heredity [noun] heredity is the passing on of qualities and characteristics from parents to children through the genes

heritage [noun] things that are passed down from previous generations, or things that have been, or should be, preserved because they provide a link with the past: *our cultural heritage*

hermit [noun: **hermits**] someone who lives all alone and doesn't have contact with other people
♦ **hermitage** [noun: **hermitages**] a place where a hermit lives or a place where someone can go to get away from the world for a while

hero [noun: **heroes**]
1 a man or boy who many people admire because of the things he has done
2 the most important male character in a story or film
♦ **heroic** [adjective]
1 very brave

Hh

Hh

2 to do with heroes or heroines

heroin [noun] heroin is a powerful illegal drug that some people take by injecting it into themselves. It is very addictive

heroine [noun: **heroines**]
1 a woman or girl who many people admire because of the things she has done
2 the most important female character in a story or film

heroism [noun] great bravery and courage that many people admire

heron [noun: **herons**] a bird with long legs and a long neck that lives near water and catches fish in its long sharp beak

herring [noun: **herring** or **herrings**] an edible sea fish with silvery-grey scales that swims in large groups

hers [pronoun] a word you use to talk about something belonging to a woman, girl or female animal that has already been mentioned or pointed out: *I gave Sandra my phone number and she gave me hers.*

ⓘ Notice that there is no apostrophe between the **r** and the **s** in **hers**.

herself [pronoun]
1 you use **herself** after a verb or preposition when the woman or girl who performs the action is affected by it: *Did Barbara hurt herself when she fell down?* • *She sang to herself as she worked.*
2 **herself** is also used to show that a girl or woman does something without any help from other people: *She always answers every fan letter herself.*
3 you can use **herself** to emphasize who you mean: *I wanted to ask Moira herself, but I couldn't get in touch with her.*

he's [short form] a short way to say and write **he is** or **he has**: *He's my brother.* • *He's done all the work.*

hesitant [adjective] if someone is hesitant, they aren't very willing to do something or they keep pausing while they are doing it: *The boy talked in a shy, hesitant way.*

hesitate [verb: **hesitates, hesitating, hesitated**]
1 to pause for a short time while you are doing something

2 to hesitate to do something is to be slightly unwilling to do it

♦ **hesitation** [noun: **hesitations**]
1 hesitating: *He did it without hesitation.*
2 a pause: *After a slight hesitation, she said she would do it.*

heterosexual [adjective] sexually attracted to people of the opposite sex [noun: **heterosexuals**] someone who is sexually attracted to people of the opposite sex

hey [interjection] an exclamation used to get someone's attention: *Hey, stop that!*

hi [interjection] a word you use to greet someone: *Hi, how are you?*

hibernate [verb: **hibernates, hibernating, hibernated**] an animal that hibernates goes into a kind of sleep for long periods during the winter when food is difficult to find

♦ **hibernation** [noun] hibernating

hiccup [noun: **hiccups**]
1 if you have hiccups, you make loud gasping noises in your throat
2 a hiccup is a small problem that causes a delay
[verb: **hiccups, hiccupping, hiccupped**] to hiccup is to make loud gasping noises that you can't control

hide[1] [verb: **hides, hiding, hid, hidden**] to put or keep someone or something in a place where they can't be seen or found easily: *You hide, and I'll come and look for you.* • *He hid behind a tree.*
➠ **hiding**[1]

hide[2] [noun: **hides**] the skin of an animal

hide-and-seek [noun] a game in which one person hides and the other players look for him or her

hideous [adjective] ugly or horrible to look at

hideout [noun: **hideouts**] a hiding place: *The gang had a secret hideout in the mountains.*

hiding[1] [noun] if someone is in hiding, they have hidden themselves in a secret place

hiding[2] [noun: **hidings**] a beating or defeat: *He gave the boy a good hiding for taking the money.*

hieroglyphics [plural noun] a form of

writing in which little pictures are used instead of letters and words. Hieroglyphics were used in ancient Egypt

hi-fi [noun: **hi-fis**] a hi-fi is a piece of equipment for playing or recording high-quality sound

[adjective] short for **high fidelity**, which means reproducing very high-quality sound

high [adjective and adverb: **higher, highest**]
1 extending far upwards, or a long way off the ground: *a high building* • *diving from the highest board*
2 having a certain height: *10 metres high* • *How high is Snowdon?*
3 near the top of a scale of measurement or list: *high marks* • *a high temperature*
4 a high sound or musical note is near the top of the range of pitch or musical notes: *the high voices of the children* • *the highest note you can sing*
5 great or large in amount or importance: *a high number*

[adverb: **higher, highest**]
1 far above in the air or a long way off the ground: *satellites orbiting high above the Earth*
2 far up a scale or ranking: *The temperature rose higher and higher.*

[noun: **highs**]
1 a peak or maximum: *Confidence was at an all-time high.*
2 if someone is **on a high**, they are feeling very excited and elated

high chair [noun: **high chairs**] a chair with long legs for a baby or young child to sit in while they are eating

high jump [noun]
1 the high jump is an athletic competition in which competitors try to jump over a horizontal pole supported on upright stands
2 if someone is **for the high jump**, they are going to get into serious trouble

highland [adjective] to do with the highlands: *a highland cottage*
♦ **highlands** [plural noun] the highlands are the mountainous areas of a country: *the Scottish Highlands*

highlight [verb: **highlights, highlighting, highlighted**] to highlight something is to make

it stand out or draw attention to it: *These figures highlight a growing problem.*

[noun: **highlights**]
1 the highlight is the best part of an event or period of time: *His singing was the highlight of the concert.*
2 highlights in your hair are streaks or parts that are a lighter colour than the rest of your hair
♦ **highlighter** [noun: **highlighters**] a pen with a special type of brightly coloured ink that you use to mark important words in a piece of writing or printing to make them stand out

highly [adverb]
1 very: *a highly infectious disease*
2 to or at a high level: *highly paid executives*
3 if you think highly of someone or something, you respect or like them a lot

highly strung [adjective] very nervous and easily upset

Highness [noun: **Highnesses**] a title you use when you are speaking about or to a prince or princess

high-rise [adjective] high-rise buildings are tall, narrow buildings with a lot of floors
[noun: **high-rises**] a very tall building, especially a tall block of flats

high school [noun: **high schools**] a secondary school

high-tech or **hi-tech** [adjective] high-tech equipment or methods use very advanced technology

highway [noun: **highways**]
1 in Britain, the highway is the public road or the main road
2 in the United States and other countries, a highway is a road that links towns and cities

Highway Code [noun] in Britain, the Highway Code is a set of official rules that tells you how to use the roads

hijack [verb: **hijacks, hijacking, hijacked**] people hijack an aeroplane or other vehicle when they take control of it by force and make it go where they want it to go
♦ **hijacker** [noun: **hijackers**] someone who hijacks an aeroplane or other vehicle

hike [verb: **hikes, hiking, hiked**]
1 to hike is to go for long walks in the countryside
2 to hike something, or **hike it up**, is to raise it

[noun: **hikes**] a long walk in the countryside
• **hiker** [noun: **hikers**] someone who goes for long walks in the countryside
• **hiking** [noun] the pastime of taking long walks in the countryside

hilarious [adjective] very funny
• **hilarity** [noun] loud laughter: *His antics caused much hilarity.*

hill [noun: **hills**]
1 a raised or high area of land, smaller than a mountain
2 a mound or heap: *a molehill*
3 someone who is **over the hill** is old
• **hilly** [adjective: **hillier, hilliest**] a hilly area has lots of hills

hilt [noun: **hilts**]
1 the handle of a sword or dagger
2 if you support or defend someone **to the hilt**, you do so as much as you possibly can

him [pronoun] a word you use to talk about a man, boy or male animal that has already been mentioned or pointed out: *I'm looking for Mr Peters. Have you seen him anywhere?*

ⓘ Try not to confuse the spellings of the pronoun **him** and the noun **hymn**.

himself [pronoun]
1 you use **himself** after a verb or preposition when the man or boy who performs the action is affected by it: *He poked himself in the eye by mistake.* • *The old man was muttering to himself.*
2 himself is also used to show that a boy or man does something without any help from other people: *Jack can tie his shoelaces himself already.*
3 you can use **himself** to emphasize who you mean: *I was surprised when Mr Blair himself answered the telephone.*

hind [adjective] an animal's hind parts are the back parts of its body: *The horse reared up on its hind legs.*

hinder [verb: **hinders, hindering, hindered**] to hinder someone or something is to delay them or stop them making progress
• **hindrance** [noun: **hindrances**] something that keeps you back and stops you making progress

hindsight [noun] knowledge you have after

some event, when you know how it has turned out and therefore how it could have been done better: *With hindsight I can see I was a fool to trust him.*

Hindu [noun: **Hindus**] a person whose religion is Hinduism
[adjective] to do with Hinduism: *The main Hindu gods are Brahma, Vishnu and Shiva.*
• **Hinduism** [noun] a religion of India and parts of South East Asia, which teaches that by a cycle of birth and rebirth, life continues forever or until the soul can be released from the cycle

hinge [noun: **hinges**] a piece of metal or plastic attaching a door to its frame, so that it can be opened and closed
[verb: **hinges, hinging, hinged**] if one thing **hinges on** another, it depends on it: *Whether he gets into university hinges on his A-level results.*

hint [noun: **hints**]
1 something that is said in a roundabout way without making the meaning absolutely clear: *She dropped a hint that something exciting was about to happen.*
2 a helpful piece of advice: *Can you give me any hints on how to grow roses?*
3 a small amount of something: *fizzy water with a hint of lemon*
[verb: **hints, hinting, hinted**] to hint is to give information in a way that is not clear or direct: *Laura hinted that she might be going to get engaged.*

hip [noun: **hips**] your hips are the parts at each side of your body, between your waist and the tops of your legs

hippo [noun: **hippos**] a hippopotamus

hippopotamus [noun: **hippopotamuses** or **hippopotami**] a large African animal with a heavy body, small rounded ears and thick legs. Hippopotamuses live near or in rivers

hire [verb: **hires, hiring, hired**]
1 you hire something when you pay to use it for a particular period of time and then return it: *On holiday, we hired bikes and cycled for miles.*
2 to hire someone is to pay them to do work
[noun] if something is **for hire**, it is available for you to hire it

Hh

hire-purchase [noun] a way of buying something by paying for it in a number of weekly or monthly payments: *We bought a new cooker on hire-purchase.*

his [pronoun] a word you use to talk about something belonging to a man, boy or male animal that has already been mentioned or pointed out: *I didn't have an umbrella so Grandad lent me his.*
[adjective] belonging to him: *Julian has left his coat behind.*

hiss [verb: **hisses, hissing, hissed**]
1 to make a noise like a long 's' sound: *The snake hissed.*
2 if someone hisses, they say something through their teeth without moving their lips: *'Quiet, everyone,' he hissed.*
[noun: **hisses**] a sound like that made by a snake

historian [noun: **historians**] someone who studies history

historic [adjective] important and likely to be remembered for a long time: *a historic agreement*
◆ **historical** [adjective] to do with history

history [noun: **histories**]
1 history is all the things that happened in the past, or the study of things that happened in the past: *local history* • *Ross is doing history at university.*
2 the history of something is where it came from and what has happened to it before now: *What's the history of this piece of furniture?*
3 a person's history is their past life

hit [verb: **hits, hitting, hit**]
1 to strike someone or something with a blow: *The lorry hit the car head-on.* • *Stop hitting your brother!*
2 an idea or feeling hits you when you realize it or feel it: *It suddenly hit me that I was quite alone.*
3 to **hit on** something is to think of it or discover it: *By sheer accident, he'd hit on the perfect solution to the problem.*
4 if two people **hit it off**, they get on well together
[noun: **hits**]
1 a blow or stroke: *a huge hit that sent the ball out of the ground*

2 a shot that strikes a target
3 a success with the public: *The show was an instant hit.*
[adjective] successful: *a hit song*

hit-and-miss or **hit-or-miss** [adjective] done without being sure what the result will be, sometimes successfully and sometimes not: *Their methods are pretty hit-and-miss.*

hit-and-run [adjective] to do with an accident in which a driver knocks someone down and doesn't stop to help or doesn't report the accident: *a hit-and-run driver*
[noun: **hit-and-runs**] an accident in which someone is knocked down in this way

hitch [noun: **hitches**] a problem that holds you up
[verb: **hitches, hitching, hitched**]
1 to fasten or attach one thing to another: *He hitched the caravan to the back of the car.*
2 to hitch a lift in someone's car is to signal to the driver to stop and give you a lift to the place you want to go
3 to **hitch up** a piece of your clothing is to pull it up: *She hitched up her skirt and climbed over the wall.*

hitchhike [verb: **hitchhikes, hitchhiking, hitchhiked**] to travel around by getting lifts in other people's cars
◆ **hitchhiker** [noun: **hitchhikers**] someone who hitchhikes

hi-tech [adjective] another spelling of **high-tech**

HIV [abbreviation] short for **human immunodeficiency virus**, the virus that causes the disease AIDS

hive [noun: **hives**] a box that bees live in and where they store their honey

HMS [abbreviation] short for **His** or **Her Majesty's Ship**, used in the names of British Royal Navy ships: *HMS Victory*

hoard [verb: **hoards, hoarding, hoarded**] to gather things and store them up in large quantities
[noun: **hoards**] a large store of things that you have gathered and kept
◆ **hoarder** [noun: **hoarders**] someone who likes saving and keeping lots of things

hoarding [noun: **hoardings**] a large board in the street for displaying advertisements

Hh

hoarse [adjective: **hoarser, hoarsest**]
1 a hoarse sound is rough and harsh
2 if you are hoarse, your voice sounds rough because your throat is sore

hoax [noun: **hoaxes**] a kind of trick in which someone says that something has happened or warns that it will happen, but they are not telling the truth
[verb: **hoaxes, hoaxing, hoaxed**] to trick people into thinking something has happened or will happen

hob [noun: **hobs**] a set of rings or plates for cooking on, either on top of a cooker or as a separate unit

hobble [verb: **hobbles, hobbling, hobbled**] to walk with short unsteady steps because your feet or legs are injured or sore

hobby [noun: **hobbies**] something you enjoy doing in your spare time

hockey [noun]
1 a game for two teams of eleven players, played with curved sticks and a ball on a field with a goal at either end
2 ice hockey

hoe [noun: **hoes**] a garden tool with a metal blade at one end, used for digging out weeds
[verb: **hoes, hoeing, hoed**] to use a hoe to dig out weeds from the soil

hog [verb: **hogs, hogging, hogged**] to hog something is to keep it for yourself and not share it with others
[noun: **hogs**]
1 another word for a pig
2 to **go the whole hog** is to leave nothing out, especially to do something in the most expensive or luxurious way possible: *We decided to go the whole hog and have brandy to finish.*

Hogmanay [noun] the name used in Scotland for December 31, or New Year's Eve, and the celebrations held that night

hoist [verb: **hoists, hoisting, hoisted**] to hoist something is to lift it up
[noun: **hoists**] a machine for lifting things

hold [verb: **holds, holding, held**]
1 to have something in your hand or hands: *He was holding a big wooden box.*
2 to keep something in a particular position for a while: *Raise your legs up and hold them there for a count of three.*

3 to contain something: *This rack holds my wine collection.*
4 a container that holds a certain amount can have that amount put into it: *It can hold 50 CDs.*
5 a place or vehicle that holds a certain number of people has enough room or seats for that number: *The stadium holds about 70,000 spectators.*
6 to hold an event or celebration, such as a party, is to organize it: *Where are the next Olympic Games going to be held?*
7 to **hold on** is to wait for a while: *Can you hold on while I get my coat?*
8 if one thing **holds up** another thing, it supports it: *The walls hold the roof up.*
9 if a robber **holds up** a person or place, they threaten the person or the people in the place with a weapon in order to rob them
10 to **hold someone** or **something up** is to delay them or it: *Sorry I'm late. I got held up in the traffic.*
[noun: **holds**]
1 a ship's hold is the space inside it where its cargo is stored
2 a grip: *Take a hold of the railing.*
3 if there are **no holds barred**, you can use any method, no matter how rough or unpleasant, to beat your opponent

holdall [noun: **holdalls**] a kind of large, soft bag that you use to carry your clothes and belongings when you are travelling

holder [noun: **holders**]
1 a container for putting or keeping something in: *a credit card holder*
2 the holder of a job, title, qualification or ticket is the person who has it

hold-up [noun: **hold-ups**]
1 a delay: *There's been a hold-up in supplies.*
2 a robbery in which guns or other weapons are used to threaten the people being robbed

hole [noun: **holes**]
1 an opening, tear or gap in something: *a hole in my sock • a hole in a tooth*
2 a pit or burrow in the ground: *They dug a deep hole to plant the rose bush in. • a rabbit hole*
♦ **holey** [adjective] full of holes: *holey socks*

holiday [noun: **holidays**]

1 a day or period of time when you don't have to work or go to school: *We're on holiday for two weeks now.*
2 a period of time spent in a place other than where you live, in order to relax or enjoy yourself: *two weeks' holiday in Spain*

holiness [noun]
1 being holy
2 a title used for the Pope, and certain other religious leaders: *His Holiness, Pope John Paul*

hollow [adjective: **hollower, hollowest**] something hollow has an empty space inside it: *hollow chocolate eggs*

holly [noun: **hollies**] an evergreen tree with sharp spiky leaves and red berries

holocaust [noun: **holocausts**]
1 a huge fire or other disaster that causes death and destruction
2 the Holocaust was the murder of millions of Jewish people by the Nazis in the 1930s and 1940s

hologram [noun: **holograms**] a photograph made using laser beams that seems to be three-dimensional when it is looked at from certain angles

holster [noun: **holsters**] a leather holder for a gun, usually worn on a belt

holy [adjective: **holier, holiest**]
1 to do with God or religion
2 pure and good and having strong religious feelings
➡ **holiness**

homage [noun] to pay homage to someone is to honour them and show or express your respect for them

home [noun: **homes**]
1 your home is the place where you live or where you were born and brought up
2 the home of something is the place where it began or was invented: *Mumbai is the home of the Indian film industry.*
3 a home is a place where people or animals with no one to look after them live and are cared for: *a children's home • an old people's home*
[verb: **homes, homing, homed**] to **home in on** something is to focus very closely on it or move directly towards it
➡ **homing**

homeopathy [noun] treating diseases by giving the patient a small amount of a natural substance that would cause the disease if it were given to them in large quantities

home page [noun: **home pages**] on the Internet, the home page of a website is the page that you start from and which gives you links to all the other parts of the site

homesick [adjective] when people who are away from their home feel homesick, they feel unhappy and want to be back at home
• **homesickness** [noun] the feeling of being homesick

homestead [noun: **homesteads**] a farmhouse, especially with land and smaller buildings around it

homewards [adverb] towards home: *trudging homewards after a hard day's work*

homework [noun] school work that you do while you are at home, especially in the evenings or at weekends

homing [adjective] a homing pigeon can find its way back home from a very long way away

homonym [noun: **homonyms**] a word spelt the same way as another word, but with a different meaning and sometimes a different sound. For example, *calf* meaning 'a young cow' and *calf* meaning 'the muscle at the back of your leg' are homonyms

ⓘ Homonyms in this dictionary are given separate entries with a small number following the word, for example **calf¹** and **calf²**.

homophone [noun: **homophones**] a word that sounds the same as another word, but has a different meaning and sometimes a different spelling. For example, *bare* and *bear*, *sea* and *see*, and *hour* and *our* are homophones

homosexual [adjective] someone who is homosexual is sexually attracted to people of the same sex
[noun: **homosexuals**] someone who is sexually attracted to people of the same sex
• **homosexuality** [noun] being sexually attracted to people of the same sex

honest [adjective] an honest person tells the truth and does not cheat or steal
• **honestly** [adverb]
1 truthfully: *Martin told me honestly what he*

Hh

thought. • I honestly didn't realize the door should have been kept locked.

2 without cheating, stealing or breaking the law

3 you say 'honestly' to show that you are annoyed or angry: Honestly, it just makes me sick!

♦ **honesty** [noun] being honest, truthful or trustworthy

honey [noun] a sweet thick liquid that bees make from the nectar of flowers and which they store in their hives

honeycomb [noun: **honeycombs**] a structure made by bees with special wax, with lots of compartments or cells in which honey is stored

honeymoon [noun: **honeymoons**] a holiday that a husband and wife take together immediately after they get married

honeysuckle [noun] a climbing plant with sweet-smelling yellow flowers

honk [noun: **honks**] a loud, short sound made by a goose or a car horn
[verb: **honks, honking, honked**] to honk is to make this sound

honorary [adjective] someone who is given an honorary title, or honorary membership of a club or organization, is given it as a mark of respect or honour

honour [noun: **honours**]
1 the respect or good reputation someone or something deserves: the honour of the family
2 something that makes you proud: It was an honour to meet him.
3 an award given to someone for good work or long service
4 to do something **in honour of** a person or event is to do it as a way of remembering that person or celebrating that event
[verb: **honours, honouring, honoured**]
1 to honour someone is to make them proud, pay them respect or give them an honour or award for good work
2 to honour a promise or agreement is to keep it

honourable [adjective] trustworthy or deserving respect
♦ **honourably** [adverb] in an honourable way

hood [noun: **hoods**]
1 a part attached to the back of a coat or jacket that you can pull up to cover the top and back of your head
2 a folding cover for something such as a pram or car

-hood [suffix] if **-hood** comes at the end of a word, it is a noun that means 'the state or time of being'. For example, childhood is the time in someone's life when they are a child, and manhood is the state of being or becoming a man

hoodwink [verb: **hoodwinks, hoodwinking, hoodwinked**] to hoodwink someone is to deceive them: The old man was hoodwinked into handing over his savings.

hoof [noun: **hooves**] the hard part of the foot of some animals, such as horses, cows or sheep

hook [noun: **hooks**]
1 a bent piece of metal or plastic that you hang things on
2 a bent piece of metal with a very sharp end used for catching fish
3 if you are **off the hook**, you do not have to do something difficult or unpleasant that you thought you would have to do
4 if a telephone is **off the hook**, the receiver has not be put back into its normal place so you can't receive calls
[verb: **hooks, hooking, hooked**]
1 to catch a fish using a hook
2 to attach something using a hook or hooks
♦ **hooked** [adjective] a hooked nose curves like a hook

hooligan [noun: **hooligans**] someone who behaves in a wild or violent way
♦ **hooliganism** [noun] the behaviour of hooligans

hoop [noun: **hoops**] a thin ring of metal, plastic or wood

hooray [interjection] another spelling of **hurrah**

hoot [noun: **hoots**]
1 the sound made by an owl or a car horn
2 a loud, sudden burst of laughter, or something that you find very amusing
[verb: **hoots, hooting, hooted**]
1 to hoot is to make the sound of an owl or a car horn

2 to hoot with laughter is to laugh very loud in sudden bursts

Hoover [noun] a machine for cleaning carpets and floors by sucking up dirt into a bag or container. This word is a trademark

⬩ **hoover** [verb: **hoovers, hoovering, hoovered**] an informal word that means to clean a carpet or floor using a vacuum cleaner

hooves [plural noun] the plural of **hoof**

hop¹ [verb: **hops, hopping, hopped**]

1 to jump on one leg

2 if you hop in, out or over somewhere, you move there quickly: *Hop in and I'll give you a lift to the station.*

[noun: **hops**]

1 a jump

2 if you **catch someone on the hop**, you surprise them by doing something they didn't expect you to

hop² [noun: **hops**] a climbing plant with fruits that are used to flavour beer

hope [verb: **hopes, hoping, hoped**] to hope for something is to think that it is possible or wish that it would happen: *I hope David manages to get home for Christmas.*

[noun: **hopes**]

1 hope is the feeling that what you want may happen: *We're not giving up hope, are we?*

2 your hopes are the things that you want to happen

hopeful [adjective] having or feeling hope: *The doctor's very hopeful that John's condition will improve.*

⬩ **hopefully** [adverb]

1 in a hopeful way: *The dog looked hopefully at the biscuits.*

2 it is to be hoped: *Hopefully, the rain will keep off.*

hopeless [adjective]

1 without any hope of succeeding: *a hopeless dream*

2 very bad: *Chris was hopeless in goal.*

⬩ **hopelessly** [adverb] in a hopeless way

horde [noun: **hordes**] a large moving crowd

horizon [noun: **horizons**] the horizon is the line where the land and sky seem to meet

horizontal [adjective] lying level or flat and not upright

hormone [noun: **hormones**] a chemical made in your body that controls things like your body's growth and development

horn [noun: **horns**]

1 horns are the hard pointed objects that grow out of some animals' heads, such as sheep, goats and cows

2 a device in a vehicle that makes a loud noise as a warning to others

3 a musical instrument that you blow into

⬩ **horned** [adjective] having horns

hornet [noun: **hornets**] a type of large wasp

horoscope [noun: **horoscopes**] your horoscope is a description of what some people believe is going to happen to you in the future depending on your sign of the zodiac

horrendous [adjective] terrible and shocking: *a horrendous crime*

horrible [adjective] very nasty, ugly or unpleasant

⬩ **horribly** [adverb] in a horrible way: *horribly disfigured*

horrid [adjective] nasty: *a horrid cold* ⬩ *a horrid man*

horrific [adjective] awful, terrifying or upsetting: *a horrific car crash*

⬩ **horrifically** [adverb] in a horrific way

horrify [verb: **horrifies, horrifying, horrified**] to shock and terrify someone

⬩ **horrifying** [adjective] shocking or terrifying

horror [noun: **horrors**]

1 horror is a feeling of great shock or alarm: *She threw up her hands in horror.*

2 if you have a horror of something, you are very afraid of it: *He has a horror of any creeping, slimy thing.*

3 horrors are very frightening, shocking or terrible experiences: *the horrors of war*

[adjective] meant to frighten you: *horror movies*

horse [noun: **horses**] a large animal with long hair on its neck and tail. Horses are used by people to ride on and to pull carts or ploughs

horseback [noun] you are **on horseback** when you are riding a horse

horse-chestnut [noun: **horse-chestnuts**] a type of tree on which large reddish-brown nuts called conkers grow

horsepower [noun] a unit for measuring the

power of engines, equal to about 746 watts

horseradish [noun] a type of plant whose root is used to make a sauce that tastes very hot

horseshoe [noun: **horseshoes**] a curved piece of iron nailed on to a horse's hoof to stop the hoof from being worn down

horticulture [noun] the science or study of growing fruit, vegetables and flowers in gardens and greenhouses

hose [noun: **hoses**] a tube made from plastic or rubber, used for carrying and spraying water

hosiery [noun] hosiery is socks and stockings

hospice [noun: **hospices**] a special type of hospital where sick people who can't be cured are cared for until they die

hospitable [adjective] welcoming to guests and strangers

hospital [noun: **hospitals**] a building where people who are sick or have been injured can go to be treated

hospitality [noun] hospitality is being welcoming and friendly to people, giving them food, entertainment or accommodation

hospitalize or **hospitalise** [verb: **hospitalizes, hospitalizing, hospitalized**] if someone is hospitalized, they are kept in a hospital for treatment

host[1] [noun: **hosts**] someone who welcomes guests, for example at a party, in a hotel or on a radio or TV show
[verb: **hosts, hosting, hosted**] to host an event is to be its host: *The city of Athens hosted the Olympics in 2004.*

host[2] [noun] a host of things is a very large number of them

hostage [noun: **hostages**] someone who is held prisoner until the people holding them get what they want

hostel [noun: **hostels**] a building with rooms that students or travellers can stay in: *a youth hostel*

hostess [noun: **hostesses**] a female host

hostile [adjective]
1 unfriendly or showing strong dislike
2 hostile forces in a war are enemy forces
◆ **hostility** [noun] unfriendliness or strong dislike

hot [adjective: **hotter, hottest**]
1 feeling very warm: *Don't touch the oven. It's very hot.*
2 spicy: *hot curries*
➞ **hotly**

hotdog [noun: **hotdogs**] a hot sausage served in a long thin roll

hotel [noun: **hotels**] a building with rooms that people pay to stay in when they are away from home

hotheaded [adjective] someone who is hotheaded is quick to get angry, or is too quick to act

hothouse [noun: **hothouses**] a heated greenhouse for growing plants that come from hot climates

hotline [noun: **hotlines**] a direct telephone line by which people can get or give information quickly in an emergency

hotly [adverb] to discuss, argue or deny something hotly is to do it in an angry or lively way

hotpot [noun: **hotpots**] a mixture of meat and vegetables cooked in the oven in a covered dish

hotseat [noun] if someone is **in the hotseat**, they are in a situation in which they have to make difficult or important decisions

hound [noun: **hounds**] a type of dog used for hunting
[verb: **hounds, hounding, hounded**] to hound someone is to go on for a long time bothering or annoying them: *celebrities hounded by the newspapers*

hour [noun: **hours**] a period of time that lasts 60 minutes. There are 24 hours in one day

hour-glass [noun: **hour-glasses**] an instrument used to measure time with two glass containers joined by a thin glass tube through which sand trickles slowly

hourly [adjective] happening once every hour or calculated by the hour: *an hourly service • an hourly rate of pay*
[adverb]
1 happening once every hour: *Buses to London leave hourly.*
2 if you are paid hourly, you earn a certain amount of money for each hour that you work

house [noun: **houses**]

Hh

1 a building in which people, especially one family, live

2 the part of a theatre or cinema where the audience sits

3 if something you are given in a restaurant, hotel or bar is **on the house**, you get it free of charge

[verb: **houses, housing, housed**]

1 to house people is to provide them with houses to live in

2 to house something such as a club or museum is to provide a place where it can operate: *The collection is housed in a pleasant old building.*

ⓘ Remember that the noun **house** is pronounced with an **ss** sound, but the verb **house** is pronounced with a **z** sound.

houseboat [noun: **houseboats**] a boat on a river with cabins for living in

housebreaker [noun: **housebreakers**] a thief who breaks into people's houses to steal things

♦ **housebreaking** [noun] the crime of breaking into people's houses

household [noun: **households**] all the people who live in the same house

♦ **householder** [noun: **householders**] someone who owns or rents a house

household name [noun: **household names**] someone or something that is a household name is famous

housekeeper [noun: **housekeepers**] someone who organizes all the work needed to run a house

house-proud [adjective] keeping the house always clean and tidy

house-trained [adjective] a house-trained pet has learnt to be clean inside the house

housewarming [noun: **housewarmings**] a party held in someone's new home

housewife [noun: **housewives**] a woman who stays at home to look after her family and do the housework, rather than going out to work

housework [noun] housework is all the work you need to do to keep a house clean and tidy

housing [noun: **housings**]

1 housing is houses of various kinds for people to live in

2 the housing for a machine is the box or structure that the machine fits into

housing association [noun: **housing associations**] an organization that builds or converts houses or flats for people to live in at a fair rent

hover [verb: **hovers, hovering, hovered**]

1 if something hovers, it stays still in the air

2 if someone hovers, they stand close to you, usually because they are watching you

hovercraft [noun: **hovercrafts**] a vehicle that travels along supported on a cushion of air

how [adverb]

1 how something is done is the way it is done or the means used to do it: *I'll show you how to tie a reef knot.* • *How will we get there?*

2 how is used in questions about measurement, extent, distance, time and age: *I don't know how old Maurice is exactly.* • *How much is that DVD player?*

3 how you are is how well or ill you feel: *Hello, how are you today?*

4 how you feel about someone or something is the feelings you have for them

5 you can also use how to show anger or for emphasis: *How dare you!* • *How sad is that?*

however [adverb]

1 no matter how: *However hard he tried, he couldn't do it.*

2 in spite of what has just been said: *Dan thinks it is a great movie. However, no one else thinks so.*

howl [noun: **howls**]

1 a long, loud, sad sound made by a wolf or dog

2 a loud shout of pain or laughter

[verb: **howls, howling, howled**]

1 a dog or wolf howls when it makes a long, loud, sad-sounding noise

2 to shout or cry loudly: *He was howling with pain.*

HQ [abbreviation] short for **headquarters**

hub [noun: **hubs**]

1 the centre part of a wheel where the axle passes through

2 the part of a place where most of the activity is: *the hub of the town*

Hh

Hh

hubbub [noun: **hubbubs**] the noise made by a lot of people talking at the same time

huddle [verb: **huddles, huddling, huddled**] people or animals huddle, or huddle together, when they move very close to each other and form a tightly packed group
[noun: **huddles**] a group of people standing or sitting very close to each other

hue [noun: **hues**] a colour or shade

hue and cry [noun] a hue and cry is a noisy fuss, often with people shouting or protesting loudly

huff [noun: **huffs**] if someone is **in a huff**, they are sulking
♦ **huffy** [adjective: **huffier, huffiest**] sulky

hug [verb: **hugs, hugging, hugged**] two people hug when they put their arms around each other's bodies in an affectionate way
[noun: **hugs**] the affectionate action of putting your arms around someone

huge [adjective] very big

hulk [noun: **hulks**]
1 a very large and clumsy person or thing
2 an old ship that is not being used
♦ **hulking** [adjective] very large and clumsy

hull [noun: **hulls**] the part of a ship or boat that sits in the water

hullabaloo [noun: **hullabaloos**] a noisy fuss

hullo [interjection] another spelling of **hello**

hum [verb: **hums, humming, hummed**] you hum when you make musical noises in your throat with your mouth closed

human [noun: **humans**] a human or a **human being** is a person
[adjective] typical of or to do with human beings: *human nature • human rights*

humane [adjective] kind and causing as little suffering as possible
♦ **humanely** [adverb] in a way that causes the least pain possible: *The dog was destroyed humanely.*

humanity [noun]
1 humanity is all human beings
2 someone who shows humanity is kind and understanding towards other people

humble [adjective: **humbler, humblest**]
1 a humble person believes they are no better than other people

2 if someone **eats humble pie**, they show that they are very sorry for a mistake they have made by admitting it and being humble

humbug [noun: **humbugs**]
1 humbug is an old-fashioned word for nonsense
2 humbugs are hard sweets made from boiled sugar that you suck

humdrum [adjective] a humdrum existence is boring because things always stay the same and nothing exciting ever happens

humid [adjective] the air or atmosphere is humid when it has a lot of moisture in it
♦ **humidity** [noun] humidity is the amount of moisture that is in the air

humiliate [verb: **humiliates, humiliating, humiliated**] to humiliate someone is to make them feel silly or ashamed, especially in front of other people
♦ **humiliating** [adjective] causing embarrassment or making you feel silly
♦ **humiliation** [noun] humiliation is being humiliated

humility [noun] being humble

humming-bird [noun: **humming-birds**] a tiny, brightly coloured bird with a long beak that feeds on nectar from flowers and beats its wings so fast they make a humming sound

humorous [adjective] funny or amusing

humour [noun] the ability someone has to be funny or amusing, or to find things funny or amusing
[verb: **humours, humouring, humoured**] to humour someone is to agree with them just to please them

hump [noun: **humps**]
1 a rounded lump on an animal's back
2 a rounded raised part on a road or other surface

humpback bridge [noun: **humpback bridges**] a bridge that is higher in the middle than at either end

hunch [noun: **hunches**] an idea you have about someone or something, which you believe but cannot prove
[verb: **hunches, hunching, hunched**] to hunch your shoulders or your back is to bring your shoulders up towards your ears so that your body is bent over at the top

hunchback [noun: **hunchbacks**] someone whose spine is bent so that there is a lump on their back

hundred [noun: **hundreds**] the number 100
+ **hundredth** [adjective and adverb] coming last in a series of one hundred things: *This is my hundredth visit here.*
[noun: **hundredths**] one of a hundred equal parts of something: *A centimetre is a hundredth of a metre.*

hung [verb] a way of changing the verb **hang** to make a past tense. It can be used with or without a helping verb: *I hung the poster on my bedroom wall.* • *He had hung the washing out before it started raining.*

hunger [noun] the feeling you get when you need to eat
[verb: **hungers, hungering, hungered**] to hunger for something is to long for it
+ **hungrily** [adverb] in a hungry way
+ **hungry** [adjective: **hungrier, hungriest**] having an empty feeling in your stomach and wanting food

hunk [noun: **hunks**] a big piece of something: *a hunk of bread and cheese*

hunt [verb: **hunts, hunting, hunted**]
1 to chase and kill animals for food or sport
2 to hunt for something is to look hard for it everywhere
[noun: **hunts**]
1 a search for something or someone: *a police hunt for the criminal*
2 an event where people search for or chase animals in order to kill them
+ **hunter** [noun: **hunters**] a person or animal that hunts
+ **hunting** [noun] chasing and killing animals

hurdle [noun: **hurdles**]
1 one of several jumps placed round a race track that athletes or horses have to jump over
2 a problem that you have to overcome
[verb: **hurdles, hurdling, hurdled**]
1 to compete in hurdle races
2 to hurdle something is to jump over it
+ **hurdler** [noun: **hurdlers**] a competitor in a race with hurdles
+ **hurdling** [noun] jumping over hurdles in a race

hurl [verb: **hurls, hurling, hurled**] to hurl something is to throw it with a lot of force

hurrah or **hooray** [interjection] an exclamation of approval or joy: *Hurrah! We've won!*

hurricane [noun: **hurricanes**] a fierce storm with very strong winds that cause serious damage

hurried [adjective] something that is hurried is done quickly: *a hurried meal*
+ **hurriedly** [adverb] quickly

hurry [verb: **hurries, hurrying, hurried**]
1 to move or go quickly
2 to **hurry up** is to move faster: *Hurry up! You're late.*
[noun]
1 hurry is trying or needing to get somewhere or get something done quickly: *in a hurry to catch the bus* • *There's no hurry.*
2 if you are **in a hurry**, you want to be quick: *I can't talk now — I'm in a hurry.*
3 if you do something **in a hurry**, you do it quickly: *The job had to be finished in a hurry.*

hurt [verb: **hurts, hurting, hurt**]
1 to hurt someone or something is to injure or damage them: *She fell and hurt her ankle.* • *Try not to hurt anyone's feelings.*
2 if something hurts, or hurts you, it is painful: *My shoulder hurts.* • *His words really hurt her.*
[adjective] injured or showing pain: *a hurt expression*
[noun] pain, injury or distress

hurtful [adjective] causing pain or distress: *a hurtful remark*

hurtle [verb: **hurtles, hurtling, hurtled**] to move very fast, often in a dangerous or uncontrolled way: *The sledge came hurtling down the bank and crashed into a tree.*

husband [noun: **husbands**] a woman's husband is the man she has married

hush [interjection] if someone says 'hush!' they want you to be quiet
[verb: **hushes, hushing, hushed**] to **hush something up** is to stop people getting to know about it
[noun] silence after there has been noise

husk [noun: **husks**] the husk of a seed is its dry outer covering

husky[1] [adjective] a husky voice is deep and rough

Hh

husky[2] [noun: **huskies**] a type of large dog with a thick warm coat that is used to pull sledges over snow in the Arctic and Antarctic

hustle [verb: **hustles, hustling, hustled**] to push someone somewhere or to hurry them along

[noun] hurried movements or actions

hut [noun: **huts**] a small building or shed made of wood, mud or metal

hutch [noun: **hutches**] a box, usually with an open front covered with wire, where pet rabbits are kept

hyacinth [noun: **hyacinths**] a plant that grows from a large bulb and has lots of small sweet-smelling flowers growing on one stem

hybrid [noun: **hybrids**] a hybrid animal or plant has been bred from two different types or species of animal or plant

hydrant [noun: **hydrants**] a pipe connected to the main water supply to which a hose can be attached to get water to put out fires

hydraulic [adjective] to do with, or powered by, the movement of liquid: *hydraulic brakes*

hydro- [prefix] if a word starts with **hydro-**, it has something to do with water. For example, *hydrogen* is one of the elements that makes water

hydrocarbon [noun: **hydrocarbons**] hydrocarbons are various chemical substances containing only carbon and hydrogen. They are found in coal and oil

hydroelectric [adjective] using or to do with electricity made by water power

◆ **hydroelectricity** [noun] electricity made by using fast flowing water whose force is converted into electrical power

hydrofoil [noun: **hydrofoils**] a fast type of boat or ship that can skim over the water on long structures shaped like an aeroplane's wings

hydrogen [noun] hydrogen is the lightest gas, which combines with oxygen to make water

hyena [noun: **hyenas**] a wild animal that lives in Africa and parts of Asia. Hyenas belong to the same family as dogs and make a howling noise that sounds like mad laughter

hygiene [noun] keeping yourself and your surroundings clean, so that you stay healthy

◆ **hygienic** [adjective] without any dirt or germs

hymn [noun: **hymns**] a religious song praising God

hype [noun] hype is publicity or advertising, especially when it makes something seem better than it is

[verb: **hypes, hyping, hyped**] to hype or **hype up** a product, TV programme or event is to advertise it a lot to make it seem more useful or interesting than it really is

hyper- [prefix] if a word starts with **hyper-**, it adds the meaning 'much bigger', 'much more' or 'too much'. For example, a *hypermarket* is much bigger than a supermarket

hyperactive [adjective] someone, especially a child, who is hyperactive is more active than normal

hyperlink [noun: **hyperlinks**] in computers, a word or picture that you can click on to move to a related document, picture or piece of information

hypertext [noun] in computers, text with hyperlinks that you can click on to move to a related document, picture or piece of information

hyphen [noun: **hyphens**] a punctuation mark (-) used to join words or parts of words together, or used at the end of a line of printed text to show that a word is split and part of it is on the next line

◆ **hyphenate** [verb: **hyphenates, hyphenating, hyphenated**] to put a hyphen in a word or to join words or parts of words with a hyphen

hypnosis [noun] if someone is under hypnosis, they have been put into a state that is similar to a deep sleep but in which they can still obey someone else's instructions

◆ **hypnotic** [adjective] having a hypnotizing effect

◆ **hypnotism** [noun] using hypnosis to put someone into a sleep-like state

◆ **hypnotist** [noun: **hypnotists**] someone who hypnotizes people, often as a public entertainment

◆ **hypnotize** or **hypnotise** [verb: **hypnotizes, hypnotizing, hypnotized**] to put someone into a sleep-like state

hypochondriac [noun: **hypochondriacs**] someone who is very worried about their health and imagines they are suffering from illnesses and diseases

hypocrisy [noun] the behaviour of someone who is not as sincere or honest as they pretend to be

• **hypocrite** [noun: **hypocrites**] someone who falsely pretends to be sincere and concerned for other people

• **hypocritical** [adjective] not having the feelings or beliefs that you pretend to have

hypothermia [noun] when someone's body temperature drops dangerously low because they are very cold

hypothesis [noun: **hypotheses**] a theory or idea that has been worked out as a possible explanation for something, but which hasn't been proved to be correct

• **hypothetical** [adjective] a hypothetical situation or example is one that is based on what might be possible, rather than fact

hysterectomy [noun: **hysterectomies**] a surgical operation to remove a woman's womb

hysteria [noun] if someone is suffering from hysteria, they become very emotional and cry or scream in a wild way

• **hysterical** [adjective]
1 suffering from hysteria
2 if you find something hysterical, you think it is very funny

• **hysterically** [adverb] in a hysterical way

• **hysterics** [plural noun] if someone has hysterics, they cry, scream or laugh in a wild and uncontrolled way

Hh

I

I [pronoun] a word you use when talking about yourself: *I like ice cream.*

-ible [suffix] look at the entry for **-able**

-ic or **-ical** [suffix] if **-ic** or **-ical** comes at the end of a word, it is an adjective that means 'like' or 'to do with'. For example, *historical* means 'to do with history'

ice [noun] frozen water
[verb: **ices, icing, iced**] to cover a cake with icing
➡ **icy**

ice age [noun] a period of time when the Earth was mostly covered with ice

iceberg [noun: **icebergs**] a large mass of ice floating in the sea

icebox [noun: **iceboxes**] the American English word for **fridge**

ice-cap [noun: **ice-caps**] a permanent covering of ice, for example at the North and South Poles

ice cream [noun: **ice creams**] a sweet frozen food made from milk or cream: *strawberry ice cream • Would you like an ice cream?*

ice hockey [noun] a sport played on ice in which two teams try to hit an object called a puck into a net

ice lolly [noun: **ice lollies**] a lump of frozen fruit-flavoured juice on a stick

ice skate [noun: **ice skates**] ice skates are boots with blades on the bottom, used for moving across ice
✦ **ice-skating** [noun] the sport or pastime of moving across ice wearing ice-skates

icicle [noun: **icicles**] a long thin piece of ice that is hanging from something

icing [noun] a mixture of sugar and water, used for decorating cakes

icon [noun: **icons**]
1 a small symbol on a computer screen that represents a program or file
2 a statue or painting of a holy person

icy [adjective: **icier, iciest**]
1 covered with ice: *icy roads*
2 extremely cold: *an icy wind*

ID [noun: **IDs**] an official document that proves who you are: *We need some ID before we can give you a library card.*

I'd [short form] a short way to say and write **I would** or **I had**: *I'd like another drink, please.* • *I'd just gone to bed when the phone rang.*

idea [noun: **ideas**]
1 a thought or plan that you have: *That's a good idea.*
2 if you **have no idea** about something, you don't know it: *I've no idea where he is.*

ideal [adjective] perfect, especially for a particular purpose: *It's an ideal house for a family.*
[noun: **ideals**]
1 an idea about what is good and right that you try to follow in how you behave: *a man of high ideals*
2 someone or something that you believe is a perfect example of something: *She's my ideal of what a woman should be.*
✦ **idealism** [noun] the belief that something perfect can be achieved, even though this is not likely
✦ **idealist** [noun: **idealists**] someone who believes that something perfect can be achieved, although it is unlikely
✦ **idealize** or **idealise** [verb: **idealizes, idealizing, idealized**] to think that something

is perfect when it really is not
◆ **ideally** [adverb] in a perfect situation: *Ideally, I'd like to finish this by tomorrow.*

identical [adjective] if two things are identical, they are exactly the same

identification [noun]
1 an official document that proves who you are
2 the process of finding out who someone is or what something is

identify [verb: **identifies, identifying, identified**]
1 to say who someone is or what something is: *Can you identify this flower?* • *She had to identify the body.*
2 if you **identify with** someone, you feel that you understand them and share their feelings

identity [noun: **identities**] who someone is or what something is: *Police are trying to discover the identity of the thief.*

idiom [noun: **idioms**] a phrase that has a special meaning. For example, 'to let the cat out of the bag' is an idiom that means 'to tell someone a secret'

idiot [noun: **idiots**] a stupid or silly person
◆ **idiotic** [adjective] extremely stupid or silly

idle [adjective]
1 someone who is idle is lazy or not doing anything useful
2 a machine or other piece of equipment that is idle is not being used
◆ **idly** [adverb] in a lazy way

ⓘ Be careful not to confuse the spellings and meanings of **idle** and **idol**.

idol [noun: **idols**]
1 a famous person who is admired by a lot of people: *a pop idol*
2 something which people worship as a god
◆ **idolize** or **idolise** [verb: **idolizes, idolizing, idolized**] to admire someone or something very much: *He idolizes his football heroes.*

ie or **i.e.** [abbreviation] You use **ie** when you are giving more information to show what you mean: *The whole trip — ie food, travel, and hotel — cost £500.*

ⓘ **ie** is short for **id est**, which is Latin for 'that is'.

if [conjunction]
1 whether: *I don't know if I can come on Thursday.*
2 used when talking about possibilities: *If we leave now, we should catch the train.* • *He will have to go into hospital if his condition gets worse.*
3 whenever: *I always call in at his house if I'm passing.*

igloo [noun: **igloos**] a hut made from blocks of snow

ignite [verb: **ignites, igniting, ignited**]
1 to ignite is to catch fire: *The paper suddenly ignited.*
2 to ignite something is to set it on fire: *Flames had ignited the curtains.*
◆ **ignition** [noun]
1 the ignition is the part of a car that ignites the petrol when you turn the key to start the engine
2 ignition is igniting something

ignorance [noun] being ignorant
◆ **ignorant** [adjective] not knowing about something: *Many people are ignorant about the dangers.*

ignore [verb: **ignores, ignoring, ignored**] to pay no attention to someone or something: *He ignored all my advice.* • *I said hello, but she just ignored me.*

iguana [noun: **iguanas**] a large lizard that lives in trees

il- [prefix] look at the entry for **in-**

ill [adjective] not well: *I was ill yesterday and had to stay off work.*
➡ **illness**

I'll [short form] a short way to say and write **I will**: *I'll see you tomorrow.*

illegal [adjective] not allowed by the law: *It's illegal to drop litter.*
◆ **illegality** [noun] being illegal
◆ **illegally** [adverb] in an illegal way: *Your car is illegally parked.*

illegible [adjective] illegible writing is so bad you cannot read it
◆ **illegibly** [adverb] in a way that is impossible to read: *You write illegibly.*

illegitimate [adjective] an illegitimate child is born to parents who are not married to each other

illiterate [adjective] not able to read or write

illness [noun: **illnesses**]
1 illness is bad health: *There is a lot of illness among the staff.*
2 an illness is a disease: *childhood illnesses*

illogical [adjective] not based on good reason or logic

illuminate [verb: **illuminates, illuminating, illuminated**] to make something brighter using lights: *We added lights to illuminate the garden.*
• **illuminated** [adjective] lit by lights
• **illumination** [noun] lighting something with lights

illusion [noun: **illusions**]
1 an idea or belief you have which is false: *He's under the illusion that it's easy to get a job.*
2 something that seems to exist but does not really exist: *an optical illusion*

illustrate [verb: **illustrates, illustrating, illustrated**] to provide pictures and photographs for a book or magazine: *a book illustrated with colour photographs*
• **illustration** [noun: **illustrations**] a picture or photograph in a book or magazine
• **illustrator** [noun: **illustrators**] someone who draws pictures for a book or magazine

ill-will [noun] bad feelings towards someone

I'm [short form] a short way to say and write **I am**: *I'm hungry.*

im- [prefix] look at the entry for **in-**

image [noun: **images**]
1 a picture that you have in your mind
2 the impression that someone or something gives to other people: *He needs to improve his image.*
3 if someone is **the image of** someone else, they look exactly like them: *Pam's the image of her mother.*
• **imagery** [noun] words that produce pictures in your mind when you are reading something or listening to something

imaginary [adjective] existing in your mind but not real: *Dragons are imaginary creatures.*

imagination [noun: **imaginations**] your ability to form pictures and ideas in your mind: *Roy has a very vivid imagination.*
• **imaginative** [adjective] using new and interesting ideas: *Paul's very imaginative.* • *an imaginative design*

imagine [verb: **imagines, imagining, imagined**]
1 to form a picture of someone or something in your mind: *I tried to imagine what he would look like.*
2 to think or believe something, especially something that is not true: *You must be imagining things.*

imam [noun: **imams**] in the religion of Islam, a man who leads the prayers in a mosque

imitate [verb: **imitates, imitating, imitated**] to copy someone or something
• **imitation** [noun: **imitations**]
1 imitation is copying someone or something
2 an imitation is a copy of something
• **imitator** [noun: **imitators**] someone who copies someone else

immaculate [adjective] spotlessly clean: *The house looked immaculate.*

immature [adjective] behaving in a silly and childish way
• **immaturity** [noun] silly and childish behaviour

immediate [adjective] happening now without any delay: *I can't give you an immediate answer.*
• **immediately** [adverb] now and without any delay: *Come here immediately!*

immense [adjective] very big: *Crime is becoming an immense problem.*
• **immensely** [adverb] extremely: *He's immensely popular.*

immerse [verb: **immerses, immersing, immersed**]
1 to put something in a liquid so it is completely covered
2 if you immerse yourself in something, you give it all of your attention
• **immersion** [noun] putting something in liquid

immigrant [noun: **immigrants**] someone from another country who has come to live in your country

immigrate [verb: **immigrates, immigrating, immigrated**] to come and live in a foreign country

◆ **immigration** [noun] coming to live in a foreign country

(i) Do not confuse this with the word **emigrate**. You **immigrate** if you come into a new country and live there, but you **emigrate** if you leave your country.

imminent [adjective] something that is imminent will happen very soon

immobile [adjective] not moving or not able to move

◆ **immobilize** or **immobilise** [verb: **immobilizes, immobilizing, immobilized**] to prevent someone or something from moving normally

immoral [adjective] wrong or bad: *immoral behaviour*

◆ **immorality** [noun] behaviour that is not good or honest

immortal [adjective] living for ever

◆ **immortality** [noun] being immortal

◆ **immortalize** or **immortalise** [verb: **immortalizes, immortalizing, immortalized**] to make someone famous for ever

immune [adjective] if you are immune to an illness, you cannot get it

◆ **immunity** [noun] your ability to avoid getting an illness

◆ **immunization** or **immunisation** [noun] putting a substance into someone's body, usually by an injection, to prevent them from getting an illness

◆ **immunize** or **immunise** [verb: **immunizes, immunizing, immunized**] to put a substance into someone's body to prevent them from getting an illness

imp [noun: **imps**]
1 an imaginary creature in stories that looks like a small man and behaves badly
2 a naughty child

impact [noun: **impacts**]
1 the strong effect that something has: *The changes will have a big impact on schools.*
2 the force of one thing hitting another thing: *The impact of the meteor left a crater on the moon.*

impair [verb: **impairs, impairing, impaired**] to damage something or make it

worse: *His hearing was impaired by the constant noise.*

◆ **impairment** [noun: **impairments**] a condition that stops part of your body from working correctly

impale [verb: **impales, impaling, impaled**] to push a sharp object through something

impartial [adjective] fair and not supporting one person more than another: *an impartial referee*

◆ **impartiality** [noun] being impartial

impatience [noun] the feeling that you want something to happen now and that you can't wait

◆ **impatient** [adjective] if you are impatient, you can't wait for something to happen

◆ **impatiently** [adverb] in a way that shows you are impatient: *'Hurry up!' she said impatiently.*

impede [verb: **impedes, impeding, impeded**] to delay the progress of someone or something

◆ **impediment** [noun: **impediments**]
1 something that delays progress
2 a problem that makes it difficult for someone to speak properly: *a speech impediment*

impending [adjective] going to happen very soon: *an impending disaster*

imperative [adjective] extremely important or necessary: *It is imperative that you reply to this letter.*
[noun: **imperatives**] a form of a verb which you use to tell someone to do something. For example, *go* in the phrase *Go away!* is imperative

imperfect [adjective] not perfect
[noun] the imperfect is the form of a verb that expresses action in the past that is not complete. For example, *The sun was shining* is in the imperfect

◆ **imperfection** [noun: **imperfections**] a fault

imperial [adjective]
1 to do with an empire: *an imperial ruler*
2 to do with a system of measuring or weighing that uses units such as gallons and ounces

impersonal [adjective] not very friendly or welcoming: *Big hotels can be a bit impersonal.*

Ii

impersonate [verb: **impersonates, impersonating, impersonated**] to copy the way someone talks and behaves, especially to entertain people

✦ **impersonation** [noun: **impersonations**] an attempt to impersonate someone: *Ben can do a brilliant impersonation of Tony Blair.*

✦ **impersonator** [noun: **impersonators**] someone who impersonates people

impertinence [noun] rude behaviour that shows you do not respect someone

✦ **impertinent** [adjective] behaving in a rude way and not showing respect: *an impertinent child*

✦ **impertinently** [adverb] in an impertinent way

implement [noun: **implements**] a tool [verb: **implements, implementing, implemented**] if you implement a new plan or system, you start using it: *The new rules will be implemented next year.*

✦ **implementation** [noun] implementing something: *the implementation of new laws*

implication [noun: **implications**]
1 a possible effect or result: *What are the implications of the President's announcement?*
2 something that is suggested and not said directly

implore [verb: **implores, imploring, implored**] to ask in a desperate way for someone to do something

imply [verb: **implies, implying, implied**] to suggest that something is true without saying it directly: *Are you implying that he lied?*
➡ **implication**

impolite [adjective] bad mannered and rude to others: *an impolite boy • an impolite way to talk*

✦ **impolitely** [adverb] in a rude way
✦ **impoliteness** [noun] rude behaviour and bad manners

import [verb: **imports, importing, imported**] to bring goods into a country from another country in order to sell them: *Many electrical goods are imported from Japan.* [noun: **imports**] something that has been imported

importance [noun] being important: *I can't*

emphasize enough the importance of education.

✦ **important** [adjective]
1 if something is important, it matters a lot: *an important meeting*
2 an important person has a lot of power

✦ **importantly** [adverb] seriously or crucially: *You must come to the class and, more importantly, you must pay attention.*

impose [verb: **imposes, imposing, imposed**]
1 to bring in a new rule or law, especially one that is not wanted: *the government imposed a new tax*
2 if you impose on someone, you expect them to do something for you that may not be convenient for them

✦ **imposing** [adjective] looking very impressive: *an imposing building*

impossibility [noun: **impossibilities**] something that is not possible

impossible [adjective] not possible: *an impossible task*

impostor [noun: **impostors**] someone who pretends to be someone else in order to deceive people

impractical [adjective] not sensible or reasonable: *an impractical suggestion*

imprecise [adjective] not exact or correct: *imprecise measurements*

impress [verb: **impresses, impressing, impressed**] if someone or something impresses you, they make you admire them: *His drawings really impressed me.*

✦ **impression** [noun: **impressions**]
1 a feeling that you get about someone or something: *I got the impression that he wasn't happy.*
2 the effect that someone or something has on you: *The film made a big impression on me.*

✦ **impressive** [adjective] making you feel admiration: *an impressive performance*

imprison [verb: **imprisons, imprisoning, imprisoned**] to put someone in prison or a place they cannot escape from

improbable [adjective] not likely to happen or be true: *an improbable story*

improper [adjective] improper behaviour is not suitable or right

improve [verb: **improves, improving, improved**]
1 to improve is to get better: *I hope the weather improves soon.*
2 to improve something is to make it better: *I want to improve my French.*
♦ **improvement** [noun: **improvements**]
1 improvement is making something better
2 an improvement is a change that makes something better: *improvements to the home*

improvise [verb: **improvises, improvising, improvised**] to use whatever is available because you do not have what you need: *They improvised a shelter from branches and blankets.*

impudence [noun] cheeky behaviour or remarks
♦ **impudent** [adjective] rude and not showing respect

impulse [noun: **impulses**] a sudden feeling you have that makes you do something
♦ **impulsive** [adjective] doing something suddenly without thinking about the possible results

impure [adjective] not pure
♦ **impurity** [noun: **impurities**] something in a substance that makes it dirty or not pure: *impurities in water*

in [preposition]
1 inside something: *He keeps his keys in the drawer.* • *The books are in my bedroom.*
2 at a place: *They live in Nottingham.*
3 at a particular time: *It's my birthday in May.*
4 after a period of time: *I'll be back in a few minutes.*
5 using a particular thing: *They were speaking in Japanese.* • *The letter was written in purple ink.*
6 wearing particular clothes: *Who's the woman in the red dress?*
[adverb]
1 at your home or place of work: *I'm sorry, Dad's not in. Can I take a message?*
2 at or into a place: *What time does your train get in?* • *Come in!*

in-, il-, im- or **ir-** [prefix]
1 if a word starts with **in-, il-, im-** or **ir-**, it can mean 'not'. For example, *inadequate* means 'not adequate', and *impossible* means 'not possible'

2 if a word starts with **in-**, it can also add the meaning 'in', 'into' or 'towards'. For example, if you move *inshore* you move towards the shore

inability [noun] the fact of not being able to do something

inaccuracy [noun: **inaccuracies**] something that is not exact or correct: *a newspaper full of inaccuracies*

inaccurate [adjective] not exact or correct: *inaccurate information*

inaction [noun] not doing anything
♦ **inactive** [adjective]
1 not doing anything
2 not working or not being used
♦ **inactivity** [noun] not doing anything

inadequacy [noun: **inadequacies**] not being good enough or not being enough: *his inadequacy as a golfer*
♦ **inadequate** [adjective] if something is inadequate, there is not enough of it or it is not good enough: *inadequate water supplies*

inadvertent [adjective] done by mistake or by accident
♦ **inadvertently** [adverb] by accident: *I had inadvertently left the door unlocked.*

inanimate [adjective] not alive: *inanimate objects like chairs and books*

inappropriate [adjective] not suitable for a particular situation or occasion: *inappropriate behaviour*
♦ **inappropriateness** [noun] being inappropriate

inattention [noun] lack of attention
♦ **inattentive** [adjective] not paying attention: *Tara is sometimes inattentive in class.*

inaugural [adjective] marking the beginning of something important: *an inaugural speech to open the new building*

inaugurate [verb: **inaugurates, inaugurating, inaugurated**] to mark the beginning or opening of something important with a ceremony
♦ **inauguration** [noun: **inaugurations**] a ceremony to mark the beginning of something important: *Clinton's inauguration as president*

incapable [adjective] not able to do something: *He seemed incapable of learning Italian.*

incapacity [noun]

1 lack of skill or ability
2 being ill or disabled: *unable to work through incapacity*

incense [noun] a substance that smells sweet when you burn it, often used in religious ceremonies

incentive [noun: **incentives**] something that encourages you to do something

incest [noun] sex between people who are too closely related to be able to get married

inch [noun: **inches**] a unit of measurement that is equal to about 2.5 centimetres

incident [noun: **incidents**] something that happens: *The incidents of the night before were still in my mind.*

♦ **incidental** [adjective] happening in connection with something else, but not intended or important

♦ **incidentally** [adverb] you say 'incidentally' when you are talking about a new subject or adding some more information: *Incidentally, did you know Jack was getting married?*

incinerate [verb: **incinerates, incinerating, incinerated**] to burn something until it becomes ashes

♦ **incinerator** [noun: **incinerators**] a container for burning waste

incisor [noun: **incisors**] one of the teeth at the front of your mouth that you use to cut food

incite [verb: **incites, inciting, incited**] to encourage people to cause trouble or fight

♦ **incitement** [noun] encouraging people to cause trouble or fight

inclination [noun: **inclinations**] a desire or tendency to do something: *Mia had no inclination to laugh now.*

incline [noun: **inclines**] a slope
[verb: **inclines, inclining, inclined**] if you are inclined to do something, you feel like doing it or have a tendency to do it: *I was inclined to tell him exactly what I thought. • He's inclined to make silly mistakes.*

include [verb: **includes, including, included**] a person or thing is included when they are part of a larger group or amount: *Did you remember to include Andy? • The price of the ticket includes dinner.*

♦ **including** [preposition] a word used to show that a person or thing is part of a larger group: *We went to all the museums, including the new one.*

♦ **inclusion** [noun] the act of including someone or something or the fact they are included

♦ **inclusive** [adjective] including everything: *From Tuesday to Thursday inclusive is three days. • a fully inclusive price*

income [noun: **incomes**] the amount of money you earn

income tax [noun] tax that you have to pay on the money you earn

incompatible [adjective]
1 if people are incompatible, they are so different that they cannot have a good relationship
2 too different to exist or be used together: *The software is incompatible with the operating system.*

incompetence [noun] being incompetent
♦ **incompetent** [adjective] not having the skill to do something, especially your job, very well

incomplete [adjective] not finished or not having all the parts it should: *an incomplete jigsaw puzzle*

incomprehensible [adjective] impossible to understand

inconsiderate [adjective] not thinking about other people's feelings

inconsistency [noun: **inconsistencies**]
1 inconsistency is behaving or doing something differently each time
2 an inconsistency is something that cannot be true if other information is true: *The report contained several inconsistencies.*

♦ **inconsistent** [adjective] doing something in a different way each time
♦ **inconsistently** [adverb] in an inconsistent way

inconsolable [adjective] so upset that no one can comfort you

inconspicuous [adjective] not easy to see

inconvenience [noun: **inconveniences**]
1 inconvenience is difficulty or problems: *We apologize for any inconvenience caused.*
2 an inconvenience is something that causes problems for you

[verb: **inconveniences, inconveniencing, inconvenienced**] to cause problems for someone

♦ **inconvenient** [adjective] causing problems: *Have I called at an inconvenient time?*

incorporate [verb: **incorporates, incorporating, incorporated**] to include something: *a television that incorporates all the latest features*

incorrect [adjective] wrong: *The answers to the sums are incorrect.*

♦ **incorrectly** [adverb] in a way that is wrong

increase [verb: **increases, increasing, increased**]

1 to increase is to become larger in size or amount: *Sales have increased over the last year.*

2 to increase something is to make it larger in size or amount: *Smoking increases the risk of lung cancer.*

[noun: **increases**] increasing or the amount by which something gets bigger: *There's been a big increase in the number of members.*

♦ **increasing** [adjective] becoming larger in size or amount: *An increasing number of people have a computer in their house.*

♦ **increasingly** [adverb] more or more: *I am becoming increasingly angry at him.*

incredible [adjective] difficult to believe: *an incredible story*

♦ **incredibly** [adverb] used for saying that something is difficult to believe: *Incredibly, no one was injured.*

incriminate [verb: **incriminates, incriminating, incriminated**] to show that someone has taken part in a crime: *All the evidence incriminated her.*

incubate [verb: **incubates, incubating, incubated**] to hatch eggs by sitting on them

♦ **incubation** [noun] incubating eggs

♦ **incubator** [noun: **incubators**]

1 a piece of hospital equipment that keeps a very small baby alive

2 a piece of equipment that keeps eggs warm until they hatch

incurable [adjective] an incurable illness cannot be cured

indecency [noun] behaviour that shocks and offends people

♦ **indecent** [adjective] shocking and offensive

♦ **indecently** [adverb] in an indecent way: *indecently dressed*

indeed [adverb] **indeed** is used to emphasize what you have just said: *He was driving very fast indeed.*

indefinite [adjective]

1 not certain: *The competition will take place on an indefinite date.*

2 not having a fixed limit: *an indefinite amount of time*

indefinite article [noun: **indefinite articles**] the name used in grammar for the words *a* and *an*

ⓘ There are two kinds of article in English grammar: **a** or **an** is the *indefinite article* and **the** is the *definite article*.

---

indefinitely [adverb] for a period of time with no fixed limits: *The match was postponed indefinitely.*

indelible [adjective] impossible to remove or forget: *indelible ink*

♦ **indelibly** [adverb] in a way that you can't forget or remove: *What happened that day is indelibly marked in my memory.*

indent [verb: **indents, indenting, indented**] to start a line of writing further from the edge of the page than other lines

♦ **indentation** [noun: **indentations**] a hollow or dent

independence [noun] being independent

independent [adjective]

1 an independent country is not controlled by another country

2 an independent person does not rely on other people for help and support

indestructible [adjective] impossible to destroy

index [noun: **indexes** or **indices**] a list in a book that tells you what page you can find information on

index finger [noun: **index fingers**] the finger that is next to your thumb

Indian summer [noun: **Indian summers**] a period of warm weather in the autumn

li

indicate [verb: **indicates, indicating, indicated**] to show something: *an arrow indicating where to go*

♦ **indication** [noun: **indications**] a sign: *Did he give you any indication when it would be finished?*

♦ **indicative** [adjective] if something is indicative of something else, it shows that it is likely to be true: *The footprints are indicative of life on the planet.*

♦ **indicator** [noun: **indicators**]
1 a flashing light on a car that shows which way the car is going to turn
2 something that is a sign of something else

indifference [noun] a lack of interest in something

♦ **indifferent** [adjective]
1 not good but not bad either: *The restaurant was nice but the food was indifferent.*
2 if you are indifferent to something, you show no interest in it or do not have any opinions on it

indigestion [noun] an uncomfortable feeling in your stomach after you have eaten

indignant [adjective] angry because you think you have been treated unfairly: *The policeman stopped his indignant protests and led him off.*

♦ **indignantly** [adverb] in an indignant way
♦ **indignation** [noun] being indignant

indirect [adjective]
1 not leading straight to a place: *an indirect route*
2 not directly caused by something or related to something: *an indirect result of his actions*
♦ **indirectly** [adverb] in an indirect way

indirect speech [noun] reporting what someone said without repeating their actual words. Look up and compare **direct speech**

indiscreet [adjective] careless in what you say or do, especially talking about something that should be secret

indispensable [adjective] someone or something that is indispensable is so useful that you cannot manage without them

indistinct [adjective] not easy to see, hear or remember

individual [adjective]
1 for one person only: *an individual slice of cake*

2 considered separately from other things: *Put a price ticket on each individual item.*
[noun: **individuals**] one person rather than a group

♦ **individuality** [noun] a quality that makes someone or something different from others

♦ **individually** [adverb] separately from other things: *Wrap each glass individually.*

indoor [adjective] inside a building: *an indoor swimming pool*

♦ **indoors** [adverb] inside a building: *Come indoors if it starts to rain.*

induction course [noun: **induction courses**] a training course for a new employee of a company to show them how the company operates

indulge [verb: **indulges, indulging, indulged**]
1 to indulge someone is to let them have or do what they want, especially something that is bad for them
2 to **indulge in** something is to allow yourself to do or have it: *We've all indulged in too much food.*

♦ **indulgence** [noun] indulging yourself or someone else

♦ **indulgent** [adjective] letting someone do what they want even if it is not good for them

industrial [adjective] relating to industry and factories: *an industrial area of town*

♦ **industrialize** or **industrialise** [verb: **industrializes, industrializing, industrialized**] to develop a lot of industry in a place

industrious [adjective] working very hard: *an industrious pupil*

industry [noun: **industries**]
1 industry is the production of goods, especially in a factory
2 an industry is a particular type of trade or production: *the steel industry*

inedible [adjective] not fit to be eaten

ineffective [adjective] not achieving anything useful

inefficiency [noun: **inefficiencies**] being inefficient, or something that is inefficient

inefficient [adjective] not working well and wasting time or money: *an inefficient use of our time*

♦ **inefficiently** [adverb] in an inefficient way

ineligible [adjective] not allowed to have or do something because of a rule or law: *You are ineligible to vote until you are 18.*

inept [adjective] having or showing no skill: *an inept performance by the actors*

inequality [noun: **inequalities**] a lack of equality

inevitable [adjective] certain to happen: *It is inevitable that it will rain on sports day.*

inexcusable [adjective] too bad to be excused

inexpensive [adjective] cheap in price

inexperience [noun] a lack of experience or knowledge

♦ **inexperienced** [adjective] not having much experience or knowledge

inexplicable [adjective] impossible to explain: *an inexplicable wish to go out in the rain*

infamous [adjective] well-known for something bad: *Dick Turpin was an infamous highwayman.*

♦ **infamy** [noun] being well-known for something bad

infancy [noun] the time when someone is a baby or very young child

♦ **infant** [noun: **infants**] a baby or very young child

♦ **infantile** [adjective]
1 to do with babies or very young children
2 infantile behaviour is very silly

infantry [noun] soldiers who fight on foot

infatuated [adjective] loving someone too much in a way that is silly and unreasonable: *She's completely infatuated with him.*

infect [verb: **infects, infecting, infected**]
1 to give someone an illness: *I am afraid I may infect you with my cold.*
2 if something infects a cut or wound, it fills it with germs that cause disease: *The wound was newly infected.*

♦ **infection** [noun: **infections**]
1 infection is becoming infected
2 an infection is an illness: *an ear infection*

♦ **infectious** [adjective]
1 an infectious illness can be spread from person to person

2 an infectious feeling or action is one that other people can't help doing: *infectious laughter*

infer [verb: **infers, inferring, inferred**] to form an opinion from information you already know

inferior [adjective] not as good as someone or something else: *Amy often felt inferior to the other women in the office.*

♦ **inferiority** [noun] being inferior to someone or something else

inferno [noun: **infernos**] a large and dangerous fire

infested [adjective] full of insects or other pests: *The whole house was infested with mice.*

infidelity [noun: **infidelities**] not being faithful to someone

infinite [adjective] without any limits or end: *The universe is infinite.*

♦ **infinitely** [adverb] very much: *This computer is infinitely better than the last one.*
➡ **infinity**

infinitive [noun: **infinitives**] the basic form of a verb that can be used to make all the other forms, for example *to play* or *to eat*

infinity [noun] space or time that has no end or limit

infirm [adjective] if someone is infirm, they are weak, especially because they are old or ill

♦ **infirmary** [noun: **infirmaries**] a hospital

♦ **infirmity** [noun: **infirmities**] a weakness

inflamed [adjective] red and swollen because of an infection

inflammable [adjective] easy to set on fire: *Paper is highly inflammable.*

inflammation [noun] swelling, pain and redness in part of your body

inflate [verb: **inflates, inflating, inflated**] to fill something with air: *The tyres need to be inflated.*

♦ **inflation** [noun]
1 filling something with air
2 when prices and wages increase

inflect [verb: **inflects, inflecting, inflected**]
1 when a word inflects, it changes its ending
2 to change the tone of your voice

♦ **inflection** [noun: **inflections**]
1 a change in the form of a word to show its tense or number

Ii

2 a word that has been changed in this way. For example, *finds, finding* and *found* are inflections of the verb *find*

3 changing the tone of your voice

inflexible [adjective]

1 stiff and unable to bend: *inflexible plastic*

2 impossible or unwilling to change

inflict [verb: **inflicts, inflicting, inflicted**] to make someone suffer something unpleasant or painful: *The home team inflicted a heavy defeat on the visitors.*

influence [noun: **influences**]

1 influence is the power to affect other people or things: *a teacher who has a lot of influence on his pupils*

2 an influence is someone or something that has an effect on other people or things: *Ann is a good influence on you.*

[verb: **influences, influencing, influenced**] to have an effect on someone or something: *His advice influenced my decision.*

♦ **influential** [adjective] having a lot of influence

influenza [noun] a formal word for **flu**

influx [noun: **influxes**] the arrival of a lot of people or things

info [noun] an informal short form of the word **information**

inform [verb: **informs, informing, informed**] to tell someone about something: *I'll inform you what my decision is.*

➡ **information, informative, informer**

informal [adjective]

1 relaxed and friendly, or suitable for relaxed occasions

2 informal language and words might be used when you are speaking to your friends, but they are not as suitable for writing

information [noun] knowledge, facts or details: *Have you got any information on things to do in the area?*

information technology [noun] the study or use of computers to store or process information

ⓘ You will often see the abbreviation of information technology, which is **IT**.

informative [adjective] giving you a lot of useful information: *an informative book*

informer [noun: **informers**] someone who gives information to the police in return for money

infra-red [adjective] infra-red light cannot be seen, but gives out heat

infrequent [adjective] not happening very often

♦ **infrequently** [adverb] not often

infuriate [verb: **infuriates, infuriating, infuriated**] to make someone very angry

♦ **infuriated** [adjective] extremely angry

♦ **infuriating** [adjective] making you extremely angry

ingenious [adjective] clever and having new ideas: *an ingenious idea* • *Oliver's very ingenious.*

♦ **ingenuity** [noun] being ingenious

ingot [noun: **ingots**] a block of metal, especially gold or silver

ingratitude [noun] being ungrateful

ingredient [noun: **ingredients**] one of the things you use to make a particular food

ingrown or **ingrowing** [adjective] an ingrown toe nail is growing into your skin

inhabit [verb: **inhabits, inhabiting, inhabited**] to live in a particular place: *the world around us and the creatures that inhabit it*

♦ **inhabitant** [noun: **inhabitants**] someone who lives in a place: *There are differences between the inhabitants of the two islands.*

♦ **inhabited** [adjective] with people living there: *A light twinkled in one of the windows, so I knew the place was inhabited.*

inhale [verb: **inhales, inhaling, inhaled**] to breathe air into your lungs through your nose and mouth. Look up and compare **exhale**

♦ **inhaler** [noun: **inhalers**] a piece of equipment for breathing in medicine, for example for asthma

inherit [verb: **inherits, inheriting, inherited**]

1 to get money or other things from someone who has died: *Imogen inherited the house from her father.*

2 to get a particular characteristic from one of your parents: *I inherited my fair hair from my mother.*

♦ **inheritance** [noun: **inheritances**] money

li

or things that you get from someone who has died

inhibit [verb: **inhibits, inhibiting, inhibited**] to prevent someone or something from doing something: *My shyness inhibits me from speaking in public.*
  ♦ **inhibited** [adjective] not feeling relaxed or confident enough to do or say what you want
  ♦ **inhibition** [noun: **inhibitions**] a feeling of worry or shyness that stops you doing or saying what you want

inhuman [adjective] extremely cruel
  ♦ **inhumanity** [noun] cruel behaviour

initial [adjective] at the beginning: *initial difficulties*
[noun: **initials**] the first letter of a word, especially someone's name
  ♦ **initially** [adverb] at first: *Initially, things were very difficult.*

initiate [verb: **initiates, initiating, initiated**]
1 to start something: *Dawn initiated a scheme to help old people with their shopping.*
2 to accept someone into a group or organization with a secret or special ceremony
  ♦ **initiation** [noun: **initiations**]
  1 initiation is initiating something or someone
  2 an initiation is a special ceremony to make someone a member of a group
  ♦ **initiative** [noun: **initiatives**]
  1 initiative is the ability to do something without waiting for someone else to tell you what to do
  2 an initiative is a new plan or process

inject [verb: **injects, injecting, injected**]
1 to put a substance into someone's body using a needle
2 to improve something by adding a particular quality to it: *Leah tried to inject some enthusiasm into her voice.*
  ♦ **injection** [noun: **injections**] putting a substance into someone's body using a needle

injure [verb: **injures, injuring, injured**] to hurt someone or something: *Matt injured his knee in a skiing accident.*
  ♦ **injured** [adjective] hurt: *Fiona was badly injured in a road accident.*
  ♦ **injury** [noun: **injuries**] a wound or damage to part of your body: *head injuries*

injustice [noun: **injustices**]
1 injustice is when people are treated unfairly
2 an injustice is an action that is unfair

ink [noun: **inks**] a black or coloured liquid used for writing or printing

inland [adjective] not by the sea
[adverb] in a direction away from the sea

Inland Revenue [noun] in Britain, the government organization that is responsible for collecting taxes

-in-law [suffix] if **-in-law** comes at the end of a word, it is a noun that refers to a person who is a relative of your husband or wife. For example, your *mother-in-law* is your husband's or wife's mother

in-laws [plural noun] the relatives of your husband or wife

inlet [noun: **inlets**] a small area of water that comes into the land

inmate [noun: **inmates**] someone who is being kept in a prison

inn [noun: **inns**] a small hotel in the country

innards [plural noun] the parts inside a person, animal or machine

inner [adjective]
1 on the inside or close to the centre of something: *She kept her purse in the inner pocket of her bag.*
2 inner feelings are ones that you keep secret

innermost [adjective] your innermost thoughts and feelings are ones that you keep secret

innings [noun] one team's turn at batting in cricket

innocence [noun]
1 when someone is not guilty of a crime: *The witnesses' stories proved his innocence.*
2 when someone does not have much experience of life and how cruel people can be: *The bully took advantage of Billy's innocence.*
  ♦ **innocent** [adjective]
  1 not guilty of a crime
  2 not having much experience of life and how cruel people can be
  ♦ **innocently** [adverb] in an innocent way: *I acted quite innocently in front of my mother.*

inoculate [verb: **inoculates, inoculating, inoculated**] to inject someone with a

Ii

substance to stop them getting a disease: *Babies are inoculated against measles.*

♦ **inoculation** [noun: **inoculations**] inoculating someone

inoffensive [adjective] not likely to offend or upset anyone

in-patient [noun: **in-patients**] someone who is staying in a hospital for treatment

input [noun]

1 energy or ideas that you put into something: *I had very little input in the project.*

2 information that is put into a computer

inquest [noun: **inquests**] a legal process to find out how someone died

inquire or **enquire** [verb: **inquires, inquiring, inquired** or **enquires, enquiring, enquired**] to ask: *He inquired how to get to the library.*

♦ **inquiry** or **enquiry** [noun: **inquiries** or **enquiries**]

1 a question you ask in order to get information

2 an official process to find out why something happened: *There was an inquiry into the children's deaths.*

inquisitive [adjective] interested in a lot of things and wanting to know more: *an inquisitive child*

♦ **inquisitively** [adverb] in an inquisitive way

insane [adjective]

1 if someone is insane, they are out of their mind or mad

2 if an action is insane, it is extremely foolish: *It is insane to run across the road without looking.*

♦ **insanity** [noun] being mad

inscribe [verb: **inscribes, inscribing, inscribed**] to cut or write words on the surface of something

♦ **inscription** [noun: **inscriptions**] writing on a piece of stone or in the front of a book: *There was an inscription on the gravestone.*

insect [noun: **insects**] a very small creature with six legs, such as an ant or wasp

insecure [adjective]

1 not safe or firm: *The ladder felt insecure.*

2 not feeling confident about your abilities or relationships

♦ **insecurity** [noun] being insecure

insensitive [adjective]

1 not noticing other people's feelings

2 not affected by physical things such as pain or cold: *He seemed to be insensitive to the noise around him.*

♦ **insensitively** [adverb] in an insensitive way

♦ **insensitivity** [noun] being insensitive

inseparable [adjective] not able to be separated or kept apart: *At school we were inseparable.*

insert [verb: **inserts, inserting, inserted**] to put something into something else: *He inserted some coins into the meter.* • *You need to insert a few more examples.*

inside [preposition and adverb] in or into something: *She put the book inside her bag.* • *Come inside, it's raining.* • *The children are playing inside.*

[adjective] in or facing the middle of something rather than outside: *the inside walls of the house*

[noun: **insides**] the inside of something is the part that is in the middle and not on the outside: *The inside of his jacket was torn.*

insight [noun: **insights**]

1 insight is the ability to understand something clearly

2 an insight is a chance to understand or learn more about something: *The book offers an insight into the mind of a killer.*

insignificant [adjective] not at all important

insincere [adjective] pretending to have a feeling that you do not really have: *insincere laughter*

♦ **insincerely** [adverb] in an insincere way

♦ **insincerity** [noun] being insincere

insist [verb: **insists, insisting, insisted**]

1 to say that something must happen or be done: *Fay insisted on paying.*

2 to keep saying in a firm way that you think something is true: *Mark insists that he hasn't done anything wrong.*

♦ **insistent** [adjective] saying that something must happen or be done: *She was insistent that we visit her.*

insolence [noun] behaviour that shows no respect or politeness

♦ **insolent** [adjective] rude and impolite

insoluble [adjective]

1 an insoluble substance cannot dissolve

2 impossible to solve: *an insoluble problem*

insomnia [noun] not being able to sleep

inspect [verb: **inspects, inspecting, inspected**]

1 to look very carefully at someone or something: *He inspected our documents closely.*

2 to officially visit somewhere to make sure that it is being run properly: *The school is to be inspected next week.*

◆ **inspection** [noun: **inspections**]

1 inspection is looking very carefully at someone or something

2 an inspection is an examination or a visit by an inspector to check something

◆ **inspector** [noun: **inspectors**]

1 someone whose job is to inspect a place such as a school or restaurant to make sure it is run properly

2 a rank of police officer above a sergeant

inspiration [noun: **inspirations**] someone or something that encourages you and gives you new ideas

◆ **inspirational** [adjective] encouraging someone and giving them new ideas: *an inspirational teacher*

inspire [verb: **inspires, inspiring, inspired**] to encourage someone by giving them confidence and new ideas: *My mother inspired me to write stories.*

◆ **inspired** [adjective] showing a lot of talent and special qualities: *an inspired performance*

install or **instal** [verb: **installs** or **instals, installing, installed**]

1 to put a piece of equipment in place and make it ready to use: *We're installing a new computer system.*

2 to install a computer program is to put it on to a computer to be used: *I installed the software and began the translation.*

3 to install someone is to put them in an important job or position

◆ **installation** [noun] installing someone or something

◆ **instalment** [noun: **instalments**]

1 one of a number of payments that you make to pay for something

2 one part of a long story that is told in a magazine or on television

instance [noun: **instances**]

1 an example of something: *an instance of John's quick thinking*

2 **for instance** means for example: *Some birds, penguins for instance, cannot fly at all.*

instant [adjective]

1 happening at once: *The film was an instant success.*

2 able to be prepared very quickly: *instant coffee*

◆ **instantaneous** [adjective] done or happening immediately or very quickly

◆ **instantly** [adverb] immediately

instead [adverb] in place of someone or something else: *Bob was ill so Joe went instead.* • *You could use a pencil instead of a pen.*

instep [noun: **insteps**] the bottom of your foot where it curves upwards

instinct [noun: **instincts**] a natural feeling or knowledge that you have without being taught

◆ **instinctive** [adjective] happening because of instinct: *Parents have an instinctive urge to protect their children.*

◆ **instinctively** [adverb] in an instinctive way: *I knew instinctively that something was wrong.*

institute [noun: **institutes**] an organization of people who want to study something, or the building they use

institution [noun: **institutions**] a large organization: *banks and other financial institutions*

instruct [verb: **instructs, instructing, instructed**]

1 to tell someone what to do

2 to teach someone

◆ **instruction** [noun: **instructions**] a piece of information that tells you how to do something: *Read the instructions before you begin.*

◆ **instructive** [adjective] providing a lot of useful information

instrument [noun: **instruments**]

1 something used for making music

2 a tool for doing something

◆ **instrumental** [adjective]

1 instrumental music is written for musical

Ii

instruments rather than singers

2 helpful in making something happen: *His wife was instrumental in his success.*

insufficiency [noun] when there is not enough of something

♦ **insufficient** [adjective] not enough: *insufficient food supplies*

insulate [verb: **insulates, insulating, insulated**] to cover something with a material that does not let electricity, heat or frost through

♦ **insulation** [noun] insulating something, or the material used to do this

insulin [noun] a hormone that controls the amount of sugar in your blood

insult [verb: **insults, insulting, insulted**] to insult someone is to say something rude to them [noun: **insults**] a rude remark

♦ **insulting** [adjective] very rude to someone

ⓘ The verb, in-**sult**, is said with the stress at the end.
The noun, **in**-sult, is said with the stress at the beginning.

insurance [noun] an arrangement in which you pay a company money each year and they pay the costs if something you own is damaged or stolen: *car insurance*

LANGUAGE FOR LIFE

insurance

There are different types of insurance.

• If you have **third-party insurance** for your car, the insurance company will pay to repair damage or injury to another person, but not to you, if you have an accident.

• If you have **comprehensive insurance** for your car, the insurance company will pay to repair all types of damage or injury if you have an accident, and will replace the car if it is destroyed or stolen.

• If you have **buildings insurance**, the insurance company will pay to repair damage to your home if there is an accident, but it will not pay if you have to repair or replace the things inside it.

• If you have **contents insurance**, the insurance company will pay to repair or replace the things inside your home if there is an accident or a burglary.

insure [verb: **insures, insuring, insured**] to pay money to a company who will pay the costs if you are injured or if things you own are damaged or stolen

ⓘ Do not confuse **insure** with **ensure**, which means 'to make sure'.

intact [adjective] not broken or damaged

intake [noun: **intakes**] the amount of people or things taken in: *this year's intake of students*

integral [adjective] forming an essential part of something: *Sport is an integral part of my life.*

integrate [verb: **integrates, integrating, integrated**]

1 to combine two or more things together to make a system

2 to mix with other groups of people

♦ **integration** [noun] integrating people or things

integrity [noun] being honest and having high moral standards

intellect [noun: **intellects**] your ability to think about things and understand them

♦ **intellectual** [adjective] relating to your intellect
[noun: **intellectuals**] someone who is intelligent and likes thinking about serious issues

intelligence [noun]

1 your ability to learn and understand things

2 secret information about other countries

♦ **intelligent** [adjective] clever and able to understand things quickly

intend [verb: **intends, intending, intended**] to plan to do something: *I intend to visit Will when I'm in Seattle.*
➡ **intent**

intense [adjective] very great: *intense heat*

♦ **intensify** [verb: **intensifies, intensifying, intensified**]

1 to intensify is to increase and become greater: *The darkness intensified.*

2 to intensify something is to make it increase and become greater: *I intensified my effort to finish on time.*

♦ **intensity** [noun] the strength of something, such as a feeling or colour

♦ **intensive** [adjective] involving a lot of effort or activity

intensive care [noun] a part of a hospital that looks after patients who need full-time care

intent [adjective]
1 if you are intent on doing something, you are determined to do it
2 doing something with a lot of attention and concentration: *an intent stare*
♦ **intention** [noun: **intentions**] the thing you plan to do: *It is my intention to finish before 5 o'clock.*
♦ **intentional** [adjective] done deliberately
♦ **intentionally** [adverb] deliberately: *You tripped me up intentionally!*
♦ **intently** [adverb] with a lot of attention and concentration

inter- [prefix] if a word starts with **inter-**, it means 'between' or 'among' a group of people or things. For example, *international* means 'among a number of nations'

interact [verb: **interacts, interacting, interacted**]
1 to talk to other people and do things with them
2 if two things interact, they have an effect on each other
♦ **interactive** [adjective] involving communication between two people or things, for example a person and a computer: *interactive television*

intercept [verb: **intercepts, intercepting, intercepted**] to stop something that is going from one place to another: *The police intercepted the parcel before it arrived at its destination.*

intercom [noun: **intercoms**] a system that allows you to talk to people who are in a different part of a building

intercourse [noun] another word for **sexual intercourse**

interest [noun: **interests**]
1 interest is a feeling that makes you think something is good and want to find out more about it: *I have no interest in cricket.*
2 an interest is something that you enjoy doing: *My main interests are sport and reading.*
3 interest is extra money that you have to pay back when you have borrowed money, or that a bank pays you for having your money

[verb: **interests, interesting, interested**] if something interests you, you think it is good and want to find out more about it
♦ **interested** [adjective] having or showing interest: *Dan is very interested in old cars.*
♦ **interesting** [adjective] making you feel interested: *an interesting story*

interface [noun: **interfaces**] something that helps a computer program work with another program

interfere [verb: **interferes, interfering, interfered**]
1 to get involved in a situation where you are not wanted: *Why do you always have to interfere?*
2 if something **interferes with** something, it prevents it from happening: *His visit interfered with my plans to go out.*
♦ **interference** [noun] interfering with something

interior [noun: **interiors**] the interior of something is the inside of it: *the interior of a house*
[adjective] on the inside of something: *an interior wall*

interjection [part of speech: **interjections**] a word or phrase used to express a strong feeling like surprise, shock or anger. For example, *Oh!* and *Hooray!* are interjections

interlude [noun: **interludes**] a short pause or interval

intermediate [adjective] if something is intermediate, it is or takes place between two other stages or levels: *an intermediate English course*

intermission [noun: **intermissions**] a short break in the middle of a play or concert

intermittent [adjective] starting and stopping again and again: *intermittent rain showers*

internal [adjective]
1 on the inside of something, especially your body: *internal injuries*
2 within an organization or country: *an internal promotion*

international [adjective] for or involving several countries: *an international sports competition*

Internet [noun] the Internet is a computer

Ii

network that allows people around the world to share information

interpret [verb: **interprets, interpreting, interpreted**]

1 to translate what someone is saying from one language to another

2 to think that something has a particular meaning: *I interpreted his silence as shyness.*

♦ **interpretation** [noun: **interpretations**] interpreting or a way of interpreting something: *What is your interpretation of the poem?*

♦ **interpreter** [noun: **interpreters**] someone whose job is to translate what someone says into another language

interrogate [verb: **interrogates, interrogating, interrogated**] to ask someone a lot of questions in order to get information

♦ **interrogation** [noun] interrogating someone

♦ **interrogator** [noun: **interrogators**] someone who is interrogating another person

interrupt [verb: **interrupts, interrupting, interrupted**]

1 to stop someone when they are in the middle of saying or doing something: *I'm sorry to interrupt, but what time do we have to leave?*

2 to stop a process or activity for a short time: *He interrupted the meeting to make a phone call.*

♦ **interruption** [noun: **interruptions**] something that stops you doing or saying something: *I can't work with all these interruptions.*

intersect [verb: **intersects, intersecting, intersected**] if lines or roads intersect, they cross each other

♦ **intersection** [noun: **intersections**] a place where lines or roads cross each other

interval [noun: **intervals**]

1 a short break in the middle of something such as a play or concert

2 a period of time between two things: *an interval of two weeks*

intervene [verb: **intervenes, intervening, intervened**] to do something to try to stop an argument or fight between other people or countries

♦ **intervention** [noun] intervening in something: *military intervention*

interview [noun: **interviews**]

1 a meeting where someone asks you questions to see if you are suitable for a job or a place on a course

2 a meeting where someone asks a famous person questions

[verb: **interviews, interviewing, interviewed**] to ask someone questions at an interview

♦ **interviewer** [noun: **interviewers**] the person who asks the questions at an interview

intestines [plural noun] the long tubes that take food from your stomach out of your body

intimate [adjective]

1 having a very close relationship with someone: *intimate friends*

2 relating to private and personal things: *intimate details*

3 an intimate knowledge of something is a very good and detailed knowledge

intimidate [verb: **intimidates, intimidating, intimidated**] to frighten someone, especially by threatening them

♦ **intimidating** [adjective] making you feel worried and less confident: *The test paper was intimidating.*

♦ **intimidation** [noun] intimidating someone

into [preposition]

1 to the inside of something: *We went into the house.*

2 used for saying how something changes: *She cut the pizza into four pieces.* • *The caterpillar changed into a butterfly.*

3 used when talking about dividing one number by another: *2 into 4 goes twice.*

intolerance [noun] being intolerant

♦ **intolerant** [adjective] not willing to accept behaviour and ideas that are different from your own

intonation [noun] the way that your voice rises and falls when you speak

intricate [adjective] containing a lot of small parts or details: *an intricate pattern*

intrigue [verb: **intrigues, intriguing, intrigued**] to make someone feel very interested or curious

[noun: **intrigues**]

1 an intrigue is a secret plan

2 intrigue is making secret plans

◆ **intriguing** [adjective] very interesting and unusual

introduce [verb: **introduces, introducing, introduced**]
1 if you introduce two people who do not know each other, you tell each of them the other person's name
2 to make something start to happen or be used: *The new law was introduced in 1999.*

◆ **introduction** [noun: **introductions**]
1 starting to use something new: *the introduction of identity cards*
2 introducing two people to each other for the first time
3 an introduction is a piece of writing at the front of a book that tells you what the book is about

◆ **introductory** [adjective] coming at the beginning

introvert or **intravert** [noun: **introverts** or **intraverts**] someone who has a quiet and thoughtful personality. Look up and compare **extrovert**

intrude [verb: **intrudes, intruding, intruded**]
1 to become involved in a situation where you are not wanted
2 to enter a place where you should not be

◆ **intruder** [noun: **intruders**] someone who enters a place where they should not be

◆ **intrusion** [noun: **intrusions**]
1 intrusion is getting involved in something where you are not wanted or entering a place where you should not be
2 an intrusion is someone or something that is not wanted in a situation

◆ **intrusive** [adjective] affecting or interrupting you in a way you do not want: *intrusive questions*

intuition [noun: **intuitions**]
1 intuition is an ability to understand or know something without thinking or being told about it
2 an intuition is an idea that something is true based on your feelings rather than facts

Inuit [noun] the Inuit are a race of people who live in Arctic areas of Canada, Greenland and Alaska

invade [verb: **invades, invading, invaded**]
to enter a country with an army to attack it or take it over

◆ **invader** [noun: **invaders**] someone who invades another country
➡ **invasion**

invalid [1] [adjective] not able to be used: *an invalid bus pass* • *invalid reasons for being late*

invalid [2] [noun: **invalids**] someone who is ill or unable to look after themselves

ⓘ The adjective **invalid** is pronounced in-**val**-id, with the stress on *val*.
The noun **invalid** is pronounced **in**-va-lid, with the stress on *in*.

invaluable [adjective] extremely useful: *an invaluable piece of advice*

invariably [adverb] always: *Dean is invariably late for everything.*

invasion [noun: **invasions**] an attack on a country by an army entering it

invent [verb: **invents, inventing, invented**]
1 to design or make something that no one else has ever made: *Thomas Edison invented the electric light bulb.*
2 to think of a story or excuse that is not true

◆ **invention** [noun: **inventions**]
1 invention is inventing something: *the invention of the wheel*
2 an invention is something someone has invented: *The Internet is a wonderful invention.*

◆ **inventive** [adjective] good at thinking of new and interesting ideas

◆ **inventor** [noun: **inventors**] someone who has invented something new

inverse [noun: **inverses**] the inverse of something is its opposite
[adjective] opposite

◆ **inversely** [adverb] in the opposite way

invert [verb: **inverts, inverting, inverted**] to turn something upside down
➡ **inverted**

invertebrate [noun: **invertebrates**] an animal that does not have a backbone, for example an insect or worm

inverted [adjective] turned upside down

inverted commas [plural noun] the symbols ' ' or " ", used in writing to show what someone says. They are sometimes called **quotation marks**

Ii

invest [verb: **invests, investing, invested**] to put money in a bank or business in order to make more money: *I invested my money in property.*
⟶ **investment, investor**

investigate [verb: **investigates, investigating, investigated**] to try to find out the truth about something: *Police are investigating the crime.*

♦ **investigation** [noun: **investigations**] a search for information about something: *a police investigation into the murder*

♦ **investigator** [noun: **investigators**] someone who is investigating something

investment [noun: **investments**]
1 investment is investing money
2 an investment is something you buy because you think it will be useful or make a profit for you: *A warm coat is a good investment.*

investor [noun: **investors**] someone who invests money in something

invigorating [adjective] making you feel full of energy: *an invigorating walk along the cliffs*

invincible [adjective] impossible to defeat

invisibility [noun] being impossible to see

invisible [adjective] impossible to see

invitation [noun: **invitations**] a written or spoken request asking you to do something or go somewhere: *I've had an invitation to Helen's party.*

invite [verb: **invites, inviting, invited**] to ask someone if they would like to do something or go somewhere: *Clare's invited me out for a drink.*

♦ **inviting** [adjective] very attractive and making you want to do something

invoice [noun: **invoices**] a piece of paper sent with things you have bought, to tell you how much you must pay
[verb: **invoices, invoicing, invoiced**] to send someone an invoice

involuntary [adjective] happening without your control: *Sneezing is an involuntary action.*

involve [verb: **involves, involving, involved**]
1 to have something as a necessary part: *The job will involve a lot of travelling.*
2 if you are involved in something, you take

part in it: *I don't want to get involved in your argument.*

♦ **involvement** [noun] being involved in something

inward [adjective]
1 inside or towards the inside of something
2 inward feelings are ones in your mind that you do not tell other people about

♦ **inwardly** [adverb] in your own mind but not told or shown to other people: *Inwardly, she felt very scared.*

♦ **inwards** [adverb] towards the inside of something: *The road curved inwards.*

ion [noun: **ions**] an atom with an electrical charge

IOU [abbreviation] short for **I owe you**. An IOU is a note that you sign to say that you owe someone money

IQ [abbreviation] short for **intelligence quotient**. Someone's IQ is a measure of how intelligent they are

ir- [prefix] look at the entry for **in-**

irate [adjective] extremely angry

iris [noun: **irises**]
1 the coloured part of your eye
2 a tall flower

iron [noun: **irons**]
1 a hard metal used for making tools
2 a piece of electrical equipment that you use for pressing the creases out of clothes
[verb: **irons, ironing, ironed**] to make clothes smooth using an iron

ironic [adjective]
1 an ironic situation is funny in a strange way: *It's ironic that we're moving to Edinburgh just as they're leaving it.*
2 saying the opposite of what you really mean: *I think he was being ironic when he said this was the happiest day of his life.*

♦ **ironically** [adverb] in a way that is ironic

ironing-board [noun: **ironing-boards**] a flat, padded board that you iron clothes on

ironmonger [noun: **ironmongers**]
1 someone whose job is to sell items such as tools and garden equipment
2 an ironmonger's is a shop selling items such as tools and garden equipment

irony [noun: **ironies**]
1 irony is using words that are the opposite of

Ii

what you really mean in order to be funny

2 an irony is a situation that is strange or funny
→ **ironic**

irregular [adjective]

1 having a shape or pattern that is not even or smooth: *an irregular pulse*

2 happening at different times so there is no pattern: *an irregular train service*

3 not obeying the usual rules: *irregular verbs*

◆ **irregularity** [noun: **irregularities**]

1 irregularity is being irregular

2 an irregularity is something that breaks a rule: *irregularities in John's behaviour*

◆ **irregularly** [adverb] in an irregular way

irrelevance [noun: **irrelevances**]

1 irrelevance is when something is not important in a situation

2 an irrelevance is someone or something that is not important in a situation: *His recent injury seemed an irrelevance when he won the race.*

◆ **irrelevant** [adjective] not important in a situation: *Your comments are irrelevant to this discussion.*

irreplaceable [adjective] too special or valuable to be replaced

irresistible [adjective] too strong or attractive to resist: *The chocolate cake looked irresistible.*

irresponsible [adjective] behaving in a silly way without thinking about the bad things that might happen as a result: *It was irresponsible to leave a six-year-old at home alone.*

◆ **irresponsibly** [adverb] in an irresponsible way

irrigate [verb: **irrigates, irrigating, irrigated**] to supply land or crops with water

◆ **irrigation** [noun] supplying land or crops with water

irritable [adjective] becoming annoyed very easily: *Jamal is irritable if he does not get enough sleep.*

◆ **irritably** [adverb] in an irritable way

irritate [verb: **irritates, irritating, irritated**]

1 to make someone feel annoyed

2 to make something such as your skin or eyes sore or itchy: *Some sun creams can irritate your skin.*

◆ **irritation** [noun: **irritations**]

1 irritation is feeling annoyed about something

2 an irritation is something that annoys you: *His constant complaints are an irritation.*

3 a sore feeling on your skin or in your eyes

is [verb]

1 the form of the verb **be** in the present tense that you use with **he, she** or **it**: *He is a fool.* • *It is too hot.*

2 is is also used as a helping verb along with a main verb: *Lisa's mother is going away for a month.*

-ise [suffix] look at the entry for **-ize**

-ish [suffix] if **-ish** comes at the end of a word, it is an adjective that means 'slightly'. For example, *greenish* means 'slightly green'

Islam [noun] the Muslim religion that was started by Mohammed

◆ **Islamic** [adjective] relating to the religion of Islam

island [noun: **islands**] an area of land surrounded by sea

isle [noun: **isles**] an island. **Isle** is used in poems or in the names of islands: *the Isles of Scilly*

-ism [suffix] if **-ism** comes at the end of a word, it is a noun that refers to a belief, principle or quality. For example, *Buddhism* is the religion started by Buddha

isn't [short form] a short way to say and write **is not**: *It isn't raining.*

isolate [verb: **isolates, isolating, isolated**] to separate or keep someone or something separate from others: *The infected animals were isolated in a field.*

◆ **isolated** [adjective]

1 feeling alone and unable to meet other people

2 a long way from anywhere else: *an isolated farmhouse*

3 happening only once and not related to other events: *This theft was an isolated incident.*

◆ **isolation** [noun] being isolated

issue [noun: **issues**]

1 a subject that people discuss: *a discussion on the issue of abortion*

2 a newspaper or magazine that is one of a number printed and sold at the same time: *Have you seen this week's issue of the magazine?*

Ii

[verb: **issues, issuing, issued**] to supply someone with something: *We were all issued with pens.*

-ist [suffix] if **-ist** comes at the end of a word, it is a noun that refers to someone who has a particular belief. For example, a *Buddhist* believes in the religion of Buddhism

IT [abbreviation] short for **information technology**

it [pronoun]
1 a word you use to talk about a thing that has already been mentioned or pointed out: *I've lost my book. Have you seen it?*
2 used for talking about the weather, time and dates: *It rained yesterday.* • *It's 3 o'clock.*
3 used for talking about a fact or opinion: *It's expensive to travel by train.* • *It's very quiet here, isn't it?*

italics [plural noun] a style of writing in which the letters slope to the right. The examples given in this book are in *italics*

itch [verb: **itches, itching, itched**] if part of your body itches, you want to scratch it
[noun: **itches**] a feeling that you want to scratch part of your body: *I've got an itch on my back.*
• **itchy** [adjective] an itchy part of your body makes you feel as though you want to scratch it

it'd [short form] a short way to say and write **it would** or **it had**: *It'd work! I know it would!* • *If you have an excuse, it'd better be good.*

item [noun: **items**] one of a number of things: *There were several items on the list.*
• **itemize** or **itemise** [verb: **itemizes, itemizing, itemized**] to list things separately, for example on a bill

-itis [suffix] if **-itis** comes at the end of a word, it is a noun that refers to an illness that causes swelling and pain in part of your body. For example, *tonsillitis* is an illness that causes the tonsils in your throat to swell and become painful

it'll [short form] a short way to say and write **it will**: *It'll all end in tears.*

its [adjective] belonging to it: *Keep the hat in its box.*

it's [short form] a short way to say and write **it is** or **it has**: *It's raining.* • *It's been a long time since I saw you.*

ⓘ Try not to confuse the spellings of **its** and **it's**.
Its is the possessive form of **it**, and tells you something belongs to **it**: *The bird built its nest.*
It's is a short form of two words put together: *I think it's going to rain.*

itself [pronoun]
1 you use **itself** after a verb or preposition when the thing that performs the action is affected by it: *The cat was washing itself.* • *The baby looked at itself in the mirror.*
2 **itself** is also used to show that something is done without any help from anything else: *The dog managed to get free all by itself.*
3 you can use **itself** to emphasize the thing you mean: *The garden is big but the house itself is quite small.*

IUD [noun: **IUDs**] short for **intrauterine device**, a contraceptive device that is put into a woman's womb

I've [short form] a short way to say and write **I have**: *I've finished my homework.*

ivory [noun] the hard white substance that an elephant's tusks are made of

ivy [noun] a plant that has leaves all year and can grow up walls

-ize or **-ise** [suffix] if a word ends in **-ize** or **-ise**, it is a verb. For example, to *televise* an event is to show it on television

J

jab [verb: **jabs, jabbing, jabbed**] to poke or prod someone or something roughly or sharply: *Jack jabbed me with his finger.*
[noun: **jabs**]
1 a quick prod or punch
2 an injection, especially one given to prevent an infectious disease: *a flu jab*

jabber [verb: **jabbers, jabbering, jabbered**] to talk nonsense, especially very fast

jack [noun: **jacks**]
1 a tool used to raise something heavy off the ground, especially a car or other vehicle
2 a playing card with a picture of a young man, also called a knave. The jack or knave comes between the queen and the ten in value
[verb: **jacks, jacking, jacked**] to jack something, or to **jack it up**, is to lift it using a jack

jackal [noun: **jackals**] a wild animal that looks like a dog or fox and is found in Africa and Asia

jackdaw [noun: **jackdaws**] a type of small black crow with a grey head

jacket [noun: **jackets**]
1 a short coat, usually with long sleeves, that reaches down to your waist or hips
2 a loose paper covering wrapped around a hardback book

jacket potato [noun: **jacket potatoes**] an unpeeled potato baked in the oven

jack-in-the-box [noun: **jack-in-the-boxes**] a doll fixed on a spring inside a box which pops up out of the box suddenly when the lid is opened

jack-knife [verb: **jack-knifes, jack-knifing, jack-knifed**] if a lorry jack-knifes, it skids out of control and the trailer swings round against the cab

jackpot [noun: **jackpots**] the jackpot in a game or lottery is the top prize made up of the money everyone else has bet and which increases until someone wins it

jade [noun] a type of hard green stone used in jewellery and for making ornaments

jaded [adjective] feeling tired and bored because you have been doing the same thing over and over again

jagged [adjective] with sharp or uneven edges or angles: *jagged rocks • a jagged tear in the tent*

jaguar [noun: **jaguars**] a large South American spotted cat, similar to a leopard, that lives in the jungle

jail [noun: **jails**] a prison
[verb: **jails, jailing, jailed**] to jail someone is to put them in prison
♦ **jailer** [noun: **jailers**] someone whose job is to watch over prisoners in a jail

jam [noun: **jams**]
1 jam is a thick sticky food made by boiling fruit with sugar
2 a jam happens when lots of vehicles or people are packed close together so that they become stuck and can't move
[verb: **jams, jamming, jammed**]
1 to push something into a space so that it fits very tightly or is difficult to get out again
2 something like a door or window jams when it becomes stuck and can't be moved
3 people or vehicles jam a place when they

crowd it so that it is difficult for any of them to move

→ **jammy**

jamboree [noun: **jamborees**] a large organized event where people from many different places gather, especially a gathering of Scouts

jammy [adjective: **jammier, jammiest**]
1 filled or covered with jam
2 an informal word meaning 'lucky'

jangle [verb: **jangles, jangling, jangled**]
1 to jangle is to make a harsh ringing sound like metal hitting metal
2 if something jangles your nerves, it gives you an unpleasant and uncomfortable sensation

janitor [noun: **janitors**] someone whose job is to look after a building, especially a school

January [noun] the first month of the year, after December and before February

jar [noun: **jars**]
1 a cylindrical container with a wide neck and no handles
2 the amount a jar will hold: *She made six big jars of marmalade from the oranges.*
3 a bump or blow that causes an unpleasant or painful vibration
[verb: **jars, jarring, jarred**]
1 to shake or hurt with an unpleasant or painful vibration: *He fell awkwardly, jarring his spine.*
2 if something jars, or it **jars on** you, it has an unpleasant effect on you: *The bird's screeching jarred on my ears.*

jargon [noun: **jargons**] the special words used by people working in a particular trade or profession, which are difficult for other people to understand: *lawyers' jargon*

jasmine [noun: **jasmines**] a shrub or climbing plant with sweetly scented white or yellow flowers

jaundice [noun] an illness that makes your skin and the whites of your eyes turn yellow, usually caused by your liver not working properly
♦ **jaundiced** [adjective]
1 having jaundice
2 feeling unhappy and bitter about life in general

jaunt [noun: **jaunts**] a trip made for pleasure: *a fishing jaunt*

♦ **jaunty** [adjective: **jauntier, jauntiest**] cheerful, confident and lively: *a jaunty manner*

javelin [noun: **javelins**] a long light spear used in ancient times as a weapon and nowadays thrown in a sporting competition

jaw [noun: **jaws**]
1 your jaw is the lower part of your face around your mouth and chin, made up of two bones that your teeth grow in
2 an animal's jaws are its mouth and teeth: *The crocodile snapped its jaws shut.*

jay [noun: **jays**] a bird with pink, grey, white and black feathers

jazz [noun] a type of music in which the musicians often change the notes or add to the music as they play
[verb: **jazzes, jazzing, jazzed**] to **jazz something up** is to make it brighter or more colourful
♦ **jazzy** [adjective: **jazzier, jazziest**] bright and colourful: *That's a very jazzy tie you have on.*

JCB [noun: **JCBs**] a large machine used for digging and moving earth and stones

jealous [adjective] feeling jealousy: *He's jealous of his brother's success.* • *She made me jealous by going out with her other friends.*
♦ **jealousy** [noun] a feeling of dislike that people have because someone else has something that they want or because they are afraid that another person will take something away from them

jeans [plural noun] jeans are casual trousers made of denim with pockets at the front and back

Jeep [noun] a type of four-wheeled vehicle that can travel over rough ground. This word is a trademark

jeer [verb: **jeers, jeering, jeered**] to jeer is to shout insults at someone and make fun of them
[noun: **jeers**] a scornful shout or laugh

Jehovah [noun] Jehovah is the name given to the Hebrew God of the Old Testament

jelly [noun: **jellies**]
1 a wobbly, sweet food made with gelatine and fruit juice
2 any wobbly substance

jellyfish [noun: **jellyfish** or **jellyfishes**] a sea animal with a soft see-through body

Jj

jemmy [noun: **jemmies**] a long iron tool used by burglars to break open locks
[verb: **jemmies, jemmying, jemmied**] to break a lock using a jemmy

jeopardize or **jeopardise** [verb: **jeopardizes, jeopardizing, jeopardized**] to jeopardize something is to put it in danger: *The injury could jeopardize her chances of winning a medal.*
♦ **jeopardy** [noun] if something is **in jeopardy**, there is a danger that it could be lost or damaged: *Her life is in jeopardy.* • *Smoking can put your health in jeopardy.*

jerk [verb: **jerks, jerking, jerked**]
1 to jerk something is to pull it with a sudden rough movement: *He jerked his hand away.*
2 to jerk is to make a short sudden movement: *The driver started the engine and the old bus jerked forward.*
[noun: **jerks**] a short sudden movement
→ **jerky**

jerkin [noun: **jerkins**] a type of short jacket or coat

jerky [adjective: **jerkier, jerkiest**] jerky movements are short and quick, and often look awkward or uncomfortable

jersey [noun: **jerseys**] a warm piece of clothing for the top part of your body

jest [verb: **jests, jesting, jested**] to joke
[noun: **jests**] a joke
♦ **jester** [noun: **jesters**] in the past, a man who was employed by a king or queen to tell jokes and amuse the court

jet¹ [noun: **jets**]
1 a powerful stream of liquid or gas forced through a narrow opening
2 a fast aeroplane with powerful engines that drive the plane forward by sucking air in at the front and forcing it out behind
[verb: **jets, jetting, jetted**] to jet somewhere is to travel there on a jet plane: *jetting off to sunny holiday destinations*

jet² [noun] jet is a black mineral that is polished and used to make jewellery

jet lag [noun] a feeling of tiredness that people get when they have made a long journey by aeroplane, because their body isn't able to adjust to the time changes from one part of the world to another

jettison [verb: **jettisons, jettisoning, jettisoned**]
1 cargo on a ship or aeroplane is jettisoned when it is thrown overboard to lighten the load, especially in an emergency
2 to jettison something is to throw it away or abandon it

jetty [noun: **jetties**] a platform built at the edge of a lake or the sea for small boats to tie up at

Jew [noun: **Jews**] someone who belongs to the Hebrew race of people or who practises the religion of Judaism
→ **Jewish**

jewel [noun: **jewels**] a precious stone, used for decoration or display
♦ **jeweller** [noun: **jewellers**] someone who makes or sells jewellery
♦ **jewellery** [noun] things that you wear to decorate your body and clothing, such as rings, earrings, bracelets, necklaces and brooches

ⓘ In the United States and Canada, **jeweller** is usually spelt **jeweler**, and **jewellery** is spelt **jewelry**.

Jewish [adjective] to do with the Hebrew people or Judaism

jib [noun: **jibs**]
1 the arm that sticks out from the upright part of a crane
2 a triangular sail at the front of some sailing boats

jibe [noun: **jibes**] a rude or insulting remark

jiffy [noun: **jiffies**] a very short time: *I'll be down in a jiffy.*

jig [noun: **jigs**] a lively dance in which people jump about

jigsaw [noun: **jigsaws**]
1 a puzzle made up of lots of different pieces that fit together to make a picture
2 a type of electric saw with a very thin blade that can cut curved and rounded shapes

jihad [noun: **jihads**] a jihad is a holy war fought by Muslims against people who do not believe in Islam

jilt [verb: **jilts, jilting, jilted**] to jilt someone you have promised to marry is to reject and abandon them

Jj

jingle [verb: **jingles, jingling, jingled**] pieces of metal jingle when they make a pleasant ringing sound as they hit each other: *coins jingling in his trouser pocket*
[noun: **jingles**]
1 a ringing sound made when small or light pieces of metal knock against each other
2 a short catchy song used in an advertisement

jinx [noun: **jinxes**] an evil spell or a person or thing that brings bad luck
♦ **jinxed** [adjective] to be jinxed is always to have bad luck

jittery [adjective] nervous

job [noun: **jobs**]
1 someone's job is the work they do regularly for pay
2 a job is a task or a piece of work: *There are plenty of jobs to do about the house.*

job centre [noun: **job centres**] a government office where jobs are advertised

job-sharing [noun] sharing one full-time job between two or more workers

jockey [noun: **jockeys**] someone who rides a horse, especially in races

jodhpurs [plural noun] trousers that are tight around the bottom part of the leg and wider near the top, worn by jockeys and other horse riders

jog [verb: **jogs, jogging, jogged**]
1 to jog is to run at a gentle pace for exercise
2 to jog someone or something is to nudge them or knock against them gently: *You jogged my elbow and made me splash the paint everywhere!*
3 to jog someone's memory is to help them remember
♦ **jogger** [noun: **joggers**] someone who jogs for exercise
♦ **jogging** [noun] running at a slowish pace for exercise

join [verb: **joins, joining, joined**]
1 to join two or more things is to put them together or connect them
2 one thing joins another when they come together or meet: *The track joins the main road just around this corner.*
3 you join a club or other organization when you become a member

[noun: **joins**] a place where two things are joined

joiner [noun: **joiners**] someone who works with wood, especially fitting together the wooden parts of houses

joint [noun: **joints**]
1 a place where two or more things join
2 your joints are the parts of your body where two or more bones meet
3 a joint of meat is a large piece of meat
[adjective] done together or shared: *a joint effort • joint responsibility*
♦ **jointly** [adverb] together

joist [noun: **joists**] a large beam that supports a floor or ceiling in a building

joke [noun: **jokes**] something that is said or done to make people laugh
[verb: **jokes, joking, joked**] to make a joke
♦ **joker** [noun: **jokers**]
1 someone who likes telling jokes or doing things to make people laugh
2 one of two cards in a pack of playing cards that have a picture of a clown. The jokers are extra cards and are only used in certain card games

jolly [adjective: **jollier, jolliest**] cheerful and happy
[adverb] very: *That was jolly unfair of you!*

jolt [noun: **jolts**]
1 a sudden sharp uncomfortable movement: *The train stopped with a jolt.*
2 an unpleasant shock: *The news gave Liam a bit of a jolt.*
[verb: **jolts, jolting, jolted**] to make a sudden sharp movement

jostle [verb: **jostles, jostling, jostled**] to push roughly: *The prime minister was jostled by an angry crowd.*

jot [verb: **jots, jotting, jotted**] to jot something down is to write it down quickly
[noun: **jots**] a small amount: *They don't care a jot what happens.*
♦ **jotter** [noun: **jotters**] a book of blank pages used for writing down notes

journal [noun: **journals**]
1 someone's journal is a book in which they write down what they have done each day
2 a magazine or newspaper
♦ **journalism** [noun] the work of journalists

Jj

• **journalist** [noun: **journalists**] someone who writes for a newspaper or magazine or for radio or TV

journey [noun: **journeys**]

1 you go on a journey when you travel from one place to another

2 a journey is the distance you travel from one place to another: *a long and difficult journey*

[verb: **journeys, journeying, journeyed**] to journey somewhere is to travel there

joust [noun: **jousts**] in medieval times, a joust was a fight between two knights on horseback who charged at each other with long lances

[verb: **jousts, jousting, jousted**] to fight, especially on horseback

jovial [adjective] cheerful and jolly

joy [noun: **joys**]

1 joy is a feeling of great happiness

2 a joy is something that gives you this feeling: *full of the joys of spring*

joyful or **joyous** [adjective] filled with or showing great happiness

joyride [noun: **joyrides**] a fast or reckless ride in a stolen car for amusement

• **joyrider** [noun: **joyriders**] someone who rides in a stolen car for amusement

joystick [noun: **joysticks**] a lever used to control an aircraft or a computer game

Jr [abbreviation] short for **Junior** and used after someone's name, as in *John Willis Jr*

jubilant [adjective] full of triumph and happiness at a success

• **jubilation** [noun] rejoicing at success

jubilee [noun: **jubilees**] a celebration made because a special event, for example a wedding or a coronation, happened a certain number of years ago

Judaism [noun] the Jewish religion which follows the teachings of the Old Testament of the Bible

judder [verb: **judders, juddering, juddered**] to vibrate or make uncomfortable shaky movements: *The old plane juddered to a halt.*

[noun: **judders**] a strong vibration or shaky movement

judge [verb: **judges, judging, judged**]

1 to judge something is to form an idea or opinion about it

2 to judge a competition is to decide which of the competitors is best

3 to judge a case in a court of law is to hear the evidence and decide on what is to be done or how someone should be punished

[noun: **judges**]

1 someone who hears cases in a law court and decides what is to be done

2 someone who judges a competition

3 someone who can decide whether something is good or bad: *a good judge of character*

• **judgement** or **judgment** [noun: **judgements** or **judgments**]

1 the ability to make decisions, especially good or sensible decisions: *She is very experienced and has excellent judgement.*

2 the decision made by a judge in a law court

3 an opinion about something: *In my judgement, it wouldn't be a very sensible thing to do.*

judicial [adjective] to do with judges, judgement or a court of justice

judicious [adjective] wise and showing good judgement

judo [noun] a Japanese form of unarmed fighting, which is played as a sport

jug [noun: **jugs**] a container for liquids with a handle and a shaped part at its top edge for pouring

juggernaut [noun: **juggernauts**] a very long or large lorry

juggle [verb: **juggles, juggling, juggled**] to juggle is to keep several things in the air by continuously throwing them up and catching them

• **juggler** [noun: **jugglers**] someone who juggles

juice [noun: **juices**]

1 juice is the liquid in fruits or vegetables

2 the juices from meat are the liquids that flow out of it while it is being cooked

• **juicy** [adjective: **juicier, juiciest**] full of juice

jukebox [noun: **jukeboxes**] a coin-operated machine that automatically plays records that you select by pressing buttons

July [noun] the seventh month of the year, after June and before August

Jj

jumble [verb: **jumbles, jumbling, jumbled**]
to jumble things up is to mix them up so that they
are out of order or in an untidy mess
[noun] a jumble is lots of things that have been
mixed up in a confused or untidy mess

jumble sale [noun: **jumble sales**] a sale
where second-hand or unwanted things are
sold to raise money

jumbo [adjective] very big: *a jumbo
crossword*
[noun: **jumbos**]
1 a jumbo jet
2 an informal name for an elephant

jumbo jet [noun: **jumbo jets**] a very big
jet aeroplane that can carry a lot of
passengers

jump [verb: **jumps, jumping, jumped**]
1 to leap off the ground: *I jumped down from
the bus, into the slush of the gutter.*
2 to jump something is to leap over it
3 to make a startled movement: *I jumped as
something crawled out from under the stone.*
4 if you jump a queue, you join it in front of other
people already in the queue
5 if you jump to do something or **jump at**
something you move quickly to do it: *I thought
you would jump at the chance.*
[noun: **jumps**]
1 a leap
2 something to be jumped over, or a distance
that has to be jumped
3 a startled movement
→ **jumpy**

jumper [noun: **jumpers**] a warm piece of
clothing with sleeves that you pull on over
your head and wear on the top half of your
body

jumpy [adjective: **jumpier, jumpiest**]
nervous and anxious: *His face was pale and
he looked jumpy.*

junction [noun: **junctions**] a place where
roads or railway lines meet and cross

June [noun] the sixth month of the year, after
May and before July

jungle [noun: **jungles**] trees and plants
growing thickly together, especially in tropical
areas of the world

junior [adjective]
1 younger: *junior members of the tennis club*

2 meant for younger people: *junior classes*
3 lower in rank: *junior staff*
[noun: **juniors**]
1 a younger pupil in a school
2 someone who is your junior is younger than
you are
3 someone who is lower in rank: *an office
junior*

juniper [noun: **junipers**] an evergreen bush
with small purple berries that are used to
flavour drinks and in cooking

junk [noun] useless or unwanted things: *What
will we do with all this old junk?*

junk food [noun] food that is not good for
your health

junk mail [noun] letters and advertisements
that people send to you although you did not
ask for them

juror [noun: **jurors**] one of the members of a
jury

jury [noun: **juries**] a group of people chosen
to decide on the evidence presented in a court
of law whether someone accused of a crime
is guilty or not guilty

just[1] [adverb]
1 exactly: *A cold drink was just what I
needed.*
2 barely: *I could only just see him.*
3 a very short time ago: *The clock's just struck
five.*
4 simply: *I just want to go home.*
5 if you have **just about** done something, you
have almost done it: *I've just about finished
here.*

just[2] [adjective]
1 fair or showing justice: *a just decision*
2 deserved: *It was a just reward for all his
efforts.*
→ **justly**

justice [noun: **justices**]
1 justice is fairness in dealing with people and
their problems
2 justice is being treated properly and fairly by
the law
3 a justice is a judge in a court of law

justifiable [adjective] able to be justified
♦ **justifiably** [adverb] in a justifiable
way

justification [noun: **justifications**] a

good reason or reasons given for doing something, showing that it is worthwhile or necessary

justify [verb: **justifies, justifying, justified**] to justify something is to give good reasons for it or to show that it is worthwhile or necessary: *She could justify her decision to leave school before she had turned sixteen.*

justly [adverb] fairly

jut [verb: **juts, jutting, jutted**] to jut, or to **jut out**, is to stick out

juvenile [adjective]
1 for or to do with young people: *a juvenile court*
2 childish: *a juvenile sense of humour*
[noun: **juveniles**] a young person or animal

Jj

K

kaleidoscope [noun: **kaleidoscopes**] a long tube that you look down, with mirrors and pieces of coloured glass at the bottom that form different patterns when you turn the tube

kangaroo [noun: **kangaroos**] an Australian animal that jumps, and that carries its babies in a pouch at the front of its body

kaput [adjective] an informal word meaning broken or not working

karaoke [noun] entertainment in which someone sings a pop song while a machine plays the backing music

karate [noun] a Japanese type of fighting in which you use your hands and feet

kayak [noun: **kayaks**] a type of canoe for one person

KB [abbreviation] short for **kilobyte**

kebab [noun: **kebabs**] a dish of meat cooked on a wooden or metal stick

keel [noun: **keels**] a long piece of wood or steel at the bottom of a ship
[verb: **keels, keeling, keeled**] to **keel over** is to fall over

keen [adjective: **keener, keenest**]
1 enthusiastic and wanting to do something or wanting something to happen: *Jim's a keen swimmer.* • *Everyone seemed very keen to help.*
2 sharp: *the eagle's keen eyes*
♦ **keenly** [adverb]
1 strongly: *The government is keenly aware of the problem.*
2 eagerly: *The match was keenly contested.*
♦ **keenness** [noun] being keen

keep [verb: **keeps, keeping, kept**]
1 to continue to have something and not give it

to anyone else: *You can keep the book.*
2 to put something in a particular place when you are not using it: *I keep my diary in a drawer.*
3 to make someone or something stay a particular way: *Keep the door closed.* • *Keep off the grass.*
4 if you keep or **keep on** doing something, you continue to do it: *I keep forgetting to phone them.*
5 if food keeps, it stays fresh: *Milk doesn't keep for very long.*
6 if you keep animals, you have them and look after them: *They keep chickens and goats.*
7 to **keep up** with someone or something is to move or do something as fast as they do: *He was running so fast that I couldn't keep up.*
♦ **keeper** [noun: **keepers**] the person who looks after something, especially animals in a zoo
♦ **keeping** [noun]
1 if something is in your keeping, it is in your care
2 if something is **in keeping with** something else, it is suitable for a particular situation

keepsake [noun: **keepsakes**] something that someone gives you so that you will remember them or an occasion

keg [noun: **kegs**] a small barrel

kennel [noun: **kennels**] a hut for a dog

kept [verb] a way of changing the verb **keep** to make a past tense. It can be used with or without a helping verb: *He kept all her letters.* • *I have kept the receipt.*

kerb [noun: **kerbs**] the edge of a pavement

kernel [noun: **kernels**] a soft substance in the shell of a nut or inside the stone of a fruit

Kk

310

kestrel [noun: **kestrels**] a small bird of the falcon family that kills other creatures for food

ketchup [noun] a sauce made from tomatoes

kettle [noun: **kettles**] a container for boiling water in

kettledrum [noun: **kettledrums**] a large drum made of a metal bowl covered with skin

key [noun: **keys**]
1 something you use for locking and unlocking something such as a door or window
2 a button on a computer keyboard or typewriter
3 one of the white or black parts you press on a piano or a similar instrument to make a sound
4 a set of musical notes: *in the key of D minor*
5 something that makes you able to understand or achieve something: *Hard work is the key to success.* • *The key to the map is over the page.*
[adjective] most important: *Dean is one of the team's key players.*

keyboard [noun: **keyboards**]
1 the set of keys on a computer or typewriter
2 the set of keys on a musical instrument such as a piano
3 an electronic musical instrument that has keys like a piano

keyhole [noun: **keyholes**] the part of a lock that you put a key into

keypad [noun: **keypads**] a small device with buttons that you push, for example on a TV remote control

kg [abbreviation] short for **kilogram** or **kilograms**

khaki [noun] a green-brown colour

kibbutz [noun: **kibbutzim**] a type of farm in Israel in which a group of people live together and share all the work

kick [verb: **kicks, kicking, kicked**]
1 to hit someone or something with your foot: *Jane kicked the ball over the fence.*
2 to move your legs strongly, for example when swimming
[noun: **kicks**]
1 a strong movement of your leg or foot
2 a feeling of pleasure or excitement: *He gets a kick out of driving fast.*

kick-off [noun: **kick-offs**] the start of a football game

kid [noun: **kids**]
1 a child
2 a young goat
[adjective] if you **treat someone with kid gloves**, you are very careful not to upset them
[verb: **kids, kidding, kidded**] to kid someone is to trick them for fun

kidnap [verb: **kidnaps, kidnapping, kidnapped**] to take someone away using force, and ask for money to return them safely
• **kidnapper** [noun: **kidnappers**] someone who kidnaps someone else
• **kidnapping** [noun: **kidnappings**] taking someone away using force and asking for money to return them: *Kidnapping is a serious crime.* • *There have been several kidnappings recently.*

kidney [noun: **kidneys**] one of the two organs in your body that remove waste from your blood and produce urine

kill [verb: **kills, killing, killed**] to make a person or animal die: *Two people were killed in the crash.*
• **killer** [noun: **killers**] a person who kills someone

killjoy [noun: **killjoys**] someone who spoils other people's enjoyment

kiln [noun: **kilns**] a large oven for baking pottery or bricks, or for drying grain

kilo- [prefix] if a word starts with **kilo-**, it adds the meaning 'one thousand'. For example, a *kilogram* is equal to 1000 grams

kilobyte [noun: **kilobytes**] a unit used to measure computer memory or data, equal to 1024 bytes. This is often shortened to **KB**

kilogram or **kilogramme** [noun: **kilograms** or **kilogrammes**] a unit for measuring weight, equal to 1000 grams. This is often shortened to **kg**

kilometre [noun: **kilometres**] a unit for measuring distance, equal to 1000 metres. This is often shortened to **km**

kilowatt [noun: **kilowatts**] a unit for measuring electrical power, equal to 1000 watts. This is often shortened to **kW**

kilt [noun: **kilts**] a pleated tartan skirt that is part of a traditional Scottish way of dressing for both men and women

kimono [noun: **kimonos**] a traditional

Kk

Japanese piece of clothing that looks like a long dress, tied round the middle

kin [noun]

1 your kin are your relatives

2 your **next of kin** is your closest relative, who would be informed if you had an accident

kind [noun: **kinds**] a type of something: *What kind of dog have you got?*

kind [adjective: **kinder, kindest**] nice, generous and wanting to make other people happy

→ **kindly, kindness**

kindergarten [noun: **kindergartens**] a school for very young children

kind-hearted [adjective] kind and generous

kindle [verb: **kindles, kindling, kindled**]

1 to light a fire

2 to start burning

♦ **kindling** [noun] pieces of wood used to start a fire

kindly [adverb]

1 in a way that shows kindness: *The teacher spoke to us kindly.*

2 you can say 'kindly' to mean 'please' when you are rather angry: *Would you kindly be quiet!*

3 if you **do not take kindly to** something, you are annoyed about it: *I do not take kindly to being called a liar.*

[adjective: **kindlier, kindliest**] kind and caring: *He was a kindly man who wished us well.*

kindness [noun] helpfulness and generosity: *an act of kindness*

kinetic [adjective] relating to or produced by movement

king [noun: **kings**]

1 a man who rules a country: *the King of Norway*

2 a playing card with a picture of an old man. The king comes between the ace and the queen in value

3 in the game of chess, a king is a piece that has a crown and has to be defended or you will lose the game

♦ **kingdom** [noun: **kingdoms**]

1 a country ruled by a king

2 one of the three divisions of the natural

world, which are the animal, vegetable and mineral kingdoms

kingfisher [noun: **kingfishers**] a brightly coloured bird that eats fish

king-size [adjective] larger than the usual size: *a king-size bed*

kink [noun: **kinks**] a bend or twist in something

kiosk [noun: **kiosks**] a small stall selling items such as newspapers and sweets

kipper [noun: **kippers**] a smoked herring

kirk [noun: **kirks**] a Scottish word for a church

kiss [verb: **kisses, kissing, kissed**] to touch someone with your lips as a sign of love: *Ellie kissed her mother.*

[noun: **kisses**] the act of kissing someone: *He gave her a kiss.*

kiss of life [noun] the kiss of life is a way of helping someone who is ill or injured to start breathing again by blowing air into their mouth

kit [noun: **kits**]

1 the clothes or tools that you need for a particular activity or job: *my football kit*

2 a set of parts that you can put together to make something: *a model boat kit*

kitchen [noun: **kitchens**] a room for preparing and cooking food

kite [noun: **kites**]

1 a toy that you fly in the air when it is windy

2 a bird from the hawk family

kitten [noun: **kittens**] a young cat

kitty [noun: **kitties**] a collection of money that a group of people regularly add money to, and use for a particular purpose

kitty [noun: **kitties**] an informal name for a cat or kitten

kiwi [noun: **kiwis**] a bird from New Zealand that can run but not fly

kiwi fruit [noun: **kiwi fruit**] a fruit with bright green flesh, black seeds and a hairy skin

klaxon [noun: **klaxons**] a loud horn that an ambulance or fire engine uses to give a warning

km [abbreviation] short for **kilometre** or **kilometres**

knack [noun: **knacks**] a special talent: *a knack for baking perfect cakes*

knapsack [noun: **knapsacks**] a bag that you carry on your back

knave [noun: **knaves**] the jack in a pack of playing cards

knead [verb: **kneads, kneading, kneaded**] to press dough or clay with your hands to make it ready to use

knee [noun: **knees**] the joint in the middle of your leg where it bends

kneecap [noun: **kneecaps**] the bone at the front of your knee

kneel [verb: **kneels, kneeling, knelt**] to move down so you are resting on your knees

knickerbockers [plural noun] trousers that fit tightly just below the knee

knickers [plural noun] a piece of underwear for women or girls, which covers their bottom

knick-knack [noun: **knick-knacks**] a small decorative object

knife [noun: **knives**] a tool used for cutting something, which has a handle and a blade [verb: **knifes, knifing, knifed**] to stab someone with a knife

knight [noun: **knights**]
1 in history, a man of a high social rank who was trained to fight
2 a man who has been given an honour by a king or queen that lets him use the title 'Sir'
3 in the game of chess, a knight is a piece which is shaped like a horse
• **knighthood** [noun: **knighthoods**] the rank or title of a knight

knit [verb: **knits, knitting, knitted**] to make something using two long needles and wool: *Sandy was knitting a scarf.* • *Do you know how to knit?*
• **knitting** [noun]
1 the activity of making things by knitting
2 something that has been or is being knitted

knitting needle [noun: **knitting needles**] one of the two long needles used for knitting

knives [noun] the plural of **knife**

knob [noun: **knobs**]
1 a round handle on a door or drawer
2 a round button used for controlling a machine
3 a lump: *a knob of butter*
• **knobbly** [adjective: **knobblier, knobbliest**] covered with lumps: *knobbly knees*

knock [verb: **knocks, knocking, knocked**]
1 to hit something so that it moves or falls: *The cat knocked the vase off the table.*
2 to hit a door or window several times with your knuckles or a knocker in order to attract attention: *Knock before you come in.*
3 to bump into something: *I knocked my elbow on the edge of the door.*
4 to **knock someone out** is to make someone become unconscious, especially by hitting them
[noun: **knocks**]
1 the sound of someone knocking on a door or window: *There was a knock at the door.*
2 a blow or injury caused by hitting something: *He's had a nasty knock on the head.*
• **knocker** [noun: **knockers**] a metal object on a door, which you knock with

knockout [noun: **knockouts**] a hit that makes someone unconscious

knoll [noun: **knolls**] a small hill

knot [noun: **knots**]
1 a join made by tying two ends of string or rope together
2 a hard lump in a piece of wood where there used to be a branch
3 a unit for measuring how fast a ship is travelling
[verb: **knots, knotting, knotted**] to tie something with a knot
• **knotty** [adjective]
1 having a lot of knots
2 difficult or complicated: *a knotty problem*

know [verb: **knows, knowing, knew, known**]
1 to have information about something: *Do you know where he lives?*
2 to have learnt about something: *I don't know much German.*
3 to be familiar with a person or place: *I didn't know anyone at the party.*
• **knowing** [adjective] showing that you know something that is supposed to be secret: *He gave me a knowing look.*

knowledge [noun] the information and understanding that you have about something: *She has a good knowledge of sport.*
• **knowledgeable** [adjective] knowing a lot about something
• **knowledgeably** [adverb] in a way that

Kk

knuckle → kW

shows you know a lot about something: *Jean spoke knowledgeably about history.*

knuckle [noun: **knuckles**] one of the parts on your hands where your fingers bend

KO [abbreviation] short for **knockout**

koala [noun: **koalas**] an Australian animal that looks like a small bear, climbs trees and eats eucalyptus leaves

Koran [noun] the holy book of the Islamic religion

kosher [adjective] kosher food is prepared according to Jewish law

kung-fu [noun] a Chinese type of fighting using your hands and feet

kW [abbreviation] short for **kilowatt** or **kilowatts**

Kk

L

l [abbreviation] short for **litre** or **litres**

label [noun: **labels**] a small note that is fixed on to something and gives information about it: *The washing instructions are on the label.* [verb: **labels, labelling, labelled**] to fix a small note to something: *All the boxes have been carefully labelled.*

laboratory [noun: **laboratories**] a room containing equipment for scientific experiments and research

labour [noun]
1 hard work
2 the process of giving birth to a baby
3 people who work: *the rising cost of labour*
[verb: **labours, labouring, laboured**] to work hard: *workers labouring in the fields*
• **labourer** [noun: **labourers**] a person who does hard physical work

labrador [noun: **labradors**] a large black or golden-coloured dog

labyrinth [noun: **labyrinths**] a network of passages that is difficult to find your way through

lace [noun: **laces**]
1 a cord for doing up shoes or other clothing: *Children often find it difficult to tie shoe laces.*
2 fabric that is made in open patterns in fine thread: *a collar trimmed with lace*
[verb: **laces, lacing, laced**]
1 to lace your shoes is to put laces in them or tie the laces in a knot or bow
2 to lace a drink is to add alcohol to it

lack [verb: **lacks, lacking, lacked**] to be completely without something or not to have enough of it: *Audrey lacks a sense of humour.*
[noun] a lack of something means not having enough of it: *Lack of sleep was making us grumpy.*

lacquer [noun: **lacquers**] a kind of varnish [verb: **lacquers, lacquering, lacquered**] to cover something with varnish to protect or decorate it

lad [noun: **lads**] a boy or young man

ladder [noun: **ladders**]
1 a set of steps that you can move around to climb up to places that you cannot normally reach
2 a long tear that has started from a hole or broken stitch in a stocking or tights
3 a system with different levels that you can progress through: *She hopes to make her way up the career ladder.*

laden [adjective] if someone or something is laden with something, they are heavily loaded with it: *He was laden with bags of shopping.* • *The tree is laden with fruit.*

ladies [noun] the ladies is a public toilet for women and girls: *Where is the ladies, please?*

ladle [noun: **ladles**] a large spoon for serving liquids, especially soup
[verb: **ladles, ladling, ladled**] to lift or serve liquid with a large spoon: *Mrs Moore was busy ladling soup into bowls.*

lady [noun: **ladies**]
1 a polite word for a woman: *Ask that lady if the seat by her is free.*
2 a woman with good manners: *Mrs Kingsley was a real lady.*
3 the title for the wife of a lord or knight or for a woman with a high social rank
➡ **ladies**

ladybird [noun: **ladybirds**] a small beetle that is usually red with black spots

lag [verb: **lags, lagging, lagged**]
1 to progress more slowly and not be as good as others: *The company is lagging a long way behind its rivals.*
2 to walk more slowly than other people you are with
3 to lag a hot water tank or pipes is to surround it with a warm covering
→ **lagging**

lager [noun: **lagers**] a light-coloured beer

lagging [noun] material for covering pipes and floors to stop heat or cold passing through them: *Lagging stops the pipes from freezing in the winter.*

lagoon [noun: **lagoons**] a shallow stretch of water inside sandbanks by the sea

laid [verb] a way of changing the verb **lay** to make a past tense. It can be used with or without a helping verb: *The hen laid three eggs.* • *Have you laid the table yet?*

laid-back [adjective] relaxed and easy-going: *a very laid-back kind of chap*

lain [verb] a form of the verb **lie** that is used with a helping verb to show that something happened in the past: *I had lain down for a moment and fallen fast asleep.*

lair [noun: **lairs**] the den of a wild animal

lake [noun: **lakes**] a large area of water that has land all around it

lamb [noun: **lambs**]
1 a young sheep
2 meat from a young sheep

lame [noun: **lamer, lamest**]
1 not able to walk properly: *Mr Harris has been lame since his accident.*
2 a lame excuse is weak and not very convincing
• **lamely** [adverb] weakly: *'I'm not coming because I just can't,' she said lamely.*

lament [noun: **laments**] a sad song or poem, especially about someone's death
[verb: **laments, lamenting, lamented**] to feel or express sadness about something: *Grandfather was lamenting the passing of the old days.*

laminated [adjective]
1 covered with thin, see-through plastic
2 made by sticking layers together: *laminated flooring*

lamp [noun: **lamps**] a piece of equipment that has a light in it: *a table lamp*

lamppost [noun: **lampposts**] a tall pillar or pole in the street with a light at the top

lance [noun: **lances**] a long spear used as a weapon

lance-corporal [noun: **lance-corporals**] a soldier ranking above a private and below a corporal

land [noun: **lands**]
1 land is the part of the Earth not covered by water
2 land is ground, especially when it is used for a particular purpose: *good land for growing crops*
3 a land is a country: *foreign lands*
[verb: **lands, landing, landed**]
1 an aircraft lands when it arrives after a flight
2 a person or a thing lands somewhere when it stops there after flying or falling: *The bird landed on a branch.* • *I slipped but managed to land on my feet.*
3 you land or are landed in or with something when you find yourself in a difficult situation, or with a difficult problem: *He's always landing me in trouble.* • *I found myself landed with a huge phone bill.*

landing [noun: **landings**]
1 the process of moving a plane down to the ground: *an emergency landing*
2 the floor at the top of a staircase or the floor between two flights of steps

landlady [noun: **landladies**]
1 a woman who owns a house that someone else pays to live in
2 a woman who runs a pub or guesthouse

landlocked [adjective] almost or completely surrounded by land: *a landlocked country*

landlord [noun: **landlords**]
1 a man who owns a house that someone else pays to live in
2 a man who runs a pub or guesthouse

landmark [noun: **landmarks**] a place, especially a building, that helps you know where you are because you can see it from all around

landscape [noun: **landscapes**] a view of a large area of land, especially a painting or photograph: *a rocky landscape* • *a landscape artist*

landslide [noun: **landslides**]
1 a large amount of the ground slipping down the side of a hill
2 a very big victory in an election

lane [noun: **lanes**]
1 a narrow road
2 a strip of a road, the air or the sea that certain vehicles should travel in: *Cyclists are allowed in the bus lanes.*

language [noun: **languages**]
1 communication in speaking and writing: *slightly formal language*
2 the words used by a particular group, such as the people that live in one country: *learn a foreign language*
3 a system of symbols or signs that give information, for example in computers

lanky [adjective: **lankier, lankiest**] tall and thin: *a lanky 15-year-old boy*

lantern [noun: **lanterns**] a case holding a light

lap [noun: **laps**]
1 the top part of a person's legs when they are sitting down
2 one round of a racecourse
[verb: **laps, lapping, lapped**]
1 to lap something is to lick it up: *a cat lapping milk from a saucer*
2 water laps when it splashes gently against rocks or on a beach
3 to lap someone is to pass them more than once as you go round a racecourse
4 to **lap something up** is to enjoy it very much: *She lapped up the compliments about her new dress.*

lapel [noun: **lapels**] the front part of a coat or jacket collar: *a flower pinned to his lapel*

lapse [noun: **lapses**]
1 a space of time: *After a lapse of ten years, Jones started to play football again.*
2 a failure to work properly for a short time: *a memory lapse*
[verb: **lapses, lapsing, lapsed**]
1 to lapse into a certain condition is to gradually pass into it: *The patient has lapsed into unconsciousness.*
2 an agreement or contract lapses when it stops being valid

laptop [noun: **laptops**] a small, portable computer that you can use, for example, when you are travelling

lard [noun] a white fat that can be used in cooking and that comes from a pig

larder [noun: **larders**] the place where food is kept in a house: *a well-stocked larder*

large [adjective: **larger, largest**]
1 big or bigger than normal: *a large man* • *a large house* • *a large increase in sales*
2 if a dangerous animal or a criminal is **at large**, they are free and have not been caught: *There is a wild animal at large in the area.*
3 people **at large** are most people rather than just some people: *The public at large don't like the idea.*
• **largely** [adverb] mainly: *The church has been largely rebuilt.*
• **largeness** [noun] the big size of something

lark [noun: **larks**]
1 a singing bird that flies high in the sky
2 a bit of fun: *We were just having a lark.*
[verb: **larks, larking, larked**] to **lark about** is to fool about or play tricks

larva [noun: **larvae**] an insect in its first stage after coming out of the egg

laryngitis [noun] an illness that makes your throat sore and makes it difficult for you to talk

lasagne or **lasagna** [noun: **lasagnes** or **lasagnas**]
1 lasagne is flat sheets of pasta
2 a lasagne is an Italian dish made up of layers of pasta, meat or vegetable sauce and cheese

laser [noun: **lasers**] a very narrow, powerful beam of light

laser printer [noun: **laser printers**] a fast printer for a computer, that uses light from a laser to make very clear letters and images

lash [noun: **lashes**]
1 a stroke made by a whip as a form of punishment: *ten lashes of the whip*
2 an eyelash
[verb: **lashes, lashing, lashed**]
1 to hit with a whipping movement: *rain that lashed against the windows*
2 to tie something up with rope or string: *The banners were lashed to the walls of the buildings.*

Ll

lass [noun: **lasses**] a girl

ⓘ **Lass** is mainly used in Scotland and Northern England.

lasso [noun: **lassoes** or **lassos**] a long rope with a loop that tightens when the rope is pulled, used especially for catching wild horses
[verb: **lassoes, lassoing, lassoed**] to throw a rope around something to catch it

last [adjective]
1 coming after all the others: *the last bus of the day*
2 the final one remaining: *my last toffee*
3 most recent: *on my last birthday*
[adverb]
1 after all the others: *She trailed in last.*
2 after everything else: *You should add the sugar last.*
3 most recently: *When did you see Anna last?*
[verb: **lasts, lasting, lasted**]
1 to continue or go on: *The lesson seemed to last for ever.*
2 to remain in good condition: *These boots have lasted well.*
[noun]
1 the final person or thing: *You are always the last to finish.*
2 if something happens **at last**, it happens in the end, especially after you have been waiting for a long time: *I've found a job at last.*
♦ **lastly** [adverb] finally: *Lastly, I just want to thank my wife.*

latch [noun: **latches**] a piece of wood or metal that rises and falls to open or fasten a door

late [adjective: **later, latest**]
1 coming after the expected time: *The bus was late.*
2 near the end of a period of time: *late afternoon • the late 18th century*
3 happening far on in a period of time: *a late movie*
4 recently dead: *our late uncle*
[adverb: **later, latest**]
1 coming after the expected time: *The train arrives later every day.*
2 far on in time: *It's getting late.*

♦ **lately** [adverb] recently: *I haven't been to many parties lately.*
♦ **lateness** [noun] being late

lathe [noun: **lathes**] a machine that turns and cuts wood or metal

lather [noun] foam that you get when you mix soap in water

Latin [noun] the language of the ancient Romans

latitude [noun] the position of a place along an imaginary line north and south of the equator. Look up and compare **longitude**

latter [adjective]
1 the latter is the second one of two people or things you are mentioning. The first one is the **former**: *If I am offered coffee or chocolate, I'll always take the latter.*
2 nearer the end of a period of time than the beginning: *the latter part of the 19th century*
♦ **latterly** [adverb] recently: *Latterly, I haven't been getting on very well at work.*

lattice [noun: **lattices**] a pattern of strips that cross over one another

laugh [verb: **laughs, laughing, laughed**] to make a sound of enjoyment when you think something is funny
[noun: **laughs**] the sound a person makes when they think something is funny

laughing stock [noun: **laughing stocks**] a person who seems ridiculous, causing people to laugh at them in an unkind way

laughter [noun] laughing: *the sound of laughter • roaring with laughter*

launch [verb: **launches, launching, launched**]
1 to put a boat or ship in the water for the first time
2 to fire a rocket off
3 to start something like a project or start to sell a new product: *The company is launching a new chocolate bar.*
[noun: **launches**] the act of launching something: *We'll be able to watch the shuttle launch on the TV.*

launch pad [noun: **launch pads**] a platform that a spacecraft is launched from

launder [verb: **launders, laundering, laundered**]
1 to launder clothes is to wash or clean them so

that they are ready to wear again
2 to launder money is to put it into legal businesses to hide the fact that it was obtained illegally

• **launderette** [noun: **launderettes**] a shop full of washing machines that you can pay to use

• **laundry** [noun: **laundries**]
1 clothes that are going to be washed, or have just been washed
2 a business where you can send washing to be done

lava [noun] the hot liquid rock that comes out of an erupting volcano and becomes solid as it cools down

lavatory [noun: **lavatories**] a toilet

lavender [noun: **lavenders**]
1 a plant with purple flowers that smell strong and sweet
2 lavender is a pale purple colour

lavish [verb: **lavishes, lavishing, lavished**] to lavish something on someone is to give them a lot, or too much of it: *Her parents had always lavished gifts on her.*
[adjective] very generous, with more than enough of everything: *a lavish dinner • lavish praise*

• **lavishly** [adverb] very generously: *a lavishly decorated room*

law [noun: **laws**]
1 a rule or set of rules for everyone in a country or state: *Driving at the age of 13 is against the law. • You could study law at university.*
2 a scientific rule that explains what always happens in certain circumstances: *The law of gravity means that the apple will fall downwards.*

lawful [adjective] allowed by the law: *The strike was not lawful.*

• **lawfully** [adverb] according to the law: *Were they lawfully married?*

lawn [noun: **lawns**] an area of short grass in a garden

lawnmower [noun: **lawnmowers**] a machine for cutting grass

lawsuit [noun: **lawsuits**] an argument that a court of law is asked to settle

lawyer [noun: **lawyers**] someone whose job is to advise people about the law

lax [adjective: **laxer, laxest**] not strict: *Discipline has been too lax recently.*

laxative [noun: **laxatives**] a drug or food that makes you pass solid waste from your body

lay [verb: **lays, laying, laid**]
1 to put something down: *lay the book on the table*
2 to arrange something: *lay the table • lay a trap*
3 to lay an egg is to produce it
4 to **lay off** something is to stop doing it or using it: *Tom's trying to lay off sweets.*
5 to **lay someone off** is to stop them working for you: *The local factories have been laying off workers.*

ⓘ Try not to confuse **lay** with **lie**. You **lay** something somewhere, whereas you **lie** somewhere:
Lay your pencils on your desks.
I am going to lie in bed for a while.
The past tenses can be confusing, too. **Lay** is also a past tense of **lie**:
The cat lay on the mat.

layabout [noun: **layabouts**] a lazy person

lay-by [noun: **lay-bys**] an area at the side of a road where drivers can stop for a while out of the way of moving traffic

layer [noun: **layers**] a covering that lies flat over something or a thickness under something: *grass covered with a layer of snow • a layer of jam in the middle of the cake*

layout [noun: **layouts**] the way things are set out or arranged: *The layout of the rooms is different.*

laze [verb: **lazes, lazing, lazed**] to be lazy and do very little: *I just like to laze around in the holidays.*

lazily [adverb] in a slow, unhurried way

lazy [adjective: **lazier, laziest**] not wanting to do anything much, especially work: *He's the laziest man I know.*

lb [abbreviation] short for **pound** or **pounds** in weight: *2lb of sugar*

lead [verb: **leads, leading, led**]
1 to show someone the way by going first: *You lead and I'll follow on my bike.*
2 to direct or control a group of people: *The*

team should be led by someone with a lot of experience.
3 to be winning in a race or competition: *Liverpool were leading 2-0 at the end of the first half.*
4 to cause someone to do something: *His expression led me to think he was lying.*
5 a road that leads somewhere goes to that place
6 to **lead your life** a certain way means to behave in that way most of the time: *We lead a pretty normal life.*
[noun: **leads**]
1 the first or front place: *Jenkins has been in the lead for most of the race.*
2 a piece of help or guidance: *Follow my lead and just do what I do.* • *The police are following up several new leads.*
3 an electrical wire or cable: *Someone had cut the lead to the alarm.*
4 a strap or chain attached to a dog's collar that you can hold when you walk with it: *Please keep your dog on its lead.*
→ **leader**

ⓘ The verb **lead**, and the nouns connected with it, are pronounced **leed**.
The noun **lead**, a kind of metal, is pronounced **led**.

lead² [noun: **leads**]
1 a soft, dark grey metal
2 the inside part of a pencil that writes, made of a soft black substance called graphite

leader [noun: **leaders**] a person who is in charge of a group of people: *the leader of the expedition* • *the Conservative Party leader*
♦ **leadership** [noun]
1 being a leader: *The club's done well under Will's leadership.*
2 the ability to lead: *He's a good worker but he lacks leadership.*

leaf [noun: **leaves**]
1 a part of a plant that grows out from the side of the stem and is usually green
2 a page of a book
3 if you **turn over a new leaf**, you change your life by starting to act in a better way

leaflet [noun: **leaflets**] a small printed sheet of paper that gives information about something

leafy [adjective: **leafier, leafiest**]
1 a leafy plant or tree has a lot of leaves
2 a leafy place has a lot of plants or trees

league [noun: **leagues**]
1 a group of people or nations who agree to work together
2 a group of teams that play sports matches against each other
3 an old measure of distance that was about 3 miles
4 two people who are **in league with** each other are working together, especially to do something bad

leak [noun: **leaks**]
1 a hole that liquid or gas can escape or enter through
2 an escape of a gas or liquid
3 an act of giving away secret information
[verb: **leaks, leaking, leaked**]
1 if gas or liquid leaks, it escapes: *Gas was leaking from somewhere under the floor.*
2 to let liquid or gas in or out through a hole: *My boots leak.*
3 to give secret information away: *This news was leaked to a newspaper yesterday.*
♦ **leakage** [noun: **leakages**] an escape of gas, a liquid or information: *We lost a lot of oil through leakage.* • *the leakage of private memos*

lean [verb: **leans, leaning, leant**]
1 to rest against something: *a boy leaning on the wall*
2 to slope over to one side: *Lean over and get the salt for me would you?*
[adjective: **leaner, leanest**] without any or much fat: *I only buy lean meat.*

leap [verb: **leaps, leaping, leapt**] to jump high or long: *dolphins leaping out of the water*
[noun: **leaps**] a big jump: *a leap over the river*

leap year [noun: **leap years**] a year that occurs every four years and has 366 days. The extra day is February 29

learn [verb: **learns, learning, learnt** or **learned**]
1 to get to know something or how to do something: *learn your lines for the play* • *learning how to swim*
2 to find out some news or information: *I was saddened to learn of his death.*

LI

◆ **learner** [noun: **learners**] a person who is finding out how to do something

◆ **learning** [noun] knowledge: *a man of great learning*

lease [noun: **leases**] an agreement to rent something like a flat or house to someone [verb: **leases, leasing, leased**] to rent something to someone

leash [noun: **leashes**] a lead for taking a dog for a walk

least [adjective] the smallest amount of anything: *The person who had the least difficulty was the tallest.*

[adverb]

1 to the smallest degree: *She chose the least expensive trousers.* • *He always turns up when you least expect him.*

2 **at least** means not less than: *She must be at least forty.* • *It will take at least two hours to get there.*

3 you say '**at least**' when adding a positive comment after you have said something negative: *She may be boring but at least she's reliable.*

4 you say '**at least**' to make something you have said seem less definite: *John has finished, at least he should have.*

leather [noun: **leathers**] a material for making shoes, bags and clothes that is made from the skin of an animal

leave [verb: **leaves, leaving, left**]

1 to go away from someone, something or somewhere: *I left the office early.*

2 to not take something with you when you go away: *Maria left her umbrella on the bus.*

3 to allow something to be in a particular position or state: *Leave the conditioner in your hair for five minutes.*

4 to not do something but do it later or let someone else do it: *I left all the driving to her.* • *I'll leave the washing up and do it in the morning.*

5 to give something to someone in your will: *Her grandmother left Joy all her jewellery.*

[noun]

1 holiday time from work: *a week's leave*

2 permission to do something

lecture [noun: **lectures**]

1 a talk by someone to an audience or a group of students

2 a long telling-off

[verb: **lectures, lecturing, lectured**]

1 to give a talk on a particular subject to a class or audience

2 to give someone a long telling-off: *'This is not good for your children,' he lectured. 'You are letting them get away with too much.'*

led [verb] a way of changing the verb **lead** to make a past tense. It can be used with or without a helping verb: *Connor led a wild life for many years.* • *Where have you led us?*

ledge [noun: **ledges**] a shelf or something that sticks out like a shelf: *a ledge of rock* • *a window ledge*

leek [noun: **leeks**] a long green and white vegetable of the onion family

left[1] [adjective] on the other side from the right side, for example, on the side of a page where you usually start reading: *Do you write with your right or left hand?*

[adverb] on or towards the other side from the right: *Now turn left.*

[noun] the left is the other side from the right side: *Can we stop just here on the left?*

left[2] [verb] a way of changing the verb **leave** to make a past tense. It can be used with or without a helping verb: *We all thanked them when they left.* • *I have left my book at home.*

left-handed [adjective]

1 preferring to use your left hand to do things, rather than your right

2 meant to be used by the left hand rather than the right: *a left-handed pair of scissors*

leftovers [plural noun] food that has not been eaten up at a meal: *Shall I put the leftovers in the fridge?*

leg [noun: **legs**]

1 one of the parts of the body that animals and humans stand and walk on

2 one half of a pair of trousers

3 one of the upright supports of a piece of furniture like a table or chair

4 one stage in a journey or a contest: *This is the second leg of the race across Europe.*

legacy [noun: **legacies**] something that someone leaves in their will

legal [adjective]

1 allowed by the law: *Is it legal to ride your bike on the pavement?*

Ll

2 to do with the law: *legal studies*

♦ **legalize** or **legalise** [verb: **legalizes, legalizing, legalized**] to legalize something is to make it allowed by law: *Most states have legalized gambling.*

legend [noun: **legends**] a traditional story that is handed down through generations

♦ **legendary** [adjective]

1 belonging to legends: *legendary knights*

2 very famous: *His goal-scoring skills were legendary.*

legibility [noun] how easy something is to read

legible [adjective] easy to read: *The letter became less legible towards the end.*

♦ **legibly** [adverb] in a way that is easy to read: *Could you write your name more legibly please?*

legion [noun: **legions**]

1 a group of several thousand Roman soldiers

2 a very big number: *his legions of fans*

legislation [noun] a law or set of laws

legitimate [adjective]

1 lawful: *the legitimate government*

2 logical and reasonable: *a legitimate complaint*

♦ **legitimately** [adverb] according to the law: *not legitimately married*

leisure [noun]

1 your leisure is your spare time

2 if you do something **at your leisure**, you do it at a time that is convenient for you: *Take the brochure home and read it at your leisure.*

♦ **leisurely** [adjective] not rushed or hurried: *walking at a leisurely pace*

lemon [noun: **lemons**]

1 an oval fruit with a hard, yellow skin and very sour juice

2 a pale yellow colour

lemonade [noun] a fizzy or still drink that has a lemon flavour

lend [verb: **lends, lending, lent**]

1 to let someone borrow something for a time

2 if you **lend a hand**, you help someone

length [noun: **lengths**]

1 how long something is from one end to the other end: *Measure the table's length.*

2 how long something is in time: *The average length of stay in hospital is four days.*

3 a length is a piece of something long and thin such as a rope or pipe: *a length of plastic piping*

4 if you talk **at length**, you talk for a long time and give a lot of details: *The doctor explained the different treatments at length.*

♦ **lengthen** [verb: **lengthens, lengthening, lengthened**]

1 to lengthen something is to make it longer: *I think you should lengthen that skirt.*

2 to lengthen is to grow longer: *a lengthening queue*

♦ **lengthy** [adjective: **lengthier, lengthiest**] taking a long time: *a lengthy delay*

lenient [adjective] not very strict in giving punishments: *The judge was too lenient.*

lens [noun: **lenses**]

1 a piece of glass that is curved on one or both sides and is used in equipment like glasses, cameras and telescopes

2 a part of your eye behind your pupil

Lent [noun] in the Christian church, the forty days before Easter when, for religious reasons, people give up something they enjoy

lent [verb] a way of changing the verb **lend** to make a past tense. It can be used with or without a helping verb: *Here's the book you lent me yesterday.* • *You haven't lent him money, have you?*

lentil [noun: **lentils**] a small orange, brown or green seed that is often cooked in soups and other dishes

leopard [noun: **leopards**] an animal of the cat family with a spotted skin

ⓘ This word is pronounced **lep**-ird.

leotard [noun: **leotards**] a tight-fitting, stretchy piece of clothing that you wear for doing exercises or dancing

leper [noun: **lepers**] someone who suffers from leprosy

leprechaun [noun: **leprechauns**] a small, magical creature in Irish folk tales that likes to cause mischief

leprosy [noun] a serious infectious skin disease that can cause damage to parts of the body

➡ **leper**

lesbian [noun: **lesbians**] a woman who is

LI

sexually attracted to other women

less [adjective and adverb] not as much: *We'll have to spend less money.* • *I exercise less nowadays.*

[noun] a smaller amount: *I've got less than he has.*

[preposition] minus: *The cost will be £100 less the discount.*

♦ **lessen** [verb: **lessens, lessening, lessened**]

1 to lessen is to become smaller in amount or importance: *My sadness lessened as the days passed.*

2 to lessen something is to make it become smaller in amount or importance: *drugs that will lessen the pain*

-less [suffix] if a word ends in **-less**, it is an adjective that means 'without'. For example, *fearless* means 'without fear'

lesson [noun: **lessons**]

1 a period of time in which someone teaches you something: *When's our next lesson?* • *a driving lesson*

2 something that you learn from life and experiences: *The war has taught us some valuable lessons.*

3 a reading from the Bible in a church service

let [verb: **lets, letting, let**]

1 to let someone do something is to allow them to do it: *Please let me go!*

2 to let a property is to rent it out

3 to **let someone down** is to disappoint them: *If she promises me something, she won't let me down.*

4 to **let someone off** is to not punish them even though they have done something wrong

5 if something **lets up**, it becomes less: *It seemed as if the rain would never let up.*

-let [suffix] if a word ends in **-let**, it is a noun that refers to something very young or very small. For example, a *piglet* is a baby pig

lethal [adjective] causing or able to cause death: *a lethal weapon* • *a lethal dose of the drug*

lethargic [adjective] lacking in energy and feeling that you do not want to do anything: *After such a huge lunch I felt very lethargic.*

♦ **lethargy** [noun] a feeling that you have no energy and do not want to do anything

let's [verb] another way of saying 'shall we?': *Let's have a game of cards.*

letter [noun: **letters**]

1 a message that you write and post to another person

2 one of the written shapes that you combine to write words, like *a*, *b* or *c*

♦ **lettering** [noun] writing, especially when it is for decoration: *The title is on the picture frame in gold lettering.*

lettuce [noun: **lettuces**] a green vegetable whose leaves are used in salads

leukaemia [noun] a kind of cancer that affects the body's white blood cells

level [adjective]

1 flat or horizontal: *a piece of level ground*

2 being as high as something else: *The picture needs to be level with the mirror next to it.*

[noun: **levels**]

1 a particular distance above or below the ground: *pictures at eye level all around the room*

2 a particular standard or grade: *It's best to start at beginners' level.*

[verb: **levels, levelling, levelled**]

1 to level something is to make it flat, smooth or horizontal: *The ground will have to be levelled before they can build on it.*

2 to level things is to make them equal: *Gray scored again to level the scores.*

3 to level a gun at someone or something is to aim it at them

4 to **level off** or **level out** is to become horizontal: *The plane levelled out at 2000 feet.*

level crossing [noun: **level crossings**] a place where a road crosses a railway track

lever [noun: **levers**]

1 a strong bar for pushing against or pulling on in order to move something heavy

2 a handle that operates a machine: *Push the lever up to start the engine.*

[verb: **levers, levering, levered**] to move something by forcing a bar under or behind it: *It should be possible to lever the door open.*

liability [noun: **liabilities**]

1 liability is responsibility for something

2 a liability is a person or thing that is likely to cause a problem for you

LI

liable [adjective]
1 very likely to: *She's liable to lose her temper very suddenly.*
2 responsible for something: *You are liable to pay for any damage.*

liaise [verb: **liaises, liaising, liaised**] to talk to other people so that you can work together effectively: *You will need to liaise with staff in other departments.*

liar [noun: **liars**] someone who tells lies

liberal [adjective]
1 broad-minded and seeing many different points of view
2 a liberal amount of something is a lot of it: *a very liberal helping of chocolate pudding*
✦ **liberally** [adverb] generously: *Pour the sauce liberally over the dish.*

liberate [verb: **liberates, liberating, liberated**] to set someone free
✦ **liberation** [noun] being set free from someone else's control

liberty [noun: **liberties**] freedom, especially to do or say what you want: *Prisoners have lost their liberty.*

librarian [noun: **librarians**] someone whose job is to look after a library

library [noun: **libraries**] a building or room that has a collection of books or recordings

lice [noun] the plural form of the word **louse**

licence [noun: **licences**] an official document that gives someone permission to do or have something: *a driving licence • a licence to fish*

ⓘ Remember that **licence** with a **c** is a noun: *a driving licence*
License with an **s** is a verb: *You are not licensed to fish here.*

license [verb: **licenses, licensing, licensed**] to allow or permit someone to do something: *a restaurant that is licensed to serve alcohol*

lichen [noun: **lichens**] a kind of mossy plant that grows on surfaces like rocks and tree trunks

ⓘ This word is pronounced the same as the verb **liken**.

lick [verb: **licks, licking, licked**] to move your tongue over something: *licking your lips*
[noun: **licks**]

1 a movement of your tongue over something: *Give the spoon one last lick.*
2 a small amount of something: *This room needs a lick of paint.*

licorice [noun] another spelling of **liquorice**

lid [noun: **lids**]
1 a cover that fits a container like a box or a pot
2 an eyelid

lie¹ [verb: **lies, lying, lied**] to say something that is not true: *I'm sure that she lies about her age.*
[noun: **lies**] a statement that is not true: *The boy's story is a pack of lies.*
➡ **liar**

lie² [verb: **lies, lying, lay, laid**]
1 to rest in a flat position: *Lie flat on your back.*
2 to be in a particular place or position: *There were clothes lying all over the floor. • The town lies to the east of Geneva.*
3 to be or remain in a particular state: *The buildings lay in ruins.*

ⓘ The past tense of **lie** when it means 'to say what is not true' is **lied**.
The past tense of **lie** when it means 'to rest flat' is **lay**.

lieutenant [noun: **lieutenants**] an officer in the army or navy

ⓘ This word is pronounced lef-**ten**-int.

life [noun: **lives**]
1 a life is the time between being born and dying: *He lived in Glasgow all his life.*
2 life is the state of being alive: *feeling her pulse for any sign of life*
3 life is energy and liveliness: *Try to put a bit more life into your singing.*
4 your life is the way you live: *Life on a boat is great fun.*
5 life is all living things: *a book about pond life*

life assurance [noun] a type of insurance scheme that will pay money to your family if you die

lifebelt [noun: **lifebelts**] a large ring that floats, which someone can hold to stop them sinking under water

lifeboat [noun: **lifeboats**] a boat for rescuing people at sea

life-cycle [noun: **life-cycles**] the different

LI

stages that a living thing goes through from its birth to its death

lifeguard [noun: **lifeguards**] someone who works at a swimming pool or on a beach to rescue people who are in danger of drowning

life-jacket [noun: **life-jackets**] a jacket filled with air that will float and stop someone from sinking

lifeless [adjective]
1 dead
2 unconscious or without any signs of life

lifelike [adjective] very like a real thing or person: *a lifelike doll*

lifeline [noun: **lifelines**]
1 a way of communicating or getting help if you need it: *The telephone is our lifeline.*
2 a rope used to rescue a person who has fallen into water

life-size [adjective] a life-size picture or statue is the same size as the real person

lifespan [noun: **lifespans**] the length of a life: *This creature has a lifespan of only one day.*

lifestyle [noun: **lifestyles**] the way that someone lives: *We try to have a healthy lifestyle.*

lifetime [noun: **lifetimes**] the time that a particular person is alive: *They've changed that law twice in my lifetime.*

lift [verb: **lifts, lifting, lifted**]
1 to lift something is to pick it up or raise it: *She lifted her hand to her forehead.*
2 to lift is to move upwards: *The fog seems to be lifting.*
3 to officially end a rule that says something is not allowed: *The ban was lifted last month.*
[noun: **lifts**]
1 a movement upwards: *ten lifts with each leg*
2 a moving platform that can take things or people between the floors of a building
3 a ride in someone's car: *Do you want a lift home?*

lift-off [noun: **lift-offs**] the time when a spacecraft leaves the ground

light [noun: **lights**]
1 light is brightness from something, such as the sun or a lamp, that allows you to see things: *The light in this room is good for painting.*
2 a light is something that gives light, such as a

lamp or a candle: *Don't forget to switch off the light.*
3 if information **comes to light**, someone discovers it
[adjective: **lighter, lightest**]
1 not dark: *It's still light enough to read.* • *Mike got up as soon as it began to get light.*
2 pale in colour: *light blue* • *You can make colours lighter by adding white to them.*
[verb: **lights, lighting, lit**]
1 to light something is to make it burn with a flame: *Let's light the fire.*
2 to light is to start burning: *Why won't the cooker light?*
3 to light a place is to make it brighter: *The stage was lit with candles.*
→ **lighten**[1], **lighter, lighting**

light[2] [adjective: **lighter, lightest**]
1 not heavy: *a light suitcase*
2 easy and not too serious: *light work* • *light music*
3 not large or strong: *a light shower*
→ **lighten**[2], **lightly**

lighten[1] [verb: **lightens, lightening, lightened**] to make something brighter

lighten[2] [verb: **lightens, lightening, lightened**] to make something less heavy

lighter [noun: **lighters**] a device with a flame or spark that can make something burn, especially a cigarette

light-hearted [adjective]
1 a light-hearted person is cheerful
2 something that is light-hearted is not very serious: *a light-hearted quiz*

lighthouse [noun: **lighthouses**] a building like a tower that has a flashing light at the top to warn or guide ships

light industry [noun] factories that produce small goods such as glass or electrical parts

lighting [noun] equipment for giving light

lightly [adverb]
1 gently: *Mum touched me lightly on the arm and smiled.*
2 not in a very serious way: *They treated the problem too lightly.*

lightning [noun] an electric flash in the sky that often happens just before a clap of thunder

LI

lightweight [adjective]
1 not very heavy: *a lightweight raincoat*
2 not very important or serious: *a lightweight comedy*

light-year [noun: **light-years**] the distance that light travels in a year, which is 6 billion miles

like [1] [preposition]
1 similar to: *Geraldine looks just like her mother.*
2 in a similar way to: *She dances like a professional.*
3 typical of: *It's not like you to be late.*
[conjunction] as if: *You look like you've seen a ghost.*
→ liken, likeness

like [2] [verb: **likes, liking, liked**] to think that something or someone is nice or good: *I like pizza.*

likeable or **likable** [adjective] a likeable person is pleasant and easy to like

likelihood [noun] if there is a likelihood of something happening, it might or will probably happen

likely [adjective] probable or expected: *It's very likely that nobody will come.*

liken [verb: **likens, likening, likened**] to say that two things are like each other: *Her writing has been likened to J. K. Rowling's.*

likeness [noun: **likenesses**]
1 something similar: *I do see a likeness between the girls.*
2 a good likeness is something that looks very similar to the real thing or person: *The portrait is an excellent likeness of Katy.*

likewise [adverb] in the same way: *Keep the trimmings and likewise any fabric left over.*

lilac [noun: **lilacs**] a bush or tree with hanging clusters of sweet-smelling white or purple flowers
[adjective] pale purple

lilt [noun: **lilts**] a light, swinging rhythm: *a Welsh lilt to her voice*

lily [noun: **lilies**] a tall plant with large white or coloured flowers that smell very sweet

limb [noun: **limbs**]
1 a leg or arm
2 a branch of a tree

limber [verb: **limbers, limbering, limbered**] to **limber up** is to stretch and warm up your muscles before doing harder exercise

lime [noun: **limes**]
1 a small fruit that looks like a green lemon
2 a large tree with yellow blossom
3 a white substance that is used for making cement and fertilizers
4 a bright green colour

limelight [noun] to be **in the limelight** is to be getting a lot of attention, especially from the public

limerick [noun: **limericks**] a kind of humorous poem with five lines

limestone [noun] a type of rock that is used in building and making cement

limit [noun: **limits**]
1 a place or point that should not, or cannot, be passed: *There's a time limit for this test.*
2 a boundary: *within the city limits*
[verb: **limits, limiting, limited**] to keep someone or something within certain amounts: *I shall have to limit you to one cake each.*
♦ limitation [noun: **limitations**] a weakness, or something that makes another thing imperfect: *Living in a city has its limitations.*
♦ limited [adjective] not great: *a limited choice*

limousine [noun: **limousines**] a large and luxurious car, especially one with a chauffeur

limp [verb: **limps, limping, limped**] to walk unevenly because of a problem with one leg or foot
[noun: **limps**] an uneven walk: *walking with a limp*
[adjective: **limper, limpest**] not stiff or firm: *a limp lettuce • a limp handshake*

limpet [noun: **limpets**] a small cone-shaped shellfish that clings to rocks

line [1] [noun: **lines**]
1 a long thin mark or stripe: *a white line in the middle of the road*
2 a row of things or people: *lines of marching soldiers • the third line down on the next page*
3 a length of rope, wire or string: *hanging the washing on the line*
4 a wrinkle, especially on someone's face
5 a railway: *the east coast line*
6 a telephone connection: *There's a strange noise on this line.*

7 a short letter: *I'll drop you a line to let you know how we get on.*

8 a subject or activity that you are interested or involved in: *What line are you in?*

[verb: **lines, lining, lined**]

1 to line something like a street is to be along both sides of it: *Police officers will line the route of the procession.*

2 to **line up** is to stand or place in a row: *Line up opposite your partners.*

3 to **line something up** is to arrange it: *Have we got anything lined up for this evening?*

line ² [verb: **lines, lining, lined**] to cover something with a layer on the inside: *a jacket lined with silk*

➞ **liner²**, **lining**

linen [noun]

1 a kind of cloth that is made from a plant called flax

2 things such as sheets or table cloths that used to be made from linen but are now often made from other fabrics

liner ¹ [noun: **liners**] a large passenger ship

liner ² [noun: **liners**] something that forms a layer inside a container and can be taken out: *a bin liner*

linesman or **lineswoman** [noun: **linesmen** or **lineswomen**] someone who judges whether a ball has crossed a line during a game such as tennis

linger [verb: **lingers, lingering, lingered**] to be slow to leave: *members of the audience lingering in the hall*

lingerie [noun] women's underwear and night clothes

linguist [noun: **linguists**] someone who knows a lot about languages

liniment [noun: **liniments**] an oil or ointment that you rub into your skin to stop your muscles or joints hurting

lining [noun: **linings**] a layer on the inside of something: *a silver box with a velvet lining*

link [noun: **links**]

1 one of the rings of a chain

2 a relationship between two things: *the link between smoking and lung cancer*

3 something that joins two places together: *a rail link between the airport and the station*

[verb: **links, linking, linked**] to connect two

things: *A footpath links the two buildings.*

linoleum or **lino** [noun] a smooth, tough covering for floors

lint [noun] a soft material for putting on wounds

lion [noun: **lions**] a powerful animal of the cat family. A male lion has a big shaggy mane

lioness [noun: **lionesses**] a female lion

lip [noun: **lips**]

1 either the upper or the lower outside edge of your mouth

2 the shaped part of the outside edge of a container such as a jug: *a saucepan with a lip for pouring*

liposuction [noun] a medical treatment that sucks fat out of someone's body to make them look thinner

lip-read [verb: **lip-reads, lip-reading, lip-read**] to understand what someone is saying by watching the way their lips are moving, rather than by listening to them

♦ **lip-reader** [noun: **lip-readers**] a person who can understand what someone is saying by watching the way their lips move

lipstick [noun: **lipsticks**] a stick of a coloured substance that you can put on your lips

liqueur [noun: **liqueurs**] a strong sweet alcoholic drink, usually drunk at the end of a meal

liquid [noun: **liquids**] a substance that can flow, such as oil or water

liquidize or **liquidise** [verb: **liquidizes, liquidizing, liquidized**] to make something into a liquid, especially a thick liquid: *Add some cream and liquidize the soup.*

♦ **liquidizer** or **liquidiser** [noun: **liquidizers**] a machine for making solid or lumpy foods into smooth liquid or paste

liquor [noun: **liquors**] alcoholic drink

liquorice or **licorice** [noun] a black, sticky sweet that is flavoured with the root of the liquorice plant

lisp [verb: **lisps, lisping, lisped**] to say *th* for *s* or *z* because you cannot say these letters properly

[noun] a speech problem that makes a person say *s* and *z* like *th*

list [noun: **lists**] a series of things like names, numbers or prices, one after another: *a shopping list*

LI

[verb: **lists, listing, listed**] to say or write a lot of words, such as names, one after another: *List the items one by one.*

listen [verb: **listens, listening, listened**] to pay attention to something that you can hear: *Listen to me.*

listless [adjective] without energy or interest: *feeling listless all day*

lit [verb] a way of changing the verb **light** to make a past tense. It can be used with or without a helping verb: *Her face lit up at the idea.* • *I haven't lit the candles yet.*

literacy [noun] being able to read and write

literal [adjective] meaning exactly what it says
 • **literally** [adverb] in a literal way: *When she told you to jump in the lake, she didn't mean it literally.*

literary [adjective] to do with books, authors and literature

literate [adjective] able to read and write
 → **literacy**

literature [noun]
 1 novels, poetry and plays: *19th-century literature*
 2 all the written information about a subject

lithe [adjective: **lither, lithest**] a lithe person is able to bend and move very easily

litre [noun: **litres**] the basic measurement of volume in the metric system, equal to about 1.76 pints. This is often shortened to **l**

litter [noun: **litters**]
 1 litter is paper and other rubbish that people have thrown on the ground in a public place
 2 a litter is a group of animals born to the same mother at the same time: *a litter of puppies*

little [adjective: **littler, littlest**] small: *a little child* • *in a little while*
 [adverb: **less, least**]
 1 a bit: *Jump up and down a little to keep warm.*
 2 not very much: *We little understood how important this was.*
 [pronoun] a small amount: *Would you like a little more milk?* • *We were a little worried by then.*

live[1] [verb: **lives, living, lived**]
 1 to be alive: *Cats don't usually live for much more than twenty years.*
 2 to have your home in a certain place: *How long have you lived in Bradford?*

3 to pass your life in a certain way: *She's used to living alone.*
 → **living**

live[2] [adjective]
 1 not dead
 2 connected to an electricity supply: *a live socket*
 3 a live broadcast or concert actually happens as you watch or listen to it

livelihood [noun: **livelihoods**] the way you earn enough money to live properly

lively [adjective: **livelier, liveliest**] cheerful and full of energy: *a lively evening with lively people*

liver [noun: **livers**] a large organ in your body that is very important for cleaning your blood

livestock [noun] farm animals

livid [adjective] extremely angry: *He was livid when she broke his camera.*

living [noun: **livings**] a way of earning money: *What do you do for a living?*

living room [noun: **living rooms**] a room for sitting and relaxing in

lizard [noun: **lizards**] a four-footed reptile with a long body and tail and a scaly skin

llama [noun: **llamas**] a South American animal like a shaggy camel without a hump, that is kept for its wool and to carry loads

load [verb: **loads, loading, loaded**]
 1 to put goods into a vehicle such a ship or lorry
 2 to load a gun is to put bullets in it
 3 to load a machine is to put something in it: *load the camera with film*
 4 to put a program into a computer's memory so you can use it
 5 to weight dice so that they always fall the same way
 [noun: **loads**]
 1 the goods that a vehicle is carrying
 2 as much as a thing or person can carry at one time: *Take another load upstairs.*
 3 a load of something is a large amount of it: *What a load of rubbish!*

loaf [noun: **loaves**] a loaf of bread has been shaped and baked in one piece
 [verb: **loafs, loafing, loafed**] to **loaf about** is to spend your time being lazy

loan [verb: **loans, loaning, loaned**] to lend something to someone: *My brother loaned me*

Ll

the money to buy a new car.
[noun: **loans**] money that you borrow

loans
You may come across these terms when you are
offered or apply for a loan:
• The **APR** or **annual percentage rate** is a
figure that shows you how much interest you
would pay over a whole year if you borrow
money. It is best to use this figure to compare the
cost of different loans, because sometimes the
other figures that lenders use are based on
shorter periods and can be misleading.
• An **instalment** is one of several regular
payments that you make to pay back the loan.
• **Interest** is extra money that you have to pay
back when you borrow money.
• The **interest rate** is the amount of extra money
you have to pay back for each £100 that you
borrow. An interest rate of 2 per cent a month
means that you have to pay an extra £2 every
month for every £100 you borrow.
• **Security** means something that you own that
you agree the person who is lending you money
can have if you cannot pay back the loan. It is
sometimes called **collateral**.

loathe [verb: **loathes, loathing, loathed**]
to hate: *Harold loathes shopping.*
lob [verb: **lobs, lobbing, lobbed**] to throw or
hit a ball high into the air
[noun: **lobs**] a hit or throw that curves high up
into the air
lobby [noun: **lobbies**] an entrance hall
lobe [noun: **lobes**]
1 the soft round part at the bottom of your ear
2 one part of a body organ that has divisions,
like the brain
lobster [noun: **lobsters**] a large sea animal
with a hard shell, two large claws and eight
legs
local [adjective] belonging to and around a
certain area: *our local library*
[noun: **locals**]
1 someone who lives within a particular area: *If
you want to know the way, you'd better ask a
local.*
2 someone's local is the pub nearest their
home

local anaesthetic [noun: **local
anaesthetics**] an injection that makes part of
your body feel numb before you have a
medical operation or dental treatment
locality [noun: **localities**] a certain place
and the area round about it
locate [verb: **locates, locating, located**]
1 to find an exact position: *He was trying to
locate the school on the map.*
2 to be located in a place is to be situated
there: *a cottage located in the Highlands*
♦ **location** [noun: **locations**]
1 a position or situation: *the exact location of
the buried treasure*
2 a film is shot **on location** when it is not filmed
in a studio, but in a real place
loch [noun: **lochs**] a lake in Scotland
lock [noun: **locks**]
1 a device that you work with a key to fasten
things such as doors and drawers
2 a small section of a canal or river with gates
at each end. The level of the water in the lock
can be changed so that boats can pass to
higher or lower sections of the canal or river
[verb: **locks, locking, locked**]
1 to lock something such as a door is to fasten it
with a key
2 something like a door locks if it is possible to
fasten it with a key: *Don't leave valuables in
this room because the door doesn't lock.*
3 to **lock something up** or **away** is to put it
somewhere that can be locked with a key: *I
locked all my jewellery away in a box.*
lock² [noun: **locks**] a lock of hair is a piece
of it
locker [noun: **lockers**] a small cupboard,
especially one that can be locked
locket [noun: **lockets**] a little case, usually of
silver or gold, on a necklace chain
locomotion [noun] the power of moving
from place to place
♦ **locomotive** [noun: **locomotives**] a
railway engine that pulls trains
locust [noun: **locusts**] a large insect like a
grasshopper that flies in large groups that eat
and destroy growing plants
lodge [verb: **lodges, lodging, lodged**]
1 to get stuck somewhere: *A piece of apple
had lodged between his front teeth.*

LI

2 to live in a room in someone else's house and pay them rent

3 to lodge a complaint is to make it officially [noun: **lodges**]

1 a small house, often at the gate of a larger property

2 a house in the country used by people who are hunting or fishing: *a hunting lodge*

✦ **lodger** [noun: **lodgers**] a person who lives in rooms that they rent in someone else's house

✦ **lodging** [noun: **lodgings**]

1 a place to stay, especially for a short time

2 lodgings are where you stay when you rent rooms in someone else's house

loft [noun: **lofts**] the space between the roof of a house and the rooms: *suitcases stored in the loft*

lofty [adjective: **loftier, loftiest**] high or tall: *lofty ceilings*

log [noun: **logs**]

1 a section of a branch or tree trunk that has been cut up

2 an official record of what happens on a journey, especially of a ship or aeroplane [verb: **logs, logging, logged**]

1 to **log in** or **log on** is to start using a computer, often by typing in a password

2 to **log out** or **log off** is to stop using a computer by clicking on something on the screen

logic [noun] a way of thinking that involves correct reasoning

✦ **logical** [adjective] following reasonably and sensibly from facts or events: *the logical thing to do next*

logo [noun: **logos**] a small design that is the symbol of a company or product

loiter [verb: **loiters, loitering, loitered**] to stand around doing nothing: *Her friends loitered at the door.*

loll [verb: **lolls, lolling, lolled**]

1 to lie or sit about lazily: *Pete's been lolling about watching football all afternoon.*

2 your head or tongue lolls when it hangs loosely

lollipop [noun: **lollipops**] a hard sticky sweet on a stick

lolly [noun: **lollies**]

1 a lollipop

2 an ice lolly

lone [adjective] a lone person or thing is all alone: *He was killed by a lone gunman.*

loneliness [noun]

1 being unhappy because you are alone

2 being a long way from anything or anyone else

lonely [adjective: **lonelier, loneliest**]

1 a lonely person feels sad because they are alone, with no friends around them

2 a lonely place has very few people living in it or visiting it: *a lonely cottage on the hillside*

long¹ [adjective: **longer, longest**]

1 big from one end to the other: *a long supermarket queue* • *a long way home*

2 lasting or taking a lot of time: *a long delay* • *the long summer holidays*

[adverb: **longer, longest**]

1 for a long time: *Have you been waiting long?* • *It won't be long till she starts school.*

2 through the whole time: *I've been looking forward to this all day long.*

➡ **length**

long² [verb: **longs, longing, longed**] to want something very much: *longing to sit down* • *longing for a rest*

✦ **longing** [noun: **longings**] a very strong wish for something: *looking at the food with longing*

longitude [noun] the position of a place east or west of an imaginary line that passes from north to south through Greenwich, London. This line is shown on maps as 0°. Look up and compare **latitude**

long jump [noun] the long jump is an athletics contest where you run up to a board and then jump forward as far as possible

long-range [adjective]

1 able to reach a great distance: *long-range missiles*

2 looking a long way into the future: *a long-range weather forecast*

long-sighted [adjective] a long-sighted person sees objects that are far away more clearly than they see things closer to them

long-term [adjective] lasting or taking place for a long time: *the long-term effects of this medicine* • *long-term plans*

loo [noun: **loos**] an informal word for a toilet

look [verb: **looks, looking, looked**]

Ll

1 to turn your eyes to see something: *She was looking at the view.*
2 to appear or seem: *You look tired.*
3 to face a certain direction: *The window looks south.*
4 to **look after** something or someone is to take care of them: *Her husband looks after the baby during the day.*
5 to **look down on** someone is to think they are not as good or important as you: *Don't look down on me just because I'm not as rich as you.*
6 to **look forward to** something is to feel happy because you know you're going to enjoy it: *looking forward to the holidays*
[noun: **looks**]
1 a glance at something or an examination of it: *Take a look at this.*
2 a certain expression on your face: *She gave me a warning look.*
3 the appearance of a thing or person: *I don't like the look of those black clouds.*

look-alike [noun: **look-alikes**] a person who looks very like someone else: *a Prince Charles look-alike*

lookout [noun: **lookouts**]
1 a person who watches for danger: *The lookout spotted a boat on the horizon.*
2 a place where someone can keep watch
3 to **keep a lookout** is to watch carefully for something
4 something that is **your lookout** is your problem or concern and nobody else's: *If you do not study for the exam, that's your own lookout.*

loom¹ [noun: **looms**] a weaving machine for making cloth

loom² [verb: **looms, looming, loomed**]
1 to appear over or in front of you, especially in a frightening way: *A shadowy figure loomed towards us.*
2 to wait in the future, especially in a worrying way: *A big decision is looming before us.*

loop [noun: **loops**] the shape of something like a thread or piece of string when it curves around and crosses over itself: *Make a loop and pull one end through it.*
[verb: **loops, looping, looped**] to twist something around loosely: *a scarf looped around her neck*

loophole [noun: **loopholes**] something that allows people to avoid doing what they are supposed to do without breaking the law: *a loophole in her contract*

loose [adjective: **looser, loosest**]
1 not tight or firmly fixed: *a loose knot*
2 not tied up or shut in: *hair hanging loose* • *Let the dogs run around loose.*
[noun] if a criminal or wild animal is **on the loose**, they have escaped and are free: *A dangerous killer is on the loose.*
♦ **loosen** [verb: **loosens, loosening, loosened**] to make something less firm, fixed or tight: *I had to loosen my belt.*

loot [noun] stolen goods or money
[verb: **loots, looting, looted**] to steal things quickly from shops, businesses or homes, especially during times of violence, like a war: *Shops were looted during the riot.*

lopsided [adjective] uneven, with one side higher or lower than the other: *a lopsided smile*

lord [noun: **lords**]
1 a man who has the title *Lord* in front of his name
2 **Lord** is used as the title of men with high social rank, judges and bishops: *Lord Asquith* • *the Lord Mayor of London*
3 **Lord** is used in prayers as a way of addressing God
4 a master or ruler: *He was lord of all he could see.*

lore [noun] all the knowledge, stories and beliefs that get handed down through the generations

lorry [noun: **lorries**] a large motor vehicle for taking heavy loads by road

lose [verb: **loses, losing, lost**]
1 to forget where you put something: *I've lost my keys.*
2 to have something taken away from you: *Fifty people have lost their jobs.*
3 to have less of something than you had before: *I'm losing patience with you all.*
4 to be beaten in a contest: *I lost by 4 games to 6.*
5 a clock or watch loses time when it goes too slowly: *My watch is losing about a minute a day.*
♦ **loser** [noun: **losers**]

Ll

1 the person who does not win an argument, contest or battle: *Even the loser will win a huge amount of money.*
2 someone who never seems to succeed at anything

loss [noun: **losses**]
1 when you cannot find something or have had something taken away: *the loss of his home in a fire*
2 having less of something than you had before: *a loss of nearly a million pounds*
3 a disadvantage: *It'll be your loss if you do not buy this wonderful car.*

lost [adjective]
1 something that is lost is missing: *The painting has been lost for centuries.*
2 someone who is lost does not know where they are: *How did you get lost when you had a map?*
3 you are lost when you are confused: *I'm lost – can you explain that last bit again?*
4 a person is lost if they are killed: *soldiers lost in battle*

lot [noun: **lots**]
1 a large number or amount: *a lot of people • lots of money*
2 a group of things or people: *Another lot of visitors will arrive tomorrow.*
3 an area of land: *a parking lot*
4 to **draw lots** is to decide who should do something by choosing a piece of paper from several that look the same
5 **the lot** is everything: *He had fifteen paintings and sold the lot.*

lotion [noun: **lotions**] a liquid for putting on your skin or hair: *a moisturizing lotion*

lottery [noun: **lotteries**] an event where people win money or prizes when their number or ticket is chosen by chance from many others

loud [adjective: **louder, loudest**]
1 making a lot of sound: *a loud noise*
2 a loud colour is very bright
[adverb: **louder, loudest**] making a lot of sound: *Could you speak a little louder please?*
➡ **loudly**

loudhailer [noun: **loudhailers**] an electronic device that you can put over your mouth to make your voice much louder so that you do not have to shout

loudly [adverb] making a lot of sound or noise: *crying loudly*

loudspeaker [noun: **loudspeakers**] the part of a sound system that the sound actually comes out of

lounge [noun: **lounges**] a sitting room [verb: **lounges, lounging, lounged**] to sit or lie around lazily: *students lounging around the common room*

louse [noun: **lice**] a small insect that lives on a person or animal

lousy [adjective: **lousier, lousiest**] very bad: *lousy weather*

lout [noun: **louts**] a young man who behaves in a rough and unpleasant way
✦ **loutish** [adjective] loutish behaviour is unpleasant and aggressive

lovable [adjective] easy to love or like a lot: *a lovable child*

love [noun: **loves**]
1 love is a deep feeling of liking something or someone very much: *the love between a husband and wife*
2 a love is something or someone that you like very much: *Her great love was music.*
3 in a game such as tennis, a score of nothing: *The score was now forty–love.*
[verb: **loves, loving, loved**] to like someone or something very much: *Greg had always loved cricket.*
➡ **lover**

loveliness [noun] how lovely a thing or person is: *gazing at her loveliness*

lovely [adjective: **lovelier, loveliest**]
1 beautiful or attractive: *lovely eyes*
2 enjoyable or pleasing: *It was lovely to see you again.*

lover [noun: **lovers**]
1 a person who is having a sexual relationship with someone else
2 someone who is very enthusiastic about something: *an art lover*

loving [adjective] full of love: *a loving look*
✦ **lovingly** [adverb] in a loving way: *He gazed lovingly at her.*

low [adjective and adverb: **lower, lowest**]
1 near to the ground: *a low hedge • clouds getting lower and lower*
2 near the bottom of something such as a list or

a scale of measurement: *Your name's quite low on the list.*

3 a low sound or musical note is near the bottom of the range of pitch or musical notes: *She spoke in a low voice.* • *the lowest note you can sing*

4 less than usual in amount or importance: *low prices* • *Soon their supplies began to run low.*

5 sad or fed up: *Are you feeling a bit low?*

lower [verb: **lowers, lowering, lowered**]
1 to move something to a position nearer the bottom of something or nearer the ground: *They lowered the boat into the water.*
2 to lower something is to reduce it in amount or degree: *They have lowered their prices.*
[adjective] below something else, especially something that is the same. Look up and compare **upper**: *the lower jaw*

lowland [adjective] to do with land that is quite flat and near sea level: *lowland farms*
◆ **lowlands** [plural noun] areas of land without mountains

lowly [adjective: **lowlier, lowliest**] having an unimportant position: *Don't ask me, I'm just a lowly assistant.*

loyal [adjective] supporting and faithful: *a loyal fan*
◆ **loyally** [adverb] in a faithful way: *I loyally voted for him every time.*
◆ **loyalty** [noun] faithful support for your friends

lozenge [noun: **lozenges**]
1 a sweet that you suck, especially to help a sore throat
2 a diamond shape

Ltd [abbreviation] short for the word **Limited** in the names of companies: *Joe Bloggs Shoes Ltd*

lubricate [verb: **lubricates, lubricating, lubricated**] to put oil or grease on something like an engine or machine, to make it run smoothly
◆ **lubrication** [noun]
1 making something move more easily by adding oil or grease
2 a substance like oil or grease that will help moving parts to work more smoothly

luck [noun]
1 the way things happen by chance: *What*

bad luck that it rained all that day!
2 something good that happens by chance: *It was a piece of luck that I found the money.*
◆ **luckily** [adverb] by a good chance: *The car hit us, but luckily, nobody was badly hurt.*
◆ **lucky** [adjective: **luckier, luckiest**] a lucky person has good things happen to them by chance: *You're lucky to live so near the school.*

lucrative [adjective] producing a profit, especially a large one: *a lucrative business*

ludicrous [adjective] completely ridiculous or silly: *a ludicrous idea*

lug [verb: **lugs, lugging, lugged**] to pull or drag something with difficulty: *lugging the suitcases up the stairs*

luggage [noun] a traveller's suitcases and bags: *Make sure all your luggage is labelled.*

lukewarm [adjective]
1 slightly warm: *The water in the shower was only lukewarm.*
2 not very interested or enthusiastic: *We got a lukewarm welcome when we arrived.*

lull [verb: **lulls, lulling, lulled**] to make someone feel calm and relaxed: *lulling the baby to sleep*
[noun: **lulls**] a time when something noisy or busy stops for a while: *a lull in the fighting*

lullaby [noun: **lullabies**] a gentle song to lull a child to sleep

lumber [verb: **lumbers, lumbering, lumbered**]
1 to move heavily, slowly and clumsily: *We saw a bear lumbering through the forest.*
2 to **be lumbered with** something is to be given something that you do not want: *I got lumbered with the washing up.*

lumberjack [noun: **lumberjacks**] someone whose job is to cut down and chop up trees

luminous [adjective] glowing in the dark: *a luminous jacket*

lump [noun: **lumps**]
1 a small, shapeless piece of something: *a lump of coal* • *I can't make custard without lumps in it.*
2 a hard swelling on your body: *She found a lump on her breast.*
[verb: **lumps, lumping, lumped**] to **lump together** people or things is to treat them all in the same way

Ll

• **lumpy** [adjective: **lumpier, lumpiest**] full of lumps: *lumpy custard*

lunacy [noun] madness

lunar [adjective] to do with the moon

lunatic [noun: **lunatics**] someone who is mad: *driving like a lunatic*
→ lunacy

lunch [noun: **lunches**] the meal that you eat in the middle of the day between breakfast and dinner

lung [noun: **lungs**] the two bag-like organs inside your chest that you use for breathing

lunge [verb: **lunges, lunging, lunged**] to make a sudden strong or violent move forwards
[noun: **lunges**] a sudden violent move forwards: *An angry customer made a lunge at the manager.*

lurch [verb: **lurches, lurching, lurched**] to move along unevenly, especially suddenly rolling to one side: *The boat lurched and we fell over.*
[noun: **lurches**] a sudden roll to one side

lure [verb: **lures, luring, lured**] to tempt a person or animal with some kind of reward: *Scraps of food are used to lure the animals out of their burrows.*
[noun: **lures**] something that tempts an animal or person to do something: *The lure of going out was too strong to resist.*

lurk [verb: **lurks, lurking, lurked**] to wait secretly where you cannot be seen, especially because you are going to do something bad: *Was there someone lurking over there in the shadows?*

luscious [adjective] sweet, delicious and juicy: *a luscious peach*

lush [adjective: **lusher, lushest**] lush plants are healthy and growing well: *cows grazing on lush farmland*

lustre [noun] a shiny appearance
• **lustrous** [adjective] shining or glossy

luxuriant [adjective] growing richly and thickly: *luxuriant forest*

luxurious [adjective] very comfortable and expensive: *The hotel room was very luxurious.*

luxury [noun: **luxuries**]
1 luxury means extremely comfortable, expensive surroundings and possessions: *living in luxury*
2 a luxury is something very pleasant, but not necessary: *We can't afford many luxuries.*

-ly [suffix] if a word ends in **-ly**, it is often an adverb that describes how something is done. For example, *quickly* means 'in a quick way'

lyric [noun: **lyrics**]
1 a lyric is a short poem about feelings and emotions
2 the lyrics of a song are its words
• **lyrical** [adjective] sounding like poetry or music: *a lyrical description of the scenery*

M

m [abbreviation] short for **metre** or **metres**, or **million**

mac [noun: **macs**] a short form of the word **mackintosh**

macabre [adjective] something that is macabre is strange and horrible, because it involves evil or death: *a macabre painting of skulls and bones*

macaroni [noun] tubes of pasta cut into short lengths

macaroon [noun: **macaroons**] a biscuit or cake made with ground almonds and sugar

machine [noun: **machines**] a device that has moving parts and is operated by some form of power, designed to do a particular job or work: *a washing machine*
[verb: **machines, machining, machined**] to machine something is to sew it, shape it, or cut it using a machine or a machine tool

machine-gun [noun: **machine-guns**] a type of automatic gun that fires bullets quickly one after the other

machinery [noun] machines: *combine harvesters and other farming machinery*

machine tool [noun: **machine tools**] a piece of equipment used to cut and shape metals

macho [adjective] a macho man behaves in a tough and aggressive way

mackerel [noun: **mackerels** or **mackerel**] a small edible sea fish with a narrow striped body

mackintosh [noun: **mackintoshes**] a waterproof coat, usually reaching down to the knees or below

mad [adjective: **madder, maddest**]
1 mentally ill: *The poor woman went mad with grief.*
2 foolish or reckless: *Swimming in shark-infested waters is a mad thing to do.*
3 very angry: *I was mad with him for lying to me.*
4 to be **mad about** someone or something is to like them or it very much: *He's mad about football.*
5 if you do something **like mad**, you do it very quickly and use a lot of effort: *She was pedalling like mad to keep up with the others.*
➡ **madden, madly, madness**

madam [noun: **madams**] a formal and polite way of addressing a woman, especially at the beginning of a letter or when serving her in a shop

madcap [adjective] foolish and reckless: *a madcap scheme*

mad cow disease [noun] the common name for **BSE**

madden [verb: **maddens, maddening, maddened**] if something maddens you, it annoys you a lot or makes you very angry
♦ **maddening** [adjective] very annoying

made [verb]
1 a way of changing the verb **make** to form a past tense. It can be used with or without a helping verb: *He made porridge for breakfast.*
• *I think you have made a mistake.*
2 if something is **made for** someone, it suits or fits them very well: *The role was just made for someone with his talents.*

madly [adverb] desperately, or in a great hurry: *We were rushing about madly trying to get ready in time.*

madness [noun] mental illness, or great foolishness

magazine [noun: **magazines**]
1 a paper published regularly, for example, once a week or once a month, and which has articles and features by various writers and usually lots of photographs or pictures: *a football magazine* • *women's magazines*
2 a place where military equipment is stored

maggot [noun: **maggots**] a fly in the worm-like stage after it has hatched out of its egg and before it develops wings

magic [noun]
1 a strange power that causes things to happen that cannot be explained
2 tricks, such as making things disappear, which seem to people watching to be impossible
3 something beautiful or wonderful: *the island's special magic*
[adjective]
1 involving tricks such as making things disappear: *magic tricks* • *a magic show*
2 able to make impossible things happen: *a magic potion*
♦ **magical** [adjective] wonderful or charming: *a magical atmosphere*
♦ **magically** [adverb] using magic or as if by magic
♦ **magician** [noun: **magicians**]
1 someone who does magic tricks to entertain people
2 someone who has magic powers, especially in stories

magistrate [noun: **magistrates**] a person who judges cases of minor crime where there is no jury

magnet [noun: **magnets**] a piece of iron or other metal which has the power to attract other pieces of metal to it and which points north to south when it hangs free
♦ **magnetic** [adjective]
1 something that is magnetic has the power to attract iron and some other metals towards it
2 someone with a magnetic personality is very popular with other people
♦ **magnetically** [adverb] using magnetism
♦ **magnetism** [noun]
1 the power that a magnet has to attract metals
2 the power some people have to attract or influence other people

♦ **magnetize** or **magnetise** [verb: **magnetizes, magnetizing, magnetized**] to magnetize a metal is to make it magnetic

magnification [noun: **magnifications**]
1 making things seem larger or closer, or making things more important than they are
2 the amount by which an instrument like a microscope or telescope makes things seem larger. For example, a magnification of 20 makes something look 20 times larger than it really is

magnificence [noun] being magnificent: *People climb the hill for the magnificence of the view from the top.*

magnificent [adjective] very impressive or splendid: *a magnificent lion* • *a magnificent achievement*
♦ **magnificently** [adverb] in an impressive way: *He coped magnificently with the crisis.*

magnified [adjective] made to seem larger or closer by using a lens, microscope or telescope: *a magnified image of a hair*

magnifier [noun: **magnifiers**] an instrument or lens that makes things look bigger than they really are

magnify [verb: **magnifies, magnifying, magnified**]
1 to make something seem bigger or closer than it really is
2 to make something seem more important or serious than it really is
➡ **magnification**

magnifying glass [noun: **magnifying glasses**] a hand-held lens that you use to look at a small object or very small writing so that you can see it more clearly

magnitude [noun] a situation's or problem's magnitude is its great size, extent or importance

magnolia [noun: **magnolias**]
1 a tree or shrub with large white, pink or purple bowl-shaped or star-shaped flowers that have a sweet scent
2 a creamy white colour, usually used when talking about a colour of paint

magpie [noun: **magpies**] a black and white bird of the crow family that likes to collect shiny objects

mahogany [noun] a hard reddish wood used to make furniture, which comes from a tree that grows in tropical parts of Central and South America

maid [noun: **maids**] a girl or woman whose job is to keep the rooms clean and tidy in a hotel or house

maiden [noun: **maidens**] an old-fashioned word for a young unmarried woman
[adjective]
1 first: *a ship's maiden voyage*
2 in cricket, a maiden over is when no runs are scored by the batting side after six balls

maiden name [noun: **maiden names**] the surname that a married woman had when she was born

mail[1] [noun] letters or parcels carried by post
[verb: **mails, mailing, mailed**] to send a letter or parcel using the postal service

mail[2] [noun] mail, or chain mail, is armour worn on the body, which is made up of lots of small connected steel rings or plates

mailbox [noun: **mailboxes**] the place on a computer where e-mail is stored

mailing list [noun: **mailing lists**] a list of the names and addresses of people that an organization or business regularly sends information to

mail order [noun] a system for buying and selling things in which the customer chooses what they want from a catalogue and the goods are delivered by post

maim [verb: **maims, maiming, maimed**] to injure a person or animal very seriously so that one or more of their limbs is crippled

main [adjective] most important or principal: *a main road* • *The main thing is to stay calm.*
[noun: **mains**] a pipe that carries water or gas into houses or buildings: *a burst gas main*
➡ **mains**

mainland [noun] the mainland of a country is its biggest single area of land rather than any island or islands that form part of the same country

mainly [adverb] mostly or in most cases: *My job mainly involves organizing conferences.*

mains [plural noun] the mains are the pipes or cables that carry water or electricity to houses and buildings: *Plug this into the mains.*

maintain [verb: **maintains, maintaining, maintained**]

1 to keep something at the same amount, or to keep it going: *The rally drivers have to maintain high speeds on dangerous and twisty roads.*
2 to keep a house or piece of equipment in good condition or working well
3 to maintain an opinion or your innocence is to keep saying it is true even if other people do not believe you
4 to maintain someone is to give them the money they need to live on
• **maintenance** [noun]
1 regular cleaning or repair done to keep something in good condition or good working order
2 money paid to someone for them to live on

maisonette [noun: **maisonettes**] a flat or apartment on two floors within a building

maize [noun] a tall cereal plant that has large seedheads called cobs. The yellow seeds, called sweetcorn, are packed tightly together on the cob

majestic [adjective] very impressive, or behaving in a very dignified or impressive way, as a king or queen might do: *a majestic cathedral* • *a majestic procession*
• **majestically** [adverb] impressively or regally

majesty [noun: **majesties**]
1 majesty is greatness and impressiveness: *the majesty of the mountains*
2 **His**, **Her**, or **Your Majesty** is a title used when speaking to or about a king or queen: *Her Majesty will be attending a thanksgiving service next week.*

major [adjective]
1 something major is very big, very serious or very important: *a major catastrophe* • *a major route into the city*
2 in music, a major scale has a semitone between the first and the third notes and between the seventh and eighth notes. A major key or chord is based on this scale
[noun: **majors**] an army officer above the rank of captain

majority [noun: **majorities**]
1 the largest number of people or things in a group: *The majority of customers leave a generous tip.*
2 the number of votes by which the winner of

Mm

an election beats the person who comes second

make [verb: **makes, making, made**]
1 to create, produce or prepare something: *She makes all her own clothes.* • *I'm making a cup of coffee.* • *a company that makes parts for cars*
2 something makes something else happen when it causes or forces that other thing to happen: *Hay always makes me sneeze.* • *He made the dog sit and stay.* • *His attitude makes me very angry.*
3 to make a point, suggestion or promise is to give it: *He made an interesting point.*
4 you make the answer to a sum a particular amount when that is the amount you calculate it to be: *I make that £1.20 you owe me.* • *What time do you make it?*
5 two or more quantities make a certain amount when they add up to that amount: *Six and six makes twelve.*
6 to make a particular place or point is to reach that place or point: *We climbed part of the way, but we didn't make the summit.* • *If we hurry, we might just make the earlier train.*
7 to make money is to earn it
8 if you **make do**, you try to manage with what you have even though it is not ideal
9 to **make for** a place is to go in that direction
10 if you **make it**, you achieve what you were trying to achieve
11 to **make off** is to run away or escape
12 to **make something out** is to be able to see it or see what it is
13 to **make something out** is to understand it
14 to **make out** a cheque or application is to complete it by writing in the details needed
15 people who have been quarrelling **make up** when they agree to become friends again
16 to **make up** something such as a story or excuse is to invent it
17 to **make up for** something that you have done wrong is to balance it by doing something good
18 to **make up your mind** is to decide

make-believe [noun] pretending or fantasy

maker [noun: **makers**] a person, business or machine that makes a particular type of thing: *a film maker* • *a coffee maker*

makeshift [adjective] made from whatever is available and used instead of the real thing or something better: *a makeshift bed of leaves and moss*

make-up [noun]
1 cosmetics that are put on the face or body
2 a person's or thing's make-up is their character or what they or it consists of

makings [plural noun] if someone or something has the makings of a particular thing, they have all the qualities needed to become that thing: *Olivia has the makings of a successful singer.*

malaria [noun] a serious disease passed to humans by the bite of a type of mosquito, which causes periods of very high fever

male [adjective]
1 a male animal is of the sex that fathers children but does not give birth: *A male swan is called a cob.*
2 to do with men or boys or the things that involve them: *It's mostly a male hobby.* • *male hormones*
[noun: **males**] a male animal

malevolent [adjective] evil and wanting to do harm to other people

malfunction [verb: **malfunctions, malfunctioning, malfunctioned**] a machine malfunctions when it stops working properly or breaks down
[noun: **malfunctions**] a fault that causes a machine to stop working properly

malice [noun] malice is a feeling of spite and wanting to harm someone else
♦ **malicious** [adjective] spiteful
♦ **maliciously** [adverb] deliberately causing harm or hurt to someone else

malignant [adjective] a malignant tumour is a cancerous lump in your body which could spread to other parts of the body

mall [noun: **malls**] a shopping centre

mallet [noun: **mallets**] a heavy wooden hammer

malnutrition [noun] someone suffering from malnutrition is ill because they have not had enough to eat or have not eaten the right foods for a long time

malt [noun] a substance in barley and other grains that is used in making beer

maltreat [verb: **maltreats, maltreating, maltreated**] to treat a person or animal badly or cruelly
♦ **maltreatment** [noun] bad or cruel treatment

mammal [noun: **mammals**] a warm-blooded animal that is not a reptile, fish or bird. Female mammals give birth to their babies, instead of laying eggs, and feed them on milk made by their own bodies

mammogram [noun: **mammograms**] an X-ray that is taken of a woman's breast, usually to see if she has breast cancer

mammoth [noun: **mammoths**] a huge hairy type of elephant that lived in prehistoric times
[adjective] huge: *a mammoth task*

man [noun: **men**]
1 an adult male human being
2 man is a word sometimes used for human beings generally: *Man is closely related to the apes.*
[verb: **mans, manning, manned**] to man something is to be the person that runs it or operates it

manage [verb: **manages, managing, managed**]
1 to manage to do something is to succeed in doing it
2 to manage something like a shop or business is to be in charge of running it
3 to survive on very little money: *I don't know how he manages on his student grant.*

manageable [adjective] something is manageable if it can be controlled or dealt with fairly easily

management [noun]
1 controlling a business or other activity: *He always wanted to go into football management.*
2 the management of a company are the people who work as its managers

manager [noun: **managers**] someone who is responsible for managing a shop or other business, or an organization

manageress [noun: **manageresses**] a woman who runs a shop, restaurant or other business

managing director [noun: **managing directors**] someone who is in overall charge of the day-to-day running of a business

mandarin [noun: **mandarins**]
1 a high-ranking government official
2 a mandarin, or mandarin orange, is a small fruit rather like an orange but easier to peel because it has a looser skin

mandolin [noun: **mandolins**] an instrument shaped like a guitar but with a rounded instead of a flat back

mane [noun: **manes**] a horse's or lion's mane is the long hair that grows on its neck

mangle [verb: **mangles, mangling, mangled**] to crush or twist something out of shape
[noun: **mangles**] an old-fashioned machine with two heavy rollers, used for squeezing water out of washed clothes

mango [noun: **mangos** or **mangoes**] a large pear-shaped fruit with orange sweet-smelling flesh and a large stone in the middle

mangy [adjective: **mangier, mangiest**]
1 suffering from mange, a skin disease of dogs and other hairy animals, which causes scabs on the skin and makes the hair fall out in patches
2 dirty and worn thin: *a mangy old rug*

manhandle [verb: **manhandles, manhandling, manhandled**] to push, pull or drag a person or thing using your hands

manhole [noun: **manholes**] a covered hole in a road big enough for a person to go down to inspect or repair underground drains

manhood [noun] being a man: *the age when a boy reaches manhood*

mania [noun: **manias**]
1 a person suffering from mania has a type of madness in which they become very excited and often violent
2 a mania is a very strong enthusiasm for something
♦ **maniac** [noun: **maniacs**] a mad or dangerous person
♦ **manic** [adjective]
1 suffering from mania
2 manic actions are done at a very fast and wild pace: *a manic dash round the shops*

manicure [verb: **manicures, manicuring, manicured**] to manicure your fingernails is to cut and polish them so that they are neat and well-shaped

Mm

339

[noun: **manicures**] you have a manicure when someone cuts and polishes your fingernails

manifesto [noun: **manifestos** or **manifestoes**] a written statement of a political party's policies

manipulate [verb: **manipulates, manipulating, manipulated**]
1 to handle something in a skilful way
2 to influence someone cleverly and make them behave in a way that suits you without them realising
+ **manipulation** [noun] manipulating something or someone

mankind [noun] all human beings

manliness [noun] being manly

manly [adjective: **manlier, manliest**] having the qualities many people expect a man to have, for example, strength and courage

mannequin [noun: **mannequins**]
1 a life-size model of a human body used to display clothes in a shop
2 an old-fashioned word for a model who shows off clothes for a fashion designer or shop

manner [noun: **manners**]
1 a way in which something is done: *They had been scattered around in a haphazard manner.*
2 the way in which a person behaves towards other people: *I thought his manner was a bit offhand.*
3 **all manner of** means 'all kinds of': *The shop stocks all manner of things.*
+ **mannerism** [noun: **mannerisms**] a person's mannerisms are their special ways of speaking or behaving that are different from other people's
+ **manners** [plural noun] to have good manners is to behave politely towards other people, and to have bad manners, or no manners, is to behave rudely towards others

manoeuvre [noun: **manoeuvres**]
1 a difficult movement that needs skill and planning
2 something that you do in a clever or skilful way that affects how a situation will develop
3 military manoeuvres are planned movements of large numbers of troops and equipment

[verb: **manoeuvres, manoeuvring, manoeuvred**]
1 to manoeuvre is to move skilfully
2 to manoeuvre something somewhere is to move it there carefully and accurately: *The prams were impossible to manoeuvre round the corner.*

manor [noun: **manors**] a name given to some large old houses, originally built for noblemen

mansion [noun: **mansions**] a large grand house

manslaughter [noun] the crime of killing someone without intending to kill them

mantelpiece [noun: **mantelpieces**] a frame around a fireplace, especially the top part that forms a shelf

mantle [noun: **mantles**] a protective covering: *The garden looked magical under its mantle of crisp white snow.*

ⓘ **Mantle** is a literary word.

manual [noun: **manuals**] a book containing information about something, for example, the parts of a machine and how to operate it
[adjective]
1 working or operated by a person rather than being automatic: *an old manual loom*
2 involving the hands or physical strength and skills: *manual labour*
+ **manually** [adverb] by hand: *manually operated machines*

manufacture [verb: **manufactures, manufacturing, manufactured**] to make things in large quantities, often in a factory
+ **manufacturer** [noun: **manufacturers**] a person or business that makes large quantities of things to sell
+ **manufacturing** [noun] the part of industry involved in making products for sale

manure [noun] a mixture containing animal dung, spread on soil to make it better for growing flowers and crops

manuscript [noun: **manuscripts**]
1 a book or document written by hand
2 an author's manuscript is his or her handwritten or typed version of a book before it is edited and printed

Manx [adjective] coming from the Isle of

Man, an island in the Irish Sea: *A Manx cat has no tail.*

many [pronoun]

1 a lot or a large number: *There were a lot of people there, but many left early.*

2 how many means 'what quantity or number': *If you take three chairs away how many will be left?*

[adjective: **more, most**] a lot or a large number: *He has many friends.* • *Many people in the world don't have enough to eat.*

Maori [noun: **Maoris**] a member of the race of people who lived in New Zealand before anyone arrived from other countries

map [noun: **maps**] a diagram of an area of land showing the position of things like hills, rivers and roads

[verb: **maps, mapping, mapped**]

1 to map an area is to make a map of it

2 to make a detailed diagram or chart of something to show the position of each of its parts: *mapping DNA*

maple [noun: **maples**] a tree with broad leaves that turn red, brown, orange and yellow in the autumn

mar [verb: **mars, marring, marred**] to mar something is to spoil it in some way

maracas [plural noun] a musical instrument made up of two hollow containers filled with small stones, which are shaken so that the stones rattle

marathon [noun: **marathons**]

1 a race in which runners cover a distance just over 26 miles or 42 kilometres

2 a long and difficult task or activity

[adjective] very long and difficult: *a marathon session at the dentist*

marauder [noun: **marauders**] someone who roams about robbing and killing people

marble [noun: **marbles**]

1 marble is a type of rock, which can be black, dark green, pink or white, and usually has veins of other colours through it. It is used for sculpture and for making fireplaces and work tops

2 marbles are small coloured glass balls used for playing a children's game

[adjective] made of marble: *a marble table top*

March [noun] the third month of the year, after February and before April

march [verb: **marches, marching, marched**]

1 soldiers march when they walk together at the same regular pace

2 people march when they walk in a large group through the streets, usually because they are protesting about something

3 to march someone somewhere is to force them to go there by holding them or walking beside them so that they do not escape

[noun: **marches**]

1 a steady walking pace or a distance covered by marching: *a slow march* • *a long march*

2 music for marching to

mare [noun: **mares**] a female horse or zebra

margarine [noun] a substance made from vegetable oils or animal fats used for cooking or for spreading on bread like butter

margin [noun: **margins**]

1 a blank area at the top, bottom or either side of a written or printed page

2 an edge or border: *reeds growing on the margins of the lake*

3 an extra amount of something: *We allowed ourselves a margin of several hours, in case we got held up anywhere.*

 • **marginal** [adjective] if something is of marginal importance it is not very important, because it is not the central or main part of something

 • **marginally** [adverb] slightly

marigold [noun: **marigolds**] a yellow or orange flower

marina [noun: **marinas**] a harbour for private boats

marine [adjective] to do with the sea or belonging to the sea: *marine life*

mariner [noun: **mariners**] someone who sails boats or ships on the sea

marital [adjective] to do with marriage: *marital status*

mark [noun: **marks**]

1 a spot or stain: *There's a dirty mark on the sofa.*

2 a written or printed sign or symbol that stands for something: *a punctuation mark*

Mm

3 a point or grade given as a reward for good or accurate work: *My son could get much higher marks if he made a bit more effort.*
[verb: **marks, marking, marked**]
1 to put a mark, scratch or stain on something
2 to look at someone's work and give it points or a grade to show how good or accurate it is
+ **marked** [adjective] noticeable or obvious: *There has been a marked improvement in her work.*
+ **marker** [noun: **markers**]
1 something used to mark the position of something
2 a pen with a thick point that is used to write on various surfaces

market [noun: **markets**]
1 a place where people sell things from a stall: *a street market • a fruit market*
2 there is a market for something when people will buy it: *There is a huge market for mobile phones.*
3 the typical place or group of people that a product is sold to: *a magazine aimed at the teenage market*
4 if something is **on the market**, it is available for people to buy: *The house has been on the market for six months.*
[verb: **markets, marketing, marketed**] to offer something for sale to the public, often using advertising to encourage people to buy it

market garden [noun: **market gardens**] a large garden where fruit and vegetables are grown to be sold

marketing [noun] the job or process of encouraging people to buy products by deciding on their price, where to sell them and how to advertise them

marksman [noun: **marksmen**] someone who can shoot very accurately

marmalade [noun] jam made from oranges or other citrus fruit and usually eaten on toast at breakfast time

maroon[1] [verb: **maroons, marooning, marooned**] to leave someone in a helpless or uncomfortable position, especially on a lonely island from which they cannot escape

maroon[2] [noun] a dark purple-red colour

marquee [noun: **marquees**] a very large tent used for circuses, weddings or parties

marriage [noun: **marriages**]
1 the ceremony in which a man and woman become husband and wife
2 the period of time when two people are married to each other: *a long and happy marriage*

married [adjective]
1 having a husband or wife: *a married man*
2 to do with marriage: *married life*

marrow [noun: **marrows**]
1 marrow is the spongy tissue inside long bones such as the ones in your leg
2 a marrow is a long rounded vegetable that grows on the ground

marry [verb: **marries, marrying, married**] to make someone your husband or wife in a special ceremony, or to perform the ceremony making two people into husband and wife
→ **marriage, married**

marsh [noun: **marshes**] an area of land that is soft and wet all the time
→ **marshy**

marshal [noun: **marshals**]
1 an official who controls the crowds at big public events like pop concerts
2 a high-ranking officer in the army, air force or navy
3 in the United States, the chief police officer or fire officer in a city or area
[verb: **marshals, marshalling, marshalled**] to marshal people or things is to gather them together in an organized way

marshmallow [noun: **marshmallows**] a very soft, spongy pink or white sweet

marshy [adjective] marshy ground is very wet and soft

marsupial [noun: **marsupials**] an animal such as the kangaroo that gives birth to partly developed babies, which then crawl into a pouch on their mother's belly where they are fed and protected until they grow bigger

martial art [noun: **martial arts**] martial arts are fighting sports or techniques of self-defence, for example, karate and judo

Martian [noun: **Martians**] in science-fiction stories, a creature from the planet Mars

martini [noun: **martinis**] a cocktail made of gin and vermouth

martyr [noun: **martyrs**] someone who is killed or tortured because they refuse to give up their beliefs
[verb: **martyrs, martyring, martyred**] to kill or torture someone for their beliefs
♦ **martyrdom** [noun: **martyrdoms**] being martyred

marvel [noun: **marvels**] an astonishing or wonderful person or thing
[verb: **marvels, marvelling, marvelled**] you marvel at something when it fills you with wonder
♦ **marvellous** [adjective] wonderful or astonishing: *She was always telling marvellous stories about dragons and sorcerers.*

marzipan [noun] a thick paste made with sugar and crushed almonds, used to make sweets and to decorate cakes

mascara [noun] make-up that is brushed on to the eyelashes to make them thicker and darker

mascot [noun: **mascots**] a person, animal or object that a person or team keeps to bring them luck

masculine [adjective]
1 to do with men, typical of men, or suitable for men
2 in English grammar, masculine forms of words refer to males. For example, *he* is a masculine pronoun
♦ **masculinity** [noun] being like a man

mash [verb: **mashes, mashing, mashed**] to crush something into a soft mass: *Mash the potatoes.*
[noun] mashed potatoes: *bangers and mash*

mask [noun: **masks**] a covering that you wear over your face to protect it or as a disguise
[verb: **masks, masking, masked**] to cover, hide or disguise something: *She sprayed air freshener to mask the cooking smells.*

mason [noun: **masons**] a craftsman who cuts and carves stone
♦ **masonry** [noun] the parts of a building that are made of stone

mass [noun: **masses**]
1 a large lump or heap of something or a large quantity gathered together: *a mass of tangled metal • a mass of blonde curls*

2 a big quantity or number: *He's got masses of toys.*
3 in science, mass is a measure of the quantity of matter in an object: *A solid rubber ball has greater mass than a hollow one of the same size.*
[adjective] made up of large quantities or numbers: *a mass meeting*
[verb: **masses, massing, massed**] people or things mass, or **mass together**, when they gather in large numbers: *soldiers massing on the border*
♦ **Mass** [noun] one of several kinds of service held in the Roman Catholic Church and some other Christian churches

massacre [noun: **massacres**] the killing of large numbers of people or animals
[verb: **massacres, massacring, massacred**] to kill large numbers of people or animals in a cruel and violent way

massage [verb: **massages, massaging, massaged**] to rub parts of the body gently but firmly to relax the muscles or treat pain and stiffness
[noun: **massages**] treatment by massaging

massive [adjective]
1 very big: *a massive amount*
2 large and heavy: *Hyenas have massive jaws for tearing flesh and crunching bones.*
♦ **massively** [adverb] hugely

mass production [noun] making goods in very large quantities, usually in a factory using machines

mast [noun: **masts**] a wooden or metal pole for holding up the sails of a boat or ship, or a radio or television aerial

mastectomy [noun: **mastectomies**] a medical operation to remove a woman's breast

master [noun: **masters**]
1 a man who owns or is in charge of something: *a dog and its master • the master of the house*
2 if someone is a master of some activity, they are very good at it: *a master of disguise*
3 in the past, **Master** was a title used for a boy: *young Master Copperfield*
[adjective] fully qualified and experienced: *a master craftsman*
[verb: **masters, mastering, mastered**]
1 to learn enough about a subject or a skill to

Mm

be able to use it or do it successfully: *Juggling needs quite a lot of practice before you master it.*

2 to master a feeling such as fear is to overcome it

♦ **masterly** [adjective] very clever or skilful: *a masterly performance*

mastermind [noun: **masterminds**] the mastermind of a clever scheme or crime is the person who thinks of it and organizes the people who carry it out
[verb: **masterminds, masterminding, masterminded**] to mastermind a scheme or crime is to think of it and do the planning or organization needed to carry it out

masterpiece [noun: **masterpieces**]
1 a book, painting, piece of music or other work of art that is one of the greatest of its kind
2 someone's masterpiece is the greatest piece of work they have done

mastery [noun]
1 great skill at something: *We were amazed at his mastery of chess at such a young age.*
2 control of something: *mastery of the seas*

mat [noun: **mats**]
1 a flat piece of material for covering or protecting part of a floor
2 a small piece of material for protecting a table's surface or for resting something on: *a table mat • a mouse mat*

matador [noun: **matadors**] the man who kills the bull in a bullfight

match¹ [noun: **matches**] a short piece of wood or other material tipped with a substance that catches fire when it is rubbed against a rough surface

match² [noun: **matches**]
1 a contest or game between two players or two teams
2 something that is similar to, or the same as, another thing, especially in its colour or pattern: *This isn't the same make of paint but it's a very good match.*
3 a person or animal who is able to equal another: *I could beat him over a mile, but I was no match for him when it came to the 100 metres.*
[verb: **matches, matching, matched**]
1 two things match when they are similar to or the same as each other

2 to match, or **match up to**, another person or thing is to be as good as them

matchbox [noun: **matchboxes**] a small cardboard box for holding matches

mate [noun: **mates**]
1 a friend or companion
2 an officer on a ship
3 an animal's mate is the male or female it mates with
[verb: **mates, mating, mated**] animals mate when a male and a female have sex so that they can produce young

material [noun: **materials**]
1 cloth or fabric: *I need ten metres of material to make the curtains.*
2 a tool or substance used for making something else: *a shop selling artist's materials*
3 information and ideas that are used to produce something such as a book or a television programme: *She used her experiences as material for her new book.*

maternal [adjective]
1 to do with, or typical of, a mother: *strong maternal feelings*
2 from your mother's side of your family: *your maternal grandmother*

maternity [noun] being a mother
[adjective] to do with pregnancy and giving birth: *a maternity dress • a maternity hospital*

math [noun] a short form of the word **mathematics** that is used mainly in the United States and Canada

mathematical [adjective] to do with or using mathematics: *a mathematical genius • a mathematical calculation*

mathematician [noun: **mathematicians**] someone who studies mathematics or is an expert in mathematics

mathematics [noun] the study of measurements, numbers, quantities and shapes

maths [noun] a short form of the word **mathematics**

matinée [noun: **matinées**] a performance at a theatre or cinema in the afternoon or morning

matrimony [noun] the state of being married

matron [noun: **matrons**]

1 an old-fashioned word for a senior nurse in charge of a hospital

2 a woman in charge of housekeeping or nursing at a hostel or boarding school

matt or **matte** [adjective] a matt surface or matt finish is dull, without any shine or gloss

matted [adjective] tangled and stuck together in a thick mass: *matted hair*

matter [noun: **matters**]

1 matter is any substance that takes up space and is part of the physical universe

2 a subject, situation or issue: *He wants to see you to discuss a personal matter.*

3 if something is the matter, something is wrong or someone is ill or has a problem: *What's the matter with Rachel? She's very quiet.*

4 as a matter of fact means 'in fact': *As a matter of fact, he's one of the wealthiest men in the country.*

5 you use **for that matter** when you are adding to something you have just said: *My sister was furious, and, for that matter, so was I.*

[verb: **matters, mattering, mattered**] to matter is to be important: *Winning matters to him more than it should.*

♦ **matter-of-fact** [adjective] a matter-of-fact person deals with or talks about an unusual or upsetting situation in a calm way, as if it was something that happened every day: *She tried hard to be matter-of-fact about it all.*

matting [noun] stiff material used to make mats

mattress [noun: **mattresses**] a thick firm layer of padding for lying on, usually as part of a bed

mature [adjective]

1 fully grown or developed: *A mature male elephant can weigh several tons.*

2 behaving in a sensible, grown-up way: *He's not very mature for his age.*

[verb: **matures, maturing, matured**] to become mature

♦ **maturity** [noun] being mature or adult

maul [verb: **mauls, mauling, mauled**] to maul a person or animal is to hurt them badly in a rough and savage attack: *The zookeeper was mauled by one of the lions.*

mauve [noun] a pale purple colour

maximum [noun and adjective] the greatest number or quantity, or the highest point: *The maximum I'm prepared to pay is £20.* • *The crime carries a maximum penalty of five year's imprisonment.*

May [noun] the fifth month of the year, after April and before June

may [verb]

1 if you may do something, there is a possibility you will do it: *I may apply for the job, but I'm not sure yet.*

2 to have permission to: *You may leave the table now.* • *May I ask what you're doing in my room?*

ⓘ **May** is the present tense form. You use **might** for the past tense.

maybe [adverb] perhaps or possibly: *Maybe you'd like to come to lunch one day?*

mayday [noun: **maydays**] a word used as an international signal of distress, especially by ships or aeroplanes in trouble

mayhem [noun] great confusion and noise

mayonnaise [noun] a smooth creamy sauce made by blending oil, egg yolks and vinegar

mayor [noun: **mayors**] a man or woman elected as the official leader of a town or city

mayoress [noun: **mayoresses**] a mayor's wife

maypole [noun: **maypoles**] a tall decorated pole with long ribbons attached at the top. People hold the ribbons as they dance round the pole in a traditional celebration of the first day of May

maze [noun: **mazes**] a confusing network of paths each with a high wall or hedge on either side, designed as a puzzle to see how well you can find your way

MB [abbreviation] short for **megabyte**

MD [abbreviation] short for **managing director**

me [pronoun] a word you use to talk about yourself: *Would you make me a cup of tea, please?* • *Lots of cakes for tea, all for you and me.*

ⓘ In a sentence in which you are doing the action, you use **I** before the verb. You use **me** after the verb or a preposition. Be careful to use **me**, not **I**, in sentences like this:

Mm

The teacher gave the best mark to Emily, Rory and **me**.
An easy way to check if you have chosen the correct word is to take away the other names, like this:
✓ *The teacher gave the best mark to* **me**.
✗ *The teacher gave the best mark to* **I**.

mead [noun] an alcoholic drink made from honey

meadow [noun: **meadows**] a field of grass

meagre [adjective] a meagre amount is a very small amount: *They can't possibly survive the winter on such meagre supplies.*

meal [noun: **meals**] a meal is food that you eat at one time, for example, breakfast, lunch or dinner

mean¹ [verb: **means, meaning, meant**]
1 a word or action means something when it shows something or you understand something from it: *The definitions in this dictionary tell you what the words mean.* • *Dark clouds usually mean rain.*
2 you mean to do something when you intend to do it: *I'm sorry. I didn't mean to stand on your foot.*
3 you mean what you say when you aren't joking or telling lies
4 something that means something to you is important to you: *That puppy means an awful lot to her.*
➡ **meaning**

mean² [adjective: **meaner, meanest**]
1 a mean person won't spend money or share what they have with others
2 if someone is mean to you, they are nasty and unkind
➡ **meanness**

mean³ [adjective]
1 a mean point or quantity is halfway between two other points or quantities
2 average: *The mean rainfall is worked out by taking a measurement every day, adding all the measurements together and dividing by the number of days.*

meander [verb: **meanders, meandering, meandered**] if a river meanders, it forms a series of bends as it flows slowly across a flat area of land

meaning [noun: **meanings**] what a word or action means

meaningful [adjective]
1 a meaningful expression or gesture is intended to show something: *a meaningful look*
2 something meaningful is useful or important: *meaningful discussions*

meaningless [adjective]
1 having no meaning: *It's just all meaningless waffle.*
2 having no purpose or importance: *He felt as if his life was meaningless.*

meanness [noun]
1 selfishness or lack of generosity
2 nastiness

means [noun]
1 a means of doing something is a way or method of doing it: *Traffic jams are so frequent, many people are looking for a different means of transport.*
2 a person's means is the money they have or earn: *Living beyond your means is spending more than you have or can earn.*
3 you use **by all means** when someone has asked your permission to do something and you want to say 'yes': *'Can I have a look at your magazine?' 'By all means.'*
4 by no means means 'in no way': *It is by no means the best film I've ever seen.*

means test [noun: **means tests**] an official inquiry into how much money someone has, to see if they qualify for financial benefits from the government

meant [verb] a way of changing the verb **mean** to form a past tense. It can be used with or without a helping verb: *I meant every word I said.* • *She had meant to tell him the news, but had forgotten.*

meantime [adverb]
1 meantime is used to refer to the time between now and some event in the future
2 in the meantime means 'for now': *We're having the car repaired but in the meantime we're borrowing my sister's.*

meanwhile [adverb] meanwhile is used to refer to something that is happening during this time or at the same time as something else is happening

measles [noun] an infectious disease, which

Mm

mostly affects children, with red spots appearing on the skin and a high fever

measly [adjective: **measlier, measliest**] small in value or amount: *All I had to eat was one measly little biscuit.*

measure [verb: **measures, measuring, measured**]
1 to measure something is to find its width, height, length, weight or amount: *She was measuring the window for some new curtains.*
2 if something measures a certain number of units, its size or amount is given in that number of units: *The room measures 3.5 metres from the door to the window.*
[noun: **measures**] a unit used in measuring: *A kilogram is a measure of weight, while a kilometre is a measure of distance or length.*
♦ **measurement** [noun: **measurements**] a size or amount found by measuring
♦ **measures** [plural noun] actions taken to achieve a particular aim: *strict measures to reduce crime*

meat [noun: **meats**] the flesh of animals used as food, for example, pork, lamb or beef
♦ **meaty** [adjective: **meatier, meatiest**] full of meat or tasting of meat: *a nice meaty pie with a crisp crust*

mechanic [noun: **mechanics**] someone whose job is to keep machinery working and repair it when it breaks down

mechanical [adjective]
1 to do with machines, or worked by machinery: *mechanical engineering • a mechanical toy*
2 mechanical behaviour or actions are done without thinking or concentrating

mechanics [noun]
1 mechanics is the study and art of building machinery: *car mechanics*
2 the mechanics of something are the details or processes involved in making it work: *the mechanics of their campaign*

mechanism [noun: **mechanisms**] a working part of a machine, or its system of working parts: *the cogs and springs that are part of the clock's mechanism*

medal [noun: **medals**] a metal disc, usually with a design or writing stamped on it, given as a prize in a competition

medallion [noun: **medallions**] a piece of jewellery with a disc like a medal hanging on a long chain that is worn around the neck

medallist [noun: **medallists**] someone who has won a medal in a competition

meddle [verb: **meddles, meddling, meddled**] to meddle is to interfere in someone else's business or to tamper with something

meddlesome [adjective] interfering

media [plural noun] the media are newspapers, television and radio or any other means of communicating information to the public

ⓘ Some people use a singular verb with **media**, as in: *The media **was** waiting when the movie star came out of the hotel.*
However, if you want to be strictly correct you should use a plural verb, as in: *The media **were** waiting when the movie star came out of the hotel.*

mediaeval [adjective] another spelling of **medieval**

medical [adjective] to do with healing and medicine or doctors and their work: *medical treatments*
[noun: **medicals**] a general examination done by a doctor to find out the state of a person's health

medical certificate [noun: **medical certificates**] an official note from a doctor stating that someone is not well enough to work

medically [adverb] by or using medicine

medicinal [adjective] to do with medicine or having an effect like medicine

medicine [noun: **medicines**]
1 the science of the treatment of illness and disease: *studying medicine*
2 any substance used to treat or prevent diseases and illnesses: *cough medicine*

LANGUAGE FOR LIFE

medicines

There are two different types of medicine, which you get in different ways.
• **Prescription-only medicines** are medicines that you can only get if your doctor signs a form.
• **Over-the-counter medicines** or **non-prescription medicines** are medicines that

Mm

you can buy at a chemist's shop without a form from your doctor.

It is very important to read the label on medicine so that you know how much to take and when to take it. You may come across these words on the labels of medicines:

• If you take a medicine **orally**, you take it through your mouth.

• The **prescribed dose** is the amount of the medicine that your doctor tells you to use each time.

• The words **use by** tell you the date when the medicine will stop being effective.

---

medieval or **mediaeval** [adjective] to do with or in the Middle Ages, the period of history from about the beginning of the 12th century to the end of the 15th century

mediocre [adjective] dull and ordinary, with no special or exciting qualities
♦ **mediocrity** [noun] being dull and ordinary

meditate [verb: **meditates, meditating, meditated**]
1 to spend time being quiet, still and relaxed, especially for spiritual or religious reasons: *He was sitting cross-legged, meditating.*
2 to think about something deeply and carefully: *She was meditating about the future.*
♦ **meditation** [noun: **meditations**] meditating or deep thought

medium [adjective] at the middle point between two ends in a range, for example, between small and large, low and high, or light and dark: *a man of medium height with medium brown hair*
[noun: **mediums** or **media**]
1 a means or substance by which something is expressed, communicated or produced: *The World Wide Web is a popular medium for advertising.*
2 someone who believes they can communicate with the dead

ⓘ Either plural, **mediums** or **media**, can be used for the first sense of the noun, but only **mediums** is used for the second sense.

medley [noun: **medleys**]
1 a mixture: *a medley of exotic fruits*
2 a piece of music combining several other pieces of music: *He played a medley of Scottish tunes.*

meek [adjective: **meeker, meekest**] a meek person is gentle and not likely to complain or argue with other people
♦ **meekly** [adjective] without complaining or arguing: *'Sorry', said Lily meekly.*
♦ **meekness** [noun] being meek

meet [verb: **meets, meeting, met**]
1 to come face to face with someone by chance: *Guess who I met in town?*
2 to come together with one other person, or a group of other people, at the same time and in the same place: *Let's meet for a coffee next week sometime.*
3 to be introduced to someone and get to know them for the first time: *Have you met my big sister, Jane?*
4 two things meet when they come together or touch: *I've got so fat, my waistband doesn't meet round my middle.*
5 to meet a challenge, or a certain attitude or response, is to face it, or be faced with it
6 to meet the cost of something is to pay for it
7 to meet a need is to provide what is needed
♦ **meeting** [noun: **meetings**] a gathering of people, usually to discuss something

mega- [prefix]
1 when **mega-** comes at the beginning of some words it means 'a million'. For example, a *megaton* is a million tons
2 when **mega-** comes at the beginning of other words it means 'huge' or 'great'. For example, if someone is called a *megastar*, they are a very big star

megabyte [noun: **megabytes**] a unit used to measure computer memory or data, equal to approximately a million bytes. This is often shortened to **MB**

megaphone [noun: **megaphones**] a device shaped like an open-ended cone that someone speaks through to make their voice sound louder

melancholy [noun] sadness
[adjective] sad and lonely, or making you feel sad: *The dog gave a melancholy howl.*

mellow [adjective: **mellower, mellowest**] soft, not strong or unpleasant: *the mellow sound of the clarinet*

[verb: **mellows, mellowing, mellowed**]
1 fruit or wine mellows when it becomes ripe or mature
2 a person mellows with age when they become more tolerant and pleasant as they get older

melodic [adjective] having a melody

melodious [adjective] a melodious sound or voice is tuneful and pleasant to listen to

melodrama [noun: **melodramas**] a style of drama with lots of exciting action that is more extreme than in real life, or a play or film in this style
♦ **melodramatic** [adjective] someone behaves in a melodramatic way when they exaggerate to make things seem more sensational or exciting than they really are

melody [noun: **melodies**] a tune, especially a pleasant-sounding one
⟶ **melodic, melodious**

melon [noun: **melons**] a large rounded fruit with a green or yellow skin, yellow or orange sweet-tasting flesh, and lots of seeds in the middle

melt [verb: **melts, melting, melted**] something melts when it becomes soft and runny as it is heated

melting point [noun: **melting points**] the temperature at which a particular substance melts when it is heated

member [noun: **members**] a person who belongs to a group, club or society
♦ **membership** [noun: **memberships**]
1 being a member: *Membership of the gym costs £600 a year.*
2 the membership of a group, club or society is all the people who are its members

membrane [noun: **membranes**]
1 a thin layer of skin that covers or connects the organs inside the body
2 any thin layer or covering

memento [noun: **mementos**] a memento is something that you buy or keep to remind you of something you have done or a place you have visited

memo [noun: **memos**] a short note or written instruction that you send to someone who works in the same company or organization as you do

ⓘ The full form of this word is **memorandum**, which has two plural forms, **memorandums** or **memoranda**.

memoirs [plural noun] someone's memoirs are a book that they write about their life's experiences

memorable [adjective] a memorable event is one that you can, or will, remember because it is special or important
♦ **memorably** [adverb] in a way that will not be forgotten

memorial [noun: **memorials**] a statue or monument put up as a way of remembering and honouring a person or event: *the Prince Albert Memorial* • *a war memorial*
[adjective] acting as a memorial: *the John Andrews memorial trophy*

memorize or **memorise** [verb: **memorizes, memorizing, memorized**] to learn something thoroughly so that you are able to remember it in every detail later on

memory [noun: **memories**]
1 memory is the power of your mind to remember things: *There are several ways to improve your memory.*
2 a memory is something you remember: *happy memories of his school days*
3 in living memory means 'from a time that people who are alive now can still remember': *Last month's storm was the worst in living memory.*
4 if you do something **in memory of** someone who has died, you do it as a way of remembering them: *a minute's silence in memory of the accident victims*

men [noun] the plural of **man**

menace [noun: **menaces**]
1 something that causes trouble or danger: *These biting flies are a real menace.*
2 threatening trouble, harm or violence: *His voice was full of menace.*
[verb: **menaces, menacing, menaced**] to threaten someone or something with trouble, harm or violence
♦ **menacing** [adjective] threatening or evil-looking

mend [verb: **mends, mending, mended**] to mend something is to repair or fix it

Mm

[noun] if someone who has been ill or injured is **on the mend**, they are starting to feel better or their injury is starting to heal

meningitis [noun] a serious and sometimes fatal infection of the brain. The main symptoms are a stiff neck, severe headache, and a dislike of light

menopause [noun] the menopause is the time in a woman's life when her periods stop and she can no longer get pregnant

menstrual [adjective] to do with menstruation

menstruation [noun] menstruation is the regular flow of blood that a woman has from her womb each month

-ment [suffix] if **-ment** comes at the end of a word, it is a noun that refers to a particular state or condition. For example, *contentment* is the state of being content

mental [adjective]
1 to do with or using the brain or intelligence: *mental ability* • *mental arithmetic*
2 an informal word for mad or suffering from an illness of the mind
 ◆ **mentality** [noun: **mentalities**] someone's mentality is the attitudes and opinions they have
 ◆ **mentally** [adverb] in or with the mind: *You must commit yourself mentally and physically when you practice yoga.*

mention [verb: **mentions, mentioning, mentioned**] to mention something is to say it to someone

menu [noun: **menus**]
1 a list of the food available in a restaurant
2 on a computer, a list of options that you can choose from by clicking with the mouse or scrolling down the list

MEP [abbreviation: **MEPs**] short for **Member of the European Parliament**, someone who has been elected to represent people in the European Parliament in Brussels

mercenary [noun: **mercenaries**] a soldier who hires himself out to any army or country that will pay him to fight

merchandise [noun] goods that are bought and sold

merchant [noun: **merchants**] someone who carries on a business buying and selling goods

merchant navy [noun: **merchant navies**] a country's merchant navy is its fleet of ships that are used to transport goods and passengers, not its fighting ships

merciful [adjective] kind and forgiving
 ◆ **mercifully** [adverb] people say 'mercifully' to show that they are glad or grateful for something: *After the heat outside, the room was mercifully cool.*

merciless [adjective] cruel and without showing any mercy: *The heat was merciless.*

mercury [noun] a silvery chemical element mostly used in liquid form in things like thermometers and barometers

mercy [noun: **mercies**]
1 someone who has or shows mercy is kind and willing to forgive someone they could punish if they wanted to
2 if you are **at the mercy of** someone or something, you are controlled by them and they have the power to harm you: *The little fishing boat was at the mercy of the weather.*

mere [adjective: **merest**] nothing more than or only: *The flight from London to Madrid cost a mere £25.*
 ◆ **merely** [adverb] only or simply: *I asked him again but he merely shrugged his shoulders.*

merge [verb: **merges, merging, merged**] two or more things merge when they combine with each other or they become mixed together: *Her work life seemed to be increasingly merging with her home life.* • *The two companies merged in 1999.*
 ◆ **merger** [noun: **mergers**] the joining of two businesses to form a single large company

meridian [noun: **meridians**] an imaginary line around the Earth passing through the north and south pole

meringue [noun: **meringues**] a mixture of whipped egg whites and sugar cooked slowly in the oven until it is dry and crisp

merit [noun: **merits**]
1 merit is value or importance
2 the merits of something are the things that make it good or valuable
[verb: **merits, meriting, merited**] to merit something is to deserve it

mermaid [noun: **mermaids**] in stories, a

Mm

beautiful creature who lives in the sea and is half woman, half fish

merrily [adverb] happily and cheerfully

merry [adjective: **merrier, merriest**] happy and cheerful

merry-go-round [noun: **merry-go-rounds**] a ride at a funfair with wooden animals and vehicles that you sit on as the ride goes round and round

mesh [noun: **meshes**] mesh is lengths of wire or thread formed into a net

mess [noun: **messes**]

1 an untidy or dirty state or sight: *The kitchen's in a mess.*

2 something that is in a confused state or that involves lots of problems: *His whole life was in a mess.*

[verb: **messes, messing, messed**]

1 to **mess about** or **mess around** is to do silly or annoying things

2 to **mess something up** is to spoil it or damage it

message [noun: **messages**] a piece of news or information sent from one person to another [verb: **messages, messaging, messaged**] to message someone is to send them a message using a mobile phone or computer

◆ **messaging** [noun] sending and receiving messages using mobile phones or computers

messenger [noun: **messengers**] someone who carries messages or letters from one person to another

messiah [noun: **messiahs**] someone who comes to save or deliver people from misery or evil

messily [adverb] sloppily or untidily

messy [adjective: **messier, messiest**] untidy or dirty: *a messy room*

met [verb] a way of changing the verb **meet** to form a past tense. It can be used with or without a helping verb: *We met yesterday.* • *I thought you two had met before.*

metal [noun: **metals**] a hard shiny material that melts when it is heated, for example iron, steel, gold, silver and tin

◆ **metallic** [adjective] hard and shiny like metal or sounding like metal when it is hit

metallurgy [noun] the study of metals

metamorphose [verb: **metamorphoses,**

metamorphosing, metamorphosed] something metamorphoses when it changes its appearance or form completely and becomes something else

◆ **metamorphosis** [noun: **metamorphoses**] a complete change made in something's appearance or form, such as happens with some living creatures, like frogs and butterflies, as they grow and develop

metaphor [noun: **metaphors**] a way of describing something in a powerful and expressive way by comparing it to something else. For example, it is a metaphor to say that someone who is very eager to do something is *straining at the leash* suggesting they are like a dog that wants to be let off the lead so that it can run free

◆ **metaphorical** [adjective] using a metaphor or metaphors

meteor [noun: **meteors**] a mass of rock travelling through space very fast, sometimes seen in the night sky as a shooting star

meteoric [adjective] very fast, like a meteor travelling through space

meteorite [noun: **meteorites**] a meteor that has fallen to Earth

meteorologist [noun: **meteorologists**] someone who studies the weather and makes weather forecasts

meteorology [noun] the study of weather

meter [noun: **meters**] an instrument that measures and records something, for example, the amount of gas or electricity used in a house

ⓘ Try not to confuse **meter** with **metre**, which is a measure of length.

methane [noun] a gas that is found in coal mines and marshes and is produced when plant material rots

method [noun: **methods**]

1 a way of doing something: *What's the best method of cleaning silver?*

2 if something you do has method, you do it in a well-planned or organized way

◆ **methodical** [adjective] well-ordered and efficient: *Let us be methodical and take one thing at a time.*

◆ **methodically** [adverb] orderly and efficiently

Mm

meths [plural noun] a short form of **methylated spirits**

methylated spirits [plural noun] a type of alcohol used as a fuel in lamps and heaters and to remove oily substances

meticulous [adjective] paying careful attention to every detail
• **meticulously** [adverb] very carefully

metre [noun: **metres**]
1 the basic measurement of length in the metric system. This is often shortened to **m**. It is equal to 39.37 inches or 1.094 yards
2 the regular rhythm of poetry or music

metric [adjective] to do with a system of measuring and weighing that uses units such as litres and grams. It is based on tens and multiples of ten

mettle [noun]
1 if something tests your mettle, it tests your courage or ability
2 if you are **on your mettle**, you are ready and prepared to do your best

mew [verb: **mews, mewing, mewed**] to make a sound like a cat
[noun: **mews**] the sound a cat makes
• **mews** [plural noun] buildings built around a yard or lane. Mews were originally stables

mg [abbreviation] short for **milligram** or **milligrams**

miaow [noun: **miaows**] the call or sound that a cat makes
[verb: **miaows, miaowing, miaowed**] a cat miaows when it makes this sound

mice [noun] the plural of **mouse**

micro- [prefix] if **micro-** comes at the beginning of a word it adds the meaning 'very small'. For example, a *microchip* is a very small silicon chip used to make computer circuits

microbe [noun: **microbes**] a tiny living creature that can only be seen under a microscope

microchip [noun: **microchips**] a very small part used in computers that has several tiny electrical circuits on it

microcomputer [noun: **microcomputers**] a small computer containing microchips or a microprocessor

microfilm [noun] film on which documents, newspapers or books are recorded in a size that is very much smaller than their actual size

microorganism [noun: **microorganisms**] a tiny living thing, such as a virus or bacterium, that can only be seen under a microscope

microphone [noun: **microphones**] an electronic instrument for picking up sound waves to be recorded or made louder

microprocessor [noun: **microprocessors**] a set of microchips that make up a computer's central processor

microscope [noun: **microscopes**] an instrument with lenses that make very tiny objects look much larger so that you can study them closely
• **microscopic** [adjective] microscopic objects are so small they can only be seen using a microscope

microwave [noun: **microwaves**]
1 a very short radio wave
2 a microwave oven

microwave oven [noun: **microwave ovens**] an oven that cooks food very quickly using electrical and magnetic waves rather than heat

mid- [prefix] if **mid-** comes at the beginning of a word it has something to do with the middle of something. For example, *midwinter* is the middle of the winter

midday [noun] noon, or the middle of the day

middle [noun: **middles**]
1 the point, position or part furthest from the sides or edges: *an island in the middle of the ocean* • *Let me sit in the middle.*
2 the point in a period of time that is halfway through that period of time: *I woke up in the middle of the night.* • *He stood up and asked a question in the middle of the meeting.*
3 your middle is your waist
[adjective] between two things or at the halfway point: *He's the middle child of a family of five boys.* • *the middle section of the book*

middle-aged [adjective] between the ages of 40 and 60

middle class [noun: **middle classes**] the middle class is the social class between the working class and the upper class, and consists of educated, professional or skilled people
[adjective] coming from, or to do with, the middle class

Mm

midge [noun: **midges**] a type of tiny biting insect

midget [noun: **midgets**] a person who is fully developed but has not grown to normal size [adjective] very small: *a midget submarine*

ⓘ Many people now consider this word to be old-fashioned and offensive. A more polite phrase to use would be a **person of restricted growth**.

midland [adjective] coming from or in the midlands
   ◆ **midlander** [noun: **midlanders**] someone who is born in or lives in the midlands
   ◆ **midlands** [plural noun] the midlands of a country are the areas in the middle of the country

midnight [noun] twelve o'clock at night

midriff [noun: **midriffs**] the area around the middle of your body just under your ribs

midst [noun]
   1 to be in the midst of several people or things is to be surrounded by them
   2 if you are in the midst of something you are in the middle of doing it

midsummer [noun] the middle of the summer

midway [adverb] at the middle point between two places

midwife [noun: **midwives**] a nurse who is specially trained to help women when they are having their babies

might[1] [verb]
   1 might is used if there is a possibility of something: *He might stay. • It might rain.*
   2 might is used as a past tense of the verb **may**: *John asked if he might come with us.*

might[2] [noun] power or strength: *He pulled with all his might.*

mightily [adverb]
   1 extremely: *He was mightily grateful for his warm snowsuit when the blizzard came.*
   2 with great strength or power: *The wind blew mightily and shook the windows and doors.*

mightiness [noun] great power or strength

mighty [adjective: **mightier, mightiest**]
   1 powerful: *Atlas took the weight of the sky on his mighty shoulders.*
   2 very great: *a mighty effort*

migraine [noun: **migraines**] a very severe headache

migrant [noun: **migrants**] migrants are people who move from place to place, usually looking for work
[adjective] moving from place to place

migrate [verb: **migrates, migrating, migrated**] birds, and sometimes animals, migrate when they travel from one region or country to another at certain times of the year

migration [noun: **migrations**] migration is when birds or animals travel from one region or country to another at certain times of the year

mike [noun: **mikes**] an informal short form of the word **microphone**

mild [adjective: **milder, mildest**]
   1 mild weather is quite warm
   2 mild things don't have a strong or powerful effect or flavour: *Use a mild soap on baby's skin. • mild cheese*
   3 a mild person is gentle and quiet
   ➡ **mildly**

mildew [noun] a disease of plants in which a spongy white fungus covers their leaves and stems

mildly [adverb]
   1 in a calm and gentle way
   2 slightly: *I was mildly amused at his antics.*
   3 you use **to put it mildly** after you have said something which you could have expressed in a much stronger way: *It was a bit of a shock, to put it mildly.*

mile [noun: **miles**] a unit of distance equal to 1760 yards or 1.6 kilometres
   ◆ **mileage** [noun] the number of miles travelled, or the number of miles a vehicle will travel on a certain amount of fuel

mileometer or **milometer** [noun: **mileometers** or **milometers**] an instrument in a car that measures the number of miles travelled

milestone [noun: **milestones**]
   1 an upright stone or post beside a road that marks the number of miles from a place
   2 an important point, especially in your life or career

militant [adjective] taking strong, sometimes violent action
[noun: **militants**] someone who takes strong,

Mm

sometimes violent action to change the political or social system

military [adjective] to do with the army, navy or air force

[noun] the military is a country's armed forces, especially its officers

milk [noun]

1 a white liquid that female mammals make in their bodies to feed their young

2 this liquid that we get from cows, goats and sheep and use to drink or to make butter and cheese

[verb: **milks, milking, milked**]

1 to milk an animal is to take milk from it

2 to milk a person or a situation is to get as much as possible from them or it, in a clever or selfish way

milkman [noun: **milkmen**] someone whose job is to deliver milk to people's houses

milkshake [noun: **milkshakes**] a drink made by blending milk, ice cream and a flavouring

milk tooth [noun: **milk teeth**] the first set of teeth that grows in a child's mouth. They fall out and are replaced by larger adult teeth at about the age of 7 or 8

milky [adjective: **milkier, milkiest**]

1 pale and cloudy, like milk: *a milky liquid*

2 containing a lot of milk: *a hot milky drink*

mill [noun: **mills**]

1 a building with machinery for grinding corn and other grain

2 a factory where goods of a particular type are made, by crushing, grinding or rolling a natural material: *a paper mill • a steel mill*

3 a machine for grinding things like coffee or pepper

[verb: **mills, milling, milled**] to mill something is to crush it or roll it between hard or heavy surfaces

➟ **miller**

millennium [noun: **millennia**] a period of a thousand years

miller [noun: **millers**] someone who grinds corn and other grain in a mill

milligram or **milligramme** [noun: **milligrams** or **milligrammes**] a unit for measuring weight, equal to one thousandth of a gram. This is often shortened to **mg**

millilitre [noun: **millilitres**] a unit for measuring the amount of a liquid, equal to one thousandth of a litre. This is often shortened to **ml**

millimetre [noun: **millimetres**] a unit for measuring length, equal to one thousandth of a metre. This is often shortened to **mm**

million [noun: **millions**] the number 1,000,000, a thousand thousand

millionaire [noun: **millionaires**] someone who has a million pounds or a million dollars or more

millipede [noun: **millipedes**] a small crawling insect with lots of pairs of legs on its long body

millstone [noun: **millstones**]

1 a heavy round stone used to grind grain

2 a problem or duty that is **a millstone round your neck** is one that prevents you from doing what you want

milometer [noun: **milometers**] look at the entry for **mileometer**

mime [noun: **mimes**] mime is acting using movements and gestures, but no words

[verb: **mimes, miming, mimed**]

1 to mime is to express something by making movements or gestures rather than using words

2 a singer mimes when they move their mouth as if they were singing, but without making a sound

mimic [verb: **mimics, mimicking, mimicked**] to mimic someone or something is to copy their actions, the way they talk, or their appearance

[noun: **mimics**] a mimic is someone who copies the way other people speak or behave, usually for fun

♦ **mimicry** [noun] mimicking

min [abbreviation: **mins**] a short form of the word **minute** used in writing: *Fry for 10–15 mins until golden brown.*

mince [noun] meat that has been cut up into very small pieces

[verb: **minces, mincing, minced**]

1 to mince meat or some other food is to cut it into very small pieces

2 if you **don't mince your words**, you say exactly what you think of someone or something

mincemeat [noun]
1 a mixture of chopped dried fruits and nuts, with suet and spices, used to fill pies
2 if you **make mincemeat of** someone, you defeat them thoroughly in a game, fight, or argument

mince pie [noun: **mince pies**] a pie filled with mincemeat, usually eaten at Christmas time

mind [noun: **minds**]
1 your mind is your brain, or your ability to think, understand or remember
2 if you are **in two minds**, you cannot decide between two alternatives
3 if you **make up your mind**, you decide
4 if you **speak your mind**, you say what you really think
[verb: **minds, minding, minded**]
1 you mind something when it upsets or annoys you
2 you ask someone if they would mind doing something, or if they would mind if you did something, when you are asking them politely to do it, or whether they object to you doing it: *Would you mind opening the window?*
3 to mind someone or something is to look after them
4 you tell someone to mind something when you are telling them to watch out for some hazard or danger: *Mind your head on that branch.*
◆ **minder** [noun: **minders**] someone who looks after another person and protects them from harm

mindless [adjective]
1 a mindless task is boring and does not need any thought or imagination
2 mindless violence or destruction is stupid and done for no purpose

mine¹ [pronoun] a word you use to talk about something belonging to yourself: *Is this book yours or mine? • a friend of mine*

mine² [noun: **mines**]
1 a place where things are dug out of the ground, for example, coal, metals and minerals, or precious stones
2 a type of bomb that is hidden in the ground or in the sea and which explodes when someone stands on it, or a ship hits it

[verb: **mines, mining, mined**]
1 to mine something like coal or gold is to dig it out of the ground
2 to mine an area of land or sea is to place explosive mines in it

minefield [noun: **minefields**]
1 an area of land with explosive mines in it
2 a situation that is full of hidden dangers or problems

miner [noun: **miners**] someone who works in a mine

mineral [noun: **minerals**] any of various substances found in the ground, such as coal, or dissolved in water, such as salt

mineral water [noun] water containing dissolved minerals thought to be good for your health

mingle [verb: **mingles, mingling, mingled**] people or things mingle when they are mixed together or move about amongst each other

mini- [prefix] if mini- comes at the beginning of a word, it means it is a small or short type of something. For example, a *minibus* is a small bus

miniature [adjective] very small
[noun: **miniatures**] a very small copy or model of a larger thing, or a very small portrait of someone

minibus [noun: **minibuses**] a small bus for around 12 to 15 passengers

minimal [adjective] something minimal is very small or the least amount possible: *Having this machine means that there is minimal effort involved in washing up.*

minimize or **minimise** [verb: **minimizes, minimizing, minimized**] to minimize something is to reduce it to the smallest size or extent possible

minimum [noun and adjective] the smallest number or quantity, or the lowest point: *The minimum contribution is £5. • They had the bare minimum of furniture in their flat.*

minister [noun: **ministers**]
1 the name given to a priest in some branches of the Christian church
2 a government minister is a politician in charge of a government department: *the Minister for Rural Affairs*
[verb: **ministers, ministering, ministered**] to minister to someone is to provide them with

Mm

some sort of help, usually because they are sick

◆ ministry [noun: **ministries**]
1 the profession of a priest or minister
2 a government department

mink [noun: **mink**]
1 a small slim animal with a pointed face, short legs and very soft fur
2 the dark-brown fur of the mink
[adjective] made from the fur of the mink: *a mink coat*

minnow [noun: **minnows**] a type of small fish that lives in fresh water

minor [adjective]
1 something minor is not very big, not very serious or not very important: *a minor problem* • *a minor road*
2 in music, a minor scale has a semitone between the second and third notes. A minor key or chord is based on this scale
[noun: **minors**] someone who is under the age when people legally become adults

minority [noun: **minorities**]
1 a small group of people which is part of a much larger group: *It was only a minority who were causing trouble.*
2 a group of people in a society that are a different race or have a different religion than most other people in the society: *ethnic minorities*

mint [noun: **mints**]
1 a plant with strong-smelling leaves used as a flavouring in cooking
2 a sweet flavoured with mint

mint [noun]
1 a place, controlled by the government, where new coins are made
2 a very large sum of money: *That fancy house must have cost a mint.*
3 something that is **in mint condition** is in perfect condition and looks as if it has just been newly made

minus [preposition]
1 taking away or subtracting: *8 minus 2 is 6*
2 without: *He came back home covered in mud and minus one shoe.*
[adjective]
1 less than zero: *minus ten degrees*
2 minus is used after a letter to show that a

mark or grade is slightly less than the grade represented by the letter alone: *My son got an A minus for his essay.*
[noun: **minuses**] a minus, or minus sign (−), is a mathematical symbol showing that a number is to be taken away from another, or that a number is less than zero

minuscule [adjective] tiny: *a minuscule spot on her blouse*

minute [noun: **minutes**]
1 sixty seconds or a sixtieth part of an hour
2 a moment or very short time: *Wait a minute while I look for my keys.*
3 the minutes of a meeting are notes taken while the meeting is going on describing what has been discussed or agreed

minute [adjective] tiny: *You only need to use a minute amount of the ointment.*

ⓘ This word is pronounced my-**nyoot**.

miracle [noun: **miracles**]
1 a wonderful act or event that cannot be explained
2 a piece of great good luck: *It's a miracle that you weren't killed running across that busy road.*
◆ miraculous [adjective] wonderful and amazing, like a miracle
◆ miraculously [adverb] amazingly: *Miraculously, he got out of the wrecked car without a scratch.*

mirage [noun: **mirages**] in deserts and hot countries, a mirage is something you see that is not really there, usually a false image of a large area of water in the distance caused by currents of hot air rising

mire [noun] deep mud or dirt

mirror [noun: **mirrors**] a piece of glass with a reflective backing that you can look at yourself in
[verb: **mirrors, mirroring, mirrored**] one thing mirrors another when it looks or behaves exactly like that other thing or like a reflection of it

mirth [noun] mirth is laughter

mis- [prefix] if **mis-** comes at the beginning of a word it adds the meaning 'bad' or 'badly', or 'wrong' or 'wrongly'. For example, to *mistreat* something is to treat it badly

Mm

misbehave [verb: **misbehaves, misbehaving, misbehaved**] to behave badly

miscarriage [noun: **miscarriages**]
1 if a pregnant woman has a miscarriage, the baby comes out of her womb too early and does not survive
2 a miscarriage of justice happens when someone is wrongly punished for a crime they did not commit

miscellaneous [adjective] a miscellaneous collection or group is one that contains many different kinds of things

mischief [noun] naughty behaviour that does not cause any serious harm: *I hope you children haven't been getting up to mischief.*
♦ **mischievous** [adjective] full of mischief

miser [noun: **misers**] someone who hates spending money, and saves as much as they can
➡ **miserly**

miserable [adjective]
1 very unhappy: *She's miserable because all her friends are away.*
2 making you feel unhappy or depressed: *What a miserable wet day it's been!*
3 sad and grumpy: *Smile! Don't be such a miserable old so-and-so!*
4 mean: *I got a miserable £2.50 for three hours work!*

miserly [adjective] very unwilling to spend money

misery [noun: **miseries**]
1 great unhappiness, or something that causes great unhappiness
2 a depressing person who spoils other people's fun

misfit [noun: **misfits**] someone whose behaviour or attitude is very different from most other people, and who does not fit in with any group well

misfortune [noun: **misfortunes**] bad luck

misgivings [plural noun] if you have misgivings about something, you have doubts about it because you think it might not work

misguided [adjective] a misguided person is lead astray by mistaken ideas, or shows bad judgement

mishap [noun: **mishaps**] an unlucky accident

mislay [verb: **mislays, mislaying, mislaid**] to mislay something is to lose it, usually because you can't remember where you put it

mislead [verb: **misleads, misleading, misled**] to mislead someone is to give them wrong information, so that they believe something is the case when it is not
♦ **misleading** [adjective] giving the wrong impression or information

misprint [noun: **misprints**] a mistake in printing: *That's definitely a misprint. It should be 10, not 1000.*

Miss [noun: **Misses**]
1 a title used for girls and unmarried women
2 a word used by schoolchildren when they are talking to a female teacher, whether she is married or not

miss [verb: **misses, missing, missed**]
1 to fail to hit or catch something you are aiming at: *The arrow missed the target.*
2 to miss an event is to be unable to attend it or watch it: *I had to miss my daughter's school concert.*
3 to miss a train, bus or plane is to not arrive in time to catch it
4 to miss a person or place is to be sad because they are not with you, or you are not at that place
5 to miss something is to realize that you do not have it or that it is lost: *When did you first miss your purse?*
6 to **miss something out** is to not include it, either by mistake or on purpose
7 if you **miss out on** something good, you do not get any of it, or you do not take part in it: *He arrived late and missed out on all the games.*
[noun: **misses**]
1 a failure to hit a target: *He scored two hits and a miss.*
2 to **give something a miss** is to not do it
➡ **missing**

missile [noun: **missiles**] a weapon or other object that is thrown or fired

missing [adjective] if someone or something is or goes missing, they are not where they should be and you do not know where they are: *He counted to see if anyone was missing.*
• *The money went missing in mysterious circumstances.*

Mm

mission [noun: **missions**]

1 a task or purpose: *astronauts on a mission to Mars*

2 a group of people representing a country or religion who are sent to another country: *a diplomatic mission*

♦ **missionary** [noun: **missionaries**] a person who goes to another country to convert the people there to a particular religion

misspell [verb: **misspells, misspelling, misspelt** or **misspelled**] to spell something in the wrong way

♦ **misspelling** [noun: **misspellings**] a word that is spelt the wrong way

mist [noun: **mists**] a thin fog, made up of tiny water droplets in the air

[verb: **mists, misting, misted**] something **mists up**, or **mists over**, when it becomes covered with tiny droplets of water or mist

→ **mistiness, misty**

mistake [noun: **mistakes**] something wrong that you do or say and which you did not mean to do or say

[verb: **mistakes, mistaking, mistook, mistaken**] to mistake one person or thing for another person or thing is to think wrongly they are that other person or thing

♦ **mistaken** [adjective] you are mistaken if you are wrong about something

♦ **mistakenly** [adverb] wrongly

Mister [noun: **Misters**] a title used for men and boys. It is usually shortened to **Mr**

mistiness [noun] being misty

mistletoe [noun] a plant with green leaves and small white berries that grows on the branches of trees. Traditionally, at Christmas time, people kiss each other under a piece of mistletoe hung up somewhere in a room

mistook [verb] a way of changing the verb **mistake** to make a past tense: *I mistook him for someone else.*

mistreat [verb: **mistreats, mistreating, mistreated**] to treat someone or something badly or cruelly

♦ **mistreatment** [noun] bad or cruel treatment

mistress [noun: **mistresses**]

1 a woman who owns or is in charge of

something: *Are you the mistress of the house?*

• *a dog and his mistress*

2 the lover of a man who is married to another woman

mistrust [verb: **mistrusts, mistrusting, mistrusted**] to mistrust a person or thing is to be suspicious of them or it

[noun] mistrust is a feeling of doubt or suspicion that people who do not trust each other have

misty [adjective: **mistier, mistiest**]

1 the weather is misty when there is mist in the air

2 your eyes are misty when you cannot see very clearly, usually because your eyes are filled with tears

→ **mistiness**

misunderstand [verb: **misunderstands, misunderstanding, misunderstood**] to think you have understood what someone has said or done, when in fact you have not understood it correctly: *I misunderstood the directions he gave and ended up in south London.*

♦ **misunderstanding** [noun: **misunderstandings**]

1 a mistake you make about what someone else means

2 a slight disagreement or argument

misuse [verb: **misuses, misusing, misused**] to misuse something is to use it in the wrong way or to treat it badly

[noun] misuse of something is using it in the wrong way

mite [noun: **mites**] a tiny creature belonging to the same family as spiders

mitt or **mitten** [noun: **mitts** or **mittens**] a type of glove without separate parts for each of the fingers

mix [verb: **mixes, mixing, mixed**]

1 to put two or more things together so that they combine or form a mass: *Mixing a little black paint into the white will give you a light grey.* • *We each took a turn to mix the Christmas cake.*

2 things mix when they combine: *Oil and water don't mix.*

3 you mix with other people when you talk to them or get to know them socially

4 if you *mix things up*, you confuse them and

think one is the other: *He said he might have got me mixed up with our Jim.*
[noun: **mixes**] a mixture: *an odd mix of comedy and horror*

♦ **mixed** [adjective] containing several different things or types of people: *a mixed grill*

♦ **mixer** [noun: **mixers**] any machine used for mixing things: *a cement mixer*

♦ **mixture** [noun: **mixtures**] a combination of several things: *cough mixture* • *a mixture of joy and sadness*

ml [abbreviation] short for **millilitre** or **millilitres**

mm [abbreviation] short for **millimetre** or **millimetres**

mnemonic [noun: **mnemonics**] a word, phrase, or poem that helps you remember something. For example, the phrase *i before e, except after c* is a mnemonic that many people use to remind them if *e* or *i* comes first in words like *relief* and *receive*

moan [verb: **moans, moaning, moaned**]
1 to make a deep noise in your throat because you are in pain or distress
2 to complain
[noun: **moans**]
1 a deep noise of pain or distress that someone makes in their throat
2 something you say that shows your dissatisfaction with something

moat [noun: **moats**] a deep ditch dug round a castle and filled with water to stop attackers being able to get to the castle walls easily

mob [noun: **mobs**] a mob is an angry crowd of people
[verb: **mobs, mobbing, mobbed**] people mob someone they want to see or meet when they crowd round that person

♦ **mobbed** [adjective] if a place is mobbed it is very crowded

mobile [adjective] something is mobile when it moves or can move around
[noun: **mobiles**]
1 a telephone that you can carry around with you
2 a hanging decoration that moves in the breeze

♦ **mobility** [noun] being able to move around

mobilize or **mobilise** [verb: **mobilizes, mobilizing, mobilized**] to mobilize people is to make them move or take action

moccasin [noun: **moccasins**] moccasins are shoes made from pieces of soft leather stitched together with thin strips of leather, worn originally by Native American people

mock [verb: **mocks, mocking, mocked**] to mock someone is to make fun of them in a cruel way, by making jokes about them or copying what they say or do
[adjective] not real or genuine: *a mock leather sofa*

♦ **mockery** [noun] mocking

mode [noun: **modes**] a way or method of doing something: *a mode of transport*

model [noun: **models**]
1 a copy of something made on a much smaller scale: *a model of the Crystal Palace*
2 a particular type or design of something that is made in large numbers: *This is our latest model of washing machine.*
3 a person who wears new clothes or fashions to show them off to possible buyers
[verb: **models, modelling, modelled**]
1 to model something in clay is to form the clay into the shape of that thing
2 to model for an artist is to sit or stand while the artist draws or paints you
3 to model a piece of clothing or jewellery is to wear it to show it off to possible buyers

modem [noun: **modems**] a device used to send information down a telephone line from a computer to other computers on a network

moderate [adjective]
1 not going to extremes: *The doctor told him to take a moderate amount of exercise every day.*
2 of medium or average quality or ability: *People of moderate intelligence find the quiz quite easy.*
[verb: **moderates, moderating, moderated**] to moderate something is to make it less extreme or less strong

♦ **moderately** [adverb] slightly, quite or fairly: *moderately cheap accommodation*

♦ **moderation** [noun] behaviour that is not too extreme

Mm

ⓘ The adjective is pronounced **mod**-i-rit. The verb is pronounced **mod**-i-rate.

modern [adjective] modern things belong to the present or recent times rather than the past: *modern technology*

+ **modernity** [noun] being modern

modernization or **modernisation** [noun: **modernizations**] the modernization of something is adding new parts or equipment to it to make it more modern

modernize or **modernise** [verb: **modernizes, modernizing, modernized**] to modernize something is to make it more up-to-date

modest [adjective]
1 a modest person does not like boasting or talking about their achievements
2 a modest amount is a small amount

modification [noun: **modifications**] a change made in something to make it work better or more efficiently

modify [verb: **modifies, modifying, modified**]
1 to modify something is to make a small change or changes in it to improve it
2 to modify your views or opinions is to change them so that they are less extreme

module [noun: **modules**]
1 a separate unit that is part of a larger unit or structure: *the space station's escape module*
2 a unit of work that forms one part of an educational course

mohair [noun] long soft hair from the angora goat, which is mixed with other types of wool to make jumpers or material for suits and jackets

moist [adjective: **moister, moistest**] slightly wet

+ **moisten** [verb: **moistens, moistening, moistened**] to make something moist: *He licked his lips to moisten them.*

+ **moisture** [noun] wetness, especially tiny drops of water in the air or condensed on a surface

moisturize or **moisturise** [verb: **moisturizes, moisturizing, moisturized**] you moisturize your skin when you put cream on it to make it feel softer

+ **moisturizer** [noun: **moisturizers**] a cream put on the skin to make it feel softer

molar [noun: **molars**] one of the large teeth at the back of your mouth that you use for chewing food

molasses [noun] molasses is a thick dark syrup left after raw sugar is refined

mole¹ [noun: **moles**] a small black or dark brown furry animal that lives underground in tunnels that it digs with its strong claws. Moles have poor eyesight but very good hearing

mole² [noun: **moles**] a small dark-coloured permanent mark or lump on someone's skin

molecular [adjective] to do with molecules: *molecular structure*

molecule [noun: **molecules**] the smallest unit that a chemical element or compound can be divided into and still remain what it is. Molecules are made up of two or more atoms

molehill [noun: **molehills**] a pile of earth that a mole pushes up on to the surface while it is digging its tunnels underground

molest [verb: **molests, molesting, molested**] to molest someone is to attack or annoy them

mollycoddle [verb: **mollycoddles, mollycoddling, mollycoddled**] to mollycoddle someone is to treat them in a fussy and over-protective way, never letting them do anything risky

molten [adjective] molten rock or metal is in a liquid state, having been melted

moment [noun: **moments**]
1 a short period of time: *Stop what you're doing for a moment.*
2 a particular point in time: *Just at that moment, she heard a door slam.*

+ **momentarily** [adverb] for a short period of time: *He was momentarily suspended in the air.*

+ **momentary** [adjective] lasting for only a moment: *There was a momentary pause, and then everyone started talking.*

momentous [adjective] very important or significant: *a momentous occasion*

momentum [noun]
1 the force that makes a moving object continue moving
2 something gains momentum when it begins

to move or develop faster and faster

monarch [noun: **monarchs**] a royal ruler of a country, especially a king or queen

♦ **monarchy** [noun: **monarchies**] a system of government in which the official head of state is a monarch, or a country with this system

monastery [noun: **monasteries**] a building where a community of monks lives

♦ **monastic** [adjective] to do with monasteries or monks

Monday [noun: **Mondays**] the day of the week after Sunday and before Tuesday

money [noun]

1 money is coins or banknotes used to buy things: *I don't have enough money to buy the jacket I want.*

2 money is wealth: *Only people with money can afford yachts and personal jets.*

mongoose [noun: **mongooses**] a small animal related to the weasel, found in South East Asia and Africa, which kills and eats snakes

mongrel [noun: **mongrels**] a dog whose parents are of different breeds

monitor [verb: **monitors, monitoring, monitored**] to monitor something is to keep a careful check on it

[noun: **monitors**]

1 an instrument used to keep a constant check on something: *a heart monitor*

2 a screen attached to a computer which displays the file or program being worked on

monk [noun: **monks**] a member of a community of men who spend their lives in religious worship in a monastery

monkey [noun: **monkeys**]

1 an animal with a long tail that walks on four legs and lives in trees

2 to **make a monkey out of someone** is to make them look foolish

[verb: **monkeys, monkeying, monkeyed**] to **monkey about** or **monkey around** is to behave in a silly or mischievous way

monkey nut [noun: **monkey nuts**] monkey nuts are peanuts in their shells

mono- [prefix] if **mono-** comes at the beginning of a word it adds the meaning 'one' or 'single'. For example, a *monologue* is a long speech made by one person

monocle [noun: **monocles**] a lens worn in front of one eye and held in place between the top and bottom of the eye socket

monopolize or **monopolise** [verb: **monopolizes, monopolizing, monopolized**] to monopolize something is to keep it all for yourself, and to exclude others: *He monopolized the conversation and no one had the chance to speak.*

monopoly [noun: **monopolies**] a business company or organization has a monopoly when it is the only company selling a particular product or providing a particular service

monorail [noun: **monorails**] a railway on which the trains run on a single rail, rather than two rails

monosodium glutamate [noun] a chemical that is added to some foods to improve their flavour

monotone [noun] if you say something in a monotone, you do not vary the tone of your voice while you are speaking

monotonous [adjective] something is monotonous when it is boring because it never varies

♦ **monotony** [noun] dullness and lack of variety

monsoon [noun: **monsoons**] the monsoon is a season in some hot countries when heavy rain falls

monster [noun: **monsters**]

1 in stories, a huge or frightening creature

2 a cruel or evil person

[adjective] enormous: *a monster truck*

monstrosity [noun: **monstrosities**] a very large and very ugly thing

monstrous [adjective]

1 extremely large: *a monstrous crocodile*

2 monstrous behaviour is very unfair and cruel

month [noun: **months**]

1 one of twelve periods that a year is divided into: *the month of May*

2 any period of approximately four weeks or 30 days: *People often have to wait several months for an appointment.*

♦ **monthly** [adjective and adverb] happening once a month or each month: *a monthly salary* • *He is paid monthly.*

monument [noun: **monuments**]

Mm

1 something that has been built in memory of a person or event: *a monument to Sir Walter Scott*
2 any building or structure that is historically important: *The Parthenon is one of Greece's ancient monuments.*
* **monumental** [adjective]
1 like a monument, or used on a monument: *monumental sculpture*
2 enormous: *I felt like a monumental idiot when I realized what I had done.*

moo [verb: **moos, mooing, mooed**] a cow moos when it makes a long low sound
[noun: **moos**] the long low sound a cow makes

mood [noun: **moods**] your mood is your feelings or temper at a particular time: *I woke up in a bad mood this morning.*
* **moodily** [adverb] in a bad-tempered way
* **moodiness** [noun] being moody
* **moody** [adjective: **moodier, moodiest**] a moody person changes their mood often or suddenly, from cheerful to grumpy and impatient

moon [noun: **moons**]
1 the large sphere that orbits the Earth once a month and which you can see in the night sky as a full circle or a partial circle depending on the time of month
2 a similar body going round certain other planets, for example, Saturn

moonbeam [noun: **moonbeams**] a shaft of moonlight

moonlight [noun] the light that seems to come from the moon, but which is really light from the sun reflected off the surface of the moon
* **moonlit** [adjective] lit by the moon: *a clear moonlit night*

moor[1] [noun: **moors**] a large area of open land with poor soil and very few, or no, trees

moor[2] [verb: **moors, mooring, moored**] to moor a boat is to tie it up using a rope, cable or anchor

mooring [noun: **moorings**] a place where a boat or ship can be tied up

moorland [noun: **moorlands**] a stretch of moor

moose [noun: **moose**] a type of large deer with large, flat, rounded horns

mop [noun: **mops**]
1 a tool for washing floors made up of a pad or mass of thick threads attached to a long handle
2 a mop of hair is a thick, often untidy, mass of hair
[verb: **mops, mopping, mopped**]
1 to mop a floor is to rub or wipe it with a mop
2 to **mop up** is to clean or wipe liquid off a surface

mope [verb: **mopes, moping, moped**] someone mopes when they are in a bored and depressed mood and do not want to do anything

moped [noun: **mopeds**] a light motorcycle with a small engine that you can also pedal like a bicycle

moral [noun: **morals**] a story or event has a moral if a lesson about how to behave is learned from it
[adjective]
1 to do with right and wrong and the way people should behave: *moral standards*
2 a moral person behaves in a way that is right, good or proper
➡ **morality, morally, morals**

morale [noun] the morale of a person or group of people is how confident they are, or how successful they think they will be

morality [noun]
1 the morality of something is whether it is right or wrong according to standards of good or bad behaviour
2 a person's morality is their standard of behaviour and the beliefs they have about what is right and wrong

morally [adverb] to behave morally is to behave in a good or proper way

morals [plural noun] someone's morals are the beliefs they have about what is right and wrong

morbid [adjective] having or showing an unhealthy interest in death or sad and unpleasant things
* **morbidity** [noun] being morbid
* **morbidly** [adverb] in a morbid way

more [adjective] a greater quantity or amount: *He has more friends than anyone else*

I know. • *Could you get me three more mugs from the cupboard?*

[pronoun]

1 a greater quantity or amount: *More than forty people turned up.*

2 an additional quantity or amount: *Is there any more jelly?*

[adverb]

1 more is used to make comparative forms of adjectives and adverbs: *He's more patient than I am.*

2 more is the comparative form of **much** and means 'to a greater degree': *At first I didn't like her much, but I'm beginning to like her more and more.*

♦ **moreish** [adjective] something is moreish if eating it makes you want more of it

moreover [adverb] you use **moreover** to mean 'besides', when you are adding information to a statement you have just made: *We came home early because it started to rain. Moreover, the children were getting tired.*

morning [noun: **mornings**] the part of the day from midnight to midday

morning sickness [noun] a feeling of sickness, or actual sickness, experienced by some women in the early stages of pregnancy

moron [noun: **morons**] a very stupid person

♦ **moronic** [adjective] very stupid

morose [adjective] silent and bad-tempered

morphine [noun] a drug used to make someone sleep or to relieve pain

morse code [noun] a code used in signalling and telegraphy, made up of long and short signals called dots and dashes

morsel [noun: **morsels**] a small piece of food: *a tasty morsel*

mortal [adjective]

1 being mortal is being certain to die at some time and unable to live forever

2 a mortal wound causes death

3 people who are mortal enemies hate each other so much they want to kill each other

[noun: mortals] a human being

♦ **mortality** [noun] being mortal

♦ **mortally** [adjective] causing, or resulting in, death: *The soldier was mortally wounded.*

mortar [noun]

1 a mixture of cement, sand and water used in building to hold bricks in place

2 a type of heavy gun that fires shells

mortarboard [noun: **mortarboards**] a cap with a square flat top worn by university graduates

mortgage [noun: **mortgages**] a type of loan made by a bank or building society to people who want to buy a house or land

LANGUAGE FOR LIFE

mortgages

There are different types of mortgage.

• If you have a **fixed-rate mortgage**, you pay the same amount every month to the bank or building society that has lent you money.

• If you have a **variable-rate mortgage**, the amount you pay every month to the bank or building society that has lent you money goes up and down according to the bank or building society's rate of interest.

• If you have a **repayment mortgage**, you keep paying back money to the bank or building society every month until you have returned all the money you borrowed and paid the interest on it.

• If you have an **endowment mortgage**, you pay money every month to buy an insurance policy, which is later used to pay off the loan from the bank or building society.

mortified [adjective] extremely embarrassed

mortise lock [noun: **mortise locks**] a lock that is fitted into a hole cut in the side edge of a door, rather than onto the door's surface

mortuary [noun: **mortuaries**] a place where dead bodies are kept before they are buried or cremated

mosaic [noun: **mosaics**] a design formed by fitting together small pieces of coloured marble or glass

Moslem [noun and adjective] another spelling of **Muslim**

mosque [noun: **mosques**] a place of worship for Muslims

mosquito [noun: **mosquitoes**] an insect found in many parts of the world, which feeds by biting and sucking blood

moss [noun: **mosses**] a small plant found in

Mm

damp places and forming a soft green mat over the ground

+ **mossy** [adjective: **mossier, mossiest**] covered with moss

most [adjective] **most** is the superlative form of **many** and **much** and means 'more than other people or things': *Who scored most goals last season?*

[pronoun]

1 nearly all, or the majority: *Most of my friends are people I know from work.*

2 the largest amount: *They both had a lot, but who had the most?*

[adverb] **most** is the superlative form of **much** and means 'to the greatest degree': *What kind of music do you like most?*

+ **mostly** [adverb] in most cases or in most parts: *They mostly play indoors.*

MOT [noun: **MOTs**] a test done in the United Kingdom on cars over three years old to find out if they are safe to drive

motel [noun: **motels**] a hotel near a main road where drivers can get rooms for the night

moth [noun: **moths**] a creature similar to a butterfly, but usually active at night, rather than during the day

mothball [noun: **mothballs**] a small ball of a strong-smelling substance that is put amongst clothes to stop moths eating them

mother [noun: **mothers**] your female parent [verb: **mothers, mothering, mothered**] to mother someone is to treat them with protective kindness, like a mother does

+ **motherhood** [noun] being a mother

mother-in-law [noun: **mothers-in-law**] the mother of your husband or wife

motherly [adjective] kind and protective

motif [noun: **motifs**] a shape or design that may be repeated to form a pattern

motion [noun: **motions**]

1 motion is moving or movement: *The motion of the waves made him sleepy.*

2 a motion is a single movement or gesture: *He flicked the fly away with a quick motion of his wrist.*

3 if you **go through the motions**, you do things but without much effort or enthusiasm

[verb: **motions, motioning, motioned**] you motion to someone when you signal to them

using your hand or some other part of your body

+ **motionless** [adjective] not moving at all

motivate [verb: **motivates, motivating, motivated**]

1 you are motivated by particular feelings or desires when they cause you to act in a certain way

2 to motivate someone is to make them feel interested and enthusiastic enough to do something

+ **motivation** [noun] something that motivates a person

motive [noun: **motives**] the reason someone has for doing something

motor [noun: **motors**] a machine, usually a petrol engine or electrical device, that provides power

[adjective] driven by an engine: *a motor mower*

motorbike [noun: **motorbikes**] a two-wheeled vehicle with a powerful engine that you sit astride like a bicycle

motor car [noun: **motor cars**] a car

motorcycle [noun: **motorcycles**] a motorbike, motor scooter or moped

+ **motorcyclist** [noun: **motorcyclists**] someone who rides a motorbike, motor scooter or moped

motorist [noun: **motorists**] someone who drives a car

motorway [noun: **motorways**] a wide fast road with several lanes going in both directions

mottled [adjective] covered with patches of different colours or shades

motto [noun: **mottoes**] a short sentence or phrase used by a person or organization as a principle to guide their behaviour: *The motto of the Scouts is 'Be prepared'.*

mould[1] [noun: **moulds**] a hollow shaped container into which a liquid is poured so that it takes on that shape when it cools and hardens: *a jelly mould*

[verb: **moulds, moulding, moulded**]

1 to form something in a mould: *The gold is moulded into ingots.*

2 to shape something using your hands: *She moulded the icing into pretty flower shapes.*

mould[2] [noun] mould is a fungus that forms

green or black patches on stale food or on damp walls and ceilings

• mouldy [adjective: **mouldier, mouldiest**] covered with mould: *a mouldy old loaf*

moult [verb: **moults, moulting, moulted**] birds and animals moult when they shed their feathers or hair, or their skin

mound [noun: **mounds**] a small hill or heap of earth or some other material

mount [verb: **mounts, mounting, mounted**]

1 to mount stairs is to go up them

2 to mount a horse or bicycle is to get on to it

3 the level of something mounts when it rises: *Fear and panic were mounting as the seconds ticked away.*

4 to mount a picture or object is to put it in a frame or to stick it on card to display it

[noun: **mounts**]

1 an animal you ride on, for example, a horse or a camel

2 Mount is used in the names of mountains: *Mount Everest*

mountain [noun: **mountains**] a very high hill

• mountaineer [noun: **mountaineers**] someone who climbs mountains using ropes and other special equipment

• mountaineering [noun] the sport or pastime of climbing mountains

• mountainous [adjective] a mountainous area has a lot of mountains

mounted [adjective] on horseback: *a mounted policeman*

Mounties [plural noun] the Canadian Mounties are the police force of Canada, who ride on horses and wear bright red jackets and wide-brimmed hats

mourn [verb: **mourns, mourning, mourned**] to mourn is to be very sad because someone has died

• mournful [adjective] full of sadness

• mourning [noun] someone who is in mourning is grieving for someone who has died

mouse [noun: **mice** or **mouses**]

1 a small animal with a long tail, bright eyes and grey or brown fur

2 a device that you move with your hand to point to places on a computer screen. It has a

button or buttons that you press to instruct the computer to do something

ⓘ The plural of **mouse** when it means 'a small animal' is **mice**.
The plural form when it is a computer device can be either **mice** or **mouses**.

mousse [noun: **mousses**]

1 a light fluffy dessert made with whipped cream and eggs: *chocolate mousse*

2 a white fluffy substance used for styling hair

moustache [noun: **moustaches**] a line of hair that some men grow above their top lip

mousy [adjective: **mousier, mousiest**]

1 a mousy person is shy and timid

2 mousy hair is a light brown colour

mouth [noun: **mouths**]

1 your mouth is the part of your face that you use to speak and eat and which contains your tongue and teeth

2 someone who is **down in the mouth** looks unhappy

[verb: **mouths, mouthing, mouthed**] to mouth words is to make the shapes of the words with your mouth without making the sounds

• mouthful [noun: **mouthfuls**] an amount you put or hold in your mouth at one time: *He took a mouthful of water and spat it out again.*

mouth-organ [noun: **mouth-organs**] an instrument that you hold to your mouth and play by blowing and sucking through the rows of reeds inside it

mouthpiece [noun: **mouthpieces**] the part of a musical instrument or telephone that you put in or close to your mouth

movable [adjective] able to be moved

move [verb: **moves, moving, moved**]

1 you move something when you take it from one place and put it in another: *Please move your bag off the kitchen table.*

2 if something moves, it changes its position: *I'm sure I saw that curtain move.*

3 to move is to change from one house or place of work to another

4 if something moves you, it makes you feel deep emotion

[noun: **moves**]

Mm

1 a change of position: *They made no move to help.*

2 the moving of a piece in a board game such as chess: *Come on, it's your move.*

3 a change to another home or another place of work

◆ **movement** [noun: **movements**]

1 changing position or a change of position

2 a division in a long piece of classical music

3 an organization or association with a common purpose or aim: *the Scout movement*

movie [noun: **movies**] a film

moving [adjective] having a strong effect on your feelings and emotions: *She made a moving speech.*

◆ **movingly** [adverb] in a moving way

mow [verb: **mows, mowing, mowed, mown** or **mowed**] to mow grass is to cut it with a mower

◆ **mower** [noun: **mowers**] a machine for cutting grass

MP [abbreviation: **MPs**] short for **Member of Parliament**, someone who has been elected to the British parliament

Mr [abbreviation] short for **Mister**, a title used before a man's name, for example, when writing his name on an envelope or at the beginning of a letter

Mrs [abbreviation] a title used before a married woman's name, for example, when writing her name on an envelope or at the beginning of a letter

MS [abbreviation] short for **multiple sclerosis**

Ms [noun] a title sometimes used before a woman's name, whether she is married or unmarried

much [adjective]

1 a lot or a large amount: *There was much laughter coming from the girls' room.*

2 much is used in questions about quantities or amounts: *How much fruit do you eat each day?*

[pronoun] a lot or a large amount: *I usually don't have much to eat at lunchtime.*

[adverb]

1 about: *Both books are much the same.*

2 greatly or a lot: *Do you miss your old school much?*

muck [noun]

1 dirt or filth: *The floor is covered in muck from your muddy boots.*

2 manure: *The farmer was spreading muck on the fields.*

[verb: **mucks, mucking, mucked**]

1 to **muck about** or **muck around** is to behave in a silly way

2 to **muck out** horses or other farm animals is to clean their stalls or pens

3 to **muck something up** is to spoil or ruin it

◆ **mucky** [adjective: **muckier, muckiest**] dirty: *Don't leave those mucky boots in the hall, please.*

mucus [noun] a thick slimy liquid that protects the delicate tissues that line certain parts of your body, for example, inside your nose

mud [noun] soft wet soil that sticks to your clothes and shoes

⇒ **muddy**

muddle [noun: **muddles**] a muddle is a confused or disorganized state

[verb: **muddles, muddling, muddled**]

1 to **muddle things up** is to mix them up so that you do not know which is which, or where they are

2 if something muddles you, it confuses you

muddy [adjective: **muddier, muddiest**] covered or filled with mud

mudguard [noun: **mudguards**] a flap over the back wheel of a car, lorry or bicycle, which stops mud from the road being splashed upwards

muesli [noun] a food eaten at breakfast time consisting of a mixture of grains, nuts and dried fruit

muff [noun: **muffs**] a tube of warm material that you put your hands in to keep them warm

[verb: **muffs, muffing, muffed**] to muff something is to do it wrong: *He muffed his lines again.*

muffin [noun: **muffins**]

1 a round flat type of bread eaten toasted or hot with butter

2 a small sweet cake that sometimes contains fruit

muffle [verb: **muffles, muffling, muffled**] to muffle a sound is to make it quieter by putting a cover over the source of the sound

◆ **muffled** [adjective] muffled sounds or

voices are low and not clear because they are heard through something that blocks out most of the sound

◆ **muffler** [noun: **mufflers**] a type of long scarf worn wrapped around the neck and the bottom of the face

mug[1] [noun: **mugs**] a cup with straight sides and a handle

mug[2] [verb: **mugs, mugging, mugged**] to mug someone is to attack and rob them in the street

◆ **mugger** [noun: **muggers**] a criminal who attacks and robs people in the street

muggy [adjective: **muggier, muggiest**] muggy weather is hot and humid

mule[1] [noun: **mules**] an animal bred from a male donkey and a female horse

mule[2] [noun: **mules**] mules are slippers with no backs

multi- [prefix] if **multi-** comes at the beginning of a word it adds the meaning 'many' to the word. For example, *multi-racial* means 'involving many races'

multicultural [adjective] involving or including people from many races and religions

multimedia [adjective] a multimedia computer can run sound and images as well as ordinary programs

multiple [adjective] involving many things of the same sort: *multiple injuries*
[noun: **multiples**] a number or quantity that contains another an exact number of times: *9 and 12 are multiples of 3*

multiple sclerosis [noun] a serious disease that affects nerve cells in the brain and spine and gradually makes it difficult for someone to walk and speak

multiplication [noun: **multiplications**] multiplying

multiply [verb: **multiplies, multiplying, multiplied**]
1 to multiply a number is to increase it by adding it to itself a certain number of times: *13 multiplied by 3 is 39*.
2 things multiply when they increase in number

multi-racial [adjective] involving or including people from many races: *a multi-racial society*

multitude [noun: **multitudes**] a huge number: *I've got a multitude of things to do before I go.*

mum[1] [noun: **mums**] an informal word for **mother**

mum[2] [adjective] to **keep mum** is to keep quiet and not speak to anyone about something that should remain a secret

mumble [verb: **mumbles, mumbling, mumbled**] to mumble is to speak without opening your mouth wide enough to make words sound separate and clear

mummify [verb: **mummifies, mummifying, mummified**] to mummify a dead body is to make it into a mummy

mummy[1] [noun: **mummies**] a child's word for **mother**

mummy[2] [noun: **mummies**] a mummy is a dead body that has been preserved and wrapped in bandages

mumps [noun] an infectious disease, mainly affecting children, in which glands in the neck become very swollen and sore

munch [verb: **munches, munching, munched**] to munch something is to chew it with regular movements of your jaws and your mouth closed

mundane [adjective] something that is mundane is dull because it is so ordinary or familiar

municipal [adjective] to do with a city or town, especially the local government of that city or town: *municipal elections*

munitions [plural noun] weapons and ammunition used in a war

mural [noun: **murals**] a picture that is painted directly on to a wall

murder [noun: **murders**] murder is the crime of killing someone deliberately
[verb: **murders, murdering, murdered**] to murder someone is to kill them deliberately

◆ **murderer** [noun: **murderers**] someone who has murdered another person

◆ **murderous** [adjective]
1 likely or intending to kill someone: *a murderous attack*
2 very angry: *a murderous look*
3 likely to kill you: *We had to escape from the murderous heat.*

Mm

murky [adjective: **murkier, murkiest**]
1 dark and difficult to see through: *murky water*
2 dishonest and sinister: *a man with a murky past*

murmur [verb: **murmurs, murmuring, murmured**] to murmur is to speak so softly that people can hardly hear you
[noun: **murmurs**]
1 a low weak voice
2 a low continuous humming noise made by voices or sounds in the distance: *the murmur of traffic in the distance*

muscle [noun: **muscles**] the parts of your body that move your limbs and organs, which you can make bigger and stronger by exercising
[verb: **muscles, muscling, muscled**] if someone **muscles in**, they involve themselves in something that is not their business
♦ **muscular** [adjective]
1 to do with the muscles
2 having big or strong muscles: *muscular arms* • *a muscular man*

museum [noun: **museums**] a place where collections of interesting things are displayed for people to see

mush [noun] mush is a soft wet mass of something: *The fruit turns into a mush as it boils.*

mushroom [noun: **mushrooms**] a type of fungus that you can eat, with a round top
[verb: **mushrooms, mushrooming, mushroomed**] something mushrooms when it increases its size very quickly

mushy [adjective: **mushier, mushiest**]
1 in a soft wet mass: *mushy peas*
2 too romantic in a way that seems silly: *The film got all mushy and I stopped watching.*

music [noun]
1 sounds arranged or combined in patterns, sung or played by instruments
2 if someone has to **face the music**, they have to accept criticism or punishment for something they have done
♦ **musical** [adjective]
1 to do with music: *musical training*
2 a musical sound is pleasant to listen to
3 someone who is musical has a talent for playing or singing music

[noun: **musicals**] a play or film in which there is lots of singing and dancing
♦ **musician** [noun: **musicians**] someone who plays music on an instrument

musk [noun] musk is a strong perfume

musket [noun: **muskets**] a type of old fashioned gun with a long barrel
♦ **musketeer** [noun: **musketeers**] a soldier who carried a musket

Muslim or **Moslem** [noun: **Muslims** or **Moslems**] a person who is a follower of Islam
[adjective] to do with Islam: *Friday is the Muslim holy day.*

muslin [noun] a thin loosely-woven cotton cloth

mussel [noun: **mussels**] a type of shellfish with two hinged black oval shells

must [verb] **must** is used with another verb to show that you have to do something or that something is certain or very likely: *You must arrive for your interview on time.* • *You must be very tired after such a long journey.*

mustard [noun] crushed seeds of the mustard plant made into a paste and used to give food a hot taste

muster [verb: **musters, mustering, mustered**]
1 to muster troops is to gather them together in a group for inspection
2 to muster something like courage is to try to find as much of it as possible
[noun] if something **passes muster**, it is acceptable to the person who is inspecting it

mustn't [short form] a short way to say and write **must not**: *You mustn't tease the cat.*

musty [adjective: **mustier, mustiest**] having a damp unpleasant smell

mute [adjective] not speaking or not able to speak
♦ **muted** [adjective]
1 muted colours are soft and not harsh or bright
2 muted voices or sounds are low or made quieter

mutilate [verb: **mutilates, mutilating, mutilated**] to mutilate something is to damage it by breaking a part off or cutting pieces off it
♦ **mutilation** [noun] being damaged

mutinous [adjective] likely to rebel, or wanting to rebel against someone in authority

mutiny [noun: **mutinies**] rebelling against someone in authority, especially sailors on a ship rebelling against their captain and officers

mutter [verb: **mutters, muttering, muttered**] to speak quietly under your breath: *Katy sighed and muttered but did as she was told.*

mutton [noun] meat from a sheep

mutual [adjective]
1 given or done by people to one another: *mutual admiration*
2 shared by two people: *Peter and Ahmed have a mutual friend who works at the library.*
♦ **mutually** [adverb] in a mutual way: *mutually involved*

muzzle [noun: **muzzles**]
1 a dog's muzzle is the part, including its nose and mouth, that sticks out from its face
2 a muzzle is a set of straps put over a dog's nose and mouth to stop it biting people
3 the muzzle of a gun is the open end of its barrel, where the bullet or shell comes out
[verb: **muzzles, muzzling, muzzled**]
1 to muzzle a dog is to put a muzzle on it
2 to muzzle someone is to do something to stop them talking

my [adjective] belonging to me: *There's my son. • Have you seen my boots anywhere?*

myriad [noun] a very great number or range of things: *a myriad of stars in the night sky*
[adjective] countless: *flowers in myriad colours and shapes*

myrrh [noun] a brown strong-smelling resin that comes from an African or Asian tree and is used in medicines and perfumes

myrtle [noun] a type of evergreen shrub with scented leaves

myself [pronoun]
1 you use **myself** after a verb or preposition when *I* is the subject of the action and is also affected by it: *I was washing myself. • I felt rather proud of myself.*
2 you also use **myself** to show that you do something without any help from anyone else: *I suppose I'll have to do it myself if no one else can be bothered.*
3 you can use the word **myself** to show more clearly who you mean: *I have not seen the film myself.*

mysterious [adjective]
1 difficult to understand or explain
2 if someone is being mysterious about something, they avoid talking about it, making you even more curious to know about it
♦ **mysteriously** [adverb] in a mysterious way: *It disappeared mysteriously in a little puff of smoke.*

mystery [noun: **mysteries**] something that you do not understand and which cannot be, or has not been, explained

mystic [noun: **mystics**] someone who tries to gain knowledge about sacred or spiritual things, usually by meditating or going into a trance
♦ **mystical** [adjective] to do with the spiritual world, or beyond ordinary human understanding

mystify [verb: **mystifies, mystifying, mystified**] if you are mystified by something, you are very puzzled by it

myth [noun: **myths**]
1 a story about ancient gods, heroes and monsters: *Greek and Roman myths*
2 something that many people believe is a fact, but which is not true or real
♦ **mythical** [adjective] existing only in myths: *mythical creatures like dragons and unicorns*
♦ **mythological** [adjective] to do with myth or mythology
♦ **mythology** [noun] stories about ancient gods and heroes

Mm

N

N [abbreviation] short for **north**

n/a [abbreviation] short for **not applicable**, something you write on forms when the form asks for information or asks a question that is not relevant to you

nab [verb: **nabs, nabbing, nabbed**]
1 to grab or take something: *Someone's nabbed all the best sandwiches already.*
2 to catch or arrest someone: *The police nabbed a man climbing out of the back window.*

naff [adjective: **naffer, naffest**] if you say something is naff you think it is not very good: *a rather naff website*

ⓘ **Naff** is a very informal word.

nag [verb: **nags, nagging, nagged**] to remind someone again and again about something they have not done: *My wife's always nagging me to paint the kitchen.*
[noun: **nags**] an informal word for a horse

nail [noun: **nails**]
1 a thin pointed piece of metal that you hit into a surface with a hammer
2 the hard covering on top of the ends of your fingers and toes
[verb: **nails, nailing, nailed**] to attach or join something by hammering it with nails: *Nail the number on the door.*

naïve [adjective] believing that things are simple and people are good when in fact life is more difficult: *She had a naïve belief that he never lied to her.*

naked [adjective]
1 without clothes: *naked children playing in the water*
2 not covered or protected: *a naked flame • a naked light bulb*

ⓘ **Naked** is pronounced with two syllables: **nay**-kid.

name [noun: **names**]
1 the word or words that you always call a certain person, place or thing: *What's your name? • I can't remember the name of the street.*
2 someone's **good** or **bad name** is their reputation: *This is how football fans get a bad name.*
[verb: **names, naming, named**] to decide on a certain word to call a person, place or thing: *They've named their son Samuel.*

nameless [adjective] without a name or with a name that is not known: *The writer of the letter wants to remain nameless.*

namely [adverb] used to give more specific details about what you have just mentioned: *Two of our members, namely the Grimes brothers, have won medals this term.*

namesake [noun: **namesakes**] your namesake is someone who has the same name as you: *Hi John, I've just been talking to your namesake in the supermarket.*

nanny [noun: **nannies**] a person whose job is to look after a child in its own home

nanny-goat [noun: **nanny-goats**] a female goat

nap [noun: **naps**] a short sleep during the day: *I sometimes have a nap in the afternoon.*
[verb: **naps, napping, napped**] to have a short sleep

nape [noun] the nape of your neck is the back of your neck

napkin [noun: **napkins**] a piece of cloth or paper that you can use during a meal to wipe your mouth or fingers

nappy [noun: **nappies**] a pad that you fasten around a baby's bottom to soak up the liquid or solid waste it produces: *I hate changing the baby's nappy.*

narcotic [noun: **narcotics**] a drug that makes you sleepy and numb
[adjective] causing sleepiness: *Alcohol can have a narcotic effect.*

nark [verb: **narks, narking, narked**] an informal word that means to annoy someone: *Her voice really narks me.*

narrate [verb: **narrates, narrating, narrated**] to tell a story: *Freddie narrated the events that led up to the explosion.*
+ **narration** [noun: **narrations**] the telling of a story: *a documentary about the war with a narration by some of the soldiers*
+ **narrator** [noun: **narrators**] the narrator of a story is the person who tells it: *We never find out the name of the narrator.*

narrow [adjective: **narrower, narrowest**]
1 not very wide: *a narrow gateway* • *The road was too narrow for overtaking.*
2 only just happening, with hardly any room or time to spare: *a narrow escape*
+ **narrowly** [adverb] closely: *We were narrowly defeated by 6 goals to 5.*

narrow-minded [adjective] not willing to consider anybody else's beliefs or ideas

nasal [adjective] to do with the nose: *a drug that relieves nasal congestion*

nasty [adjective: **nastier, nastiest**]
1 very unpleasant or unkind: *a nasty taste in my mouth* • *saying nasty things about her family*
2 serious: *a nasty injury*

nation [noun: **nations**]
1 a country with its own government
2 the people of a country: *Today the nation is voting for a new government.*
+ **national** [adjective] to do with a whole country: *the local, national and international news*

national anthem [noun: **national anthems**] the official song of a country

National Insurance [noun] money that you pay to the government while you are working so that the government can pay money to people who are sick, unemployed or retired

nationalism [noun]
1 the belief that the people of a country should have their own government
2 a great love for your own country
+ **nationalist** [noun: **nationalists**]
1 someone who wants their country to have its own government
2 someone with a great love for their own country
[adjective] wanting your country to have its own government: *nationalist beliefs*

nationality [noun: **nationalities**] your nationality is your membership of a nation: *Louis has dual nationality because his mother is French and his father is American.*

nationalize or **nationalise** [verb: **nationalizes, nationalizing, nationalized**] to nationalize an industry is to bring it under the control of the government: *The railways in many countries have been nationalized for years.*

national park [noun: **national parks**] an area of countryside that the government controls in order to protect it

nationwide [adjective] in every area throughout a country: *a nationwide search for the robbers*

native [adjective]
1 your native country is the one you were born in
2 your native language is the first one you learnt
[noun: **natives**] a native of a country is someone who was born there

Native American [noun: **Native Americans**] a person from the race of people who lived in North or South America before the Europeans arrived there

natural [adjective]
1 to do with or made by nature, not by people or machines: *the natural world* • *An earthquake is an example of a natural disaster.*
2 natural behaviour is what you do normally without thinking: *It's only natural to be a little nervous before a test.*

natural gas [noun] gas that comes from under the sea or underground and can be used as fuel

natural history [noun] studying plants, animals and rocks

Nn

naturalist [noun: **naturalists**] a person who studies plants or animals

naturalize or **naturalise** [verb: **naturalizes, naturalizing, naturalized**] a person is naturalized when they become a legal citizen of a country they were not born in

naturally [adverb]
1 you can say 'naturally' to mean 'of course': 'Will you take me with you?' 'Naturally.'
2 in a way that is normal: Joe began to relax and behave a bit more naturally.
3 without help from anything artificial: Let the skin heal naturally.

natural resources [plural noun] things that people use and that exist naturally, like forests, coal and water

nature [noun: **natures**]
1 everything in the world that was not made or changed by people: I love watching programmes about nature.
2 what something is basically like: the nature of the business
3 the kind of person someone is: It's not in her nature to be unkind.

nature reserve [noun: **nature reserves**] an area of land that is kept separate to protect the plants and animals that live there

nature trail [noun: **nature trails**] a path through the countryside where you can see particularly interesting plants and wildlife

naughtiness [noun] bad behaviour or disobedience

naughty [adjective: **naughtier, naughtiest**] a naughty child does things they should not do

nausea [noun] the feeling that you are about to be sick

♦ **nauseating** [adjective] something nauseating makes you feel sick: a nauseating smell

nautical [adjective] to do with ships and the sea

naval [adjective] to do with the navy

navel [noun: **navels**] the small hollow in the centre of your stomach where a cord connected you to your mother before you were born

navigate [verb: **navigates, navigating, navigated**] to decide which way to go in a vehicle such as a car, aeroplane or ship: My mother always drove and my father had to navigate.

♦ **navigation** [noun] deciding which way to go in a vehicle such as a car, plane or boat

♦ **navigator** [noun: **navigators**] a person who decides which direction a vehicle should go in

navy [noun: **navies**] the part of a country's armed forces that works at sea

navy blue [noun] a dark blue colour

NB [abbreviation] you can write **NB** at the start of a sentence to make someone pay particular attention to it

ⓘ **NB** is short for **nota bene**, which is Latin for 'note well'.

near [preposition] not far away: the shop near our house
[adverb: **nearer, nearest**] close by a thing or person: Stand a little nearer and you'll be able to see better.
[adjective: **nearer, nearest**] not far away: the near future • a near neighbour
[verb: **nears, nearing, neared**] to approach or get close to something: As we neared the building, the faces at the window became clearer.

nearby [adjective and adverb] quite close to where you are or the place you are talking about: We went to a nearby restaurant for dinner. • Do you live nearby?

nearly [adverb] almost but not completely: We're nearly there. • Nearly everyone had a good time.

neat [adjective: **neater, neatest**]
1 clean and tidy: a neat bedroom
2 done skilfully: a neat shot into the corner of the goal
3 a liquid, especially a drink, is neat when it is not mixed with anything: She was drinking neat whisky.

necessarily [adverb] for certain: Men aren't necessarily stronger than women.

necessary [adjective] needed in order to get a result: Is it necessary for everyone to fill in their own form? • We can stay a bit longer if necessary.

necessity [noun: **necessities**] something

that is needed or that must happen: *A warm coat is a necessity in this weather.*

neck [noun: **necks**]
1 the part of your body between your head and your shoulders
2 the opening in a piece of clothing that you put your head through
3 the narrow part of a bottle near its opening
4 if two people in a race or competition are **neck and neck**, they are level with each other and it is difficult to know who will win

necklace [noun: **necklaces**] a piece of jewellery for wearing around your neck, for example, a string of beads or jewels or a chain

nectar [noun] the sweet liquid that bees collect from flowers to make honey

nectarine [noun: **nectarines**] a fruit very similar to a peach but with a smooth skin

née [adjective] née is used before the surname that a woman had when she was born: *Mrs Janet Carter, née Tindale*

need [verb: **needs, needing, needed**]
1 to have to do something: *We all need to eat and drink.*
2 to be without something that would be helpful or useful: *What I need here is a sharp knife.*
[noun: **needs**]
1 you have a need for something when you want it but do not have it: *If you feel the need of some company, just give me a call.*
2 if there is no need to do something, it is not necessary: *There's no need to shout.*
3 your needs are the things that it is necessary for you to have
➞ **needless, needy**

needle [noun: **needles**]
1 a small pointed piece of metal used for sewing
2 a long thin piece of wood, metal or plastic that is used for knitting
3 an instrument for giving injections of medicine
4 a moving pointer, especially on a dial, for example on a compass

needless [adjective] not necessary: *a needless waste of money*

needy [adjective: **needier, neediest**] poor: *help for needy families who have lost their homes*

negative [adjective]
1 a negative answer or response says or means *no*: *We got a very negative reaction.*
2 to have a negative attitude is to feel uncertain and not very hopeful
3 a negative number is one that is less than zero, for example −5
[noun: **negatives**]
1 a film before it is printed, where light objects appear dark and dark objects appear light
2 in grammar, a negative is a word or phrase that means 'not' or 'no', for example *I am not ready*

negative equity [noun] the situation when your house is worth less than the amount you owe to the organization that provided you with the mortgage on it

neglect [verb: **neglects, neglecting, neglected**]
1 to not give a thing or person proper care and attention: *I've been neglecting the housework because I've been so busy.*
2 to forget to do something: *I neglected to lock the door and found it wide open when I got home.*
[noun] lack of proper care: *All the houseplants had died from neglect.*

negligence [noun] not doing the things you should do, or not doing them carefully enough
✦ **negligent** [adjective] careless about the things you should do carefully

negligible [adjective] so small that you can ignore it: *negligible differences between the two stories*

negotiable [adjective] a negotiable price, offer or contract is one that you can discuss and change before you agree on it

negotiate [verb: **negotiates, negotiating, negotiated**]
1 to try to reach an agreement with someone by having discussions with them: *Employees are currently negotiating with managers over a pay rise.*
2 to go along a path or way successfully: *We just managed to negotiate the last corner and came in third.*
✦ **negotiation** [noun: **negotiations**] discussion of a subject in order to reach an agreement on it

Nn

Nn

◆ **negotiator** [noun: **negotiators**] a person who tries to make people come to an agreement by having discussions

neigh [verb: **neighs, neighing, neighed**] to make the noise that a horse makes
[noun: **neighs**] the noise that a horse makes

neighbour [noun: **neighbours**] someone who lives near you or next door to you

◆ **neighbourhood** [noun: **neighbourhoods**] an area of a town or city: *This is a pretty neighbourhood with a lot of trees and parks.*

◆ **neighbouring** [adjective] next or nearby: *the mayors of all the neighbouring towns*

neither [adjective and pronoun] not either: *Neither woman seemed to understand English.* • *Neither of us can go.*
[conjunction] neither is often used with **nor** to show negative possibilities: *I neither know, nor care, where he is.*

ⓘ You can say either *Neither of us **is** able to be there* or *Neither of us **are** able to be there.*

neon [noun] a gas that shines very brightly when electricity passes through it

nephew [noun: **nephews**] your nephew is the son of your brother or sister, or the son of your wife or husband's brother or sister

nerve [noun: **nerves**]
1 a nerve is one of the tiny thread-like connections that carry messages about feelings and movements between your brain and other parts of your body
2 nerve is a kind of boldness or courage: *I didn't have the nerve to jump.*
3 if someone or something **gets on your nerves**, they annoy you

nerve-racking [adjective] making you feel extremely anxious or worried

nerves [plural noun] a nervous feeling: *Breathe deeply before the performance to try to calm your nerves.*

nervous [adjective]
1 worried or frightened: *I get terribly nervous just before I go on stage.* • *a nervous laugh*
2 to do with the nerves in your body: *nervous disorders*

nervous breakdown [noun: **nervous breakdowns**] a mental illness in which someone is so anxious, unhappy and exhausted that they are unable to deal with their normal life

nervously [adverb] in a worried, rather scared way: *She answered nervously, wondering why they were asking her.*

nervousness [noun] a worried, rather scared feeling

nervous system [noun: **nervous systems**] the body's nervous system is its network of nerves and the way they link to the brain to send messages about feeling and movement

-ness [suffix] if **-ness** comes at the end of a word, it is a noun that refers to a particular state or condition. For example, *sadness* is the condition of being sad

nest [noun: **nests**] a place where birds or some kinds of insects and animals live and bring up their young
[verb: **nests, nesting, nested**] to build a place to live, especially from twigs and leaves, in a tree

nestle [verb: **nestles, nestling, nestled**]
1 to nestle somewhere is to settle yourself in a warm and comfortable place or position
2 to be in a partly hidden, sheltered place: *a cottage nestling at the edge of the wood*

net [noun: **nets**]
1 net is a material made by crossing and knotting threads and making a pattern of holes
2 a net is made from crossed and knotted threads and is used for catching things like fish or in sports like tennis, football or basketball
3 the Net is the Internet: *I found some good information about Sweden on the Net.*

net [adjective]
1 a net profit is the money you have made after you have paid all your expenses
2 the net weight of something is its weight without its packaging

netball [noun] a game where teams of players throw a ball to each other and try to score goals by putting the ball through a high loop surrounded by a net at the end of a court. It is similar to basketball but players may not run with the ball

nettle [noun: **nettles**] a wild plant that stings if you touch its leaves

network [noun: **networks**]
  1 an arrangement of lines that cross and connect with one another: *a railway network*
  2 a system of something like computers or radio stations that are all connected together

neurologist [noun: **neurologists**] a doctor who specializes in diseases which affect your nervous system

neurology [noun] the study of the body's nervous system and the diseases which affect it

neuter [verb: **neuters, neutering, neutered**] to carry out an operation on an animal so that it cannot breed

neutral [adjective]
  1 a person who is neutral in an argument does not support either side
  2 a neutral colour is not strong or noticeable
  3 an engine's neutral gear is not connected to its forward or backward driving parts
  ✦ **neutralize** or **neutralise** [verb: **neutralizes, neutralizing, neutralized**] to prevent something from having an effect

never [adverb] not ever, or not at any time: *I've never been abroad.* • *It's never too late to learn.*

nevertheless [adverb] however or anyway: *I couldn't swim; nevertheless I jumped in to try to save him.*

new [adjective: **newer, newest**]
  1 not existing or known about before: *a new discovery*
  2 just bought, made or received: *a new jacket*
  3 different: *Take this book back and get a new one from the library.*

newcomer [noun: **newcomers**] a person who has recently arrived

newfangled [adjective] new and complicated in a way that annoys you: *a newfangled washing machine*

newly [adverb] only recently: *a newly painted room*

news [noun]
  1 information about something that has just happened: *Have you heard the news about Raj?*
  2 a radio or television report about recent events: *listening to the news at 10 o'clock*

newsagent [noun: **newsagents**]
  1 someone who sells newspapers and magazines
  2 a newsagent's is a shop that sells newspapers and magazines and usually other things like sweets and stationery: *She bought some envelopes at the newsagent's.*

newsletter [noun: **newsletters**] a sheet or booklet containing news and information, given regularly to members of an organization

newspaper [noun: **newspapers**] a collection of reports and pictures about recent events that is published daily or weekly on a set of folded sheets of paper

newt [noun: **newts**] a small animal like a lizard that lives both in water and on land

next [adjective] the one that follows immediately after: *What's the next name on the list?* • *Let's meet next week.*
  [adverb] after the present thing, person or time: *Who's coming next?* • *What will happen next?*

next of kin [noun] your next of kin is your closest relative, who would be informed if you had an accident

NHS [abbreviation] short for **National Health Service**, the system which provides free medical treatment for people in the UK: *He had the operation done on the NHS.*

NI [abbreviation] short for **National Insurance**

nib [noun: **nibs**] the point of a pen

nibble [verb: **nibbles, nibbling, nibbled**] to take little bites of something: *A mouse had nibbled right through the wires.*
  [noun: **nibbles**] a small bite or several small bites out of something

nice [adjective: **nicer, nicest**]
  1 pleasant, good or attractive: *We'll find somewhere nice to sit, out in the fresh air.*
  2 kind or friendly: *James is quite nice really, once you get used to him.*
  ✦ **nicely** [adverb]
  1 in a pleasant way: *Ask the lady nicely.*
  2 well: *A cheque will do nicely, thank you.*
  ✦ **niceness** [noun] being pleasant or attractive

niche [noun: **niches**]
  1 a hollow space in a wall for a statue
  2 a situation that you fit into very comfortably:

Nn

She seems to have found her niche in life.

nick [noun: **nicks**]
1 a small cut
2 an informal word for a police station
[verb: **nicks, nicking, nicked**]
1 to make a very small cut in something
2 an informal word that means to steal something: *Who's nicked my pen?*
3 an informal word that means to arrest someone

nickel [noun: **nickels**]
1 a white metal that is often mixed with other metals
2 an American or Canadian coin worth 5 cents

nickname [noun: **nicknames**] a name that you use for someone that is not their real name
[verb: **nicknames, nicknaming, nicknamed**] to call someone a name that is not their real one: *They nicknamed him 'Scottie'.*

nicotine [noun] the poisonous substance that is contained in tobacco

niece [noun: **nieces**] your niece is the daughter of your brother or sister, or the daughter of your wife's or husband's brother or sister

nifty [adjective: **niftier, niftiest**] neat and clever: *You should have seen his nifty footwork when he got near the goal.*

niggle [verb: **niggles, niggling, niggled**] to worry or irritate you slightly, but continually
♦ **niggling** [adjective] a niggling doubt or worry is a small one that will not go away

night [noun: **nights**] the time of darkness between the sun going down in the evening and rising again in the morning
⇒ **nightly**

nightclub [noun: **nightclubs**] a place where people can go to drink and dance late at night

nightdress or **nightgown** [noun: **nightdresses** or **nightgowns**] a loose dress that a woman or girl sleeps in

nightfall [noun] the time when it starts to get dark in the evening: *We arranged to meet at nightfall.*

nightingale [noun: **nightingales**] a small bird that sings beautifully

nightly [adjective and adverb] every night: *nightly visits to the cinema • adverts that you see at least twice nightly*

nightmare [noun: **nightmares**]
1 a frightening dream
2 a very unpleasant experience: *The journey turned out to be a complete nightmare.*

night shift [noun: **night shifts**]
1 a period of time during the night when you have to go to work: *I'm doing night shifts this week.*
2 the group of people who work in a place at night

nightshirt [noun: **nightshirts**] a long loose shirt for sleeping in

nil [noun] a score of nothing in a game or sport: *The score was eight-nil.*

nimble [adjective: **nimbler, nimblest**]
1 a nimble movement is quick, quiet and easy
2 a nimble person moves quickly and neatly
♦ **nimbly** [adverb] in a quick neat way: *He jumped nimbly aside and let the bike pass.*

nine [noun: **nines**] the number 9

nineteen [noun: **nineteens**] the number 19

nineteenth [adjective and adverb] after eighteenth and before twentieth: *the nineteenth day of the month*

ninetieth [adjective and adverb] after eighty-ninth and before ninety-first: *It's my grandfather's ninetieth birthday tomorrow.*

ninety [noun: **nineties**] the number 90

ninth [adjective and adverb] after eighth and before tenth: *I came ninth out of ten — it could have been worse!*
[noun: **ninths**] the fraction $\frac{1}{9}$, which means one of nine equal parts of something

nip [verb: **nips, nipping, nipped**]
1 to nip someone is to pinch them, squeeze them sharply, or bite them
2 to go somewhere quickly or for a short time: *I must just nip to the shops.*
[noun: **nips**]
1 a small bite or pinch
2 a cold feeling: *a nip in the air that feels like winter*
♦ **nipper** [noun: **nippers**] an informal word for a child

nipple [noun: **nipples**] the pointed part of a breast that a baby sucks milk from

nippy [adjective: **nippier, nippiest**]

1 cold or frosty: *It's a bit nippy out today.*

2 a nippy car is easy to turn and move quickly

nit [noun: **nits**]

1 the egg of a louse or other small insect which is sometimes found in people's hair

2 an informal word for a person who you think is stupid

nitrogen [noun] a colourless gas that makes up about four-fifths of the air we breathe

no [interjection] a word that you use to express things like refusing, denying or disagreeing: *'Are you alright?' 'No.'*

[adjective] not any: *They have no money.*

[adverb] not at all: *She's no better.*

No. or **no.** [abbreviation: **Nos.**] short for **number**

nobility [noun]

1 people in the highest classes of society, for example royalty

2 being noble

noble [adjective: **nobler, noblest**]

1 brave, fine and good: *making a noble effort to be nice*

2 belonging to a high social class: *coming from a noble family*

nobleman [noun: **noblemen**] a man of high rank in society

noblewoman [noun: **noblewomen**] a woman of high rank in society

nobody [pronoun] not any person: *Nobody tells me what to do! • There was nobody at home.*

[noun: **nobodies**] a person who is not at all important: *He's just a nobody who thinks he's somebody.*

nocturnal [adjective] nocturnal animals are active at night-time

nod [verb: **nods, nodding, nodded**] to move your head up and down as if you were agreeing or saying 'yes'

[noun: **nods**] an up-and-down movement of your head

no-fault [adjective]

1 a no-fault insurance policy is one that is valid whether an accident is your fault or not

2 a no-fault divorce is one in which neither person has to prove that the other person caused the marriage to fail

noise [noun: **noises**]

1 a noise is a sound: *Did you hear a noise outside?*

2 noise is sound that you do not like: *Could you please make a little less noise?*

• **noisy** [adjective: **noisier, noisiest**] making a lot of sound that you do not like: *a noisy party • The fridge seems very noisy — is there something wrong with it?*

nomad [noun: **nomads**] a person who wanders from place to place, rather than living in the same place all the time

nominate [verb: **nominates, nominating, nominated**] to nominate someone to do something is to suggest that they should do it: *Charles nominated Peter as leader of the group.*

• **nomination** [noun: **nominations**] a suggestion that a certain thing or person should be chosen for something: *We've had several nominations, so we'll have to have a vote.*

• **nominee** [noun: **nominees**] a person who has been suggested for a job or prize

non- [prefix] you can add **non-** to the beginning of many words to make them mean the opposite, or 'not', for example, *non-smokers* are people who do not smoke

non-contributory [adjective]

1 a non-contributory pension scheme is one that your employer pays for and you do not have to pay anything

2 a non-contributory state benefit is one that you can get even if you have not paid National Insurance contributions

none [pronoun] not one: *None of them are going to admit to being wrong. • We looked for more biscuits but there were none left.*

[adverb] not at all: *I heard the answer but I'm none the wiser.*

non-existent [adjective] not existing: *Many types of butterfly are almost non-existent in this area.*

nonplussed [adjective] puzzled and confused

nonsense [noun]

1 something that does not make sense: *His theory is a load of nonsense.*

2 silly behaviour: *Stop your nonsense now please.*

Nn

non-stop [adjective and adverb] without a break or a pause: *There was non-stop hammering from the room above.* • *It's rained non-stop for three days.*

noodle [noun: **noodles**] noodles are long thin pieces of pasta

nook [noun: **nooks**] a corner or a space, especially where someone or something can be hidden

noon [noun] twelve o'clock in the day: *We'll have our lunch at noon.*

no one or **no-one** [pronoun] not any person: *No one's in at the moment.*

noose [noun: **nooses**] a loop of rope that tightens when the end is pulled

nor [conjunction] a word that is used with **neither**, before a second negative possibility: *Neither Jack nor Jenny is at home.*

ⓘ You use **or** when you start with **either**: *Either he goes or I do.*
You use **nor** when you start with **neither**: *Neither you nor I will ever understand this.*

norm [noun: **norms**] the norm is what people usually do or what usually happens: *It has become the norm to send young children to nursery school.*

normal [adjective] usual and expected: *It's normal to feel hungry at lunchtime.*

◆ **normality** [noun] the state of things as they usually are: *After all the excitement it was good to return to normality.*

◆ **normally** [adverb]
1 usually: *We normally go to bed pretty early.*
2 in the usual way: *This plant has developed normally, but this one is diseased.*

north [noun]
1 the direction a compass needle points, opposite to south
2 the part of a country or the world that is in the north
[adjective] in, from, or towards the north: *the cold North wind* • *the north wall of the building*
[adverb] to the north: *travelling north on the motorway*

north-east [noun] the area midway between north and east: *the north-east of Scotland*

northerly [adjective] coming from, or going towards, the north: *a northerly breeze* • *going in a northerly direction* • *the island's most northerly point*
[noun: **northerlies**] a wind that comes from the north

northern [adjective] belonging to, or coming from, the north: *the cold northern climate* • *Northern districts will have some rain.*

northward or **northwards** [adverb] to or towards the north: *We cycled northwards for several miles.*

north-west [noun] the area midway between north and west: *the north-west of England*

nose [noun: **noses**]
1 the part of your face that you breathe and smell through
2 the front part of something that sticks out, for example, the front of an aircraft

nosedive [noun: **nosedives**] a dive straight downwards
[verb: **nosedives, nosediving, nosedived**] to dive down headfirst: *The rocket flew straight up and then nosedived straight down again.*

nosey [adjective] look at the entry for **nosy**

nostalgia [noun] a feeling of sadness when you remember happy times in the past
◆ **nostalgic** [adjective] thinking of, or reminding you of, happy times in the past: *a nostalgic evening of black and white movies*

nostril [noun: **nostrils**] your nostrils are the two openings in your nose that you breathe and smell through

nosy or **nosey** [adjective: **nosier, nosiest**] always wanting to find out about other people and what they are doing

not [adverb] a word that is used to express negatives and opposites. It often becomes **n't** when it is added to verbs: *I'm not going.* • *It isn't fair.* • *I can't hear you.*

notable [adjective] important and worth remembering: *The most notable part of the evening was the music.*
◆ **notably** [adverb] particularly: *I loved the old buildings, notably the palace.*

notch [noun: **notches**] a small, V-shaped cut: *We cut notches in a stick as the days passed.*
[verb: **notches, notching, notched**] to make a V-shaped cut in something

Nn

note [noun: **notes**]
1 a word or sentence to tell or remind someone of something: *They've left a note to say that dinner's in the oven.*
2 a short letter: *This is just a quick note to let you know we're well.*
3 a written comment: *a note at the bottom of the page*
4 a piece of paper money: *a five pound note*
5 a single musical sound or the sign that stands for it
6 a piano key
[verb: **notes, noting, noted**] to pay attention to something so that you remember it: *I noted that she always wore red, and wondered why.*

notebook [noun: **notebooks**]
1 a small book that you use to write things down in
2 a very small computer that you can carry around

notepaper [noun] plain paper that you use for writing letters on

nothing [pronoun] not anything: *There was nothing in the cupboard.* • *Nothing's the matter with me.*
♦ **nothingness** [noun] complete emptiness

notice [verb: **notices, noticing, noticed**] to realize something because you see, hear, feel, smell or taste it: *I noticed a funny smell in the hall.* • *Did you notice the way George was looking at Emily?*
[noun: **notices**]
1 an announcement: *a notice pinned on the board*
2 something **comes to your notice** when you realize it: *It's come to our notice that you are always late.*
3 you **give someone notice** of something happening when you warn them about it: *Please give me notice if you plan to visit.*

noticeable [adjective] obvious or easy to see: *a noticeable difference in his appearance*
♦ **noticeably** [adverb] that you can easily see: *We were all noticeably more relaxed after dinner.*

notification [noun] notification is when someone officially tells you something: *You will receive notification of any changes to payments made to you.*

notify [verb: **notifies, notifying, notified**] to tell someone about something in an official way: *Please notify the chairperson if you are not able to attend this meeting.*

notion [noun: **notions**] an idea, a belief or an understanding: *I had a notion that this wouldn't really matter to you.*

notorious [adjective] famous for something bad: *a notorious criminal*
♦ **notoriously** [adverb] well known to be something bad: *That model is notoriously unreliable.*

nougat [noun] a sticky kind of sweet that contains nuts

nought [noun: **noughts**]
1 nothing
2 the figure 0: *Write twenty as a two and a nought.*

noun [part of speech: **nouns**] a word that refers to a person or a thing. For example, *tree, Sue,* and *idea* are nouns

nourish [verb: **nourishes, nourishing, nourished**] to provide people, animals or plants with what they need to keep them healthy
♦ **nourishment** [noun] healthy food and drink

novel [noun: **novels**] a book that tells a story that is not true: *a romantic novel*
[adjective] completely new and original: *What a novel idea!*

November [noun] the eleventh month of the year, after October and before December

novice [noun: **novices**] a beginner, who is only just learning how to do something: *Don't ask me for advice — I'm just a novice at this.*

now [adverb]
1 at the present time: *It is now five o'clock.*
2 immediately: *I'll do it now.*
3 **just now** means 'a moment ago': *I saw Jim outside just now.*
4 **just now** also means 'at this moment': *I can't come out, I'm busy just now.*
5 if something happens **now and again** or **now and then**, it happens occasionally: *I see him walking his dog now and again.*

nowadays [adverb] these days:

Nn

Nowadays, women usually have their babies in hospital.

nowhere [adverb] not anywhere: *We've got nowhere to go.*

noxious [adjective] harmful or poisonous: *noxious gases leaking from factories*

nozzle [noun: **nozzles**] a part at the end of a pipe that controls how fast a liquid comes out of it

nuclear [adjective] to do with the reaction that occurs when atoms are split apart or forced together: *a nuclear power station*

nuclear energy [noun] the energy that is created when atoms are split apart or forced together

nuclear weapon [noun: **nuclear weapons**] a weapon that uses the power from nuclear reactions to create a very powerful explosion

nucleus [noun: **nuclei**] the central part of an atom

nude [adjective] not wearing any clothes: *a nude woman*
[noun: **nudes**] a nude is a picture or statue of someone without clothes on
➜ **nudity**

nudge [verb: **nudges, nudging, nudged**] to give someone a gentle push, especially with your elbow: *I nudged him and he began to speak.*
[noun: **nudges**] a gentle push, especially with your elbow: *Give him a nudge or he'll fall asleep.*

nudity [noun] not having any clothes on

nugget [noun: **nuggets**] a small lump of something, especially gold or chicken

nuisance [noun] a thing or person that annoys you: *That cat is a dreadful nuisance, scratching at the door to get in.*

numb [adjective: **number, numbest**] a part of your body is numb when you cannot feel it properly: *I was so cold my hands had gone completely numb.*
➜ **numbness**

ⓘ Remember there is a *b* in **numb** that you do not pronounce.

number [noun: **numbers**]
1 a word or figure showing how many of something there are or in what position

something is in a series: *the number four • Please write down any three figure number.*
2 a group or collection of people or things: *a large number of animals*
3 a popular song or piece of music: *a catchy number*
[verb: **numbers, numbering, numbered**]
1 to give a thing or person a number as part of a series: *The boxes are all clearly numbered.*
2 a group that numbers a certain quantity is made up of that many: *The crowd numbered many thousands.*

numbness [noun] when you lose the feeling in a part of your body

numeral [noun: **numerals**] a symbol that stands for a number: *a Roman numeral*

numerate [adjective] a numerate person knows how to use numbers to do calculations

numerical [adjective] to do with numbers: *Put the cards into numerical order.*

numerous [adjective] many: *Numerous people have had the same experience.*

nun [noun: **nuns**] a member of a religious group of women who live in a convent

nurse [noun: **nurses**] a person whose job is to look after people when they are ill or injured, especially in a hospital
[verb: **nurses, nursing, nursed**] to look after someone when they are ill or injured: *He had nursed her back to health over several weeks.*

nursery [noun: **nurseries**]
1 a place where parents can take their children to be looked after while they are at work
2 a room for young children
3 a place where plants are grown and sold

nursery school [noun: **nursery schools**] a school for children between three and five years old

nursing [noun] the job of looking after people who are ill or injured

nursing home [noun: **nursing homes**] a small private hospital or home, especially for old people

nurture [verb: **nurtures, nurturing, nurtured**] to look after a person, animal or plant so that they grow healthily

nut [noun: **nuts**]
1 a fruit from certain trees that has a hard shell and a firm inside that you can eat

Nn

2 a small piece of metal with a hole in the middle of it for screwing onto the end of a bolt ⇒ **nutty**

nutmeg [noun: **nutmegs**] a hard seed that is grated or used as a brown powder to flavour food

nutrient [noun: **nutrients**]
1 a substance in food that gives you energy and makes you healthy
2 a substance in the soil that helps plants to grow healthily

nutrition [noun] eating healthy food: *Good nutrition is necessary for a quick recovery.*
♦ **nutritious** [adjective] healthy for you to eat or drink: *a nutritious meal*

nutshell [noun] to **put something in a nutshell** is to say it using as few words as possible: *To put it in a nutshell, we must stop spending so much money.*

nutty [adjective: **nuttier, nuttiest**]
1 containing nuts or tasting of nuts
2 silly or crazy

nuzzle [verb: **nuzzles, nuzzling, nuzzled**] an animal nuzzles you when it rubs its nose gently against you

nylon [noun: **nylons**] nylon is a strong fabric that is made in a factory
♦ **nylons** [plural noun] stockings that are made of nylon

Nn

oaf [noun: **oafs**] a stupid or clumsy person: *That big oaf is always knocking things over.*

oak [noun: **oaks**] a large tree with hard wood and seeds called acorns

OAP [abbreviation] short for **old age pensioner**

oar [noun: **oars**] a long piece of wood with a flat end, used to row a boat

oasis [noun: **oases**] a place in a desert where there is water and where trees grow: *The travellers stopped at an oasis.*

oath [noun: **oaths**]
1 a solemn promise: *He swore an oath to support the king.*
2 a swear word: *curses and oaths*

oatmeal [noun] oats that have been ground to a powder

oats [plural noun] oats are the grain of a type of grassy plant that is used as food: *Horses eat oats.*

obedience [noun] being willing to do what you are told: *Teachers expect obedience from their pupils.*
 • obedient [adjective] ready to do what you are told: *an obedient child*

obese [adjective] very fat

obey [verb: **obeys, obeying, obeyed**] to do what you are told to do: *I obeyed the order.*
 ➡ **obedience**

obituary [noun: **obituaries**] an announcement in a newspaper that someone has died, often with a short account of their life

object [noun: **objects**]
1 something that can be seen or felt: *There were various objects on the table.*
2 an aim or purpose: *His main object in life was to become rich.*

3 the word or words in a sentence that stand for the person or thing that the verb affects, for example *me* in *He hit me*
[verb: **objects, objecting, objected**] to **object to** someone or something is to say that you do not like them or do not agree with them: *I object to her rudeness.* • *Jack objected to the proposal.*
 • objection [noun: **objections**]
1 objecting to something: *His view is open to objection.*
2 a reason for objecting: *My objection is that he is too young.*

ⓘ The noun is pronounced **ob**–jikt, with the stress at the beginning.
The verb is pronounced ob–**jekt**, with the stress at the end.

objective [noun: **objectives**] an aim or purpose: *His objective was to score more than one goal.*
[adjective] if you are objective, you are fair and try to look at things from different points of view

obligation [noun: **obligations**] a promise or duty: *You are under no obligation to buy this.*

obligatory [adjective] something that is obligatory must be done: *It is obligatory to pay tax.*

oblige [verb: **obliges, obliging, obliged**]
1 to oblige someone is to do something to help them: *Could you oblige me by carrying this, please?*
2 to oblige someone to do something is to force them to do it: *I was obliged to invite him to my party.*

◆ **obliged** [adjective] grateful: *I am obliged to you for all your help.*

◆ **obliging** [adjective] ready to help others: *a most obliging man*

oblique [adjective]
1 sloping: *an oblique line*
2 not direct or not saying exactly what is meant: *an oblique reply*

obliterate [verb: **obliterates, obliterating, obliterated**] to destroy something completely: *The house was obliterated by an earthquake.*

oblivious [adjective] not aware of what is happening: *I was oblivious to her exhaustion.*

oblong [noun: **oblongs**] a shape with four straight sides that is longer than it is wide [adjective] shaped like an oblong: *an oblong table*

obnoxious [adjective] very unpleasant and annoying: *an obnoxious remark*

oboe [noun: **oboes**] a woodwind musical instrument

obscene [adjective] disgusting: *obscene photographs*

◆ **obscenity** [noun: **obscenities**]
1 obscenity is being obscene: *the obscenity of war*
2 an obscenity is a word or act that is obscene: *The youths shouted obscenities at the police.*

obscure [adjective]
1 not easy to see or understand: *an obscure outline • obscure references to Shakespeare*
2 not famous or well-known: *an obscure poet* [verb: **obscures, obscuring, obscured**] to hide something: *Thick clouds obscured the sun.*

◆ **obscurity** [noun] being obscure: *the obscurity of his poems • an old actor who slipped into obscurity*

observant [adjective] good at noticing things

observation [noun: **observations**]
1 observation is noticing or watching: *He has been kept in hospital for observation.*
2 an observation is a remark or comment: *She made a couple of observations about the weather.*

observatory [noun: **observatories**] a place with large telescopes for studying the stars or weather

observe [verb: **observes, observing, observed**]
1 to observe something is to notice it: *I observed her smiling face.*
2 to observe something is to watch it carefully: *The police continued to observe his actions with interest.*
3 to observe something is to obey or keep it: *observe the rules • observe a tradition*
4 to observe is to remark: *'It's a lovely day,' he observed.*

◆ **observer** [noun: **observers**] someone who observes

obsess [verb: **obsesses, obsessing, obsessed**] if something obsesses you, it fills your mind completely

◆ **obsessed** [adjective] always thinking about something: *obsessed by football • obsessed with his work*

◆ **obsession** [noun: **obsessions**]
1 an obsession is a feeling or idea that you cannot stop thinking about: *his obsession with motorbikes*
2 obsession is being obsessed: *David's tidiness borders on obsession.*

obsolete [adjective] out of date or no longer in use: *The steam locomotive has become obsolete.*

obstacle [noun: **obstacles**] something that stands in your way and stops you from doing something

obstinacy [noun] being obstinate

obstinate [adjective] refusing to give in to someone or something: *I've asked her to change her mind, but she's very obstinate.*

◆ **obstinately** [adverb] in an obstinate way: *Anil obstinately refused to speak to me.*

obstruct [verb: **obstructs, obstructing, obstructed**]
1 to obstruct something is to block it: *The road was obstructed by a fallen tree.*
2 to obstruct someone or something is to stop them from getting past or to hold them back: *The crashed lorry obstructed the traffic.*

◆ **obstruction** [noun: **obstructions**] blocking or preventing something: *an obstruction in the pipe • the obstruction of justice*

Oo

obtain [verb: **obtains, obtaining, obtained**] to get something: *He obtained a large sum of money by selling houses.*

obvious [adjective] easily seen or understood: *It was obvious that she was ill.* • *an obvious reason*

♦ **obviously** [adverb] clearly: *Obviously, I'll need some help.*

occasion [noun: **occasions**]
1 a particular time when something happens: *I've met him on several occasions.*
2 a special event: *The Queen's birthday was a great occasion.*

♦ **occasional** [adjective] happening now and then: *occasional outings to the seaside*

♦ **occasionally** [adverb] now and then: *I occasionally go to the theatre.*

occult [noun] **the occult** refers to secret practices such as magic and witchcraft

occupant [noun: **occupants**] someone who lives or works in a place: *the occupants of the flat*

occupation [noun: **occupations**]
1 a person's occupation is their job
2 an occupation is something that you do in your free time: *Reading is his favourite occupation.*
3 occupation is the occupying of territory: *the Roman occupation of Britain*

occupier [noun: **occupiers**] the person who lives in a particular house or flat

occupy [verb: **occupies, occupying, occupied**]
1 to occupy a space is to fill it: *A table occupied the centre of the room.*
2 to occupy a house or building is to live or work there: *The family used to occupy a small flat.*
3 to occupy yourself or your time is to keep busy: *He occupied himself with the garden.*
4 to occupy territory is to capture it: *Soldiers were occupying the town.*

occur [verb: **occurs, occurring, occurred**]
1 to happen: *The accident must have occurred last night.*
2 to exist or be found: *Dragons only occur in fairy tales.*
3 if something occurs to you, it comes into your mind: *It never occurred to me that he was unhappy.*

♦ **occurrence** [noun: **occurrences**] something that happens

ocean [noun: **oceans**]
1 the ocean is the salt water that covers most of the Earth's surface
2 an ocean is one of the five large areas of sea in the world, for example the Atlantic Ocean

o'clock [adverb] o'clock is used after a number to say what time of day it is: *five o'clock in the afternoon*

octave [noun: **octaves**] a range of eight musical notes, for example from one C to the next C above or below it

October [noun] the tenth month of the year, after September and before November

octopus [noun: **octopuses**] a sea creature with eight long arms

OD [abbreviation] short for **overdose**

odd [adjective: **odder, oddest**]
1 unusual or strange: *He's wearing very odd clothes.*
2 an odd number is one that cannot be divided exactly by 2: *5 and 7 are odd numbers.*
3 not one of a matching pair or group: *an odd shoe*
4 left over: *Have you got any odd bits of wood I could use?*
5 not part of a regular routine: *doing odd jobs around the house*

♦ **oddity** [noun: **oddities**] a strange or unusual person or thing: *He's always been a bit of an oddity.*

♦ **oddly** [adverb] strangely: *You're behaving very oddly.*

oddments [plural noun] scraps or pieces left over from something else: *She made the jacket from oddments of material.*

oddness [noun] being odd: *the oddness of the situation*

odds [plural noun]
1 the chances of something happening: *The odds are that he will win.*
2 difference: *It makes no odds.*
3 **odds and ends** are small objects of different kinds

odour [noun: **odours**] a smell, especially an unpleasant one: *the odour of cigarette smoke*

Oo

of [preposition]
1 belonging to: *a friend of mine* • *Where is the lid of this box?*
2 away from: *within two miles of his home*
3 from among: *one of my friends*
4 made from or out of: *a house of bricks*
5 used to show an amount or measurement of something: *a gallon of petrol*
6 about: *stories of his adventures in India*
7 containing: *a box of chocolates*
8 used to show the cause of something: *She died of hunger.*
9 used to show a removal or taking away: *robbed of her jewels*

off [adverb]
1 away from a place or position: *He marched off down the road.* • *Take your shoes off.*
2 not working or in use: *Switch off the light.*
3 completely: *Finish off your work.*
[adjective]
1 cancelled: *The holiday is off.*
2 gone sour or rotten: *This milk is off.*
3 not being used: *The radio was off.*
4 if you are **badly off**, you are poor
5 if you are **well off**, you are rich
[preposition]
1 away from or down from: *a mile off the coast* • *It fell off the table.*
2 out of a vehicle: *We got off the bus.*
3 taken away from: *There is £10 off the usual price.*
4 not wanting something: *Jane is not well and is off her food.*

offence [noun: **offences**]
1 a crime: *The police charged him with several offences.*
2 a feeling of hurt, anger or annoyance: *His rudeness caused offence.*

offend [verb: **offends, offending, offended**]
1 to offend someone is to make them feel upset or angry: *She will be offended if you don't go to her party.*
2 to offend is to do wrong or break a law: *young people who offend again and again*
♦ **offender** [noun: **offenders**] a person who has committed a crime
♦ **offensive** [adjective]
1 insulting: *even more offensive remarks*
2 disgusting: *an offensive smell*
3 used for attacking: *offensive weapons*
[noun: **offensives**] an attack: *a military offensive*

offer [verb: **offers, offering, offered**]
1 to offer someone something is to ask if they would like it: *She offered me more tea.*
2 to offer to do something is to say that you will do it: *No one offered to help me carry the bags.*
3 to offer an amount of money is to say how much you are willing to pay for something: *I'll offer you £50 for the picture.*
[noun: **offers**]
1 an act of offering: *an offer of help*
2 an amount of money offered: *They made an offer of £100,000 for the house.*

offhand [adjective] if you are offhand with someone, you do not treat them with courtesy and respect: *You were a bit offhand with her at the meeting.*
[adverb] without having or taking time to think carefully: *Can you tell me offhand how much it might cost?*

office [noun: **offices**]
1 a building or set of rooms in which the business of a company is done: *Our head office is in London.*
2 the room in which a particular person works: *the bank manager's office*
3 a room or building used for a particular purpose: *the lost property office*
4 an important job or position: *the office of President*

officer [noun: **officers**]
1 a person in the army, navy or air force who is in charge of ordinary soldiers
2 a policeman or policewoman

official [adjective]
1 done or given out by people in power: *an official announcement*
2 making up part of the tasks of a job or office: *official engagements*
[noun: **officials**] a person who holds a job with authority: *government officials*
♦ **officially** [adverb]
1 as an official: *He attended the ceremony officially.*
2 formally: *The new library is now officially open.*

Oo

385

off-peak [adjective] when there is lowest demand for something: *The train fare is less if you travel during off-peak periods.*

off-putting [adjective] making you think badly of something: *His description of the hotel was a bit off-putting.*

offset [verb: **offsets, offsetting, offset**] one thing offsets another when it balances it out or makes up for it: *The price rises will be offset by tax cuts.*

offshore [adjective]
1 in or on the sea, not far from the coast: *offshore oilrigs*
2 blowing away from the coast, out to sea: *offshore breezes*

offside [adjective] in a position not allowed by the rules of a game such as football: *The goal was disallowed because Smith was offside.*

offspring [noun: **offspring**] a child or baby animal: *How many offspring does a cat usually have at one time?*

often [adverb] many times: *I often go to the cinema.*

ogre [noun: **ogres**]
1 a frightening cruel giant in fairy tales
2 a frightening person: *Her boss is a bit of an ogre.*

oh [interjection] a cry of surprise, admiration, pain or annoyance: *Oh, what a lovely present!* • *Oh no, I've forgotten my keys.*

oil [noun: **oils**]
1 a greasy liquid that will not mix with water: *olive oil* • *vegetable oil*
2 a substance, also called **crude oil** or **petroleum**, made from the remains of dead animals and plants. It can be taken out of the ground and used as fuel
[verb: **oils, oiling, oiled**] to put oil on or into something: *The machine will work better if it's oiled.*

oilfield [noun: **oilfields**] a place where oil is found in the ground or under the sea: *the oilfields of the North Sea*

oil paint [noun: **oil paints**] paint made with oil

✦ oil painting [noun: **oil paintings**] a picture painted with oil paints

oil rig [noun: **oil rigs**] a structure set up for drilling an oil well

oil well [noun: **oil wells**] a hole that is drilled into the ground or seabed in order to get oil

oily [adjective: **oilier, oiliest**] like, or covered with, oil: *an oily liquid* • *an oily rag*

oink [noun: **oinks**] the sound made by a pig [verb: **oinks, oinking, oinked**] to make the sound of a pig: *pigs oinking noisily in the farmyard*

ointment [noun: **ointments**] a greasy substance that is rubbed on the skin to soothe or heal it

OK or **okay** [interjection, adjective and adverb] an informal way of saying 'all right': *OK! I'll do it!* • *an okay song* • *Do I look OK?*

old [adjective: **older, oldest**]
1 having lived or existed a long time: *an old man* • *an old building*
2 having a particular age: *nine years old*
3 belonging to times long ago: *the good old days*
4 worn-out or no longer used: *She threw away her old clothes.*
5 former or previous: *I preferred my old job to this one.*

old age [noun] the later part of a person's life: *He wrote poems in his old age.*

old age pensioner [noun: **old age pensioners**] an old person, especially one who has retired from work and gets money to live on from the government

old-fashioned [adjective] of a kind that was usual some time ago: *old-fashioned clothes*

olive [noun: **olives**]
1 a small oval fruit with a hard stone, used to make cooking oil
2 the tree on which it grows
3 a yellow-green colour

Olympic games or **Olympics** [plural noun] a sports competition held once every four years for sportsmen and sportswomen from all over the world

ombudsman [noun: **ombudsmen**] a person who investigates complaints that people make against the government or other official bodies

omelette or **omelet** [noun: **omelettes** or **omelets**] a dish made of eggs beaten and fried, sometimes with a filling: *a cheese omelette*

Oo

omen [noun: **omens**] a sign of future events: *The storm was a bad omen.*

◆ **ominous** [adjective] giving a warning about something bad that is going to happen: *ominous clouds*

omission [noun: **omissions**]

1 omission is the leaving out of something: *the omission of his name from the list*

2 an omission is something that has been left out: *There are omissions in his report.*

omit [verb: **omits, omitting, omitted**]

1 to omit something is to leave it out: *You can omit the last chapter of the book.*

2 to omit to do something is to fail to do it: *I omitted to tell him about the meeting.*

omni- [prefix] if **omni-** appears at the start of a word it means 'all', 'every' or 'everywhere'. For example, *omniscient* means knowing everything, and *omnipresent* means present everywhere

omnibus [noun: **omnibuses**] something such as a TV programme or book that is made up of a number of individual episodes or stories

omnivore [noun: **omnivores**] an animal that eats all kinds of food, including plants and meat. Look up and compare **carnivore** and **herbivore**

◆ **omnivorous** [adjective] eating all kinds of food: *Human beings are omnivorous.*

on [preposition]

1 touching, fixed to or covering the upper or outer side of something: *on the table*

2 supported by: *standing on one leg*

3 during a certain day: *on Friday*

4 about: *a book on Scottish history*

5 with: *Do you have a pen on you?*

6 near or beside: *a shop on the main road*

7 taking part in: *He is on the committee.*

[adverb]

1 so as to be touching, fixed to or covering the upper or outer side of something: *Put your coat on.*

2 forwards or onwards: *They moved on.*

3 working or being used: *Switch the light on.*

[adjective]

1 working or being used: *The television is on.*

2 planned: *Do you have anything on this evening?*

3 not cancelled: *Is the party still on?*

once [adverb]

1 a single time: *He only did it once.*

2 at a time in the past: *People once lived in caves.*

[conjunction] when or as soon as: *Once you've finished, you can go.*

oncoming [adjective] moving towards you: *oncoming traffic*

one [noun: **ones**] the number 1: *One and one is two.*

[pronoun]

1 a single person or thing: *One of my friends called round.*

2 a rather formal word for **anyone** or **you**: *One can see the sea from here.*

3 you use **one another** after a verb or preposition when an action takes place between two or more people: *They embraced one another.* • *great respect for one another*

[adjective] a single: *We had only one reply.*

oneself [pronoun]

1 you use **oneself** after a verb or preposition when *one* is the subject of the action and is also affected by it: *One should wash oneself every day.*

2 you also use the word **oneself** for emphasis to show more clearly who you mean: *One always has to do these things oneself.*

one-sided [adjective]

1 with one person or side having a big advantage over the other: *a one-sided contest*

2 showing only one view of a subject: *a one-sided discussion*

one-way [adjective] a one-way street is one in which traffic can move in one direction only

ongoing [adjective] continuing: *ongoing talks*

onion [noun: **onions**] a round vegetable that has a strong taste and smell

online [adjective and adverb] using or involving the Internet: *online shopping* • *Our telephone banking service went online in April.*

onlooker [noun: **onlookers**] someone who watches something happening: *A crowd of onlookers had gathered.*

only [adverb]

1 not more than: *There are only two weeks left.*

Oo

2 alone: *Only you can do it.*

3 not longer ago than: *I saw her only yesterday.*

[adjective] without any others of the same type: *the only book of its kind*

[conjunction] but or however: *I'd like to come, only I have to work.*

onset [noun: **onsets**] the onset of something is the beginning of it: *the onset of a cold*

onto [preposition]

1 so as to be on the top or surface of something: *I climbed onto the roof.*

2 if you are onto someone, you are aware or suspicious of their bad behaviour: *I tried to hide the tickets, but I think Harry may be onto us.*

onward [adjective] going forward in place or time: *their onward journey* • *the onward march of science*

◆ **onwards** or **onward** [adverb] forward: *He led them onward through the night.* • *from nine o'clock onwards*

ooze [verb: **oozes, oozing, oozed**] to flow slowly: *The glue oozed out of the tube.*

opal [noun: **opals**] a precious stone that is milky in colour, with traces or streaks of other colours

opaque [adjective] not able to be seen through: *an opaque liquid*

open [adjective]

1 not shut: *The door is wide open.*

2 allowing the inside to be seen: *an open book*

3 not enclosed: *open countryside*

4 honest: *He was very open with me about his work.*

5 not yet decided: *The matter is still open for discussion.*

6 if you are **open to** something, you are likely or willing to receive it: *open to attack* • *open to suggestions*

[verb: **opens, opening, opened**]

1 to open something is to make it open: *He opened the door.*

2 to open is to become open: *The door opened.*

3 to open something is to begin it: *He opened the meeting with a speech of welcome.*

◆ **opener** [noun: **openers**] something that opens something else: *a tin opener*

◆ **opening** [noun: **openings**]

1 a hole or space: *an opening in the fence*

2 a beginning: *the opening of the film*

3 a chance, especially for a job: *There is an opening in the sales team.*

◆ **openly** [adverb] without trying to hide anything: *She talked openly about her illness.*

open-minded [adjective] ready to take up new ideas

opera [noun: **operas**] a musical play in which the words are sung: *an opera by Verdi*

operate [verb: **operates, operating, operated**]

1 to operate is to work: *The printer doesn't seem to be operating properly.*

2 to operate a machine is to make it work: *How do you operate this computer?*

3 to operate on someone is to perform a surgical operation on them: *The surgeon operated on the man's heart.*

◆ **operation** [noun: **operations**]

1 a carefully planned action: *a rescue operation*

2 the process of working: *Our plan is now in operation.*

3 something done to a person's body, usually by a surgeon, in order to remove part of it or to treat a disease: *an operation for appendicitis*

◆ **operator** [noun: **operators**]

1 someone who works a machine: *a lift operator*

2 someone who connects telephone calls: *Ask the operator to put you through to that number.*

opinion [noun: **opinions**] what you think or believe: *My opinions about education have changed.*

opinion poll [noun: **opinion polls**] a survey of what people think, made by questioning a certain number of them

opponent [noun: **opponents**] someone who is against you, for example in a war or competition: *He beat his opponent by four points.*

opportunity [noun: **opportunities**] a chance to do something: *I'd like to have an opportunity to go to Paris.*

oppose [verb: **opposing, opposes, opposed**] to oppose someone or something is to be against them: *We opposed the*

Oo

government on this question. • *Who is opposing him in the election?*
→ **opponent, opposition**

opposite [adjective]
1 on the other side of something: *on the opposite side of town*
2 completely different: *They walked off in opposite directions.*
[preposition and adverb] facing: *the house opposite mine* • *Who lives in the house opposite?*
[noun: **opposites**] one thing is the opposite of another if it is completely different from it: *Hot is the opposite of cold.*

opposition [noun]
1 opposition is resisting or fighting against someone or something: *There is a lot of opposition to his new ideas.*
2 opposition can also be the people you are fighting or competing against: *a strong opposition*
3 the Opposition is the main political party that opposes the party in government

oppress [verb: **oppresses, oppressing, oppressed**]
1 to oppress someone is to govern or treat them cruelly: *The king oppressed his people.*
2 if something oppresses you, it worries or distresses you: *The heat oppressed her.*
 ♦ **oppression** [noun]
1 cruel treatment
2 worry or distress
 ♦ **oppressive** [adjective]
1 cruel and harsh: *oppressive government*
2 causing worry: *an oppressive situation*
3 unpleasantly hot: *the oppressive heat of the desert*

opt [verb: **opts, opting, opted**]
1 to **opt for** something is to choose it: *I opted for the strawberry gateau.*
2 to **opt to** do something is to decide to do it: *She opted to stay on at college.*
3 to **opt out** is to decide not to do something: *I opted out of the trip.*

optical [adjective] to do with the eyes or sight: *an optical aid*

optical illusion [noun: **optical illusions**] something which deceives the eye, often making you think you can see something that is

not actually there: *The water he thought he could see was actually an optical illusion caused by the light.*

optician [noun: **opticians**] someone who tests your eyesight and makes and sells spectacles

LANGUAGE FOR LIFE
opticians
There are two different types of optician.
• An **ophthalmic optician** or **optometrist** tests your eyes and tells you which glasses or lenses you need.
• A **dispensing optician** fits and sells glasses, but is not qualified to test your eyes and tell you which glasses or lenses you need.

optimism [noun] the habit of expecting things to turn out well: *full of optimism.* Look up and compare **pessimism**
 ♦ **optimist** [noun: **optimists**] someone who usually expects or hopes that something good will happen
 ♦ **optimistic** [adjective] hoping or believing that something good will happen: *an optimistic person*
 ♦ **optimistically** [adverb] in an optimistic way: *'She might still come,' he said optimistically.*

option [noun: **options**]
1 choice: *You have no option.*
2 a thing that you choose or that may be chosen: *There are several options open to me.*
 ♦ **optional** [adjective] a matter of choice, not compulsory: *Music was optional at my school.*

or [conjunction]
1 used to show choices or alternatives: *Would you prefer tea or coffee?*
2 because if not: *I'd better go or I'll miss the last bus.*

-or [suffix] look at the entry for **-er²**

oral [adjective]
1 spoken, not written: *an oral examination*
2 to do with the mouth: *oral hygiene*
 ♦ **orally** [adverb]
1 by speaking: *I prefer to communicate orally rather than by e-mail.*
2 by mouth: *medicine to be taken orally*

orange [noun: **oranges**]
1 an orange is a juicy citrus fruit with a thick skin

Oo

of a colour between red and yellow

2 orange is the colour of this fruit

orang-utan [noun: **orang-utans**] a large man-like ape

orbit [noun: **orbits**] the path along which something moves around a planet or other body in space: *The spaceship is in orbit round the moon.*

[verb: **orbits, orbiting, orbited**] to go round something in space: *The spacecraft is orbiting Earth.*

orchard [noun: **orchards**] an area where fruit trees are grown: *a cherry orchard*

orchestra [noun: **orchestras**] a large group of musicians playing together

orchid [noun: **orchids**] a plant with brightly-coloured flowers

ordain [verb: **ordains, ordaining, ordained**] to ordain someone is to make them a priest or minister: *Some Christian churches have decided to ordain women.*

ordeal [noun: **ordeals**] a difficult or painful experience: *Going to the dentist can be quite an ordeal.*

order [noun: **orders**]

1 an instruction to do something: *The soldier was given the order to shoot.*

2 an instruction to supply something: *The waiter came to take our order.*

3 the way things are arranged: *alphabetical order*

4 peaceful conditions and behaviour: *law and order*

5 an organized state when things are in their proper places: *It was time to bring some order into my life.*

[verb: **orders, ordering, ordered**]

1 to order someone to do something is to tell them to do it: *The doctor ordered her to rest for a few days.*

2 to order something is to ask for it to be supplied: *I ordered some magazines from the newsagent.*

✦ orderly [adjective]

1 well-behaved, quiet: *Please form an orderly queue.*

2 in proper order: *an orderly arrangement of objects*

ordinary [adjective] normal and not very

special: *an ordinary Monday morning*

ore [noun: **ores**] solid material, for example rock, from which a metal is obtained: *iron ore*

organ [noun: **organs**]

1 a part of your body that has a special purpose: *Eyes are the organs that we use to see.*

2 a musical instrument with keys like a piano

organic [adjective]

1 to do with the organs of the body

2 found in or made by living things: *organic fertilizers*

3 organic food is produced without using chemicals: *I only buy organic vegetables.*

✦ organically [adverb] in an organic way: *vegetables that are organically grown*

organism [noun: **organisms**] any living thing

organist [noun: **organists**] someone who plays the organ

organization or **organisation** [noun: **organizations**]

1 an organization is a group of people who work together for a purpose: *a business organization*

2 organization is the organizing of something: *The success of the project depends on good organization.*

organize or **organise** [verb: **organizes, organizing, organized**]

1 to arrange and prepare something: *We've organized a surprise party for his birthday.*

2 to put something in order: *He organized all the papers on his desk.*

✦ organizer or **organiser** [noun: **organizers** or **organisers**] someone who organizes something

orgasm [noun: **orgasms**] the climax of sexual excitement

orgy [noun: **orgies**] a wild party or celebration

oriental [adjective] in or from the east, especially China and Japan: *oriental art*

orienteering [noun] a sport in which you run across country, finding your way with a map and a compass

origami [noun] the Japanese art of making objects by folding pieces of paper

origin [noun: **origins**] the place from which

Oo

someone or something comes: *the origins of the English language*

◆ **original** [adjective]
1 existing from the start, first: *The original story had been changed over the centuries.*
2 not copied, new: *an original design* • *original ideas*
3 done by the artist himself or herself: *The original painting is in the museum, but there are hundreds of copies.*
[noun: **originals**] the earliest version of a piece of art: *The original of this painting is in Florence.*

◆ **originally** [adverb]
1 in or from the beginning: *His family comes from Scotland originally.*
2 in a new and different way: *She dresses very originally.*

originate [verb: **originates, originating, originated**] to originate is to start or come into being: *This style of painting originated in China.*

ornament [noun: **ornaments**] an object used to decorate something: *fine ornaments on the mantelpiece*
[verb: **ornaments, ornamenting, ornamented**] to decorate something: *The ceiling was richly ornamented.*

◆ **ornamental** [adjective] for decoration: *an ornamental pond*

◆ **ornamentation** [noun] things added to something to decorate it

ornate [adjective] decorated with a complicated design: *an ornate doorway*

ornithologist [noun: **ornithologists**] someone who studies or is an expert on birds

◆ **ornithology** [noun] the study of birds

orphan [noun: **orphans**] a child whose parents are both dead

◆ **orphanage** [noun: **orphanages**] a home for orphans

orthodox [adjective] having beliefs that have traditionally been thought correct and generally accepted: *orthodox Jews* • *orthodox medical treatment*

orthopaedic [adjective] orthopaedic surgery involves correcting damaged bones and joints

osprey [noun: **ospreys**] a type of eagle that feeds on fish

osteopath [noun: **osteopaths**] someone whose job is to treat damaged bones and joints by manipulating them with the hands and massaging muscles

ostrich [noun: **ostriches**] a large bird which cannot fly but runs very fast

other [adjective]
1 the second of two: *Where is my other glove?*
2 the rest: *Jack is here and the other children are at school.*
3 different or extra: *There must be some other reason.*
4 recently past: *just the other day*
[pronoun] the second of two: *Here's one sock, but where is the other?*
[adverb] **other than** means 'except': *There was no one there other than an old woman.*

◆ **others** [pronoun] the others are the additional or remaining ones: *Joe is here, but where are the others?*

◆ **otherwise** [adverb]
1 or else: *You can't leave now, otherwise you'll always wonder what it would've been like.*
2 in any other way: *One person raised his hand. Otherwise, no one stirred.*
3 in a different way: *He must have asked somebody because he couldn't possibly know otherwise.*

otter [noun: **otters**] a small furry river animal that feeds on fish

ouch [interjection] a word that people shout when they feel a sudden pain

ought [verb]
1 ought is used to show what you should do: *You ought to help them.*
2 ought is also used to show what is likely to happen: *The weather ought to be fine.*

ounce [noun: **ounces**] a unit of measurement of weight, equal to $\frac{1}{16}$ of a pound or 28.35 grams: *You need five ounces of flour to make this cake.*

our [adjective] belonging to us: *That is our car.*

ours [pronoun] a word you use to talk about something belonging to us: *That car is ours.* • *These books are ours.*

ourselves [pronoun]
1 you use **ourselves** after a verb or

Oo

preposition when *we* is the subject of the action and is also affected by it: *We saw ourselves in the mirror.* • *We should keep some of the money for ourselves.*

2 ourselves is also used to show that you have done something without any help from other people: *We painted the room ourselves.*

3 you can use **ourselves** to emphasize who you mean: *We ourselves played no part in this.*

-ous [suffix] if **-ous** comes at the end of a word, it is an adjective that means 'like' or 'having'. For example, if something is *spacious* it has plenty of space

out [adverb]

1 into or towards the open air: *go out for a walk*

2 from inside something: *She opened her bag and took out an umbrella.*

3 away from a place, for example, your home or your office: *I'm afraid he's out at the moment.*

4 loudly: *shout out the answer*

5 completely: *tired out*

6 no longer hidden or secret: *The secret is out.*

7 dismissed from a game: *The batsman is out.*

8 if something is **out of date**, it is old or old-fashioned: *This telephone directory is out of date.*

out-and-out [adjective] complete: *an out-and-out liar*

outback [noun] the remote parts in the middle of Australia where few people live

outbreak [noun: **outbreaks**] a sudden beginning, usually of something unpleasant: *the outbreak of war*

outburst [noun: **outbursts**] an explosion, especially of angry feelings: *a sudden outburst of rage*

outcast [noun: **outcasts**] someone who has been driven away by their friends, family or society

outcome [noun: **outcomes**] a result: *What was the outcome of your discussion?*

outcry [noun: **outcries**] a strong reaction or protest by a large number of people: *The decision caused a public outcry.*

outdo [verb: **outdoes, outdoing, outdid, outdone**] to outdo someone is to do better than them: *The girls tried to outdo each other in their kindness.*

outdoor [adjective] outside or for use outside: *an outdoor swimming pool* • *outdoor shoes*

✦ outdoors [adverb] outside: *She sat outdoors in the sun.* • *Don't go outdoors if it's raining.*

outer [adjective] nearer the outside: *outer space* • *outer layers*

outfit [noun: **outfits**] a set of clothes worn together: *a wedding outfit*

outgrow [verb: **outgrows, outgrowing, outgrew, outgrown**] to outgrow something is to grow too big or too old for it: *She has outgrown all her clothes.* • *Babies quickly outgrow their toys.*

outhouse [noun: **outhouses**] a small building such as a shed which is attached to or close to a larger building

outing [noun: **outings**] a short trip made for pleasure: *an outing to the seaside*

outlaw [noun: **outlaws**] someone who is given no protection by the law in their country because they are a criminal

[verb: **outlaws, outlawing, outlawed**] to outlaw something is to make it illegal: *The sale of alcohol was outlawed.*

outlay [noun] money that is spent, especially in order to start a business or a project: *The scheme required an initial outlay of £50,000.*

outlet [noun: **outlets**]

1 a way of letting something out: *an outlet from the main tank* • *an outlet for his energy*

2 a place to sell goods: *We must find new outlets for this product.*

outline [noun: **outlines**]

1 the line forming the outside of something: *First he drew the outline of the face, then added the features.*

2 a short description of something: *Just give me an outline of the facts.*

[verb: **outlines, outlining, outlined**]

1 to outline something is to draw a line showing the outside of it

2 to outline a plan or story is to give a short description of it

outlook [noun: **outlooks**]

1 a view: *Their house has a wonderful outlook.*

2 the way that a person thinks about things: *He has a strange outlook on life.*

Oo

3 what seems likely to happen: *the weather outlook*

outlying [adjective] far from a town or city: *a small outlying village*

outnumber [verb: **outnumbers, outnumbering, outnumbered**] to outnumber something is to be more in number than it: *The boys outnumber the girls by three to two.*

out-patient [noun: **out-patients**] someone who comes to a hospital for treatment but does not stay overnight

outpost [noun: **outposts**]
1 a small military camp far away from the main army, built especially to protect it from a surprise attack
2 a settlement far from where most people live

output [noun: **outputs**]
1 a quantity of goods produced or an amount of work done: *The output of this factory increased last year.*
2 the information produced by a computer [verb: **outputs, outputting, output**] in computing, to output data is to cause it to be produced

outrage [noun: **outrages**] a shocking or cruel action: *The decision to close the hospital is an outrage.*
[verb: **outrages, outraging, outraged**] to outrage someone is to hurt, shock or insult them: *Fay was outraged by his remarks.*
♦ **outrageous** [adjective] shocking, terrible: *outrageous behaviour*

outright [adverb] completely: *We won outright.*
[adjective] complete: *an outright fool*

outset [noun] the beginning: *The project was in difficulty from the outset.*

outside [noun: **outsides**] the outer surface of something: *The outside of the house was painted white.*
[adjective]
1 of, on or near the outer part of anything: *the outside edge*
2 slight: *an outside chance of winning*
[adverb] on or to the outside, outdoors: *Let's eat outside.*
[preposition] on the outer side of, not inside: *He was standing outside the gate.*

♦ **outsider** [noun: **outsiders**]
1 someone not included in a particular group: *I have lived here for ten years, but I still feel like an outsider.*
2 a horse or person not expected to win a race or contest

outsize [adjective] bigger than the largest standard size: *outsize clothing*

outskirts [plural noun] the outer parts, especially of a town or city: *He lives on the outskirts of Edinburgh.*

outspoken [adjective] saying exactly what you mean, even if it upsets people: *She makes enemies because she is so outspoken.*

outstanding [adjective]
1 excellent: *an outstanding student*
2 not yet paid or done: *You must pay all outstanding bills.*

outward [adjective]
1 on or towards the outside: *She shows no outward sign of unhappiness.*
2 away from a place: *the outward voyage*
♦ **outwardly** [adverb] on the outside so you can see: *Outwardly they were cheerful.*
♦ **outwards** [adverb] towards the outside: *a window that opens outwards*

outweigh [verb: **outweighs, outweighing, outweighed**] to outweigh something is to be more important than it: *The advantages outweigh the disadvantages.*

outwit [verb: **outwits, outwitting, outwitted**] to outwit someone is to defeat them by being cleverer than they are: *She outwitted the police and managed to escape.*

oval [adjective] shaped like an egg but flat: *an oval table*
[noun: **ovals**] an oval shape: *He drew an oval.*

ovary [noun: **ovaries**]
1 the part of a woman's body where eggs are formed
2 the part of a flower where seeds are formed

oven [noun: **ovens**] an enclosed space, usually part of a cooker, for cooking and heating food

over [preposition]
1 higher than, above: *Hang that picture over the fireplace.*
2 more than: *He's over 90 years old.*
3 across: *We ran over the bridge.*

Oo

4 about: *They quarrelled over the children.*
5 by means of: *We often talk over the telephone.*
[adverb]
1 across: *He walked over to speak to them.*
2 downwards: *The baby's fallen over.*
3 above in number: *children aged seven and over*
4 left or remaining: *There were two cakes left over.*
5 through: *Read the passage over.*
[adjective] finished: *The match is already over.*
[noun: **overs**] in cricket, an over is a series of six balls bowled by the same bowler from the same end of the pitch
→ **overly**

over- [prefix] **over-** at the start of a word means 'too' or 'too much'. For example, to *overeat* is to eat too much, and *overcareful* means too careful

overall [noun: **overalls**] a piece of clothing worn over ordinary clothes to protect them: *She wears an overall when cleaning the house.*
[adjective] including everything: *the overall cost*

overalls [plural noun] trousers or a suit made of hard-wearing material worn by workmen to protect their clothes

overarm [adjective and adverb] with the hand and arm raised above the level of the shoulder and coming down in front of the body: *an overarm throw • Try throwing it overarm.*

overbearing [adjective] bossy and too confident: *I can't stand his overbearing manner.*

overboard [adverb] over the side of a ship or boat and into the water: *He jumped overboard.*

overcast [adjective] dark with clouds: *The sky was overcast but it didn't rain.*

overcoat [noun: **overcoats**] a heavy coat worn over all other clothes

overcome [verb: **overcomes, overcoming, overcame, overcome**]
1 to overcome someone or something is to defeat them eventually: *She overcame her fear of the dark.*

2 to be overcome by something is to become helpless because of it: *overcome with grief • overcome by fumes*

overdo [verb: **overdoes, overdoing, overdid, overdone**]
1 to overdo something is to do it too much: *It's good to work hard, but don't overdo it.*
2 to overdo food is to cook it for too long: *The meat was rather overdone.*

overdose [noun: **overdoses**] more of a drug or medicine than is safe: *an overdose of sleeping pills*
[verb: **overdoses, overdosing, overdosed**] to overdose is to take too much of a drug or medicine

overdraft [noun: **overdrafts**] if you have an overdraft with a bank, the bank allows you to take out more money than you have put in: *I had to pay interest on my overdraft.*
♦ **overdrawn** [adjective] having taken more money out of the bank than you have put in

overdrive [noun] an extra high gear on a motor vehicle: *She put the car into overdrive.*

overdue [adjective]
1 not yet paid, done or delivered although the time for doing this has passed: *overdue library books*
2 late: *The train is overdue.*

overflow [verb: **overflows, overflowing, overflowed**]
1 liquid overflows when it reaches the top of a container and starts to spill over the sides: *The river overflowed its banks.*
2 a container overflows when it is so full that its contents spill out: *boxes overflowing with toys*

overgrown [adjective] full of plants that have grown too large and thick: *The back garden is completely overgrown with weeds.*

overhang [verb: **overhangs, overhanging, overhung**] to overhang something is to stick out or hang over it: *The stream was overhung by the branches of a tree.*

overhaul [verb: **overhauls, overhauling, overhauled**] to overhaul something is to examine it carefully and repair any faults: *He had his car overhauled at the garage.*
[noun: **overhauls**] a thorough examination

and repair: *The mechanic gave the car a complete overhaul.*

overhead [adverb] above your head: *A plane was flying overhead.*
[adjective] placed high above the ground: *overhead cables*

overheads [plural noun] the money that a business has to spend regularly on things like rent and electricity

overhear [verb: **overhears, overhearing, overheard**] to hear something when you were not meant to: *I overheard them talking about me.*

overjoyed [adjective] very happy: *We were overjoyed to hear that he was safe.*

overland [adverb and adjective] across land, rather than by sea or air: *travelling overland across America • an overland safari*

overlap [verb: **overlaps, overlapping, overlapped**]
1 to overlap something is to cover a part of it: *Each roof-tile overlaps the one below it.*
2 if things overlap, they lie partly over each other: *The curtains should be wide enough to overlap.*
[noun: **overlaps**] the amount by which something overlaps: *an overlap of half an hour between the two programmes*

overlook [verb: **overlooks, overlooking, overlooked**]
1 to overlook something such as a place is to look down on it: *The house overlooks the river.*
2 to overlook something is to fail to see or notice it: *You have overlooked one important detail.*
3 to overlook something such as a fault is to take no notice of it: *I shall overlook your lateness this time.*

overly [adverb] too much: *an overly possessive mother*

overnight [adjective and adverb]
1 for the night: *an overnight bag • We stayed in London overnight.*
2 sudden or suddenly: *an overnight success • He became a hero overnight.*

overpower [verb: **overpowers, overpowering, overpowered**] to overpower someone is to defeat them through being stronger: *He was overpowered by two policemen.*

♦ **overpowering** [adjective] very strong: *an overpowering smell • overpowering sadness*

overrated [adjective] something that is overrated is thought to be better than it really is: *His new film is overrated.*

overrun [verb: **overruns, overrunning, overran, overrun**]
1 to overrun a place is to spread quickly all over it: *The house is overrun with mice.*
2 if something overruns, it goes on for longer than it should: *The programme overran by half an hour.*

overseas [adjective and adverb] abroad: *an overseas job • They went overseas.*

oversee [verb: **oversees, overseeing, oversaw, overseen**] to oversee something is to watch over or supervise it: *His job is to oversee the factory workers.*

overshadow [verb: **overshadows, overshadowing, overshadowed**] to overshadow someone or something is to seem much more successful or important than them or it: *Clare was always overshadowed by her brilliant sister.*

oversight [noun: **oversights**] a mistake, especially one that you make because you have not noticed something: *It was a serious oversight on his part.*

overtake [verb: **overtakes, overtaking, overtook, overtaken**] to overtake a vehicle is to catch up with and pass it: *He overtook a police car.*

overthrow [verb: **overthrows, overthrowing, overthrew, overthrown**] to overthrow someone is to force them out of power: *The government has been overthrown.*

overtime [noun] time spent working outside your normal hours

overture [noun: **overtures**]
1 a piece of music played at the start of an opera or ballet
2 a friendly attempt to start a discussion or relationship: *overtures of peace*

overturn [verb: **overturns, overturning, overturned**]
1 to overturn an object such as a chair or table is to turn it upside down

Oo

2 to overturn a decision is to cancel it: *The ruling was overturned by the court of appeal.*

overweight [adjective] too heavy: *I'm about half a stone overweight.*

overwhelm [verb: **overwhelms, overwhelming, overwhelmed**]

1 to overwhelm someone is to defeat them completely: *Our soldiers were overwhelmed by the enemy.*

2 to overwhelm someone is to load them with too much of something: *overwhelmed with work*

3 to overwhelm someone is to have a strong and sudden effect on them: *overwhelmed with joy*

♦ **overwhelming** [adjective] very great or strong: *an overwhelming victory* • *overwhelming relief*

overwork [verb: **overworks, overworking, overworked**]

1 to overwork is to work too hard

2 to overwork someone is to make them work too hard

[noun] the act of working too hard: *Overwork made him ill.*

♦ **overworked** [adjective] made to work too hard: *The staff are overworked.*

owe [verb: **owes, owing, owed**]

1 to owe someone something is to be in debt to them: *I owe Val £10.*

2 to owe something to someone is to have them to thank for it: *He owes his success to his family.*

owl [noun: **owls**] a bird that hunts at night and feeds on small birds and animals

own [verb: **owns, owning, owned**]

1 you own something if it belongs to you: *I own a car.*

2 to **own up** is to admit that you did something: *No one owned up to breaking the window.*

[adjective] belonging to the person mentioned: *all his own work*

[pronoun]

1 own is used for something belonging to a person: *I lent him a pencil, because he forgot to bring his own.*

2 if you **get your own back**, you take revenge

3 if you do something **on your own**, you do it without help: *Did he do it all on his own?*

4 if you are **on your own**, you are alone: *Please don't leave me on my own.*

♦ **owner** [noun: **owners**] a person who owns something

ownership [noun] owning something: *The shop is under new ownership.*

own goal [noun: **own goals**] in sport, an own goal is a goal someone scores by mistake against their own side

ox [noun: **oxen**] a bull used for pulling loads

oxygen [noun] a gas that has no taste, colour or smell, and forms part of the air

oyster [noun: **oysters**] a type of shellfish that can be eaten

oz [abbreviation] short for **ounce** or **ounces**

ozone [noun] a form of oxygen with a strong smell

ozone layer [noun] the layer of ozone that is part of the Earth's atmosphere and that protects the planet from the radiation of the Sun

Oo

P

p [abbreviation] short for **page** or **pence**

PA [abbreviation: **PAs**] short for **personal assistant**

pace [verb: **paces, pacing, paced**] to walk backwards and forwards because you are worried or impatient: *She was pacing up and down, waiting for the phone to ring.*
[noun: **paces**]
1 a step, or a speed of walking or running: *Take four paces forward.* • *a slow pace*
2 a rate at which something happens or moves forward: *the pace of change*

pacemaker [noun: **pacemakers**] a small device, fitted by a surgeon, that keeps someone's heart beating at the correct rhythm

pacifist [noun: **pacifists**] someone who believes war is wrong and should be avoided

pacify [verb: **pacifies, pacifying, pacified**] to pacify someone is to calm them down

pack [noun: **packs**]
1 things that are tied together or put in a bag, so that you can carry them
2 a packet: *a pack of chewing gum*
3 a set of 52 playing cards: *Who's going to shuffle the pack?*
4 a group of certain animals, especially animals of the dog family: *a pack of hyenas*
[verb: **packs, packing, packed**]
1 to put your belongings into a bag or suitcase for a journey: *She packed hurriedly and caught the next train.*
2 if people pack a place, they fill it so that there is very little, or no, space left
3 if someone is **packed off** somewhere, they are sent there, often without having any choice about it

4 to **pack something in** is to stop doing it

package [noun: **packages**]
1 a parcel that has been wrapped up for sending by post
2 a number of things that are sold or used together: *a software package*
[verb: **packages, packaging, packaged**] to package something, or **package it up**, is to put it in a parcel, wrapping or bundle

package holiday [noun: **package holidays**] a holiday in which all the travel and accommodation is arranged for you by a travel agent

packaging [noun] the wrapping or container that something comes in

packet [noun: **packets**] a container made of paper or cardboard, or the container with its contents: *a packet of biscuits*

pact [noun: **pacts**] an agreement or treaty between two people, groups or countries: *They made a pact always to look out for each other.*

pad [noun: **pads**]
1 a cushion-like object made of a soft material
2 a soft cushion-like part on the paw of some animals, for example, dogs
3 a book of several sheets of paper fixed together at one edge and used for writing on
4 a platform for launching rockets
[verb: **pads, padding, padded**]
1 to pad something is to stuff or protect it with soft material
2 to **pad out** an essay or speech is to add extra and unnecessary material to it to make it longer
3 to pad is to walk softly making little or no sound

✦ **padding** [noun]
1 material used for stuffing chairs or cushions
2 extra and unnecessary material added to an essay or speech

paddle [verb: **paddles, paddling, paddled**]
1 you paddle when you walk about in shallow water
2 to paddle a boat or canoe is to move it through the water using a paddle
[noun: **paddles**] a short oar, often with a wide part at one or both ends, used for paddling a small boat or canoe

paddock [noun: **paddocks**] a grassy field with a fence around it where horses and other animals are kept

paddy field [noun: **paddy fields**] a field used to grow rice. Paddy fields are usually flooded with a few centimetres of water because rice needs wet and muddy conditions to grow

padlock [noun: **padlocks**] a lock with a U-shaped bar which hinges to one side and can be passed through a ring or chain and locked in position

paediatrician [noun: **paediatricians**] a doctor who deals with illnesses affecting children

paedophile [noun: **paedophiles**] a person who is sexually attracted to children

pagan [noun: **pagans**] someone who believes in a religion that is not one of the world's main religions
[adjective] to do with pagans or paganism: a pagan festival celebrating the coming of Spring

✦ **paganism** [noun] pagan beliefs and practices

page[1] [noun: **pages**] one side of a sheet of paper in a book, newspaper or magazine, or one of the sheets of paper that make up a book, newspaper or magazine: The information can be found on page 135.

page[2] [noun: **pages**] a small boy who helps a bride at her wedding
[verb: **pages, paging, paged**] to page someone is to call them by sending a message to their electronic pager

pageant [noun: **pageants**]

1 a type of outdoor entertainment or parade with people dressed up in colourful costumes and often acting out scenes from history
2 any splendid and colourful show or display

✦ **pageantry** [noun] splendid and colourful display that forms part of a grand ceremony or parade

pager [noun: **pagers**] an electronic device used to call someone, for example a doctor in a hospital, through a small radio receiver that they carry with them and that beeps to get their attention

pagoda [noun: **pagodas**] a Chinese temple, with several storeys or levels and overhanging roofs

pail [noun: **pails**] a bucket, or its contents: a milk pail • a pail of water

pain [noun: **pains**]
1 an unpleasant uncomfortable feeling in your body, because you have been hurt or are ill: He's broken his leg in three places and is in great pain. • He had pains in his chest.
2 a feeling of being very unhappy or upset: the pain of leaving loved ones behind

✦ **pained** [adjective] if someone has a pained expression, their face shows that they are upset or offended

painful [adjective]
1 sore, or causing pain or distress: Is your knee still painful? • Will the treatment be painful?
2 involving a lot of hard work or effort: Their progress up the steep mountain was slow and painful.

✦ **painfully** [adverb] in a painful or distressing way: The poor little dog was painfully thin.

painkiller [noun: **painkillers**] a drug or medicine that takes away pain

painless [adjective] causing no pain

painstaking [adjective] paying careful attention to every detail, or needing a lot of careful attention to detail: It's painstaking work building a model out of matchsticks.

✦ **painstakingly** [adverb] very carefully or thoroughly

paint [noun: **paints**] a coloured substance that you put on a surface to change its colour or to make a picture
[verb: **paints, painting, painted**]

1 to put paint on walls and other parts of a building

2 to make a picture using paint

✦ **painter** [noun: **painters**]

1 a person whose job is to put paint on walls and other parts of buildings

2 an artist who makes pictures using paint

✦ **painting** [noun: **paintings**]

1 painting is the activity of painting walls or pictures

2 a painting is a picture made using paints

pair [noun: **pairs**]

1 two things of the same kind used or kept together: *a pair of socks • a pair of china dogs*

2 a single thing made up of two parts: *a pair of trousers*

[verb: **pairs, pairing, paired**]

1 to pair things is to form them into pairs or sets of two

2 people **pair off** when they form pairs or couples

ⓘ Try not to confuse the spelling of **pair** with **pear**, which is a fruit.

pal [noun: **pals**] your pals are your friends

palace [noun: **palaces**] a large and magnificent house, especially one for a king, queen or emperor

palate [noun: **palates**]

1 your palate is the top part of the inside of your mouth. The front part feels hard and bony and the part further back is soft

2 a person's palate is their particular taste or liking, especially for certain kinds of food: *dishes to suit every palate*

ⓘ Try not to confuse the spelling of **palate** with **palette** and **pallet**.

pale [adjective: **paler, palest**]

1 light in colour: *pale blue • the pale light of dawn*

2 someone who is pale has less colour in their skin than normal, often because they are ill or have had a shock: *What's the matter? You've gone pale all of a sudden.*

palette [noun: **palettes**] a small flat piece of wood on which artists mix their colours

ⓘ Try not to confuse the spelling of **palette** with **palate** and **pallet**.

pall [noun: **palls**] a pall of smoke is a cloud of smoke that hangs over something

[verb: **palls, palling, palled**] if something palls, it begins to bore you, usually because you have done or seen it too often

pallet [noun: **pallets**] a wooden tray or platform on which things are stacked so that they can be lifted or moved by a fork-lift truck

ⓘ Try not to confuse the spelling of **pallet** with **palate** and **palette**.

pallid [adjective] unnaturally or unhealthily pale in colour: *There were tears running down his pallid cheeks.*

pallor [noun] unnatural or unhealthy paleness of the skin

palm [noun: **palms**]

1 the inner surface of your hand between your wrist and fingers

2 a tropical tree with very large leaves which spread out from the top of the trunk

[verb: **palms, palming, palmed**]

1 to palm an object is to hide it in the palm of your hand

2 to **palm off** an unwanted thing on someone is to get rid of it by giving it to them

palmistry [noun] palmistry is telling fortunes by looking at the pattern of lines or markings on a person's hand

palpitations [plural noun] if you have palpitations, your heart beats too quickly

paltry [adjective] very small or unimportant, or not enough to be useful: *a paltry sum of money*

pamper [verb: **pampers, pampering, pampered**] to pamper someone is to spoil them by doing too much for them

pamphlet [noun: **pamphlets**] a thin book with a paper cover

pan [noun: **pans**]

1 a metal container with a handle or handles, used for cooking food

2 a toilet bowl

[verb: **pans, panning, panned**]

1 to pan is to move a film, television or video camera to the left or right to give a wider view of a scene

2 the way something **pans out** is the way it turns out

Pp

pancake [noun: **pancakes**] a thin cake made by frying a mixture of milk, flour and eggs in a pan

pancreas [noun: **pancreases**] a gland just behind the stomach that produces substances which help in digestion

panda [noun: **pandas**] a large and rare black and white bear-like animal that lives in the mountains of China and eats bamboo

pandemonium [noun] wild and noisy confusion

pander [verb: **panders, pandering, pandered**] to **pander to** someone is to do things their way, or to always try to please them

p & p [abbreviation] short for **postage and packing**, used to show how much money you need to pay to have something sent to you by post

pane [noun: **panes**] a flat piece of glass used in a window

panel [noun: **panels**]
1 a flat rectangular piece of wood or other material, often set into a door or wall
2 a group of people chosen to judge a contest or take part in a quiz or other game
3 the part of a machine where the switches are: *a control panel*
♦ **panelling** [noun] wood or other material used for panels in walls and doors
♦ **panellist** [noun: **panellists**] one of the members of a panel in a contest or game

pang [noun: **pangs**] a sudden sharp or painful feeling: *pangs of hunger*

panic [noun] panic is sudden great fear, especially the kind that spreads through a crowd and causes people to scream or rush about not knowing what to do
[verb: **panics, panicking, panicked**] to panic is to become so frightened that you lose the power to think clearly
♦ **panicky** [adjective] tending to panic

panic-stricken [adjective] filled with terror and anxiety

panorama [noun: **panoramas**] a wide view in all directions, usually of a large area of land, or of a city and the surrounding landscape

pansy [noun: **pansies**] a small garden flower

with large flat rounded petals, usually white, yellow or shades of purple

pant [verb: **pants, panting, panted**]
1 to pant is to gasp for breath
2 to say something while gasping for breath: *'I've just sprinted two miles to catch this train,' he panted.*

panther [noun: **panthers**] a leopard, especially one that is black rather than having a spotted coat

pantomime [noun: **pantomimes**] a show put on at Christmas time, often based on a popular fairy tale, and including singing, dancing and comedy acts

pantry [noun: **pantries**] a small room near a kitchen, used for storing food

pants [plural noun]
1 a piece of underwear that covers your bottom
2 the American English word for **trousers**

papal [adjective] to do with the pope: *a papal visit*

papaya [noun: **papayas**] a large yellow fruit with sweet orange flesh, which grows on a tropical tree. Another name for the papaya is the **pawpaw**

paper [noun: **papers**]
1 paper is a material made from wood pulp or rags and used for writing, printing and wrapping things in
2 a paper is a newspaper: *Have you read today's paper?*
3 paper is wallpaper *She chose a floral paper with little rosebuds.*
4 a paper is a piece of paper with things written or printed on it: *a briefcase full of legal papers • an examination paper • identity papers*
[verb: **papers, papering, papered**] to paper a wall or room is to put wallpaper on it

paperback [noun: **paperbacks**] a book with a cover that can bend easily, made of very thin card. Look up and compare **hardback**

paperwork [noun] work that involves filling in forms and writing letters and reports: *The job involves a lot of paperwork.*

par [noun]
1 in golf, par is the number of strokes that a

good golfer should take to complete a hole, or all the holes on the golf course

2 something that is **below par** does not reach the standard required

3 if you are feeling **below par**, you are feeling slightly ill

4 if something is **on a par** with something else, the two things are equal in size or importance: *The salary is on a par with the salary of a senior civil servant.*

parable [noun: **parables**] a story, especially in the Bible, that is told to teach people something, especially a moral or religious lesson

paracetamol [noun] a drug that you take to reduce pain and lower a high temperature

parachute [noun: **parachutes**] an umbrella-shaped piece of light material attached to a person or object so that, when they are dropped from a plane, they fall slowly to the ground

[verb: **parachutes, parachuting, parachuted**] to parachute is to jump from a plane and fall slowly to the ground supported by a parachute

• **parachutist** [noun: **parachutists**] someone who parachutes

parade [noun: **parades**]

1 a line of people or vehicles moving forward in a procession, often as a celebration of some event

2 soldiers are **on parade** when they are gathered together in formal rows or ranks for marching or to be inspected

[verb: **parades, parading, paraded**] to parade is to march in line or move forward in a procession

paradise [noun]

1 paradise is heaven: *eternal paradise*

2 any place that has everything you want can be called a paradise: *The island is a paradise for bird watchers.*

paradox [noun: **paradoxes**] a statement or situation in which two things that seem to contradict each other are combined, but which is true or real despite this

• **paradoxical** [adjective] combining two things that seem to contradict each other

paraffin [noun] a type of oil that is made

from coal or petroleum and is used as a fuel in heaters and camping stoves

paragraph [noun: **paragraphs**] a section of a piece of writing, which has its first sentence starting on a new line

parallel [adjective] parallel lines go in the same direction and are always the same distance apart along their length

paralyse [verb: **paralyses, paralysing, paralysed**]

1 something paralyses a person or animal when it stops the normal movement in their body, or part of their body: *He had been paralysed by a stroke.*

2 to make something come to a complete stop where no movement is possible: *Heavy snow falls paralysed the road and rail network.*

• **paralysis** [noun] paralysis is loss of the power of movement in a part of the body, or loss of the ability to move or work

paramedic [noun: **paramedics**] a person who is not a doctor but who is trained to give emergency medical treatment

paramilitary [adjective] paramilitary organizations operate like an army but are not part of a country's official army

paramount [adjective] more important than anything else: *The children's safety is paramount.*

paranoia [noun]

1 paranoia is a form of mental illness in which someone imagines that other people are trying to harm them

2 paranoia is a tendency some people have to worry that other people do not like them and want to treat them badly

• **paranoid** [adjective] suffering from paranoia: *He was paranoid about getting caught.*

parapet [noun: **parapets**] a low wall along the edge of a bridge, balcony or roof

paraphernalia [noun] paraphernalia is a large number of different objects and pieces of equipment: *Kevin packed all his fishing paraphernalia into the back of the car.*

paraphrase [noun: **paraphrases**] a paraphrase of something is a different way of saying or writing it

[verb: **paraphrases, paraphrasing,**

Pp

paraphrased] to paraphrase something is to express it in a different way

parasite [noun: **parasites**] an animal or plant that lives on, and gets its food from, another animal or plant

parasol [noun: **parasols**] a light umbrella used to give shade from the sun

paratrooper [noun: **paratroopers**] a soldier trained to drop by parachute into enemy country

♦ **paratroops** [plural noun] a group of these soldiers

parcel [noun: **parcels**] something wrapped in paper or cardboard and tied with string or sticky tape

parched [adjective]
1 if you are parched, you are very thirsty
2 parched land has been dried by the sun so that there is no moisture for plants to grow

parchment [noun: **parchments**]
1 parchment is a material made from animal skin, used long ago for writing on
2 a parchment is a piece of this with writing on

pardon [verb: **pardons, pardoning, pardoned**]
1 to forgive or excuse someone for a fault they have or a crime they have committed
2 some people say 'pardon' or 'pardon me', either because they haven't heard what has been said, or they want to apologize for something they have done
[noun: **pardons**] if someone who has been sentenced to be punished for a crime receives a pardon, their punishment is cancelled

pare [verb: **pares, paring, pared**] to pare something is to cut or trim it, layer by layer

parent [noun: **parents**] your parents are your mother and father

♦ **parentage** [noun] a person's or animal's parentage is who or what each of their parents are

♦ **parental** [adjective] to do with a parent or parents: *parental responsibilities*

➡ **parenthood**

parenthesis [noun: **parentheses**] parentheses are curved brackets put round information that adds to the main point but is not an essential part of a sentence

parenthood [noun] the condition of being

or becoming a parent: *the responsibilities of parenthood*

parish [noun: **parishes**] a district or area with its own church and priest or minister

♦ **parishioner** [noun: **parishioners**] someone who lives in a parish, especially someone who goes to services in the parish church

park [noun: **parks**] a piece of land in a town or city that has grass and trees and where people can go for fresh air or leisure
[verb: **parks, parking, parked**] to park a vehicle is to stop it somewhere, for example, by the side of the road or in a driveway or car park

parka [noun: **parkas**] a type of long warm jacket with a hood

parking lot [noun: **parking lots**] the American term for a **car park**

parking meter [noun: **parking meters**] a metal box on a pole that has a slot where you can put coins to pay for parking your car in the space next to the meter

Parkinson's disease [noun] a serious disease that affects someone's brain and causes them to shake and have difficulty in walking

parliament [noun: **parliaments**] a group of people, usually politicians, who meet to discuss and make a particular country's laws: *the new parliament of Scotland*

♦ **parliamentary** [adjective] to do with a parliament: *a parliamentary debate*

parlour [noun: **parlours**]
1 a shop selling a particular product or service: *an ice-cream parlour* • *a beauty parlour*
2 an old-fashioned word for the room where you sit or receive guests in a house

parody [noun: **parodies**] a parody is an imitation of an author's, artist's or musician's work or style, done to make fun of them
[verb: **parodies, parodying, parodied**] to parody someone or their work is to imitate them or their style in an amusing way

parole [noun] a criminal on parole has been allowed out of prison before their sentence is finished on condition that they behave well

parrot [noun: **parrot**]
1 a bird with a strong curved beak, beady

Pp

eyes, and brightly coloured or grey feathers, that can be taught to imitate human speech and is often kept as a pet

2 if you learn or repeat something **parrot fashion**, you learn or repeat it exactly, but without really thinking about what it means

parsley [noun] a type of herb with curly or flat green leaves, used to add flavour in cooking

parsnip [noun: **parsnips**] a vegetable, similar in shape to a carrot, which is a pale cream colour and grows underground

parson [noun: **parsons**] any Christian priest, especially one belonging to the Church of England

+ **parsonage** [noun: **parsonages**] a parson's house

part [noun: **parts**]

1 a division or piece of something: *The pizza is cut into six equal parts.* • *a part for the engine* • *part of the day*

2 a character in a play or film, or the words or actions that a character has to say or do in a play or film: *a leading part in the musical* • *He's learned his part well.*

3 to **take part** in an activity is to do it or be involved in it: *She wanted to take part in all the festivities.*

[verb: **parts, parting, parted**]

1 people or things part when they separate and move away from each other or out of each other's company

2 to **part with** something is to give it away, sell it, or let it be taken away from you

➡ **parting, partly**

part exchange [noun] a way of buying something in which you give something you own as part of the payment, for example trading in your old car as part of the payment for a new one

partial [adjective]

1 not complete: *a partial success*

2 to be **partial to** something is to be fond of it: *She's very partial to chocolate.*

3 to be partial is to prefer or favour one person or side over another in an unfair way: *She's too partial to be a good judge.*

+ **partiality** [noun] preferring one side over another, for example in a competition or trial

+ **partially** [adverb] partly: *a partially eaten biscuit*

participant [noun: **participants**] someone who takes part in something with other people

participate [verb: **participates, participating, participated**] to participate in something is to take part in it: *Most of the staff participated in the charity event.*

+ **participation** [noun] taking part

participle [noun: **participles**] a participle is a word formed from a verb and used as an adjective, or to form different tenses of the verb. For example, *spending*, *looking* and *passing* are called **present participles** and *canned*, *stolen* and *dealt* are called **past participles**

particle [noun: **particles**] a very small piece that you can hardly see: *a particle of dust*

particular [adjective]

1 you use 'particular' to show that you are talking about one specific person or thing that should not be confused with any other: *On that particular day I was early.* • *Is there a particular person I should speak to about this?*

2 especially great: *He took particular care when writing the letter.*

3 someone who is particular has strong ideas about what they like and do not like, and is very difficult to please

[noun: **particulars**]

1 your particulars, or the particulars of a situation, are your personal details, or the details of that situation

2 **in particular** means 'especially': *I enjoy reading novels, romantic fiction in particular.*

parting [noun: **partings**]

1 leaving someone or saying goodbye to them

2 you have a parting in your hair when it has been brushed or combed in opposite directions on either side of a line across your head

partition [noun: **partitions**]

1 a partition is a thin wall, used to divide up a room, but not usually reaching up as far as the ceiling

2 partition is dividing something into parts

partly [adverb] in some ways or to a certain extent: *I was partly to blame for the mix-up.*

partner [noun: **partners**]

Pp

1 one of two people who do something together, like dance or play in a game
2 people who are business partners share the ownership of a business
3 someone's partner is the person they are married to or have a sexual relationship with
♦ **partnership** [noun: **partnerships**] being a partner

part of speech [noun: **parts of speech**] in grammar, the parts of speech are the various groups that words belong to depending on the job they do. The parts of speech you will find in this dictionary are noun, pronoun, verb, adjective, adverb, preposition, conjunction and interjection

partridge [noun: **partridges**] a small plump grey and brown wild bird that nests on the ground and is hunted for sport and food

part-time [adjective and adverb] if you work part-time or have a part-time job, you work for only part of a full working day or week

party [noun: **parties**]
1 a party is an event where people gather to celebrate something or to enjoy each other's company
2 a political party is an organized group of people who share the same political beliefs
3 a party of people is a group of people travelling or doing something together

pass [verb: **passes, passing, passed**]
1 to pass is to move towards and then go beyond something: *The procession passed in front of the town hall.* • *The lorry passed us on a bend.*
2 to pass something to someone is to hand it to them or give it to them: *Pass me the butter, please.*
3 to pass a test or exam is to be successful in it
4 something passes when it ends or goes away: *The storm passed and the sun came out again.*
5 to pass a law is to make it a law
6 if someone **passes away**, they die
7 to **pass out** is to faint or become unconscious
8 to **pass something up** is to decide not to take it or use it
[noun: **passes**]

1 a ticket or card that allows you to get into a place or to travel somewhere
2 in games like football, hockey and rugby, a pass is a kick, hit or throw that sends the ball from one player to another in the same team
3 a successful result in an exam
4 a narrow gap between mountains

passable [adjective]
1 if something is passable, it is of quite a good standard but is not the best
2 a road is passable if it is not completely blocked

passage [noun: **passages**]
1 a narrow corridor
2 a tube from an opening in the body: *Your nasal passages are connected to your nose.*
3 a part or section in a piece of writing or music: *Read the next passage aloud.*
4 a journey in a ship
5 passing: *the passage of time*

passageway [noun: **passageways**] a way through between walls or other barriers

passenger [noun: **passengers**] someone travelling in a car, bus, ship or plane who is not the driver or one of the crew

passer-by [noun: **passers-by**] someone who is passing in the street when something happens

(i) Remember that you make this word plural by adding the s to *passer*, not to *by*.

passion [noun: **passions**] very strong feeling or emotion, especially anger or love
♦ **passionate** [adjective] showing strong emotions

passive [adjective]
1 someone who is passive stays or lies still and does not react to anything
2 in grammar, a passive verb is the form of a verb used when the person or thing that is the subject of the verb does not do the action but has something done to them, for example in the sentence *The leaves are being eaten by caterpillars.*
♦ **passively** [adverb] in a passive way

passive smoking [noun] passive smoking is when you breathe in the smoke from other people's cigarettes

Passover [noun] a Jewish festival held in

Pp

March or April celebrating the freeing of the Jews from slavery in Egypt

passport [noun: **passports**] a document with your photograph and personal details that you must carry when you are travelling abroad

password [noun: **passwords**] a secret word or phrase that you have to know before you are allowed into a place, or which you must type into a computer before you can see the information in it

past [noun]
1 the past is the time before the present
2 someone's past is what they have done in their life before the present time
[adjective] over or ended: *in the past year* • *Summer is nearly past and autumn is on the way.*
[preposition]
1 up to and beyond: *She dashed past me, gasping as she ran.*
2 later than: *It's past eight o'clock.*

pasta [noun] a food made from a special type of flour, water and eggs and formed into lots of different shapes, all of which have special names, for example, spaghetti, macaroni and lasagne

paste [noun: **pastes**]
1 a soft moist mixture
2 a type of glue for sticking paper together or for fixing wallpaper to walls
[verb: **pastes, pasting, pasted**] to paste something is to stick it with glue

pastel [adjective] pastel colours are pale and contain a lot of white: *pastel blue*
[noun: **pastels**] pastels are chalky crayons used to draw and colour with

pasteurization or **pasteurisation** [noun] a process which involves heating milk to kill all the bacteria in it
♦ **pasteurize** or **pasteurise** [verb: **pasteurizes, pasteurizing, pasteurized**] to pasteurize milk is to heat it so that all the bacteria in it are killed

pastille [noun: **pastilles**] a small sugary sweet, often sucked as a medicine for sore throats or coughs

pastime [noun: **pastimes**] something you enjoy spending your time doing

pastor [noun: **pastors**] a religious minister or priest

pastoral [adjective]
1 to do with the countryside or country life: *a pastoral scene*
2 the pastoral work of a priest or teacher involves people's social needs rather than their religion or education

past participle [noun: **past participles**] the form of a verb used after a helping verb such as *has* or *was* to show that something happened in the past. For example, *fought* in *I have fought with my brother* is a past participle

pastry [noun: **pastries**]
1 pastry is a mixture of flour and fat used to make pies and cakes
2 a pastry is a cake made with pastry

past tense [noun] a form of a verb that you use when you are talking about what has happened in the past. For example, *relaxed* in *I relaxed after the race* is a past tense

pasture [noun: **pastures**] a field with grass for cattle and other animals to eat

pasty¹ [adjective: **pastier, pastiest**] having unhealthily pale skin, especially on the face

pasty² [noun: **pasties**] a small pie made with pastry filled with chopped meat and vegetables

ⓘ **Pasty**¹ is pronounced **paste**-y.
Pasty² is pronounced **pass**-ty.

pat [verb: **pats, patting, patted**] to pat someone or something is to hit them or it gently with your hand, usually as a sign of affection
[noun: **pats**] a light, gentle blow or touch, usually with the palm of your hand

patch [noun: **patches**]
1 a piece of material sewn on to a piece of clothing to cover a hole or tear
2 a piece of material worn over a damaged or blind eye
3 a small area of something: *a patch of grass*
4 if someone or something is **not a patch on** someone or something else, they are not nearly as good: *He's a good player, but not a patch on Gordon.*
[verb: **patches, patching, patched**]
1 to patch something is to repair a tear or hole in it by sewing a piece of material over it

2 to **patch something up** is to mend it, and to **patch someone up** is to treat their injuries
3 to **patch up** a quarrel is to end it and be friendly again

patchwork [noun] small pieces of fabric sewn together in a decorative pattern

patchy [adjective: **patchier, patchiest**]
1 existing in some places but not in others: *patchy fog*
2 good sometimes but not always: *The standard of cooking can be a bit patchy.*

pâté [noun: **pâtés**] a smooth or lumpy paste made by chopping and blending meat, fish or vegetables with flavourings

patent [noun: **patents**] a licence from the government that gives one person or company the right to make and sell a product and to stop others from copying it
[verb: **patents, patenting, patented**] to patent something you have invented or developed is to get a licence for it from the government
[adjective] obvious: *his patent lack of enthusiasm*
♦ **patently** [adverb] very clearly: *It's patently obvious he had no intention of doing it.*

ⓘ The adjective is pronounced **pay**-tent. The noun and verb can be pronounced **pay**-tent or **pa**-tent.

paternal [adjective]
1 to do with, or behaving like, a father: *He showed off his daughter's trophy with paternal pride.*
2 from your father's side of the family: *my paternal grandparents*

paternity [noun] being a father
[adjective] to do with being or becoming a father: *paternity leave • a paternity test to discover whether he was the child's father*

path [noun: **paths**]
1 a track across a piece of land made or used by people or animals walking
2 the line along which something travels
3 a particular course of action or way of doing something

pathetic [adjective]
1 something pathetic causes you to feel pity or sadness: *the pathetic cries of a lost kitten*

2 if you say a person or thing is pathetic you think they are useless or hopeless: *This knife is pathetic. It won't even cut butter!*

pathway [noun: **pathways**] a route from one place to another that people or things travel along

patience [noun]
1 the ability or willingness to stay calm: *You need to have a lot of patience when dealing with young children.*
2 a card game played by one person
♦ **patient** [adjective] a patient person is able to stay calm and self-controlled, especially when they have to wait a long time for something
[noun: **patients**] someone being seen or treated by a doctor, or being treated for a particular illness: *The nurse called, 'Next patient, please.' • cancer patients*
♦ **patiently** [adverb] in a patient way: *waiting patiently for a bus*

patio [noun: **patios**] a paved area beside or at the back of a house, used for sitting outdoors in good weather

patriot [noun: **patriots**] someone who loves and is loyal to his or her country
♦ **patriotic** [adjective] loving, and being loyal to, your country
♦ **patriotism** [noun] being patriotic

patrol [verb: **patrols, patrolling, patrolled**] to patrol an area is to go around it looking out for trouble or making sure no one is there who should not be
[noun: **patrols**]
1 a police or army patrol is the group of soldiers or police officers who patrol an area
2 someone **on patrol** is walking around a building or area making sure there is no trouble or no one is trying to get in without permission

patron [noun: **patrons**]
1 if an artist or musician has a patron, they have someone who supports them and buys their work
2 a patron of a charity is someone, usually someone well-known, who gives it their public support
3 a shop's or business's patrons are its customers

♦ patronage [noun] support or money given by a patron to the arts or to a charity

patron saint [noun: **patron saints**] a saint who is believed to protect a place, activity or trade: *the patron saint of Scotland*

patter[1] [verb: **patters, pattering, pattered**] to make quick, light, tapping sounds: *rain pattering on the windows*
[noun] a series of quick, light, tapping sounds: *the patter of mice as they scurried around in the attic*

patter[2] [noun] patter is fast talk, especially the fast persuasive talk of someone who is trying to sell you something

pattern [noun: **patterns**]
1 a guide used for making something: *a sewing pattern*
2 a design that is repeated over and over again, for example on a piece of fabric or on wallpaper
3 the way in which something happens or is organized: *the pattern of the seasons*
♦ patterned [adjective] having a pattern

patty [noun: **patties**] a small flat cake made with chopped meat or vegetables and usually fried

pause [verb: **pauses, pausing, paused**] to pause is to stop what you are doing for a short time
[noun: **pauses**] a short stop

pave [verb: **paves, paving, paved**] to pave an area is to lay paving stones or some other hard material on it

pavement [noun: **pavements**] a raised path beside a road used by pedestrians to walk along

pavilion [noun: **pavilions**]
1 a building at a sports ground where players change their clothes and keep their equipment
2 a large building or tent

paw [noun: **paws**] an animal's foot
[verb: **paws, pawing, pawed**] an animal paws something when it feels or touches it with its paw

pawn [verb: **pawns, pawning, pawned**] to pawn something valuable is to give it to someone in exchange for a loan. If the loan is repaid, the article is given back to the person who has pawned it

[noun: **pawns**] in the game of chess, a pawn is one of the small, least important pieces

pawnbroker [noun: **pawnbrokers**] someone who runs a shop where valuable objects can be pawned

pawpaw [noun] look at the entry for **papaya**

pay [verb: **pays, paying, paid**]
1 to pay for something is to give money in exchange for it: *I'll pay for the meal.*
2 to pay someone is to give them money for something or for doing something for you: *I need the money to pay the builder.*
3 it pays to do something if it brings you a benefit of some sort: *Crime does not pay.*
4 to pay for something you have done is to suffer because of it: *I paid for my laziness when I failed the test.*
5 to pay attention or a compliment is to give it
6 if someone has done something bad to you and you **pay them back**, you do something bad to them in return
7 something you do **pays off** if it brings a good result, or a profit: *I hope your hard work pays off and you do well at school.*
8 if a company or employer **pays off** workers, the workers lose their jobs
[noun] someone's pay is the amount of money they are paid by their employer

LANGUAGE FOR LIFE
pay
You may come across a number of different terms that measure your pay.
• Your **basic pay** is the amount you are usually paid for doing your job before any bonus payments are added onto it for things like overtime work.
• Your **net pay** is the amount that you actually receive for your work, after you have paid tax and National Insurance.
• Your **taxable pay** is the part of your pay that is used to work out how much tax you have to pay the government. Your taxable pay will be less than your total pay, because you are allowed to earn a certain amount of money before you pay any tax.
• Your **total pay**, sometimes called **gross pay**, is all the money that you earn, including your basic

Pp

pay and any bonuses, before tax is taken out of it.
• In some jobs, you may come across the expression **OTE** or **on-target earnings**. This is the money you are supposed to be able to earn if you do your work successfully, for example if you manage to sell a lot of goods.
You should also look at the information after the entry for **payslip**.

PAYE [abbreviation] short for **pay as you earn**, a system of paying income tax in which your employer takes money from your wages and gives it to the government

payment [noun: **payments**]
1 a payment is a sum of money paid for something: *All payments will be made to your bank account.*
2 payment is paying money or being paid: *prompt payment of bills*

payroll [noun: **payrolls**] a list of all the people that a company employs and the money that they earn

payslip [noun: **payslips**] a piece of paper that shows how much money you have earned and how much money has been taken away for things such as tax

LANGUAGE FOR LIFE

payslips

Here are some important words you may see on a payslip:
• **Deductions** or **adjustments** are amounts that are taken out of your pay for things such as tax or your pension.
• **NI** stands for **National Insurance**. This is money that you and your employer give to the government to pay for things such as healthcare and old-age pensions.
• **PAYE** stands for **Pay As You Earn**. This means that your employer takes money and gives it to the government to pay tax for you.
• Your **tax code** is a group of letters and numbers used by the government to tell them how much tax you have to pay on the money you earn.
You should also look at the information after the entry for **pay**.

PC [abbreviation: **PCs**]
1 short for **personal computer**

2 short for **police constable**, used before a police officer's name: *PC Evans*

PE [abbreviation] short for **physical education**

pea [noun: **peas**] a small round green vegetable that grows in pods on a climbing plant

peace [noun] there is peace when there is no war, or everything is quiet and calm: *The two countries have been at peace for 50 years.* • *I want a little peace to get on with my homework.*
◆ **peaceful** [adjective]
1 a peaceful place is quiet and calm
2 a peaceful nation does not try to go to war with other countries
◆ **peacefully** [adverb] quietly and calmly

peach [noun: **peaches**] a soft round fruit with a velvety skin, pale orange flesh and a large stone inside

peacock [noun: **peacocks**] a large bird belonging to the same family as pheasants. The male bird's tail, which he can raise and spread out like a fan, has long blue and green feathers with round black markings at the ends

peak [noun: **peaks**]
1 a peak is the pointed top of a mountain or hill, or anything that looks like this: *snow-covered peaks* • *Beat the egg whites until they form soft peaks.*
2 the peak of something is its highest, greatest or busiest point or time: *the peak of the holiday season*
3 the peak of a cap is the front part that sticks out and shades the eyes
[verb: **peaks, peaking, peaked**] something peaks when it reaches its highest, greatest or busiest point or time: *Traffic usually peaks about 5 or 6 o'clock.*

peal [noun: **peals**]
1 a sound made by one or more large bells ringing together
2 a loud rolling noise, made by something such as thunder
[verb: **peals, pealing, pealed**]
1 bells peal when they ring loudly together
2 thunder peals when it makes a loud continuous noise

peanut [noun: **peanuts**] a kind of nut that

Pp

grows underground in a shell similar to a pea pod

peanut butter [noun] a thick paste made with crushed peanuts that you spread on bread

pear [noun: **pears**] a fruit which is round at the bottom and narrows towards the stem at the top

pearl [noun: **pearls**]
1 a valuable, white, rounded stone formed by oysters and some other shellfish inside their shells
2 something valuable: *pearls of wisdom*

peasant [noun: **peasants**] someone who lives and works on the land, especially a farmer who owns a small piece of land that he works on himself

ⓘ **Peasant** is used mainly about people in very poor countries or about people in history.

peat [noun: **peats**] material formed in the ground over many years as layers of dead plants rot down, and used for gardening and as a fuel for burning

pebble [noun: **pebbles**] a small stone that has been made smooth by water

pebble dash [noun] a covering made of cement with lots of tiny stone chips or pebbles stuck in it, used on the outside of some houses

peck [verb: **pecks, pecking, pecked**] a bird pecks when it taps or hits something, or picks something up, with its beak
[noun: **pecks**]
1 a tap or bite with the beak
2 a quick light kiss: *a peck on the cheek*

peckish [adjective] slightly hungry: *I'm a bit peckish. Are there any biscuits left?*

peculiar [adjective]
1 strange or odd: *a very peculiar smell*
2 something that is peculiar to a person, place or thing, belongs to, or is found in, that particular person, place or thing, and no other: *habits peculiar to cats*
  ◆ **peculiarity** [noun: **peculiarities**]
  1 an odd or strange thing, or the quality of being odd or strange
  2 a distinctive feature or characteristic
  ◆ **peculiarly** [adverb]
  1 strangely: *behaving very peculiarly*

2 in a distinctive way: *a peculiarly British habit*

pedal [noun: **pedals**] a lever that you work with your foot, such as on a bicycle, piano or organ
[verb: **pedals, pedalling, pedalled**] to pedal a bike is to make it move forward by pressing down on the pedals

peddle [verb: **peddles, peddling, peddled**] to peddle goods is to go from place to place or house to house selling them
➞ **pedlar**

pedestal [noun: **pedestals**]
1 the base that something stands on, for example a statue or wash hand basin
2 if you **put someone on a pedestal**, you admire them so much that you think they have no faults

pedestrian [noun: **pedestrians**] someone who is walking along a road rather than travelling in a vehicle

pedigree [noun: **pedigrees**]
1 if an animal has a pedigree, there is a record showing that its parents and other ancestors were all of the same breed
2 your pedigree is your background or the people you are descended from
[adjective] having a pedigree: *a pedigree cow*

pedlar [noun: **pedlars**] a person who travels round selling small objects, usually from door to door

peek [verb: **peeks, peeking, peeked**] to peek is to look, especially when you should not be looking: *He peeked inside the box.*
[noun: **peeks**] a quick look

ⓘ Try not to confuse the spelling of **peak**, which is the top of something, with **peek**.

peel [verb: **peels, peeling, peeled**]
1 to peel a fruit or vegetable is to take off its skin or outer covering
2 paint or skin peels when it comes off in small pieces
[noun] peel is the skin of some fruits and vegetables

peep [verb: **peeps, peeping, peeped**] to peep is to look through a narrow opening or from behind something: *A child's face was peeping from behind the curtain.*

[noun: **peeps**] a quick look at something

peer [verb: **peers, peering, peered**] to peer at something is to look at it with your eyes narrowed because you cannot see very clearly

[noun: **peers**]

1 your peers are the people who are the same age, class or status as you

2 in Britain, peers are members of the nobility or people who have been awarded a title

peg [noun: **pegs**]

1 a wooden, plastic or metal clip used for hanging clothes on a washing line

2 a hook for hanging coats, hats or jackets on

3 a piece of wood or metal driven into the ground to secure a tent, or as a marker

Pekinese or **Pekingese** [noun: **Pekineses** or **Pekingeses**] a type of small dog with long silky hair, large eyes, and a small wrinkled nose

pelican [noun: **pelicans**] a large white bird found in tropical parts of the world, which dives for fish and stores the ones it catches in a pouch under its beak

pelican crossing [noun: **pelican crossings**] a road crossing for pedestrians with lights that are operated by the people waiting to cross

pellet [noun: **pellets**] a small hard round object formed by pressing and rolling material into a tightly-packed ball

pelmet [noun: **pelmets**] a long narrow piece of cloth or wood fitted along the top of a window to hide the curtain rail

pelt [verb: **pelts, pelting, pelted**]

1 to pelt someone with things is to throw things at them one after the other

2 rain pelts down when it falls fast and heavily

3 to pelt is to run or move very fast: *He came pelting down the road on his bike.*

[noun: **pelts**] the skin from an animal: *beaver pelts*

pelvis [noun: **pelvises**] your pelvis is the bowl-shaped bone at your hips

pen[1] [noun: **pens**] an instrument for writing or drawing in ink

pen[2] [noun: **pens**] a small area of land surrounded by a fence and used for keeping animals in

[verb: **pens, penning, penned**]

1 to pen an animal is to put it in a pen

2 to **pen someone in** is to surround them or shut them in so that they cannot move or escape

pen[3] [noun: **pens**] a female swan

penalize or **penalise** [verb: **penalizes, penalizing, penalized**] to penalize someone is to punish them for doing something that is against the rules

penalty [noun: **penalties**]

1 a punishment for doing wrong

2 in games like football, rugby and hockey, a penalty is a free shot at goal given because a player in the other team has broken a rule of the game

penance [noun] if someone does penance they suffer a punishment willingly to make up for doing something wrong

pence [noun] a plural of **penny**

pencil [noun: **pencils**] an instrument made up of a wooden shaft containing a stick of a soft black substance called graphite, or coloured chalk, and used for writing or drawing

pendant [noun: **pendants**] an ornament that hangs from a chain or necklace

pendulum [noun: **pendulums**] a weight that swings from side to side and operates the mechanism of a clock

penetrate [verb: **penetrates, penetrating, penetrated**]

1 to get into or through something: *Rain could not penetrate those thick trees.*

2 if something you have been told penetrates, you understand it: *The news didn't penetrate at first.*

✦ **penetrating** [adjective]

1 a penetrating voice or sound seems to carry for a long distance

2 if someone gives you a penetrating look, they look at you hard as if they are searching your mind

✦ **penetration** [noun] going into or through something

pen-friend [noun: **pen-friends**] a friend you exchange letters with, but do not meet

penguin [noun: **penguins**] a bird that cannot fly but which uses its wings like flippers to swim underwater. Penguins are found in the Antarctic

penicillin [noun] a drug used to treat infections caused by bacteria

peninsula [noun: **peninsulas**] a piece of land surrounded by water on every side except the end where it joins a larger land mass

♦ **peninsular** [adjective] to do with, or formed like, a peninsula

penis [noun: **penises**] the organ male animals use to urinate and reproduce

penknife [noun: **penknives**] a small knife with blades that fold into the handle and which you can carry in your pocket

pennant [noun: **pennants**] a small narrow flag that tapers to a point at one end

penniless [adjective] if someone is penniless, they have no money

penny [noun: **pennies**] a small bronze British coin worth one hundredth of £1

pension [noun: **pensions**] a sum of money paid regularly to a person who has retired from work

♦ **pensioner** [noun: **pensioners**] a retired person who is receiving a pension

LANGUAGE FOR LIFE

pensions

There are different types of pension.
• An **occupational pension**, sometimes called a **company pension**, is arranged by a company and offered to its employees. Often the company as well as the employee will contribute to the pension.
• A **personal pension**, sometimes called a **private pension**, is one which someone sets up by themselves, using a company that provides pension schemes. Only the person who sets up a private pension contributes to it.
• A **state pension**, sometimes called a **government pension**, is paid by the government from funds raised by taxes and National Insurance contributions.

pentathlon [noun: **pentathlons**] an athletics competition that consists of five different kinds of sporting contest

penultimate [adjective] the penultimate thing is the last but one in a series

people [noun: **peoples**]
1 people are men, women and children

2 a people is one of the races of human beings: *all the peoples of the world*
3 the plural of **person**: *a small flat suitable for one person or perhaps two people*
[verb: **peoples, peopling, peopled**] a place is peopled by a certain group if they are the people who live there

ⓘ Except when it means 'a race', the noun **people** always takes a plural verb, for example: *People **are** always happy to go on holiday.*

pepper [noun: **peppers**]
1 pepper is a hot-tasting powder made by grinding dried seeds called peppercorns
2 a pepper is a red, yellow, orange or green hollow fruit used as a vegetable
⟶ **peppery**

peppermint [noun: **peppermints**]
1 peppermint is a strong flavouring obtained from a type of mint plant, used in sweets and toothpaste
2 a peppermint is a sweet flavoured with peppermint
[adjective] flavoured with peppermint: *peppermint toothpaste*

peppery [adjective] hot-tasting, like pepper

per [preposition]
1 for every or for each: *The meal will cost £15 per person.*
2 in every or in each: *sixty kilometres per hour*

perceive [verb: **perceives, perceiving, perceived**]
1 to perceive something is to notice it with one of your senses: *I perceived that something was troubling her.*
2 to perceive something is to understand or think about it in a particular way: *How do you perceive your role?*
⟶ **perception, perceptive**

ⓘ The first sense of **perceive** is a formal word.

per cent [adverb] in or for every 100: *forty per cent*

♦ **percentage** [noun: **percentages**]
1 a number or amount in each hundred, written as a fraction with that number over a hundred, for example $\frac{35}{100}$. It can also be written with a percentage sign, for example 35%
2 a part or proportion of something: *A high percentage of students got top grades.*

Pp

perception [noun: **perceptions**]
1 the ability to see, hear or understand
2 your perception of something is the way you see or understand it

perceptive [adjective] a perceptive person is good at noticing or understanding things

perch [verb: **perches, perching, perched**]
1 a bird perches when it sits or stands on a branch or some other place above the ground
2 to perch somewhere high or narrow is to sit there
[noun: **perches**] a branch or other place above the ground that a bird sits or stands on

percolator [noun: **percolators**] a pot for making coffee with ground coffee beans in a small container at the top that boiling water bubbles through

percussion [noun] musical instruments, such as drums, cymbals, tambourines and triangles, that you play by hitting them with your hands or with sticks, or by shaking them

perfect [adjective]
1 without any mistakes or faults: a perfect score
2 exact: a perfect circle
3 complete: a perfect stranger
[verb: **perfects, perfecting, perfected**] to perfect something is to make it perfect, without any faults
♦ **perfection** [noun] making perfect or being perfect
♦ **perfectly** [adverb]
1 without any mistakes or faults: She did the pirouette perfectly.
2 exactly: perfectly square
3 completely: perfectly ridiculous

ⓘ The adjective is pronounced **per**-fikt, with the stress at the beginning.
The verb is pronounced pir-**fekt**, with the stress at the end.

perforate [verb: **perforates, perforating, perforated**] to perforate something is to pierce it and make a small hole in it
♦ **perforated** [adjective] pierced with a hole or a series of holes
♦ **perforation** [noun: **perforations**] a small hole made in something, especially the series of small holes made around the edges of stamps so that they can be torn from the sheet

perform [verb: **performs, performing, performed**]
1 to perform something such as a play, piece of music or a dance is to do it in front of an audience
2 to perform something is to do it or carry it out: Surgeons perform operations.
♦ **performance** [noun: **performances**]
1 something performed in front of an audience
2 a level of success achieved in doing something: a brilliant performance
♦ **performer** [noun: **performers**] someone who does an act in front of an audience

perfume [noun: **perfumes**]
1 a perfume is a smell, especially a pleasant one
2 perfume is a pleasant smelling liquid or cream that you put on your body to make it smell nice
[verb: **perfumes, perfuming, perfumed**] to perfume something is to put perfume on it or fill it with a pleasant smell

perhaps [adverb] possibly or maybe: He's late again. Perhaps he's got held up in traffic.

peril [noun: **perils**] danger: the perils of sailing round the world alone • The business's future was in peril.
♦ **perilous** [adjective] very dangerous or full of danger: a perilous journey on foot across miles of desert

perimeter [noun: **perimeters**] the perimeter of an area is its outer edge or boundary

period [noun: **periods**]
1 a period of time is a length of time: a period of several weeks
2 a stage or phase in history: the Regency period • one of the earliest geological periods
3 the flow of blood each month from the body of a woman who is not pregnant
[adjective] from or in the style of a period in history: period costumes
♦ **periodic** [adjective] for a certain length of time and at regular intervals: He gets periodic bouts of asthma.
♦ **periodical** [noun: **periodicals**] a magazine that is published regularly, for example once a week or once a month

Pp

periscope [noun: **periscopes**] an instrument consisting of a special arrangement of angled mirrors in a tube, which makes it possible for you to look at things over the top of a barrier in front of you. Periscopes are used in submarines

perish [verb: **perishes, perishing, perished**] to perish is to die, especially in a war or from extreme cold

periwinkle [noun: **periwinkles**] a shellfish that looks like a small snail and clings to rocks

perjury [noun] the crime of telling a lie in court after you have sworn an oath to tell the truth

perk [verb: **perks, perking, perked**] if you **perk up**, you feel more lively and cheerful [noun: **perks**] a perk is an extra benefit or advantage that someone gets from their job

perm [noun: **perms**] a chemical treatment for hair that gives a long-lasting curly hairstyle [verb: **perms, perming, permed**] to perm hair is to treat it with chemicals so that it stays in a curly style for a long time

permanent [adjective]
1 lasting for ever, or for a long time: *Will the scar be permanent?*
2 a permanent job is one that is expected to last for a long time, rather than being temporary
3 never changing: *a permanent state of chaos*
◆ **permanently** [adverb] for ever

permissible [adjective] something that is permissible is allowed

permission [noun] you get or are given permission to do something when someone says you are allowed to do it

permit [verb: **permits, permitting, permitted**] to permit something is to allow it to happen
[noun: **permits**] an official document allowing a person to do something: *a fishing permit*

ⓘ The verb is pronounced pir-**mit**, with the stress at the end.
The noun is pronounced **per**-mit, with the stress at the beginning.

perpendicular [adjective]
1 standing straight upwards: *a perpendicular line*
2 touching another line to make a right angle. For example, the touching lines in a rectangle are perpendicular to each other

perpetual [adjective] never ending or continuous: *perpetual darkness* • *a perpetual noise*

perplex [verb: **perplexes, perplexing, perplexed**] if something perplexes you, it puzzles or baffles you
◆ **perplexed** [adjective] puzzled: *a perplexed expression*
◆ **perplexity** [noun] being perplexed: *'Hum!' said he, scratching his chin in some perplexity.*

persecute [verb: **persecutes, persecuting, persecuted**] to persecute someone is to make them suffer, especially because of their opinions or beliefs
◆ **persecution** [noun] being persecuted

perseverance [noun] continuing with something even though it is difficult

persevere [verb: **perseveres, persevering, persevered**] to persevere is to continue with something even though it is difficult

persist [verb: **persists, persisting, persisted**]
1 if something persists, it continues for a long time
2 you persist with something when you keep on doing it and refuse to give up
3 to keep talking about something: *'It was you,' I persisted.*
◆ **persistence** [noun] continuing with something in spite of people saying you should not
◆ **persistent** [adjective]
1 refusing to give up: *Even though I said I wasn't interested, the salesman was very persistent.*
2 continuing without a break: *persistent rain*

person [noun: **people** or **persons**]
1 a human being
2 if you do something **in person**, you do it by going to a place or person rather than by writing or by sending someone else to do it

personal [adjective]
1 belonging to, or done by, one particular person and no one else: *a personal opinion* • *a personal appearance*
2 private: *It's personal and none of your business.*

Pp

personal assistant [noun: **personal assistants**] a secretary who helps someone who has an important job. This is often shortened to **PA**

personal computer [noun: **personal computers**] a computer that is designed to be used by one person. This is often shortened to **PC**

personality [noun: **personalities**]
1 your personality is your character and the qualities you have
2 someone with personality behaves in a way that has a strong impression on you
3 a personality is a famous person

personally [adverb]
1 you say 'personally' when you are giving your own opinion about something: 'Personally, I would have ignored it.'
2 done by you and not by anyone else: He wrote to everyone personally.

personnel [noun]
1 the personnel in a business or organization are the people employed in it or who are part of it
2 personnel is the department in a company that keeps records of all the people who work there and chooses new workers. A personnel department may also be called a **human resources** department

perspective [noun: **perspectives**]
1 the technique of drawing solid objects on a flat surface, so that they appear to have the correct shape and distance from each other
2 if you get a situation into perspective, you do not make it more important than it is
3 a point of view

perspiration [noun] sweat

perspire [verb: **perspires, perspiring, perspired**] to sweat

persuade [verb: **persuades, persuading, persuaded**] to persuade someone is to give them good reasons why they should, or should not, do something
+ **persuasion** [noun] persuading
+ **persuasive** [adjective] a persuasive person or argument can change your mind or make you decide to do something

perturb [verb: **perturbs, perturbing, perturbed**] something perturbs you when it makes you feel uncomfortable and worried
+ **perturbed** [adjective] worried

pessimism [noun] the habit of expecting things to turn out badly. Look up and compare **optimism**
+ **pessimist** [noun: **pessimists**] someone who usually expects bad things to happen
+ **pessimistic** [adjective] expecting that things will turn out badly: a pessimistic outlook

pest [noun: **pests**]
1 a pest is an insect that eats crops and garden plants, or an animal that destroys things
2 someone who is a pest is a nuisance

pester [verb: **pesters, pestering, pestered**] to pester someone is to annoy them continually

pesticide [noun: **pesticides**] a substance used to kill insects that eat or destroy plants and crops

pet [noun: **pets**] a tame animal that you keep in your home
[verb: **pets, petting, petted**] to pet an animal is to pat it and stroke it

petal [noun: **petals**] one of the coloured parts of a flower

peter [verb: **peters, petering, petered**] if something **peters out**, it gradually comes to an end or stop

petite [adjective] a girl or woman who is petite is attractively small or slim

petition [noun: **petitions**] a request for something, especially one signed by many people and sent to a government or someone in authority

petrify [verb: **petrifies, petrifying, petrified**] if something petrifies you, it terrifies you so much that you cannot move

petrochemical [noun: **petrochemicals**] a chemical made from petroleum or natural gas

petrol [noun] a fuel for engines, made from oil

petroleum [noun] an oil found underground or under the seabed and used to make petrol

petticoat [noun: **petticoats**] a piece of clothing that a woman wears under her skirt

petty [adjective: **pettier, pettiest**]
1 having very little importance: petty details
2 if someone is being petty, they concentrate on or criticize small unimportant details

petty cash [noun] small sums of money spent or received by a company or business

Pp

petulance [noun] being petulant
  ◆ **petulant** [adjective] someone who is
petulant is bad-tempered, impatient and huffy,
like a spoilt child
pew [noun: **pews**] a long wooden bench in a
church
pewter [noun] a dull grey metal made from a
mixture of lead and tin
PG [abbreviation] short for **parental
guidance**, a film classification used in Britain
which means that a child can only be allowed
to see the film if an adult is with them
phantom [noun: **phantoms**] a ghost
pharaoh [noun: **pharaohs**] one of the
powerful rulers of ancient Egypt
pharmacist [noun: **pharmacists**] someone
who prepares and sells medicines
  ◆ **pharmacy** [noun: **pharmacies**] a shop
where medicines are prepared and sold
phase [noun: **phases**] a stage in someone's
or something's development or progress
[verb: **phases, phasing, phased**]
1 to **phase something in** is to introduce it
gradually or in stages
2 to **phase something out** is to get rid of it
gradually or in stages
pheasant [noun: **pheasants**] a large bird
with a long tail, that is hunted for sport and
eaten
phenomenal [adjective] extraordinary or
amazing: *The show has been a phenomenal
success.*
  ◆ **phenomenally** [adverb] in a phenomenal
way
phenomenon [noun: **phenomena**]
something that is seen to happen or exist,
especially something that is interesting or
unusual
philosopher [noun: **philosophers**]
someone who studies philosophy
philosophical [adjective]
1 to do with philosophy
2 if you are philosophical about something
such as a disappointment, you stay calm and
are not upset by it
philosophy [noun: **philosophies**]
1 philosophy is the search for knowledge and
truth about the universe and human beings and
their behaviour

2 a philosophy is a set of beliefs
phobia [noun: **phobias**] an unreasonable
fear or hatred of something
phoenix [noun: **phoenixes**] in stories and
myths, a bird that burns itself on a fire and is
born again from its own ashes
phone [noun: **phones**] a telephone
[verb: **phones, phoning, phoned**] to phone
someone is to call them on the telephone
phonecard [noun: **phonecards**] a card that
you use instead of money in a public phone box
phoney or **phony** [adjective: **phonier,
phoniest**] fake or false: *a phoney French
accent*
photo [noun: **photos**] a photograph
photo- [prefix] if a word starts with **photo-**, it
has something to do with light, or photography.
For example, *photosensitive* means sensitive to
light, and *photojournalism* is using pictures or
photographs to report stories that are in the
news
photocopier [noun: **photocopiers**] a
machine that copies a document by taking a
photograph of it
photocopy [noun: **photocopies**] a copy of
a document that you make using a
photocopier
[verb: **photocopies, photocopying,
photocopied**] to make a copy of a document
using a photocopier
photograph [noun: **photographs**] a
picture taken by a camera
[verb: **photographs, photographing,
photographed**] to photograph something is
to take a picture of it using a camera
  ◆ **photographer** [noun: **photographers**]
someone who takes photographs, either as a
hobby or as a profession
  ◆ **photography** [noun] the art of taking
photographs
phrase [noun: **phrases**] a group of words
expressing a single meaning or idea and that is
used on its own or as part of a sentence
physical [adjective]
1 to do with the body: *physical pain*
2 to do with things that you can see or touch,
rather than things that exist only in your mind
physical education [noun] a school
subject in which children learn sports, games

Pp

and exercises and how to keep their bodies fit

physicist [noun: **physicists**] someone who studies physics

physics [noun] the scientific study of things that occur naturally, for example, heat, light, sound, electricity and magnetism

physiotherapist [noun: **physiotherapists**] someone trained in physiotherapy

♦ **physiotherapy** [noun] the treatment of injuries and diseases by physical exercise and massage, rather than drugs

pianist [noun: **pianists**] a musician who plays the piano

piano [noun: **pianos**] a stringed instrument that you sit at and play by pressing the black and white keys on a long keyboard

piccolo [noun: **piccolos**] a type of small flute with a high-pitched sound

pick [verb: **picks, picking, picked**]
1 to pick a person or thing is to choose them
2 to pick something, or **pick it off**, is to lift it off, using your finger and thumb
3 to pick fruit or flowers is to break or pull them off the plant or tree they are growing on
4 to pick a lock is to use a piece of wire to open it
5 to pick a fight or quarrel is to deliberately get someone to fight or quarrel with you
6 to **pick on someone** is to bully them or treat them unkindly
7 to **pick someone up** is to go and fetch them from the place where they are waiting to be collected
8 to **pick something up** is to lift it using your fingers or hands
9 to **pick something up** is to learn it by watching or listening rather than being taught in a lesson
[noun: **picks**]
1 if you have, or take, your pick of things, you choose whichever you like
2 the pick of a group of people or things are the best in that group
→ **picky**

picket [verb: **pickets, picketing, picketed**] to stand outside a factory or other place of work in order to protest about something and to persuade other workers not to go in

pickpocket [noun: **pickpockets**] a criminal who steals things from people's pockets

picky [adjective: **pickier, pickiest**] a person who is picky is fussy and difficult to please

picnic [noun: **picnics**] a meal that you have outdoors
[verb: **picnics, picnicking, picnicked**] to have a picnic
♦ **picnicker** [noun: **picnickers**] people who are having a picnic

pictorial [adjective] having lots of pictures or using pictures to show something

picture [noun: **pictures**]
1 a painting, drawing or photograph
2 an image: *He had a picture in his mind of what he wanted to do.* • *television pictures*
[verb: **pictures, picturing, pictured**] to picture something is to form an image of it in your mind
[adjective] with a picture or pictures: *a picture postcard* • *a picture book*

picturesque [adjective] attractive or interesting to look at: *a picturesque old castle*

pie [noun: **pies**] food baked in a covering of pastry

piebald [adjective] having patches of two different colours, especially black and white: *a piebald horse*

piece [noun: **pieces**]
1 a part or bit of something: *a jigsaw with 300 pieces* • *a piece of cake*
2 something that has been written or composed: *There's a short piece in the paper about our company.* • *He played one of the more romantic pieces.*
3 one of the objects you move about the board in games like chess
4 a coin of a particular value: *a 50p piece*
[verb: **pieces, piecing, pieced**] to **piece things together** is to fit them together to try to make something that is complete

ⓘ Try not to confuse the spelling of **piece** with **peace**, which is quietness and calmness.

piecemeal [adjective] doing things a little bit at a time and in no particular order: *a piecemeal approach to policy-making*

pier [noun: **piers**]
1 a platform of stone or wood by a lake or the

sea, where boats and ships can tie up

2 a long platform built out over the sea that people can walk along at a seaside town

pierce [verb: **pierces, piercing, pierced**] a sharp object pierces something when it goes in or through it

♦ **piercing** [adjective] a piercing sound is very sharp and seems to travel through solid objects

pig [noun: **pigs**] an animal with a broad heavy body, small eyes and a snout

pigeon [noun: **pigeons**] a bird with a plump body and a small head, often seen in towns and cities or kept for racing

pigeon-hole [noun: **pigeon-holes**] one of a series of boxes or compartments, each for a different person, used to put their letters or messages in

[verb: **pigeon-holes, pigeon-holing, pigeon-holed**] to pigeon-hole someone is to decide what type of person they are without taking the time to consider them properly

piggy-back [noun: **piggy-backs**] someone gives you a piggy-back when they carry you on their back with their arms supporting your legs

pig-headed [adjective] a pig-headed person will not change their opinions even if it is obvious that they are not right

piglet [noun: **piglets**] a baby pig

pigment [noun: **pigments**]

1 any substance used for colouring or making paint or dye

2 the substance in your skin that gives it its colour

pigmy [noun: **pigmies**] another spelling of **pygmy**

pigsty [noun: **pigsties**]

1 an enclosure where pigs are kept

2 a dirty or very untidy place

pigtail [noun: **pigtails**] hair that has been plaited and hangs down at the side or back of the head

pike [noun: **pike** or **pikes**] a large fish that lives in freshwater lakes

pilchard [noun: **pilchards**] a small sea fish rather like a herring, that you eat fresh or buy packed in tins

pile [noun: **piles**]

1 a heap or stack of things one on top of the other

2 piles of something means a lot of it: *I've got piles of work to do.*

[verb: **piles, piling, piled**] to put things one on top of the other in a heap or stack

piles [plural noun] painful swollen veins in your bottom

ⓘ **Piles** is quite an informal word. The word that a doctor would use is **haemorrhoids**.

pilfer [verb: **pilfers, pilfering, pilfered**] to pilfer is to steal small amounts or small items

pilgrim [noun: **pilgrims**] a person who is travelling to a holy place

♦ **pilgrimage** [noun: **pilgrimages**] a journey that someone makes to a holy place

pill [noun: **pills**]

1 a small tablet of medicine

2 **the pill** is a tablet that some women take every day to stop themselves becoming pregnant: *women who are on the pill*

pillage [verb: **pillages, pillaging, pillaged**] when invaders or enemies pillage they steal things from the place they have invaded or conquered

[noun] pillage is taking things from people or places during an invasion or war

pillar [noun: **pillars**] an upright post used in building as a support or decoration

pillarbox [noun: **pillarboxes**] a metal container in the street for posting letters in

pillion [noun: **pillions**] a seat for a passenger behind the rider of a bicycle or motorbike

pillow [noun: **pillows**] a large soft cushion that you lay your head on when you are in bed

pillowcase or **pillowslip** [noun: **pillowcases** or **pillowslips**] a cloth covering for a pillow

pilot [noun: **pilots**] someone who flies a plane, or who guides a ship into and out of a harbour

[verb: **pilots, piloting, piloted**] to pilot a plane is to operate its controls

pilot light [noun: **pilot lights**] a flame that burns inside a gas boiler or water heater and which ignites gas burners when the boiler or heater is in use

Pp

pimple [noun: **pimples**] a raised spot on the skin

PIN [abbreviation] short for **personal identification number**, which is a secret number that every person with a card for an automatic cash machine is given so that they can get money out of their bank account

pin [noun: **pins**] a short thin pointed piece of metal for pushing through fabric or paper to hold it in place
[verb: **pins, pinning, pinned**]
1 to pin something is to fasten it or hold it in place with a pin: *She pinned the map to the wall.*
2 to pin someone somewhere is to hold them firmly so that they cannot move: *They pinned me to the ground.*

pinafore [noun: **pinafores**] a sleeveless dress, worn over a blouse or jumper

pinball [noun] a game played on a slot machine in which a ball is struck by little paddles and runs down a sloping board between obstacles into holes

pincers [plural noun]
1 a tool for gripping things tightly
2 a lobster's or crab's claws

pinch [verb: **pinches, pinching, pinched**]
1 to pinch someone is to squeeze their skin or flesh tightly between your thumb and forefinger
2 if a shoe or piece of clothing pinches, it hurts you because it is too small or tight
3 to pinch something is to steal it
[noun: **pinches**]
1 a small amount that you can pick up between your finger and thumb: *add a pinch of salt*
2 a nip with the thumb and forefinger
3 if someone **feels the pinch**, they are having problems because they do not have enough money
• **pinched** [adjective] if someone's face is pinched, it looks thin and pale because of cold or illness

pine [noun: **pines**] a tall evergreen tree with cones and needle-like leaves
[adjective] made from the wood of a pine tree: *pine furniture*

pine [verb: **pines, pining, pined**]
1 to **pine for** something is to long for it

2 to **pine away** is to become weaker and weaker because of grief for a person or thing you have lost

pineapple [noun: **pineapples**] a large fruit with sweet firm yellow flesh and a tough brown skin divided into small diamond shapes

ping [verb: **pings, pinging, pinged**]
1 to make a noise like a small hard object bouncing off metal
2 to ping something like a wire or piece of elastic is to pull it so that it bends or stretches, and then let it go suddenly so that it makes a sharp noise
[noun: **pings**] a pinging noise: *electronic pings and bleeps*

ping-pong [noun] another name for the game of table-tennis

pink [noun] a pale red colour with a lot of white in it

pinnacle [noun: **pinnacles**]
1 a high pointed rock or mountain, or a tall thin spire built on the roof of a church or castle
2 the highest point of something: *the pinnacle of his acting career*

pint [noun: **pints**] a measurement of liquid equal to 0.57 of a litre. There are 8 pints in a gallon

pioneer [verb: **pioneers, pioneering, pioneered**] to pioneer something is to be the first to do or make it
[noun: **pioneers**]
1 someone who is one of the first people to go to a new country to live and work there
2 a person who is the first to develop a new skill or method

pious [adjective] a pious person takes religious rules and morals very seriously and always thinks and acts in a good and religious way

pip [noun: **pips**] a small seed from fruits like apples and oranges

pipe [noun: **pipes**]
1 a metal or plastic tube through which water or gas can flow
2 a tube with a hollow bowl at one end used for smoking tobacco
3 an instrument that you play by blowing air into one end of a hollow tube
[verb: **pipes, piping, piped**]

Pp

1 to pipe liquid or gas is to carry it from one place to another through pipes
2 to play a pipe or bagpipes
3 to **pipe down** is to be quiet
4 someone **pipes up** when they suddenly say something after they have been quiet for a while

pipeline [noun: **pipelines**]
1 a long pipe that crosses the land or sea and carries oil or gas
2 if something is **in the pipeline**, it is being dealt with or is going to happen

piper [noun: **pipers**] someone who plays a pipe or bagpipes

piping [noun] piping is playing the bagpipes

piping hot [adjective] boiling or nearly boiling: a bowl of piping hot soup

piracy [noun]
1 illegal copying of things such as CDs, DVDs and computer software
2 robbery from ships while they are sailing

piranha [noun: **piranhas**] a small fierce fish that lives in rivers in South America

pirate [noun: **pirates**]
1 someone who robs ships while they are sailing
2 someone who makes illegal copies of things such as CDs, DVDs and computer software
➡ **piracy**

pirouette [noun: **pirouettes**] a dance movement in which you spin round very fast while standing on one leg
[verb: **pirouettes, pirouetting, pirouetted**] to pirouette is to spin your body in a full circle once or several times

pistol [noun: **pistols**] a small gun that is held in one hand

piston [noun: **pistons**] a round piece of metal that fits inside a cylinder in an engine and moves up and down or backwards and forwards inside it

pit [noun: **pits**]
1 a large deep hole in the ground
2 a deep mine, especially a coal mine
3 **the pits** is the place at the side of a motor-racing track where the cars can stop to get fuel or have their tyres changed
[verb: **pits, pitting, pitted**] to **pit someone against** another person is to make them fight or compete with each other

pitch[1] [noun: **pitches**]
1 an area of ground, often with special lines marked on it, used to play games like football, rugby or cricket
2 a sound's pitch is how high or low it is
3 the level or intensity that something reaches: The excitement reached fever pitch when Zidane headed the ball into the net.
[verb: **pitches, pitching, pitched**]
1 to pitch a tent is to erect it and set up camp
2 to pitch something at a particular level is to set it or direct it at that level: She pitched her voice low. • The programme is pitched at children under 2.
3 to pitch forward is to fall forward suddenly
4 if a ship pitches, it goes up and down from front to back as it moves forward
5 in baseball, you pitch when you are the player who throws the ball at the batting team
6 to **pitch in** is to join in or make a contribution to something

pitch[2] [noun] pitch is a black sticky substance made from tar
[adjective] it is pitch dark when it is very dark and you can see nothing

pitched battle [noun: **pitched battles**] a pitched battle is a fierce fight or argument

pitcher [noun: **pitchers**] a large jug

pitchfork [noun: **pitchforks**] a tool with two prongs and a long handle, used to lift hay and straw

pitfall [noun: **pitfalls**] a possible danger or difficulty, or a mistake that can be made easily

pith [noun] pith is the white layer between the skin and the flesh of an orange or other citrus fruit

pitiful [adjective]
1 sad and pathetic: a pitiful sight
2 of such poor quality that it makes you feel contempt: a pitiful excuse

pittance [noun] a very small sum of money

pitted [adjective] covered with small dents

pity [noun]
1 pity is sorrow you feel for other people's troubles or difficulties
2 you say that something is a pity if you are sorry about it: It's a pity that John can't come.
3 to **take pity on someone** is to feel so sorry

Pp

for them that you help them or give them something

[verb: **pities, pitying, pitied**] to pity someone is to feel sorry for them

pivot [noun: **pivots**] a pin or centre on which something balances and turns

[verb: **pivots, pivoting, pivoted**] to pivot is to turn or revolve while balancing on a central point

pixel [noun: **pixels**] one of the tiny elements that pictures on a computer or TV screen are made up of, with each pixel occupying a unit of computer memory

pixie [noun: **pixies**] in stories, a small good fairy or elf

pizza [noun: **pizzas**] a flat round piece of dough topped with cheese, tomatoes and herbs and baked in an oven

placard [noun: **placards**] a board with a notice or message on it that is carried by someone in public

place [noun: **places**]

1 a particular area or position: *a place by the sea* • *Put the books back in their proper place on the shelf.* • *I imagine Beijing is a very interesting place.*

2 a seat, or a space at a table for someone to sit and eat: *Please go back to your places and sit down.*

3 a position in an order, series or queue: *She was in first place after the second round.*

4 in place of means 'instead of': *Kelly's here in place of John who is ill.* • *You could use plain yogurt in place of cream.*

5 you feel **out of place** when you feel that you do not fit in with the people or things around you

6 something is **out of place** when it is not in its usual position: *The books were all out of place.*

[verb: **places, placing, placed**]

1 to place something somewhere is to put it there

2 to place someone in a certain position is to put them there: *He had placed me in a very awkward spot by promising that I would go to the party.*

3 to place a bet or an order is to make a bet or an order

placement [noun: **placements**] a

temporary job that allows someone to get experience of working

placid [adjective] gentle and calm

plague [noun: **plagues**]

1 a large number of insects or other pests that suddenly appear and cause damage or a nuisance

2 the plague is a disease that spreads rapidly and kills many people

[verb: **plagues, plaguing, plagued**] something plagues you when it causes you a lot of discomfort or annoyance

plaice [noun: **plaice**] a type of flat fish found in the sea

plaid [noun: **plaids**] a long piece of cloth, especially with a tartan pattern, that people in Scottish Highland costume wear over their shoulders

plain [adjective: **plainer, plainest**]

1 without any decoration or without a pattern: *a plain white room*

2 simple or ordinary: *good plain cooking*

3 easy to see or understand: *He made it quite plain that he didn't like me.*

4 straightforward: *That's just plain nonsense.*

[noun: **plains**] a large flat area of land

plait [noun: **plaits**] lengths of something such as hair or straw that are twisted over each other in turn

[verb: **plaits, plaiting, plaited**] to twist strands of hair or straw in this way

plan [verb: **plans, planning, planned**]

1 to plan something is to work out how it may be done or make the arrangements to do it

2 to plan something such as a building is to design it

3 to plan to do something is to decide to do it at some time before you actually do it

[noun: **plans**]

1 an idea of how to do something or a method worked out for doing it

2 a drawing showing the layout of a building or town as if you are looking at it from above

plane[1] [noun: **planes**] an aeroplane

plane[2] [noun: **planes**]

1 a carpenter's tool with a cutting blade set in a frame, used for making a level or smooth surface

2 a flat or level surface: *A cube has six planes.*

[verb: **planes, planing, planed**] to plane wood is to make it smooth and level using a plane

ⓘ Be careful not to confuse the spelling of **plane** with **plain**, which means ordinary.

planet [noun: **planets**] any of the large objects in space that orbit round a sun. The planets that orbit round our sun are Mercury, Venus, Earth, Mars, Jupiter, Saturn, Uranus, Neptune and Pluto
• **planetary** [adjective] to do with the planets, especially those in our own solar system

plank [noun: **planks**] a long flat piece of wood

plant [noun: **plants**]
1 any living thing that grows from the ground and has a stem, roots and leaves
2 a factory or industrial building
[verb: **plants, planting, planted**]
1 to plant seed or plants is to put them in the ground so that they grow
2 to plant something is to place or fix it firmly: *He planted his feet on either side of the rope and pulled as hard as he could.*

plantation [noun: **plantations**] a piece of land where a certain crop is grown or where trees are planted

plaque [noun: **plaques**]
1 a plaque is a metal plate with writing on it, fixed to a wall and usually put up to remember a famous person or event
2 plaque is a substance that forms on teeth and can cause tooth decay

plasma [noun] the clear liquid part of blood

plaster [noun: **plasters**]
1 plaster is a thin paste put on walls that dries to form a hard smooth surface
2 a plaster is a sticky dressing that you put over a scratch or wound to protect it from germs
[verb: **plasters, plastering, plastered**]
1 to apply plaster to walls
2 to plaster a surface is to cover it with thick liquid: *paper plastered with paint*
➡ **plasterer**

plaster cast [noun: **plaster casts**] a hard casing put around a broken limb to support it while the bone heals

plasterer [noun: **plasterers**] someone whose job is to plaster walls

plaster of Paris [noun] a type of white plaster that dries out quickly and is used to make models or plaster casts for broken bones

plastic [noun: **plastics**] a substance made from chemicals that can be moulded while it is still soft and stretched to make objects
[adjective] made from plastic: *plastic toys*

plastic surgery [noun] an operation to improve a patient's appearance or to repair scars

plate [noun: **plates**]
1 a shallow dish for holding food
2 a thin flat sheet of metal or some other hard substance
3 a large picture or photograph in a book
4 one of the large areas of rock that make up the Earth's surface and that move very slowly under or over each other
[verb: **plates, plating, plated**] to plate an object is to cover it with a thin layer of metal, for example, silver or tin

plateau [noun: **plateaus** or **plateaux**] a broad, fairly flat area of land that is higher than the land around it on at least one side

plate-glass [noun] glass made in thick sheets and used for shop windows and mirrors

platform [noun: **platforms**]
1 a raised floor from which performers or speakers can be seen by an audience
2 a raised area beside the tracks at a railway station, where passengers can get on and off trains
3 a floating structure used as a base for drilling for oil

platinum [noun] a silvery-white precious metal

platoon [noun: **platoons**] a group of soldiers

platter [noun: **platters**] a large flat dish used for serving food

play [verb: **plays, playing, played**]
1 to play is to spend time amusing yourself with games or toys: *The children were playing in the garden.*
2 you play a game when you take part in it: *He plays cricket on Saturdays.*
3 to play a musical instrument is to make music with it

Pp

4 to play a DVD, CD or tape is to put it into the player and listen to it or watch it
5 an actor plays a particular part when he or she acts that part
6 to **play a part in** something is to be one of the people involved in it
7 to **play down** a success or a problem is to make it seem less impressive or serious
8 to **play safe** is to take no risks
9 a child **plays up** when they behave badly
10 a part of your body **plays up** when it is causing you pain: *My back's playing up again.*
11 a machine **plays up** when it is not working properly
[noun: **plays**]
1 play is having fun with games and toys: *learning through play*
2 play is the action that goes on in a sports game: *Rain stopped play.*
3 a play is a story acted out in the theatre or on TV or radio
+ **player** [noun: **players**]
1 someone who plays a game
2 a machine for playing DVDs, CDs, tapes or records
+ **playful** [adjective] full of fun or wanting to play
playground [noun: **playgrounds**] an area, for example beside a school or in a public park, where children can play
playgroup [noun: **playgroups**] an organized group where very young children can play and learn together
playing-card [noun: **playing-cards**] a card from a set of 52, made up of four suits of 13 cards: clubs, diamonds, hearts and spades
playmate [noun: **playmates**] someone a child plays with
play-off [noun: **play-offs**] an extra match or game played to decide the winner from two players or teams with equal points in a competition
playschool [noun: **playschools**] a nursery school or playgroup
playwright [noun: **playwrights**] someone who writes plays
plc [abbreviation: **plcs**] short for **public limited company**, a company with shares that people can buy

plea [noun: **pleas**]
1 an urgent and emotional request for something
2 someone charged with a crime makes a plea when they state to a court whether they are guilty or not guilty
plead [verb: **pleads, pleading, pleaded** or **pled**]
1 to plead is to try to persuade someone in an urgent and emotional way, because you want something very much
2 to plead in a court is to answer a charge, saying 'guilty' or 'not guilty'
pleasant [adjective]
1 something pleasant gives you a feeling of enjoyment and happiness
2 a pleasant person has a friendly and likeable manner
+ **pleasantly** [adverb] in a pleasant way: *His laugh was pleasantly like a chuckle.*
please [verb: **pleases, pleasing, pleased**]
1 to please someone is to do what they want or to give them pleasure or satisfaction
2 to do **as you please** is to do exactly as you want, not thinking what other people may want
[adverb and interjection] a polite word you use when you are asking for something or accepting an offer: *Please don't park in front of the driveway.* • *'Would you like another biscuit?' 'Yes, please.'*
+ **pleasing** [adjective] giving pleasure or satisfaction: *a pleasing result*
pleasurable [adjective] giving pleasure or enjoyment
pleasure [noun: **pleasures**]
1 a feeling of enjoyment or satisfaction, or something that gives you this feeling
2 pleasure is time spent enjoying yourself rather than working: *Is your trip business or pleasure?*
pleat [noun: **pleats**] a fold sewn or pressed into a piece of cloth
+ **pleated** [adjective] having folds or folded lines: *a pleated skirt*
plectrum [noun: **plectrums**] a small hard piece of plastic or metal used to pick the strings of a guitar
pledge [noun: **pledges**] a solemn promise
[verb: **pledges, pledging, pledged**] to

Pp

pledge to do something is to promise solemnly to do it

plentiful [adjective] something is plentiful when there is a good supply of it or it exists in large amounts

plenty [noun]

1 as much as you need: *You have plenty of time to complete the test.*

2 a large amount or number: *There's plenty more bread in the freezer if we run out.*

ⓘ If the noun with **plenty** is singular, you use a singular verb: *Plenty of money **is** being made available to spend on computer equipment.* If the noun is plural, you use a plural verb: *There **are** plenty of people who don't have access to a computer.*

pliable [adjective] easy to bend or shape without breaking

pliant [adjective] easy to bend, or easy to influence

pliers [plural noun] pliers are a tool with two flat surfaces that come together to grip things

plight [noun: **plights**] a bad condition or situation

plimsolls [plural noun] light rubber-soled canvas shoes worn for gymnastics

plod [verb: **plods, plodding, plodded**]

1 to walk slowly as if your feet and legs are heavy

2 to work slowly but steadily, especially on a job that you find boring

plonk [noun: **plonks**] a sound made by something dropping heavily

[verb: **plonks, plonking, plonked**] to plonk something somewhere is to put it down heavily: *He plonked himself down on the sofa and turned on the telly.*

plop [noun: **plops**] the sound of a small or light object dropping into water: *The frog jumped back into the pond with a plop.*

[verb: **plops, plopping, plopped**] to plop is to fall or drop making this sound

plot [noun: **plots**]

1 a secret plan, especially for doing something illegal or evil

2 the story of a play, novel or film

3 a small piece of land to be used as a

gardening area or for building a house on: *a vegetable plot*

[verb: **plots, plotting, plotted**]

1 to plan to do something illegal or evil

2 to plot things on a graph is to mark them as points on the graph and then make a connecting line between the points

plough [noun: **ploughs**] a farm tool with a heavy blade which is pulled through the top layer of the soil to turn it over or break it up

[verb: **ploughs, ploughing, ploughed**]

1 to plough is to turn over soil with a plough

2 to **plough through** work is to do your work slowly and with difficulty until you reach the end

plover [noun: **plovers**] a wading bird that nests on open ground

ploy [noun: **ploys**] a carefully thought-out plan or method of achieving something

pluck [verb: **plucks, plucking, plucked**]

1 to pluck something is to take hold of it and pull it sharply so that it comes out or off

2 to pluck a chicken or turkey is to pull its feathers off before cooking it

[noun] a rather old-fashioned word for courage

♦ **plucky** [adjective: **pluckier, pluckiest**] having courage

plug [noun: **plugs**]

1 an object attached to an electrical appliance by a wire and which you fit into a socket in the wall so that an electric current can reach the appliance

2 an object that you use for blocking a hole, especially in a bath or sink to stop the water from running away

[verb: **plugs, plugging, plugged**]

1 to plug a hole or gap is to push something into it to block it

2 to plug something new is to mention it so that people know about it: *The author plugged his new book during the interview.*

plum [noun: **plums**] a soft red or yellow fruit with a smooth skin and a stone in the centre

plumage [noun] a bird's plumage is its covering of feathers

plumb [noun: **plumbs**] a small weight that is hung on a string and used to test if a wall or other upright structure is straight

[verb: **plumbs, plumbing, plumbed**]
1 to **plumb the depths** of something is to reach its deepest or lowest point
2 to **plumb in** something such as a washing machine is to connect it to the water supply
[adjective] perfectly straight or vertical

plumber [noun: **plumbers**] someone whose job is to fit and repair water, gas and sewage pipes

◆ **plumbing** [noun]
1 the work of a plumber
2 the plumbing in a building is the system of pipes that carry water and gas

plume [noun: **plumes**] a long broad feather, or something that has the shape of a long broad feather: *ostrich plumes* • *a plume of smoke*
➡ **plumage**

plummet [verb: **plummets, plummeting, plummeted**] to plummet is to fall very fast

plump [adjective: **plumper, plumpest**] fat or rounded, in a pleasant way: *plump rosy cheeks*
[verb: **plumps, plumping, plumped**]
1 to **plump up** cushions or pillows is to squash and shake them so that they become rounded
2 to **plump for** something is to choose it

plunder [verb: **plunders, plundering, plundered**] to plunder is to rob or steal from a place, especially taking everything valuable that is there
[noun] plundering, or the things got by plundering

plunge [verb: **plunge, plunging, plunged**]
1 to plunge is to dive: *He plunged off the high board.* • *She plunged into the crowd, pushing her way through.*
2 to plunge something into water is to push it quickly into the water so that it is covered
3 to plunge something into something else is to push it violently or suddenly into that thing: *The pirate plunged his dagger into the sack, spilling the contents all over the deck.*
[noun: **plunges**] a dive

plural [noun: **plurals**] a plural is the form of a noun, pronoun or verb that you use when there is more than one of something. For example, *feet* is the plural of *foot* and *toes* is the plural of *toe*
[adjective] in the plural form

plus [preposition]
1 adding: *8 plus 2 is 10*
2 as well as: *There are six children, plus two adults.*
[adjective]
1 more than zero: *plus ten degrees*
2 plus is used after a letter or number to show that a mark or number is more than the mark or number indicated by the letter or number alone: *He got a B plus for his project.* • *You have to be 60 plus to join the club.*
[noun: **pluses**] a plus, or plus sign (+), is a mathematical symbol showing that a number is to be added to another

plush [adjective: **plusher, plushest**] plush places are very smart, elegant and expensive

ply [noun: **plies**]
1 a thickness of yarn or rope, measured by the number of strands it is made of: *two-ply wool*
2 plywood

plywood [noun] a material made up of thin layers of wood glued together

PM [abbreviation] short for **Prime Minister**

pm or **p.m.** [abbreviation] **pm** is added after the time to show that the time is in the afternoon or evening rather than the morning, for example *2pm.* Look up and compare **am**²

ⓘ **pm** is short for **post meridiem**, which is Latin for 'after midday'.

PMT or **PMS** [abbreviation] short for **pre-menstrual tension** or **pre-menstrual syndrome**, the unpleasant feelings that some women have every month before their period

pneumatic [adjective]
1 filled with air: *pneumatic tyres*
2 worked by air pressure or compressed air: *a pneumatic drill*

pneumonia [noun] a serious infection of the lungs which makes breathing difficult and painful

poach [verb: **poaches, poaching, poached**]
1 to hunt and kill fish, birds or animals without permission on someone else's land
2 to poach food is to cook it by heating it gently in water or some other liquid

◆ **poacher** [noun: **poachers**] someone who hunts and kills fish or game illegally

pocket [noun: **pockets**]
1 an extra piece of cloth sewn into a piece of clothing and used for keeping small items in, like money or keys
2 any pouch-like container, for example, in a suitcase or car door, or at the sides of a snooker table
3 the amount of money you have or can afford: *presents to suit every pocket*
4 a small isolated area or group: *pockets of mist*
5 if you are **out of pocket**, you have lost money as the result of a deal
[verb: **pockets, pocketing, pocketed**] to pocket something is to put it in your pocket, or to take it and keep it for yourself, especially dishonestly

pocket-book [noun: **pocket-books**] the American English word for a **wallet**

pocket money [noun] an allowance of money that parents give their children to buy small things such as sweets or magazines

pockmark [noun: **pockmarks**] a scar or dent left in the skin by a disease or spots

pod [noun: **pods**] a long narrow seed case that grows on plants like peas and beans

podgy [adjective: **podgier, podgiest**] slightly fat

podium [noun: **podiums**] a small platform that someone stands on, for example an orchestra's conductor or a speaker at a public meeting

poem [noun: **poems**] a piece of writing in imaginative language arranged in patterns of lines and sounds, often, but not always, rhyming

poet [noun: **poets**] someone who writes poetry
♦ **poetic** [adjective] written in verse, or having qualities of beauty and imagination like poetry
♦ **poetry** [noun] poems as a group or as a form of literature. Look up and compare **prose**

poignant [adjective] something poignant makes you feel great sadness or pity

point [noun: **points**]
1 a sharp end: *the point of a needle*
2 a small dot (.) used in decimal fractions
3 a particular place or a particular moment:

the highest point on the British mainland • *At that point, we all burst out laughing.*
4 a mark used to score a competition, game or test: *Who got the highest number of points?*
5 your good points and bad points are your personal qualities or characteristics
6 a fact, idea or opinion that is a part of an argument or discussion, or the most important part of what is being said: *What's your point?*
7 the point of doing something is its purpose: *What's the point of going home if you just have to go straight back out again?*
[verb: **points, pointing, pointed**]
1 to point is to stretch your finger in the direction of something to show other people what or where you mean
2 to point something is to aim it in a particular direction: *He pointed the gun at the target.*
3 to **point to** something is to show that it is true or to explain it: *All the evidence points to an inside job.*

point-blank [adjective and adverb]
1 in an abrupt or rude way: *She refused point-blank to come.*
2 very close: *The gun was fired at point-blank range.*

pointed [adjective] with a sharp end: *a pointed stick*

pointer [noun: **pointers**]
1 a long instrument used to point at things, for example on a wall map or blackboard
2 the needle on a dial

pointless [adjective] having no purpose or meaning: *a pointless argument*

point of view [noun: **points of view**] your point of view is your opinion or judgement about something

poise [noun]
1 to have poise is to have dignity and self-confidence
2 poise is a graceful way of moving, sitting or standing
[verb: **poises, poising, poised**] to be poised somewhere is to balance there ready to move or take off: *He was poised on the edge of the diving board.*
♦ **poised** [adjective] someone who is poised is dignified and self-confident

poison [noun: **poisons**] any substance that

Pp

causes death or illness when taken into your body

[verb: **poisons, poisoning, poisoned**]

1 to poison a person or animal is to kill or harm them with poison

2 to poison something is to add poison to it

✦ poisonous [adjective]

1 a poisonous substance causes illness or death when taken into your body: *This cleaning liquid is poisonous.*

2 producing poison: *a poisonous snake*

poke [verb: **pokes, poking, poked**]

1 to poke someone or something is to push something sharp into them: *He poked me in the ribs.*

2 to poke something through a gap or hole is to stick it through: *She poked her head through the hatch.*

[noun: **pokes**] a sharp prod

✦ poker [noun: **pokers**]

1 a poker is a heavy metal rod used for moving wood or coal about in a fire

2 poker is a card game played for money

poky [adjective: **pokier, pokiest**] a poky place is small and uncomfortable

polar [adjective] at or to do with the north or south pole

polar bear [noun: **polar bears**] a large white bear that lives in the Arctic

Polaroid [noun] a type of photograph that is developed inside the camera. This word is a trademark

pole¹ [noun: **poles**] a long thin rounded piece of wood or metal

pole² [noun: **poles**]

1 the north and south poles are the two points on the Earth at the north and south end of its axis

2 either of the opposite ends of a magnet

polecat [noun: **polecats**] an animal like a large weasel

pole vault [noun: **pole vaults**] an athletic event in which competitors try to jump over a high bar by pushing themselves up and over it with a long flexible pole

police [noun] the police are the people whose job is to prevent crime, keep order and make sure that laws are obeyed

policeman [noun: **policemen**] a male police officer

police officer [noun: **police officers**] a member of the police, both the uniformed officers and detectives in plain clothes

police station [noun: **police stations**] a building where the police have their offices and where people are taken when they are arrested

policewoman [noun: **policewomen**] a female police officer

policy [noun: **policies**]

1 a planned or agreed course of action: *government policies*

2 a contract between you and an insurance company: *The policy covers theft and damage to your car.*

polio [noun] polio is a serious disease that affects the nerves and muscles and can cause paralysis. Nowadays, polio is very rare because most children are vaccinated against it

polish [verb: **polishes, polishing, polished**]

1 to polish something is to rub it until it shines

2 to **polish something off** is to eat or drink it until it is completely finished: *She polished off the chocolate cake.*

[noun: **polishes**] a substance used to polish wood or metal

polite [adjective: **politer, politest**] a polite person has good manners

✦ politely [adverb] in a well-mannered way: *'Would you like a seat?' he asked her politely.*

✦ politeness [noun] being polite

political [adjective] to do with politics, politicians or government

politician [noun: **politicians**] someone involved in politics, especially someone who has been elected to a parliament or local council

politics [noun] politics is the study of the ways in which countries are governed, or the work of governing a country

polka [noun: **polkas**] a kind of fast lively dance, or music for this dance

poll [noun: **polls**]

1 a political election in which people vote, or the number of votes cast in an election

2 a poll is a survey of people picked at random

to find out what the general public opinion of something is

pollen [noun] the powder, often yellow, that a flower releases and which fertilizes the female part of the plant

pollinate [verb: **pollinates, pollinating, pollinated**] a plant is pollinated when pollen fertilizes it and its fruit and seeds begin to form
• **pollination** [noun] when pollen from a male flower lands on the female part of a plant and fruit and seeds begin to form

polling station [noun: **polling stations**] the building where you go to vote in an election

pollute [verb: **pollutes, polluting, polluted**] to pollute the air, the soil or a river is to release harmful substances into it
• **pollution** [noun] the release of harmful chemicals and other substances into the air, water or soil

polo [noun] a game played on horseback by two teams of players who hit a ball along the ground using long-handled hammers called mallets

polo neck [noun: **polo necks**] a jumper with a high round neck

poltergeist [noun: **poltergeists**] a type of ghost that is believed to move or throw objects around, or cause strange things to happen in a house

poly- [prefix] if a word starts with **poly-**, it adds the meaning 'many' to the word. For example, a *polygon* is a figure with many sides and angles

polyester [noun] polyester is a man-made fabric used for making clothes

polystyrene [noun] a very light plastic substance like stiff foam, used for packaging and insulation

polythene [noun] a very thin plastic material used for making bags, light containers and protective coverings

pomp [noun] pomp is solemn and splendid display or ceremony

pompous [adjective] a pompous person is too full of their own importance

poncho [noun: **ponchos**] a loose piece of clothing covering the shoulders and top half of the body which has a hole for your head to go through

pond [noun: **ponds**] a small area of water, smaller than a lake and larger than a pool

ponder [verb: **ponders, pondering, pondered**] to think about something carefully and for a long time

pontoon [noun] a card game where you try to collect cards that add up to 21

pony [noun: **ponies**] a type of small horse

pony-tail [noun: **pony-tails**] a hairstyle in which the hair is gathered up at the back of the head and tied so that it hangs down like a tail

pony-trekking [noun] travelling across the countryside, often for quite long distances, on ponies

poodle [noun: **poodles**] a breed of dog with curly hair, often clipped in a fancy way

pool[1] [noun: **pools**]
1 a pond or puddle, or any other small area of still water
2 a swimming pool

pool[2] [noun: **pools**]
1 a group of people or things shared by several people: *a typing pool • a car pool*
2 the money played for in a gambling game
[verb: **pools, pooling, pooled**] to pool things is to put them all together into one large fund or group that everyone can use or benefit from

poor [adjective: **poorer, poorest**]
1 a poor person has very little money or property
2 of a low standard: *a poor imitation*
3 you call a person or animal 'poor' when you think they deserve pity or sympathy: *The poor little thing is all wet.*
• **poorly** [adverb] badly: *a poorly lit passage*
[adjective: **poorlier, poorliest**] ill: *Grant's feeling a bit poorly today.*

pop[1] [noun: **pops**]
1 a pop is a sudden sound like a small explosion
2 pop is a fizzy drink
[verb: **pops, popping, popped**]
1 to pop is to make a sudden sound like a small explosion
2 something pops out when it comes out suddenly

pop[2] [noun] popular music

popadom or **popadum** or **poppadom** [noun: **popadoms** or **popadums** or **poppadoms**] in Indian cookery, a very thin circle of dough fried in oil until it is crisp

popcorn [noun] the seeds of maize that burst open into crisp fluffy balls when they are heated

pope [noun: **popes**] the head of the Catholic Church

poppy [noun: **poppies**] a tall flower that grows wild in fields and has broad, flat, red petals

popular [adjective] something that is popular is liked by a lot of people: *a popular make of car*
+ **popularity** [noun] the popularity of something is how many people like it
+ **popularize** or **popularise** [verb: **popularizes, popularizing, popularized**] to popularize something is to make it popular

populate [verb: **populates, populating, populated**] people or animals populate an area when they live there
+ **populated** [adjective] a populated area has a lot of people living in it
+ **population** [noun: **populations**] the population of an area is the number or type of people living in it

porcelain [noun] a type of fine china used to make crockery and ornaments
[adjective] made from porcelain: *a porcelain doll*

porch [noun: **porches**] a small roofed entrance to a building

porcupine [noun: **porcupines**] an animal that has lots of long sharp spines called quills growing on its back

pore[1] [noun: **pores**] one of the tiny holes in your skin that sweat comes out of

pore[2] [verb: **pores, poring, pored**] to **pore over** books or documents is to read them very closely and carefully, giving them your full attention

pork [noun] meat from a pig

porn [noun] an informal word for **pornography**
[adjective] an informal word for **pornographic**

pornographic [adjective] pornographic pictures, magazines and films show sexual activities in a very obvious way which is intended to make you feel sexually excited

pornography [noun] pornographic pictures, magazines and films

porous [adjective] a porous material lets liquids and gases pass through it

porpoise [noun: **porpoises**] a large sea mammal, similar to a dolphin but with a shorter and rounder nose

porridge [noun] a food made by boiling oats in water or milk, often eaten for breakfast

port [noun: **ports**]
1 a place where ships can load and unload, or shelter during stormy weather
2 a town or city with a harbour
[adjective] the port side of a ship or aircraft is the left side when you are facing the front. Look up and compare **starboard**

portable [adjective] something portable can be carried around: *a portable television*

porter [noun: **porters**]
1 someone whose job is to carry baggage for people at railway stations or on long treks
2 a caretaker at a college, office or factory

portfolio [noun: **portfolios**]
1 a flat case for carrying papers or drawings
2 an artist's portfolio is a collection of drawings, paintings or sketches that represent their work

porthole [noun: **portholes**] a round window in the side of a ship

portion [noun: **portions**] a portion of something is one of several pieces or parts it can be or is divided into: *a portion of land*

portly [adjective: **portlier, portliest**] a portly person is rather fat, especially round their middle

portrait [noun: **portraits**]
1 a painting, drawing or photograph of a person
2 a description in words of a person, place or thing

portray [verb: **portrays, portraying, portrayed**]
1 to portray a person or thing is to make a picture or written description of them or it
2 an actor portrays a person or an emotion

Pp

when they act the part of that person or act out that emotion

◆ **portrayal** [noun: **portrayals**] a description or representation of something, especially in words

pose [verb: **poses, posing, posed**]

1 to pose for a photo or portrait is to stay in a particular position so that the photographer or artist can take or paint your picture

2 to **pose as** something is to pretend to be that person or thing: *a thief posing as a gas repair man*

3 to pose a question or problem is to ask a question or put a problem to someone

[noun: **poses**]

1 a particular position into which you put your body

2 pretence or exaggerated behaviour intended to impress people: *He's not tough at all. It's all just a pose.*

◆ **poser** [noun: **posers**]

1 a poser is a question or problem that is difficult to answer or solve

2 someone who pretends to be something they are not, just to impress other people

posh [adjective: **posher, poshest**]

1 a posh place is very smart and expensive: *a posh hotel*

2 a posh person is from a high social class

position [noun: **positions**]

1 a place or situation: *The house is in a lovely position on the edge of the lake.* • *This puts me in a very difficult position.*

2 a way of standing, sitting or lying: *sleeping in an awkward position*

3 a job or post: *He applied for a position as a butler.*

[verb: **positions, positioning, positioned**] if you position an object, or yourself, somewhere, you put it, or yourself, there

positive [adjective]

1 you are positive about something when you are very sure about it

2 a positive answer or response means or says 'yes'

3 to have a positive attitude is to feel hopeful and confident

4 a positive number is one that is greater than zero

◆ **positively** [adverb] completely or absolutely: *He was positively seething with rage.*

posse [noun: **posses**] a group of people who are doing the same thing: *There was a posse of journalists waiting outside the house.*

possess [verb: **possesses, possessing, possessed**] to possess something is to have it or own it

◆ **possessed** [adjective] someone who is possessed is being controlled by an emotion or an evil spirit

◆ **possession** [noun: **possessions**]

1 possession is having or owning something

2 your possessions are the things you have or own

◆ **possessive** [adjective] a possessive person is not willing to share the things they have with other people

[noun: **possessives**] in grammar, a possessive is a word that shows who or what a person or thing belongs to. For example, *my, yours* and *theirs*, and nouns with *'s* added at the end, are possessives

possibility [noun: **possibilities**] something that is possible

possible [adjective]

1 something that is possible can happen, or may happen: *It isn't possible to see the doctor today.*

2 something that is possible may be true: *It's possible I made a mistake.*

◆ **possibly** [adverb] perhaps: *Possibly I was wrong.*

post [1] [noun: **posts**] a long piece of wood or metal fixed upright in the ground

post [2] [noun] the postal service, which collects and delivers letters and parcels, or the letters and parcels sent or delivered by this service: *I sent it by post, not by fax.* • *Has the morning post arrived yet?*

[verb: **posts, posting, posted**] to post a letter or parcel is to send it by the postal service, for example by taking it to the post office or putting it in a postbox

➡ **postage, postal**

post [3] [noun: **posts**]

1 a job: *He was dismissed from his post.*

2 a place where someone such as a soldier or security guard is on duty

Pp

429

[verb: **posts, posting, posted**] if someone is posted somewhere they are sent there for a while to work

post- [prefix] if a word starts with **post-**, it adds the meaning 'after' to the word. For example, *postwar* means 'after a war'

postage [noun] the amount of money you have to pay to send a letter or parcel through the post

postage stamp [noun: **postage stamps**] a small printed label stuck on letters and parcels to show that the postage has been paid

postal [adjective] to do with the service that collects and delivers letters and parcels

postal order [noun: **postal orders**] a piece of paper that you buy at the post office which represents a certain sum of money, and which is a safe way of sending money through the post

postbox [noun: **postboxes**] a box in a public place where letters can be posted

postcard [noun: **postcards**] a card for writing messages on that you can send through the post without an envelope

post code [noun: **post codes**] a special series of letters and numbers at the end of an address that helps the postal service to sort letters and parcels

postdate [verb: **postdates, postdating, postdated**] to write a date on something such as a cheque or letter, which is later than the real date

poster [noun: **posters**] a large notice in a public place advertising something or giving information

posterior [adjective] at the back or rear: *in a posterior position*
[noun: **posteriors**]
1 the back of something
2 your posterior is your bottom

postman [noun: **postmen**] someone who delivers letters and parcels to people's houses or businesses

postmark [noun: **postmarks**] the postmark on a letter or parcel is a stamp put on it by the post office showing the date when it was posted and the place where it was posted

postmaster [noun: **postmasters**] a man who is in charge of running a post office

postmistress [noun: **postmistresses**] a woman who is in charge of running a post office

post mortem [noun: **post mortems**] a medical examination of a dead body to find out the cause of death

postnatal [adjective] to do with the time just after a woman has given birth to a baby: *postnatal depression*

post office [noun: **post offices**] a place where you can post letters and parcels, buy stamps and use various other postal services

postpone [verb: **postpones, postponing, postponed**] to postpone something is to put it off until a later time

• **postponement** [noun: **postponements**] putting something off until a later time

postscript [noun: **postscripts**] if a letter has a postscript, it has an extra message under the writer's signature, usually with the abbreviation **PS** before it

posture [noun: **postures**] your posture is the way you usually stand, sit or walk

posy [noun: **posies**] a small bunch of flowers

pot [noun: **pots**] a deep container, often with a lid, used for cooking, for holding liquids, for storing things like jam, or for growing plants in

potassium [noun] potassium is a soft, silvery–white metallic element

potato [noun: **potatoes**] a round white or yellow vegetable that grows underground

potency [noun] power or strength

potent [adjective] powerful or strong: *a potent drug*

potential [adjective] capable of becoming a particular thing: *a potential customer*
[noun] your potential is the qualities you have that can be developed successfully

pothole [noun: **potholes**] a hole in the road

potion [noun: **potions**] a drink containing medicine or poison, or having a magic effect

pot-luck [noun] if you **take pot-luck**, you decide to accept whatever is available or being offered, without knowing exactly what you will get

potter[1] [verb: **potters, pottering, pottered**] to wander about doing small jobs or nothing very important

potter[2] [noun: **potters**] someone who makes things out of clay

pottery [noun: **potteries**]
1 pottery is things such as jugs, bowls and ornaments made out of baked clay
2 a pottery is a workshop or factory where things are made out of baked clay

potty[1] [noun: **potties**] a container that a small child sits on to go to the toilet

potty[2] [adjective: **pottier, pottiest**] someone who is potty is mad

pouch [noun: **pouches**]
1 a small bag
2 the fold of skin that a female kangaroo carries her baby in

pouffe [noun: **pouffes**] a low soft seat with no back or arms

poultry [noun] birds such as chickens and turkeys that are raised for us to eat

pounce [verb: **pounces, pouncing, pounced**] to jump forward suddenly to attack or catch hold of something: *The cat pounced on the mouse.*

pound [noun: **pounds**]
1 the main unit of money in Britain, made up of 100 pence and usually written £
2 a measure of weight, equal to 0.454 kilograms
[verb: **pounds, pounding, pounded**] to pound something is to hit it hard: *Someone was pounding at the door trying to get in.*

pour [verb: **pours, pouring, poured**]
1 to pour a liquid is to make it flow out of a container: *She poured the orange juice into a glass.*
2 to pour is to flow out fast and in large quantities: *Water was pouring through the ceiling.*
3 people pour somewhere when they go there in large numbers: *Crowds of people poured out of the stadium.*
4 if it is pouring, it is raining heavily

pout [verb: **pouts, pouting, pouted**] if someone pouts, they push out their lips, or only their lower lip, because they are annoyed

poverty [noun] being poor

powder [noun: **powders**]
1 a substance in the form of a fine dry dust
2 powder is a cosmetic that some women pat

on their skin to make it look smooth
♦ **powdered** [adjective] dried and made into a powder: *powdered milk*
♦ **powdery** [adjective] made up of very small pieces or particles, like powder: *powdery snow*

power [noun: **powers**]
1 power is strength or force
2 to have power is to have the ability or authority to control people or things: *political power*
3 to have the power to do something is to have the ability to do it: *He's lost the power of speech.*
4 power is any form of energy used to drive machines: *wind power • The power was cut off in the storm.*
[verb: **powers, powering, powered**] to power something is to provide it with the energy to work: *a machine powered by steam*

power cut [noun: **power cuts**] a period when there is no electricity because of a fault in the supply

powerful [adjective] strong or having the ability to control other people

powerless [adjective] unable to control or affect things

power station [noun: **power stations**] a building where electricity is made from coal, oil, gas or nuclear power

PR [abbreviation] short for **public relations**

practical [adjective]
1 something that is practical is useful or efficient: *a very practical solution to the problem*
2 a practical person is good at doing things rather than thinking about them
[noun: **practicals**] an examination that tests practical ability and skill rather than theory

practical joke [noun: **practical jokes**] a trick played on someone that makes them look silly

practically [adverb] almost: *It was practically full.*

practice [noun: **practices**]
1 practice is doing something often so that you get better at it: *He'll soon get the hang of the violin with a bit more practice.*
2 to put a theory, plan or idea into practice is to do it

Pp

3 a doctor's or lawyer's practice is the place where they work

practise [verb: **practises, practising, practised**]

1 to practise something is to do it again and again so that you get better at it

2 to practise something is to make it a habit or to do it: *He practises yoga.*

3 a doctor or lawyer practises when they do their professional work

ⓘ Remember that **practice** with a **c** is a noun: *I need some **practice**.*
Practise with an **s** is a verb: *You must **practise** often.*

prairie [noun: **prairies**] a large area of flat grassy land in North America

praise [verb: **praises, praising, praised**] to praise someone or something is to say how well they have done
[noun: **praises**] praise is saying how good someone is or how well they have done

praiseworthy [adjective] something is praiseworthy if it deserves praise

pram [noun: **prams**] a small wheeled vehicle that a baby sits or lies in and which is pushed by someone walking

prance [verb: **prances, prancing, pranced**] to prance is to dance or jump about

prank [noun: **pranks**] a trick or practical joke

prattle [verb: **prattles, prattling, prattled**] to talk in a silly or meaningless way

prawn [noun: **prawns**] a shellfish you can eat that looks like a large shrimp

pray [verb: **prays, praying, prayed**]
1 to speak to God
2 to pray for something is to hope for it: *We were praying for a nice sunny day.*

✦ **prayer** [noun: **prayers**]
1 prayer is praying: *They knelt in prayer.*
2 a prayer is the words that you use when you pray

ⓘ Try not to confuse the spelling of **pray** with **prey**, which is the creatures an animal hunts.

pre- [prefix] if a word starts with **pre-**, it adds the meaning 'before' to the word. For example, *prehistoric* times are the times before history was written down

preach [verb: **preaches, preaching, preached**]
1 to talk about right and wrong, often as part of a religious service
2 to preach a particular thing is to speak in favour of it: *He preached patience and understanding.*

✦ **preacher** [noun: **preachers**] someone who preaches or gives sermons

precarious [adjective] a precarious state or position is risky or dangerous: *Abruptly the path became steep and the footing became more precarious.*

precaution [noun: **precautions**] something you do to avoid an accident or problem happening

precede [verb: **precedes, preceding, preceded**] one thing precedes another when it comes before that other thing

✦ **precedence** [noun] one person or thing takes precedence over another when they come before, or have the right to come before, the other

✦ **precedent** [noun: **precedents**] something that has happened in the past that guides or provides a rule for what should happen now or in the future

✦ **preceding** [adjective] coming before

precinct [noun: **precincts**]
1 an area of shops in the centre of a town or city where no cars or motor vehicles are allowed
2 the precincts of a building are the areas within its boundaries or inside its walls: *the cathedral precincts*

precious [adjective]
1 valuable or highly valued by someone: *precious stones • His books are very precious to him.*
2 **precious little** or **precious few** means very little or very few

precipice [noun: **precipices**] a very steep cliff

precise [adjective]
1 exact: *At that precise moment, the bell rang.*
2 careful and accurate: *Her work is very precise.*

✦ **precisely** [adverb] exactly: *Precisely when did he give you the letter?*

• **precision** [noun] being exact and accurate: *He hit the target again and again with precision.*

precocious [adjective] a precocious child is more advanced than is usual for his or her age

predator [noun: **predators**] an animal that hunts and eats other animals

• **predatory** [adjective] hunting, killing and eating other animals

predecessor [noun: **predecessors**] someone's predecessor in a job is the person who had the job before them

predicament [noun: **predicaments**] if someone is in a predicament they are in a difficult situation

predict [verb: **predicts, predicting, predicted**] to predict something is to say that it will happen before it actually does happen

• **predictable** [adjective] something that is predictable can be predicted

• **prediction** [noun: **predictions**] predicting, or something that is predicted

predominant [adjective] the predominant person or thing in a group is the one that stands out most: *The predominant colour in his paintings is blue.*

• **predominantly** [adjective] mostly or mainly: *The trains are predominantly old, out-of-date models.*

preen [verb: **preens, preening, preened**]
1 a bird preens when it smoothes and cleans its feathers
2 you preen yourself when you stroke your hair or adjust your appearance

preface [noun: **prefaces**] the preface to a book is a short section at the beginning that introduces the rest of the book or the story

prefect [noun: **prefects**] a senior pupil in a school who has been given some powers to help in the running of the school

prefer [verb: **prefers, preferring, preferred**] if you prefer something, you like it better than something else

• **preferable** [adjective] if one thing is preferable to another, you like it, or would like it, better than the other thing

• **preference** [noun: **preferences**] your preferences are the things you like or prefer

prefix [noun: **prefixes**] a letter or a group of letters that is added to the beginning of a word to make another word

pregnancy [noun: **pregnancies**] being pregnant, or the time when a woman or female animal is pregnant

• **pregnant** [adjective] a woman or female animal is pregnant when she is carrying an unborn baby in her womb

preheat [verb: **preheats, preheating, preheated**] to preheat an oven is to switch it on until it reaches a particular temperature before you put the food in it

prehistoric [adjective] belonging to the time before history was written down: *prehistoric cave paintings*

prejudice [noun: **prejudices**] an unfair opinion or dislike of a person or thing without trying to understand that person or thing
[verb: **prejudices, prejudicing, prejudiced**] one thing prejudices another when it harms it or puts it in danger

• **prejudiced** [adjective] having a prejudice or prejudices against a person or thing

preliminary [adjective] preliminary things are said or done to prepare for a main event or what is to come next
[noun: **preliminaries**] preliminaries are things said or done to prepare for a main event

premature [adjective]
1 a premature baby is born before the time it should have been born
2 an action is premature when it is done too early

premier [adjective] leading or most important: *France's premier resort*
[noun: **premiers**] a prime minister

première [noun: **premières**] the première of a film or play is its first public showing or performance

premises [plural noun] the premises of a company or business are the buildings and land it uses

premium [noun: **premiums**]
1 a premium is a regular amount paid to an insurance company for insurance cover
2 if something is **at a premium**, it is difficult to get and so is more expensive

premonition [noun: **premonitions**] a strange feeling that something is going to happen before it actually does happen

Pp

preoccupation [noun: **preoccupations**] something you think about all or most of the time

♦ **preoccupied** [adjective] thinking so much about one thing that you do not pay enough attention to other things

♦ **preoccupy** [verb: **preoccupies, preoccupying, preoccupied**] something preoccupies you when you think about it a lot

prepaid [adjective] paid for in advance: *prepaid postage*

preparation [noun: **preparations**]
1 preparation is getting ready for something
2 preparations are things you do to get ready for something: *preparations for the wedding*

preparatory [adjective] preparing for something that comes later

prepare [verb: **prepares, preparing, prepared**]
1 to prepare is to get ready for something or get into a fit state to deal with it or do it
2 to prepare food is to do whatever is needed to make it ready for eating

♦ **prepared** [adjective]
1 made ready in advance
2 you are prepared for something, or prepared to do something, when you are ready for it, or are willing to do it

preposition [part of speech: **prepositions**] a word put before a noun or pronoun to show how it is connected to another word in the same sentence. For example, in the sentence *I put my keys in my bag*, the word *in* is a preposition

prepossessing [adjective] attractive: *It's not a very prepossessing building.*

preposterous [adjective] ridiculous: *What a preposterous suggestion!*

prescribe [verb: **prescribes, prescribing, prescribed**] a doctor prescribes a drug for a patient when he or she tells the patient which drug to take

prescription [noun: **prescriptions**] an instruction from a doctor to a pharmacist stating what medicine should be prepared for a particular patient

presence [noun]
1 your presence somewhere is your being there

2 to do something in someone's presence is to do it while they are there

present[1] [noun: **presents**] something given as a gift
[verb: **presents, presenting, presented**]
1 to present someone with something is to give it to them, usually as an award for good work or high achievement
2 you present one person to another when you introduce them
3 someone presents a radio or TV show when they introduce it
4 you present information when you communicate it to other people
5 something presents a problem when it becomes difficult to deal with
6 you present yourself somewhere when you go there and let someone know you have arrived

present[2] [noun] the present is the time now
[adjective]
1 someone is present somewhere when they are there
2 to do with the time now: *the present day* • *pupils past and present*

ⓘ The noun and adjective are pronounced **prez**-ent, with the stress at the beginning. The verb is pronounce pri-**zent**, with the stress at the end.

presentation [noun: **presentations**] the presenting of something such as a gift or a talk

presently [adverb]
1 an old-fashioned word meaning 'soon': *The bus should be here presently.*
2 just now: *Are you employed presently?*

present participle [noun: **present participles**] the form of a verb used after a helping verb such as *is* or *was* to show that something is or was taking place at that time. For example, *going* in *I am going to the shops* is a present participle

present tense [noun] the present tense of a verb is the form used to show that the action of the verb is happening here and now. For example, *throw* and *throws* in *I throw the ball and he throws it back* are present tense forms of the verb *throw*

preservation [noun] preserving: *preservation of the rainforest*

preservative [noun: **preservatives**] a substance that is put in food or on wood to stop it rotting

preserve [verb: **preserves, preserving, preserved**] to preserve something is to keep it as it is and stop it being lost or destroyed
[noun: **preserves**] a food such as jam or bottled fruit that has been boiled with sugar to stop it going bad

preside [verb: **presides, presiding, presided**] to preside over a meeting or formal event is to be in overall charge of it

presidency [noun: **presidencies**] the position of being a president or the time when someone is a president

president [noun: **presidents**]
1 a president is the elected head of a country that has no king or queen
2 the president of a company or organization is the person with the top job in that company or organization

press [verb: **presses, pressing, pressed**]
1 to press something is to push it or squeeze it
2 you press clothes when you iron them
3 to **press for something** is to be forceful in trying to get someone to agree to it
[noun: **presses**]
1 a pressing action
2 a press is a printing machine
3 the press are newspapers and journalists

pressing [adjective] a pressing problem is one that needs to be dealt with now or very soon

press-up [noun: **press-ups**] a floor exercise in which you push the top half of your body up off the floor by pressing down with your hands and arms

pressure [noun: **pressures**]
1 the force on or against a surface by something pressing on it: *air pressure*
2 pressure is strong persuasion: *He put me under pressure to agree.*
3 pressures are the stresses and strains of life
• pressurize or **pressurise** [verb: **pressurizes, pressurizing, pressurized**]
1 to pressurize an aeroplane or a diving bell is to keep the air pressure the same as that on the ground or at sea level

2 to pressurize someone into doing something is to force them to do it

prestige [noun] someone has prestige when they are highly thought of or have influence because of their rank or success

presumably [adverb] you say 'presumably' when you suppose something is true: *Presumably someone will be arranging the chairs before the concert.*

presume [verb: **presumes, presuming, presumed**] to presume something is to believe that it is true without having any proof
• presumption [noun: **presumptions**] presuming, or something presumed
• presumptuous [adjective] a presumptuous person takes too much for granted and behaves in a bold way

pretence [noun] pretending something

pretend [verb: **pretends, pretending, pretended**]
1 to try to make someone believe something that is not true: *She closed her eyes and pretended she was asleep.*
2 to imagine that something is true as part of a game: *The children were pretending to be submarine captains.*

pretext [noun: **pretexts**] to do something on a pretext is to give a false reason for doing it

prettiness [noun] being pretty

pretty [adjective: **prettier, prettiest**] attractive to look at: *pretty flowers • a pretty little girl*
[adverb]
1 quite: *a pretty good mark*
2 pretty much, pretty well and **pretty nearly** mean 'almost': *The building work is pretty much finished.*

prevail [verb: **prevails, prevailing, prevailed**] to prevail is to win a contest or battle
• prevailing [adjective] the prevailing winds are winds that blow most frequently in a part of the world

prevalence [noun] how prevalent something is
• prevalent [adjective] common and widespread

prevent [verb: **prevents, preventing, prevented**] to prevent something happening is to stop it happening

Pp

◆ **prevention** [noun] preventing something

◆ **preventive** [adjective] a preventive medicine stops you getting a disease or illness

preview [noun: **previews**] a viewing of something such as a film or exhibition before it is released or shown to the general public

previous [adjective] happening earlier or at some time in the past: *I had met him on a previous occasion.*

◆ **previously** [adverb] before or earlier

prey [noun] the creatures a predator hunts, kills and eats are its prey: *Small birds are the usual prey of the sparrowhawk.*

[verb: **preys, preying, preyed**]

1 to **prey on** something is to hunt it and kill it

2 if something **preys on your mind**, you cannot stop thinking or worrying about it

price [noun: **prices**] the price of something is the amount of money it costs: *What price are your apples today?* • *Prices in the shops were rising.*

[verb: **prices, pricing, priced**] to price things is to find out how much they cost or to mark a price on them

◆ **priceless** [adjective]

1 a priceless item is so valuable that it is not possible to put a price on it

2 very funny: *The surprised expression on his face was priceless.*

◆ **pricey** [adjective: **pricier, priciest**] expensive: *Petrol is getting very pricey.*

prick [verb: **pricks, pricking, pricked**] if something sharp pricks you, it sticks into your skin, hurting you

prickle [noun: **prickles**] a short sharp spine, as on a hedgehog's back or on a bramble's stems

[verb: **prickles, prickling, prickled**] if something prickles, it pricks or makes your skin feel as if it is being pricked by lots of sharp little points

◆ **prickly** [adjective: **pricklier, prickliest**] covered in prickles or feeling like lots of sharp little spines

pride [noun: **prides**]

1 pride is the feeling you get when you know you have done something well, or when someone you are connected with has done something well: *His heart swelled with pride.*

2 pride is self-respect: *taking pride in her appearance*

3 a pride of lions is a family group of lions

priest [noun: **priests**]

1 a person who is qualified to conduct services in one of the Christian churches

2 a person with official duties of various kinds in other religions

◆ **priestess** [noun: **priestesses**] a female priest in certain ancient or non-Christian religions

◆ **priesthood** [noun] the position of being a priest, or priests as a group

prig [noun: **prigs**] a rather old-fashioned word for someone who always behaves correctly and tends to find fault with other people's behaviour

◆ **priggish** [adjective] behaving like a prig

prim [adjective: **primmer, primmest**] very formal and correct and easily shocked by rudeness

primary [adjective] first or most important: *the primary route into the city*

primary colour [noun: **primary colours**] the primary colours are the colours red, blue and yellow. All other colours can be made by mixing two or more of the primary colours

primary school [noun: **primary schools**] a school for children between the ages of 4 and 11

primate [noun: **primates**]

1 primates are animals that belong to the group that includes monkeys, apes and humans

2 an archbishop

prime [adjective] greatest or of the best quality: *a matter of prime importance* • *a prime cut of beef*

[noun] someone is in their prime when they are at the time of their life when they are at their best because they are experienced and wise and are still physically fit

[verb: **primes, priming, primed**] to prime something is to make it ready for the next stage: *Prime the wood before painting.*

prime minister [noun: **prime ministers**] the leader of the government in Britain and in many other countries of the world

primitive [adjective]

1 belonging to the earliest stages of development: *primitive man* • *a primitive kind of computer*
2 rough and unsophisticated: *The accommodation was pretty primitive.*

primrose [noun: **primroses**] a wild plant with small pale yellow flowers

prince [noun: **princes**] the son or grandson of a king or queen, or the ruler of a small state or country

princess [noun: **princesses**] the daughter or granddaughter of a king or queen, or the wife of a prince

principal [adjective] most important: *Steelmaking was the principal industry in the area.*
[noun: **principals**] the head of a school, college or university
♦ **principally** [adverb] mainly or mostly: *She collects old toys, principally dolls.*

principle [noun: **principles**]
1 a principle is a general rule that something is based on: *We follow the principle of first come, first served.*
2 your principles are the rules of behaviour that you live by: *It was against his principles to borrow money.*
3 if you agree to something **in principle**, you agree to it in a general way although you may not agree with all the details
4 if you do something **on principle**, you do it because you believe it is morally right

ⓘ Try not to confuse the spelling of **principal** with **principle**.

print [verb: **prints, printing, printed**]
1 to print a book or newspaper is to publish it
2 you print when you write words with each letter separate from the one next to it, not joined up: *Print your name at the top of the form.*
3 to print something, or to **print it out** from a computer, is to make a copy of it using a printing machine or a computer printer
[noun: **prints**]
1 print is the words in a book or newspaper that have been made by a printing machine
2 a print is a mark, picture or design made by something pressing down on a surface
♦ **printer** [noun: **printers**]

1 a machine that prints words and pictures
2 a person or company whose business is printing documents, books and newspapers

printout [noun: **printouts**] a paper copy of something that is on a computer screen

prior [adjective] earlier or previous: *I couldn't go because I had a prior engagement.*

priority [noun: **priorities**] something that has to be dealt with before other things

priory [noun: **priories**] a building where a group of monks or nuns lives

prise [verb: **prises, prising, prised**] to prise something is to force it open, off or out, often using a flat tool as a lever: *He prised open the lid with a knife.*

prison [noun: **prisons**] a building where criminals are kept
♦ **prisoner** [noun: **prisoners**]
1 someone who is kept in prison as a punishment
2 someone who is locked up or kept from moving about freely, against their will

pristine [adjective] something pristine is in perfect condition, shiny and new-looking

privacy [noun] being private: *A higher fence will give us a bit more privacy.*

private [adjective]
1 belonging to and used by only one person, or a small group of people: *a private beach*
2 kept secret or away from people in general: *Our discussions must be strictly private.*
3 owned and run by individual people or companies, not by the government: *private industry*
[noun: **privates**] an ordinary soldier in the army
♦ **privately** [adverb]
1 secretly: *Privately, he thought they were all fools.*
2 away from other people: *Can we talk privately?*

privatization or **privatisation** [noun] the process by which a business owned and controlled by the government is sold to private individuals and companies

privatize or **privatise** [verb: **privatizes, privatizing, privatized**] to privatize a government-owned business is to sell it to private individuals and companies

privet [noun] a plant used in hedges

Pp

privilege [noun: **privileges**] a special right or advantage given to only one person, or to only a few people

• **privileged** [adjective] having advantages or privileges that other people do not have

prize [noun: **prizes**] something won in a competition or given as a reward for good work

[verb: **prizes, prizing, prized**] to prize something is to value it very much

pro [noun: **pros**] a short form of the word **professional**: *a golf pro*

pro- [prefix]

1 if a word starts with **pro-**, it often has something to do with 'beginning' or 'forward'. For example, a *prologue* is the part at the beginning of a play, and to *proceed* is to go forward

2 if a word starts with **pro-**, it can also have something to do with supporting someone or something. For example, to be *pro-Europe* is to support the European Union

probability [noun: **probabilities**] the probability of something happening is how likely it is to happen: *What's the probability of seeing the eclipse clearly?*

probable [adjective] likely: *A lit cigarette was the probable cause of the fire.*

• **probably** [adverb] likely to be the case, or likely to happen: *It's probably just a cold, rather than flu.* • *The weather forecast said we'd probably get rain in the afternoon.*

probation [noun] if someone is on probation, they are being watched to see if they behave or do a job well

probe [noun: **probes**]

1 an investigation

2 a spacecraft with no people aboard that is sent into space to investigate things

[verb: **probes, probing, probed**] to investigate a matter thoroughly by asking questions and examining evidence

problem [noun: **problems**]

1 a situation, matter or person that causes difficulties, or is difficult to deal with: *There's a problem with the car. It won't start.*

2 a puzzle or question that has to be solved: *maths problems*

• **problematic** [adjective] causing problems

procedure [noun: **procedures**] a way of doing something or the order in which things are done: *What's the procedure for logging on to the Internet?*

proceed [verb: **proceed, proceeding, proceeded**] to proceed is to go on or go forward: *Let's proceed to the next chapter.*

• **proceedings** [plural noun] things done or said: *A power cut interrupted proceedings.*

• **proceeds** [plural noun] the proceeds from a sale or fund-raising event are all the money made from it

process [noun: **processes**]

1 the series of stages or events that have to be gone through to achieve or do something

2 to be in the process of doing something is to be in the middle of doing it

[verb: **processes, processing, processed**] to process something is to deal with it in a number of stages

• **procession** [noun: **processions**] a line of people or vehicles moving along one behind the other

proclaim [verb: **proclaims, proclaiming, proclaimed**] to proclaim something is to announce it publicly

• **proclamation** [noun: **proclamations**] a public announcement of something important

prod [verb: **prods, prodding, prodded**] to prod something is to poke at it roughly

prodigal [adjective] to be prodigal is to spend or waste money

prodigy [noun: **prodigies**] a wonderfully clever or talented person, especially a young person

produce [verb: **produces, producing, produced**]

1 to produce something is to make, grow or create it: *factories producing goods for export* • *Will the tree produce fruit this year?* • *The sun produces both light and heat.*

2 to produce something is to bring it out or bring it forward so that people can see it: *The conjuror produced a rabbit from a hat.*

3 to produce a film or play is to arrange for it to be made and shown to the public

[noun] produce is things grown or produced on farms

+ **producer** [noun: **producers**]
1 someone who arranges for a film, television programme or play to be made, by organizing all the equipment, sets and actors, and the money to pay for them
2 someone who makes products or grows produce to be sold: *meat producers*

ⓘ The verb **produce** is pronounced pro-**dyoos**, with the stress at the end. The noun is pronounced **prod**-yoos, with the stress at the beginning.

product [noun: **products**]
1 something that is produced, either by manufacturing it or growing it on a farm
2 one thing is the product of another when it is the result of that other thing
+ **production** [noun: **productions**]
1 production is making, growing or producing something, or the amount that is produced
2 a production is a version of a play, opera or ballet
+ **productive** [adjective]
1 producing a lot: *a productive piece of land*
2 giving good or useful results: *a productive meeting*
+ **productivity** [noun] the rate at which goods are made or produced, or the rate at which one person works to produce something

profession [noun: **professions**] a profession is a job or occupation that needs special qualifications and training, for example, medicine, law, teaching and engineering
+ **professional** [adjective]
1 to do with a profession: *professional training*
2 doing something for money rather than as a hobby or as an amateur: *a professional footballer*
3 someone who is professional does their job with skill and care: *She is always very calm and professional.*
+ **professionally** [adverb] in a professional way, or for money rather than as an amateur: *a professionally qualified accountant* • *He used to play football professionally.*
professor [noun: **professors**]

1 the head of a university department
2 in the United States, a professor is a teacher in a university or college
proficiency [noun] the level of skill you have reached in doing something
+ **proficient** [adjective] good at something that needs skill or practice: *He's proficient in several languages.*
profile [noun: **profiles**]
1 a person's profile is the shape of their face seen from the side
2 a profile of someone is a short description of their life
profit [noun: **profits**] to make a profit is to make money by selling something for more than you paid for it
[verb: **profits, profiting, profited**] to profit from something is to benefit from it
+ **profitable** [adjective] making a profit
profound [adjective]
1 very great: *profound changes*
2 profound feelings are very strong and deep: *a profound sense of guilt*
3 something said or written is profound if it shows great knowledge and deep thought: *profound comments*
+ **profoundly** [adverb] deeply: *I was profoundly shocked by what she said.*
program [noun: **programs**] a set of coded instructions put into a computer that allows the computer to perform a task
[verb: **programs, programming, programmed**] to program a computer is to put a program into it which will control how it works or what it does with data
programme [noun: **programmes**]
1 a show on TV or radio
2 a leaflet or thin book that gives information and details about an event
3 a list of planned events or actions: *a programme of exercise*
progress [noun]
1 progress is forward movement: *The bus made very slow progress on the wet and winding roads.*
2 progress is improvement: *Freya has made a lot of progress in the last year.*
[verb: **progresses, progressing, progressed**]

Pp

1 to go forward: *They progressed slowly up the icy ridge.*
2 to develop or improve: *Things are progressing nicely.*
♦ **progression** [noun] going forward, or forward movement
♦ **progressive** [adjective] progressive ideas look forward to the future

ⓘ The noun is pronounced **proh**-gres, with the stress at the beginning.
The verb is pronounced pro-**gres**, with the stress at the end.

prohibit [verb: **prohibits, prohibiting, prohibited**] to prohibit something is to forbid it
♦ **prohibition** [noun: **prohibitions**] a law or order forbidding something
♦ **prohibitive** [adjective] the cost of something is prohibitive if it is so expensive you cannot buy it

project [noun: **projects**]
1 a piece of work done by a pupil or student, often involving study and research
2 a plan: *What's his next project going to be?*
[verb: **projects, projecting, projected**]
1 to stick or jut out
2 to project a film is to show it by running it through a projector
3 to project your voice is to make it carry over a long distance, especially to the back of a theatre
♦ **projection** [noun: **projections**]
1 a projection is something that sticks or juts out
2 projection is projecting something, especially films

ⓘ The noun is pronounced **proj**-ekt, with the stress at the beginning.
The verb is pronounced pro-**jekt**, with the stress at the end.

projectionist [noun: **projectionists**] someone who operates a film projector, especially in a cinema
projector [noun: **projectors**] a machine used to project films on to a screen by focusing a beam of light behind the film through a lens
prologue [noun: **prologues**] a short introductory part at the beginning of a play, story or poem

prolong [verb: **prolongs, prolonging, prolonged**] to prolong something is to make it go on for longer
prom [noun: **proms**] a promenade
promenade [noun: **promenades**] a broad path or pavement for people to walk along, especially on the sea front in a town by the sea
prominence [noun] being prominent, or something that is prominent
♦ **prominent** [adjective]
1 standing out or easily seen: *prominent teeth*
• *a prominent landmark*
2 a prominent person is famous: *a prominent writer*
promise [verb: **promises, promising, promised**]
1 you promise when you say that you will, or will not, do something: *I promise I'll pay you back.*
2 you promise something to someone when you say that you will give them something or help them in some way: *Sorry, you can't borrow this book. I promised it to Vishal.*
3 something promises something good when it shows signs of being good or successful: *It promises to be another lovely day tomorrow.*
[noun: **promises**]
1 something promised: *Make me a promise that you won't be late.*
2 if someone or something shows promise they show signs of future success
♦ **promising** [adjective] showing promise: *a promising young tennis player*
promote [verb: **promotes, promoting, promoted**]
1 to promote someone is to move them to a higher-ranking job
2 to promote something is to work to spread and encourage it, or to make it popular: *His aim was to promote peace amongst nations.* • *This month, we're promoting a new range of make-up.*
♦ **promotion** [noun: **promotions**]
1 if someone gets a promotion they are given a higher-ranking job
2 special advertising designed to make a product popular
prompt [adjective] doing something or happening without delay: *a prompt reply*

[verb: **prompts, prompting, prompted**]

1 to prompt someone to do something is to cause or encourage them to do it

2 to prompt an actor is to tell them the line that they have to say next

+ **promptly** [adverb] without delay
+ **promptness** [noun] being prompt

prone [adjective]

1 you are prone to something if you are likely to suffer from it: *He's prone to headaches.*

2 someone who is prone is lying flat, especially face down

prong [noun: **prongs**] a spike of a fork

+ **pronged** [adjective] having prongs

pronoun [part of speech: **pronouns**] a word that can be used in place of a noun. For example, in the sentence *Gary ate the ice cream cone*, *Gary* and *the ice cream cone* could be changed to pronouns and the sentence would be *He ate it*

pronounce [verb: **pronounces, pronouncing, pronounced**]

1 to pronounce words or letters is to say them: *The two 'z's in pizza are pronounced 'tz'.*

2 to pronounce something is to declare it formally and publicly

+ **pronounced** [adjective] noticeable: *He had a pronounced limp.*

➡ **pronunciation**

pronto [adverb] to do something pronto is to do it as fast as possible

pronunciation [noun: **pronunciations**] pronouncing words, or the way a word is pronounced

proof [noun: **proofs**] evidence that shows definitely that something is true

-proof [suffix] if **-proof** comes at the end of a word, the word is an adjective that means 'protected against'. For example, a *waterproof* or *showerproof* coat does not let in water or rain

prop [noun: **props**]

1 a heavy piece of wood or metal used to hold a building or other structure up

2 props are the pieces of furniture and other objects used on a stage or on a film set to help make a scene look real

[verb: **props, propping, propped**]

1 to prop something against an upright surface is to lean it there

2 to **prop something up** is to use a prop or props to stop it falling down

3 you **prop yourself up** when you support yourself, for example, with your elbows or with a pillow

propaganda [noun] propaganda is ideas, news or opinions that are spread by a political group or by one side in a war, in order to influence people

propel [verb: **propels, propelling, propelled**] to propel something is to drive it forward, often using an engine or some other source of power

+ **propeller** [noun: **propellers**] a shaft with revolving blades that drives a ship or aeroplane forward

proper [adjective]

1 right or correct: *Is this the proper way to fold a shirt?*

2 complete or thorough: *She gave the house a proper spring-clean.*

3 well-mannered and well-behaved: *a very proper young man*

+ **properly** [adverb] correctly: *Sit up properly in your chair.*

proper noun [noun: **proper nouns**] a noun that names a particular person, place or thing. Proper nouns usually begin with a capital letter, for example *Marianne, Mauritius, Mississippi* and *March*

property [noun: **properties**]

1 your property is something that belongs to you

2 a property is a house and the land it is on: *residential properties*

prophecy [noun: **prophecies**] if someone makes a prophecy they say that something will happen at some time in the future

prophesy [verb: **prophesies, prophesying, prophesied**] to say what will happen in the future

prophet [noun: **prophets**]

1 someone who claims to be able to predict what will happen in the future

2 prophets are believed by some to be people chosen by God to communicate God's will to the people on Earth

proportion [noun: **proportions**]

1 a proportion of an amount or total is part of it

Pp

2 the proportion of one thing to another is how much there is of one compared with the other
3 something's proportions are its size and measurements
• **proportional** [adjective] one thing is proportional to another when it matches or corresponds with it by the same amount

proposal [noun: **proposals**]
1 a plan or suggestion
2 when someone asks another person to marry them

propose [verb: **proposes, proposing, proposed**]
1 to propose something is to suggest it: *He proposed that we spend a long weekend in the country.*
2 if you propose to do something you intend to do it: *I don't propose to spend any time in Birmingham. I'll just be passing through.*
3 to propose to someone is to ask them to marry you

proprietor [noun: **proprietors**] the proprietor of a shop or business is its owner

prose [noun] writing that is not in verse

prosecute [verb: **prosecutes, prosecuting, prosecuted**] to prosecute someone is to accuse them of a crime and take them to court
• **prosecution** [noun: **prosecutions**]
1 the process of taking someone to court
2 the lawyer or team of lawyers who try to prove that someone is guilty in a court of law

prospect [noun: **prospects**]
1 a view of something into the future
2 your prospects are what you are likely to do in the future
[verb: **prospects, prospecting, prospected**] to prospect for gold and other precious metals is to search for it in the earth

ⓘ The noun is pronounced **pros**–pekt, with the stress at the beginning.
The verb is pronounced pro–**spekt**, with the stress at the end.

prospectus [noun: **prospectuses**] a booklet that gives you information about a school, college or university and the courses it offers

prosper [verb: **prospers, prospering, prospered**] to do well, especially by making money
• **prosperity** [noun] success, especially having plenty of money
• **prosperous** [adjective] a prosperous person has done well, especially by making a lot of money in business

prostate [noun: **prostates**] a gland in a man's body near the bladder

prostitute [noun: **prostitutes**] someone who has sex with people in return for money
[verb: **prostitutes, prostituting, prostituted**] if you prostitute your talents, you use them in a way that is not worthy

prostrate [adjective] lying flat

protect [verb: **protects, protecting, protected**] to protect someone or something is to guard them from harm and keep them safe: *Protect the young plants from frost.*
• **protection** [noun]
1 protecting
2 safety or shelter: *The boats were heading for the protection of the harbour.*
• **protective** [adjective] providing protection
• **protector** [noun: **protectors**] someone who protects another person

protein [noun: **proteins**] a substance found in foods like eggs, meat and milk that is necessary for strength and growth

protest [verb: **protests, protesting, protested**] to protest about something is to say publicly that you think it is wrong
[noun: **protests**] a strong statement saying that something is wrong or an organized demonstration against something

ⓘ The noun is pronounced **proh**–test, with the stress at the beginning.
The verb is pronounced pro–**test**, with the stress at the end.

Protestant [noun: **Protestants**] a member of one of the Christian churches that broke away from the Catholic Church at the time of the Reformation
[adjective] to do with the Protestant church, or Protestants

prototype [noun: **prototypes**] the first built version of a new design, for example, for a new

Pp

model of car, used to test how well it works before it is manufactured in large numbers

protrude [verb: **protrudes, protruding, protruded**] to protrude is to stick out from something

♦ **protrusion** [noun: **protrusions**] something that sticks or is pushed out

proud [adjective: **prouder, proudest**]
1 feeling pleased about your achievements or possessions or about the achievements of people you are connected to: *I was very proud when my son got the award.*
2 behaving as though you think you are better than other people
3 a proud person does not like other people to think they are weak and does not like to ask for help

prove [verb: **proves, proving, proved**] to prove something is to show that it is true by providing evidence
➡ **proof**

proverb [noun: **proverbs**] a wise saying that gives advice or makes a statement about something that is true
♦ **proverbial** [adjective] well-known, like a proverb

provide [verb: **provides, providing, provided**]
1 to provide something is to give or supply it
2 to provide for someone is to supply the money and other things they need to live
➡ **provision**

province [noun: **provinces**]
1 a division of a country, usually with its own local government
2 the provinces are the parts of a country away from the capital
♦ **provincial** [adjective] belonging to the provinces or typical of the provinces

provision [noun: **provisions**]
1 providing something
2 to **make provision for** something is to prepare for it
➡ **provisions**

provisional [adjective]
1 intended to be temporary: *a provisional driving licence*
2 a provisional offer or arrangement is not yet definite but is likely to become definite in the

future: *He's been offered a provisional place at college.*

provisions [plural noun] food and other items you need, for example, if you go on a long journey

provocation [noun: **provocations**] provoking someone, or something that provokes them

provoke [verb: **provokes, provoking, provoked**] to provoke someone is to make them angry deliberately

prow [noun: **prows**] the prow of a boat is the raised part at the front or bows

prowl [verb: **prowls, prowling, prowled**] to wander about, especially in a secretive way
♦ **prowler** [noun: **prowlers**] someone who wanders about an area, keeping themselves hidden and watching people or their houses

proximity [noun] nearness: *People living in such proximity can get on each other's nerves.*

proxy [noun: **proxies**] a person who you have officially chosen to vote or do something official on your behalf: *She voted by proxy.*

prudence [noun] being prudent
♦ **prudent** [adjective] careful and wise, and not taking any risks, especially with money

prune[1] [verb: **prunes, pruning, pruned**] to prune a plant or tree is to cut bits off it to make it smaller

prune[2] [noun: **prunes**] a dried plum

pry [verb: **pries, prying, pried**] to try to find out things that people do not want you to know

PS [abbreviation] short for **postscript**. PS is written before an extra bit that you add to the end of a letter, after your signature

psalm [noun: **psalms**] a holy song, especially one from the Bible

pseudonym [noun: **pseudonyms**] a name that someone, especially a writer, uses instead of their real name

psychiatric [adjective] to do with psychiatry or mental illness
♦ **psychiatrist** [noun: **psychiatrists**] a doctor who treats mentally ill people
♦ **psychiatry** [noun] the branch of medicine that studies and treats mental illness

psychic [adjective] someone who is psychic is believed to have special powers such as

Pp

telepathy and the ability to see into the future

psychological [adjective] to do with the mind

♦ **psychologist** [noun: **psychologists**] someone who has studied psychology and human behaviour

♦ **psychology** [noun] the study of the mind and how it affects the way humans and animals act

PTO [abbreviation] short for **please turn over**, written at the bottom of a page to tell someone that you want them to turn the page over and read the other side

pub [noun: **pubs**] a place where you can buy and drink alcoholic drinks

puberty [noun] the time when a child's body begins to change into an adult's

public [noun]
1 the public are people generally
2 to do something **in public** is to do it where anyone can see it or take part
[adjective]
1 to do with, or for, all the people of a country or community, or all people: *public opinion • a public park*
2 known by everyone: *It's public now that they're getting engaged.*
3 a public figure is someone who is well known and appears in newspaper or news reports a lot

publication [noun: **publications**] something such as a magazine or newspaper that is printed and sold

publicity [noun]
1 advertising or anything done to make the public aware of something
2 public interest or attention: *The affair attracted a lot of publicity.*

publicize or **publicise** [verb: **publicizes, publicizing, publicized**] to publicize something is to advertise it or make it known publicly

public relations [noun] the job of making something such as a company, organization or famous person seem good to the public. This is often shortened to **PR**

publish [verb: **publishes, publishing, published**] to publish something is to print it in a book, newspaper or magazine

♦ **publisher** [noun: **publishers**] a person or company that publishes books, newspapers or magazines

♦ **publishing** [noun] the work or business of printing books, newspapers and magazines

puck [noun: **pucks**] the hard disc hit by the players in ice hockey

pucker [verb: **puckers, puckering, puckered**] to form into, or create, folds or wrinkles

pudding [noun: **puddings**] a sweet dish that you eat as the last course at dinner

puddle [noun: **puddles**] water filling a shallow hole in the ground

puff [verb: **puffs, puffing, puffed**]
1 to puff smoke or steam is to blow it out
2 you puff when you breathe quickly because you have been exercising
3 to **puff something out**, or **puff something up**, is to make it swell or become larger
[noun: **puffs**] a small amount of breath, wind, air or smoke

puffin [noun: **puffins**] a sea bird rather like a parrot that has a black and white body, and white, red and blue markings on its beak and face

puffy [adjective: **puffier, puffiest**] swollen: *puffy eyes*

pull [verb: **pulls, pulling, pulled**]
1 to pull something is to take hold of it and bring it towards you
2 if you pull a muscle you stretch it or strain it so that it is painful
3 to **pull a face** is to twist your face into an ugly or funny shape
4 a driver **pulls in** when they move to the side of the road and stop
5 to **pull something off** is to manage to do it successfully
6 a driver **pulls out** when they move out of a side road on to a main road, or they move to an outer lane to overtake another vehicle
7 to **pull out** of an arrangement is to stop taking part in it
8 someone who has been dangerously ill **pulls through** when they recover
9 a driver **pulls up** when they slow down and stop
10 if you **pull yourself together**, you start to

get control of your emotions after you have been very upset, angry or shocked
[noun: **pulls**] a pulling movement

pulley [noun: **pulleys**] a device for lifting or lowering heavy loads, which consists of a wheel with a rope in a groove around its edge

pullover [noun: **pullovers**] a knitted piece of clothing for the top half of your body that you pull on over your head

pulp [noun]
1 the soft flesh of certain fruits and vegetables
2 a substance that has been mashed into a thick, soft mass: *paper made from wood pulp* • *Mash the raspberries to a pulp.*

pulpit [noun: **pulpits**] a high platform where a minister stands to give the sermon in a church

pulsate [verb: **pulsates, pulsating, pulsated**] to vibrate or move in and out with a regular beat or rhythm

pulse[1] [noun: **pulses**] your pulse is the regular beat that you feel on your wrist or neck caused by the heart pumping blood through your arteries
[verb: **pulses, pulsing, pulsed**] something that pulses vibrates or moves with a regular rhythm

pulse[2] [noun: **pulses**] pulses are seeds you can eat, for example, peas, beans and lentils

pulverize or **pulverise** [verb: **pulverizes, pulverizing, pulverized**] to pulverize something is to crush it to dust or powder

puma [noun: **pumas**] a large, wild, cat–like animal found in North America

pumice [noun] a light kind of rock formed from lava that has gone solid, used to smooth hard skin

pummel [verb: **pummels, pummelling, pummelled**] to pummel someone or something is to beat them or it hard and repeatedly with your fists

pump [noun: **pumps**] a device or machine used to force or drive liquids or gases in, through or out of something: *a bicycle pump*
[verb: **pumps, pumping, pumped**] to pump liquid or gas is to force it up, through or out of something using a pump

pumpkin [noun: **pumpkins**] a large

rounded vegetable with thick yellow skin and soft orange flesh

pun [noun: **puns**] a joke using words that have more than one meaning, or words that sound the same but have different meanings. For example: *Two pears make a pair.*

punch [verb: **punches, punching, punched**] to hit someone or something with the fist or fists
[noun: **punches**]
1 a blow with the fist
2 a machine for making holes

punchline [noun: **punchlines**] the punchline of a joke or funny story is the part containing the point that makes you laugh

punchy [adjective: **punchier, punchiest**] having a forceful or striking effect: *a punchy performance*

punctual [adjective] a person or thing that is punctual arrives exactly on time, not early or late
‣ **punctuality** [noun] being punctual
‣ **punctually** [adverb] arriving on time

punctuate [verb: **punctuates, punctuating, punctuated**]
1 to punctuate written work is to put commas, full stops and other punctuation marks in it
2 if something is punctuated with things, these things happen or are done all through it or during it: *Her story was punctuated by little squeaks and giggles.*
‣ **punctuation** [noun] the process of putting commas, full stops and other punctuation marks in writing

punctuation mark [noun: **punctuation marks**] any of the special marks such as full stops and commas used in writing to mark off pauses or breaks in what has been written

puncture [noun: **punctures**] a hole made right through the outer surface of something, especially a tyre
[verb: **punctures, puncturing, punctured**] to puncture something is to make a hole in its outer skin or covering

pungent [adjective] a pungent smell is very strong and noticeable

punish [verb: **punishes, punishing, punished**] to punish someone is to make them suffer for something they have done wrong

Pp

◆ **punishable** [adjective] having a particular punishment: *The crime of murder is punishable by death in many countries.*

◆ **punishment** [noun: **punishments**]
1 punishing someone, or being punished
2 a particular method of making someone suffer for something they have done wrong

punk [noun: **punks**]
1 rock music played in a very loud and aggressive way
2 a young person with a style of dressing and behaving meant to shock people. Punks often wear black or ripped clothes with chains and have a spiky hairstyle

punnet [noun: **punnets**] a small light box made of cardboard or plastic and used to hold soft fruits like strawberries or raspberries

punt [noun: **punts**] a boat with a flat bottom that is moved along on rivers by someone standing upright and pushing with a long pole
[verb: **punts, punting, punted**] to punt is to travel on a river in a punt

puny [adjective: **punier, puniest**] weak and small

pup [noun: **pups**] a young dog or a young seal

pupil [noun: **pupils**]
1 a child or adult who is being taught
2 the pupil of your eye is the round opening in the middle of your eye through which light passes

puppet [noun: **puppets**] a doll that can be moved by wires or strings, or fitted over your hand and moved by your fingers

◆ **puppeteer** [noun: **puppeteers**] someone who operates puppets

puppy [noun: **puppies**] a baby dog

purchase [verb: **purchases, purchasing, purchased**] to purchase something is to buy it
[noun: **purchases**] something you have bought

◆ **purchaser** [noun: **purchasers**] a buyer

purdah [noun] purdah is the Muslim or Hindu tradition of keeping women hidden from men or strangers. Women in purdah cover their heads, bodies and faces when they are in public

pure [adjective: **purer, purest**]
1 not mixed with anything else: *pure gold • pure greed*
2 clean: *pure water*

3 a pure person is innocent and does not do any wrong things

◆ **purely** [adverb] only or simply: *Our meeting was purely accidental.*

→ **purify, purity**

purge [verb: **purges, purging, purged**] to purge people or things is to get rid of them because they are not wanted
[noun: **purges**] the act of getting rid of people or things that are not wanted

purify [verb: **purifies, purifying, purified**] to purify something is to make it clean or pure

purity [noun] being pure

purl [noun: **purls**] a stitch used in knitting

purple [noun] a dark reddish-blue colour

purpose [noun: **purposes**]
1 you have a purpose when you have an aim or goal
2 something's purpose is the job or role it is intended for
3 if you do something **on purpose**, you do it intentionally

◆ **purposeful** [adjective] determined and having an aim: *a purposeful walk to the shops*

◆ **purposefully** [adverb] in a determined way: *Sarah began to walk purposefully towards the house.*

◆ **purposely** [adverb] on purpose

purr [verb: **purrs, purring, purred**] a cat purrs when it makes a low vibrating noise because it is happy
[noun: **purrs**] the noise a cat makes when it is contented

purse [noun: **purses**] a small container for money, that you carry in a handbag or pocket
[verb: **purses, pursing, pursed**] you purse your lips when you draw them together into a round shape with your mouth tightly shut

pursue [verb: **pursues, pursuing, pursued**]
1 to pursue someone is to follow or chase them, usually in order to catch them
2 to pursue an activity or aim is to be involved in it or work hard at it

◆ **pursuer** [noun: **pursuers**] someone who is trying to catch the person or thing in front

◆ **pursuit** [noun: **pursuits**]
1 pursuing someone or something: *a pack of dogs in pursuit of a hare*
2 trying to achieve an aim or goal

3 an activity that interests you or that you do as a hobby: *My favourite pursuits are football and reading.*

pus [noun] a thick yellow liquid that forms in infected wounds

push [verb: **pushes, pushing, pushed**]

1 to push something is to press against it with your hands or body, so that it moves

2 to push someone is to try hard to make them do something: *He wouldn't do any work if he wasn't pushed.*

3 to **push someone around** is to bully them

4 push off is a slang term for 'go away' [noun: **pushes**] a pushing movement

pushchair [noun: **pushchairs**] a small folding chair on wheels used for pushing a young child around

pushy [adjective: **pushier, pushiest**] a pushy person behaves in a forceful way, determined to get their own way or to get attention

puss or **pussy** [noun: **pusses** or **pussies**] a name people often call their pet cat

put [verb: **puts, putting, put**]

1 to put something somewhere is to move it or place it there: *Put the shopping over there.* • *He put his hand over his eyes.*

2 to put something is to say or to write it: *I wouldn't put it like that.* • *I had to write a message in the card but I didn't know what to put.*

3 something that causes you to feel a certain way puts you in that mood

4 to **put someone down** is to criticize them or make them feel unimportant

5 to **put something off** is to delay it until a later time

6 if something **puts you off** doing something, it makes you not want to do it

7 if someone or something **puts you out**, they cause you inconvenience or trouble

8 to **put up with** someone or something is to tolerate them or it

putrid [adjective] rotten and smelling bad

putt [noun: **putts**] in golf, a gentle hit of the ball that you make so that it will go into the hole [verb: **putts, putting, putted**] in golf, to hit a ball gently so that it rolls forward on the green towards the hole

◆ **putter** [noun: **putters**] a golf club used for putting

putty [noun] an oily grey or white paste used for fixing glass in window frames

puzzle [noun: **puzzles**]

1 a game or toy that gives you a problem to solve

2 something that is a puzzle is hard to understand

[verb: **puzzles, puzzling, puzzled**] something puzzles you if you do not understand it or you cannot decide what it means

PVC [abbreviation] short for **polyvinyl chloride**, which is a type of plastic

pygmy or **pigmy** [noun: **pygmies**] a member of an African tribe of very small people

[adjective] small: *a pygmy hippopotamus*

pyjamas [plural noun] a suit with a top and matching trousers that you wear in bed

pylon [noun: **pylons**] a tall metal tower that supports electric power cables

pyramid [noun: **pyramids**]

1 a solid shape, with flat triangular sides, that comes to a point at the top

2 a tomb with this shape built for one of the ancient Egyptian pharaohs

pyre [noun: **pyres**] a fire in which a dead body is burned

python [noun: **pythons**] a large snake that kills its prey by winding itself around it and crushing it in its powerful coils

Pp

Q

quack [noun: **quacks**] the sound made by a duck
[verb: **quacks, quacking, quacked**] to make the sound of a duck: *The ducks quacked noisily as they swam across the pond.*

quad [noun: **quads**] a short form of the word **quadruplet**

quadruped [noun: **quadrupeds**] an animal that has four feet: *Cows, goats and sheep are all quadrupeds.*

quadruple [adjective]
1 four times as much or as many
2 made up of four parts
[verb: **quadruples, quadrupling, quadrupled**]
1 to quadruple something is to make it four times greater: *The shopkeeper had quadrupled the price.*
2 to quadruple is to become four times greater: *The river quadrupled in size during the rainy season.*

quadruplet [noun: **quadruplets**] one of four children born at one time to the same mother

quagmire [noun: **quagmires**] wet boggy ground: *Heavy rain had turned the garden into a quagmire.*

quail [noun: **quails**] a type of small bird like a partridge

quaint [adjective: **quainter, quaintest**] old-fashioned and pleasant: *quaint customs*

quake [verb: **quakes, quaking, quaked**] to quake is to tremble or shake: *The ground quaked under their feet.*
[noun: **quakes**] an informal word for an earthquake

qualification [noun: **qualifications**] an exam you have passed or a skill that you have that makes you suitable for a job or type of work: *What qualifications do you need for this job?*

qualify [verb: **qualifies, qualifying, qualified**]
1 to qualify for something such as a job is to be suitable for it: *He is too young to qualify for a place in the team.*
2 to qualify as something such as a doctor or a lawyer is to pass all the exams that are needed to do the job
3 to qualify something such as a statement or a remark is to make it less strong by adding or changing words

quality [noun: **qualities**]
1 how good or bad something is: *cloth of poor quality*
2 a part of someone's character that makes them behave in a particular way: *Her best qualities are her kindness and honesty.*

quantity [noun: **quantities**] amount or number: *a small quantity of paper • large quantities of tinned food*

quarantine [noun] if a person or animal is in quarantine they are kept away from other people or animals because they have or might have a disease that they could pass on

quarrel [verb: **quarrels, quarrelling, quarrelled**] to quarrel with someone is to argue angrily with them: *I've quarrelled with my brother. • We often hear them quarrelling next door.*
[noun: **quarrels**] an angry argument: *I've had a quarrel with the manager.*

• **quarrelsome** [adjective] quarrelling a lot: *quarrelsome children*

quarry [noun: **quarries**]
1 a place where stone is dug out of the ground
2 an animal that is being hunted

quart [noun: **quarts**] a measure of liquids, the same as 1.136 litres or 2 pints

quarter [noun: **quarters**]
1 a quarter is one of four equal parts that together make up the whole of something: *We cut the cake into quarters.*
2 the fraction $\frac{1}{4}$, equivalent to the decimal fraction 0.25, and equal to one divided by four
3 one fourth of a year, three months: *In the first quarter of the year the company made a profit.*
[verb: **quarters, quartering, quartered**] to divide something into four equal parts: *She quartered the melon.*

quarter-final [noun: **quarter-finals**] the third-last round in a competition, immediately before the semi-final

quarterly [adjective] happening every three months (quarter of a year): *quarterly payments*
[adverb] every three months: *We pay our gas bill quarterly.*
[noun: **quarterlies**] a magazine that is published every three months

quarters [plural noun] a place to stay, especially for soldiers

quartet [noun: **quartets**]
1 a group of four musicians or singers
2 a piece of music written for four musicians or singers

quartz [noun] a hard substance found in rocks in the form of crystals that can be used in electronic clocks and watches

quash [verb: **quashes, quashing, quashed**]
1 to quash something such as a protest is to stop it from continuing
2 to quash a judge's decision is to officially say that it is no longer valid or correct

quaver [verb: **quavers, quavering, quavered**] to shake or tremble: *Her voice quavered with fright as she spoke.*
[noun: **quavers**] a trembling: *He tried to sound brave but there was a quaver in his voice.*

quay [noun: **quays**] the edge of a harbour where ships are loaded or unloaded

(i) This word is pronounced the same as **key**.

queasy [adjective: **queasier, queasiest**] feeling sick: *The motion of the boat made her queasy.*

queen [noun: **queens**]
1 a woman who rules a country: *Queen Elizabeth II*
2 the wife of a king: *the king and his queen*
3 a playing card with a picture of a woman. The queen comes between the king and the jack in value
4 in the game of chess, the queen is a piece that has a crown and can move in any direction
5 a female bee, ant or wasp that lays eggs

queen mother [noun] the mother of the present king or queen who was once queen herself

queer [adjective: **queerer, queerest**] odd or strange: *queer behaviour*

quench [verb: **quenches, quenching, quenched**]
1 to quench your thirst is to drink until you no longer feel thirsty
2 to quench a fire is to put it out

query [noun: **queries**]
1 a question: *Please phone me if you have any queries.*
2 a question mark
[verb: **queries, querying, queried**] to query something is to question whether it is correct or true: *I rang the gas company to query my bill.*

quest [noun: **quests**] a search, especially a long one: *his quest for the truth*

question [noun: **questions**]
1 what you ask when you want to know something: *After the talk, some people asked questions.*
2 something you have to write an answer to in an exam: *I didn't have time to answer all the questions.*
3 a subject for discussion: *There is the question of how much to pay him.*
4 a suggestion or possibility: *There's no question of him leaving.*
5 if something is **out of the question**, it is impossible or not allowed so there is no point in discussing it: *It is quite out of the question for you to go out tonight.*

Qq

questionable [adjective] that may not be good or proper: *Her reasons seem questionable.*

question mark [noun: **question marks**] the mark (?) that you write after a sentence which is a question

questionnaire [noun: **questionnaires**] a list of questions to be answered by several people to get information for a survey

queue [noun: **queues**] a line of people waiting for something: *There was a long queue outside the cinema.*
[verb: **queues, queuing, queued**] to stand in a line waiting for something: *We had to queue for three hours to get the tickets.*

quibble [verb: **quibbles, quibbling, quibbled**] to quibble is to argue over or complain about details that are not important
[noun: **quibbles**] an argument over or complaint about small or unimportant details

quiche [noun: **quiches**] an open tart filled with beaten eggs, cheese and other savoury fillings

quick [adjective: **quicker, quickest**]
1 fast: *a quick walker*
2 done in a short time: *a quick trip into town*
3 doing something without delay: *She's always quick to help.*
[adverb] quickly: *Come quick!*
[noun] a tender area of skin under the nails
◆ **quickly** [adverb] if someone does something quickly, they do it rapidly or at great speed: *Come quickly! Someone's fallen in the river!*
◆ **quickness** [noun] being quick: *the quickness of his reply*

quicksand [noun: **quicksands**] loose wet sand that sucks in anything that lands on it

quicksilver [noun] an old-fashioned word for the metal **mercury**

quick-tempered [adjective] if someone is quick-tempered, they are easily made angry

quid [noun: **quid**] a pound (£1): *He paid fifty quid for the jacket.*
ⓘ This is a slang word.

quiet [adjective: **quieter, quietest**]
1 not loud: *a quiet voice*
2 calm and peaceful: *a quiet life*

[noun] a quiet state or time: *in the quiet of the night*
[verb: **quiets, quieted, quieting**]
1 to quiet something or someone is to make them quiet or calm: *quiet the baby*
2 to quiet is to become quiet or calm: *The teacher told the class to quiet down.*
◆ **quieten** [verb: **quietens, quietening, quietened**]
1 to quieten something or someone is to make them quiet: *He mother was trying to quieten her.*
2 to quieten or **quieten down** is to become quiet: *Things seem to have quietened down.*
◆ **quietly** [adverb] with little or no sound: *She slipped quietly from the room.*
◆ **quietness** [noun] being quiet: *the quietness of early morning*

quiff [noun: **quiffs**] a tuft of hair at the front of the head, especially one brushed up above the forehead

quill [noun: **quills**] a large feather of a goose or other bird, made into a pen

quilt [noun: **quilts**] a warm cover for a bed, filled with feathers or some other material
◆ **quilted** [adjective] made of two layers of material with padding between them: *a quilted jacket*

quin [noun: **quins**] a short form of the word **quintuplet**

quintet [noun: **quintets**]
1 a group of five musicians or singers
2 a piece of music written for five musicians or singers

quintuplet [noun: **quintuplets**] one of five children born at one time to the same mother

quip [noun: **quips**] a witty remark or reply
[verb: **quips, quipping, quipped**] to make a witty remark: *'Flattery will get you everywhere,' she quipped.*

quirk [noun: **quirks**]
1 something strange or unusual in a person's behaviour: *Wearing odd socks is just one of his little quirks.*
2 a strange happening: *By a quirk of fate, they met again years later.*
◆ **quirky** [adjective: **quirkier, quirkiest**] full of sudden and unexpected qualities: *a quirky sense of humour*

quit [verb: **quits, quitting, quit** or **quitted**]
1 to quit doing something is to stop it: *I'm going to quit smoking.*
2 to quit something is to leave it: *He's quit his job.*
➡ **quits, quitter**

quite [adverb]
1 rather: *I'm quite hungry but I don't mind waiting.*
2 completely: *I'm afraid I'm not quite ready.*

quits [adjective] if two people are quits, they do not owe each other anything, especially money: *I've paid for the damage to your car – now we're quits.*

quitter [noun: **quitters**] someone who gives up too easily

quiver[1] [verb: **quivers, quivering, quivered**] to tremble or shake: *Her lip quivered and her eyes filled with tears.*
[noun: **quivers**] a quivering sound or movement

quiver[2] [noun: **quivers**] a carrying case for arrows

quiz [noun: **quizzes**] a competition in which you have to answer questions on different subjects: *a TV quiz show*
[verb: **quizzes, quizzing, quizzed**] to quiz someone is to ask them lots of questions

quoits [noun] a game in which heavy flat rings called quoits are thrown onto small pegs

quota [noun: **quotas**] the part or share given to each member of a group: *Each school has received its quota of funds.*

quotation [noun: **quotations**]
1 quotation is the act of repeating something said or written by someone else
2 a quotation is a set of words taken from a speech or piece of writing: *a quotation from Shakespeare*
3 a quotation is the price estimated for doing a job: *I'd like a quotation for replacing these missing roof tiles.*

quotation marks [plural noun] the symbols ' ' or " " which are used in writing to show that someone's words are being repeated exactly. They are sometimes called **inverted commas**

quote [verb: **quotes, quoting, quoted**]
1 to quote someone is to repeat their words exactly as they said or wrote them
2 to quote words is to use them in a quotation
3 to quote a price is to say how much money you will charge for doing something: *He quoted a price for repairing the bicycle.*

Qur'an [noun] another spelling of **Koran**

Qq

R

rabbi [noun: **rabbis**] a Jewish religious leader

rabbit [noun: **rabbits**] a long-eared furry animal that lives in holes in the ground that are called burrows

rabble [noun] a noisy, uncontrolled crowd of people

rabid [adjective] affected with rabies

rabies [noun] a disease that causes madness and then death. Humans catch rabies if they are bitten by an animal that has it

raccoon or **racoon** [noun: **raccoons** or **racoons**] a small furry animal from North America that has a bushy striped tail

race [noun: **races**]
1 a competition to see who can get somewhere fastest: *a two-mile horse race* • *Lewis won the race.*
2 a competition to be the first to do something: *the race to put the first man on the moon*
[verb: **races, racing, raced**]
1 to try to do something first, before anyone else: *I'll race you to the postbox.*
2 to go very fast: *The car raced along the narrow lanes.* • *I could feel my heart racing with excitement.*

race [noun: **races**] a large group of people who have the same ancestors and look the same in some ways, for example in the colour of their skin or their hair

racecourse [noun: **racecourses**] the track that horses race on

racial [adjective] to do with a person's race or different races of people: *efforts to stop racial prejudice*

racism [noun] disliking people, or treating them badly or unfairly, only because they belong to a different race

racist [adjective] to do with racism: *racist remarks*
[noun: **racists**] someone who dislikes people or treats them badly, only because they belong to a different race

rack [noun: **racks**] a framework with rails, shelves or hooks, for holding or storing things: *a mug rack*
[verb: **racks, racking, racked**] to **rack your brains** is to try as hard as you can to think of something

racket¹ [noun: **rackets**] an oval frame with strings stretched across it that you use for hitting the ball in games like tennis and squash

racket² [noun: **rackets**]
1 a loud and disturbing noise: *Will you turn that racket down?*
2 an illegal scheme for making money

radar [noun] a system that uses radio waves that bounce off solid objects to find the position of aeroplanes or ships

radiance [noun] happiness that shows on your face
✦ **radiant** [adjective] showing a lot of happiness: *a picture of the radiant bride*

radiate [verb: **radiates, radiating, radiated**]
1 to radiate heat or light is to send it out
2 things radiate from a central point when they form a pattern of lines like spokes in a wheel
✦ **radiation** [noun] radioactive energy that can harm or kill people if they are exposed to it
✦ **radiator** [noun: **radiators**]

1 part of a central heating system that releases heat into a room

2 part of an engine that keeps it cool

radical [adjective] a radical idea is one that involves big, important changes

radio [noun: **radios**]

1 radio is a system of broadcasting that uses sound waves instead of wires to send messages

2 a radio is a piece of electrical equipment that receives or sends messages as sound waves

[verb: **radios, radioing, radioed**] to communicate with someone by radio: *Tell them to radio for help.*

radioactive [adjective] giving off rays that can be dangerous, even in very small amounts

♦ **radioactivity** [noun] the energy, that may be harmful, that is produced by the atoms of some substances, such as uranium

radiographer [noun: **radiographers**] someone whose job is to carry out X-rays in a hospital

♦ **radiography** [noun] the job or science of carrying out X-rays

radiotherapy [noun] the use of X-rays and other forms of radiation to treat diseases such as cancer

radish [noun: **radishes**] a small round vegetable with a red skin and strong taste that is eaten raw in salads

radius [noun: **radii**] an area that covers a particular distance from a central point: *We deliver anywhere within a ten-mile radius of the store.*

raffia [noun] strips of palm-tree leaf that are used in weaving things like hats and mats

raffle [noun: **raffles**] a lottery to win a prize: *a book of raffle tickets*

[verb: **raffles, raffling, raffled**] to offer something as a prize in a lottery: *Fran only bought one ticket and won the car they were raffling.*

raft [noun: **rafts**] a simple boat made from pieces of wood tied together to form a platform to sit on

rafter [noun: **rafters**] one of the sloping pieces of wood that form the framework inside a roof

rag [noun: **rags**] an old piece of cloth: *dressed in rags* • *Polish the wood with a soft rag.*

rage [noun]

1 rage is violent anger

2 a rage is an outburst of violent anger: *I've never seen him fly into a rage like that before.*

3 if something is **all the rage**, it is very fashionable: *Flares were all the rage.*

ragged [adjective] torn and untidy: *ragged clothes*

ⓘ **Ragged** is pronounced with two syllables: **rag**-id.

raid [noun: **raids**]

1 a sudden unexpected attack: *a bombing raid*

2 a sudden unexpected visit from the police, who force their way into a building and search it

[verb: **raids, raiding, raided**]

1 to attack a place suddenly, without warning

2 to visit a place unexpectedly and search it

♦ **raider** [noun: **raiders**] a person who attacks, searches for something and removes it

rail [noun: **rails**]

1 a bar for hanging things on: *a towel rail*

2 a long steel bar that is one of the tracks that a train runs on

3 rail travel or travel by rail is travelling by train

♦ **railing** [noun: **railings**] one of the vertical bars that make up a fence: *He was leaning on the railings.*

railroad [noun: **railroads**] the American word for **railway**

railway [noun: **railways**] a track for trains to travel on

rain [noun] drops of water falling from the clouds: *a heavy shower of rain*

[verb: **rains, raining, rained**]

1 it is raining when drops of water fall from the clouds

2 an event such as a sports match is **rained off** if rain stops it from happening

rainbow [noun: **rainbows**] an arch of different colours that can often be seen in the sky when it is raining and the sun is shining at the same time

raincoat [noun: **raincoats**] a light waterproof coat

Rr

rainfall [noun] the amount of rain that falls in a particular place over a particular period of time

rainforest [noun: **rainforests**] an area of thick tropical forest with very tall trees and a high rainfall

rainy [adjective: **rainier, rainiest**] a rainy day is one when it rains a lot

raise [verb: **raises, raising, raised**]
1 to lift something up: *Raise your hand if you know the answer.* • *The wreck was slowly raised from the seabed.*
2 to increase an amount or number: *They've raised the rent again.*
3 to mention a new subject in a discussion: *I want to raise a matter that we all care very much about.*
4 to raise money is to get money together for a particular reason: *We're raising money for charity.*
5 to raise children is to look after them until they are grown up
6 to raise crops is to grow them
[noun: **raises**] a pay increase

ⓘ The noun **raise** is more common in American English. The usual British word is **rise**.

raisin [noun: **raisins**] a dried grape

rake [noun: **rakes**] a gardening tool like a large comb with a long handle
[verb: **rakes, raking, raked**]
1 to use a rake, usually to collect leaves or smooth the soil
2 to **rake in** money is to get a lot of it easily: *We were raking the money in from everyone at the sale.*

ⓘ **Rake in** is a very informal phrase.

rally [noun: **rallies**]
1 a large meeting of people, especially for an outdoor meeting
2 a car race on a course that includes ordinary roads and forest tracks
3 in sports like tennis, a rally is series of strokes and returns that make up one point
[verb: **rallies, rallying, rallied**]
1 to feel better and improve after being ill or suffering a setback: *The team have rallied now and will probably win.*

2 to rally or **rally round** is to come together to support someone: *We're hoping to rally all our members to vote.*

RAM [noun] short for **Random Access Memory**, which is a type of computer memory

ram [noun: **rams**] a male sheep
[verb: **rams, ramming, rammed**] to push one thing very hard into another: *The boat was clearly going to ram the pier.*

Ramadan [noun] the ninth month of the Islamic calendar, when Muslims fast during the day

ramble [verb: **rambles, rambling, rambled**]
1 to walk about the countryside for pleasure
2 to ramble or **ramble on** is to speak or to write a lot without keeping to the subject
[noun: **rambles**] a long walk in the countryside
◆ **rambler** [noun: **ramblers**] someone who enjoys walking in the countryside

ramp [noun: **ramps**] a sloping surface: *We should be able to get the wheelchair up the ramp quite easily.*

rampage [verb: **rampages, rampaging, rampaged**] people or animals rampage when they rush about wildly or violently
[noun] if a group of people **go on the rampage**, they behave in a violent way and cause damage to a lot of things

rampart [noun: **ramparts**] a mound or wall that is built around a castle or town as a defence

ramshackle [adjective] a ramshackle building is in very bad condition and falling apart

ran [verb] a way of changing the verb **run** to make a past tense: *I ran all the way here.*

ranch [noun: **ranches**] a large farm, especially one in North America, where they keep cattle and horses

rancid [adjective] rancid food tastes or smells unpleasant because the fat in it is no longer fresh: *rancid butter*

random [adjective] done without a plan or a system: *a random selection*

range [noun: **ranges**]
1 a number of different things that are of the same type: *a huge range of evening wear*
2 the distance that something can travel:

Spectators have to stand well out of range of the arrows.

3 the distance between the top and bottom notes of a voice or musical instrument

4 an area where you can practise hitting golf balls or shooting: *a firing-range*

5 a group of hills or mountains: *a mountain range in the distance*

6 an old-fashioned kitchen stove

[verb: **ranges, ranging, ranged**]

1 to range between two things is to include a variety of different things in addition to the two things mentioned: *holidays ranging from hostels to luxury hotels • We were quoted prices ranging from £200 to £1000 for doing the job.*

2 to wander around or over a place: *We ranged over the hills for days.*

• **ranger** [noun: **rangers**] someone whose job is to look after a forest or park

rank [noun: **ranks**] someone's position, grade or level in an organization or in society: *A private is the lowest rank in the British army. • A duchess has a very high social rank.*

[verb: **ranks, ranking, ranked**] to have a certain position amongst other things: *He ranks as one of the world's best actors.*

ransack [verb: **ransacks, ransacking, ransacked**] to search a place violently, without caring about damaging or destroying things in it: *The inspector came home to find his flat had been ransacked.*

ransom [noun: **ransoms**] a ransom is the money that kidnappers demand before they will give back someone they have taken hostage

rant [verb: **rants, ranting, ranted**] to speak in a loud, angry, uncontrolled way

rap [verb: **raps, rapping, rapped**]

1 to hit something quickly and sharply

2 to perform a song by speaking the words in rhythm

[noun: **raps**]

1 a quick, sharp tap or hit: *a rap at the door*

2 a pop song with words that are spoken in rhythm

rape [noun: **rapes**] the crime of violently forcing someone to have sex with you when they do not want to: *He was accused of rape.*

[verb: **rapes, raping, raped**] to violently force someone to have sex with you when they do not want to

➞ **rapist**

rapid [adjective] moving, acting or happening very quickly: *a rapid response to the emergency situation*

• **rapidly** [adverb] very quickly: *moving rapidly on to the next question*

• **rapids** [plural noun] parts of a river where the water flows very quickly, usually over dangerous rocks

rapist [noun: **rapists**] someone who has committed the crime of violently forcing someone to have sex with them

rare [adjective: **rarer, rarest**]

1 not often done or found, or not occurring often: *a rare example of a blue diamond • It's rare to find a vase like this in perfect condition.*

2 rare meat is only lightly cooked and often still has blood in it: *I always order a rare steak.*

• **rarely** [adverb] not very often: *I rarely go out.*

• **rarity** [noun: **rarities**]

1 a rarity is something that is not found very often: *This map is truly a rarity.*

2 rarity is unusualness: *very expensive because of its rarity*

rascal [noun: **rascals**]

1 a cheeky or naughty child

2 a dishonest person

rash [1] [adjective: **rasher, rashest**] a rash person does foolish things quickly without thinking first

rash [2] [noun: **rashes**] an area of red spots on your skin, caused by an illness or allergy: *Measles causes a rash.*

rasher [noun: **rashers**] a rasher of bacon is a thin slice of it

rasp [verb: **rasps, rasping, rasped**] to make a rough grating noise

[noun: **rasps**] a rough grating sound: *the loud rasp of the old hinges moving*

raspberry [noun: **raspberries**] a red berry that you can eat and that grows on bushes.

rat [noun: **rats**] a small furry animal like a large mouse with a long tail

rate [noun: **rates**]

1 how fast or often something happens: *The*

Rr

rate of progress has been very slow. • The disease is spreading at a tremendous rate.
2 at any rate means 'anyway': He's gone to see his cousin or someone - a relative at any rate.
[verb: **rates, rating, rated**] to decide how good or bad something is: How do you rate him as a player?

♦ **rates** [plural noun] a tax that businesses must pay to a local council for the buildings and land they use. In the past, people had to pay this tax on their house too

rather [adverb]
1 a bit or somewhat: It's rather cold in here, isn't it?
2 more correctly: I've already agreed; or rather, I haven't said 'no'.
3 you **would rather** do something if you would prefer to do it: I would rather talk about this later if you don't mind.

ratio [noun: **ratios**] the relationship between two numbers or amounts. For example, if you say The child-to-teacher ratio is five to one then you mean there are five children to every teacher

ration [noun: **rations**] your ration of something is how much of it you are allowed to have: I ate my ration of biscuits for the day before lunchtime.
[verb: **rations, rationing, rationed**] to limit the amount of something that people are allowed because there is not a lot available: Sugar was rationed during the war.

rational [adjective] reasonable and sensible: a rational decision
♦ **rationally** [adverb] thinking reasonably and sensibly

rattle [verb: **rattles, rattling, rattled**]
1 to rattle is to make lots of short, sharp, hard sounds: a closed door rattling in the wind
2 to rattle something is to shake it so that it makes a noise: a person rattling a box and asking for money
3 to rattle a person is to worry them or make them nervous: A police warning had rattled the gang.
[noun: **rattles**]
1 a baby's toy that makes a noise when you shake it

2 the noise something hard and loose makes when it is shaken: There's a bad rattle coming from the engine.

rattlesnake [noun: **rattlesnakes**] a poisonous snake that lives in America. Its tail makes a rattling sound when it gets angry

raucous [adjective] a raucous sound is rough and loud: raucous laughter

ravage [verb: **ravages, ravaging, ravaged**] to damage something until it is almost destroyed
♦ **ravages** [plural noun] the ravages of something, such as time, are its damaging effects

rave [noun: **raves**] a large party held in a large building where people dance to very loud music
[verb: **raves, raving, raved**]
1 to talk about something very enthusiastically: The newspapers have been raving about this programme.
2 someone is raving when they talk in an uncontrolled way, as if they were mad

raven [noun: **ravens**] a large black bird like a crow

ravenous [adjective] very hungry

ravine [noun: **ravines**] a deep narrow valley with steep sides

ravioli [noun] an Italian dish made up of small cases of pasta with savoury fillings

raw [adjective: **rawer, rawest**]
1 raw food is not cooked: a salad of raw vegetables
2 a raw substance is in its natural state before it is used for anything or put through any processes: raw cotton
3 a raw recruit is someone who has no training or experience
4 a raw wound is sore where the skin has been damaged
5 cold, wet and windy: raw weather conditions

raw material [noun: **raw materials**] a natural substance that other things are made from

ray [noun: **rays**] a beam of light: a few rays of sunshine

razor [noun: **razors**] an instrument with a sharp blade that is used to shave hair

Rd [abbreviation] short for **road**

re- [prefix]

1 if a word starts with **re-**, it often has something to do with something happening again. For example, to *reappear* is to appear again

2 if a word starts with **re-**, it can also have something to do with something moving or being sent back. For example, to *refund* money is to give it back

reach [verb: **reaches, reaching, reached**]

1 to reach a place is to arrive there: *We didn't reach the cottage till long after dark.*

2 to be able to reach something is to be able to touch or get hold of it: *I can't reach the top shelf.*

3 to reach someone is to be able to contact them, especially by telephone: *I've been trying to reach you all day.*

4 to reach to somewhere is to extend as far as that: *Charlotte's hair reaches right down her back.*

[noun] something is **within** or **out of reach** if you can or cannot touch it or get to it

react [verb: **reacts, reacting, reacted**] to do something as a result of something else happening: *How did Helen react when she heard the news?*

♦ **reaction** [noun: **reactions**]

1 behaviour that is a direct result of something else: *Did you see his reaction when he found out?*

2 a bad response by your body to something such as a food you have eaten or a drug you have taken: *He had an allergic reaction to the drug.*

read [verb: **reads, reading, read**]

1 to look at something such as writing and understand it: *Read a book.* • *I'd like to learn to read music.*

2 to say aloud what is written or printed: *I always read a story to the children at bedtime.*

3 an instrument reads something when that is what it shows: *The thermometer reads 31 degrees.*

[noun: **reads**] a **good read** is a book that is enjoyable to read

♦ **readable** [adjective] easy or enjoyable to read

♦ **reader** [noun: **readers**] a person who reads, especially a particular book or newspaper: *Regular readers will recognize this name.*

→ **reading**

readily [adverb]

1 something is readily available if it is easy to get

2 you do something readily if you do it willingly: *The whole family readily agreed to help.*

readiness [noun] being ready and prepared for something: *The car had been filled with petrol in readiness for the journey.*

reading [noun: **readings**]

1 reading is looking at and understanding written words

2 a reading is a part of a book that someone reads to an audience

3 a reading is a measurement on a gauge

ready [adjective]

1 prepared for something: *Are the children ready for bed?* • *Dinner's ready.*

2 willing: *Are you sure you're ready to give up chocolate for a whole week?*

→ **readily, readiness**

real [adjective]

1 actually existing, not invented or imaginary: *real people with real problems*

2 genuine, not a copy: *The seats are made of real leather.*

→ **really**

realism [noun] the style that tries to show things as they really are, especially in art, books and films

♦ **realist** [noun: **realists**] someone who deals with situations as they really are, rather than pretending that they are different

♦ **realistic** [adjective]

1 very like real life: *The fight scenes were very realistic.*

2 dealing with the real situation in a sensible way: *a realistic outlook on life*

♦ **realistically** [adverb]

1 in a way that is very like real life: *The grapes were realistically painted.*

2 seeing things as they really are: *Realistically, there was no chance that he could win.*

realization or **realisation** [noun:

Rr

realizations] when you suddenly realize something: *The realization that they were sinking caused instant panic.*

realize or **realise** [verb: **realizes, realizing, realized**] to know and understand something: *I suddenly realized that he wasn't joking.*

really [adverb]
1 actually, in fact: *We're in the same class but we're not really friends.*
2 very: *a really lovely day*
3 certainly: *We'll really have to work hard to finish on time.*

realm [noun: **realms**]
1 an area of activity, study or interest: *the realm of general science*
2 a country that is ruled by a king or queen

reap [verb: **reaps, reaping, reaped**]
1 to cut and gather a crop such as corn
2 to **reap the benefit** of something is to gain from something you did earlier: *He passed the exam so he's reaped the benefits of all that hard work.*
◆ **reaper** [noun: **reapers**] a person or machine that brings in the harvest

rear [noun: **rears**]
1 the rear is the back part of something: *seats towards the rear of the plane*
2 your rear is the part of your body that you sit on
[verb: **rears, rearing, reared**]
1 to rear children or animals is to look after them as they grow
2 a horse or other animal rears or **rears up** when it rises up on its back legs

reason [noun: **reasons**]
1 the reason for something is why it happened or exists: *No one knows the reason for his disappearance.*
2 your reason is your ability to think clearly and form opinions: *Will you please listen to reason?*
◆ **reasonable** [adjective]
1 sensible and not foolish: *I suppose it's a reasonable decision.* • *Any reasonable person would agree with that.*
2 a reasonable amount of something is quite a lot of it

reassurance [noun: **reassurances**]

something that stops someone from feeling worried

reassure [verb: **reassures, reassuring, reassured**] to say something to stop someone from feeling worried and to give them hope: *He tried to reassure me that everything would be all right.*
◆ **reassuring** [adjective] helping to make a person feel confident and happy or safe: *a reassuring look*

rebate [noun: **rebates**] part of a payment, especially a tax, that someone gets back because they paid, or were charged, too much

rebel [verb: **rebels, rebelling, rebelled**] to refuse to obey someone: *Teenagers often rebel against their parents.*
[noun: **rebels**] a person who fights against, or simply does not obey, people in authority, especially their government
◆ **rebellion** [noun: **rebellions**]
1 rebellion is when people refuse to do what they are told
2 a rebellion is a fight against an authority such as a government
◆ **rebellious** [adjective] difficult to control and not wanting to obey: *a rebellious child*

ⓘ The verb **rebel** is pronounced ri–**bel**, with the stress at the end.
The noun **rebel** is pronounced **reb**–il, with the stress at the beginning.

reboot [verb: **reboots, rebooting, rebooted**] to start a computer up again: *You'll have to reboot to save these changes.*

rebound [verb: **rebounds, rebounding, rebounded**] to bounce back again: *The ball hammered against the crossbar, and rebounded into the net.*

rebuke [verb: **rebukes, rebuking, rebuked**] to tell someone off for doing something wrong
[noun: **rebukes**] a telling–off

recall [verb: **recalls, recalling, recalled**]
1 to remember: *Do you recall how we used to play here as children?*
2 to order someone to come back: *The government has recalled all its diplomats.*
3 if a store or manufacturer recalls a product,

they ask for people to return it because there is something wrong with it

recap [verb: **recaps, recapping, recapped**] to go back over something that you have already said or heard: *To recap, this button switches it on, and this one controls volume.*

recapture [verb: **recaptures, recapturing, recaptured**]
1 to catch a person or animal that has escaped
2 to bring back a feeling or experience from another place or time: *The film perfectly recaptures the atmosphere of 1940s Hollywood.*

recede [verb: **recedes, receding, receded**] to move backwards or into the distance
♦ **receding** [adjective] someone's hairline is receding if they are going bald at the front

receipt [noun: **receipts**]
1 a receipt is a piece of paper you get when you pay money or hand something over to someone
2 receipt is the fact that you have received something: *On receipt of the card, you must sign it.*

receive [verb: **receives, receiving, received**]
1 to get something that someone gives or sends to you: *Did you receive my last letter?*
2 to receive guests is to greet and welcome them: *The mayor stood near the door and received his guests personally.*
♦ **receiver** [noun: **receivers**]
1 the part of a telephone that you hear through
2 equipment that picks up radio or television signals
➡ **receipt, reception, recipient**

recent [adjective] happening only a short time ago: *a recent rise in prices* • *These changes are all quite recent.*
♦ **recently** [adverb] a short time ago: *I saw Ann quite recently.*

reception [noun: **receptions**]
1 a reception is a formal party, for example for a wedding
2 reception is the place where visitors arrive and are welcomed in hotels, office buildings or hospitals: *The people at reception will tell you which room to go to.*

3 how someone reacts to something: *I got a pretty cool reception when I asked the boss for more money.*
4 how clear the sound or picture is that you get on your radio or television: *Our reception up here in the hills is not always very good.*
♦ **receptionist** [noun: **receptionists**] someone whose job is to welcome people who arrive in a building and answer enquiries

recess [noun: **recesses**]
1 a place where a wall is set back a bit to make a small space: *The post office has a recess with a small shelf where you can write a note.*
2 recess is a time when parliament or law courts do not work
♦ **recession** [noun: **recessions**] a country is in recession when its businesses are not doing well and unemployment is increasing

recipe [noun: **recipes**] a set of instructions on how to prepare or cook a particular dish and a list of its ingredients: *a recipe for chocolate-chip cookies*

recipient [noun: **recipients**] a person who receives something

recital [noun: **recitals**] a public performance of music, songs or poetry, usually by one person

recite [verb: **recites, reciting, recited**] to say something, such as a poem, aloud from memory

reckless [adjective] doing things without caring or thinking about the results of your actions: *reckless driving*
♦ **recklessly** [adverb] carelessly and possibly dangerously
♦ **recklessness** [noun] behaving carelessly and possibly causing harm or damage

reckon [verb: **reckons, reckoning, reckoned**]
1 to suppose or believe: *I reckon they're in love.*
2 to calculate: *Do you reckon we'll be finished on time?*

recline [verb: **reclines, reclining, reclined**] to lie or sit leaning back or sideways

recluse [noun: **recluses**] a person who lives alone and prefers not to mix with other people

recognition [noun] recognizing someone or something: *a smile of recognition*

Rr

recognizable or **recognisable**
[adjective]
1 someone or something that is recognizable is easy to identify because you have seen them before: *He is barely recognizable since he shaved off his beard.*
2 easy to see or notice: *a recognizable difference*

recognize or **recognise** [verb: recognizes, recognizing, recognized]
1 to know who or what you are seeing or hearing because you have seen or heard them before: *I recognized you from your photo.*
2 to accept that something is true: *I recognize that this isn't your fault.*

recoil [verb: recoils, recoiling, recoiled] to move back suddenly from a thing or person because you are afraid or disgusted: *Bill recoiled from the hand that tried to catch hold of him.*

recollect [verb: recollects, recollecting, recollected] to remember: *I recollect that it was a cold Tuesday morning.*
• **recollection** [noun: recollections] something that you remember: *I have absolutely no recollection of what happened.*

recommend [verb: recommends, recommending, recommended]
1 to advise someone to do something: *The doctor has recommended that the whole family takes a holiday.*
2 to suggest to someone that something would be good or suitable for them: *My friend recommended this book to me.*
• **recommendation** [noun: recommendations] something that a person suggests would be good or suitable for someone else: *a list of recommendations from the tourist board*

reconcile [verb: reconciles, reconciling, reconciled]
1 to accept that you will have to do or deal with something unpleasant: *He isn't reconciled to the idea of spending six weeks in hospital.*
2 you are reconciled with someone when you are friendly with them again after an argument
• **reconciliation** [noun] being friendly with someone again after an argument or disagreement

reconstruction [noun: reconstructions] a reconstruction of something like a crime, is when people try to act out how it happened

record [verb: records, recording, recorded]
1 to record something, such as music or a television programme, is to copy it on to a tape so that it can be played again later: *The band recorded their first album in 1982.*
2 to record a piece of information is to write it down
[noun: records]
1 a piece of information that has been written down and stored: *We have a record of all the names of the past members.*
2 a round flat piece of plastic that music and speech can be stored on: *a pile of old jazz records*
3 the highest, lowest, best or worst level or performance: *Denise is determined to beat her own record on this jump.*
• **recorder** [noun: recorders]
1 a machine that copies sounds or pictures, such as a tape recorder or video recorder
2 a simple wind instrument with holes that you cover with your fingers as you blow
• **recording** [noun: recordings] a tape or video of sounds or pictures

ⓘ The verb **record** is pronounced ri-**kord**, with the stress at the end.
The noun **record** is pronounced **rek**-ird, with the stress at the beginning.

recover [verb: recovers, recovering, recovered]
1 to get better after being ill, injured or upset: *My aunt is recovering from a short illness.*
2 to get something back that has been lost, stolen or used up: *The wreck has been recovered from the seabed.* • *The patient has not yet recovered consciousness.*
• **recovery** [noun: recoveries]
1 when someone gets better: *97% of our patients make a full recovery.*
2 getting something back: *the recovery of stolen goods*

recreation [noun] enjoyable things that you do in your spare time: *Shopping is my favourite form of recreation.*

recruit [verb: **recruits, recruiting, recruited**] to take on new staff or get someone to join an organization: *The company recruits a few school-leavers each year.*
[noun: **recruits**] a person who joins an organization: *a line of new recruits*
 • **recruitment** [noun] taking on new staff or getting people to join an organization
rectangle [noun: **rectangles**] a four-sided shape with opposite sides that are of equal length and four right angles
 • **rectangular** [adjective] with two pairs of straight sides and four right angles: *a rectangular table*
recuperate [verb: **recuperates, recuperating, recuperated**] to get better after being ill
 • **recuperation** [noun] getting better after being ill
recur [verb: **recurs, recurring, recurred**] to happen again, either once or several times: *There is a possibility that this situation will recur.*
 • **recurrence** [noun: **recurrences**] when something happens again: *a recurrence of the same problem*
 • **recurring** [adjective] happening again, and possibly again: *a recurring illness*
recycle [verb: **recycles, recycling, recycled**]
1 to save or process something so that it can be used again: *I keep the bags in this drawer and recycle them.* • *Most plastics can be recycled.*
 • **recycled** [adjective] not made from new materials, but from something that has been saved and used again: *cardboard made from recycled paper*
 • **recycling** [noun] saving things so that they can be used again, either as they are, or in another production process
red [noun]
1 the colour of blood, or any similar shade
2 an orange-brown hair colour
3 if someone **sees red**, they suddenly get very angry: *The way she looked at me just made me see red.*
redeem [verb: **redeems, redeeming, redeemed**]

1 to redeem something is to get it back by paying some money: *You can redeem your coat from the cloakroom with this ticket.*
2 to redeem a person is to save them from sin and evil, especially in the Christian religion
 • **redeemer** [noun] another name for Jesus Christ
 • **redemption** [noun]
1 when a thing is paid for and returned to its owner
2 when a person is saved from sin and evil, especially in the Christian religion
red-handed [adjective] to **catch someone red-handed** is to catch them as they are doing something wrong or illegal
red herring [noun: **red herrings**] something designed to make someone believe the wrong thing or to give them the wrong idea about something
red-letter [adjective] a **red-letter day** is a day that is especially happy or important
reduce [verb: **reduces, reducing, reduced**] to make something smaller or less: *We have reduced the number of classes to four.* • *Prices have been reduced.*
 • **reduction** [noun: **reductions**] when something is made smaller or less: *We're offering massive price reductions.*
redundancy [noun: **redundancies**] when a person is not needed to do their job any more: *A company losing money often means redundancy for many workers.*
 • **redundant** [adjective] to be **made redundant** is to be told that you no longer have a job because the company is reducing staff numbers
reed [noun: **reeds**]
1 a tall stiff grass that grows in or near water. Reeds are used to make baskets
2 a part of the mouthpiece of some wind instruments
reef [noun: **reefs**] a chain of rocks or a bank of sand just above or below the surface of the sea
reek [verb: **reeks, reeking, reeked**] to smell terrible: *His clothes reeked of fish.*
reel [noun: **reels**]
1 a cylinder that turns to wind up anything long and untidy, such as thread or film

Rr

2 a lively Scottish or Irish dance
[verb: **reels, reeling, reeled**]
1 to walk unsteadily
2 to **reel something off** is to say a long list of things quickly, without having to think

ref[1] [noun: **refs**] a short form of the word **referee**

ref[2] [abbreviation] short for **reference**

refer [verb: **refers, referring, referred**]
1 to refer to something is to mention it: *They referred to the letter I had written them last week.*
2 to refer a person to someone else or to a place is to direct them there to get more help: *My doctor referred me to the hospital to get an X-ray.*
→ **referral**

referee [noun: **referees**] in some sports, the person who makes sure the players obey the rules
[verb: **referees, refereeing, refereed**] to carefully watch the players and make decisions about whether a game is being played correctly

reference [noun: **references**]
1 a mention of something: *She made no reference to what had happened the day before.*
2 a direction that tells you where else to look for information: *a reference in the dictionary to another entry*
3 a written report on your character that someone reads before offering you a job: *You'll need a reference from your previous employer.*

reference book [noun: **reference books**] a book that you look in for information

referendum [noun: **referenda** or **referendums**] a chance for the people of a country to vote on whether they agree with something their government is suggesting

referral [noun: **referrals**] if your doctor gives you a referral, he or she sends you to see a specialist doctor at a hospital

refill [verb: **refills, refilling, refilled**] to fill something again: *We'll need to refill the tank before we go much further.*
[noun: **refills**] a full container to replace one that is empty of something that has been used

up: *Can you buy refills for that kind of pen?*

refine [verb: **refines, refining, refined**] to make a substance pure
• **refined** [adjective] a refined substance such as oil has been through a process that removes all dirt or other waste material from it
• **refinery** [noun: **refineries**] a factory where raw materials such as oil or foods are purified
• **refining** [noun] the process of purifying substances like oil or food

refit [verb: **refits, refitting, refitted**] to repair and improve the condition of a vehicle such as a ship
[noun: **refits**] a time when a ship is repaired and put back into good condition

reflect [verb: **reflects, reflecting, reflected**]
1 something is reflected when you can see an image of it in a surface like a mirror
2 to reflect something is to be a sign of it happening or existing: *Her face reflected how she felt inside.*
3 to reflect or to reflect on something is to think about it calmly
• **reflection** [noun: **reflections**]
1 an image that you can see in a surface like a mirror
2 a sign of something being responsible: *Your bad manners are a reflection on your parents.*
3 your reflections are your thoughts: *I wrote my reflections in my diary.*
• **reflective** [adjective] a reflective person thinks deeply about things
• **reflector** [noun: **reflectors**] a piece of shiny metal, especially on a vehicle or bicycle, that throws back light from other vehicles

reflex [noun: **reflexes**]
1 an automatic uncontrollable movement that you make in a certain situation: *The doctor will check your reflexes by tapping your knee with a small hammer.*
2 you have good reflexes if you can react quickly and well when something unexpected and sudden happens

reflexive [adjective] to do with words that show that the subject of a verb is the same as its object. For example, in the sentence *He* *washed himself, wash* is a **reflexive verb** and *himself* is a **reflexive pronoun**

reflexologist [noun: **reflexologists**] someone who treats medical conditions by pressing on particular places on the soles of your feet

◆ **reflexology** [noun] the work of a reflexologist

reform [verb: **reforms, reforming, reformed**]

1 to reform something is to make big changes to improve it

2 to reform is to stop doing bad things: *David decided to reform and not smoke any more.*

[noun: **reforms**] big changes that improve something: *reforms in the health service*

◆ **reformation** [noun] change in order to make an improvement

◆ **reformer** [noun: **reformers**] someone who makes changes to improve things

refrain [verb: **refrains, refraining, refrained**] to stop yourself doing something: *Please refrain from talking in the library.*

[noun: **refrains**] the chorus of a song

refresh [verb: **refreshes, refreshing, refreshed**]

1 to make you feel like you have new energy: *a rest to refresh you*

2 to make you feel cooler: *a drink that refreshes*

3 to refresh your memory is to remind yourself of something

◆ **refreshing** [adjective] making you feel more energetic again: *a refreshing cup of tea*

◆ **refreshment** [noun: **refreshments**] food and drink

refrigerate [verb: **refrigerates, refrigerating, refrigerated**] to make and keep food or drink cold to stop it going off

◆ **refrigeration** [noun] keeping things at a low temperature

◆ **refrigerator** [noun: **refrigerators**] a machine that you can store food or drink in to keep it cold and fresh

refuel [verb: **refuels, refuelling, refuelled**] to fill up with fuel again: *stopping on the motorway to refuel*

refuge [noun: **refuges**] a place where someone can feel safe from danger

◆ **refugee** [noun: **refugees**] a person who looks for protection in another country because they are not safe in their own country any more

refund [verb: **refunds, refunding, refunded**] to give someone back some money that they have paid: *We'll refund your money if you're not completely satisfied.*

[noun: **refunds**] money that you have paid and then get back

refusal [noun: **refusals**]

1 a decision not to accept something: *three refusals and twenty acceptances for our party invitations*

2 a decision not to do something that you are asked to do: *a refusal to shake hands*

refuse[1] [verb: **refuses, refusing, refused**]

1 to decide not to take something that you are offered: *Gerry refused a cup of tea but took a glass of water.*

2 to decide not to do something that you are asked to do: *He refused to help me.*

refuse[2] [noun] rubbish that people throw away

ⓘ **Refuse** meaning 'not to take' is pronounced ri–**fuze**, with the stress at the end.
Refuse meaning rubbish is pronounced **ref**–yoos, with the stress at the beginning.

regain [verb: **regains, regaining, regained**] to get something back: *Can the team regain the cup?*

regal [adjective] royal, like a king or queen

regard [verb: **regards, regarding, regarded**]

1 to regard a person or thing as something is to think about them like that: *My mother still regards me as a child.*

2 to regard a thing or person is to study the way they look: *He regarded me for a moment, smiled, and patted me on the head.*

[noun] regard is consideration: *They went ahead without regard for our opinion.* • *The professor's work is held in high regard.*

◆ **regarding** [preposition] about: *I'd like to talk to you regarding next weekend.*

◆ **regardless** [adverb] without paying any attention to something: *Regardless of the cost, I'm determined to take this holiday.*

Rr

+ **regards** [plural noun] your regards are your best wishes: *Give my regards to Fiona when you see her.*

regatta [noun: **regattas**] a series of yacht races

regenerate [verb: **regenerates, regenerating, regenerated**] to regenerate something is to make it return to its original good state: *The council is regenerating old housing.*

+ **regeneration** [noun] making or growing again in good condition: *the regeneration of damaged skin*

reggae [noun] a Jamaican style of music that has strong rhythms

regime [noun: **regimes**]
1 a system of government: *a communist regime*
2 a routine: *a strict regime of diet and exercise*

regiment [noun: **regiments**] a part of an army commanded by a colonel

+ **regimental** [adjective] to do with an army regiment

region [noun: **regions**]
1 a large area of land such as a part of a country: *the wine-making regions of Spain*
2 **in the region of** means 'approximately': *Repairs will cost in the region of £500.*

+ **regional** [adjective] to do with or coming from a particular region of a country: *a regional accent*

register [verb: **registers, registering, registered**]
1 to put your name down for something: *We registered for the new term's swimming class.*
2 to have a name added to an official list of records: *You must register your son's birth in the next week.*
3 information registers with someone if they understand it and take it in: *She certainly heard the news but I don't know if it really registered.*
4 an instrument registers a measurement when it shows it: *Earthquakes are measured by what they register on the Richter scale.*
[noun: **registers**] a list of names: *the attendance register • a register of births and deaths*

+ **registrar** [noun: **registrars**] a person whose job is to keep a record of births, marriages and deaths

+ **registration** [noun: **registrations**] putting your name down for something: *registration for next term's classes*

+ **registry** [noun: **registries**] an office or building where official records are kept

registry office or **register office** [noun: **registry offices** or **register offices**] the place where you go to register a birth or a death, and also a place where people can get married

regret [verb: **regrets, regretting, regretted**] to regret something is to wish it had not happened: *Yes I'm sorry, I regret saying that.*
[noun: **regrets**] a sad feeling: *Marion had no regrets about leaving home.*

+ **regretful** [adjective] feeling sad about something that has happened

+ **regrettable** [adjective] something is regrettable if you wish it had not happened: *a regrettable accident*

regular [adjective]
1 happening after intervals of the same length of time: *a regular heartbeat • eating regular meals*
2 usual or normal: *our regular teatime*
3 of a standard size: *a regular portion of French fries*

+ **regularity** [noun] when something happens repeatedly after gaps of similar length: *check the regularity of his pulse*

+ **regularly** [adverb] repeatedly: *We regularly have to call the police on a Saturday night.*

regulate [verb: **regulates, regulating, regulated**] to adjust a machine so that it works just as you want it to: *regulate the temperature of the central heating*

+ **regulation** [noun: **regulations**] a rule or law: *We can't allow that — it's against the regulations.*

rehearsal [noun: **rehearsals**]
1 a rehearsal is a practice of a performance: *the dress rehearsal*
2 rehearsal is practising: *Regular rehearsal will help you to get it right.*

rehearse [verb: **rehearses, rehearsing, rehearsed**] to practise performing something: *Can we rehearse that last bit again?*

rehouse [verb: **rehouses, rehousing, rehoused**] to provide someone with somewhere else to live

reign [verb: **reigns, reigning, reigned**] to rule over a country as a king or queen: *Queen Victoria reigned for over sixty years.*
[noun: **reigns**] the time when someone is the king or queen of a country: *in the reign of King John*

reimburse [verb: **reimburses, reimbursing, reimbursed**] to give someone back the money they have paid out: *The theatre will reimburse everyone who had tickets for the cancelled performance.*

reindeer [noun: **reindeer**] a large deer with large horns that lives in Arctic regions

reinforce [verb: **reinforces, reinforcing, reinforced**] to make something stronger: *reinforced glass*
  ♦ **reinforcement** [noun: **reinforcements**]
  1 anything that makes something stronger
  2 reinforcements are extra military troops

reins [plural noun] straps attached to a horse's head that the rider uses to control it

reject [verb: **rejects, rejecting, rejected**]
  1 to refuse to accept something: *The machine rejected my coin.*
  2 you are rejected if you apply for a job and do not get it
  [noun: **rejects**] a product that is not good enough to sell
  ♦ **rejection** [noun: **rejections**] when a thing or person is not accepted: *I didn't apply because I was afraid of rejection.*

ⓘ The verb **reject** is pronounced ri-**jekt**, with the stress at the end.
The noun **reject** is pronounced **ree**-jekt, with the stress at the beginning.

rejoice [verb: **rejoices, rejoicing, rejoiced**] to feel or show great happiness

relate [verb: **relates, relating, related**]
  1 to relate to something is be connected or linked with it: *Is violent crime related to violence on TV?*
  2 to relate a story is to tell it: *They related their strange experience to their friends.*
  3 to relate to someone is to understand how they feel

♦ **related** [adjective]
  1 to be related to someone is to belong to the same family: *We have the same surname, but we're not related.*
  2 to be related is to be linked or connected in some way

♦ **relation** [noun: **relations**]
  1 a relation between things is some kind of connection: *the relation between smoking and lung cancer*
  2 a relation is someone in your family: *all our friends and relations*

♦ **relationship** [noun: **relationships**]
  1 the way people feel about each other is their relationship: *Anne felt she had a good relationship with her brother.*
  2 the way things are when you consider them together: *What's the relationship between these numbers?*
  3 a love affair: *He's having a relationship with a younger woman.*

relative [noun: **relatives**] a member of your family
  [adjective] compared with normal: *She lives in relative luxury.*
  ♦ **relatively** [adverb] fairly or quite: *That suit's relatively cheap.*

relax [verb: **relaxes, relaxing, relaxed**]
  1 to become less tense, worried or stressed: *A short holiday will help you relax.*
  2 to rest completely: *The family spent the afternoon relaxing in the garden.*
  3 to relax something like a rule is to make it less strict
  ♦ **relaxation** [noun] rest from work or worrying things

relay [verb: **relays, relaying, relayed**] to pass on to someone else what has been passed to you: *She relayed the information to the others.*
  [noun: **relays**] a **relay race**

relay race [noun: **relay races**] a race for teams where a runner or swimmer takes over when the previous team member stops running or swimming

release [verb: **releases, releasing, released**]
  1 to let someone or something go: *Release the handbrake slowly. • Three more prisoners have been released.*

Rr

2 a film or book is released when the public are allowed to see it

[noun: **releases**]

1 when someone or something is set free: *the release of the hostages*

2 something like a film or book that has been made available to the public: *the band's latest release*

relegate [verb: **relegates, relegating, relegated**] to move someone down to a lower grade or level: *My team has been relegated to the third division.*

♦ **relegation** [noun] being moved down to a lower position

relent [verb: **relents, relenting, relented**] to give in a bit when you have been very strict

♦ **relentless** [adjective] never letting up: *the relentless heat of the desert sun*

relevance [noun] how much something has to do with anything or anyone else: *What possible relevance can this have to me?*

♦ **relevant** [adjective] something is relevant if it has something to do with what is happening or being discussed: *Is this answer relevant to the question?*

reliability [noun] how much you can depend on or trust a thing or person: *the reliability of the witness*

reliable [adjective]

1 a reliable person is someone you can depend on

2 reliable information is probably true or correct

3 a reliable machine does not often break down

reliance [noun] the way you rely on a thing or person: *Our reliance on cars these days is frightening.*

♦ **reliant** [adjective] you are reliant on a thing or person when you depend on them and cannot manage without them: *a charity totally reliant on donations from the public*

relic [noun: **relics**] an object from the past

relief [noun]

1 a good feeling caused by a bad thing stopping or not happening: *It was a relief to be outside in the fresh air again.*

2 relief is help for a large group of people in need, especially in the form of food and medicine: *relief for flood victims*

relieve [verb: **relieves, relieving, relieved**]

1 to relieve pain or suffering is to make it less or stop it completely: *pills to relieve a headache*

2 to relieve someone of something is to take it away from them: *Let me relieve you of that heavy suitcase.*

♦ **relieved** [adjective] feeling good because something bad that you were expecting has not happened: *I'm so relieved that you're home safely.*

religion [noun: **religions**] belief in, or the worship of, a god or gods

♦ **religious** [adjective]

1 to do with belief in a god or gods: *a religious service*

2 a religious person has strong beliefs about a god or gods

relish [verb: **relishes, relishing, relished**] to enjoy something very much: *Ben relishes singing in public.*

[noun: **relishes**]

1 a relish is a spicy kind of food that you eat together with other food for extra flavour

2 relish is enjoyment: *watching the film with obvious relish*

reluctance [noun] being unwilling to do something: *disappointed by their reluctance to help*

♦ **reluctant** [adjective] unwilling to do something: *I'm reluctant to do any more.* • *three reluctant helpers*

rely [verb: **relies, relying, relied**]

1 to rely on someone is to need them or depend on them: *We rely on the help of parents and friends.*

2 if you can rely on someone, you can trust them to do what they say they will do

➞ **reliability, reliable, reliance**

remain [verb: **remain, remaining, remained**]

1 to be left when everything else or everyone else has gone: *All that remains in the fireplace is a pile of ash.*

2 to stay in the same place or the same way, without changing: *The building remains in ruins to this day.*

♦ **remainder** [noun] the remainder of something is what is left of it after some of it has gone

remake [noun: **remakes**] a new version of an old film, that usually has the same title

remark [verb: **remarks, remarking, remarked**] to say something: *Tim remarked that he liked Di's hat.*

[noun: **remarks**] something someone says, such as an opinion or a thought: *He made a nasty remark about my writing.*

♦ **remarkable** [adjective] surprising, interesting or impressive: *It's remarkable how often you can see the same film and not get bored.*

remedy [noun: **remedies**] something that gets rid of a problem: *a remedy for spots*

[verb: **remedies, remedying, remedied**] to put a situation right

remember [verb: **remembers, remembering, remembered**]

1 to have something in your mind from the past: *How much of what you saw can you remember?* • *Can you remember the colour of his jacket?*

2 not to forget to do something: *Remember to take your key with you.*

♦ **remembrance** [noun] if you do something **in remembrance** of a person who has died, you do it to show that you have not forgotten them

remind [verb: **reminds, reminding, reminded**] to make someone remember something: *Remind me to close the window before I go out.* • *That picture reminds me of our holiday last year.*

♦ **reminder** [noun: **reminders**] a note that helps someone remember to do something

remittance [noun: **remittances**] money that you send to make a payment for something

remnant [noun: **remnants**] a small piece of something that is left after the rest has been used, lost or destroyed: *We can used the remnants of the curtains to make cushion covers.*

remorse [noun] a deep feeling of guilt about something bad or wrong that you have done: *a confession full of remorse*

remorseful [adjective] feeling very guilty and sorry

♦ **remorsefully** [adverb] in a way that

shows that you feel very guilty about having done something bad or wrong

remorseless [adjective]

1 a remorseless person does not feel sorry or guilty at all

2 not ending: *the remorseless increase in crime*

remote [adjective: **remoter, remotest**]

1 a remote place is very far away from other places: *a remote Highland village*

2 a remote chance is very slight: *There's not even a remote possibility that we'll win.*

remote control [noun: **remote controls**]

1 remote control is controlling something from a distance by using an electronic device

2 a remote control is a device for controlling something, for example a television set, from a distance

remotely [adverb] at all: *I'm not even remotely interested.*

removal [noun: **removals**] taking something away: *the removal of a bad stain*

remove [verb: **removes, removing, removed**]

1 to take something away or get rid of it: *The police have removed the car that was dumped here.*

2 to remove clothes is to take them off: *Please remove your shoes at the door.*

render [verb: **renders, rendering, rendered**] to put a thing or person into a certain state or condition: *His cheek rendered me speechless.*

rendezvous [noun: **rendezvous**] an arranged meeting, especially a secret one

renew [verb: **renews, renewing, renewed**]

1 to renew something like a licence is to pay for it to be valid again after it runs out: *You can renew your bus pass at the office.*

2 to start something or doing something again: *We'll renew our attempt to get the rules changed.*

renounce [verb: **renounces, renouncing, renounced**] to give up something or a belief in something: *trying to persuade the rebels to renounce violence*

renovate [verb: **renovates, renovating, renovated**] to do up a building so that it can be used again

♦ **renovation** [noun: **renovations**] repairs

Rr

to a building that restore it to good condition

renown [noun] fame: *a man of great renown*

✦ **renowned** [adjective] famous: *a woman renowned for her stirring political speeches*

rent [verb: **rents, renting, rented**]

1 to pay someone money so that you can use their property, especially a house or flat: *a rented flat*

2 to rent something or **rent something out** is to let other people use it if they pay you: *We'll rent the house to students while we're away.*

[noun: **rents**] money you pay to the owner of a house or other building so that you can live in it or use it

✦ **rental** [noun: **rentals**]

1 renting things out to people: *a car rental business*

2 the amount of rent you pay

repair [verb: **repairs, repairing, repaired**]
to fix something that is damaged or not working: *Can the washing-machine be repaired?*

[noun: **repairs**]

1 something you do to fix something

2 **good** or **bad repair** is good or bad condition: *The car is in remarkably good repair for its age.*

repay [verb: **repays, repaying, repaid**]

1 to give back money that you have borrowed

2 to do something for somebody in return for something they did for you: *How can we ever repay this kindness?*

✦ **repayment** [noun: **repayments**] one of several amounts of money that you pay back until you have paid back all the money you borrowed

repeat [verb: **repeats, repeating, repeated**]

1 to say something again: *Could you repeat your name please?* • *Don't you dare repeat this to your friends.*

2 to do something again: *I hope this mistake will never be repeated.*

[noun: **repeats**] something that happens again, especially a broadcast: *watching repeats of old comedy shows*

✦ **repeatedly** [adverb] again and again
➠ **repetition**

repel [verb: **repels, repelling, repelled**]

1 to force a thing or person away: *This material repels water and is used for rainwear.*

2 to be repelled by something is to be disgusted by it

✦ **repellent** [noun: **repellents**] a chemical that you use to keep something away: *an insect repellent*

[adjective] disgusting or very unpleasant: *a repellent sight*

repent [verb: **repents, repenting, repented**] to be sorry for something that you have done

✦ **repentance** [noun] being sorry for what you have done

✦ **repentant** [adjective] sorry

repetition [noun: **repetitions**]

1 repetition is saying or doing things again: *learning by repetition*

2 a repetition of something is when it is said or done again: *We don't want a repetition of yesterday's argument.*

✦ **repetitive** [adjective] boring because the same thing is repeated many times

replace [verb: **replaces, replacing, replaced**]

1 to put something back in its previous or proper position: *Make sure you replace the books in exactly the right order.*

2 to take the place of another thing or person: *The company bought new computers to replace the old ones.*

✦ **replacement** [noun: **replacements**] a person or thing that is in the place of a previous one: *This is broken so I'd like a replacement, please.*

replay [verb: **replays, replying, replayed**]
a sports match is replayed when it is played again, usually because there was no clear winner the first time.

[noun: **replays**]

1 a sports match that is played a second time: *He scored in the second-round replay.*

2 an incident in a sports match that is shown again during a broadcast: *an instant action replay*

ⓘ The verb **replay** is pronounced ree-**play**, with the stress at the end.
The noun **replay** is pronounced **ree**-play, with the stress at the beginning.

replica [noun: **replicas**] a model of something, usually much smaller than the original

reply [verb: **replies, replying, replied**] to answer: *You haven't replied to my question yet.* [noun: **replies**] an answer: *We've had a number of replies to our advertisement.* • *In reply, Phoebe gave a nod.*

report [noun: **reports**]
1 an account of something that has happened: *Reports of an accident are just coming in.*
2 a description of someone's progress: *a school report*
[verb: **reports, reporting, reported**]
1 to tell people about what has happened: *Did you report the incident to the police?* • *The whole story was reported in the papers.*
2 to make a complaint about something that someone has done: *I reported the bus driver for not stopping.*
3 to go to a place and tell them that you have arrived: *Please report to reception when you enter the building.*

reported speech [noun] another name for **indirect speech**, where you report what someone has said without using their exact words

reporter [noun: **reporters**] a person who writes articles and reports for newspapers or television or radio news programmes

repossess [verb: **repossesses, repossessing, repossessed**] to take back something, especially a car or a house, that someone has bought, but that they cannot finish paying for

represent [verb: **represents, representing, represented**]
1 to represent people is to speak or act on their behalf: *Our MPs represent us in our government.*
2 to represent a thing is to be a symbol of it: *The crown represents the king or queen.*
3 to represent something in a certain way is to describe it that way: *The children in the picture were all represented as angels.*
◆ **representative** [noun: **representatives**]
1 someone who acts or speaks on behalf of other people

2 someone whose job is to sell the products of the company they work for: *a sales representative*

repress [verb: **represses, repressing, repressed**] to keep people down or under control, by force
◆ **repression** [noun] very strict controlling of people, not allowing them to do things such as vote in elections
◆ **repressive** [adjective] a repressive government controls the people of a country very strictly

reprieve [noun: **reprieves**] an order to cancel or delay a punishment or other unpleasant event
[verb: **reprieves, reprieving, reprieved**] when someone is reprieved, something unpleasant that was due to happen to them is cancelled or delayed

reprimand [noun: **reprimands**] a telling-off
[verb: **reprimands, reprimanding, reprimanded**] to tell someone off

reprint [noun: **reprints**] a new copy of something like a photograph or a book
[verb: **reprints, reprinting, reprinted**] to print more copies of a book

reprisal [noun: **reprisals**] something that is done against a person or group of people because of what they had done previously: *The country will suffer reprisals for their attacks.*

reproach [verb: **reproaches, reproaching, reproached**] to tell someone that you think they have behaved or are behaving badly: *The teacher reproached the pupils for being noisy.*
[noun] criticism: *a look of reproach*
◆ **reproachful** [adjective] criticizing someone's behaviour: *reproachful words*

reproduce [verb: **reproduces, reproducing, reproduced**]
1 to reproduce something is to make or produce it again or copy it: *The child had reproduced his father's signature.*
2 to reproduce is to have babies
◆ **reproduction** [noun: **reproductions**]
1 copying things, especially works of art
2 the process in which people, animals and

Rr

plants produce others like themselves
[adjective] produced by copying styles of
things such as art or old furniture: *reproduction furniture*

reptile [noun: **reptiles**] a cold-blooded
animal such as a snake or lizard

republic [noun: **republics**] a country with no
king or queen, that is ruled by an elected
government and usually has a president

♦ **republican** [adjective] belonging to a
republic or wanting to see your own country as
a republic

repulsive [adjective] disgusting

reputation [noun: **reputations**] the opinion
that most people have of a thing or person: *a
restaurant with a very good reputation* • *He
has a reputation for being a very tough player.*

request [verb: **requests, requesting,
requested**] to ask for something: *Can I
request a taxi for eight o'clock?*
[noun: **requests**]
1 something that someone asks: *I've got a
request to make.* • *hundreds of requests for
information*
2 something that someone asks for, especially
a piece of music on the radio: *Tell me the title of
your request.*

requiem [noun: **requiems**] a religious piece
of music that is played or sung at a Christian
service for someone who has died

require [verb: **requires, requiring,
required**]
1 to need something: *Do you require any
further information?*
2 to be required to do something is to have to
do it: *All staff are required to dress
appropriately.*

♦ **requirement** [noun: **requirements**]
something that is needed: *Write a list of your
requirements and we'll design the kitchen for
you.*

rerun [noun: **reruns**] a repeated television
programme

rescue [verb: **rescues, rescuing, rescued**]
to save someone from danger: *Firefighters
rescued the people from the burning house.*
[noun: **rescues**] when someone is saved from
danger: *stranded on an island with no hope of
rescue*

♦ **rescuer** [noun: **rescuers**] a person who
saves someone from a dangerous situation

research [noun: **researches**] to **do** or **carry
out** research is to investigate a subject and
study what you find out: *money for research
into causes of cancer*
[verb: **researches, researching,
researched**] to carry out an investigation into
a certain subject

♦ **researcher** [noun: **researchers**] a person
who finds out and studies background
information about a subject: *a television
documentary researcher*

resemblance [noun: **resemblances**]
something similar about things or people,
especially in the way they look: *Can you see
the resemblance between the brothers?*

resemble [verb: **resembles, resembling,
resembled**] to be similar in some way,
especially in looks: *Tom resembles his father.*

resent [verb: **resents, resenting, resented**]
to be irritated, angry or bitter about something:
I resent the way nobody asked me how I felt.

♦ **resentful** [adjective] feeling irritated,
angry or bitter: *a resentful look*

♦ **resentment** [noun] a feeling of bitterness
and anger about something

reservation [noun: **reservations**]
1 a reservation is a booking for something like
a table in a restaurant, a hotel room, a theatre
ticket or a ticket to travel somewhere: *I'd like to
make reservations for two double rooms
please.*
2 to **have reservations** about something is to
be unsure about how good or sensible it is:
Peter had reservations about moving abroad.
• *We supported his ideas without reservation.*

reserve [verb: **reserves, reserving,
reserved**]
1 to keep something to use later: *Mix in half the
sugar, reserving the rest for the icing.*
2 to reserve something such as a hotel room or
a ticket is to book it: *I'd like to reserve a table for
dinner tonight, please.*

♦ **reserved** [adjective]
1 something like a table in a restaurant is
reserved when it is being kept for someone in
particular
2 if a person is reserved, they are quiet and shy

reservoir [noun: **reservoirs**] a large lake, often man-made, where water is collected and stored

reshuffle [noun: **reshuffles**] a rearrangement of people doing different jobs within a group: *another cabinet reshuffle by the Prime Minister*

reside [verb: **resides, residing, resided**] to live in a place

♦ **residence** [noun: **residences**] a residence, or a place of residence, is where someone lives: *one of the queen's official residences • What is your country of residence?*

♦ **resident** [noun: **residents**] a resident of a place is someone who lives there: *a letter to all the residents in the street*

♦ **residential** [adjective]
1 a residential area is mostly made up of housing, not offices or factories
2 a residential activity is one where you live and work in the same place: *a residential course for teachers*

residue [noun: **residues**] an amount left after the rest has gone or been used up

resign [verb: **resigns, resigning, resigned**] to give up your job: *Harry resigned after a row with the manager.*

♦ **resignation** [noun: **resignations**]
1 to hand in your resignation is to give up your job
2 resignation is accepting something unpleasant and putting up with it: *a look of resignation*

resigned [adjective] if you are **resigned to** an unpleasant situation, you accept it even though you do not like it

resilience [noun] resilience is a quality that things or people can have that means they are not easily damaged or hurt

♦ **resilient** [adjective] resilient things or people are able to survive hard treatment without being badly affected

resin [noun] a sticky substance produced by certain trees

resist [verb]
1 to resist something like change is to try to stop it happening
2 to resist someone is to try to stop them doing something

3 you resist a temptation when you do not give in to it

♦ **resistance** [noun] an attempt to stop someone or something: *the body's resistance to disease*

♦ **resistant** [adjective]
1 not harmed or affected by something: *a water-resistant watch*
2 opposed to something: *people who are resistant to change*

resit [verb: **resits, resitting, resat**] to take an exam again
[noun: **resits**] a chance to take an exam again

resolute [adjective] very determined not to give up or change your mind

♦ **resolutely** [adverb] very firmly: *We have resolutely refused to do extra work.*

♦ **resolution** [noun: **resolutions**]
1 a firm decision to do something: *a New Year's resolution*
2 the solving of a problem

resolve [verb: **resolves, resolving, resolved**]
1 to resolve to do something is to make a firm decision to do it: *We have resolved to try harder next time.*
2 to resolve a problem is to solve it or deal successfully with it
[noun] great determination: *I have always admired his resolve.*

resort [verb: **resorts, resorting, resorted**] you resort to doing something when everything else you have tried has failed: *The worst thing would be to resort to violence.*
[noun: **resorts**]
1 a place where people go for their holidays: *a popular seaside resort*
2 a **last resort** is something you would prefer not to do, but you do because everything else has failed: *I suppose we could borrow the money as a last resort.*

resound [verb: **resounds, resounding, resounded**] to echo around

resource [noun: **resources**] resources are substances or qualities that you have and are able to use: *natural mineral resources such as coal • We'll need all our resources of patience to put up with this.*

♦ **resourceful** [adjective] good at finding

Rr

ways of doing things, especially of solving problems

respect [noun: **respects**]

1 a feeling that a thing or person deserves your attention, admiration or consideration

2 a way of looking at things: *The plan was good in every respect.*

[verb: **respects, respecting, respected**] to treat someone with kindness and attention

respectability [noun] being good, honest and decent

respectable [adjective]

1 decent and honest: *Simon comes from a perfectly respectable family.*

2 fairly good or, at least, not bad: *Now he's beginning to earn a respectable amount of money.*

◆ **respectably** [adverb] quite well

respectful [adjective] showing respect: *a respectful attitude*

◆ **respectfully** [adverb] in a way that shows respect: *Everyone respectfully bowed their heads as the coffin went past.*

respective [adjective] to do with each thing that has been mentioned: *David and Diane are each good at their respective jobs.*

◆ **respectively** [adverb] according to the order of things already mentioned: *Colin, Jane and Ian were given £5, £3 and £1 respectively.*

respiration [noun] breathing

◆ **respirator** [noun: **respirators**] a machine that helps someone to breathe when they are too ill to do it naturally

resplendent [adjective] very bright and splendid-looking

respond [verb: **responds, responding, responded**] to answer or react: *If someone hits you, you tend to respond by hitting back.*

◆ **response** [noun: **responses**] an answer or reaction: *His response was a shake of his head.*

responsibility [noun: **responsibilities**]

1 responsibility for something is a duty that you must do or deal with properly: *The manager has responsibility for all the business.*

2 a responsibility is a job or duty that you are trusted to do: *It's my responsibility to make sure all the doors are locked.*

3 responsibility is being able to sensibly do things that you are trusted with: *I am not ready for the responsibility of having children.*

responsible [adjective]

1 to be responsible for something is to be the person whose job or duty that thing is: *Who is responsible for keeping the money?*

2 to be responsible for something like a mistake is to be the person whose fault it is

3 a responsible job is one that includes important duties and decisions

4 a responsible person is someone you can trust

rest [verb: **rests, resting, rested**]

1 to spend time doing very little, or nothing, in order to relax: *You should rest every few minutes when you're lifting such heavy weights.*

2 to rest against something is to lean against it: *a spade resting against a wall*

3 to rest one thing on something else is to put it there gently: *Mo rested her hands on the piano keys for a moment.*

[noun: **rests**]

1 a time when you relax or sleep: *I need a rest before I can work any more.*

2 a rest is something that is used as a support: *an adjustable rest for the arms*

3 the rest of something is what is left or remaining: *I don't want to spend the rest of my life here.* • *The rest of the country will have showers.*

restaurant [noun: **restaurants**] a place where you can buy and eat a meal

restful [adjective] making you feel calm and relaxed: *restful music* • *a restful afternoon*

restless [adjective] not able to stay still or quiet because you are nervous and worried or bored: *The audience began to get restless after about an hour.*

◆ **restlessly** [adverb] in an uncomfortable, agitated way: *standing and waiting restlessly by the door*

◆ **restlessness** [noun] an uncomfortable feeling that makes you want to move about or do something active

restoration [noun] putting something back the way it was before: *After the fire, the restoration of the church took three years.*

Rr

restore [verb: **restores, restoring, restored**] to put something back the way it was before: *The house had been restored to its former glory.*

restrain [verb: **restrains, restraining, restrained**]
1 to control someone's physical movements: *One of the children got very excited and had to be restrained by a parent.*
2 to stop yourself from doing something: *We had to restrain ourselves from laughing.*
✦ **restraint** [noun: **restraints**]
1 a restraint is something that prevents you from doing something: *A lack of money is a restraint on our holiday plans.*
2 restraint is self-control: *She behaved with amazing restraint considering how insulting Vera was being.*

restrict [verb: **restricts, restricting, restricted**] to limit or control something: *We are restricting people to one ticket each.*
✦ **restriction** [noun: **restrictions**] a limit or control: *Are there any parking restrictions on this road?*
✦ **restrictive** [adjective] preventing normal behaviour: *restrictive laws*

restructuring [noun] the reorganization of a business or company in order to make it more efficient or to reduce costs

result [noun: **results**]
1 the result of something is what happens because of it: *He died as a result of the accident.*
2 the result of a contest is the number of points each team or contestant won
3 a student's exam results are the marks or grades they got
[verb: **results, resulting, resulted**] to happen because of something else: *The fire apparently resulted from a cigarette not being put out properly.*

resume [verb: **resumes, resuming, resumed**] to start again: *Normal services will resume next week.*
✦ **resumption** [noun] when something starts again: *the resumption of peace talks*

resurrect [verb: **resurrects, resurrecting, resurrected**] to bring someone back to life or bring something back into use: *We've*

resurrected the old custom of gathering the family together for dinner.
✦ **resurrection** [noun]
1 bringing back to life or use
2 the Resurrection is the Christian belief that Jesus Christ rose again three days after his death

resuscitate [verb: **resuscitates, resuscitating, resuscitated**] to make an unconscious person start to breathe again
✦ **resuscitation** [noun] making an unconscious person start to breathe again

retail [noun] selling goods to members of the public
✦ **retailer** [noun: **retailers**] a person who sells goods to the public, usually in a shop

retain [verb: **retains, retaining, retained**] to keep something: *A smaller house would retain heat better in the winter.*
✦ **retention** [noun] keeping something and not letting it go

retina [noun: **retinas** or **retinae**] the back of your eyeball, where images that you see are picked up by your brain

retinue [noun: **retinues**] a group of people who travel along with an important or famous person: *The princess and her retinue are staying at the Victoria Hotel.*

retire [verb: **retires, retiring, retired**] to stop working because you are old enough to get a pension: *I want to retire next year.*
✦ **retired** [adjective] no longer working because you are old enough to get a pension: *a retired teacher*
✦ **retirement** [noun] the time when you stop working and get a pension: *I hope you enjoy your retirement.*
✦ **retiring** [adjective] quiet and shy

retort [verb: **retorts, retorting, retorted**] to make a quick reply
[noun: **retorts**] a sharp answer: *an angry retort*

retrace [verb: **retraces, retracing, retraced**] to **retrace your steps** is to go over the same route that you took earlier

retrain [verb: **retrains, retraining, retrained**] to learn new skills or do a course so that you can get a different job: *I want to retrain to be a plumber.*

Rr

473

retreat [noun: **retreats**] a movement backwards
[verb: **retreats, retreating, retreated**] to move back or move away because you do not want to fight

retrieve [verb: **retrieves, retrieving, retrieved**] to get something back after leaving it somewhere: *Can you help me retrieve my pen from the back of the sofa?*
✦ **retriever** [noun: **retriever**] a kind of large light-brown or black dog that hunters use to fetch birds or animals that have been shot

return [verb: **returns, returning, returned**]
1 to return is to go back to a place: *We fly out on Friday and return the following Wednesday.* • *The search will continue as soon as daylight returns.*
2 to return something is to give it, put it, or send it back: *Please return your books by Friday.*
3 to return something like a look or a smile is to do it to someone who does it to you: *I hope I can return the favour one day.*
[noun: **returns**]
1 a time when you come or go back again: *On my return to the house, I found the door wide open.*
2 a **return ticket**: *Do you want a single or a return?*
3 something that is given or sent back
4 a shot that someone hits back in tennis or a similar game: *a wonderful return of service*
5 a statement of the money you have earned and spent, used for calculating how much tax you must pay: *a tax return*

return ticket [noun: **return tickets**] a ticket that allows you to travel to a place and back again

reunion [noun: **reunions**] a meeting of people such as friends or family members who have not seen each other for a long time: *a reunion of the class of 1982*
✦ **reunite** [verb: **reunites, reuniting, reunited**] people are reunited when they meet again after not seeing each other for a long time

Rev [abbreviation] short for **Reverend** when it is written down: *the vicar, Rev Pat Green*

rev [noun: **revs**] a revolution of an engine, which is one turn of its pistons

[verb: **revs, revving, revved**] to press the accelerator of a car to make the engine go faster

reveal [verb: **reveals, revealing, revealed**]
1 to reveal something is to allow it to be seen
2 to reveal information is to tell it to someone: *The newspaper is claiming that it can reveal all the details.*
➡ **revelation**

revel [verb: **revels, revelling, revelled**]
1 to celebrate in a jolly way: *friends revelling the night away*
2 to revel in something is to enjoy it very much: *Maxine revelled in all the attention she got at her birthday party.*
➡ **reveller**

revelation [noun: **revelations**] something unexpected that becomes known: *an article full of revelations about his private life*

reveller [noun: **revellers**] someone having a good time at a party

revenge [noun] to get revenge on someone who has harmed you is to harm them in return

revenue [noun] money that is given as payment to a business or organization: *Most of the government's revenue comes from taxes.*

reverberate [verb: **reverberates, reverberating, reverberated**] to produce several loud echoes: *the sounds of gunfire reverberating along the valley*
✦ **reverberation** [noun: **reverberations**] a repeated echo

revere [verb: **reveres, revering, revered**] to respect and admire someone very much
✦ **reverence** [noun] great respect
✦ **Reverend** [noun] the title that comes before the name of a Christian minister: *Reverend Frances Cook*

reversal [noun: **reversals**] a reversal is when a change or decision that has been made is cancelled

reverse [verb: **reverses, reversing, reversed**]
1 to reverse is to move backwards
2 to reverse a vehicle is to drive it backwards
3 to reverse a decision is to cancel it
✦ **reversible** [adjective]

1 a decision or process that is reversible can be cancelled

2 a reversible garment can be worn with either side in or out

revert [verb: **reverts, reverting, reverted**] to go back to the way something was before: *Many ex-prisoners revert to a life of crime.*

review [verb: **reviews, reviewing, reviewed**]

1 to check the way something works, to see if any changes need to be made

2 to say what you thought of something like a book or a performance

[noun: **reviews**]

1 a check on the way something such as a process works, to see if it needs changing: *a review of the education system* • *All our contracts are under review.*

2 a critic's opinion of something such as a book or a performance: *The play received some wonderful reviews.*

• **reviewer** [noun: **reviewers**] a person who gives their opinion about a book, a play, a piece of music or a performance

revise [verb: **revises, revising, revised**]

1 to revise a written work is to make changes to improve it: *The revised edition of the dictionary has hundreds of new words in it.*

2 to revise is to study for an exam by looking again at the work you have done

• **revision** [noun: **revisions**]

1 a revision is a new version of an old text, with improvements made

2 revision is studying that you do before an exam, by looking at work you have done

revival [noun: **revivals**] when something becomes active or popular again: *a revival of an old children's TV programme*

revive [verb: **revives, reviving, revived**]

1 to revive someone is to bring them back to consciousness again

2 to revive something is to become interested in it again or make it popular again: *reviving some of the traditional customs of the countryside*

revolt [noun: **revolts**] an attempt by the people to take power in a country by violence and force

[verb: **revolts, revolting, revolted**]

1 to rise up and try to seize power in a country

2 to disgust someone: *The very idea revolted me.*

• **revolting** [adjective] disgusting

revolution [noun: **revolutions**]

1 when people use force and violence to overturn a government and take power

2 a complete change in something such as an industry or society: *the industrial revolution of the nineteenth century*

3 a complete turn of something such as a wheel

• **revolutionary** [adjective] completely new and different, and so bringing about a complete change: *revolutionary computerized machines in our factories*

[noun: **revolutionaries**] a person who is involved in or who is in favour of overturning a government

• **revolutionize** or **revolutionise** [verb: **revolutionizes, revolutionizing, revolutionized**] to introduce a lot of new and different methods or ideas so that something changes completely: *The silicon chip has revolutionized computers.*

revolve [verb: **revolves, revolving, revolved**] to turn round and round a central point: *a revolving door* • *The Earth revolves around the sun.*

• **revolver** [noun: **revolvers**] a pistol that has a cylinder of bullets in it that turns after each shot

reward [noun: **rewards**] something you get for doing something good or useful: *a £300 reward for any information that helps catch the criminal*

[verb: **rewards, rewarding, rewarded**] to give someone something for being good or useful: *He was rewarded for all his hard work.*

rewind [verb: **rewinds, rewinding, rewound**] to wind a tape or cassette backwards to the beginning or an earlier place

rewrite [verb: **rewrites, rewriting, rewrote, rewritten**] to write something again: *You'll have to rewrite this because it is full of mistakes.*

[noun: **rewrites**] a second version of something that has been written before

rhapsody [noun: **rhapsodies**] a poem or a

Rr

piece of music that expresses strong feelings or enthusiasm

rheumatism [noun] a disease that causes painful swelling in a person's joints and muscles

rhino [noun: **rhinos**] a short form of the word **rhinoceros**

rhinoceros [noun: **rhinoceroses**] a large animal from Africa and Asia that has thick grey skin and one or two horns on its nose

rhododendron [noun: **rhododendrons**] a large bush that has evergreen leaves and large flowers

rhubarb [noun] a plant that has red stems that are cooked and eaten as a fruit

rhyme [verb: **rhymes, rhyming, rhymed**] to sound like another word, especially at the end. For example, *ghost* rhymes with *toast*.
[noun: **rhymes**]
1 a rhyme is a word that sounds like another, or a pair of words that have a similar sound: *I don't think there is a rhyme for 'orange'.*
2 rhyme is poetry that uses similar-sounding words at the end of the lines

rhythm [noun: **rhythms**] a repeated pattern of sounds or movements
♦ **rhythmic** [adjective] a rhythmic sound or movement has a repeated pattern

rib [noun: **ribs**] one of the curved bones in your chest, around your heart and lungs

ribbon [noun: **ribbons**] a long narrow strip of fabric that you can use as a decoration for clothes, hair or parcels

rice [noun] brown or white grains that are cooked and used as food: *a bowl of boiled rice*

rice paper [noun] thin edible paper that can be put under something like a cake that is baked, to prevent it from sticking to the tin

rich [adjective: **richer, richest**]
1 a rich person has a lot of money or possessions
2 rich food contains a lot of sugar or fat
3 rich soil contains a lot of things that make plants grow well
4 rich colours are strong and bright
5 anything rich is full of a lot of good things: *fruit juices rich in vitamins* • *the city's rich history*

Richter scale [noun] a way of measuring how strong earthquakes are: *Earthquakes can measure anything between 0 and 8 on the Richter scale.*

rickshaw [noun: **rickshaws**] a kind of two-wheeled cart for passengers that is pulled by one or more people and used in East Asia

ricochet [verb: **ricochets, ricocheting, ricocheted**] to bounce or rebound off a surface

ⓘ **Ricochet** is pronounced **rik**-oh-shay.

rid [verb: **rids, ridding, rid**] to clear or empty a place of something: *Scientists are working to rid the world of this virus.*
[adjective]
1 to **get rid of** something is to throw it or give it away: *We got rid of the old sofa and bought a new one.*
2 to **get rid of** someone is to make them go away: *He arrived at 7 o'clock and we couldn't get rid of him.*
♦ **riddance** [noun] **good riddance** is a phrase you can use when you are glad that someone or something has gone

riddle [noun: **riddles**]
1 a word puzzle
2 a mystery that is difficult to solve: *How the burglar got into the house is a bit of a riddle.*

riddled [adjective] something is riddled with holes if it has holes all over it

ride [verb: **rides, riding, rode, ridden**]
1 to travel on a horse or bicycle: *I never learnt to ride a bike.*
2 to travel in or on a vehicle: *She had been riding around in the car all day.*
[noun: **rides**] a journey in or on a vehicle: *a bus ride into town*
♦ **rider** [noun: **riders**] someone sitting on and controlling a bike or horse

ridge [noun: **ridges**]
1 a narrow strip of land that is higher than the ground on either side of it, for example along the top of a mountain
2 the top edge of something where two sloping surfaces meet: *the ridge of the roof*

ridicule [verb: **ridicules, ridiculing, ridiculed**] to make fun of a thing or person
♦ **ridiculous** [adjective] very silly: *She looked totally ridiculous in that hat.*

rife [adjective] something is rife when it is all

over the place: *Rumours about the affair were rife.*

rifle [noun: **rifles**] a powerful gun with a long barrel that you hold against your shoulder to fire
[verb: **rifles, rifling, rifled**] to **rifle through** something is to search through it quickly: *I caught him rifling through the papers on my desk.*

rift [noun: **rifts**]
1 a break in a friendship between people because of a disagreement: *a rift between the two families that lasted for years*
2 a large long crack in the land

rig [verb: **rigs, rigging, rigged**]
1 to fix something dishonestly so that you get the results that you want: *Everyone agreed that the election must have been rigged.*
2 to **rig something up** is to make, fix or build something in a hurry with whatever things you have available: *We rigged up a new aerial using a wire coat hanger.*
[noun: **rigs**] a large platform that supports the equipment that can get oil or gas from under the ground or the sea
• **rigging** [noun] the system of ropes that support and control the sails of a ship

right [adjective]
1 correct: *I got most of the answers wrong, but a couple were right.*
2 good and proper: *It doesn't seem right that so many people in the world are hungry.*
3 on the other side from the left side: *I write with my right hand.*
[adverb]
1 on or towards the other side from the left: *Now turn right.*
2 exactly: *Don't move; stay right there.*
3 immediately: *I'll be right there.*
4 all the way: *This road goes right round the outside of the park.*
5 correctly: *Can't you do anything right?*
[noun]
1 the right is the opposite side to the left side: *There's a chemist over there on the right.*
2 a right is something that you should be allowed to: *Everyone has a right to a decent education.*
3 if you are something **in your own right**, you

have achieved it by your own ability and not because of anyone else: *His father is well known, but Michael is a famous actor in his own right.*

right angle [noun: **right angles**] an angle of 90 degrees, like the corner of a square
righteous [adjective] a righteous person is a very good person
• **righteousness** [noun] being very good and doing the right thing
rightful [adjective] proper and as it should be: *return the stolen goods to their rightful owners*
• **rightfully** [adverb] properly and fairly: *She lives in the house which rightfully belongs to her.*

right-handed [adjective]
1 preferring to use your right hand to do things, rather than your left: *It's not fair that most of these gadgets are designed for right-handed people.*
2 meant to be used by the right hand rather than the left: *a right-handed pair of scissors*
rightly [adverb] correctly or fairly: *Phil has rightly pointed out that we should include Robert.*

rigid [adjective]
1 stiff and impossible to bend: *The girl stood in the doorway, rigid with fear.*
2 rigid rules are very strict and cannot be changed
• **rigidity** [noun] being very stiff or strict
• **rigidly** [adverb] stiffly or strictly
rigorous [adjective] very careful, strict and thorough: *ready for the rigorous training that you get in the army • rigorous checks on all the equipment*

rim [noun: **rims**]
1 the top edge of a container such as a cup or bowl
2 the outside edge of something like a wheel
rind [noun: **rinds**]
1 the hard outside edge of cheese or bacon
2 the skin or peel of fruit such as lemons
ring[1] [noun: **rings**]
1 anything in the shape of a circle: *The children sit in a ring around the story-teller. • The curtains are attached to rings on a pole.*
2 a small circle of something such as gold or

Rr

silver, that you wear on your finger as jewellery: *a wedding ring*

3 an enclosed area where a performance takes place: *a boxing ring • a circus ring*

ring [noun: **rings**]

1 the sound a bell makes: *Did I hear a ring at the door?*

2 a telephone call: *I'll give you a ring tomorrow.*

[verb: **rings, ringing, rang, rung**]

1 to make a sound like a bell: *I think I heard the doorbell ring.*

2 to telephone someone: *Can I ring you back later?*

ringleader [noun: **ringleaders**] the leader of a gang of criminals or troublemakers

ringlet [noun: **ringlets**] a long curl of hair

ringmaster [noun: **ringmaster**] the person in charge at a circus, who introduces the performers

ring road [noun: **ring roads**] a road that goes right around a town or city

rink [noun: **rinks**] a large area of ice for skating on

rinse [verb: **rinses, rinsing, rinsed**] to wash something with clean water

[noun: **rinses**]

1 a wash with clean water

2 a liquid hair dye

riot [noun: **riots**] a crowd of people behaving noisily and violently in the streets

[verb: **riots, rioting, rioted**] to behave noisily and violently with a lot of other people in the street

♦ **rioter** [noun: **rioters**] a person who is part of a violent crowd in the street

♦ **riotous** [adjective] noisy and uncontrolled

RIP [abbreviation] short for **rest in peace**, a phrase that is often written on gravestones

rip [verb: **rips, ripping, ripped**]

1 to tear something roughly: *ripping sheets into strips for bandages • Steve had ripped his trousers on the barbed wire.*

2 to snatch something from someone: *A reporter ripped the notebook right out of my hand.*

3 to **rip someone off** is to cheat them out of some money, especially by charging too much for something: *You're bound to get ripped off if you shop there.*

[noun: **rips**] a rough tear: *There was a rip in my sleeve where the handlebars had caught it.*

ripe [adjective: **riper, ripest**] ready to be picked or eaten: *Slightly green bananas will soon be completely ripe.*

♦ **ripen** [verb: **ripens, ripening, ripened**] to ripen is to become ready to pick or eat: *The apples are ripening quickly this year.*

♦ **ripeness** [noun] how completely ready a growing food is to pick or eat: *Check the ripeness of the fruit by squeezing it very gently.*

ripple [noun: **ripples**] a tiny wave on the surface of water

rise [verb: **rises, rising, rose, risen**]

1 to go upwards: *a column of smoke rising through the air • Ahead, the ground rose steeply. • The sun rises in the east.*

2 to increase: *Prices have risen this year.*

3 to get up: *We all rose when the judge entered. • His habit was to rise early for breakfast.*

4 to **rise up** is to rebel in protest

[noun: **rises**]

1 an increase: *a pay rise*

2 if something **gives rise to** something else, it causes it: *The accident has given rise to worries about safety.*

risk [noun: **risks**] a possibility that something bad will happen: *There's a risk that the whole project might be called off. • Do we want to take this risk?*

[verb: **risks, risking, risked**] to take a chance of damaging or losing something: *Soldiers are risking their lives every day.*

♦ **risky** [adjective: **riskier, riskiest**] dangerous: *a risky route to the top of the mountain*

risotto [noun] an Italian dish of rice, often with meat or seafood

rite [noun: **rites**] a ceremony, especially one to do with a religion

ritual [noun: **rituals**] a set of actions that are part of a ceremony for certain occasions

rival [noun: **rivals**] a person or organization that competes with another: *a match between fierce rivals*

[verb: **rivals, rivalling, rivalled**] to be as good, or nearly as good, as something or someone else: *Shop-bought vegetables*

can't rival the ones you grow yourself.
 • **rivalry** [noun] when people or organizations compete against each other: *There's a lot of rivalry between the twins.*

river [noun: **rivers**] a large stream of water that flows across land: *the River Thames*

rivet [noun: **rivets**] a kind of short nail that holds pieces of metal together
 [verb: **rivets, riveting, riveted**] to **be riveted by** something is to be very interested in it
 • **riveting** [adjective] holding all your attention: *The last half hour of the film was simply riveting.*

road [noun: **roads**] a hard, level surface for vehicles to travel along: *The British drive on the left-hand side of the road.*

road rage [noun] angry or violent behaviour by drivers on the road

road tax [noun] money that you must pay the government each year if you want to drive a car on the roads

roadworthy [adjective] if a vehicle is roadworthy, it is in good enough condition to drive on the roads

roam [verb: **roams, roaming, roamed**] to travel or wander around: *There wasn't anything else to do but roam the streets.*

roar [verb: **roars, roaring, roared**] to make a loud, angry sound like a lion: *traffic roaring past in the street below*
 [noun: **roars**] a loud noise like the sound a lion makes

roast [verb: **roasts, roasting, roasted**] to cook or be cooked in an oven or over a fire: *Roast the potatoes at the same time as the turkey.*
 [noun: **roasts**] a piece of meat that has been cooked in the oven
 [adjective] cooked in the oven: *roast potatoes* • *roast beef*

rob [verb: **robs, robbing, robbed**] to rob someone is to steal something from them: *I've been robbed!* • *They stole thousands of pounds when they robbed the bank.*
 • **robber** [noun: **robbers**] a person who steals
 • **robbery** [noun: **robberies**] when something is stolen: *a bank robbery*

robe [noun: **robes**] a long loose piece of clothing: *The mayor wears a chain and a robe on special occasions.*

robin [noun: **robins**] a small brown bird with a red breast

robot [noun: **robots**] a machine that can do things like a person

rock [noun: **rocks**]
 1 rock is the hard stone substance that the Earth is made of
 2 a rock is a large stone
 3 rock is a sweet that is sold at tourist attractions. It is usually in the form of a long stick
 ➡ **rocky^1**

rock^2 [verb: **rocks, rocking, rocked**]
 1 to rock is to move or swing gently backwards and forwards or from side to side
 2 to rock something is to make it move backwards and forwards or from side to side: *She was rocking the baby in her arms.*
 [noun] a type of loud music with a deep beat
 • **rocker** [noun: **rockers**] the curved part of a chair or cradle that it can move backwards and forwards on
 ➡ **rocky^2**

rockery [noun: **rockeries**] a place where people grow small plants among rocks and stones

rocket [noun: **rockets**]
 1 a spacecraft for travelling from Earth into space
 2 a large missile
 3 a kind of firework that explodes high in the sky
 [verb: **rockets, rocketing, rocketed**] to go upwards very quickly: *rocketing prices*

rocking horse [noun: **rocking horses**] a child's toy horse that they can sit on and rock backwards and forwards

rocky^1 [adjective: **rockier, rockiest**] full of or covered with rocks

rocky^2 [adjective: **rockier, rockiest**] shaky, unsteady or uncertain: *Their relationship got off to a rocky start when she didn't even recognize him.*

rod [noun: **rods**] a long thin pole or bar, especially made of wood or metal

rode [verb] a way of changing the verb **ride** to make the past tense: *I rode my bike for hours at a time in those days.*

Rr

rodent [noun: **rodents**] any kind of small furry animal with sharp teeth, such as a mouse, rat or rabbit

rodeo [noun: **rodeos**] a show of riding and other skills by cowboys

roe [noun: **roes**]
1 roe is the eggs of a fish
2 a roe or a **roe deer** is small deer

rogue [noun: **rogues**] a cheating and dishonest person
♦ **roguish** [adjective] mischievous: *a roguish twinkle in his eye*

role [noun: **roles**]
1 the part that someone plays in a play or film: *a starring role in a new British film*
2 the purpose or reason for what something or someone does: *A parent's role is to provide a safe background to a child's life.*

roll [verb: **rolls, rolling, rolled**]
1 to move along, turning over and over: *a ball rolling down a slope*
2 to move along on wheels: *Take the brake off and let the car roll forwards.*
3 to form something into the shape of a ball or cylinder: *Roll the sleeping bag up tightly and tie the string around it.*
4 to roll something is to make it flat by crushing it under a rolling cylinder: *I am going to roll the lawn.* • *rolled metal*
5 to rock from side to side: *In rough weather, the ship rolls a bit.*
6 to **roll up** is to arrive: *Some guests were only just rolling up when the first ones started to leave.*
[noun: **rolls**]
1 a very small loaf of bread: *a cheese roll for lunch*
2 a cylinder shape made from a large flat piece of something like carpet or paper: *We'll need 12 rolls of wallpaper for this room.*
3 an official list of names, for example the names of students at a school or the people who can vote in an election
4 a long rumbling sound: *a drum roll* • *a roll of thunder*

rollcall [noun: **rollcalls**] when someone calls out the names from a list

roller [noun: **rollers**]
1 something in the shape of a cylinder that

turns like a wheel, and is often used to flatten things
2 an object like a cylinder that you can wind hair around when it is wet, to make it curl
3 a long heavy wave on the sea

Rollerblades [plural noun] boots used for skating, each with a single row of wheels on the bottom. This word is a trademark

rollerskate [noun: **rollerskates**] a boot with two pairs of wheels on the bottom

rolling pin [noun: **rolling pins**] a thick round stick that you roll over pastry to flatten it

ROM [abbreviation] short for **Read Only Memory**, a type of memory in a computer that allows you to see information, but not change it

romance [noun: **romances**]
1 romance is the exciting emotions people feel when they are falling in love
2 a romance is a love affair: *his first romance*
3 a romance is a love story: *Betty used to read mainly romances.*
♦ **romantic** [adjective] to do with love: *a romantic relationship* • *a romantic dinner for two*
♦ **romantically** [adverb] in a way that suggests love or a love affair: *She's not romantically involved with anyone just now.*

romp [verb: **romps, romping, romped**] to play in a lively way
[noun: **romps**] a fast-moving, lively game

roof [noun: **roofs**]
1 the part that covers the top of a building or vehicle: *The house has a red tiled roof.*
2 the top inside surface of your mouth

rook [noun: **rooks**]
1 a large black bird like a crow
2 in the game of chess, a rook is a piece which is shaped like a castle

room [noun: **rooms**]
1 one of the areas a building is divided into inside: *We have three rooms downstairs and four upstairs.*
2 enough space for something: *Is there room for a grand piano on the stage?*
♦ **roomy** [adjective: **roomier, roomiest**] having a lot of space

roost [noun: **roosts**] the place where a bird rests at night
[verb: **roosts, roosting, roosted**] if a bird

Rr

roosts somewhere, it sits or sleeps there at night

+ **rooster** [noun: **roosters**] a cockerel

root [noun: **roots**]

1 the underground part of a plant

2 the part of a tooth or hair that attaches it to your body

3 the basic cause of a problem: *The root of all our troubles is that we don't have enough money.*

4 your roots are your family connections and where you come from

[verb: **roots, rooting, rooted**]

1 to grow roots: *The seedlings rooted nicely when I planted them in the compost.*

2 to **root around** is to search roughly and untidily for something: *Who's been rooting around in my desk?*

3 to be **rooted to the spot** is not to be able to move, for example because you are surprised or afraid

4 to **root something out** is to find something and get rid of it

rope [noun: **ropes**] a very thick twisted cord: *an anchor tied on the end of a long piece of rope*

rose¹ [noun: **roses**]

1 a garden plant with prickly stems and sweet-smelling flowers

2 a pink colour

→ **rosy**

rose² [verb] a way of changing the verb **rise** to make a past tense: *The temperature in the room rose steadily as the day wore on.*

rosehip [noun: **rosehips**] the fruit of a rose

rosemary [noun] an evergreen plant that has sweet-smelling leaves that can be used to flavour food in cooking

rosette [noun: **rosettes**] a round decoration or a badge made of gathered ribbon. Rosettes may be given as prizes or worn to show that you support a particular group or party

rostrum [noun: **rostrums**] a platform that someone stands on to make a speech

rosy [adjective: **rosier, rosiest**]

1 a pink colour: *rosy cheeks*

2 hopeful or cheerful: *The future certainly looks rosy for Hugh.*

rot [verb: **rots, rotting, rotted**] to go rotten

and decay: *The leaves fall on the forest floor and gradually rot into the soil.*

[noun]

1 decay where something is going rotten: *They've discovered some rot in the roof timbers.*

2 nonsense: *You do talk such rot!*

→ **rotten, rotter**

rota [noun: **rotas**] a list of people who take turns to do a job

rotary [adjective] going round and round like a wheel

rotate [verb: **rotates, rotating, rotated**]

1 to turn or spin like a wheel: *Each wheel rotates on its own axle.*

2 to go through a series of changes and then start again at the beginning: *Rotating the different kinds of vegetables we grow keeps the soil healthy.*

+ **rotation** [noun: **rotations**]

1 going around like a wheel: *The rotation of the blades keeps the air moving.*

2 working through a series of changes and then beginning again

rotor [noun: **rotors**] a part of a machine that turns round, especially a helicopter blade

rotten [adjective]

1 going bad or decaying: *John stepped on a rotten floorboard and it gave way beneath him.*

2 bad quality: *a rotten meal*

3 unfair or unkind: *That was a rotten thing to say.*

rotter [noun: **rotters**] a person who behaves badly towards someone else

rough [adjective: **rougher, roughest**]

1 not smooth: *a rough track along the side of the field • rough skin on the bottom of your feet*

2 violent: *Rugby is such a rough game, some schools refuse to play it.*

3 not exact: *a rough sketch of the building*

→ **roughen, roughly, roughness**

roughage [noun] another name for the **fibre** in fruit, vegetables and whole grains, that you should eat to help your body deal with your food well

roughen [verb: **roughens, roughening, roughened**] to remove the smoothness of something: *Roughen the edges before you apply the glue to them.*

Rr

roughly [adverb]
1 in a quick way, without being careful or gentle: *If you handle the flowers roughly, you'll damage them.*
2 approximately: *There were roughly ten thousand people in the stadium.*

roughness [noun]
1 not being gentle
2 not being smooth

roulette [noun] a gambling game in which a ball is dropped on to a spinning wheel that has sections with different numbers on them

round [adjective: **rounder, roundest**]
1 of the same shape as a circle: *a round table*
2 of the same shape as part of a circle: *a round archway*
3 of the same shape as a ball: *The Earth is round.*

[adverb and preposition]
1 around or on all sides: *I glanced round at the pictures on the walls.* • *The Moon goes round the Earth.*
2 from one person or place to another: *The news got round pretty quickly.* • *Please pass the wine round all the guests.*

[noun: **rounds**]
1 a burst of something like laughing, cheering, clapping or firing: *Let's give him a round of applause.*
2 a route of calls that someone makes: *We're always last on the postman's round.*
3 a level in a contest: *the second round of the FA Cup*
4 a single bullet or shell for a gun
5 a song in which each singer begins the tune a little after the previous one

[verb: **rounds, rounding, rounded**]
1 to go around a corner: *As I rounded the corner, I came face to face with Sharon.*
2 to round a number up or down is to make it a whole number: *Round the fractions up to the nearest whole number.*
3 to **round on** someone is to attack them suddenly: *She rounded on me as if I'd hit her.*
4 to **round up** people or animals is to collect them together: *Farmers are rounding the animals up for the winter.*

roundabout [noun: **roundabouts**]
1 a circular platform in a playground or a funfair that turns while you ride on it
2 a road junction where several roads meet and the traffic must travel around a central island before continuing

rounders [noun] a team game similar to baseball

roundly [adverb] plainly and thoroughly: *We were roundly criticized for failing to finish.*

rouse [verb: **rouses, rousing, roused**] to wake someone up
• **rousing** [adjective] exciting and making people feel enthusiastic: *a rousing march from the brass band*

rout [noun: **routs**] a complete defeat

route [noun: **routes**] a way of getting somewhere: *Which route do you take to work?*

routine [noun: **routines**]
1 a fixed order of doing things: *Our daily routine includes three good meals and plenty of exercise.*
2 a dance routine is a fixed set of dance steps
[adjective] a routine job or task is an ordinary one that is done regularly: *a routine inspection*

rove [verb: **roves, roving, roved**] to wander around: *Harry has been roving about the world.*
• **rover** [noun: **rovers**] a wanderer or unsettled person

row[1] [noun: **rows**]
1 a number of things arranged beside each other in a line: *the front row of seats* • *Sow the seeds in a straight row.* • *a row of figures*
2 if events happen **in a row**, they happen one after another: *They've lost five matches in a row.*

row[2] [verb: **rows, rowing, rowed**] to pull a boat through water using oars

row[3] [noun: **rows**]
1 a noisy argument or a fight
2 a loud unpleasant noise: *Why are the children making such a row?*
[verb: **rows, rowing, rowed**] to argue noisily: *They were always rowing and falling out.*

ⓘ **row**[1] and **row**[2] rhyme with **low**. **row**[3] rhymes with **how**.

rowdy [adjective: **rowdier, rowdiest**] noisy and rough: *a rowdy party*

rowing boat [noun: **rowing boats**] a small boat that you row with oars

royal [adjective] to do with a king or queen or their family: *a royal wedding*
* **royalty** [noun] all the members of the king or queen's family

RSVP [abbreviation] People write **RSVP** on an invitation in order to ask for a reply

ⓘ **RSVP** is short for **répondez s'il vous plaît**, which is French for 'please reply'.

rub [verb: **rubs, rubbing, rubbed**]
1 to move your hand backwards and forwards over a surface, usually pressing down at the same time: *He lowered his head and rubbed his eyes.*
2 to press against something and move backwards and forwards: *My shoes are rubbing and giving me blisters.*
[noun: **rubs**] a backwards and forwards movement of your hand while pressing down: *Let me give your neck a rub where it's aching.*

rubber [noun: **rubbers**]
1 rubber is a strong substance that stretches and can be man-made or made from tree juices: *rubber-soled shoes*
2 a rubber is a small block that you can use to rub on pencil marks to get rid of them

rubber stamp [noun: **rubber stamps**] a small tool for printing numbers or short words on paper

rubbish [noun]
1 things that have been thrown away or should be thrown away: *Put the rubbish in the bin.*
2 complete nonsense: *Her new chat show is utter rubbish.*

rubble [noun] the broken pieces that are left when a building falls down

ruby [noun: **rubies**] a dark red stone that is used as a jewel

rucksack [noun: **rucksacks**] a bag that you carry on your back, especially when you are walking or climbing

rudder [noun: **rudders**] the flat piece of wood or metal at the back of a boat, under the water, that moves to steer it in a different direction. An aeroplane also has a rudder on its tail

ruddy [adjective: **ruddier, ruddiest**] pink and healthy looking: *a ruddy complexion*

rude [adjective: **ruder, rudest**]
1 not polite: *a rude answer*
2 embarrassing and not proper in a polite situation: *rude jokes*
3 rough and basic: *a rude stable*
* **rudely** [adverb] in a bad-mannered way, without being polite: *'Not likely!' he said rudely.*
* **rudeness** [noun] bad manners or not being polite: *I apologize for my friend's rudeness.*

rueful [adjective] feeling sorry about something and wishing it had not happened: *a rueful smile*

ruff [noun: **ruffs**] a pleated frill that was worn round the neck in the past

ruffian [noun: **ruffians**] a person who behaves in a rough violent way

ruffle [verb: **ruffles, ruffling, ruffled**]
1 to disturb something such as a hairstyle by making it untidy: *A small bird sat on the fence, ruffling its feathers.*
2 to annoy or upset someone: *She never seems to get ruffled.*

rug [noun: **rugs**] a large mat on the floor

rugby [noun] a game played by two teams on a large field with an oval ball that the players must try to take over a line at the end of the pitch

rugged [adjective] rough or unevenly shaped: *rugged countryside* • *The man had a really rugged face.*

ruin [verb: **ruins, ruining, ruined**] to destroy something: *The rain ruined my hairstyle.*
[noun: **ruins**]
1 a ruin is something such as a building that has fallen to pieces: *a Roman ruin*
2 ruin is when someone has lost all the money they had: *If this plan did not work, he would be facing certain ruin.*
3 to be **in ruins** is to be destroyed: *a city in ruins after the earthquake* • *All our plans were in ruins now that Bob had walked out.*
* **ruined** [adjective] destroyed: *a ruined castle*

rule [noun: **rules**]
1 an instruction about what is or what is not allowed: *It's against the rules to move your feet when you're holding the ball.*

Rr

2 government or control by politicians or a king or queen: *a country under the rule of the military*

3 the way things usually happen: *As a rule, more people go to work by car when it's raining.*

[verb: **rules, ruling, ruled**]

1 to rule something such as a country is to control it

2 to make an official decision: *The judge has ruled that the prisoner can go free.*

3 to rule a line is to draw a straight line: *a pad of ruled paper*

4 to **rule something out** is to decide that it is not a possibility: *The police have ruled out the suggestion that his death was an accident.*

♦ **ruler** [noun: **ruler**]

1 a person who controls or governs a country

2 a strip of wood, plastic or metal that can be used to help you to draw a straight line or for measuring short lengths

♦ **ruling** [noun: **rulings**] a decision by someone like a judge: *The committee's ruling is that the race was a draw.*

rum [noun] a strong alcoholic drink made from sugar cane

[adjective] strange or peculiar

rumble [verb: **rumbles, rumbling, rumbled**] to make a low continuous sound: *tanks rumbling along the road*

[noun: **rumbles**] a long low sound like thunder

rummage [verb: **rummages, rummaging, rummaged**] to search for something by untidily moving things out of the way: *rummaging in her handbag for a pen*

rummy [noun] a card game where each player has seven cards and tries to collect sets of three or more by changing some cards

rumour [noun: **rumours**] information that people pass to each other, although it may not be true: *There's a rumour going round that Steve and Julie are having an affair.*

[verb: **rumours, rumouring, rumoured**] something is rumoured if people say it is true, although it may not be

rump [noun: **rumps**] the area around an animal's tail or above its back legs

rumpus [noun] a disturbance when people are arguing noisily

run [verb: **runs, running, ran, run**]

1 to move with very fast steps: *We had to run for the bus.*

2 to follow a certain route: *The number 5 bus runs every 10 minutes.* • *This road runs over the hill to the next village.*

3 to run someone somewhere is to give them a lift: *I run the children to school if it's raining.*

4 a liquid runs when it flows easily: *tears running down my face* • *Your nose is running.*

5 an engine or other machinery runs, or you run it, when it works or operates: *The engine runs on diesel oil.*

6 a scheme or system runs, or you run it, when it happens or works: *We're running a new course in the spring.*

7 to continue: *The film runs for 2 hours.*

8 to run your hand or finger over something is to pass your hand or finger across its surface: *Grace ran her finger down the list.*

9 to compete for an important job or award: *Mr Bush was running for president.*

10 to **run a risk** is to take a chance that something bad might happen: *If we don't leave now, we'll run the risk of missing the train.*

11 to **run away** is to leave somewhere in secret

12 to **run out of something** is to use it all up: *We've run out of milk.*

[noun: **runs**]

1 a fast movement, quicker than a walk: *break into a run and get there faster*

2 a race or period of exercise: *a cross-country run*

3 a trip or journey in a vehicle: *a quick run into town to do the shopping*

4 a point that a player wins in a game like cricket by running a certain distance after hitting the ball

5 a period of time during which something is repeated: *a run of bad luck*

6 a long fenced area where animals are kept: *a chicken run*

➡ **runner, running, runny**

runaway [noun: **runaways**] someone who has run away from home

[adjective] a runaway vehicle is out of control and moving very fast

run-down [adjective]

Rr

1 continually feeling tired and not very healthy
2 a run-down building is not kept in good condition

rung¹ [noun: **rungs**] a step on a ladder

rung² [verb] a form of the verb **ring** that is used with a helping verb to show that something happened in the past: *I've rung all my friends and can't get anyone to go with me.*

runner [noun: **runners**]
1 a person or animal that runs: *a fast runner*
2 the blade of a skate or sledge

runner-up [noun: **runners-up**] the person who finishes in second place in a competition

running [noun]
1 organization and management: *You'll be responsible for the running of the shop.*
2 to be **in** or **out of the running** for something is to have, or not have, the chance of winning it: *Henman is still in the running for the championship.*
[adjective] continuing without a break: *a running commentary on the events*
[adverb] one after the other: *for three days running*

runny [adjective: **runnier, runniest**]
1 like a liquid: *Heat the jam until it is runny.*
2 if you have a runny nose, you need to blow it frequently

runway [noun: **runways**] the long road-like surface at an airport that aircraft take off from and land on

rupture [verb: **ruptures, rupturing, ruptured**] to break: *a patient with an appendix that has ruptured*
[noun: **ruptures**] a break or tear, especially in a muscle or joint

rural [adjective] to do with the countryside

rush [noun: **rushes**]
1 a hurry: *We were just in time but it had been a dreadful rush.*
2 a large number of people trying to get to the same place at the same time: *a rush for the door*

[verb: **rushes, rushing, rushed**]
1 to go somewhere in a hurry: *I rushed downstairs as soon as I heard the thump.*
2 to rush someone somewhere is to take them there very quickly: *Fletcher was rushed to hospital in an ambulance.*
3 to do something too quickly or in a hurry: *Don't rush it or you'll just make a mistake.*
4 to attack someone suddenly, hoping to surprise them

rusk [noun: **rusks**] a hard dry biscuit that babies eat

russet [noun] a reddish-brown colour

rust [noun] a reddish-brown substance that forms on iron and other metals if they are exposed to air and wetness
[verb: **rusts, rusting, rusted**] to become rusty
➡ **rusty**

rustle [verb: **rustles, rustling, rustled**] to make a soft sound like dry leaves rubbing together: *people rustling sweet papers*
[noun: **rustles**] a soft sound like dry leaves: *the rustle of a silk dress*

rusty [adjective: **rustier, rustiest**]
1 rusty metal has a reddish-brown substance on it that makes it weak and brittle
2 a person's knowledge of something is rusty if it is not as good as it used to be: *My French is a bit rusty, but it'll come back to me with practice.*

rut [noun: **ruts**]
1 a deep track made by a wheel
2 a boring routine: *I'm in a rut and the only way out is to change my job.*

ruthless [adjective] a ruthless person does what they think they must do without caring how cruel or kind they are being
◆ **ruthlessly** [adverb] without taking into account how kind or cruel you are being
◆ **ruthlessness** [noun] doing things without thinking about how kind or cruel you are being

rye [noun] a kind of grain that is used for making flour and whisky

Rr

S

S [abbreviation] short for **south**

Sabbath [noun] the day of the week set aside for rest and worship in certain religions. The Jewish Sabbath is Saturday, for Muslims it is Friday and for most Christians, it is Sunday

sabotage [noun]
1 deliberate damage that someone does to buildings or equipment in secret
2 secret action that is intended to wreck someone's plan or system
[verb: **sabotages, sabotaging, sabotaged**] to deliberately damage an enemy's equipment or plans

sac [noun: **sacs**] any part of a plant or animal that is like a bag, especially one that contains liquid

saccharin [noun] a very sweet chemical that can be used instead of sugar
♦ **saccharine** [adjective] very sweet or sickly

sachet [noun: **sachets**] a small plastic or paper packet containing a small amount of a liquid or powder: *a handy sachet of shampoo for your suitcase*

sack [noun: **sacks**]
1 a sack is a very large bag used for carrying or storing things
2 **the sack** is when you are dismissed from your job: *That new boy got the sack for stealing coins from the till.*
[verb: **sacks, sacking, sacked**] to dismiss someone from their job, usually because they are not good at the job or have done something wrong: *He was sacked for being late all the time.*

sacrament [noun: **sacraments**] any of

several important Christian ceremonies such as baptism and communion

sacred [adjective]
1 holy, or to do with a god
2 to do with religion or worship: *a CD of sacred music*

sacrifice [noun: **sacrifices**]
1 something that is killed and offered to a god in the hope that something good will then happen: *Ancient peoples killed small and large animals in this place as sacrifices to their gods.*
2 giving up something for the sake of someone or something else: *We didn't earn much and we had to make a lot of sacrifices to afford a house.*
[verb: **sacrifices, sacrificing, sacrificed**]
1 to kill something and offer it to a god
2 to give something up for the sake of someone or something else: *The boy bravely sacrificed his life to save his sister.*

sad [adjective: **sadder, saddest**]
1 feeling unhappy: *a sad look*
2 making you feel unhappy: *a sad film*
3 boring and not fashionable: *You're sad if you think that party was good.*
♦ **sadden** [verb: **saddens, saddening, saddened**] you are saddened if something makes you feel unhappy: *We were greatly saddened by the news.*
➡ **sadly, sadness**

saddle [noun: **saddles**] a seat for a rider of a horse or a bicycle
[verb: **saddles, saddling, saddled**]
1 to put a seat on a horse so that you can ride it
2 to **saddle someone with something** is to give them a job that nobody wants to do: *They've saddled me with organizing the cleaning rota.*

sadism [noun] enjoying being cruel or hurting other people
  ◆ **sadist** [noun: **sadists**] someone who enjoys hurting other people
  ◆ **sadistic** [adjective] a sadistic person enjoys hurting other people
sadly [adverb]
  1 unfortunately: *Sadly, we must say goodbye to Mrs Green today.*
  2 unhappily: *She looked up sadly and tried to smile.*
sadness [noun] a feeling of unhappiness or pity
sae [abbreviation] short for **stamped addressed envelope**
safari [noun: **safaris**] an expedition or tour when people hunt or watch wild animals, especially in Africa
safari park [noun: **safari parks**] a large area of land where wild animals are kept for visitors to see
safe [adjective: **safer, safest**]
  1 not harmed: *Thank goodness you're safe!*
  2 not involving danger or risk: *the safest way to travel long distances • That ladder doesn't look very safe to me.*
  [noun: **safes**] a strong metal box that you can lock valuables in: *The safe had been blown open with dynamite.*
safeguard [noun: **safeguards**] protection against danger or harm: *The double lock is a safeguard against theft.*
  [verb: **safeguards, safeguarding, safeguarded**] to protect something from danger: *Vaccinations should safeguard our children from these deadly diseases.*
safely [adverb] without risk or danger: *getting everyone home safely • safely tucked up in bed*
safe sex [noun] sex in which people are careful not to get sexual diseases, for example by using a condom
safety [noun] being safe: *Everyone dived for safety. • We must put the safety of our passengers first.*
safety belt [noun: **safety belts**] a strap in a car or plane that stops you being thrown out of your seat if there is a crash
safety pin [noun: **safety pins**] a pin with a

guard that covers the sharp point when it is closed
sag [verb: **sags, sagging, sagged**] to sag is to droop or not to be firm: *a mattress that has begun to sag in the middle*
saga [noun: **sagas**] a long story, especially one about several generations of a family
sage [noun: **sages**]
  1 a sage is a wise man
  2 sage is a herb that is used in cooking to add flavour
said [verb] a way of changing the verb **say** to make a past tense. It can be used with or without a helping verb: *They said I can come back any time. • I've told you everything he said.*
sail [verb: **sails, sailing, sailed**]
  1 to travel in a ship or a boat: *My ambition is to sail across the Atlantic on an ocean liner.*
  2 to start a journey in a ship: *The ferry sails at noon.*
  3 to **sail through something** is to do it quickly and easily: *Amy sailed through her exams with no bother.*
  [noun: **sails**]
  1 a sheet of canvas attached to a mast on a boat that catches the wind and carries the boat along
  2 a broad flat blade that turns on a windmill
  ◆ **sailor** [noun: **sailors**] someone who works on a ship
saint [noun: **saints**]
  1 someone that the Christian church believes was especially holy
  2 a particularly good and kind person
  ◆ **saintly** [adjective] very good or very holy
sake [noun: **sakes**]
  1 for someone's sake is for them or for their benefit: *For his mother's sake, he didn't want to make a fuss. • Please don't go to any trouble just for my sake.*
  2 to do something **for the sake of it** is to do it simply because you want to: *I'm sure she argues with me just for the sake of it.*
  3 to do something **for the sake of something** is to do it because you want to achieve that thing: *I gave in for the sake of peace.*
salad [noun: **salads**] a mixture of mostly raw

Ss

vegetables that sometimes includes other foods like ham or cheese

salami [noun] a type of spicy sausage that is usually served cold in thin slices

salary [noun: **salaries**] an amount of money that a person is paid for doing their job for a year. It is usually broken down into twelve monthly payments

sale [noun: **sales**]
1 when something is sold for money: *a sale of quality carpets* • *a house for sale* • *This week's edition is on sale now.*
2 an occasion when goods in a shop are sold at cheaper prices than usual: *the January sales*

salesman [noun: **salesmen**] a man whose job is to sell goods to customers

saleswoman [noun: **saleswomen**] a woman whose job is to sell goods to customers

saline [adjective] containing salt

saliva [noun] the watery liquid produced in your mouth

sallow [adjective: **sallower, sallowest**] a person with a sallow complexion has pale, yellow-brown, unhealthy-looking skin

sally [verb: **sallies, sallying, sallied**] to rush out suddenly
[noun: **sallies**]
1 a sudden rush or attack
2 a witty remark

salmon [noun: **salmon**]
1 a salmon is a large sea fish with a silvery skin, that swims up rivers to lay its eggs
2 salmon is the orange-pink flesh from this fish that people eat as food
3 salmon is an orange-pink colour

salmonella [noun] a type of bacteria that can cause food-poisoning

salon [noun: **salons**] a shop where services such as hairdressing or beauty treatments take place

saloon [noun: **saloons**]
1 a bar where alcoholic drinks are served
2 a car with a hard roof, several seats and a separate space for luggage
3 a dining-room for passengers on a ship

salt [noun: **salts**] salt is small white crystals that come from the ground (**rock salt**) or the sea (**sea salt**) and are used for flavouring food

[verb: **salts, salting, salted**] to put salt on something, usually on food for flavour, or on roads to stop ice forming

◆ **salty** [adjective: **saltier, saltiest**] containing salt or tasting very strongly of salt: *I thought the soup was awfully salty.*

salute [verb: **salutes, saluting, saluted**]
1 to greet someone with a formal gesture. Soldiers salute their officers by standing still and raising one hand to their forehead
2 to praise someone or what they have done: *Today we salute the brave people of this town.*
[noun: **salutes**] a movement that shows respect to someone you meet, especially a military officer

salvage [verb: **salvages, salvaging, salvaged**] to rescue what you can after a disaster of some kind, especially the sinking of a ship: *some furniture that was salvaged from the building after the fire*

salvation [noun] being saved or saving someone or something

same [adjective] exactly alike or very similar: *I was wearing the same jacket as Barbara.* • *The two cases are exactly the same.*
[pronoun]
1 something that is alike or similar: *You know I'd do the same for you.*
2 all the same means 'anyway' or 'in spite of something': *The flight might be delayed but you have to check in now all the same.*

sample [noun: **samples**] a small part of something that shows what the rest is like
[verb: **samples, sampling, sampled**] to take or test a small part of something: *Would you like to sample our new product?*

sanatorium [noun: **sanatoriums** or **sanatoria**] a hospital that cares for people who need treatment or rest for a long time

sanctuary [noun: **sanctuaries**]
1 a holy place, for example in a church, mosque or temple
2 a safe place: *refugees seeking sanctuary* • *a bird sanctuary*

sand [noun: **sands**] tiny grains of rock that are found on beaches, on river-beds and in deserts
[verb: **sands, sanding, sanded**] to make a rough surface smooth by rubbing it with

sandpaper: *The wood looked very different after it had been sanded down and varnished.*
➞ **sandy**

sandal [noun: **sandals**] sandals are light open shoes with straps for wearing in warm weather

sandbag [noun: **sandbags**] a small sack filled with sand. Sandbags are used to build walls to keep out flooding water or bullets

sand dune [noun: **sand dunes**] a hill of sand on or near a beach

sandpaper [noun] strong paper with a layer of sand glued to one side, used for smoothing wood or rough metal surfaces

sandstone [noun] a type of soft rock that is often used in building

sandwich [noun: **sandwiches**] two slices of bread with a filling between them: *a ham sandwich*
[verb: **sandwiches, sandwiching, sandwiched**] to be sandwiched between things or people is to be squashed between them: *I was sandwiched between the backs of two huge people.*

sandy [adjective: **sandier, sandiest**]
1 containing or covered with sand: *sandy soil*
2 light reddish-brown: *a sandy-haired child*

sane [adjective: **saner, sanest**]
1 not mad or mentally ill: *The judge was told that Foster was sane at the time of the murder.*
2 sensible: *She seems like a sane enough person.*
➞ **sanity**

sang [verb] a way of changing the verb **sing** to make a past tense: *We sang folk songs all evening to Gerry's guitar.*

sanitary [adjective] to do with keeping clean and healthy: *Diseases spread quickly where sanitary conditions are poor.*

sanitary towel [noun: **sanitary towels**] a pad that a woman wears to absorb the blood when she is having her period

sanitation [noun] ways of protecting people's health by providing clean water and getting dirty water and waste away from buildings

sanity [noun] not being mad or mentally ill

sank [verb] a way of changing the verb **sink** to make a past tense: *Many ships sank without trace in those days.*

sap [noun] the juice inside plants and trees
[verb: **saps, sapping, sapped**] to sap your strength or energy is to gradually make you feel more and more tired: *The terrible heat sapped our energy by lunchtime.*

sapling [noun: **saplings**] a young tree

sapphire [noun: **sapphires**] a dark blue precious stone that is used in jewellery

sarcasm [noun] saying one thing when you actually mean the opposite. People often use sarcasm when they are trying to be funny
• **sarcastic** [adjective] meaning the exact opposite in order to hurt or amuse someone: *When we told Marge we liked her hat, she didn't know if we were being sarcastic or not.*

sardine [noun: **sardines**] a type of small sea fish that is either eaten fresh or packed tightly in small tins

sari [noun: **saris**] a long piece of fabric that is worn like a dress by Hindu women. It is wound round the waist and the end is draped over one shoulder or over the head

sarong [noun: **sarongs**] a wide piece of fabric that covers the lower part of the body. It is wound round the waist or under the arms

sash [noun: **sashes**] a strip of cloth worn around the waist or over one shoulder, usually as part of a uniform

sat [verb] a way of changing the verb **sit** to make a past tense. It can be used with or without a helping verb: *He sat on a chair.* • *I've sat here for an hour waiting for you!*

satchel [noun: **satchels**] a small bag with a shoulder strap that is used to carry schoolbooks

satellite [noun: **satellites**]
1 a natural object in space, such as the moon, that moves around a planet or star
2 a piece of equipment that is sent into space to travel around the Earth in order to send and receive information

satellite dish [noun: **satellite dishes**] a saucer-shaped dish that is attached to the side of a building to pick up signals for satellite television

satellite television [noun] broadcasts

Ss

that are sent and received using satellites that are designed for that purpose

satin [noun] a fabric with a shiny surface
[adjective] made from satin: *satin sheets*

satisfaction [noun] a contented feeling after getting or doing what you wanted: *I get a lot of satisfaction out of baking my own bread.*

satisfactory [adjective]
1 good enough, but not outstanding: *The work was of a satisfactory standard.*
2 right or wanted: *a very satisfactory result*

satisfy [verb: **satisfies, satisfying, satisfied**]
1 to be satisfied is to be happy or contented: *I'm afraid I'm not satisfied with the way we've been treated.*
2 to satisfy someone is to give them what they want or need: *I don't think a biscuit will satisfy a boy who's been playing football all afternoon.*

satsuma [noun: **satsumas**] a fruit like a small orange with no pips

saturate [verb: **saturates, saturating, saturated**] to be saturated is to be soaking wet

Saturday [noun: **Saturdays**] the day of the week after Friday and before Sunday

sauce [noun: **sauces**]
1 a liquid that food is cooked in or served with: *I like plenty of tomato sauce with my chips.*
2 cheeky remarks: *That's enough of your sauce!*

saucepan [noun: **saucepans**] a deep round cooking pot that usually has a long handle and a lid

saucer [noun: **saucers**] a small shallow dish that you put under a cup

saucy [adjective: **saucier, sauciest**] cheeky

sauna [noun: **saunas**] a steam bath where you sit in a room filled with the steam produced by throwing cold water on hot coals

saunter [verb: **saunters, sauntering, sauntered**] to walk slowly in a relaxed way: *people sauntering round the park on a warm evening*
[noun: **saunters**] a gentle stroll: *a saunter along the seafront*

sausage [noun: **sausages**] meat that is minced and stuffed into a skin to make long tube shapes

sauté [verb: **sautés, sautéing, sautéed**] to fry something quickly in a small amount of butter or oil
[adjective] fried quickly in a small amount of butter or oil: *sauté potatoes*

savage [adjective] fierce and cruel: *a savage attack by a stray dog*
[verb: **savages, savaging, savaged**] to be savaged by an animal is to be attacked and badly injured by it
[noun: **savages**] an uncivilized person
✦ **savagely** [adverb] fiercely and cruelly

save [verb: **saves, saving, saved**]
1 to save someone or something is to rescue them from something unpleasant: *The firefighters saved everyone in the building.* • *We saved our photographs, but everything else in the loft was wrecked by the leaking water.*
2 to save someone's life is to prevent them from dying: *There's no doubt that the safety belts saved our lives.*
3 to save something is to store it for later: *Save the data on your files on a backup disk if you can.* • *Save any leftover food and heat it up later.*
4 to save time or money is to use less time or money than you would normally do: *Save 20% on all our products this week.* • *You can save 40 minutes by going along the motorway.*
[noun: **saves**] when a goalkeeper prevents the other team from scoring a goal: *a brilliant save, just in front of the goalpost*
✦ **savings** [plural noun] money that you collect and keep to use at some time in the future: *Colin's going to spend all his savings on a drum kit.*
✦ **saviour** [noun: **saviours**]
1 a person who rescues someone or something from danger
2 the Saviour, in Christian religions, is Jesus Christ

savour [verb: **savours, savouring, savoured**] to eat or drink something slowly in order to enjoy it for longer: *We ate the cakes slowly, savouring every mouthful.*
✦ **savoury** [adjective] not sweet or containing sugar: *savoury snacks such as crisps and nuts*

saw[1] [noun: **saws**] a tool with a thin notched blade that can cut through wood or metal [verb: **saws, sawing, sawed, sawed** or **sawn**] to cut through wood or metal using a saw

saw[2] [verb] a way of changing the verb **see** to make a past tense: *I know you were there because I saw you with my own eyes.*

sawdust [noun] the thick dust that is created when wood is cut with a saw

sawmill [noun: **sawmills**] a place where timber is taken to be cut before being used, for example, in building

saxophone [noun: **saxophones**] a wind instrument with a long curved metal body. You play it by blowing it and pressing different keys

say [verb: **says, saying, said**]
1 to speak words out loud: *I was just going to say 'hello'.*
2 to express in written words: *What does the notice say?*
[noun] to **have a say** or to **have your say** is to be able to give your opinion: *The others all decided to go and I didn't even have a say in the matter.*
◆ **saying** [noun: **sayings**] a phrase or sentence that people often use and sometimes gives wise advice: *Gran's favourite saying was 'an apple a day keeps the doctor away'.*

scab [noun: **scabs**] a crust of dried blood that forms over a wound as it heals
◆ **scabby** [adjective: **scabbier, scabbiest**]
1 covered in scabs: *a scabby knee*
2 not in good condition or nice-looking: *a scabby old hairbrush*

scaffold [noun: **scaffolds**] a platform used in the past to execute criminals on

scaffolding [noun] a framework of poles and planks for workmen to stand on when they are working on the outside of a tall building

scald [verb: **scalds, scalding, scalded**] to be scalded is to be burnt by very hot liquid or steam
[noun: **scalds**] a burn caused by hot liquid or steam

scale [noun: **scales**]
1 a series of marks or divisions used for measuring something: *an earthquake that measured 3.2 on the Richter scale*

2 the size of something such as a model or a map, compared to the actual size of the thing it represents: *A scale of 10:1 means the model is ten times bigger than the real thing.*
3 the general size of something: *steel production on a huge scale*
4 a sequence of musical notes, especially between notes that are octaves apart: *the scale of G major*
5 one of the small thin flakes covering the skin of a fish or snake
[verb: **scales, scaling, scaled**] to scale something is to climb up it
◆ **scales** [plural noun] an instrument for weighing: *a set of kitchen scales*
➞ **scaly**

scallop [noun: **scallops**] a shellfish that you can eat and that lives inside two hinged fan-shaped shells

scalp [noun: **scalps**] the skin on top of your head where your hair grows

scalpel [noun: **scalpels**] a small knife, used especially by surgeons, with a very sharp thin blade

scaly [adjective: **scalier, scaliest**] covered with small, dry, flaky particles

scamp [noun: **scamps**] a mischievous child

scamper [verb: **scampers, scampering, scampered**] to run quickly, taking short steps

scampi [plural noun] large prawns that are usually fried in oil in batter or breadcrumbs

scan [verb: **scans, scanning, scanned**]
1 to scan something such as a page of writing is to read it very quickly: *Lou scanned the jobs section of the paper, looking for anything suitable.*
2 to scan an area is to look all around it from one position
3 to scan something with a scanner is to pass the scanner over it to take a picture: *You can scan the picture, and then send it to me in an e-mail.*
4 a poem scans when it has a rhythmic pattern
[noun: **scans**]
1 a quick look through a piece of writing or around an area
2 a process that produces an image on a screen by directing beams of light or sound at

Ss

an object: *The doctor sent Amy for a brain scan.*

scandal [noun: **scandals**]

1 a scandal is a disgraceful or shocking situation: *a political scandal*

2 scandal is information about other people that is considered shocking: *Heard any juicy scandal recently?*

♦ **scandalous** [adjective] disgraceful or outrageous: *It's scandalous that we can't do more to help these people.*

scanner [noun: **scanners**]

1 a machine that copies a picture or document into a computer

2 a machine that produces a picture of the inside of a part of someone's body as part of a medical test

3 a machine that can read information such as the bar code on a product

scant [adjective: **scanter, scantest**] very little or hardly enough: *She had paid scant attention so I wasn't surprised when she looked at me blankly.*

♦ **scanty** [adjective: **scantier, scantiest**] very small or hardly big enough: *a scanty nightshirt*

scapegoat [noun: **scapegoats**] a person who is forced to take the blame for something that was not all their fault

scar [noun: **scars**] a mark that is left on skin after a wound has healed

[verb: **scars, scarring, scarred**] to be scarred is to have permanent marks where you were injured: *He was scarred for life in the accident.*

scarce [adjective: **scarcer, scarcest**] difficult to get: *Food was scarce in wartime.*

♦ **scarcely** [adverb] hardly, or almost not at all: *Carmen's throat was so sore she could scarcely speak.*

♦ **scarcity** [noun: **scarcities**] a shortage of something

scare [verb: **scares, scaring, scared**] to be scared is to be frightened by something: *Some of the younger children were scared by the screeching fireworks.*

[noun: **scares**]

1 a scare is a fright: *It gave us àll a bit of a scare when Mother fainted.*

2 a scare is a sudden worry that lots of people have about something: *a bomb scare*

➝ **scary**

scarecrow [noun: **scarecrows**] a simple model of a person in a field, set up to frighten birds and stop them from eating crops

scarf [noun: **scarves**] a long strip or square of cloth that you wear around your neck, shoulders or head to keep warm or for decoration

scarlet [noun] a bright red colour

scarper [verb: **scarpers, scarpering, scarpered**] to run away

scary [adjective: **scarier, scariest**] making you feel frightened: *It was scary when the doors suddenly blew open.*

scatter [verb: **scatters, scattering, scattered**]

1 to scatter a thing or things is to spread them in lots of places over a wide area: *Scatter the seeds evenly over the prepared soil.*

2 a group of people scatter when they run away in different directions

scavenge [verb: **scavenges, scavenging, scavenged**] to search amongst rubbish for things that can be used or eaten: *stray dogs scavenging food from the dustbins*

♦ **scavenger** [noun: **scavengers**] a wild bird or animal that feeds mainly on the flesh of dead animals and on other waste material

scenario [noun: **scenarios**] a situation that might happen, or one in a play, film or book: *The worst scenario would be if the two countries declare war.* • *I'm thinking about a couple of scenarios for a new story.*

scene [noun: **scenes**]

1 the setting that an event takes place in: *the scene of the crime*

2 a small section of a play, a book or a film: *We'll have to film the ball scene next.*

3 a place or situation as someone sees it: *Before me was a scene of celebration.* • *The scene in the town square is just the same as yesterday.*

4 to **make a scene** is to make an embarrassing fuss

♦ **scenery** [noun] the countryside around you: *You get to see some wonderful scenery from the train.*

scenic [adjective] with pleasant things to look at: *a scenic route*

scent [noun: **scents**]
1 a perfume: *The scent of lilies can fill a whole room.*
2 the smell of an animal that other animals can follow
[verb: **scents, scenting, scented**] to discover by smell: *A hungry animal will scent food long before it sees it.*

sceptic [noun: **sceptics**] a person who has doubts about things that other people are sure about: *Of course the sceptics said the photographs of the aliens were fakes.*
• sceptical [adjective] doubting that something is true: *Ken thinks it'll work, but I'm still sceptical.*

sceptre [noun: **sceptres**] a rod that a king or queen carries at official ceremonies

schedule [noun: **schedules**]
1 a plan or timetable that shows when certain things should happen or be done: *a flight schedule*
2 if something is **on schedule**, it happens at the time it was planned to happen: *The building work finished on schedule.*
[verb: **schedules, scheduling, scheduled**] to plan for something to happen at a particular time: *The meeting has been scheduled for next Wednesday.*

scheme [noun: **schemes**] a plan of action: *a new scheme to build a car park on the old playing field*
[verb: **schemes, scheming, schemed**] to make secret plans, especially to cause harm or damage
• scheming [adjective] crafty or cunning

schizophrenia [noun] a severe mental illness in which the way that someone thinks and feels is not connected with what is really happening
• schizophrenic [adjective] suffering from, or to do with schizophrenia
[noun: **schizophrenics**] someone who is suffering from schizophrenia

scholar [noun: **scholars**] a person who studies and knows a lot about a particular subject: *a scholar of Greek*
• scholarly [adjective] showing a deep knowledge of a subject: *a scholarly work about Victorian art*

• scholarship [noun: **scholarships**]
1 a scholarship is money for a student to study at a school or university: *There are several scholarships available for very bright students.*
2 scholarship is serious study of a subject

school [noun: **schools**]
1 a place where children and teenagers go to be educated: *You'll go to school when you're five years old.*
2 all the pupils and teachers in a school: *The whole school was in the playground, watching the fire.*
3 a large number of fish or dolphins that swim together in a group
[verb: **schools, schooling, schooled**] to school someone to do something is to train them to do it: *The boys have been schooled to be polite to visitors.*

schoolchildren [plural noun] children who go to school

schooling [noun] your schooling is the education you receive, especially at school

schoolteacher [noun: **schoolteachers**] a teacher in a school

schooner [noun: **schooners**] a sailing ship with two masts

sciatica [noun] pain in your lower back and the back of your thigh, caused by pressure on a nerve

science [noun: **sciences**]
1 studying the natural world and the things that happen in it
2 a particular study about the natural world, especially chemistry, physics or biology

science fiction [noun] stories and films that are set in the future or in other parts of the universe

scientific [adjective]
1 to do with science: *scientific research*
2 based on expert knowledge or a system of rules and tests, like the study of a science: *Jeremy's explanation of why my seeds didn't come up wasn't very scientific – he said it was because they were mine!*
• scientifically [adverb] according to the rules of science: *a scientifically proven law*

scientist [noun: **scientists**] a person who

Ss

studies science or whose work involves science: *a laboratory where scientists test bacteria found in food*

scissors [plural noun] a cutting tool that has two blades joined in the middle. You use scissors by opening and closing the blades with the fingers and thumb of one hand

scoff [verb: **scoffs, scoffing, scoffed**]
1 to **scoff at** a thing or person is to think that they do not deserve your serious attention: *The president scoffed at the idea of a revolution in his country.*
2 to scoff something is to eat it very fast

scold [verb: **scolds, scolding, scolded**] to tell someone off for doing something wrong
✦ **scolding** [noun: **scoldings**] a telling-off

scone [noun: **scones**] a small, round, plain cake that is often eaten with butter and jam

scoop [verb: **scoops, scooping, scooped**] to lift something with your hands cupped like a spoon
[noun: **scoops**]
1 a hollow instrument like a bowl or shovel for lifting liquid or loose substances like sand or ice cream
2 a news story that a newspaper prints before other newspapers do: *This story was a wonderful scoop for the Evening Mail.*

scooter [noun: **scooters**]
1 a type of vehicle that looks like a motorbike but is less powerful
2 a child's toy with two wheels at either end of a board, and a tall handle. You ride it by standing on the board with one foot and pushing the ground with the other

scope [noun]
1 the whole range of things that a subject deals with: *I'm afraid your question falls outside the scope of this meeting.*
2 freedom or opportunity to do something: *There's plenty of scope for improving these plans.*

scorch [verb: **scorches, scorching, scorched**] to burn the surface of something by touching it with something hot and leaving a brown mark
✦ **scorching** [adjective] very hot: *It was a scorching day.*

score [verb: **scores, scoring, scored**]

1 to get a point in a game, test or competition: *Hamilton has scored again for the Rovers.* • *Jenny was first in the maths test because she scored 19 out of 20.*
2 to keep a record of the points that are won in a game or competition: *Who's scoring?*
3 to scratch a surface with something sharp: *Score a straight line across the card and fold it carefully.*
[noun: **scores**]
1 the number of points that you get in a game, test or competition: *What's the final score?* • *On this test, a score of more than 15 is good.*
2 an old word for twenty

scorn [verb: **scorns, scorning, scorned**] to refuse to accept something such as an idea or suggestion because you think they are bad or worthless: *The family scorned everyone's attempts to help them.*
[noun] a feeling that someone or something is bad or worthless and should not be respected
✦ **scornful** [adjective] showing that you think someone or something is bad or worthless and should not be respected: *scornful remarks*
✦ **scornfully** [adverb] in a superior, mocking way: *He laughed scornfully.*

scorpion [noun: **scorpions**] a small creature like an insect with four pairs of legs and a long tail with a sting on the end

scot-free [adverb] without being punished: *The girls got off scot-free because nobody had seen them.*

scoundrel [noun: **scoundrels**] a man who cheats and behaves dishonestly

scour [verb: **scours, scouring, scoured**]
1 to clean a surface by scraping and rubbing hard: *The saucepans needed scouring.*
2 to search a large area thoroughly: *Teams of villagers scoured the hillside for the missing climber.*

scout [noun: **scouts**]
1 a scout is a person who is sent out to gather information, especially one who is sent ahead of a group on an expedition
2 a Scout is a young person who is a member of the Scout Association
[verb: **scouts, scouting, scouted**] to **scout around** for something is to go looking for it: *I'll scout around for a chair that matches the others.*

scowl [verb: **scowls, scowling, scowled**] to lower your eyebrows in an angry or puzzled way: *What are you scowling at?*
[noun: **scowls**] an angry or puzzled look

scramble [verb: **scrambles, scrambling, scrambled**]
1 to climb using your hands and feet: *scrambling up the hillside*
2 to push and shove with other people to get to something: *people scrambling to get to the bargains before anyone else*
3 to scramble eggs is to mix them together and cook them
4 to scramble a broadcast or message is to code it so that it cannot be understood easily
[noun: **scrambles**]
1 a difficult climb over rough ground
2 a struggle to get to something before other people
3 a motorbike race over rough ground

scrap [noun: **scraps**]
1 a scrap is a small piece of something bigger: *a scrap of paper to write your address on* • *There isn't a scrap of evidence against us.*
2 scrap is rubbish, especially waste metal that could be used again
3 a scrap is a fight
[verb: **scraps, scrapping, scrapped**]
1 to decide not to use something such as a plan or system because it is not practical: *Let's just scrap the whole idea now.*
2 to scrap something such as machine or vehicle is to get rid of it and use the parts or waste for something else
→ **scrappy**

scrapbook [noun: **scrapbooks**] a book with blank pages that you can fill up with cuttings or pictures that you want to keep together

scrape [verb: **scrapes, scraping, scraped**]
1 to remove something from a surface by using something such as a knife or stick: *I'll have to scrape the mud off this window before I clean it.*
2 to scrape something is to damage or hurt it slightly by rubbing it along something rough: *Lydia had scraped her elbow when she fell off her bike.*

3 to **scrape through** an exam is to pass it, but only just
4 to **scrape together** money is to just manage to collect enough money from different people or places
[noun: **scrapes**]
1 when something hard or rough is rubbed or scratched against a surface
2 a difficult or embarrassing situation: *You expect boys to get into scrapes when they're young.*

scrappy [adjective: **scrappier, scrappiest**] not well put together or organized: *a scrappy piece of writing*

scratch [verb: **scratches, scratching, scratched**]
1 to make a mark on a surface with something sharp or pointed: *Mick scratched the car when he brushed the wall.* • *Generations of students had scratched their names on these desks.*
2 to rub your nails on your skin, usually because you feel itchy: *Try not to scratch the spots.*
[noun: **scratches**]
1 a mark left on a surface by something sharp
2 if you do something **from scratch**, you do it from the very beginning, often for the second time: *Let's just start again from scratch.*
3 if something is **up to scratch**, it is good enough: *The work was not up to scratch.*

scrawl [verb: **scrawls, scrawling, scrawled**] to write in a very untidy way
[noun] very untidy handwriting

scrawny [adjective: **scrawnier, scrawniest**] very thin and bony

scream [verb: **screams, screaming, screamed**] to make a long high-pitched cry because you are frightened, angry or in pain: *Everyone screamed on the roller coaster.*
[noun: **screams**] a loud and high-pitched cry: *The neighbours came running when they heard the screams.*

screech [noun: **screeches**] a sudden, harsh, high-pitched sound: *the screech of an owl in the night* • *a screech of tyres as the car sped away*
[verb: **screeches, screeching, screeched**] to make a sudden, harsh, high-pitched sound

screen [noun: **screens**]

Ss

1 the part of a computer, television or cinema that you look at to see images: *You should be sitting at least two metres away from the screen.*
2 an upright frame or panel that protects people from something or makes a more private area in a room: *You have to go behind the screen to be examined.*
[verb: **screens, screening, screened**]
1 to show a television programme or film: *They are screening the whole series for the third time.*
2 to hide something from view or shelter it: *This part of the garden is screened by a high fence.*
3 to test lots of people for a particular illness: *All the workers here should be screened for the virus.*

screen saver [noun: **screen savers**] a computer program that makes a computer screen blank or show a picture when the screen is on but not being used. It is designed to prevent the screen from damage

screw [noun: **screws**] an object like a nail with a slot in its head and a spiral ridge all the way down it
[verb: **screws, screwing, screwed**]
1 to fix a screw into something: *Screw the bits of wood together.*
2 to fit something with a turning movement: *Screw the lid on tightly.*

screwdriver [noun: **screwdrivers**] a tool with a metal stick that fits into the head of a screw so that when you turn it, the screw also turns

scribble [verb: **scribbles, scribbling, scribbled**]
1 to write very quickly and untidily: *I scribbled his name down before I forgot it.*
2 to draw meaningless lines in an untidy way: *The baby had a pen and was scribbling on the wall.*
[noun: **scribbles**]
1 handwriting that is very untidy
2 meaningless untidy lines that someone has drawn

scrimp [verb: **scrimps, scrimping, scrimped**] to spend as little money as possible by living cheaply: *After scrimping and saving for a year, we had enough money for a short holiday.*

script [noun: **scripts**]
1 the words of a film or play: *The actors were reading from their scripts at rehearsal.*
2 a way of writing down language: *To us, the Russian language is written in an unfamiliar script.*

scripture [noun: **scriptures**] the holy writings of a religion, for example the Bible

scroll [noun: **scrolls**] a long roll of paper with writing on it
[verb: **scrolls, scrolling, scrolled**] to move text up or down on a computer screen so that you can see other parts of a file

scrounge [verb: **scrounges, scrounging, scrounged**] an informal word meaning to get the things you want by asking for them from other people: *You should buy your own cigarettes instead of scrounging off me all the time.*
◆ **scrounger** [noun: **scroungers**] a person who gets what they want by asking other people instead of buying their own things

scrub [verb: **scrubs, scrubbing, scrubbed**] to rub something hard to get it clean: *We'll need to scrub these stains off the floor.*

scruff [noun: **scruffs**]
1 a scruff is a person who looks very untidy
2 by the scruff of the neck means by the collar or the back of a person's or animal's neck: *The mother cat lifts her kittens in her mouth by the scruff of the neck.*
◆ **scruffy** [adjective: **scruffier, scruffiest**] untidy and dirty

scrum [noun: **scrums**] the part of a rugby game where groups of players from both teams form a circle by joining arms with their heads down and try to win the ball by pushing against the players of the other team

scrumptious [adjective] delicious

scrunch [verb: **scrunches, scrunching, scrunched**]
1 to crush or crumple something
2 to make the noise of something hard being crushed: *The gravel scrunched under our feet.*
[noun: **scrunches**] the noise of something hard being crushed: *a horrible scrunch as the car hit the wall*
◆ **scrunchie** [noun: **scrunchies**] a piece of elastic covered in cloth that you can use to hold long hair back from your face

Ss

scuba diving [noun] swimming underwater while breathing air through a pipe and mouthpiece connected to tanks fixed on the swimmer's back

scuffle [noun: **scuffles**] a fight involving a small number of people

scull [verb: **sculls, sculling, sculled**] to row a boat using small paddles

scullery [noun: **sculleries**] a small room by a kitchen in a big old house, where the washing-up is done and food is cleaned before being used

sculpt [verb: **sculpts, sculpting, sculpted**] to carve or make models of objects or figures using materials such as clay or stone

♦ **sculptor** [noun: **sculptors**] an artist who makes models of objects or figures

♦ **sculpture** [noun: **sculptures**]
1 a sculpture is a model of an object or figure that an artist carves or makes out of a material like stone, wood or clay
2 sculpture is the work of an artist who creates models: go to art college to study sculpture

scum [noun]
1 a layer of dirt or dust floating on the surface of a liquid
2 a very informal and impolite word for a person or people that you find disgusting

scurry [verb: **scurries, scurrying, scurried**] to move in a hurry with a lot of short steps

scurvy [noun] a disease caused by not eating enough fresh fruit and vegetables

scuttle [verb: **scuttles, scuttling, scuttled**]
1 to scuttle is to move along with lots of short fast steps: a beetle scuttling away
2 to scuttle a boat is to purposely make a hole in it to sink it

scythe [noun: **scythes**] a tool with a handle and a long curved blade that is used for cutting long grass or harvesting crops

sea [noun: **seas**]
1 the salt water that covers most of the Earth's surface: Australia is completely surrounded by sea.
2 a large lake of salt water: the Dead Sea

seabed [noun] the floor of the sea: a wreck on the seabed

seafarer [noun: **seafarers**] a sailor or a person who travels by sea

♦ **seafaring** [adjective] used to travelling by or working at sea: a seafaring nation

seafood [noun] fish and things such as prawns and mussels which you can eat

seafront [noun] a seashore, or a road or path along it

seagull [noun: **seagulls**] a sea bird with webbed feet, short legs and long wings with grey, black or white feathers

sea-horse [noun: **sea-horses**] a type of small fish that swims upright and has a horse-like head and neck

seal[1] [verb: **seals, sealing, sealed**] to close something firmly: Don't seal the envelope yet. [noun: **seals**]
1 anything that keeps something firmly closed: Break the seal with scissors before opening the box. • We need a new seal on the washing-machine door.
2 an official mark stamped on a piece of wax and attached to a document to show that it is genuine

seal[2] [noun: **seals**] an animal with a small head and a shiny coat that lives mainly in the sea.

sealant [noun: **sealants**] a substance or material used for closing a gap, for example to prevent water leaking

sea lion [noun: **sea lions**] a type of large seal

seam [noun: **seams**]
1 a join between two edges: the trousers have split down the back seam
2 a seam of coal is a band or layer of it in the ground

seaman [noun: **seamen**] a sailor who is not an officer

seaplane [noun: **seaplanes**] an aircraft that is designed to take off from and land on water

sear [verb: **sears, searing, seared**] to hurt or burn

search [verb: **searches, searching, searched**] to search is to look carefully for a thing or person: I've searched everywhere for my keys.
[noun: **searches**] an attempt to find something: They made a thorough search for the missing child.

searchlight [noun: **searchlights**] a strong

Ss

beam of light that can pick out distant objects at night: *A figure running across the field was caught in the searchlight.*

seashore [noun] the land next to the sea, especially the rocky or sandy parts that the sea covers when the tide is high

seasick [adjective] if you are seasick, you feel or are sick when you are on a boat, because of its movement on the sea

◆ **seasickness** [noun] feeling or being sick when you are on a boat because of its movement on the sea

seaside [noun] a place beside the sea where people go on holiday

season [noun: **seasons**]
1 one of the four main periods that the year is divided into: *Spring is my favourite season.*
2 the period of the year that a particular activity takes place: *the football season*
[verb: **seasons, seasoning, seasoned**] to flavour food by putting salt, pepper or other herbs and spices into it

◆ **seasonal** [adjective] happening only at certain times of the year

◆ **seasoning** [noun: **seasonings**] salt, pepper and other herbs and spices that you use to flavour food

season ticket [noun: **season tickets**] a ticket that you can use as often as you want for a certain period of time

seat [noun: **seats**]
1 a piece of furniture for sitting on: *a garden seat • a theatre seat*
2 the part of your body that you sit on: *There's a rip in the seat of my skirt.*
3 a position in parliament or on a committee: *The party lost three seats in the election.*
[verb: **seats, seating, seated**]
1 to seat a person is to give them somewhere to sit: *The host and hostess were seated at opposite ends of the table.*
2 to seat a certain number of people is to have enough room for them all to sit down: *The new theatre seats twice as many people as the old one did.*

seat belt [noun: **seat belts**] a strap attached to a seat in a vehicle that prevents a passenger from being thrown forward in a crash: *Please fasten your seat belts now.*

seaweed [noun] a type of plant that grows in the sea

seaworthy [adjective] a boat that is seaworthy is in good enough condition to be sailed on the sea

secateurs [plural noun] a small tool like a pair of scissors, used for cutting plants and bushes

secluded [adjective] a secluded place is quiet, private and hidden from view: *a secluded corner of the garden*

◆ **seclusion** [noun] peacefulness and privacy

second [adjective and adverb] next after the first: *Julia is their second daughter. • Craig came second in the race.*
[noun: **seconds**]
1 a thing or person that is number two in a series: *This programme is the second in a series of three.*
2 one sixtieth of a minute or a very short time: *one minute and thirty seconds • Just wait a second.*
3 a product that has been made with a fault and so is not perfect: *The factory shop sells seconds at very cheap prices.*
[verb: **seconds, seconding, seconded**]
1 to second a fighter is to be an attendant and support them
2 to second an idea or plan is to support it and agree when someone suggests it

◆ **secondary** [adjective]
1 to do with a development from something that came first or before: *Freddie had measles and then developed a secondary infection.*
2 of less importance than something else: *Your health comes first. Money is only secondary.*

secondary school [noun: **secondary schools**] a school for pupils between the ages of 11 and 18, that you go to after primary school

second-class [adjective and adverb] to do with a standard of the mail service that is cheaper and not as quick as first-class: *a second-class stamp • I sent the letter second-class.*

second-hand [adjective and adverb] not new because of being owned before by someone else: *Our car was second-hand when we bought it. • Kathryn buys all her clothes second-hand.*

secondly [adverb] a word that you use to introduce the second thing in a list: *And secondly, I'd like to thank Mrs Ambrose for all her help.*

second nature [noun] a firmly fixed habit that you do not think about: *I took a long time to learn to drive but it's second nature to me now.*

secrecy [noun] being secret: *The mission must be carried out in total secrecy.*

secret [noun: **secrets**]
1 a piece of information that must not be told to anyone else: *The birthday party was a well-kept secret.*
2 something that nobody knows or understands: *looking for the secret of eternal youth*
[adjective] not to be told or shown to other people: *a secret passage • secret government files*

secretarial [adjective] to do with the job of a secretary

secretary [noun: **secretaries**]
1 a person whose job is to type letters, keep files and take notes at business meetings for another person or a group of people: *Please leave a message with my secretary if I'm out.*
2 a person who is in charge of a government department

secrete [verb: **secretes, secreting, secreted**] to make and release a substance: *The plant secretes a sticky liquid that attracts flies.*
♦ **secretion** [noun: **secretions**] a substance that a part of a plant or animal makes and releases

secretive [adjective] liking to keep secrets from people: *Logan was very secretive about his past.*
♦ **secretively** [adverb] so that nobody else knows or finds out

secret service [noun: **secret services**] a government department that deals with spying: *a secret service agent*

sect [noun: **sects**] a small group of people within a larger group, who have certain different opinions about things, especially about their religion

sectarian [adjective] to do with there being different small groups within a larger one, each with different opinions and beliefs, especially about religion

section [noun: **sections**]
1 a part or a division of something: *The table has three sections that fit together. • The novels will be in the fiction section of the library.*
2 the side view of something when it is cut right through or across: *a section showing the inside of a plant stem*

sector [noun: **sectors**] a part of any kind of area: *the American sector of the city • the business sector of the community*

secure [adjective]
1 safe, happy and not worried about any danger: *a secure family background*
2 safe against attack or harm: *Locks that keep your house secure against burglars.*
3 firmly fixed or fastened: *Check that the ropes are secure.*
[verb: **secures, securing, secured**]
1 to fix or fasten something firmly: *The tent was secured with ropes and pegs.*
2 to get something for sure: *Sheila has secured a place at the best college in the country.*
3 to legally promise that if you cannot pay back a loan you will give the lender goods or property of the same value instead: *a secured loan*

♦ **security** [noun]
1 being protected from harm or any danger: *matters of national security • the security of a loving family*
2 the staff in an organization whose job is to protect buildings and workers: *Call security if you see anything suspicious.*
3 property or goods that you legally promise to give someone if you cannot pay back a loan: *He used his house as security on the loan.*
[adjective] to do with the safety of someone or something: *a security guard • The airport needs to improve security measures. • a security risk*

sedate [verb: **sedates, sedating, sedated**] to give someone a drug to make them feel calmer and less nervous or excited
[adjective] quiet, calm and dignified
♦ **sedation** [noun] giving someone a drug to make them feel calmer
♦ **sedative** [noun: **sedatives**] a medicine that helps you feel calm

Ss

sediment [noun] the solid grains that settle at the bottom of a liquid

see [verb: **sees, seeing, saw, seen**]
1 to look at something and notice it: *The dog goes mad whenever he sees a cat.* • *We're going to London to see the sights.*
2 to meet someone or spend time with them: *Have you seen Peter much lately?*
3 to understand something: *Now I see what you mean.*
4 to see someone as something is to imagine them like it: *I can't see him as a father.*
5 to see someone somewhere is to go there with them: *I'll see you to the door.*
6 to see that something happens is to make sure that it happens
7 to **see through** a thing or person is to know what they are up to when they are trying to trick you
8 to **see to** something is to deal with it: *Don't you worry about the travel arrangements — I'll see to them.*

seed [noun: **seeds**] a thing that a plant produces and that new plants grow from: *Sow the seeds about two inches deep in the soil.*
♦ **seedling** [noun: **seedlings**] a very young plant

seek [verb: **seeks, seeking, sought**]
1 to search for something: *They sought in vain for a place to stay.*
2 to try to get or achieve something: *She's seeking fame and fortune.*
3 to ask for something: *You should seek the advice of a doctor.*

seem [verb: **seems, seeming, seemed**] to appear to be something or to give the impression of being something: *You didn't seem to be interested.* • *Things seem calm at the moment.*
♦ **seemingly** [adverb] apparently: *The queue to get in was seemingly endless.*
♦ **seemly** [adjective] decent or suitable: *seemly behaviour*

seen [verb] a form of the verb **see** that is used with a helping verb to show that something happened in the past: *I haven't seen you for ages.* • *I wouldn't have seen that if you hadn't pointed it out.*

seep [verb: **seeps, seeping, seeped**] to leak or flow slowly through something: *Water was seeping through the ceiling.*

seesaw [noun: **seesaws**] a playground toy that children sit on either end of, pushing off the ground with their feet and alternately swinging up and down

seethe [verb: **seethes, seething, seethed**] to be extremely angry

see-through [adjective] so thin that you can see what is on the other side: *a blouse with see-through sleeves*

segment [noun: **segments**] a section or a division of something: *Divide the orange into segments.*

segregate [verb: **segregates, segregating, segregated**] to keep one kind of person or animal separate from another kind: *The young bulls are segregated from the cows.*
♦ **segregation** [noun] separating different kinds of animals or people from each other

seismic [adjective] to do with earthquakes

seize [verb: **seizes, seizing, seized**]
1 to grab something: *Joel seized my hand and shook it.*
2 to **seize up** is to stop moving easily: *I knelt on the floor so long that my knees seized up.*
♦ **seizure** [noun: **seizures**] a sudden attack of an illness, for example, a heart attack

seldom [adverb] rarely or not often: *I seldom go out in the evenings any more.*

select [verb: **selects, selecting, selected**] to choose from several things or people that are available: *Gail has been selected for the Olympic hockey team.*
♦ **selection** [noun: **selections**]
1 a range of things that you can chose from: *a wide selection of boots and shoes*
2 something that has been chosen from amongst others: *Bring your selection to the cash desk at the door.*

self [noun: **selves**] the real you: *Actors try to forget their true selves.*
⇒ **selfish, selfless**

self-assurance [noun] being confident about your own talents and abilities
♦ **self-assured** [adjective] confident

self-catering [adjective] a self-catering holiday is one in which you cook your own meals

self-centred [adjective] thinking only about yourself and not other people

self-confident [adjective] believing in your own ability and sure that you will succeed

self-conscious [adjective] feeling nervous and uncomfortable when you are with other people because you feel they are looking at you and criticizing you

self-defence [noun] trying to defend yourself from someone who is attacking you: *classes in self-defence* • *He said he fired the gun in self-defence.*

self-employed [adjective] working for yourself rather than being employed by someone else: *a self-employed painter and decorator*

• **self-employment** [noun] the situation when you work for yourself and are not employed by someone else

self-esteem [noun] thinking well of yourself: *Robert lacks self-esteem.*

self-importance [noun] thinking too well of yourself and that you are more important than other people

self-indulgent [adjective] always ready to allow yourself things that you like or want

selfish [adjective] thinking only about yourself and not what other people might want or need: *It would be selfish not to offer to help.*

• **selfishly** [adverb] thinking only about yourself: *He selfishly finished the food before we'd taken any.*

• **selfishness** [noun] thinking only about yourself

selfless [adjective] thinking about other people's wants or needs before your own

• **selflessly** [adverb] thinking about other people before yourself: *George selflessly looked after his parents at home.*

self-portrait [noun: **self-portraits**] a drawing or painting that an artist makes of himself or herself

self-raising flour [noun] flour that is used in baking and that includes an ingredient that makes the mixture rise when it is cooked

self-reliance [noun] the ability to manage alone, without asking for help from other people

• **self-reliant** [adjective] not needing the help of other people because you can manage by yourself

self-respect [noun] respect for yourself and concern for your own character

self-righteous [adjective] thinking that you are a very good person because you do not do bad things

self-satisfied [adjective] irritatingly pleased with yourself and your achievements: *a self-satisfied grin*

self-service [noun] a system in a shop or restaurant where customers serve themselves and, usually, pay at a checkout

self-sufficient [adjective] able to provide everything you need for yourself: *If we were a self-sufficient country, we would never need to import any food at all.*

sell [verb: **sells, selling, sold**]
1 to give somebody something in exchange for money: *Nigel sold his car and bought a motorbike.*
2 to have something available for people to buy: *Do you sell batteries?*

sell-by date [noun: **sell-by dates**] a date stamped on packets of food to show when they are no longer fit to be sold: *The sausages were past their sell-by date.*

seller [noun: **sellers**] a person who has something for sale

Sellotape [noun] Sellotape is a see-through sticky tape that is used especially for sticking pieces of paper together. This word is a trademark

semaphore [noun] a way of signalling using your arms in different positions to signal different letters

semi [noun: **semis**] a house that is joined to another house on one side

semi- [prefix] if a word starts with **semi-**, it adds the meaning 'half' or 'partly' to the word. For example, *semi-conscious* means not fully conscious

semicircle [noun: **semicircles**] half a circle

semicolon [noun: **semicolons**] a punctuation mark (;) that separates items in a list or different parts of a sentence, for example in *Several things need to be done: the menu; a seating plan; tickets.*

semi-detached [adjective] joined to

Ss

another house on one side: *Houses that are semi-detached may share a driveway.*

semi-final [noun: **semi-finals**] one of the two matches in a competition just before the final, which is a match for the winners of the two semi-finals: *Sweden reached the semi-final of the 1994 World Cup.*

seminar [noun: **seminars**]
1 a meeting to discuss a particular subject: *a marketing seminar*
2 a class in a university or college where a small number of students discuss a subject with a tutor

semi-skilled [adjective]
1 a semi-skilled person has less training than is needed for more specialized work
2 a semi-skilled job needs less training than that needed for specialized work

semitone [noun: **semitones**] the difference between two notes that are next to each other on the piano

semolina [noun] grains of wheat that are used for making pasta and milky puddings

senate [noun: **senates**] the highest-ranking part of parliament in some countries, for example, the United States and France
• **senator** [noun: **senators**] a member of a senate

send [verb: **sends, sending, sent**]
1 to post something somewhere
2 to arrange for something to be taken somewhere: *Our luggage was sent on the next flight.*
3 to tell someone to go somewhere: *The doctor took one look and sent me straight to hospital.*
• **sender** [noun: **senders**] the person that a letter or parcel comes from: *If this letter is undelivered, please return it to the sender.*

senile [adjective] weak and confused because of old age

senior [adjective]
1 higher in rank or more powerful: *You must salute when you meet a more senior officer.*
2 older: *senior members of the family*

senior citizen [noun: **senior citizens**] a person who has passed the usual retiring age

seniority [noun] how old or powerful a person is: *We sat along the table in order of seniority.*

sensation [noun: **sensations**]
1 a physical feeling: *a burning sensation in his chest*
2 a state of excitement or shock: *The announcement caused quite a sensation.*
• **sensational** [adjective]
1 wonderful and impressive: *Kate looked sensational in her new dress.*
2 causing a lot of excitement, shock or horror: *sensational news*

sense [noun: **senses**]
1 one of the five powers of sight, touch, taste, hearing and smell: *Janet lost her sense of smell after an illness.*
2 an ability to understand or appreciate something: *I don't think he has much of a sense of humour.*
3 a feeling: *People need work that gives them a sense of achievement.*
4 sense is the ability to make sensible decisions: *Someone had the sense to call an ambulance.*
5 a meaning: *A single English word can have lots of different senses.* • *You only have to understand the general sense of the passage.*
[verb: **senses, sensing, sensed**] to become aware of something although it is not very obvious: *I sensed that not many people agreed with what I was saying.*
• **senseless** [adjective]
1 unconscious or stunned: *A firemen was knocked senseless by a falling lamppost.*
2 foolish and with no purpose: *a senseless battle over a piece of useless ground*
• **senselessness** [noun] not having any good or sensible purpose: *the senselessness of war*

sensible [adjective] not foolish, but showing common sense: *the most sensible thing to do* • *It would be sensible to get that promise in writing.*
• **sensibly** [adverb] using your common sense: *Jeff very sensibly kept the receipt.*

sensitive [adjective]
1 very quickly and easily affected by anything: *skin that is very sensitive to the sun* • *The alarm is very sensitive and is sometimes set off by birds or cats.*
2 very easily hurt or upset: *Brian's very sensitive about being bald.*

◆ **sensitively** [adjective] in a way that carefully considers how people are feeling: *The matter has been dealt with very sensitively.*

◆ **sensitivity** [noun] how easily something or someone is affected by something

sensor [noun: **sensors**] a device that notices things such as heat, light or movement: *A sensor on the front of the camera measures how much light is available.*

sent [verb] a way of changing the verb **send** to make a past tense. It can be used with or without a helping verb: *The judge sent Jenkins to prison for ten years.* • *I've sent ten e-mail messages this morning.*

sentence [noun: **sentences**]
1 a sequence of words that usually includes a verb and expresses a statement, a question or a command
2 the punishment that a judge gives a person who has been found guilty of a crime: *Floyd received a five year prison sentence.*
[verb: **sentences, sentencing, sentenced**] to tell a person who has been found guilty of a crime what their punishment will be: *The whole gang was sentenced to life imprisonment.*

sentiment [noun: **sentiments**] a view or feeling about a subject: *Several other people share these sentiments.*

◆ **sentimental** [adjective]
1 feeling or making you feel too much emotion: *a sentimental love story*
2 to do with emotions: *I know the ring is not valuable but I love it for sentimental reasons.*

sentry [noun: **sentries**] a soldier who guards an entrance

separable [adjective] able to be separated from each other or from the main part of something: *a coat with a separable hood*

separate [adjective] different and not joined or connected: *This is a completely separate matter.* • *The farm is separate from the rest of the estate.*
[verb: **separates, separating, separated**]
1 to split up the people in a group or the parts of something that can be divided: *Could we please separate the boys from the girls for this exercise?* • *The north and the south are separated by a range of high mountains.*

2 to decide to live apart: *They are not divorced but they separated some time ago.*

◆ **separately** [adverb] not together: *Each of the suspects was interviewed separately by the police.*

◆ **separation** [noun: **separations**]
1 when people are apart from each other: *Lily found the separation from her family very difficult while she was working abroad.*
2 keeping things apart: *I firmly believe in the separation of work from family life.*

ⓘ The adjective and the verb **separate** are pronounced differently. The adjective is pronounced **sep**-er-it. The verb is pronounced **sep**-a-rate.

September [noun] the ninth month of the year, after August and before October

septic [adjective] full of poisonous germs: *If the cut goes septic, you will have to take a course of antibiotics.*

sequel [noun: **sequels**] a book, play or film that continues an earlier story

sequence [noun: **sequences**]
1 a series of things that follow each other: *a remarkable sequence of events*
2 a short section of something like a dance or a film: *an opening sequence that involves the whole cast*
3 a series of things that follow each other in a particular order: *a sequence of numbers that starts 1,4,9*

sequin [noun: **sequins**] a small shiny disc that can be sewn on clothes as a decoration

serenade [noun: **serenades**] a song or other piece of music that, according to tradition, is performed at night, beneath a woman's window by a man who wants to be her lover
[verb: **serenades, serenading, serenaded**] to sing or play music for someone

serene [adjective] calm and peaceful: *a serene smile*

sergeant [noun: **sergeants**]
1 a soldier who has a higher rank than a private or a corporal
2 a police officer who has the rank between constable and inspector

sergeant-major [noun: **sergeant-**

Ss

majors] an army rank above sergeant

serial [noun: **serials**] a story in parts that you read, see or listen to at different times

series [noun: **series**]
1 a number of similar things that happen or are done one after the other: *a series of accidents*
2 a set of television or radio programmes with the same subject and characters: *a nature series* • *an old series of 'Cheers'*

serious [adjective]
1 important and needing proper attention: *a more serious matter*
2 very bad: *a serious accident*
3 not joking: *I can never tell when he's joking and when he's being serious.*

sermon [noun: **sermons**] a talk such as the ones preachers give in church

serpent [noun: **serpents**] an old word for a snake

servant [noun: **servants**] a person whose job is to do things for someone else, such as clean their house and cook for them

serve [verb: **serves, serving, served**]
1 to work for someone: *Brown had served the family for fifty years.* • *Johnson served his country in two world wars.*
2 to hand people things they want to buy in a shop or what they want to eat: *Are you being served?* • *I'll serve the soup and you can give out the spoons.*
3 to have a certain purpose or use: *The cave served as a shelter for the night.*
4 to serve time or a prison sentence is to stay in prison as a punishment for committing a crime
5 to serve in tennis or some other games is to start play by throwing the ball up and hitting it
6 if something bad that happens **serves someone right**, you think that they deserve it: *If you're sick, it serves you right for eating too much chocolate.*
[noun: **serves**] throwing the ball up and hitting it to start playing a point in tennis: *a very fast serve*

✦ **server** [noun: **servers**]
1 a central computer that gives out and stores information from lots of smaller computers
2 the person who starts playing a point in tennis

service [noun: **services**]

1 working for someone or something: *resigning after 25 years' service to the company* • *He received an award for his services to the community.*
2 an industry that does things for people rather than producing goods: *the health service* • *Postal services are more frequent now.*
3 the help that someone gives you in a place such as a hotel or shop: *I loved the things they sell but the service in that shop is awful.*
4 a regular check of a car or other machine to keep it working properly: *I'm taking my car in for a service.*
5 the services are a country's army, navy and air force
6 a religious ceremony, especially in a church: *a service of remembrance*
7 a set of matching plates and bowls or cups and saucers: *a dinner service* • *a china tea service*
8 throwing the ball up and hitting it to start playing a point in tennis: *a terrible first service*
9 if something such as a machine or vehicle is **in service** or **out of service**, it is being used or no longer being used by an organization: *These aircraft have now been taken out of service.*
[verb: **services, servicing, serviced**] to service a vehicle or machine is to check it to make sure it is working properly and to make any necessary small repairs

service charge [noun: **service charges**] an amount of money that is added on to a bill in a restaurant to cover the cost of service by a waiter or waitress

service station [noun: **service stations**] a place where you can buy petrol

serviette [noun: **serviettes**] a table napkin

sesame [noun] a plant that produces seeds that are eaten and also used for making an edible oil

session [noun: **sessions**]
1 a period of time that you do something for: *Next session we'll be able to decorate the work you've done today.*
2 a meeting or a series of meetings: *the next session of Parliament*
3 a term of a school or college

set [verb: **sets, setting, set**]

1 to place something somewhere: *Set the tray down on the table.* • *a house that was set back from the road*
2 to adjust a clock or control so that it is ready to work: *Don't forget to set the video to record.*
3 to become hard or firm: *Wait an hour or so for the jelly to set.*
4 the sun sets when it goes down: *watching the setting sun*
5 to set words to music is to compose music to go with them
6 to set someone doing something is to start them doing it: *His comment set me thinking.*
7 to set someone something to do is to give it to them to do: *The teacher doesn't set my children enough homework.*
8 to **set about** doing something is to start to do it: *It's time we set about learning our lines for the play.*
9 to **set in** is to begin: *It looks like winter has set in.*
10 to **set the table** is to put things such as knives, forks and plates on it so that it is ready for you to eat a meal
[adjective]
1 fixed: *a set menu*
2 compulsory, not something you can choose: *a set piece for this year's music exam*
3 ready or prepared: *Are we all set to go?*
[noun: **sets**]
1 a number of things or people that have something in common or are used together: *a set of chairs* • *a chess set* • *the set of odd numbers*
2 a radio or television: *We have a technical problem; please do not adjust your set.*
3 the scenery and furniture where actors perform in a play or film, on a stage or in a studio
4 a series of games that form part of a tennis match
⇒ **setting**

setback [noun: **setbacks**] a problem that stops you making progress for a while

settee [noun: **settees**] a comfortable chair for two or more people

setting [noun: **settings**]
1 the position of the controls of a machine or instrument: *What setting did you have the oven on?*
2 the background for something such as a building or some sort of action, either in real life or in a story: *a beautiful setting for a hotel* • *The setting of the play is important.*
3 a place setting or a table setting is the cutlery and crockery for one person at a meal

settle [verb: **settles, settling, settled**]
1 to decide or agree on something: *Can you settle this argument for us?* • *Have you settled a date for the wedding yet?*
2 to become relaxed and comfortable in a certain situation or position: *We settled into army life very easily.* • *Harry settled into his armchair and fell asleep.*
3 to go somewhere and make your home there: *The family settled in New South Wales.*
4 to land and rest somewhere: *A fly settled on the picture frame for a moment.* • *Shake the bottle, then wait while the flakes inside settle.*
5 to pay a bill or debt: *The bill can be settled in cash or with a cheque.*

♦ **settlement** [noun: **settlements**]
1 an agreement: *a new peace settlement*
2 a place where people arrived and set up their homes: *an ancient riverside settlement*
3 payment of a bill or debt: *Please accept this cheque as settlement of the bill.*

♦ **settler** [noun: **settlers**] a person who goes to live in a new country or an area that has few or no people living in it

seven [noun: **sevens**] the number 7
seventeen [noun] the number 17
seventeenth [adjective and adverb] after sixteenth and before eighteenth: *my sister's seventeenth birthday*
seventh [adjective and adverb] after sixth and before eighth: *the seventh day of the week* [noun: **sevenths**] the fraction $\frac{1}{7}$, which means one of seven equal parts of something: *There are seven of us, so divide the pie into sevenths.*
seventieth [adjective and adverb] after sixty-ninth and before seventy-first
seventy [noun: **seventies**] the number 70
sever [verb: **severs, severing, severed**] to cut through something or cut something off: *The phone cables were severed in the high winds.*

Ss

several [adjective] more than two but not very many: *Several people stopped to look in the window.* • *I've asked him several times but he hasn't repaid the money.*

severe [adjective]
1 extremely bad: *severe weather conditions* • *a severe punishment*
2 stern and not gentle or kind: *a severe expression as she concentrated*
♦ **severity** [noun] extreme seriousness: *I don't think you understand the severity of the situation.*

sew [verb: **sews, sewing, sewed, sewn**] to use a needle and thread or a sewing machine to join fabric with stitches: *Could you teach me to sew?* • *I'll need some red thread to sew that button back on.*

sewage [noun] waste matter that is carried away from toilets in buildings

sewer [noun: **sewers**] a large pipe or underground channel for carrying away waste matter from drains in and near buildings

sex [noun: **sexes**]
1 either of two groups that humans are divided into: males and females
2 sex is the act in which a man puts his penis into a woman's vagina
[adjective] to do with the act that a man and woman perform to make a baby or for enjoyment: *sex education* • *sex drive*

sexism [noun] the belief that men and women should be treated differently and that they should do different types of jobs and have different positions in society: *sexism in the workplace*

sexist [noun: **sexists**] a person who believes that men and women should be treated differently and that they should do different types of jobs and have different positions in society
[adjective] to do with or involving sexism: *sexist attitudes* • *a sexist remark*

sexual [adjective] to do with sex: *the body's sexual organs*

sexual intercourse [noun] the act in which a man puts his penis into a woman's vagina

sexually transmitted disease [noun: **sexually transmitted diseases**] any disease that can be passed from one person to another when they are having sex. This is often shortened to **STD**

shabby [adjective: **shabbier, shabbiest**] old and worn: *a shabby house full of shabby furniture*

shack [noun: **shacks**] a roughly-built hut or shed

shackle [noun: **shackles**] shackles are a pair of metal rings, joined by a chain, that are locked around a prisoner's wrists or ankles
[verb: **shackles, shackling, shackled**] to shackle someone is to lock them in chains to stop them from moving freely

shade [noun: **shades**]
1 an area of slight darkness caused by blocking sunlight: *sitting in the shade of a tree* • *plants that grow in shade*
2 an object that prevents a light being too bright: *a lampshade*
3 a colour that is a bit lighter or darker than a similar colour: *a darker shade of lipstick*
4 a very small amount or difference: *Can you make it a shade looser?*
[verb: **shades, shading, shaded**]
1 to block bright light from an area: *a row of trees shading the path*
2 to draw or paint an area of a picture to make it look darker
→ **shady**

shadow [noun: **shadows**]
1 a shadow is a dark shape on a surface caused when an object is between the surface and a bright light: *There was a shadow on the wall.*
2 shadow is an area darkened by the blocking out of light: *I couldn't see his face because it was in shadow.*
♦ **shadowy** [adjective] like a shadow, not easy to see clearly: *The shadowy figures moved in and out of the trees.*

shady [adjective: **shadier, shadiest**]
1 a shady place is out of bright sunlight
2 a shady person or business does not seem to be very honest

shaft [noun: **shafts**]
1 the long straight part of a tool or weapon
2 a bar or rod in a machine that turns round to make other parts of the machine move: *The engine's drive shaft is twisted.*

3 a long narrow passage in the ground or in a building: *a lift shaft* • *a mine shaft*
4 a shaft of light is a ray or beam of light

shaggy [adjective: **shaggier, shaggiest**] shaggy hair is thick and untidy

shake [verb: **shakes, shaking, shook, shaken**]
1 to move quickly or unsteadily with very small movements: *The earth shook when the bomb landed.* • *Mina was shaking with fear.*
2 to move something quickly from side to side or backwards and forwards: *The wind shook the trees and rattled the windows.*
3 to shock or upset someone: *We were terribly shaken by the news of his death.*
[noun: **shakes**]
1 a quick movement from side to side or backwards and forwards: *Give the bottle a quick shake.*
2 a very quick moment: *I'll be there in two shakes.*
3 a drink of milk and some sort of flavouring
♦ **shakily** [adverb] in an unsteady way: *a new lamb walking shakily round its mother*
♦ **shaky** [adjective: **shakier, shakiest**] trembling: *Her voice was shaky as she tried to explain how she fell.*

shale [noun] a soft grey type of rock that breaks easily into flaky layers

shall [verb] a helping verb that is used along with a main verb to make future tenses when the subject of the verb is **I** or **we**: *I shall never forget this moment.*

ⓘ **Shall** is the present tense form. You use **should** for the past tense.

shallow [adjective: **shallower, shallowest**] not deep: *a shallow lake*

sham [noun] a person or thing is a sham if they are not what they pretend to be or seem to be: *Her niceness was just a sham; she was really cruel.*

shamble [verb: **shambles, shambling, shambled**] if someone shambles, or shambles along, they walk slowly and awkwardly without lifting their feet properly: *The old man shambled along, leaning on his stick.*

shambles [noun] if something is a shambles, it is completely disorganized or in a terrible mess: *The attic was a shambles, full of broken furniture.*

shame [noun]
1 an embarrassing feeling of guilt or foolishness, especially because you have done something wrong
2 if you say something is a shame, you mean it is a pity: *What a shame that you can't come to the party.*
3 if something **brings shame on** or **to** people, it brings them disgrace because it is bad or morally wrong
4 to **put someone to shame** is to do something much better than they do, so that they look foolish or a failure
[verb: **shames, shaming, shamed**] to shame someone is to make them feel ashamed or embarrassed
♦ **shameful** [adjective] disgraceful: *shameful behaviour*
♦ **shamefully** [adverb] disgracefully
♦ **shameless** [adjective] someone who is shameless feels no shame, although they have done something that other people think is wrong or immoral
♦ **shamelessly** [adverb] without feeling shame: *He lied shamelessly.*

shampoo [noun: **shampoos**] a soapy liquid for washing your hair, or for cleaning carpets [verb: **shampoos, shampooing, shampooed**] to shampoo your hair, or a carpet, is to wash it using shampoo

shamrock [noun: **shamrocks**] a plant like clover with rounded leaves in three parts. It is the national emblem of Ireland

shank [noun: **shanks**]
1 the long straight part of a nail, screw or tool
2 the part of the leg, especially an animal's leg for eating, between the knee joint and the foot

shan't [short form] a short way to say and write **shall not**: *I shan't be late.*

shanty [noun: **shanties**] a roughly-built hut or shack

shape [noun: **shapes**]
1 something's shape is its outline or form: *a mountain in the shape of a crown*
2 shapes are things like squares, circles, rectangles, diamonds and triangles
3 the shape that a person or thing is in is their

Ss

condition: *The team is in good shape for Saturday's match.*

4 if a piece of clothing is **out of shape**, it has been stretched so that it is no longer the shape it should be

5 if a person is **out of shape**, they are not as fit as they once were

6 things **take shape** when they start to develop a form that you can recognize or start to become organized
[verb: **shapes, shaping, shaped**]

1 to shape something is to form it or model it into a certain shape: *He shapes the clay pots on the potter's wheel.*

2 to **shape up** is to develop in a satisfactory way

♦ **shapeless** [adjective] having no particular shape: *a shapeless old cardigan*

♦ **shapely** [adjective] having an attractive shape or figure

share [verb: **shares, sharing, shared**]

1 to share something is to divide it among a number of people so that each person gets some: *Are you going to eat that whole pizza yourself, or are you going to share it?*

2 to share something with other people is to allow them to use it too: *There aren't enough books to go round so some of you will have to share.* • *I have my own bedroom but share a bathroom.*

3 to share experiences or interests with other people is to have the same experiences or interests as they have: *They shared an obsession with golf.*
[noun: **shares**]

1 a share is one of the parts of something that has been, or is to be, divided among several people

2 someone's share in an activity or project which involves several people is the part they play in it

3 one of the equal parts of a company that you can buy as a way of investing money: *She's bought some shares in the bank.*

shareholder [noun: **shareholders**] someone who owns shares in a company

shark [noun: **sharks**] a large fish whose mouth is full of rows of very sharp teeth.

sharp [adjective: **sharper, sharpest**]

1 a sharp object has a thin edge that can cut, or a point that can pierce: *a sharp knife*

2 a sharp fall or increase is sudden and steep: *a sharp rise in crime*

3 sharp images are clear and distinct with no blurred edges

4 a sharp pain is sudden and stabbing

5 a person or animal with sharp hearing or eyesight is good at hearing or seeing

6 something that tastes sharp tastes bitter, like lemon juice

7 someone who is sharp is very quick to understand or react
[adverb]

1 punctually: *He was to be there at 5 o'clock sharp.*

2 with a sudden or abrupt change of direction: *Turn sharp left at the next set of traffic lights.*
[noun: **sharps**] in written music, a sign (♯) that makes a note higher by another half tone

♦ **sharpen** [verb: **sharpens, sharpening, sharpened**] to sharpen something is to make it sharp or sharper: *The leopard was sharpening its claws on a tree.*

♦ **sharpener** [noun: **sharpeners**] a device that you use to sharpen pencils or knives

shatter [verb: **shatters, shattering, shattered**]

1 to shatter is to break into lots of tiny pieces: *He dropped the glass and it shattered.*

2 if something shatters you, it upsets you a lot or makes you very tired

shave [verb: **shaves, shaving, shaved**]

1 to shave is to use a razor to cut away hair that is growing on your face or body

2 to shave something is to cut or scrape thin layers off it with a sharp blade

♦ **shaver** [noun: **shavers**] an electrical tool for shaving hair

♦ **shavings** [plural noun] very thin strips of wood or metal that have been cut off a surface with a plane or other sharp tool

shawl [noun: **shawls**] a large rectangular piece of cloth for covering your shoulders

she [pronoun] a word you use to talk about a woman, girl, female animal, or boat that has already been mentioned or pointed out for the first time: *Madeleine is funny. She tells jokes* *and imitates people. • This boat is great for racing and she can turn on a sixpence.*

sheaf [noun: **sheaves**] a bundle, especially a bundle of ripe corn that has been cut and tied together

shear [verb: **shears, shearing, sheared, sheared** or **shorn**]
1 to cut wool from a sheep using shears
2 if a piece of metal, such as a bolt, **shears off**, it breaks off
◆ **shears** [plural noun] a tool with two large sharp-edged blades which move over each other, used for cutting sheep's wool, or for trimming hedges

sheath [noun: **sheathes**]
1 a long narrow case for holding or carrying a sword or dagger
2 a condom
◆ **sheathe** [verb: **sheathes, sheathing, sheathed**] to sheathe a sword is to put it into a sheath

shed [noun: **sheds**] a simple wooden or metal building used for working in or for storing things [verb: **sheds, shedding, shed**]
1 people shed their clothes, reptiles shed their skins, and birds shed their feathers when they take or cast them off and get rid of them
2 a tree sheds its leaves when they drop off in the autumn
3 to shed tears or blood is to have tears flowing from your eyes or blood flowing from a wound

she'd [short form] a short way to say and write **she had** or **she would**: *She'd forgotten her umbrella. • She'd rather not say.*

sheen [noun] a soft shine or glossiness on a surface

sheep [noun: **sheep**] a medium-sized farm animal with a thick wool fleece

sheep-dip [noun: **sheep-dips**] a chemical solution into which sheep are put so that any bacteria on their wool are killed

sheepdog [noun: **sheepdogs**] a dog bred or trained to round up and move sheep

sheepish [adjective] if someone looks sheepish, they look embarrassed

sheer [adjective]
1 a sheer cliff or rock face is vertical
2 a sheer fabric is so thin you can see through it

3 pure or complete: *He ate four bags of crisps. It was just sheer greed.*

sheet [noun: **sheets**]
1 a large broad thin piece of fabric, metal or glass: *I'll just change the sheets on your bed.*
2 a single piece of paper used for writing or printing on
3 a continuous layer of ice

sheikh [noun: **sheikhs**] an Arab chief or ruler

shelf [noun: **shelves**]
1 a board fixed horizontally to a wall or as part of a cupboard, used for putting things on
2 a part of the landscape or seabed that is formed like a shelf, with a flat top
➡ **shelve**

shell [noun: **shells**]
1 a hard covering on an egg or a nut, or protecting the soft bodies of creatures like snails, crabs, shellfish and tortoises
2 an explosive missile or cartridge fired from a large gun
3 the framework of a building or other structure

she'll [short form] a short way to say and write **she will** or **she shall**: *She'll be back in a minute.*

shellfish [noun: **shellfish**] shellfish are creatures with a hard outer shell that live in fresh water or the sea

shelter [noun: **shelters**]
1 a shelter is a building or other structure that provides protection from harm or bad weather
2 to **take shelter** is to go somewhere that gives protection from danger or bad weather [verb: **shelters, sheltering, sheltered**]
1 to shelter somewhere is to stay in a place where you are protected from harm or bad weather
2 to shelter someone or something is to protect them

shelve [verb: **shelves, shelving, shelved**]
1 to shelve a cupboard is to put up shelves in it
2 to shelve a plan is to decide not to carry it out or decide to do it at a later date

shepherd [noun: **shepherds**] someone who looks after sheep
[verb: **shepherds, shepherding, shepherded**] to shepherd people somewhere is to keep them in a group and direct them in or into a place

Ss

sherbet [noun: **sherbets**] sherbet is a sharp-tasting powder with a fruit flavour

sheriff [noun: **sheriffs**]

  1 in the United States, a sheriff is the head of police in a particular county

  2 in England and Wales, a sheriff is the representative of the king or queen in a particular county, who has mostly ceremonial duties

  3 in Scotland, a sheriff is a county judge who tries cases in local courts

sherry [noun] sherry is a type of strong wine that has had brandy added to it

she's [short form] a short way to say and write **she is** or **she has**: *She's my friend.* • *She's always been my friend.*

shield [noun: **shields**]

  1 a piece of armour that is used to block an attack by a sword or other weapon

  2 a competition trophy in the shape of this piece of armour

  3 a protection from harm or danger: *The spacecraft has a heat shield for when it re-enters the Earth's atmosphere.*

  [verb: **shields, shielding, shielded**] to shield someone or something is to protect them from harm or danger: *He had his hand over his eyes, shielding them from the strong sun.*

shift [verb: **shifts, shifting, shifted**] if you shift something or it shifts, you move it or it changes its position

  [noun: **shifts**]

  1 a move or change to another position: *a slight shift in speed*

  2 the period of time a worker does his or her job: *on the early shift*

  3 a loose dress

shifty [adjective: **shiftier, shiftiest**] a shifty person looks or behaves in a way that makes you distrust them and think they are dishonest

shilling [noun: **shillings**] an old British coin worth five pence

shimmer [verb: **shimmers, shimmering, shimmered**] to shine with a quivering light

shin [noun: **shins**] the front of your leg below your knee

shine [verb: **shines, shining, shone**]

  1 something shines when it gives off or reflects light

  2 you shine a light on something when you point the light in its direction

  3 you shine something when you polish it

  4 if you shine at something, you are so good at it you stand out from everyone else

  ➟ **shining, shiny**

shingle [noun] shingle is a mass of small pebbles on a seashore or river bank

shingles [noun] a painful infection that causes blisters on a particular part of your skin where there is a nerve

shining [adjective]

  1 having a shine

  2 a shining example of something is one that stands out because it is so good

shiny [adjective: **shinier, shiniest**] reflecting light or polished so as to reflect light

ship [noun: **ships**] a large boat that carries passengers or cargo, or both, on long sea journeys

  [verb: **ships, shipping, shipped**] to ship something somewhere is to have it carried on a ship

-ship [suffix]

  1 if **-ship** comes at the end of a word, the word is a noun that refers to a particular state or condition. For example, *friendship* is the condition of being friends

  2 when **-ship** comes at the end of other words, the word is a noun that refers to a particular skill. For example, *craftsmanship* is having the skill of a craftsman

shipment [noun: **shipments**] a load of goods sent by ship

shipping [noun] the business of carrying goods, especially by ship, or ships travelling from place to place

shipshape [adjective] tidy and in good order

shipwreck [noun: **shipwrecks**] a ship that has been destroyed or sunk, especially by hitting rocks

shipyard [noun: **shipyards**] a place where ships are built

shirk [verb: **shirks, shirking, shirked**] to shirk something is to avoid doing something that you should be doing

  ✦ **shirker** [noun: **shirkers**] someone who avoids work, a responsibility or a duty

shirt [noun: **shirts**] a piece of clothing for the top half of your body, with long or short sleeves, a collar, and buttons down the front

shiver [verb: **shivers, shivering, shivered**] to tremble or quiver because you are cold or frightened
[noun: **shivers**] a trembling feeling that goes through your body when you get cold or get a fright
  ♦ **shivery** [adjective] having shivers

shoal [noun: **shoals**] a shoal of fish is a large group of them swimming together

shock [noun: **shocks**]
1 shock, or a shock, is a strong and unpleasant reaction you get when you have had a fright or a bad injury
2 a sudden bump or jolt that comes with great force: The shock of the impact threw us all forward.
3 if you get an electric shock, a current of electricity passes through your body
[verb: **shocks, shocking, shocked**] if something shocks you, it upsets or horrifies you

shock absorber [noun: **shock absorbers**] a device in a car that stops it bouncing too much when it goes over bumps

shocking [adjective] upsetting or horrifying

shoddy [adjective: **shoddier, shoddiest**] not very well made or made with poor quality materials

shoe [noun: **shoes**] shoes are things made of leather or a similar material that you wear on your feet

shoehorn [noun: **shoehorns**] a long hard curved object that you use to get shoes on, by slipping it between your heel and the back of the shoe

shoelace [noun: **shoelaces**] a thin piece of cord or leather threaded through the holes of a lace-up shoe to fasten it

shoestring [noun] to do something **on a shoestring** is to do it for very little money

shone [verb] a way of changing the verb **shine** to make a past tense. It can be used with or without a helping verb: The sun shone all day. • It had shone all week.

shoo [interjection] you say 'shoo!' when you want to chase a person or animal away

shook [verb] a way of changing the verb **shake** to make a past tense: He shook his head sadly.

shoot [verb: **shoots, shooting, shot**]
1 to shoot a gun or other weapon is to fire it: I shot an arrow in the air.
2 to shoot someone or something with a gun or other weapon is to kill or wound them with it
3 a person or thing shoots somewhere when they travel there very fast: He shot past me in his new red sports car. • Pain shot through his body.
4 in games like football and hockey, a player shoots when they kick or hit the ball at the goal
5 to shoot a scene for a film is to record it on film
6 if a something such as a price, rate, or amount **shoots up**, it increases very quickly: Prices shot up overnight.

ⓘ Be careful not to confuse the spelling of **shoot** with **chute**, which is a sloped channel.

shooting star [noun: **shooting star**] a meteor that burns up in the Earth's atmosphere, making a trail of bright light in the night sky

shop [noun: **shops**] a place where goods are sold or a particular service is provided: a flower shop • a betting shop
[verb: **shops, shopping, shopped**] to shop is to buy things in shops

shop assistant [noun: **shop assistants**] someone who serves customers in a shop

shopkeeper [noun: **shopkeepers**] someone who owns a shop

shoplifter [noun: **shoplifters**] someone who steals things from shops
  ♦ **shoplifting** [noun] the crime of stealing things from shops

shopper [noun: **shoppers**] someone who shops or is shopping: crowds of Saturday shoppers

shopping [noun]
1 the activity of going round shops to buy things: Let's go shopping for new clothes.
2 the things you buy at the shops: She carried all the shopping in to the kitchen.

shore [noun: **shores**] the area of land beside the sea or beside a lake

shorn [verb] a way of changing the verb **shear** to make a past tense. It is used with a helping verb: The farmer had shorn the sheep.

Ss

short [adjective: **shorter, shortest**]
1 not very long: *a short skirt • a short speech*
2 small, not tall: *a short man*
3 if something is short, or in short supply, there is less than there should be, or there is not enough of it to go round: *We are two players short.*
4 if someone is short with you, they are rude and abrupt in the way they talk to you
5 to be **short of** something is to not have enough of it: *I'm a bit short of money at the moment.*
[noun] if you call someone something **for short**, you call them that as a shortened form of their real name: *I'm Alisdair, you can call me Al for short.*
[adverb]
1 if something **falls short**, it is not as good or as big as it should be
2 to **stop short** is to stop suddenly just before reaching a particular point: *My ball stopped slightly short of the last hole.*

◆ **shortage** [noun: **shortages**] a lack of something: *food shortages*

shortbread [noun] a rich sweet biscuit made from flour, sugar and butter

short-circuit [verb: **short-circuits, short-circuiting, short-circuited**] a piece of electrical equipment short-circuits when the electric current is carried away from its normal path by something breaking the normal electrical circuit

shortcoming [noun: **shortcomings**] a fault or weakness a person has

shortcut [noun: **shortcuts**] a quicker route between two places, or a quicker way of doing something

shorten [verb: **shortens, shortening, shortened**] to shorten something is to make it shorter: *I couldn't bring myself to shorten such a lovely name.*

short form [noun: **short forms**] a word made from two words that have been joined together and some letters missed out. An apostrophe replaces the missing letters. For example, *don't* is a short form of 'do not'

shorthand [noun] shorthand is a fast way of writing what someone is saying

short list [noun: **short lists**] a list of the best people for a job

short-lived [adjective] lasting only for a short time: *Mandy's quarrels with Jenny, though frequent and explosive, were usually short-lived.*

shortly [adverb]
1 soon: *We'll be arriving at Waverley Station shortly.*
2 not long: *The bomb exploded shortly before midday.*

shorts [plural noun] shorts are a piece of clothing for the bottom half of your body, with short legs that reach down to the tops of your thighs or as far down as your knees

short-sighted [adjective]
1 a short-sighted person cannot see things clearly unless the object is very close
2 an idea that is short-sighted does not take into account what is likely to happen in the future

short-tempered [adjective] a short-tempered person loses their temper easily

short-term [adjective] lasting or taking place for only a short time: *a short-term solution to the problem*

shot [verb] a way of changing the verb **shoot** to make a past tense. It can be used with or without a helping verb: *The ships shot at each other using large cannons. • Nelson's battleships had shot the rigging from most of the enemy ships.*
[noun: **shots**]
1 the sound of a gun being fired: *I heard a shot and ran to see what had happened.*
2 an attempt to kick or hit a ball towards the place where you can score: *It was an excellent shot that just missed the goal.*
3 a photograph: *I managed to get some good shots of the mountains.*

shotgun [noun: **shotguns**] a type of long gun with one or two barrels, which fires little metal pellets

should [verb]
1 **should** is used as a past tense of the verb **shall**: *He said that we should all go home.*
2 ought to: *I wonder whether or not I should go.*
3 used to say what is likely to happen: *The train should be arriving in a couple of minutes.*
4 sometimes used in formal situations with *I* or

we to express a wish: *I should love to come to your party.*

5 should is also used to refer to an event that is rather surprising: *There was a little tap on the door, and who should pop his head round but George.*

shoulder [noun: **shoulders**] one of the top parts of your body between your neck and the tops of your arms
[verb: **shoulders, shouldering, shouldered**]
1 to shoulder something is to carry it on your shoulder or shoulders
2 to shoulder a responsibility is to accept it as something you must do

shoulderblade [noun: **shoulderblades**] one of the two flat bones at the top of your back on either side of your spine

shouldn't [short form] a short way to say and write **should not**: *You shouldn't have waited out in the rain.*

shout [verb: **shouts, shouting, shouted**] to say something very loudly
[noun: **shouts**] a loud cry or call

shove [verb: **shoves, shoving, shoved**]
1 to shove something is to push it hard or roughly
2 if someone tells another person to **shove off**, they are telling that person rudely to go away
[noun: **shoves**] a hard or rough push

shovel [noun: **shovels**] a tool like a spade that can be small with a short handle or large with a long handle
[verb: **shovels, shovelling, shovelled**] to shovel things is to scoop them up and move them using a shovel

show [verb: **shows, showing, showed, shown**]
1 to show something is to allow it or cause it to be seen: *Show me your new bike.* • *There's a cartoon showing at the local cinema.*
2 something shows if it can be seen: *The scar hardly shows.*
3 to show someone something is to point it out to them or demonstrate it to them: *Can you show me how to tie a reef knot?*
4 to show someone somewhere is to guide them in that direction: *The steward showed us to our seats.*
5 something shows something, such as a

particular quality, when it makes it clear or proves that it is true: *His actions showed great courage.* • *The evidence shows that he couldn't have committed the crime.*
6 to **show off** is to behave in a way that attracts attention
7 to **show up** is to arrive
8 if someone **shows you up**, they embarrass you in front of other people
[noun: **shows**]
1 an entertainment in the theatre or on radio or TV
2 an event where people or businesses can exhibit their goods or produce to the public
3 a show of something is a sign of it or a demonstration of it: *There was no show of support for Tom's idea.*
4 if people do things for show, they do them to impress other people
→ **showy**

show business [noun] show business is the entertainment industry, including films, theatre, radio and television

ⓘ **Show business** is often shortened to **showbiz**.

shower [noun: **showers**]
1 a short fall of rain, snow or sleet: *sunshine and showers*
2 a sudden burst or fall of things: *a shower of sparks*
3 a device that sends out water in a stream or spray and that you stand under to wash your body
[verb: **showers, showering, showered**]
1 to wash your body under a shower
2 someone is showered with gifts or compliments when they are given lots of them at the same time
• **showery** [adjective] showery weather is when showers of rain fall between periods when it is dry

shown [verb] a form of the verb **show** that is used with a helping verb to show that something happened in the past: *Niall had shown us how well he could act.*

showroom [noun: **showrooms**] a place where goods are displayed for people to see: *a car showroom*

Ss

showy [adjective: **showier, showiest**] showy things attract attention because they are big and bright, although they may not be beautiful or in good taste

shrank [verb] a way of changing the verb **shrink** to make a past tense: *The hot wash shrank my jersey.*

shrapnel [noun] shrapnel is pieces of metal from the case of an exploding bomb or shell that fly out in all directions

shred [noun: **shreds**]
1 a long thin strip: *His shirt was torn to shreds.*
2 a shred of something is a very small amount of it: *They didn't have a shred of evidence to link him to the crime.*
[verb: **shreds, shredding, shredded**] to tear into shreds

shrew [noun: **shrews**] a tiny animal, similar to a mouse, but with a long pointed nose

shrewd [adjective: **shrewder, shrewdest**] wise and showing good judgement: *a shrewd politician* • *a shrewd guess*

shriek [verb: **shrieks, shrieking, shrieked**] to give a piercing scream or to speak in a loud shrill voice
[noun: **shrieks**] a piercing scream

shrill [adjective] high-pitched, clear and piercing: *a shrill voice*
♦ **shrilly** [adverb] with a shrill sound or voice: *A child was calling shrilly for its mother.*

shrimp [noun: **shrimps** or **shrimp**] a small shellfish with a long tail that turns pink when it is cooked and is similar to, but smaller than, a prawn

shrine [noun: **shrines**] a sacred place where people go to worship, often because it has something to do with a holy person

shrink [verb: **shrinks, shrinking, shrank, shrunk**]
1 to get smaller
2 you **shrink from** something when you move away from it in horror or disgust, or when you want to avoid it

shrivel [verb: **shrivels, shrivelling, shrivelled**] to become smaller and wrinkled

shroud [noun: **shrouds**] a cloth wrapped around a dead body
[verb: **shrouds, shrouding, shrouded**] to shroud something is to cover it completely: *hills shrouded in mist*

shrub [noun: **shrubs**] a small bush
♦ **shrubbery** [noun: **shrubberies**] an area in a garden where shrubs are grown

shrug [verb: **shrugs, shrugging, shrugged**]
1 to raise and lower your shoulders in a movement that shows you do not know something or that you do not care about it
2 to **shrug something off** is to get rid of it easily: *He's fit enough to shrug off colds.*
[noun: **shrugs**] a quick raising and lowering movement of the shoulders

shrunk [verb] a way of changing the verb **shrink** to make a past tense. It is used with a helping verb: *The hot water had shrunk my jersey.*

shrunken [adjective] having shrunk or having been shrunk: *a small, shrunken old man*

shudder [verb: **shudders, shuddering, shuddered**] you shudder when your whole body shakes for a moment because you have seen or heard something shocking or disgusting: *She shuddered when she heard the bad news.*
[noun: **shudders**] a sudden shaking movement of your body

shuffle [verb: **shuffles, shuffling, shuffled**]
1 to slide your feet along the ground without lifting them
2 to shuffle things, such as playing-cards, is to mix them up so that they are in random order

shun [verb: **shuns, shunning, shunned**] to deliberately ignore someone

shunt [verb: **shunts, shunting, shunted**]
1 to shunt railway engines or carriages is to move them from one track to another
2 to shunt people or things about or around is to move them from place to place

shut [verb: **shuts, shutting, shut**]
1 to shut something is to close it or move it to a position where it covers an opening, or where its opening is covered
2 a shop or other business shuts when it stops being open or the staff stop working and go home
3 to **shut down** a machine or factory is to stop it working
4 to **shut off** a machine is to stop it working, and to **shut off** power or water is to stop it flowing

5 to **shut up** is to be quiet or stop talking [adjective] closed: *All the shops are shut after 6 o'clock.*
♦ **shutter** [noun: **shutters**]
1 a wooden cover for a window that hinges from the side
2 the moving cover over the lens of a camera, which opens when a photograph is taken

shuttle [noun: **shuttles**]
1 in weaving, the shuttle is the part that carries the thread backwards and forwards across the loom
2 a shuttle is an air, train or other transport service that operates backwards and forwards between two places
[verb: **shuttles, shuttling, shuttled**] to shuttle between places is to travel to and fro between them

shuttlecock [noun: **shuttlecocks**] an object made of plastic feathers that you hit in the game of badminton

shy [adjective: **shyer, shyest**] a shy person feels very uncomfortable when they have to speak or do something in front of other people, or when they meet new people
[verb: **shies, shying, shied**]
1 if a horse shies, it turns to the side suddenly because it has been frightened
2 to **shy away** from something is to avoid it or move away from it quickly

Siamese cat [noun: **Siamese cats**] a breed of cat with a slim body, blue eyes and grey-brown fur

Siamese twins [plural noun] twins that are joined together at some part of their body when they are born. Another name for them is **conjoined twins**

sibling [noun: **siblings**] a person's siblings are their brothers and sisters

sick [adjective: **sicker, sickest**]
1 if you feel sick, you feel like vomiting
2 you are sick when you vomit
3 sick people or animals are ill
4 to do with time that you take off work because you are ill: *sick leave • sick pay*
5 if you are **sick of** something or someone, you are very tired of or fed up with them
♦ **sicken** [verb: **sickens, sickening, sickened**]

1 if someone sickens, they become ill
2 if something sickens you, it disgusts you or makes you feel like vomiting
♦ **sickening** [adjective] disgusting
♦ **sickly** [adjective: **sicklier, sickliest**]
1 someone who is sickly is often ill or gets ill easily: *a sickly child*
2 something sickly is unhealthy looking or makes you want to vomit: *a sickly green colour • a sickly smell*
♦ **sickness** [noun: **sicknesses**] an illness or disease

side [noun: **sides**]
1 the side of something is the part at or near its edge: *a house by the side of the river • at the side of the garden*
2 one of two or more surfaces of a figure, shape or structure, especially one of the surfaces that is not the top, bottom, front or back: *A cube has six sides. • Put the label on the side of the box.*
3 your sides are the left and right parts of your body: *I've got a pain in my left side.*
4 one of the two teams playing in a match, or one of the two groups of people involved in an argument or battle
5 **on all sides** means 'all around'
6 **side by side** means 'next to each other': *The two men were sitting side by side.*
7 to **take sides** is to support one person, or group of people, who is arguing or fighting with another person or group of people
[verb: **sides, siding, sided**] to **side with** someone is to support them against another person or group in an argument

sideboard [noun: **sideboards**] a piece of furniture with cupboards and drawers, usually for storing things such as plates and glasses in a dining room

sidecar [noun: **sidecars**] a small vehicle that is attached to the side of a motorbike for a passenger

side effect [noun: **side effects**] if something, especially a medicine, has side effects, it has effects that are additional to the effect it is supposed to have

sideline [noun: **sidelines**]
1 an extra job apart from your normal work
2 on a sports pitch, the sidelines are the lines

Ss

along both sides of the pitch marking the outer edges of the playing area

sidelong [adjective] a sidelong look is made sideways

sideshow [noun: **sideshows**] a small show that is part of a larger more important show

sidetrack [verb: **sidetracks, sidetracking, sidetracked**] if you are sidetracked by something, it makes you turn away from what you are doing or saying

sidewalk [noun: **sidewalks**] the American English word for a **pavement**

sideways [adverb] something that goes sideways goes towards the side, or with its side facing the direction it is moving

siding [noun: **sidings**] a short stretch of railway track where trains and carriages are shunted off the main track when they are not being used

sidle [verb: **sidles, sidling, sidled**] to move sideways, especially in a cautious way, so that you are not noticed

siege [noun: **sieges**]
1 a situation in which a town is completely surrounded by an enemy army that prevents supplies from getting in
2 a situation in which police with guns surround a building to try and force a criminal to give himself or herself up

siesta [noun: **siestas**] a short sleep or nap, especially in hot countries when the sun gets very hot in the afternoon

sieve [noun: **sieves**] a bowl with a bottom made of fine mesh, used to separate liquids from solids, or small fine pieces from larger ones

sift [verb: **sifts, sifting, sifted**]
1 to sift a substance is to pass it through a sieve to separate out lumps or larger pieces
2 to sift things is to go through them, examining each one carefully

sigh [verb: **sighs, sighing, sighed**] to take a long, deep breath and breathe out noisily, because you feel tired, relieved or unhappy
[noun: **sighs**] a long, deep breath in which you breathe out noisily, because you feel tired, relieved or unhappy

sight [noun: **sights**]
1 sight is the power of seeing things: A very

young kitten's sight is not very good.
2 a sight is something that you see or something that is worth seeing: It was a sight I'll never forget. • We are going out today to look at the sights of London.
3 something that is **in sight** can be seen, and something that is **out of sight** cannot be seen
4 a person or thing that looks ridiculous, unusual or shocking: What a sight she is with that bright blue hair!
5 if you **set your sights on** something, you decide that is what you want
6 a sight for sore eyes is a person or thing that is very funny or unpleasant to look at

ⓘ Be careful not to confuse the spelling of **sight** with **site**, which is a place where something is.

sight-read [verb: **sight-reads, sight-reading, sight-read**] if someone can sight-read music, they can play it or sing it by reading the notes printed on a sheet of music, even if they have never heard the music before

sightseeing [noun] sightseeing is travelling around looking at interesting things and places
✦ sightseer [noun: **sightseers**] someone who travels round looking at interesting things

sign [noun: **signs**]
1 a mark or gesture with a special meaning: He gave the sign to join him.
2 a notice that gives information to the public: The sign said 'No parking'.
3 one thing is **a sign of** another when it shows what is happening or what will happen: Leaves falling are a sign of autumn.
[verb: **signs, signing, signed**]
1 you sign something or sign your name on something when you write your signature on it
2 to sign someone, especially a professional player in certain sports, is to sign a contract with them, making them part of your team
3 to sign to someone is to make a sign or gesture to them: He signed to me to come in.
4 to **sign up** for something is to decide to join in with that thing

signal [noun: **signals**]
1 a sign, a gesture, a light or a sound giving a command, warning or other message
2 a radio or TV signal is the wave of sound or

light received by a radio or TV: *a strong clear signal*
[verb: **signals, signalling, signalled**]
1 to send information by signals
2 to signal to someone is to make a signal or signals to them
signalman [noun: **signalmen**] someone whose job is to control railway signals
signature [noun: **signatures**] your name, written by you, for example on the bottom of a letter
signature tune [noun: **signature tunes**] a tune that is used to identify a TV or radio series, usually played at the beginning and end of the programme
significance [noun] meaning or importance: *a matter of great significance*
 ◆ **significant** [adjective] important or meaning something: *a very significant remark*
 ◆ **significantly** [adverb] in a significant way
signify [verb: **signifies, signifying, signified**] to have a certain meaning: *A symbol of a skull and crossbones signifies a poison.*
sign language [noun] a system of gestures made with the hands and fingers used to communicate with deaf people
signpost [noun: **signposts**] a post by a road showing which direction to go to get to a particular place
Sikh [noun: **Sikhs**] someone whose religion is Sikhism
[adjective] to do with Sikhs or Sikhism: *the Sikh temple at Amritsar*
 ◆ **Sikhism** [noun] a religion believing in one God, founded by Guru Nanak in Punjab in North India
silence [noun: **silences**]
1 silence is complete quietness when no sound can be heard
2 a silence is a time when there is no sound or no one speaks
[verb: **silences, silencing, silenced**]
1 to silence someone is to stop them speaking
2 to silence something is to stop it making a noise
 ◆ **silencer** [noun: **silencers**]
1 a device on a car exhaust that reduces noise
2 a device used on a gun to lessen the sound made when it is fired

 ◆ **silent** [adjective] completely quiet
 ◆ **silently** [adverb] without making any sound
silhouette [noun: **silhouettes**] the shape of a person or thing seen against a light background with just an outline filled with shadow
silicon [noun] a substance in the form of grey crystals or brown powder, used in electronic devices
silicon chip [noun: **silicon chips**] a tiny piece of silicon with very small electrical circuits printed on it, used in computers and other electronic devices
silk [noun: **silks**] very soft fine fibres made by silkworms, or a soft smooth fabric with a slight sheen that is made from these
[adjective] made of silk: *a silk kimono*
 ◆ **silken** [adjective] soft, fine and slightly shiny
silkworm [noun: **silkworms**] a type of moth whose caterpillar spins fine silk threads which are used to make silk
silky [adjective: **silkier, silkiest**] soft and smooth, like silk: *silky hair*
sill [noun: **sills**] a horizontal piece of wood or stone at the bottom part of the opening of a window or door
silliness [noun] silly behaviour
silly [adjective: **sillier, silliest**] foolish or stupid
silt [noun] fine sand and mud that is carried along and left behind by flowing water
silver [noun]
1 a shiny grey precious metal
2 a shiny grey colour
3 things made of silver or a silvery grey metal, such as cutlery and coins
[adjective] silver-coloured or made of silver: *a silver cup* • *silver hair*
silver medal [noun: **silver medals**] a medal made of silver awarded to the person who comes second in a sporting event
silver wedding [noun: **silver weddings**] a couple who celebrate their silver wedding have been married for 25 years
silvery [adjective] like silver in colour: *Birch trees have silvery bark.*
similar [adjective] two things are similar

Ss

517

when they are quite like each other but not exactly the same: *An alligator is similar to a crocodile, but smaller.*

♦ **similarity** [noun: **similarities**] the way one thing is like another thing

♦ **similarly** [adverb] in the same or a similar way

simile [noun: **similes**] a sentence or phrase in which one thing is described by being compared with another, usually with *as* or *like*. For example, *Its fleece was white as snow* and *He ran like a hare* are similes

simmer [verb: **simmers, simmering, simmered**]

1 to simmer food is to cook it slowly over a low heat or to boil it very gently

2 someone who has been angry **simmers down** when they become calm again

simper [verb: **simpers, simpering, simpered**] to smile or speak in a silly unnatural way

simple [adjective: **simpler, simplest**]

1 straightforward or very easy to do: *simple instructions* • *a simple sum*

2 plain or basic: *a simple design*

♦ **simplicity** [noun] being simple and uncomplicated

simplification [noun] making something less complicated and therefore easier to do or understand

simplify [verb: **simplifies, simplifying, simplified**] to simplify something is to make it simpler and therefore easier to do or understand

simply [adverb]

1 in a straightforward, uncomplicated way: *I'll explain it simply so that you all understand.*

2 only: *Now, it's simply a question of waiting until something happens.*

3 completely or absolutely: *The concert was simply fantastic.*

simulate [verb: **simulates, simulating, simulated**] to simulate a real thing is to create another thing that looks or seems like the real thing

♦ **simulation** [noun: **simulations**] simulating something, or something that simulates the real thing

♦ **simulator** [noun: **simulators**] a machine

that creates the conditions of a real situation, especially the flight of an aeroplane

simultaneous [adjective] happening or done at exactly the same time: *a simultaneous broadcast on radio and TV*

♦ **simultaneously** [adverb] at exactly the same time

sin [noun: **sins**] a wicked act, especially one that breaks a religious law

➝ **sinful, sinner**

since [conjunction]

1 since is used when you are giving a reason for something and has more or less the same meaning as **because**: *I decided to go shopping, since I had some free time.*

2 after a particular event or time: *He's been a lot happier since he changed jobs.* • *He's grown a lot since you saw him last.*

[preposition] from the time of something in the past until the present time: *Theresa has been dancing since she was three.*

[adverb]

1 from the time that has already been mentioned onwards: *She joined the choir last month and has been going to practice regularly since.*

2 at a later time than the time first mentioned: *They were enemies for years, but they have since become friends.*

sincere [adjective]

1 a sincere person is honest and means what they say

2 a sincere feeling is real and not faked

♦ **sincerely** [adverb] honestly and truly

♦ **sincerity** [noun] being sincere

sinew [noun: **sinews**] a type of strong body tissue like cord that joins your muscles to your bones

sinful [adjective]

1 sinful behaviour is bad or wicked, especially because it breaks a religious law

2 a sinful person has committed a sin or sins

♦ **sinfulness** [noun] being sinful

sing [verb: **sings, singing, sang, sung**]

1 people sing when they make musical sounds with their voices

2 birds and some other animals sing when they make musical calls

➝ **singer, singing**

singe [verb: **singes, singeing, singed**] to singe something is to burn its surface or edge slightly by touching it with something hot: *I singed the tablecloth with the iron.*

(i) Be careful not to confuse the spelling of **singeing** with **singing**.

singer [noun: **singers**] a person who sings

singing [noun] singing is making musical sounds with your voice

single [adjective]
1 a single thing is only one and no more
2 someone who is single is not married
3 for use by one person: *a single room*
[noun: **singles**]
1 a ticket for a journey you make in one direction but not back again
2 a recording of a song that is released on its own, and not as part of an album
3 in games like tennis and badminton, you play singles when you play against only one other person
[verb: **singles, singling, singled**] to **single out** a person or thing is to pick them in particular from a group of people or things

single-handed [adjective] without anyone else's help

single-minded [adjective] a single-minded person sticks in a determined way to one aim or purpose

single parent [noun: **single parents**] a mother or father who is bringing up a child on their own

singly [adverb] one at a time or one by one: *You usually see tigers singly, but sometimes you will see a small family group.*

sing-song [adjective] a sing-song voice goes up and down like someone singing

singular [adjective]
1 in grammar, a singular form of a word is the form used to refer to one person, thing or group, rather than two or more
2 very noticeable or out of the ordinary: *a poem of singular beauty*
[noun] the form of a noun, pronoun, adjective or verb that you use when it expresses the idea of one person, thing or group, rather than two or more: *The singular is 'sheep' and the plural is also 'sheep'.*

♦ **singularly** [adverb] remarkably: *He was singularly unprepared for life in the outback.*

sinister [adjective] threatening evil or harm: *a sinister black figure with a large hood covering the face*

sink [verb: **sinks, sinking, sank, sunk**]
1 to drop below the surface of water and go on moving downwards to the bottom: *The boat sank in a storm.*
2 to go down or get lower: *The sun was sinking towards the horizon.* • *He sank to his knees.*
3 to sink into something is to push or go deeply into it or pass through its surface: *The rainwater sank into the soil.* • *The dog sank its teeth into the postman's leg.*
4 if information you are given **sinks in**, you understand it properly
[noun: **sinks**] in a kitchen or bathroom, a large fixed container with taps and a drain, used for washing

sinner [noun: **sinners**] someone who has committed a sin

sinuous [adjective] with lots of curves or bends: *the sinuous movement of a snake*

sinus [noun: **sinuses**] an air-filled hollow in the bones of your skull that connects with your nose

♦ **sinusitis** [noun] an infection in which your sinuses become very painful

sip [verb: **sips, sipping, sipped**] to sip a drink is to drink it slowly taking only a little mouthful at a time
[noun: **sips**] a small amount of a drink that you take into your mouth: *She took a sip of water.*

siphon or **syphon** [noun: **siphons** or **syphons**] a bent pipe or tube through which a liquid is drawn from one container into a second container placed at a lower level

sir [noun: **sirs**]
1 a polite way of addressing a man, for example at the beginning of a letter or when serving him in a shop
2 a title used before the name of a knight: *Sir Paul McCartney*

sire [noun: **sires**]
1 the father of an animal, especially an animal bred on a farm
2 a title that was sometimes used in the past when talking to a king

Ss

siren [noun: **sirens**] a device that makes a very loud noise to warn people of something: *The ambulance came hurtling along the road with its siren on.*

sirloin [noun: **sirloins**] a cut of beef from the top of the back leg, or loin

sister [noun: **sisters**] your sister is a girl or woman who has the same parents as you do

♦ **sisterhood** [noun: **sisterhoods**]
1 sisterhood is a feeling of friendship among women and girls
2 a sisterhood is a group of women, especially nuns

sister-in-law [noun: **sister-in-laws**] your brother's wife, or your husband or wife's sister

sit [verb: **sits, sitting, sat**]
1 you sit or **sit down** when you have your weight supported on your bottom rather than your feet
2 you sit or **sit down** when you lower yourself into this position so that your bottom is resting on a surface
3 something sits in the place where it is resting or lying: *There was a big parcel sitting on the kitchen table.*
4 you sit an exam when you do the exam

sitcom [noun: **sitcoms**] short for **situation comedy**, a television comedy series that is set in the same place and includes the same characters in each episode

site [noun: **sites**] a place where something was, is, or is to be situated or located, or a place used for a certain purpose: *the site of a battle* • *a good site to build a house*

sitting-room [noun: **sitting-rooms**] a room where people can sit down and relax

sitting tenant [noun: **sitting tenants**] someone who is renting a flat or house at the time when it is bought by someone else

situate [verb: **situates, situating, situated**] something is situated in a certain place or position when it is put or placed there

♦ **situation** [noun: **situations**]
1 a place where something stands or is located: *Plant the sunflowers in a sunny situation.*
2 a set of circumstances or a state of affairs: *The situation in the areas affected by the drought is getting more and more difficult every day.*

six [noun: **sixes**] the number 6

sixteen [noun] the number 16

sixteenth [adjective and adverb] after fifteenth and before seventeenth

sixth [adjective and adverb] after fifth and before seventh
[noun: **sixths**] the fraction $\frac{1}{6}$, which means one of six equal parts of something

sixtieth [adjective and adverb] after fifty-ninth and before sixty-first: *her sixtieth birthday*

sixty [noun: **sixties**] the number 60

size [noun: **sizes**]
1 how big or small something is, or how long, wide, high, and deep it is
2 a shoe or clothes size is one that is made to fit a certain size of feet or body
[verb: **sizes, sizing, sized**] to **size up** a person or thing is to study them to find out what they are like

♦ **sizeable** or **sizable** [adjective] fairly big

sizzle [verb: **sizzles, sizzling, sizzled**] to make a hissing noise like the sound of food frying

skate [noun: **skates**]
1 a boot with a blade fitted to the bottom, used for gliding smoothly over ice
2 a **rollerskate**
[verb: **skates, skating, skated**] to move over ice wearing skates on your feet, or to move over the ground with rollerskates on your feet

skateboard [noun: **skateboards**] a long narrow board with wheels fitted to the bottom, for riding on in a standing or crouching position

♦ **skateboarding** [noun] riding on skateboards

skater [noun: **skaters**] someone who skates on ice

skating [noun] the sport or pastime of moving over the surface of ice wearing skates

skeleton [noun: **skeletons**] the frame of bones inside your body that supports all your muscles and organs

skeleton key [noun: **skeleton keys**] a key that will open several different locks

sketch [noun: **sketches**]
1 a drawing that is done quickly, often as a guide for a more detailed picture or plan
2 a very short funny play

[verb: **sketches, sketching, sketched**] to sketch something is to draw it quickly

skew [verb: **skews, skewing, skewed**] something is skewed when it is at an angle

skewer [noun: **skewers**] a long thin pointed piece of metal or wood that is pushed through small pieces of food so that they can be cooked under a grill or on a barbecue

ski [noun: **skis**] skis are two long narrow strips of wood or metal used for gliding over snow and which you attach to special boots
[verb: **skis, skiing, skied** or **ski'd**] to move over snow with a pair of long narrow strips of wood or metal attached to your boots
➡ **skiing**

skid [verb: **skids, skidding, skidded**] to slide over a surface in an uncontrolled way

skiing [noun] the sport of gliding over snow on skis

skilful [adjective] having a lot of skill
♦ **skilfully** [adverb] with skill
♦ **skilfulness** [noun] being skilful

skill [noun: **skills**]
1 to have skill is to be clever or expert at doing something
2 a skill is a talent that you develop through training and practice: *football skills*
♦ **skilled** [adjective]
1 a skilled person is expert at what they do: *a skilled pianist*
2 a skilled job needs training and practice

skim [verb: **skims, skimming, skimmed**]
1 something skims a surface when it travels along just above the surface
2 to skim something floating on the top of a liquid is to remove it
♦ **skimmed** [adjective] skimmed milk has had all or almost all of the cream removed

skimpy [adjective: **skimpier, skimpiest**] skimpy clothes do not cover much of your body

skin [noun: **skins**]
1 the tissue that covers the outer surface of the bodies of humans and animals
2 the thin outer covering on fruit and some vegetables
3 a layer that forms on the top of some liquids
4 if you manage to do something **by the skin of your teeth**, you only just manage to do it

[verb: **skins, skinning, skinned**] to skin something is to remove its skin

skinflint [noun: **skinflints**] a person who is very mean with money

skinny [adjective: **skinnier, skinniest**] thin

skint [adjective] an informal way of saying you have no money: *I can't afford the ticket. I'm totally skint.*

skip [verb: **skips, skipping, skipped**]
1 to move forward springing or hopping from one foot to the other as you go
2 to jump over a skipping rope
3 to skip something is to leave it out and go on to the next thing
4 to skip something such as a meeting or lesson is to not attend it when you should do
[noun: **skips**] a skipping movement

skipper [noun: **skippers**] the captain of a ship, aircraft or sports team

skipping rope [noun: **skipping ropes**] a rope that you jump over and which is swung round repeatedly by two people holding it at either end, or which you hold and swing over and under your own body

skirmish [noun: **skirmishes**] a short battle or fight

skirt [noun: **skirts**] a piece of clothing for girls or women that hangs from the waist
[verb: **skirts, skirting, skirted**]
1 to go around the border or edge of something: *A dense wood skirted the grounds.*
2 you skirt around something when you avoid it by going around it

skirting or **skirting board** [noun: **skirtings** or **skirting boards**] a length of wood fixed to the bottom of an inside wall where it meets the floor

skittle [noun: **skittles**] one of several bottle-shaped objects that you try to knock down with a ball in the game of skittles

skive [verb: **skives, skiving, skived**] to avoid doing the work you should be doing
♦ **skiver** [noun: **skivers**] someone who avoids work

skulk [verb: **skulks, skulking, skulked**] to wait somewhere, hidden from view

skull [noun: **skulls**] the bony part of your head that contains your brain and forms a framework for your face

Ss

skull and crossbones [plural noun] a flag or sign with a black skull and two crossed thighbones on a white background. In the past it was used as a symbol of pirates and is now used as a warning of possible death or danger

skullcap [noun: **skullcaps**] a small round hat that fits tightly round the top part of the head

skunk [noun: **skunks**] a small North American animal with black–and–white fur and a long bushy tail, that defends itself by spraying a stinking liquid at its attacker

sky [noun: **skies**] the area of space above the Earth where you can see the sun, moon, stars and clouds

sky-diving [noun] a sport in which people jump out of aeroplanes and let themselves fall for quite a while before they open their parachutes to land

skylark [noun: **skylarks**] a small brown bird that flies upwards and hovers in the sky singing a sweet song

skylight [noun: **skylights**] a window set into a roof

skyline [noun] the line where the sky seems to meet the land or sea at the horizon

skyscraper [noun: **skyscrapers**] a tall building with lots of storeys

slab [noun: **slabs**] a thick flat slice of something: *an enormous slab of chocolate cake*

slack [adjective: **slacker, slackest**]
1 not stretched tight or fitting snugly: *These trousers are too slack around the waist.* • *The rope was too slack.*
2 careless or lazy: *slack discipline* • *She's slack about her work and doesn't show much interest.*
3 if business is slack, there are not many customers and not much is being sold
[verb: **slacks, slacking, slacked**] to do less work than you should
♦ **slacken** [verb: **slackens, slackening, slackened**]
1 to slacken something is to loosen it
2 the pace or strength of something slackens when it gets slower or weaker
♦ **slackness** [noun] being lazy
♦ **slacks** [plural noun] slacks are smart but loose casual trousers

slalom [noun: **slaloms**] a type of course in which skiers or canoeists move in a zigzag pattern around upright posts

slam [verb: **slams, slamming, slammed**]
1 to slam something, such as a door, is to shut it with a bang
2 to slam something is to hit it or put it down hard

slang [noun] very informal words or expressions that you use in everyday speech, but not in writing or when you are being polite

slant [verb: **slants, slanting, slanted**] to slope or move diagonally
[noun: **slants**]
1 a slope or diagonal direction
2 someone's slant on something is their particular point of view

slap [noun: **slaps**]
1 a blow made with the palm of your hand or anything flat
2 a sound made by something hitting a flat surface
[verb: **slaps, slapping, slapped**] to hit with the palm of your hand or something flat

slapdash [adjective] careless: *slapdash work*

slapstick [noun] a type of comedy in which actors or comedians get laughs by behaving in a silly way, for example by falling over

slash [verb: **slashes, slashing, slashed**]
1 to slash something is to cut it with a sharp blade swung in a quick movement
2 to slash things like prices is to cut them by a large amount
[noun: **slashes**]
1 a long cut made by a sharp blade
2 one of two punctuation marks (/) or (\), used especially in computing and in website addresses

slat [noun: **slats**] a long strip of plastic or wood put together with others to form something such as a window blind or bench

slate [noun: **slates**]
1 slate is a type of stone that can be split into thin pieces along natural lines in the stone
2 a slate is a rectangular piece of this rock used for roofing, or in the past, for schoolchildren to write on with chalk

slaughter [verb: **slaughters,**

slaughtering, slaughtered] to slaughter people or animals is to kill them in large numbers
[noun] the killing of large numbers of people or animals
slaughterhouse [noun: **slaughterhouses**] a place where animals are killed for food
slave [noun: **slaves**] a person who is owned by another person and who is usually made to work hard for little or no pay
[verb: **slaves, slaving, slaved**] to work very hard
• **slavery** [noun]
1 buying, selling, and using slaves
2 very hard work for very little reward
slay [verb: **slays, slaying, slew, slain**] to kill a person or animal: *The dragon was slain by Saint George.*

ⓘ **Slay** is used mainly in old stories.

sled or **sledge** [noun: **sleds** or **sledges**]
1 a small vehicle with metal runners underneath or with a flat underside that you sit on to slide over snow
2 a vehicle with ski-like runners underneath that is pulled over snow by dogs or horses
sledgehammer [noun: **sledgehammers**] a large heavy hammer that you swing with both arms
sleek [adjective: **sleeker, sleekest**] smooth, soft and glossy: *A mink has sleek dark-brown fur.*
• **sleekness** [noun] being sleek
sleep [noun: **sleeps**]
1 sleep is rest that you have with your eyes closed and in a natural state of unconsciousness
2 a sleep is a period of time when you rest in this way
3 when you **go to sleep**, you fall asleep
4 if something such as your leg or arm **goes to sleep**, you lose the feeling in it, for example because you have been sitting or lying on it
[verb: **sleeps, sleeping, slept**]
1 to rest with your eyes closed and in a state of unconsciousness
2 if you **sleep in**, you sleep for too long so that you are late for something

• **sleeper** [noun: **sleepers**]
1 someone who sleeps
2 a carriage on a train where you can sleep
3 one of the heavy wooden or metal beams that a railway track is laid on
sleepily [adverb] in a tired or sleepy way
• **sleepiness** [noun] being sleepy
sleeping bag [noun: **sleeping bags**] a large sack made of layers of warm fabric and used for sleeping in, especially by someone who is camping
sleepless [adjective] if you have a sleepless night you are unable to go to sleep at all
• **sleeplessness** [noun] being unable to sleep
sleepwalker [noun: **sleepwalkers**] someone who walks about while they are sleeping
• **sleepwalking** [noun] walking about in an unconscious state, as if sleeping
sleepy [adjective: **sleepier, sleepiest**] feeling tired and wanting to sleep
sleet [noun] a mixture of rain and snow
sleeve [noun: **sleeves**] the part of a piece of clothing that covers your arm or part of your arm
• **sleeved** [adjective] having sleeves
• **sleeveless** [adjective] having no sleeves
sleigh [noun: **sleighs**] a large sledge pulled by a horse or horses
sleight-of-hand [noun] moving your hands quickly and skilfully so that people cannot see what you are doing, as a conjuror does when performing magic tricks
slender [adjective]
1 slim or thin, especially in an attractive way: *a tall slender tree*
2 small or slight: *His chances of winning are extremely slender.*
slept [verb] a way of changing the verb **sleep** to make a past tense. It can be used with or without a helping verb: *He slept for ten hours.* • *He had slept all morning and afternoon.*
sleuth [noun: **sleuths**] an old-fashioned word for a detective
slice [noun: **slices**] a thin or smaller piece cut from a larger piece of food: *a slice of cake*
[verb: **slices, slicing, sliced**]
1 to slice something, or **slice it up**, is to cut it into slices

Ss

2 to slice something is to cut it with a sharp blade or knife: *The knife slipped and sliced my finger.*

slick [adjective: **slicker, slickest**]
1 a slick performance is done well without seeming to involve much effort
2 a slick talker is clever at persuading people
[noun: **slicks**] a layer of oil that has been spilt on the surface of the sea
◆ **slickly** [adverb] efficiently and effortlessly

slide [verb: **slides, sliding, slid**]
1 to slip or move over a surface quickly and smoothly
2 to move downwards or get worse: *She's let standards slide since we were last here.*
[noun: **slides**]
1 an apparatus with a smooth sloping surface, for children to slide down
2 a small clear glass or plastic plate on which specimens are put so that they can be looked at under a microscope
3 a small transparent photograph that you put in a projector to be viewed on a screen

slight [adjective: **slighter, slightest**]
1 small or not great: *a slight increase in temperature* • *a slight problem* • *Lewis has a slight cold.*
2 slim and light: *He has a slight build.*
3 not in the slightest means 'not at all': *I'm not worried in the slightest by the news.*
◆ **slightly** [adverb] by only a small amount

slim [adjective: **slimmer, slimmest**]
1 thin or slender: *slim fingers*
2 small or slight: *The chances of winning the lottery are very slim.*
⟶ **slimness**

slime [noun] a soft, sticky, half-liquid substance that looks a bit like thin jelly
⟶ **slimy**

slimness [noun] being thin or slender

slimy [adjective: **slimier, slimiest**] covered with, or feeling like, slime

sling [verb: **slings, slinging, slung**]
1 to sling something is to throw it hard
2 to sling something over your shoulder is to throw it over your shoulder so that it hangs down
[noun: **slings**]
1 a bandage that is hung from someone's neck or shoulder to support an injured arm

2 a strong band of material that is used to support something that is being lifted or to throw stones

slink [verb: **slinks, slinking, slunk**] to move quietly, trying not to be noticed

slip [verb: **slips, slipping, slipped**]
1 to slide accidentally and lose your balance
2 to slip something somewhere is to slide it there or put it there quickly
3 to **slip in** or **out** of a place, or to **slip away**, is to go in or out, or go away, quietly and without anyone noticing you
4 to **slip up** is to make a mistake or do something wrong
[noun: **slips**]
1 an accidental slide
2 a small mistake
3 a small piece of paper: *Fill in the green slip and give it back to me.*
4 a piece of thin underclothing that a girl or woman wears under her dress or skirt
5 if you **give someone the slip**, you escape from them without them noticing
⟶ **slippery**

slipped disc [noun: **slipped discs**] you have a slipped disc when one of the layers of body tissue between the joints of your spine moves out of place

slipper [noun: **slippers**] a soft shoe for wearing indoors

slippery [adjective] smooth, wet or shiny and not easy to balance on or hold

slip road [noun: **slip roads**] a narrower road used by traffic going on to or leaving a motorway

slipshod [adjective] careless and untidy

slit [noun: **slits**] a long cut or narrow opening
[verb: **slits, slitting, slit**] to slit something is to make a long narrow cut in it

slither [verb: **slithers, slithering, slithered**] to slide or slip: *The ice cubes slithered off the table.*
◆ **slithery** [adjective] smooth and slippery: *a slithery path to the water's edge*

sliver [noun: **slivers**] a long thin piece cut or broken from something: *slivers of glass*

slobber [verb: **slobbers, slobbering, slobbered**] a person or animal slobbers when saliva dribbles out of their mouth

slog [verb: **slogs, slogging, slogged**] to work very hard

slogan [noun: **slogans**] a phrase that is easy to remember and is often repeated, used especially in advertising

slop [verb: **slops, slopping, slopped**] liquid slops when it moves around or splashes or spills

slope [verb: **slopes, sloping, sloped**] to be at an angle that is not level or straight but at an upward or downward slant
[noun: **slopes**]
1 an upward or downward slant
2 the side of a hill

sloppy [adjective: **sloppier, sloppiest**]
1 careless: *sloppy work*
2 showing love in a way that is silly and embarrassing

slot [noun: **slots**] a small narrow opening, especially one that you put coins into
[verb: **slots, slotting, slotted**] to **slot someone** or **something in** is to fit them into a small space or gap

sloth [noun: **sloths**]
1 a sloth is a South American animal that lives mostly in trees and moves very slowly
2 sloth is laziness
 ✦ **slothful** [adjective] lazy and slow-moving

slot machine [noun: **slot machines**] a machine that you work by putting in a coin or a token

slouch [verb: **slouches, slouching, slouched**] to move, stand or sit with your shoulders rounded and your head hanging forward

slovenly [adjective] dirty or untidy: *slovenly work*

slow [adjective: **slower, slowest**]
1 not fast or not moving quickly: *a slow march • Our progress was slow.*
2 if a clock or watch is slow, it shows a time earlier than the correct time
[verb: **slows, slowing, slowed**] to slow, or to **slow down**, is to become slower, or make something slower

slowcoach [noun: **slowcoaches**] someone who takes a long time to move or do something

slowly [adverb] in a slow way: *He walks very slowly.*

slow-motion [adjective] a slow-motion scene in a film has the action slowed down to slower than its real speed

sludge [noun] thick soft slimy mud or any substance that is like this

slug [noun: **slugs**] a creature with a long soft body like a snail, but with no shell

slum [noun: **slums**] a building or part of a town or city where the conditions are dirty and overcrowded

slumber [verb: **slumbers, slumbering, slumbered**] to sleep
[noun: **slumbers**] sleep

ⓘ **Slumber** is used mainly in poetry.

slump [verb: **slumps, slumping, slumped**]
1 to fall or sink: *Business has slumped in the last few months.*
2 you slump, or **slump down**, when your body sinks so that you are lying heavily against something: *He was slumped over his desk, fast asleep.*
[noun: **slumps**] a period when businesses are not selling many goods

slung [verb] a way of changing the verb **sling** to form a past tense. It can be used with or without a helping verb: *He slung his backpack over his shoulder. • They had slung all their coats into a corner without hanging them up.*

slunk [verb] a way of changing the verb **slink** to form a past tense. It can be used with or without a helping verb: *The fox slunk away into the bushes. • He had slunk up behind me and shouted 'Boo!'.*

slur [verb: **slurs, slurring, slurred**] to pronounce words unclearly, especially because you are drunk or ill
[noun: **slurs**] an insult that is likely to damage someone's reputation

slurp [verb: **slurps, slurping, slurped**] to drink very noisily

slush [noun] partly melted snow on the ground
 ✦ **slushy** [adjective: **slushier, slushiest**]
1 soft and almost liquid, like partly melted snow
2 romantic in a silly way: *a slushy novel*

sly [adjective: **slyer** or **slier, slyest** or **sliest**] cunning and good at deceiving others
 ✦ **slyly** [adjective] in a sly way
 ✦ **slyness** [noun] being sly

Ss

smack [verb: **smacks, smacking, smacked**]

1 to smack someone is to slap them

2 to smack your lips is to make a loud sucking noise by bringing your lips together tightly and then opening your mouth again quickly

[noun: **smacks**] a slap, or the sound made by a slap

small [adjective: **smaller, smallest**]

1 little: *a small country* • *This coat is too small for you.* • *a small problem*

2 if something makes you feel small, it makes you feel silly and unimportant

3 a small voice is soft and difficult to hear

smallholding [noun: **smallholdings**] an area of land used for farming on a small scale

small-minded [adjective] someone who is small-minded has a limited view of the world and does not want to learn about different ways of doing things

smallness [noun] how small something is compared to other things

small print [noun] the details of a contract that are often printed in very small letters: *You should always read the small print before signing anything.*

smart [adjective: **smarter, smartest**]

1 neat: *my smartest clothes*

2 clever and quick: *a smart answer*

3 fast: *a smart pace*

[verb: **smarts, smarting, smarted**] to feel a sharp stinging pain

♦ **smarten** [verb: **smartens, smartening, smartened**]

1 to smarten something, or **smarten something up**, is to make it look better: *They smartened up the room with a coat of paint.*

2 to **smarten up** is to make yourself look neater: *I'd like to smarten up before we go out.*

♦ **smartly** [adverb]

1 neatly and fashionably: *smartly dressed businessmen*

2 quickly or briskly: *You'll have to walk pretty smartly if you want to catch the train.*

♦ **smartness** [noun] being smart

smash [verb: **smashes, smashing, smashed**]

1 to smash something is to break it into pieces, for example by dropping it: *I've smashed one of the best glasses.*

2 to smash is to break into pieces: *The vase fell off the table and smashed.*

3 to smash something, or smash into it, is to hit or crash into it with great force

[noun: **smashes**]

1 the sound of something breaking

2 a road accident in which two vehicles hit each other and are damaged

♦ **smashing** [adjective] great or splendid: *That was a smashing film.*

smear [verb: **smears, smearing, smeared**] to spread a surface with something sticky or oily

smear test [noun: **smear tests**] a regular medical test for women, in which cells are taken from the neck of their womb to check for cancer

smell [noun: **smells**]

1 smell is the power or sense of being aware of things through your nose

2 a smell is something you notice using this sense: *a strong smell of garlic*

3 a sniff at something: *Have a smell of this milk and tell me if you think it's off.*

[verb: **smells, smelling, smelled** or **smelt**]

1 to smell something is to notice it through your nose

2 something that smells gives off a smell of some kind

♦ **smelly** [adjective: **smellier, smelliest**] giving off a strong or bad smell

smelt [superscript 1] [verb: **smelts, smelting, smelted**] to melt rock or other material that contains metal to separate the metal from the rest of the material

smelt [superscript 2] [verb] a way of changing the verb **smell** to make a past tense. It can be used with or without a helping verb: *He smelt the rose.* • *He had never smelt one so sweet.*

smile [verb: **smiles, smiling, smiled**] to show pleasure or amusement by turning up the corners of your mouth

[noun: **smiles**] an expression of pleasure or amusement in which you turn up the corners of your mouth

smirk [verb: **smirks, smirking, smirked**] to

smile in a self-satisfied, cheeky or silly way
[noun: **smirks**] a self-satisfied, cheeky or silly
smile

smithereens [plural noun] something that is
smashed to smithereens is broken into lots of
tiny pieces

smitten [adjective] to be smitten by someone
is to be strongly attracted to them

smock [noun: **smocks**] a loose piece of
clothing worn over other clothes to protect
them

smog [noun] smoke from car exhausts and
chimneys mixed with fog which hangs over
some cities and towns

smoke [noun] the cloud of gases and bits
of soot given off by something that is
burning
[verb: **smokes, smoking, smoked**]
1 something smokes when it gives off smoke
2 someone who smokes puts a lit cigarette,
cigar or pipe in their mouth and breathes in the
smoke
♦ **smoker** [noun: **smokers**] someone who
smokes cigarettes, cigars or a pipe
♦ **smoking** [noun] the habit of smoking
cigarettes, cigars or a pipe
♦ **smoky** [adjective: **smokier, smokiest**]
1 filled with smoke
2 like smoke: *a smoky grey colour*

smooth [adjective: **smoother, smoothest**]
1 something smooth has an even surface that is
not rough or bumpy
2 a smooth substance has no lumps
3 a smooth ride or smooth progress has no
jerks, stops or problems
[verb: **smoothes, smoothing, smoothed**] to
smooth something is to make it smooth or flat:
*She smoothed the bed covers and tidied her
bedroom.*
♦ **smoothly** [adverb] in a smooth way
♦ **smoothness** [noun] being smooth

smother [verb: **smothers, smothering,
smothered**]
1 if someone is smothered, they die because
something is over their nose and mouth and
they cannot breathe
2 to smother flames is to cover them so that no
oxygen gets to the fire and it goes out

smoulder [verb: **smoulders, smouldering,**

smouldered] to burn slowly, without a flame

smudge [noun: **smudges**] a mark made by
rubbing something across a surface or
pressing something greasy against it
[verb: **smudges, smudging, smudged**] to
smudge something is to rub something across it
so that it smears

smug [adjective: **smugger, smuggest**]
showing in an irritating way that you are very
pleased with your own abilities and
achievements
➡ **smugly, smugness**

smuggle [verb: **smuggles, smuggling,
smuggled**]
1 to bring things into a country secretly and
illegally
2 to smuggle something somewhere is to take it
there secretly: *He smuggled the puppy into his
room without his parents knowing.*
♦ **smuggler** [noun: **smugglers**] someone
who smuggles goods into a country

smugly [adverb] in an irritating way that
shows you are too pleased with your own
abilities and achievements: *He smiled smugly
when he heard he had won.*

smugness [noun] being irritatingly pleased
with your own abilities and achievements

snack [noun: **snacks**] a small meal, or
something like a biscuit or piece of fruit that
you eat between meals

snag [noun: **snags**] a small problem
[verb: **snags, snagging, snagged**] to snag
your clothing is to catch or tear it on something
sharp or rough

snail [noun: **snails**] a small creature with a
soft body and a shell on its back that it can
draw its body into for protection

snake [noun: **snakes**] a type of reptile with a
long thin body and no legs, which moves along
the ground with twisting movements

snap [verb: **snaps, snapping, snapped**]
1 to break with a sudden sharp noise
2 something snaps shut when it closes with a
sudden sharp noise
3 you snap your fingers when you rub your
thumb and finger together in a quick
movement, making a cracking noise
4 if someone snaps at you, they suddenly
speak to you in an angry way

Ss

5 an animal snaps when it makes a biting movement with its jaws
[noun: **snaps**]
1 the sound of something breaking or of an animal bringing its teeth together quickly
2 a photograph
♦ **snappily** [adverb]
1 quickly
2 in a bad-tempered way
♦ **snappy** [adjective: **snappier, snappiest**]
1 if someone is snappy, they speak to people in a bad-tempered way
2 if someone tells you to **make it snappy**, they mean you should be quick

snapshot [noun: **snapshots**] a photograph taken quickly

snare [noun: **snares**] a kind of trap for catching animals
[verb: **snares, snaring, snared**] to trap an animal

snarl [verb: **snarls, snarling, snarled**] an animal, such as a dog or wolf, snarls when it growls in a threatening way
[noun: **snarls**] an angry-sounding growl

snatch [verb: **snatches, snatching, snatched**]
1 to snatch something is to grab it suddenly
2 to snatch something, like a sleep or a meal, is to take it quickly when you have time or the chance
[noun: **snatches**] a short piece of music or conversation

sneak [noun: **sneaks**] someone who tells tales or is deceitful
[verb: **sneaks, sneaking, sneaked**]
1 to go somewhere quietly and secretly
2 to tell someone in authority something behind a person's back
3 to **sneak up on** someone is to creep up behind them, to surprise or frighten them
♦ **sneakily** [adverb] in a sneaky way
♦ **sneaky** [adjective: **sneakier, sneakiest**] deceitful or secretive

sneer [verb: **sneers, sneering, sneered**]
1 to raise your top lip at one side in a kind of smile that shows you think you are better than someone else
2 to **sneer at** something is to speak in an unpleasant way about it that shows you do not

respect it: *John sneered at my attempt to write a story.*
[noun: **sneers**] a sneering expression or remark

sneeze [verb: **sneezes, sneezing, sneezed**] to suddenly and uncontrollably blow out air from your nose and mouth
[noun: **sneezes**] the action and sound of sneezing

snide [adjective] spiteful in an almost hidden way: *snide remarks*

sniff [verb: **sniffs, sniffing, sniffed**] to breathe in air through your nose with a small noise, or to draw air into your nose so that you can smell something
[noun: **sniffs**] a quick loud breath taken in through your nose

sniffle [verb: **sniffles, sniffling, sniffled**] to sniff over and over again, especially because you have a cold or are crying

snigger [verb: **sniggers, sniggering, sniggered**] to laugh quietly in an unpleasant and cruel way
[noun: **sniggers**] a quiet unpleasant laugh

snip [verb: **snips, snipping, snipped**] to snip something is to cut small pieces off it using scissors
[noun: **snips**] a quick cutting action made with a pair of scissors

sniper [noun: **snipers**] a person armed with a gun who shoots at people from a hiding place

snippet [noun: **snippets**] a small piece of something such as news, information or conversation: *a snippet of information*

snivel [verb: **snivels, snivelling, snivelled**] to cry and sniff weakly and in a way that does not make other people feel sympathy for you

snob [noun: **snobs**] someone who admires people of high social class, or things that are of high quality, and despises people who are of a lower class than they are, or does not like the things that ordinary people like
♦ **snobbery** [noun] the behaviour of snobs
♦ **snobbish** [adjective] being a snob

snooker [noun] a game for two players played on a large table, with several coloured balls which have to be hit into pockets at the side of the table using a long stick called a cue

snoop [verb: **snoops, snooping, snooped**]

to try to find out things in a secretive way: *Jane was snooping around to try to find my diary.*

✦ **snooper** [noun: **snoopers**] someone who snoops

snooty [adjective: **snootier, snootiest**] behaving in a rude and unfriendly way because you think you are better than other people

snooze [noun: **snoozes**] a short light sleep [verb: **snoozes, snoozing, snoozed**] to sleep, especially not very deeply or for a short time

snore [verb: **snores, snoring, snored**] to make a noise like a snort while you are sleeping, when you breathe in

snorkel [noun: **snorkels**] a tube that allows an underwater swimmer to breathe, with one end sticking out above the water to let in air [verb: **snorkels, snorkelling, snorkelled**] to swim underwater using a snorkel to breathe

snort [verb: **snorts, snorting, snorted**]
1 to make a noise by pushing air out through your nostrils: *The horses snorted, stamping their hooves.*
2 to make this noise because you are angry, disagree, or think something is funny: *'Don't be stupid!' she snorted.*
[noun: **snorts**] a loud noise made by breathing out through your nose: *a snort of laughter*

snout [noun: **snouts**] the mouth and nose of a pig or animal like that

snow [noun] water that has frozen into soft white pieces that fall from the sky: *Thick snow had blocked the road.*
[verb: **snows, snowing, snowed**] if it snows, snow falls from the sky: *It's been snowing all night.*

snowball [noun: **snowballs**] a ball of snow that children make and throw at each other: *a snowball fight*
[verb: **snowballs, snowballing, snowballed**] if a situation or a problem snowballs, it grows quickly and becomes more difficult to deal with: *The strike snowballed and soon all the post offices were closed.*

snowboarding [noun] a sport in which you move quickly down hills over snow on a flat plastic board called a snowboard

snowdrift [noun: **snowdrifts**] a lot of snow

that the wind has blown into a pile

snowdrop [noun: **snowdrops**] a small white flower that grows from a bulb in the early spring

snowman [noun: **snowmen**] a figure of a person, made of snow

snowplough [noun: **snowploughs**] a large vehicle that clears snow from the roads

snowy [adjective: **snowier, snowiest**]
1 covered with snow
2 perfectly white: *a fat gentleman with a snowy beard*

snub [verb: **snubs, snubbing, snubbed**] to treat someone in a rude or insulting way: *I tried to speak to him but he just snubbed me and turned away.*
[adjective] a snub nose is small and turns up at the end

snuff or **snuff out** [verb: **snuffs, snuffing, snuffed**] to put out a candle flame, often with your fingers
[noun] a type of tobacco in the form of a powder

snuffle [verb: **snuffles, snuffling, snuffled**] to make sniffing noises, especially because you have a cold

snug [adjective: **snugger, snuggest**] warm and cosy: *We were all quite snug in our sleeping bags.*

snuggle or **snuggle up** [verb: **snuggles, snuggling, snuggled**] to curl up and get warm: *Sam snuggled closer to his mother and soon fell asleep.*

so [adverb]
1 to such an extent or to a great extent: *I was so relieved to hear her voice.* • *The box was so heavy he could not lift it.* • *Thank you so much for all your help.*
2 you can use **so** when you are talking about something mentioned or something shown by a gesture: *a little boy about so high* • *'I feel sick after all those sweets.' 'I told you so, didn't I?'* • *'Are you coming to the party?' 'I hope so.'*
3 also: *She's tired and so am I.*
4 in this way or that way: *Stretch your leg out so.*
5 so as to means 'in order to': *We got there early so as to get good seats.*
6 so far means 'up to now': *I'm enjoying the job so far.*

Ss

529

7 and so forth is a phrase that you use after you have given a list of things, to say that the list could be continued with more similar things: *pens, pencils, paper and so forth*

8 so what? is something you say to show that you think what has just been mentioned is not important: *He ignored you. So what?*

[conjunction]

1 therefore: *He asked me to come, so I did.* • *So they got married and lived happily ever after.*

2 so or **so that** means 'in order that': *I've washed my jeans so (that) I can wear them tomorrow.*

soak [verb: **soaks, soaking, soaked**]

1 to soak something is to cover it in liquid and leave it there: *If you soak your blouse, the stain might come out.*

2 to soak someone is to make them very wet

3 if a piece of cloth or paper **soaks up** a liquid, it sucks it up or absorbs it: *I used a towel to soak up the spilt milk.*

♦ **soaking** or **soaking wet** [adjective] very wet: *Take your clothes off — they're soaking.*

so-and-so [noun]

1 someone whose name you cannot remember: *She's always gossiping about so-and-so getting married or so-and-so's new job.*

2 a word you use instead of saying something rude: *She can be a real so-and-so!*

soap [noun: **soaps**]

1 a substance that you use to wash yourself and other things: *a bar of soap*

2 another word for **soap opera**

soap opera [noun: **soap operas**] a television series about a group of families and their daily lives

soapy [adjective: **soapier, soapiest**] covered in or full of soap bubbles: *soapy water*

soar [verb: **soars, soaring, soared**]

1 to fly high up into the air: *An eagle soared high above their heads.*

2 if prices soar, things become much more expensive very quickly: *The price of petrol has soared over the last ten years.*

sob [verb: **sobs, sobbing, sobbed**] to cry

noisily: *Lisa lay on her bed, sobbing.*

[noun: **sobs**] the sound of someone sobbing

sober [adjective]

1 not drunk

2 serious: *a sober man*

3 plain and not brightly coloured: *sober colours*

♦ **soberly** [adverb] in a sober way: *soberly dressed* • *a soberly worded message*

♦ **soberness** [noun] being sober: *the soberness of the mood*

sob story [noun: **sob stories**] a story that you tell someone to make them feel sorry for you: *He gave me some sob story about his mother being ill.*

so-called [adjective] called by this name, often mistakenly: *your so-called friend, Mr Williams*

soccer [noun] another word for **football**

sociable [adjective] friendly and enjoying being with other people

social [adjective]

1 to do with society or a community: *social problems such as bad housing*

2 social animals live in groups

3 to do with meeting and being friendly with other people: *a social club*

socialism [noun] the belief that a country's main industries and land should be owned by the government and not by individual people

♦ **socialist** [noun: **socialists**] someone who believes in socialism

[adjective] believing in or to do with socialism: *a socialist state*

social security [noun] money that the government pays to people who are old, ill, or unemployed

social services [plural noun] the department or system provided by a local council to help people who are old or have family problems

social work [noun] work that the government pays for to help people who are poor, ill, or have problems

♦ **social worker** [noun: **social workers**] someone who is paid by the government, whose job is to help people who are poor, ill, or have problems

society [noun: **societies**]

1 all the people in the world in general: *Drugs are a huge danger to society.*
2 a particular group of people, especially fashionable and wealthy people: *high society*
3 a social club with a particular interest: *the debating society*
4 a formal word meaning 'being with other people': *I've always enjoyed the society of people older than myself.*

sociologist [noun: **sociologists**] someone who studies how human societies are organized and how people behave
• **sociology** [noun] the study of human behaviour and societies

sock [noun: **socks**]
1 a covering for your foot that you wear inside your shoe: *a pair of socks*
2 if you **pull your socks up**, you try harder to improve your behaviour or your work: *You'll have to pull your socks up if you want to get a promotion.*

socket [noun: **sockets**]
1 a piece of plastic with holes in it, fitted to a wall, that you plug electrical equipment into: *an electric socket*
2 a hollow structure that something fits into: *She nearly pulled my arm out of its socket.*

sod [noun: **sods**] a piece of earth with grass growing on it

soda or **soda-water** [noun: **sodas** or **soda-waters**] fizzy water that is usually mixed with alcoholic drinks

sodden [adjective] very wet: *The ground's sodden after all that rain.*

sodium [noun] a silvery white element that is part of many substances, for example sodium chloride or salt

sofa [noun: **sofas**] a long comfortable chair for two or three people

sofa bed [noun: **sofa beds**] a sofa that you can make into a bed

soft [adjective: **softer, softest**]
1 not hard or firm: *a nice soft cushion* • *soft silky hair*
2 not strict or tough: *He's far too soft with his children.* • *Ben's too soft to get into a fight.*
3 not loud: *a soft voice*
4 not too bright: *Her bedroom is decorated in soft pastel colours.*

soft drink [noun: **soft drinks**] a drink that does not contain alcohol

soften [verb: **softens, softening, softened**]
1 to soften something is to make it become soft: *Soften the clay by working it with your hands.*
2 to soften is to become soft: *Her voice softened as she looked at the baby.*

softly [adverb] gently or quietly: *Snow was falling softly in the moonlight.* • *She stroked the cat softly.*

softness [noun] being soft, gentle or quiet: *the softness of the pillows*

software [noun] computer programs. Look up and compare **hardware**

soggy [adjective: **soggier, soggiest**] wet and soft: *soggy ground*

soil [noun] the top layer of the ground, that you can grow plants in: *sandy soil*
[verb: **soils, soiling, soiled**] to soil something is to make it dirty: *soiled linen*

solar [adjective] relating to or powered by energy from the sun: *solar panels*

solar power [noun] electricity that is made using the sun's light and heat

solar system [noun] the sun and the planets that move around it

sold [verb] a way of changing the verb **sell** to make a past tense. It can be used with or without a helping verb: *Tom sold me his old bike.* • *Have you sold your house yet?*

solder [verb: **solders, soldering, soldered**] to join two pieces of metal with metal that has been melted
[noun] melted metal used to join pieces of metal together

soldier [noun: **soldiers**] someone who is in the army

sole [adjective]
1 only: *Her sole ambition was to be famous.*
2 belonging to one person alone: *He has sole ownership of the company.*

sole [noun: **soles**]
1 the underside of your foot
2 the underside of your shoe: *The sole came off my shoe as I was running.*

sole [noun: **soles** or **sole**] a flat fish that people can eat

solely [adverb] only or alone: *You are solely responsible for your own actions.*

Ss

solemn [adjective]
1 serious: *a solemn expression* • *a rather solemn little boy*
2 a solemn occasion is celebrated in a dignified way with a lot of ceremony
• **solemnity** [noun] being solemn
• **solemnly** [adverb] in a solemn way

solicitor [noun: **solicitors**] someone whose job is giving advice about the law system to people, for example when they buy a house or a business, or if the police arrest them

solid [adjective]
1 with a fixed shape, not in the form of a liquid or a gas
2 not hollow: *a solid chocolate teddy*
3 firm and strong: *a solid piece of furniture*
4 a solid shape has length, width, and height: *A cube is a solid figure.*
5 with no pauses in between: *I've been working for six solid hours.*
[noun: **solids**]
1 something that is not a liquid or a gas
2 a shape that has length, width, and height
• **solidify** [verb: **solidifies, solidifying, solidified**]
1 to solidify is to become solid
2 to solidify something is to make it become solid
• **solidly** [adverb]
1 strongly or firmly: *a solidly built structure*
2 continuously: *We've been working solidly since nine o'clock this morning.*

solitary [adjective] lonely or alone: *a solitary figure*

solitude [noun] when you are alone

solo [noun: **solos**] a piece of music or a song for one person to play or sing: *Emma sang a solo in the Christmas concert.*
[adjective] alone: *a solo flight*
[adverb] alone: *It's the first time he's flown solo.*
• **soloist** [noun: **soloists**] someone who sings or plays a musical instrument solo

solstice [noun: **solstices**] the **summer solstice** is the day of the year when there are most hours of daylight and the **winter solstice** is the day when there are most hours of darkness

soluble [adjective]
1 a soluble substance will dissolve in water: *soluble aspirin*
2 a soluble problem can be solved

solution [noun: **solutions**]
1 an answer to a problem, question, or puzzle
2 the act of solving a problem or puzzle
3 a liquid with a substance dissolved in it: *a salt-water solution*

solve [verb: **solves, solving, solved**]
1 to work out the answer to a problem or puzzle: *Solve the riddle to win a prize.*
2 to understand and explain how a mystery happened or a crime took place

solvent [noun: **solvents**] something that dissolves another substance

sombre [adjective]
1 dark and gloomy: *sombre colours*
2 serious and sad: *a sombre mood*

sombrero [noun: **sombreros**] a Mexican hat with a broad brim

some [adjective]
1 a number or amount that you do not specify: *It's all right; I've got some money.* • *Some people agreed but others didn't.*
2 a number or amount that is fairly large: *It was some time before I noticed.*
3 used to mean a person or thing when you do not say exactly which: *You're just like your father in some ways.*
[pronoun] part of a number or amount: *I've made a cake — would you like some?*

somebody or **someone** [pronoun]
1 a person that you do not know or name: *Somebody knocked at the door.*
2 an important person: *He really thinks he's somebody in that big car.*

somehow [adverb] in some way: *Don't worry, we'll manage somehow.*

somersault [noun: **somersaults**] a jump in which you turn over forwards or backwards in the air
[verb: **somersaults, somersaulting, somersaulted**] to do a somersault: *She somersaulted neatly into the water.*

something [pronoun]
1 a thing that is not known or stated: *Let's have something to eat before we go.*
2 a slight truth or importance: *There is something in what he says.*
3 you say '**or something**', when you have just

said something but are not sure about it: *I think he's an actor or something.*

sometimes [adverb] at times: *I still see him sometimes.* • *Sometimes I feel like giving up my job and moving away.*

somewhat [adverb] rather: *a somewhat lonely man*

somewhere [adverb]
1 in or to some place: *They live somewhere near Oxford.*
2 used when you are not sure of an amount, time, or number: *She must be somewhere between 35 and 40.*

son [noun: **sons**] someone's male child

sonar [noun] special equipment that uses sound waves to find out where things are under water

song [noun: **songs**]
1 a song is a piece of music with words that you can sing: *a pop song*
2 song is the activity of singing: *A blackbird suddenly burst into song.*

songbird [noun: **songbirds**] a bird that sings

sonic [adjective] relating to sound: *a sonic boom*

son-in-law [noun: **sons-in-law**] your daughter's husband

sonnet [noun: **sonnets**] a type of poem that has fourteen lines

soon [adverb: **sooner, soonest**]
1 in a short time from now: *It will soon be Christmas.*
2 early: *It's too soon to tell whether she'll recover.*
3 if you would **as soon** do something, you would prefer to do it: *I'd just as soon stay in this evening.*
4 as soon as is a phrase meaning 'when': *We ate as soon as they arrived.*
◆ **sooner** [adverb]
1 rather or more willingly: *I'd sooner do it myself than ask her to help.*
2 if something will happen **sooner or later**, it will certainly happen at some time in the future: *You're bound to bump into him sooner or later.*

soot [noun] the black powder that collects in chimneys
➡ **sooty**

soothe [verb: **soothes, soothing, soothed**]

1 to make someone feel calmer or happier: *The little boy was so upset that it took his mother nearly an hour to soothe him.*
2 to make pain less strong: *I bathed to soothe my sore muscles.*
◆ **soothing** [adjective]
1 making you feel calmer or happier
2 making pain less strong

sooty [adjective: **sootier, sootiest**] covered in soot or like soot

sophisticated [adjective]
1 a sophisticated person knows a lot about the world and about what is fashionable
2 sophisticated ideas, machines and processes are complicated and well-developed
◆ **sophistication** [noun] being sophisticated

sopping [adjective] very wet

soppy [adjective: **soppier, soppiest**] too sentimental in a way that seems silly: *a soppy love song*

soprano [noun: **sopranos**]
1 a very high singing voice
2 a woman or young boy with a high singing voice

sorcerer [noun: **sorcerers**] a man who can make magic spells work

sorceress [noun: **sorceresses**] a woman who can make magic spells work

sorcery [noun] magic or the ability to make magic spells work

sore [adjective: **sorer, sorest**] red and painful: *a sore finger*
[noun: **sores**] a red, painful spot on your skin: *The horse had a nasty sore on its leg.*
◆ **sorely** [adverb] very much or a lot: *Mr Watson will be sorely missed by his colleagues.*
◆ **soreness** [noun] being sore

sorrow [noun: **sorrows**] grief or sadness because you are disappointed or someone has died: *I couldn't find the words to comfort her in her sorrow.*
◆ **sorrowful** [adjective] feeling or showing sorrow: *a long, sorrowful face*

sorry [adjective: **sorrier, sorriest**]
1 sorry is a word you use when you are apologizing or saying you regret something:

Ss

I'm sure Tim is sorry he upset you. • Sorry, I didn't mean to hurt you.

2 if you are **sorry for** someone, you feel pity for them: I felt so sorry for Lizzie when she failed her driving test.

3 bad or unfortunate: the sorry plight of the refugees

sort [noun: **sorts**]

1 a type or kind of person or thing: What sort of books do you read? • You meet all sorts of people in this job.

2 if you feel **out of sorts**, you do not feel well

3 sort of is a phrase that means 'slightly': It was sort of strange when the children left home.

[verb: **sorts, sorting, sorted**]

1 to separate people or things into different groups according to their type: Can you sort the washing into whites and coloureds?

2 if you **sort out** one type of thing from a group of things, you separate it from them: Sort out the books that have to go back to the library.

3 if you **sort out** a problem or difficult situation, you solve it or deal with it: There are a lot of things to sort out before we go on holiday.

SOS [noun] a signal that a ship or aircraft sends to ask for help

so-so [adjective] not particularly good: The restaurant looked nice but the meal was so-so.

sought [verb] a way of changing the verb **seek** to make a past tense. It can be used with or without a helping verb: He sought his boss's permission. • I have sought to solve this problem.

soul [noun: **souls**]

1 the part of a person that is not their body but is their spirit, which some people believe lives on after they die

2 a person: The poor old soul got an awful shock.

sound [noun: **sounds**]

1 something that you can hear: There isn't a sound coming from the children's bedroom. • the sound of breaking glass

2 the way that something such as a description or piece of news seems from what you have

heard: I don't much like the sound of your new boss.

[verb: **sounds, sounding, sounded**]

1 if something sounds good or bad, it seems that way from what you have heard about it: Tom's holiday sounds wonderful.

2 if something sounds like something else, the two sounds are very similar: That sounds like Zoe's voice in the kitchen.

3 to sound something is to make a noise with it: Sound your horn before you turn the corner.

4 if you **sound someone out**, you talk to them to find out their opinion: Could you sound John out about my suggestion?

[adjective: **sounder, soundest**]

1 strong, firm, or healthy: The walls of the old church were still sound. • a sound heart

2 a sound sleep is deep and difficult to wake up from

3 thorough and complete: a sound knowledge of French

[adverb] if someone is **sound asleep**, they are sleeping very deeply: At ten o'clock I was still sound asleep.

sound barrier [noun] if a plane breaks the sound barrier, it begins to go faster than the speed that sound travels at

soundproof [adjective] a soundproof material, structure, or room is made so that sound cannot pass through it

soundtrack [noun: **soundtracks**] a recording of the music from a film or television programme

soup [noun: **soups**] a liquid food made from meat, fish, or vegetables

sour [adjective: **sourer, sourest**]

1 sour food has a bitter taste like a lemon, sometimes because it is going bad: sour plums • The milk had gone sour in the sun.

2 bad-tempered and unpleasant: a sour face

source [noun: **sources**]

1 the place where something begins or is naturally present: a rich source of gas

2 a spring that is the start of a river

south [noun]

1 the direction on your right when you are facing towards the rising sun

2 the part of a country or the world that is in the south

[adjective] in, from, or towards the south: *the south coast* • *the south wind*

[adverb] to the south: *The river flows south into the sea.*

south-east [noun] the area midway between south and east: *another sunny day in the south-east*

southerly [adjective] coming from, or going towards, the south

[noun: **southerlies**] a wind that comes from the south

southern [adjective] belonging to, or coming from, the south: *the southern states of the USA*

southward or **southwards** [adverb] to or towards the south: *We were soon heading southward down the motorway.*

south-west [noun] the area midway between south and west: *the south-west of France*

souvenir [noun: **souvenirs**] something that you buy to remind you of a particular place or occasion: *We brought back some shells as souvenirs of our holiday.*

sou'wester [noun: **sou'westers**] a waterproof hat that people sometimes wear in very heavy rain

sovereign [noun: **sovereigns**]
1 a king or queen
2 an old gold coin
[adjective] a sovereign state has its own government

sow [verb: **sows, sowing, sowed, sown**] to scatter seeds on or in the ground so that they will grow

ⓘ This meaning of **sow** is pronounced **so**.

sow [noun: **sows**] a female pig

ⓘ This meaning of **sow** rhymes with **how**.

soya bean or **soy bean** [noun: **soya beans** or **soy beans**] a type of bean that contains a lot of protein

spa [noun: **spas**] a place where people go to drink or bathe in water that comes out of the ground at a natural spring

space [noun: **spaces**]
1 a space is a gap or empty place: *a parking space* • *Fill in the spaces on your answer sheet.*
2 space is the area available to use or do something: *There isn't enough space to hold a party here.* • *Can you make space for one more person?*
3 space is the empty area beyond the Earth's atmosphere, where the planets and stars are: *Another rocket was launched into space yesterday.*
[verb: **spaces, spacing, spaced**] if you space things or **space them out**, you leave gaps between them: *Try to space your work out neatly.*

spacecraft [noun: **spacecraft** or **spacecrafts**] a vehicle that can travel into space

spaceship [noun: **spaceships**] a vehicle that can travel into space

space shuttle [noun: **space shuttles**] a vehicle like a plane that can travel into space and come back to Earth to be used again

spacesuit [noun: **spacesuits**] a set of clothes worn by someone in a spaceship

spacious [adjective] with a lot of room: *a spacious apartment*

spade [noun: **spades**]
1 a tool with a broad blade that you use for digging
2 spades is one of the four suits of playing cards, which have the symbol ♠ printed on them: *the ace of spades*
3 if you **call a spade a spade**, you say exactly what you think and do not worry about whether you are being polite

spaghetti [noun] a type of pasta that is like long thin string: *a plate of spaghetti with tomato sauce*

span [noun: **spans**] the length of time that something lasts: *The country had changed completely within the span of twenty years.*
[verb: **spans, spanning, spanned**] to span something is to stretch across it: *An old wooden bridge spans the river.*

spangle [noun: **spangles**] a small sparkling piece of metal used as a decoration on clothes

• **spangly** [adjective] covered with spangles: *a spangly scarf*

spaniel [noun: **spaniels**] a type of dog with long ears that hang down

Ss

spank [verb: **spanks, spanking, spanked**] to hit someone on the bottom with your hand flat, especially as a punishment
[noun: **spanks**] a hit on someone's bottom with your hand flat

spanner [noun: **spanners**] a tool used for tightening or loosening nuts or screws

spar [verb: **spars, sparring, sparred**] to fight or argue with someone

spare [adjective]
1 a spare room or thing is extra and is not being used at the moment: *a spare tyre* • *I've got a spare ticket for Saturday's concert, if you'd like it.*
2 spare time is time when you are free to do what you want
[verb: **spares, sparing, spared**]
1 if you can spare something or someone, you can manage without them: *We can't spare anyone to help out today.*
2 if you can spare the time to do something, you have enough time to do it: *I'm sorry, but I can't spare the time to go out tonight.*
3 to avoid hurting someone or making things difficult for them: *Break the news gently to spare her as much pain as possible.*
4 if you have time or money **to spare**, you have more than you need
[noun: **spares**] a spare part for a car or piece of equipment
◆ **sparing** [adjective] careful or using very little of something

spark [noun: **sparks**]
1 a very small burning piece thrown out of a fire or when two hard surfaces are rubbed together: *Sparks were shooting out of the bonfire.*
2 a small amount of something such as enthusiasm or interest: *There seemed to be no spark of life in the old woman.*
[verb: **sparks, sparking, sparked**]
1 to make a spark
2 to spark something is to start or cause it: *Her remark sparked off a huge argument.*

sparkle [verb: **sparkles, sparkling, sparkled**] to glitter or shine: *Her jewels sparkled in the firelight.*
◆ **sparkling** [adjective]
1 shining or glittering: *sparkling lights*

2 a sparkling drink has bubbles of gas in it: *sparkling mineral water*

spark-plug or **sparking-plug** [noun: **spark-plugs** or **sparking-plugs**] a small part in a car engine that produces a spark to light the gases that make it start

sparrow [noun: **sparrows**] a small brown bird

sparse [adjective: **sparser, sparsest**] if something is sparse, there is not much or not enough of it: *sparse hair*

spasm [noun: **spasms**] a sudden movement of your muscles that you cannot control: *The muscles of his leg had gone into spasm.*

spate [noun] a sudden large number or amount: *a spate of burglaries*

spatter [verb: **spatters, spattering, spattered**] if you spatter something, you splash it with small drops of liquid: *His hair was spattered with paint.*

spatula [noun: **spatulas**] a kitchen tool with a broad, flat blade, used for spreading or lifting things

spawn [noun] the eggs of frogs, toads or fish: *frog spawn*
[verb: **spawns, spawning, spawned**]
1 if fish or frogs spawn, they lay eggs
2 to spawn something is to cause or produce it: *the small businesses spawned by this new development*

speak [verb: **speaks, speaking, spoke, spoken**]
1 to say something: *Could I speak to you for a moment?* • *She was so tired she could hardly speak.*
2 to be able to talk in a particular language: *Do you speak Greek?*
3 to make a speech: *She spoke for almost an hour about her work abroad.*
4 if you **speak up**, you speak more loudly: *Speak up, we can't hear you at the back.*
◆ **speaker** [noun: **speakers**]
1 someone who is speaking
2 a piece of equipment that increases the sound coming out of a radio, CD-player, or cassette player

spear [noun: **spears**] a long thin weapon with a metal point
[verb: **spears, spearing, speared**] to push a

long thin point into something: *He speared a piece of meat with his fork.*

special [adjective]

1 unusual and different from others: *We've been saving this wine for a special occasion.* • *the special relationship between parents and their children*

2 meant for or having a specific purpose: *Special trains will take fans to the match.* • *a special tool for making rugs*

♦ **specialist** [noun: **specialists**] someone who knows a lot about a particular subject, especially a doctor who has special training in diseases affecting a particular part of the body: *My GP has referred me to a heart specialist.*

♦ **speciality** [noun: **specialities**] something that someone does particularly well: *Birthday cakes are my speciality.*

specialization or **specialisation** [noun] study of a particular subject or work at a particular job

♦ **specialize** or **specialise** [verb: **specializes, specializing, specialized**] to give all of your attention to studying one particular subject or working in one particular area: *Jessica's decided to specialize in Paediatrics.*

specially [adverb] with one particular purpose: *Jo's had her costume specially made for the party.*

ⓘ Remember the difference between **specially** and **especially**:
specially means 'for a special purpose': *I cooked this meal **specially** for you.*
especially means 'particularly': *I like all of the characters but **especially** Harry.*

species [noun: **species**] a group of animals or plants whose members have many of the same features

specific [adjective]

1 giving all the details about something in a clear way: *Sarah's directions weren't very specific.*

2 exactly as someone stated or described: *We each have our own specific jobs to do.*

♦ **specifically** [adverb]

1 for one particular purpose and no other: *flats designed specifically for the elderly*

2 clearly and exactly: *I specifically told you not to go out tonight.*

specification [noun: **specifications**] a clear description of the details of something such as a plan, contract, or machine: *The car was built to his own specifications.*

specify [verb: **specifies, specifying, specified**] to specify what you want is to state it clearly: *Please specify the colour and size your require on the order form.*

specimen [noun: **specimens**] something that is a sample of a particular group or kind of thing: *The specimens were arranged in cases, clearly labelled.*

speck [noun: **specks**]

1 a very small piece of something: *a speck of dust*

2 a small spot: *a speck of paint*

speckle [noun: **speckles**] a small coloured spot: *The egg was covered with speckles.*

♦ **speckled** [adjective] covered in speckles: *a speckled hen*

spectacle [noun: **spectacles**] a wonderful or impressive sight: *The royal wedding was a great spectacle.*

♦ **spectacles** [plural noun] glasses that you wear to help you see properly: *a pair of spectacles*

spectacular [adjective] very impressive: *a spectacular firework display* • *The scenery was absolutely spectacular.*

♦ **spectacularly** [adverb] impressively or by a very large amount: *a spectacularly successful film*

spectator [noun: **spectators**] someone who is watching an event

spectre [noun: **spectres**] a ghost

spectrum [noun: **spectra** or **spectrums**]

1 all the different colours produced when light passes through glass or water

2 all the different types or forms of something: *a broad spectrum of opinions*

speculate [verb: **speculates, speculating, speculated**] to guess: *I wouldn't like to speculate about what might have happened to him.*

♦ **speculation** [noun: **speculations**]

1 speculation is guessing something

2 a speculation is a guess

Ss

sped [verb] a way of changing the verb **speed** to make a past tense. It can be used with or without a helping verb: *A bullet sped past his ear.* • *The holidays have just sped by.*

speech [noun: **speeches**]
1 speech is the ability to speak: *He seemed to have lost the power of speech.*
2 the way that you speak: *She was so tired that her speech was slurred.*
3 a speech is a talk that you give in front of a lot of people: *The bride's father usually makes a speech.*
• **speechless** [adjective] if you are speechless, you cannot talk because you are so surprised or shocked: *His remarks left her speechless.*

speed [noun: **speeds**]
1 the rate at which someone or something is moving: *He was driving at a speed of about 30 miles per hour.*
2 quickness: *Speed is important in this job.*
[verb: **speeds, speeding, sped** or **speeded**]
1 to move quickly or hurry: *He sped off down the road on his bike.*
2 to drive faster than the law says you can: *I really didn't think I was speeding until I saw the police car.*
• **speeding** [noun] the offence of driving faster than the law says you can: *He's been fined for speeding three times.*

speedometer [noun: **speedometers**] a piece of equipment in a car that measures how fast you are travelling

speedway [noun: **speedways**] the sport of motor-cycle racing, or the track that is used for this

speedy [adjective: **speedier, speediest**] quick: *Thanks for the speedy reply to my letter.*

spell[1] [verb: **spells, spelling, spelt** or **spelled**]
1 to say or write the letters of a word in the correct order: *Could you spell your name for me?*
2 to make up a word: *L-i-g-h-t spells 'light'.*

spell[2] [noun: **spells**] a short period of time: *The weather will be dull, with sunny spells.*

spell[3] [noun: **spells**] a set of words that are supposed to make something magic happen: *The wicked witch cast a spell on Snow White.*

spelling [noun: **spellings**]
1 a spelling is the way that a word is spelt: *'Donut' is the American spelling of 'doughnut'.*
2 spelling is the ability to spell well: *Your spelling is terrible.*

spend [verb: **spends, spending, spent**]
1 to use money to buy things: *We spend a lot of money on food.*
2 to use a lot of time, energy or effort doing something: *I used to spend hours reading in my room.*

spent [verb] a way of changing the verb **spend** to make a past tense. It can be used with or without a helping verb: *I spent weeks making that sweater.* • *Have you spent your birthday money yet?*

sperm [noun: **sperm** or **sperms**] a cell from a man that joins with the egg from a woman to make a baby

sphere [noun: **spheres**] a solid object that is the shape of a ball
• **spherical** [adjective] shaped like a ball

spice [noun: **spices**] any substance that adds flavour to food: *herbs and spices* • *Ginger is a spice.*
• **spiciness** [noun] being spicy: *the spiciness of the sauce*
• **spicy** [adjective: **spicier, spiciest**] tasting hot on your tongue: *spicy chilli tortillas*

spider [noun: **spiders**] a small creature with eight legs that spins a web made of very fine threads
• **spidery** [adjective] spidery handwriting is untidy with long, thin strokes

spike [noun: **spikes**] a hard, thin point: *There were sharp spikes on top of the wall.*
• **spiky** [adjective: **spikier, spikiest**] with sharp points: *a spiky hairstyle*

spill [verb: **spills, spilling, spilt** or **spilled**]
1 to spill a liquid is to let it run out accidentally: *Careful! You're going to spill your tea.*
2 if a liquid spills, it flows out accidentally: *The milk spilled all over the floor.*

spin [verb: **spins, spinning, spun**]
1 to turn round and round very quickly: *The ballerina spun round and round on her toes.*
2 to make long, thin threads out of cotton, wool, or another material by pulling it and twisting it

spinach [noun] a vegetable with large flat green leaves

spinal [adjective] to do with your spine: *a spinal injury*

spinal cord [noun: **spinal cords**] the nerve cells inside your spine

spindle [noun: **spindles**] the pin that something turns on, for example a knob on a radio or a bobbin of thread
  ◆ **spindly** [adjective: **spindlier, spindliest**] long and thin: *a creature with long, spindly arms*

spin drier [noun: **spin driers**] a machine that you put wet clothes into to dry them

spine [noun: **spines**]
  1 the line of bones down the back of a person or animal
  2 a stiff spike that grows on animals such as the hedgehog or on plants: *the spines of a cactus*
  → **spinal**

spinning wheel [noun: **spinning wheels**] a piece of equipment for spinning thread, with a large wheel that turns and makes spindles move

spinster [noun: **spinsters**] a woman who is not married

spiral [adjective] coiled or winding round and round: *a spiral staircase*
  [noun: **spirals**] something with a spiral shape: *The shell formed a perfect spiral.*
  [verb: **spirals, spiralling, spiralled**]
  1 to move in a spiral
  2 to increase very quickly: *House prices have spiralled recently.*

spire [noun: **spires**] a tall pointed roof on a church tower

spirit [noun: **spirits**]
  1 your soul, which some people believe lives on after you die: *Some villagers thought the graveyard was haunted by evil spirits.*
  2 bravery or liveliness: *a horse with spirit*
  3 a strong alcoholic drink: *whisky, vodka and other spirits*
  4 a general feeling or attitude: *team spirit* • *a town with a strong community spirit*
  ◆ **spirited** [adjective] lively and with a lot of personality: *a spirited performance*

spirit level [noun: **spirit levels**] a tool that you use to test whether a surface is level

spiritual [adjective] to do with someone's soul or to do with ghosts: *a spiritual experience*

spit [noun: **spits**]
  1 the watery liquid inside your mouth
  2 a metal bar that you put meat on to roast
  [verb: **spits, spitting, spat**] if you spit, you push liquid or food out of your mouth: *She took one mouthful and then spat it out on to her plate.*

spite [noun]
  1 a feeling of wanting to offend or upset someone: *He threw my picture away out of spite.*
  2 if you do something or something happens **in spite of** something else, the first thing does not prevent the other: *We decided to go to the seaside in spite of the rain.*
  ◆ **spiteful** [adjective] doing or saying something nasty just to upset someone: *It isn't like Maddy to be spiteful.* • *a spiteful remark*
  ◆ **spitefully** [adverb] in a way that aims to upset people
  ◆ **spitefulness** [noun] being spiteful

spitting image [noun: **spitting images**] someone who looks exactly like someone else: *Tara's the spitting image of her mother.*

spittle [noun] the liquid inside your mouth. It is also called **saliva**

splash [verb: **splashes, splashing, splashed**]
  1 if you splash someone with a liquid, or splash a liquid over someone, you throw drops of it over them: *Kate quickly splashed her face with water.* • *The car drove off, splashing mud all over my new coat.*
  2 if a liquid splashes somewhere, it flies there in drops: *The water splashed over the edge of the pan.*
  3 if you splash or splash a part of your body in water, you move the water around in a noisy way: *The baby was splashing happily in his bath.*
  [noun: **splashes**]
  1 the water sent up when something moves through it, or the noise this makes: *He fell into the pool with a loud splash.*
  2 a mark made on something where liquid has fallen on it: *jeans covered in splashes of paint*
  3 a splash of colour is a bright patch of it

Ss

splay [verb: **splays, splaying, splayed**] to spread your legs, arms, or fingers out wide

spleen [noun: **spleens**] an organ near your stomach which controls the quality of your blood

splendid [adjective]
1 magnificent, rich, or grand: *The king was a splendid sight in his robes.*
2 very good: *What a splendid meal!*
✦ **splendour** [noun] when something looks very grand or magnificent: *the splendour of the royal palaces*

splint [noun: **splints**] a piece of wood used to keep a broken arm or leg in the right position

splinter [noun: **splinters**] a small piece of wood or glass that breaks off from a large piece: *She got a splinter in her hand from the broken fence.*
[verb: **splinters, splintering, splintered**] if a piece of wood splinters, small thin pieces of it break off

split [verb: **splits, splitting, split**]
1 if something splits, it breaks or tears apart: *Your trousers have split down the back.*
2 if you split something, you break it or tear it apart: *The lightning had split the tree in two.*
3 to divide a group of people into smaller groups: *I split the children into two groups.*
4 if two people who have a relationship **split up**, they stop going out together: *Did you know Katy's split up with her boyfriend?*
[noun: **splits**]
1 a crack, tear, or break in something: *There's a long split in the box.*
2 if you **do the splits**, you sit on the floor with one leg stretched straight out in front of you and one behind

split second [noun] a split second is a very short time, less than a second: *For a split second I thought something awful had happened.*

splutter [verb: **splutters, spluttering, spluttered**] to make spitting noises when you talk because you are excited, angry, or shocked: *'I don't know what you're talking about!' he spluttered.*

spoil [verb: **spoils, spoiling, spoilt** or **spoiled**]
1 to spoil something is to damage or ruin it: *He*

spilled a drink on the picture and spoiled it. • *Not even the rainy weather could spoil our fun.*
2 if food spoils, it starts to go bad: *If you don't put it in the fridge it will spoil.*
3 to spoil someone is to give them too much of what they want so that they no longer appreciate it

spoil-sport [noun: **spoil-sports**] someone who refuses to join in other people's fun: *Come on, Barry, don't be such a spoil-sport!*

spoke [1] [noun: **spokes**] one of the thin pieces that come out from the centre of the wheel to the edge

spoke [2] [verb] a way of changing the verb **speak** to make a past tense: *He spoke so fast that I couldn't understand him.*

spoken [verb] a form of the verb **speak** that is used with a helping verb to show that something happened in the past: *I've spoken to my boss about it.*

spokesman [noun: **spokesmen**] someone who speaks on behalf of other people

spokeswoman [noun: **spokeswomen**] a woman who speaks on behalf of other people

sponge [noun: **sponges**]
1 a soft object, made from natural or artificial material, that you use to wash your body
2 a light cake or pudding made by mixing and baking eggs, flour, sugar, and sometimes butter: *a sponge pudding*
[verb: **sponges, sponging, sponged**]
1 to wash something with a sponge
2 to try to get money from people
✦ **spongy** [adjective] feeling soft like a sponge: *a spongy texture*

sponsor [verb: **sponsors, sponsoring, sponsored**]
1 to pay some or all of the cost of an event or project: *A local company sponsors my son's football team.*
2 to promise to pay someone a sum of money, that they will give to charity, if they do a particular thing: *a sponsored swim*
[noun: **sponsors**] a person or company that sponsors someone or something: *official sponsors of the 2002 World Cup*
✦ **sponsorship** [noun] the money someone pays to sponsor an event or a person

spontaneity [noun] being spontaneous

spontaneous [adjective]
1 natural: *a spontaneous laugh*
2 not planned: *a spontaneous offer of help*

spoof [noun: **spoofs**] a trick or joke

spook [noun: **spooks**] a ghost
♦ **spooky** [adjective: **spookier, spookiest**] frightening because it makes you think of ghosts: *a spooky ghost story* • *spooky music*

spool [noun: **spools**] a cylindrical object that film or thread is wound around: *a spool of cotton*

spoon [noun: **spoons**] an object with a thin handle and a shallow bowl at one end that you use for eating or serving food
[verb: **spoons, spooning, spooned**] to lift up food on a spoon: *She was slowly spooning the cereal into the baby's mouth.*
♦ **spoonful** [noun: **spoonfuls**] the amount a spoon will hold

spore [noun: **spores**] a tiny cell like a seed that mushrooms and some other plants produce

sporran [noun: **sporrans**] a type of bag that men wear hanging from their waists when they wear a kilt

sport [noun: **sports**]
1 sport is games and physical activities like football, tennis, and swimming: *Adam loves all kinds of sport.*
2 a sport is a particular game or activity: *Alex particularly enjoys winter sports.*
3 a sport is a kind and helpful person: *Max'll give us a hand — he's a good sport.*
♦ **sporting** [adjective] playing fair: *a very sporting player*

sports car [noun: **sports cars**] a fast car that has only two seats and no roof

sportsman [noun: **sportsmen**] a man who takes part in sport

sportswoman [noun: **sportswomen**] a woman who takes part in sport

spot [noun: **spots**]
1 a small mark or stain on something: *There were spots of paint all over the table.*
2 a round shape that is part of a pattern: *a pink dress with white spots*
3 a red raised mark on your skin: *Teenagers often suffer from spots.*
4 a place: *a lovely spot for a picnic* • *X marks the spot where the treasure is buried.*
[verb: **spots, spotting, spotted**] to notice something or someone: *I suddenly spotted Ian over by the window.*

spotless [adjective] totally clean: *a spotless white handkerchief*
♦ **spotlessly** [adverb] something that is spotlessly clean is very clean
♦ **spotlessness** [noun] being very clean

spotlight [noun: **spotlights**] a small bright light, for example on a stage

spotty [adjective: **spottier, spottiest**]
1 someone who is spotty has a lot of spots: *a spotty face*
2 covered in round shapes of a different colour: *a spotty scarf*

spouse [noun: **spouses**] your spouse is your husband or wife

spout [noun: **spouts**]
1 the long thin part of a teapot or kettle that you pour the water out of
2 a jet of water
[verb: **spouts, spouting, spouted**] to come out in a fountain: *The oil came spouting up out of the ground.*

sprain [verb: **sprains, spraining, sprained**] to twist one of the joints in your body and hurt yourself: *a sprained ankle*
[noun: **sprains**] a painful injury when you twist a joint such as your ankle or wrist: *Her wrist isn't broken; it's just a bad sprain.*

sprang [verb] a way of changing the verb **spring** to make a past tense: *The cat sprang on to the mouse.*

sprawl [verb: **sprawls, sprawling, sprawled**]
1 to sit, lie, or fall with your legs and arms spread out: *Tony lay sprawled at full length on the sofa.*
2 if a town, building, or group of buildings sprawls, it covers a large area in an untidy way: *a large, sprawling old house*

spray [noun: **sprays**]
1 a fine mist of liquid: *The spray from the waterfall wet their hair.*
2 a device with a lot of little holes that produces a mist of liquid: *a perfume spray*
3 a liquid that you spray on to something: *a hair spray*

Ss

[verb: **sprays, spraying, sprayed**] to cover something with a mist of fine drops of liquid: *A sprinkler was spraying water on to the lawn.*

spread [verb: **spreads, spreading, spread**]
1 to put a layer of something onto a surface: *She spread her toast thickly with butter.* • *Tom was carefully spreading cream onto the top of the cake.*
2 to open something out flat or to cover a surface: *Spread the map out so that we can look at it.* • *Ann spread all her shopping out on her bed.*
3 if news spreads, it becomes known by a lot of different people: *Rumours spread very quickly in this little village.*
4 to be spaced out over a period of time: *Luckily, the exams were spread out over two whole weeks.*
[noun: **spreads**]
1 the area, time, or range that something covers: *the spread of a disease*
2 a type of paste that you spread on bread: *chicken spread*

spread-eagled [adjective or adverb] if someone is spread-eagled, their arms and legs are spread out wide

spreadsheet [noun: **spreadsheets**] a computer program that can calculate numbers entered into a table, used for planning and keeping financial accounts

spree [noun: **sprees**] a burst of doing something: *a shopping spree*

sprig [noun: **sprigs**] a small branch of a plant: *a sprig of holly*

sprightly [adjective] a sprightly person is lively and moves quickly: *She's very sprightly for 85.*

spring [verb: **springs, springing, sprang, sprung**]
1 to jump quickly, usually up: *He's the type who just springs out of bed in the morning.*
2 to develop from something else: *His confidence springs from his loving family background.*
[noun: **springs**]
1 a coil of wire: *a chair with a broken spring*
2 the season of the year between winter and summer when plants start to grow: *the first day of spring*

3 a jump or quick movement
4 a small stream that flows up out of the ground: *a mountain spring*
[adjective] happening after winter and before summer: *spring flowers*

springboard [noun: **springboards**] a type of board that divers can jump from into the water

spring-cleaning [noun] thorough cleaning of your house, especially in the spring

springy [adjective: **springier, springiest**] a springy surface or substance easily springs back into its original shape: *a springy mattress* • *springy floorboards*

sprinkle [verb: **sprinkles, sprinkling, sprinkled**] to scatter small drops or pieces of something over a surface: *She sprinkled chocolate chips onto the trifle.*
◆ **sprinkler** [noun: **sprinklers**] a device that you use to sprinkle something, especially water on to a garden

sprint [verb: **sprints, sprinting, sprinted**] to run fast for a short distance: *He sprinted down the street after her.*
[noun: **sprints**] a short running race: *the 100 metre sprint*
◆ **sprinter** [noun: **sprinters**] an athlete who is good at running fast for short distances

sprout [verb: **sprouts, sprouting, sprouted**]
1 to produce new leaves and shoots: *Buds were sprouting on the sycamore tree.*
2 to grow or appear: *New cafés are sprouting up everywhere.*
[noun: **sprouts**]
1 a new shoot: *bean sprouts*
2 a **Brussels sprout**

spruce[1] [noun: **spruces**] a type of fir tree
spruce[2] [adjective: **sprucer, sprucest**] neat and smart: *You're looking very spruce in your new suit.*

sprung [verb] a form of the verb **spring** that is used with a helping verb to show that something happened in the past: *James had sprung to his feet when she came in.*

spud [noun: **spuds**] an informal word for a potato

spur [noun: **spurs**]
1 a small pointed object that a rider wears on

his heel to stick into his horse to make it go faster

2 anything that makes someone try harder

3 if you do something **on the spur of the moment**, you do it suddenly without planning it first: *On the spur of the moment, he decided to take a day off work.*

[verb: **spurs, spurring, spurred**] if something **spurs someone on**, it encourages them to do something: *Winning the prize spurred her on to try even harder.*

spurn [verb: **spurns, spurning, spurned**] to reject someone or something unkindly: *He spurned all her efforts to be friendly.*

spurt [verb: **spurts, spurting, spurted**] to pour out in a heavy flow: *Blood was spurting from a wound on his head.*

[noun: **spurts**]

1 a sudden burst of a liquid: *a spurt of blood*

2 a sudden increase of effort, energy, or feeling: *We'll have to put a spurt on if we want to catch that train.*

spy [noun: **spies**] someone who is employed by the government of their country to secretly find out information about another country

[verb: **spies, spying, spied**]

1 to work as a spy

2 to see or notice someone or something: *He suddenly spied a man hiding behind the door.*

squabble [verb: **squabbles, squabbling, squabbled**] to argue about something that is not important: *Stop squabbling and eat your tea.*

[noun: **squabbles**] an argument about something that is not important

squad [noun: **squads**] a small group of people who are doing a job together: *a squad of bricklayers*

squadron [noun: **squadrons**] a group of people in the army, navy, or air force

squalid [adjective] dirty and poor: *a squalid room in a hostel*

squall [noun: **squalls**] a sudden strong wind

♦ **squally** [adjective] stormy: *a squally night at sea*

squalor [noun] very dirty living conditions: *The old man had been living alone in squalor.*

squander [verb: **squanders, squandering, squandered**] to waste time or

money: *He squandered all his money on gambling.*

square [noun: **squares**]

1 a flat shape with four equal sides and four right angles

2 an open space with buildings on all four sides: *a tree-lined square* • *Trafalgar Square*

[adjective]

1 shaped like a square: *a square table*

2 measuring a particular amount on each side: *The room was about 3 metres square.*

3 a square measurement is one used to measure area. For example, a square metre is a space one metre long and one metre wide.

4 a square number is a number that has been multiplied by itself, for example 3×3, which is written as 3^2

5 with equal scores or amounts: *The two teams were all square at half-time, at 3–3.* • *If you pay for the coffee, we'll be square.*

6 straight or level: *Keep the paper square with the edge of the table.*

[verb: **squares, squaring, squared**]

1 to make something have a square shape: *Square off the end of the piece of wood.*

2 to square a number is to multiply it by itself: *Four squared is sixteen.*

squash [verb: **squashes, squashing, squashed**] to press, squeeze, or crush someone or something: *We were all squashed together in the back of the car.*

[noun: **squashes**]

1 a squash is a situation when people or things are squashed: *It was a bit of squash fitting everything in his suitcase.*

2 squash is a drink with a fruit flavour: *an orange squash*

3 squash is a game in which you hit a small rubber ball against the walls of a court with a racket

squat [verb: **squats, squatting, squatted**]

1 to crouch down on your heels: *He squatted on the ground to eat his lunch.*

2 to live in a building without having permission to be there

[adjective] short and fat: *a rather squat little man*

♦ **squatter** [noun: **squatters**] someone who lives in a building without permission

Ss

squawk [verb: **squawks, squawking, squawked**] to make a loud, high-pitched cry [noun: **squawks**] a loud, high-pitched cry: *The hen gave a squawk.*

squeak [verb: **squeaks, squeaking, squeaked**] to make a small, high-pitched sound: *That door squeaks when you open it.* [noun: **squeaks**] a small, high-pitched sound
♦ **squeaky** [adjective: **squeakier, squeakiest**] making a noise like a squeak: *a squeaky floorboard*

squeal [verb: **squeals, squealing, squealed**] to give a loud, shrill cry: *The baby squealed with delight when he saw his mother.* [noun: **squeals**] a loud, shrill cry: *a squeal of pain*

squeamish [adjective] easily shocked or made to feel sick: *I've always been squeamish about blood.*

squeeze [verb: **squeezes, squeezing, squeezed**]
1 to press something tightly: *She squeezed my hand encouragingly.*
2 to force something into or out of a small space or container: *The cat tried to squeeze itself under the sofa.* • *He was trying to squeeze the last of the toothpaste out of the tube.*
[noun: **squeezes**]
1 the action of squeezing or pressing something
2 a tight fit: *We all got into the car, but it was a tight squeeze.*

squelch [noun: **squelches**] the noise you make when you move through something thick and sticky like mud

squid [noun: **squids**] a sea creature with tentacles

squiggle [noun: **squiggles**] a short, wavy line

squint [verb: **squints**]
1 to half-close your eyes when you are looking at something: *She looked up at him, squinting in the sunlight.*
2 to have eyes that look in different directions
[noun: **squints**] a problem with your eyes that makes them look in different directions

squirm [verb: **squirms, squirming, squirmed**] to wriggle or twist your body because you are embarrassed or in pain: *She squirmed when she remembered how rude she had been.*

squirrel [noun: **squirrels**] a small reddish-brown or grey animal with a bushy tail that lives in trees and eats nuts

squirt [verb: **squirts, squirting, squirted**] to shoot out a jet of liquid: *The kids were squirting each other with water.*

St [abbreviation] short for **Saint** or **Street**

stab [verb: **stabs, stabbing, stabbed**]
1 to kill or injure someone by pushing a knife or other sharp object into them: *The woman was stabbed with a knife.*
2 to push something sharp into something else: *She stabbed the pin into the cushion angrily.*
[noun: **stabs**]
1 a sharp feeling: *a stab of pain*
2 if you **have a stab at something**, you try to do it: *I'd love to have a stab at running my own business.*

stability [noun] being steady and balanced

stabilize or **stabilise** [verb]
1 to stabilize is to become balanced or steady: *She's been very ill but her condition has stabilized.*
2 to stabilize someone or something is to make them balanced or steady: *Put a book under the table leg to stabilize it.*

stable [adjective]
1 firm and steady: *This bracket will help to keep the shelf stable.*
2 a stable relationship is one that has lasted for some time and will probably continue
3 a stable person is sensible and calm
[noun: **stables**] a building to keep a horse in

stack [noun: **stacks**] a large pile of things: *a stack of books*
[verb: **stacks, stacking, stacked**] to pile things up neatly: *Stack the dishes in the sink and I'll wash them later.*

stadium [noun: **stadiums** or **stadia**] a large sports ground with seats for people to watch: *a football stadium*

staff [noun: **staffs**]
1 the people who work in a particular place: *The company has a staff of 150.* • *Six new members of staff are joining the school this term.*
2 a stick

staff nurse [noun: **staff nurses**] a qualified nurse

stag [noun: **stags**] a male deer

stage [noun: **stages**]

1 the raised platform in a theatre where the actors perform

2 a step in a process or series of developments: *The work is still in its early stages.* • *It's hard to predict what will happen at this stage.*

[verb: **stages, staging, staged**] to put a play or other performance on in a theatre: *an opera staged in Verona*

stagger [verb: **staggers, staggering, staggered**]

1 to walk unsteadily, swaying from side to side: *He staggered across the room and fell into a chair.*

2 to amaze someone: *I was staggered when they got married.*

3 to arrange events so that they do not all happen at the same time: *We have to stagger our lunch breaks to cover the phones.*

♦ **staggering** [adjective] very surprising: *The amount of money collected was absolutely staggering.*

stagnant [adjective] stagnant water is dirty and unhealthy because it does not flow: *a stagnant pond*

staid [adjective] serious and not keen to try new things

stain [verb: **stains, staining, stained**]

1 to leave a permanent coloured mark on something: *The coffee you spilt has stained the carpet.*

2 to dye wood a different colour

[noun: **stains**] a dirty mark that is hard to remove from something: *overalls covered in oil stains*

stained glass [noun] a glass panel made up of pieces of differently coloured glass that form a picture

stainless steel [noun] a type of steel that does not rust: *stainless steel cutlery*

stair or **stairs** [noun: **stairs**]

1 a set of steps that lead to another level in a building: *A flight of stairs led down to the cellar.*

2 one of these steps

staircase [noun: **staircases**] a set of stairs: *a marble staircase*

stake [noun: **stakes**]

1 a strong pointed stick, for example to support a fence

2 an amount of money that you bet on something: *a £5 stake*

3 if something is **at stake**, you risk losing it: *She felt that her whole future was at stake in the competition.*

[verb: **stakes, staking, staked**] to bet an amount of money on something: *I'll stake £10 on Paul winning.*

stale [adjective: **staler, stalest**] not fresh but dry and tasteless: *stale bread* • *The air smelt stale inside the room.*

stalemate [noun]

1 a situation in which progress is impossible because the people or groups involved do not agree

2 a situation in the game of chess in which neither person can make a move and therefore neither person can win

stalk [noun: **stalks**] the stem of a flower, leaf, or fruit: *an apple stalk*

[verb: **stalks, stalking, stalked**]

1 to walk proudly and stiffly: *He was stalking angrily up and down.*

2 to hunt an animal quietly, trying to keep hidden: *a tigress stalking her prey*

3 to follow and watch someone in a way that they find threatening: *people who stalk celebrities*

♦ **stalker** [noun: **stalkers**] someone who develops an unhealthy interest in someone else and follows and watches them in a threatening way

stall [noun: **stalls**]

1 a table or open-fronted shop where things are laid out to be sold: *a market stall*

2 a compartment for one animal in a cowshed or barn

3 the stalls are the lower floor of a theatre, where the audience sit

[verb: **stalls, stalling, stalled**]

1 if a vehicle stalls or someone stalls it, its engine suddenly stops while you are driving

2 to delay doing something: *I wish he'd stop stalling and give me an answer.*

stallion [noun: **stallions**] a male horse

stamina [noun] the strength to keep doing

Ss

something for a long time: *exercises to increase your stamina*

stammer [verb: **stammers, stammering, stammered**]
1 to have a speech problem that makes it difficult for you to pronounce the first letters of some words
2 to speak like this because you are frightened or nervous: *'I'm s-s-sorry,' he stammered.*
[noun: **stammers**] a speech problem that makes it difficult for you to pronounce the first letters of some words

stamp [verb: **stamps, stamping, stamped**]
1 to bring your foot down firmly on the ground: *She stamped her feet to keep them warm.*
2 to stick a stamp on a letter
3 to print letters, numbers, or a design on something: *Each letter is stamped with the date we receive it.* • *a file stamped 'Urgent'*
4 if you **stamp something out**, you try to stop it happening: *a plan to stamp out crime*
[noun: **stamps**]
1 a postage stamp: *first-class stamps*
2 the movement or sound of a foot being brought down hard on the ground
3 an object that you put into ink and press onto a surface to print words, numbers, or a design: *a date stamp*
4 a design or mark that you make with this object: *a manufacturer's stamp*

stamp duty [noun] tax that you have to pay for some legal documents, especially documents that show you have bought a house

stamped addressed envelope [noun: **stamped addressed envelopes**] an envelope that you write your name and address on and stick a stamp on. You send it with a letter so a reply can be sent to you. This is often shortened to **sae**

stampede [noun: **stampedes**] a sudden wild rush of animals or people: *a buffalo stampede* • *The bell went and there was a stampede for the door.*
[verb: **stampedes, stampeding, stampeded**] to rush in a stampede: *The noise of the gun made the elephants stampede.*

stance [noun: **stances**]
1 the way someone stands

2 an attitude or set of opinions: *What's the company's stance on working from home?*

stand [verb: **stands, standing, stood**]
1 to be upright on your feet, not sitting or lying: *I was so tired I could barely stand.*
2 to get up onto your feet: *The whole class used to stand when a teacher came into the room.* • *Stand up and let me look at you.*
3 to be or stay in a particular position: *The train stood outside Waterloo for nearly an hour.* • *Durham stands on the River Wear.*
4 to continue to apply or be valid: *The judge ordered that the sentence should stand.*
5 to bear: *I can't stand her brother, Mark.* • *Marie couldn't stand hearing her parents arguing any more.*
6 if particular letters **stand for** particular words, they are short for them: *UN stands for United Nations.*
7 if you **stand in for someone**, you take their place for a short time: *Emma will stand in for Mrs Harris while she is on holiday.*
8 if you **stand up for someone**, you defend or support them: *My big sister, Fran, always stood up for me.*
9 if you **stand up to someone**, you fight back when they attack you: *You've got to learn to stand up to bullies.*
[noun: **stands**]
1 something that an object stands on: *a television stand* • *a large mirror on a stand*
2 rows of seats where people sit to watch a game or event: *Spectators were cheering from the stands.*
3 someone's opinion about something: *a tough stand on crime*

standard [noun: **standards**]
1 a level that you can judge things against: *a restaurant with very high standards*
2 an official rule for measuring things: *The kilogram is the international standard of weight.*
[adjective] normal or usual: *the standard charge for postage*
• **standardize** or **standardise** [verb: **standardizes, standardizing, standardized**] to make or keep things all the same shape or size as it is more convenient: *We're trying to standardize the filing system.*

Ss

standard lamp [noun: **standard lamps**] a lamp on a tall base that stands on the floor

standby [noun]

1 something or someone that is available to be used when they are needed: *I always keep some long-life milk as a standby.*

2 if someone or something is **on standby**, they are ready to travel or ready to do something if needed

standing order [noun: **standing orders**] an instruction that you give to your bank to tell them to regularly pay a particular amount of money from your account to someone else

standstill [noun] a complete stop: *Icy roads brought traffic to a standstill.*

stank [verb] a way of changing the verb **stink** to make a past tense: *The dirty fish tank really stank.*

staple [staple: **staples**] a type of food or product that you use a lot of: *There's a village shop for staples such as milk and butter.*
[adjective] a staple food or product is one of the most basic and important ones: *Their staple diet is rice.*

staple [noun: **staples**] a piece of wire that you force through papers to fasten them together: *a box of staples*
[verb: **staples, stapling, stapled**] to fasten papers together with a staple
♦ **stapler** [noun: **staplers**] a small tool for stapling papers together

star [noun: **stars**]

1 a mass of burning gas in the sky that you can see at night as a point of light

2 a shape with five or six points

3 a famous actor, singer or performer: *a film star* • *a pop star*
[adjective] involving or typical of a famous actor, singer or performer: *a star performance*
[verb: **stars, starring, starred**]

1 if an actor stars in something, he or she plays one of the main parts in it: *Tom Cruise is to star in the sequel.*

2 if a film or play stars someone, they have one of the main parts in it: *the new film starring Kate Winslet*
➡ **stardom, starry**

starboard [adjective] the starboard side of a ship or aircraft is the right side when you are facing the front. Look up and compare **port**

starch [noun: **starches**]

1 a white carbohydrate found in foods such as potatoes, pasta and bread

2 a powder used to make clothes stiff
♦ **starchy** [adjective] containing a lot of starch

stardom [noun] being a famous performer: *She shot to stardom after appearing on a TV talent show.*

stare [verb: **stares, staring, stared**] to look at someone or something for a long time: *Gemma spends her days staring out of the window.* • *What are you staring at?*
[noun: **stares**] a fixed look

starfish [noun: **starfishes**] a sea creature with five points or arms

stark [adjective: **starker, starkest**]

1 plain and bare: *a stark, barren landscape*

2 complete: *The cool indoors was in stark contrast to the heat outside.*
[adverb] if someone is **stark naked**, they are not wearing any clothes at all
♦ **starkly** [adverb] in a stark way: *a starkly furnished room* • *The figures starkly show the financial problems we are facing.*

starling [noun: **starlings**] a common bird with dark, shiny feathers

starry [adjective: **starrier, starriest**] full of stars or shining like stars: *a starry sky* • *starry eyes*

start [verb: **starts, starting, started**]

1 to begin: *Suddenly, a bird started to sing.* • *What time did you start working this morning?* • *She started her own business.*

2 to make a machine begin to work: *Start the car and drive off.*

3 to jump because you are surprised: *The thunder made me start.*
[noun: **starts**]

1 the beginning: *Right from the start, I knew I'd be happy here.* • *The runners lined up for the start of the race.*

2 a sudden movement or shock: *Her news gave me quite a start.*

3 in a race or chase, the advantage of starting earlier or further forward than others: *We gave Amy a bit of a start as she's the youngest.*
♦ **starter** [noun: **starters**]

Ss

1 the first course of a meal: *We had soup as a starter.*

2 an electric device that starts a car's engine. It is also called a **starter motor**

startle [verb: **startles, startling, startled**] to give someone a shock or surprise: *Oh, you startled me!*

♦ **startling** [adjective] shocking because unusual or unexpected: *startling news*

starvation [noun] when people are very hungry and have not got enough to eat: *Thousands are dying of starvation every year.*

starve [verb: **starves, starving, starved**]

1 to die or suffer because you have not got enough to eat: *If we don't get food aid into the country, these people are going to starve to death.*

2 to starve someone is to not give them enough to eat: *They were accused of starving their prisoners.*

3 an informal way of saying you are very hungry: *What's for supper? I'm starving.*

state [noun: **states**]

1 the condition that someone or something is in: *people in a poor state of health* • *She's always complaining about the state of our public transport.*

2 a government or a country: *The state should provide for the sick and elderly.*

3 a part of a country that has its own government: *The law differs from state to state in America.*

4 if someone is in a state, they are upset and worried: *There's no point getting in a state about things.*

[verb: **states, stating, stated**] to say or write something: *The letter clearly states that you must bring some identification with you.*

stately [adjective] dignified and impressive: *a stately procession of lords*

stately home [noun: **stately homes**] a large country house where a noble family lived, especially one that people can pay to look round

statement [noun: **statements**]

1 something that you say or write: *The police asked me to make a written statement of what I saw.*

2 a piece of paper that the bank sends you

that shows how much money you have in your account and what you have spent

statesman [noun: **statesmen**] an important political leader

static [adjective] not moving or changing: *Temperatures should stay static for the next few days.*

[noun] tiny sparks of electricity caused by rubbing two surfaces together: *You get static when you comb your hair with a plastic comb.*

station [noun: **stations**]

1 a building where trains, buses, or coaches stop to let people get on or off

2 a place where police officers, fire officers, or ambulance drivers work: *a police station*

3 a radio or television station is a company which makes or broadcasts programmes

[verb: **stations, stationing, stationed**] to put someone in a particular position: *They stationed a guard at each door.*

♦ **stationary** [adjective] not moving: *a stationary vehicle*

stationery [noun] paper, pens, crayons, and other things you use to write or draw with

statistical [adjective] to do with statistics: *All the statistical evidence supports our case.*

♦ **statistically** [adverb] using statistics: *His views have not been statistically proven.*

statistics [plural noun] figures and facts about a particular subject: *Statistics show that more babies were born this year than last year.*

statue [noun: **statues**] a figure of a person or animal carved out of stone, metal or wood: *a statue of Napoleon*

stature [noun]

1 size or height: *He was small in stature but had a strong personality.*

2 importance: *a politician of great stature*

status [noun: **statuses**] someone's position or rank in a society: *She achieved high status in her work.*

statutory [adjective] required or controlled by law: *statutory employment rights*

staunch [adjective: **stauncher, staunchest**] loyal and faithful: *a staunch supporter of the team*

stave [noun: **staves**] the set of spaced lines that musical notes are written on

[verb: **staves, staving, staved**] if you **stave**

Ss

something off, you delay it happening: *We had a packet of crisps to stave off our hunger.*

stay [verb: **stays, staying, stayed**]
1 to remain in a place: *I stayed in Padua for three years.* • *Would you like to stay for dinner?*
2 to continue to be in a particular condition: *She tried to stay calm as they waited.*
[noun: **stays**] time spent in a place: *The trip includes an overnight stay in Bangkok.*

STD [abbreviation: **STDs**] short for **sexually transmitted disease**

steadfast [adjective] firm and never changing: *a steadfast friend*

steadily [adverb] in a continuous and gradual way: *His performance has improved steadily.*

steady [adjective: **steadier, steadiest**]
1 firm and not wobbling or shaking: *This table isn't very steady.*
2 happening in a continuous and gradual way: *We're making steady progress.*
[verb: **steadies, steadying, steadied**]
1 to steady something is to stop it from moving or wobbling: *She tried to steady the tray.*
2 to steady is to stop moving or changing: *House prices have begun to steady.*
3 if you do something to **steady your nerves**, you do it to make yourself feel calmer: *I took several deep breaths to steady my nerves.*

steak [noun: **steaks**]
1 a steak is a thick slice of meat or fish: *a fillet steak* • *two tuna steaks*
2 steak is good quality beef

steal [verb: **steals, stealing, stole, stolen**]
1 to take something without the owner's permission: *The thieves stole money and jewellery.* • *It's wrong to steal.*
2 to move quietly: *She stole out to the garden.*

stealth [noun] action or movement that is secret or quiet: *the stealth of a hungry lion*
♦ **stealthy** [adjective: **stealthier, stealthiest**] done secretly or quietly: *stealthy footsteps*

steam [noun]
1 the clouds of tiny drops of liquid that rise from boiling water
2 power produced by steam: *Diesel fuel replaced steam on the railways.*

[verb: **steams, steaming, steamed**]
1 to give off steam: *A kettle was steaming on the stove.*
2 to move by means of steam: *The ship steamed across the bay.*
3 to steam food is to cook it using steam: *steamed vegetables*
4 to **steam up** is to become covered with steam: *My glasses steamed up and I couldn't see a thing.*

steam engine [noun: **steam engines**] an engine, especially a railway engine, that is driven by steam

steamer [noun: **steamers**] a ship that is driven by steam

steamroller [noun: **steamrollers**] a type of vehicle which has large, heavy wheels and is used to flatten the surface of newly-made roads

steel [noun] a very hard metal that is a mixture of iron and carbon. Steel is used to make tools, vehicles and many other things
[adjective] made of steel: *steel knives*
[verb: **steels, steeling, steeled**] if you **steel yourself**, you prepare yourself for something unpleasant: *She steeled herself for the test results.*
♦ **steely** [adjective: **steelier, steeliest**] hard or cold or strong like steel: *a steely gaze*

steep [adjective: **steeper, steepest**] a steep hill or slope rises sharply: *It was a steep climb.* • *The path was too steep for me to cycle up.*

steeple [noun: **steeples**] a tall tower that comes to a point, especially one that is part of a church

steeplechase [noun: **steeplechases**] a race for horses or people in which obstacles must be jumped

steer [verb: **steers, steering, steered**] to steer a vehicle is to control the direction it is going in: *He steered the car through the narrow streets.* • *The captain steered out of the harbour.*

steering wheel [noun: **steering wheels**] the wheel inside a vehicle that the driver uses to control the direction it is moving in

stem [noun: **stems**]
1 the part of a plant from which the leaves and flowers grow

Ss

2 the narrow part of various objects, for example of a wine glass

[verb: **stems, stemming, stemmed**]

1 to stem something is to stop it: *He used his scarf to stem the flow of blood.*

2 to **stem from** something is to come from it or be caused by it: *Her problems stem from childhood.*

stench [noun: **stenches**] a strong bad smell: *the stench of stale cigarette smoke*

stencil [noun: **stencils**]

1 a piece of paper, metal or plastic with pieces cut out of it, which is coloured or painted over to produce a design on a surface

2 a design produced in this way

[verb: **stencils, stencilling, stencilled**] to use a stencil or stencils to decorate a surface: *We decided to paint the walls white then stencil them.* • *Why don't you stencil some flowers round the doorway?*

step [noun: **steps**]

1 the action of lifting your foot off the ground and putting in down again in walking, running or dancing: *He took a step forward.*

2 the sound made by someone's foot coming down on the ground when they walk or run: *I'm sure I heard steps outside.*

3 a particular movement of the feet, for example in dancing: *Try to learn these simple steps.*

4 the flat part of a stair that you put your foot on when going up or down: *The postman left the parcel on the front step.*

5 one of a series of actions involved in doing or achieving something: *the first step to becoming an actor* • *I shall take steps to prevent this happening again.*

[verb: **steps, stepping, stepped**]

1 to step is to take a step: *He opened the door and stepped out.*

2 to step is also to walk: *Please step this way.*

3 to **step something up** is to increase it: *Brian stepped up his speed and won the race.*

step- [prefix] if a word starts with **step-**, it shows that people are related not by blood but by a second marriage. For example, your *stepfather* is a man who is married to your mother but is not your own father

stepfather [noun: **stepfathers**] your stepfather is a man who is married to your mother but is not your own father

stepladder [noun: **stepladders**] a small ladder that can be folded up

stepmother [noun: **stepmothers**] your stepmother is a woman who is married to your father but is not your own mother

stepping-stone [noun: **stepping-stones**]

1 a stone that rises above the surface of water and can be used for crossing over to the other side of a stream or river

2 anything that helps you make progress: *Think of your Saturday job as a stepping-stone to better things.*

stereo [adjective] short for **stereophonic**: *stereo sound*

[noun: **stereos**] a CD, cassette or record player which plays the sound through two speakers

stereophonic [adjective] a stereophonic system uses two speakers so that the listener feels surrounded by sound

sterile [adjective]

1 not able to produce babies, seeds or crops: *sterile land*

2 completely clean and free from germs: *A surgeon's instruments must be sterile.*

♦ **sterility** [noun] being sterile: *the sterility of the soil*

sterilization or **sterilisation** [noun: **sterilizations**]

1 the treatment of food or surgical instruments in order to destroy germs

2 an operation that is carried out on people or animals so that they cannot have babies

♦ **sterilize** or **sterilise** [verb: **sterilizes, sterilizing, sterilized**]

1 to make something completely free from germs, for example by boiling it in water

2 to make a person or animal sterile by means of an operation

sterling [noun] the money used in Great Britain: *She changed her euros into sterling.* [adjective] of good quality: *He has done some sterling work.*

stern[1] [noun: **sterns**] the back part of a ship

stern[2] [adjective: **sterner, sternest**]

1 looking or sounding angry, serious or unfriendly: *He looked rather stern.* • *a stern voice*

2 harsh or severe: *a stern prison sentence*
• **sternly** [adverb] in a stern way

steroid [noun: **steroids**] a drug that doctors give people to treat swelling, or one that some people take illegally to improve their sports performance

stethoscope [noun: **stethoscopes**] an instrument used by a doctor to listen to your heartbeat or breathing

stew [verb: **stews, stewing, stewed**] to stew something is to cook it by boiling it slowly: *First she stewed the apples.*

[noun: **stews**] a mixture of vegetables, or meat and vegetables, cooked slowly together in liquid in a pan: *beef stew and dumplings*

steward [noun: **stewards**]
1 a man whose job is to look after passengers on an aircraft or a ship
2 a person who is an official at events such as races and concerts

stewardess [noun: **stewardesses**] an old-fashioned word for a woman whose job is to look after passengers on an aircraft or a ship

stick[1] [noun: **sticks**]
1 a branch or twig from a tree: *We searched for sticks to make a fire.*
2 a long thin piece of wood shaped for a special purpose: *a walking-stick* • *a hockey-stick* • *a drumstick*
3 a long piece of something: *a stick of rhubarb* • *a stick of rock*

stick[2] [verb: **sticks, sticking, stuck**]
1 to stick something in or into something is to push it in: *Stop sticking your elbows into me!* • *Stick the knife in your belt.*
2 to stick something is to fix it with something like glue: *Never mind, we can always stick the pieces back together.*
3 to stick is to become fixed and unable to move: *The car stuck in the mud.*
4 to stick to something is to become attached firmly to it: *These seeds stick to your clothes.*
5 to stick to something such as a decision is to keep it: *We've decided to stick to our original plan.*
6 if something **sticks out**, it pushes out and stays there: *A nail stuck out from the plank.*
7 if someone or something **sticks out**, you notice them immediately: *Her bright red hair*

makes her stick out in a crowd.
8 to **stick up for someone** is to defend them: *Maya sticks up for her best friend even when she is wrong.*
➡ **sticky**

sticker [noun: **stickers**] a label or sign with a design or message, for sticking on something

stick insect [noun: **stick insects**] an insect with a long thin body and legs, that look like twigs

sticky [adjective: **stickier, stickiest**]
1 designed or likely to stick to another surface: *Mend the book with some sticky tape.* • *sticky fingers*
2 difficult: *They found themselves in a sticky situation.*

stiff [adjective: **stiffer, stiffest**]
1 difficult to bend or move: *stiff cardboard* • *a stiff neck* • *I can't turn the tap on — it's too stiff.*
2 difficult to do: *a stiff test*
3 a stiff wind is very strong: *a stiff breeze*
4 not relaxed or friendly: *She replied with stiff politeness.*
• **stiffen** [verb: **stiffens, stiffening, stiffened**]
1 to stiffen something is to make it stiff: *stiffen cotton with starch*
2 to stiffen is to become stiff: *She suddenly stiffened in fright.*
• **stiffly** [adverb] in a stiff way: *Grandad got up stiffly from his chair.* • *'No thank you,' she replied stiffly.*
• **stiffness** [noun] being stiff

stifle [verb: **stifles, stifling, stifled**]
1 to be stifled is to be prevented from breathing: *stifled by the fumes*
2 to stifle something is to keep it back: *She stifled a giggle.*
• **stifling** [adjective] very hot and stuffy: *stifling heat*

stigma [noun: **stigmas**] shame or disgrace: *There used to be a lot of stigma attached to being unemployed.*

stile [noun: **stiles**] a step or a set of steps for climbing over a wall or fence

still [adjective: **stiller, stillest**]
1 without movement or noise: *Keep still while I brush your hair!* • *The city seems very still in the early morning.*

Ss

2 a still drink is not fizzy: *still lemonade* [adverb]

1 up to the present time or the time mentioned: *Are you still working for the same company?* • *By Sunday she still hadn't replied to the invitation.*

2 even so, nevertheless: *It's difficult but we must still try.*

3 even: *Still more people were arriving.*

[verb: **stills, stilling, stilled**]

1 to still something is to make it calm or quiet: *It was time to still the rumours.*

2 to still is to become calm or quiet: *Darkness fell and the forest stilled.*

♦ **stillness** [noun] being still: *the stillness of early morning*

stilts [plural noun]

1 a pair of poles with supports for your feet, that you can stand on and walk about

2 tall poles to support a house built over water

stimulant [noun: **stimulants**] something, such as a drug or medicine, that makes you feel more active: *Caffeine and nicotine are stimulants.*

stimulate [verb: **stimulates, stimulated, stimulating**]

1 to stimulate someone is to encourage or excite them: *After seeing the concert, he was stimulated to take up the violin again.*

2 to stimulate something is to make it more active: *changes designed to stimulate growth*

♦ **stimulation** [noun] being stimulated: *stimulation of the senses*

♦ **stimulus** [noun: **stimuli**] something that makes a living thing do something: *Light is the stimulus that causes a flower to open.*

sting [noun: **stings**]

1 the part of some animals and plants, such as the wasp or nettle, which can prick your skin and cause pain or irritation: *Bees usually leave their stings in the wound.*

2 the wound, swelling or pain caused by a sting: *Use vinegar to soothe a wasp sting.*

[verb: **stings, stinging, stung**]

1 if an insect or plant stings you, they prick your skin and put poison into the wound: *The child was badly stung by nettles.* • *Do these insects sting?*

2 if something stings, it is painful: *The shampoo made his eyes sting.*

stingy [adjective: **stingier, stingiest**] mean, not generous: *A very stingy person is sometimes called a Scrooge.*

stink [noun: **stinks**] a bad smell: *the stink of rotting fish*

[verb: **stinks, stinking, stank** or **stunk, stunk**] to have a bad smell: *The house stinks of cats.*

stir [verb: **stirs, stirring, stirred**]

1 to stir something is to mix it with a circular movement: *He put sugar in his tea and stirred it.*

2 to stir is to move slightly: *The baby stirred in its sleep.*

3 to stir something is to make it move slightly: *The breeze stirred her hair.*

4 to **stir something up** is to cause trouble, problems or arguments: *You're always trying to stir up trouble.*

[noun: **stirs**]

1 an act of stirring: *Now give the paint a stir.*

2 a fuss: *Their arrival caused quite a stir.*

stir-fry [verb: **stir-fries, stir-frying, stir-fried**] to cook small pieces of food very quickly in hot oil in a wok or large pan: *stir-fried vegetables*

[noun: **stir-fries**] a meal made by stir-frying vegetables and sometimes meat

stirring [adjective] exciting: *stirring tales of knights and their heroic deeds*

stirrup [noun: **stirrups**] a metal loop hanging from a horse's saddle, that you put your foot in when riding

stitch [noun: **stitches**]

1 the loop you make in thread or wool, using a needle, when you are sewing or knitting: *She sewed the hem with small neat stitches.*

2 a sharp pain in your side, especially when you are running

[verb: **stitches, stitching, stitched**] to sew: *I stitched the button on to my coat.*

stoat [noun: **stoats**] a small fierce animal similar to a weasel.

stock [noun: **stocks**]

1 a store of goods, for example in a shop or warehouse: *Buy now while stocks last!*

2 stock is the animals of a farm: *The farmer goes to market to buy more stock.*

3 stocks are shares in companies that people can buy through a stock exchange
4 liquid in which meat or vegetables have been cooked, used for example for making soup: *chicken stock*
5 a type of sweet-smelling garden flower
6 a person's stock is their family origins: *of peasant stock*
[verb: **stocks, stocking, stocked**]
1 to stock something is to keep a supply of it for sale: *Most supermarkets now stock organic products.*
2 to stock a place with something is to fill it or supply it with something: *He stocked the fridge with plenty of beers.*

stockade [noun: **stockades**] a fence of strong posts put up round an area or building to protect or defend it

stock car [noun: **stock cars**] a car that has been strengthened to take part in a type of racing where cars deliberately collide with each other

stock exchange [noun: **stock exchanges**] a place where stocks and shares in companies are bought and sold

stocking [noun: **stockings**] a close-fitting covering for the leg and foot, made of fine nylon and worn by women

stockpile [noun: **stockpiles**] a large store of something: *She keeps a stockpile of flour in her cupboard.*
[verb: **stockpiles, stockpiling, stockpiled**]
to stockpile something is to build up a store of it: *There are reports that weapons are being stockpiled.*

stocktaking [noun] the process of counting all the goods in a shop or factory at a particular time: *The shop is closed for stocktaking.*

stocky [adjective: **stockier, stockiest**] a stocky person is short and strongly built

stodgy [adjective: **stodgier, stodgiest**]
1 stodgy food is heavy and filling: *a stodgy pudding*
2 a stodgy book or person is dull and boring

stoke [verb: **stokes, stoking, stoked**] to stoke a fire is to put coal, wood or other fuel on it

stole [noun: **stoles**] a length of material, such as fur or silk, worn by women around their shoulders

stole [verb] a way of changing the verb **steal** to make a past tense: *How can you be sure that she stole the money?*

stomach [noun: **stomachs**]
1 the part inside your body where food goes when it is swallowed, and where it is digested
2 courage: *I don't have the stomach for dangerous sports.*
[verb: **stomachs, stomaching, stomached**]
to bear or put up with: *I can't stomach TV programmes that show real operations.*

stomp [verb: **stomps, stomping, stomped**]
to walk heavily and noisily: *He stomped off to his room in a temper.*

stone [noun: **stones** or **stone**]
1 stone is the hard material that rocks are made of: *a house built of stone*
2 a stone is a piece of this: *The boys were throwing stones into the water.*
3 a piece of this shaped for a special purpose, for example a tombstone or paving stones
4 a gem or jewel: *diamonds, rubies and other stones*
5 the hard shell around the seed in some fruits, for example peaches and cherries
6 a measure of weight equal to 14 pounds or 6.35 kilograms: *I weigh twelve stone.*
[verb: **stones, stoning, stoned**]
1 to stone someone is to throw stones at them
2 to stone fruit is to take the stones out of it
[adjective] made of stone: *stone tools*
♦ **stony** [adjective: **stonier, stoniest**]
1 hard like stone
2 full of, or covered with, stones: *a stony beach*
3 hard and cold in manner: *He gave me a stony stare.*

(i) The plural of the noun is **stones**, except when it means a measure of weight. Then the plural **stone** is used.

stood [verb] a way of changing the verb **stand** to make a past tense. It can be used with or without a helping verb: *She stood quietly in the corner.* • *He had stood there all day.*

stool [noun: **stools**]
1 a seat without a back
2 a word sometimes used by doctors for the

Ss

solid waste that comes out of your bottom: *The doctor asked me to give a stool sample.*

stoop [verb: **stoops, stooping, stooped**]
1 to bend your body forward and downward: *The doorway was so low that she had to stoop to get through it.*
2 to **stoop to** doing something is to be wicked or bad enough to do it: *Surely he wouldn't stoop to stealing.*
[noun: **stoops**] a forward bend of your body: *The old man walked with a stoop.*

stop [verb: **stops, stopping, stopped**]
1 to stop is to come to a halt or come to an end: *The car stopped in front of our house.* • *The rain stopped.*
2 to stop something is to bring it to a halt or bring it to an end: *Stop the car now!* • *Please stop this nonsense.*
3 to stop doing something is to finish doing it or not do it any longer: *We stopped talking and listened.*
4 to stop someone doing something is to prevent them from doing it: *Can't you stop her working so hard?*
5 to stop something or **stop something up** is to block it or close it up: *He stopped his ears with his hands.* • *Stop up the hole with newspaper.*
[noun: **stops**]
1 the act of stopping: *We made two stops on our journey.*
2 a place where something, such as a bus, stops
3 a full stop: *All sentences should end with a stop.*

stopcock [noun: **stopcocks**] a tap that you turn to stop the flow of water or gas into a pipe

stoppage [noun: **stoppages**]
1 a period when workers refuse to work because they are angry about something
2 a blockage in a narrow part of something

stopper [noun: **stoppers**] something, such as a cork, that is put into the neck of a bottle or jar to close it

stop press [noun] the most recent news, put into a newspaper after printing has started

stopwatch [noun: **stopwatches**] a watch that can be stopped and started, used for timing races

storage [noun]
1 the storing of something: *the storage of goods*
2 if you put something in storage, you pay for it to be stored somewhere

store [noun: **stores**]
1 a supply of goods from which things are taken as they are needed: *Squirrels keep a store of food.*
2 a place where things are kept: *a store for books*
3 a shop: *the village store* • *a department store*
[verb: **stores, storing, stored**] to store something is to keep it somewhere for use in the future: *Store the wine in a cool dry place.*

store card [noun: **store cards**] a credit card that you can only use in one chain of shops

storey [noun: **storeys**] one of the floors or levels in a building: *a house with two storeys*

stork [noun: **storks**] a wading bird with a long bill, neck and legs

storm [noun: **storms**]
1 a sudden burst of bad weather with strong winds, rain or snow, and sometimes thunder and lightning
2 a violent outburst: *a storm of protests* • *a storm of applause*
[verb: **storms, storming, stormed**]
1 to storm is to shout or move in an angry way: *She stormed out of the room.* • *'How dare you!' he stormed.*
2 to storm a place is to attack it suddenly and violently in order to capture it: *Troops stormed the embassy.*

• **stormy** [adjective: **stormier, stormiest**]
1 stormy weather is weather with strong winds, rain or snow, and sometimes thunder and lightning
2 full of anger: *a stormy meeting* • *a stormy relationship*

story [noun: **stories**] a description of an event or events, which can be real or invented: *The book is the story of his life.* • *She loves to write adventure stories.*

stout [adjective: **stouter, stoutest**]
1 fat: *a rather stout middle-aged man*
2 brave: *stout resistance*
3 thick and strong: *stout walking-boots*

* **stoutly** [adverb] in a stout way
* **stoutness** [noun] being stout

stove [noun: **stoves**] a device for cooking or for heating a room: *a gas stove*

stow [verb: **stows, stowing, stowed**]
1 to stow something is to pack it or put it away: *The sailor stowed his belongings in his locker.*
2 to **stow away** is to hide yourself on a vehicle such as a ship or aeroplane before its departure so that you can travel without paying

stowaway [noun: **stowaways**] a person who hides on a ship or aircraft so that they can travel without paying

straddle [verb: **straddles, straddling, straddled**] to straddle something is to stand or sit with one leg on each side of it

straggle [verb: **straggles, straggling, straggled**] to walk too slowly to keep up with others: *Some of the younger children were straggling behind.*
* **straggler** [noun: **stragglers**] a person who walks too slowly and gets left behind the main group
* **straggly** [adjective: **stragglier, straggliest**] growing untidily: *straggly hair*

straight [adjective: **straighter, straightest**]
1 not bent, curved or curly: *a straight line* • *straight hair*
2 honest: *Give me a straight answer!*
3 in the proper position, not crooked: *That picture isn't straight.*
4 tidy, sorted out: *I'll never get this room straight* • *Now let's get the facts straight!*
5 not smiling or laughing: *You should keep a straight face when you tell a joke.*
[adverb]
1 in a straight line, without changing direction: *Turn right, then go straight on.*
2 at once, without any delay: *I came straight here.*
3 honestly: *You're not playing straight.*
4 straight away means 'immediately': *Could you sign this for me straight away?*
* **straighten** [verb: **straightens, straightening, straightened**]
1 to straighten is to become straight: *The road curved then straightened.*

2 to straighten something is to make it become straight: *He straightened his tie.*

straightforward [adjective]
1 easy: *a straightforward task*
2 honest: *a nice straightforward boy*

strain [verb: **strains, straining, strained**]
1 to strain a muscle or other part of your body is to injure it through too much use: *You'll strain your eyes reading in the dark.*
2 to strain to do something is to make a great effort to do it: *He strained to reach the rope.*
3 to strain something is to force it to be used beyond a normal or acceptable limit: *Your constant demands are straining my patience.*
4 to strain a mixture is to separate the liquid from it by passing it through a sieve: *Now strain the water off the vegetables.*
[noun: **strains**]
1 a strain is an injury to a muscle or other part of your body caused by straining it: *eye strain*
2 strain is the bad effects on your mind and body of too much work and worry: *suffering from strain*
3 too great a demand on something: *You children are a strain on my patience!*
* **strainer** [noun: **strainers**] a sieve for separating liquids from solids: *a tea-strainer*

strait [noun: **straits**]
1 a narrow strip of sea between two pieces of land: *the Straits of Gibraltar*
2 if someone or something is **in dire straits**, they are in an extremely bad or difficult situation

strand [noun: **strands**] a length of something soft and fine, for example hair or thread

stranded [adjective]
1 a ship is stranded if it is stuck on sand or rocks: *The ships were stranded in shallow water.*
2 a person is stranded if they are left helpless: *She was left stranded without money or passport.*

strange [adjective: **stranger, strangest**]
1 unusual or odd: *a strange noise coming from the engine*
2 not familiar, not known or seen before: *a strange land*
* **strangely** [adverb] in a strange way: *She looked at me strangely.*

Ss

♦ **strangeness** [noun] being strange: *the strangeness of the situation*

♦ **stranger** [noun: **strangers**]
1 a person you do not know: *Children should never talk to strangers.*
2 a person who is in a place they do not know: *I'm afraid I don't know where the station is. I'm a stranger here myself.*

strangle [verb: **strangles, strangling, strangled**] to strangle someone is to kill them by squeezing their throat tightly

strap [noun: **straps**] a long narrow piece of leather or cloth used to hold things, fasten things or hang things on: *a watch-strap • a bag with a shoulder strap*
[verb: **straps, strapping, strapped**] to strap something is to fasten it with a strap: *I usually strap my bag to my bike.*

strategy [noun: **strategies**] planning that is designed to achieve something

straw [noun: **straws**]
1 straw is dried stalks of grain: *The cows need fresh straw.*
2 a straw is a thin tube, usually made of plastic, for sucking up a drink
[adjective] made of straw: *a straw hat*

strawberry [noun: **strawberries**] a soft red fruit with many tiny seeds on its skin

stray [verb: **strays, straying, strayed**] to wander or get lost: *Be careful not to stray from the path. • The farmer was searching for some sheep that had strayed.*
[adjective]
1 wandering or lost: *stray dogs*
2 happening here and there, scattered: *The sky was clear except for a few stray clouds.*
[noun: **strays**] a cat or dog that has no home

streak [noun: **streaks**]
1 a long thin line or mark: *hair with blonde streaks • dirty streaks on the window • a streak of lightning*
2 a trace of something that can be seen in a person: *He has a cowardly streak.*
[verb: **streaks, streaking, streaked**]
1 to streak something is to mark it with streaks: *tears streaking her face*
2 to streak is to move very fast: *The runner streaked round the race track.*

♦ **streaked** [adjective] having streaks: *a beard streaked with grey*

♦ **streaky** [adjective: **streakier, streakiest**] marked with streaks: *Her face was all streaky with crying.*

stream [noun: **streams**]
1 a very narrow river
2 a flow of something: *streams of people • a stream of traffic*
[verb: **streams, streaming, streamed**] to flow: *Tears streamed down her face • The workers streamed out of the factory gates.*

♦ **streamer** [noun: **streamers**] a long narrow strip of paper or ribbon, used as a decoration

streamline [verb: **streamlines, streamlining, streamlined**]
1 to streamline something such as a vehicle is to shape it in such a way that it will cut through air or water as easily as possible
2 to streamline something is to make it more efficient, especially by making it simpler: *The company streamlined its production methods.*

street [noun: **streets**] a road with buildings such as houses and shops on one or both sides: *I live at 32 Montgomery Street. • the main shopping street*

strength [noun: **strengths**]
1 strength is being strong: *He didn't have the strength to lift the box.*
2 a person's strengths are the good things about them: *Her greatest strength is her sense of humour.*

♦ **strengthen** [verb: **strengthens, strengthening, strengthened**]
1 to strengthen something is to make it strong or stronger: *He did exercises to strengthen his muscles.*
2 to strengthen is to become strong or stronger: *The wind strengthened.*

strenuous [adjective] needing or using a lot of effort or energy: *Squash is a strenuous game. • The plans met strenuous resistance.*

stress [noun: **stresses**]
1 a physical force that may bend or break something: *metal that bends under stress*
2 stress is the effect on your mind or body of working or worrying too much: *headaches caused by stress*

3 special importance that is attached to something: *The General laid particular stress on the need for secrecy.*

4 extra weight that is put on a part of a word: *In the word 'bedroom' the stress is on 'bed'.*

[verb: **stresses, stressing, stressed**]

1 to stress someone is to make them suffer stress: *Many of the pressures of everyday life can stress us.*

2 to stress something is to place special importance on it: *Her speech stressed the need for change.*

3 to stress part of a word is to place extra weight on it: *When 'object' is a noun you stress the 'ob'.*

stressful [adjective] causing you to feel nervous, worried and anxious: *Starting a new job can be stressful.*

stretch [verb: **stretches, stretching, stretched**]

1 to stretch something is to make it longer or wider, especially by pulling: *Stretch this rope between the two posts.*

2 to stretch is to become longer or wider: *This material stretches.*

3 to stretch from one place to another is to cover the distance between them: *The mountains stretch from the north to the south of the country.*

[noun: **stretches**]

1 the action of stretching: *I always have a good stretch when I get out of bed.*

2 a length in distance or time: *a dangerous stretch of road* • *a three-year stretch*

♦ **stretcher** [noun: **stretchers**] a light folding bed with handles for carrying a sick or wounded person

♦ **stretchy** [adjective: **stretchier, stretchiest**] able to stretch: *stretchy fabric*

strew [verb: **strews, strewing, strewed, strewn**] to scatter things untidily: *She has strewn paper all over the floor.* • *The ground was strewn with rubbish.*

strict [adjective: **stricter, strictest**]

1 someone who is strict expects other people to obey rules: *a strict teacher*

2 something that is strict is meant to be obeyed: *strict rules* • *under strict orders*

3 exact: *the strict sense of the word*

stride [verb: **strides, striding, strode, stridden**] to walk with long steps: *He strode up the path.*

[noun: **strides**]

1 a long step you take when you walk

2 if you **get into your stride**, you start to feel comfortable doing something and can then do it continuously and well

3 if you **take something in your stride**, you cope with it very well even if it is difficult or unpleasant: *He's taken all his health problems in his stride.*

strife [noun] fighting or quarrelling

strike [verb: **strikes, striking, struck**]

1 to strike someone or something is to hit them or it: *He struck me in the face with his fist.* • *My head struck the table.*

2 to strike is to attack: *The enemy troops struck at dawn.*

3 to strike a match is to light it

4 to strike is to produce a strong clear sound: *The clock struck three.*

5 something strikes you when it suddenly comes into your mind or when it impresses you: *It suddenly struck me that I was completely wrong.* • *He was struck by her beauty.*

6 workers strike when they stop work as a protest against something or in an attempt to get something: *The men were striking for higher wages.*

7 to strike oil or gold is to discover it

[noun: **strikes**]

1 the stopping of work as a protest or in an attempt to get something: *The strike lasted for ten days.*

2 a sudden attack, especially a military one: *repeated air strikes*

3 a discovery of oil or gold

♦ **striker** [noun: **strikers**]

1 a worker who strikes

2 in football, a player whose job is to try to score goals

♦ **striking** [adjective] if you find something striking, you notice it or are impressed by it: *a striking resemblance* • *striking beauty*

Strimmer [noun] an electrical garden tool for trimming long grass or grass at the edge of a lawn. This word is a trademark

string [noun: **strings**]

Ss

1 string is thick thread used for tying things: *a ball of string*

2 the strings of a musical instrument, such as a guitar, are the pieces of wire or other material that are stretched across it

3 a string of things is a number of things coming one after the other: *a string of disasters*

[verb: **strings, stringing, strung**]

1 to string something is to tie it and hang it with string: *Coloured lights were strung across the ceiling.*

2 to string something such as beads is to put them on a string: *She took the pearls to a jeweller to be strung.*

3 to string a musical instrument is to put strings on it

◆ **stringy** [adjective: **stringier, stringiest**]

1 something that is stringy is long and thin and looks like string: *stringy hair*

2 meat that is stringy is full of tough chewy bits

strip [noun: **strips**]

1 a long narrow piece: *a strip of paper*

2 an outfit worn by a sports team: *a red football strip*

strip[2] [verb: **strips, stripping, stripped**]

1 to strip something is to take the covering off it: *I always strip the beds on Mondays.*

2 to strip is to undress: *He stripped and dived into the water.*

3 to strip someone of something is to take it away from them: *The officer was stripped of his rank.*

stripe [noun: **stripes**] a band of colour: *a blue suit with thin white stripes*

◆ **striped** [adjective] having stripes: *striped wallpaper*

◆ **stripy** [adjective: **stripier, stripiest**] having stripes: *a stripy T-shirt*

strive [verb: **strives, striving, strove, striven**] to try very hard: *We strive very hard to please our customers.*

strobe [noun: **strobes**] a light that flashes rapidly

strode [verb] a way of changing the verb **stride** to make a past tense: *He strode up the hill.*

stroke [noun: **strokes**]

1 a movement or hit made by swinging your arm or arms while holding an oar, a golf club, a

tennis racket, or a long-handled weapon: *He felled the tree with one stroke of the axe.*

2 a stroke in swimming is one of the ways that you can move your arms and legs to travel through the water: *breast stroke*

3 the sound made by a clock when it strikes the hour: *We arrived on the stroke of midnight.*

4 a sudden illness in the brain that can leave a person unable to move or speak

[verb: **strokes, stroking, stroked**] to rub something gently: *She was stroking the cat.*

stroll [verb: **strolls, strolling, strolled**] to walk in a slow, relaxed way

[noun: **strolls**] a relaxed walk

strong [adjective: **stronger, strongest**]

1 powerful, not weak: *a strong young man* • *a strong wind* • *a strong smell*

2 not easily worn away or broken: *strong cloth* • *fastened with a strong chain*

3 in number: *a workforce 500 strong*

➡ **strongly**

stronghold [noun: **strongholds**] a fortress or castle built to survive attacks

strongly [adverb]

1 in a strong way: *The boxer fought back strongly.*

2 very much: *I strongly recommend that you follow the instructions.*

struck [verb] a way of changing the verb **strike** to make a past tense. It can be used with or without a helping verb: *Her head struck the wall.* • *Lightning has struck the building.*

structural [adjective] to do with the structure of something: *Gales caused structural damage to many buildings.*

structure [noun: **structures**]

1 the way that the parts of something are arranged: *the structure of the story*

2 something that is built or constructed: *The bridge was a massive steel structure.*

struggle [verb: **struggles, struggling, struggled**]

1 to turn and twist your body and try to escape: *The child struggled in his arms.*

2 to struggle to do something is to try hard to do it: *She struggled to finish the work on time.*

3 to fight against difficulty: *All his life he has struggled against poverty.* • *struggling through the mud* [noun: **struggles**] a fight: *They got their money back after a long struggle.*

strum [verb: **strums, strumming, strummed**] to play a musical instrument such as the guitar with sweeping movements of your fingers

strut [verb: **struts, strutting, strutted**] to walk in a stiff, proud way: *The cock strutted round the farmyard.*

[noun: **struts**]
1 a proud way of walking
2 a bar made of wood or metal which supports something

stub [noun: **stubs**] a short piece of something such as a cigarette or pencil which is left over when the rest has been used up

[verb: **stubs, stubbing, stubbed**]
1 to stub your toe is to knock it painfully against something hard
2 to **stub out** a cigarette is to put it out by pressing it against something

stubble [noun]
1 the short stalks of corn left standing in the fields after the crop has been harvested
2 short coarse hairs growing on a man's face when he has not shaved

stubborn [adjective] a stubborn person refuses to do what other people tell them to do, or to follow advice: *a silly, stubborn child*
✦ **stubbornly** [adverb] in a stubborn way: *She stubbornly refused to listen to my advice.*
✦ **stubbornness** [noun] being stubborn

stuck [verb] a way of changing the verb **stick** to make a past tense. It can be used with or without a helping verb: *He stuck the stamp on the envelope.* • *I've stuck the broken vase together again.*

stud [noun: **studs**] a piece of metal with a large head, used as a fastener or decoration on clothes or on the soles of boots or shoes: *jeans with copper studs* • *I need new studs for my football boots.*

student [noun: **students**] someone who is studying, especially at a college or university
[adjective]
1 intended for students: *student loans* • *student accommodation*
2 studying to become something: *a student nurse*

studio [noun: **studios**]
1 the room that an artist or photographer works in
2 a place where films are made
3 a room from which radio or television programmes are broadcast

studious [adjective] a studious person spends a lot of time studying

study [verb: **studies, studying, studied**]
1 to study is to spend time learning about a subject: *I'm studying French.* • *She's studying to be a teacher.*
2 to study something is to look at it carefully: *He studied the railway timetable.* • *We must study the problem in detail.*

[noun: **studies**]
1 study is reading and learning about something: *the study of history*
2 a study is a room used for studying or quiet work

stuff [noun]
1 a substance or material of any kind: *What's that black oily stuff on the beach?*
2 things or objects: *There's far too much stuff in this cupboard.*

[verb: **stuffs, stuffing, stuffed**]
1 to stuff something is to pack it or fill it tightly: *She used feathers to stuff the cushions.* • *We need to stuff the turkey before we cook it.*
2 to stuff something into a place is to push it in carelessly: *He stuffed the papers into his pocket.*
✦ **stuffed** [adjective] a stuffed animal or bird has had its skin filled after it has died so that it looks like it did when it was alive
✦ **stuffing** [noun: **stuffings**]
1 material used for stuffing things such as cushions or soft toys
2 a savoury mixture used to stuff meat such as turkeys and chickens before cooking: *sage and onion stuffing*

stuffy [adjective: **stuffier, stuffiest**]
1 a place that is stuffy lacks fresh air: *How can you sit in this stuffy office all day?*
2 a person who is stuffy is dull and old-fashioned

stumble [verb: **stumbles, stumbling, stumbled**]
1 to trip and nearly fall: *She stumbled over the edge of the carpet.*

Ss

2 to walk with difficulty, nearly falling over: *He stumbled along the track in the dark.*
3 to make mistakes or hesitate: *She stumbled over the difficult words when reading.*
4 to **stumble across** or **stumble on** something is to find it by chance: *I stumbled across this book today.*

stump [noun: **stumps**]
1 the part of something such as a tree, limb or tooth left after the main part has been taken away
2 in cricket, one of the three wooden sticks which make up a wicket
[verb: **stumps, stumping, stumped**]
1 to stump the person batting in cricket is to put them out by touching the stumps with the ball
2 if something stumps you, it is too hard for you: *Those exam questions stumped us all.*
♦ **stumpy** [adjective: **stumpier, stumpiest**] short and thick: *The dog had a stumpy tail.*

stun [verb: **stuns, stunning, stunned**]
1 to stun someone is to make them unconscious, usually by a blow on the head: *The punch stunned him.*
2 to stun someone is also to surprise or shock them greatly: *We were all stunned by the news of the accident.*

stung [verb] a way of changing the verb **sting** to make a past tense. It can be used with or without a helping verb: *The wasp stung him on the finger.* • *Ouch! It's stung me.*

stunk [verb] a way of changing the verb **stink** to make a past tense. It can be used with or without a helping verb: *The room stunk of cigar smoke.* • *If the dead mouse hadn't stunk so much, I'd never have found it.*

stunt [noun: **stunts**] something daring or unusual that someone does to attract attention: *He's always doing stunts on his motorbike.* • *The whole event was a big publicity stunt.*

stunt [verb: **stunts, stunting, stunted**] to stunt something is to stop its growth or development: *Lack of water stunted the plants.*
♦ **stunted** [adjective] small and badly shaped: *trees with stunted branches*

stupendous [adjective] wonderful, amazing: *It was a stupendous concert.*

stupid [adjective: **stupider, stupidest**] not

clever: *a stupid mistake* • *You stupid boy!*
♦ **stupidity** [noun] being stupid: *His stupidity cost us first prize.*
♦ **stupidly** [adverb] in a stupid way: *Stupidly, I agreed to do it.*

sturdy [adjective: **sturdier, sturdiest**] strong, well built: *a sturdy body* • *sturdy furniture*

stutter [verb: **stutters, stuttering, stuttered**] to keep repeating parts of words, especially the first part
[noun: **stutters**] a speech problem that makes you repeat parts of words: *That child has a bad stutter.*

sty [noun: **sties**] a place where pigs are kept
sty or **stye** [noun: **sties** or **styes**] a painful swelling on your eyelid

style [noun: **styles**]
1 a way of doing something such as writing, acting or speaking: *I like the style of her writing.*
2 a style is a fashion: *a new style of shoe*
3 style is being elegant: *She's got style.*
[verb: **styles, styling, styled**] to style something such as hair or clothes is to give them a certain style: *I'm having my hair cut and styled.* • *clothes styled for comfort*
♦ **stylish** [adjective] smart, elegant and fashionable: *stylish clothes*

sub- [prefix] if a word starts with **sub-**, it adds the meaning 'below' or 'under' to the word. For example, a *submarine* is a type of ship that is able to travel under water

subconscious [noun] the part of your mind of which you yourself are not aware but which makes you feel certain things and behave in certain ways
[adjective] which exist in the subconscious: *subconscious fears*
♦ **subconsciously** [adverb] in a subconscious way: *Subconsciously she wanted to be famous.*

subdivide [verb: **subdivides, subdividing, subdivided**] to subdivide something is to divide the parts it has already been divided into, making even smaller parts: *Each class is subdivided into groups according to ability.*
♦ **subdivision** [noun: **subdivisions**] a part made by subdividing

Ss

subdue [verb: **subdues, subduing, subdued**] to subdue someone is to overpower them or bring them under control: *After months of fighting the rebels were subdued.*

♦ **subdued** [adjective] quiet, in low spirits: *subdued voices* • *You seem very subdued today.*

subheading [noun: **subheadings**] a heading that is less important than the main heading in a piece of writing

subject [noun: **subjects**]

1 something that you learn about, for example science or mathematics: *My favourite subject at school was French.*

2 the subject of something such as a story or conversation is the person or thing that it is about: *Can we change the subject, please?*

3 the subject of a sentence is the word or words that stand for the person or thing doing the action of the verb, for example *He* in *He hit me*

4 a person who is under the power of someone or something else: *the king's subjects*

[verb: **subjects, subjecting, subjected**] to subject someone to something is to make them suffer it: *He was subjected to cruel treatment.*

ⓘ The noun is pronounced **sub**-jikt, with the stress at the beginning.
The verb is pronounced sub-**jekt**, with the stress at the end.

subjective [adjective] resulting from your own thoughts and feelings: *a subjective opinion*

sublet [verb: **sublets, subletting, sublet**] to sublet a house or flat is to rent it out when you are renting it from someone else

sublime [adjective] very great or beautiful: *It was a sublime moment in my life.*

submarine [noun: **submarines**] a ship that can travel under water

submerge [verb: **submerges, submerging, submerged**]

1 to submerge something is to cover it with water: *Entire villages had been submerged.*

2 to submerge is to go under water: *I watched the whale submerge.*

♦ **submergence** or **submersion** [noun] submerging or being submerged

submission [noun: **submissions**]

1 submission is the action of submitting: *forced into submission*

2 a submission is something such as an idea or plan that is offered to someone to be considered by them

submissive [adjective] willing to obey: *a submissive servant*

submit [verb: **submits, submitting, submitted**]

1 to submit is to give in: *The rebels were ordered to submit.* • *I refuse to submit to his control.*

2 to submit something such as a plan or idea is to offer it to someone to be considered by them: *All competition entries must be submitted by Friday.*

subordinate [adjective] lower in rank or less important: *his subordinate officers* [noun: **subordinates**] someone who is lower in rank or less important than someone else: *She always tries to help her subordinates.*

subordinate clause [noun: **subordinate clauses**] a clause which cannot stand on its own as a sentence, for example *that I got for my birthday* in the sentence *The book that I got for my birthday was boring.*

subscribe [verb: **subscribes, subscribing, subscribed**]

1 to subscribe to a charity or other cause is to give money to it: *We each subscribed £5 towards the cost of the clock.*

2 to subscribe to something such as a magazine is to promise to take and pay for a certain number of issues

♦ **subscriber** [noun: **subscribers**] someone who subscribes to something

♦ **subscription** [noun: **subscriptions**] money paid to subscribe to something

subsequent [adjective] following or coming after something else: *The story tells of the soldier's capture and subsequent escape.*

♦ **subsequently** [adverb] later: *She ate the shellfish and subsequently became ill.*

subside [verb: **subsides, subsiding, subsided**]

1 if land or a building subsides, it starts to sink gradually into the ground: *When buildings*

Ss

subside, cracks usually appear in the walls.

2 to become less or quieter: *Let's stay here until the wind subsides.*

✦ subsidence [noun] when land or a building starts to sink lower into the ground

subsidiary [noun: **subsidiaries**] a company that is controlled by a larger company

subsidize or **subsidise** [verb: **subsidizes, subsidizing, subsidized**]

1 to subsidize someone or something is to give them money as a help: *The government subsidizes the mining industry.*

2 to subsidize something is to pay part of the cost so that the customer pays less: *The company subsidizes meals in its canteen.*

subsidy [noun: **subsidies**] money given to help someone or something or to keep prices low

substance [noun: **substances**]

1 a substance is a material that you can touch and see: *Glue is a sticky substance.*

2 the substance of something is its general meaning: *The substance of her argument was that women are more intelligent than men.*

substantial [adjective]

1 solid and strong: *a substantial table*

2 large: *a substantial sum of money*

✦ substantially [adverb]

1 a lot: *Profits have increased substantially.*

2 mostly: *These two items are substantially the same.*

substitute [verb: **substitutes, substituting, substituted**] to substitute something for something else is to use it instead of something else: *I substituted your name for mine on the list.* [noun: **substitutes**] a person or thing used instead of another: *Use lemons as a substitute for limes.* • *Our goalkeeper is injured. We need to bring on a substitute.*

✦ substitution [noun: **substitutions**] substituting something or someone else, or being substituted

subtitle [noun: **subtitles**]

1 a second title of something such as a book or film

2 a translation of a film that is in a foreign language, appearing at the bottom of the screen: *a French film with English subtitles*

subtle [adjective: **subtler, subtlest**]

1 slight, difficult to describe or explain: *There is a subtle difference between these two shades of blue.*

2 clever or cunning: *He has a subtle mind.*

✦ subtlety [noun: **subtleties**] being delicate: *the subtlety of the colours in the painting*

subtotal [noun: **subtotals**] the total of one set of figures within a larger group

subtract [verb: **subtracts, subtracting, subtracted**] to take one number away from another: *If you subtract 4 from 6, you get 2.*

✦ subtraction [noun: **subtractions**] the act of taking one number away from another

suburb [noun: **suburbs**] an area of houses at the edge of a town or city: *a suburb of Liverpool*

✦ suburban [adjective] to do with suburbs: *suburban housing*

succeed [verb: **succeeds, succeeding, succeeded**]

1 to succeed is to manage to do what you have been trying to do: *If you try hard, I'm sure you'll succeed.* • *She succeeded in getting the job.*

2 to succeed someone is to take their place: *He succeeded his father as manager of the company.*

success [noun: **successes**]

1 success is managing to do something you have been trying to do: *Have you had any success in finding a job?*

2 a success is someone who does well or something that turns out well: *She's a great success as a teacher.* • *The party was a great success.*

✦ successful [adjective]

1 a successful person has managed to do something, or has done very well in a particular way: *Were you successful in passing the test?* • *a successful artist*

2 a successful event is one that goes well: *We had a successful meeting with the boss.*

✦ successfully [adverb] in a successful way

succession [noun: **successions**]

1 the right to succeed to a throne or title: *He is third in succession to the throne.*

2 a number of things coming one after the

Ss

other: *a succession of failures*

3 if things happen **in succession**, they happen one after another: *three sneezes in quick succession*

♦ **successive** [adjective] following one after the other: *The team won three successive matches.*

♦ **successively** [adverb] one after the other

successor [noun: **successor**] someone who has a particular job or title after someone else: *Who will be appointed as the head teacher's successor?*

succulent [adjective] juicy and delicious: *succulent peaches*

succumb [verb: **succumbs, succumbing, succumbed**] to succumb to something is to give in to it: *She succumbed to temptation.*

such [adjective]

1 of a kind already mentioned: *Such things are difficult to find.*

2 of the same kind: *doctors, nurses and such people*

3 so great or so much: *His excitement was such that he shouted out loud.* • *It's such a disappointment!*

such-and-such [adjective] any: *Let's suppose that you go into such-and-such a shop.*

[noun] any person or thing: *Then you ask for such-and-such.*

suck [verb: **sucks, sucking, sucked**]

1 to take something into your mouth by drawing in air: *She was sucking lemonade through a straw.*

2 to hold something in your mouth while making pulling movements with your lips and tongue: *My daughter still sucks her thumb.* • *If your throat's sore, try sucking this sweet.*

3 to **suck something in** or **suck something up** is to draw it in: *The vacuum cleaner sucked up the crumbs.* • *She sucked in her cheeks.*

[noun: **sucks**] the action of sucking: *She took a suck of her lollipop.*

♦ **sucker** [noun: **suckers**] a rubber or plastic pad that can be pressed on to a surface and sticks there

♦ **suckle** [verb: **suckles, suckling, suckled**] to feed a baby or young animal from the breast or udder: *The cow suckled her calf.*

♦ **suction** [noun] reducing the air in a place, and so producing a vacuum which draws in other air or things to fill the space

sudden [adjective] happening quickly without being expected: *a sudden attack*

sudden infant death syndrome [noun] the sudden and unexpected death, often during the night, of a baby that seems to be healthy

suddenly [adverb] quickly and unexpectedly: *He suddenly woke up.*

suddenness [noun] being sudden: *We were shocked by the suddenness of his death.*

suds [plural noun] soap bubbles

sue [verb: **sues, suing, sued**] to sue a person or organization is to start a law case against them, usually to try to get money from them

suede [noun] a kind of leather with a soft, dull surface which feels like velvet

[adjective] made of suede: *a suede jacket*

suet [noun] a kind of hard animal fat used to make pastry and puddings

suffer [verb: **suffers, suffering, suffered**]

1 to feel pain or misery: *She suffered a lot of pain after the accident.*

2 to suffer from an illness or condition is to have it: *She suffers from headaches.*

♦ **suffering** [noun] pain and misery

sufficiency [noun] enough of something: *a sufficiency of food*

♦ **sufficient** [adjective] enough: *We haven't sufficient food for all these people.*

♦ **sufficiently** [adverb] to a sufficient degree: *I have not learned the song sufficiently to sing it in the concert.*

suffix [noun: **suffixes**] a letter or group of letters that is added to the end of a word to make another word. For example, the suffixes –*ly* and –*ness* can be added to the word *kind* to make *kindly* and *kindness*

suffocate [verb: **suffocates, suffocating, suffocated**]

1 to suffocate someone is to kill them through lack of oxygen: *The thick black smoke was suffocating him.*

2 to suffocate is to die through lack of oxygen: *Babies can suffocate if they sleep with a pillow.*

♦ **suffocation** [noun] suffocating or being

Ss

suffocated: *The cause of death was suffocation.*

sugar [noun] white or brown grains that you add to food and drink to make them taste sweeter: *Do you take sugar in your coffee?*
♦ **sugary** [adjective] very sweet: *a cup of hot, sugary tea*

suggest [verb: **suggests, suggesting, suggested**]
1 to suggest something is to put it forward as an idea or a possibility: *He suggested a picnic.* • *I suggest that we have lunch now.*
2 to suggest something is to hint at it: *Are you suggesting that I'm too old for the job?*
♦ **suggestion** [noun: **suggestions**]
1 an idea put forward: *What a clever suggestion!*
2 a suggestion of something is a hint or trace of it: *There was a suggestion of anger in her voice.*

suicide [noun: **suicides**] killing yourself deliberately: *He committed suicide by jumping off a bridge.*

suit [noun: **suits**]
1 a set of clothes, for example a jacket and trousers, made to be worn together: *He was wearing a suit and tie.*
2 a piece of clothing worn for a particular activity: *a bathing-suit*
3 one of the four sets (spades, hearts, diamonds, clubs) of playing-cards
4 a case in a law court: *He won his suit.*
[verb: **suits, suiting, suited**]
1 something such as a colour, hairstyle or piece of clothing suits you when it makes you look nice: *Blue really suits her.*
2 something suits you when you are happy to agree to it: *Would it suit you if I called round this evening?*
♦ **suitability** [noun] being suitable: *I am not sure of his suitability for the job.*
♦ **suitable** [adjective] something is suitable when it is right for a purpose or occasion: *High-heeled shoes aren't suitable for walking in the country.* • *What would be a suitable time for our meeting?*

suitcase [noun: **suitcases**] a container with flat sides and a handle, to put your clothes in when you are travelling

suite [noun: **suites**]
1 a set of rooms: *a hotel suite*
2 a set of furniture: *a three-piece suite* • *a bathroom suite*
3 a set of short pieces of music to be played one after the other

suitor [noun: **suitors**] an old-fashioned word for a man who wants to marry a woman

sulk [verb: **sulks, sulking, sulked**] to show that you are angry by being silent: *He's sulking because I said he couldn't go out.*
♦ **sulky** [adjective: **sulkier, sulkiest**]
1 sulking: *She's in a sulky mood.*
2 tending to sulk: *a sulky girl*

sullen [adjective] angry and silent: *a sullen young man*

sulphur [noun] a solid yellow substance found in the ground, which burns with a blue flame and an unpleasant smell and is used to make matches and gunpowder

sultan [noun: **sultans**] a ruler in certain Muslim countries: *the Sultan of Brunei*

sultana [noun: **sultanas**]
1 a light-coloured seedless raisin
2 a sultan's wife

sum [noun: **sums**]
1 the total made by two or more things or numbers added together: *The sum of 2, 3 and 4 is 9.*
2 a calculation in which you add and take away numbers: *I was never any good at sums.*
3 an amount of money: *It will cost an enormous sum to repair the roof.*
[verb: **sums, summing, summed**] to **sum up** is to give the main points of something such as a discussion or evidence given in court: *So, to sum up, my main points were as follows ...*

summarize or **summarise** [verb: **summarizes, summarizing, summarized**] to give a shortened version of something: *He summarized the arguments.*

summary [noun: **summaries**] a shortened form of something, giving only the main points: *A summary of his speech was printed in the newspaper.*

summer [noun: **summers**] the warmest season of the year, between spring and autumn
[adjective] happening or used after spring and

before autumn: *summer clothes* • *summer holidays*

summit [noun: **summits**]
  1 the top of a hill or mountain
  2 a meeting between heads of governments

summon [verb: **summons, summoning, summoned**]
  1 to summon someone is to order them to come: *The boss summoned me to his office.*
  2 to **summon up** something such as strength or courage is to gather it: *At last I summoned up the courage to tell him.*
  ✦ **summons** [noun: **summonses**] an order to appear in court

sun [noun: **suns**]
  1 the star in the sky that you see as a huge yellow disc, and which gives light and heat to the Earth: *The Earth goes round the sun.*
  2 sunshine: *We sat in the sun.*

sunbathe [verb: **sunbathes, sunbathing, sunbathed**] to lie or sit in the sun in order to get a suntan

sunbeam [noun: **sunbeams**] a ray of light from the sun

sunblock [noun: **sunblocks**] a cream that you put on your skin to stop yourself from being burned by the sun

sunburn [noun] redness and soreness of the skin caused by being out in the sun for too long

sundae [noun: **sundaes**] a portion of ice-cream served with fruit, syrup or cream

Sunday [noun: **Sundays**] the day of the week after Saturday and before Monday: *I always go to church on Sundays.*

sundial [noun: **sundials**] an instrument that uses sunlight to cast a shadow and show the time

sunflower [noun: **sunflowers**] a tall yellow flower whose seeds provide oil

sung [verb] a form of the verb **sing** that is used with a helping verb to show that something happened in the past: *I've sung in several choirs.*

sunglasses [plural noun] dark glasses which protect your eyes from bright sunlight

sunk [verb] a form of the verb **sink** that is used with a helping verb to show that something happened in the past: *The ship had sunk in minutes.*
  ✦ **sunken** [adjective]

  1 under water: *sunken treasure*
  2 lower than the surrounding area: *a sunken bath*

sunlight [noun] the light of the sun: *Bright sunlight shone in through the window.*
  ✦ **sunlit** [adjective] lit up by the sun: *a sunlit room*

sunny [adjective: **sunnier, sunniest**]
  1 full of sunshine: *It's a lovely sunny day.*
  2 cheerful: *her sunny nature*

sunrise [noun: **sunrises**] the rising of the sun in the morning, or the time of this: *a spectacular sunrise* • *I was up at sunrise.*

sunroof [noun: **sunroofs**] a window in the roof of a car which you can open to let air in

sunset [noun: **sunsets**] the setting of the sun in the evening, or the time of this: *a beautiful golden sunset* • *The younger children were in bed by sunset.*

sunshine [noun] the light and heat of the sun: *The cat was enjoying the warm sunshine.*

sunstroke [noun] an illness caused by staying out in hot sun for too long

suntan [noun: **suntans**] a brown colour of the skin, caused by the sun

super [adjective] extremely good or excellent: *We had a super time at the funfair.*

super- [prefix] if a word starts with **super-**, it adds the meaning 'above' or 'beyond' to the word. For example, someone who is *superhuman* has abilities which are beyond those of a normal person

superannuation [noun]
  1 an amount that is taken from your wages and put towards a company pension for when you retire
  2 money that you receive from your former employer after you retire

superb [adjective] magnificent or excellent: *The view from our balcony was superb.*

superficial [adjective]
  1 affecting the surface only: *The wound is only superficial.* • *The building suffered superficial damage.*
  2 not deep or detailed: *a superficial knowledge of history*

superglue [noun] very strong and fast-acting glue

superintendent [noun: **superintendents**]

Ss

1 a senior police officer

2 someone who is in charge of something such as a building or department

superior [adjective]

1 higher in rank, better or greater: *Is a captain superior to a commander in the navy?* • *With his superior strength he defeated his opponent.*

2 thinking yourself better than others: *I can't stand her superior attitude.*

[noun: **superiors**] a person who is better than, or has a higher rank than, others: *You should always respect your superiors.*

♦ **superiority** [noun] being superior: *his superiority over others*

superlative [noun: **superlatives**] in grammar, the superlative form of an adjective or adverb is the form that usually ends with –*est* or is formed with *most*. For example, *hardest*, *worst* and *most difficult* are superlative forms

supermarket [noun: **supermarkets**] a large self-service shop that sells food and other goods

supernatural [adjective] not natural or normal and impossible to explain: *supernatural happenings*

supersonic [adjective] faster than the speed of sound: *a supersonic aeroplane*

superstition [noun: **superstitions**]

1 belief in magic and other strange powers

2 an example of this kind of belief: *There is an old superstition that walking under a ladder will bring you bad luck.*

♦ **superstitious** [adjective] a superstitious person believes in superstitions

supervise [verb: **supervises, supervising, supervised**] to supervise something or someone is to be in charge of them: *Who supervises this department?* • *His job is to supervise the factory workers.*

♦ **supervision** [noun] the act of supervising: *The prisoner was kept under close supervision.*

♦ **supervisor** [noun: **supervisors**] someone whose job is to make sure that other people's work is done properly

supper [noun: **supper**] a meal that you eat in the evening

supple [adjective] a supple person is able to bend and stretch easily

➡ **suppleness**

supplement [noun: **supplements**]

1 something that you have to make something complete or make up for something that is lacking: *I always take a vitamin supplement.*

2 an extra section added to a book: *The supplement to the dictionary contains hundreds of new words.*

3 an extra part of a newspaper or magazine that comes with the main part

[verb: **supplements, supplementing, supplemented**] to supplement something is to make it bigger by adding something else: *He supplements his wages by working in the evening.*

♦ **supplementary** [adjective] extra or additional: *a few supplementary questions*

suppleness [noun] being able to bend and stretch easily

supply [verb: **supplies, supplying, supplied**] to supply something is to give or provide it: *The shop was unable to supply what she wanted.* • *I can supply you with more paper if you want.*

[noun: **supplies**]

1 supply is supplying something: *The company is involved in the supply of weapons to the Middle East.*

2 a supply is a stock or store: *a supply of food*

[adjective] a supply teacher takes another teacher's place for a time

support [verb: **supports, supporting, supported**]

1 to support something is to carry its weight: *That chair won't support him.*

2 to support someone is to provide the money that they need to live: *He has a wife and two children to support.*

3 to support someone or something is to help and encourage them: *His family supported his decision.*

4 to regularly watch a particular sports team and want them to win: *Which football team do you support?*

[noun: **supports**]

1 support is the action of supporting

2 a support is something such as a column or pillar which takes the weight of something else: *One of the supports of the bridge collapsed.*

♦ **supporter** [noun: **supporters**] someone

who supports something, especially a sports team: *a Liverpool supporter*

suppose [verb: **supposes, supposing, supposed**]
1 to believe that something is probably so: *I suppose you'll be going to the concert.*
2 to consider something as a possibility: *Suppose you had £100 — what would you buy?*
♦ **supposed** [adjective]
1 believed to be so even if it is not true: *her supposed generosity*
2 you are **supposed to** do something when people expect you to do it: *I was supposed to go to the meeting but I didn't bother.*
♦ **supposedly** [adverb] so it is believed: *He is supposedly one of the best doctors in the country.*

suppress [verb: **suppresses, suppressing, suppressed**]
1 to keep back something such as a feeling, laugh or yawn: *She suppressed a laugh.*
2 to defeat something such as a rebellion
♦ **suppression** [noun] the act of suppressing something

supremacy [noun] being the most powerful: *the supremacy of the president*

supreme [adjective]
1 most powerful: *the supreme ruler*
2 greatest: *supreme courage*

surcharge [noun: **surcharges**] an extra amount of money that you have to pay, especially because you were late in paying a bill

sure [adjective]
1 you are sure of something when you have no doubts about it: *I'm sure I gave him the book.*
2 certain to do or get something: *He's sure to win.*
3 able to be trusted: *a sure way to cure hiccups*
[adverb] an informal way of saying 'of course' or 'certainly': *Sure I'll help you!*
♦ **surely** [adverb]
1 surely is used to express a little doubt: *Surely you won't tell him.*
2 an old-fashioned way of saying 'certainly', 'without doubt': *If you go near the pond you will surely fall in.*

surf [noun] the foam made when waves break on rocks or on the shore
[verb: **surfs, surfing, surfed**]
1 to ride on waves towards the shore, standing or lying on a surfboard
2 to surf the Internet is to browse through it looking at different websites
➡ **surfer, surfing**

surface [noun: **surfaces**] the outside or top part of something: *This road has a very bumpy surface.*
[verb: **surfaces, surfacing, surfaced**]
1 to surface is to come up to the surface of water: *The submarine surfaced close to the ship.*
2 to surface something such as a road or path is to put a hard top layer on it
[adjective] travelling on the surface of land or water: *surface mail*

surfboard [noun: **surfboards**] a long narrow board used in surfing

surfer [noun: **surfers**] a person who surfs

surfing [noun] the sport of balancing on a surfboard and riding on waves towards the shore

surge [verb: **surges, surging, surged**] to suddenly move forward or upward: *The crowd surged towards the fire exit.*
[noun] a sudden rush: *He felt a surge of affection for her.*

surgeon [noun: **surgeons**] a doctor who carries out operations

surgery [noun: **surgeries**]
1 surgery is the work of a surgeon, carrying out operations: *heart surgery*
2 a surgery is the room where a doctor or dentist examines their patients

surgical [adjective] to do with a surgeon or his work: *surgical techniques*
♦ **surgically** [adverb] by means of an operation: *The lump will have to be surgically removed.*

surly [adjective: **surlier, surliest**] bad-tempered and rude: *He spoke in a surly voice.*

surname [noun: **surnames**] your last name or family name: *Smith is a common English surname.*

surpass [verb: **surpasses, surpassing,**

Ss

surpassed] to be or do better than: *His work surpassed my expectations.*

surplus [noun: **surpluses**] an amount left over after what is needed has been taken away: *This country produces a surplus of grain.*
[adjective] extra, left over: *We have surplus food.*

surprise [noun: **surprises**]
1 something sudden or unexpected: *Your letter was a nice surprise.*
2 the feeling caused by something sudden or unexpected: *He stared at her in surprise.*
[verb: **surprises, surprising, surprised**]
1 to surprise someone is to cause them to feel surprise: *The news surprised me.*
2 to surprise someone is to come upon them suddenly and without warning: *They surprised the enemy from the rear.*

surrender [verb: **surrenders, surrendering, surrendered**]
1 to surrender is to give up: *They surrendered to the enemy.*
2 to surrender something is to give it up or hand it over: *He was forced to surrender his passport.*
[noun] an act of surrendering

surround [verb: **surrounds, surrounding, surrounded**]
1 to surround someone or something is to be or come all round them: *The city is surrounded by hills.* • *Fans surrounded the players.*
2 if police or soldiers surround a place, they position themselves around it so that people cannot get in or out
• **surroundings** [plural noun] the area around a person or place: *The hotel is set in beautiful surroundings.* • *He was glad to be back in his own surroundings.*

survey [verb: **surveys, surveying, surveyed**] to survey something is to look at it or inspect it: *She surveyed her garden from the window.*
[noun: **surveys**]
1 an investigation into what people think: *Would you mind answering some questions? I'm doing a survey.*
2 an inspection of a building in order to see its condition and value, especially when someone wants to buy it

• **surveyor** [noun: **surveyors**] someone whose job is to examine the condition of a building or to look at the details of an area of land

ⓘ The verb is pronounced sur-**vay**, with the stress at the end.
The noun is pronounced **sur**-vay, with the stress at the beginning.

survival [noun] staying alive: *His survival depended on finding fresh water.*

survive [verb: **survives, surviving, survived**] to stay alive: *He didn't survive long after the accident.*
• **survivor** [noun: **survivors**] someone who stays alive: *the only survivor of the crash*

suspect [verb: **suspects, suspecting, suspected**]
1 to suspect someone is to think that they have done something wrong: *He's suspected of murdering two women.*
2 to suspect something is to think that it is likely: *I suspect that she is hiding her true feelings.*
[noun: **suspects**] someone who is thought to have done something wrong: *There are three suspects in this murder case.*

ⓘ The verb is pronounced sus-**pekt**, with the stress at the end.
The noun is pronounced **sus**-pekt, with the stress at the beginning.

suspend [verb: **suspends, suspending, suspended**]
1 to suspend something is to hang it: *The meat was suspended from a hook.*
2 to suspend something is to stop it for a while: *All business will be suspended until after New Year.*
3 to suspend someone is to stop them doing their job or taking part in an activity for a time because they have done something wrong: *suspended from the team for bad behaviour*

suspense [noun] a state of feeling uncertain and anxious: *We waited in suspense for the result.*

suspension [noun]
1 suspending something or someone: *a two-week suspension from school*
2 the system of springs that supports a motor

vehicle, making it more comfortable to ride in

suspension bridge [noun: **suspension bridges**] a type of bridge that is suspended from cables hanging from towers

suspicion [noun: **suspicions**]
1 a thought or feeling that something is likely: *I have a suspicion she is not telling the truth.*
2 a feeling of doubting on not trusting: *They looked at each other with suspicion.*
 ✦ **suspicious** [adjective]
1 feeling or showing suspicion: *She gave him a suspicious glance.*
2 causing suspicion: *He died in suspicious circumstances.*
 ✦ **suspiciously** [adverb] in a suspicious way: *She looked at him suspiciously.* • *acting suspiciously*

sustain [verb: **sustains, sustaining, sustained**]
1 to sustain someone is to give help and strength to them: *a few sandwiches to sustain you during the journey*
2 to sustain an injury is to suffer it: *He sustained head injuries in the crash.*
3 to sustain something is to keep it up or keep it going: *It would be difficult to sustain such a fast pace.*
 ✦ **sustenance** [noun] food and drink: *We need sustenance if we are to carry on.*

swab [noun: **swabs**]
1 a piece of cotton wool used, for example, to clean wounds or soak up blood
2 a sample of fluid taken from the body for examination: *The doctor took a swab from her throat to check for infection.*

swagger [verb: **swaggers, swaggering, swaggered**] to walk as though pleased with yourself, swinging your arms and body: *He swaggered along the street in his new suit.*
[noun: **swaggers**] a proud and confident way of walking

swallow[1] [verb: **swallows, swallowing, swallowed**]
1 to swallow food or drink is to make it pass down your throat to your stomach: *Try to swallow the pill.*
2 to swallow something such as a lie or an insult is to accept it without question: *She'll never swallow that story!*

3 to **swallow something up** is to make it disappear: *The increase in profits has been swallowed up by rising wage bills.*
[noun: **swallows**] an act of swallowing

swallow[2] [noun] a small bird with long pointed wings and a forked tail

swamp [noun: **swamps**] a piece of wet, marshy ground
[verb: **swamps, swamping, swamped**]
1 to swamp something is to flood it: *A great wave swamped the deck.*
2 to swamp someone is to overload them with something: *I'm swamped with work.*

swan [noun: **swans**] a large, usually white, water bird with a long neck

swap [verb: **swaps, swapping, swapped**] to exchange one thing for another: *They swapped books with each other.* • *I took the dress back to the shop and swapped it for a bigger size.*

swarm [noun: **swarms**] a large number of insects flying or moving together: *a swarm of bees*
[verb: **swarms, swarming, swarmed**]
1 to move in great numbers: *Crowds swarmed through the streets.*
2 to be swarming with something is to be crowded with it: *streets swarming with tourists*

swarthy [adjective: **swarthier, swarthiest**] dark-skinned

swashbuckling [adjective] full of adventure and excitement: *a swashbuckling story of buccaneers*

swastika [noun: **swastikas**] a cross with its arms bent at right angles, used as the sign of the former German Nazi party

swat [verb: **swats, swatting, swatted**] to swat a fly is to crush it
[noun: **swats**] a device for crushing flies, usually with a long handle and a flat end

sway [verb: **sways, swaying, swayed**]
1 to sway is to move from side to side with a swinging action: *She swayed in time to the music.*
2 to sway someone is to persuade or influence them: *She's too easily swayed by her friends' opinions.*

swear [verb: **swears, swearing, swore, sworn**]

Ss

1 to promise: *I swear to tell the truth.*
2 to use words that are offensive: *He swore under his breath.*
3 to **swear by** something is to believe that it is very good and effective: *He swears by this diet.*
4 to **swear someone to secrecy** is to make them give a promise that they will not tell anyone something: *The children were sworn to secrecy.*

sweat [noun] the salty liquid that comes out of your skin when you are hot: *He was dripping with sweat after his run.*
[verb: **sweats, sweating, sweated**] to give out sweat: *Exercise makes you sweat.*
♦ **sweater** [noun: **sweaters**] a jersey or pullover

sweatshirt [noun: **sweatshirts**] a type of thick cotton jersey

sweaty [adjective: **sweatier, sweatiest**] wet with sweat: *I feel all sweaty.*

swede [noun: **swedes**] a kind of large round yellow vegetable like a turnip

sweep [verb: **sweeps, sweeping, swept**]
1 to sweep something is to clean it using a brush or broom: *He swept the floor.*
2 to sweep is to move quickly or forcefully: *The disease is sweeping through the country.* • *She swept into my room without knocking.*
3 to sweep someone or something is to move them with a sweeping movement: *The wind nearly swept me off my feet.* • *Whole villages were swept away by the flood.*
[noun: **sweeps**]
1 the action of sweeping: *She gave the room a sweep.*
2 a sweeping movement: *He indicated the damage with a sweep of his hand.*
3 a person who cleans chimneys
♦ **sweeper** [noun: **sweepers**] in football, a defensive player who stays behind the other defenders

sweepstake [noun: **sweepstakes**] a system of gambling in which the prize money is the sum of the money gambled by all those taking part

sweet [adjective: **sweeter, sweetest**]
1 tasting like sugar: *strong sweet tea*
2 pleasant in smell or sound: *the sweet smell of*

flowers • *the sweet song of the nightingale*
3 attractive or nice: *My baby brother is very sweet.*
[noun: **sweets**]
1 a small piece of sweet food, for example chocolate or toffee: *a packet of sweets*
2 something sweet served at the end of a meal: *Would you like to see the sweet menu?*

sweetcorn [noun] sweetcorn is the yellow grains of a cereal crop called maize, that are eaten as a vegetable

sweeten [verb: **sweetens, sweetening, sweetened**]
1 to sweeten something is to make it sweet: *Sweeten the raspberries with sugar.*
2 to sweeten is to become sweet: *Her smile sweetened.*
♦ **sweetener** [noun: **sweeteners**] a substance that is used instead of sugar to sweeten food and drinks, often used by people who are trying to lose weight

sweetheart [noun: **sweethearts**] a boyfriend or girlfriend: *They were childhood sweethearts.*

sweetly [adverb] in a sweet way: *She smiled sweetly.*

sweetness [noun] being sweet

sweet pea [noun: **sweet peas**] a climbing flower with a sweet smell, grown in gardens

sweet tooth [noun] a liking for things that taste sweet: *She never refuses chocolate — she has a very sweet tooth.*

swell [verb: **swells, swelling, swelled, swollen**]
1 to swell is to get bigger: *The wasp sting made her finger swell.*
2 to swell something is to make it bigger: *Heavy rain had swollen the river.*
[noun] swell is the up and down movement of the sea when there are no breaking waves
♦ **swelling** [noun: **swellings**] a swollen part of the body: *She had a swelling on her arm where she had been stung.*
→ **swollen**

swelter [verb: **swelters, sweltering, sweltered**] to be too hot: *I'm sweltering in this heat!*
♦ **sweltering** [adjective] very hot: *It's sweltering today.*

swept [verb] a way of changing the verb **sweep** to make a past tense. It can be used with or without a helping verb: *He swept up the crumbs.* • *She has swept the floor.*

swerve [verb: **swerves, swerving, swerved**] to turn quickly to one side, especially to avoid hitting something: *The driver had to swerve to miss the dog.*
[noun: **swerves**] a quick turn to one side, especially to avoid hitting something

swift [adjective: **swifter, swiftest**] fast or quick: *a swift recovery*
[noun: **swifts**] a small bird rather like a swallow
♦ **swiftly** [adverb] quickly: *'No way,' she answered swiftly.*
♦ **swiftness** [noun] being swift

swill [verb: **swills, swilling, swilled**] to swill something is to wash it out: *He swilled out the cups.*
[noun] leftover food mixed with water, given to pigs to eat

swim [verb: **swims, swimming, swam, swum**]
1 to swim is to move through water: *I learned to swim when I was five.*
2 to swim something is to cross it by swimming: *Her ambition is to swim the Channel.*
3 to be swimming in a liquid is to be covered with it: *meat swimming in grease*
4 if your head swims, you feel dizzy
[noun: **swims**] an act of swimming: *I think I'll go for a swim.*
♦ **swimmer** [noun: **swimmers**] someone or something that swims: *Penguins are excellent swimmers.*

swimming baths [plural noun] a place with a pool or pools of water, where people can go and swim

swimming costume [noun: **swimming costumes**] a piece of clothing worn for swimming, usually by women and girls

swimming pool [noun: **swimming pools**] an indoor or outdoor pool for swimming in

swimsuit [noun: **swimsuits**] a piece of clothing worn for swimming, usually by women and girls

swindle [verb: **swindles, swindling, swindled**] to swindle someone is to cheat them, especially out of money: *That*

shopkeeper has swindled me out of £2!
[noun: **swindles**] an act of swindling: *I paid £20 for this watch and it doesn't work. What a swindle!*
♦ **swindler** [noun: **swindlers**] a person who swindles others

swine [noun: **swine**]
1 an old word for a pig
2 a rude word for someone who treats others badly: *He left me to pay the bill, the swine!*

swing [verb: **swings, swinging, swung**]
1 to move from side to side, or forwards and backwards from a fixed point: *You swing your arms when you walk.* • *The children were swinging on a rope hanging from a tree.*
2 to turn suddenly: *He swung round and stared at us.*
[noun: **swings**]
1 a seat hanging from ropes or chains, that children sit on and swing
2 a swinging movement: *the swing of a pendulum*
3 if an event or process is **in full swing**, it is happening and everyone involved is very busy: *The party was in full swing.*

swipe [verb: **swipes, swiping, swiped**]
1 to swipe someone or something is to hit them with a heavy sweeping blow: *She swiped me across the face.*
2 to swipe a credit card or a debit card is to pass it through an electronic device that reads the details on the card
[noun: **swipes**] a heavy sweeping blow: *He took a swipe at the ball.*

swipe card [noun: **swipe cards**] a plastic card, for example a credit card or debit card, that can be read by swiping it through an electronic device

swirl [verb: **swirls, swirling, swirled**] to move quickly round in circles: *Leaves swirled along the ground.*
[noun: **swirls**] a swirling movement

swish [verb: **swishes, swishing, swished**] to move with a rustling sound: *Her long skirt swished as she danced.*
[noun: **swishes**] a swishing sound

switch [noun: **switches**]
1 a device for turning power on and off: *I can't find the light-switch.*

Ss

2 a change: *After several switches of direction they were at last on the right road.*

[verb: **switches, switching, switched**]

1 to switch something on or off is to turn it on or off using a switch

2 to switch something is to change it: *Jane switched her job to become a driver.*

switchboard [noun: **switchboards**] a board with lots of switches for making connections by telephone

swivel [verb: **swivels, swivelling, swivelled**]

1 to swivel or swivel round is to turn round: *I swivelled round to look at him.*

2 to swivel something or swivel something round is to turn it round: *She swivelled her chair round to face the desk.*

swollen [adjective] bigger than usual because of swelling: *He had a swollen ankle after falling downstairs.*

[verb] a form of the verb **swell** that is used with a helping verb to show that something happened in the past: *Her face had swollen up with crying.*

swoon [verb: **swoons, swooning, swooned**] an old-fashioned word that means to faint

[noun: **swoons**] an old word for a faint: *She fell into a swoon.*

swoop [verb: **swoops, swooping, swooped**] to rush or fly downwards: *The owl swooped down on its prey.*

[noun: **swoops**] a sudden downward rush

swop [verb: **swops, swopping, swopped**] another spelling of **swap**

sword [noun: **swords**] a weapon with a long blade

swordfish [noun: **swordfish** or **swordfishes**] a type of large fish with a long pointed upper jaw like a sword

swore [verb] a way of changing the verb **swear** to make a past tense: *She swore to tell the truth.*

sworn [verb] a form of the verb **swear** that is used with a helping verb to show that something happened in the past: *He has sworn he will never tell anyone.*

[adjective] promised always to be something: *They are sworn enemies.*

swot [verb: **swots, swotting, swotted**] to study hard: *She has been swotting for her exams.*

[noun: **swots**] a person who studies hard or too hard

sycamore [noun: **sycamores**] a type of large tree with winged seeds

syllable [noun: **syllables**] a word or part of a word that is a single sound. For example, *pen* has one syllable, *pen-cil* has two and *com-pu-ter* has three

syllabus [noun: **syllabuses** or **syllabi**] a list of things to be studied by a class

symbol [noun: **symbols**]

1 a mark or sign that is used as a short form of something, for example + meaning *plus* and O meaning *oxygen*

2 something that stands for something else: *The dove is a symbol of peace.*

♦ **symbolic** [adjective] used as a sign or symbol of something: *The gift was a symbolic gesture of friendship.*

♦ **symbolize** or **symbolise** [verb: **symbolizes, symbolizing, symbolized**] to symbolize something is to be a symbol of it: *A ring symbolizes everlasting love.*

symmetrical [adjective] having symmetry: *The two sides of a person's face are never completely symmetrical.*

♦ **symmetry** [noun] when two parts or halves are exactly the same but the opposite way round, as if one were a mirror image of the other

sympathetic [adjective] feeling or showing sympathy: *a sympathetic smile*

♦ **sympathetically** [adverb] in a sympathetic way: *She patted his hand sympathetically.*

sympathize or **sympathise** [verb: **sympathizes, sympathizing, sympathized**] to sympathize with someone is to feel or show sympathy for them: *I sympathize with your trouble.* • *I'm afraid I cannot help, I can only sympathize.*

sympathy [noun: **sympathies**]

1 the feeling of being sorry for someone who is upset or suffering: *She received many letters of sympathy when her husband died.*

2 loyal support for a group, organization or

belief: *Are you in sympathy with the strikers?*

symphony [noun: **symphonies**] a long piece of music to be played by an orchestra

symptom [noun: **symptoms**] a symptom of an illness is a sign that someone has that illness: *Sore throat, blocked nose, and sneezing are the usual symptoms of a cold.*

synagogue [noun: **synagogues**] a Jewish place of worship

syndrome [noun: **syndromes**] a group of symptoms which are the sign of a particular illness

synonym [noun: **synonyms**] a word that means the same, or nearly the same, as another word. For example, *angry* and *cross* are synonyms

synthesis [noun: **syntheses**]
  1 the making of a product by combining different chemical substances: *Plastic is produced by synthesis.*
  2 a mixture: *His latest plan is a synthesis of old and new ideas.*

♦ **synthesizer** or **synthesiser** [noun: **synthesizers**] an electronic musical instrument that makes the sounds of various other musical instruments

♦ **synthetic** [adjective] not real: *synthetic leather*

syringe [noun: **syringes**] a small instrument shaped like a cylinder with a needle attached to it, used for injecting liquids into your body or for taking blood out of your body

syrup [noun: **syrups**] a thick sticky liquid made by boiling water or fruit juice with sugar: *hot pancakes covered with syrup*

system [noun: **systems**]
  1 an arrangement of many parts that work together: *the railway system*
  2 a way of organizing something: *a system of education*

♦ **systematic** [adjective] well planned and following a system: *a systematic search of the area*

Ss

T

ta [interjection] an informal word for 'thank you'

tab [noun: **tabs**] a small piece of fabric, metal or paper attached to something and used to hang it up, identify it, open it, or hold it by

tabby [noun: **tabbies**]
1 a cat with grey or brown fur marked with darker stripes
2 a female cat

table [noun: **tables**]
1 a piece of furniture with a flat top that is supported on legs
2 figures or words laid out in rows and columns
3 to **turn the tables on someone** is to change the situation around completely so that they are in the position, usually a bad or uncomfortable one, that they had put you in before

tablecloth [noun: **tablecloths**] a cloth for covering a table

tablespoon [noun: **tablespoons**] a large size of spoon, often used for measuring cooking ingredients
◆ **tablespoonful** [noun: **tablespoonfuls**] the amount that a tablespoon will hold

tablet [noun: **tablets**]
1 a pill
2 a flat solid piece of something, such as soap or chocolate
3 a flat surface, usually made of stone or wood, with words carved on it

table tennis [noun] an indoor game for two or four players in which a light hollow ball is hit with small rounded bats across a net on a table

tabloid [noun: **tabloids**] a newspaper with pages that are smaller than some other papers. They often have lots of pictures and news about famous people

taboo [noun: **taboos**] a taboo is anything people are not allowed to do, especially for religious or social reasons
[adjective] not allowed for social or religious reasons: *a taboo subject*

tack [noun: **tacks**]
1 a short nail with a broad flat head and a sharp point
2 a course of action or way of approaching something: *We aren't getting anywhere, so we need to try a different tack.*
[verb: **tacks, tacking, tacked**]
1 to tack something is to fasten it with tacks
2 to tack pieces of fabric is to sew them together with large loose temporary stitches

tackle [verb: **tackles, tackling, tackled**]
1 you tackle a job or problem when you try to deal with it
2 you tackle someone when you ask them directly about something they have done wrong or about something that they should have done but have not done
3 in games like football and rugby, you tackle a player in the other team when you try to get the ball from them
[noun: **tackles**]
1 tackle is equipment: *fishing tackle • lifting tackle*
2 a tackle is the movement a rugby, football or hockey player makes to try to get the ball from a player in the other team

tacky [adjective: **tackier, tackiest**]
1 if glue is tacky, it is still rather sticky because it hasn't dried completely

2 cheap and badly made or in bad taste

tact [noun] the ability to be careful in what you do or say so that you do not upset or offend someone

　　✦ **tactful** [adjective] careful in what you do or say so that you do not upset or offend someone

　　✦ **tactfully** [adverb] in a tactful way

　　➟ **tactless**

tactic [noun: **tactics**] someone's tactics are the things they do or the methods they use to get what they want or to help them win

　　✦ **tactical** [adjective] a tactical action or move is cleverly worked out to achieve the best result

tactless [adjective] thoughtless and not considering other people's feelings: *a tactless remark*

tadpole [noun: **tadpoles**] a young frog or toad with a rounded head and long tail, which eventually disappears as it develops legs

taffeta [noun] a stiff shiny silk fabric or a silky fabric with raised ridges on its surface

tag [noun: **tags**] a label with information such as someone's name printed on it

[verb: **tags, tagging, tagged**]

　　1 to tag something is to put a tag or label on it

　　2 if someone **tags along** with another person, they go with that person somewhere, often without being invited

tail [noun: **tails**]

　　1 an animal's, bird's or fish's tail is the part of its body that sticks out from the end of its spine or at the end of its body

　　2 any part that sticks out, or hangs down, at the back of an object: *The aeroplane had a red and black symbol painted on its tail.* • *His shirt tail was hanging out.*

[verb: **tails, tailing, tailed**]

　　1 to tail someone is to follow them, usually to watch what they do or where they go

　　2 if something **tails off**, it gets less and less, or smaller and smaller, until it eventually disappears

tailor [noun: **tailors**] someone whose job is making suits, coats or other pieces of clothing

[verb: **tailors, tailoring, tailored**]

　　1 to tailor clothes is to make them so that they fit well

2 to tailor something for a particular purpose is to design it specially for that purpose

tails [plural noun] the side of a coin opposite the side that has the head on it: *Call heads or tails.*

taint [verb: **taints, tainting, tainted**] to taint something is to add something bad or unpleasant to it so that it is spoiled

take [verb: **takes, taking, took, taken**]

　　1 you take something when you reach out and get it or get it for yourself: *Take my hand.* • *I'm taking piano lessons.* • *Someone's taken my ruler.*

　　2 to take someone or something to a place is to bring them or it with you when you go there: *I'm taking the children to school.* • *I took the parcel to the post office.*

　　3 you take one number from another when you subtract the first one from the second one: *If you take 5 from 16, you are left with 11.*

　　4 you take something when you eat it, drink it or swallow it: *You must take your medicine if you want to get better quickly.*

　　5 to take something is to accept it: *Take my advice. Wear a warm jumper when you go out.* • *He cannot take criticism.*

　　6 to take something such as a form of transport or a route is to use it: *We usually take the bus rather than the train.* • *Take the next left after the town hall.*

　　7 you take an exam or test when you do it

　　8 to take a photograph is to use a camera to record an image

　　9 something takes a certain length of time if it lasts for that length of time or you need that amount of time to do it: *The journey took four hours.*

　　10 if a space or container takes a certain amount, it has enough room for it: *This jug takes nearly two pints.*

　　11 take is used with nouns to refer to actions: *Let's take a look at that sore leg of yours.* • *He took a leap.*

　　12 to **take someone in** is to deceive them

　　13 a plane **takes off** when it leaves the ground at the beginning of a flight

　　14 to **take over** from someone is to replace them and do what they had been doing

　　15 to **take up** a hobby or other activity is to start doing it

Tt

take-away [noun: **take-aways**] a cooked meal that you buy at a shop or restaurant and take away with you to eat somewhere else

take-off [noun: **take-offs**] the moment when an aeroplane leaves the ground at the beginning of a flight

takings [plural noun] the amount of money that is taken in a shop, or at a concert or other event that people pay to see or take part in

talc [noun] talcum powder

talcum powder [noun] a fine powder with a pleasant scent, that people put on their bodies

tale [noun: **tales**] a story: *tales of great adventures*

talent [noun: **talents**] you have talent, or a talent, when you have special skill or natural ability to do something well
♦ **talented** [adjective] having the skill or ability to do something well: *a talented young artist*

talk [verb: **talks, talking, talked**]
1 to say words out loud
2 to talk to someone is to have a conversation with them
3 to **talk something over** with someone is to discuss it with them
[noun: **talks**]
1 talk is speech or conversation
2 if someone gives a talk, they talk about a subject to an audience
♦ **talkative** [adjective] a talkative person talks a lot

tall [adjective: **taller, tallest**]
1 big, or bigger than average, in height: *He's tall for his age.* • *a tall building*
2 how big someone or something is in height: *He's only three feet tall.*
3 a **tall story** is difficult to believe

tally [noun: **tallies**] a tally of things is a record you keep so that you can work out the total, for example, of points scored or money spent
[verb: **tallies, tallying, tallied**] two or more things tally when they match or are the same: *His answer tallied with mine.*

Talmud [noun] a book of religious laws written by rabbis, used by members of the Jewish faith

talon [noun: **talons**] a long hooked claw on an eagle's or other large bird of prey's foot

tambourine [noun: **tambourines**] an instrument that you play by shaking and hitting it. It is a circular frame with skin stretched tightly across it and small round pieces of metal set into the frame in pairs

tame [adjective: **tamer, tamest**] a tame animal is used to being with humans and is not dangerous
[verb: **tames, taming, tamed**] to tame a wild animal is to train it so that it is used to living or working with humans

tamper [verb: **tampers, tampering, tampered**] to tamper with something is to interfere with it, especially in a way that causes it not to work properly

tampon [noun: **tampons**] something that a woman puts inside her vagina to absorb the blood when she is having her period

tan [noun: **tans**]
1 you get a tan when your skin is turned browner by the sun
2 tan is a yellow-brown colour
[verb: **tans, tanning, tanned**]
1 your skin tans when it is turned a darker colour by the sun
2 animal hides are tanned when they are treated with chemicals to make them into leather

tandem [noun: **tandems**]
1 a type of long bicycle for two riders that has two seats and two sets of pedals
2 people or things work or go **in tandem** when they work or go along together

tang [noun: **tangs**] a strong or sharp taste or flavour

tangerine [noun: **tangerines**] a type of small orange with skin that is loose and easy to peel

tangle [noun: **tangles**]
1 a tangle is an untidy twisted mass of something, such as rope, wire or hair
2 if you get in a tangle, you get into a confused or disorganized state
[verb: **tangles, tangling, tangled**]
1 to tangle is to become entwined
2 to tangle something is to twist it or disorganize it

Tt

tank [noun: **tanks**]
1 a large container for holding liquids
2 a large heavy army vehicle covered with metal plates and with a long gun on the top

tankard [noun: **tankards**] a large metal mug, usually with a handle and sometimes a hinged lid, used for drinking beer

tanker [noun: **tankers**] a ship or lorry used to carry oil or other liquids

tanner [noun: **tanners**] someone whose job or business is to tan leather
  ◆ **tannery** [noun: **tanneries**] a place where animal skins are made into leather

tantalize or **tantalise** [verb: **tantalizes, tantalizing, tantalized**] if something tantalizes you, it makes you feel frustrated because you want it but cannot have it
  ◆ **tantalizing** or **tantalising** [adjective] something that is tantalizing torments you because you are tempted by it, but cannot have it

tantrum [noun: **tantrums**] if someone has or **throws a tantrum**, they suddenly start to shout, scream or kick in a furious and uncontrolled way

tap¹ [noun: **taps**]
1 a device fitted to a water or gas pipe used to turn the water or gas on and off and control the flow
2 if something is **on tap**, there is a supply of it available when you need it
[verb: **taps, tapping, tapped**]
1 to tap a source or supply of something is to use it
2 to tap someone's phone is secretly to put a device in their phone that lets you hear their telephone conversations

tap² [noun: **taps**] a light quick knock
[verb: **taps, tapping, tapped**] to tap is to knock lightly: *He tapped on the window to get my attention.*

tapdance [verb: **tapdances, tapdancing, tapdanced**] to dance in special shoes with metal pieces on the toes and heels that make tapping noises as your feet hit the ground

tape [noun: **tapes**]
1 tape is a long narrow ribbon or strip of material, used for tying or sticking things
2 the strip of material across a finishing line on a race track: *She was the first through the tape at the finish.*
3 a tape is a length of magnetic tape wound on a cassette, for recording sounds or pictures
[verb: **tapes, taping, taped**]
1 to tape sounds or images is to record them on tape
2 to **tape something up** is to fasten it with sticky tape

tape-measure [noun: **tape-measures**] a long thin piece of metal or fabric marked with units of measurement that you use to find out the length of things

taper [verb: **tapers, tapering, tapered**]
1 to get gradually thinner or narrower at one end
2 something **tapers off** when it decreases gradually
[noun: **tapers**] a long thin candle used for lighting other candles and fires

tape-recorder [noun: **tape-recorders**] a machine that records sounds on magnetic tape and plays recordings back

tapestry [noun: **tapestries**] a piece of cloth with a design or picture sewn on it in wool or thick thread

tapeworm [noun: **tapeworms**] a long flat worm that lives in the guts of animals, including humans, as a parasite

tapioca [noun] a starchy food in the form of white grains that are cooked in milk and eaten as a pudding

tar [noun] a thick dark sticky liquid made from coal or wood, which goes hard when it gets cold and is used in making roads

tarantula [noun: **tarantulas**] a large hairy spider that has a poisonous bite

target [noun: **targets**]
1 a mark or object that people aim at when they are shooting
2 something or someone being aimed at: *The company won't reach its sales targets.* • *He was the target of everyone's jokes.*
[verb: **targets, targeting, targeted**] to target someone or something is to aim at them

tariff [noun: **tariffs**] a list of prices or charges

Tarmac [noun] a short form of the word **tarmacadam**, used as a trademark

tarmacadam [noun] a mixture of small

Tt

stones and tar used to make road surfaces

tarnish [verb: **tarnishes, tarnishing, tarnished**]

1 if metal tarnishes, it becomes dull and stained

2 something tarnishes a person's reputation when it spoils or damages it

tarot [noun] tarot is a way of telling people's fortunes using cards with pictures that are supposed to predict what is going to happen in the future

tarpaulin [noun: **tarpaulins**] a tarpaulin is a piece of strong waterproof canvas

tarry [verb: **tarries, tarrying, tarried**] an old-fashioned word which means to linger or wait: *O let us be married! Too long we have tarried: but what shall we do for a ring?*

tart[1] [noun: **tarts**] a pastry case with a sweet filling of custard, jam or fruit

tart[2] [adjective: **tarter, tartest**] sour-tasting

tartan [noun: **tartans**] woollen cloth with a check pattern made up of horizontal and vertical stripes of different colours

task [noun: **tasks**]

1 a job or duty that you have to do

2 to **take someone to task** is to criticize them because they have done something wrong

task force [noun: **task forces**] a group of people or soldiers with a special task to do

tassel [noun: **tassels**] a bunch of threads tied firmly together at one end and used as decoration

taste [noun: **tastes**]

1 taste is the sense by which you recognize different flavours or foods when you touch them with your tongue

2 something's taste is the particular flavour it has when it touches your tongue

3 to have a taste of something is to put a little bit of it in your mouth to find out what its flavour is like

4 your taste or tastes are the kinds of things you like

[verb: **tastes, tasting, tasted**]

1 you taste something when you put it in your mouth so that you can find out what sort of flavour it has: *Have you tasted this cheese?*

2 food tastes a certain way if it has that flavour: *This sauce tastes salty.*

3 if you taste something, you experience it

briefly: *They'd tasted victory for the first time and wanted more.*

♦ **tasteful** [adjective] showing good taste and judgement

♦ **tastefully** [adverb] in a tasteful way

♦ **tasteless** [adjective]

1 having no flavour

2 vulgar or showing lack of taste and judgement

♦ **tasty** [adjective: **tastier, tastiest**] having a good flavour

tattered [adjective] tattered clothing is torn and ragged

tatters [plural noun]

1 clothes that are **in tatters** are badly torn

2 something that is **in tatters** is ruined: *Their holiday plans were in tatters.*

tattoo[1] [noun: **tattoos**] a pattern or picture marked on someone's skin by making little holes in the surface of the skin and filling the holes with ink

[verb: **tattoos, tattooing, tattooed**] to tattoo someone is to put a tattoo on their skin

tattoo[2] [noun: **tattoos**] an outdoor military display with music

tatty [adjective: **tattier, tattiest**] scruffy, old and worn: *tatty old jeans*

taught [verb] a way of changing the verb **teach** to make a past tense. It can be used with or without a helping verb: *Who taught you how to do magic tricks?* • *She had taught several classes that day.*

taunt [verb: **taunts, taunting, taunted**] to taunt someone is to say cruel and hurtful things to them

[noun: **taunts**] a cruel or hurtful remark

taut [adjective: **tauter, tautest**] pulled or stretched tight

tavern [noun: **taverns**] an old-fashioned word for an inn or pub

tawdry [adjective: **tawdrier, tawdriest**] cheap or cheap-looking and of bad quality

tawny [adjective] something that is tawny has a yellow-brown colour: *a tawny owl*

tax [noun: **taxes**] a charge made by the government on a person's income or on the price of goods to help pay for the running of the country

[verb: **taxes, taxing, taxed**]

1 to tax income or goods is to charge tax on them

2 if something taxes you, you find it hard work or a strain

♦ **taxable** [adjective] if something is taxable, you have to pay tax on it: *taxable income*

♦ **taxation** [noun] the system of taxing income or goods, or the amount of money the government gets by charging taxes

➡ **taxpayer, tax year**

taxi [noun: **taxis**] a car with a driver that you can hire to take you from one place to another [verb: **taxis, taxiing, taxied**] an aeroplane taxis when it moves slowly forward along the ground, after it has landed or when it is getting into position to take off

taxpayer [noun: **taxpayers**] someone who has to pay tax on the money they earn

tax year [noun: **tax years**] a period of twelve months that is used for working out the tax you have to pay

TB [abbreviation] short for **tuberculosis**

tbsp [abbreviation] short for **tablespoon**. It is an abbreviation that is usually used in recipe books

tea [noun: **teas**]

1 a drink made by pouring boiling water on dried leaves that come from a small tree or shrub that grows in Asia

2 a cup of tea: *Two teas and a coffee, please.*

3 a light meal, with tea and sandwiches, that some people have between lunch and dinner

4 the name some people give to the meal that they have in the early evening

teabag [noun: **teabags**] a small bag of thin paper containing tea leaves that you put in a pot or cup and pour boiling water over to make tea

teach [verb: **teaches, teaching, taught**]

1 to teach is to pass the knowledge and experience you have on to other people to help them learn new things: *Will you teach me how to sail a dinghy?* • *He taught in the local school.*

2 to teach a particular subject is to give people lessons in that subject: *He teaches Maths.*

♦ **teacher** [noun: **teachers**] someone who teaches, usually as their job

♦ **teaching** [noun] the work of a teacher

teacup [noun: **teacups**] a cup used for drinking tea

teak [noun] a type of hard yellow-brown wood

team [noun: **teams**]

1 a group of people who form one side in a game: *the England cricket team* • *Which football team do you support?*

2 a group of people working together: *a team of engineers*

[verb: **teams, teaming, teamed**] to **team up** with other people is to join them so that you can do something together

ⓘ Be careful not to confuse **team** and **teem**.

teapot [noun: **teapots**] a pot with a spout and a handle, used for making and pouring tea

tear [superscript 1] [verb: **tears, tearing, torn**]

1 to tear something is to make a hole or split in it: *You've torn your sleeve on that barbed wire.*

2 to tear something is to pull it using force: *The old buildings were torn down and new ones built in their place.*

3 to tear somewhere is to rush there

[noun: **tears**] a hole or split made in something

tear [superscript 2] [noun: **tears**]

1 a drop of liquid that forms in, and drops from, your eyes when you cry

2 if someone is **in tears**, they are crying or weeping

♦ **tearful** [adjective] crying or in tears

tear gas [noun] a gas which stings people's eyes and makes them stream with tears

tease [verb: **teases, teasing, teased**]

1 to tease a person or animal is to annoy them or it on purpose: *Stop teasing the dog!*

2 to tease someone is to make fun of them or joke with them: *I didn't mean what I said. I was only teasing.*

♦ **teaser** [noun: **teasers**] a problem or puzzle

teaspoon [noun: **teaspoons**] a small spoon used for stirring tea or for measuring small amounts of ingredients when you are cooking

♦ **teaspoonful** [noun: **teaspoonfuls**] the amount a teaspoon will hold

teat [noun: **teats**]

1 the part of a female animal that its babies suck at to get milk

Tt

2 the rubber part on a feeding bottle that a baby sucks at to get milk

technical [adjective] to do with technology or practical skills: *Does he have any technical training?*

♦ **technicality** [noun: **technicalities**] a technicality is a detail of the law or any other set of rules

♦ **technically** [adverb] according to the rules, or according to technical or scientific methods

technician [noun: **technicians**] someone whose job is to do practical work in a laboratory or deal with technical equipment

technique [noun: **techniques**] a particular method of doing something

technological [adjective] involving technology

technology [noun: **technologies**] the study of the way things are made and work

teddy or **teddy bear** [noun: **teddies** or **teddy bears**] a toy bear with soft fur

tedious [adjective] long and boring

♦ **tedium** [noun] boredom

tee [noun: **tees**]

1 an area of level ground from which a golf ball is hit at the beginning of a hole

2 a small plastic peg pushed into the ground and used to rest a golf ball on before it is hit from this flat area of ground

[verb: **tees, teeing, teed**] a golfer **tees off** when he or she hits the ball from the tee at the start of a hole

teem [verb: **teems, teeming, teemed**]

1 if a place teems with people or animals, there are crowds or large numbers of them moving around there

2 it is teeming with rain when rain is falling very fast and heavily

teenage [adjective] suitable for or to do with teenagers: *teenage magazines*

♦ **teenager** [noun: **teenagers**] someone who is aged between 13 and 19

♦ **teens** [plural noun] your teens are the years of your life between the ages of 13 and 19

teeny [adjective: **teenier, teeniest**] very small

tee-shirt or **T-shirt** [noun: **tee-shirts** or **T-shirts**] a loose cotton top with short sleeves

that you pull on over your head

teeter [verb: **teeters, teetering, teetered**] to move about unsteadily and be just about to fall over: *The vase was teetering on the edge of the shelf.*

teeth [noun] the plural of **tooth**: *He got fillings in one front tooth and two back teeth.*

teethe [verb: **teethes, teething, teethed**] a baby teethes when its first teeth start to come through its gums

teetotal [adjective] someone who is teetotal does not drink any alcohol

♦ **teetotaller** [noun: **teetotallers**] someone who does not drink alcohol

tele- [prefix] if a word starts with **tele-**, it adds the meaning 'at or over a distance'. For example, *television* is pictures sent over a long distance between a transmitter and the sets that receive the pictures

telebanking [noun] a system in which you use your telephone to transfer money into and out of your bank account

telecommunications [plural noun] sending information over long distances by telephone, radio or television

telegram [noun: **telegrams**] a message sent by telegraph

telegraph [noun: **telegraphs**] an old-fashioned system of sending messages over long distances using radio signals or electrical signals sent along wires

♦ **telegraphic** [adjective] using telegraph

♦ **telegraphy** [noun] the system used for sending messages by telegraph

telepathic [adjective] someone who is telepathic can communicate with another person's mind without speaking, writing or using gestures

♦ **telepathy** [noun] communicating by thought alone

telephone [noun: **telephones**] a device which allows you to speak to someone at a distance, using electrical wires or radio

[verb: **telephones, telephoning, telephoned**] to telephone someone is to contact them using the telephone

♦ **telephonist** [noun: **telephonists**] someone who operates a telephone switchboard

telescope [noun: **telescopes**] an instrument with lenses and mirrors inside that make distant objects seem closer or larger
  ◆ **telescopic** [adjective]
  1 to do with telescopes
  2 having sliding parts that can be pushed inside each other

teletext [noun] a service that provides news and information that is regularly updated and which can be viewed in written form on a TV screen

televise [verb: **televises, televising, televised**] to televise something is to film it and show it on television

television [noun: **televisions**]
  1 television is a system for sending images and sounds in the form of electrical signals from a transmitter to a receiver, which changes the signals back into pictures and sounds
  2 a television, or television set, is the equipment which receives these pictures and sounds

tell [verb: **tells, telling, told**]
  1 to tell someone something is to give them information by speaking to them: *Why won't you tell me your name?*
  2 to tell someone to do something is to order them to do it: *I won't tell you again to be quiet.*
  3 if you can tell what something is or what is happening, you know what it is or understand what is happening: *I couldn't tell if he was joking or not.*
  4 to tell the truth or a lie is to give true or untrue information to someone
  5 someone who tells gives away a secret
  6 if someone **tells you off**, they talk to you in an angry way because you have done something wrong
  ◆ **teller** [noun: **tellers**] someone who works in a bank and whose job is to pay out and take in money from the bank's customers

tell-tale [noun: **tell-tales**] a child who tells an adult what another child has done wrong, even if it is not true
  [adjective] a tell-tale sign is a sign that shows where or what something that was secret or hidden is

telly [noun: **tellies**] an informal word for **television**

temp [noun: **temps**] someone who has a job in an office for a short period of time
  [verb: **temps, temping, temped**] to work in an office for a short period of time

temper [noun: **tempers**]
  1 a person's mood: *Don't ask him until he's in a better temper.*
  2 if you **lose your temper**, you get angry

temperament [noun: **temperaments**] your temperament is your nature, which affects the way you think and behave
  ◆ **temperamental** [adjective] a temperamental person changes their mood suddenly and gets upset or excited easily

temperate [adjective] a temperate climate never gets very cold or very hot

temperature [noun: **temperatures**]
  1 something's temperature is how hot or cold it is
  2 if someone has a temperature, their body is hotter than it should be because they are ill

tempest [noun: **tempests**] a word used in stories and poems for a very violent storm, with strong winds
  ◆ **tempestuous** [adjective] full of very strong emotions: *a tempestuous relationship*

template [noun: **templates**] a pattern that you can use to make the same shape many times

temple [1] [noun: **temples**] a building in which the members of some religions worship

temple [2] [noun: **temples**] your temples are the areas on either side of your forehead between your hairline and the sides of your eyes

tempo [noun: **tempos** or **tempi**] the tempo of a piece of music is its speed and rhythm

temporarily [adverb] for a short or limited time only: *He'd repaired the roof temporarily with a piece of plastic.*

temporary [adjective] lasting or used only for a short or limited time: *a temporary job • temporary repairs*

tempt [verb: **tempts, tempting, tempted**] to tempt someone is to make them want to do something or have something, especially something that they should not do or have
  ◆ **temptation** [noun: **temptations**] a feeling that you want to do something that you know is wrong or that might harm you

Tt

◆ **tempting** [adjective] something tempting is attractive and makes you want to do it or have it: *The cake looks very tempting.* ◆ *a tempting offer*

ten [noun: **tens**] the number 10
→ **tenth**

tenancy [noun: **tenancies**] the time when someone is a tenant or the agreement that makes someone a tenant

tenant [noun: **tenants**] someone who pays rent to the owner of a house, building or land in return for being able to use the house, building or land

tend [verb: **tends, tending, tended**] to tend someone or something is to look after them: *doctors and nurses tending the sick and injured*

tend [verb: **tends, tending, tended**] something tends to happen when it is likely to happen, or often happens: *She tends to be a bit moody.*

◆ **tendency** [noun: **tendencies**] if someone or something has a tendency to do something, they are likely to behave in that way

tender [adjective]
1 meat that is tender is easy to chew
2 showing gentle love: *a tender smile*
3 sensitive and delicate: *These plants are too tender to be grown outside.*

◆ **tenderly** [adjective] gently and lovingly: *He smiled at her tenderly.*

◆ **tenderness** [noun] being tender

tendon [noun: **tendons**] a type of strong body tissue that attaches your muscles to your bones

tendril [noun: **tendrils**]
1 a long, thin, curling stem with which a climbing plant fastens itself to something
2 a long curling section of hair

tenement [noun: **tenements**] a building with several floors that contain flats or apartments

tenner [noun: **tenners**] an informal word for ten pounds or a ten pound note

tennis [noun] a game played on a court that has a net stretched across the middle. Tennis is played by two or four players who use rackets to hit a ball to and fro across the net

tenor [noun: **tenors**]
1 a high male singing voice

2 a man who has this singing voice
[adjective] a tenor instrument plays notes at the lower end of the range: *a tenor saxophone*

tenpin bowling [noun] an indoor game in which a large heavy ball is rolled along a polished wooden track towards ten skittles or tenpins at the end of the track with the aim of knocking them down

tense [noun: **tenses**] a verb's tense is the form of the verb that shows whether the action of the verb happens here and now (the **present tense**), in the past (the **past tense**), or in the future (the **future tense**)

tense [adjective: **tenser, tensest**]
1 if you feel tense, you feel nervous and unable to relax
2 a tense situation makes people feel nervous and worried
3 your muscles are tense when they are stretched so that they feel tight

◆ **tension** [noun: **tensions**]
1 tension is nervousness or worry about something unpleasant that might happen
2 the tension of a piece of wire, rope or wool is how tightly it is stretched or twisted

tent [noun: **tents**] a temporary shelter made of canvas or nylon supported by a frame

tentacle [noun: **tentacles**] tentacles are the long, thin, flexible parts on the body of an octopus and some other sea animals

tenth [adjective and adverb] after ninth and before eleventh: *October is the tenth month of the year.* ◆ *He came tenth out of twenty in the singing competition.*
[noun: **tenths**] the fraction $\frac{1}{10}$, which means one of ten equal parts of something: *a tenth of a litre*

tepee [noun: **tepees**] a sort of tent used by Native American people in the past, made by tying poles together in a cone shape and covering them with animal skins

tepid [adjective] tepid liquid is slightly warm

term [noun: **terms**]
1 one of the periods of time that the school or college year is divided into: *the autumn term*
2 any limited period of time: *the president's term of office*
3 a word or expression with a particular meaning or used in a particular subject area:

Tt

What is the term for someone who collects old coins? • *complicated medical terms*
4 the terms of a contract or other agreement are the individual points or conditions it contains
5 people who are on goods terms, or who are on bad terms, have a good, or bad, relationship with each other
[verb: **terms, terming, termed**] what something is termed is what it is named or called: *Dogs that are used for hunting are often termed 'hounds'.*

terminal [noun: **terminals**]
1 a building at an airport where passengers arrive or depart
2 the place or building where rail, bus or boat journeys begin or end: *a ferry terminal*
3 a place or point where a connection is made to an electrical circuit
4 a computer terminal is one of several visual display units or monitors connected to one large central computer
[adjective]
1 a terminal illness is one that cannot be cured and that causes death
2 of or at the end

terminate [verb: **terminates, terminating, terminated**] to end or come to a stop
♦ **termination** [noun] the ending of something

terminus [noun: **termini** or **terminuses**] a place or building at the end of a railway or bus route

termite [noun: **termites**] a small pale-coloured insect that eats wood

terrace [noun: **terraces**]
1 a row of houses that are connected to each other
2 a raised level area, usually with paving, beside a house
3 a raised bank of earth with a level top
4 the terraces at a football or rugby ground are the sloping banks or tiers of seats where spectators stand or sit

terrain [noun] terrain is land, especially a particular type of land: *hilly terrain*

terrapin [noun: **terrapins**] a type of small turtle that lives in freshwater ponds and rivers

terrestrial [adjective] from the Earth, rather than from space or another planet

terrible [adjective] very bad: *a terrible smell* • *a terrible shock* • *Your writing is really terrible.*
♦ **terribly** [adverb] extremely: *I'm terribly sorry I broke your vase.* • *I feel terribly guilty about it.*

terrier [noun: **terriers**] any of various breeds of small dog

terrific [adjective]
1 excellent: *The party was terrific.*
2 very great or powerful: *a terrific wind*
♦ **terrifically** [adverb] extremely or very greatly: *We were terrifically pleased to get the award.*

terrify [verb: **terrifies, terrifying, terrified**] if something terrifies you, it frightens you very much

territorial [adjective] to do with territory: *a territorial dispute*

territory [noun: **territories**]
1 the land that a country or ruler owns or controls: *on British territory*
2 an area or region: *They were travelling on foot across mountainous territory.*

terror [noun: **terrors**]
1 terror is great fear
2 a terror is something that makes you very frightened
➞ **terrify**

terrorism [noun] the use of violence by small or illegal political organizations with the aim of forcing a government or society to accept their demands
♦ **terrorist** [noun: **terrorists**] someone who uses terrorism
♦ **terrorize** or **terrorise** [verb: **terrorizes, terrorizing, terrorized**] to terrorize people is to frighten them by using, or threatening to use, violence

test [noun: **tests**]
1 a set of questions or a short examination to find out your ability or knowledge: *a spelling test*
2 something done to find out whether something is in good condition or whether someone is healthy: *medical tests*
[verb: **tests, testing, tested**] to test someone or something is to give them a short examination or to carry out tests on them

testament [noun: **testaments**]

Tt

1 a written statement, especially of what someone wants to happen to their property when they die

2 proof or evidence of something: *Her success is testament to all her hard work.*

3 the **Old Testament** and the **New Testament** are the two parts of the **Bible**

testicle [noun: **testicles**] one of two glands in a man's body where sperm is made

◆ **testicular** [adjective] to do with the testicles: *testicular cancer*

testify [verb: **testifies, testifying, testified**] to give information or evidence, especially in a law court

testimonial [noun: **testimonials**]

1 a written statement about someone's character, skills and abilities

2 a gift given to someone as a way of thanking them for service they have given in the past

testimony [noun: **testimonies**] a witness's testimony is the statement they make in a law court

test match [noun: **test matches**] one of a series of matches played between two international teams, especially cricket teams

test tube [noun: **test tubes**] a thin glass tube, closed at one end and open at the other, used in chemical experiments

testy [adjective: **testier, testiest**] easily irritated or made angry

tetanus [noun] a disease caused by bacteria that get into a cut on your skin. It causes a stiff neck and jaw and can cause death

tether [verb: **tethers, tethering, tethered**] to tether an animal is to tie it with a rope to a post or bar

text [noun: **texts**]

1 the written or printed words in a book

2 a written message sent to a mobile phone [verb: **texts, texting, texted**] to text someone is to send a written message to their mobile phone

textbook [noun: **textbooks**] a book containing information on a particular subject, used by students in schools or colleges

textile [noun: **textiles**] a cloth or fabric made by weaving

texture [noun: **textures**] something's texture is the way it feels when you touch it

than [conjunction] **than** is used when you are making comparisons: *The test was easier than I thought it would be.* ◆ *He can swim better than me.*

thank [verb: **thanks, thanking, thanked**] you thank someone when you let them know you are grateful for something they have done for you or have given you

◆ **thankful** [adjective] happy, relieved and grateful

◆ **thankfully** [adverb] happily or gratefully

◆ **thankless** [adjective] a thankless job or task is one for which you get no thanks or appreciation

◆ **thanks** [plural noun]

1 you say 'thanks' to someone, or express your thanks to them, when you express your gratitude or appreciation

2 if something happens **thanks to** someone or something, they were responsible for it happening: *We finished the project on time, thanks to everyone's hard work.*

3 if something bad happens **thanks to** someone or something, they were responsible for it happening: *We were stuck in the airport all day, thanks to the strike.*

thanksgiving [noun] a church service giving thanks to God

◆ **Thanksgiving** [noun] a public holiday held on the fourth Thursday in November in the United States and the second Monday in October in Canada

thank you [interjection] something you say to someone when you are grateful for something they have done or given you: *Thank you for the flowers. They're beautiful.*

that [adjective: **those**] the word **that** is used before a noun to refer to a person or thing that is some distance away from you, or that has already been mentioned: *Who is that girl over there?* ◆ *Pass me that towel, please.*

[pronoun: **those**] the word **that** is used instead of a noun to refer to a person or thing that is some distance away from you, or that has already been mentioned: *I don't want to know that.* ◆ *Who is that at the door?*

[adverb] to the extent or degree mentioned: *I didn't think I'd run that far.* ◆ *The film wasn't that bad.*

[conjunction] **that** is used after verbs that have to do with saying, thinking or feeling, and to connect clauses: *He said that he hated sports.* • *I'm afraid that I can't offer you much help.*

thatch [noun] thatch is reeds, rushes or straw used as a roofing material for houses
[verb: **thatches, thatching, thatched**] to thatch a roof is to cover it with reeds, rushes or straw

that'd [short form] a short way to say and write **that had** or **that would**: *That'd better be the pizza delivery. I'm starving!* • *That'd be nice.*

that'll [short form] a short way to say and write **that will**: *That'll be the day!*

that's [short form]
1 a short way to say and write **that is**: *That's not what I meant.*
2 if someone says **that's that**, they mean that there is no more to be done or said about something: *I'm not going and that's that.*

thaw [verb: **thaws, thawing, thawed**] something that has been frozen thaws when it starts to melt or the ice in it melts

the [adjective] **the** is used before nouns to refer to a particular person, thing or group: *The bus arrived late, as usual.* • *Is it on the right or the left side of the road?* • *The men rode on horses and the women rode in carriages.*

theatre [noun: **theatres**]
1 a building where plays, operas or musicals are performed
2 theatre is the acting profession or the dramatic arts
3 a room where operations are done in a hospital
  ◆ **theatrical** [adjective] to do with plays or acting

thee [pronoun] an old-fashioned word for **you**: *I tell thee again, eye of my eye, this hunting is ended.*

theft [noun: **thefts**] stealing: *car thefts*

their [adjective] belonging to them: *Do you know their address?*
  ◆ **theirs** [pronoun] a word you use to talk about something belonging to a group of people or things that have already been mentioned: *They say it belongs to them, but I know it's not theirs.*

ⓘ Be careful not to confuse the spellings of **their, they're**, and **there**.
Their is the possessive form of **they**, and shows you someone owns something: *They have brought **their** exercise books.*
They're is short for **they are**: *They're late.*
There points something out: *Put this box over **there**.* • *There is nothing to do here.*

them [pronoun] a word you use to talk about two or more people or things that have already been mentioned: *The girls waved to me and I waved back to them.* • *'Do you like your new boots?' 'Yes, I like them a lot.'*

theme [noun: **themes**] the main idea, subject, or melody in a piece of writing, a talk, or a piece of music

theme park [noun: **theme parks**] an amusement park with activities connected to a particular subject or theme

themselves [pronoun]
1 you use **themselves** after a verb or preposition when the people who perform the action are affected by it: *They'd made themselves a cosy little shelter.*
2 **themselves** is also used to show that a group of people do something without any help from other people: *They'll have to work it out for themselves.*
3 you can use **themselves** to show more clearly who you mean: *They themselves are innocent.*

then [adverb]
1 at that time, in the past or future: *I didn't know you then.* • *The rest of the kids should be here by then.*
2 after that time, or next: *I went for a swim, and then I went home.*
[conjunction] as a result, or in that case: *If you have been eating sweets, then you must brush your teeth.*

theology [noun] the study of God and religion

theoretical [adjective] something that is theoretical is based on theory and ideas rather than practical knowledge or experience: *a theoretical risk*
  ◆ **theoretically** [adverb] possibly but not absolutely certain

Tt

theory [noun: **theories**]
1 a theory is an idea or suggested explanation that has not yet been proved
2 theory is the ideas and principles of an art or science rather than its practice

therapist [noun: **therapists**] someone who is an expert in therapy of a particular sort: *a speech therapist*

therapy [noun: **therapies**] the treatment of diseases or disorders, usually without surgery or drugs

there [adverb] at, in, or to that place: *Don't stop there. I was just beginning to enjoy the story.* • *I know someone who lives there.* • *I'm going there tomorrow.*
[pronoun] you use **there** with *is* or *are* to draw attention to what is going to follow: *There is a mouse somewhere in this house.*

thereabouts [adverb] approximately: *It will cost £50 or thereabouts.*

thereby [adverb] in that way: *We cut down all the trees, thereby letting more light into the house and providing wood for the fire.*

therefore [adverb] for that reason or because of that: *She had been awake all that night and therefore was very tired the next day.*

therm [noun: **therms**] a unit of heat used for measuring gas
♦ **thermal** [adjective]
1 using heat or to do with heat: *thermal energy*
2 thermal clothes keep you warm by preventing heat escaping from your body

thermometer [noun: **thermometers**] an instrument for measuring how hot or cold something is

Thermos [noun] a container made with a special double layer of glass and metal, used for keeping hot liquids hot and cold liquids cold. This word is a trademark

thermostat [noun: **thermostats**] a device that controls the temperature in a room or of a heating system
♦ **thermostatically** [adverb] using a thermostat

thesaurus [noun: **thesauri** or **thesauruses**] a book that lists groups of words that have similar meanings and can be used instead of each other

these [adjective] **these** is used before a noun to refer to people or things nearby or which are being mentioned: *Both these cups are dirty.* • *On these cold winter days, you have to wrap up warmly.* • *Can you make me a pair of these gloves?*
[pronoun] **these** is used instead of a noun to refer to people or things nearby or which are being mentioned: *Are these the same as the ones you had yesterday?* • *These are difficult times for everyone.*

they [pronoun] you use **they** to talk about two or more people or things that have already been mentioned or pointed out for the first time: *Apes are not monkeys. They don't have tails.* • *What did they think of your idea?*

they'd [short form] a short way to say and write **they had** or **they would**: *They'd all had their lunch.* • *They'd be better off selling that old house.*

they'll [short form] a short way to say and write **they will** or **they shall**: *They'll not be hungry again until supper time.*

they're [short form] a short way to say and write **they are**: *They're going for a drink after work.*

they've [short form] a short way to say and write **they have**: *They've never been skating before.*

thick [adjective: **thicker, thickest**]
1 quite wide from one side to the other: *a thick piece of rope*
2 something is a certain measurement thick when it measures that distance between one side and the other: *The ice was two feet thick.*
3 made up of parts that are very close together or densely packed: *thick wool*
4 not having a lot of liquid in it or not flowing easily: *thick gravy*
5 thick smoke or fog is dense and difficult to see through
[noun]
1 if you are **in the thick of something**, you are in the middle of it or in the place where all the action is happening
2 **through thick and thin** means 'even when there are difficulties': *We've been together through thick and thin.*
♦ **thicken** [verb: **thickens, thickening,**

thickened] to make thick or thicker
➟ **thickness**

thicket [noun: **thickets**] a mass of bushes growing together

thickness [noun: **thicknesses**] how thick something is, especially compared with other things

thick-skinned [adjective] a thick-skinned person does not get upset when they are insulted or criticized

thief [noun: **thieves**] someone who steals things
• **thieve** [verb: **thieves, thieving, thieved**] to steal
• **thieving** [noun] stealing
➟ **theft**

thigh [noun: **thighs**] your thighs are the parts of your legs between your hips and your knees

thimble [noun: **thimbles**] a metal cover for your finger used when you are sewing to help push the needle through the fabric

thin [adjective: **thinner, thinnest**]
1 not wide from one side to the other: *thin strips of paper*
2 a thin person doesn't have much fat on their body
3 not dense or thick: *His hair is getting a bit thin.* • *a thin porridge*
[verb: **thins, thinning, thinned**] to make a substance thin or thinner, for example by adding water or liquid to it

thing [noun: **things**]
1 an object, or something that is not alive: *I bought a few things for the party when I was in town.* • *Where's the thing for opening bottles?*
2 a fact, item, action or event: *We've got lots of things to discuss.* • *I hope I haven't done the wrong thing.*

think [verb: **thinks, thinking, thought**]
1 to think is to have or form ideas in your mind: *Don't disturb him. He's thinking.*
2 what you think about something is the opinion you have of it: *I don't think much of their new album.*
3 if you are thinking of doing something, you are considering doing it: *I'm thinking of applying for a new job.*

third [adjective and adverb] after second and before fourth: *That's the third time he's called today.*
[noun: **thirds**] the fraction $\frac{1}{3}$, which means one of three equal parts of something: *The bottle holds a third of a litre.*

third-party [adjective] third-party insurance covers damage or injury caused to someone else by the person who has the insurance policy

Third World [noun] the Third World is the name given to nations of the world that have not reached an advanced state of development and are fairly poor

ⓘ This phrase is now sometimes considered old-fashioned and offensive. **Developing World** is the term that many people prefer.

thirst [noun] thirst is the feeling that you must have something to drink
• **thirsty** [adjective: **thirstier, thirstiest**] feeling you must have something to drink

thirteen [noun] the number 13

thirteenth [adjective and adverb] after twelfth and before fourteenth: *You become a teenager on your thirteenth birthday.*

thirtieth [adjective and adverb] after twenty-ninth and before thirty-first: *February does not have a thirtieth day.*

thirty [noun: **thirties**] the number 30

this [adjective: **these**] the word **this** is used before a noun to refer to a person or thing nearby or which is being mentioned: *This apple is sour.* • *I have a meeting this afternoon.*
[pronoun] the word **this** is used instead of a noun to refer to a person or thing nearby or which is being mentioned: *I can't eat this.* • *Where are you going after this?*
[adverb] to the extent or degree mentioned: *It was this long and this wide.* • *We've come this far. Don't let's give up now.*

thistle [noun: **thistles**] a plant with prickly leaves and purple flowers

thorn [noun: **thorns**] a hard sharp point that sticks out from the stems of some plants
• **thorny** [adjective: **thornier, thorniest**]
1 covered with thorns
2 a thorny problem or question is difficult to solve or deal with

thorough [adjective]

Tt

1 you are thorough when you do something carefully, paying attention to every detail: *He made a thorough search.*

2 complete: *It was a thorough nuisance.*
➡ **thoroughly**

thoroughbred [noun: **thoroughbreds**] a horse bred from parents that both have pedigrees

thoroughfare [noun: **thoroughfares**] a public road or street that anyone can travel along

thoroughly [adverb]

1 with great care and attention to every detail: *Clean all the kitchen surfaces thoroughly.*

2 completely: *She was feeling thoroughly fed-up with the whole thing.*

those [adjective] **those** is used before a noun to refer to people or things at a distance from you or which are being mentioned: *Who are those two boys?* • *In those days, people didn't have cars.*

[pronoun] **those** is used instead of a noun to refer to people or things at a distance from you, or which are being mentioned: *What are those?* • *Those are just some of the coins in his collection.*

thou [pronoun] an old-fashioned word for **you**

though [conjunction] in spite of the fact that: *We only waited for half an hour, though it seemed like hours.* • *He went out, though I told him not to.*

[adverb]

1 however: *It's a pity we didn't win. It was an exciting match, though.*

2 as though means 'in a way that makes something seem to be true': *He looked as though he was going to cry.*

thought [verb] a way of changing the verb **think** to make a past tense. It can be used with or without a helping verb: *I thought I heard a noise.* • *He had thought about the problem all day.*

[noun: **thoughts**]

1 thought is thinking

2 a thought is an idea or something you think
♦ **thoughtful** [adjective]

1 if someone looks thoughtful, they look as if they are thinking

2 a thoughtful person is kind and thinks of other people
♦ **thoughtfully** [adverb] in a thoughtful way: *'I just can't work this out,' he said, scratching his head thoughtfully.* • *She'd very thoughtfully left drinks and sandwiches on the kitchen table for us.*
♦ **thoughtless** [adjective] a thoughtless person does things without first thinking about how they or other people will be affected by their actions

thousand [noun: **thousands**] the number 1000
♦ **thousandth** [adjective and adverb] coming last in a series of one thousand things: *the thousandth customer in the shop today*
[noun: **thousandths**] one of a thousand equal parts of something

thrash [verb: **thrashes, thrashing, thrashed**]

1 to thrash someone is to beat them very easily in a game

2 to thrash someone or something is to hit them very hard many times

3 to thrash or **thrash about** is to make wild violent movements

thread [noun: **threads**] a thin strand of cotton, wool or silk used for sewing
[verb: **threads, threading, threaded**] to thread a needle is to push a strand of thread through the hole in the top of a sewing needle

threadbare [adjective] a threadbare carpet or other piece of fabric has been worn thin by use

threat [noun: **threats**] a warning that someone is going to hurt you or harm you, especially if you do not do what they say
♦ **threaten** [verb: **threatens, threatening, threatened**] to threaten someone is to say that they will be harmed or hurt if they do not do something

three [noun: **threes**] the number 3

three-dimensional [adjective] a three-dimensional shape is solid and has length, breadth and height that you can measure

three-point turn [noun: **three-point turns**] a movement to turn a car round in which you go forward, reverse, and go forward again

thresh [verb: **threshes, threshing, threshed**] to thresh corn is to beat it so that the grain is separated from the straw

threshold [noun: **thresholds**]
1 a piece of wood or stone on the floor at a door
2 to be **on the threshold** of something is to be just about to begin it or enter it

threw [verb] a way of changing the verb **throw** to make a past tense: *He threw the ball hard.*

thrift [noun] being careful about money, saving as much as you can, and not wasting any
♦ **thrifty** [adjective: **thriftier, thriftiest**] using money and other things carefully, without wasting any

thrill [verb: **thrills, thrilling, thrilled**] something thrills you when it makes you feel excited and very pleased
[noun: **thrills**] something that gives you a glowing feeling of excitement and pleasure
♦ **thriller** [noun: **thrillers**] a book, film or play with an exciting plot, full of danger and frightening events
♦ **thrilling** [adjective] very exciting

thrive [verb: **thrives, thriving, thrived** or **throve, thrived** or **thriven**] if a person or thing thrives, they grow strong and healthy, or become successful: *The business is thriving.* • *a plant that thrives in sunlight*

throat [noun: **throats**]
1 your throat is the top part of the tube that goes from your mouth down to your stomach
2 your throat is also the front part of your neck

throb [verb: **throbs, throbbing, throbbed**]
1 something throbs when it beats regularly, as your heart or pulse does
2 an injured part of your body throbs when you feel pains in it that come and go like the regular beat of your pulse

throne [noun: **thrones**]
1 a special chair that a king or queen, or a bishop, sits on
2 the throne is the position or power of a monarch

throng [noun: **throngs**] a large crowd or gathering

throttle [noun: **throttles**] the throttle in a car or machine is the part of their engine through which petrol or steam can be turned on or off
[verb: **throttles, throttling, throttled**] to throttle someone is to grip them by their throat and strangle them

through [preposition]
1 entering at one side and coming out at the other: *He walked through the door.*
2 from end to end: *She was flicking through a magazine.*
3 because of, or by means of: *He ended up in hospital through his own stupidity.* • *I heard about it through a friend.*
[adverb]
1 entering at one side and coming out at the other: *He opened the hatch and stuck his head through.*
2 from end to end: *You're wet through.* • *Take this booklet away and read it through.*
[adjective]
1 a through route is one that gets you from one place to another and is not blocked anywhere along the way
2 a through train does not stop between the place it leaves from and the end of the line

ⓘ Try not to confuse this spelling with **threw**, the past tense of **throw**.

throughout [preposition] all the way through or in every part: *It rained throughout June and July.* • *There will be regular news bulletins throughout the day.*
[adverb] all the way through or in every part: *The show was a great success, and the children behaved themselves throughout.*

throw [verb: **throws, throwing, threw, thrown**]
1 to throw something is to send it through the air with force: *He threw the ball into the scrum.* • *She threw her bag down and rushed to switch on the TV.*
2 a horse throws its rider when it makes the rider fall off its back
3 if something throws you, it confuses you
[noun: **throws**] a throwing movement: *That was a great throw!*

thrush [1] [noun: **thrushes**] a wild bird with brown feathers and a speckled breast

thrush [2] [noun] an infection caused by a

Tt

fungus which affects your mouth and throat or a woman's vagina

thrust [verb: **thrusts, thrusting, thrust**] to thrust something is to push it quickly and violently: *He thrust his hands into his coat pockets.*

[noun: **thrusts**] a quick and violent push forward: *With a thrust of his sword, he scored the winning point.*

thud [noun: **thuds**] a dull sound made by something heavy hitting the ground

[verb: **thuds, thudding, thudded**] to thud is to make this sound

thug [noun: **thugs**] a violent man

thumb [noun: **thumbs**]

1 the short thick finger that is at a different angle from the other four fingers on your hand

2 if you are **under someone's thumb**, they control you completely and you are not allowed any freedom

thump [verb: **thumps, thumping, thumped**]

1 to fall with a loud heavy noise

2 to thump someone is to hit them hard

[noun: **thumps**]

1 the dull sound of something falling to the ground

2 an act of hitting someone hard

thunder [noun] the loud and deep rumbling sound that you hear after a flash of lightning

[verb: **thunders, thundering, thundered**] to make a loud rumbling sound, or to talk in a very loud, angry voice

thunderbolt [noun: **thunderbolts**]

1 a flash of lightning that is followed immediately by thunder

2 if something hits you like a thunderbolt, it has a sudden violent and disturbing effect on you

thunderclap [noun: **thunderclaps**] a sudden loud noise made by thunder

thunderous [adjective] very loud, like thunder: *thunderous applause*

thunderstorm [noun: **thunderstorms**] a storm with thunder and lightning

thundery [adjective] the weather is thundery when there are dark clouds and thunder

Thursday [noun: **Thursdays**] the day of the week after Wednesday and before Friday

thus [adverb]

1 as a result of that: *The heating has broken down; thus everyone is being sent home early.*

2 in this or that way: *The poem begins thus: 'I must go down to the sea again.'*

thwart [verb: **thwarts, thwarting, thwarted**] to thwart someone is to stop them from doing what they want to do

thy [adjective] an old-fashioned word for **your**: *Thy will be done.*

thyme [noun] a herb with lots of tiny leaves and flowers

ⓘ This word is pronounced **time**.

thyroid or **thyroid gland** [noun: **thyroids** or **thyroid glands**] an organ in your neck that gives out chemical substances which control how your body grows and functions

tiara [noun: **tiaras**] a piece of jewellery like a small crown

tick [noun: **ticks**]

1 a small mark (✓) used to show that something is correct or to mark off the things on a list that you have dealt with

2 the soft regular tapping or clicking noise that a clock makes

3 a very short time: *Can you wait a tick while I get my coat?*

[verb: **ticks, ticking, ticked**]

1 to tick something is to mark it with a tick

2 a clock ticks when it makes regular tapping or clicking noises

tick² [noun: **ticks**] a small insect that burrows into an animal's skin and sucks its blood

ticket [noun: **tickets**]

1 a small piece of printed paper or card that shows you have paid a fare on a bus, train or aeroplane, or that allows you to get into a concert or other event

2 an official notice saying that you have done something wrong while driving, such as parking in an illegal place or driving too fast

tickle [verb: **tickles, tickling, tickled**]

1 to tickle someone is to touch part of their body lightly so that they get a tingling or prickly feeling that makes them laugh

2 something tickles when it causes this tingling or prickly feeling on your skin

[noun: **tickles**] a tickling movement

♦ **ticklish** [adjective] if you are ticklish, you are sensitive to tickling

♦ **tickly** [adjective: **ticklier, tickliest**] causing a tingling or prickly feeling

tidal [adjective] affected by tides or to do with tides

tidal wave [noun: **tidal waves**] a huge wave, often caused by a volcano erupting under the sea or by unusually high tides

tiddler [noun: **tiddlers**] a very small fish

tiddlywinks [noun] a game played with small round coloured discs, in which you press one disc down on another making it flip upwards and fall into a cup

tide [noun: **tides**] the regular rise and fall of the level of the sea
[verb: **tides, tiding, tided**] if you have or get something to **tide you over**, it helps you get through a difficult time, especially one when you don't have enough money
➡ **tidal**

tidily [adverb] neatly

tidiness [noun] being tidy or neat

tidings [plural noun] an old-fashioned word for **news**: *glad tidings*

tidy [adjective: **tidier, tidiest**]
1 a place is tidy when it is neat and everything is in its proper place
2 a tidy person likes to keep things neat and in their proper place
[verb: **tidies, tidying, tidied**] to put things back in their proper places and make everything neat
➡ **tidily, tidiness**

tie [verb: **ties, tying, tied**]
1 to tie one thing to another is to join them or fasten them together, using string, rope or wire
2 to tie a knot or bow is to make loops that you twist round each other to form a knot or bow
3 two teams or competitors tie when they each have the same number of points: *They tied for second place.*
[noun: **ties**]
1 a narrow strip of material that goes round your neck under your shirt collar and is tied in a knot just under your chin
2 a situation in which two teams or competitors each have the same number of points
3 a match between two teams in a competition

tie-breaker [noun: **tie-breakers**] an extra question or test that will decide the winner in a contest where two people or teams have the same score

tier [noun: **tiers**] a row or layer, with another row or layer above or below it: *a wedding cake with three tiers*

tiff [noun: **tiffs**] an argument, especially one that is not very serious

tiger [noun: **tigers**] a large striped wild animal related to the cat

tight [adjective: **tighter, tightest**]
1 fitting very closely or too closely: *a tight shirt*
• *The top on this jar is very tight.*
2 very firm: *Have you got a tight grip on that rope?*
3 not leaving much room or space for movement: *a tight bend*
♦ **tighten** [verb: **tightens, tightening, tightened**] to make or become tight or tighter
♦ **tightly** or **tight** [adverb]
1 closely: *She held her purse tight.*
2 firmly: *Hold tight. It's going to be a bumpy ride.*
3 fully stretched: *Make sure that rope is pulled tight.*

tightrope [noun: **tightropes**] a long piece of rope stretched tightly between supports, which an acrobat walks along

tights [plural noun] tights are a one-piece covering for your feet, legs and bottom made of thin stretchy material

tigress [noun: **tigresses**] a female tiger

tile [noun: **tiles**] a piece of baked clay of various sizes, used for putting on roofs, walls or floors
[verb: **tiles, tiling, tiled**] to tile a roof, wall or floor is to put tiles on it

till [noun: **tills**] a machine in a shop used for counting up what customers have bought, and which has a drawer for the money

till [verb: **tills, tilling, tilled**] to till soil is to prepare it for crops or other plants by ploughing it or turning the soil over

till [preposition and conjunction] until

tiller [noun: **tillers**] a long piece of wood attached to the rudder at the back of a boat and which you use to steer the boat

tilt [verb: **tilts, tilting, tilted**] to lean over to one side

Tt

timber [noun]
1 wood that is used for building things such as houses
2 trees that can be used to provide wood for building

timbre [noun: **timbres**] the timbre of someone's voice or of a musical instrument is the quality of sound it makes

ⓘ This word is pronounced **tam**-bir.

time [noun: **times**]
1 time is the passing of days, weeks, months and years: *People say that time heals most things.*
2 the time is the hour of the day: *What's the time?*
3 the time of something is when it happens or is done: *Do you know the times of the trains to Edinburgh?*
4 the number of minutes, hours, days or years that something takes to do or happen: *It takes a long time for water to wear down rocks.*
5 one of several occasions: *They've won the cup four times.*
6 a particular period: *in olden times*
7 a suitable or right moment: *Now is not a good time to ask for more money.*
8 things happen or are done **from time to time** if they happen or are done occasionally, but not all the time
9 to be **in time** is to be early enough to do something or early enough for something to happen: *We arrived in time to see the fireworks.*
10 to be **on time** is to happen or arrive at the right time and not be late: *The train was on time.* • *We finished the work on time.*
[verb: **times, timing, timed**]
1 to time something is to use a clock or watch to find out how long it takes or when it will be ready
2 to time something well is to choose a good time to do it
♦ **timely** [adjective] something that is timely happens at just the right time: *a timely reminder*
♦ **timer** [noun: **timers**] a device for timing something
➡ **timing**

times [preposition] **times** is used in multiplication between the numbers you are multiplying: *Two times four is eight.*

time scale [noun: **time scales**] the time during which an event or process happens: *Evolution happens over a time scale of thousands of years.*

timetable [noun: **timetables**] a table listing the times when things should or will happen

timid [adjective] nervous, shy and easily frightened: *a timid child* • *a timid smile*
♦ **timidity** [noun] being nervous and shy
♦ **timidly** [adverb] in a shy, nervous way

timing [noun] choosing just the right moment to do or say something: *All comedians need to learn good timing.* • *The timing of the event is very important.*

timpani [plural noun] the large metal drums that are usually part of a symphony orchestra

tin [noun: **tins**]
1 tin is a soft, silvery metal
2 a sealed metal container for preserving food: *a tin of baked beans*
3 a metal container with a lid, which you store food in: *a tin of biscuits*

tinder [noun] dry material, especially small bits of wood, that can be used to light a fire

tinfoil [noun] thin metal wrapping for food

tinge [noun: **tinges**] a slight amount of something, especially a colour or feeling: *white with a tinge of pink* • *a tinge of sadness in her voice*

tingle [verb: **tingles, tingling, tingled**] to prickle, tickle or sting slightly: *My face was tingling in the cold night air.*
[noun: **tingles**] a prickling, tickling feeling: *I felt a tingle of excitement as the curtain went up.*
♦ **tingly** [adjective] feeling excited about something that is about to happen

tinker [verb: **tinkers, tinkering, tinkered**] to try to repair or improve a machine by making small changes: *Phil loves spending hours tinkering with his motorbike.*
[noun: **tinkers**] a person who used to travel around mending pots and pans for people

tinkle [verb: **tinkles, tinkling, tinkled**] to make a sound like small bells ringing
[noun: **tinkles**] a small, repeated ringing sound: *the tinkle of the bell on the cat's collar*

Tt

tinnitus [noun] a constant ringing or buzzing sound in your ears

tinny [adjective: **tinnier, tinniest**]
1 a tinny sound is thin, hard and high
2 a tinny object is made of thin or bad quality metal

tinsel [noun] strands of shiny, glittery material that are used as a Christmas decoration

tint [noun: **tints**] a small amount of colour: *a blue tint in her green eyes*
[verb: **tints, tinting, tinted**] to colour something slightly

tiny [adjective: **tinier, tiniest**] very, very small: *a baby's tiny hands and feet* • *the tiniest handwriting you ever saw*

tip [noun: **tips**] the point at the end or the top of something: *arrows with poison tips* • *Point to it with the tip of your finger.*

tip [verb: **tips, tipping, tipped**]
1 to tilt: *Tip the chairs forward against the tables.*
2 to spill the contents of a container: *They just tip the rubbish over the side of the ship.* • *Kitty tipped all her toys on to the floor.*
[noun: **tips**]
1 a rubbish dump: *taking the old carpet to the tip*
2 a very untidy place: *Your bedroom's a tip.*

tip [noun: **tips**]
1 a small extra amount of money for someone who has done a job for you: *They left almost ten dollars tip.*
2 a small piece of helpful advice: *useful tips on laying floor tiles*
[verb: **tips, tipping, tipped**] to give someone a small gift of money when they have done a good job for you: *How much did you tip the taxi-driver?*

tiptoe [verb: **tiptoes, tiptoeing, tiptoed**] to walk somewhere very quietly or carefully on your toes: *tiptoeing along the corridor, trying not to wake the other guests*
[noun] if you are **on tiptoe**, you are standing or walking balanced on your toes: *I can just see the sea if I stand on tiptoe.*

tire [verb: **tires, tiring, tired**]
1 to run out of energy and need a rest: *Auntie tires easily nowadays and has a rest every afternoon.*

2 to get bored with something: *I'm beginning to tire of Nigel's stories.*

♦ **tired** [adjective]
1 needing a rest: *You must be tired after your journey.*
2 bored: *I'm tired of wearing the same clothes every day.*

♦ **tireless** [adjective] having a lot of energy and never needing a rest: *her tireless efforts to raise money for charity*

♦ **tiresome** [adjective] annoying or boring: *Mona has a tiresome habit of finishing my sentences for me.*

♦ **tiring** [adjective] making you feel that you need a rest or sleep: *a tiring climb up the hill*

ⓘ Be careful not to confuse the spellings of **tire** and **tyre**, which is the covering of a wheel. However, in North America these words are both spelt **tire**.

tissue [noun: **tissues**]
1 a tissue is a paper handkerchief
2 tissue is very thin paper that is used for protecting delicate objects
3 tissue is the substance that animals and plants are made of: *muscle tissue* • *plant tissue*

tit [noun: **tits**] a type of small bird

titbit [noun: **titbits**]
1 a small tasty bit of food
2 a small but interesting bit of gossip

title [noun: **titles**]
1 the name of something such as a book, song or film: *What's the title of your poem?*
2 a word that you can use before your name: *Her title is 'Doctor', not 'Mrs'.*

titter [verb: **titters, tittering, tittered**] to laugh in a silly, nervous or embarrassed way
[noun: **titters**] a silly, nervous laugh

to [preposition]
1 towards: *walking to the shops*
2 as far as: *a mile from the house to the station*
3 compared with: *win by two goals to one*
[adverb]
1 almost closed: *Would you pull the door to?*
2 awake: *He came to in a few moments.*
3 **to and fro** means backwards and forwards: *He was rocking to and fro.*

toad [noun: **toads**] an animal that looks like a large frog

Tt

toadstool [noun: **toadstools**] a fungus that looks like a large mushroom and is often poisonous

toast [noun: **toasts**]
1 toast is bread that has been made crisp by being sliced and heated: *toast and marmalade for breakfast*
2 a toast is when people drink together to express a good wish for someone: *I'd like to propose a toast to the bride and groom.*
[verb: **toasts, toasting, toasted**]
1 to toast food is to cook it under a grill or at a fire
2 to toast a person is to have a drink and wish them well
✦ **toaster** [noun: **toasters**] a machine for heating slices of bread to make them crisp to eat

tobacco [noun] a type of plant whose leaves are dried and used for smoking or chewing
✦ **tobacconist** [noun: **tobacconists**]
1 someone whose job is selling cigarettes, cigars and pipes and sometimes sweets and newspapers
2 a tobacconist's is a shop that sells cigarettes, cigars and pipes and sometimes sweets and newspapers

toboggan [noun: **toboggans**] a sledge

today [noun] this day: *Today is Tuesday.*
[adverb]
1 on this day: *I can't come today.*
2 nowadays, at the present time: *People are taller today than they were a hundred years ago.*

toddler [noun: **toddlers**] a very young child who has just learned to walk

toe [noun: **toes**]
1 one of the five jointed parts at the end of your foot: *reach up high, standing on your toes*
2 the closed end of a shoe or sock: *a hole in the toe of my sock*

toffee [noun: **toffees**] a sticky sweet that may be chewy or hard: *a piece of toffee • a bag of toffees*

tog [noun: **togs**] a way of measuring how warm something such as a duvet is. The higher the number, the warmer it is: *a 10.5 tog duvet*

together [adverb] with each other: *We often go for a drink together. • Mix the sugar and eggs together in a bowl.*

toggle [noun: **toggles**] a small bar of wood or plastic that passes through a loop to fasten a coat or jacket

toil [verb: **toils, toiling, toiled**] to work hard for a long time
[noun] hard work that takes a long time

toilet [noun: **toilets**]
1 a large bowl-shaped piece of furniture where human waste can be washed away
2 a room with a toilet in it
✦ **toiletries** [plural noun] products that people use to keep clean and to look and smell nice: *Perfume, toothpaste, shaving cream and hair spray are all toiletries.*

token [noun: **tokens**]
1 a plastic or metal disc or a coupon or voucher that can be used instead of money: *a book token worth £10 • You need to buy special tokens to make the machine work.*
2 a sign of something: *I've got a bracelet as a token of our friendship.*

told [verb] a way of changing the verb **tell** to make a past tense. It can be used with or without a helping verb: *He told us a very interesting story. • Has Sarah told you her news yet?*

tolerable [adjective] something is tolerable if you can put up with it

tolerance [noun] patience and willingness to accept other people's ideas and behaviour

tolerant [adjective] willing to accept that other people have different opinions from yours

tolerate [verb: **tolerates, tolerating, tolerated**] to put up with something: *I can't tolerate this noise for much longer.*

toll¹ [noun: **tolls**]
1 a fee you must pay to cross a bridge or use certain roads
2 the loss or damage caused in a disaster: *The death toll was highest in the city centre.*

toll² [verb: **tolls, tolling, tolled**] to ring a bell slowly

tomato [noun: **tomatoes**] a juicy red-skinned fruit that is used like a vegetable in salads, sauces and sandwiches

tomb [noun: **tombs**] a place like a room where a dead body is buried

tombola [noun: **tombolas**] a kind of lottery

Tt

where certain numbered tickets win prizes

tomboy [noun: **tomboys**] a girl who likes rough, energetic activities

tombstone [noun: **tombstones**] a piece of stone with a dead person's name written on it that stands at the end of that person's grave

tomcat [noun: **tomcats**] a male cat

tomorrow [noun] the day after today: *Tomorrow is Wednesday.*
[adverb] on the day after today: *Let's have our meeting tomorrow.*

ton [noun: **tons**]
1 a measure of weight that is about 1016 kilograms or 2240 pounds in Britain or about 907 kilograms or 2000 pounds in America
2 tons of things or people are a very many of them: *She's got tons of clothes to choose from.*

tone [noun: **tones**]
1 the sound of something: *I could tell she was angry from the tone of her voice.* • *a cello with a soft gentle tone*
2 a brighter or darker version of a certain colour: *several tones of blue*
[verb: **tones, toning, toned**]
1 to tone or **tone in** with something is to match it or look good with it: *The red scarf tones in with the plum-coloured coat.*
2 to tone or **tone up** your body or muscles is to do exercises to become fitter

tongs [plural noun] a tool with two arms that are joined at one end and are squeezed together to pick something up

tongue [noun: **tongues**]
1 the soft thing inside your mouth that you can move and that you use to lick, speak, eat and taste
2 a language: *speaking in a foreign tongue*
3 the leather flap underneath the opening of a shoe or boot

tongue-tied [adjective] too nervous, shy or embarrassed to speak

tongue-twister [noun: **tongue-twisters**] a phrase or sentence that is difficult to say quickly

tonic [noun: **tonics**]
1 something that makes you feel stronger or gives you energy
2 tonic, or tonic water, is a clear, fizzy, bitter-tasting drink

tonight [noun] the night or evening of today: *I'll have to miss tonight's class, I'm afraid.*
[adverb] on the night or evening of today: *I'm going to bed early tonight.*

tonne [noun: **tonnes**] a metric unit of weight of 1000 kilograms or about 2205 pounds

tonsil [noun: **tonsils**] either of the soft lumps on either side of the back of your throat
♦ **tonsillitis** [noun] an infection that causes your tonsils to swell and hurt

too [adverb]
1 also: *Can I come too?*
2 more than necessary or more than is sensible: *If the water is too hot, add some cold.* • *You're driving much too fast!*

took [verb] a way of changing the verb **take** to make a past tense: *Fran took me to a concert on my birthday.* • *The shopping took all morning.*

tool [noun: **tools**] a piece of equipment that you use to do a certain job: *plumbing tools*

toot [verb: **toots, tooting, tooted**] to toot a horn is to make it sound
[noun: **toots**] the noise a horn makes

tooth [noun: **teeth**]
1 one of the hard, white bony parts in your mouth that you use for biting and chewing
2 one of the sharp points of something such as a saw or a comb

toothache [noun] a pain in or near your tooth

toothpaste [noun] a cream that you use to clean your teeth

top[1] [noun: **tops**]
1 the highest point or part of something: *climbing to the top of the tower* • *waiting at the top of the steps* • *distant mountain tops* • *Start reading at the top of the page.*
2 the upper surface of something: *a vase on the top of the television*
3 the lid or cap of a container: *Screw the top back on tightly.*
4 a piece of clothing for the upper half of your body: *green trousers and a black top*
[adjective] highest or most important: *My office is on the top floor.* • *a top fashion designer*
[adverb] with the highest marks or score: *He always came top in exams at school.*

Tt

[verb: **tops, topping, topped**]
1 to cover the upper surface of something: *Top the cake with fruit and whipped cream.*
2 to come first in a list: *This album is expected to top the charts next week.*
3 to **top something up** is to fill it up again: *Can I top up your drink for you?*
top [noun: **tops**] a toy that spins around on a point

topaz [noun] a type of precious stone that is often yellow

top hat [noun: **top hats**] a tall hat with a flat top that men often wore in the past

topic [noun: **topics**] a subject or theme to study, write or talk about: *an interesting topic for an article*

topless [adjective] without any clothes on the top half of your body

topmost [adjective] right at the top: *in the topmost branches of the tree*

topple [verb: **topples, toppling, toppled**] to wobble and fall over

top-secret [adjective] very secret: *a spy passing on information that should have been top-secret*

topsy-turvy [adjective and adverb] turned upside down

Torah [noun] the holy book of the Jewish people

torch [noun: **torches**]
1 a small electric light that you hold in your hand. It uses batteries for power
2 a big stick with something burning on the end that is carried as a light in a procession

tore [verb] a way of changing the verb **tear** to make a past tense: *Heidi tore the parcel open to see what was inside.*

torment [verb: **torments, tormenting, tormented**]
1 to treat someone cruelly or annoy them in a spiteful way
2 to be tormented by something is to suffer for a long time because of it: *still tormented by bad dreams*
[noun: **torments**] very great pain or worry that goes on for a long time
♦ **tormentor** [noun: **tormentors**] a person who makes a person or animal suffer on purpose

ⓘ The noun is pronounced **tor**-ment, with the stress on *tor*.
The verb is pronounced tor-**ment**, with the stress on *ment*.

torn [verb] a form of the verb **tear** that is used with a helping verb to show that something happened in the past: *The photograph had been torn right down the middle.*

tornado [noun: **tornadoes**] a violent storm with a whirling wind that causes a lot of damage

torpedo [noun: **torpedos** or **torpedoes**] a long thin bomb that moves quickly under water and explodes when it hits its target, which is usually a ship or submarine
[verb: **torpedoes, torpedoing, torpedoed**] to fire a torpedo at something

torrent [noun: **torrents**] a lot of water rushing or falling down quickly
♦ **torrential** [adjective] torrential rain is very heavy rain

torso [noun: **torsos**] the main part of your body, not including your arms, legs or head

tortoise [noun: **tortoise**] a slow-moving animal with a hard shell that covers its body

tortoiseshell [noun] the brown and yellow shell of a sea turtle that has been used to make things like combs or jewellery

torture [verb: **tortures, torturing, tortured**] to hurt someone on purpose, usually either as a punishment or to get some information out of them
[noun: **tortures**] hurting someone as a punishment or to get information from them: *an instrument of torture*
♦ **torturer** [noun: **torturers**] a person who hurts another person on purpose for some reason

Tory [noun: **Tories**] someone who supports or is a member of the Conservative Party
[adjective] to do with or supporting the Conservative Party: *Tory policies* • *Tory councillors*

toss [verb: **tosses, tossing, tossed**]
1 to throw something lightly into the air: *Toss the keys over here, would you?*
2 to move from side to side again and again when you are lying down: *tossing and turning in her bed all night*

3 to throw a coin up in the air to see which side it lands on: *We decided to toss for the front seat.*

total [noun: **totals**] the number you get when you add everything together: *We've got a total of fifteen cats.* • *thirty people in total*
[verb: **totals, totalling, totalled**] to come to a particular amount when added together: *Our collection totalled £320.*
[adjective] complete or absolute: *a total eclipse of the sun* • *The job must be done in total secrecy.*
♦ **totally** [adverb] completely: *Is she totally deaf?* • *I agree with you totally.*

totem pole [noun: **totem poles**] a tall wooden pole with carvings and paintings made by Native Americans

totter [verb: **totters, tottering, tottered**] to walk unsteadily and with small steps as if you are about to fall over

touch [verb: **touches, touching, touched**]
1 to put your hand or fingers on something: *Please do not touch the items on the shelf.* • *Can you touch the ceiling?*
2 to make contact with a thing or person: *We stood in a long line with our shoulders touching.* • *The car came close, but fortunately didn't actually touch us.*
3 to interfere with something: *Don't let anyone touch my desk while I'm away.*
4 to be touched by something is to be affected emotionally by it: *I was touched by your kind letter.*
5 to **touch something up** is to make small changes to something to improve it: *We decided to touch up the living room walls before we sold the house.*
[noun: **touches**]
1 touch is the sense that tells you what things feel like: *The fur was smooth to the touch.*
2 putting a hand or finger on something: *You can start the engine at the touch of a button.*
3 a touch is a small thing that you add to improve something: *She added the finishing touches to the display.*
4 communication with someone: *Get in touch with me.* • *I have lost touch with Sally.*

touch-and-go [adjective] very uncertain or risky: *It was touch and go whether she'd survive.*

touching [adjective] making you feel sympathy: *a touching story about a lost puppy*

touchy [adjective: **touchier, touchiest**]
1 easily annoyed: *What's she so touchy about today?*
2 needing to be dealt with carefully because people are likely to become annoyed or upset: *a touchy subject*

tough [adjective: **tougher, toughest**]
1 strong and not easily worn out: *You'll need a tough pair of shoes for climbing.*
2 strong, fit and not easily beaten: *a tough businesswoman*
3 difficult to deal with: *a tough customer* • *a tough decision*
4 hard to chew: *tough meat*
5 firm or strict: *It's time to get tough with football hooligans.*
♦ **toughen** [verb: **toughens, toughening, toughened**] to toughen or **toughen up** a thing or person is to make them stronger
♦ **toughness** [noun] being strong and not easily beaten or worn out

tour [noun: **tours**] a visit somewhere, stopping several times at points of interest: *a coach tour of the Lake District* • *a tour of the cathedral*
[verb: **tours, touring, toured**] to go round a place, stopping at points of interest on the way: *We're going to tour the wine-making regions of France.* • *We've hired a car to tour the city.*
♦ **tourism** [noun]
1 travelling to and visiting places for enjoyment
2 the industry that is involved in providing holidays and leisure activities for people
♦ **tourist** [noun: **tourists**] a person who is travelling for enjoyment or on holiday

tournament [noun: **tournaments**] a series of matches that make up a big competition

tour operator [noun: **tour operators**] a company that organizes holidays for people

tousled [adjective] tousled hair is untidy and looks tangled

tout [noun: **touts**] a person who tries to sell something, especially very expensive tickets for popular events

tow [verb: **tows, towing, towed**] to pull something behind you with a rope or chain: *The car broke down and we had to be towed home.*

Tt

[noun: **tows**] pulling something behind you with a rope or chain

towards or **toward** [preposition]
1 in a certain direction: *walking towards the gate* • *leaning over towards Bill*
2 in connection with: *Nothing has been done towards organizing the prize-giving.*
3 helping to pay for something: *a donation towards the new roof*

towel [noun: **towels**] a piece of thick cloth for drying yourself: *a bath towel*
[verb: **towels, towelling, towelled**] to dry a thing or person with a towel: *Towel your hair dry before applying the conditioner.*
• **towelling** [noun] thick cotton material that absorbs water well and so is good for drying things: *a bath robe made of towelling*

tower [noun: **towers**] a tall narrow building or part of a building: *the tower of the church* • *the Eiffel Tower*
[verb: **towers, towering, towered**] to be much taller than other things or people: *William towers over all his colleagues.*
• **towering** [adjective] very tall: *towering office blocks*

town [noun: **towns**] a place where people live and work, that has streets, buildings and a name

town hall [noun: **town halls**] a building that has council offices in it and, usually, a hall for public events

towpath [noun: **towpaths**] a path beside a canal or river

toxic [adjective] poisonous: *polluting the rivers with toxic waste*

toy [noun: **toys**] an object made for a child to play with
[verb: **toys, toying, toyed**]
1 to **toy with** something is to push it around for no real reason: *toying with her food but not eating it*
2 to **toy with** an idea is to consider it, but not very seriously

trace [verb: **traces, tracing, traced**]
1 to find someone or something by following information about where they have been: *The man has been traced to a village in the south of the country.*
2 to make a copy of a picture by covering it with a sheet of thin paper and drawing over the lines you can see through it
[noun: **traces**]
1 a mark or sign that someone or something leaves behind: *traces of footsteps in the sand* • *He vanished without trace.*
2 a very small amount of something: *traces of gunpowder on his shoes*

tracing paper [noun] very thin paper that you can see the lines of a picture through

track [noun: **tracks**]
1 a mark on the ground left by a person, animal or thing that has passed: *following the bear's tracks through the forest*
2 a rough path or road: *a narrow track around the edge of the field*
3 an area of ground with a circular course on it, used for racing
4 a set of rails that a train or tram runs on
5 one of the songs or pieces of music on a CD, tape or record
6 a heavy strip linking the wheels of a vehicle such as a tank
7 to **keep track of** someone or something is to make sure you know where they are and what is happening to them
[verb: **tracks, tracking, tracked**]
1 to follow the marks that an animal, person or thing leaves as they pass: *It was impossible to track anyone over such stony ground.*
2 to **track someone** or **something down** is to find them after a long search: *I'm trying to track down an old friend.* • *The shop has tracked down the book you ordered.*

tracksuit [noun: **tracksuits**] a warm suit with a loose top and trousers that you can wear when exercising or to keep your body warm before or after exercise

tract[1] [noun: **tracts**]
1 a large area of land
2 a system of tubes and organs in the body: *the digestive tract*

tract[2] [noun: **tracts**] a leaflet or a short essay

traction [noun] pulling or dragging

tractor [noun: **tractors**] a slow vehicle with two large rear wheels that is used for pulling heavy loads, for example, on a farm

trade [noun: **trades**]

Tt

1 buying, selling or exchanging things or services: *foreign trade*
2 a job or occupation, especially when it involves skill and training: *a young joiner who is still learning his trade*
[verb: **trades, trading, traded**]
1 to buy, sell or exchange things or services: *The government wants companies to trade outside Europe.*
2 to **trade something in** is to give it as part of the price of a new one: *We traded in our old car for the latest model.*

trademark [noun: **trademarks**] a name, word or symbol that a company uses to identify its products

trader [noun: **traders**] a person or company that buys and sells things

tradesman [noun: **tradesmen**]
1 a person who has been trained in a particular skill as their job
2 a shopkeeper

trade union [noun: **trade unions**] an organization of workers who are involved in similar work

tradition [noun: **traditions**]
1 a tradition is a custom that has been passed down from one generation to the next: *Having special birthday meals is a family tradition.*
2 tradition is passing down beliefs and customs from one generation to the next
♦ **traditional** [adjective] existing for a long time and being done by many generations: *traditional Christmas carols*

traffic [noun]
1 travelling vehicles: *There was a lot of traffic this morning* • *air traffic*
2 trade that is illegal
[verb: **traffics, trafficking, trafficked**] to buy and sell things illegally: *drug trafficking*

traffic lights [plural noun] a set of red, amber and green lights that controls traffic at road junctions

tragedy [noun: **tragedies**]
1 a very sad event: *The driver avoided a tragedy by his quick reaction.*
2 a story that has a sad ending, especially when the main character dies: *Shakespeare wrote comedies, histories and tragedies.*

♦ **tragic** [adjective] very sad or to do with suffering: *a tragic mistake*
♦ **tragically** [adverb] very sadly: *The poet died tragically young.*

trail [noun: **trails**]
1 a series of signs that you follow to find a thing or person: *The children in the story left a trail of paper when they got lost.*
2 a path or track through rough or wild country
[verb: **trails, trailing, trailed**]
1 to trail is to drag loosely behind someone: *Her long coat trailed on the floor.*
2 to trail something is to pull it loosely behind you: *Children trailed their boats through the water.*
3 to walk slowly because you are tired: *children trailing along behind their parents*
4 to be behind the winner of a competition: *The English team are trailing by 5 points.*
5 a plant that trails grows across and down, rather than upwards: *roses trailing over the wall*
♦ **trailer** [noun: **trailers**]
1 a container on wheels that is pulled behind another vehicle: *a tent in a trailer*
2 a short part of a film or programme that is used as an advertisement for it: *We saw some trailers for new films.*

train [superscript]1[/superscript] [noun: **trains**]
1 a series of railway carriages or trucks that are pulled by an engine
2 the back part of a long dress that trails on the floor: *The bride's gown had a long train made of lace.*

train [superscript]2[/superscript] [verb: **trains, training, trained**]
1 to teach a person or animal to do something: *Veronica has trained her dog to carry her handbag.*
2 to train as something is to learn to do that job: *Andrew trained as a nurse as soon as he left school.*
3 to prepare for a sporting event: *The team trains for three hours every day.*
4 to point a camera or gun in a certain direction: *The enemy's guns are trained on the airport.*
♦ **trainee** [noun: **trainees**] someone who is being trained to do a particular job
♦ **trainer** [noun: **trainers**]

Tt

1 a person who teaches people or animals to improve their skills
2 trainers are soft shoes that are designed for sports use

♦ **training** [noun]
1 practice and instruction in doing a certain job: *training in computing*
2 preparation for a sports event: *The team will be in training for the next year.*

traitor [noun: **traitors**] a person who is not loyal to their friends or country

tram [noun: **trams**] a type of electric bus that runs on rails in the street

tramp [noun: **tramps**] a person without a fixed home or job who walks from place to place
[verb: **tramps, tramping, tramped**] to walk with slow, firm, heavy footsteps

trample [verb: **tramples, trampling, trampled**] to tread on something heavily and roughly: *The sheep have trampled all over the wheat.* • *If you stand there you'll get trampled on.*

trampoline [noun: **trampolines**] a piece of canvas that is stretched across a frame for acrobats, gymnasts and children to jump on

trance [noun: **trances**] a state like sleep when you are awake, but not aware of what is going on around you

tranquil [adjective] quiet, calm and peaceful
♦ **tranquillity** [noun] calm and peacefulness
♦ **tranquillize** or **tranquillise** [verb: **tranquillizes, tranquillizing, tranquillized**] to give a person or animal a drug to make them calmer and more relaxed or to help them to sleep
♦ **tranquillizer** or **tranquilliser** [noun: **tranquillizers**] a drug that makes people feel calmer and more relaxed

trans- [prefix] if a word starts with **trans-**, it has something to do with moving across, through or over to the other side. For example, *transport* means 'to carry over' to another place

transaction [noun: **transactions**] a business deal or one that involves money

transatlantic [adjective] involving crossing the Atlantic Ocean: *a transatlantic flight*

transfer [verb: **transfers, transferring, transferred**]
1 to transfer a person or thing is to move it from one place to another: *transferring computer files to a floppy disk* • *George has been transferred to our London office.*
2 to change to a different vehicle or transport system: *At Kings Cross, transfer to the Northern Line.*
[noun: **transfers**]
1 moving a thing or person from one place to another: *The sergeant has asked for a transfer.*
2 a piece of paper with a design on one side that can be ironed or rubbed on to another surface
♦ **transferable** [adjective] a transferable ticket can be used by someone else or can also be used on a different transport system

transfix [verb: **transfixes, transfixing, transfixed**] to frighten or shock someone so much that they cannot move

transform [verb: **transforms, transforming, transformed**] to change something completely: *We could transform this room with a few tins of paint.*
♦ **transformation** [noun: **transformations**] a complete change in the way a thing or person looks
♦ **transformer** [noun: **transformers**] a device that changes an electric current from one voltage to another

transfusion [noun: **transfusions**] a blood transfusion is when blood that has been taken from one person is given to another person

transistor [noun: **transistors**]
1 a small piece of electronic equipment used in radios and televisions to make the sound louder
2 a transistor or a transistor radio is a small radio that you can carry around easily

transit [noun] to be **in transit** is to be travelling between one place and another: *The luggage has been lost in transit.*

transition [noun] a change from one state or place to another: *the transition from spring to summer*
♦ **transitional** [adjective] to do with changing or developing from one state to

Tt

another: *a transitional period of a few weeks when the old computer system is replaced*

translate [verb: **translates, translating, translated**] to put something into a different language: *Can you translate this into French?*

• **translation** [noun: **translations**]

1 a translation is writing or speech that has been put into a different language: *a new translation of an old book*

2 translation is changing speech or writing into a different language: *I'm no good at translation although I can understand what's going on.*

• **translator** [noun: **translators**] someone who puts speech or writing into a different language

translucent [adjective] not transparent, but shiny because light is reflected or can get through

transmission [noun: **transmissions**]

1 a television or radio broadcast: *a transmission that will be heard by millions all over the world*

2 broadcasting television and radio signals: *a transmission breakdown*

transmit [verb: **transmits, transmitting, transmitted**] to send out the signals for television or radio programmes

• **transmitter** [noun: **transmitters**] a piece of equipment that sends and receives signals for television and radio programmes

transparent [adjective] see-through: *The box is made of transparent plastic so that you can see all the wires inside.*

transplant [verb: **transplants, transplanting, transplanted**]

1 to remove a part from one person's body and put it in someone else's

2 to move a plant that is growing in one place to somewhere else: *The seedlings can be transplanted when they have four leaves.*

[noun: **transplants**] an operation to put an organ from one person's body into someone else: *a heart transplant*

transport [noun]

1 the vehicles that you travel in, such as cars, trains, aircraft and boats: *travel by public transport*

2 moving people or things from one place to

another: *This includes the cost of transport.*

[verb: **transports, transporting, transported**] to move something from one place to another

• **transportation** [noun] moving people or things

ⓘ The noun is pronounced **trans**-port, with the stress on *trans*.
The verb is pronounced trans-**port**, with the stress on *port*.

---

transporter [noun: **transporters**] a long vehicle that is usually used for taking a number of large objects, such as cars, to another place

trap [noun: **traps**]

1 a piece of equipment for catching animals

2 a plan to trick someone into doing or saying something or to catch them doing something wrong: *a speed trap to catch people driving too fast*

3 a small, two-wheeled carriage pulled by a horse

[verb: **traps, trapping, trapped**]

1 to catch an animal in a trap

2 to trick someone into doing or saying something: *The suspect was trapped into admitting that he had been there.*

3 to put someone in a situation that they cannot escape from: *One passenger was trapped in the crashed car until the fire brigade could cut him free.*

trapdoor [noun: **trapdoors**] a door in a floor or a ceiling

trapeze [noun: **trapezes**] a short bar hanging between two ropes high up from the ground, that gymnasts or acrobats swing on

trash [noun] rubbish: *a lot of trash in the newspapers*

• **trashy** [adjective: **trashier, trashiest**] of very bad quality: *trashy novels*

trauma [noun: **traumas**] a very upsetting, unpleasant experience that has a lasting effect: *suffering the trauma of going to war*

• **traumatic** [adjective] very upsetting, unpleasant or frightening: *a traumatic event*

travel [verb: **travels, travelling, travelled**] to go from one place to another, especially abroad or far from home: *Holly spent the*

Tt

summer travelling in the United States. • *How fast does sound travel?*

[noun: **travels**]

1 travel is going from one place to another, especially far from home

2 your travels are the journeys you make: *Did you have good weather on your travels?*

travel agent [noun: **travel agents**] a person or company whose job is to help people arrange holidays

traveller [noun: **travellers**]

1 a person who is on a journey: *a hostel for travellers*

2 a person who lives in a vehicle and does not stay in one place

traveller's cheque [noun: **traveller's cheques**] a cheque for a fixed amount that you can change for local money when you are on holiday in a foreign country

trawl [verb: **trawls, trawling, trawled**] to fish by dragging a net along behind a boat

• **trawler** [noun: **trawlers**] a fishing boat that drags a large net deep in the sea behind it

tray [noun: **trays**] a flat piece of something like wood or plastic with raised edges, for carrying food and drink

treacherous [adjective]

1 a treacherous person is someone who betrays people they should be loyal to

2 treacherous things or places are very dangerous: *The rain made the road treacherous.*

• **treachery** [noun] doing something that might harm your country or someone who trusts you

treacle [noun] a sweet, thick, sticky liquid made from sugar

tread [verb: **treads, treading, trod, trodden**]

1 to tread on something is to walk or step on it: *I accidentally trod on the dog's tail.* • *Don't tread on the flowers.*

2 to walk in a certain way: *We trod carefully around the broken glass.*

[noun: **treads**]

1 the sound you make when you walk: *the heavy tread of their boots on the bridge*

2 the tread of a tyre is the raised pattern on its surface that grips the road: *The tread on this tyre is completely worn away in parts.*

treason [noun] the crime of not being loyal to your country and possibly causing it harm, for example, by giving away secret information

treasure [noun: **treasures**]

1 treasure is valuable things, especially if they have been hidden: *looking for where the treasure is buried*

2 a precious thing: *the treasures in our museums*

[verb: **treasures, treasuring, treasured**] to think that something is very precious: *These are memories which I shall always treasure.*

• **treasurer** [noun: **treasurers**] a person who looks after the money of a club or society

• **treasury** [noun: **treasuries**] the part of a government that is responsible for a country's money

treat [verb: **treats, treating, treated**]

1 to deal with someone or behave towards them in a certain way: *I think Debbie treated Steve really badly.* • *You should not treat a mistake like this as a joke.*

2 to give a person who is ill some medicine or medical help: *Doctors use all the latest methods to treat their patients.*

3 to apply some sort of layer or protection to a surface: *The material is treated with a waterproofing spray.*

4 to pay for something special for someone else: *I treated the children to a pizza on the way home.*

[noun: **treats**]

1 an unexpected present for someone that you pay for: *How would you like a treat?*

2 an enjoyable outing that someone organizes for you: *We went to the theatre as a treat.*

• **treatment** [noun: **treatments**]

1 the way you deal with someone or behave towards them: *Will I get special treatment if I offer to pay more?*

2 the medical care that a patient gets: *My treatment will last for about a month.*

treaty [noun: **treaties**] an agreement between countries or governments: *a peace treaty*

treble [adjective] three times bigger or three times as much: *House prices are treble what they were ten years ago.*

[verb: **trebles, trebling, trebled**]

Tt

1 to multiply something by three
2 to become or to make something three times as big or as much: *Her pay has trebled over the last year.*
[noun: **trebles**]
1 in music, the treble is the higher range of notes: *Can you turn up the treble any more?*
2 a musical instrument with a high tone: *a treble recorder*
3 a boy with a high singing voice

treble clef [noun: **treble clefs**] a sign (𝄞) that is usually written before musical notes that are higher than middle C

tree [noun: **trees**] a tall plant with a hard trunk and branches

trek [verb: **treks, trekking, trekked**] to go on a long and difficult journey on foot: *They trekked over the mountains to the sea.*
[noun: **treks**] a long hard journey, usually on foot

trellis [noun: **trellises**] a frame of narrow wooden strips that is used to support climbing plants

tremble [verb: **trembles, trembling, trembled**]
1 to shake because you are cold or frightened: *Joe's hand trembled as he dialled the number.*
2 to sound unsteady: *I heard a trembling voice outside the window.*

tremendous [adjective]
1 very great: *a tremendous amount of work • travelling at a tremendous speed*
2 very good: *That's tremendous news!*

tremor [noun: **tremors**]
1 a shaking or quivering: *Was there a slight tremor in his voice?*
2 a small earthquake

trench [noun: **trenches**] a long narrow hole dug in the ground

trend [noun: **trends**]
1 a new fashion: *the latest trend in trousers*
2 the way things are going or developing: *There's a new trend towards healthier eating.*

• trendy [adjective: **trendier, trendiest**] fashionable: *trendy people • trendy clothes*

trespass [verb: **trespasses, trespassing, trespassed**] to enter or go on someone else's land or property without permission: *No trespassing! This is private property.*

• trespasser [noun: **trespassers**] a person who enters someone else's land or property without permission: *Trespassers will be prosecuted.*

trestle [noun: **trestles**] a wooden support with legs that is usually used for holding up the end of a table

tri- [prefix] if **tri-** comes at the start of a word, it adds the meaning 'three' or 'three times' to the word. For example, a *triangle* is a shape with three sides and three angles

trial [noun: **trials**]
1 a test that you do to make sure something works properly or that someone can do something properly: *We're carrying out trials on new products.*
2 a legal process where a jury decides whether or not a person is guilty of a crime: *a fair trial • The suspect will now have to stand trial.*

triangle [noun: **triangles**]
1 a flat shape with three sides and three angles: *a right-angled triangle*
2 a musical instrument that is a three-sided metal bar that you tap with a short metal stick

• triangular [adjective] in the shape of a triangle: *a triangular scarf*

triathlon [noun: **triathlons**] a sports contest that has three events, usually swimming, running and cycling

tribal [adjective] belonging to or done by a tribe or tribes: *tribal ceremonies*

tribe [noun: **tribes**] a group of families who live together and are ruled by a chief

tribesman [noun: **tribesmen**] a man who belongs to a particular tribe

tribeswoman [noun: **tribeswomen**] a woman who belongs to a particular tribe

tribulation [noun: **tribulations**] a great sorrow or great suffering: *a life of tribulation*

tribunal [noun: **tribunals**] a court or a group of people whose job is to investigate a particular thing and make a legal judgement on it: *an employment tribunal*

tributary [noun: **tributaries**] a stream or river that flows into a larger river or lake

tribute [noun: **tributes**] a speech or action that shows praise, thanks or respect for someone: *The film will be shown as a tribute to its star who died last week.*

Tt

trick [noun: **tricks**]

1 something that you do or say to fool someone: *a nasty trick to get all her money* • *a card trick*

2 a clever special way of doing something: *There's a trick to opening that door quietly.*

[adjective] a **trick question** is cleverly worded so that you probably give the wrong answer

[verb: **tricks, tricking, tricked**] to fool someone, especially when you make them do something they do not want to do: *They tricked her into agreeing to help.*

◆ **trickery** [noun] using cheating to get what you want

➡ **tricky**

trickle [verb: **trickles, trickling, trickled**] to flow in a slow, thin stream: *tears trickling down her face*

[noun: **trickles**] a slow, thin stream of liquid: *The waterfall has become a trickle because there's been so little rain.*

tricky [adjective: **trickier, trickiest**] difficult to deal with: *a tricky question*

tricycle [noun: **tricycles**] a vehicle that you pedal, with two wheels at the back and one at the front

tried [verb] a way of changing the verb **try** to make a past tense. It can be used with or without a helping verb: *I've tried and tried, but I still don't understand.* • *Rita tried not to giggle.*

trifle [noun: **trifles**]

1 a cold pudding made from sponge, custard, fruit and cream

2 a small amount: *It's a trifle hot in here.*

3 something that is not important or valuable

[verb: **trifles, trifling, trifled**] to **trifle with** someone or something is to deal with them in a light, thoughtless way: *It can be hurtful if someone trifles with your feelings.*

◆ **trifling** [adjective] not at all important: *a trifling matter*

trigger [noun: **triggers**] the small lever that you squeeze to fire a gun

[verb: **triggers, triggering, triggered**] to trigger something or to **trigger something off** is to set it off: *A dusty room always triggers my sneezing off.*

trill [noun: **trills**] the repeated sound of two

notes next to each other being played or sung alternately

[verb: **trills, trilling, trilled**] to sing repeated high notes: *birds trilling in the high branches*

trillion [noun: **trillions**]

1 a trillion in Britain and Europe is a million million millions

2 a trillion in the United States and in Canada is a million millions

3 an informal word for a very large number: *There are trillions of things we could do.*

trilogy [noun: **trilogies**] a series of three plays, novels, poems or operas that have the same subject

trim [verb: **trims, trimming, trimmed**]

1 to cut a little bit off something to make it tidy: *Get your hair trimmed.* • *You'll need to trim that photo to get it into the frame.*

2 to decorate the edges of something: *a coat trimmed with white fur*

[noun: **trims**] cutting a small amount off something: *Ask the hairdresser for a quick trim.*

◆ **trimming** [noun: **trimmings**]

1 a ribbon or lace that is used to decorate clothes or furnishings

2 the trimmings are the sauces and vegetables that usually go with a certain meal: *roast turkey and all the trimmings*

trinket [noun: **trinkets**] a small cheap ornament or piece of jewellery

trio [noun: **trios**]

1 a group of three people or things, especially musicians

2 a piece of music for three players or singers

trip [noun: **trips**] a short journey to a place and back again: *a shopping trip* • *a trip to the zoo*

[verb: **trips, tripping, tripped**]

1 to catch your foot on something and fall, or nearly fall over: *Caroline tripped over the edge of the carpet.* • *Mind you don't trip on the step.*

2 to make someone fall or stumble: *One of the boys tripped me up.*

3 to **trip along** is to walk or run along quickly and lightly

tripe [noun]

1 parts of the stomach of a cow or sheep, used as food

2 an informal word for rubbish or nonsense

triple [adjective]
1 three times as much or as many: *We had triple the number of entries this year.*
2 made up of three parts: *triple-glazed windows* • *a triple somersault*
[verb: **triples, tripling, tripled**] to become or to make something three times as big: *The number of students has tripled this year.*

triplet [noun: **triplets**] one of three children born to the same mother at the same time

tripod [noun: **tripods**] a stand with three legs for supporting something like a camera

triumph [noun: **triumphs**] a great victory or success: *another triumph for the champions* • *a shout of triumph*
[verb: **triumphs, triumphing, triumphed**] to win or succeed: *a man who triumphed over the hardships of a poor background*
• **triumphant** [adjective] very happy after winning or succeeding: *the triumphant medal-winners*

trivia [noun] details and small matters that are not important
• **trivial** [adjective] small and not important: *a trivial mistake*

trod [verb] a way of changing the verb **tread** to make a past tense: *Hey, you trod on my toe just then!*

trodden [verb] the form of the verb **tread** that is used with a helping verb to show that something happened in the past: *A lot of feet have trodden on these steps in the past.*

troll [noun: **trolls**] an imaginary, ugly, bad-tempered, human-like creature that is either a dwarf or a giant

trolley [noun: **trolleys**]
1 a basket on wheels: *a supermarket trolley*
2 a table on wheels

trombone [noun: **trombones**] a brass instrument that you blow. You change the notes by pushing a sliding tube in and out

troop [noun: **troops**]
1 a troop is a group of people: *a troop of children on a school outing*
2 troops are soldiers: *troops advancing from the west*
[verb: **troops, trooping, trooped**] to go somewhere in a large group: *tourists trooping around all the art galleries*

trophy [noun: **trophies**] a prize such as a cup or medal for winning a competition: *Helen won the junior tennis trophy three years running.*

tropic [noun: **tropics**]
1 either of two imaginary circles around the Earth. The **Tropic of Cancer** is 23 degrees north of the equator, and the **Tropic of Capricorn** is 23 degrees south
2 either of the hot regions to the north or south of the equator
• **tropical** [adjective] to do with, in or from the tropics: *a tropical rainforest*

trot [verb: **trots, trotting, trotted**] to run fairly fast with small steps
[noun: **trots**]
1 a jogging kind of run
2 if things happen or you do things **on the trot**, they happen or you do them one after another: *The team have had three wins on the trot.*
• **trotters** [plural noun] the feet of pigs or sheep, used as food

trouble [noun: **troubles**]
1 something that gives you a lot of work or problems: *A washing-machine would save you a lot of trouble.* • *You'd have no trouble finding a better job.*
2 your troubles are your worries and problems
[verb: **troubles, troubling, troubled**]
1 to trouble someone is to bother or disturb them: *I'm sorry to trouble you, but can you help me please?*
2 to trouble to do something is to make an effort or be bothered to do it: *He didn't even trouble to say where he was going.*
3 to be troubled by something is to worry about it or to suffer from it: *What's troubling you?*
• **troublesome** [adjective] causing worry or problems

trough [noun: **troughs**] a long narrow container that animals eat or drink from

trounce [verb: **trounces, trouncing, trounced**] to trounce someone in a game is to beat them easily

troupe [noun: **troupes**] a group of performers who work together: *a troupe of acrobats*

Tt

trousers [plural noun] a garment for the lower half of your body that covers each leg separately

trout [noun: **trout** or **trouts**] a kind of fish that lives in rivers and lakes

trowel [noun: **trowels**] a tool like a small spade

truancy [noun] being absent from school without permission

   • **truant** [noun: **truants**]

   1 a pupil who stays away from school without permission

   2 to **play truant** is to stay away from school without permission

truce [noun: **truces**] an agreement to stop fighting for a while

truck [noun: **trucks**]

   1 a lorry

   2 an open railway wagon for transporting goods or animals

trudge [verb: **trudges, trudging, trudged**] to walk with tired, heavy, slow steps: *trudging along in the snow*

true [adjective: **truer, truest**]

   1 real and not invented: *a true story*

   2 real and not pretend or supposed: *Are these your true feelings?* • *a true friend*

   → **truly, truth**

truffle [noun: **truffles**]

   1 a kind of chocolate with a soft creamy centre

   2 a rare fungus that grows underground and is used as food

truly [adverb] really: *Tell me what you truly want to do.* • *I'm truly sorry.*

trump [noun: **trumps**] trumps are the suit of cards that has been chosen to be worth more than the others in a card game

[verb: **trumps, trumping, trumped**] to trump a card is to beat it by playing a card that has a higher value in that game

trumped-up [adjective] deliberately made up in order to make someone seem guilty: *trumped-up evidence*

trumpet [noun: **trumpets**] a brass musical instrument that you blow into to make a loud, high, clear sound

[verb: **trumpets, trumpeting, trumpeted**] an elephant trumpets when it makes a loud noise

truncheon [noun: **truncheon**] a short, thick, heavy stick carried by police officers

trundle [verb: **trundles, trundling, trundled**]

   1 to trundle is to move heavily and slowly along on wheels: *lorries trundling through the empty streets*

   2 to trundle something with wheels is to push or pull it slowly: *Gordon trundled the wheelbarrow round to the back of the house.*

trunk [noun: **trunks**]

   1 the main stem of a tree, without its branches or roots

   2 an elephant's long nose

   3 a large box or chest for storing or transporting clothes and other possessions

   4 the main part of a person's body, not including their head, arms or legs

   5 the American English word for the **boot** of a car

trunk call [noun: **trunk calls**] a long-distance telephone call

trunk road [noun: **trunk roads**] a main road

trunks [plural noun] trunks are short trousers worn by men or boys for swimming

trust [verb: **trusts, trusting, trusted**]

   1 to believe that someone is honest and loyal: *The colonel picked out ten men he knew he could trust.*

   2 to rely on someone to do something properly and not cause damage: *I know I can trust you not to make any mistakes.* • *Can I trust you with my new camera?*

   3 to expect and believe that something is so: *I trust that all is well with you?*

[noun]

   1 the belief that someone is honest and loyal: *It can be difficult to get a new pet's trust.*

   2 a responsibility to look after something or do something properly: *The children had been placed in my trust.*

   3 a legal arrangement in which one person looks after and controls money for someone else

   • **trustee** [noun: **trustees**]

   1 someone who looks after and controls someone else's money

   2 one of a group of people who manage a

Tt

company or organization such as a school or hospital

+ **trusting** [adjective] believing that other people are honest and good: *a very trusting person*
+ **trustworthy** [adjective] honest
+ **trusty** [adjective] reliable: *my trusty friend*

truth [noun: **truths**]

1 what is true and real: *Please try to tell the truth.* • *The truth is that she never really loved him.*

2 being true: *There is no truth in his story.*

+ **truthful** [adjective]

1 a truthful person tells the truth

2 truthful information is not false

+ **truthfully** [adverb] without lying: *Answer the questions as truthfully as you can.*

try [verb: **tries, trying, tried**]

1 to make an effort or an attempt to do something: *Please try to understand.* • *I'm trying to call John but he's not answering the phone.*

2 to do or use something to see if you like it or if it is good: *Try this powder for a cleaner wash.*

3 to find out if someone committed a crime by hearing all the evidence in a court: *They will be tried in the European Court of Human Rights.*

[noun: **tries**]

1 an attempt to do something: *That was a good try. Better luck next time.*

2 in rugby, a successful attempt to put the ball over the other team's goal line

→ **trial**

tsar or **czar** [noun: **tsars** or **czars**] the male ruler of Russia before 1917

tsarina or **czarina** [noun: **tsarinas** or **czarinas**] the wife of the ruler, or the female ruler of Russia before 1917

T-shirt [noun: **T-shirts**] another spelling of **tee-shirt**

tsp [abbreviation] short for **teaspoon**. It is an abbreviation that is usually used in recipe books

tsunami [noun: **tsunamis**] a very high, fast-moving wave that is caused by an earthquake under the sea

tub [noun: **tubs**]

1 a round container for liquid or creamy substances: *a tub of ice-cream* • *a tub that will hold 20 litres of water*

2 a bath: *a long soak in the tub*

tuba [noun: **tubas**] a large brass musical instrument that you blow. It usually plays very low notes

tubby [adjective: **tubbier, tubbiest**] slightly fat

tube [noun: **tubes**]

1 a long, thin, hollow pipe: *a rubber tube that carries the gas into the other bottle*

2 a long hollow container: *a cardboard tube for storing posters* • *a tube of toothpaste*

3 an underground railway system, especially in London: *We can easily get there by tube.*

tuber [noun: **tubers**] a swollen plant root that new plants can grow from: *Potatoes are tubers that you can eat or plant again.*

tuberculosis [noun] a serious infectious disease that affects your lungs and makes it difficult to breathe. This is often shortened to **TB**

tuck [noun: **tucks**] a fold in cloth that is fixed, usually with stitching: *a blouse with tucks down the front* • *We can make a small tuck in the waist to make it fit.*

[verb: **tucks, tucking, tucked**]

1 to hide an edge or loose end inside or under something else to make it firm or tidy: *Tuck your shirt in.* • *Tuck the flap into the envelope and seal it with tape.*

2 to **tuck in** is to eat with enjoyment: *The kids tucked in without waiting for the adults to arrive.*

3 to be **tucked up** in bed is to be snug and comfortable under the bedclothes

Tuesday [noun: **Tuesdays**] the day of the week after Monday and before Wednesday

tuft [noun: **tufts**] a bunch of something, such as grass or hair, that grows from the same place

tug [verb: **tugs, tugging, tugged**] to pull something suddenly or strongly towards you: *The children were tugging each other's hair.*

[noun: **tugs**]

1 a sudden hard pull towards you: *I gave his arm a tug and he looked at me crossly.*

2 a short form of the word **tugboat**

tugboat [noun: **tugboats**] a small powerful boat that is used for towing ships

Tt

tug-of-war [noun] a contest in which the winners are the team that can pull their end of a rope over a line

tuition [noun] teaching or instruction in how to do something: *driving tuition*

tulip [noun: **tulips**] a type of flower with a straight stem and a cup-shaped flower that grows from a bulb in the spring

tumble [verb: **tumbles, tumbling, tumbled**]

1 to fall down and over

2 to **tumble to** something is to realize or suddenly understand it: *We finally tumbled to the fact that he was lying.*

[noun: **tumbles**] a fall: *Lucy had taken a tumble over the doorstep.*

tumbledown [adjective] a tumbledown building is falling to pieces

tumble-dry [verb: **tumble-dries, tumble-drying, tumble-dried**] to dry clothes in a machine

♦ **tumble-dryer** or **tumble-drier** [noun: **tumble-dryers** or **tumble-driers**] a machine that uses hot air to dry clothes in a drum that turns around and around

tumbler [noun: **tumblers**] a large drinking glass with straight sides

tummy [noun: **tummies**] a word children use for their stomach

tumour [noun: **tumours**] a lump in or on your body. Some types can make you ill

tumult [noun: **tumults**] a loud or confused noise made by a crowd

♦ **tumultuous** [adjective] noisy and confused: *a tumultuous welcome*

tuna [noun: **tuna**] a large fish whose flesh is sold in cans and eaten as food

tune [noun: **tunes**]

1 a series of musical notes that sound nice together

2 a musical note is **in tune** if it is exactly the right note

3 an instrument is **in tune** if it produces the right notes

[verb: **tunes, tuning, tuned**]

1 to adjust a musical instrument so that it sounds right

2 to adjust a television or radio to a certain channel or station

3 to adjust an engine so that it works smoothly

♦ **tuneful** [adjective] having a pleasant melody

tunic [noun: **tunics**]

1 a loose piece of clothing with no sleeves

2 the top half of a policeman's or soldier's uniform

tunnel [noun: **tunnels**] a long underground passage

[verb: **tunnels, tunnelling, tunnelled**] to make an underground passage: *Will they tunnel under the river or build a bridge over it?*

turban [noun: **turbans**] a long piece of cloth that is wrapped round and round the head to make a kind of hat. Sikh men wear a turban

turbine [noun: **turbines**] a machine or engine that is driven by a flow of water or gas

turbulence [noun] disturbance in the water or air that makes ships or aircraft shake

♦ **turbulent** [adjective] disturbed or confused: *a turbulent week for the government*

turf [noun] short thick grass

turkey [noun: **turkeys**] a large farmyard bird that is eaten as food

turmoil [noun] a state of worry and confusion: *Her mind was in turmoil.*

turn [verb: **turns, turning, turned**]

1 to turn is to move to face in another direction: *He turned and walked away.*

2 to turn something is to move it so that it faces in another direction: *Why have you turned that picture towards the wall?*

3 to spin around or twist: *a turning wheel* • *Turn the handle to the right.*

4 to change and become something: *She took one look and turned pale.* • *The frog turned into a prince.*

5 to **turn something** or **someone down** is to refuse an offer they make: *He asked her to marry him but she turned him down.*

6 to **turn something down** is to reduce the amount of light, heat or sound that something produces: *Turn that radio down, will you?*

7 to **turn in** is to go to bed

8 to **turn someone in** is to hand them over to the police

9 to **turn out** a certain way is to finish or end up like that: *How did the experiment turn out?*

10 to **turn out** is to come out to see or do

something: *Not many people turned out for the local election.*

11 to **turn up** is to appear or arrive: *To our surprise over twenty people turned up.*

12 to **turn something up** is to increase the amount of light, heat or sound that something produces: *Can you turn the volume up a bit?*

[noun: **turns**]

1 a curve, bend or change of direction: *Take the first turn on the right.*

2 something that people do one after the other: *It's your turn next.*

3 a short performance in a show: *Jolly Jack will be the star turn at the Christmas show this year.*

4 a **good turn** is a favour that you do for someone

5 if you do things **in turn**, you do them one after the other

turncoat [noun: **turncoats**] a person who changes sides in an argument

turnip [noun: **turnips**] a hard, round, white vegetable that grows under the ground

turnover [noun: **turnovers**]

1 the value of the goods and services that a company sells during a particular period

2 the rate at which people leave and join a company or organization: *a company with a high turnover of staff*

3 a small sweet pie made of a piece of folded pastry with a fruit filling

turnpike [noun: **turnpikes**] a road in America which travellers pay to use

turnstile [noun: **turnstiles**] a gate that turns, allowing one person to go through at a time

turntable [noun: **turntables**] a turning platform

turpentine [noun] an oily liquid used for things like making paint thinner and cleaning paintbrushes

turquoise [noun: **turquoises**]

1 a green-blue precious stone

2 a green-blue colour

turtle [noun: **turtles**] a large reptile that usually lives in the sea, with a hard shell and flippers for swimming

tusk [noun: **tusks**] a long curved pointed tooth that sticks out of the mouth of some animals, such as the elephant and walrus

tussle [noun: **tussles**] a struggle with someone to get something

[verb: **tussles, tussling, tussled**] to argue or struggle with someone over something you both want

tutor [noun: **tutors**]

1 a private teacher who teaches individual pupils at home

2 a university or college teacher who teaches students in small groups or gives them advice

[verb: **tutors, tutoring, tutored**] to tutor someone is to teach them

✦ **tutorial** [noun: **tutorials**] a lesson at a university or college for an individual student or a small group

tutu [noun: **tutus**] a ballet dancer's dress that has a stiff, sticking-out skirt

TV [noun: **TVs**]

1 a TV is a television set: *We've got a new TV.*

2 TV is television broadcasts: *I think the children watch too much TV.*

tweak [verb: **tweaks, tweaking, tweaked**] to pull something with a small jerk: *He tweaked my hair roughly.*

[noun: **tweaks**] a small pull at something to make a small change: *The tablecloth needs a bit of a tweak.*

tweed [noun: **tweeds**] thick, rough, woollen cloth that is often used for making clothing

tweezers [plural noun] a small tool for gripping very thin things such as hairs

twelfth [adjective and adverb] after the eleventh and before the thirteenth: *the twelfth day of May*

twelve [noun: **twelves**] the number 12

twentieth [adjective and adverb] after the nineteenth and before the twenty-first: *the twentieth day of April*

twenty [noun: **twenties**] the number 20

twice [adverb] two times: *He sneezed twice.* • *I could eat twice that amount.*

twiddle [verb: **twiddles, twiddling, twiddled**] to twist or twirl something round and round: *Try twiddling some knobs to try to make it work.*

twig [noun: **twigs**] a small thin piece that grows from a branch of a tree or bush: *We need a pile of dry twigs to start the fire.*

[verb: **twigs, twigging, twigged**] an

Tt

informal word that means to suddenly realize something: *Then I twigged what he was really talking about.*

twilight [noun] the time after the sun sets when it is not quite dark

twin [noun: **twins**] one of two children born to the same mother at the same time: *Paul and Jo are twins.* • *Yes, I'm a twin.*
[adjective] belonging to a pair of things that are very similar: *twin beds* • *a car with twin exhaust pipes*

twine [noun] strong string
[verb: **twines, twining, twined**] to twist around something: *twining a lock of hair round her finger.*

twinge [noun: **twinges**] a sudden unpleasant feeling: *a twinge of toothache* • *a twinge of guilt*

twinkle [verb: **twinkles, twinkling, twinkled**]
1 lights twinkle when they glitter brightly: *lights twinkling along the shoreline*
2 someone's eyes twinkle when they are bright with excitement or humour
[noun: **twinkles**] a bright shining light

twirl [verb: **twirls, twirling, twirled**]
1 to twirl is to spin round quickly
2 to twirl something is to spin it round quickly: *The leaders of the parade twirled their batons.*
[noun: **twirls**] a fast turn or spin around

twist [verb: **twists, twisting, twisted**]
1 to wind something or turn it round: *Her hair was tangled and twisted around the clip.* • *Twist the handle hard and then pull it to open the door.*
2 to turn the top half of your body: *Gregory twisted round in his chair to look at me.*
3 to bend something out of its proper shape: *After twisting my ankle, I developed a bad limp.* • *The front wheel of the bike twisted when it hit the wall.*
4 to wind from side to side: *a road that twists*
[noun: **twists**]
1 a turn round: *Give the lid a good hard twist.*
2 the shape of something that has been turned or wound around: *a twist of wire*
3 a change in the way something happens: *an unusual twist at the end of the story*

twitch [noun: **twitches**] a jerky movement

[verb: **twitches, twitching, twitched**]
1 to move jerkily: *Her eyelid twitched.*
2 to move something sharply or jerkily: *people twitching curtains to look outside*

twitter [verb: **twitters, twittering, twittered**] to make a lot of high-pitched noises: *birds twittering in the trees*

two [noun: **twos**] the number 2

two-dimensional [adjective] a two-dimensional shape is flat and has length and width you can measure, but not height or depth

two-faced [adjective] not honest or not acting in the same way with everyone

tycoon [noun: **tycoons**] a rich and powerful businessman or businesswoman

type [noun: **types**]
1 a sort or kind of thing or person: *What type of person would write a letter like this?* • *Choose the right type of shampoo.*
2 letters and figures that are used in printing: *The title should be in bold type.*
[verb: **types, typing, typed**] to write using a keyboard on a typewriter or computer: *Type your name and then your password.*
➜ **typist**

typewriter [noun: **typewriters**] a machine that you can use to produce printed text

typhoon [noun: **typhoons**] a violent storm

typical [adjective]
1 having the usual qualities of a certain type of thing or person: *typical holiday weather*
2 just as you expect from a certain thing or person: *That's typical of Nick.*

◆ **typically** [adverb]
1 in most cases: *An insect typically has six legs and two pairs of wings.*
2 as you would expect from a certain person or thing: *Tracy was typically late.*

typist [noun: **typists**] someone whose job is to type, especially in an office

tyrannical [adjective] cruel and not fair towards people: *a tyrannical leader*

tyranny [noun: **tyrannies**] a cruel and unfair way of using power

tyrant [noun: **tyrants**] a ruler who has complete power and who uses it cruelly

tyre [noun: **tyres**] a thick rubber ring that is usually filled with air and covers the edge of a wheel: *a flat tyre*

Tt

U

udder [noun: **udders**] the part like a bag that hangs under a cow and supplies milk

UFO [abbreviation: **UFOs**] short for **unidentified flying object**, which is something seen in the sky and nobody knows what it is

ugliness [noun] being ugly

ugly [adjective: **uglier, ugliest**] not very nice to look at: *an ugly man* • *an ugly building*

UHT [abbreviation] short for **ultra-heat treated**, which describes a type of milk that you can keep for a long time

ukulele [noun: **ukuleles**] a musical instrument like a small guitar with four strings

ulcer [noun: **ulcers**] a sore on your skin or inside your body

ultimate [adjective] happening at the end of a process: *an ultimate aim*
  ✦ **ultimately** [adverb] finally

ultimatum [noun: **ultimatums** or **ultimata**] if you give someone an ultimatum, you say that you will take a certain action unless they do something by a certain time

ultra- [prefix] if a word starts with **ultra-**, it adds the meaning 'very' or 'beyond a particular limit'. For example, *ultra-careful* means 'extremely careful'

ultrasound [noun] a way of producing an image of an unborn baby by using sound waves with a very high frequency

ultraviolet [adjective] ultraviolet light is light you cannot see and which turns the skin darker

umbilical cord [noun: **umbilical cords**] the cord that connects a baby to its mother before it is born

umbrella [noun: **umbrellas**] something you put up and shelter under when it rains, which consists of a frame with cloth over it

umpire [noun: **umpires**] someone who watches a game such as tennis or cricket and makes sure that the rules are not broken

umpteen [adjective] an informal word for a large number: *I've told you umpteen times you should quit smoking.*

un- [prefix] if a word starts with **un-**, it adds the meaning 'not'. For example, *untidy* means 'not tidy'

ⓘ There are many other words that begin with **un-** besides the ones that are listed in this dictionary. If a word that begins with **un-** is not listed here, you should be able to work out its meaning by looking up the definition of the word without **un-** and adding 'not' to it.

unable [adjective] not having enough time, strength or skill to do something: *He stood mesmerized, quite unable to take his eyes off the bear.*

unaccustomed [adjective] if you are unaccustomed to something, you are not used to it

unanimous [adjective] agreed by everyone: *a unanimous decision*
  ✦ **unanimously** [adverb] in a way that is unanimous: *He was elected unanimously.*

unarmed [adjective] without weapons: *unarmed combat* • *an unarmed policeman*

unaware [adjective] not knowing about something: *We were unaware of the danger.*
  ✦ **unawares** [adverb] when not expected: *Their arrival caught me unawares.*

unbearable [adjective] too painful or annoying to deal with

Uu

611

♦ **unbearably** [adverb] in a way that is difficult to bear: *It is unbearably hot outside.*

unbelievable [adjective]
1 difficult to believe: *an unbelievable excuse*
2 a word used to emphasize how bad, good or big something is: *an unbelievable success*
♦ **unbelievably** [adverb] in a way that is unbelievable: *She's unbelievably rich.*

uncalled [adjective] if an action is **uncalled for**, it is not fair or not necessary: *That remark was completely uncalled for.*

uncanny [adjective] strange and difficult to explain

uncertain [adjective]
1 having doubt about something: *I was uncertain about what to do next.*
2 not definitely known: *The future is uncertain.*

uncle [noun: **uncles**]
1 the brother of one of your parents
2 your aunt's husband

unclean [adjective] dirty or soiled: *unclean clothes*

uncomfortable [adjective] not comfortable
♦ **uncomfortably** [adverb] in an uncomfortable way: *Tom shifted uncomfortably in his seat.*

uncommon [adjective] unusual or rare
♦ **uncommonly** [adverb] extremely: *uncommonly talented*

unconscious [adjective]
1 in a state like sleep where you are not aware of what is happening around you, because you are seriously ill or injured: *A brick fell on his head and he was knocked unconscious.*
2 an unconscious feeling is one that you are not aware of having
3 if you are unconscious of something, you do not notice it: *He was unconscious of the danger.*
♦ **unconsciously** [adverb] in an unconscious way
♦ **unconsciousness** [noun] being unconscious

uncover [verb: **uncovers, uncovering, uncovered**]
1 to remove a cover from something
2 to discover something that had been secret: *uncover the truth*

undecided [adjective] not able to decide about something

undeniable [adjective] true or certain: *It is undeniable that the Earth goes round the sun.*
♦ **undeniably** [adverb] in a way that is true or certain

under [preposition]
1 below or beneath: *The bag is under the table.*
2 less than an amount: *All the clothes are under £20.*
3 working for someone: *a manager with three members of staff under her*
4 if something gets **under way**, it starts
[adverb]
1 in or to a lower place: *We watched the divers go under.*
2 if a business **goes under**, it fails and has to stop trading

underarm [adjective and adverb] done with your hand kept below your shoulder, moving up and forward: *an underarm throw* • *He rolled the ball back underarm.*

underclothes [plural noun] clothes you wear next to your skin and under your other clothes

undercover [adjective] working or done secretly: *an undercover police operation*

underdeveloped [adjective] an underdeveloped country is not modern and does not have many industries

underdog [noun: **underdogs**] the weaker person or team in a competition

underdone [adjective] not cooked enough

underfoot [adverb] on the ground where you are walking: *The stones underfoot grew slippery in the rain.*

undergo [verb: **undergoes, undergoing, underwent, undergone**] if you undergo something, you experience it: *He underwent an operation to mend his broken leg.*

undergraduate [noun: **undergraduates**] someone who is studying at a university and has not yet been awarded a degree

underground [adjective and adverb]
1 below the surface of the ground: *Moles live underground.* • *an underground stream*
2 existing or done secretly: *an underground organization*

Uu

[noun: **undergrounds**] a railway that is under the ground, usually in a large city

undergrowth [noun] bushes and plants that cover the ground

underhand [adjective] secret and not honest: *underhand business deals*

underline [verb: **underlines, underlining, underlined**]

1 to draw a line underneath something

2 to emphasize that something is important or true: *She underlined the need to be careful crossing the road.*

undermine [verb: **undermines, undermining, undermined**] to undermine someone or their plans is to make them weaker

underneath [adjective and preposition] under something: *Look underneath the table!* • *He was wearing a jumper with a shirt underneath.*

undernourished [adjective] someone who is undernourished does not eat enough healthy food

underpants [plural noun] underwear that men and boys wear under their trousers

underpass [noun: **underpasses**] a road or path under another road

underprivileged [adjective] having less money and fewer opportunities than other people

underskirt [noun: **underskirts**] a thin skirt that women and girls wear under another skirt

understand [verb: **understands, understanding, understood**]

1 to know what something means: *I can't understand the instructions.* • *Do you understand German?*

2 to know about something: *Doctors still don't understand how the disease is spread.*

3 to understand someone is to know why they behave and feel the way they do: *I'll never understand him.*

4 to think something is true: *I understood that you weren't coming.*

✦ **understandable** [adjective] reasonable in a particular situation: *His disappointment at not getting promoted was understandable.*

✦ **understanding** [adjective] able to understand other people's feelings
[noun: **understandings**]

1 the ability to see the meaning of something: *I have no understanding of chemistry.*

2 an agreement: *We have an understanding that we will stand up for each other.*

understudy [noun: **understudies**] someone who learns the part of another actor so they can play that part if the actor is ill

undertake [verb: **undertakes, undertaking, undertook, undertaken**] to undertake a task is to accept it and do it: *I undertook to make all the travel arrangements.*

undertaker [noun: **undertakers**] someone whose job is to arrange funerals

underwater [adjective and adverb] under the surface of water: *an underwater creature* • *Can you swim underwater?*

underwear [noun] clothes you wear next to your skin and under your other clothes

underweight [adjective] not heavy enough

underworld [noun]

1 in stories, the place where people go when they die

2 the underworld is criminals and the crimes they commit

undesirable [adjective] not wanted

undivided [adjective]

1 not split into separate parts or groups

2 complete: *You must give me your undivided attention.*

undo [verb: **undoes, undoing, undid, undone**]

1 to open something that is fastened: *He undid his jacket.*

2 to cancel out the effect of something: *She's undone all the good work of the previous manager.*

undoubted [adjective] certain: *Ellie has undoubted talent as a singer.*

✦ **undoubtedly** [adverb] a word you use to emphasize that something is true: *You are undoubtedly correct.*

undress [verb: **undresses, undressing, undressed**] to take your clothes off

✦ **undressed** [adjective] not wearing any clothes: *He was getting undressed.*

undue [adjective] more than is necessary: *undue alarm*

Uu

unduly [adverb] more than is necessary: *He did not seem unduly worried.*

unearth [verb: **unearths, unearthing, unearthed**]
1 to find something by digging in the ground
2 to discover something: *Someone had unearthed some unpleasant facts about him.*

unearthly [adjective] strange and a bit frightening: *an unearthly sound*

uneasily [adverb] in a way that shows you are worried or uncomfortable: *John looked uneasily at his watch, knowing he was late.*

uneasiness [noun] a feeling of slight worry

uneasy [adjective] slightly worried or unhappy

unemployed [adjective] without a job
 • **unemployment** [noun]
1 not having a job: *the misery of unemployment*
2 the number of people who do not have a job: *Unemployment has risen again.*

unequal [adjective] different in size, amount or position: *an unequal share of money*

uneven [adjective]
1 not level or smooth: *an uneven road*
2 not all of the same quality: *Your work has been uneven this year.*
 • **unevenly** [adverb] in an uneven way

unexpected [adjective] surprising because you were not expecting it: *an unexpected visitor* • *an unexpected development*
 • **unexpectedly** [adverb] in a way that you were not expecting

unfair [adjective] not right or not fair: *an unfair advantage* • *It's unfair to make her pay for everything.*
 • **unfairly** [adverb] in a way that is unfair: *We have been very unfairly treated.*
 • **unfairness** [noun] being unfair

unfaithful [adjective] not loyal or not keeping your promises

unfamiliar [adjective] not known or seen before: *an unfamiliar feeling* • *an unfamiliar face*

unfasten [verb: **unfastens, unfastening, unfastened**] to open something that was fastened: *She unfastened her coat.*

unfavourable [adjective] not good, and likely to cause problems: *The weather was unfavourable for our barbecue.*

unfit [adjective: **unfitter, unfittest**]
1 not suitable or not good enough: *water that's unfit to drink*
2 someone who is unfit is not in good physical condition, especially because they do not do enough exercise

unfold [verb: **unfolds, unfolding, unfolded**]
1 to spread out something that was folded
2 to become known or make something known through a gradual process: *The details of what happened began to unfold.*

unforgettable [adjective] impossible to forget

unforgivable [adjective] unforgivable behaviour is so bad that you cannot forgive the person who has done it
 • **unforgivably** [adverb] in a way that is unforgivable: *You were unforgivably rude to my friend.*

unfortunate [adjective]
1 caused by bad luck: *an unfortunate accident*
2 causing regret: *an unfortunate choice of words*
 • **unfortunately** [adverb] a word you use to show that you wish something had not happened: *Unfortunately, I lost the ring.*

unfurnished [adjective] an unfurnished house or room has no furniture in it

ungainly [adjective] not graceful

ungrateful [adjective] not showing or saying thanks when someone does something for you or gives you something
 • **ungratefully** [adverb] in a way that is ungrateful

unhappily [adverb]
1 in a way that is not happy
2 a word you use to show that something makes you sad or disappointed: *Unhappily, things did not work out as I planned.*

unhappiness [noun] being unhappy

unhappy [adjective: **unhappier, unhappiest**]
1 sad: *Ben has been feeling unhappy for a long time.*
2 not pleased or not satisfied: *We were unhappy with the result of the meeting.*
3 unfortunate: *an unhappy coincidence*

unhealthy [adjective: **unhealthier, unhealthiest**]
1 someone who is unhealthy does not have good health
2 something that is unhealthy is bad for your health: *an unhealthy lifestyle*

unicorn [noun: **unicorns**] in stories, an animal like a white horse with a horn on its head

uniform [noun: **uniforms**] a set of clothes that shows you belong to a particular organization, profession or school: *a bus-driver's uniform*

unify [verb: **unifies, unifying, unified**] to combine things so they become one

unimportance [noun] the fact of not being important
♦ **unimportant** [adjective] not important

uninhabited [adjective] an uninhabited place does not have people living in it

unintentional [adjective] done by accident and not deliberately
♦ **unintentionally** [adverb] in an unintentional way

uninterested [adjective] not interested: *I am uninterested in sport.*
♦ **uninteresting** [adjective] boring

uninterrupted [adjective]
1 not stopped by anything: *an uninterrupted conversation*
2 an uninterrupted view is not blocked by anything

union [noun: **unions**]
1 another word for a **trade union**
2 a group of states or countries that work together
♦ **unionist** [noun: **unionists**]
1 a member of a trade union
2 someone who believes that their country or a part of it should be joined to another

unique [adjective] completely different from anyone or anything else

unisex [adjective] intended for either men or women: *unisex clothes*

unison [noun] if people do something **in unison**, they all do it together

unit [noun: **units**]
1 a single thing, person or group that can be part of a larger thing: *an army unit • The book is divided into ten units.*

2 a fixed quantity that is used for measuring something: *A metre is a unit of length.*
3 a department in a hospital that provides a particular type of treatment: *a burns unit*

unite [verb: **unites, uniting, united**]
1 if people or things unite, they join together
2 to unite two or more things is to join them together

universal [adjective] something that is universal affects or includes everyone: *English may become a universal language that everyone can learn and use.*

universe [noun] everything that exists anywhere, including the Earth, the sun and all the other planets and stars in space: *Somewhere in the universe there might be another world like ours.*

university [noun: **universities**] a place where you go to study at the highest level after leaving school

unjust [adjective] not fair: *an unjust punishment*
♦ **unjustly** [adverb] not fairly: *He was unjustly punished.*

unkempt [adjective] not tidy: *unkempt hair*

unkind [adjective: **unkinder, unkindest**] cruel and not kind: *It was unkind of you to tease her.*
♦ **unkindly** [adverb] in an unkind way: *They treated me unkindly.*
♦ **unkindness** [noun] being unkind

unknown [adjective]
1 not known: *The man's whereabouts are unknown.*
2 not well known: *an unknown actor*

unleaded [adjective] unleaded petrol does not have lead added to it and therefore causes less harm to the environment

unleash [verb: **unleashes, unleashing, unleashed**] if you unleash an animal or an attack, you release it: *She unleashed a furious outburst.*

unless [conjunction] except when or except if: *We always go for a walk on Sundays, unless it's raining. • Don't come unless I phone you.*

unlike [preposition]
1 different from: *I never saw twins who were so unlike each other.*
2 not usual for someone: *It's unlike her to be so bad-tempered.*

Uu

unlikely [adjective]
1 not likely or expected to happen: *It's unlikely that she'll come.*
2 probably not true: *an unlikely tale*

unload [verb: **unloads, unloading, unloaded**] to unload something such as a ship or vehicle is to remove all the things that it is carrying: *After we got back from the trip, our first job was to unload the car.*

unlock [verb: **unlocks, unlocking, unlocked**] to open something that is locked: *Unlock this door now!*
♦ **unlocked** [adjective] not locked

unluckily [adverb] I am sorry to say: *Unluckily, he is injured and can't play in the match.*

unlucky [adjective] having, or coming from, bad luck: *I'm very unlucky at cards.* • *It was an unlucky defeat.*

unmask [verb: **unmasks, unmasking, unmasked**]
1 to unmask someone is to take away their mask or disguise: *The policeman unmasked the robber.*
2 to unmask someone is to show what they are really like: *He was unmasked as a liar and a cheat.*

unmistakable [adjective] not able to mistaken for anything else: *the unmistakable sound of a Ferrari*
♦ **unmistakably** [adverb] in an unmistakable way: *It was unmistakably his handwriting.*

unnatural [adjective] not natural or not normal: *an unnatural silence*
♦ **unnaturally** [adverb] in an unnatural way

unnecessarily [adverb] when it is not necessary: *We spent all that money unnecessarily.*

unnecessary [adjective] not necessary or not needed: *It is unnecessary to eat so much.*

unoccupied [adjective] empty and not lived in: *These houses have been unoccupied for years.*

unpack [verb: **unpacks, unpacking, unpacked**] to take things out of a suitcase or bag: *I've unpacked my case.* • *Have you unpacked yet?* • *He still hasn't unpacked his clothes.*

unpleasant [adjective] nasty and not pleasant: *an unpleasant smell*
♦ **unpleasantly** [adverb] in an unpleasant way
♦ **unpleasantness** [noun] being unpleasant

unplug [verb: **unplugs, unplugging, unplugged**]
1 to unplug something electrical is to take its plug out of a socket
2 to unplug something is to remove a blockage from it: *It will not be easy to unplug the pipe.*

unpopular [adjective] not popular or not liked: *His attitude makes him very unpopular with his workmates.*

unprotected [adjective]
1 not protected from attack or disease
2 if you have unprotected sex, you do not use a condom to prevent infection or pregnancy

unravel [verb: **unravels, unravelling, unravelled**]
1 to unravel something is to unwind it or take the knots out of it: *He could not unravel the tangled thread.*
2 to unravel something puzzling is to solve it: *She was determined to unravel the mystery.*

unreal [adjective] not actually existing

unreasonable [adjective] asking too much, and not fair: *It's unreasonable to expect students to do so much homework.*
♦ **unreasonably** [adverb] in an unreasonable way

unrest [noun] trouble and discontent among people: *unrest all over the country*

unruly [adjective] badly behaved and difficult to control: *an unruly child* • *unruly behaviour*

unscathed [adjective] without being harmed: *They escaped from the burning building unscathed.*

unscrew [verb: **unscrews, unscrewing, unscrewed**]
1 to loosen or remove something by taking out a screw or screws: *Jean unscrewed the cupboard door.*
2 to loosen or remove something with a twisting action: *Joe unscrewed the lid from the bottle and took a drink.*

unseemly [adjective] not suitable or not proper: *unseemly behaviour*

unseen [adjective] not seen or not noticed: *He managed to leave the house unseen.*

unselfish [adjective] generous and thinking of others
+ **unselfishly** [adverb] in an unselfish way
+ **unselfishness** [noun] being unselfish

unsettled [adjective]
1 if the weather is unsettled, it changes a great deal
2 if a bill is unsettled, it has not been paid

unsightly [adjective] ugly and not nice to look at: *The new office block is very unsightly.*

unsound [adjective] not safe or not reliable: *The bridge is structurally unsound.* • *His evidence is unsound.*

unspeakable [adjective] too bad to describe in words: *unspeakable rudeness*

unsteadily [adverb] in an unsteady way

unsteady [adjective] likely to fall and not firm: *After the operation she was very unsteady on her feet.*

unstoppable [adjective] not able to be stopped or prevented: *an unstoppable wave of protest*

unstuck [adjective] if a person or plan **comes unstuck**, they go wrong and are not successful: *My plan for a quick getaway came unstuck when I couldn't find a taxi.*

unsuccessful [adjective] not managing to do something you have been trying to do: *She tried to find him but was unsuccessful.*
+ **unsuccessfully** [adverb] in an unsuccessful way: *I tried unsuccessfully to speak to her.*

unsuitable [adjective] not right for a purpose or occasion: *These shoes are unsuitable for dancing.*

unsung [adjective] not praised or not recognized: *an unsung hero*

unthinkable [adjective] too bad or too unlikely to be thought about: *It is unthinkable that he would steal from his own family.*

untidiness [noun] being untidy

untidy [adjective: **untidier, untidiest**] not neat or not well organized: *His flat is always untidy.*

untie [verb: **unties, untying, untied**] to loosen or unfasten something that is tied: *He untied his shoelaces.*

until [preposition] up to the time of: *We waited until ten o'clock.*
[conjunction] up to the time when: *Keep walking until you come to the station.*

untimely [adjective] happening too soon or at a time that is not suitable: *his untimely death* • *her untimely return*

untold [adjective]
1 not yet told: *the untold story*
2 too great to be counted or measured: *untold riches*

untoward [adjective] unlucky or unfortunate: *If nothing untoward happens, I should be there by lunchtime.*

untrue [adjective]
1 false, not true: *His story is completely untrue.*
2 not faithful or not loyal
+ **untruth** [noun: **untruths**] a lie: *telling untruths*
+ **untruthful** [adjective] not honest: *She was being untruthful when she said she didn't care.*
+ **untruthfully** [adverb] in an untruthful way

unused [adjective]
1 that has not been used: *an unused stamp*
2 if you are unused to something, you do not know it very well or have not done it very often: *I'm unused to spicy food.* • *He was unused to having to cook his own meals.*

unusual [adjective] not normal or not ordinary: *It's unusual for him to arrive late.* • *That's an unusual necklace.*
+ **unusually** [adverb] to an unusual degree: *unusually cold for the time of year*

unveil [verb: **unveils, unveiling, unveiled**]
1 to unveil something is to take a cover away from it as part of a ceremony: *The Prime Minister unveiled the new statue.*
2 to reveal something: *The minister has unveiled plans for a shorter working day.*

unwell [adjective] not in good health: *I feel slightly unwell this morning.*

unwieldy [adjective] large and awkward to carry or manage: *This suitcase is too unwieldy for me.*

unwilling [adjective] not wanting to do something: *He's unwilling to accept the money.*
+ **unwillingness** [noun] being unwilling

Uu

unwind [verb: **unwinds, unwinding, unwound**]

1 to unwind something is to undo it from a wound position: *He unwound the bandage from his ankle.*

2 to unwind is to come undone from a wound position: *The snake slowly unwound from the branch.*

3 to relax: *Having a bath is a good way to unwind.*

unwise [adjective] not sensible: *It was rather unwise not to bring an umbrella with you.*

unworthy [adjective]

1 not deserving: *It's unworthy of attention.*

2 less good than is usually expected from someone: *Such bad behaviour is unworthy of him.*

unwrap [verb: **unwraps, unwrapping, unwrapped**] to open something that is wrapped: *She carefully unwrapped the present.*

unzip [verb: **unzips, unzipping, unzipped**] to undo the zip of something: *He unzipped his bag and took out a book.*

up [adverb]

1 towards or in a higher position: *Prices have gone up again.* • *Stand up!*

2 completely, so as to finish: *Drink up your milk.*

3 out of bed: *I got up at five o'clock this morning.*

4 as far as: *He came up to me and shook my hand.*

[preposition]

1 to or at a higher part of something: *He climbed up the tree.* • *She's up the ladder.*

2 along: *walking up the road*

[adjective]

1 going up: *the up escalator*

2 out of bed: *He's not up yet.*

3 ahead: *two goals up at the end of the first half*

4 if the sun is up, it has risen

5 finished: *Your time is up.*

6 an informal way of saying 'wrong': *What's up with you today?*

7 if you are **up to** something, you are doing that thing, especially in a secretive way: *My brother is up to no good again.*

8 if you are **up to** a task, then you have the

ability to do it: *Do you think you are up to winning the race?*

9 if a choice is **up to** you, then you have to decide what to do or have: *Whether we stay or go home is up to you.*

10 if something is **up to date**, it has all the information or features available just now: *I want to bring my diary up to date.* • *My computer is an old model and not up to date.*

[noun: **ups**] **ups and downs** are good and bad times

upbringing [noun: **upbringings**] the process of bringing up a child: *We had a strict upbringing.*

update [verb: **updates, updating, updated**]

1 to update someone is to give them the latest information: *Could someone update me on what's been happening here?*

2 to update something is to make it more modern: *I need to update my computer.*

[noun: **updates**]

1 bringing someone or something up to date: *I need an update on what is happening.*

2 an updated version of something: *an update of the news*

upgrade [verb: **upgrades, upgrading, upgraded**]

1 to upgrade something such as machinery or a computer is to improve it, especially by adding or replacing parts

2 to upgrade someone is to promote them

[noun: **upgrades**] in computing, a newer version of a software program

upheaval [noun: **upheavals**] a great change or disturbance: *the upheaval of moving house*

uphill [adjective]

1 going upwards: *an uphill part of the track*

2 difficult: *This will be an uphill struggle.*

[adverb] up a slope: *We travelled uphill for several hours.*

uphold [verb: **upholds, upholding, upheld**] to uphold something such as a decision is to support it or agree with it: *The court upheld his complaint.*

upholstery [noun] the coverings and cushions of a seat: *car upholstery*

upkeep [noun]

1 the keeping of something, such as a house or car, in good condition
2 the cost of keeping something such as a house or car in good condition

uplifting [adjective] if something is uplifting, it cheers you up and makes you feel more hopeful: *an uplifting song*

up-market [adjective] high in quality and price: *an up-market housing estate*

upon [preposition] a more formal word for **on**: *a castle upon a high cliff*

upper [adjective] above something else, especially something that is the same. Look up and compare **lower**: *the upper floors of the building*
[noun: **uppers**] the part of a shoe above the sole: *These shoes have leather uppers.*

uppermost [adjective] highest: *the uppermost room of the house*

upright [adjective]
1 standing straight up: *a row of upright posts*
2 fair and honest: *an upright man*
[noun: **uprights**] a vertical post or pole, especially one that supports something such as a fence

uprising [noun: **uprisings**] a fight or rebellion against a government

uproar [noun: **uproars**] a noisy disturbance: *The room was in an uproar.*

uproot [verb: **uproots, uprooting, uprooted**]
1 to pull a plant out of the ground together with its roots
2 to make people move away from their homes: *Thousands of people were uprooted by the war.*

upset [verb: **upsets, upsetting, upset**]
1 to make someone sad, angry or worried: *His friend's death upset him very much.*
2 to knock something over: *The dog upset a vase of flowers.*
3 to spoil something: *Her illness has upset our holiday plans.*
[adjective]
1 sad, angry or worried: *Are you very upset about the news?*
2 slightly disturbed: *an upset stomach*
[noun: **upsets**]

1 sadness or worry: *Her sudden departure caused a lot of upset.*
2 something that causes a surprise: *Losing the match to such a poor team was quite an upset.*
3 a slight disturbance: *a stomach upset*

upshot [noun] the final result of something: *The upshot of all of the delays was that we decided not to go at all.*

upside down [adjective and adverb]
1 with the top part where the bottom should be and the bottom part where the top should be: *He was holding the book upside down.*
2 in or into confusion: *The burglars turned the house upside down.*

upstairs [adverb] to or on a higher floor: *I went upstairs to get changed.*
[adjective] on a higher floor: *an upstairs bedroom*

upstream [adverb] further up a river or stream towards its source, against the direction in which it flows: *Salmon swim upstream to lay their eggs.*

uptake [noun] if someone is **quick** or **slow on the uptake**, they are quick or slow to understand or realize something: *He's a bit slow on the uptake, but he's OK once he knows what he's doing.*

uptight [adjective] nervous or anxious: *You seem a bit uptight today.*

up-to-date [adjective]
1 new or modern: *up-to-date technology*
2 having the latest information: *an up-to-date news story*

upward [adjective] towards a higher place or position: *an upward climb*
♦ **upwards** or **upward** [adverb] moving or leading towards a higher place or position: *He looked upwards and saw the sun.*

uranium [noun] a radioactive metal that is used to make nuclear energy

urban [adjective] to do with a town or city: *urban life* • *urban traffic*

urchin [noun: **urchins**] a dirty child with ragged clothes

urge [verb: **urges, urging, urged**]
1 to urge someone to do something is to try to persuade them to do it: *He urged her to drive carefully.*

Uu

2 to **urge someone on** is to encourage them to carry on: *He urged his followers on.*

[noun: **urges**] a sudden feeling of wanting to do something: *I felt an urge to hit him.*

urgency [noun] being urgent: *I didn't realize the urgency of the situation.*

♦ **urgent** [adjective] needing attention immediately: *I have an urgent message from the boss.*

♦ **urgently** [adverb] immediately or desperately: *Medical supplies are needed urgently.*

urinate [verb: **urinates, urinating, urinated**] to pass urine out of your body

urine [noun] the waste liquid passed out of the bodies of humans and animals

urn [noun: **urns**]

1 a sort of vase for holding the ashes of a dead person who has been cremated

2 a large metal container with a tap, used for heating water or for making large amounts of tea or coffee

us [pronoun] a word you use when you are talking about yourself and at least one other person: *His happy face surprised all of us.* • *Do you want to come with us?*

use [verb: **uses, using, used**]

1 to use something is to put it to a purpose: *Use a knife to open it.* • *Use your common sense!*

2 if you are **used to** something, you know it well, or to have done it lots of times: *She soon got used to her new job.*

3 if you **used to** do something, you did it often or regularly in the past: *We used to go to the seaside every summer.*

4 to **use something up** is to use all of it so that there is none left: *He used up all the milk.*

[noun: **uses**]

1 the using of something: *We cannot allow the use of guns.*

2 the purpose for which something can be used: *This knife has a lot of uses.*

3 the value or advantage of something: *Is this coat of any use to you?* • *What's the use of crying?*

♦ **used** [adjective] not new: *He sells used cars.*

♦ **useful** [adjective] helpful or able to do what needs doing: *She made herself useful by washing the dishes.* • *a useful tool*

♦ **usefulness** [noun] being useful

♦ **useless** [adjective] having no use, or not doing what it is supposed to do: *This knife's useless — it's completely blunt.* • *I tried to stop the baby crying, but it was useless.*

user [noun: **users**] a person who uses something: *users of public transport*

user-friendly [adjective] easy to use or understand: *Modern computers need to be user-friendly.*

usher [noun: **ushers**] someone who shows people to their seats in a cinema or theatre, or at a wedding

[verb: **ushers, ushering, ushered**] to go with someone and show them the way: *The waiter ushered him to a table.*

usherette [noun: **usherettes**] a woman who shows people to their seats in a cinema or theatre

usual [adjective] done or happening most often: *I took my usual walk this morning.* • *He was late as usual.*

♦ **usually** [adverb] normally, on most occasions: *We usually go on holiday in June.*

utensil [noun: **utensils**] a tool or container, especially one for everyday use in the home: *knives, pans, and other utensils*

uterus [noun: **uteri**] a more technical word for the **womb**, the part of a woman's or female animal's body where babies grow until they are born

utility [noun: **utilities**]

1 usefulness: *a tool of little utility*

2 a company which supplies gas, electricity, water or another service

utilize or **utilise** [verb: **utilizes, utilizing, utilized**] to make use of: *Old newspapers can be utilized for making recycled paper.*

utmost [adjective] greatest possible: *You must take the utmost care.*

[noun] if you **do your utmost**, you make the biggest possible effort: *She has done her utmost to help him.*

utter [verb: **utters, uttering, uttered**] to utter a sound is to make it with your voice: *She uttered a sigh of relief.* • *She didn't utter a single word.*

Uu

utter[2] [adjective] complete or total: *utter silence*

◆ **utterly** [adverb] completely or totally: *I feel utterly exhausted.*

◆ **uttermost** [adjective] another word for **utmost**

U-turn [noun: **U-turns**]

1 a turn in the shape of a U, made by a driver to go back the way he or she has just come

2 a complete change of plan or ideas: *a U-turn in government policy*

UV [abbreviation] short for **ultraviolet**, a type of light from the sun that you cannot see and which turns the skin darker. Too much of this can be harmful

Uu

V

vacancy [noun: **vacancies**]
1 a room in a hotel that is available: *Sorry, we have no vacancies.*
2 a job that is available
♦ **vacant** [adjective] not being used: *a vacant seat*

vacate [verb: **vacates, vacating, vacated**] to leave a place empty: *He led me back to the chair I had vacated.*
♦ **vacation** [noun: **vacations**] an American English word for a **holiday**: *a two-week vacation*

vaccinate [verb: **vaccinates, vaccinating, vaccinated**] to put a substance into someone's body to protect them from a disease
♦ **vaccination** [noun: **vaccinations**] the process of vaccinating someone

vaccine [noun: **vaccines**] a substance containing bacteria or a virus, which can be injected into a person's body and can protect against a disease

vacuum [noun: **vacuums**] a space with nothing in it
[verb: **vacuums, vacuuming, vacuumed**] to clean something using a vacuum cleaner

vacuum cleaner [noun: **vacuum cleaners**] an electrical machine that sucks dust up from the floor

vacuum flask [noun: **vacuum flasks**] a container that has a vacuum between its inside and outside coverings, and which keeps drinks hot or cold

vagina [noun: **vaginas**] the passage that connects a woman's womb to the outside of her body

vagrant [noun: **vagrants**] someone who has no permanent place to live

vague [adjective: **vaguer, vaguest**] not very clear or definite: *I have a vague idea where he lives.*
♦ **vaguely** [adverb] not clearly or precisely: *He looked vaguely familiar.*

vain [adjective: **vainer, vainest**]
1 too proud of yourself and thinking too much about the way you look
2 useless: *He made a vain attempt to get up.* [noun] if you do something **in vain**, you do it without success: *He tried in vain to get out through the bars of the cage.*
♦ **vainly** [adverb] without achieving what you want to do: *I tossed about in bed, vainly trying to get comfortable.*
➡ **vanity**

valentine [noun: **valentines**]
1 a card that you send on Saint Valentine's Day (14 February) to show that you love someone
2 the person you send a valentine to

valet [noun: **valets**] a male servant who works for another man and looks after his clothes
[verb: **valets, valeting, valeted**] to clean out a car

ⓘ The noun is pronounced **va**-lay, with a silent t.

valiant [adjective] brave: *She made a valiant attempt to rescue the cat.*
♦ **valiantly** [adverb] in a brave way

valid [adjective]
1 legally or officially acceptable and able to be used: *a valid passport*
2 reasonable and acceptable: *a valid excuse*

* **validate** [verb: **validates, validating, validated**] to validate something such as a ticket is to make it valid
* **validity** [noun] being valid

valley [noun: **valleys**] a stretch of low land between hills, often with a river running through it

valour [noun] bravery or courage, for example in a battle

valuable [adjective]
1 worth a lot of money: *a valuable diamond*
2 very useful: *She's a valuable member of the team.*
* **valuables** [plural noun] things, especially things that you own, that are worth a lot of money

valuation [noun: **valuations**]
1 the act of deciding how much something is worth
2 an estimated price or value

value [noun: **values**]
1 the amount that something is worth
2 usefulness and importance
[verb: **values, valuing, valued**]
1 to think something is important or worthwhile: *I value my free time.*
2 to say how much something is worth: *The jewels were valued at three thousand dollars.*

valve [noun: **valves**] something that opens and shuts to control the flow of liquid, air or gas through a pipe

vampire [noun: **vampires**] in stories, a dead person who comes out at night and sucks people's blood

van [noun: **vans**] a road vehicle, smaller than a lorry, for carrying goods

vandal [noun: **vandals**] someone who deliberately damages things for no good reason
* **vandalism** [noun] the crime of deliberately damaging something such as a public building
* **vandalize** or **vandalise** [verb: **vandalizes, vandalizing, vandalized**] to damage something deliberately

vanilla [noun] a flavouring that comes from the pods of a plant: *vanilla ice-cream*

vanish [verb: **vanishes, vanishing, vanished**] to disappear and leave nothing behind

vanity [noun] taking too much pride in the way you appear to other people

vapour [noun: **vapours**] a mist or smoke that is produced by small drops of liquid in the air

variable [adjective] changing often and never staying the same

variant [noun: **variants**] a different form or version of something
* **variation** [noun: **variations**] a change in the amount or level of something: *variations in temperature*

varicose [adjective] varicose veins are abnormally swollen and twisted

varied [adjective] of many different types: *He has varied interests, from reading to outdoor sports.*

variety [noun: **varieties**]
1 if something has variety, it has many different things in it: *I wanted a bit of variety in my life.*
2 a variety is an example of something that is different from other similar things: *a new variety of rose*
3 a variety of things is a collection of different types of the same thing: *The chairs are available in a variety of colours.*
4 variety is a type of entertainment with singing, dancing and comedy: *He was invited to appear in variety at the London Palladium.*

varifocals [plural noun] glasses that allow you to focus on objects over a wide range of distances. Look up and compare **bifocals**

various [adjective] different: *There were various things to choose from.*

varnish [noun: **varnishes**] a liquid that gives a shiny surface to wood when it dries
[verb: **varnishes, varnishing, varnished**] to put varnish on wood

vary [verb: **varies, varying, varied**]
1 to vary is to change: *The weather varies a lot.*
2 to vary something is to change it slightly
➡ **variable, variant, varied, variety**

vase [noun: **vases**] a decorative container for flowers

vasectomy [noun: **vasectomies**] an operation that involves cutting a tube to stop a man from fathering children

vast [adjective] extremely big: *vast deserts*
* **vastly** [adverb] much: *vastly different*

VAT [abbreviation] short for **value-added**

Vv

tax, which is a tax you pay on things you buy

vat [noun: **vats**] a large container for liquids

vault [noun: **vaults**] an underground room for dead bodies or for storing valuable things

VCR [abbreviation] short for **videocassette recorder**

VDU [abbreviation] short for **visual display unit**

veal [noun] meat from a calf

Veda [noun] the most ancient holy writings of the Hindu religion

veer [verb: **veers, veering, veered**] to change direction: *The car suddenly veered to the left.*

vegan [noun: **vegans**] someone who does not eat anything that comes from an animal

vegetable [noun: **vegetables**] a plant that you can eat, especially one that is not sweet: *Potatoes and carrots are vegetables.*

vegetarian [noun: **vegetarians**] someone who does not eat meat or fish
[adjective] not containing meat or fish: *vegetarian foods*

vegetate [verb: **vegetates, vegetating, vegetated**] to lead a dull life

♦ **vegetation** [noun] plants, especially plants that grow in a particular area

vehicle [noun: **vehicles**] something that carries people or goods, for example a car or lorry

veil [noun: **veils**] a piece of material that covers a woman's head and face

vein [noun: **veins**] one of the very thin tubes inside your body that carry blood to your heart

Velcro [noun] a material made up of tiny hooks and loops that can join together, used to fasten things. This word is a trademark

velocity [noun: **velocities**] the speed at which something moves

velvet [noun] a type of cloth with a surface that is covered with short hairs and feels very soft

♦ **velvety** [adjective] feeling like velvet

vendetta [noun: **vendettas**] a bitter disagreement that lasts for a long time

vending machine [noun: **vending machines**] a machine that you can buy things from

vendor [noun: **vendors**] someone who is selling something: *an ice-cream vendor*

veneer [noun: **veneers**] a thin layer that provides an attractive surface to something

venereal disease [noun: **venereal diseases**] any disease that is spread through sexual intercourse

Venetian blind [noun: **Venetian blinds**] a device that hangs in front of a window and consists of long thin pieces of metal, plastic or wood that can be pulled together or turned to let in or keep out light

vengeance [noun] punishment that you give to someone who has harmed you

♦ **vengeful** [adjective] wanting to punish someone because they have hurt you

venison [noun] meat from a deer

venom [noun]
1 the poison that some snakes produce
2 deep hatred: *letters full of venom*

♦ **venomous** [adjective] poisonous

vent [noun: **vents**]
1 a small opening to allow air or smoke to pass through
2 if you **give vent to** a feeling such as anger, you express it freely

ventilate [verb: **ventilates, ventilating, ventilated**] to let fresh air into a room or building

♦ **ventilation** [noun] letting fresh air into a room or building

♦ **ventilator** [noun: **ventilators**]
1 a machine that helps someone to breathe by pumping air into and out of their lungs
2 an opening or piece of equipment that lets air into a room or building

ventriloquism [noun] the skill of speaking without moving your lips and making it look as though a puppet is speaking

♦ **ventriloquist** [noun: **ventriloquists**] someone who has the skill of ventriloquism

venture [noun: **ventures**] an activity or project: *his latest business venture*
[verb: **ventures, venturing, ventured**] to go somewhere unknown to you, which may be dangerous or unpleasant

venue [noun: **venues**] the place where an event takes place

veranda [noun: **verandas**] a terrace with a roof, attached to a house

verb [part of speech: **verbs**] the word in a sentence that tells you what someone or something does. For example, *eat* and *speak* are verbs

verbal [adjective] spoken rather than written: *a verbal promise*

verdict [noun: **verdicts**] a decision made in a court of law whether someone is guilty or not guilty of committing a crime

verge [noun: **verges**]
1 the grassy area at the edge of a road
2 if you are **on the verge of** doing something, you are almost doing it or just about to do it: *Sanjay was on the verge of tears.*

verify [verb: **verifies, verifying, verified**] to prove or say for definite that something is true

vermin [noun] animals or insects such as rats or fleas, which people think are pests

vermouth [noun: **vermouths**] an alcoholic drink consisting of wine flavoured with herbs

verruca [noun: **verrucas**] a wart on someone's foot

versatile [adjective]
1 useful for many different things: *versatile clothes*
2 able to do many different things: *a versatile actor*
◆ **versatility** [noun] being versatile

verse [noun: **verses**]
1 verse is poetry rather than writing
2 a verse is a set of lines that form one part of a song or poem

version [noun: **versions**]
1 a description of events from one person's point of view: *I seriously doubt your version of what happened.*
2 a type of something that is slightly different from the original form: *Have you heard the new version of the song?*

versus [preposition] against. Versus is used when saying who is playing in a sports game: *It's Scotland versus France tonight.*

vertebra [noun: **vertebrae**] one of the bones that form your backbone

vertebrate [noun: **vertebrates**] an animal that has a backbone

vertical [adjective] standing upright and straight: *vertical lines*

vertigo [noun] a feeling of dizziness when you are in a very high place

verve [noun] excitement and energy

very [adverb] to a great degree: *I'm very tired.*
[adjective] exact: *At that very moment, the telephone rang.*

vessel [noun: **vessels**]
1 a large boat or ship
2 a container for liquids
3 a tube that carries blood through your body

vest [noun: **vests**]
1 a piece of underwear that covers the top part of your body
2 the American English word for a **waistcoat**

vet [noun: **vets**] someone whose job is to treat animals that are ill or injured

veteran [noun: **veterans**]
1 someone who has a lot of experience at something
2 someone who fought in a war

veterinary surgeon [noun: **veterinary surgeons**] someone whose job is to treat animals that are ill or injured. This is usually shortened to **vet**

veto [verb: **vetoes, vetoing, vetoed**] to stop something from happening: *The president vetoed the plan to lower taxes.*
[noun: **vetoes**]
1 the power to stop a law from being passed or a decision from being made
2 an occasion when someone does not let something go ahead

vex [verb: **vexes, vexing, vexed**] to annoy someone
◆ **vexation** [noun] feeling annoyed

VHF [abbreviation] short for **very high frequency**

via [preposition] travelling through a place: *The train goes to London via Birmingham.*

viable [adjective] a viable plan or proposal has a chance of being successful

viaduct [noun: **viaducts**] a bridge that takes a railway over a road or river

vibrant [adjective] exciting and full of life: *a vibrant city*

vibrate [verb: **vibrates, vibrating, vibrated**] to shake very quickly
◆ **vibration** [noun: **vibrations**]

Vv

1 vibration is shaking very quickly

2 a vibration is a quick shaking movement

vicar [noun: **vicars**] someone who is in charge of a parish in the Church of England

vice[1] [noun: **vices**]

1 a vice is a bad habit

2 vice is behaviour that is bad or not decent

vice[2] [noun: **vices**] a tool for holding objects firmly while you work on them

vice- [prefix] if a word starts with **vice-**, it refers to someone who is next in importance. For example, a *vice-president* is someone who is next in rank to a president and takes their place if they are not available

vice versa [adverb] the other way around: *I needed his help and vice versa.*

vicinity [noun] the area around a place: *There are no schools in the vicinity.*

vicious [adjective] extremely cruel and wanting to hurt people: *a vicious attack*

vicious circle [noun: **vicious circles**] a situation in which one problem causes another problem which makes the first problem worse

victim [noun: **victims**] someone who is harmed by a bad situation or bad event: *victims of crime*

 victimize or **victimise** [verb: **victimizes, victimizing, victimized**] to treat someone in an unfair way and make them a victim

victor [noun: **victors**] the person who has won a game or competition

victorious [adjective] successful in a battle or competition

victory [noun: **victories**] the winning of a battle or competition: *victory in the Cup Final*

video [noun: **videos**]

1 a recording of a film or television programme made on videotape

2 a recording of an event on a videocassette that has been made using a video camera

3 a machine for playing videos

[verb: **videos, videoing, videoed**]

1 to record a television programme onto videotape

2 to film an event using a video camera

video camera [noun: **video cameras**] a piece of equipment that you use to record events onto a videocassette

videocassette [noun: **videocassettes**] a plastic case that contains videotape

videocassette recorder or **video recorder** [noun: **videocassette recorders** or **video recorders**] a machine for recording and playing videos

videotape [noun: **videotapes**] magnetic tape that pictures and sounds can be recorded on

view [noun: **views**]

1 the things you can see from a place: *There's a fantastic view from the top of the hill.*

2 your ability to see things from a place: *The pillar spoilt my view of the concert.*

3 someone's opinion: *What's your view on the new school uniform?*

4 if you do something **in view of** another thing, you do it after taking that other thing into consideration: *In view of the weather, we have cancelled the game.*

5 if something is **on view**, it is being shown for people to look at: *Several classic cars will be on view.*

6 if you do something **with a view to** a second thing, you do it with the intention of achieving the second thing: *He's moving to London with a view to finding a job.*

[verb: **views, viewing, viewed**]

1 to look at something: *People came from all over the country to view his work.*

2 to think about someone or something in a particular way: *The painting was viewed as very unusual.*

 viewer [noun: **viewers**] someone who watches television: *The programme attracted less than a million viewers.*

viewpoint [noun: **viewpoints**]

1 a place from which you look at something: *a good viewpoint at the top of a hill*

2 a way of thinking about something: *Try looking at what happened from my viewpoint.*

vigil [noun: **vigils**] a time when people stay awake at night in order to pray, protest or watch someone who is ill

vigilance [noun] being careful to notice any trouble or problems

 vigilant [adjective] watching things carefully in order to notice any trouble or problems: *Police have urged people to be vigilant after a series of thefts.*

vigorous [adjective] very active or strong: *vigorous defence*

♦ **vigorously** [adverb] in an active or strong way: *We argued vigorously.*

vigour [noun] strength and energy

vile [adjective: **viler, vilest**] extremely unpleasant: *a vile taste*

villa [noun: **villas**] a large house, especially one used for holidays

village [noun: **villages**] a small place in a country area, which is not as big as a town

♦ **villager** [noun: **villagers**] someone who lives in a village

villain [noun: **villains**] a bad person or a criminal

♦ **villainous** [adjective] behaving like a villain

vindictive [adjective] wanting to harm someone because they have done harm to you

vine [noun: **vines**] the plant that grapes grow on

vinegar [noun] a sour liquid used for flavouring food

vineyard [noun: **vineyards**] a place where grapes are grown to produce wine

vintage [noun: **vintages**]
1 the wine that is produced in a particular year or place
2 the time that something is from
[adjective] typical of a particular time in the past: *vintage clothing*

vintage car [noun: **vintage cars**] a car made between 1917 and 1930 that is still in very good condition

viola [noun: **violas**] a musical instrument that looks like a big violin and is played in the same way

violate [verb: **violates, violating, violated**]
1 to violate a law or rule is to break it
2 to violate someone's rights is to not respect them
3 to violate a special place is to damage or destroy it

♦ **violation** [noun: **violations**] violating something

violence [noun] behaviour that is rough and intended to hurt someone

♦ **violent** [adjective]
1 behaving in a rough way that is intended to hurt someone
2 very sudden and strong: *a violent storm*

♦ **violently** [adverb] in a violent way

violet [noun: **violets**]
1 a small purple flower
2 a purple colour

violin [noun: **violins**] a musical instrument with four strings, which you hold under your chin and play by drawing a bow across the strings

♦ **violinist** [noun: **violinists**] someone who plays the violin

VIP [abbreviation] short for **very important person**

viper [noun: **vipers**] a small poisonous snake

virgin [noun: **virgins**] someone who has never had sexual intercourse

virile [adjective] strong and manly

virtual [adjective]
1 almost a particular thing: *He was a virtual prisoner in his own home.*
2 using computer images that make something seem real: *a virtual tour of the museum*

♦ **virtually** [adverb] almost: *Virtually all her friends are unemployed.*

virtual reality [noun] pictures and sounds that seem real but are actually created by computer software

virtue [noun: **virtues**]
1 virtue is goodness
2 a virtue is a good quality in a person's character

♦ **virtuous** [adjective] behaving in a very good way

virus [noun: **viruses**]
1 a germ that causes illnesses such as a cold or chickenpox
2 a computer program that can send itself to many computers, for example by e-mail, and can destroy files on those computers

visa [noun: **visas**] a document that you need to travel to and work in some countries

visibility [noun]
1 how far and well you can see because of conditions such as the weather: *poor visibility*

Vv

2 the fact of being easy to see: *Visibility is important for cyclists.*

visible [adjective] able to be seen: *The house is not visible from the road.*
* **visibly** [adverb] in a way that is easy to see: *He was visibly shaken.*

vision [noun: **visions**]
1 your vision is your ability to see
2 a vision is something that you see or imagine might happen: *One ghastly vision after another swam through his brain.*

visit [verb: **visits, visiting, visited**] to go and see a place or person
[noun: **visits**] the act of visiting a place or person: *I'm going to pay him a visit.*
* **visitor** [noun: **visitors**] someone who visits a person or place

visor [noun: **visors**] the clear part of a helmet that covers someone's face

visual [adjective] to do with seeing: *visual aids*

visual display unit [noun: **visual display units**] a screen that you use with a computer

visualize or **visualise** [verb: **visualizes, visualizing, visualized**] to form a picture of something in your mind: *I remember his name, but I can't visualize him.*

visually [adverb] in a way that involves your ability to see

vital [adjective] necessary or extremely important: *vital information*
* **vitality** [noun] liveliness and enthusiasm
* **vitally** [adverb] extremely: *vitally important*

vitamin [noun: **vitamins**] a substance in food that you need to stay healthy: *Oranges contain vitamin C.*

LANGUAGE FOR LIFE

vitamins
There are many different types of vitamin. Each one is known by a letter.
• **Vitamin A** is found in eggs and dairy products, and is required for healthy growth and vision.
• **Vitamin B** covers a wide range of different substances found especially in vegetables, yeast, and liver. A lack of this vitamin can cause certain diseases.

• **Vitamin C** is found in fruit and vegetables and is important for healthy bones and teeth.
You may also come across vitamins called **Vitamin D, Vitamin E, Vitamin H, Vitamin K, Vitamin L** and **Vitamin P.**

vivacious [adjective] lively and full of energy

vivid [adjective]
1 producing very clear ideas and pictures in your mind: *vivid memories*
2 very bright: *vivid colours*
* **vividly** [adverb] in a very clear way: *I vividly remember meeting him.*

vivisection [noun] doing experiments on animals that are alive, for medical research

vixen [noun: **vixens**] a female fox

vocabulary [noun: **vocabularies**] the range of words that someone knows and uses: *a child with a good vocabulary*

vocal [adjective] to do with your voice
* **vocalist** [noun: **vocalists**] a singer, especially in a rock band

vocation [noun: **vocations**]
1 a job or way of life that you feel is very right for you
2 a belief that you should do a particular job or live in a particular way

vodka [noun] a strong clear alcoholic drink

vogue [noun] a current fashion: *a vogue for Spanish films*

voice [noun: **voices**]
1 the sound you make when you speak or sing: *'Hello!' he said in a loud voice.*
2 your ability to make speaking or singing sounds: *I had a sore throat and lost my voice.*
[verb: **voices, voicing, voiced**] to voice something such as an opinion is to express it: *Many people have voiced their concerns.*

void [adjective] not valid or legally binding: *The contract was declared void.*

volatile [adjective]
1 a volatile person is likely to change their mood very quickly
2 a volatile situation could change very suddenly
3 a volatile liquid changes quickly to a gas

volcanic [adjective] relating to volcanoes

volcano [noun: **volcanoes**] a mountain that

Vv

sometimes sends out hot lava through a hole in its top

vole [noun: **voles**] a small animal similar to a mouse or rat

volley [noun: **volleys**]

1 a lot of bullets or weapons that are fired or thrown at the same time

2 in some sports such as tennis and soccer, a volley is hitting the ball before it hits the ground

[verb: **volleys, volleying, volleyed**] in tennis, to hit the ball before it hits the ground

volt [noun: **volts**] a unit for measuring how strong an electric current is

♦ **voltage** [noun] the amount of electrical force something has

volume [noun: **volumes**]

1 the space that something takes up or the amount of space that a container has

2 the amount of sound that something makes: *Can you turn the volume down on the TV, please?*

3 the amount of something: *The volume of trade has increased.*

4 a book, especially a book that is part of a set

voluntary [adjective]

1 done by choice and not because you have to

2 done without payment: *voluntary work*

volunteer [noun: **volunteers**] someone who offers to do something: *Do I have any volunteers to help me tidy up?*

[verb: **volunteers, volunteering, volunteered**]

1 to offer to do something: *Dana volunteered to take the children swimming.*

2 to give information or make a suggestion without being asked for it

vomit [verb: **vomits, vomiting, vomited**] to bring food back up from your stomach through your mouth

[noun] food that a person or animal has

brought back from their stomach through their mouth

vote [verb: **votes, voting, voted**]

1 to choose someone for an official job or choose something by secretly marking a piece of paper or putting your hand up to be counted: *Which party did you vote for?*

2 to decide something by voting: *He was voted best actor.*

[noun: **votes**]

1 a choice you make by marking a piece of paper or putting your hand up to be counted

2 the right you have to vote in elections: *They campaigned to be given the vote.*

♦ **voter** [noun: **voters**] someone who votes in an election

vouch [verb: **vouches, vouching, vouched**] to **vouch for** someone or something is to say that they are good or true

voucher [noun: **vouchers**]

1 a piece of paper that can be used instead of money to pay for something

2 a piece of paper that lets you pay less than usual for something

vow [verb: **vows, vowing, vowed**] to promise in a very serious way

[noun: **vows**] a serious promise

vowel [noun: **vowels**]

1 one of the letters **a, e, i, o** or **u**

2 a speech sound you make that does not use your lips, teeth, or tongue to stop the flow of air

voyage [noun: **voyages**] a long journey by sea or in space

vulgar [adjective] extremely rude and having very bad manners

vulnerable [adjective] weak and likely to be harmed or damaged: *Old people are especially vulnerable.* • *a place that is vulnerable to attack*

vulture [noun: **vultures**] a large bird that eats dead animals

Vv

W

W [abbreviation]
1 short for **west**
2 short for **watt** or **watts**

wad [noun: **wads**]
1 a pad of loose material such as cloth or paper pressed together into one piece: *She cleaned the wound with a wad of cotton wool.*
2 a roll or bundle of bank notes

waddle [verb: **waddles, waddling, waddled**] to walk moving from side to side, like a duck

wade [verb: **wades, wading, waded**]
1 to walk through water or mud: *The stream had flooded and we had to wade across.*
2 if you **wade through** something, you find it difficult to do and it takes a long time: *wading through a pile of paperwork*
♦ **waders** [plural noun] very high waterproof boots that you wear when you are fishing

wafer [noun: **wafers**] a very thin flat biscuit, often eaten with ice cream

waffle [noun: **waffles**]
1 a waffle is a type of thick pancake with a pattern of squares on it
2 waffle is talk that goes on for a long time but does not say anything interesting
[verb: **waffles, waffling, waffled**] to talk for a long time without saying anything interesting

waft [verb: **wafts, wafting, wafted**] to float through the air: *The smell of freshly baked bread came wafting out of the window.*

wag [verb: **wags, wagging, wagged**] to move a part of your body or a tail from side to side: *The dog ran backwards and forwards, wagging its tail.* • *Don't you wag your finger at me!*

wage [noun: **wages**] a wage or wages are money that you are paid for doing your job: *We collect our wages from the office every Friday afternoon.*
[verb: **wages, waging, waged**] to wage a war is to carry it on

wager [noun: **wagers**] a bet
[verb: **wagers, wagering, wagered**] to make a bet

waggle [verb: **waggles, waggling, waggled**] to move something from side to side or up and down: *Can you waggle your ears?*

wagon or **waggon** [noun: **wagons** or **waggons**]
1 a vehicle or cart with four wheels that is used for carrying heavy loads: *a hay wagon*
2 a type of railway truck with no roof, used for carrying things: *a coal wagon*

waif [noun: **waifs**] a child who has no home or family, and looks poor

wail [verb: **wails, wailing, wailed**] to cry loudly: *A small child was wailing in the next room.*
[noun: **wails**] a loud cry or long noise like a cry: *the wail of a siren*

waist [noun: **waists**] the narrow part of your body between your chest and your hips

waistband [noun: **waistbands**] the part of a pair of trousers or a skirt that fits around your waist

waistcoat [noun: **waistcoats**] a short jacket with no sleeves and usually with buttons up the front

wait [verb: **waits, waiting, waited**]
1 to wait or **wait for** someone or something is to stay in a place until they arrive: *Several*

people were already waiting for the bus.
2 to wait or wait until something happens is to not do an action until that thing happens: *I will wait until it stops raining before I leave.*
3 if someone **waits on** people, they serve them food and drinks: *There are six waitresses to wait on the guests.*
[noun: **waits**] a delay or period of waiting: *a long wait for the bus*
waiter [noun: **waiters**] a man who serves people with food in a restaurant
waiting list [noun: **waiting lists**] a list of people who are waiting for something: *There's a long waiting list for tickets.*
waiting room [noun: **waiting rooms**] a room where people can wait, for example in a station or a doctor's surgery
waitress [noun: **waitresses**] a woman who serves people with food in a restaurant
waive [verb: **waives, waiving, waived**] to give up a claim or right to something
wake[1] [verb: **wakes, waking, woke, woken**]
1 if you wake or **wake up**, you stop sleeping: *She suddenly woke up and looked around.*
2 to wake someone is to make them stop sleeping: *Please don't wake the baby!*
wake[2] [noun: **wakes**]
1 the strip of disturbed water left behind a moving boat
2 if something happens **in the wake of** something else, it happens after or because of it: *Many airlines went bankrupt in the wake of the disaster.*
waken [verb: **wakens, wakening, wakened**]
1 to waken is to stop sleeping
2 to waken someone is to make them stop sleeping: *A loud sound wakened me.*
walk [verb: **walks, walking, walked**]
1 to move on foot fairly slowly: *The door opened and Simon walked in.* • *I think I'll walk to work today.*
2 to travel on foot for pleasure: *We usually go walking on the moors every weekend.*
3 if a group of workers **walk out**, they leave work suddenly, often as a protest: *Council workers walked out in a dispute about pay.*
[noun: **walks**]

1 a journey on foot: *It's just a short walk to the newsagent's.*
2 a way of walking: *I recognised Ann by her walk.*
3 a path that you can walk along for pleasure: *a book of walks in the Lake District*
• **walker** [noun: **walkers**] someone who walks, especially for pleasure
walkie-talkie [noun: **walkie-talkies**] a radio that you can carry with you to send and receive messages
walking stick [noun: **walking sticks**] a stick that you can use to help you walk: *Ellen needs to use a walking stick since she had her fall.*
walkover [noun: **walkovers**] a game or race that is easy to win: *The score was 3–1 but it was no walkover.*
wall [noun: **walls**]
1 a structure made of brick or stone that separates or goes around an area: *Hadrian's Wall* • *A high wall surrounds the school.*
2 any of the sides of a room or building: *She hung the new clock on the kitchen wall.*
[verb: **walls, walling, walled**] to surround or enclose something with a wall: *a walled garden*
wallaby [noun: **wallabies**] an animal like a small kangaroo
wallet [noun: **wallets**] a small folding holder for banknotes and cards: *a leather wallet*
wallflower [noun: **wallflowers**]
1 a spring flower with a sweet smell
2 someone who does not have a partner to dance with
wallop [verb: **wallops, walloping, walloped**] to hit someone or something hard: *He walloped his head on the door as he came into the room.*
[noun: **wallops**] a hard hit: *She fell off her bike with quite a wallop.*
wallow [verb: **wallows, wallowing, wallowed**] to roll about in mud or water and enjoy it: *The hippos were wallowing in the mud.*
wallpaper [noun: **wallpapers**] paper that you can use to cover and decorate the walls of a room
walnut [noun: **walnuts**] a large nut with a hard, round shell

Ww

walrus [noun: **walruses**] a sea animal like a large seal with very big teeth called tusks

waltz [noun: **waltzes**] an old-fashioned dance for couples, to music with three beats in every bar
[verb: **waltzes, waltzing, waltzed**] to dance a waltz

wand [noun: **wands**] a long thin stick used when doing magic spells or tricks

wander [verb: **wanders, wandering, wandered**]
1 to go from one place to another without any definite plan: *We spent the summer wandering all around southern Italy.*
2 to wander or **wander off** is to go away from where you should be: *Their little boy had wandered off and could not find them.*
◆ **wanderer** [noun: **wanderers**] someone who wanders

ⓘ Try not to confuse the spelling of **wonder**, which means to be curious or surprised, with **wander**.

wane [verb: **wanes, waning, waned**]
1 to become less strong: *Support for the government is waning fast.*
2 if the moon wanes, it seems to become smaller. Look up and compare **wax²**
[noun] if something is **on the wane**, it is becoming smaller or less powerful: *I think his interest in politics is on the wane.*

wangle [verb: **wangles, wangling, wangled**] to achieve or obtain something by being clever or crafty: *Do you think you could wangle me a couple of free tickets to the concert?*

want [verb: **wants, wanting, wanted**]
1 to wish for something: *Do you want some cake? • Someone wants to speak to you. • I'll stay here with you, if you want.*
2 to need or lack something: *Your hands want a good wash.*
[noun: **wants**]
1 a want is something that you want: *a long list of wants*
2 want is the state of being very poor: *families living in severe want*
3 a lack of something: *He failed the test, but not for want of trying.*

◆ **wanted** [adjective]
1 someone who is wanted is being searched for by the police: *Pictures of the wanted man appeared in all the newspapers.*
2 loved, needed, and cared for: *Make your pet feel wanted by giving it plenty of attention.*
◆ **wanting** [adjective] lacking or missing something: *found wanting*

war [noun: **wars**] armed conflict between two countries or groups: *the war in Afghanistan • War broke out between neighbouring tribes.*
[verb: **wars, warring, warred**] to fight in a war: *The two countries have been warring against each other for centuries.*
→ **warrior**

warble [verb: **warbles, warbling, warbled**] to sing like a bird

ward [noun: **wards**]
1 a room with beds in it in a hospital: *the children's ward*
2 someone who is looked after by an adult who is not their parent, or by a court of law
[verb: **wards, warding, warded**] if you **ward something off**, you fight to keep it away from you: *He covered his head with his arms to ward off the blows.*

warden [noun: **wardens**]
1 someone who is in charge of a place, for example an old people's home, hostel or caravan site: *All visitors should report to the warden.*
2 someone who is responsible for looking after or controlling something: *a traffic warden • a game warden*

warder [noun: **warders**] someone who guards the prisoners in a prison

wardrobe [noun: **wardrobes**]
1 a tall cupboard that you can hang clothes inside
2 all of the clothes someone owns: *her summer wardrobe*

warehouse [noun: **warehouses**] a large building where businesses store things: *a furniture warehouse*

wares [plural noun] things that are for sale: *The large shop windows are used to display our wares.*

Ww

warfare [noun] fighting in a war: *modern warfare*

warhead [noun: **warheads**] the part of a missile that contains the explosive: *a nuclear warhead*

warily [adverb] cautiously: *He eyed the guard dog warily.*

warlike [adjective] a warlike country or person enjoys fighting

warm [adjective: **warmer, warmest**]
1 pleasantly hot: *a warm bath* • *As the sun rose we began to feel a little warmer.*
2 warm clothes make you feel warm: *a warm winter coat*
3 kind and friendly: *a warm welcome* • *Shilpa is a warm, kind-hearted person.*
[verb: **warms, warming, warmed**]
1 to make someone or something feel warm: *She warmed her hands on the radiator.*
2 to warm or **warm up** is to become warm: *I'll put the heating on and the house'll soon warm up.*
3 if you **warm up** before an event, you prepare for it by practising or doing gentle exercises: *The players were on the pitch, warming up.*

warm-blooded [adjective] a warm-blooded animal has a temperature that is higher than the air around it

warmly [adverb] in a warm way: *Make sure you're warmly dressed for the hike.* • *She smiled warmly.*

warmth [noun]
1 pleasant heat, or the state of being pleasantly warm: *the warmth of the fire*
2 being kind, friendly and affectionate: *the warmth of her welcome*

warm-up [noun: **warm-ups**] a set of gentle exercises that you do before playing a sport, dancing or running

warn [verb: **warns, warning, warned**] to tell someone that something is dangerous or bad before it happens: *I warned her about the icy roads.*
• **warning** [noun: **warnings**] an event or something that you say to warn someone: *The volcano erupted without any warning.*

warp [verb: **warps, warping, warped**] to become or make something twisted and out of shape: *This drawer has warped and is hard to open.* • *The wet weather had warped the back door.*

warpath [noun] if someone is **on the warpath**, they are in the type of mood to have an argument or fight with someone: *I'd avoid Maurice — he's on the warpath today.*

warrant [noun: **warrants**] a document that gives the police the right to arrest someone or search their property
[verb: **warrants, warranting, warranted**] to be a good reason or excuse for something: *He was in the wrong, but it did not warrant such a harsh punishment.*

warranty [noun: **warranties**] a promise that something will be repaired if it goes wrong

warren [noun: **warrens**] a network of tunnels called burrows that rabbits live in

warrior [noun: **warriors**] a soldier or fighter

warship [noun: **warships**] a ship with a lot of guns used for fighting at sea

wart [noun: **warts**] a small hard lump on the skin

wary [adjective] cautious: *a wary glance* • *I'd be very wary of lending her money.*
→ **warily**

was [verb] a way of changing the verb **be** that you use with **I**, **he**, **she** or **it** to make a past tense: *I was surprised to see Rosie there.* • *Mr Brock was my favourite teacher.*

wash [verb: **washes, washing, washed**]
1 to clean something with water and soap: *Wash your hands and face before we eat.*
2 if water washes against something, it flows against it: *Gentle waves were washing against the boat.*
3 if something such as a building, tree or car is **washed away**, the force of the water carries it away: *Whole houses were washed away in the storm.*
4 if you **wash up**, you wash the dishes after you have eaten: *It's your turn to wash up, Adam.*
[noun: **washes**]
1 if you have a wash or give something a wash, you wash yourself or it
2 all the clothes that need to be washed: *Your red shirt is in the wash.*
3 the waves that a boat causes as it moves

Ww

washer [noun: **washers**]
1 a flat ring made of metal or rubber that you put under a screw to keep it tightly in place
2 a washing machine

washing [noun] all the clothes that need to be washed: *a pile of dirty washing*

LANGUAGE FOR LIFE

washing

There are different ways of washing clothes, depending on the material they are made from.

• A **hand wash** involves washing clothes in a basin or a sink rather than in a washing machine.

• A **machine wash** involves washing clothes in a washing machine.

• **Dry cleaning** is a way of cleaning clothes with special chemicals instead of water. Clothes that need to be dry-cleaned have to be taken to a shop to be cleaned.

It is important to read the labels on clothes so that you know whether you can wash them in a machine and what temperature you can wash them at.

washing machine [noun: **washing machines**] a piece of electrical equipment that you wash clothes in

washing-up [noun]
1 all the dishes that need to be washed: *How come there's so much washing-up tonight?*
2 the activity of washing dishes: *You sit down and relax while I do the washing-up.*

wasn't [short form] a short way to say and write **was not**: *Are you sure Mark wasn't joking?*

wasp [noun: **wasps**] an insect with a thin black and yellow striped body that can sting you

waste [verb: **wastes, wasting, wasted**]
1 to use more of something than you need: *I'm trying not to waste any paper.*
2 if you waste time or money, you spend it in a way that is not useful: *You're wasting your time trying to fix the television.*
[noun: **wastes**]
1 waste is rubbish or useless material: *industrial waste*
2 a waste is a bad use of something: *The computer turned out to be a waste of money.*

3 a large area of land that is not cultivated: *the frozen wastes of Siberia*
[adjective]
1 waste products or materials are useless and thrown away: *waste paper*
2 waste land has no buildings or crops on it

wasteful [adjective] involving or causing waste: *It's very wasteful, throwing all these apples away.*

watch [verb: **watches, watching, watched**]
1 to look at someone or something: *Roy's watching the football match in the other room.*
2 to be careful about something: *Watch you don't trip over that step.*
3 to look after someone or something: *Could you watch the baby for me while I go to the shop?*
[noun: **watches**]
1 a small clock that you wear on your wrist
2 a time when someone keeps guard: *Two guards kept watch over the prisoners.*

watchdog [noun: **watchdogs**] a dog that is trained to guard a building

watchful [adjective] careful to notice what is happening: *Sue kept a watchful eye on her little sister.*

watchman [noun: **watchmen**] a man whose job is to guard a building: *a night watchman*

water [noun] a clear liquid with no taste that falls from the sky as rain: *a glass of water*
[verb: **waters, watering, watered**]
1 to water a plant is to give water to it so it will grow
2 if your eyes water, they produce tears: *The thick smoke made her eyes water.*
3 if your mouth waters, it produces saliva because you see something good to eat
4 if you **water down** a drink, you add water to it so that it is not as strong

watercolour [noun: **watercolours**]
1 a type of paint that is mixed with water, not oil: *a box of watercolours*
2 a painting done with watercolour paints: *a watercolour of a thatched cottage*

watercress [noun] a plant that grows in water and has rounded leaves that taste peppery

Ww

waterfall [noun: **waterfalls**] a place where a river or stream falls over a high rock or cliff

waterlogged [adjective] waterlogged ground is so wet that it cannot take in any more water: *The match was cancelled because the pitch was waterlogged.*

watermark [noun: **watermarks**] a faint design that you can see in a piece of paper or banknote when you hold it up against the light

watermelon [noun: **watermelons**] a large round fruit with a hard green skin and red juicy flesh

waterproof [adjective] waterproof material does not allow water through it [noun: **waterproofs**] a coat or other piece of clothing made of waterproof material: *The fishermen were wearing bright yellow waterproofs.*

watershed [noun: **watersheds**] an important event after which everything is different: *a watershed in India's history*

watertight [adjective] a watertight join or seal does not let liquid in or out

waterway [noun: **waterways**] a river or canal that a boat can travel along

waterworks [noun] a waterworks is a place where water is cleaned and stored

watery [adjective]
1 like water: *watery soup*
2 full of water: *watery eyes*

watt [noun: **watts**] a unit of electrical power. This is often shortened to **W**
• **wattage** [noun] electric power measured in watts

wave [noun: **waves**]
1 a moving ridge of water in the sea: *Surfers were jumping into the waves.*
2 a curving shape in your hair: *Your hair has a natural wave.*
3 a vibration that travels through the air and carries something such as sound or light: *radio waves*
4 a movement of the hand to say hello or goodbye or to attract someone's attention: *She gave a cheery wave as the train pulled out of the station.*
5 a rush of a feeling or emotion: *The pain seemed to come in waves.*
[verb: **waves, waving, waved**]

1 to move your hand backwards and forwards: *We waved goodbye to the children.*
2 to move in the wind: *flags waving in the breeze*
3 hair that waves or is waved is slightly curly: *Mel's hair waves naturally.*

wavelength [noun: **wavelengths**]
1 the distance between one point on a radio wave and the next
2 the length of radio wave that a radio or television station uses to broadcast on. These are marked on radios so that you can find them: *Which wavelength is that station on?*

wavy [adjective: **wavier, waviest**]
1 a wavy line goes up and down in gentle curves
2 wavy hair has gentle curls in it

wax¹ [noun] a sticky, fatty substance such as the one that bees make their cells out of or the one that forms in your ears
[verb: **waxes, waxing, waxed**] to polish wood with wax

wax² [verb: **waxes, waxing, waxed**] if the moon waxes, it seems to grow bigger. Look up and compare **wane**

waxy [adjective: **waxier, waxiest**] like wax: *a waxy substance*

way [noun: **ways**]
1 a method or manner of doing something: *She's got a funny way of walking.* • *The best way to make new friends is to join a club.*
2 a road or path: *22 Purley Way*
3 a route or direction: *Could you tell me the way to the cinema?*
4 a distance: *It's quite a long way to the coast.*
5 if you **get your own way**, things happen in the way that you want them to: *You should not let children always get their own way.*
6 if something is **in the way**, it is blocking your progress or movement: *Am I in your way if I sit here?*

wayward [adjective] a wayward person tends to break rules and not obey other people

WC [noun] a toilet

ⓘ **WC** is short for **water closet**, an old-fashioned word for a toilet.

Ww

we [pronoun] a word you use when you are talking about yourself and at least one other person: *We left home at about nine o'clock.*

weak [adjective: **weaker, weakest**]

1 feeble and not physically strong: *His illness has left him feeling very weak.* • *a weak heart*
2 not strong in character: *She's too weak to stand up to her boss.* • *a weak excuse*
3 someone who is weak at a subject or activity is not good at it: *I was always weak at maths.*
4 a weak drink or mixture has too much water in it: *a cup of weak tea*

♦ **weaken** [verb: **weakens, weakening, weakened**]

1 to weaken is to become weak: *His determination to leave weakened when Jenny arrived.*
2 to weaken something or someone is to make them weaker: *The bout of flu had weakened her severely.*

♦ **weakling** [noun: **weaklings**] a weak person

♦ **weakly** [adverb] in a way that is not strong or determined: *She smiled weakly at his joke.*

♦ **weakness** [noun: **weaknesses**]

1 lack of strength: *the weakness of my argument*
2 something that is not good but you cannot help liking: *Chocolate is my only weakness.*

wealth [noun]

1 wealth is riches: *a businessman of great wealth*
2 a wealth of something is a lot of it: *a sports team with a wealth of talent*

♦ **wealthy** [adjective: **wealthier, wealthiest**] rich: *a wealthy landowner*

wean [verb: **weans, weaning, weaned**] to gradually start feeding a baby on food rather than only on its mother's milk

weapon [noun: **weapons**] something that you use to fight someone: *weapons of war* • *Our best weapon was surprise.*

wear [verb: **wears, wearing, wore, worn**]

1 to be dressed in clothes or carrying something on your body: *Ann was wearing a red hat.* • *How long have you worn glasses?*
2 to arrange your hair in a particular style: *She usually wears her hair in a ponytail.*
3 to have a particular expression on your face: *Ted wore an angry frown.*

4 if a material or surface wears, it gradually becomes thinner because of being used or rubbed: *His sleeves had worn through at the elbows.*
5 if something wears a material or surface, it gradually makes it thinner: *The pressure of the waves slowly wears away the rocks.*
6 if an effect **wears off**, it gradually becomes less: *The anaesthetic should soon wear off.*
7 if time **wears on**, it passes slowly: *As the day wore on, we got bored.*
8 if you **wear something out**, it becomes too old or worn for you to use: *Ben seems to wear out a pair of shoes every three months.*
9 to **wear someone out** is to make them very tired: *Walking so far completely wore me out.*

[noun]

1 clothes: *evening wear*
2 damage caused by being used or rubbed: *The carpet was showing signs of wear.*

♦ **wearer** [noun: **wearers**] someone who is wearing something

wearily [adverb] in a weary way: *The old man sighed wearily.*

weary [adjective: **wearier, weariest**] tired: *He finally got home, weary after a long day.*

weasel [noun: **weasels**] a small wild animal with a long thin body

weather [noun] the weather means how hot, cold, wet or dry it is outside: *The weather's very warm for October.*

[verb: **weathers, weathering, weathered**] to survive a bad situation safely: *She felt that she had weathered the storm.*

weatherbeaten [adjective] rougher and darker because of being outside in all types of weather: *a weatherbeaten face*

weathervane [noun: **weathervanes**] a piece of metal that swings in the wind to show which direction the wind is coming from

weave [verb: **weaves, weaving, wove** or **weaved, woven** or **weaved**]

1 to pass threads under and over each other on a frame called a loom to make cloth
2 to move in and out between objects: *a car weaving through the traffic*

♦ **weaver** [noun: **weavers**] someone who weaves

ⓘ The past tense of **weave** when it means 'to make cloth' is **wove**: *She wove fine materials.* The past tense of **weave** when it means 'to move in and out' is **weaved**: *She weaved through the crowd.*

web [noun: **webs**]
1 a spider's web is a type of net it makes to catch insects
2 Web is a shortened form of **World Wide Web**
◆ **webbed** [adjective] webbed feet have skin joining the toes together

web page [noun: **web pages**] a page on a website

website [noun: **websites**] a collection of linked pages on the World Wide Web about a subject or an organization

wed [verb: **weds, wedding, wedded**] to wed someone is to marry them
→ **wedding**

we'd [short form] a short way to say and write **we had** or **we would**: *We'd better hurry up or we'll be late.* • *We'd buy a new car if we had the money.*

wedding [noun: **weddings**] a marriage ceremony: *I met her at Lucy and John's wedding.*

wedge [noun: **wedges**]
1 a piece of hard material that is thick at one end and thin at the other and is used to hold something in place
2 something shaped like a wedge: *He cut himself a thick wedge of chocolate cake.*
[verb: **wedges, wedging, wedged**] to hold something in place or in a space: *She wedged the door open with a piece of cardboard.* • *Sally found herself wedged in a corner.*

wedlock [noun] the state of being married

Wednesday [noun: **Wednesdays**] the day of the week after Tuesday and before Thursday

wee [adjective] an informal word which some people use to mean very small: *a wee boy*

weed [noun: **weeds**] a wild plant that is growing where you do not want it to: *The garden was overgrown with weeds.*
[verb: **weeds, weeding, weeded**] to remove the weeds from a place: *I spent an hour weeding the garden.*

◆ **weedy** [adjective: **weedier, weediest**]
1 full of weeds
2 someone who is weedy is thin and weak

week [noun: **weeks**]
1 a period of seven days, often from Sunday to Saturday: *Debbie teaches aerobics twice a week.*
2 the five days from Monday to Friday when many people go to work: *I don't go out much during the week.*

weekday [noun: **weekdays**] any of the days from Monday to Friday: *The office is only open on weekdays.*

weekend [noun: **weekends**] Saturday and Sunday: *We're going to Oxford for the weekend.*

weekly [adjective] happening or produced once every week: *a weekly magazine*
[adverb] once every week: *In those days I used to get paid weekly.*

weep [verb: **weeps, weeping, wept**] to cry tears: *Mother wept when she heard the terrible news.*

weigh [verb: **weighs, weighing, weighed**]
1 to measure how heavy something is by putting it on a scale: *Brenda weighs herself every day.*
2 to have a particular heaviness: *My suitcase weighed 15 kilograms.*
3 if something **weighs you down**, it is heavy or difficult for you to deal with: *I am weighed down with problems.*

◆ **weight** [noun: **weights**]
1 the amount that something or someone weighs: *What weight are you?*
2 a piece of solid material that is used to hold things down or weigh things on scales
3 a load or burden: *Getting a job took a weight off his mind.*
[verb: **weights, weighting, weighted**] to add a weight to something: *The base is weighted with lead.*

◆ **weightless** [adjective] floating in the air because there is no gravity

◆ **weightlessness** [noun] being weightless

◆ **weighty** [adjective: **weightier, weightiest**]
1 heavy: *a weighty volume of magic spells*
2 important: *discussing some weighty problems*

Ww

weir [noun: **weirs**] a low dam across a river

weird [adjective: **weirder, weirdest**]
strange or mysterious: *a weird light in the sky*
- **weirdly** [adverb] in a weird way: *weirdly dressed*
- **weirdness** [noun] being weird

welcome [adjective]
1 if someone or something is welcome, you are happy to accept or receive them: *Joe's parents always make us very welcome.* • *a welcome gift*
2 if someone is welcome to do something, you are happy to let them do it: *You're welcome to borrow the car if I'm not using it.*
3 you say '**you're welcome**' after someone has thanked you for something: *'Thank you for all your help.' 'You're welcome.'*
[noun: **welcomes**] the way you receive a visitor: *Her fans gave her a warm welcome.*
[verb: **welcomes, welcoming, welcomed**]
1 to meet someone and make them feel that you are happy to see them: *The whole family turned out to welcome us at the airport.*
2 to accept something gladly: *I would welcome the chance of a different job.*

weld [verb: **welds, welding, welded**] to join together pieces of metal by heating them until they melt
- **welder** [noun: **welders**] someone whose job is to weld metals
- **welding** [noun] the activity of joining metal by heat

welfare [noun] health, comfort and happiness: *parents concerned for the welfare of their children*

welfare state [noun] a system in which a government provides services such as free health care and money for the unemployed

well¹ [adverb: **better, best**]
1 in a satisfactory, successful or correct way: *Janet speaks French very well.*
2 thoroughly: *Mix the butter and sugar well before adding the flour.*
3 as well means 'too': *I'd like an ice cream as well.*
[adjective: **better, best**]
1 healthy: *I don't feel well today.*
2 good or pleasing: *All is not well at home.*

well² [noun: **wells**] a deep hole in the ground where you can get water, oil or gas: *an oil well*
[verb: **wells, welling, welled**] if tears **well up** in your eyes, they begin to flow

we'll [short form] a short way to say and write **we will**: *I'm sure we'll meet again.*

well-being [noun] health and happiness

wellingtons or **wellington boots**
[plural noun] high rubber boots that cover your lower leg

well-off [adjective: **better-off, best-off**]
1 rich: *Only the better-off kids had bicycles.*
2 fortunate: *The trouble is, you don't realize when you're well-off.*

well-to-do [adjective] rich: *Our customers are mostly quite well-to-do.*

went [verb] a way of changing the verb **go** to make a past tense: *Bill went out at about 6 o'clock.*

wept [verb] a way of changing the verb **weep** to make a past tense. It can be used with or without a helping verb: *I could have wept when I saw the state of the house.* • *A woman wept openly in the corner.*

were [verb] the past tense of the verb **be** that you use with **you**, **we** or **they**: *We were so relieved to see him.* • *The children were playing in the garden when we arrived.*

we're [short form] a short way to say and write **we are**: *We're so pleased you could come.*

weren't [short form] a short way to say and write **were not**: *Weren't the acrobats amazing?*

werewolf [noun: **werewolves**] in stories, a werewolf is a person who changes into a wolf when there is a full moon

west [noun]
1 the direction in which the sun sets, opposite to east: *the west of England*
2 the West is a name for the countries in Europe and North America
[adjective] in, from, or towards the west: *the west coast of America*
[adverb] to the west: *We travelled west as far as the motorway.*
- **westerly** [adjective] coming from, or going towards, the west: *a westerly breeze*
- **western** [adjective] belonging to, or coming from, the west: *the western hills*

[noun: **westerns**] a book or film about cowboys in North America

♦ **westward** or **westwards** [adverb] to or towards the west: *We travelled westwards.*

wet [adjective: **wetter, wettest**]

1 full of water or covered with water: *wet clothes* • *It's easy to skid on wet roads.*

2 not dried: *wet paint*

3 rainy: *a wet afternoon*

[verb: **wets, wetting, wet**] to wet something is to make it wet: *He wet his hair to flatten it down.*

wet suit [noun: **wet suits**] a rubber suit that you wear to keep you warm when you swim underwater

we've [short form] a short way to say and write **we have**: *We've got something to tell you.*

whack [verb: **whacks, whacking, whacked**] to hit someone or something hard with a loud noise: *He whacked his brother on the head with a book.*

[noun: **whacks**] a hard loud hit: *Jim gave him a whack across the shoulders.*

whale [noun: **whales**]

1 a very large mammal that lives in the sea

2 if you have **a whale of a time**, you enjoy yourself very much

♦ **whaler** [noun: **whalers**] a ship or person that goes out hunting whales

♦ **whaling** [noun] hunting and killing whales

wharf [noun: **wharfs** or **wharves**] a platform where ships stop to be loaded and unloaded

what [adjective and pronoun]

1 what is used to ask questions about things: *What day is it today?* • *What's your brother's name?*

2 you can say **what** in exclamations to emphasize something: *What a beautiful view!*

3 the thing or things: *I hope you find what you're looking for.* • *This bag is just what I wanted.*

whatever [adjective and pronoun]

1 any, anything or any amount: *I can give you whatever money you need.* • *Choose whatever you like from the menu.*

2 no matter what: *You know we'll always love you whatever happens.*

whatsoever [adjective] at all: *Your problems are nothing whatsoever to do with me.*

wheat [noun] a type of grain that is used to make flour

wheatgerm [noun] the centre of a grain of wheat

wheedle [verb: **wheedles, wheedling, wheedled**] to beg or persuade someone to do something, often by flattering them: *I managed to wheedle some money out of my dad.*

wheel [noun: **wheels**]

1 one of the round things under a vehicle that turns around as it moves: *The spare wheel is in the boot.*

2 anything that goes around like a wheel: *a potter's wheel*

[verb: **wheels, wheeling, wheeled**]

1 to wheel something is to push it along on wheels: *He got a puncture and had to wheel his bike home.*

2 to move in a wide curve: *Vultures were wheeling overhead.*

3 to turn round quickly: *Kay wheeled around when she heard his voice.*

wheelbarrow [noun: **wheelbarrows**] a small cart with only one wheel at the front and with handles that you use to push it

wheelchair [noun: **wheelchairs**] a seat with wheels used by people who are ill or cannot walk

wheeze [verb: **wheezes, wheezing, wheezed**] to breathe with a rough, gasping or whistling sound

[noun: **wheezes**]

1 a rough, gasping or whistling breath

2 a clever or cunning idea: *his latest wheeze for raising money*

whelk [noun: **whelks**] a small snail-like sea creature that lives inside a hard shell

when [adverb] at what time: *When did you arrive home?*

[conjunction]

1 at the time at which, or during the time at which: *I was just going out when the phone rang.*

2 in spite of the fact that: *How could he say he was busy when the office was closed?*

Ww

whenever [conjunction]
1 at any time that: *You can borrow my book whenever you want to.*
2 at every time that: *They go swimming whenever they get the chance.*

where [adverb] to, from or in what place: *Where are we going?* • *Where did you get that hat?*
[conjunction] to, from or in what place: *I have no idea where we are.*

whereabouts [noun] the whereabouts of a person or thing is the place where they are or it is: *Do you know the whereabouts of your cousin?*
[adverb] near or in what place: *Whereabouts in Texas do you come from?*

whereas [conjunction] but: *They thought he was a bit strange, whereas he was simply quiet and shy.* • *He wanted to go to the cinema, whereas I wanted to go swimming.*

where's [short form] a short way to say and write **where is** or **where has**: *Where's the cat?* • *Where's he gone?*

whereupon [conjunction] at or immediately after which: *His boss told him he was sacked, whereupon he flew into a rage.*

wherever [adverb and conjunction] to, or in, any place or every place: *He follows me wherever I go.* • *Wherever he is, I am sure he will come back soon.*
[adverb] a more emphatic way of saying 'where': *The cat's disappeared. Wherever can he be?*

wherewithal [noun] the **wherewithal** is the things that are necessary: *We don't have the wherewithal to complete the project.*

whet [verb: **whets, whetting, whetted**]
1 to whet the blade of a knife is to sharpen it
2 if something **whets your appetite**, it makes you want to eat, or it makes you want to do something: *He'd seen a clip of the film, which had whetted his appetite to see more.*

whether [conjunction] **whether** is used to show that there is a choice between two possibilities: *Whether we like it or not, we have to get up early.*

whey [noun] whey is the watery part of milk that is left after separating out the solid curds which make cheese

which [adjective] what one or ones: *Which hand do you think the coin is in?*
[pronoun]
1 what one or ones: *Which of these books is yours and which is mine?*
2 you use **which** to talk about a thing that has been mentioned in the earlier part of a sentence: *I had two apples which I had bought at the market.*

whichever [adjective and pronoun] that or any one: *Come on whichever day suits you.* • *You can come round on Monday or Tuesday, whichever suits you.*

whiff [noun: **whiffs**] a smell or scent which you notice as it is carried in the air to your nose: *a whiff of garlic*

while [conjunction]
1 during the time that: *Will you be going to Disneyland while you are in Florida?*
2 although: *While I understand why you got angry, I think you should try to control your temper.*
[noun] a period of time: *We waited inside for a while, but the rain didn't stop.*
[verb: **whiles, whiling, whiled**] to **while away** time is to pass the time doing something: *We whiled away the journey talking about our holidays.*

whilst [conjunction] while: *You could look at these magazines whilst you're waiting.*

whim [noun: **whims**] a sudden idea or a sudden desire to do something

whimper [verb: **whimpers, whimpering, whimpered**] to make a series of low weak crying sounds, showing pain or fear
[noun: **whimpers**] a low weak crying or whining sound

whimsical [adjective] a whimsical thought or idea is humorous and playful, and not made for any obvious reason

whine [verb: **whines, whining, whined**]
1 a dog or other animal whines when it makes a long high sound
2 a person whines when they talk in a complaining voice
[noun: **whines**]
1 the sound a dog or animal makes when it whines
2 a complaining voice

whinge [verb: **whinges, whingeing, whinged**] to complain in a way that other people find annoying
[noun: **whinges**] a complaint, especially one made in an irritating way about something unimportant

whinny [noun: **whinnies**] a gentle series of sounds a horse or pony makes
[verb: **whinnies, whinnying, whinnied**] a horse or pony whinnies when it makes a gentle series of sounds

whip [noun: **whips**] a piece of leather or cord fastened to a handle and used to hit animals or people
[verb: **whips, whipping, whipped**]
1 to whip an animal or person is to hit them with a whip
2 to whip liquids like cream or eggs is to beat them so that they form a froth or become thick and stiff
3 to **whip something out**, or **whip it away**, is to take it out or take it away very quickly, or in one quick movement
4 to **whip up** something to eat is to prepare it quickly
5 to **whip up** a particular feeling or reaction is to encourage that feeling or reaction in other people

whippet [noun: **whippets**] a breed of dog with a slim head and body, like a small greyhound

whirl [verb: **whirls, whirling, whirled**] to turn or spin very quickly
[noun: **whirls**]
1 a very fast turning or spinning movement
2 if you **give something a whirl**, you try it out

whirlpool [noun: **whirlpools**] a place in a river or in the sea where a current of water swirls round and round and is sometimes strong enough to drag things down

whirlwind [noun: **whirlwinds**] a column of wind that swirls round and round in a spiral as it moves across the land

whirr [verb: **whirrs, whirring, whirred**] something whirrs when it turns or moves quickly making a buzzing sound
[noun: **whirrs**] the buzzing sound made by something turning quickly through the air

whisk [noun: **whisks**] a piece of kitchen equipment made up of loops of wire and used for mixing things like cream or eggs
[verb: **whisks, whisking, whisked**]
1 to whisk foods like cream or eggs is to beat them with a whisk so that they are well mixed or become thick
2 to **whisk someone** or **something away** is to take them quickly, or with a quick movement

whisker [noun: **whiskers**]
1 one of the long stiff hairs that grow on the faces of animals like mice, cats and dogs, and which are sensitive to touch
2 the hair that grows on a man's face is sometimes called his whiskers

whisky [noun: **whiskies**] a strong alcoholic drink made from grain or barley, especially in Scotland

whisper [verb: **whispers, whispering, whispered**] to talk very quietly under your breath so that only people near you can hear what you are saying
[noun: **whispers**] a very quiet voice: She answered in a whisper.

whistle [verb: **whistles, whistling, whistled**]
1 to make a high-pitched sound or a musical note by blowing air through your teeth and lips
2 if something whistles, it makes a high-pitched sound
[noun: **whistles**]
1 a whistling sound
2 a device or simple instrument that you blow into to make a high-pitched sound

white [noun: **whites**]
1 the very pale colour of milk or snow
2 the white of an egg is the clear substance around the yolk which turns white if it is cooked

white-hot [adjective] something that is white-hot is so hot it is glowing with white light

whiten [verb: **whitens, whitening, whitened**] to make something white or whiter

whitewash [noun] a thin white liquid, containing lime, used to paint on walls and ceilings to make them white
[verb: **whitewashes, whitewashing, whitewashed**] to paint whitewash on walls or ceilings

Whitsun [noun] the seventh Sunday after Easter

Ww

whizz [verb: **whizzes, whizzing, whizzed**] to move very quickly
[noun: **whizzes**] someone who is a whizz at something is an expert at it

who [pronoun]
1 which person or people: *Who is your favourite actor?*
2 you use **who** when you want to say something else about a person or people you have just mentioned, or to explain which person you mean: *Emily, who lives next door, is 12 years old.* • *It was Malcolm who told me the news.*

who'd [short form] a short way to say and write **who had** or **who would**: *It was my Dad who'd said I should be a photographer.* • *Who'd like another biscuit?*

whoever [pronoun]
1 the person that has done something: *Would whoever it was that left the gate open, please go and close it.*
2 any person: *Bring whoever you like to the party.*

whole [adjective] containing all of something: *a whole day*
[noun] a whole is a complete thing, especially one that is made up of different parts: *Two halves make a whole.*
➡ **wholly**

wholehearted [adjective] wholehearted support or agreement is complete and sincere

wholemeal [adjective] wholemeal bread or biscuits are made from flour that uses whole grains of wheat

wholesale [adjective]
1 wholesale goods are bought in large amounts by a business which then sells them in smaller amounts to shops or smaller businesses
2 total or complete: *the wholesale destruction of the rainforests*

wholesome [adjective] healthy and good for you

who'll [short form] a short way to say and write **who will** or **who shall**: *Who'll help me to carry this box?*

wholly [adverb] completely: *They were wholly committed to the team.*

whom [pronoun] **whom** is used as the object of a verb or preposition, and means the same as **who**: *He phoned his friend Andrew, whom he hadn't seen for years.* • *To whom should I address the letter?*

ⓘ Nowadays, people often use **who** instead of **whom** as the object of a verb, as in: *He phoned his friend Andrew, **who** he hadn't seen for years.*
However, you should always use **whom** after a preposition:
✗ *To who should I address the letter?*
✓ *To **whom** should I address the letter?*

whoop [verb: **whoops, whooping, whooped**] to give a loud shout of joy or excitement

whooping cough [noun] a disease which makes it difficult to breathe and causes a painful cough

whopper [noun: **whoppers**] something that is extremely big: *That fish was an absolute whopper.*

whopping [adjective] extremely big: *a whopping 20% pay rise*

whore [noun: **whores**] a prostitute

who's [short form] a short way to say and write **who is** or **who has**: *Who's coming for a walk?* • *Who's got the TV guide?*

whose [adjective]
1 you use **whose** before a noun when you are asking which person or people something belongs to: *Whose bike is this?*
2 you use **whose** before a noun to mean 'of which' or 'of whom': *the boy whose family owns the farm*
[pronoun] you use **whose** when you are asking or talking about which person or people something belongs to: *Whose is this?* • *It must be someone's dog, but I don't know whose.*

ⓘ Try not to confuse the spellings of **whose** and **who's**.
Whose is the possessive form of **who**, and tells you something belongs to someone: ***Whose** shoes are these?*
Who's is a short form of two words put together: ***Who's** in the bathroom?*

why [adverb] for what reason: *Why did it have to rain today?*

wick [noun: **wicks**] the string in a candle or lamp which you light

wicked [adjective]
1 very bad or evil: *a wicked old witch*
2 mischievous: *Don't tip your cup upside-down, you wicked little monkey!*
3 a very informal word for **excellent**: *That's a wicked new haircut you've got there!*

wicker or **wickerwork** [noun] reeds or strips of cane that have been woven together to make things like baskets

wicket [noun: **wickets**] in cricket, a set of three upright wooden sticks with two horizontal rods across the top in front of which the batsman stands

wide [adjective: **wider, widest**]
1 measuring a great distance from side to side: *across the wide Missouri river*
2 having a certain width: *The river is nearly a mile wide at some points.*
3 covering a great range or amount: *a wide knowledge of history*
[adverb: **wider, widest**]
1 with a great distance from top to bottom or side to side: *The tiger opened his mouth wide, showing his enormous fangs.*
2 if you are wide awake, you are completely awake and alert
3 something that is wide of its target is a long distance away from the target
4 if you search or travel **far and wide**, you search or travel over a large area
♦ **widely** [adverb] something that is widely known or widely admired is known or admired by a lot of people
♦ **widen** [verb: **widens, widening, widened**] to make or cause to be wide or wider
➡ **width**

widespread [adjective] found in a lot of places or among a lot of people: *widespread rumours*

widow [noun: **widows**] a woman whose husband has died

widower [noun: **widowers**] a man whose wife has died

width [noun: **widths**] the width of something is how much it measures from side to side: *This curtain material comes in several different widths.*

wield [verb: **wields, wielding, wielded**]

1 to wield a tool or a weapon is to hold it and use it: *pictures of Vikings wielding axes and swords*
2 to wield something such as power is to use it

wife [noun: **wives**] a man's wife is the woman he has married

wig [noun: **wigs**] a covering of false hair that is worn on the head

wiggle [verb: **wiggles, wiggling, wiggled**] to move from side to side, or backwards and forwards: *Harriet was wiggling her loose tooth.*
[noun: **wiggles**]
1 a movement from side to side or backwards and forwards
2 a line that has lots of bends and curves
♦ **wiggly** [adjective: **wigglier, wiggliest**]
1 a wiggly line has lots of bends and curves
2 something wiggly moves, or can be moved, by wiggling: *a wiggly tooth*

wigwam [noun: **wigwams**] a cone-shaped tent that Native American people used as shelter in the past

wild [adjective: **wilder, wildest**]
1 wild animals or plants live in their natural surroundings and are not kept by human beings: *a wild goat • wild rice*
2 a wild area of land is in a natural state and has not been farmed or built on by human beings
3 wild behaviour is not controlled, and is sometimes violent: *The fans went wild with excitement.*
4 wild weather is windy and stormy
5 a wild idea is a bit crazy and isn't very likely to work
6 if you make a wild guess, you guess completely at random
7 if you are **wild about** something or someone, you are very keen on them
[noun: **wilds**] animals that live in the wild live in their natural environment and are not kept as pets or in zoos

wilderness [noun: **wildernesses**] a desert or wild area of a country with very few people living in it

wildfire [noun] if something spreads **like wildfire**, it spreads over a large area very quickly

Ww

643

wild-goose chase [noun: **wild-goose chases**] you are on a wild-goose chase if you are searching for something but have no hope of finding it

wildlife [noun] wild animals, birds and insects

wile [noun: **wiles**] a crafty trick used to deceive people
→ **wily**

wilful [adjective]

1 a wilful person is determined to do exactly what they want, not what other people think they should do

2 deliberate: *wilful damage*

♦ **wilfully** [adverb] in a wilful way

will [verb]

1 will is used to talk about the future: *It will be winter soon.*

2 you use **will** to ask someone to do something, or to tell them to do something, or to ask them what they would like: *Will you hold this for me?* • *Will you please stop making that racket!* • *Will you have tea or coffee?*

ⓘ **Will** is the present tense form. You use **would** for the past tense.

will [noun: **wills**]

1 your will is the control you have over your own actions and decisions

2 your will is what you want to do and your desire or determination to do it

3 a will is a legal document written by someone saying who they want their property and money to be given to after their death

[verb: **wills, willing, willed**] if you will something to happen, you try to make it happen by using the power of your thoughts

willing [adjective] if you are willing, you are ready or happy to do what is asked or needed: *a willing helper* • *He's willing to work hard.*

♦ **willingly** [adverb] if you do something willingly, you do it happily and eagerly

♦ **willingness** [noun] being willing

willow [noun: **willows**] a tree with long thin branches that often grows near water

willpower [noun] willpower is the determination and discipline you need to achieve something

wilt [verb: **wilts, wilting, wilted**]

1 if plants wilt, their stems get weak and hang down towards the ground

2 if a person wilts, they become weak or tired

wily [adjective: **wilier, wiliest**] crafty

wimp [noun: **wimps**] an insulting word for someone who is not strong or brave

win [verb: **wins, winning, won**]

1 to win is to beat all the others in a competition and get first place or first prize

2 to win something is to get it as a prize

3 to **win someone over** is to succeed in getting them to agree with you or be on your side

[noun: **wins**] a victory
→ **winning, winnings**

wince [verb: **winces, wincing, winced**] to make a small, quick, jerking movement with your face or head in pain or embarrassment: *He winced when I reminded him of his mistake.*

winch [noun: **winches**] a piece of equipment used for lifting or pulling something heavy by attaching it to a rope which is wound around a cylinder

[verb: **winches, winching, winched**] to winch something is to lift it or pull it using a winch

wind [noun: **winds**]

1 wind, or a wind, is a strong current of air

2 if someone has wind, they have gas trapped in their stomach, which makes them feel uncomfortable

3 your wind is your breath or your ability to breathe easily
→ **windy**

ⓘ This word rhymes with **pinned**.

wind [verb: **winds, winding, wound**]

1 to wind something is to twist it round and round in loops or coils: *A turban is a long piece of cloth that is wound round the head.*

2 to wind or **wind up** a watch or clock is to turn the screw or key that tightens the spring inside and makes it work

3 a road, path or river winds if it twists and turns

4 to **wind down** is to get slower and slower, or less and less active

5 to **wind up** somewhere is to end up in that place or situation, especially one that is unpleasant or uncomfortable

Ww

6 to **wind something up** is to finish it or end it

7 to **wind someone up** is to make them believe something is true when it isn't, as a joke or to annoy them

(i) This word rhymes with **find**.

windfall [noun: **windfalls**] something, especially money, that you get without expecting it

wind instrument [noun: **wind instruments**] an instrument in an orchestra that is played by blowing air into it

windmill [noun: **windmills**] a building with large sails on the outside which are turned by the wind and provide power for grinding corn

window [noun: **windows**]

1 an opening in the wall of a building or in a vehicle, with glass fitted in it so that you can see through it, and which can usually be opened to let in air

2 an area on a computer screen where you can view or work with information or a computer file

windpipe [noun: **windpipes**] the tube that goes from your mouth down your throat and into your lungs

wind power [noun] power that is generated by the wind and which can be turned into electricity or used to make machines work

windscreen [noun: **windscreens**] the clear screen at the front of a car or other vehicle

windshield [noun: **windshields**] another word for a **windscreen**, used especially in the United States and Canada

windsurfing [noun] the sport of moving across the surface of water standing on a narrow board with a sail attached to it

windswept [adjective]

1 a windswept place is exposed to strong winds

2 people look windswept when their hair is untidy from being blown about by the wind

windward [adjective and adverb] facing into the wind

windy [adjective: **windier, windiest**] if the weather is windy, there is a wind blowing: *a windy day with the white clouds flying*

wine [noun: **wines**] an alcoholic drink usually made from grapes, but which can also be made from the juice of other types of fruit

wing [noun: **wings**]

1 a bird's or insect's wings are the parts of its body that it uses to fly with

2 an aeroplane's wings are the two long flat parts that stick out at either side of its body

3 a wing of a building is a part that sticks out from the main building

4 in games like football and hockey, the wings are the two long sides of the pitch, or the players whose position is at either side of the field: *He's dribbling the ball down the wing.* • *She's the best right wing we've ever had in our team.*

5 a wing of a political party or other organization is a group within it that has its own particular role or its own set of ideas and policies: *the right wing of the Labour Party*

6 in a theatre, the wings are the areas on either side of the stage that are hidden from the audience

• **winged** [adjective] having wings: *a winged insect*

• **winger** [noun: **wingers**] a player in a sports team whose place is on one of the wings

wink [verb: **winks, winking, winked**]

1 to shut one of your eyes and open it again quickly, as a friendly or secret sign to someone

2 lights wink when they twinkle or go off and on again quickly

[noun: **winks**] a sign you make by closing and opening one of your eyes quickly

winkle [noun: **winkles**] a small edible sea snail that lives inside a spiral shell

[verb: **winkles, winkling, winkled**] to **winkle something out** is to get it out with a lot of difficulty and effort

winning [adjective]

1 the winning team, entry, shot or goal is the one that wins a competition or match

2 someone who has a winning smile, or winning ways, makes people like them or cooperate with them

winnings [plural noun] all the money that someone wins from bets or gambling

winter [noun: **winters**] the coldest season of the year, between autumn and spring

Ww

[adjective] happening or used during winter: *a warm winter coat* • *the winter months*

♦ **wintry** [adjective] cold, like winter

wipe [verb: **wipes, wiping, wiped**]

1 to wipe something is to rub its surface to clean it or dry it

2 to wipe a computer disk, or a sound or video tape, is to remove or erase all the information, sound or images on it

3 to **wipe something** or **someone out** is to destroy them and get rid of them completely

[noun: **wipes**]

1 an act of wiping: *I need to give my glasses a wipe.*

2 a piece of cloth or tissue used to wipe things with

♦ **wiper** [noun: **wipers**] a piece of rubber on a metal support that moves to and fro and clears water from a vehicle's windscreen

wire [noun: **wires**]

1 metal that has been pulled into a long narrow strand that bends easily

2 a length of wire, or several pieces of it twisted into a cable for carrying electricity or telephone signals

[verb: **wires, wiring, wired**]

1 to wire a house is to fit the cables that are needed to carry electricity to lights and plugs

2 to wire or **wire up** a piece of equipment is to fit it with electrical cables or a plug so that it can be connected to the power supply

wireless [noun: **wirelesses**] an old-fashioned word for a radio

wiry [adjective: **wirier, wiriest**]

1 someone who is wiry has a slim but strong body

2 wiry hair is strong and curly

wisdom [noun] being able to make sensible decisions about things, based on your knowledge and experience

wisdom tooth [noun: **wisdom teeth**] your wisdom teeth are the big teeth at the back of your mouth that grow when you are an adult

wise [adjective: **wiser, wisest**]

1 able to make sensible decisions and judgements

2 if you are **wise to** something, you are not fooled by it

-wise [suffix]

1 if **-wise** comes at the end of a word, it is an adverb that means 'in the direction of'. For example, *clockwise* means in the direction that the hands of a clock move

2 if **-wise** comes at the end of other words, it may be an adverb that means 'with regard to'. For example, you might say *How are we getting on time-wise?*

wish [verb: **wishes, wishing, wished**]

1 to want something and hope that it will happen: *I wish it would stop raining.* • *What did you wish for when you blew out the candles on your cake?*

2 to want to do something or want it to be done: *Do you wish to pay now or later?*

3 you wish someone something when you say that you hope they will have it: *We all wish you luck.*

[noun: **wishes**] something you wish for or want: *Make a wish.*

wishbone [noun: **wishbones**] the thin V-shaped bone at the top of a chicken's or other bird's breast. The wishbone is often pulled apart by two people, and the person who gets the bigger piece makes a wish

wishy-washy [adjective] wishy-washy colours are pale and uninteresting

wisp [noun: **wisps**] a wisp of smoke or hair is a long, thin, delicate piece of it

♦ **wispy** [adjective: **wispier, wispiest**] wispy hair or smoke forms wisps

wistful [adjective] if you are wistful, you long sadly for something that you know you cannot have

♦ **wistfully** [adverb] in a wistful way: *She gazed wistfully at the beautiful sports car.*

wit [noun: **wits**]

1 intelligence and common sense

2 wit is a clever sense of humour

3 if you **have your wits about you**, you are alert and ready to deal with anything that happens

→ **witty**

witch [noun: **witches**] a woman or girl who is supposed to have special magic powers

♦ **witchcraft** [noun] the magic and spells that witches do, especially to make something bad happen

witch doctor [noun: **witch doctors**] in

Ww

some cultures, a witch doctor is a man who uses magic to heal people in his tribe

with [preposition]
1 in the company of or in the same place as: *Come with me.* • *She keeps her diary on the shelf with her other books.*
2 using: *stuck down with glue*
3 having: *a house with a green door*
4 going in the same direction: *drifting with the tide*
5 as the result of: *He was doubled up with pain.*
6 against: *They've argued with each other since they were children.*
7 with is used after verbs about covering, filling or mixing: *He covered the table with a sheet.* • *Mix the dry ingredients with the milk in a large bowl.*
8 with is used after verbs about separating or finishing: *I parted with them at the station.* • *Have you finished with this magazine?*

withdraw [verb: **withdraws, withdrawing, withdrawn**]
1 to withdraw is to retreat or move back or away
2 to withdraw something is to remove it or take it back: *I would like to withdraw what I said earlier.* • *He withdrew all the money from his bank account.*
  ◆ **withdrawal** [noun: **withdrawals**]
1 withdrawing from something or somewhere
2 a sum of money that you take out of your bank account

wither [verb: **withers, withering, withered**] a plant withers when it shrinks and dries up

withhold [verb: **withholds, withholding, withheld**] to withhold something is to refuse to give it to someone

within [preposition]
1 inside: *They took cover within the castle walls.*
2 in no more than, or less than: *We'll be home within the hour.*
3 not beyond: *A place in the final is within your reach.*
[adverb] inside: *The notice on the restaurant window said: 'Waiters wanted. Apply within.'*

without [preposition] not with or not having: *They left without me.* • *Do you take coffee with or without milk?*

withstand [verb: **withstands, withstanding, withstood**] to withstand something is to bear it successfully: *The buildings are specially designed to withstand earthquakes.*

witness [noun: **witnesses**]
1 someone who sees an event happening and can tell other people about it: *Were there any witnesses to the accident?*
2 someone who is a witness in a court case gives evidence about the facts of the case
[verb: **witnesses, witnessing, witnessed**] to witness something is to see it happening

witter [verb: **witters, wittering, wittered**] if someone witters or **witters on**, they talk endlessly about things that are not important

wittily [adverb] in a clever and amusing way

witty [adjective: **wittier, wittiest**] a witty person, or a witty comment, is clever and funny

wives [plural noun] the plural of **wife**: *Henry the Eighth had six wives.*

wizard [noun: **wizards**] a man or boy who is supposed to have special magic powers
  ◆ **wizardry** [noun]
1 magic performed by a wizard
2 clever or surprising things, especially done using machines: *technical wizardry*

wobble [verb: **wobbles, wobbling, wobbled**] to rock or move from side to side unsteadily
  ◆ **wobbly** [adjective: **wobblier, wobbliest**] something that is wobbly shakes or moves about unsteadily

woe [noun: **woes**]
1 woe is sorrow, grief or misery
2 a woe is something that causes grief or misery: *He told me all his woes.*
  ◆ **woeful** [adjective]
1 miserable or unhappy
2 feeble or useless: *a woeful attempt to be funny*
  ◆ **woefully** [adverb] miserably or unhappily

wok [noun: **woks**] a type of pan shaped like a large bowl, used to cook Chinese-style food

woke [verb] a way of changing the verb **wake** to make a past tense: *He woke with a start.*

Ww

woken [verb] the form of the verb **wake** that is used with a helping verb to show that something happened in the past: *He had woken with a start.*

wolf [noun: **wolves**] a wild animal like a dog, which lives in family groups called packs [verb: **wolfs, wolfing, wolfed**] to **wolf down** food is to eat it very quickly and greedily

woman [noun: **women**] an adult female human being
+ **womanhood** [noun] being a woman
+ **womanly** [adjective] like a woman or having the qualities people expect a woman to have

womb [noun: **wombs**] the organ inside a woman's or female animal's body where her babies grow until they are ready to be born

wombat [noun: **wombats**] an Australian animal like a small bear that has dark brown fur and short strong legs

won [verb] a way of changing the verb **win** to make a past tense. It can be used with or without a helping verb: *We won the cup.* • *We had won it for four years running.*

wonder [verb: **wonders, wondering, wondered**]
1 you wonder about things when you are curious about them or cannot decide about them: *I wonder what Jack has bought me for Christmas.*
2 you **wonder at** something when you are surprised by it
3 you can say 'I wonder if' when you are asking someone politely about or for something: *I wonder if you could tell me where the post office is?*
[noun: **wonders**]
1 wonder is the feeling you get when you see something extraordinary or surprising: *The comet filled people who saw it with wonder.*
2 a wonder is something unexpected or extraordinary: *It's a wonder you didn't freeze to death out in that blizzard.*
+ **wonderful** [adjective] extraordinary or marvellous: *a wonderful view of the mountains*
+ **wonderfully** [adverb] in a marvellous way: *The concert went wonderfully.*

+ **wondrous** [adjective] astonishing or impressive: *a wondrous sight*

ⓘ Try not to confuse the spelling of **wander**, which means to roam, with **wonder**.

won't [short form] a short way to say and write **will not**: *He won't tell me what he saw.*

woo [verb: **woos, wooing, wooed**] if you woo someone, you try to gain their affection or their support

wood [noun: **woods**]
1 wood is the hard material that forms the trunks and branches of trees, and is cut up to make furniture, buildings and paper
2 a wood or the woods is an area of forest or woodland
+ **wooded** [adjective] a wooded area has trees growing on it
+ **wooden** [adjective]
1 made of wood: *wooden toys*
2 a wooden action or expression or wooden behaviour is stiff and unnatural: *The actress who played Juliet was rather wooden.*

woodland [noun: **woodlands**] land covered with trees

woodlouse [noun: **woodlice**] a small creature similar to a beetle that lives in rotten wood or damp areas

woodpecker [noun: **woodpeckers**] a wild bird that uses its strong beak to peck holes in trees to find the insects it eats

woodwind [noun] the instruments in an orchestra that are made from wood, such as the oboe, clarinet and bassoon

woodwork [noun] making objects out of wood, using tools like saws, planes and chisels

woodworm [noun: **woodworm**] a young form of a type of beetle which eats wood

woof [noun: **woofs**] the barking sound that a dog makes
[verb: **woofs, woofing, woofed**] a dog woofs when it makes a barking sound

wool [noun]
1 the soft fibre that grows on the bodies of sheep
2 a thread made from this fibre, used for knitting and making cloth: *a ball of wool*
+ **woollen** [adjective] made of wool: *a woollen blanket*

♦ **woollens** [plural noun] jumpers and cardigans made of wool, especially knitted wool

♦ **woolly** [adjective: **woollier, woolliest**] covered with wool or with hair that is dense and curly like wool

word [noun: **words**]

1 a unit of language that is written as a group of letters with spaces on either side

2 to get word about something is to get news about it

3 if you give your word, you give your solemn promise that you will do something

[verb: **words, wording, worded**] you word something in a certain way when you choose certain words to express it

♦ **wording** [noun] the wording of something is the way words have been used to express it: *We argued about the precise wording of the letter.*

word processing [noun] using a word processor or a computer to create documents

♦ **word processor** [noun: **word processors**] an electronic machine, with a keyboard and a screen, used to type letters and other documents

wordy [adjective: **wordier, wordiest**] using a lot of words, especially too many words: *a long wordy explanation of what happened*

wore [verb] a way of changing the verb **wear** to make a past tense: *She wore an old pair of jeans.*

work [noun: **works**]

1 someone's work is their job or employment: *My wife leaves for work about 8 o'clock in the morning.*

2 work is something you do that needs effort: *It was hard work climbing to the top with heavy packs on our backs.*

3 your work is what you create by working

4 a work is something produced by an artist or composer

5 a works is a factory or workshop

6 the works of a machine or clock are the parts inside it that make it operate

7 someone who does good work does good deeds for other people

[verb: **works, working, worked**]

1 you work when you do something that needs effort or energy

2 people who work have a job or are employed

3 a machine that works operates properly

4 a plan works when it is successful

5 to work something such as a machine is to make it operate

6 if something works loose, it slackens or becomes loose slowly

7 you **work out** something such as a problem when you think about it carefully until you find the answer

8 something **works out** a certain way when it turns out that way at the end

9 if someone **works out**, they do exercises to make themselves stronger and fitter

♦ **worker** [noun: **workers**]

1 someone who works for a living, especially in a particular industry: *steel workers*

2 a bee, ant, or termite that does the work in the colony, for example feeding the queen and looking after the eggs

workforce [noun: **workforces**] the workforce is all the people who work in a particular place, such as a factory

working class [noun: **working classes**] the working class is the people in society who do manual or factory work, or similar jobs

workman [noun: **workmen**] a man who works with his hands, especially doing building work

♦ **workmanship** [noun] workmanship is the skill that a craftsman has in making things

workout [noun: **workouts**] a period of time when you do exercises to make you stronger and fitter

workplace [noun: **workplaces**] a building or room where people perform their jobs

workshop [noun: **workshops**] a place or business where things are built, made or repaired

world [noun: **worlds**]

1 the Earth or all the people living on it: *The whole world is affected by global warming.*

2 a planet: *a creature from another world*

3 an area of life or activity: *the world of antiques*

♦ **worldly** [adjective: **worldlier, worldliest**]

Ww

1 to do with the Earth and life on Earth

2 your worldly goods are all the things that belong to you

3 a worldly person is only interested in things like money and possessions, not in the spirit or the soul

worldwide [adjective] everywhere in the world

World Wide Web [noun] the World Wide Web is a huge network of computers all round the world where you can find information about a lot of things

worm [noun: **worms**] a small creature with a soft body and no backbone or legs
[verb: **worms, worming, wormed**]
1 to worm your way somewhere is to get there by wriggling through small spaces
2 to **worm something out of** someone is to get information from them gradually and with great difficulty

worn [verb] the form of the verb **wear** that is used with a helping verb to show that something happened in the past: *She had worn the dress before.*
[adjective]
1 worn things are damaged by rubbing or wearing: *The carpet is worn and dirty.*
2 if you are **worn out**, you are very tired

worried [adjective] anxious

worrier [noun: **worriers**] a person who worries, especially all the time

worry [verb: **worries, worrying, worried**]
1 to worry about a problem is to keep thinking about it in an anxious way because you are not sure how to deal with it or how it will turn out
2 to worry someone is to disturb them and make them anxious or upset
[noun: **worries**]
1 worry is being anxious
2 a worry is something that makes you anxious

worse [adjective] **worse** is the comparative form of the adjective **bad**, which you use when you are comparing how bad things are: *My brother's house is a worse mess than mine.*
[adverb] more badly, or more severely: *It was raining worse than ever.*
♦ **worsen** [verb: **worsens, worsening, worsened**]

1 something worsens when it becomes worse than it was before
2 to worsen something is to make it worse
➡ **worst**

worship [verb: **worships, worshipping, worshipped**]
1 to honour a god or gods by praising them and praying to them
2 to love or admire someone or something, especially in a way that stops you seeing their faults
[noun] religious services and other ways of worshipping: *a place of worship*
♦ **worshipper** [noun: **worshippers**] someone who worships, especially in a church or temple

worst [adjective] worst is the superlative form of the adjective **bad**, which you use when you are describing something as worse than all the rest: *It was the worst storm we'd ever seen.*
[adverb] in the most unpleasant or unsuccessful way: *The car handles worst in icy conditions.* • *I scored worst in the test.*
[pronoun] the person or thing that is worse than all the others: *His asthma seems to be at its worst on cold mornings.*

ⓘ **Bad** and **good** are two of the adjectives in English that have what are called **irregular** comparative and superlative forms. So something is **bad**, or **worse**, or **worst** (not bad, badder, baddest), and something is **good**, or **better**, or **best** (not good, gooder, goodest). Remember also that you cannot describe something as more bad or more good, or most bad or most good.

worth [noun]
1 something's worth is its value or importance
2 someone's worth is their usefulness or value
[adjective]
1 what something is worth is how much money it is valued at: *The ring is worth £1000.*
2 if something is worth doing or worth considering, it is useful or deserves to be considered
♦ **worthless** [adjective] a worthless person or thing has no value or use

worthwhile [adjective] something that is worthwhile is worth doing or getting involved in, because it results in something good

worthy [adjective: **worthier, worthiest**]
1 to be worthy of something is to deserve it
2 a worthy person, or a worthy cause, deserves to be given respect or support

would [verb]
1 a way of changing the verb **will** to make a past tense: *She said she would be in touch later.*
2 you use **would** to ask people if they want something or if they will do something: *Would you like a new coat for your birthday?* • *Would you close the door behind you, please.*

wouldn't [short form] a short way to say and write **would not**: *She wouldn't go.*

wound[1] [verb] a way of changing the verb **wind** to make a past tense. It can be used with or without a helping verb: *She wound a long, red, knitted scarf around her neck.* • *He had wound the old grandfather clock in the hall.*

ⓘ This word rhymes with **found**.

wound[2] [noun: **wounds**] an injury to a person's or animal's body in which the skin has been damaged by a cut or blow
[verb: **wounds, wounding, wounded**]
1 to wound a person or animal is to cause an injury to their body
2 to wound someone is to hurt their feelings
♦ **wounded** [adjective] a wounded soldier or animal has been injured by a blow from a weapon

ⓘ This word rhymes with **spooned**.

wove [verb] a way of changing the verb **weave** to make a past tense: *She wove flowers into her hair.*

woven [verb] the form of the verb **weave** that is used with a helping verb to show that something happened in the past: *The scarves were woven from wool.*

WPC [abbreviation: **WPCs**] short for **woman police constable**, used before a female police officer's name: *WPC Hobbs*

wrap [verb: **wraps, wrapping, wrapped**]
1 to wrap something, or to **wrap something up**, is to put a covering of paper or other material round it
2 to put something like paper or cloth round another thing to cover it: *She wrapped the bandage round my knee.*

♦ **wrapper** [noun: **wrappers**] a piece of paper or cardboard that something is wrapped in

wrath [noun] great anger

wreak [verb: **wreaks, wreaking, wreaked**] to wreak something, such as havoc, damage or revenge, is to cause it

wreath [noun: **wreaths**] an arrangement of flowers and leaves in the shape of a ring, which is put on a dead person's coffin or grave, or hung up on a door at Christmas

wreathe [verb: **wreathes, wreathing, wreathed**] one thing is wreathed in another when it is covered or surrounded by that other thing

wreck [verb: **wrecks, wrecking, wrecked**]
1 to wreck something is to destroy it
2 a ship is wrecked when it is badly damaged, for example by hitting rocks, and can no longer sail
[noun: **wrecks**] a badly damaged ship or an aeroplane or vehicle that has crashed
♦ **wreckage** [noun] the broken or damaged pieces left after something has been wrecked

wren [noun: **wrens**] a tiny wild bird with brown feathers and a short tail

wrench [verb: **wrenches, wrenching, wrenched**] to pull or twist something very hard so that it comes out of its position
[noun: **wrenches**]
1 a hard pull or twist
2 a tool used to turn things

wrestle [verb: **wrestles, wrestling, wrestled**]
1 to wrestle with someone is to fight with them by gripping them and trying to throw them over or hold them down on the ground
2 to wrestle with a problem is to try very hard to solve it
♦ **wrestler** [noun: **wrestlers**] someone who fights by wrestling
♦ **wrestling** [noun] the sport of fighting using special holds and movements to throw your opponent to the ground and to hold him or her there

wretch [noun: **wretches**] a very wicked or very miserable person
♦ **wretched** [adjective]
1 very poor and miserable: *They lived in a*

Ww

wretched little shack in the woods.

2 very annoying: *Where's that wretched cat?*

wriggle [verb: **wriggles, wriggling, wriggled**] to twist about: *Stop wriggling about in your chair and sit still!*

wring [verb: **wrings, wringing, wrung**]

1 to twist or squeeze a wet cloth or wet washing so that all or most of the water is forced out

2 to wring something such as someone's hand is to twist or squeeze it hard

wrinkle [noun: **wrinkles**]

1 wrinkles are lines and creases that form in your skin as you get older

2 a wrinkle is a crease or ridge in the surface of something

[verb: **wrinkles, wrinkling, wrinkled**] you wrinkle your forehead or your nose when you screw it up so that the skin forms into little creases or lines

♦ **wrinkly** [adjective: **wrinklier, wrinkliest**] having lots of wrinkles

wrist [noun: **wrists**] your wrist is the part of your body where your arm joins your hand

write [verb: **writes, writing, wrote, written**]

1 to form letters and words usually on paper using a pen or pencil

2 you write to someone when you write or type a letter and send it to them

3 to write a story, article, play or music is to create it and write it down

4 to **write something off** is think of it as being lost or too damaged to be used again

♦ **writer** [noun: **writers**] someone who writes books, plays, film scripts or newspaper articles

♦ **writing** [noun: **writings**]

1 writing is forming letters and words on paper or some other surface so that they can be read

2 your writing is the way you write

3 an author's writings are the things he or she has written

♦ **written** [adjective]

1 a written agreement or application is set down in writing or print

2 a written exam is one in which you have to write something

wrong [adjective]

1 not right or not satisfactory: *Is there something wrong with David? He doesn't look happy.* • *Stealing is wrong.*

2 not correct: *That was the wrong answer.*

3 not suitable: *He has decided he's in the wrong job.*

[adverb] wrongly or incorrectly: *I think I have spelt your name wrong.*

♦ **wrongly** [adverb] not correctly or accurately: *The plug had been fitted wrongly so the machine did not work.*

wrote [verb] a way of changing the verb **write** to make a past tense: *He wrote an e-mail to his friend.*

wrung [verb] a way of changing the verb **wring** to make a past tense. It can be used with or without a helping verb: *The woman wrung her hands.* • *He had wrung all the water out of the mop.*

wry [adjective: **wryer, wryest**] a wry smile, comment or sense of humour is one that shows gentle amusement at something that has gone wrong

WWW or **www** [abbreviation] short for **World Wide Web**

Ww

Xmas [noun] an informal short spelling of **Christmas**

X-ray [noun: **X-rays**] a special kind of photograph that shows the bones inside someone's body

xylophone [noun: **xylophones**] a musical instrument made up of a set of wooden bars that make different notes when you hit them with hammers

Y

yacht [noun: **yachts**] a sailing boat that you use for racing or for pleasure trips

yachtsman [noun: **yachtsmen**] a man who sails a yacht

yachtswoman [noun: **yachtswomen**] a woman who sails a yacht

yak [noun: **yaks**] a type of ox with long hair that comes from Tibet

yam [noun: **yams**] a root vegetable like a potato that grows in tropical countries

yank [verb: **yanks, yanking, yanked**] to pull something sharply and roughly: *He yanked the book out of my hand.*
[noun: **yanks**] a sudden sharp pull

yap [verb: **yaps, yapping, yapped**] if a dog yaps, it makes a high-pitched bark
[noun: **yaps**] a high-pitched bark

yard¹ [noun: **yards**] a unit of measurement of length, equal to 0.914 metres or 3 feet

yard² [noun: **yards**]
1 an enclosed area of land used for a particular purpose: *a builders' yard*
2 an American English word for **garden**

yarn [noun: **yarns**]
1 wool or cotton that has been spun into thread
2 a story that includes things that are not true: *I began the whole story over again, spinning as long a yarn as possible.*

yashmak [noun: **yashmaks**] a type of veil that some Muslim women wear

yawn [verb: **yawns, yawning, yawned**]
1 to open your mouth very wide and breathe in, because you are feeling tired or bored
2 if a hole yawns, it is wide open: *The mouth of the cave yawned below them.*
[noun: **yawns**] the sound or action of someone yawning

ye [pronoun] an old-fashioned word for **you**

year [noun: **years**] a period of 365 or 366 days, marking the length of time it takes for the Earth to go around the sun, especially the period from 1 January to 31 December
  ◆ **yearly** [adjective] happening every year: *our yearly holiday*

yearn [verb: **yearns, yearning, yearned**] to yearn for something is to want it very much: *Harry yearned to play the guitar.*

yeast [noun] a substance that you add to dough to make bread rise

yell [verb: **yells, yelling, yelled**] to shout or scream: *'Let me go!' she yelled.*
[noun: **yells**] a shout or scream

yellow [noun] the colour of the sun or the middle of an egg

yelp [verb: **yelps, yelping, yelped**] if a dog yelps, it makes a short, high sound because it is in pain
[noun: **yelps**] a short, high sound

yes [adverb] a word you say when you agree with someone or something: *'Are these shoes all right?' 'Yes,' I said. 'They're all right.'*

yesterday [noun] the day before today
[adverb] on the day before today: *We went shopping yesterday.*

yet [adverb]
1 by now, by this time: *Have you read her new book yet?*
2 before something is finished, still: *We might win this game yet.*

Yeti [noun: **Yetis**] a hairy creature like a big

man who is supposed to live in the Himalayan mountains

yew [noun: **yews**] a tree with very dark green leaves

yield [verb: **yields, yielding, yielded**]
1 to give in or surrender: *The army yielded to enemy forces.*
2 to give way to pressure or force: *The door suddenly yielded and he fell into the room.*
3 to produce an amount of something such as a crop
[noun: **yields**] the amount of something that is produced: *cows with a high milk yield*

yob [noun: **yobs**] a young man who behaves in a rough and unpleasant way

yodel [verb: **yodels, yodelling, yodelled**] to sing in a way that involves changing back and forth between your normal singing voice and a very high voice

yoga [noun] a type of exercise in which you stretch your muscles whilst taking deep breaths. Yoga also involves meditation, which is thinking deeply

yogurt or **yoghurt** [noun: **yogurts** or **yoghurts**] a runny food with a slightly sour taste that is made from milk

yoke [noun: **yokes**]
1 a wooden frame that you put around the necks of a pair of oxen when they are pulling a cart
2 something that stops people from being free: *the yoke of slavery*
3 the part of a dress or blouse that fits over your shoulders and neck: *a blouse with an embroidered yoke*
[verb: **yokes, yoking, yoked**] to fasten two things together with a yoke

yolk [noun: **yolks**] the yellow part in the middle of an egg

Yom Kippur [noun] a Jewish religious day when people do not eat. It is also called the Day of Atonement

yonder [adverb] an old-fashioned word for 'in that place'
[adjective] over there: *Take my sword, and go with it to yonder river.*

you [pronoun] a word you use to the person or people that you are talking to: *Do you like pizza?* • *I'll ring you tomorrow night.* • *Max is taller than you.*

you'd [short form] a short way to say or write **you had** or **you would**: *You'd better be careful.* • *You'd be sorry if she left.*

you'll [short form] a short way to say and write **you will**: *You'll never guess what happened next!*

young [adjective: **younger, youngest**] not old: *a young boy*
[noun]
1 the babies that an animal or bird has: *a sparrow feeding its young*
2 **the young** are young people
♦ **youngster** [noun: **youngsters**] a young person

your [adjective] belonging to the person or people you are talking to: *Can I borrow your pen?*

ⓘ Try not to confuse the spellings of **your** and **you're**.
Your is the possessive form of **you**, and shows that someone owns something: *I like your shoes.*
You're is short for **you are**: *You're my best friend.*

you're [short form] a short way to say and write **you are**: *You're a better singer than he is.*

yours [pronoun] a word you use to talk about something belonging to the person or people you are talking to: *Which glass is yours?*

LANGUAGE FOR LIFE

yours

You use **yours** as part of a phrase at the end of a formal letter before signing your name.
• If you have addressed the person as 'Dear Sir' or 'Dear Madam', you should write **Yours faithfully** or **Yours truly** before you sign your name.
• If you have addressed the person by their name, you should write **Yours sincerely** or **Yours truly** before you sign your name.

yourself [pronoun: **yourselves**]
1 you use the words **yourself** or **yourselves** after a verb or preposition when the person or people you are talking to perform an action and are affected by it: *Careful you don't cut yourself on that knife.* • *You'll have to dry yourselves on your T-shirts.*

Yy

---

2 you can use **yourself** or **yourselves** to show that someone does something without any help from anyone else: *Did you really make that skirt yourself?*

3 you can use **yourself** or **yourselves** to show more clearly who you mean: *You cannot film it yourselves, but you can buy a video.*

youth [noun: **youths**]

1 the time in your life when you are young: *She spent most of her youth abroad.*

2 a boy aged between about 15 and 20: *a gang of youths*

3 young people as a group: *the youth of today*

• **youthful** [adjective] young: *a youthful-looking fifty-year-old*

ⓘ You only use the plural **youths** when you are talking about teenage boys.

youth hostel [noun: **youth hostels**] a place where young people can stay overnight quite cheaply when they are on holiday

you've [short form] a short way to say and write **you have**: *You've left the door open again.*

yo-yo [noun: **yo-yos**] a toy that is made up of a circular object on a piece of string that you have to try to keep spinning up and down

Yule [noun] an old-fashioned word for **Christmas**

Yy

Z

zany [adjective: **zanier, zaniest**] crazy or funny: *a zany sense of humour*

zap [verb: **zaps, zapping, zapped**]
1 to shoot or kill something, especially in a computer game: *You have to zap all the aliens before they catch you.*
2 to move quickly through or between things: *zapping through the TV channels*

ⓘ This is a slang word.

zeal [noun] enthusiasm and keenness
 ♦ **zealous** [adjective] very enthusiastic about something: *a zealous supporter of the football team*

zebra [noun: **zebras**] an animal like a horse with black and white stripes

zebra crossing [noun: **zebra crossings**] a place where you can cross a road, marked in black and white stripes

zenith [noun] the highest point in something: *Scoring those five goals was the zenith of his career.*

zero [noun: **zeros**]
1 nothing or the number 0: *There are six zeros in one million.*
2 the point on a scale where you start measuring things, for example on a thermometer: *It was three degrees below zero.*

zest [noun] a lot of enjoyment: *Joe had a great zest for life.*

zigzag [adjective] with lots of sharp bends from left to right: *a zigzag pattern*
[verb: **zigzags, zigzagging, zigzagged**] to have a lot of sharp bends from left to right: *The path zigzagged up the hillside.*

Zimmer [noun] a metal frame that old people

sometimes use to help them walk. This word is a trademark

zinc [noun] a blue-white metal

zip [noun: **zips**] a fastener on clothes or bags that has two rows of metal or plastic teeth that fit tightly together when a sliding piece is pulled along them
[verb: **zips, zipping, zipped**]
1 to fasten something with a zip: *Zip up your jacket; it's cold.*
2 to move somewhere very quickly: *The bullet zipped by his head.*
3 to make the information on a computer file fit into a much smaller space, so that it uses up less memory

zip code [noun: **zip codes**] the American word for **post code**

zodiac [noun] in astrology, an imaginary strip in the sky that has 12 parts that are named after constellations, for example *Capricorn* and *Aquarius*

zombie [noun: **zombies**]
1 a dead body that is supposed to come back to life through witchcraft
2 someone who seems to be very slow or stupid

zone [noun: **zones**] an area or part of a place that people set aside and use for a particular purpose: *a no-parking zone*

zoo [noun: **zoos**] a place where people keep wild animals to breed them and study them, and where you can go to see these animals

zoological [adjective] relating to animals

zoology [noun] the study of animals

Zz

zoom [verb: **zooms, zooming, zoomed**]

1 to go somewhere very fast, especially with a loud buzzing noise: *The rocket zoomed up into the air.*

2 if a camera **zooms in**, it makes the thing that is being filmed or photographed look much bigger

zoom lens [noun: **zoom lenses**] a lens on a camera that can make things look bigger or smaller